A DICTIONARY OF

Literary Terms and Literary Theory

THIRD EDITION

A DICTIONARY OF Literary Terms and Literary Theory

THIRD EDITION

J. A. CUDDON

Blackwell Reference

First published in Great Britain by André Deutsch Ltd 1977
First published in the United States of America
by Doubleday & Company Inc., 1977
Revised edition published in Great Britain
by André Deutsch Ltd 1979
Revised edition published in the United States of America
by Doubleday & Company Inc., 1980

Third revised edition published 1991
by Basil Blackwell Ltd
108 Cowley Road, Oxford OX4 1JF
Basil Blackwell Inc.,
3 Cambridge Center, Cambridge, MA 02142, USA

British Library Cataloguing in Publication Data
Cuddon, J. A. (John Anthony) 1928–
A dictionary of literary terms. – 3rd rev. ed.
1. Literature
I. Title
803

ISBN 0–631–17214–9

Library of Congress Cataloging-in-Publication Data
Cuddon, J. A. (John Anthony) 1928–
A dictionary of literary terms / by J. A. Cuddon – 3rd ed.
p. cm.
1. Literature—Dictionaries. I. Title.
PN41.C83 1991 90–49943
803—dc20

ISBN 0–631–17214–9

Typest in Garamond
by Hope Services, Abingdon
Printed in Great Britain by
Billing & Sons Ltd., Worcester

THE TO THE MASTER AND FELLOWS
OF MAGDALENE COLLEGE, CAMBRIDGE,
IN GRATITUDE FOR THEIR KINDNESS
AND HOSPITALITY

ACKNOWLEDGMENTS

A. Alvarez, pastiche in the preface to *The New Poetry* (1961), by permission of the author.

Kingsley Amis, extract from 'Beowulf' by permission of the author.

W. H. Auden, 'If I could tell you' and extracts from *Letter to Lord Byron* from *Collected Poems*, by permission of Faber & Faber and Random House Inc.

Nicolas Bentley, two clerihews by permission of the author.

John Berryman, extract from 'The Dispossessed' from *Homage to Mistress Bradstreet* by permission of Faber & Faber and Harcourt Brace Jovanovich Inc.

John Betjeman, extract from 'In Westminster Abbey' from *Collected Poems* by permission of the author and John Murray Ltd.

Roy Campbell, 'The Seventh Sword' from *Mithraic Emblems*, by permission of The Bodley Head.

Charles Causley, extracts from 'Mother, Get Up, Unbar the Door', 'The Prisoners of Love', 'Timothy Winters' and 'The Life of the Poet', by permission of the author and David Higham Associates Ltd.

J. R. Clark Hall, extracts from translation of *Beowulf* by permission of George Allen & Unwin Ltd and Barnes & Noble.

Jack Clemo, extract from 'The Plundered Fuchsias' from *The Map of Clay*, by permission of Methuen & Co USA Ltd.

Wendy Cope, for 'Valentine' by permission of the author.

John Crowe Ransom, extract from 'Dog' from *Selected Poems*, by permission of Laurence Pollinger Ltd and Alfred A. Knopf, Random House Inc.

C. Day Lewis, extract from 'Sing We the Two Lieutenants' from *A Time to Dance* in *Collected Poems 1954*, by permission of the Executor of the Estate of C. Day Lewis, Hogarth Press and Jonathan Cape Ltd.

T. S. Eliot, extracts from 'The Love Song of J. Alfred Prufrock', 'The Waste Land', 'Ash Wednesday', Little Gidding', and 'Dry Salvages' from *Collected Poems 1909–1962*; UK: by permission of Faber & Faber and USA: 'from *Collected Poems 1909–1962* by T. S. Eliot, copyright 1963, 1964, by T. S. Eliot. Reprinted by permission of Harcourt Brace Jovanovich Inc.'

D. J. Enright, extract from 'The Laughing Hyena by Hokusai' from *Selected Poems*, by permission of Chatto & Windus and Bolt & Watson.

Geoffrey Hill, extract from 'God's Little Mountain' from *For the Unfallen* by permission of the author and André Deutsch Ltd.

David Holbrook, 'Living? Our Supervisors will do that for Us' reprinted by permission of the author.

Ted Hughes, extracts from 'February', 'View of a Pig', and 'Thrushes' from *Lupercal*, by permission of the author, Faber & Faber and Harper & Row.

Robinson Jeffers, extract from 'Hurt Hawks' from *The Selected Poetry of Robinson Jeffers*, by permission of Alfred A. Knopf, Random House Inc.

David Jones, extracts from 'Middle Sea and Lear Sea' from *Anathemata*, by permission of Faber & Faber and the Chilmark Press.

James Kirkup, extracts from 'Four Haiku on the Inland Sea', from *Paper Windows*, by permission of the author and Curtis Brown Ltd.

Philip Larkin, extract from 'The Whitsun Weddings', by permission of the author and Faber & Faber.

D. H. Lawrence, 'Kangaroo' and 'Snake'; UK: by permission of Laurence Pollinger Ltd; USA: 'From the *Complete Poems of D. H. Lawrence* edited by Vivian de Sola Pinto and F. Warren Roberts, copyright 1964, 1971, by Angelo Ravagli and C. M. Weekley. Executors of the Estate of Frieda Lawrence Ravagli. All rights reserved. Reprinted by permission of the Viking Press Inc.'

Robert Lowell, extracts from 'Our Lady of Walsingham', 'Mr Edwards and the Spider', 'The Holy Innocents', and 'Man and Wife' from *Lord Weary's Castle* in *Poems 1938–49*, by permission of Faber & Faber and Harcourt Brace Jovanovich Inc.

George MacBeth, extracts from 'The God of Love' by permission of the author.

Hugh Macdiarmid, extract from 'On a Raised Beach' by permission of the author.

Norman McCaig, extract from 'Mutual Life' by permission of the author and Granada Publishing Ltd.

Roger McGough, extract from 'Hoarding' from *Watchwords* by

permission of the author, Jonathan Cape Ltd and Hope Leresche & Steele.

John Masefield, extract from 'Cargoes' by permission of the Society of Authors and Macmillan Publishing Company Inc.

Ogden Nash, 'Reflections on Ice Breaking' from *Verses from 1929 On* (plus extra lines 'pot/is not'), 'What's the Use?' copyright Ogden Nash 1931 and 'Requiem', copyright Ogden Nash 1938 by permission of A. P. Watt & Son and Little, Brown & Co.

Sylvia Plath, extract from 'The Moon and the Yew Tree' by permission of Miss Olwyn Hughes and Harper & Row.

Ezra Pound, extracts from 'The Seafarer'; UK: Faber & Faber; USA: 'Ezra Pound. PERSONAE. Copyright 1926 by Ezra Pound. Reprinted by permission of New Directions Publishing Corporation.'

Peter Redgrove, extracts from 'Lazarus and the Sea' and 'The Archaeologist' from *The Collector and Other Poems* by permission of the author and Routledge Kegan Paul Ltd.

Dylan Thomas, 'Vision and Prayer' from *Collected Poems*; UK: J. M. Dent and the Trustees for the copyrights of the late Dylan Thomas; USA: '*The Poems of Dylan Thomas.* Copyright 1946 by New Directions Publishing Corporation. Reprinted by permission of New Directions Publishing Corporation.'

R. S. Thomas, extracts from 'The Welsh Hill Country', 'Song at the Year's Turning', and 'A Blackbird Singing' from *Poetry for Supper*, by permission of the author and Granada Publishing Ltd.

Vernon Watkins, extract from 'The Ballad of the Mari Lwyd' by permission of Faber & Faber.

W. B. Yeats, extracts from 'Sailing to Byzantium' and 'Among School Children' from *The Collected Poems of W. B. Yeats*, by permission of M. B. Yeats, Miss Anne Yeats and Macmillan of London and Basingstoke.

ABBREVIATIONS

A – Arabic
abbrev. – abbreviation, -ated
AL – Anglo-Latin
AN – Anglo-Norman
Ar – Armenian
c. – century, or centuries
c. – *circa* (as in *c.* 1150, meaning the approximate date)
cf. – *confer* 'compare'
Ch – Chinese
Du – Dutch
e.g. – *exempli gratia* 'for example'
Eng – English
et al. – *et alii* 'and others'
F – French
fl. – *floruit* 'he flourished'
G – German
Gk – Greek
Heb – Hebrew
HG – High German
i.e. – *id est* 'that is'
It – Italian
J – Japanese
K – Korean
L – Latin
LDu – Low Dutch
LG – Low German
LL – Late Latin
MDu – Middle Dutch
ME – Middle English
MedL – Medieval Latin
MHG – Middle High German
MLG – Middle Low German

ModL – Modern Latin
NGk – Neo-Greek
OE – Old English
OF – Old French
OHG – Old High German
ON – Old Norse
P – Persian
Pg – Portuguese
pl. – plural
Pr – Provençal
Pt – Part
publ. – published
qq.v. – *quae vide* 'which see' (pl.)
q.v. – *quod vide* 'which see' (sing.)
R – Russian
S – Serbian
sing. – singular
Skt – Sanskrit
Sp – Spanish
Sw – Swedish
T – Turkish
trans. – translation, -ated
viz. – *videlicet* 'namely'
W – Welsh

PREFACE

As is usual in the making of anything, one of the main problems at the outset in compiling this dictionary was to decide what to put in and what to omit. In the first place, it is not easy to decide what a literary term really is, because, by most standards, it is a vague classification. Epic is one, hexameter is, and so is elegy. But are pornography, patter-song and apocrypha? In the *Shorter Oxford Dictionary* the main definition of 'literary' runs thus: 'Of or pertaining to, or of the nature of, literature, polite learning, or books and written compositions; pertaining to that kind of written composition which has value on account of its qualities of form.' If we accept this as a working indication of what is meant by 'literary', then what is to be done about the terms (and there are many) used by printers and compositors? What about the language of grammarians and the proliferating terminology of linguisticians? Most or all of these are related, however tenuously in some cases, to the literary, and to literature. After a good deal of deliberation on these matters, I decided to be judiciously selective and include a few terms of printers, grammarians, philologists and linguisticians. So, for instance, I have included **quarto** and **folio** but left out **line-block** and **galley**. **Paragraph** and **loose** and **periodic sentence** are in; **supine** and **declension** are not. **Keneme** and **morpheme** are in; **diphthong** and **labial** are not.

Another poser was whether to include all literary terms from all or most languages and literatures and to provide illustrations and examples, but this would surely have seemed like assuming the function of the encyclopaedist, and greatly lengthened the book. In any case, some terms are so obscure (and rare) as to be of interest only to the specialist.

What I have endeavoured to do, then, is to provide a serviceable and fairly comprehensive dictionary of those literary terms which are in regular use in the world today; terms in which intelligent people may be expected to have some interest and about which they may wish to find out something more. If by any chance they do not know (or have forgotten) what a *haiku* is, or *verso tronco*, or how blue-stockings came to be so named, then I hope that this dictionary will provide them with the basic information.

I say 'fairly comprehensive' because any work of orismology is bound to be limited by the author's reading and knowledge. No man or woman can be expected to have read even a tithe of everything. I am familiar with Classical, European, Slavonic and Near Eastern literatures and have some knowledge of the literatures of North America and of Commonwealth nations. But my knowledge of Oriental literatures and those of Spanish America and South America is limited. There are, therefore, inevitably, considerable gaps.

Most of the terms are drawn from Greek, Latin, English, French, German, Spanish, Italian, Russian, Arabic, Japanese, Old French, Old Provençal and Old Norse. A few are Serbian, Chinese, Persian, Turkish, Welsh and Korean.

Twelve main categories can be distinguished at the outset, as follows:

1. Technical terms (e.g. iamb, pentameter, metonymy, *ottava rima*).
2. Forms (e.g. sonnet, *villanelle*, limerick, *tanka*, clerihew).
3. Genres or kinds (e.g. pastoral, elegy, *fabliau*, *Märchen*, *conte*).
4. Technicalities (e.g. pivot word, tenor and vehicle, communication heresy, aesthetic distance).
5. Groups, schools and movements (e.g. Pléiade, Parnassians, Pre-Raphaelites, School of Spenser).
6. Well-known phrases (e.g. willing suspension of disbelief, negative capability, *discordia concors*, *in medias res*, *quod semper quod ubique*).
7. -isms (e.g. realism, primitivism, Platonism, plagiarism, structuralism, orientalism).
8. Motifs or themes (e.g. *ubi sunt*, *carpe diem*, Faust-theme, *leitmotif*).
9. Personalities (e.g. *scop*, *jongleur*, villain, *gracioso*, *guslar*).
10. Modes, attitudes and styles (e.g. *dolce stil nuovo*, irony, Marinism, grotesque, sentimental comedy).
11. Objects/artefacts (e.g. *coranto*, holograph, manuscript, gazette, buskin, book).
12. Concepts (e.g. sincerity, the sublime, concrete universal, noble savage, decorum).

These twelve categories account for a fair proportion of literary terms but there are scores which do not belong to any particular family or phylum, and any kind of taxonomical approach soon breaks down as one begins to classify. The following haphazard list suggests the difficulty of satisfactory division: abstract, *belles lettres*, brief, censorship, forgery, Freytag's pyramid, *hamartia*, inspiration, juvenilia, Grub Street, palindrome, quotation titles – to mention no others.

The plan of the dictionary is simple. It is alphabetical and runs from Abbey Theatre (though it would have been more suitable to start with *ab ovo*) to zeugma; and, so to speak, from epic to limerick. Each term is given a brief description or definition. In some cases, but by no means always, when I thought it might be helpful and/or of interest, I give some brief etymology of the term. This is particularly necessary when a term comes from one thing but now denotes another. For instance, the Spanish *estribillo*: the word signifies 'little stirrup', being the diminutive of *estribo* 'stirrup'. It here denotes a refrain or chorus (also a pet word or phrase) and is a theme, verse or stanza (of from two to four lines) of a *villancico*; and there is more to it than that. *Fit* (a division of a poem, a canto or stave) and *slang* are other interesting examples.

Many indications of origin are added in brackets. Where it was not possible to do this in a simple fashion I have shown the history at greater length within the definition of the term. Often this description explains the etymology and what the term denotes. For literary forms and genres I have provided a *résumé* of origins, history and development, and I have also provided details of notable examples and distinguished practitioners. I have not included bibliographies; to have done so would have been to lengthen the book by perhaps a third as much again. But, where appropriate, I have referred to the classic work on a particular theme or subject (e.g. C. S. Lewis's *The Allegory of Love*, A. O. Lovejoy's *The Great Chain of Being*, Maud Bodkin's *Archetypal Patterns in Poetry*).

I would have liked to provide an example in full to illustrate every poetic form and genre (e.g. **rondeau, ode, elegy, lyric**), but this was not feasible either. I would also have liked to include a quotation for every kind of metrical scheme, but this again would have expanded the book inordinately. It would have entailed quoting in at least sixteen different languages and this would have required translation in many instances. Moreover, it would have involved using seven alphabets (Greek, Japanese, Hebrew, Arabic, Cyrillic, Sanskrit and Chinese) in addition to the Roman. Thus, in the interests of simplicity and brevity, I have settled, whenever possible, for a quotation in English verse.

Apropos versification I am obliged to mention the matter of terms used in Classical prosody. Miscellaneous hierophants have pointed out that Classical prosody, its systems and classifications, bear little relationship to English verse. This may well be so, but we have inherited the terms (as have other nations and languages); they have been in use for some hundreds of years; and it will be found that the vast majority of poets have a very thorough knowledge and understanding of them. Moreover, if in doubt about their utility, one might ask: is it easier to say (or write) 'an iambic pentameter', or 'a line of verse consisting of five feet with a rising rhythm in which the first syllable of each foot is unstressed and the second stressed'? The Greeks in fact *did* have a word for almost everything and we have inherited these terms whether we like them or not. And it seems to me much simpler to understand and use them rather than to pretend they do not exist, or find verbose alternatives.

Some entries were peculiarly difficult to condense, and none more so than **novel**. The chief problem here was what to include out of the thousands of possible examples. In the end I decided to go by that principle which guided me throughout the making of the dictionary and to include only those writers whose books I am familiar with and which have seemed to me to be of particular merit. Naturally enough, the selection must often coincide with what, in all probability, most other people would choose. Some novelists have to go in whether you like them or not because the general consensus over the years has confirmed that their novels are outstanding or at any rate of notable quality. On the whole, as far as the novel is concerned, I have mentioned most of those who I believe are major novelists, and I have provided a selection of minor novelists. Inevitably, the treatment of the novel (like the treatment of travel books, short stories, detective stories, spy, ghost and horror stories) has involved long lists.

I have some misgivings about the lists but I have kept them fairly detailed in order to be fair, as it were, and also in the hope that the browser or reader may encounter things that they have not met before or which they have forgotten existed. For instance, the works of some authors of distinction have, unhappily, sunk leaving few traces. A mention of their neglected books may help to revive interest.

With regard to works of fiction in general, I would have liked to include more evaluative comments, however brief, but to have done this would have been to double or even triple the length of the entries.

As for dates – these, as we all know, can become boring. On the other hand, their absence can be frustrating. Accordingly, I have attempted a compromise. It seemed otiose to put in the dates of every author each time I referred to him or her, especially the famous. There are, for instance, many references to Aristotle, Plato, Horace, Dante,

Chaucer, Sir Philip Sidney, Shakespeare, Molière, Dryden, Pope, Goethe, Keats, Thomas Mann, James Joyce, W. B. Yeats and T. S. Eliot – to cite only a handful. When referring to the famous I assume that the reader is familiar with the approximate period in which they flourished. When referring to the not-so-famous, but, nonetheless, important (e.g. Archilochus, Lucian, Cavalcanti, Dunbar, Clément Marot, Thomas Campion, Tieck, Lady Winchilsea, James Sheridan Knowles, Théophile Gautier, Queiros) I have, in many instances, included some indication of their dates. In any event it is clear as a rule when they lived because I refer to the century, or I give the dates of their works whenever it is helpful or necessary to do so. The dates given refer, unless otherwise indicated in the text, to the first performance of plays, the first publication in one volume of prose works, and the first collected publication of poems. I diverge from this system only where it might be misleading. I have cited in English those titles of works which are less familiar in their original form to an English-speaking reader. The dates give in such cases refer to the first publication in the original language.

The whole dictionary is cross-referenced so that the user can move easily from one entry to another. The references are the plumbing and wiring of the book. If, for example, you look up **ballad** you will be referred to REFRAIN, ORAL TRADITION, HOMERIC EPITHET, KENNING, INCREMENTAL REPETITION, NARODNE PESME, BROADSIDE, FOLKSONG, LAY and NARRATIVE VERSE.

In the fourteen years since this book was first published a great deal has happened in the world of literature. Thousands of novels have been published in many languages, thousands of short stories, poems, biographies and autobiographies; several hundred new plays have been produced – and so on. Since the early 1970s the full impact of structuralist theory has been experienced and has been succeeded or added to by post-structuralism of which deconstruction is a vital part. Feminist criticism has burgeoned; so, to a lesser extent, have Marxist criticism and psychoanalytic and Freudian criticism. Reader-response and reception theories have developed. Such concepts as narratology and grammatology have become established. Indeed, literary theory has proliferated, sometimes counter-productively in so far as there are commentaries about commentaries about commentaries so that we approach that state of affairs so vividly predicted by E. M. Forster in his admonitory short story *The Machine Stops*. A select bibliography of books, essays and miscellaneous discourses concerned with literary theory during the last fifteen to twenty years (in the major languages of the world) may run to five hundred or more entries.

With the theories and the theories about theories have come a considerable number of what might be called 'technical terms' (e.g. *aporia*, *différance*, dissemination, *écriture feminine*, indeterminacy, intertextuality, logocentrism, metalanguage, phallogocentrism, *plaisir/jouissance*, readerly/writerly, *supplément*, *qq.v.*).

In this revised and considerably expanded edition I have attempted a *résumé* and clarification of these matters which, very often, are extremely complex and not infrequently abstruse to the point of being arcane: to such an extent, in fact, that sometimes one is reminded of 'the lone scholars' sniping at each other from the walls of learned periodicals.

However, the *raison d'être* of a dictionary is, I take it, to provide information – be it commonplace or recondite. A decent dictionary of geography, for instance, will tell us what exfoliation, jungle and *Karst* are. It should also inform us about katabatic winds, *poljes* and diastrophism. So, in this edition, in response to quite a large number of letters (one from a man who requested a list of *all* the rare technical terms left out of earlier editions) I have included a good many esoteric technical terms and semi-technical terms, plus information about important theatres and theatrical companies which have had a potent influence in the world of drama.

I have also devoted a good deal of space to some of the more 'popular' forms or modes. In earlier editions there were no entries for **ghost story** or **horror story**. In view of the wide and apparently increasing interest in these I have now included quite long accounts. The original entry for **detective story** was totally inadequate and that has been much expanded. I have also expanded the entries on, for example, **gothic novel**, **limerick**, **nonsense**, **spy story** and **thriller**, and included entries for, among other things, **censorship**, **literary forgery**, **literary prizes**, **police procedural**, **roman policier** and **Western**.

I should also add that, as this is a personal book, I have, occasionally, spread myself with entries on subjects of particular interest to me; for example, conceit, *danse macabre*, the limerick, nonsense, primitivism, revenge tragedy and table talk – to name but a few. But every author and reader has his or her favourite themes and subjects. It is probable that, from time to time, I have allowed my opinions (and perhaps some prejudices) an easy rein; but when one has read many thousands of volumes of verse, plays and fiction, essays, discourses, sermons, courtesy books, encyclopaedias, *novelle*, *Festschriften*, tracts and interpretations (and what not?) perhaps one is entitled to ventilate a few opinions. They are unlikely, I feel, to do any harm in such circumstances, and they may have the beneficial effect of provoking argument, comment or disagreement.

I have also taken the liberty of contributing a few items of my own: firstly, a double-dactyl verse – under that heading; secondly an example of synthetic rhyme – under that heading; and thirdly, three neologisms – namely *birocrat*, *sufferingette* and *verbocrap* (all under **neologism**). At any rate, I put in a modest claim for having devised these ghost-words.

I wrote above that this is a 'personal' book, but, naturally, in the course of making it, I have consulted a number of friends and I would like to take this opportunity of thanking them for giving me the benefit of their knowledge and advice. They are: Mrs Heywood, Margaret J. Miller, Mr John Basing, Dr Derek Brewer, Mr Paul Craddock, Mr Vincent Cronin, Professor Ian Jack, Mr Kevin Jackson, Dr Harry Judge, Mr Paul Moreland, Mr T. R. Salmon, Mr Philip Warnett, Professor and Mrs Singmaster, Mr and Mrs McNally, Dr David Stockton, Mr Hardcastle, Mr Clive Wilmer, Mr Bill Smith, Mr Michael Charlesworth, Mr Alastair Ogilvie, Mr Colin Chambers, Mr Steve Gooch, Mr Andrew Brown, Mr Stuart Thomson, Mr Harry Jackson, Mr Barry Duesbury and Mr Kenneth Lowes.

I remain much indebted to my original editors in the Language Library Series, the late Professor Simeon Potter and the late Eric Partridge. Professor Potter showed much patience and gave me the unstinting help of his wide learning and experience; Eric Partridge, often by means of his famous postcards, sustained my sometimes flagging spirits with help, praise and encouragement.

I am also much indebted to Mr Martin Wright who devoted many hours to checking the manuscript of this edition and to making suggestions for improving it, and to Mr Michael Rossington who also gave much time and thought to many entries. Finally, my thanks also to my current editors for their help: Mr Alyn Shipton, Mr Philip Cartwright, Miss Helen Jeffrey and Miss Caroline Richmond.

A

Abbey Theatre The most famous of Irish theatres and one of the most famous in the British Isles, if not in Europe. It was the centre of the Irish Dramatic movement founded in 1899 by W. B. Yeats and Lady Gregory. The aim of the movement was to present Irish plays on Irish subjects performed by Irish actors. The building itself was the result of a conversion of the old theatre of the Mechanics' Institute in Abbey Street and the old city morgue next to it. Its creation was made possible through the munificence (and tea) of Annie Horniman (1860–1937), who was later the pioneer of the Manchester School (*q.v.*). It was opened in 1904 and in the next eighty-five years was to bring forward plays by almost all Irish dramatists of any note. Apart from Annie Horniman, the main moving spirits of the Abbey were W. B. Yeats, J. M. Synge and Lady Gregory, plus the Fay brothers. The first plays presented were *On Baile's Strand* and *Cathleen ni Houlihan* by Yeats and *Spreading the News* by Lady Gregory. Later came Synge's *The Playboy of the Western World* (1907), which caused riots because Irish morality was offended by a reference in the text to a woman's shift (i.e. a chemise). The fortunes of the theatre declined somewhat with the removal of Annie Horniman's financial support. Synge died in 1909 and Yeats resigned as a result of a dispute with Lady Gregory, who was to continue until she retired in 1928. Among distinguished Irish playwrights to have their plays produced at the Abbey in its earlier years were Padraic Colum (1881–1972), St John Greer Ervine (1883–1971) and Lennox Robinson (1886–1958), who was manager of the Abbey from 1910 to 1923 (apart from a short break), in which year he became director. After the First World War there were more financial troubles, which were partly relieved by three famous plays by Sean O'Casey (1880–1964): namely, *Shadow of a Gunman* (1923), *Juno and the Paycock* (1924) and *The Plough and the Stars* (1926). In 1925 the Abbey received a government grant and became the first state-subsidized theatre in the English-speaking world. After O'Casey's departure for England (the Abbey rejected *The Silver Tassie* in 1928 and O'Casey was deeply offended) the theatre was sustained by a number of fine plays by George Shiels (1886–1949). There was also emphasis on plays in Gaelic. The theatre burned down in 1951; a new one opened in 1966. *See* CELTIC REVIVAL; CELTIC TWILIGHT.

abecedarius See ACROSTIC.

Abenteuerroman (G 'adventure novel') A form of fiction (related to the *Schelmenroman* or picaresque novel) primarily intended as entertainment but sometimes with a serious purpose. It appears to be traceable to medieval verse tales (of the *Spielmannsdichtung*, *q.v.*, variety) such as *Herzog Ernst*, *König Rother* and *Salman und Morolf*, and also to tales in prose of the 16th c. of the *Volksbücher* kind. Georg Wickram's *Der Goldtfaden* (1557) is an example. There was also the *Volksbuch Fortunatus* (1509), which became widely known in Europe in several languages. Thomas Dekker wrote an agreeable comedy titled *Old Fortunatus* (1600). A notable example of the fully fledged *Abenteuerroman* was Johann Grimmelhausen's *Der abenteuerliche Simplicissimus* (1669). Johann Beer (1655–1700) also wrote some. Later derivatives, in the 18th c., were the *Schauerromane* (*q.v.*) and the *Ritter- und Räuberromane* (*q.v.*). *See also* GOTHIC NOVEL/FICTION; PICARESQUE NOVEL; ROBINSON-ADE; VOLKSBUCH.

ab ovo (L 'from the egg') This term may refer to a story which starts from the beginning of the events it narrates, as opposed to one which starts in the middle – *in medias res* (*q.v.*). Horace used the expression in *Ars Poetica.*

abridged edition An abbreviated or condensed version of a work. Abridgement may be done in order to save space or to cut out passages which are thought unsuitable for some sections of the reading public. School editions of Shakespeare were often abridged (and still are occasionally) lest the sensibilities of adolescents be offended. *See also* BOWDLERIZE.

absence/presence Terms or concepts given a particular meaning by the French philosopher Jacques Derrida (1930–). Speech and the spoken word imply the immediate presence of somebody: a speaker, orator, actor or politician, for example. Writing does not require the writer's presence. Thus, the originator of the word is absent.

absolutism The principle or doctrine that there are immutable standards by which a work of art may be judged. The absolutist contends that certain values are basic and inviolable. *See* RELATIVISM.

abstract (a) A summary of any piece of written work; (b) Not concrete. A sentence is abstract if it deals with a class of things or persons: for example: 'All men are liars'. On the other hand 'Smith is a liar' is a concrete statement. The subject of a sentence may also be an abstraction, as in 'The wealth of the ruling classes'. Something may be said to be abstract if it is the name for a quality, like heat or faith. Critics use the terms abstract and concrete of imagery. For instance, Pope's:

> Hope springs eternal in the human breast,
> Man never is, but always to be, blest.

is abstract; whereas the following by the same poet is concrete:

> Fair tresses man's imperial race insnare
> And beauty draws us with a single hair.

In poetics the concrete has tended to be valued above the abstract. Sidney, for example, in *Apologie for Poetrie* (1595), praised poetry's concreteness. Neoclassical thought preferred generality. A preference, in theory, for concreteness reappears with Wordsworth, Coleridge and Shelley. In the 20th c. the distinction between concrete and abstract has undergone further change. Ezra Pound and T. E. Hulme attempted to formulate a theory of concrete poetry. Eliot reinforced this with his 'objective correlative' (*q.v.*).

For the most part poetry is the language of concreteness; prose that of the abstract. At any rate prose tends to be better able to deal with the abstract because it is more precise; not necessarily, therefore, more accurate. *See also* ABSTRACT POEM; IMAGISTS; NEOCLASSICISM.

abstract poem Edith Sitwell used this term for verses which depend primarily on their sound for meaning. In their more extreme forms sense is almost completely sacrificed to aural effects. Edith Sitwell herself was a gifted practitioner of such poetry, especially in the collection *Façade*. Gerard Manley Hopkins also made daring use of onomatopoeic and melopoeic devices; so did the French poet Rimbaud. Among writers using English Roy Campbell (1901–57) was perhaps the most outstanding and prolific experimenter. This example is taken from his series *Mithraic Frieze*, published in *Mithraic Emblems*:

> Of seven hues in white elision,
> the radii of your silver gyre,
> are the seven swords of vision
> that spoked the prophets' flaming tyre;
> their sistered stridencies ignite
> the spectrum of the poets' lyre
> whose unison becomes a white
> revolving disc of stainless fire,
> and sights the eye of that sole star
> that, in the heavy clods we are,
> the kindred seeds of fire can spy,
> or, in the cold shell of the rock,
> the red yolk of the phoenix-cock
> whose feathers in the meteors fly.

See also ABSTRACT.

abusio *See* CATACHRESIS.

academic Four basic meanings may be distinguished: (a) that which belongs to the school of thought of Plato – from academy (*q.v.*); (b) a person or work that is scholarly and erudite; (c) concerned with the rules of composition rather than with the result of the act of creation; (d) of little importance or note. In the second and fourth senses the word is often used pejoratively.

academic drama Plays, considerably under the influence of Roman comedy, which were performed in schools and colleges in England early in the 16th c. The works of Terence and Plautus were particularly popular. Eventually, original plays, based on Classical models, appeared in English. An early – possibly *the* earliest – example is *Ralph Roister Doister* (written *c.* 1553, printed *c.* 1567), a knockabout comedy by Nicholas Udall, written for the boys of Westminster School. It follows Roman prototypes in divisions and unities (*q.v.*), in motivation and plot (*q.v.*). *See also* COMEDY; JESUIT DRAMA; SCHOOL DRAMA; SENECAN TRAGEDY.

academy The word is derived from the name of a park near Athens where Plato's Academy was situated from 387 BC to AD 529. The name was adopted in Italy by scholars during the Renaissance and now usually applies to some sort of institution devoted to learning, even if it be only the trade of war – as at the Royal Military Academy. There are a large number of academies scattered round the world. Most of them are concerned with research and culture and have limited memberships. Some are very exclusive. Probably the most famous is the Académie Française, founded by Richelieu in 1635. This is primarily a literary academy, one of whose main tasks is the compilation and revision of a dictionary of the French language. The British Academy was founded in 1902 for the promotion of moral and political sciences. The exclusiveness of many academies may account for the pejorative use of the word 'academic' (*q.v.*). The Académie Française, for instance, has been described as the 'hôtel des invalides de la littérature'. The pejorative use may equally derive from the anti-intellectualism of modern literary culture. *See also* ACADEMIC.

acatalectic (Gk 'not lacking a syllable in the last foot') It denotes, therefore, a metrical line which is complete. If a line lacks one or more unaccented syllables, it is truncated (*see* CATALEXIS). If a line contains an extra syllable it is then hypercatalectic (or hypermetrical, redundant or extrametrical). In the following stanza from William Blake's *Art and Artists* the first line is catalectic, the third acatalectic, and the fourth hypercatalectic:

> When Sr Joshua Reynolds died
> All Nature was degraded;
> The King dropp'd a tear into the Queen's Ear,
> And all his Pictures Faded.

See BRACHYCATALECTIC; CATALEXIS; DICATALECTIC.

accent The emphasis or stress (*q.v.*) placed on a syllable, especially in a line of verse. It is a matter of vocal emphasis. Where the accent comes will depend on how the reader wishes to render the sense. In the following lines the metrical stress is fairly clear, but the accents can be varied:

> All human things are subject to decay,
> And, when Fate summons, Monarchs must obey.

The variables are 'all', 'human', 'and', 'when', 'Fate', 'Monarchs', 'must', and 'obey'. At least half a dozen emphases are possible. Obviously, where the metrical scheme is very strict, then accent variation is limited. In blank verse (*q.v.*), however, many subtleties of accent are possible. *See* BEAT; HOVERING ACCENT; ICTUS; LEVEL STRESS; LOGICAL STRESS; QUANTITY.

accentual verse *See* METER.

accidence That branch of grammar which deals with 'accidents'; that is, the inflexions or the variable endings of words.

acclamatio *See* EPIPHONEMA.

acephalous (Gk 'headless') A metrical line whose first syllable, according to strict meter, is wanting. An iambic line with a monosyllabic first foot would be acephalous.

acervatio *See* POLYSYNDETON.

acmeism The Acmeists were a group or school of Russian poets, who, early in the 20th c., began a new anti-symbolist movement. Much of their work and their theories were published in the magazine *Apollon*. They were in favour of an Apollonian (*q.v.*) lucidity and definiteness and strove for texture (*q.v.*) in their verse. The movement did not last very long (it seems to have faded out by *c.* 1920) but it included some distinguished poets: principally, Nikolai Gumilyev (1886–1921), Osip Mandelstam (1891–1940?) and Anna Akhmatova (1889–1967), who is still highly regarded as a writer of lyric (*q.v.*) poems.

acroama (Gk 'something heard') Two meanings may be distinguished: (a) a dramatic entertainment or a recital, during a meal or on some such occasion; (b) a lecture to the initiated; for instance, a discourse given by a *guru*, professor or comparable Gamaliel.

acronym (Gk *acron* 'tip, end' + *onyma* 'name') A word formed from or based on the initial letters or syllables of other words. For example: ENSA (*E*ntertainments *N*ational *S*ervices *A*ssociation); NAAFI (*N*avy, *A*rmy and *A*ir*f*orce *I*nstitute); NATO (*N*orth *A*tlantic *T*reaty *O*rganization); NIMBY (*N*ot *I*n *M*y *B*ack *Y*ard); OPEC (*O*rganization of *P*etroleum *E*xporting *C*ountries; PEN (*P*oets, Playwrights, *E*ditors, Essayists and *N*ovelists); RADAR (*Ra*dio *D*etection *a*nd *R*anging).

acrostic Apart from puzzles in newspapers and magazines the commonest kind of acrostic is a poem in which the initial letters of each line make a word or words when read downwards. An acrostic might also use the middle (mesostich) or final (telestich) letter of each line. In prose the first letter of each paragraph or sentence might make up a word.

The acrostic may have been first used as a kind of mnemonic device to aid oral transmission. In the Old Testament most of the acrostics belong to the alphabetical or abecedarian kind. The forming of words from the initials of words is also a form of acrostic. Chaucer used a simple acrostic device in *ABC*, a twenty-four stanza poem in which the first letter of the first word in each stanza is the appropriate letter of the alphabet, from A to Z. Some dramatists have put the titles of their plays in acrostic verses which give the argument (*q.v.*) of the play. A well-known instance is Ben Jonson's *Argument* prefacing *The Alchemist*.

A famous example of an 'all round' acrostic, which is a form of palindrome (*q.v.*), is the Cirencester word square, Roman in origin:

ROTAS
OPERA
TENET
AREPO
SATOR

There has been much learned debate as to the possible meanings of this acrostic, which is known in a second form from an Egyptian papyrus of the late 4th or early 5th c. AD, thus:

SATOR
AREPO
TENET
OPERA
ROTAS

Various permutations suggest that one meaning may be: 'the sower Arepo holds the wheels carefully'.

This, like many acrostics, may have magic and/or religious significance. In Ethiopia in the 6th c. the five words, corrupted to Sador, Alador, Danet, Adera and Rodas, were used as the names of the five nails of Christ's Cross.

The word square is known to have been used in France as a form of charm (*q.v.*); a citizen of Lyon was cured of madness by eating three crusts of bread (each inscribed with the square) while making five recitations of the Pater Noster in remembrance of the five wounds of Christ and the five nails. In the 19th c. in South America it was used as a charm against snake bites and also to aid childbirth. *See also* LOGOGRIPH.

acryology *See* EUPHEMISM.

act A major division in a play. Each act may have one or more scenes. Greek plays were performed as continuous wholes, with interpolated comment from the Chorus (*q.v.*). Horace appears to have been the first to insist on a five-act structure. At some stage during the Renaissance the use of five acts became standard practice among French dramatists. Plays by Shakespeare and his contemporaries have natural breaks which can be taken as act divisions. In shaping their plays Elizabethan dramatists were influenced by Roman models (e.g. Seneca). The act divisions were marked as such by later editors. Ben Jonson was largely responsible for introducing the five-act structure in England. From the second half of the 17th c. the vast majority of plays were in five acts. The introduction of the proscenium and the curtain (unknown in the Elizabethan theatre) during the Restoration period (*q.v.*) had some influence on structure. In the Restoration period the curtain rose at the end of the prologue (which was spoken on the forestage) and stayed out of sight until the end of the play. By *c.* 1750 the curtain was dropped regularly to mark the end of an act. Ibsen (1828–1906) cut the number of acts to four. Dramatists like Chekhov (1860–1904) and Pirandello (1867–1936) also used four. Since early in the 20th c. most playwrights have preferred the three-act form, though the two-act play is not uncommon. In modern productions, especially in the cases of five- and four-act plays, there is only one curtain-drop and interval. Thus the first three or two acts are run together without a break. Many modern plays are written and presented in a sequence of scenes. Pirandello, Shaw, Brecht and Beckett, among others, have been responsible for an increased flexibility. T. W. Baldwin gives an illuminating account of Elizabethan methods in *Shakespeare's Five-Act Structure* (1947). *See* SCENE.

actant *See* NARRATOLOGY.

action Two basic meanings may be distinguished: (a) the main story (in cinematic jargon 'story-line') of a play, novel, short story, narrative poem, etc.; (b) the main series of events that together constitute the plot (*q.v.*). Action is fundamental to drama, and implies motion forward. Much action is achieved without physical movement on stage, or even without anything being said. An essential part of action is the unfolding of character and plot. *See* CONFLICT.

activism At the end of the First World War activism (in German *Aktivismus*) denoted active political commitment or engagement among and by intellectuals. Historically it is closely associated with expressionism (*q.v.*), and as far as drama was concerned it required realistic solutions to social problems. It is particularly associated with Kurt Hiller, who organized the Neuer Club for expressionist poets, and with the magazine *Aktion*, founded in 1911 by Franz Pfempfert. Now, activism is predominantly a political term.

actual reader *See* IMPLIED READER/ACTUAL READER.

adage A maxim or proverb (*qq.v.*). A well-known collection of adages was made by Erasmus and published as *Adagia* (1500).

adaptation Broadly speaking, the re-casting of a work in one medium to fit another, such as the re-casting of novels and plays as film or television scripts. For example, *Stephen Hero*, *A Passage to India*, *The Prime of Miss Jean Brodie* and *Les Liaisons dangereuses* as stage plays; *The Forsyte Saga*, *Daniel Deronda*, *War and Peace*, *Brideshead Revisited* and *The Jewel in the Crown* as television dramas. Sometimes a cycle or sequence is adapted: for instance, the dramatization (*q.v.*) of some of the *Canterbury Tales* as a musical comedy (1967). Short stories and poems are often equally suitable.

As an extension there are works like the TV version of *Peyton Place* and *Colditz* of which episodes continued to be presented long after the original stories had been used up.

addendum (L 'something to be added') An addition or an appendix to a book (pl. addenda).

Addisonian In the manner or style of Joseph Addison (1672–1719): equable, relaxed, good-humoured and urbane. Some would also add complacent. Addison is chiefly famous for his contributions to the periodical essay (*q.v.*).

address A statement or speech of some formality, which may be delivered or written. It also denotes the kind of audience or reader an author intends. He may be self-communing or addressing a single person or a group of people.

adjunctio *See* ZEUGMA.

adnominatio *See* POLYPTOTON.

adonic A line consisting of a dactyl (*q.v.*) followed by a spondee (*q.v.*). The fourth and last line of the Sapphic (*q.v.*) is usually adonic.

adonius *See* ADONIC.

adversaria (L *adversaria scripta* 'things written on the side') Miscellaneous collections of notes. The kind of things that most writers accumulate in a notebook, day book, journal or diary. *See* ANNOTATION; DIARY AND JOURNAL.

advertiser A journal or newspaper which publishes advertisements, like *The Advertiser's Weekly*.

adynaton (Gk 'not possible') A form of hyperbole (*q.v.*) which involves the magnification of an event by reference to the impossible. There are famous examples in Marvell's poem *To His Coy Mistress* and his *The Definition of Love*, which begins:

My Love is of a birth as rare
As 'tis for object strange and high:
It was begotten by despair
Upon Impossibility.

ae freislighe In Irish prosody (*q.v.*), a quatrain (*q.v.*) of seven-syllable lines, rhyming abab. The poem should end with the same first syllable, line or word with which it begins.

Aeolic The name derives from the Greek dialect which Alcaeus and Sappho used for their poetry. Thus it applies to particular meters in which dactyls and trochees (*qq.v.*) are brought close together so that the choriambs (*q.v.*) are very noticeable. *See* ALCAICS; SAPPHIC ODE.

Aeschylean In the manner or style of Aeschylus (525–456 BC), the first of the great Greek tragedians. Thus – sombre, magnificent, lofty, possessing grandeur.

aesopic language A name invented by Mikhail Saltykov (1826–89) to describe the language of dissident political writing. It was a form of literary disguise to pass the censorship. So named after Aesop (6th c. BC), the Greek fabulist who is sometimes thought of as making political points. Much aesopic writing is circumlocutory or cast in fable (*q.v.*) form. The reader has to read between the lines and interpret the hints and allusions. Saltykov himself wrote a large number of satirical sketches couched in such language. *See* DISSIDENT WRITERS.

aesthetic distance The term implies a psychological relationship between the reader (or viewer) and a work of art. It describes the attitude or perspective of a person in relation to a work, irrespective of whether it is interesting to that person. A reader may dislike a poem, for instance, for subjective reasons but this should not vitiate his objective reaction. The reader or critic has at once to be involved with – and detached from – what he is concentrating on. The work is 'distanced' so that it may be appreciated aesthetically and not confused with reality. The writer bears the responsibility for gauging and determining the distance (not in any spatial sense) at which his work should be viewed. If he bullies the reader into attending, then his reader may be repelled. Conversely, if he undertakes too much, then his reader may not get the point.

The concept of aesthetic distance has become established in the 20th c., though it appears to be inherent in 19th c. aesthetics; and, as long ago as 1790, Kant, in his *Critique of Judgement*, had already described the distinterestedness of our contemplation of works of art. In 1912, E. Bullough published an essay entitled *Psychical Distance as a Factor in Art and an Aesthetic Principle* (*British Journal of Psychology*, V) in which he defined 'psychical distance'. This is an important essay in the history of the concept. Since Bullough a number of critics have addressed themselves to the matter, including David Daiches in *A Study of Literature for Readers and Critics* (1948). More recently, Hans Robert Jauss, in developing his theory of the 'horizon of expectations' (*q.v.*), has given the term a very different additional significance. In his theory literary value is measured according to 'aesthetic distance', the degree to which a work departs from the 'horizon of expectations' of its first readers. *See* ALIENATION EFFECT; SUBJECTIVITY AND OBJECTIVITY; VIEWPOINT.

aestheticism A complex term 'pregnant' with many connotations. The actual word derives from Greek *aisthēta* 'things perceptible by the senses'; and the Greek *aisthētēs* denotes 'one who perceives'. In 1750 A. T. Baumgarten published *Aesthetica*, a treatise (*q.v.*) on the criticism of taste considered as a philosophical theory. Gradually, the term *aesthetic* has come to signify something which pertains to the criticism of the beautiful or to the theory of taste. An *aesthete* is one who pursues and is devoted to the 'beautiful' in art, music and literature. And *aestheticism* is the term given to a movement, a cult, a mode of sensibility (a way of looking at and feeling about things) in the 19th c. Fundamentally, it entailed the point of view that art is self-sufficient and need serve no other purpose than its own ends. In other words, art is an end in itself and need not be (or should not be) didactic, politically committed, propagandist, moral – or anything else but itself; and it should not be judged by any non-aesthetic criteria (e.g. whether or not it is useful).

The origins of this movement or cult are to be found in the work of several German writers of the Romantic period (*q.v.*) – notably Kant, Schelling, Goethe and Schiller. They all agreed that art must be autonomous (that is, it should have the right of self-government) and from this it followed that the artist should not be beholden to anyone. From this, in turn, it followed that the artist was someone special, apart from others. Tennyson expressed the post-Romantic idea that the poet was superior to ordinary mortals:

Vex not thou the poet's mind
  With thy shallow wit:
Vex not thou the poet's mind;
  For thou canst not fathom it.

This attitude helps to explain why, later in the 19th c., the artist developed the image of being a Bohemian and a non-conformist. This was the long-term result of Romantic subjectivism and self-culture; of the cult of the individual ego and sensibility.

The influence of the Germans referred to above was very considerable, especially that of Goethe. Their ideas were diffused in Britain by Coleridge and Carlyle; in America by Edgar Allan Poe and Ralph Waldo Emerson; and in France by what we would now call 'culture vultures' in the shape of Madame de Staël, Victor Cousin and Théophile Jouffroy.

Approximately concurrent with the new aesthetic (or 'science of beauty') we have the doctrine of 'art for art's sake' (*q.v.*), and the movement known as Parnassianism.

Gautier's Preface to *Mademoiselle de Maupin* (1835) is often quoted as one of the earliest examples of a new aesthetic point of view. Thereafter, Poe and Baudelaire between them (and later Flaubert and Mallarmé) virtually launched aestheticism as a cult and their combined influence on the *symboliste* poets in France was very great (*see* SYMBOL AND SYMBOLISM). In England aestheticism was the result of French influence and native ideas.

The major implication of the new aesthetic standpoint was that art had no reference to life, and therefore had nothing to do with morality (Poe, for instance, had condemned the 'heresy of didacticism'), and in the later Victorian period we find Swinburne (who was much influenced by Baudelaire) proclaiming the art for art's sake theory. Walter Pater advocated the view that life itself should be treated in the spirit of art. His collection of essays *The Renaissance* (1873) had a deep influence on the poets of the 1890s, especially Wilde, Dowson, Lionel Johnson and Symons.

Art, not life. Art instead of life, or as an alternative to life. Life as art, or as a work of art. The outstanding example of the aesthete's withdrawal from life is J-K. Huysman's *A rebours* (1884), in which the hero, Des Esseintes, seeks to create an entirely artificial life. The work 'illustrates' Wilde's flippant dictum that 'The first duty in life is to be as artificial as possible. What the second duty is no one has yet discovered'. Much of the attitude was neatly summarized by Villiers de l'Isle-Adam when he has his hero in *Axel* (1890) say: 'Live? Our servants will do that for us'.

In part aestheticism seems to have been a kind of reaction against the materialism and capitalism of the later Victorian period; and also against the Philistines who embodied what has been described as the 'bourgeois ethos'. Certainly one can detect a widespread disenchantment in the literature of the 'aesthetes', and especially in their poetry. By contrast it is noticeable that many novelists of the period (e.g. Dickens, Zola, Gissing and Samuel Butler) *were* dealing with reality in a forthright and unsqueamish fashion.

Aestheticism in poetry (as in art) is closely identified with the Pre-Raphaelites (*q.v.*) and shows a tendency to withdrawal or aversion. Many poets of the period strove for beautiful musical effects in their verses rather than for sense. They aspired to sensuousness and to what has become known as 'pure poetry' (*q.v.*). They also revived archaistic modes and archaic language (in this respect they were heavily influenced by Spenser and Keats) and revived an extensive use of Classical mythology as a framework for expressing ideas. Medievalism (*q.v.*) and the interest in chivalry and romance was an important part of the aesthetic cult. Tennyson, William Morris, D. G. Rossetti and Swinburne are the major writers in these respects. Tennyson's *The Lotos-Eaters* embodies many of the feelings inherent in the aesthetic ideal. Ah, why *should* life all labour be?

Among English artists Burne-Jones, D. G. Rossetti, William Morris, James McNeill Whistler and Aubrey Beardsley were the main exponents of aestheticism. It should also be noted that George Moore (an enthusiast for pure poetry), Arthur Symons and Edmund Gosse did much to popularize the works of French poets and painters in England in the 1890s.

Aestheticism is particularly associated with that decade; with Aubrey Beardsley, with Oscar Wilde (long the 'folk hero' or 'cult hero' of the aesthetic movement), with *The Yellow Book* (*q.v.*), with dandyism, with affectation, and with Max Beerbohm. But by the 1890s it was becoming less intense. As Beerbohm drolly observed: 'Beauty had existed long before 1880. It was Oscar Wilde who managed her début'. With this period, too, are associated ideas about the Bohemian and immoral life of the artist. The cult of Bohemianism (itself a kind of rejection of a commercially orientated society) had been influenced earlier in the century by Henri Murger's *Scènes de la vie de Bohème* (1851).

At its best aestheticism was a revitalizing influence in an age of ugliness, brutality, dreadful inequality and oppression, complacency, hypocrisy and Philistinism (*q.v.*). It was a genuine search for beauty and a realization that the beautiful has an independent value. At its worst it deteriorated into posturing affectation and mannerism, to vapid idealism and indeed to a kind of silliness which is not wholly dead. Nothing could be more 'Bohemian' than the post-war cultural revolution of the so-called 'freaked out' society. 'Pop' is another kind of aestheticism, another kind of reaction against a corrupt and commercial world. *See* DECADENCE; PARNASSIANS.

affectation The adoption of a mode or style of writing unsuited to the matter, form or occasion. In the 18th c. writers were particularly sensitive to inappropriateness of this kind. *See* DECORUM.

affective fallacy A term defined by Wimsatt and Beardsley (*The Verbal Icon*, 1954) as 'a confusion between the poem and its results (what it is and what it does)'. It is said to be a critical error of evaluating a work of art in terms of 'its results in the mind of the audience'. It would be a mistake, therefore, for a reader to conclude that Spenser's *Faerie Queene* was a bad poem because it inspired in him a repugnance to Protestantism. The principles involved in this fallacy can also be applied to prose works. *See* INTENTIONAL FALLACY.

affective stylistics *See* READER-RESPONSE THEORY.

afflatus (L 'blown upon') As far as poetry is concerned, the equivalent of inspiration (*q.v.*). The usual phrase is 'divine afflatus'. The implications are that a writer's inspiration is vouchsafed to him by some supranormal or supernatural power, like a Muse (*q.v.*) or the gods. *See* DONNEE; FANCY AND IMAGINATION; INVENTION; LIGNE DONNEE.

after-piece A short play, often a one-act farce or comedy (*qq.v.*), presented after the main play in a programme, and regardless of whether that play was a tragedy or comedy or any other form of drama. They became popular in the 18th c. as a result of the introduction of the half-price system – an entrance fee for late-comers. Theatrical managers had to pad out a programme for these patrons and felt justified in charging them. Originally, they had been allowed in for nothing. The half-price arrangement prevailed in London and elsewhere until at least the 1870s. In the 18th c. not a few playwrights wrote notable after-pieces. David Garrick (1717–79), Samuel Foote (1720–77) and Arthur Murphy (1727–1805) excelled at them. Murphy wrote some very good two-act after-pieces, including *The Apprentice* (1756), *The Upholsterer* (1758), *The Citizen* (1761) and *What We Must All Come To* (1764). *See* CURTAIN RAISER.

agent, literary The first agents began to appear towards the end of the 19th c. and A. P. Watt (1834–1914) is often taken to have been the first. Among his clients were Thomas Hardy, Rudyard Kipling and Rider Haggard. Other notable agents were J. B. Pinker (1863–1922), Curtis Brown (1866–1945) and John Farquharson. For many years there was a good deal of opposition to agents, and authors were by no means in agreement as to their desirability and usefulness. Nowadays it is rare to find an author who has not got one. As in any other line of business (including publishing) there are some who are unscrupulous or plain crooked. An agent's job is many-sided and includes the placing of manuscripts with publishers/ editors/theatrical managements etc., negotiating contracts and rights, dealing with legal matters and advising in general. It has been said that a successful relationship between author and agent is comparable to a successful marriage.

age of reason A term applied to the Restoration and Augustan periods (*qq.v.*). So named because it was a period when the workings of reason were revered. Form, balance, restraint, harmony, decorum (*q.v.*) and order are some of the main characteristics of the literature of the period. *See* NEOCLASSICISM.

agitprop drama The term 'agitprop' is a conflation of the words 'agitation' and 'propaganda' (*q.v.*) and derives from the name of the Department of Agitation and Propaganda created in September 1920 as part of the Central Committee Secretariat of the Soviet Communist Party. The Bolsheviks wished to use art as a weapon in the revolutionary struggle, and the agitprop department mobilized culture across the vast and largely illiterate country to stimulate people's understanding of and involvement in such important matters as health, sanitation, literacy or the military situation. Cine-trains and boats showed short agitational films and colourful posters carried stirring slogans (*q.v.*). In drama, the Blue Blouse movement, named after the industrial clothes a worker would wear, drew on these visual forms, on traditional folk art and on *avant-garde* (*q.v.*) techniques to develop its own accessible and popular forms of agitprop.

Blue Blouse troupes usually performed away from conventional theatres, in pubs and clubs, on wagons or platforms. They used colloquial language and music in cartoon-style Living Newspapers (*q.v.*) and revues (*q.v.*) that featured political analysis of a single topic presented in a montage of effects. This new form was physical, flexible and mobile. It relied on striking but simple costume, minimal props and little or no scenery. The troupes worked collectively and attempted to create a new style of performance to match their new form of non-literary, non-naturalistic drama. They were predominantly amateur and reached the height of their influence in the mid-1920s, but were eclipsed by the rise of official, dogmatic socialist realism (*q.v.*).

In the wake of the Russian Revolution, agitprop drama spread to Europe, Scandinavia and America through visits abroad of Soviet companies and by way of the international Communist movement, particularly during its extreme sectarian period at the end of the 1920s and the beginning of the 1930s. Agitprop was seen as a proletarian antidote to bourgeois drama and in each country it evolved as a mix of the imported model and indigenous traditions. Outside the Soviet Union, Germany had the most powerful agitprop movement until Nazism suppressed it. The German troupes were noted for their cabaret forms and mass or choral speaking and were associated with, among others, Erwin Piscator (1893–1966) and Bertolt Brecht (1898–1956), whose film *Kühle Wampe* shows an agitprop group in performance. Agitprop influenced the development of epic theatre and the *Lehrstück* (*qq.v.*) or didactic play and in the long run affected techniques of dramatic presentation. Britain and the USA had numerically smaller agitprop groups, but each played a vital role in animating drama when the Communist Left sought to build alliances in the Popular Front period up to the Second World War.

The American Workers' Theatre was absorbed by the government-financed Federal Theatre Project (*q.v.*) in 1935 and had direct links with the Group Theatre and the plays of Clifford Odets (1906–63). The British Workers' Theatre spawned the influential amateur Unity Theatre (*q.v.*) movement, and, after the war, the professional Theatre Workshop (*q.v.*) of Joan Littlewood (1914–) and Ewan MacColl (1915–89).

Hard-hitting agitprop linked to workers' campaigns resurfaced in Europe and America at another period of international and political turmoil in the late 1960s and 1970s, by which time the term agitprop was being applied loosely to any drama that was seen to place ideology above aesthetics. A new movement came and went as it had forty years previously but again was marked by innovation, energy and far left views. *See also* DOCUMENTARY THEATRE.

agnominatio *See* PUN.

agon (Gk 'contest') In Greek drama a verbal conflict between two characters, each one aided by half the Chorus (*q.v.*). *See* ANTAGONIST; PROTAGONIST.

agrarian movement A 'back to grass roots', 'back to the soil', and 'back to nature' cult that had some vogue in Germany and America early in the 20th c. Sherwood Anderson was one of its examplars. *See* NEW CRITICISM.

aiodos An itinerant Greek singer of songs and poems. *See also* GUSLAR; MINNESINGER; SCOP; SKALD; TROUBADOUR; TROUVERE.

air It usually denotes a song (*q.v.*), tune or melody, or all three. Frequently used in the late 16th c. and during the 17th when many collections were published. For example: John Dowland's *Second Book of Airs* (1600); Robert Jones's *First Book of Songs and Airs* (1600). Cowper suggests the general sense when, in *A Winter Walk at Noon*, he writes:

> There is in souls a sympathy with sounds;
> And, as the mind is pitch'd the ear is pleased
> With melting airs, or martial, brisk, or grave:
> Some chord in unison with what we hear,
> Is touch'd within us, and the heart replies.

See also MOTET.

akhyana An Indian beast-fable or folk tale (*qq.v.*) in prose. The central part, or that which deals with the climax, is in verse.

Alazon The braggart in Greek comedy. Other examples of the type in drama are the *miles gloriosus* of Plautus, Molière's Tartuffe and, conceivably, Falstaff. *See also* BRAGGADOCIO; STOCK CHARACTER.

alba Spanish for aubade (*q.v.*).

album (L *albus* 'white') For the Roman an *album* was a white tablet or register on which the praetor's edicts and other such public notices were recorded. The modern album dates from the 16th c. and comprises a blank book for the insertion of photographs, autographs, newspaper cuttings, excerpts, etc. In short, it is a kind of scrap book. One of the earliest examples is the *Album Amicorum*.

Alcaics A four-lined stanza or strophe (*qq.v.*) named after the Greek poet Alkaios (Alcaeus, a native of Lesbos, late 7th to early 6th c. BC). The arrangement, predominantly dactylic, is:

> ⏑̄ / ⏑ / ⏑̄ / ⏑ ⏑ / ⏑ ⏑
> ⏑̄ / ⏑ / ⏑̄ / ⏑ ⏑ / ⏑ ⏑
> ⏑̄ / ⏑ / ⏑̄ / ⏑ / ⏑̄
> / ⏑ ⏑ / ⏑ ⏑ / ⏑ / ⏑̄

The mark indicating an unstressed syllable placed above a stress mark denotes a possible variation.

The scheme was often used between the 16th and 18th c. by Italian poets, but has seldom been popular in England. However, Swinburne, Clough, Tennyson and R. L. Stevenson experimented with alcaics. A well-known example is Tennyson's sixteen-line poem on Milton which begins:

Ó míghtў- | moúthĕd ĭn | véntŏr ŏf | hármŏniĕs,
Ó skílled to síng ŏf | Tíme ŏr Ĕ | térnĭtў,
Gód-gíftĕd | órgăn- | vóice ŏf | Énglănd,
Míltŏn, ă | náme tŏ rĕ | sóund fŏr | ágĕs.

Less well known is Stevenson's *Alcaics: to H. F. B.*, whose first stanza runs:

Bráve láds | ĭn óldĕn | músĭcăl | céntŭriĕs
Sáng, níght | bў níght, ă | dórăblĕ | chórŭsĕs,
Sát láte bў | álehŏuse | dóors ĭn | Áprĭl
Cháuntĭng ĭn | jóy ăs thĕ | móon wăs | rísĭng.

See AEOLIC; DACTYL; SAPPHIC ODE.

Alcmanic verse A metrical form used by and named after Alcman (7th c. BC). It consists of a dactylic tetrameter (*q.v.*) line. It was used in Greek dramatic poetry, and is occasionally found in Latin dramatic poetry. The alcmanic strophe (*q.v.*) combines a dactylic hexameter (*q.v.*) with an archilochian (*q.v.*) verse. *See* DACTYL.

aleatory writing (L *aleatorius*, from *aleator*, *alea* 'dice') 'Aleatory' means depending on the throw of a die, and it here refers to writing (as well as to the composition of music, sculpture and painting) achieved by some random means, by leaving things to chance or accident. No doubt many creative artists have depended on the element of luck and chance, the totally unexpected; and the history of inspiration (*q.v.*) provides many instances of fortuitous experience which have helped in the creative act. In fact, one might go so far as to say that it may be a fundamental part of the process of inspiration and invention.

Those who practise aleatoric techniques are somewhat more deliberate. They do not leave things to chance; they create the opportunities of chance. There is a certain 'method' in their 'madness', as it were. For example, a writer may write down a large number of words on different pieces of paper, throw the pieces of paper into the air, see how (like dice) they fall – and then join the words together according to their random disposition. Or, he might shuffle them like cards and then record the sequence that ensues. There are a number of ways of setting about it.

William Burroughs, for example, is well known for his 'cut-up' technique in which he snips up pages and allows the random fall of the words and phrases to guide him. B. S. Johnson composed *The Unfortunates* – a 'novel in a box'. It consists of a box of separately bound chapters which the reader is invited to rearrange as he or she pleases and to read in any order. Tom Phillips's *Humument* is the result of taking a Victorian novel called *A Human Document* by W. H. Mallock and inking out words and letters to find a book within a book. Ian Hamilton Finlay has also made various experiments of an aleatory kind in the creation of concrete poetry (*q.v.*). Mallarmé's *Coup de dés* is a good example of a poem which at any rate *appears* to be the result of aleatoric techniques. It is a long poem about a shipwreck in which phrases are repeated in lines stretched right across the page; the original version was printed on very large pages. Dream sequences have also been used as aleatoric guides. De Chirico's novel *Hebdomeros* comprises a series of linked dream sequences. Many other experimental efforts might be cited. In music and painting, too, we find aleatoric methods. The composer John Cage has been successful with them; Jackson Pollock tried them with many paintings. *See also* ALTERNATIVE LITERATURE; ANTI-NOVEL; POST-MODERNISM.

alejandrino A Spanish verse form of two hemistichs (*q.v.*) with seven syllables each. It derives from Alexander the Great, whose legendary deeds were celebrated in this meter in the *Libro de Alejandre* (*c.* 1240), a *mester de clerecía* (*q.v.*) poem.

aleluyas (Heb *hallelu* 'praise ye' + *Jāh* 'Jehovah') Thus *hallelujah*, *alleluiah*. A Spanish term for verses printed below wood-block prints or other illustrations on broadsheets or broadsides (*q.v.*). At first they were basically religious; later they became secular. They were popular from the end of the 15th c. until some way into the 19th c. *See also* PLIEGO SUELTO.

Alexandrianism The term refers to the works, styles and critical principles of the Alexandrian (Greek) writers who flourished between *c.* 325–30 BC. Some of the main forms they used were: elegy, epigram, epyllion, lyric (*qq.v.*). They also wrote drama. Much of their work was marked by ornateness and obscurity (*q.v.*).

alexandrine In French prosody a line of twelve syllables and known as *tétramètre* (*q.v.*). It has been the standard meter of French poetry since the 16th c., especially in dramatic and narrative forms. The equivalent in English verse is the iambic hexameter (*q.v.*). The earliest alexandrines occur in *Le Pèlerinage de Charlemagne à Jérusalem*, an early 12th c. *chanson de gestes* (*q.v.*), but the term probably takes its name from a later poem – the *Roman d'Alexandre* (towards the end of the 12th c.). The meter was used by Ronsard and members of the Pléiade (*q.v.*) and was perfected by the great 17th c. French dramatists. These two lines are from Racine's *Andromaque* (I, ii, 173–4):

> La Grèce en ma faveur est trop inquiétée:
> De soins plus importants je l'ai crue agitée.

It has never been a popular meter in English verse, largely because it is rather unwieldy, just a little too long; though Spenser used it to good effect for the last line of his Spenserian stanza (*q.v.*) in *The Faerie Queene*. Other English poets to use it fairly successfully were Drayton in *Polyolbion*, Browning in *Fifine at the Fair*, and Bridges in *The Testament of Beauty*. A classic example of its use occurs in Pope's *Essay on Criticism*:

> A needless Alexandrine ends the song,
> Thát, líke | ă wóund|ĕd snáke, | drágs ĭts | slów léngth ălóng.

See TRIMETRE.

alienation effect Often abbreviated to A-effect. An important element in Brecht's theory of drama; in German, *Verfremdungseffekt*. Brecht's view was that both audience and actors should preserve a state of critical detachment from the play and its presentation in performance. He required the audience to be reminded from time to time that they were only watching a play, a representation of life, and therefore they should control their identification with the characters and action. Likewise the actors should keep a kind of distance from the parts they are interpreting; they should have *an attitude towards* the character rather than try to efface themselves within it. *See also* COMMITMENT; CONVENTION; EPIC THEATRE; ESTRANGEMENT; ILLUSION; SOCIALIST REALISM.

aljamiado A Spanish composition written in Arabic characters.

allegory The term derives from Greek *allēgoria* 'speaking otherwise'. As a rule, an allegory is a story in verse or prose with a double meaning: a primary or surface meaning; and a secondary or under-the-surface meaning. It is a story, therefore, that can be read, understood and interpreted at two levels (and in some cases at three or four levels). It is thus closely related to the fable and the parable (*qq.v.*). The form may be literary or pictorial (or both, as in emblem-books, *q.v.*). An allegory has no determinate length.

To distinguish more clearly we can take the old Arab fable of the frog and the scorpion, who met one day on the bank of the River Nile, which they both wanted to cross. The frog offered to ferry the scorpion over on his back provided the scorpion promised not to sting him. The scorpion agreed so long as the frog would promise not to drown him. The mutual promises exchanged, they crossed the river. On the far bank the scorpion stung the frog mortally.

'Why did you do that?' croaked the frog, as it lay dying.

'Why?' replied the scorpion. 'We're both Arabs, aren't we?'

If we substitute for the frog a 'Mr Goodwill' or a 'Mr Prudence', and for the scorpion 'Mr Treachery' or 'Mr Two-Face' and make the river any river and substitute for 'We're both Arabs . . .' 'We're both men . . .' we can turn the fable into an allegory. On the other hand, if we turn the frog into a father and the scorpion into a son (boatman and passenger) and we have the son say 'We're both sons of God, aren't we?', then we have a parable (if rather a cynical one) about the wickedness of human nature and the sin of parricide.

The best known allegory in the English language (if not in the world) is Bunyan's *Pilgrim's Progress* (1678). This is an allegory of Christian Salvation. Christian, the hero, represents Everyman. He flees the terrible City of Destruction and sets off on his pilgrimage. In the course of it he passes through the Slough of Despond, the Interpreter's House, the House Beautiful, the Valley of Humiliation, the Valley of the Shadow of Death, Vanity Fair, Doubting Castle, the Delectable Mountains, and the country of Beulah, and finally arrives at the Celestial City. On the way he meets various characters, including Mr Worldly Wiseman, Faithful, Hopeful, Giant Despair, the fiend Apollyon, and many others. In the second part of the book Christian's wife and children make their pilgrimage accompanied by Mercy. They are helped and escorted by Great-heart who destroys Giant Despair and other monsters. Eventually they, too, arrive at the Celestial City.

The whole work is a simplified representation or similitude (*q.v.*) of the average man's journey through the trials and tribulations of life on his way to Heaven. The figures and places, therefore, have an arbitrary existence invented by the author; and this distinguishes them from symbols (*q.v.*) which have a real existence.

The origins of allegory are very ancient, and it appears to be a mode of expression (a way of feeling and thinking about things and seeing them) so natural to the human mind that it is universal. Its fundamental origins are religious. Much myth (*q.v.*), for example, is a form of allegory and is an attempt to explain universal facts and forces. The myth of Orpheus and Eurydice, for instance, is a notable example of the allegory of redemption and salvation. In fact, most Classical myth is allegorical.

Early examples of the use of allegory in literature are to be found in Plato's *Timaeus*, *Phaedrus* and *Symposium*. The myth of the Cave in Plato's *Republic* is a particularly well-known example.

In the lost sixth book of *De Republica* by Cicero (1st c. BC) there is a dream narrative (usually known as the *Somnium Scipionis*) in which Scipio Aemilianus makes a journey through the spheres and from this vantage point sees the shape and structure of the universe. Later (*c.* AD 400) Macrobius Theodosius compiled a commentary on the *Somnium Scipionis* which was to have a considerable influence in the Middle Ages.

The journey through the underworld and the journey through the spheres are recurrent themes in European literature.

Another example in Classical literature is *The Golden Ass* (2nd c. AD) of Apuleius. The fourth, fifth and sixth books deal with the allegory of Cupid and Psyche. A further key-work for an understanding of Graeco-Roman allegory is *About Gods and the World* (4th c. AD) by Sallustius. But perhaps the most influential of all is Prudentius's *Psychomachia* (4th c. AD), which elaborates the idea of the battle within, the conflict between personified vices and virtues for the possession of the soul. It is thus a kind of psychological allegory and establishes themes which were used again and again during the Middle Ages as we can readily verify by examination of sermon literature, homilies, theological handbooks, exempla and works of moral counsel and edification. Above all, we find the themes in the Morality Plays (*q.v.*) which in their turn had a deep influence on the development of comedy (*q.v.*) and especially comedy of humours (*q.v.*).

Allegory, largely typological, pervades both the Old and the New Testaments. The events in the Old Testament are 'types' or 'figures' of events in the New Testament. In *The Song of Solomon*, for instance, Solomon is a 'type' of Christ and the Queen of Sheba represents the Church: later explained by Matthew (12: 42). The Paschal Lamb was a 'type' of Christ.

Scriptural allegory was mostly based on a vision of the universe. There were two worlds: the spiritual and the physical. These corresponded because they had been made by God. The visible world was a revelation of the invisible, but the revelation could only be brought about by divine action. Thus, interpretation of this kind of allegory was theological. St Thomas Aquinas analysed this in some detail in his *Summa* (13th c.) in terms of fourfold allegory; thus having four levels of meaning (*q.v.*). This exegetical method can be applied, for instance, to the City of Jerusalem. On the literal level, it is the Holy City; allegorically, it stands for the Church militant; morally or as a trope, it signifies the just soul; and anagogically, it represents the Church triumphant. In his *Convivio* Dante elaborated this theory in terms of poetry.

Some notable instances of allegory in European literature are: Bernadus Sylvestris's *De Mundi Universitate* (12th c.); Alan of Lille's *Anticlaudianus* (12th c.); the *Roman de la Rose* (13th c.) by Guillaume de Lorris, and later continued by Jean de Meung; Dante's *Divina Commedia* (13th c.); Langland's *Piers Plowman* (14th c.); Tasso's *Gerusalemme Liberata* (1574); Spenser's *Faerie Queene* (1589, 1596); Bunyan's *The Life and Death of Mr Badman* (1680) and *The Holy War* (1682); Dryden's allegorical satires *Absalom and Achitophel* (1681), *Mac Flecknoe* (1684) and *The Hind and the Panther* (1687); Swift's *Tale of a Tub* (1704) and *Gulliver's Travels* (1726); William Blake's prophetic books (late 18th c.); Hawthorne's *The Marble Faun* (1860); Samuel Butler's *Erewhon* (1872) and *Erewhon Revisited* (1901); C. S. Lewis's *Pilgrim's Regress* (1933); Virginia Woolf's *Between the Acts* (1941); and George Orwell's *Animal Farm* (1945). More recent developments of allegory in the novel have been Robert Coover's *The Universal Baseball Association, Inc., J. Henry Waugh, Prop.* (1968), which uses baseball as a kind of metaphor to satirize religious attitudes in America; and Richard Adams's story of a group of rabbits in *Watership Down* (1972).

Allegorical drama, since the demise of the Morality Plays, has been rare. Two interesting modern examples are Karel Čapek's *The Insect Play* (1921) and Edward Albee's *Tiny Alice* (1964). *See* BEAST EPIC; MOCK-EPIC.

allegro A musical term which, when used as a literary term, means much the same thing: in a lively and brisk manner. The rhythm and movement of Milton's *L'Allegro*, from which these lines are taken, indicate the meaning:

> Haste thee nymph, and bring with thee
> Jest and youthful Jollity,
> Quips and cranks, and wanton wiles,
> Nods, and becks, and wreathèd smiles,
> Such as hang on Hebe's cheek,
> And love to live in dimple sleek;
> Sport that wrinkled Care derides,
> And Laughter holding both his sides.
> Come, and trip it as you go
> On the light fantastic toe.

alliteration (L 'repeating and playing upon the same letter') A figure of speech in which consonants, especially at the beginning of words, or stressed syllables, are repeated. It is a very old device indeed in English verse (older than rhyme) and is common in verse generally. It is used occasionally in prose. In OE poetry alliteration was a continual and essential part of the metrical scheme and until the late Middle Ages was often used thus. However, alliterative verse (*q.v.*) becomes increasingly rare after the end of the 15th c. and alliteration – like assonance, consonance and onomatopoeia (*qq.v.*) – tends more to be reserved for the achievement of the special effect.

There are many classic examples, like Coleridge's famous description of the sacred river Alph in *Kubla Khan*:

> Five miles meandering with a mazy motion

Many others less well known, like this from the beginning of Norman MacCaig's poem *Mutual Life*:

> A wild cat, fur-fire in a bracken bush,
> Twitches his club-tail, rounds his amber eyes
> At rockabye rabbits humped on the world. The air
> Crackles about him. His world is a rabbit's size.

And this, from the first stanza R. S. Thomas's *The Welsh Hill-Country*:

> Too far for you to see
> The fluke and the foot-rot and the fat maggot

Gnawing the skin from the small bones,
The sheep are grazing at Bwlch-y-Fedwen,
Arranged romantically in the usual manner
On a bleak background of bald stone.

Alliteration is common in nonsense verse (*q.v.*):

Be lenient with lobsters, and ever kind to crabs,
And be not disrespectful to cuttle-fish or dabs;
Chase not the Cochin-China, chaff not the ox obese,
And babble not of feather-beds in company with geese.

in tongue-twisters (*q.v.*):

Betty Botter bought some butter,
But, she said, the butter's bitter;
If I put it in my batter
It will make my batter bitter,
But a bit of better butter,
That would make my batter better.

in jingles (*q.v.*):

Dingle dingle doosey,
The cat's in the well,
The dog's away to Bellingen
To buy the bairn a bell.

and in patter (*q.v.*), beloved of drill sergeants and the like:

Now then, you horrible shower of heathens, have I your complete hattention? Hotherwise I shall heave the whole hairy lot of you into the salt box where you will live on hopeful hallucinations for as long as hit pleases God and the commanding hofficer.

See also ASSONANCE; CACOPHONY; INTERNAL RHYME.

alliterative prose A good deal of OE and ME prose alliterates and uses some of the techniques of alliterative verse (*q.v.*). In OE Aelfric (*c.* 955–*c.* 1010) and Wulfstan (d. 1023) wrote outstanding alliterative prose. Notable instances in ME belong to what is called 'The Katherine Group': five works of devotional prose, in MS Bodley 34, dating from *c.* 1190–1225. They are *Seinte Marherete*, *Seinte Iuliene*, *Seinte Katerine* (hence the group name), *Sawles Warde* and *Hali Meiohad*. They come from Herefordshire.

alliterative revival A general term for a collection of poems composed in the second half of the 14th c. Alliteration had been the basic device in OE poetry and was then again used, especially by Langland in *Piers Plowman* and by the author of *Sir Gawain and the Green Knight*. *See* ALLITERATION; ALLITERATIVE VERSE.

alliterative verse Alliterative meter is an essential feature of Germanic prosody. Alliteration (*q.v.*) was a basic part of the structure. Nearly all OE verse is heavily alliterative, and the pattern is fairly standard – with either two or three stressed syllables in each line alliterating. This example is from *Beowulf* (8th c.):

> þa waes on burgum Beowulf Scyldinga,
> leof leodcyning longe þrage
> folcum gefræge fæder ellor hwearf,
> aldor of earde—, oþ þaet him eft onwoc
> heah Healfdene.

In succeeding centuries the systematic pattern is gradually loosened. These lines from the beginning of Passus III of Langland's *Piers Plowman* (14th c.) show some of the changes:

> Now is Mede þe Mayde · and namo of hem alle
> With bedellus & wiþ bayllyues brouȝt bifor þe kyng.
> The kyng called a clerke can I nouȝt his name,
> To take Mede þe mayde and make hire at ese.

Another but similar alliterative style is adopted in *Sir Gawain and the Green Knight* (*c.* 1350–75):

> The brygge watȝ brayde doun, and þe brode ȝateȝ
> Vnbarred and born open vpon boþe halue.
> Þe burne blessed hym bilyue, and þe bredeȝ passed;
> Prayses þe porter bifore þe prynce kneled.

The poem *Pearl* (*c.* 1375) is also elaborately alliterative, and many of the Medieval Mystery Plays (*q.v.*) were written in rough alliterative verse. These lines come from the start of the York version of *The Harrowing of Hell*:

> ⟨Iesus. M⟩anne on molde, be meke to me,
> And haue thy Maker in þi mynde,
> And thynke howe I haue tholid for þe
> With pereles paynes for to be pyned.

The use of alliteration dwindled steadily during the 15th c. and the only notable poet to make much use of it in Tudor times was John Skelton. Shakespeare used it occasionally, as in Sonnett XXX:

When to the sessions of sweet silent thought
I summon up remembrance of things past,
I sigh the lack of many a thing I sought,
and with old woes new wail my dear time's waste.

It was not until late in the 19th c. that Gerard Manley Hopkins revived the alliterative tradition. He experimented a great deal. These lines from *Spring* suggest how:

Nothing is so beautiful as Spring –
  When weeds, in wheels, shoot long and lovely and lush;
  Thrush's eggs look little low heavens, and thrush
Through the echoing timber does so rinse and wring
The ear, it strikes like lightnings to hear him sing;

Later Ezra Pound also experimented with it. In 1912 he published *Ripostes* which contained a fine rendering of the OE elegiac lyric *The Seafarer.* These are the opening lines:

May I for my own self song's truth reckon,
Journey's jargon, how I in harsh days
Hardship endured oft.
Bitter breast-cares have I abided,
Known on my keel many a care's hold,
And dire sea-surge, and there I oft spent
Narrow nightwatch nigh the ship's head
While she tossed close to cliffs.

Three other poets in recent years have shown mastery of this form: Richard Eberhart, C. Day Lewis and W. H. Auden. Eberhart's *Brotherhood of Men* is a distinguished experiment, so are C. Day Lewis's *As One Who Wanders into Old Workings* and *Flight to Australia.* The latter, particularly, shows the influence of the OE meter and the style of Langland. The third stanza runs:

Fog first, a wet blanket, a kill-joy, the primrose-of-morning's
  blight,
Blotting out the dimpled sea, the ample welcome of land,
The gay glance from the bright
Cliff-face behind, snaring the sky with treachery, sneering
At hope's loss of height. But they charged it, flying blind;
They took a compass-bearing against that dealer of doubt,
As a saint when the field of vision is fogged gloriously steels

His spirit against the tainter of air, the elusive taunter:
They climbed to win a way out,
Then downward dared till the moody waves snarled at their
wheels.

W. H. Auden made skilful use of alliterative meters, as in *The Age of Anxiety*:

For the others, like me, there is only the flash
Of negative knowledge, the night when, drunk, one
Staggers to the bathroom and stares in the glass
To meet one's madness, when what mother said seems
Such darling rubbish and the decent advice
Of the liberal weeklies as lost an art
As peasant pottery, for plainly it is not.
To the Cross or to *Clarté* or to Common Sense
Our passions pray but to primitive totems
As absurd as they are savage; science or no science,
It is Bacchus or the Great Boyg or Baal-Peor,
Fortune's Ferris-wheel or the physical sound
Of our own names which they actually adore as their
Ground and goal.

allœostrophe (Gk 'irregular strophe') A rare term. Used by Milton in his preface to *Samson Agonistes* to describe verses composed in stanzas of irregular length; verses not in the traditional strophic form. *See* STROPHE.

allonym Someone else's name used by an author. *See* PSEUDONYM.

allusion Usually an implicit reference, perhaps to another work of literature or art, to a person or an event. It is often a kind of appeal to a reader to share some experience with the writer. An allusion may enrich the work by association (*q.v.*) and give it depth. When using allusions a writer tends to assume an established literary tradition, a body of common knowledge with an audience sharing that tradition and an ability on the part of the audience to 'pick up' the reference. The following kinds may be roughly distinguished: (a) a reference to events and people (e.g. there are a number in Dryden's and Pope's satires); (b) reference to facts about the author himself (e.g. Shakespeare's puns on Will; Donne's pun on Donne, Anne and Undone); (c) a metaphorical allusion (there are many examples in T. S. Eliot's work); (d) an imitative allusion (e.g. Johnson's to Juvenal in *London*).

almanac A book or table which comprises a calendar (*q.v.*) of the year which shows: days, weeks and months; a register of feast days and saints' days; a record of astronomical phenomena. Sometimes it contains meteorological forecasts and agricultural advice on seasonal activities. The word may be connected with late Greek *almenikhiaká* and we find it in medieval Latin as *almanac*. In Roger Bacon's *Opus Majus* (*c.* 1367) the term denoted permanent tables which showed the apparent movements of the stars and planets.

Among the earliest were the 'clog' almanacs of the Danes and Normans. These crude tables consisted of blocks of wood on which the days of the year were notched. The first printed almanac dates from 1457. Most English almanacs were published by the Stationers' Company, and they became very popular in 17th c. England, especially in the period 1640–1700. Besides astronomical and astrological tables they contained a wide range of information, including feast days, agricultural notes, prophecies and verses. Particularly well-known compilers and publishers were Richard Allestree, John Gadbury and William Lilly (1602–81), the astrologer, who published almanacs for some forty years. These often sold in huge quantities (up to 300,000 per year). The best known to us now is the *Vox Stellarum* (1700) of Francis Moore (1657–1714), a physician and astrologer. This was a collection of weather predictions and was intended to promote the sales of his pills. It survives as *Old Moore's Almanac* and still sells in large numbers. *Whitaker's Alamanack* (first published in 1868) is a compendious volume of general information about the world.

A different kind is the *Almanach de Gotha*, which has been published annually since 1763. It gives royal and aristocratic genealogies and statistics of the world.

a lo divino (Sp 'in religious terms') A literary treatment through which popular secular themes were transformed into religious themes by the use of Christian allegory, metaphor or symbol (*qq.v.*). It was particularly common during the Golden Age (*q.v.*).

als ob (G 'as if') In 1876 Hans Vaihinger put forward the idea that it was a prerequisite of any idealism that we must act on the assumption that something presented as art is as it appears. Thus it is *as if* we were watching a real representation. *See* WILLING SUSPENSION OF DISBELIEF.

altar poem Also known as a *carmen figuratum* (L 'shaped poem'), it is a poem in which the verses or stanzas are so arranged that they form a design on the page and take the shape of the subject of the poem. The device is believed to have been first used by Persian poets of the 5th c. and it was revived during the Renaissance period when it was practised by a number of poets – including Wither, Quarles, Benlowes, Herrick and Herbert. Puttenham, in his *The Arte of English Poesie* (1589), devoted a complete chapter to the shaped poem and provided a number of interesting illustrations. Herbert's *The Altar* and his *Easter Wings* are two particularly well-known instances. The latter is arranged thus:

Lord, who createdst man in wealth and store,
Though foolishly he lost the same,
Decaying more and more,
Till he became
Most poore:
With thee
O let me rise
As larks, harmoniously,
And sing this day thy victories:
Then shall the fall further the flight in me.

The second stanza is arranged in the same fashion.

A well-known recent example is Dylan Thomas's *Vision and Prayer*, a series of twelve devotional poems; but the device has been exploited with other motifs. Rabelais, for example, wrote a bottle-shaped song, his *epilenie*, in honour of Bacchus; and Apollinaire wrote a poem called *Il pleut* (in *Calligrammes*) which was printed so that the letters trickled down the page like falling tears. *See also* CONCRETE POETRY; EMBLEM-BOOK; PATTERN POETRY.

altercatio (L 'argument') A Roman legal term signifying rapid cross-questionings and replies. Applied to literature, it refers to a series of short questions and answers. Common in drama, dialogue and debate. *See* STICHOMYTHIA.

alternance des rimes In French prosody the term refers to the rules regulating the alternation of masculine and feminine rhymes (*qq.v.*). The principles were more or less established in the 16th c. and were accepted until well on in the 19th c. *Les symbolistes* tended to ignore them. In the 20th c. they have often been ignored. One of the more rigid rules was that in alexandrine verse a couplet with a masculine rhyme must be followed by a couplet with feminine rhyme (or vice versa). Also known as *rimes plates* or *rimes suivies*.

See also ALEXANDRINE; RHYME; RIMES CROISEES; RIMES EMBRASSEES; RIMES MELEES.

alternate rhyme The rhyme of the stanza form abab. *See* QUATRAIN.

alternative literature A vague and loose term usually used to describe literature which does not belong to the 'mainstream'. Whether or not such literature actually exists is open to doubt. If it does, then broadly speaking it appears to be anti-traditional, anti-establishment, way-out, off-beat and possibly the product of the literate or semi-literate members of the so-called alternative society and its sub-cultures (*q.v.*). Had the term existed in the 1920s it might have been applied to poetry composed during the worst excesses of the Futurist revolution, or that composed by the Smithy Poets (*q.v.*) or those suffering from imaginism (*q.v.*). By the same token, in the 1950s, it might have referred to the poetry of the Beat generation (*q.v.*), much of whose best work has long since been 'mainstream'. Some forms of anti-novel (*q.v.*) might be described as alternative literature. *See also* ALEATORY WRITING; ALTERNATIVE THEATRE; POST-MODERNISM.

alternative theatre A term loosely applied to any kind of dramatic presentation which is basically non-conformist and non-traditional and thus outside the standard repertory productions one would expect to find in the West End of London, on Broadway, in boulevard theatres or in regional theatres in cities and large towns. It tends to be *avant-garde* (*q.v.*), experimental and off-beat. *See* AGITPROP DRAMA; CELEBRATORY THEATRE; FRINGE THEATRE; OFF-BROADWAY; THIRD THEATRE; TOTAL THEATRE.

ambiguity Ever since William Empson published *Seven Types of Ambiguity* (1930) this term has had some weight and importance in critical evaluation. In brief, Empson's theory was that things are often not what they seem, that words *connote* at least as much as they *denote* – and very often more. Empson explained thus: 'We call it ambiguous . . . when we recognize that there could be a puzzle as to what the author meant, in that alternate views might be taken without sheer misreading . . . An ambiguity, in ordinary speech, means something very pronounced, and as a rule witty or deceitful'. He uses the word in an extended sense and finds relevance in any 'verbal nuance, however slight, which gives room for alternative reactions to the same piece of language'. 'The machinations of ambiguity', he says, 'are among the very roots of poetry'.

He distinguishes seven main types, which may be summarized as follows:

1. When a detail is effective in several ways simultaneously.
2. When two or more alternative meanings are resolved into one.
3. When two apparently unconnected meanings are given simultaneously.
4. When alternative meanings combine to make clear a complicated state of mind in the author.
5. A kind of confusion when a writer discovers his idea while actually writing. In other words, he has not apparently preconceived the idea but come upon it during the act of creation.
6. Where something appears to contain a contradiction and the reader has to find interpretations.
7. A complete contradiction which shows that the author was unclear as to what he was saying.

In varying degrees Gerard Manley Hopkins's poem *The Bugler's First Communion* exemplifies all seven types. *See also* ALLUSION; ASSOCIATION; CONNOTATION; DENOTATION; PLURISIGNATION.

amblysia (Gk 'blunting') A device related to euphemism (*q.v.*) where language is reduced or modified by way of preparation for the announcement of something tragic or alarming. Often used by the bearers of bad news, it is the equivalent of saying 'I am afraid you must prepare yourself for a shock'. In Classical tragedy the Messenger had the task. Two good examples are Ross (in *Macbeth*) making ready to break the news to Macduff of the murder of the latter's wife and children; and the Messenger in Milton's *Samson Agonistes* gradually working his way up to the description of how Samson destroyed the temple.

amoebean (Gk 'interchanging') This term relates to verses, couplets or stanzas spoken alternately by two speakers. A device very similar to *stichomythia* (*q.v.*) and highly effective in creating tension and conflict. It is common in pastoral (*q.v.*) and not unusual in drama. A good example is to be found in *October*, the tenth Eclogue in Spenser's *Shepheard's Calendar*, where Piers and Cuddie have a debate. Such an exchange (at its best the amoebean verse involves competition) is reminiscent of the *débat* and poetic contest (*qq.v.*).

amour courtois *See* COURTLY LOVE.

ampersand A corruption of *and per se and. Per se* means 'standing by itself'. Thus: 'and', standing by itself, means 'and'. Ampersand is the old way of naming and spelling the sign & (formerly &), the ligature of *et*.

amphiboly (Gk 'thrown on both sides') An ambiguity (*q.v.*) produced either by grammatical looseness or by double meaning. For example: (a) He spoke to the man laughing; (b) The article in question is the thirty-ninth. *See* DOUBLE ENTENTE.

amphibrach (Gk 'short at both ends') A metrical foot consisting of a stressed syllable flanked by two unstressed ones: ∪ / ∪. It is not common in English verse and very seldom indeed functions as the main foot of a poem. However, occasional amphibrachs (mixed with other feet) occur quite often in stress groups. Matthew Prior's *Jinny the Just* is a fairly well-known instance of a poem which has a basis of amphibrachs. This is the first verse:

Rĕléas'd frŏm | thĕ nóise ŏf | thĕ Bútchĕr | ănd Bákĕr
Whó, mȳ óld | Friénds bĕ thánked, | dĭd séldŏm | fŏrsáke hĕr,
Ănd fróm thĕ | sŏft Dúns ŏf | mȳ Lándlŏrd | thĕ Quákĕr,

Many three syllable words in English are amphibrachs. For example: dĕpéndĕnt, ărrángemĕnt, cŏntúsiŏn. *See also* AMPHIMACER.

amphigory (Gk 'circle on both sides') The term has come to mean a kind of burlesque or parody (*qq.v.*), especially a kind of nonsense verse (*q.v.*) which appears to be going to make sense but does not. A well-known example is Swinburne's *Nephelidia*.

amphimacer (Gk 'long at both ends') The opposite of an amphibrach (*q.v.*), thus: / ∪ /. Also known as the Cretic foot, it is believed to have originated with the Cretan poet Thaletas (7th c. BC). Rare in English verse, except when mixed with other feet. Tennyson used it in *The Oak*:

Líve thȳ Lífe,
Yóung ănd óld,
Líke yŏn óak,
Bríght ĭn spríng,
Lívĭng góld.

And Coleridge described and imitated it:

Fírst ănd Lást | béiñg lóng, | míddlĕ, shórt | Ámphĭmácĕr
Stríkes hĭs thún | dĕriñg hoóves | lĭke ă próud | hígh-bréd Rácĕr.

In the second line the pattern is not so regular, and unless 'like a' is counted as one syllable and '-bred' is unstressed the meter does not really fit.

amphisbaenic rhyme The term derives from the Greek word *amphisbaina* 'a monster with a head at each end'. It denotes a backward rhyme. For example: liar/rail. A rare poetical device.

amplification A device in which language is used to extend or magnify or emphasize. A part of rhetoric (*q.v.*) and common in oratory. Often used to attain a particular effect, as in this passage from *Our Mutual Friend* by Dickens:

> Mr and Mrs Veneering were bran-new people in a bran-new house in a bran-new quarter of London. Everything about the Veneerings was spick and span new. All their furniture was new, all their friends were new, all their servants were new, their plate was new, their carriage was new, their harness was new, their horses were new, their pictures were new, they themselves were new, they were as newly-married as was lawfully compatible with their having a bran-new baby, and if they had set up a great-grandfather, he would have come home in matting from the Pantechnicon, without a scratch upon him, French-polished to the crown of his head.

-ana As in Holmesiana, Victoriana, etc. A suffix adopted in continental literature and deriving from the neuter plural of Latin adjectives ending in *-anus*. Johnson defined '-ana' in his *Dictionary* thus:

> Books so called from the last syllables of their titles; as Scaligerana, Thuaniana; they are loose thoughts, or casual hints, dropped by eminent men, and collected by their friends.

A particularly important example is *Thraliana*, a mixed bag of poems, jokes, diary entries and anecdotes, compiled by Mrs Hester Thrale, Dr Johnson's dear friend, between 1776 and 1809. This collection was edited and published in 1942. Other examples are *Baconiana* (1679); *Blackguardiana* (c. 1785); *Addisoniana* (1803);

Boxiana (1818–29); *Feminiana* (1835). *See* ANECDOTE; BIOGRAPHY; TABLE-TALK.

anabasis (Gk 'a going up') The rising of an action to a climax or dénouement (*qq.v.*). In drama, for instance, the approach to the climax in *Othello* when the Moor murders Desdemona (V).

anachorism (Gk 'something misplaced') Action, scene or character placed where it does not belong. *See* ANACHRONISM.

anachronism (Gk 'back-timing') In literature anachronisms may be used deliberately to distance events and to underline a universal verisimilitude and timelessness – to prevent something being 'dated'. Shakespeare adopted this device several times. Two classic examples are the references to the clock in *Julius Caesar* and to billiards in *Antony and Cleopatra*. Shaw also does it in *Androcles and the Lion* when the Emperor is referred to as 'The Defender of the Faith'. *See* ANACHORISM.

anaclasis (Gk 'back bending') The interchange of a long and a short syllable in verse.

anacoluthon (Gk 'lacking sequence') Beginning a sentence in one way and continuing or ending it in another. 'You know what I – but let's forget it!'

anacreóntica A Spanish poetic genre named after the Greek poet Anacreon of Teos (6th c. BC). It was a kind of pastoral (*q.v.*) or nature poem particularly popular in the 18th c. *See* ANACREONTIC VERSE.

anacreontic verse Named after Anacreon of Teos (6th c. BC). The *Anacreontea* or *Anacreontics* consist of sixty-odd short poems on love, wine and song. They had a considerable influence on Ronsard and Belleau in France; on Tasso, Parini and Leopardi in Italy; and on some 18th c. German lyricists. There are not many examples in English literature, though Abraham Cowley wrote some *Anacreontiques*, and so did Thomas Moore in a translation called the *Odes of Anacreon*. But this example is by Thomas Campion (1567–1620):

Follow, follow,
Though with mischief
Armed, like whirlwind
Now she flies thee;
Time can conquer
Love's unkindness;
Love can alter
Time's disgrace;
Till death faint not
Then but follow.
Could I catch that
Nimble traitor,
Scornful Laura,
Swiftfoot Laura,
Soon then would I
Seek avengement.
What's th'avengement?
Even submissely
Prostrate then to
Beg for mercy.

See ANACREONTICA.

anacrusis (Gk 'striking up') One or more initial syllables in a line of verse which are unaccented, as in Blake's *The Tyger*:

When the stars threw down their spears
And watered heaven with their tears.

The 'and' is unaccented.

anadiplosis (Gk 'doubling') The repetition of the last word of one clause at the beginning of the following clause to gain a special effect. For example, Samson at the beginning of Milton's *Samson Agonistes*:

I seek
This unfrequented place to find some ease,
Ease to the body some, none to the mind
From restless thoughts.

It is not uncommon in prose, as in this instance from Dr Johnson's *Rambler* No. 21: 'Labour and care are rewarded with success, success produces confidence, confidence relaxes industry, and negligence ruins the reputation which diligence had raised'. *See* EPANADOS; EPANALEPSIS.

anagnorisis (Gk 'recognition') A term used by Aristotle in *Poetics* to describe the moment of recognition (of truth) when ignorance gives way to knowledge. According to Aristotle, the ideal moment of anagnorisis coincides with peripeteia (*q.v.*), or reversal of fortune. The classic example is in *Oedipus Rex* when Oedipus discovers he has himself killed Laius. *See* TRAGEDY.

anagram (Gk 'writing back or anew') The letters of a word or phrase are transposed to form a new word. For instance, the word 'Stanhope' can be turned into the word 'phaetons'. A common feature of crosswords. Samuel Butler's title *Erewhon* is an anagram of 'nowhere'.

analects (Gk 'things gathered up')A collection of passages, *obiter dicta* (*q.v.*), *pensées* (*q.v.*) taken from an author. They are crumbs or gleanings. Confucius, though he is supposed to have written nothing, is credited with the authorship of analects. A well-known Confucian example is: 'Do not do unto others what you would not wish done unto you'. There are also a number of ribald Confucianisms. *See* TABLE-TALK.

analogue A word or thing similar or parallel to another. As a literary term it denotes a story for which one can find parallel examples in other languages and literatures. A well-known example is Chaucer's *The Pardoner's Tale*, whose basic plot and theme were widely distributed in Europe in the Middle Ages. The tale is probably of oriental origin and a primitive version exists in a 3rd c. Buddhist text known as the *Jatakas*; but the version usually taken to be the closest analogue to Chaucer's tale is in the Italian *Libro di Novelle e di Bel Parlar Gentile* (1572) which is nearly two hundred years later than Chaucer's story.

analysed rhyme Also known as suspended rhyme, this is usually the use of two or more types of rhyme. A common arrangement is assonantal and consonantal rhyme; for example: *fun/runt*; *bin/stint*. Another combination is a mixture of pure and consonantal rhymes; for instance: *fair/lyre*; *pair/dire*. In the following extract from Peter Porter's *John Marston Advises Anger* we have a mixture of pure, consonantal and assonantal rhyme:

All the boys are howling to take the girls to bed.
Our betters say it's a seedy world. The critics say
Think of them as an Elizabethan Chelsea set.
Then they've never listened to our lot – no talk
Could be less like – but the bodies are the same:
Those jeans and bums and sweaters of the King's Road
Would fit Marston's stage. What's in a name,
If Cheapside and the Marshalsea mean Eng. Lit.
And the Fantasie, Sa Tortuga, Grisbi, Bongi-Bo
Mean life? A cliché? What hurts on paper,
Fades to classic pain. Love goes as the MG goes.

Same and *name* are pure rhymes; *set* and *Lit.* are consonantal; *bed* and *set* are assonantal – as are *say* and *same*, *Road*, *-Bo* and *goes*. *See* ASSONANCE; CONSONANCE; EYE-RHYME; HALF-RHYME; VOWEL RHYME.

analysis A detailed splitting up and examination of a work of literature. A close study of the various elements and the relationship between them. An essential part of criticism. As T. S. Eliot put it, the tools of the critic are comparison and analysis. Analytical criticism helps to make clear an author's meaning and the structure of his work. It is argued that analysis spoils an intuitive and spontaneous response to a work of literature. Those in favour of 'deep' analysis contend that, on the contrary, it enhances the reader's enjoyment.

anamnesis (Gk 'recalling to mind') The recollection of ideas, people or events (in a previous existence). This is common in memoirs and autobiography (*qq.v.*), but it may also pervade a work of fiction or a poem. It is a special kind of harking back, and the maieutic processes of the writer often involve it. Proust's *A la recherche du temps perdu* is a good example in fiction. Among poets, the anamnesic element is particularly noticeable in the work of W. B. Yeats, Ezra Pound, T. S. Eliot and W. H. Auden.

ananym (Gk 'behind name') A name or word written backwards. *See* BACK SLANG.

anapaest (Gk 'beaten back') A metrical foot comprising two unstressed syllables and one stressed: ◡ ◡/. The opposite of a dactyl (*q.v.*). It is a running and galloping foot and therefore used to create the illusion of swiftness and action. As Coleridge illustrates it in *Metrical Feet*:

> Wĭth ă leáp | ănd ă boúnd | thĕ swĭft Á | năpaĕsts thróng.

Originally it was a martial rhythm used in Greek verse, and was adapted by the Romans for drama. In English literature it is mostly found in popular verse until early in the 18th c. Thereafter it was used fairly frequently for 'serious' works by poets like Cowper, Scott, Byron, Morris and Swinburne. In the 20th c. Belloc, Chesterton, Masefield and Betjeman have all employed it successfully. Most poets at some time or another have occasion to use anapaests in combination with other feet. A famous anthology piece which illustrates the anapaestic rhythm is Byron's *Destruction of Sennacherib*. The following example comes from William Morris's *The Message of the March Wind*:

> Bŭt ló, | thĕ ŏld ínn, | ănd thĕ líghts, | ănd thĕ fíre
> Ănd thĕ fídd|lĕr's ŏld túne | ănd thĕ shúff|lĭng ŏf feét;
> Sóon fŏr ús | shăll bĕ quí|ĕt ănd rést | ănd dĕsíre,
> Ănd tŏmór|rŏw's ŭprí|sĭng tŏ déeds | shăll bĕ swéet.

anaphora (Gk 'carrying up or back') A rhetorical device involving the repetition of a word or group of words in successive clauses. It is often used in ballad and song, in oratory and sermon (*qq.v.*), but it is common in many literary forms. A fine example in verse occurs six verses from the end of Chaucer's *Troilus and Criseyde*:

> Swich fyn hath, lo, this Triolus for love!
> Swich fyn hath al his grete worthynesse!
> Swich fyn hath his estat real above,
> Swich fyn his lust, swich fyn hath his noblesse!
> Swich fyn hath false worldes brotelnesse!
> And thus bigan his lovyng of Criseyde,
> As I have told, and in this wise he deyde.

An equally fine instance in prose is the lament for Lancelot in Malory's *Le Morte Darthur*:

> Said Sir Ector . . . Sir Launcelot . . . thou wert never matched of earthly knight's hand; and thou wert the courteoust knight that ever bare shield; and thou wert the truest friend to thy lover that ever bestrad horse; and thou wert the truest lover of a sinful man that ever loved woman; and thou wert the kindest man that ever struck with sword; and thou wert the goodliest person that ever

> came among press of knights; and thou wert the meekest man and the gentlest that ever ate in hall among ladies; and thou wert the sternest knight to thy mortal foe that ever put spear in the rest.

See also INCREMENTAL REPETITION.

anastrophe (Gk 'turning back') The inversion of the normal order of words for a particular effect. The word order in these lines, from the beginning of Belial's speech in the Council of Pandemonium in *Paradise Lost*, is deliberately confused to suggest Belial's speciousness:

> I should be much for open war, O Peers,
> As not behind in hate, if what was urged
> Main reason to persuade immediate war
> Did not dissuade me most, and seem to cast
> Ominous conjecture on the whole success.
> When he who most excels in fact of arms,
> In what he counsels and in what excels
> Mistrustful, grounds his courage on despair
> And utter dissolution, as the scope
> Of all his aim, after some dire revenge.

Anastrophe is also common in prose. This example comes from Richard Whateley's *Elements of Rhetoric* (1828): 'The question between preaching extempore and from a written discourse, it does not properly fall within the province of this discourse to discuss on any but what may be called rhetorical principles'.

anatomy (Gk 'cutting up') A detailed analysis of a subject; an exhaustive examination. Well-known examples are: Lyly's *Euphues or the Anatomy of Wit* (1579); Philip Stubbes's *Anatomie of Abuses* (1583); Thomas Nashe's *Anatomie of Absurditie* (1589), a reply to Stubbes; Robert Burton's *Anatomy of Melancholy* (1621), perhaps the most famous of all. Among more recent instances one should mention Rosamund Harding's *Anatomy of Inspiration* (1940). In his *Anatomy of Criticism* (1957) Northrop Frye treats 'anatomy' as a form of fiction associated with Menippean Satire (*q.v.*), and thus a compendious, if not encyclopaedic, satirical analysis of human behaviour, attitudes and beliefs.

ancients and moderns The phrase refers to two literary parties which grew up in France and England in the late 17th c. Originally, in

France, there were arguments over the relative merits of French and Latin for literary purposes, an issue discussed by du Bellay long before in his *Deffense et Illustration* (1549). The increasing influence of the French Academy in the 17th c. helped to provoke further argument. Fundamentally, it was a case of progress and the modern rationalistic spirit of inquiry versus reverence for Classical rules and precepts. Some moderns thought they were better than the ancients; others did not. A number of distinguished writers joined the fray, including Perrault, Bayle, La Fontaine and Boileau. By 1700 the quarrel was over, but the issues were still unresolved. Neoclassicism (*q.v.*) was to prevail in France for a very long time (far longer than anywhere else) and the moderns did not really gain their victory until the 19th c. was well advanced.

In England the *casus belli* was an essay by Sir William Temple, published in 1690, on the comparative merits of ancient and modern learning. Temple praised ancient learning at the expense of the moderns. In so doing he praised the spurious *Epistles* of Phalaris. This provoked the indignation and criticism of William Wotton and Richard Bentley.

However remote and even esoteric such intellectual and literary fracas may now seem, this one at any rate had good side-effects. Among other things it produced Swift's *The Battle of the Books* (1704), a prose satire in which the ancients have the advantage.

anecdote A brief account of or a story about an individual or an incident. The anecdotal digression is a common feature of narrative in prose and verse. In the history of English literature and of literary characters the anecdote has a specific importance. In his *Dictionary* Johnson defined the term as 'something yet unpublished; secret history'. During the 18th c. an interest in 'secret' histories increased steadily, and no doubt there is some connection between this and the growing popularity of -ana, table-talk and biography (*qq.v.*) at that time. During the second half of the 18th c. there was almost a 'craze' for 'secret' histories. In the last thirty years of it over a hundred books of anecdotage were published in England. Isaac Disraeli, father of Benjamin, became one of the best known and most assiduous gleaners of anecdotes. In 1791 he published three volumes titled *Curiousities of Literature, consisting of Anecdotes, Characters, Sketches, and Observations, Literary, Historical and Critical.* These he followed with other collections: *Calamities of Authors* (1812–13) in two volumes, and *Quarrels of Authors* (1814) in three volumes. In 1812 John Nichols published the first of nine volumes in a series titled *Literary Anecdotes of the 18th c.* Such works remained popular during the Victorian period. Nor is the appetite for collections of anecdotes assuaged. In 1975 there was *The Oxford Book of Literary Anecdotes.*

Anglo-Saxon period (or Old English period) The period from the invasion of Celtic England by the Angles, Saxons and Jutes in the first half of the 5th c. up till the conquest in 1066 by William of Normandy. After their conversion to Christianity in the 7th c. the Anglo-Saxons began to develop a written literature (prior to that period it had been oral). The Benedictine monastic foundations played an important part in the development of culture, literacy and learning. Two outstanding scholars of the period were the Venerable Bede (*c.* 673–735) and Alcuin (*c.* 735–804). From the Anglo-Saxon period dates what is known as Old English literature (composed in the vernacular Anglo-Saxon). It includes the epic (*q.v.*) *Beowulf* and some fine lyric poems such as *The Wanderer*, *The Seafarer* and *Deor*. Much of the literature that survives is anonymous, but the names of two poets are known: Caedmon (fl. late 7th c.) and Cynewulf (late 8th and early 9th c.). They wrote on biblical and religious themes. Alfred the Great (*c.* 848–99), who was king of Wessex, 871–99, was largely responsible for the restoration of learning in England after the Viking invasions. He translated into Old English various books in Latin and is believed to have been responsible for planning the *Anglo-Saxon Chronicle* which continued from his reign, in the Peterborough version, until 1134. This is written in Old English prose and is an invaluable source of Anglo-Saxon history.

angry young man The term or phrase seems to have been first used as the title of an autobiography by Leslie Paul published in 1951. It became a catch-phase in Britain in the middle and late 1950s, and by 1960 at the latest was a much used cliché. Apart from the journalists, the writer mainly but indirectly responsible for its popularity was John Osborne whose play *Look Back in Anger* (1957) spoke for a generation of disillusioned and discontented young men who were strongly opposed to the establishment; to its social and political attitudes and *mores*, and indeed to the whole 'bourgeois ethic'. Jimmy Porter, the anti-hero (*q.v.*) of Osborne's play, was really the prototypal modern 'angry young man'. In a short time all such vocal protesters were classified as 'angry young men' or as 'the young angries'. Osborne's excellent play survives;

the cliché is now hardly ever used. *See also* BEAT GENERATION; KITCHEN-SINK DRAMA.

anisometric (Gk 'of unequal lengths') A stanza composed of lines of unequal lengths; as in the first stanza of John Donne's *The Message*:

Send home my long strayd eyes to mee,
Which (Oh) too long have dwelt on thee;
Yet since there they have learn'd such ill,
  Such forc'd fashions,
  And false passions,
    That they be
    Made by thee
Fit for no good sight, keep them still.

annals (L 'year books') Notable examples are: the *Anglo-Saxon Chronicle*, made in a number of recensions, of which seven survive, from the 9th c. to the middle of the 12th; and the *Annales Cambriae*, the ancient annals of Wales whose earliest extant manuscript dates from the second half of the 10th c. *See also* CHRONICLE; YEAR BOOK.

annotation Textual comment in a book. It may consist of a reader's comment in the margin, hence the term marginalia (*q.v.*), or printed explanatory notes provided by an editor. *See also* ADVERSARIA.

anomoiosis *See* CONTRAST.

anonymous There is a great body of anonymous literature, especially that belonging to early or primitive societies, most of which is of the oral tradition (*q.v.*). Much Homeric poetry was anonymous in origin, so was OE poetry (of which *Beowulf* is a notable example), and the South Slav *narodne pesme* (*q.v.*). Folk literature of all kinds tends to be anonymous; so are many sagas, ballads, medieval *chansons de gestes, fabliaux*, proverbs, nursery rhymes, etc. (*qq.v.*). *See also* PSEUDONYMOUS LITERATURE.

anonymuncule (L 'nameless little man') A derogatory term for a petty type of anonymous writer. A mean, shifty writer who hides behind anonymity.

antagonist In drama or fiction the antagonist opposes the hero or protagonist (*q.v.*). In *Othello* Iago is antagonist to the Moor. In *The Mayor of Casterbridge*, Farfrae is antagonist to Henchard.

antanaclasis (Gk 'breaking back against') A figurative device in which a word is used twice or more in two or more of its possible senses. When Othello is about to murder Desdemona (*Othello*, V, ii) he says: 'Put out the light, and then put out the light'. The first 'light' refers to a candle or taper; the second to Desdemona's life.

anthimeria (Gk *anthos* 'flower' + *meros* 'part') The substitution of one part of speech for another; often a form of metaphor (*q.v.*). The term carries with it the idea of 'flowerizing' or 'making decorative'. This example comes from Shakespeare's *Coriolanus* (V, i, 5):

> A mile before his tent fall down, and *knee*
> The way into his mercy.

And this from Edward Young's *Complaint, or Night Thoughts*:

> That ghastly thought would drink up all your joy,
> And quite *unparadise* the realms of light.

anthology (Gk 'collection of flowers') in Classical times anthologies tended to be collections of epigrams, elegiac and otherwise, and date back to the *Garland of Meleager* (*c.* 60 BC). Philippus of Thessalonica (*c.* AD 40) made a further collection of Greek epigrams. The first major anthology is known as the *Palatine* or the *Greek Anthology*, compiled *c.* 925 by Constantinus Cephalas, a Byzantine Greek. In the 16th c. anthologizing became commonplace. From this period date two important Latin anthologies: *Catalecta veterum poetarum* (1573) and *Epigrammata et poemata vetera* (1590). In England several notable collections appeared: Tottel's Miscellany (*Songes and Sonettes*) (1557); *Very Pleasaunt Sonettes and Storyes in Myter* (1566); *The Paradice of Dainty Devices* (1576); *A Gorgious Gallery of Gallant Inventions* (1578); *The Phoenix Nest* (1593); *Englands Parnassus* (1600); *Englands Helicon* (1600); *Poetical Rhapsody* (1602); then little of note until Percy's *Reliques* (1765). In 1831 Southey put out *Select Works of the British Poets*, and in 1861 came Palgrave's *Golden Treasury*, probably the most famous of all English anthologies. Others worthy of mention are T. H. Ward's *English Poets* (1883) and Arther Quiller-Couch's *Oxford Book of English Verse* (1900). In the last fifty years anthologies have proliferated endlessly, especially anthologies of verse. Many are little more than commercial publishing packages which provoke the invention of anaemic academic 'joke' titles such as *The Oxford Book of Cambridge Light*

Verse, The Cambridge Book of Oxford Light Verse, The Oxbridge Book of Heavy Verse – and so forth.

antibacchius *See* PALIMBACCHIUS.

anticlimax According to Dr Johnson's definition (and he appears to have been the first to record the word) it is 'a sentence in which the last part expresses something lower than the first'. In fact, a bathetic declension from a noble tone to one less exalted. The effect can be comic and is often intended to be so. A good example occurs in Fielding's burlesque (*q.v.*), *Tom Thumb*:

King [Arthur, to his queen Dolallola]
. . . Whence flow those Tears fast down thy blubber'd
cheeks,
Like swoln Gutter, gushing through the Streets?

The effect can also be unintentionally comic. There is a well-known example in Crashaw's *Saint Mary Magdalene, or the Weeper*:

And now where e'er He strays,
Among the Galilean mountains,
Or more unwelcome ways,
He's followed by two faithful fountains;
Two walking baths; two weeping motions;
Portable, & compendious oceans.

See BATHOS.

anti-hero A 'non-hero', or the antithesis of a hero of the old-fashioned kind who was capable of heroic deeds, who was dashing, strong, brave and resourceful. It is a little doubtful whether such heroes have ever existed in any quantity in fiction except in some romances (*q.v.*) and in the cheaper kind of romantic novelette (*q.v.*). However, there have been many instances of fictional heroes who have displayed noble qualities and virtuous attributes. The anti-hero is the man who is given the vocation of failure.

The anti-hero – a type who is incompetent, unlucky, tactless, clumsy, cack-handed, stupid, buffoonish – is of ancient lineage and is to be found, for instance, in the Greek New Comedy (*q.v.*). An early and outstanding example in European literature is the endearing figure of the eponymous knight of *Don Quixote* (1605,

1615). But perhaps the first anti-hero who fits the modern image is Hylas, in d'Urfé's very successful *Astrée* (1627), who is a contrast to the conventional hero Céladon. Another notable instance is Tristram Shandy – in Sterne's *Tristram Shandy* (1760–67). One can find isolated representatives in European literature from the 18th c. onwards, for example Hašek's Schweik in *The Good Soldier Schweik* (1920–23). A case could be argued that Leopold Bloom in Joyce's *Ulysses* (1922) is a kind of anti-hero. Camus's Meursault in *L'Etranger* (1942) is an example. Charles Lumley in John Wain's *Hurry on Down* (1953) is another. When Kingsley Amis created Jim Dixon in *Lucky Jim* (1954) the post-war anti-hero type was established, and the anti-hero Jimmy Porter of John Osborne's play *Look Back in Anger* (1957) produced a succession of personalities of the same kind. Other examples are Sebastien in J. P. Donleavy's *The Ginger Man* (1955), Herzog in Bellow's *Herzog* (1964), and Yossarian in Joseph Heller's *Catch-22* (1961). The principal male characters in several of Graham Greene's novels are also anti-heroes. *See* ANGRY YOUNG MAN; ANTI-NOVEL; NOUVEAU ROMAN.

anti-literature A term coined by the poet David Gascoyne (1916–) in 1935 to describe literature which turns traditional rules and conventions upside down. Gascoyne was a staunch advocate of surrealism (*q.v.*) and in 1935 published *A Short Survey of Surrealism*. *See also* ALTERNATIVE LITERATURE; ANTI-HERO; ANTI-NOVEL.

antilogy (Gk 'against knowledge') An illogicality or contradiction in terms.

anti-masque An innovation by Ben Jonson in 1609. It took the form of either a buffoonish and grotesque episode before the main masque (*q.v.*) or an interlude, similarly farcical, during it. When performed beforehand, it was known as an ante-masque. One form of it was a burlesque (*q.v.*) of the masque itself, in which case it had some affinity with the Greek satyr play (*q.v.*).

antimetabole (Gk 'opposite change/variety') The repetition of words in successive clauses, in reverse grammatical order. As in this example by Dr Johnson in one of his *Rambler* essays: 'It ought to be the first endeavour of a writer to distinguish nature from custom, or that which is established because it is right from that which is right only because it is established'. *See also* CHIASMUS.

antinomy (Gk 'contradictory law') A kind of division or contradiction between laws or principles, yet the term also contains the idea that the contradictions are reconcilable. For instance, Kant proposes that, on the subject of taste (*q.v.*), there can be no argument, and at the same time there can be. *See* APOLLONIAN/DIONYSIAN; CLASSICISM/ROMANTICISM; HEBRAISM/HELLENISM; NAIV UND SENTIMENTALISCH.

anti-novel This kind of fiction tends to be experimental and breaks with the traditional story-telling methods and form of the novel (*q.v.*). Often there is little attempt to create an illusion of realism or naturalism (*qq.v.*) for the reader. It establishes its own conventions and a different kind of realism which deters the reader from self-identification with the characters, yet at the same time persuades him to 'participate' but not vicariously. One has only to compare novels by, say, Thomas Hardy and Henry James, with those by, say, Nabokov and Samuel Beckett, to see how the work of the latter writers comes into the anti-novel category; though anti-novel is a thoroughly misleading term.

We can see the process of anti-novel innovation at work in the major experiments of James Joyce in *Ulysses* and *Finnegans Wake*, in several novels by Virginia Woolf (e.g. *Mrs Dalloway*, *The Waves*, and *To the Lighthouse*) and in the early fiction of Samuel Beckett (e.g. *Molloy* and *Murphy*). However, it may be that the possibilities were perceived long before by Laurence Sterne. *Tristram Shandy* (1760–67) might be cited as a kind of anti-novel. Horace Walpole described it as 'a kind of novel . . . the great humour of which consists in the whole narration always going backwards'.

Some of the principal features of the anti-novel are: lack of an obvious plot; diffused episode; minimal development of character; detailed surface analysis of objects; many repetitions; innumerable experiments with vocabulary, punctuation and syntax; variations of time sequence; alternative endings and beginnings.

Some of the more extreme features are: detachable pages; pages which can be shuffled like cards; coloured pages; blank pages; collage effects; drawings; hieroglyphics.

Of notable and influential contributions to the anti-novel – apart from those referred to above – one should mention Sartre's *La Nausée* (1938); Flann O'Brien's *At Swim-Two-Birds* (1939);

Nathalie Sarraute's *Tropismes* (1939) and her *Le Planétarium* (1959); Maurice Blanchot's *Thomas l'obscur* (1941), *Aminadab* (1942), *Le Très-Haut* (1948); Camus's *L'Etranger* (1942); Philip Toynbee's *Tea with Mrs Goodman* (1947); Robbe-Grillet's *La Jalousie* (1957); Butor's *L'Emploi du temps* (1957) and *La Modification* (1957); Nabokov's *Pale Fire* (1962); Rayner Heppenstall's *The Connecting Door* (1962) and *The Shearers* (1969); Christine Brooke-Rose's *Out* (1964), *Such* (1966) and *Between* (1968); Claude Simon's *La Route des Flandres* (1960).

It is worth noting that as far back as 1627 Charles Sorel subtitled his novel *Le Berger extravagant* an *anti-roman*. *See also* ANTI-HERO; AVANT-GARDE; EXPRESSIONISM; FABULATION; NOUVEAU ROMAN; NOUVELLE VAGUE; STREAM OF CONSCIOUSNESS.

antiphon Either a hymn (*q.v.*) in alternative parts or a lyric (*q.v.*) containing responses, as in this example from George Herbert, which again is a kind of hymn:

CHORUS Let all the world in every corner sing, My God
and King.
VERSICLE The heavens are not too high,
His praise may thither fly;
The earth is not too low,
His praises there may grow.
CHORUS Let all the world in every corner sing, My God
and King.
VERSICLE The church with psalms must shout,
No door can keep them out:
But above all, the heart
Must bear the longest part.
CHORUS Let all the world in every corner sing, My God
and King.

The Divine Office is sung antiphonally.

antiphrasis (Gk 'expressed by the opposite') The use of a word in a sense opposite to its proper meaning. Common in irony and litotes (*qq.v.*).

anti-play A dramatic work which not only ignores the traditional conventions but actively distorts them. There is no observable plot and little development of character. Dialogue is often inconsequential or totally disconnected. Playwrights of the Theatre of the Absurd (*q.v.*) have used anti-play techniques. Sometimes they have been very successful. *See* HAPPENING.

antipophora (Gk 'against answer') A figurative device in which a person (or character) asks a question of himself and then answers it himself. There is a succession of them in Falstaff's famous disquisition on 'honour' in *Henry IV*, Pt I (V, i). *See* RHETORICAL QUESTION.

antisagoge (Gk 'leading into against') A complex figurative device in which an order or precept is given and a reward offered if it is obeyed, and punishment threatened if it is ignored. As when Leontes speaks to Camillo in *The Winter's Tale* (I, ii):

> Do't, and thou hast the one half of my heart;
> Do't not, thou split'st thine own.

antispast (Gk 'drawn in the contrary direction') A metrical foot comprising two stressed syllables flanked by two unstressed ones: ∪ / / ∪. In other words, an iamb and a trochee (*qq.v.*). It is by no means certain if this foot (*q.v.*) actually existed in Classical prosody.

antistoichon (Gk 'balanced opposition of ideas') An antithetical device in which statements counterbalance each other. *See* ANTITHESIS.

antistrophe (Gk 'counter-turning') In Greek drama the return movement of the Chorus from left to right. It also refers to the choric song accompanying this movement. It was also the second of a pair of movements or stanzas in an ode (*q.v.*), exactly the same metrically as the preceding strophe (*q.v.*). *See also* EPODE.

antisyzygy *See* OXYMORON.

anti-theatre The term was devised some time in the 1950s and denotes any form of drama which is not naturalistic, traditional, conventional or 'legit'; thus, theatre which disobeys or actively goes against accepted laws and rules of dramaturgy. It has been used to describe the Theatre of the Absurd (*q.v.*). *See also* AGITPROP DRAMA; ALTERNATIVE THEATRE; ANTI-HERO; ANTI-LITERATURE; ANTI-NOVEL; THIRD THEATRE.

antithesis (Gk 'opposition') Fundamentally, contrasting ideas sharpened by the use of opposite or noticeably different meanings. For example, Bacon's apophthegm (*q.v.*): 'Crafty men contemn studies; simple men admire them; and wise men use them'.

It is common in rhetoric (*q.v.*) and was particularly favoured by the Augustan poets and users of the heroic couplet (*q.v.*). These lines from Dryden's *Absalom and Achitophel* are strongly antithetical:

Rais'd in extremes, and in extremes decry'd;
With Oaths affirm'd, with dying Vows deny'd.
Not weighed, or winnow'd by the Multitude;
But swallow'd in the Mass, unchew'd and Crude.
Some Truth there was, but dash'd and brew'd with Lyes;
To please the Fools, and puzzle all the Wise.
Succeeding times did equal folly call,
Believing nothing, or believing all.

Pope was an expert at the antithetical, as this compact example in his *Moral Essays* shows:

Les wit than mimic, more a wit than wise.

It is also used frequently in prose to telling effect, as in this example from Dr Johnson (in the *London Chronicle*, May 2nd, 1769) on the character of the Reverend Zacariah Mudge: 'Though studious, he was popular; though argumentative, he was modest; though inflexible, he was candid; and though metaphysical, yet orthodox'. *See* EPIGRAM; OXYMORON.

antode (Gk 'opposite song') In Greek Old Comedy (*q.v.*), during the parabasis (*q.v.*) the antode was the lyric song sung by one half of the Chorus in response to the ode (*q.v.*) sung earlier by the other half.

antonomasia (Gk 'naming instead') A figure of speech in which an epithet, or the name of an office or dignity, is substituted for a proper name. So 'the Bard' for Shakespeare, 'a Gamaliel' for a wise man; 'a Casanova' for a womanizer; and 'a Hitler' for a tyrant. *See also* AUNT EDNA; METONYMY; SYNECDOCHE.

antonym A word of opposite meaning to another: fierce/mild; ugly/beautiful; abstract/concrete. *See* SYNONYM.

anxiety of influence *See* FREUDIAN CRITICISM/PSYCHOANALYTIC CRITICISM.

aphaeresis (Gk 'a taking away') The suppression of an initial, unstressed syllable, usually a vowel: ''mongst' for *amongst*; ''mid' for *amid*; ''tween' for *between*. *See also* APHESIS.

aphesis (Gk 'letting go') The loss of an unstressed initial vowel: 'squire' from *esquire*. *See also* APHAERESIS.

aphorism (Gk 'marking off by boundaries') A terse statement of a truth or dogma; a pithy generalization, which may or may not be witty. The proverb (*q.v.*) is often aphoristic; so is the maxim (*q.v.*). A successful aphorism exposes and condenses at any rate a part of the truth, and is an aperçu or insight. For instance, the anonymous 'Conscience is a cur that will let you get past it, but that you cannot keep from barking'.

The aphorism is of great antiquity, timeless and international. The Classical, Hebraic and Oriental worlds have all made great contributions, and the common stock of wisdom and knowledge everywhere has scattered these nuggets of truth in the writings and sayings of many civilizations. Of the thousands who have added to the store the following deserve special mention: Aristotle, Plato, St Augustine; Montaigne, Pascal, La Rochefoucauld, Chamfort, La Bruyère, Vauvenargues, Joubert, de Tocqueville, Valéry, de Chazal, Remy de Gourmont, Proust, Camus; Chaucer, Francis Bacon, Sir Thomas Browne, George Halifax, Pope, Dr Johnson, Lord Chesterfield, William Blake, Coleridge, Walter Bagehot, Hazlitt, Samuel (*Erewhon*) Butler, Oscar Wilde, Bernard Shaw, A. N. Whitehead, W. H. Auden; Ralph Waldo Emerson, Thoreau; Goethe, Schopenhauer, Lichtenberg, Nietzsche, Karl Kraus; Kierkegaard; Chekhov; Cesare Pavese; Ortega y Gasset; Santayana. John Stuart Mill composed a short piece on aphorisms and John Morley wrote a brief discourse on them. Two valuable modern collections are *The Faber Book of Aphorisms* (1964) compiled by W. H. Auden and *The Oxford Book of Aphorisms* (1983) compiled by John Gross. *See also* SENTENTIA.

apocalyptic literature The term 'apocalyptic' derives from Greek *apocalypse* 'to disclose', and Apocalypse is the name given to the last book of the New Testament, *The Revelation of St John*. Such literature comprises prophetic or quasi-prophetic writings which tend to present doom-laden visions of the world and sombre and minatory predictions of mankind's destiny. An early example is Wulfstan's homily (or address) to the English (*c.* 1014). In the later

Middle Ages chiliastic movements in Europe evoked a large number of diatribes against the wickedness of humanity and the imminence of the end of the world. Sermon literature abounds in apocalyptic visions. But it is a very general term quite often used loosely. It might certainly be applied to a good deal of Blake's poetry, and to such works as James Thomson's despairing poem *The City of Dreadful Night* (1874), H. G. Wells's profoundly depressing *Mind at the End of Its Tether* (1945) and perhaps Orwell's *Nineteen Eighty-Four* (1949). Latterly, such novels as *The Drowned World* (1962) by J. G. Ballard, *The Armies of the Night* (1968) by Norman Mailer and *The Four-Gated City* (1969) by Doris Lessing have been deemed to possess apocalyptic characteristics.

apocope (Gk 'cutting off') The dropping of a letter or letters from the end of a word. Fairly common in verse to achieve an elision, especially with the word 'the'. Other examples are: taxi(cab); edit(or); curio(sity); cinema(tograph). *See* BACK-FORMATION.

apocrypha (Gk 'things hidden') Writings of unknown or uncertain authorship. Fourteen books of the Greek version of the Old Testament, contained in the *Septuagint* but not in the Hebrew Bible, were rejected from the Canon (*q.v.*). Writings ascribed on insufficient evidence to certain authors (e.g. Chaucer and Shakespeare) are also called apocryphal.

Apollonian/Dionysian Terms derived from the names of the Greek gods Apollo and Dionysus. Apollo was the messenger of the gods, and the presiding deity of music, medicine, youth and light, and was sometimes identified with the sun. Dionysus was the god of vegetation and wine and, it might be said, of 'permissiveness'. Nietzsche used the terms in *The Birth of Tragedy out of the Spirit of Music* (1872). He was making a distinction between reason and instinct, culture and primitive nature; possibly brains as opposed to loins and heart. Apollonian is also often thought to signify 'sunny' and 'serene', whereas the Dionysian means 'stormy' and 'turbulent'. Nietzsche argued that these elements formed a unity in Greek tragedy where dialogue provided the Apollonian element and the dithyrambic choral songs the Dionysiac. In the 19th c. this antinomy (*q.v.*) was much elaborated, particularly in the work of Schopenhauer, but it was Schiller who originally made the distinction between *naiv* and *sentimentalisch* (*q.v.*). Among more modern writers D. H. Lawrence was deeply interested in it. He might be described as a Dionysiac writer whereas Stendhal and André Gide were Apollonian. Of course, a combination is possible, as in Shakespeare's sonnets, or the love poems of Donne and Burns. *See also* CLASSICISM/ROMANTICISM; EMOTIVE LANGUAGE; HEBRAISM/HELLENISM.

apologue *See* FABLE.

apology (Gk 'defence') A work written to defend a writer's opinions or to elaborate and clarify a problem. A well-known example is Plato's *Apology* in which Socrates defends himself against the governing body of Athens. Another notable instance is Sir Philip Sidney's *Apologie for Poetrie*, or *Defence of Poesie* (1595), an essay which examines the art of poetry and discusses the state of English poetry at the time. Shelley also wrote a *Defence of Poetry* (1821), a remarkable achievement in which he vindicates his views on the elements of love and imagination in poetry. A very different work was Lamennais's apologia, *Paroles d'un Croyant* (1834), a 'reply' to a Papal Encyclical. The most famous example of more recent times is John Henry Newman's *Apologia Pro Vita Sua* (1864): a masterly exposition of Newman's beliefs, and a refutation of Charles Kingsley's accusation that Newman did not regard truth as a necessary virtue.

apophasis (Gk 'from speaking') Affirming by apparent denial, a stressing through negation. A famous example is contained in Hamlet's parting words to Gertrude at the end of the 'bedroom scene' (III, iv):

> Not this, by no means, that I bid you do:
> Let the bloat King tempt you again to bed;

He goes on to emphasize a series of injunctions.

apophthegm (Gk 'speaking out plainly') A terse, pithy saying – akin to proverb, maxim and aphorism (*qq.v.*). A well-known collection from antiquity was the *Apophthegmata Patrum*, a compilation of anecdotes and sayings from the Egyptian Desert Fathers. The work was probably compiled late in the 5th c. Francis Bacon made a collection entitled *Apophthegms New and Old* (1624), which contained the saying 'Hope is a good breakfast, but it is a bad supper'. *See also* GNOMIC VERSE; SENTENTIA.

aporia (Gk 'impassable path') A term used in the theory of deconstruction (*q.v.*) to indicate a kind of impasse or insoluble conflict between rhetoric and thought. *Aporia* suggests the 'gap' or lacuna between what a text means to say and what it is constrained to mean. It is central to Jacques Derrida's theory of *différance* (*q.v.*). In his excellent book on Derrida's critique of philosophy (*Derrida*, 1987) Christopher Norris discusses this central feature of deconstruction as 'the seeking-out of those "aporias", blindspots or moments of self-contradiction where a text involuntarily betrays the tension between rhetoric and logic, between what it manifestly means to say and what it is nonetheless constrained to mean'.

aposiopesis (Gk 'becoming silent') A rhetorical device in which speech is broken off abruptly and the sentence is left unfinished. A memorable example occurs in a speech by King Lear (II, iv) in which he fulminates against Regan and Goneril:

> – No, you unnatural hags,
> I will have such revenges on you both,
> That all the world shall – I will do such things, –
> What they are, yet I know not; but they shall be
> The terrors of the earth.

apostrophe (Gk 'turning away') A figure of speech in which a thing, a place, an abstract quality, an idea, a dead or absent person, is addressed as if present and capable of understanding. Classic instances are Goldsmith's opening of *The Deserted Village*: 'Sweet Auburn, loveliest village of the plain. . .'; Antony's cry in *Julius Caesar*: 'O Judgement! thou art fled to brutish beasts . . .'; and Wordsworth's passionate appeal in *London 1812*: 'Milton! Thou should'st be living at this hour . . .'.

appositum *See* EPITHET.

aptronym A name that fits the nature and character of a person and/or their occupation. This is how names were originally acquired or bestowed (e.g. Hunter, Farmer, Cooper, Smith, Mason, Miller, Draper). Aptronymic titles have often been used in literature as a kind of label (William Archer called them 'label names'). They were common in the Morality Plays (*q.v.*), in allegories like Spenser's *Faerie Queene* and Bunyan's *Pilgrim's Progress*, in novels (especially those of Fielding, Dickens and Thackeray) and in dramatic comedy (e.g. plays by Jonson, Congreve, Sheridan and Goldsmith). Famous instances are Mr Worldly Wiseman, Mrs Malaprop and Mr Gradgrind. *See* ALLEGORY; COMEDY OF HUMOURS; HUMOURS.

Arcadia Originally a mountainous district in the Peloponnese. For Classical poets Arcadia was the symbol of rural serenity, the harmony of the legendary Golden Age. Virgil's *Eclogues* illustrate an ideal way of pastoral life in Arcadia, where shepherds and shepherdesses, removed from 'real life', devote themselves to their flocks and their songs. During the Renaissance the idea was popularly revived by a number of writers, especially Sannazzaro, who published a series of verses linked by prose called *L'Arcadia* (1501), and by Sir Philip Sidney who published a prose romance, also called *Arcadia* (1590). Spenser's pastoral (*q.v.*) poems also depict this ideal existence.

archaism This term denotes what is old or obsolete. Its use was common in poetry until the end of the 19th c. The reasons are various. Sometimes the older form of a word was more suitable metrically. Many archaisms were used because of their associations with the past, especially those linked to the age of chivalry and romances (*q.v.*). Spenser, who much admired Chaucer, was the person chiefly responsible for the fashion – particularly in *The Faerie Queene* (1589, 1596). Spenser, in order to try to re-create the spirit and atmosphere of chivalry and devotion in the Middle Ages (as seen from his point of view), used a sort of poetic diction (*q.v.*) which was partly archaic and partly of his own devising. Milton, who greatly admired Spenser, used them sparingly; but in Milton we find a different kind of archaism – namely the use of a syntax and word order characteristic of Latin which was by his day a dead language. The 18th c. 'Spenserians' continued the tradition; so did Keats (much influenced by Spenser), Coleridge and William Morris. Tennyson used archaisms for the same purposes as Keats and Spenser. Late in the 19th c. Gerard Manley Hopkins also resuscitated a number of archaisms, but they were seldom of the Spenserian type. He was interested in 'working' words, rather than the decorative or atmospheric.

This stanza from Thomas Parnell's *A Fairy Tale* (*c.* 1700) illustrates a grotesque use of the Spenserian variety:

With that Sir Topaz, hapless youth!
In accents faultering, ay for *ruth*
  Intreats them pity *graunt*;
For *als* he been a mister *wight*,
Betray'd by wandering in the night
To tread the circled haunt.

The italicized words were all archaisms by the time this was written.

On the other hand, in Keats's *The Eve of Saint Mark* (*c.* 1819) we find a deliberate archaism to suggest something written in the 14th c. The maiden fair Bertha is reading the 'legend page' of 'Holy Mark':

'Gif ye wol stonden hardie wight –
Amiddes of the blacke night –
Righte in the churche porce, pardie
Ye wol behold a companie
Appouchen thee full dolourouse
For sooth to sain from everich house
Be it in city or village
Wol come the Phantom and image
Of ilka gent and ilka carle
Whom coldè Deathè hath in parle
And wol some day that very year
Touchen with foulè venime spear
And sadly do them all to die –

And so on for a further nineteen lines before he reverts to normal language thus:

At length her constant eyelids come
Upon the fervent martyrdom;
Then lastly to his holy shrine,
Exalt amid the tapers' shine
At Venice, –

Except in parody (*q.v.*), archaism is rare in prose. A noteworthy example is C. M. Doughty's *Travels in Arabia Deserta* (1888). In this extraordinary work Doughty used a mixture of Chaucerian and Elizabethan English combined with Arabic.

archetypal criticism The investigation and analysis of archetypal and mythical narrative patterns, character types, themes and motifs in literature and their recurrence in literature. It owes much to the original work of the school of comparative anthropology at Cambridge, to J. G. Frazer's monumental study *The Golden Bough* (1890–1915), which traces elemental patterns of myth and ritual, and to the depth psychology of C. G. Jung. The term has often been used since Maud Bodkin's remarkable book *Archetypal Patterns in Poetry* (1934). Northrop Frye's *Anatomy of Criticism* (1957) is perhaps the classic work. *See* ARCHETYPE; MYTH; NARRATOLOGY.

archetype (Gk 'original pattern') A basic model from which copies are made; therefore a prototype. In general terms, the abstract idea of a class of things which represents the most typical and essential characteristics shared by the class; thus a paradigm or exemplar. An archetype is atavistic and universal, the product of 'the collective unconscious' and inherited from our ancestors. The fundamental facts of human existence are archetypal: birth, growing up, love, family and tribal life, dying, death, not to mention the struggle between children and parents, and fraternal rivalry. Certain character or personality types have become established as more or less archetypal. For instance: the rebel, the Don Juan (womanizer), the all-conquering hero, the braggadocio (*q.v.*), the country bumpkin, the local lad who makes good, the self-made man, the hunted man, the siren, the witch and *femme fatale*, the villain, the traitor, the snob and the social climber, the guilt-ridden figure in search of expiation, the damsel in distress, and the person more sinned against than sinning. Creatures, also, have come to be archetypal emblems. For example, the lion, the eagle, the snake, the hare and the tortoise. Further archetypes are the rose, the paradisal garden and the state of 'pre-Fall' innocence. Themes include the arduous quest or search, the pursuit of vengeance, the overcoming of difficult tasks, the descent into the underworld, symbolic fertility rites and redemptive rituals.

The archetypal idea has always been present and diffused in human consciousness. Plato was the first philosopher to elaborate the concept of archetypal or ideal forms (Beauty, Truth, Goodness) and divine archetypes. Since the turn of the 19th c. the idea and subject have been explored extensively. Practitioners of the two sciences of comparative anthropology and depth psychology have made notable contributions. The major works in this venture of discovery include: J. G. Frazer's *The Golden Bough* (1890–1915); C. G. Jung's 'On the Relation of Analytical Psychology to Poetic

Art' (1922) in *Contributions to Analytical Psychology* (1928) and 'Psychology and Literature' in *Modern Man in Search of a Soul* (1933); Sigmund Freud's *A General Introduction to Psychoanalysis* (1920); Maud Bodkin's *Archetypal Patterns in Poetry* (1934); G. Wilson Knight's *Starlit Dance* (1941); E. Cassirer's *Language and Myth* (trans. 1946); Robert Graves's *The White Goddess* (1948); Richard Chase's *Quest for Myth* (1949); J. Campbell's *The Hero with a Thousand Faces* (1949); Philip Wheelwright's *The Burning Fountain* (1954) and his *Metaphor and Reality* (1962); B. Seward's *The Symbolic Rose* (1960); Northrop Frye's *Anatomy of Criticism* (1957) and 'The Archetypes of Literature' in *Fables of Identity* (1963), plus several other inquiries. *See also* IMAGERY; MYTH; STOCK CHARACTER; STOCK RESPONSE; STOCK SITUATION; SYMBOL AND SYMBOLISM.

archi-écriture *See* PHONOCENTRISM.

Archilochian verse So called after the Greek satirist Archilochus (*c.* 700 BC). He is believed to have invented lines or couplets in which different meters were combined. The main forms are: Greater Archilochian – a dactylic tetrameter (*q.v.*) plus a trochaic tripody (*q.v.*); and the Lesser Archilochian – a dactylic trimeter catalectic. He also used the dactylic tetrameter catalectic, the iambelegus and the elegiambus. In addition he is credited with four different kinds of strophe (*q.v.*). His work had a major influence on Horace. *See* CATALEXIS; DACTYL; TROCHEE.

archive (Gk 'public office') Archives are either the repository of public records, or the records themselves.

argot A French word of unknown origin. It means slang or cant (*qq.v.*) and usually refers to the slang used by social outcasts or those who are disapproved of socially. Much abstruse *argot* of this kind has been assembled by Auguste le Breton in *Langue verte et noirs desseins* (1960). *See also* BACK SLANG; PATOIS; RHYMING SLANG.

argument (a) In literary use an abstract or summary of a plot prefacing a work. For instance, each book of *Paradise Lost* is preceded by an explanation of what is going to happen. This used to be common practice with a long poem, a novel or a treatise of some length and substance. The practice survives in the summaries sometimes found in the contents pages of a book; (b) An argument is also a division of a speech; (c) The term is also used to describe the dialectic (*q.v.*) in a poem. The argument in this fine poem by Thomas Beedome, for instance, is set forth in four different but interlocked statements and is concluded in the resolution of the final couplet:

The Question and Answer

When the sad ruines of that face
In its owne wrinkles buried lyes
And the stiffe pride of all its grace,
By time undone, fals slack and dyes:
Wilt thou not sigh, and wish in some vext fit,
That it were now as when I courted it?

And when thy glasse shall it present,
Without those smiles which once were there,
Showing like some stale monument,
A scalpe departed from its haire,
At thy selfe frighted wilt not start and sweare
That I belied thee, when I call'd thee faire?

Yes, yes, I know thou wilt, and so
Pitty the weaknesse of thy scorne,
That now hath humbled thee to know,
Though faire it was, it is forlorne,
Love's sweetes thy aged corps embalming not,
What marvell if thy carkasse, beauty, rot?

Then shall I live, and live to be
Thy envie, thou my pitty; say
When e're thou see mee, or I thee,
(Being nighted from thy beautie's day),
'Tis hee, and had my pride not wither'd mee,
I had, perhaps, beene still as fresh as hee.

Then shall I smile, and answer: 'True thy scorne
Left thee thus wrinkled, slackt, corrupt, forlorne.'

argumentum ad (L 'appeal to') There are several phrases: (a) *ad baculum* ('to the stick', and thus the argument according to force); (b) *ad crumenam* ('to the wallet', the argument which appeals to a person's material instincts); (c) *ad hominem* ('to the man', that is, personal); (d) *ad ignorantiam* ('to ignorance', that is, the argument which depends upon the person being ignorant or uninformed); (e) *ad populum* ('to the people', that is the argument which is intended to rouse the feelings of the crowd); (f) *ad verecundiam* ('to modesty', that is an argument so constructed that the other person has to make a cautious reply in order to avoid being indecorous).

ars est celare artem (L 'art is to conceal art') The implication is that the best art seems spontaneous though in all probability it is the outcome of extremely hard work. Or 'hard writing makes easy reading'. *See* INSPIRATION; SPONTANEITY.

arsis and thesis (Gk 'lifting up' and 'setting down') The terms describe the upward and downward beat keeping time in Greek verse. The long syllable of a dactyl (*q.v.*) was the *thesis*; the *arsis* comprised the two short beats. *See* THESIS.

arte mayor (Sp 'major art') In the first place an eight-syllable verse in stanzas of eight lines; later of twelve syllables. It was usually employed for longer poems and there were several variations on the basic form. The twelve-syllable line would have a caesura (*q.v.*) after the sixth syllable and therefore this scheme amounted to a pair of *versos de redondilla menor.* But whereas the latter was only stressed on the fifth syllable, in *arte mayor* there is a stress on the second syllable. The rhyme scheme was usually abba acca. Intimations of *arte mayor* begin with Juan Ruiz, the Archpriest of Hita (*c.* 1280–*c.* 1351) and stories in the *Conde Lucanor.* Juan de Mena (1411–56) brought a new seriousness to Spanish poetry and was one of the masters of *arte mayor.* *See* ARTE MENOR; REDONDILLA.

arte menor (Sp 'minor art') A Spanish metrical term denoting lines of two to eight syllables with accent on the penultimate, and either assonance or rhyme. This type of line being relatively easy to compose *arte menor* can be said to be a rather vague term. Popular poetry of many types falls readily into this category. It is found in traditional narrative poetry, popular song, and dramatic work. *See* ARTE MAYOR.

art for art's sake The phrase connotes the idea that a work of art has an intrinsic value without didactic or moral purpose. This concept seems to have been first put forward by Lessing in *Laokoon* (1766), and became something of an artistic battle-cry or slogan (*q.v.*) following the publication of Gautier's Preface to *Mademoiselle de Maupin* (1835). Throughout the 19th c. it became a guiding principle for many writers. Oscar Wilde was one of its leading advocates. *See* AESTHETICISM; DECADENCE; PARNASSIANS; REALISM.

articulus *See* BRACHIOLOGY.

artificial comedy *See* COMEDY OF MANNERS.

art nouveau (F 'new art') Primarily a style of architecture and decoration which had a wide vogue in Europe and America in the 1890s and up to *c.* 1914. It was ornate, decorative, asymmetrical and somewhat fantastic. As far as the literary scene is concerned it had a considerable influence on book production and periodicals in the 1890s, a decade which saw such productions as *The Century Guild Hobby Horse* (1884), *The Dial* (1889–97), *The Yellow Book* (1894–7) and *The Savoy* (1889–97). The *art nouveau* book was adorned by distinguished illustrators: principally, Aubrey Beardsley (1872–98), Charles Ricketts (1860–1931), Laurence Housman (1865–1959), Charles Conder (1868–1909) and Thomas Sturge Moore (1870–1940).

arts, the seven liberal *See* QUADRIVIUM.

Arzamas A short-lived Russian literary group which flourished 1815–18. Its members were in favour of literary and stylistic reforms and included Karamzin, Zhorkiski, Batynashkov, Vyazemski and Pushkin.

ascending rhythm *See* RISING RHYTHM.

Asclepiad A meter named after the Greek poet Asclepiades (*c.* 290 BC) of Samos. It comprised one spondee, two or three choriambs and one iamb (*qq.v.*). It was used for lyric and tragic verse and was much employed by Horace. It is rare in English verse. W. H. Auden was probably the first poet since Campion to use accentual Asclepiads (in *In Due Season*).

aside In drama a few words or a short passage spoken in an undertone or to the audience. It is a theatrical convention and by convention the words are presumed inaudible to other characters on stage; unless of course the aside be between two characters and therefore clearly not meant for anyone else who may be present. It was in continual use until early in this century (especially in comedy and melodrama, *qq.v.*). The advent of 'naturalistic drama' (*q.v.*) led to its almost complete exclusion. However, it is still liberally used in pantomime (*q.v.*) and in farce (*q.v.*).

association The shared connection between an object and ideas. Coleridge spoke of it in *Biographia Literaria*: 'Ideas by having been together acquire a power of recalling each other; or every partial representation awakes the total representation of which it had been a part'.

Any sensory perception or idea may be associated with something from the past. Proust's *A la recherche du temps perdu* is a sustained exercise in the use of associations. Nearly all poetry is strongly associative. *See* AMBIGUITY; CONNOTATION; DISSOCIATION OF SENSIBILITY; SUGGESTION.

assonance Sometimes called 'vocalic rhyme', it consists of the repetition of similar vowel sounds, usually close together, to achieve a particular effect of euphony (*q.v.*). There is a kind of drowsy sonority in the following lines from Tennyson's *Lotos-Eaters* which is assonantal:

The Lotos blooms below the barren peak:
The Lotos blows by every winding creek:
All day the wind breathes low with mellower tone
Thro' every hollow cave and alley lone,
Round and round the spicy downs the yellow Lotos-dust is blown.

In *Strange Meeting* Wilfred Owen uses a vocalic or half rhyme (*q.v.*) to similar effect:

It seemed that out of battle I escaped
Down some profound dull tunnel, long since scooped
Through granites which titanic wars had groined.
Yet also there encumbered sleepers groaned,
Too fast in thought or death to be bestirred.

See also ALLITERATION; CONSONANCE; EUPHONY; MELOPOEIA; ONOMATOPOEIA; PHANOPOEIA; VOWEL RHYME.

asteismus (Gk 'clever talk, wit') A contrived turning or twisting of the meaning of something said so that it implies something else. Related to the *double entente* and pun (*qq.v.*).

astracanada A form of Spanish farce (*q.v.*), often broad and bawdy. It developed *c.* 1900 and remains popular. Two playwrights were largely responsible for the creation of this genre: Pedro Muñoz Seca (1881–1936) and Enrique García Álvarez (1873–1931).

asynartete (Gk 'disconnected') Applied to a poem whose divisions have different rhythms and meters. The creator of this sort of verse was Archilochus (7th c. BC) who used dactylic, trochaic and iambic verse. Hence the term Archilochian verse (*q.v.*).

asyndeton (Gk 'unconnected') A rhetorical device where conjunctions, articles and even pronouns are omitted for the sake of speed and economy. Puttenham, in *The Arte of English Poesie* (1589), calls it 'loose language', but it has been particularly popular in modern poetry (e.g. the work of W. H. Auden, Robert Lowell and John Berryman) as a means of achieving compact expression. Milton often used it, in *Paradise Lost* especially:

> The first sort by their own suggestion fell
> Self-tempted, self-depraved; man falls, deceived
> By the other first; man therefore shall find grace,
> The other none . . .

See ELLIPSIS.

asyntactic (Gk 'not arranged') Applied to prose or verse which is loose, ungrammatical in structure and therefore which breaks the normal conventions governing word order. *See* SYNTAX.

Atellan fables *See* FABULA.

atmosphere The mood and feeling, the intangible quality which appeals to extra-sensory as well as sensory perception, evoked by a work of art. For instance, the opening scene in *Hamlet* where the watch is tense and apprehensive, even 'jumpy'. By contrast, the beginning of Ben Jonson's *The Alchemist* indicates clearly that the play is going to be comic to the point of knockabout. An excellent example in the novel is Hardy's depiction of Egdon Heath in *The Return of the Native*.

atmosphere of the mind A phrase invented by Henry James to denote what the subjective writer of the novel tries to convey to the reader. After a time we in a sense 'inhabit' the writer's mind, breathe that air and are permeated by his vision.

atonic (Gk 'without tone or stress') Generally used to describe the unaccented syllables of a word; or, in verse, the unstressed syllables of a word or foot (*q.v.*).

Atticism A style adopted by Greek and Roman orators; distinguished by its simplicity and directness and by its lack of rhetorical device.

aubade (F 'dawn song') The Provençal and German equivalents are *alba* and *Tagelied* (*q.v.*) respectively. The dawn song is found in almost all the world's early literatures and expresses the regret of parting lovers at daybreak. The earliest European examples date from the end of the 12th c. There is a theory that the *aubade* grew out of the night watchman's announcement from his tower of the passing of night and the renewal of day. The exchange between Romeo and Juliet at the end of their wedding night is a good example. Perhaps the most beautiful and moving one in English literature occurs in Book III of Chaucer's *Troilus and Criseyde*:

> Myn hertes lif, my trist, and my plesaunce,
> That I was born, allas, what me is wo,
> That day of us moot make disseveraunce!
> For tyme it is to ryse and hennes go,
> Or ellis I am lost for evere mo!
> O nyght, allas! why nyltow over us hove,
> As longe as whan Almena lay by Jove?

Thus Criseyde begins when she hears the cock crow, and the exchange continues between the lovers for a further fourteen stanzas. An interesting modern example is William Empson's *Aubade* (1940).

au-dessus de la mêlée (F 'above the battle') The expression had some vogue during the First World War (1914–18), as the title of an article in the *Journal de Génève* (Sept. 1914) and also of a pamphlet. This comprised articles by Romain Rolland (1866–1944), who was sympathetically inclined to German literature and music. Rolland was in effect making a plea for tolerance and peace. However, among writers, only Hermann Hesse (1877–1962) agreed with

Rolland's attitude. Most people strongly disapproved. The expression came to stand for indifference and unacceptable detachment.

audition colorée *See* SYNAESTHESIA.

Aufklärung A German term for Enlightenment (*q.v.*).

Augustan age During the reign of the Emperor Augustus (27 BC–AD 14) many distinguished writers flourished, notably Virgil, Horace, Ovid and Tibullus. The term has been applied to that period of English history in which Dryden, Pope, Addison, Swift, Goldsmith, Steele and, to some extent, Johnson lived and imitated their style: that is the final decades of the 17th c. and the first half of the 18th c. So the phrase suggests a period of urbane and classical elegance in writing, a time of harmony, decorum (*q.v.*) and proportion. Goldsmith contributed an essay to *The Bee* on 'the Augustan Age in England', but he confined it to the reign of Queen Anne (1702–14). In French literature the term is applied to the age of Corneille, Racine and Molière. *See also* ENLIGHTENMENT; NEOCLASSICISM.

Aunt Edna The typical theatre-goer invented by Terence Rattigan and called by Kenneth Tynan 'a mythical, middle-class admirer . . . backbone of the theatre . . . she follows, never leads, intelligent taste.' An instance of antonomasia (*q.v.*).

aureate language A kind of poetic diction (*q.v.*) used by Scottish and English poets in the 15th c. It was a rather ornate and ornamental language, often consisting of vernacular coinages from Latin words. It is particularly noticeable in the poems of Dunbar and Henryson in Scotland, and Lydgate, Hawes and King James I of Scotland (1394–1437). James I was detained in England for nineteen years and there composed *The Kingis Quair* (written 1423–4) in aureate style. However, Dunbar was probably its best exponent. These lines by Dunbar give some indication of the style:

Hale, sterne superne, hale in eterne
  In Godis sicht to schyne;
Lucerne in derne for to discerne
  Be glory and grace devyne:
Hodiern, modern, sempitern,
  Angelicall regyne,

Our tern inferne for to dispern,
  Helpe, rialest rosyne.
    Ave Maria, gracia plena,
  Haile, fresche floure femynyne;
Yerne us, guberne, virgin matern,
  Of reuth baith rute and ryne.

author, death of In *The Death of the Author*, an essay first published in *Mantéia V* in 1968, Roland Barthes attacks the common and traditional view of the author as the ultimate 'explanation' of a work. Barthes (and post-structuralist theory) contends that the author can no longer be regarded as the omniscient and all-pervading presence and influence in a work of literature; indeed, he implies that the reader takes over as the prime source of power in a text. At the end of the essay Barthes suggests that 'the birth of the reader must be at the cost of the death of the Author'. The author becomes little more than an hypothesis, a 'person' projected by the critic from the text, and a convenient catch-all for the critic, whereas the reader is at liberty to see the plurality of the text.

Barthes explains the idea of 'the death of the author' via a specific French literary tradition – that of Mallarmé and Valéry. Mallarmé's poetics consists in suppressing the author in the interests of writing. In a memorable phrase, he wrote of the poet's role being to 'cede the initiative to words'. Barthes also refers to the 'modern scriptor' implying a comparison between 'classic realist' and 'modern/post-modern' fiction. It should be remembered that his essay (1968) is close to *S/Z* (1970) and the essay *From Work to Text* (1971), which are, *inter alia*, critiques of bourgeois ideology.

Readers have become conditioned by the idea and 'construct' of an Author – be the author dead or alive. Barthes is at pains to dismantle this idea; and deconstructive practice, for example, has shown anyway that authors are extremely unreliable; they often do not know what they are doing; and there is a big discrepancy between intention and result. Authorial authority is highly questionable.

A key passage in Barthes's essay is:

> the image of literature one can find in contemporary culture is tyrannically centred around the author, his person, his history, his tastes, his passions; criticism still consists for the most part in saying that Baudelaire's *œuvre* is the failure of Baudelaire the man, that Van Gogh's *œuvre* is his madness, and Tchaikovsky's

> his vice: the explanation of the *œuvre* is always sought on the side of the man who has produced it as if, through the more or less transparent allegory of the fiction, it was always in the end the voice of one person alone, the author, who was giving us his confidences.

Foucault's essay *What is an Author?* (1969) should also be noted. Foucault historicizes the notion of authorship in a sceptical way and envisages anonymous texts at the end. But this is distinct from Barthes's point of view.

Finally, it should be said that, arguably, the 'death of the author' was initiated in Anglo-American literary criticism by the New Critics (*see* NEW CRITICISM), who, like deconstructionists, advocated the primacy of the text (though with totally different results). Barthes has argued that the New Critics have consolidated the position of the author. *See* DECONSTRUCTION.

autobiographical novel Many novels are in part autobiographical. Some are more obviously so than others. Fairly well-known representative examples are: Goethe's *Die Leiden des jungen Werthers* (1774), E. J. Trelawny's *The Adventures of a Younger Son* (1831), Thomas Aldrich's *The Story of a Bad Boy* (1870), Somerset Maugham's *Of Human Bondage* (1915), Gertrude Stein's *The Autobiography of Alice B. Toklas* (1933), Henry Miller's *Tropic of Cancer* (1934) and Maureen Duffy's *That's How It Was* (1962). The most famous instance in English literature is probably Joyce's *A Portrait of the Artist as a Young Man* (1916), which developed from *Stephen Hero* begun by Joyce *c.* 1904 (publ. 1944). *See* MEMOIR-NOVEL; NOVEL; WERTHERISM.

autobiography An account of a person's life by him- or herself. The term appears to have been first used by Southey in 1809. In Dr Johnson's opinion no man was better qualified to write his life than himself, but this is debatable. Memory may be unreliable. Few can recall clear details of their early life and are therefore dependent on other people's impressions, of necessity equally unreliable. Moreover, everyone tends to remember what he wants to remember. Disagreeable facts are sometimes glossed over or repressed, truth may be distorted for the sake of convenience or harmony and the occlusions of time may obscure as much as they reveal.

An autobiography may be largely fictional. Rousseau's *Confessions* (published posthumously in 1781 and 1788) are a case in point.

They are unreliable as literal truth; they have a different literary value.

From Classical times little in the way of autobiography survives, and it is likely that little was written. Then history and autobiography were almost the same thing – as we can see from the *Histories* of Herodotus, Xenophon's *Anabasis* and Caesar's *Commentaries.* Tacitus reports that Rutilius Rufus and Emilius Scaurus both wrote autobiographies, but they are not extant. The nearest we get to the modern conception of autobiography at this period is the *Meditations* of Marcus Aurelius, and these are of the 2nd c. AD.

The first autobiography of any note was St Augustine's *Confessions* of the 4th c.: an intensely personal account of spiritual experience and an extraordinary instance of deep psychological self-analysis of a kind that has become commonplace only in modern times.

In his *Ecclesiastial History*, Bede (*c.* 673–735) gave a brief account of his own life. Thereafter, there is little of note until the 15th c. when we find an unusual kind of spiritual autobiography in the shape of *The Book of Margery Kempe (c* 1420) by the mystic Margery Kempe (*c.* 1373–*c.* 1439). It was not until the 16th c. that autobiographies started to become common. The sculptor Benvenuto Cellini (1500–71) was the author of one of the most vivid autobiographies ever written. Another important instance was the *De Vita Propria Liber* by Cardan (1501–76), an extremely personal account. A curiosity of that period is Thomas Whythorne's account of his life, which, despite its title of *A Book of Songs and Sonetts*, is autobiographical. This work was discovered in 1955 and published in 1961. Much more remarkable is the autobiography of John Gerard, SJ, an account of his life as a hunted priest in England. He began it *c.* 1609, but it was not translated from the Latin and published until 1951. In 1580 the first *Essais* by Montaigne appeared – thoughtful and analytical excursions into his own self. It seems that the cult of anthropocentric humanism during the Renaissance period encouraged people to explore and analyse themselves in greater detail. The analysis of character and personality in plays, essays and character sketches became frequent. Increasing subjectivity was almost bound to produce autobiography.

From early in the 17th c. it became more and more the practice to keep a diary or a journal (*q.v.*), and to compile memoirs and soon the more or less 'straight' autobiographical narrative became commonplace. Notable instances were: Thomas Bodley's brief account of his own life published in 1647; Margaret Cavendish's *True Relation of My Birth, Breeding and Life* (1656); John

Bunyan's *Grace Abounding to the Chief of Sinners* (1666) and Richard Baxter's *Reliquiae Baxterianae* (1696). During the same period Evelyn and Pepys were compiling their famous diaries. Sir Thomas Browne's *Religio Medici* (1642) was a highly self-revealing form of autobiography.

Some autobiographies written in the 17th c. were not published until much later for political reasons. Three such distinguished examples were Lord Herbert of Cherbury's account of his life up until 1624 which was eventually printed by Horace Walpole in 1764, Sir Kenelm Digby's *Private Memoirs* which were not published until 1827–8, and Clarendon's *Life of Clarendon* which came out in 1759.

At the end of the 17th c. George Fox published his *Journal* (1694), a fascinating document. It set something of a vogue for 18th and 19th c. Quakers like Ellwood, Woolman, Pearson and Shilleto. John Wesley and fellow Wesleyans, too, wrote similar kinds of 'confessional' biographies. Wesley's *Journal* came out in 1771–4. Later Silas Todd and William Black published their lives.

Several other such works of great merit appeared during the 18th c. For example, Colley Cibber's *Apology for the Life of Colley Cibber* (1740), believed to be the first 'theatrical' autobiography; David Hume's *My Own Life* (1777); and Edward Gibbon's *Memoirs* (1796), which were put together by Lord Sheffield. Apart from these and Boswell's copious *Journals*, the two most famous personal accounts of the 18th c. were Benjamin Franklin's *Autobiography* (1766) and Rousseau's *Confessions* (1781 and 1788), the latter being one of the most influential books ever written.

During the 18th c. we find there is some connection between autobiography and the then relatively new form of the novel. For example, Defoe's *Robinson Crusoe* (1719) and Sterne's *Sentimental Journey* (1768) are taken to be a kind of autobiographical fiction, or fictionalized autobiography. A good deal of fiction since has been fairly thinly disguised autobiography; and there has been an enormous quantity of it in the last fifty years owing, in considerable measure, to the development of the stream of consciousness (*q.v.*) technique. Very occasionally, too, the long poem has been used for autobiography. The classic instance is Wordsworth's *The Prelude* completed in 1805, and published posthumously in 1850.

From early in the 19th c. autobiography of almost every kind (factual, detached narrative; self-communing narrative; 'progress of the soul' narrative) has proliferated. Some of the most notable works are: Goethe's *Die Wahlverwandtschaften* (1809); Leigh

Hunt's *Autobiography* (1850); Benjamin Haydon's *Autobiography* and *Journals* (1853); George Sand's *Histoire de ma vie* (1854–5); Sergei Aksakov's *A Family Chronicle* (1856), *Recollections* (1856) and *The Childhood Years of Bagrov Grandson* (1858); Cardinal Newman's *Apologia Pro Vita Sua* (1864); Alfred de Vigny's *Journal d'un poète* (1867); John Stuart Mill's *Autobiography* (1873); Carlyle's *Reminiscences* (1881); Mark Twain's *Life on the Mississippi* (1883); Trollope's *Autobiography* (1883); Renan's *Souvenirs d'enfance et de jeunesse* (1883); Ruskin's *Praeterita* (1886); Darwin's *Life and Letters of Charles Darwin* (1887); George Moore's *Confession of a Young Man* (1888), and in his later trilogy *Hail and Farewell* (1911–14); Stendhal's *Journal* (1888), covering the years 1801–18, and his *Vie de Henri Brûlard* (1890) and *Souvenirs d'égotisme* (1892), which covers the period 1822–30; Herbert Spencer's *Autobiography* (1904); Oscar Wilde's *De Profundis* (1905); A. R. Wallace's *My Life* (1905); Edmund Gosse's *Father and Son* (1907); W. H. Davies's *The Autobiography of a Super-Tramp* (1908); Gorki's *Childhood* (1913), which he was later to follow with *Among People* (1915) and *My Universities* (1923).

The First World War produced a number of a very fine autobiographical records: T. E. Lawrence's *Seven Pillars of Wisdom* (1926); Robert Graves's *Good-Bye to All That* (1927); Edmund Blunden's *Undertones of War* (1928); and Siegfried Sassoon's *Memoirs of an Infantry Officer* (1930). Sassoon also gave us *The Memoirs of a Fox-Hunting Man* (1928); *Sherston's Progress* (1930–36); *The Old Century* (1938); *The Weald of Youth* (1942); and *Siegried's Journey* (1945).

Other notable examples after the First World War have been: Barbellion's *Journal of a Disappointed Man* (1919); Forrest Reid's *Apostate* (1926); Vera Brittain's *Testament of Youth* (1933); Edith Wharton's *A Backward Glance* (1934); H. G. Wells's *Experiment in Autobiography* (1934); J. M. Barrie's *The Greenwood Hat* (1937); Frank Swinnerton's *An Autobiography* (1937); Havelock Ellis's *My Life* (1940); A. L. Rowse's *A Cornish Childhood* (1942); George Bernard Shaw's *Sixteen Self-Sketches* (1948); Sir Harold Acton's *Memoirs of an Aesthete* (1948), which he followed with *More Memoirs* (1970); James Agate's autobiographical diary in nine volumes titled *Ego* (1935–48); and Sir Osbert Sitwell's *Left Hand! Right Hand!* (1944–50), the first and title volume of a five-volume account of his life. This is one of the longest autobiographies ever written. Two copious collections of autobiographical journals stretch over the inter-war period and indeed began before the First

World War. They are Arnold Bennett's *Journals*, which he began in 1896 and eventually published in 1932–3, and André Gide's *Journals*, which he kept over much of his life – the 1885–1939 period being published in 1939, the 1939–42 period in 1946, and the 1942–9 period in 1950.

From *c.* 1950 autobiography started to proliferate on a huge scale and here it is possible to mention only a few of the many worth reading: Roy Campbell's *Light on a Dark Horse* (1951); Stephen Spender's *World Within World* (1951); Conrad Aiken's *Ushant* (1952); Carl Sandburg's *Always the Young Strangers* (1953); Brendan Behan's *Borstal Boy* (1958); Primo Levi's *Se questo è un uomo* (1958), which he was to follow with *La tregua* (1963); Simone de Beauvoir's *Mémoires d'une jeune fille rangée* (1959) and her later *La Force de l'âge* (1965) – she published four volumes of autobiography altogether; Gerald Brenan's *A Life of One's Own* (1962), which he was to follow with *Personal Record* (1974); P. J. Kavanagh's *The Perfect Stranger* (1963); Sir Herbert Read's *The Contrary Experience* (1963); Elmer Rice's *Minority Report* (1963); André Malraux's *Antimémoires* (1967) – a remarkable work and very different in method from most autobiographies; V. S. Pritchett's *The Cab at the Door: Early Years* (1968), which he was to follow with *Midnight Oil* (1971); Storm Jameson's *Journey from the North* (1967); Vernon Scannell's *The Tiger and the Rose* (1971); Graham Greene's *A Sort of Life* (1971), which he was to follow with *Ways of Escape* (1980); Naomi Mitchison's *Small Talk* (1973), *All Change Here* (1975) and *You May Well Ask* (1979); Peter Quennell's *The Marble Foot* (1975); Edward Lucie-Smith's *The Burnt Child* (1975); John Mortimer's *Clinging to the Wreckage* (1982); Sir Geoffrey Keynes's *The Gates of Memory* (1983); Peter Levi's *The Flutes of Autumn* (1983); V. S. Naipaul's *Finding the Centre* (1984).

There was also an extensive work by Leonard Woolf in the shape of a five-volume life: *Sowing* (1960), *Growing* (1961), *Beginning Again* (1964), *Downhill All the Way* (1967) and *The Journey not the Arrival Matters* (1969); the third volume gives an interesting account of the Bloomsbury Group (*q.v.*). There is also Sir Compton Mackenzie's marathon *My Life and Times* (1963–71), in ten octaves; a work which could have been cut heavily to its advantage.

To these might be added six highly individual and readable books of an autobiographical nature: namely, W. H. Hudson's *Far Away and Long Ago* (1918); Winston Churchill's *My Early Life* (1930);

Christopher Isherwood's *Lions and Shadows* (1938); Denton Welch's *Maiden Voyage* (1943); Flora Thompson's *Lark Rise to Candleford* (1945) and *Still Glides the Stream* (1948); Richard Church's *Over the Bridge* (1945), to which *The Golden Sovereign* (1957) was a less successful sequel; and John Lehmann's autobiographical trilogy: *The Whispering Gallery* (1955); *I am My Brother* (1960); *The Ample Proposition* (1966).

Since the Second World War almost anyone who has achieved distinction in life – and many who have not – has written an account of his life; especially politicians, statesmen and high-ranking members of the services. *See also* CONFESSIONAL LITERATURE; SUBJECTIVITY AND OBJECTIVITY.

autoclesis (Gk 'self-invitation') A rhetorical device by which an idea is introduced in negative terms in order to call attention to it and arouse curiosity. A classic example is Mark Antony's use of the will in *Julius Caesar* (III, ii) in order to rouse the mob's interest.

automatic writing Writing which is attempted without conscious control. It is more likely to be possible in states of hypnosis or under the influence of drugs. When dadaism and surrealism (*qq.v.*) were fashionable, the disciples of the creeds 'went in for' automatic writing. It produced the equivalent of a 'happening' (*q.v.*). Nothing of any importance survives.

autos sacramentales An allegorical and didactic genre of Spanish religious drama intended to expound the doctrines of the Church. The allegories were taken from biblical, Classical and historical themes. The plays were put on by the civic authorities and staged with pomp. Calderón (1600–81), the most famous of the playwrights who composed them, is credited with over eighty. *Autos* were performed until 1765, when they were banned by Charles III. *See also* ALLEGORY; MYSTERY PLAY.

autotelic (Gk 'self-completing') A jargon term employed in the New Criticism (*q.v.*) to denote that a poem, for instance, has no other end or purpose but to *be*; therefore it has no didactic, moral or any other additional purpose. The origins of the idea are found in the work of the 18th c. Swiss critics J. J. Bodmer and Breitinger. It helped to promote the doctrine of art for art's sake (*q.v.*) and also seems to have influenced those involved in the *avant-garde* (*q.v.*) *creacionismo* (*q.v.*) movement which developed *c.* 1916 in the

Spanish-speaking world and in France. The main theorist was Vicente Huidobro (1893–1948), the Chilean poet, who had some influence on the development of concrete poetry (*q.v.*). In France, Pierre Reverdy, a friend of Huidobro, was the main theorist.

auxesis *See* AMPLIFICATION.

avant-garde An important and much used term in the history of art and literature. It clearly has a military origin ('advance guard') and, as applied to art and literature, denotes exploration, pathfinding, innovation and invention; something new, something advanced (ahead of its time) and revolutionary.

In 1845, Gabriel-Désiré Laverdant published a work called *De la mission de l'art et du rôle des artistes.* In it he wrote:

> Art, the expression of society, manifests, in its highest soaring, the most advanced social tendencies: it is the forerunner and the revealer. Therefore, to know whether art worthily fulfils its proper mission as initiator, whether the artist is truly of the avant-garde, one must know where Humanity is going, what the destiny of the human race is . . .

In 1878 Bakunin founded and published for a short time a periodical devoted to political agitation called *L'Avant-garde*. Even at this period it is rare to find the term applied to art and literature alone. Baudelaire treats it with scorn. In his personal notebook, *Mon cœur mis à nu*, he refers to 'les littérateurs d'avant-garde', and elsewhere he speaks of 'la presse militante' and 'la littérature militante'. He is referring to radical writers, to writers of the political left.

During the last quarter of the 19th c. the term and concept appear in both cultural and political contexts. Gradually the cultural-artistic meaning displaced the socio-political meaning. For a long time it has been commonplace to refer to *avant-garde* art or literature. Nowadays we are accustomed to think of the symbolist poets Verlaine, Rimbaud and Mallarmé as the first members of the *avant-garde*; likewise the playwrights of the Theatre of the Absurd (*q.v.*) and novelists like Alain Robbe-Grillet, Michel Butor, Nathalie Sarraute. *See* ANTI-NOVEL; NOUVEAU ROMAN; NOUVELLE VAGUE.

aversio *See* APOSTROPHE.

awdl Originally this Welsh term was a variant of *odl* and came to acquire several meanings in succession: a stave (*q.v.*) bearing the rhyme, a series of monorhymes, a poem in monorhyme (*q.v.*), a poem in particular *awdl* meters, and then a poem of some length in *cynghanedd* (*q.v.*) and in one of the strict meters (*q.v.*). In Wales an *awdl* is regarded as the summit of bardic achievement. *See* BARD; EISTEDDFOD.

B

bacchius A metrical foot consisting of one unstressed syllable followed by two stressed ones: ∪//. The name may derive from the use of the foot in Greek drinking songs and verses devoted to the god Bacchus. Rare in English verse; not many three-syllable words take such quantities. *See* PALIMBACCHIUS.

back-formation The formation of what *appears* to be a root-word from a word which might be (but is not) a derivative of it. For example: *burgle* from *burglar*; *edit* from *editor*. *See* APOCOPE.

back slang A simple form of cryptic slang which consists merely of reversing words and saying them backwards. Thus, 'There aren't any apples for sale today' becomes 'Ereth tonera yna selppa rof elas yadot'. Cockneys are believed to be the originators of it and it can still be heard occasionally in London markets. It enables stallholders to communicate with one another without bystanders or customers understanding. *See* ARGOT; PATOIS; SLANG.

Baconian theory The theory that Francis Bacon (1561–1626) wrote the plays ascribed to Shakespeare. This hypothesis began to achieve some vogue in the middle of the 19th c. but is not now taken seriously.

In 1920 the unfortunately named T. J. Looney identified Edward de Vere, 17th Earl of Oxford (1550–1604), as the author of Shakespeare's plays. Since then the so-called 'Oxfordians' have tried to promote the claim.

bailes (Sp 'dances') A term used in Golden Age (*q.v.*) literature to denote compositions for music, song and dance, usually performed between the second and third acts of three-act *comedias*. A notable example is *Las flores* by Alonso de Olmedo, used as an interlude (*q.v.*) in Calderón's *Hado y divisa* (1680). *Bailes* were composed by many authors.

Bakhtinian *See* CARNIVALIZATION/CARNIVALESQUE; HETEROGLOSSIA.

balada A dance song of Provençal origin. It was not a fixed form but it had a refrain (*q.v.*) that was often repeated.

ballad Like *ballade* (*q.v.*) and ballet, the word derives from the late Latin and Italian *ballare* 'to dance'. Fundamentally a ballad is a song that tells a story and originally was a musical accompaniment to a dance. We can distinguish certain basic characteristics common to large numbers of ballads: (a) the beginning is often abrupt; (b) the language is simple; (c) the story is told through dialogue and action; (d) the theme is often tragic (though there are a number of comic ballads); (e) there is often a refrain (*q.v.*). To these features we may add: a ballad usually deals with a single episode; the events leading to the crisis are related swiftly; there is minimal detail of surroundings; there is a strong dramatic element; there is considerable intensity and immediacy in the narration; the narrator is impersonal; stock, well-tried epithets are used in the oral tradition (*q.v.*) of kennings and Homeric epithets (*qq.v.*); there is frequently incremental repetition (*q.v.*); the single line of action and the speed of the story preclude much attempt at delineation of character; imagery is sparse and simple.

We may distinguish further between two basic kinds of ballad: the folk or traditional ballad and the literary ballad. The former is anonymous and is transmitted from singer to singer by word of mouth. It thus belongs to oral tradition (*q.v.*). In this manner ballads have been passed down from generation to generation over centuries. Inevitably, this has led to many variations of one particular story. The folk ballad has tended to flourish among illiterate or semi-literate peoples in rural environments, and is still a living tradition in northern Greece, in parts of the central Balkans (e.g. Bosnia-Hercegovina, Montenegro and Serbia) and in Sicily. Faroese and Icelandic ballad-makers continue to add to the corpus of traditional ballads. The latter kind of ballad is not anonymous and is written down by a poet as he composes it. These considerations apart, ballads of both traditions have distinct similarities. Here are two examples: firstly a traditional oral ballad; secondly a literary ballad by a modern poet, Charles Causley.

The Twa Corbies

As I was walking all alone,
  I heard twa corbies making a mane;
The tane unto the t'other say,
  'Where sall we gang and dine to-day?'

'In behint yon auld fail dyke,
  I wot there lies a new-slain knight;
And naebody kens that he lies there,
  But his hawk, his hound and his lady fair.

His hound is to the hunting gane,
  His hawk, to fetch the wild-fowl hame,
His lady's ta'en another mate,
  So we may mak our dinner sweet.

Ye'll sit on his white hause-bane,
  And I'll pike out his bonny blue een.
Wi'ae lock o' his gowden hair,
  We'll theek our nest when it grows bare.

'Mony a one for him makes mane,
  But nane sall ken whare he is gane;
O'er his white banes, when they are bare,
  The wind sall blaw for evermair.'

Mother, Get Up, Unbar the Door

Mother, get up, unbar the door,
Throw wide the window-pane,
I see a man stand all covered in sand
Outside in Vicarage Lane.

His body is shot with seventy stars,
His face is as cold as Cain,
His coat is a crust of desert dust
And he comes from Alamein.

He has not felt the flaking frost,
He has not felt the rain,
And not one blow of the burning snow
Since the night that he was slain.

O mother, in your husband's arms
Too long now you have lain,
Rise up, my dear, your true-love's here
Upon the peaceful plain.

Though, mother, on your broken brow
Forty long years are lain,
The soldier they slew at twenty-two
Never a one does gain.

I will unlock the fine front door
And snap the silver chain,
And meek as milk in my skin of silk
I'll ease him of his pain.

My breast has been for years eighteen
As white as Charles's wain,
But now I'm had by a soldier lad
Whistling *Lili Marlene*.

Farewell to Jack, farewell to Jim,
And farewell Mary Jane,
Farewell the good green sisterhood
Knitting at purl and plain.

Go wash the water from your eye,
The bullet from your brain.
I'm drowned as a dove in the tunnel of love
And I'll never come home again.

Many historians and critics distinguish a third kind of ballad – the popular. This has much in common with the traditional or folk ballad. However, it tends to be associated with semi-literate or literate *urban* rather than rural communities, and is often very realistic, unheroic and comic or satirical (e.g. *The Darlaston Dogfight*, *Wednesbury Cocking*). Occasionally it may be tragic: for example, *The Gresford Disaster* and *The Sorrowful Lamentation, Confession and Last Farewell to the World of John Lomas*. It is sometimes called the broadside ballad (see below) or street ballad and, like the traditional ballad, has influenced many poets (e.g. Pope, Byron, Wordsworth, Blake, Coleridge, Shelley and Oscar Wilde).

Ballad is a poetic form of great antiquity. Apart from those ballads which we may presume were the main materials for Homer's epics, the main ballad tradition in Europe begins to be evident in the late Middle Ages: in Denmark in the 12th c., in Russia in the 13th, in Spain, Scotland and England in the 14th. By the end of the 14th c. the ballad tradition was already well established in Scandinavia and in South Slav countries.

The ballad poet drew his materials from community life, from local and national history, from legend and folklore. His tales are usually of adventure, war, love, death and the supernatural. A very notable cycle combining all these themes and elements is the group of epic ballads or *narodne pesme* (*q.v.*) which grew up in Serbia as a result of the battle of Kosovo in 1389. In the British Isles the border conflicts between English and Scots produced many splendid ballads. Further important sources of balladry in England were the stories and legends of Robin Hood.

Among traditional ballads on various themes one should mention particularly *The Elfin Knight*; *The Twa Sisters*; *Lord Randal*; *The Cruel Mother*; *The Three Ravens*; *Clerk Colvill*; *Young Beichan*; *The Wife of Usher's Well*; *The Bailiff's Daughter of Islington*; *The Gypsy Laddie*; *James Harris*; *The Demon Lover*; and *Get up and Bar the Door.*

Of the Robin Hood and Border Ballads the following are among the better known: *Robin Hood and the Monk*; *Robin Hood's Death*; *Chevy Chase*; *Johnnie Armstrong*; *Johnnie Cock*; and *Captain Car.*

In the 18th c. the ballad tradition was particularly alive in Scotland, from which period survive *Edward*, *Sir Patrick Spens*, *Thomas Rymer*, *Tam Lin*, *Geordie* and *Marie Hamilton.*

There are also a number of famous broadside (*q.v.*) ballads, some of which are anonymous and some of which are ascribed to authors. For instance: *A Ballade of the Scottyshe Kynge* (1513) by John Skelton; *The Journey into France*; *A Ballade Upon a Wedding* by Sir John Suckling; *On the Lord Mayor and Court of Alderman* (1674) by Andrew Marvell; *Clever Tom Clinch going to be hanged* (1726) by Swift; *Newgate's Garland* (1725) by John Gay; *The Fine Old English Gentleman* (1841) by Charles Dickens; *Wednesbury Cocking*; *Miss Bailey's Ghost*; and *Danny Deever* by Rudyard Kipling.

There are also many fine Irish traditional ballads, particularly: *Brian O'Linn*; *Dunlavin Green*; *Brennan on the Moor*; *The Rocky Road to Dublin*; *The Night before Larry was Stretched*; *Mrs McGrath*; *The Old Orange Flute*; *Kevin Barry*; *The Ballad of Persse O'Reilly*, and *Van Diemen's Land.*

Among Australian and American ballads the following are more or less famous: *The Wild Colonial Boy*; *The Death of Morgan*; *Stir the Wallaby Stew*; *Barbara Allen*; *The Jam on Jerry's Rock*; *The Dying Cowboy*; *Blow the Candle Out*.

Among ballads in the literary tradition there are several distinguished works, especially Coleridge's *Rime of the Ancient Mariner*; Keats's *La Belle Dame Sans Merci*; Wilde's *The Ballad of Reading Gaol*; W. S. Gilbert's *Bab Ballads*; Chesterton's *Ballad of the White Horse*; Kipling's *Barrack Room Ballads*; and Masefield's *Salt-water Ballads*. To these should be added works which are in the ballad style. For instance, Scott's *Lay of the Last Minstrel* and *Lochinvar*; Macaulay's *Lays of Ancient Rome*; and a number of works by Alfred Noyes (especially *The Highwayman*). Robert Service also wrote many poems which owe much to the traditional ballad – particularly *The Shooting of Dan MacGrew*. More recently the tradition of balladry has been sustained with many good poems by Charles Causley. Vernon Watkins's long narrative peom *The Ballad of the Mari Lwyd* also shows how alive and flexible this form still is.

Since early in the 18th c. there have been several important collections of ballad literature, namely: Allan Ramsay's *The Tea-table Miscellany* (3 vols., 1724–32); Percy's *Reliques of Ancient English Poetry* (1765); J. Ritson's *Pieces of Ancient Popular Poetry* (1791); Walter Scott's *Minstrelsy of the Scottish Border* (3 vols., 1802–3); F. J. Child's *The English and Scottish Popular Ballads* (8 vols., 1857–9, 1882–98); B. H. Bronson's *The Traditional Tunes of the Child Ballads* (3 vols., 1959–66); A. Clark's *The Shirburn Ballads* (1907); Cecil Sharp's *Folk Songs of England* (5 vols., 1908–12); A. Quiller-Couch's *The Oxford Book of Ballads* (1910); *The Faber Book of Ballads* (1965). *See also* BALLAD METER; BALLAD OPERA; FOLKSONG; LAY; NARRATIVE VERSE.

ballade An OF verse form, particularly popular during the 14th and 15th c. The commonest type consists of three eight-line stanzas rhyming ababbcbc, with a four-line *envoi* (*q.v.*) rhyming bcbc. The last line of the first stanza serves as the refrain (*q.v.*) repeated in the last line of each stanza and of the *envoi*. Its rhyming complexity makes the *ballade* a difficult form.

The *ballade* was standardized by the 14th c. French poets like Guillaume de Machaut and Eustache Deschamps, and perfected in the next century, principally by Villon (especially in, for instance, *Ballade des pendus* and *Ballade des dames du temps jadis*). By the 17th c. there was little regard for the form; it was mocked by Molière and Boileau.

Medieval English poets (especially Chaucer and Gower) occasionally imitated it but it never became popular. It was not until the 19th c. that English poets – notably Dobson, Lang, W. E. Henley and Swinburne – revived it with mixed success. Since then the few who have attempted it include Chesterton, Belloc and Sir John Squire. *See also* BALLAD; BALLAD METER; CHANT ROYAL; TERN.

ballad meter Traditionally a four-line stanza or quatrain (*q.v.*) containing alternating four-stress and three-stress lines. The rhyme scheme is usually abcb; sometimes abab. A refrain (*q.v.*) is common. Here is the opening stanza of *Earl Brand*:

> Rise up, rise up, my seven brave sons,
> And dress in your armour so bright;
> Earl Douglas will hae Lady Margaret awa
> Before that it be light.

ballad opera It may be considered an early form of musical (*q.v.*). It combines dialogue in dramatic prose (which is spoken rather than 'sung' or chanted in any way) with music and songs, usually set to traditional and contemporary melodies. It was virtually invented by John Gay when he composed *The Beggar's Opera* (1728), a play with music and songs interpolated (the music was arranged by J. C. Pepusch). This has remained a regular favourite with amateur and professional theatre companies (cf. Alan Ayckbourn's *Chorus of Disapproval*, 1987). There were many imitations of Gay's work in the 18th c. and ballad opera was very popular for some twenty years. Gay wrote a sequel, *Polly*, to *The Beggar's Opera*, and this was eventually produced in 1777. Other 18th c. works of note which are very like ballad opera were Arne and Bickerstaffe's *Thomas and Sally* (1760) and *Love in a Village* (1762). Sheridan also made a contribution to this form with *The Duenna* (1775). In the 20th c. Bertolt Brecht experimented with the form and produced one outstanding example in the shape of *The Threepenny Opera* (1928), a reworking of Gay's theme and story. Thereafter the main practitioner was Ewan MacColl (1915–89), who wrote several. His *Johnny Noble* (1945) was particularly fine. *See* BALLAD; OPERA.

barbarism An impropriety of language. The term includes a mistake in the form of a word and the unwarranted use of foreign words.

barcarole (It *barca* 'boat') A poem or song whose subject matter is in some way connected with boats or water; also one whose aural effects can suggest the movement of water. Dates from the Middle Ages.

bard (Welsh, *bardd*; Irish, *bard*) Among the ancient Celts a bard was a sort of official poet whose task it was to celebrate national events – particularly heroic actions and victories. The bardic poets of Gaul and Britain were a distinct social class with special privileges. The 'caste' continued to exist in Ireland and Scotland, but nowadays are more or less confined to Wales, where the poetry contests and festivals, known as the Eisteddfodau, were revived in 1822 (after a lapse since Elizabethan times). In modern Welsh a *bardd* is a poet who has taken part in an Eisteddfod (*q.v.*). In more common parlance the term may be half seriously applied to a distinguished poet – especially Shakespeare.

baroque The term probably derives from the word *baroco*, often used in the late Middle Ages to describe any form of grotesque pedantry. It is a term more commonly used of the visual arts (and music) than literature, but it may be used judiciously to describe a particularly ornate or sumptuous style. It can be applied, for example, to the prose of Sir Thomas Browne and to the more extravagant conceits (*q.v.*) of Crashaw and Cleveland, all writers who flourished in the Baroque period. *See* EUPHUISM; GONGORISM; MANNERISM; MARINISM; SECENTISMO.

barzelletta (It 'joke, funny story') An Italian verse form. Originally it was a mixture of disconnected and nonsensical matter presented in variable meters and rhymes. It the 14th c. it denoted epigram and didactic verse. Later it was used by love poets but seems to have remained a very flexible form with which a poet might do much as he pleased. *See also* NONSENSE.

basic English A language devised by Ogden and Richards and presented in 1930. Its carefully selected vocabulary consisted of only 830 words – of which 600 were nouns, and 150 were adjectives. The remainder were what they called 'operators': that is, verbs, adverbs, prepositions and conjunctions. Though the range of expression was limited it was serviceable.

batch An early English word for a stanza (*q.v.*). *See also* FIT; STAVE.

bathos (Gk 'depth') In a mock critical treatise called *Peri Bathous, or, Of the Art of Sinking in Poetry* (1728), Pope assures the reader that he will 'lead them as it were by the hand . . . the gentle downhill way to Bathos; the bottom, the end, the central point, the non plus ultra, of true Modern Poesy!'

Bathos is achieved when a writer, striving at the sublime, overreaches himself and topples into the absurd. Pope illustrates bathos himself with the lines:

> Ye Gods! annihilate but Space and Time
> And make two lovers happy.

There is a fine collection of the bathetic in *The Stuffed Owl* (1930, rev. ed. 1948), an anthology of bad verse selected by Wyndham Lewis and C. Lee. *See* ANTICLIMAX.

battle of the books *See* ANCIENTS AND MODERNS.

beast epic An allegorical tale, often, but by no means always, long, in which animals are characters and in which the style is pseudo-epic. The 1st c. collection of Latin fables made by Phaedrus was, after Aesop, the source and inspiration of a very large number of fables in European literature. The prototypal beast epic is almost certainly *Roman de Renart*, composed late in the 12th c. by Pierre de Saint-Cloud. The first episode is the Chanticleer story later used by Chaucer in the *Nun's Priest's Tale* (*c.* 1395). Spenser continued the tradition in *Mother Hubbard's Tale* (1590). Goethe used it in his *Reineke Fuchs* (1794). The intention of this form was often satirical, like many fables. Orwell's *Animal Farm* (1945) is in the same tradition. *See also* ALLEGORY; BESTIARY; EPIC; FABLE; MOCK-EPIC.

beat Metrical emphasis in poetry, sometimes used as a synonym for stress (*q.v.*). *See also* ACCENT; METER.

beat generation The term 'beat', in this restricted sense, is generally believed to have been devised by Jack Kerouac (1922–69). It bears connotations of down-beat, off-beat, down-and-out, drop-out and beatitude, and denotes a group of American writers (especially poets) who became prominent in the 1950s. They are particularly associated with San Francisco, USA, and their generally accepted father-figures were Kenneth Rexroth, Henry Miller and William Burroughs. The beat writers (and many of the 'beat generation') developed their own slang and a highly idiosyncratic style. Their convictions and attitudes were unconventional, provocative, anti-intellectual, anti-hierarchical and anti-middle-class (the 'squares'). They were influenced by jazz, by Zen Buddhism and by American Indian and Mexican Peyote cults, and their Bohemian lifestyle was popularly associated with drugs, 'free' sex, drink and permissive living in general. It was in some respects anarchic and provoked considerable hostility. Allen Ginsberg's *Howl and Other Poems* (1956) represents as well as anything the disillusionment of the beat movement with modern society, its materialism and militarism and its outmoded, stuffed-shirt, middle-class values and mores. Ginsberg's *Kaddish* (1960), an elegy for his mother, and *Reality Sandwiches* (1963) were other important publications. So were Lawrence Ferlinghetti's *Pictures of the Gone World* (1955) and *A Coney Island of the Mind* (1958), Gregory Corso's *Gasoline* (1958) and *Bomb* (1959), and Gary Snyder's collection of work songs and *haikus* (*q.v.*) in *Riprap* (1959). Jack Kerouac himself made memorable contributions to the beat movement and literature with his prose works *On the Road* (1957), *The Dharma Bums* (1958) and *Big Sur* (1962). The novels of William Burroughs (e.g. *Junkie*, 1953, *The Naked Lunch*, 1959, *Minutes to Go*, 1960) and John Clellon Holmes (e.g. *Go*, 1952, *The Horn*, 1958) are also closely associated with the beat movement, whose influence was to go far beyond the English-speaking world. It is discernible, for instance, in the work of the Russians Yevtushenko and Voznesensky. It created a cult and affected pop culture. *See also* BLACK MOUNTAIN POETS; JAZZ POETRY; SUB-CULTURE.

beginning rhyme This is rare. An example occurs in Thomas Hood's *Bridge of Sighs*:

> *Mad* from life's history,
> *Glad* to death's mystery.

belles lettres (F 'fine letters') The term is the literary counterpart of *beaux arts*. Formerly, it was the equivalent of the 'humanities' or *literae humaniores* (literally, 'the more human letters'). Swift appears to have been the first to use the term in English literature, in *Tatler* No. 230 (1710), where he refers to '. . . Traders in History and Politicks, and the Belles lettres'. Now it is applied almost exclusively to literary studies, the aesthetics of literature and, conceivably, what may be described as 'light' literature, but not fiction or poetry. Often the essay (*q.v.*) is the favoured form of the belle-lettrist. The works of Max Beerbohm provide good examples. So do those of Aldous Huxley, many of whose collections of essays (*Themes and Variations*, *Vulgarity in Literature*, *Music at Night*, etc.) are listed as *belles lettres*. They are witty, elegant, urbane and learned – the characteristics one would expect of *belles lettres.*

bergette A single strophe (*q.v.*) *rondeau* (*q.v.*) without a refrain (*q.v.*). Now used sometimes for light verse (*q.v.*).

Berliner Ensemble An important and influential theatrical company founded in East Berlin in 1949. It moved to the Theater am Schiffbauerdamm in 1954. A new theatre was opened in 1980. Bertolt Brecht was a vital influence on its work and many of his plays were performed by it; Brecht's wife, the actress Helene Weigel, made an invaluable contribution. Manfred Wekwerth (1929–) has been its most notable director.

Besserungsstück (G 'recovery' or 'improvement' play) A minor dramatic genre of Viennese provenance which was popular in the early part of the 19th c. The themes of such plays were concerned with the remedy and cure of some evil or malady or grave shortcoming in the main character. Among notable examples are *Die Musikanten am hohen Markt* (1815) and *Der Berggeist* (1819), both by Joseph Gleich (1772–1841). *See also* LOKALPOSSE; VOLKSSTUCK.

bestiary A medieval didactic genre in prose or verse in which the behaviour of animals (used as symbolic types) points a moral. The prototype is very probably the Greek *Physiologus* (2nd–4th c. AD), a compendium of some fifty fabulous anecdotes. This was widely translated, especially into Latin. During the 12th c. additions were made to Latin versions, and these derived from the *Etymologiae* of Isidore of Seville (570–636). The period of greatest popularity for bestiaries in Europe was from the 12th to the 14th c., especially in French. The development and combination of story and moral in the bestiaries had some influence on the evolution of the *exemplum* and the fable (*qq.v.*). Literary sleuths have surmised that such stories as Orwell's *Animal Farm* (1945) and Richard Adams's *Watership Down* (1972) are modern developments of the bestiary. *See also* BEAST EPIC.

best-seller This term first came into frequent use in the 1920s, and in its proper sense denotes a book that at any given time (in a particular country) is selling more copies than any other work. It is one that captures popular interest and imagination; for example, Voltaire's *Candide* (1759) or Byron's *Don Juan* (1819). More recent instances are Remarque's *All Quiet on the Western Front* (1929), Margaret Mitchell's *Gone with the Wind* (1936), Nicholas Monsarrat's *The Cruel Sea* (1951) and John Le Carré's *The Spy Who Came in from the Cold* (1963). *Jane's Fighting Ships*, *Aircraft Recognition* and the Bible are perennial best-sellers.

bhakti (Skt 'serve, enjoy') The term denotes popular religious poetry in the vernacular languages of medieval India.

bibelot A French word for a very small book.

biblio- A number of words, apart from bibliography (*q.v.*), which relate to literature, are built on this stem. The main ones are: BIBLIOCLASM (Gk 'breaking of a book'): the destruction of a book or books for religious, ideological or other reasons; BIBLIOCLAST: a destroyer of books; BIBLIOGONY (Gk 'book making'): the production of books; BIBLIOLATRY (Gk 'book worship'): an excessive devotion to or reverence for a book or books. (The bibliophile (*q.v.*) is susceptible to it; so are worshippers of the Bible and other sacred books (*q.v.*).); BIBLIOMANCY (Gk 'divination by book'): the practice of opening the Bible or a comparable work at random and interpreting the first verse or verses as a form of prophecy or precognition; BIBLIOMANIA (Gk 'book madness'): a manic devotion to the collection and possession of books; BIBLIOPHILE (Gk 'book lover'): one who collects, cherishes and preserves books for their value as physical objects, as well as for other reasons; BIBLIOPOLE (Gk 'book merchant'): a book-seller or book dealer; BIBLIOTAPH (Gk 'book' and 'tomb'): a burier of books; a concealer and hoarder; one who keeps them under lock and key; BIBLIOTECHA (Gk 'book' and 'repository'): a collection of books; a library; a bibliographer's catalogue.

bibliography (Gk 'book writing') A list of books, essays and monographs on a subject; or a list of the works of a particular author. More strictly the historical study of the make-up and form of books as physical objects. The study of printing and the physical composition, format, of books is known as 'analytical' or 'critical bibliography'; the detailed and formal description of books is 'descriptive bibliography'; and the application of the methods and the evidence to textual criticism (*q.v.*) is 'textual bibliography'.

Biedermeier In the first place this was a grotesque figure who originated in *Fliegende Blätter*, the German *Punch*. The caricature symbolized narrow-minded Philistinism and a head-in-the-sand attitude. Ludwig Eichrodt parodied the type in nonsense verses published in 1869 as *Biedermeiers Liederlust*. Later the name *Biedermeierstil* was given to the type of early Victorian furniture and décor common in Germany between 1815 and 1848. The term was also extended to describe painting, sculpture, music and literature. *See also* GROBIANISM.

bienséances, les A French term closely related to *vraisemblance* (*q.v.*), which means and implies appropriate decorum, of which there are two kinds: external and internal. The former requires that a character behave as his rank, position, title, etc. demand; the latter that a character behave in character as he or she is depicted within the play, novel or story. *See also* CONSISTENCY; VERISIMILITUDE.

Bildergedicht (G 'picture poem') *See* ALTAR POEM; CONCRETE POETRY/VERSE; LETTRISM; MERZ; PATTERN POETRY.

Bildungsroman (G 'formation novel') This is a term more or less synonymous with *Erziehungsroman* – literally an 'upbringing' or 'education' novel (*q.v.*). Widely used by German critics, it refers to a novel which is an account of the youthful development of a hero or heroine (usually the former). It describes the processes by which maturity is achieved through the various ups and downs of life. The earliest example is usually taken to be Wieland's *Agathon* (1765–6). The most famous (and most often imitated) examples are Goethe's *Die Leiden des jungen Werthers* (1774) and his *Wilhelm Meisters Lehrjahre* (1795–6) – which became well known in Britain through Thomas Carlyle's translation of 1824. Other celebrated examples in German are Tieck's *Sternbalds Wanderungen* (1798), Keller's *Der grüne Heinrich* (1854), Freytag's *Soll und Haben* (1855), Stifter's *Der Nachsommer* (1857), and Raabe's *Der Hungerpastor* (1864). Plus, in the 20th c., Thomas Mann's *Königliche Hoheit* (1904), *Der Zauberberg* (1924) and *Joseph und seine Brüder* (1933–42). In France Flaubert's *L'Education sentimentale* (1869) is an instance.

Novels in English that might be put into this category are Defoe's *Moll Flanders* (1722), Fielding's *Tom Jones* (1749), Jane Austen's *Emma* (1816), Dickens's *David Copperfield* (1849–50), Meredith's *The Adventures of Henry Richmond* (1871) and Samuel Butler's *The Way of All Flesh*, though autobiography, too (1903). Joyce's *A Portrait of the Artist as a Young Man* (1916) has also been so classified but Germans would call this a *Künstlerroman* (*q.v.*), or 'artist novel'. A recent instance is Doris Lessing's five-volume work *Children of Violence* (1952–69), whose heroine is Martha Quest. *See also* AUTOBIOGRAPHICAL NOVEL; ZEITROMAN.

binary opposition The term 'binary' denotes 'composed of two', 'twofold'; as in a binary star, 'one of a pair of stars held together by gravitation'. Language, too, has countless binary oppositions: up/down; slow/fast; sense/nonsense; truth/falsehood; black/white; man/woman – and so on. The concept of binary opposition is central to structuralism (*q.v.*) and structuralist practice. As a structuralist concept it derives especially from Lévi-Strauss's studies of mythology. Linguistics and structuralist analysis use the notion of binary opposition not only in terms of words or concepts but in terms of the conventions or codes of a text. For deconstruction, and post-structuralism (*qq.v.*), the notion of binary opposition is unsatisfactory because it represents a nostalgia for 'self-presence' or 'centring'. Derrida's *Structure, Sign and Play in the Discourse of the Human Sciences* (1966) criticizes Lévi-Strauss's hankering for essences in his interpretation of myth. The very idea of a binary opposition implies a centring or imposition of order: such binary signification is stable and systematic to structuralists, and unstable and decentred to post-structuralists. Deconstructive practice seeks to undermine, loosen, such analogical oppositions (which tend to oversimplify meaning) and reveal how a text undermines the imposition of binary structure on it through *apòria* and indeterminancy (*qq.v.*) and through its inherent 'disseminations' (i.e. the 'surplus' or 'overspill' of meaning). *See* DISSEMINATION.

biography An account of a person's life, and a branch of history. Dryden defined it as the 'history of particular men's lives'. As a literary form it has become increasingly popular since the second half of the 17th c., before which period it is rare.

Almost any form of material is germane to the biographer's purpose: the subject's own writings (especially diaries and letters), his laundry bills, official archives, memoirs of contemporaries, the memories of living witnesses, personal knowledge, other books on the subject, photographs and paintings.

The origins of biography are no doubt to be found in the early accounts of monarchs and heroes; in, for example, the Old Testament stories, in the Greek, Celtic and Scandinavian epics and sagas. The sayings of wise and holy men are also a branch of biography; and we can learn a lot about Socrates, for instance, from Plato's teaching; as we can from Xenophon's *Memorabilia*. However, the Roman historians Plutarch, Tacitus and Suetonius were the pioneers of the form. Plutarch's *Parallel Lives* (1st c. AD) covered twenty-three Greeks and twenty-three Romans, arranged in pairs. They proved an important source of plots for many plays, including some by Shakespeare. Sir Thomas North produced a version of them from a French translation in 1579. Incidentally, Plutarch seems to have been the first writer to distinguish between biography and history. The main biographical work of Tacitus is contained in his *Histories* (*c.* 104–9) which deal with the reigns of the emperors from Galba to Domitian. An outstanding work by Tacitus is his account of Agricola, his father-in-law. Suetonius wrote *Lives of the Caesars* (from Julius Caesar to Domitian) and also lives of Terence, Horace and Lucan. The lives of the Caesars are particularly readable because they are full of gossip and scandal, but as history they are unreliable.

There was little in the way of biography in the Middle Ages, for, with few exceptions, the lives of the saints were idealized according to predictable patterns. However, hagiology does contain some notable instances of good biography. One should mention especially Bede's account of St Cuthbert and St Adamnan's account of St Columba. Eadmer wrote an admirable biography of St Anselm. Secular biographies from the Middle Ages include Asser's Life of Alfred (*c.* 900); Aelfric's lives of St Oswald and St Edmund; and various lives of Edward the Confessor in both prose and verse. A remarkable work dating from the later Middle Ages is Boccaccio's *De Casibus Virorum et Feminarum Illustrium* (late 14th c.).

At the Renaissance biography, like autobiography (*q.v.*), acquired considerable interest. Notable achievements in the 16th c. were Sir Thomas More's *Life of John Picus, Earl of Mirandola* (1510) and his *History of Richard III* (1543, 1557); Vasari's important *Lives of the Painters* (1550, 1568); Thomas Cavendish's *Life of Cardinal Wolsey* (a contemporary account but not published until 1641); and William Roper's *The Life of Sir Thomas More* (written *c.* 1558 but not published until 1626). To these should be added John Leland's huge collection of lives of English authors which John Bale was to make use of.

The Elizabethan period in England produced some notable translations of Classical biographers and also Bacon's *The History of Henry VII* (not published until 1622). Like Plutarch, Bacon made clear distinctions between biography and history.

The 17th c. was the most important period for the development of English biography. From this age date Aubrey's *Brief Lives* (not published until 1813) and Izaak Walton's *Lives* of Donne, Sir Henry Wotton, Richard Hooker, George Herbert and Robert Sanderson (the first four were written over a long period and published in one volume in 1670; the last appeared in 1678). These works are major contributions to the course of biography. Less important but notable are Bishop Burner's *Life and Death of John, Earl of Rochester* (1680), Sprat's *Life of Cowley* (1688), and Dryden's biography of Plutarch, which prefaced his translation of Plutarch's *Lives* published in 1683. Dryden clearly understood the business of the biographer better than most.

In the 18th c. the principal works are Roger North's *The Lives of the Norths* (1740–44), Mason's *Life of Gray* (1774), Johnson's *Lives of the Poets* (1779–81) and Boswell's *Life of Johnson* (1791). Johnson was one of the most influential and accomplished of biographers. Before him many biographies had been ruined by excessive adulation and, in some cases, indiscriminate panegyric. Johnson changed all this. He was not interested in what he described as 'honeysuckle lives' but in presenting a rounded and detailed portrait of a person. His life of Savage is an outstanding example of his method. Many think that Boswell's *Life of Johnson* is still the supreme example in this genre. Between them, Johnson and Boswell virtually decided the course of biography in the early 19th c., when biographies began to appear in great numbers: Southey's *Life of Nelson* (1813) and his *Life of Wesley* (1820); Moore's *Life and Letters of Byron* (1830); Hogg's *Early Life of Shelley* (1832); and Lockhart's *Life of Sir Walter Scott* (1838).

In the mid-Victorian period a certain prudishness and gentility pervaded biographical works for the worse. The truth was glozed by the need for 'respectability' and reticence candied over anything scandalous or disagreeable. However, there were honourable exceptions, like Carlyle's portrait of Abbot Samson in *Past and Present* (1843) and his account of *The Life and Times of Frederick the Great* (1858–65). Earlier, in 1824, Carlyle had published a good biography of Schiller. Mrs Gaskell's *Life of Charlotte Brontë* (1857) is also a distinguished work; as is Forster's *Life of Charles Dickens* (1872–4). Eventually Carlyle's friend and disciple Froude produced a major biography of Carlyle himself (1882–4). Other notable works from the second half of the 19th c. are Masson's *Milton* (1859–80), Morley's *Voltaire* (1872) and his *Rousseau* (1876), plus a large number of works by various authors in the Series *English Men of Letters* and *Heroes of the Nations*.

Soon after the First World War Lytton Strachey brought about something of a revolution in the art of biography. Like Carlyle and Froude, he despised panegyric and prolixity. He did not hesitate to be selective. His method was to criticize and expose, often irreverently. He wrote with elegance, ironic wit and acute perception. His biographies are supreme of their kind and include *Eminent Victorians* (1918), *Queen Victoria* (1921), *Books and Characters* (1922), *Elizabeth and Essex* (1928) and *Portraits in Miniature* (1931).

Apart from Strachey, during the 20th c., among English biographers Harold Nicolson is generally regarded as one of the ablest. His most notable works are *Tennyson* (1923), *Byron, the Last Journey* (1924), *Lord Carnock* (1930), *Curzon, the Last Phase* (1934) and *Helen's Tower* (1937). Hesketh Pearson, a contemporary of Nicolson, wrote several very readable and popular biographies: on Hazlitt (1934), Sydney Smith (*The Smith of Smiths*, 1934), George Bernard Shaw (1942), Oscar Wilde (1946), Beerbohm Tree (1956), plus a very entertaining one on Arthur Conan Doyle (1943).

Since the 1950s the art of biography has burgeoned, and biography has become a major publishing industry. Scores of new biographies appear each year. There is a vast quantity of historical and political biography, and the majority of those who have become prominent in the performing arts and in sport have also had biographies written about them. Literary biography has become immensely popular. In fact, there appears to be no foreseeable end to the making of biographies. There are also critical books about the biographies and biographies of the biographers – and so on.

A handful of the most eminent and monumental works since the 1950s are: George Painter's two volumes on Proust (1959, 1965); Leon Edel's four volumes on Henry James (1953–72); Robert Gittings's book on John Keats (1968) and his two-volume life of Thomas Hardy (1975, 1978); Richard Ellman's classic works on W. B. Yeats (1948), James Joyce (1959) and Oscar Wilde (1987); Michael Holroyd's two volumes on Lytton Strachey (1967, 1968), his two volumes on Augustus John (1974, 1975) and the first volume of his three-volume life of George Bernard Shaw, which appeared in 1988.

These apart, during the last twenty-odd years there has been a steadily increasing number of literary biographies. Here there is space to mention but a few of the more notable (the biographers are in alphabetical order and followed by author subject in brackets): Kingsley Amis (Rudyard Kipling); Jocelyn Baines (Joseph Conrad); Sybille Bedford (Aldous Huxley); Quentin Bell (Virginia Woolf); Vincent Brome (J. B. Priestley); Humphrey Carpenter (W. H. Auden and J. R. R. Tolkien); Michael Coren (G. K. Chesterton); Bernard Crick (George Orwell); Victoria Forde (Basil Bunting); P. N. Furbank (E. M. Forster); Victoria Glendinning (Rebecca West, Vita Sackville-West and Edith Sitwell); John Halpern (George Gissing); Ian Hamilton (Robert Lowell); Ronald Hayman (Jean-Paul Sartre); Richard Holmes (Shelley and Coleridge); John Lehmann (Christopher Isherwood); Maynard Mack (Alexander Pope); Michael Meyer (Strindberg); Nigel Nicolson (*Portrait of a Marriage* – an experimental biography about Vita Sackville-West and Harold Nicolson); V. S. Pritchett (Chekhov); Jean-Paul Sartre (Flaubert); Samuel Schoenbaum (Shakespeare); Norman Sherry (Graham Greene); Hilary Spurling (Ivy Compton-Burnett); Christopher Sykes (Evelyn Waugh); Ann Thwaite (Edmund Gosse); Claire Tomalin (Katherine Mansfield); Philip Walker (Zola); Fay Weldon (Rebecca West).

Outside England biography has flourished in many countries, particularly France where the form was already established in the Middle Ages – for instance, de Joinville's life of St Louis written in the 13th c. Later Jacques Amyot translated Plutarch's *Lives* (1559). This work evoked great interest in biography in Europe. Towards the end of the 17th c. Fontenelle published his *éloges*, a remarkable collection of sketches of sixty-nine members of the Académie des Sciences. In 1731 Voltaire published a highly successful life of Charles XII, and later in the century Condorcet wrote two outstanding biographies, namely *Vie de Turgot* (1786) and *Vie de Voltaire* (1787). Among other French biographers some of the best known are Emile Legouis, Anatole France, Romain Rolland and André Maurois. Maurois is particularly well known in England because of his excellent portraits of English authors: *Ariel, ou la Vie de Shelley* (1923), *Disraeli* (1927), *Byron* (1930) and *Dickens* (1934).

German biographies are less eminent, but a German classic is Eckermann's *Conversations with Goethe* (*Gespräche mit Goethe*, 1836). A classic in Spanish literature is Guzmán's *Generaciones y*

Semblanzas (15th c.). Early biographies in Italian were written by Boccaccio and Bruni on Dante (14th c.). Probably the most distinguished of modern Italian biographers is Pasquale Villari who wrote great works on Savonarola and Macchiavelli.

Among biographical collections some of the more valuable and important works are: the *Legenda Aurea* (13th c.) of Jacobus a Voragine, later a source for Caxton's *The Golden Legend*; the *Acta Sanctorum* (1654); *Dictionnaire Historique et Critique* (1694); *Biographia Britannica* (1744); *Biographie Universelle Ancienne et Moderne* (1843–65); *Nouvelle Biographie Générale* (1852–66); and *Dictionary of National Biography* (1885–1900) with later Supplements. *See also* -ANA; ANECDOTE; TABLE-TALK.

black comedy The term is a translation of *comédie noire* which we owe to Jean Anouilh (1910–88), who divided his plays of the 1930s and 1940s into *pièces roses* and *pièces noires*. It is more than likely that the term also in part derives from André Breton's *Anthologie de l'humeur noire* (1940), which is concerned with the humorous treatment of the shocking, horrific and macabre. Black comedy is a form of drama which displays a marked disillusionment and cynicism. It shows human beings without convictions and with little hope, regulated by fate or fortune or incomprehensible powers. In fact, human beings in an 'absurd' predicament. At its darkest such comedy is pervaded by a kind of sour despair: we can't do anything so we may as well laugh. The wit is mordant and the humour sardonic.

This form of drama has no easily perceptible ancestry, unless it be tragi-comedy (*q.v.*) and the so-called 'dark' comedies of Shakespeare (for instance, *The Merchant of Venice*, *Measure for Measure*, *All's Well that Ends Well* and *The Winter's Tale*). However, some of the earlier works of Jean Anouilh (the *pièces noires*) are blackly comic: for example, *Voyageur sans bagage* (1936) and *La Sauvage* (1938). Later he wrote what he described as *pièces grinçantes* (grinding, abrasive), of which two notable examples are *La Valse des toréadors* (1952) and *Pauvre Bitos* (1956). Both these plays could be classified as black comedy. So might two early dramatic works by Jean Genet: *Les Bonnes* (1947) and *Les Nègres* (1959). Edward Albee's *Who's Afraid of Virginia Woolf?* (1962), Pinter's *The Homecoming* (1965) and Joe Orton's *Loot* (1965) are other examples of this kind of play. The television dramatist Giles Cooper also made a very considerable contribution.

In other forms of literature 'black comedy' and 'black humour' (e.g. the 'sick joke') have become more and more noticeable in the 20th c. It has been remarked that such comedy is particularly prominent in the so-called 'literature of the absurd'. Literary historians have found intimations of a new vision of man's role and position in the universe in, for instance, Kafka's stories (e.g. *The Trial*, *The Castle*, *Metamorphosis*), in surrealistic art and poetry and, later, in the philosophy of existentialism (*q.v.*). Camus's vision of man as an 'irremediable exile', Ionesco's concept of life as a 'tragic farce', and Samuel Beckett's tragi-comic characters in his novels are other instances of a particular Weltanschauung (*q.v.*). A baleful, even, at times, a 'sick' view of existence, alleviated by sardonic (and, not infrequently, compassionate) humour is to be found in many works of 20th c. fiction; in Sartre's novels, in Genet's non-dramatic works also, in Günter Grass's novels, in the more apocalyptic works of Kurt Vonnegut (junior). One might also mention some less famous books of unusual merit which are darkly comic. For example, Serge Godefroy's *Les Loques* (1964), Thomas Pynchon's *V* (1963) and his *The Crying of Lot 49* (1966), Joseph Heller's *Catch-22* (1961), D. D. Bell's *Dicky, or The Midnight Ride of Dicky Vere* (1970) and Mordecai Richler's *St Urbain's Horseman* (1966). *See* NONSENSE; SURREALISM; THEATRE OF CRUELTY; THEATRE OF THE ABSURD.

Black Mountain poets So called after Black Mountain College in North Carolina, USA. In the early 1950s the college became a centre for 'poetics' and also for a 'school' of poets. Charles Olson, Rector of the college from 1951 to 1956, encouraged a new approach to writing poetry. In 1950 Olson published *Projective Verse*, a statement of aims of Black Mountain poetics: anti-academic, anti-intellectual, anti-traditional; pro-spontaneity and pro the dynamism that may derive from using breathing exercises. Robert Creeley and Robert Duncan have been among the more celebrated poets in this 'school'. The quality of the work produced by the Black Mountain poets has been variable. It may be assessed in the magazine *Origin* (1951–56) and in the *Black Mountain Review* (1954–57).

black theatre Drama which, initially, was concerned with the consciousness and identity of black Americans, and a kind of movement which has had considerable influence outside America and which has in turn been affected by the Black Power and the Civil Rights movements. During the 1960s the black theatre movement became progressively more radical and there was an increasing tendency among black playwrights to dissociate themselves from the white American theatre and put on performances for black audiences only. A kind of side effect has been the use of all-black casts for plays by Shakespeare and other dramatists, including Beckett (*Waiting for Godot*, for instance). The movement had some influence in England, for example at the Dark and Light Theatre in Brixton, London. The first major work by a black dramatist is generally reckoned to be Hansberry's *A Raisin in the Sun* (1959). Other black playwrights of note have been James Baldwin, Le Roi Jones (who changed his name to Amamu Amiri Baraka) and Ed Bullins. West African dramatists – especially Wole Soyinka – have also made a contribution, as has Aimé Césaire, the Martinique-born writer. *See also* NEGRITUDE.

blank verse This was introduced by the Earl of Surrey in the 16th c. in his translation of the *Aeneid* (*c.* 1540) and consists of unrhymed five-stress lines; properly, iambic pentameters (*q.v.*). Surrey probably took the idea from the *versi sciolti* ('freed verse') of Molza's Italian translations of the *Aeneid* (1539). It has become the most widely used of English verse forms and is the one closest to the rhythms of everyday English speech. This is one of the reasons why it has been particulary favoured by dramatists. It was almost certainly first used for a play by Sackville and Norton in *Gorboduc* (1561), and then became the standard verse for later Tudor and Jacobean dramatists who made it a most subtle and flexible instrument: for instance, Thomas Heywood in *A Woman Killed with Kindness* (1603):

O speak no more!
For more than this I know, and have recorded
Within the red-leaved table of my heart.
Fair, and of all beloved, I was not fearful
Bluntly to give my life into your hand,
And at one hazard all my earthly means.
Go, tell your husband; he will turn me off,
And I am then undone. I care not, I:
'Twas for your sake. Perchance in rage he'll kill me,
I care not, 'twas for you. Say I incur
The general name of villain through the world,
Of traitor to my friend; I care not, I.

Beggary, shame, death, scandal, and reproach,
For you I'll hazard all: why, what care I?
For you I'll live, and in your love I'll die.

Thereafter it was used a great deal for reflective and narrative poems, notably by Milton in *Paradise Lost* (1667). During the late 17th c. and the first half of the 18th c. it was used much less often. Dryden, Pope, indeed the majority of 18th c. poets, preferred the heroic couplet (*q.v.*). However, Thomson used it in *The Seasons* (1726–30), so did Young in *Night Thoughts* (1742) and Cowper in *The Task* (1785). Wordsworth especially, and Coleridge, made much use of it. All the poets of the Romantic period (*q.v.*) wrote blank verse extensively, and so did most of the great poets of the 19th c. It is still quite widely practised today and dramatists like Maxwell Anderson and T. S. Eliot have experimented with it in freer forms in their plays.

blazon (F 'coat-of-arms' or 'shield') As a literary term it was used by the followers of Petrarchism (*q.v.*) to describe verses which dwelt upon and detailed the various parts of a woman's body; a sort of catalogue of her physical attributes. Such a catalogue was a convention established in the 13th c. by Geoffrey of Vinsauf and often used after Marot published his *Blason du Beau Tétin* (1536). Elizabethan sonneteers and lyric poets frequently listed the physical beauties of their mistresses. A well-known instance occurs in Spenser's *Epithalamion* (1595):

Her goodly eyes like sapphires shining bright,
Her forehead ivory white,
Her cheeks like apples which the sun hath rudded,
Her lips like cherries charming men to bite,
Her breast like to a bowl of cream uncrudded,
Her paps like lilies budded,
Her snowy neck like to a marble tower,
And all her body like a palace fair.

Such inventories or litanies are also to be found in Thomas Watson's *Hekatompathia* (1582), Sir Philip Sidney's *Astrophil and Stella* (1591) and Thomas Lodge's *Phillis* (1593). As a rule, there was nothing original in this form of conceit (*q.v.*). Most of the images were used long before by the elegiac Roman poets and the Alexandrian Greek poets.

Almost inevitably the convention became a cliché and we find poets parodying this kind of conceit in the *contreblazon*. Sir Philip Sidney, for example, copied Francesco Berni's device of using conventional descriptions for the 'wrong' parts of the body, thus producing a sort of grotesque mutant. Mopsa's forehead is 'jacinth-like', her cheeks are opal, her twinkling eyes are 'bedeckt with pearl' and her lips are 'sapphire blue'. Shakespeare turned the *blazon* upside down in his famous sonnet which begins: 'My mistress' eyes are nothing like the sun'; and Greene, in *Menaphon* (1589), reduced the *blazon* to absurdity:

> Thy teeth like to the tusks of fattest swine,
> Thy speech is like the thunder in the air:
> Would God thy toes, thy lips, and all were mine.

It was only a few years earlier that Sidney had written one of the most famous *blazons* of all, beginning:

> What tongue can her perfections tell?

See also CATALOGUE VERSE.

Bloomsbury group A *coterie* of writers who lived in the Bloomsbury area, London, before, during and after the First World War. The main figures were Virginia Woolf, Leonard Woolf, Lytton Strachey, Clive Bell, Vanessa Bell, Roger Fry, Duncan Grant, Maynard Keynes, E. M. Forster and David Garnett. Indirectly (they did *not* form a 'school') they had a considerable influence in the world of letters, art and philosophy.

blue blouse movement *See* AGITPROP DRAMA.

blue book A cheap (blue-covered) kind of thriller (*q.v.*), spine-chiller, shocker, horror story, romance (*q.v.*) which sold in large quantities at the end of the 18th c. and the beginning of the 19th. A relation of the penny dreadful, the dime novel (*qq.v.*), and others. Also, most commonly, a Parliamentary report.

blues, the Solo Negro folksongs. Not to be confused with Negro spirituals (*q.v.*). Many blues songs are based on a three-line lyric and are often expressive of despair, grief, and a general feeling of hopelessness and oppression; hence suffering from 'the blues'.

blues stanza a form of triplet (*q.v.*) stanza (*q.v.*) which derives from traditional jazz among black Americans. Customarily, the mood is one of lament or complaint (*qq.v.*). The first two lines are identical rhymes (e.g. dark/dark). A line usually comprises a flexible iambic pentameter (*qq.v.*) measure, with incremental repetition (*q.v.*) of the first line in the second.

blue stocking circle/society The Blue Stockings were a group of intelligent, well-educated and gifted women who, from early in the 1750s, held receptions or soirées, in the French salon (*q.v.*) tradition, at their homes in London, and continued to do so through most of the second half of the 18th c. The first hostess was almost certainly Mrs Vesey. Other regular hostesses were Mrs Montagu, Mrs Carter, Mrs Chapone, Mrs Boscawen, Mrs Delaney and, later, Hannah More, who wrote an agreeable poem, *Bas bleu* (1786), which described the pleasures and activities of the Blue Stocking Society. Those who attended the meetings were fashionable and literary and included a number of famous men such as: Joshua Reynolds, David Garrick, Horace Walpole, James Boswell, James Beattie, Samuel Richardson, George Lyttleton and Dr Johnson. Members of the aristocracy were frequent attenders. The main object of the meetings was conversation; there were no cards and no alcohol, and politics, swearing and scandal were forbidden. Their title derives from the worsted blue stockings of Bishop Benjamin Stillingfleet. He could not afford evening clothes and attended in his ordinary everyday gear. Traditionally it was Admiral Boscawen who nicknamed the group thus. When used pejoratively, as it often has been (and was in the 18th c.), the term 'bluestocking' denotes a woman who affects literary tastes and behaves in a dilettante fashion; a female pedant. Henry James described George Eliot as 'a horse-faced bluestocking'.

blurb A brief description of the contents of a book printed on the dust jacket. Often couched in enthusiastic and, at times, extravagant terms. The word is believed to have been coined by the American author Gelett Burgess who defined it as 'a sound like a publisher'. Earlier the term 'puff' was used, probably after Mr Puff in Sheridan's *The Critic* (1779). *See also* PUFFERY.

boasting poem Common in oral literatures in many parts of the world, especially in the epic and ballad (*qq.v.*) traditions. A warrior or hero 'blows his own trumpet' about his exploits. It is debatable whether there is an example of a boasting poem in English literature, though there are instances of something akin to it in

Beowulf – especially the slanging match between Unferth and Beowulf himself, when Unferth taunts the hero at being defeated by Breca in a seven-day swimming match at sea. Beowulf defends himself by giving the true account of the Breca episode. A further example occurs when Beowulf tells Hygelac how he overcame the monster Grendel. *See also* FARSA; GIERASA.

bob and wheel A metrical device found in alliterative verse (*q.v.*). The first short line of a group of rhyming lines is known as the 'bob', and the following four as the 'wheel'. Often the group ends a strophe (*q.v.*). The bob contains one stress preceded by one and sometimes two unstressed syllables. Each line of the wheel contains three stresses. The device is used throughout *Sir Gawain and the Green Knight*. For example:

> On many bonkkes ful brode Bretayn he setteȝ
> wyth wynne,
> Where werre and wrake and wonder
> Bi syþeȝ hatȝ wont þerinne,
> And oft boþe blysse and blunder
> Ful skete hatȝ skyfted synne.

Here 'wyth wynne' is the bob; the final four lines form the wheel.

Boedo Street group A literary group of the 1920s named after a lower-class area in Buenos Aires largely inhabited by Creole immigrants. Little of the writers' work survives. *See* FLORIDA STREET GROUP.

Boerde A MDu term for tales which tend to be bawdy or satirical, akin to the French *fabliau* (*q.v.*) and the Italian *novelle* (*q.v.*), and the kind of tale that Chaucer and Boccaccio delighted in. Many of them hail from Indian and Arabic legends.

bombast Originally the word described the cotton or horse-hair used in tailoring for padding. The term came to mean inflated and extravagant language. In *Othello* (I, i), Iago, complaining to Roderigo of how the Moor has passed him over for promotion, says:

> But he, as loving his own pride and purposes,
> Evades them [i.e. three great ones of the city] with a
> bombast circumstance

Horribly stuff'd with epithets of war;
And in conclusion
Nonsuits my mediators.

There are many instances of ranting and bombastic speeches in late Tudor drama (especially in Marlowe's plays) and few better than Hotspur's tirade in *Henry IV*, Pt I (I, iii):

By heaven methinks it were an easy leap
To pluck bright honour from the pale-fac'd moon

But Shakespeare burlesqued bombast in the play in *Hamlet*. Sometimes bombast has been used for humorous effect, as in Fielding's *Tom Thumb* (1730). *See also* FUSTIAN; HYPERBOLE; RODOMONTADE.

bonnes lettres, la société des There were several such societies after the restoration of the monarchy in France and their members were mostly young men who had religious and monarchical sympathies. They had literary as well as political and altruistic interests and they had quite close links with the *Congrégations* (the lay and clerical associations which originated from the Jesuits in the 16th c., were suppressed during the Revolution, and were regarded with some suspicion when they were revived during the Empire).

book The word probably derives from *boks* 'beech' (Germanic), the wood of that tree usually providing the tablets on which runes (*q.v.*) were carved (cf. 'Barbara fraxineis pingatur runa tabellis', Venantius Fortunatus VI). A book is either a written document or a record; or a written or printed literary composition. It may also be a volume of accounts or notes. It has a further meaning when it denotes a sub-division of a work (e.g. *Paradise Lost* is made up of twelve books). Occasionally, novels are divided into separate books, or parts. *See also* LEDGER; MANUSCRIPT; ROLL.

Booker McConnell Prize A prize for fiction in English. It was founded in 1969 and is financed by Booker McConnell, a multinational conglomerate. It is awarded annually by a panel of judges for what, in their opinion, is the best full-length novel published in the previous twelve months. The award is accompanied by considerable publicity and media razzmatazz. It has become the best known literary prize in Britain; but some other literary prizes are deemed more prestigious. The first winner was P. H. Newby.

Since 1969 the following have won it: 1970 – Bernice Rubens; 1971 – V. S. Naipaul; 1972 – John Berger; 1973 – J. G. Farrell; 1974 – Nadine Gordimer and Stanley Middleton; 1975 – Ruth Prawer Jhabvala; 1976 – David Storey; 1977 – Paul Scott; 1978 – Iris Murdoch; 1979 – Penelope Fitzgerald; 1980 – William Golding; 1981 – Salman Rushdie; 1982 – Thomas Keneally; 1983 – J. M. Coetzee; 1984 – Anita Brookner; 1985 – Keri Hulme; 1986 – Kingsley Amis; 1987 – Penelope Lively; 1988 – Peter Carey; 1989 – Kazuo Ishiguro; 1990 – A. S. Byatt.

book of hours *See* CALENDAR.

boulevard drama In 1791 the French theatres were given their freedom, the Boulevard du Temple became a centre of theatrical activity and many theatres were opened. Popular drama was presented, often of a melodramatic kind. Guilbert de Pixerécourt (1773–1844), who wrote at least fifty melodramas, was one of the most prolific and popular dramatists. Alexandre Dumas (*père*, 1802–70), was another. Many of the melodramas presented were about contemporary crime. Boulevard drama also fostered the Romantic movement in the French theatre. Eventually boulevard drama became a generic term for popular French drama from the mid-19th c. onwards. The plays consisted for the most part of farce and domestic comedy (*qq.v.*) and were a distinctly commercial entertainment. Two of the best known dramatists were Eugène Labiche (1815–88) and Ludovic Halévy (1834–1908). *See* MELODRAMA.

bourgeois drama Now a slightly pejorative term describing modern naturalistic drama (*q.v.*) concerned with middle-class social problems. Many dramatists were engaged in writing this kind of play during the first forty years or so of this century. An outstanding example was Galsworthy, especially such works of his as *Strife* (1909), *Justice* (1910), *The Skin Game* (1920) and *Loyalties* (1922).

boustrophedon (Gk 'ox-turning' when ploughing up and down a field) Lines written alternately from right to left and left to right, as in ancient Greek inscriptions.

bouts-rimés (F 'rhymes without lines') A versifying game which appears to have originated in 17th c. Paris. It became a vogue and spread to England. The idea was, given certain rhymes, to compose lines for them and make up a poem which was natural. For instance, given the rhyming words 'might', 'dog', 'sleight' and 'fog', compose a four-line poem. The diversion remained fashionable in France, England and Scotland until the 19th c.

bowdlerize Derived from the name of Thomas Bowdler, MD (1754–1825), who in 1818 produced *The Family Shakespeare.*

Bowdler removed from the plays whatever in his opinion was 'unfit to be read by a gentleman in the company of ladies'. Other editors, for example A. W. Verity, when producing school editions of Shakespeare, cut out passages which they regarded as indecent. *See also* ABRIDGED EDITION.

boys' companies Companies of boy actors which flourished during the 16th c. Early records show that the choristers of the Chapel Royal had performed plays by 1516. Choristers at St Paul's also performed them *c.* 1525. In 1576 Richard Farrant, Master of the Children of the Chapel at Windsor, leased premises in the Blackfriars to present commercial theatrical performances. The Marprelate controversy in 1588–9 led to the prohibition of the companies in the 1590s. However, at the beginning of the 17th c. they were revived and a number of well-known dramatists composed plays for them, including Beaumont and Fletcher, Chapman, Dekker, Ben Jonson, Marston, Middleton and Webster. By *c.* 1613 they were again falling into desuetude. *See also* JESUIT DRAMA; SCHOOL DRAMA.

brachiology (Gk 'short speech') Terse and condensed expression. Characteristic of the heroic couplet (*q.v.*). *See* ASYNDETON.

brachycatalectic (Gk 'short left off') A metrical line which lacks two syllables or a foot and is therefore an incomplete line. *See* ACATALECTIC.

Bradleyan Characteristic of the method and style of A. C. Bradley's criticism of Shakespeare's plays, as typified in his celebrated book *Shakespearean Tregedy* (1904). Bradley (1851–1935), who displayed remarkable insight and perception, tended to a naturalistic interpretation, treating characters as if they were real people and ignoring dramatic and stage convention (*q.v.*). Later criticism, more concerned with myth, symbol, patterns of imagery (*qq.v.*), etc., and with convention, was a reaction against his approach.

braggadocio The term came into English *c.* 1590 from the verb *to brag*, to which the Italian augmentative suffix was added. It denotes a swaggering, idle man; usually a coward. Spenser created a character called Braggadochio in *The Faerie Queene*, a typical braggart who is finally shown to be what he really is. Falstaff is probably the most famous *braggadocio* type in English Literature. *See also* ALAZON; MILES GLORIOSUS.

Bread and Puppet Theatre founded in 1961 by Peter Schumann, who regarded bread and theatre as equally sacramental and distributed home-made bread to the audiences. The type of work presented was close to performance art (*q.v.*) and visual impact was all-important, not least in the use of huge puppets (up to twenty feet high). Anti-materialist in spirit, Schumann's presentations were often in the open air. Notable productions were: *A Man Says Goodbye to His Mother* (1968), *The Cry of the People for Meat* (1969), *A Monument for Ishi* (1975) and *Ave Maris Stella* (1978).

Brechtian Characteristic of the style and technique of the plays of Bertolt Brecht (1898–1956), the German poet, playwright and director. He is particularly associated with the alienation effect, epic theatre, *Lehrstück* and the Berliner Ensemble (*qq.v.*).

bref double In French prosody, a fixed form (*q.v.*) and a kind of quatorzain (*q.v.*). It may be an ancestor of the sonnet (*q.v.*) and is a fourteen-line poem, in three quatrain stanzas ending with a couplet (*qq.v.*). There are only three rhymes in such a poem but every line is rhymed. The *a* rhyme appears somewhere in the three quatrains and once in the couplet. Likewise, the *b* rhyme. Rhyme *c* ends each quatrain.

breve *See* MORA.

breviary (L 'summary, abridgement') The book contains the Divine Office for each day and is used by Roman Catholic priests. It contains: Calendar; Psalter; Proprium de Tempore (i.e. collects and lessons); Proprium de Sanctis (i.e. collects for Saints' Days); Hours of the Virgin; burial services.

brief We may distinguish the following meanings: (a) a summary; (b) a list or memorandum; (c) a letter; (d) a Papal communication on disciplinary matters; (e) a summary of a law case prepared for counsel.

Briefroman (G 'letter novel') In Germany there were two kinds of epistolary novel (*q.v.*): (a) those in which all the letters are by one person; (b) those in which the letters are by two or more people (though most of them are by the main character). Examples of (a) are: Goethe's *Die Leiden des jungen Werthers* (1774), Hölderlin's *Hyperion* (1797, 1799) and the anonymously published *Briefe die ihn nicht erreichten* (1903) – which was written by Baroness von Heyking. Examples of (b) are: Johann Hermes's *Sophiens Reise von Memel nach Sachsen* (1769–73) and Sophie von La Roche's *Geschichte des Fräuleins von Sternheim* (1771).

broadsheet *See* BROADSIDE.

broadside A sheet of paper printed on one side only and usually distributed by hand. Broadsides were used largely for disseminating news and information and also for the publication of songs and ballads. They were hawked about Britain from early in the 16th c. until the 1920s. *See also* BALLAD.

brochure A pamphlet or comparably short work which is stitched, not bound. Nowadays brochures are mostly used for a variety of commercial and advertising purposes.

broken rhyme This occurs when a word is 'broken' or split in order to get a rhyme. Not unusual in light verse or for some comic effect, but rare in serious verse. However, Gerard Manley Hopkins uses it successfully in several poems. This example comes from *To what serves Mortal Beauty?*:

> To what serves mortal beauty | – dangerous; does set danc-
> ing blood – the O-seal-that-so | feature, flung prouder form
> Than Purcell tune lets tread to? | See: it does this: keeps warm
> Men's wits to the things that are; | what good means – where a glance
> Master more may than gaze, | gaze out of countenance.

brut A transferred use, in French or in Welsh, of *Brutus*, the name of the legendary and eponymous founder of Britain and the reputed grandson of Aeneas. The *Roman de Brut* and Laȝamon's *Brut* (of the late 12th c.) were well-known accounts of English history that went back to Brutus. Thus, a chronicle (*q.v.*).

bucolic *See* PASTORAL.

bucolic diaeresis So called because it was so common in bucolic poetry and occurred after a dactyl (*q.v.*)in the fourth foot. *See* DIAERESIS.

bugarštice The term probably derives from the Serbo-Croatian word *bugariti* 'to chant' and denotes a long line of verse of fifteen or sixteen syllables, with a caesura (*q.v.*) usually after the seventh. They were used in the composition of heroic songs or epic ballads which for the most part dealt with combat against the Turks in Dalmatia and other parts of what is now Jugoslavia from the 15th c. onwards. *See* GUSLAR; NARODNE PESME; PEVACI.

bull (L 'bubble, round object') The lead seal on an official document, especially one of papal origin and thus the document itself. It is also used to denote a tall story (*q.v.*), or a story which strains credulity; for example, a cock-and-bull story (*q.v.*). More generally it may apply to a literary incongruity or howler.

bululú A single ambulatory actor in 16th and 17th c. Spain. In some respects a descendant of the *juglar* or *jongleur* (*q.v.*). Where two travelled and played as a pair they were known as *ñaque*; if four as a *gangarilla*; and there was a standard company of six – five men and one woman – known as a *cambaleo*. The *cambaleo* has been recorded as late as the 1930s.

bunkum Originally non-sensical oratory; now applicable to almost anything said or written if it is regarded as rubbish. It derives from the name of Buncombe County in North Carolina, because a member of that district, while attending the 16th Congress debate on the 'Missouri Question', persistently declared, when pressed for a 'Question', that he was obliged to make a speech for Buncombe.

burden (or bourdon or burthen) The word probably derives from the late Latin *burdo* 'drone bee'. The term denotes either the refrain (*q.v.*) or chorus (*q.v.*) of a song, or its theme or principal sentiment.

bürgerliches Trauerspiel A genre of German dramatic tragedy (*q.v.*) – the term originated mid-18th c. to describe the kind of play which did not deal with the fall of nobles and princes but rather with that of middle-class people (burghers) in a middle-class environment (i.e. *bürgerlich*). Such plays were written in prose. Probably the earliest example is Lessing's *Miss Sara Sampson* (1755). Lessing was influenced by George Lillo's tragedy *The London Merchant* (1731), a rarity then because it made ordinary commercial life the theme of tragedy. Diderot was also influenced by it in his *Le Fils naturel* (1757). *See* DOMESTIC TRAGEDY.

burlesque The term derives from the Italian *burlesco*, from *burla* 'ridicule' or 'joke'. It is a derisive imitation or exaggerated 'sending up' of a literary or musical work, usually stronger and broader in tone and style than parody (*q.v.*). For the most part burlesque is associated with some form of stage entertainment. Aristophanes used it occasionally in his plays. The satyr plays (*q.v.*) were a form of burlesque. Clowning interludes in Elizabethan plays were also a type.

An early example of burlesque in England is the play of Pyramus and Thisbe performed by Bottom and his companions in *A Midsummer Night's Dream* (*c.* 1595). Here Shakespeare was making fun of the Interludes (*q.v.*) of earlier generations. A few years later Francis Beaumont created one of the first full-length dramatic burlesques – namely *The Knight of the Burning Pestle* (*c.* 1607). In 1671 George Villiers, Duke of Buckingham, had produced *The Rehearsal*, generally regarded as an outstanding example of a full-scale dramatic burlesque. In it he ridiculed contemporary actors and dramatists as well as the heroic tragedies of the period. Later Henry Carey did the same thing with his *Chrononhotonthologos* (1734). He also burlesqued contemporary opera in *The Dragon of Wantley* (1734). Fielding did much the same thing with *Tom Thumb* (1730) and his *Historical Register for the Year 1736*. Samuel Foote employed the same kind of caustic, but his plays and sketches ridiculed people rather than contemporary drama. One of the most famous works in this genre is Gay's *The Beggar's Opera* (1728), in part a burlesque of Italian opera. His work anticipates the kind of entertainment that became popular in the 19th c. in the hands of Gilbert and Burnand. Other dramatic burlesques of note from this period are: *The What d'ye Call it* (1715) by Gay; *Three Hours After Marriage* (1717) by Gay, Pope and John Arbuthnot; *The Covent Garden Tragedy* (1732) by Henry Fielding; *Distress upon Distress* (1752) by George Alexander Stevens; *The Critic* (1779) by Sheridan; *The Rovers* (1798) by George Canning, John Hookham

Frere and George Ellis; and *Bombastes Furioso* (1810) by William Rhodes. In the USA a theatrical burlesque is an entertainment with songs, dances, routines and extensive use of a chorus line and leg-show.

Burlesque was not confined to drama. In the mid-17th c. the French dramatist Scarron wrote a burlesque in verse called *Virgile travestie* (1648), and a little later Samuel Butler published *Hudibras* (1662), a mock-heroic (*q.v.*) poem ridiculing romance, chivalry and Puritanism. In 1674 Boileau wrote a famous mock-epic (*q.v.*), *Le Lutrin*, in which, with much irony and grave epic decorum (*q.v.*), he made fun of Classical epic. Dryden burlesqued the animal fable in *The Hind and the Panther* (1687); and, later, Pope showed great mastery of the possibilities of burlesque in his mock-epic *The Rape of the Lock* (1714) and in *The Dunciad* (1728, 1742, 1743). From this period also dates an agreeable burlesque by Swift – *Baucis and Philemon* (1709). A curiosity is William Blake's fragment *An Island in the Moon* (originally untitled) which he wrote *c.* 1784–5, a kind of 'send-up' of cultural and scientific pretensions. In fiction, Peacock came close to burlesque of the Gothic novel (*q.v.*) with his *Nightmare Abbey* (1818). *See also* ANTI-MASQUE; CARICATURE; FARCE; IRONY; INVECTIVE; SATIRE.

burletta Like burlesque (*q.v.*), the term derives from the Italian *burla*, 'joke' or 'fun'. A *burletta* is a comic play with music, or a play spoken to music, popular in the 18th and 19th c. theatre. It is of minor importance in the history and development of drama, except that, in company with musical burlesques and the later musical comedies, it may well have had some influence on the conception of the modern musical.

Burns stanza Also known as Burns meter, 'Scottish stanza' and 'Habbie stanza'. In fact, Burns did not invent it. It has been found in 11th c. Provençal poems and in medieval English romances. However, it takes its name from the frequent use Burns made of it. It comprises a six-line stanza rhyming aaabab. The first, second, third and fifth lines are tetrameters (*q.v.*) and the others dimeters (*q.v.*) as in *To a Mountain Daisy*:

> Ev'n thou who mourn'st the Daisy's fate,
> That fate is thine – no distant date;
> Stern Ruin's ploughshare drives elate
>   Full on thy bloom

Till crush'd beneath the furrow's weight
Shall be thy doom.

buskin The derivation is disputed, but it occurs in a number of European languages. It denotes a thick-soled half boot (*cothurnus*) worn by actors in Athenian tragedy, and contrasted with the low shoes (*soccus*) or 'sock' worn by comic actors. Thus it describes figuratively the spirit or style of tragedy. There is a famous reference in Ben Jonson's poem of praise to Shakespeare:

To hear thy buskin tread,
And shake a stage: or, when thy socks were on,
Leave thee alone, for the comparison
Of all, that insolent Greece, or haughty Rome
Sent forth, or since did from their ashes come.

Milton, in *L'Allegro*, refers to Jonson's 'Learned sock'.

Butzenscheibenpoesie (G 'archery target poetry') A type of late 19th c. poetry which displays a kind of decadent or degenerate romanticism (*q.v.*) with an emphasis on medieval themes and nationalistic attitudes and values. Prominent practitioners were J. V. von Scheffel, Rudolf Baumbach and Julius Wolff. *Butzenscheibenpoesie* was a derogatory term invented by Paul Heyse (1830–1914).

bylina (R *byl* 'that which happened') A type of Russian epic (*q.v.*) folksong and poetry often associated with an historical event or movement. The term *bylina* is of academic provenance and came into use in the 1830s; the peasants use the word *starina* ('what is old'). These songs are mostly about the exploits of the *bogatyrs*, warrior heroes at the court of Prince Vladimir (978–1015) in Kiev, and the very earliest examples may pre-date Vladimir's era. For many centuries they belonged to oral tradition (*q.v.*). People were beginning to write them down in the 16th and 17th c. Possibly the first collector was an Englishman, Richard James, who was chaplain to the English embassy in Moscow in 1619. The main garnering belongs to the 19th c. when, anyway, there was widespread interest in Europe in collecting and studying these ballad and epic forms of verse. In fact, many *byliny* still belong to oral tradition among peasants, particularly in areas where literacy is minimal. The same is true of the *narodne pesme* (*q.v.*) among the South Slavs.

Byliny vary in length from, say, a hundred lines to a thousand or more. There are two basic categories: (a) the heroic, concerned with deeds of valour; (b) the romantic, concerned with love, deceit, infidelity, magic and wealth. The former far outnumber the latter. Traditionally, they are sung or chanted, without musical accompaniment, by specialist narrators/singers called *skaziteli* ('narrators'). Some *skaziteli* are blind and in many respects are close kin of the Anglo-Saxon *scopas*, the Scandinavian *skalds* and the South Slav *guslari*. Like these bards of honoured and ancient vocation, the *skaziteli* are often poets as well as reciters, and a skilled one will amplify, embellish and improvise on traditional material with words, phrases and lines of his own devising. The verse tends to be free, with a pattern of a fairly fixed number of stresses and considerable flexibility in the number of unstressed or 'slack' syllables. Rhyme is occasional. Strong, plain similes, of the 'white as a swan', 'brown as a berry', 'fresh as a daisy' ilk, are a conspicuous feature. Fixed or Homeric epithets (*q.v.*) are frequent and obligatory. Incremental repetition (*q.v.*) is also common; as are periphrastic figures, and figures comparable to the kenning (*q.v.*) of skaldic and Old English verse. *See also* BALLAD; DUMY; GUSLAR; SKAZ.

byr a thoddaid In Welsh prosody a quatrain (*q.v.*) stanza which combines a couplet (*q.v.*) of eight syllables per line with another couplet of ten syllables in the first line and six in the second. In the ten-syllable line the main rhyme comes before the end of the line and the syllables that follow the main rhyme are linked by alliteration, assonance (*qq.v.*) or secondary rhyme with the early syllables of the first part of the six-syllable line.

Byronic stanza *See* OTTAVA RIMA.

Byzantine age A period which runs approximately from the beginning of the 6th c. until 1453, the year in which Constantinople fell to the Turks.

C

caccia (It 'hunt') An Italian verse form which may have evolved from the madrigal (*q.v.*). A poem of short lines with a refrain (*q.v.*) but no rhyme. The name suggests that at some stage the subjects of the *caccia* were connected with hunting. The form was used mostly in the 14th and 15th c.

cacoethes scribendi (Gk 'evil disposition' + L 'of writing') This phrase goes back to Juvenal's *insanabile* (incurable) *scribendi cacoethes* (*Satires*, VII, 52).

cacophony Gk 'dissonance') The opposite of euphony (*q.v.*). Harsh sounds are sometimes used deliberately by writers, especially poets, to achieve a particular effect. A well-known example occurs in Tennyson's *Morte D'Arthur*:

> Dry clashed his harness in the icy caves
> And barren chasms, and all to left and right
> The bare black cliff clanged round him, as he based
> His feet on juts of slippery crag that rang
> Sharp-smitten with the dint of armed heels –
> And on a sudden, lo! the level lake,
> And the long glories of the winter moon.

The alliteration and assonance (*qq.v.*) of the first five lines are self-evidently rough; the last two lines, containing the same devices, are mellifluously smooth and euphonious. *See also* ONOMATOPOEIA.

cadence In particular it refers to the melodic pattern preceding the end of a sentence; for instance, in an interrogation or an exhortation; and also the rhythm of accented units. In more general terms it refers to the natural rhythm of language, its 'inner tune', depending on the arrangement of stressed and unstressed syllables; so, now, a rising and falling. It is present in prose as well as verse. Almost every writer with any individuality of style at all has particular cadences which are really his own 'voice', the inherent and intrinsic melody of linked syllables and words, of phrases, sentences and paragraphs, which at once transcends and supports the meaning. Sense and sound are inseparable. The cadences of prose writers as various as Sir Thomas Browne, Edward Gibbon, Jack London and Samuel Beckett are instantly apparent. In verse, even within traditional metrical arrangements, differing cadences are apparent, especially in free verse (*q.v.*). *See* RHYTHM.

caesura (L 'a cutting') A break or pause in a line of poetry, dictated, usually, by the natural rhythm of the language. If near the beginning of the line it is called the initial caesura; near the middle, medial; near the end, terminal. The commonest is the medial. A masculine caesura follows the accented syllable; a feminine, the unaccented. A line may have more than one caesura or none at all. It is often marked by punctuation. In OE verse the caesura was used rather monotonously to indicate the half line:

> Đa waes on burgum || Beowulf Scyldinga
> leof leodcyning || longe þrage.

So long as alliterative verse (*q.v.*) was the favoured form, there was not a great deal of variation, as these lines from Langland's *Piers Plowman* show:

> Loue is leche of lyf || and nexte owre lorde selue,
> And also þe graith gate || þat goth in-to heuene.

The development of the iambic pentameter (*q.v.*) in Chaucer's hands produced much more subtle varieties:

> With him ther was his sone, || a yong Squier
> A lovyere || and a lusty bacheler,
> With lokkes crulle || as they were leyd in presse.
> (*Prologue to the Canterbury Tales*)

Blank verse (*q.v.*) allowed an even wider range in the preservation of speech rhythms, as these lines from Shakespeare suggest:

> I have ventur'd
> Like little wanton boys || that swim on bladders,
> This many summers || in a sea of glory;
> But far beyond my depth. || My high-blown pride

At length broke under me, || and now has left me,
Weary and old with service, || to the mercy
Of a rude stream || that must for ever hide me.
(*King Henry VIII*, III, ii, 359)

For the most part it is more regular in the heroic couplet (*q.v.*) as Dryden shows:

In squandering wealth || was his peculiar art:
Nothing went unrewarded, || but desert.
Beggar'd by fools, || whom still he found too late:
He had his jest, || and they had his estate.
(*Absalom and Achitophel*, Pt I, 559)

In more modern verse there is a great deal of variation in the placing of the caesura, as can be seen in the work of outstanding innovators like Gerard Manley Hopkins, W. B. Yeats, Ezra Pound and T. S. Eliot. Take, for instance, these lines from Yeats:

That is no country for old men. || The young
In one another's arms, || birds in the trees
– Those dying generations – || at their song,
The salmon-falls, || the mackerel-crowded seas,
Fish, flesh, or fowl, || commend all summer long
Whatever is begotten, || born, || and dies
Caught in that sensual music || all neglect
Monuments of unageing intellect.
(*Sailing to Byzantium*)

It will be noticed that the last line has no caesura.

It can be seen from these few examples that the caesura is used, basically, in two contrary ways: (a) to emphasize formality and to stylize; and (b) to slacken the stiffness and tension of formal metrical patterns.

Calderonian honour *El honor calderiano* implies an exaggerated concept of honour. A product of 17th c. Spanish drama, and particularly of the plays of Calderón (1600–81). The following are especially noteworthy: *El médico de su honra, A secreto agravio, secreta venganza, El Pintor de su deshonra, El mayor monstruo, los celos.* The usual situation is that the play's climax centres on the sacrifice of the wife who is either really or supposedly unfaithful. The atmosphere of the dénouement (*q.v.*) is harsh and even bloody. For instance, in the first of the above four plays the jealous husband engages a blood-letter to perform the deed in his wife's bedroom where she is apparently ill, thus purging his own besmirched honour by 'surgery'.

calendar The term derives from Latin *calendae* (calends, or kalends), the first day of the month and the date on which accounts were due. Hence Latin *calendarium* 'an account book'. The ordinary calendar is a table giving the divisions of the year. Some of the major calendars are: the Julian, the Gregorian, the Jewish, the Chinese, the French Republican and the Mohammedan. The perpetual calendar provides the year, the dominical letter (i.e. the *dies dominica*, Latin for 'Sunday'; a convention adopted in tables to indicate that day in January on which the first Sunday falls in any particular year), followed by the regnal years, their beginning and ending. It also shows the fixed feasts and saints' days which are important in the dating of documents.

Another kind of calendar is the book of hours (*les heures*), an illustrated prayer-book based on the priest's breviary (*q.v.*) and ordered according to the hours of the Divine Office in monasteries. Such books made their appearance in the 12th c. and quite soon became popular, especially in France and the Netherlands. Some of them were of remarkable beauty and exquisitely illustrated. A very well-known example is the Duc de Berry's *Très Riches Heures* of the 15th c. which was illustrated by the Limbourg brothers. Such a work contains the usual *calendarium*, the Little Office of Our Lady, the Penitential Psalms, the Litanies, the Office for the Dead, The Adoration of the Cross, Devotions to the Holy Ghost, and others.

A notable instance of the form of the calendar being used for a poetic work is Spenser's *Shepheard's Calendar* (1579) which comprises twleve eclogues – one for each month of the year. John Clare attempted something similar in *The Shepherd's Calendar* (1827).

Another type of calendar is a sort of register (*q.v.*). An unusual example is *The Newgate Calendar, or Malefactors' Bloody Register* (*c.* 1774), a work which gave an account of the more infamous crimes perpetrated from 1700 to 1774. A further series came out *c.* 1826.

A curiosity in the genre is Nicholas Breton's *The Fantasticks* (1626), a collection of observations arranged in calendar form according to hours, days and seasons. *See* ALMANAC.

calligramme A design using the letters of a word; more particularly a poem written and printed in a specific shape. Guillaume Apollinaire (1880–1918) published *Calligrammes* (1918), which contains the well-known *Il pleut*, printed with letters trickling down the page like 'tears'. Rabelais had done something comparable with his *epilenie*: a song in honour of Bacchus printed in the shape of a bottle. *See* ALTAR POEM; CONCRETE POETRY/VERSE.

calypso Usually an improvised song or ballad (*qq.v.*) composed and sung by West Indians on festive and public occasions – like carnivals, elections and test matches. The word happens to be the same as the name of the nymph who detained Ulysses on the island of Ogygia, but there appears to be no connection.

Cambridge Festival Theatre This theatre existed from 1926 to 1933 and became a centre of innovative theatre design and production in Britain. Notable features were its thrust stage and revolving stage and remarkable experiments with lighting. The inspiration of the enterprise was Terence Gray, assisted by Harold Ridge. Gray's other collaborators included Ninette de Valois, his cousin. The Festival Theatre was eventually sold to the Cambridge Arts Theatre, founded by J. M. Keynes.

campus novel A novel which has a university campus as its setting. The majority have been written by those who were or are academics. Notable instances are: *Pictures from an Institution* (1954) by Randall Jarrell; *Lucky Jim* (1954) by Kingsley Amis; *The War between the Tates* (1974) by Alison Lurie; *Changing Places* (1975) by David Lodge; and *The History Man* (1975) by Malcolm Bradbury. *See* NOVEL.

canción The term is now generally applied to any Spanish poem consisting of strophes (*q.v.*) with alternate lines of eleven and seven syllables. This, the Italianate *canción* was introduced into Spain near the middle of the 16th c. *See* LIRA; REMATE; SILVA.

cancioneiros Portuguese songbooks and, in particular, collections of medieval Galician and Portuguese poems extant in three manuscripts – namely *Cancioneiro de Ajuda*, *Cancioneiro da Vaticana* and *Colocci-Brancuti*. They cover the period from late in the 12th c. to the middle of the 14th c. These collections contain mostly love lyrics and satires. The later *Cancioneiro Geral* (1516) is a huge anthology (*q.v.*) which contains verses written by court poets. Many of the poems are also love lyrics.

cancrine (L 'crab-wise') Verses that read both ways, and which thus form a palindrome (*q.v.*).

canon A body of writings established as authentic. The term usually refers to biblical writings accepted as authorized – as opposed to the *Apocrypha* (*q.v.*). The term can also apply to an author's works which are accepted as genuine. For example: the Shakespeare Canon.

canso Also *chanso* and *chanson* (*q.v.*) A Provençal love-song or lyric (*q.v.*). The lyrical *canso* has five or six stanzas with an *envoi* (*q.v.*). Metrical virtuosity in the *canso* was much prized. The themes were almost invariably those of courtly love (*q.v.*). *See* ODE; SONNET.

cant The jargon or slang (*qq.v.*) of a particular class, group, trade, calling or profession. Usually associated with pedlars, thieves, gipsies, tinkers and vagabonds. Professional tramps or roadmen, for instance, have a variety of cant terms – like: *blagging hard* – travelling fast; *castle* – the house, flat or office of a wealthy person; *croker* – fourpence; *dead hard mark* – a place only approachable by an expert tramp; *dollcie* – well-off; *front the gaff* – call at the entrance of a large house; *gry* – a horse (of Romany origin); *lurk* – a tramp's favourite stopping place; *mark* – a house, its resident or the sign outside; *merry* – a girl; *postman* – a fast-moving tramp; *sham* – a gentleman; *steamer* – a mug, a simpleton; *top-cock* – a master tramp; *wheeler* – a pauper who circles near institutions and who is despised by the real roadmen or 'pikers' who refer to the road as 'the stem', 'the grit', 'the white'.

cantar In Spanish literature the word has often been used vaguely to denote words for a song. In modern times it has come to mean an octosyllabic quatrain (*q.v.*), with certain characteristics: assonance (*q.v.*) and, occasionally, consonance (*q.v.*) in the even-numbered lines, and unrhymed oxytones (*q.v.*) in the odd ones.

cantar de gesta (Sp 'song of deeds') The Spanish equivalent of the French *chanson de gestes* (*q.v.*), but differing in some respects from the French *chansons* which tend to be in assonanced *laisses* (*q.v.*) of ten syllables whereas the Spanish type is usually in longer lines, but of varying length with a leaning towards fourteen syllables, in four-accent *laisses* with all four having the same assonance. The most complete and most famous *cantar de gesta* is the *Poema de mío Cid* (*c.* 1140) whose composer probably had the advantage of reading the French *chansons*, including *Roland*.

cantar de pandeiro A Galician folksong in the three-lined tercet (*q.v.*) form, sung to the accompaniment of the *pandeiro* or timbrel; sometimes written in groups and interconnected in theme.

cantares Spanish narrative poems of the epic (*q.v.*) genre which derive from oral tradition (*q.v.*), originally sung or accompanied by music. Two notable examples of *cantares de gesta* are *Poema de mío Cid* (*c.* 1140) and *Bernardo del Carpio* (*c.*1200 AD). During the Romantic period there was renewed interest in this genre. *See also* ROMANTIC REVIVAL.

cante jondo An Andalusian term for *cante hondo* 'deep song'; also called a *cante flamenco*. A type of folksong which is typical of southern Spain. Traditional subjects are love, its loss, and death.

cantica de serrana In the 14th c. book called *Libro de buen amor*, by Juan Ruiz, the Archpriest of Hita, the *canticas de serrana* are pastoral lyrics intended for singing. The *serrana* is a shepherdess or cow-girl.

canticle A form of hymn (*q.v.*) with biblical words, other than those from the Psalms.

canticum In Roman drama that part of a play which was declaimed or sung, as opposed to the *diverbium* (*q.v.*) or spoken dialogue. There are a large number of *cantica* in the plays of Plautus; few in Terence.

cantiga The term usually refers to Iberian folksongs and to the collection of Galician and Portuguese lyrics of the Middle Ages which are contained in the *Cancioneiros* (*q.v.*).

canto (It 'song') A sub-division of an epic (*q.v.*) or narrative poem; comparable to a chapter in a novel. Outstanding examples of its use are to be found in Dante's *Divina Commedia*, Spenser's *Faerie Queene*, Pope's *The Rape of the Lock* and Byron's *Childe Harold*.

canzone An Italian and Provençal form of lyric (*q.v.*) which consists of a series of verses in stanza form but without a refrain (*q.v.*). Usually written in hendecasyllabic lines with end-rhyme (*q.v.*). There were three main styles: tragic, comic and elegiac. William Drummond of Hawthornden was one of the few British writers to use it. The *canzone* had considerable influence on the evolution of the sonnet (*q.v.*). *See* CANZONET; OTTAVA RIMA.

canzonet *Canzonetta* is a diminutive of the Italian *canzone* (*q.v.*), and a *canzonet* is 'a little song'; a light-hearted song akin to the madrigal (*q.v.*).

capa y espada (Sp 'cloak and sword') The term describes 16th and 17th c. comedies about more or less melodramatic love and conspiracy among the aristocracy. Two of the main playwrights were Lope de Vega and Calderón. *See also* CLOAK-AND-DAGGER STORY; COMEDY; COMEDY OF INTRIGUE.

capitolo (It 'chapter') An Italian verse form which is either an imitation or a parody (*q.v.*) of Dante's *terza rima* (*q.v.*). It has all the characteristics of that form and has been widely used since the 15th c., especially for satire (*q.v.*).

capsule criticism A term used by Alexander Woollcott (1887–1943) as the title of an essay on dramatic criticism. It denotes a clever, witty, epigrammatic one-liner (usually damning). Examples are: 'I watched this play at a disadvantage; the curtain was up'; 'A bad play saved by a bad performance'; 'Business was so bad they were shooting deer in the balcony'.

caricature In literature (as in art) a portrait which ridicules a person by exaggerating and distorting his most prominent features and characteristics. Quite often the caricature evokes genial rather than derisive laughter. English literature is exceptionally rich in examples. The following are a few of the more outstanding: Sir Andrew Aguecheek, Malvolio and Sir Toby Belch (*Twelfth Night*); Pistol and Fluellen (*Henry V*); Falstaff (*Henry IV* and *The Merry Wives of Windsor*) – all by Shakespeare. Other examples are Sir Giles Overreach in Massinger's *A New Way to Pay Old Debts*; Sir Epicure Mammon in Ben Johnson's *The Alchemist*; and Jonson's Volpone in *Volpone*; Sir Fopling Flutter in Etherege's *The Man of Mode*; Captain Brazen in Farquhar's *The Recruiting Officer*; Sir

Lucius O'Trigger in Sheridan's *The Rivals*; Tony Lumpkin in Goldsmith's *She Stoops to Conquer*; Lady Bracknell in Wilde's *The Importance of Being Earnest*; Drinkwater in Shaw's *Captain Brassbound's Conversion*.

There are many in satirical poems: for instance, Dryden's caricature of Shadwell in *Mac Flecknoe*; and Pope's of Cibber in *The Dunciad*.

There are so many in novels that the list would be almost endless. The works of Fielding, Smollett, Dickens, Thackeray and Surtees are especially rich in them.

On the whole caricature belongs to the province of comedy (*q.v.*). However, a caricature is occasionally to be found in tragedy – among minor characters. For instance, the weak and gullible Roderigo in *Othello*; and Osric, the pansy courtier, in *Hamlet*.

carmen (L 'song') Usually a song or lyric (*qq.v.*) but the word has been applied to a wide variety of forms ranging from epic (*q.v.*) to legal formula. Now almost an archaism (*q.v.*) and, if used, likely to be very nearly facetious, except when referring to Catullus's *Carmina* or Horace's *Odes* or a *carmen figuratum* (*q.v.*).

carmen figuratum *See* ALTAR POEM.

Carmina Burana A collection of Goliardic poems from the Benedictine monastery of Benedictbeuern in Bavaria. *See* GOLIARDIC VERSE; SONGBOOK.

carnivalization/carnivalesque Originally, a carnival was a feast observed by Roman Catholics before the Lenten fast began. The word *carnival* derives, apparently, from the Latin *carnem levare* 'to put away flesh'. Traditionally, meat was not eaten during the Lenten fast; thus, a carnival would be the last occasion on which meat was permissible before Easter. Broadly speaking, a carnival is an occasion or season or revels, of merrymaking, feasting and entertainments (e.g. a Spanish fiesta). In times past there were carnivals which were symbolic of the disruption and subversion of authority; a turning upside down of the hierarchical scale (e.g. the Feast of Fools, the Abbot of Misrule, the Boy Bishop). Mikhail Bakhtin (1895–1975) coined the word 'carnivalization' (he introduces it in the chapter 'From the Prehistory of Novelistic Discourse', in his book *The Dialogic Imagination* – translated in 1981) to describe the penetration or incorporation of carnival into everyday life, and its shaping effect on language and literature.

Early examples of literary 'carnival' are the Socratic dialogues (in which what appears to be logic is stood on its head and shown to be illogical) and Menippean satire (*q.v.*). A carnivalesque element is also characteristic of burlesque, parody and personal satire. Bakhtin puts forward the theory that the element of carnival in literature is subversive; it disrupts authority and introduces alternatives. It is a kind of liberating influence and he sees it as part of the subversion of the sacred word in Renaissance culture. He cites Rabelais as an example of a writer who used carnival (e.g. in *Gargantua and Pantagruel*, 1532–46).

In his book *Problems of Dostoievski's Poetics* (1929) he develops the idea of the carnivalesque in making a contrast between the novels of Tolstoy and Dostoievski. In Tolstoy's fiction he sees a type of 'monologic' novel where all is subject to the author's controlling purpose and hand, whereas Dostoievski's fiction is 'dialogic' or 'polyphonic'. Many different characters express varying, independent views which are not 'controlled' by the author to represent the author's viewpoint (*q.v.*). They are 'not only objects of the author's word, but subjects of their own directly significant word as well'. Bakhtin sees this quality as a kind of dynamic and liberating influence which, as it were, conceptualizes reality, giving freedom to the individual character and subverting the type of 'monologic' discourse characteristic of many 19th c. novelists (including Tolstoy).

Dostoievski's tale *Bobok* (1873) is a particularly good example of carnival. The dead, disencumbered of natural laws, can say what they like and speak the truth for fun. But Bakhtin does not pretend that an author is not still in control of his material while allowing his characters to be subversive. He acknowledges the role of the author as directing agent. *See* AUTHOR, DEATH OF; DIALOGIC/MONOLOGIC.

carol The word derives from the Italian *carola*. It seems very probable that originally a carol was a kind of ring or round dance, then the song accompanying the dance. Now a carol denotes a light-hearted song sung in a spirit of joy at Christmas time (and also, occasionally, at Easter). Thus, a festive religious song. It appears to have been an ancient practice in the Church to sing carols, and throughout the Middle Ages the clergy wrote many of them – usually in sequences like the *Laetabundus*. Most of the carols we know today are not earlier than the 15th c. In 1521 Wynkyn de Worde, a pupil of Caxton, printed the first collection of Christmas carols. Counterparts of the carol elsewhere are the *noël* in France (dating from the 16th c.), and the *Weihnachtslied* in Germany. After the Reformation the practice of composing carols dwindled, though in the 17th c. several poets (Southwell, Herbert, Vaughan, Crashaw and Milton) wrote poems and songs which belong to the carol genre. Milton's *Nativity* hymn is an outstanding example; so is Southwell's *The Burning Babe*. Among well-known carols mention should be made of *The Seven Joys of Mary*; *I saw Three Ships*; *God Rest You Merry, Gentlemen*; *The Virgin Unspotted*; *Jesus Born in Bethlehem*; and *The Twelve Days of Christmas*. Other kinds of carol have moral and satirical themes. There are also love carols. *See also* LYRIC; SONG.

Caroline period Of the time of Charles I (1625–49), from the Latin *Carolus* 'Charles'. During this period the Civil War was fought and a large number of distinguished writers were active. The following were pre-eminent: Donne, Burton, Shirley, Massinger, Milton, Edward and George Herbert, Sir Thomas Browne, Thomas Carew, Crashaw, Vaughan, Quarles, Thomas Killigrew (the elder), Herrick, Sir John Suckling and Lovelace. *See also* CAVALIER DRAMA; CAVALIER POETS.

carpe diem (L 'snatch the day') The phrase occurs in Horace's *Odes* (I, xi):

> *Dum loquimur, fugerit invida*
> *Aetas: carpe diem, quam minimum credula postero.*

In short: 'Enjoy yourself while you can'. Horace elaborates on the motif (*q.v.*) in *Odes* III, xxix. It is found in Greek as well as Latin poetry, recurs frequently in many literatures and obviously arises from the realization of the brevity of life and the inevitability of death. It might be assessed as the motto of epicureanism.

At some point, possibly in the work of the 4th c. Roman poet Ausonius, the rose became the symbol (*q.v.*) of the beauty and transitoriness of life, a thought finely expressed by Ausonius in *De Rosis Nascentibus*. Whatever its origin the symbolism persisted through the Middle Ages and is to be found associated with the *carpe diem* motif in Goliardic verse (*q.v.*) and in much French and English poetry. At some stage the rose came to represent virginity; and its death, loss of virginity. The 15th and 16th c. love poets incorporated both theme and symbolism in their appeals to their mistresses not to deny them or disdain them. The Cavalier poets (*q.v.*) were among the last to elaborate the idea (for example, Herrick's poem *To the Virgins, to Make Much of Time* begins: 'Gather ye Rose-buds, while ye may'), but it has never entirely lost its hold on the poet's imagination – as is evident in the work, for instance, of Yeats.

The *carpe diem* motif, in more specifically Christian and didactic writings, appears in many sermons and much devotional literature during the Middle Ages and thereafter, but the import tends to be admonitory: life is short – prepare to meet thy doom. However, it is the more pagan and epicurean spirit of the motif that has made the greatest appeal to writers, and in few places is it better expressed than in a poem about a Syrian dancing girl, in the *Appendix Vergiliana*, which concludes:

> *Pone merum et talos, pereat qui crastini curat.*
> *Mors aurem vellens, 'vivite', ait, 'venio'.*

See also UBI SUNT.

casbairdne In Irish prosody, a quatrain (*q.v.*) stanza of heptasyllabic lines. The second and fourth lines rhyme and the first and third lines consonate with them. There are at least two cross-rhymes in each couplet (*q.v.*).

catachresis (Gk 'misuse') The misapplication of a word, especially in a mixed metaphor (*q.v.*). Puttenham, in *The Arte of English Poesie* (1589), described catachresis as a figure of 'plain abuse, as he that bade his man go into his library to fetch his bow and arrows'. A famous instance occurs in Milton's *Lycidas*:

> Blind mouths! that scarce themselves know how to hold
> A sheep-hook, or have learned aught else the least
> That to the faithful herdman's art belongs!

catalects Literary works which are detached (or detachable) from the main body of a writer's work. *See* ANALECT.

catalexis The omission of the last syllable or syllables in a regular metrical line. Often done in trochaic and dactylic verse to avoid monotony. The second and fourth lines of this verse from Hood's *The Bridge of Sighs* illustrate the point:

Óne mŏre ŭn | fórtŭnăte,
Wéarў ŏf | breáth,
Ráshlў ĭm | pórtŭnăte,
Góne tŏ hĕr | deáth!

It may, however, be argued that the second and fourth lines are choriambic feet. *See* ACATALECTIC; CHORIAMBUS.

catalogue raisonné A descriptive and annotated catalogue of books or works of art. Often divided into subject groups.

catalogue verse The term describes a list of people, things, places or ideas. It is a device of ancient origin and found in many literatures. Sometimes its function has been didactic. In any event its usual object is to reinforce by elaboration. There are many instances in epic (*q.v.*) poetry, like this from Milton's *Paradise Lost* (X, 695):

now from the north
Of Norumbega, and the Samoed shore
Bursting their brazen dungeon, armed with ice
And snow and hail and stormy gust and flaw,
Boreas, and Caecias and Argestes loud
And Thrascias rend the woods and seas upturn;
With adverse blasts upturns them from the south
Notus and Afer black with thunderous clouds
From Serraliona; thwart of these as fierce
Forth rush the Levant and the ponent winds
Eurus and Zephir, with their lateral noise,
Sirocco, and Libecchio

See also BLAZON; EPIC SIMILE.

catastasis Two meanings may be distinguished: (a) the narrative part that comes in the introduction of a speech (*q.v.*); (b) the third of the four divisions of a tragedy (*q.v.*) – the first, second and fourth being *protasis, epitasis* and *catastrophe* (*qq.v.*). *See also* FREYTAG'S PYRAMID.

catastrophe (Gk 'overturning') The tragic dénouement (*q.v.*) of a play or story. For example, the Moor's murder of Desdemona and his own suicide at the climax (*q.v.*) of *Othello*. *See* CATASTASIS; FREYTAG'S PYRAMID.

catch In verse the term denotes an extra unstressed syllable at the beginning of a line when the regular meter requires a stress. A famous example occurs in Gray's poem *On Vicissitude*:

New-born flocks, in rustic dance,
  Frisking ply their feeble feet;
Forgetful of their wintry trance,
  The birds his presence greet –

In contrast to 'new-born' and 'frisking', the word 'forgetful' takes a stress on the second syllable.

A catch is also a 'round' for three or more voices. A singer starts a line, another follows him. They take each other up and harmonize. A good example occurs in *Twelfth Night* (II, iv) when Sir Toby Belch, Sir Andrew Aguecheek and Feste are fooling about and getting drunk.

catharsis (Gk 'purgation') Aristotle uses the word in his definition of tragedy (*q.v.*) in Chapter VI of *Poetics*, and there has been much debate (still inconclusive) on exactly what he meant. The key sentence is: 'Tragedy through pity and fear effects a purgation of such emotions'. So, in a sense, the tragedy (*q.v.*), having aroused powerful feelings in the spectator, has also a therapeutic effect; after the storm and climax there comes a sense of release from tension, of calm.

cauda (L 'tail') The short line or tail which, in a stanza (*q.v.*) of longer lines, usually rhymes with another short line. The use of *caudae* was common in medieval metrical romances (*q.v.*). *See also* TAIL-RHYME.

caudate sonnet A form of sonnet (*q.v.*) in which the normal pattern of fourteen lines is modified by one or more *codas* or 'tails'. The practice is believed to originate from Francesco Berni, the 16th c. Italian poet. The form is rare in English verse, though it has been used for satirical purposes: for instance, Milton's poem *On the New Forces of Conscience Under the Long Parliament*. *See* TAIL-RHYME.

causerie (F *causer* 'to talk, converse') It denotes an informal talk, essay or article particularly on literary topics. The term comes from Sainte-Beuve's *Causeries du lundi*, his contributions to *Le Globe* and *Le Constitutionnel* in the 19th c. *See also* ESSAY; PROPOS.

Cavalier drama In the 1630s the Queen gave patronage to a type of court play called Cavalier drama. It was a decadent form, artificial and ponderous in style, unoriginal in subject matter. The main playwrights were Sir John Suckling, James Shirley and Thomas Killigrew. The Civil War put an end to it.

Cavalier poets A group of English lyric poets who were active, approximately, during the reign of Charles (1625–49). The label is much later than the 17th c., but it is fair to include in the group Lovelace, Sir John Suckling, Herrick, Carew and Waller; plus some minor ones like Godolphin and Randolph. These poets virtually abandoned the sonnet (*q.v.*) form which had been the favoured medium for love poems for a century. They were considerably influenced by Ben Jonson. Their lyrics are light, witty, elegant, and, for the most part, concerned with love. They show much technical virtuosity. Good representative examples are: Suckling's *Why so pale and wan, fond lover*?; Herrick's *Delight in Disorder*; Lovelace's *To Althea, from Prison*. *See* CAROLINE PERIOD.

celebratory theatre A form of festive and popular theatrical entertainment which may celebrate and dramatize some important event or events. It may combine elements of pageant, tableau, *son et lumière* (*qq.v.*), the circus and the tattoo. It may also include song, music, dance, mime, acrobatics and ritual. There is an emphasis on spectacular and ceremonial presentation. A notable example was the celebration of the French Revolution in Le Théâtre du Soleil's *1789*, created by Ariane Mnouchkine in 1970. Peter Brook (1925–) has been a pioneer of celebratory theatre in Britain and abroad. *See also* CARNIVALIZATION/CARNIVALESQUE; LIVING THEATER.

Celtic revival A recrudescence of interest in culture, myth, legend and literature of Celtic people took place in the second half of the 18th c. and was to continue through the Romantic period, and indeed on into the 20th c. Interest in the Gothic and in early Celtic culture was becoming apparent by *c.* 1760. It is evident in, for example, Thomas Gray's Pindaric ode *The Bard* (1757) and in *The Triumphs of Owen* (1768). Gray was influenced by a big collection of Welsh poetry, namely *Some Specimens of the Poetry of the Ancient Welsh Bards. Translated into English . . .* (1764) by Ieuan Brydydd. Interest was also stimulated by James Macpherson's Ossianic poems, which were forgeries (*see* LITERARY FORGERIES) but which were enormously popular and widely influential. In the 19th c. a number of translations of Celtic works began to appear, including Charlotte Guest's version of the *Mabinogion* (1838–49) and Hersart de la Villemarqué's *Barzaz Breiz* (1839) and *Les Bardes bretons du sixième siècle* (1850). In 1854 Ernest Renan published his celebrated study *La Poésie des races celtiques*, which may have caught the attention of Matthew Arnold. In 1865–6 Arnold delivered a series of lectures on Celtic literature at Oxford; this linked all Celtic literatures and helped to promote the foundation of a Chair of Celtic at Oxford in 1877. During the 19th c. several English writers were affected by Celtic culture; notable instances are Thomas Love Peacock, Tennyson and Gerard Manley Hopkins. So, too, were Welsh, Scottish and Irish writers. Among the Scots we should mention particularly the novelist William Black (1841–98) and the poet and novelist William Sharp (1855–1905), whose verse and prose romances on Celtic themes were published under the pen-name Fiona Macleod, a literary *alter ego* or heteronym (*q.v.*). Irish writers of the Irish literary renaissance (*see* CELTIC TWILIGHT) looked back to Celtic origins. In 1893 W. B. Yeats published *The Celtic Twilight*, a collection of stories in folklore. The creation of the Abbey Theatre (*q.v.*) and its promotion of Irish plays by Irish dramatists can be considered as an aspect of the Celtic revival. Renewed interest in the study of Gaelic was another aspect, and continues to be.

Celtic twilight A vague term used to describe that atmosphere, that romantic and somewhat dreamy sense and evocation of the past, which was cultivated and admired in Ireland towards the end of the 19th c. Irish writers, in what has been called the Irish literary Renaissance, wishing to dispel the influence of English literature, turned to their own heritage in search of myth and legend and the glories of a putative 'golden age' represented by such heroic figures as Finn MacCool. It was an attempt, partially successful, at a revival of Irish Celtic culture.

Three influential works in this recrudescence were : O'Grady's *History of Ireland: Heroic Period* (1878); W. B. Yeats's *The Wanderings of Oisin* (1889) and his *The Celtic Twilight* (1893). Yeats, with other distinguished writers, founded the Irish Literary Society in London and The Irish National Literary Society in Dublin. In 1899 he, George Moore and Edwin Martin founded the Irish Literary Theatre; and, in 1901, the Abbey or National Theatre Society was established. Yeats, Lady Gregory and Synge supported it. As the movement gained popularity, libraries were created, books on Irish subjects published, lectures delivered and the Gaelic language revived. Other notable writers assocated with the movement were: 'AE' (pseudonym of George William Russell), Oliver St John Gogarty, Sean O'Casey and James Stephens. Many people ridiculed the movement and James Joyce dismissed it with a scornful phrase 'cultic twalette'.

cénacle (F 'supper room') The *cénacles* were groups or coteries which formed round the early leaders of the Romantic movement. The first is believed to have been formed in the *salon* of Charles Nodier (1780–1844) at the Bibliothèque de l'Arsenal. The second gathered at Victor Hugo's house. Later a group of 'disciples' sat at the feet of Sainte-Beuve.

censorship Forms of censorship began to be introduced very soon after the invention of printing. Rulers, governments and the Church quickly realized the power of the printed word to spread sedition and heresy. Proclamations against seditious and heretical works began in England under Henry VIII in 1529. In 1538 laws were introduced that books must be licensed for printing by Privy Council or other royal nominees. Thereafter, throughout the 16th c., there was a series of proclamations and prohibitions. British monarchs were particularly concerned about the importation of foreign books. In Europe there were similar measures. Underground and illegal printing presses were soon in operation. Thus a pattern was set for the next 450 years.

In 1557 there was an important development when the Stationers' Company got a 'charter of incorporation', after which only members of the company (or others holding a special patent) were allowed to print any work for sale in the kingdom. In 1586 the Star Chamber devised an ordinance which directed that no printing press might be set up in any place other than London – apart from one each in the university towns of Oxford and Cambridge. The Star Chamber continued to exercise considerable power and in 1637 imposed harsh penalties on offending printers. The Star Chamber was abolished by the Long Parliament in 1641, but this did not mean the press was liberated. In fact restrictions and controls became, if anything, even tougher. During the 1640s there were numerous suppressions, prosecutions and imprisonments. In 1655 Cromwell stopped all unofficial periodicals (e.g. the *corantos*, *q.v.*, and other forms of newsletter). The Rump Parliament of 1659 permitted licensed newsbooks but their issue was restricted.

During the Restoration period (*q.v.*) control and licensing of the press continued. In 1662 a Licensing Act was passed in Parliament, initially for two years; it was renewed and extended to 1679. In that year it lapsed, to be renewed in 1685. In 1694 Parliament declined to renew again. Later, the Secretary of State was responsible for dealing with any libellous or offensive matter. This covered anything published which might constitute a breach of the peace, or bring king, government or Parliament or the administration of justice into contempt. The authorities had wide-ranging powers. Offenders might be imprisoned and prosecuted. Standard punishments were the pillory, imprisonment and fines. Not a few writers, journalists and printers fell foul of the law. In 1719 John Mathews was hanged for high treason because of his pamphlet *Vox Populi Vox Dei.* In 1703 Daniel Defoe was arrested, imprisoned and pilloried for his pamphlets on ecclesiastical issues. During the 18th c. interference with and restrictions on the press were gradually reduced but there were a number of celebrated controversies, particularly those in which John Wilkes was concerned. People still had to be careful what they wrote and published. When Thomas Paine published *The Rights of Man* (1791–2) both he and his book were regarded as subversive and he had to flee the country. In 1810 William Cobbett was sent to prison for two years and fined £1,000 (a huge sum in those days) because he denounced flogging in the army. During the 19th c. restrictions on the press in Britain were further lessened and the Stamp Duty (introduced under the Stamp Act of 1712) was abolished in 1855.

Censorship and control of the theatre, plays and performers were established in the 16th c. Some companies of players were attached to the court and to noble households, and there were also wandering troupes of players who had no patrons. In the interests of public order some controls over stage performances were in operation by *c.* 1550. The licensing of individual plays began in 1549 (or earlier). By an act in 1572 all players (actors) were deemed 'rogues and vagabonds' unless they belonged to a baron of the realm (or somebody of higher rank), or were licensed by two justices. Plays were popular at court (Queen Elizabeth herself enjoyed them), but the civic authorities of London were basically not in favour of them. The Corporation produced an act of Common Council which required all players (and all plays) to be licensed by the Corporation. There were ways of evading these regulations. For example, the first theatre to be built in London was in Finsbury Fields (an area outside the Lord Mayor's control). In *c.* 1574 the post of Master of the Revels was created. He was a court official and no play could be performed in England without his licence. In 1581 he was given powers to imprison offenders. From 1606 he had the power to license the printing as well as the performance of plays. During the reigns of James I and Charles I the London theatrical companies worked under royal patents. The authorities were concerned with matters of religion and government, but not morals.

The Puritans were hostile to all forms of theatre and regarded the stage as immoral. In 1642 the Long Parliament prohibited all dramatic performances. The theatres were closed. Even so, there were various evasions, such as the drolls (*q.v.*). At or after the Restoration Charles II issued patents (*see* PATENT THEATRES) to Davenant and Thomas Killigrew (the Elder). These patents allowed them to form two companies of actors with the right to perform in London and Westminster. However, many disputes ensued – not least with the Master of the Revels – and eventually Killigrew was appointed to this post. Gradually censorship became very slack. Scurrility, indecency and licentiousness became rife. What came to be known as Restoration comedy (*q.v.*) no doubt reflected the manners and morals of the period, but some of it caused offence. Matters of religion and politics were also treated in an offensive fashion. A reaction set in. In 1698 Jeremy Collier published his celebrated diatribe (*q.v.*) on the 'profaneness and immorality of the stage'. The following year a royal order forbade the presentation of anything contrary to religion and good manners and the Master of the Revels was prohibited from licensing plays which might offend propriety. Here, perhaps, we see an aspect of the Augustan Age's regard for decorum and good taste.

In due course it became the Lord Chamberlain's job to exercise controls. During the first thirty-odd years of the 18th c. some dramatic performances gave offence (e.g. John Gay's *The Beggar's Opera* and *Polly*, and Fielding's *Pasquin* and *The Historical Register for the Year 1736*). The government and the King were touchy about political and social satire. In 1737 the Licensing Act was passed. This was the result of Walpole's efforts and was intended to control dramatic performance. It was more positive and comprehensive then earlier measures. The Lord Chamberlain became licenser of theatres in London and Westminster, but his powers (at any rate in theory) covered Great Britain. If a new play was to be performed then the Lord Chamberlain had to receive a copy of it. Moreover, the Lord Chamberlain had an official at his disposal in the shape of an 'Examiner of Plays'. Like many such measures the Licensing Act was unpopular, and there were not a few evasions. There were also some fairly absurd prohibitions and censorings. In the 19th c. one of the better known Examiners of Plays was George Colman (the Younger), himself a dramatist and poet, who had the post from 1824 to 1836. Charles Kemble, the actor, succeeded him and he in turn was succeeded by his son. Various nonentities followed.

In 1832 a select committee of the House of Commons, under the direction of Edward Bulwer Lytton, was set up to look into the provisions of the 1737 Act. Out of this came another Act (in 1843), which was more or less a case of *Plus ça change* . . . Censorship of drama remained the Lord Chamberlain's job and he had powers to prohibit the performance of any play (or part of a play) whenever, in his view, it might be contrary to the preservation of good manners, decorum or 'the public peace'. This was on a par with the famous clause in King's Regulations for the army about behaviour contrary to good order and military discipline. There continued to be much criticism of the Lord Chamberlain's role and powers (this criticism was to continue until the 1960s). In 1909 another select committee (this time drawn from the House of Lords *and* the House of Commons) reviewed the whole situation. There was no legislative action as a result of the committee's submissions. It was recommended by the committee that the Lord Chamberlain should continue to be the licenser of players, but that unlicensed plays might be performed and theatre managements would apply for a licence if they wished to.

Eventually, in 1968, the Theatres Act was passed. This abolished the Lord Chamberlain's job as licenser of plays and thereafter it was no longer necessary to get a licence. In effect, matters were at last left to the good judgement, intelligence and artistic integrity of all those who were involved in putting on a play.

It is of some historical interest that in 1982 a private prosecution was brought against the National Theatre in London. This concerned Howard Brenton's play *The Romans in Britain*. The prosecution alleged that the director had 'procured an act of gross indecency' (in this case the simulation, on stage, of a homosexual rape). The prosecution's case foundered on technical grounds.

In general, Britain may be said to have escaped fairly lightly in matters of censorship. However, in the 1920s DORA (Defence of the Realm Act) had some influence. Clauses in this Act provided for forms of censorship, which, in the hands of a reactionary or puritanical Home Secretary, might be invoked.

Elsewhere, during the 20th c., censorship controls of the most stifling kind have been imposed by all totalitarian and repressive régimes. Censorship departments in Communist-bloc countries (especially the USSR, Czechoslovakia, Hungary, Rumania and Albania) were extremely careful about what they would allow to be published, and equally careful in their control of the importation of foreign books, papers and magazines. In the 19th c. Russian writers had long been accustomed to rigorous censorship under the Czarist régime.

It is worth noting that in 1972 a periodical named *Index on Censorship* was founded by Writers and Scholars International: a group of writers, scholars, intellectuals and artists. This group was formed primarily at the instigation of the English poet and critic Stephen Spender and the Soviet dissident Pavel Litvinov. The group is concerned with the promotion of intellectual freedom in countries which suffer from repressive régimes, and the periodical publishes work by writers who are restricted or suppressed in their own countries. It also contains accounts of censorship and the imprisonment of authors. *See* PROPAGANDA; SAMIZDAT.

cento (L 'patchwork') A collection of bits and pieces from various writers. A patchwork poem made up of verses by different writers. Such works were common in later antiquity (e.g. Falconia Proba dedicated to Honorius a *Cento Vergilianus* dealing with events of the Old and New Testaments). Perhaps the most outstanding example of a *cento* is that by Decimus Magnus Ausonius (*c.* AD 310–90). His *Cento Nuptialis* runs to 131 lines, the lines or half lines being taken from, variously, Virgil's *Aeneid*, *Georgics* and *Eclogues*. He derives the term from Greek *kentrōn*, and in his introductory exposition to Paulus defines and explains it:

> It is a poem compactly built out of a variety of passages and different meanings, in such a way that either two half-lines are joined together to form one, or one line and the following half with another half. For to place two (whole) lines side by side is weak, and three in succession mere trifling. But the lines [i.e. the lines of the poet from whose works the *cento* is compiled] are divided at any of the caesurae which heroic verse admits, so that either a penthemimeris can be linked with an anapaestic continuation, or a trochaic fragment with a complementary section, or seven half-feet with a choric anapaest, or after a dactyl and a half-foot is placed whatever is needed to complete the

hexameter: so that you may say it is like the puzzle which the Greeks have called *ostomachia*.

(*Ostomachia* is a puzzle in which fourteen different pieces of bone representing different geometrical shapes are placed in combinations to represent various objects.) Ausonius's poem is a kind of epithalamion (*q.v.*). These are the opening lines (with references):

> Accipite haec animis laetasque advertite mentes,[1]
> ambo animis, ambo insignes praestantibus armis;[2]
> ambo florentes,[3] genus insuperabile bello.[4]

(1. *Aeneid*, V, 1. 304; 2. *Aeneid*, XI, 1. 291; 3. *Eclogues*, VII, 1. 4; 4. *Aeneid*, IV, 1. 40.)

An ingenious modern example is that by A. Alvarez in his introduction to *The New Poetry* (rev. ed. 1966). The synthesis contains lines from eight different modern poets:

> Picture of lover or friend that is not either
> Like you or me who, to sustain our pose,
> Need wine and conversation, colour and light;
> In short, a past that no one now can share,
> No matter whose your future; calm and dry,
> In sex I do not dither more than either,
> Nor should I now swell to halloo the names
> Of feelings that no one needs to remember:
> The same few dismal properties, the same
> Oppressive air of justified unease
> Of our imaginations and our beds.
> It seems the poet made a bad mistake.

See COLLAGE; PASTICHE.

Centre 42 A scheme which was the brain-child of Arnold Wesker (1932–), the dramatist. He planned to create an arts centre supported by the trade unions and Labour movement. In 1960 the Trades Union Congress passed a resolution (No. 42) by which the arts should be supported. Festivals were held in 1962 and for a while it was hoped that the Round House in London would be the centre. Eventually, lack of money meant the whole plan was aborted. *See also* THEATRE WORKSHOP.

centres dramatiques Theatres (in some cases combined with a drama school) established in the purlieus of Paris and some provincial towns from 1945. The ideas was to take theatre and drama 'to the people': to the workers and those of the lower-middle-class bracket. Work done by the directors had discernible leftist tendencies and many of the directors belonged to the Left. A number of these centres were combined with *maisons de la culture* and not a few were highly successful. In Britain they have had counterparts comparable in some respects. For instance, the Unity Theatre, Centre 42, Theatre Workshop (*qq.v.*).

chain verse A rhyming scheme, like *rime riche* (*q.v.*), where the last syllable of a line is repeated in the first syllable of the next line; but though the sound is the same, the sense is different. It is rare in English verse.

The term is also applied to a verse in which the last line of each stanza becomes the first line of the next. Again, this is rare. *See* VILLANELLE.

chair ode That ode which, at the Eisteddfod (*q.v.*), gains the prize of a carved oaken chair.

change of heart A term associated in the 18th c. with sentimental comedy (*q.v.*). By 'a change of heart' the 'baddies' became 'reformed characters' so that sentiments might not be offended and all should look well. Basically, a rather crude theatrical contrivance – often totally implausible.

changga (K 'long poem') A 'popular' Korean verse form, usually of ten or more lines or stanzas with refrains. A frequent theme was love.

chanson A form of love-song, particularly among the Provençal troubadour (*q.v.*) poets. The *chanson* had five or six stanzas, all of the same construction, and an *envoi* (*q.v.*) or *tornada* (*q.v.*). A high degree of originality and technical virtuosity was required, but the themes and subjects were usually the same: devotion to a lady or mistress in the courtly love (*q.v.*) tradition.

chanson à danser Song from the Middle Ages (the earliest extant dates from the first half of the 13th c.) composed as an accompaniment to dance. The metrical forms varied considerably. The principal dance was the *carole*, from which evolved the poetic form *rondet de carole* – similar to a *triolet* (*q.v.*). The *ballette* was another dance song consisting of three stanzas and a refrain (*q.v.*). *See also* CAROL; VIRELAI.

chanson à personnages Medieval song in dialogue form. Popular themes were a dispute between husband and wife, an exchange between lovers parting at dawn, a meeting between a knight and a shepherdess. *See* AUBADE; DEBAT; PASTOURELLE; REVERDIE.

chanson de gestes (F 'song of deeds') OF epic poems which relate the heroic deeds of Carolingian noblemen and other feudal lords. Some describe wars against the Saracens; others are devoted to intrigue, rebellion and war among the nobles. They exhibit a combination of history and legend (*q.v.*) and also reflect a definite conception of religious chivalry. There are three main cycles: the cycle of Guillaume d'Orange; the cycle of Charlemagne; the third mostly develops the themes of a lord's revolt against his *seigneur*. They were very popular (a literature of entertainment) between the 11th and 14th c. and over eighty survive. Easily the most famous is the *Chanson de Roland* (The Song of Roland), probably composed in the second half of the 11th c. *See also* EPIC; NARRATIVE VERSE; ROMANCE.

chanson de toile *Toile* is 'linen, canvas, cloth'. The *chansons de toile* are associated particularly with northern medieval France, the idea being that they were sung by women while they were sewing, spinning or the like. They were short poems in the form of monorhyme stanzas with a refrain (*q.v.*) and related some love episode or sorrow. They tended to be simple, and touching by their immediacy of feeling.

chansonnier A collection of Provençal troubadour (*q.v.*) poems in manuscript form.

chant (OF *chanter*, L *cantare* 'to sing') The term may denote almost any song or melody, particularly the melody to which the Psalms are sung. It may denote the Psalm itself. Chants are commonest in liturgical services. Gregorian plain song or *cantus firmus* is the most famous form of chant and has been the most influential. Anglican chant and the chants of the Orthodox churches are also notable. When a poem is chanted the musical elements are subordinate to the verbal. This produces a stylized quality, noticeable in the recitation of the choral pieces in Classical drama, or choral pieces modelled on the Classical style. Also in the recitation of epic ballads. The *guslari* (*q.v.*) for instance, chant their poems to the accompaniment of a one-string fiddle called a *gusle*.

chante fable (Pr) A romance (*q.v.*) of adventure composed of alternating prose and verse. *Aucassin and Nicolette* (early 13th c.) is believed to be the only survivor of a genre which probably had some popularity in the 12th and 13th c.

chantey *See* SHANTY.

chant royal A metrical and rhyming scheme related to *ballade* (*q.v.*) forms. It consists of five eleven-line stanzas rhyming ababccddedE, followed by an *envoi* (*q.v.*) rhyming ddedE. It also has a refrain (*q.v.*) as indicated by the capital letters, at the end of each stanza and including the last line of the *envoi*. A further complication is that no rhyme word may be used twice except in the *envoi*. The formidable technical difficulties involved make it a rare form except in the 14th c. when distinguished poets like Eustache Deschamps, Charles d'Orléans and Jean Marot used it.

chapbook A form of popular literature hawked by pedlars or chapmen, mostly from the 16th to the 18th c. Chapbooks consisted of ballads, pamphlets, tracts, nursery rhymes and fairy stories (*qq.v.*). They were often illustrated with wood-blocks and were sold at a penny to sixpence. Old romances like *Bevis of Hampton* and *Guy of Warwick* were favourites.

chapka (K 'miscellaneous songs') Long narrative poems sung by professional Korean minstrels.

character, the A literary genre which became popular early in the 17th c. At this time there was an increasing interest in the analysis of character (we may have here the beginning of the novelist's approach to character) but the 'Character' had already a long history, in one form or another, in European literature: in *exemplum*, allegory, fable, tale (*qq.v.*) (for instance, the character studies in Chaucer's *General Prologue to the Canterbury Tales*), and in the dramatic and psychological doctrine of humours (*q.v.*), influenced by Horace's precepts on dramatic types. Moreover, it seems there was a disposition towards and an interest in Charactery because of the by then well-established idea that man in little was an embodiment of the universe.

In his *Advancement of Learning* (1605) Francis Bacon discusses the ancient opinion that 'man was *microcosmus*, an abstract or model of the world'. And in his *History of the World* (1614) Sir Walter Ralegh wrote '. . . because in the little frame of man's body there is a representation of the Universal; and (by allusion) a kind of participation of all the parts there, therefore was man called *Microcosmos*, or the little World'. Later, Sir Thomas Browne, in *Religio Medici* (1642), observed: 'We carry within us the wonders we seek without us: there is all Africa and her prodigies in us; we are that bold and adventurous piece of Nature, which he that studies wisely learns in a *compendium* what others labour at in a divided piece and endless volume'.

Writers and thinkers of the period were very attracted to the microcosm/macrocosm concept, but the popularity of the 'Character' may also be attributed to the publication in 1592 of a Latin translation, by Isaac Casaubon, of the *Characters* of Theophrastus of Lesbos (371–287 BC) – the prototypal work – which was followed in 1593 by an English version of Casaubon's Latin by John Healey. Other works which very probably had some influence were pamphlets by Nashe and Greene and Nicholas Breton's *The Fantasticks* (1626).

The first major collection of character studies was Joseph Hall's *Characters of Virtues and Vices* (1608). A minor work by 'W.M.' called *The Man in the Moon* came out in 1609. The next major work was Sir Thomas Overbury's *Characters* (1614), some of which are believed to have been written by Webster, Dekker and Donne. Another minor work was Geffray Mynshul's *Essays and Characters of Prison and Prisoners* (1617). By now the connection between the essay (*q.v.*) and the 'Character' is becoming clear, and one may suppose that the influence of Montaigne is to be detected here. Then, in 1628, John Earle published *Microcosmographie*. Earle is the truest descendant of Theophrastus and his characters are generally thought to be the best.

The subjects of Characterology fall into roughly three categories: (a) a type – a self-conceited man, a blunt man; (b) a social type – an antiquary, an old college butler; (c) a place or scene: a tavern or cockpit. The idea was to create an individual while formulating a type. There was usually an attempt at universality. For instance, a pretender to learning might be found in any part of the world at any time. The miniature portraits were aphoristically terse, a style particularly congenial in the 17th c.

Hall, Overbury and Earle had many imitators. The more notable authors and works were: Donald Lupton's *Long and Country Carbonadoed* (1632); Richard Flecknoe's *Enigmatical Characters* (1658); Francis Osborn's *A Miscellany of Sundry Essays* (1659). An elaborate extension of the whole idea of 'charactery' is George Halifax's *The Character of a Trimmer* (1688).

One of the most famous of all such collections was La Bruyère's *Les Caractères* (1688), in the great French tradition of Montaigne, Pascal and La Rochefoucauld. He combined translations of Theophrastus with his own observations – which are shrewd, tartly laconic, aphoristic (like La Rochefoucauld's *Maxims*) and presented with Baconian terseness.

The practice of 'charactery' was carried on in the following century in the periodical essay (*q.v.*), especially by Steele, Addison, Goldsmith and Johnson. They took the process a stage further by naming the characters (for instance, Sir Andrew Freeport, Will Honeycomb, Dick Minim), and these essay characters, though types, were also particular individuals. The essay character gave place to and made possible the character of the novel (*q.v.*), as can be seen in Fielding's novels *Joseph Andrews* (1742) and *Tom Jones* (1749).

Modern 'charactery' tends to be the portrayal of individuals, though many of Dickens's characters are also typical – just as virtues and vices are typical in most parts of the world. Something in between the characters of Earle and the novel character is to be found in such works as Dickens's *Sketches by Boz* (1839), Thackeray's *Book of Snobs* (1848) and George Eliot's *Theophrastus Such* (1879). *See also* MAXIM; PENSEE.

charm A spell or incantation which may consist of song, verse or mere mumbo jumbo and abracadabra to invoke supernatural or supranormal powers. It is one of the earliest forms of written literature and appears to be almost universal. The OE *Charms* are among the first extant written works in our language. There are several: For a sudden stitch; Against a dwarf; Against wens; For taking a swarm of bees; A land remedy; A journey spell; Against the theft of cattle; The nine herbs charm. Examples of charms incorporated in a more literary context are to be found in Elizabethan and Jacobean plays. Famous instances are the Weird Sisters' charms in *Macbeth* (*c.* 1606). Quite as good are those in Ben Jonson's *The Masque of Queens* (1609), and the lyric of Campion's which begins:

> Thrice toss these oaken ashes in the air;
> Thrice sit thou mute in his enchanted chair;
> Then thrice three times tie up this true love's knot,
> And murmur soft: 'She will, or she will not.'

See INCANTATION.

chastushka (R 'part-song') A form of Russian folksong. It usually consists of two, four or six lines (four being the commonest) which rhyme. Often humorous and epigrammatic, most of them are love-songs. Some *chastushki* are concerned with political events such as the Revolution, the Second World War, and not a few express anti-Soviet attitudes. As a kind of brief lyric poetry, they are sung solo or chorally and may be accompanied by guitar, balalaika or accordion.

Chaucerian stanza *See* RHYME ROYAL.

cheville (F 'peg, pin, bolt, plug') A French term for an expression or phrase which serves to round off a verse.

Chevy Chase stanza *See* BALLAD METER.

chiasmus (Gk 'a placing crosswise') A reversal of grammatical structures in successive phrases or clauses. As in this example from Dr Johnson's *The Vanity of Human Wishes*:

> By the day the frolic, and the dance by night.

And this from Pope's *Essay on Man* (Epistle I):

> His time a moment, and a point his space.

The device is related to antithesis (*q.v.*). *See also* ANTIMETABOLE; ZEUGMA.

Chicago critics A group of critics associated with the University of Chicago who in 1952 published *Critics and Criticism: Ancient and Modern*, ed. R. S. Crane.

children's books Until about the middle of the 18th c. there was little in the way of books specifically for children, except for didactic works of one sort and another like text books, books of etiquette and works of moral edification. For entertainment and diversion they had Aesop's *Fables*, romances, travel books, chapbooks, broadside ballads (*qq.v.*) and any 'adult' reading they could lay their hands on. Notable examples of this are Bunyan's *Pilgrim's Progress* (1678), Defoe's *Robinson Crusoe* (1719) and Swift's *Gulliver's Travels* (1726). In France children had been a little better off because of Fénelon's *Télémaque* (1699), Perrault's fairy tales, and *The Arabian Nights* which came to England via a French translation early in the 18th c.

In England one of the first people to realize that there was a demand for children's books was John Newbery (1713–67), a book-seller who issued a variety of works illustrated with wood-cuts or engravings at low prices. His two best known publications were *A Little Pretty Pocket-Book* (1744) and *The History of Little Goody Two-Shoes* (1765?).

Apart from imitations of *Robinson Crusoe* (e.g. *The Hermit, or . . . The Adventures of Mr Philip Quarll*, 1727) there was still not much available until the latter half of the 18th c. when a number of writers (among them several women) produced juvenile literature. Some of the better known works are *The History of Sandford and Merton* (1783–9) by Thomas Day, *Fabulous Histories* (1786) by Sarah Trimmer, *Evenings at Home* (1792–6) by John Aikin and Mrs Barbauld, and *The Parent's Assistant* (1796–1801) Maria Edgeworth, the novelist.

Early in the 19th c. Charles and Mary Lamb wrote their famous *Tales From Shakespeare.*

A certain amount of verse specifically for children was written in the 18th c., notably Isaac Watts's *Divine Songs for Children* (1715), Cotton's *Visions in Verse* (1751), and Christopher Smart's *Hymns for the Amusement of Children* (1775). There were also a large number of ballads (*q.v.*) in circulation and nursery rhymes (*q.v.*). In 1804–5 there came out *Original Poems for Infant Minds*, a collection of moral verses; and in 1807 William Roscoe published *The Butterfly's Ball and the Grasshopper's Feast* which was very popular.

From this point on we find an ever increasing number of publications for children in Europe and America. Outstanding works are: Grimm's *Fairy Tales* (1823), Catherine Sinclair's *Holiday House* (1839), Edward Lear's *A Book of Nonsense* (1846), Hans Andersen's *Fairy Tales*, which were translated into English in 1846, Lane's version of *The Arabian Nights* (1839–41), Ruskin's *King of the Golden River* (1851), Thackeray's *The Rose and the Ring* (1855), Kingsley's *Water Babies* (1863), Jean Ingelow's *Mopsa the Fairy* (1869), George Macdonald's *At the Back of the North Wind* (1871). Probably none of these is as famous as Lewis Carroll's *Alice's Adventures in Wonderland* (1865) and *Through the Looking-Glass* (1872). Other works of importance in the 19th c. are Lang's collections of fairy tales, Hawthorne's *Tanglewood Tales* (1851) and Kingsley's *Heroes* (1856).

School stories have also proved a very popular form of fiction among children and adolescents. A few of the more or less classic works in this field are: Sarah Fielding's *Governess* (1749); Harriet Martineau's *Crofton Boys* (1841); Thomas Hughes's *Tom Brown's Schooldays* (1857); Dean Farrer's *Eric or Little by Little* (1858); Talbot Baines Reed's *The Fifth Form at St Dominic's* (1887); Kipling's *Stalky & Co.* (1899); Richmal Crompton's *Just William* (1922), which she followed up with thirty or more 'William' books; and the famous Billy Bunter stories by Frank Richards which first appeared in *The Gem* and *The Magnet* and were then gathered into volume form as *Billy Bunter of Greyfriars' School* (1947).

The fairy tale (*q.v.*) is a widespread form of fiction for children. Again there are a number of classic works, like *The Arabian Nights*, Perrault's tales, the stories by the Grimm brothers and Hans Andersen, Chandler Harris's *Uncle Remus* (1880), Lewis Carroll's *Alice's Adventures in Wonderland* (1865), A. A. Milne's *Winnie the Pooh* (1926) and *The House at Pooh Corner* (1928), Carlo Lorenzini's *Pinocchio* (1883), Waldemar Bonsels's *Maja* (1912) and Selma Lagerlöf's *Nils Holgersson* (1906–7).

There are also a large number of what may be described as animal stories. Notable instances are Anna Sewell's *Black Beauty* (1877), Kipling's *Jungle Books* (1894–5), J. W. Fortescue's *Story of a Red Deer* (1897), various stories by Grey Owl and Frances Pitt. In this field Henry Williamson wrote two classic works in the shape of *Tarka the Otter* (1927), which was not, in fact, intended as a children's story, and *Salar the Salmon* (1935).

Other children's stories of note are: Elizabeth Wetherell's *The Wide, Wide World* (1850); Charlotte M. Yonge's *The Daisy Chain* (1856); Richard Jefferies's *Bevis* (1882); Frances Hodgson Burnett's *Little Lord Fauntleroy* (1886) and *The Secret Garden* (1911); Edith Nesbitt's *The Story of the Treasure Seekers* (1899), and *The Phoenix and the Carpet* (1904); Noel Streatfield's *Ballet Shoes* (1936); and a number of very good books by Arthur Ransome.

Some notable instances of children's verse are Christina Rossetti's *Sing-Song* (1872); R. L. Stevenson's *A Child's Garden of Verses* (1885); Hilaire Belloc's *The Bad Child's Book of Beasts* (1896) and his *Cautionary Tales* (1908); T. S. Eliot's *Old Possum's Book of Practical Cats* (1939). This last is a kind of nonsense verse (*q.v.*), a genre to which (for children) several famous writers have made outstanding contributions – especially Lewis Carroll and A. A. Milne. Walter de la Mare and Eleanor Farjeon have also written some fine poetry for children. Robert Graves, Charles Causley and Ted Hughes have also written excellent verse specifically for children; and Roald Dahl's poetry for children has been immensely popular, particularly his two collections *Revolting Rhymes* (1982) and *Dirty Beasts* (1984). In recent years Puffin has published some of the best anthologies of children's verse, namely, *Junior Voices* (in four different books) and *Voices* (in three books).

In the 20th c. there are a number of works in the fairy tale category which have become classics. Obvious examples are: J. M. Barrie's *Peter Pan* (1904); Kipling's *Just So Stories* (1902), *Puck of Pook's Hill* (1906) and *Rewards and Fairies* (1910); A. A. Milne's Christopher Robin series (begun in the 1920s); Hugh Lofting's Dr Dolittle series (also begun in the 1920s). To these should be added Kenneth Grahame's *Wind in the Willows* (1908), and the many Beatrix Potter stories, the first being published in 1902.

Adventure stories, most of which have been intended for boys, first became popular in the 19th c. An early and well-known example is Marryat's *Masterman Ready* (1841–2). R. M. Ballantyne's *The Coral Island* (1858) is a classic of the genre. So are Stevenson's *Treasure Island* (1881–2) and Rider Haggard's *King Solomon's Mines* (1885). Early science fiction (*q.v.*) written by Jules Verne and H. G. Wells was immensely popular and of a high order. W. E. Johns's Biggles stories had a great vogue from the 1920s onwards.

Most crime and detective story (*q.v.*) novels have been written for adults, but have proved very popular among children; especially Conan Doyle's Sherlock Holmes stories and G. K. Chesterton's Father Brown stories. A classic in crime fiction aimed primarily at children is Erich Kästner's *Emil and the Detectives*, and many works by Enid Blyton.

Outside English literature some of the other better known outstanding works are: the Comtesse de Ségur's *Les Malheurs de Sophie* (1864); Louisa M. Alcott's *Little Women* (1868–9); Hector Malot's *Sans Famille* (1878); Mark Twain's *Adventures of Tom Sawyer* (1876) and his *Adventurers of Huckleberry Finn* (1884); Johanna Spyri's *Heidi* (1880–81); and L. M. Montgomery's *Anne of Green Gables* (1908).

Since the 1950s literature intended specifically for children has become a publishing industry in its own right. There are specialist guides, and, in the more reputable newspapers, specialist reviewers. The whole approach has become highly professional. Different age groups are carefully catered for, and so are the sexes. Close attention has been given to racism and sexism, and also to what is acceptable or unacceptable politically and ideologically. Not a few prize awards have been created: for example, the Kate Greenaway Medal for illustration, the Newbery Medal, the Eleanor Farjeon Medal and the Carnegie Medal.

Some authors have become enormously popular and have what is almost a cult following. A notable example is J. R. R. Tolkien (1892–1973), who published *The Hobbit* in 1937 and followed this with *The Lord of the Rings* in three volumes (1954–5) and *The Silmarillion* (1977). C. S. Lewis (1898–1963) has been equally popular and is considered by many to be a far better writer. Apart from his science fiction novels, he wrote the Narnia series: seven stories beginning with *The Lion, the Witch and the Wardrobe* (1950) and ending with *The Last Battle* (1956). In the 1970s the author and illustrator Raymond Briggs (1914–) achieved fame with a series of outstanding stories; principally, *Jim and the Beanstalk* (1970), *Father Christmas* (1973), *Father Christmas Goes on Holiday* (1975), *Fungus the Bogeyman* (1977) and *The Snowman* (1979). This last inspired a brilliant short film. Besides his verse for children Roald Dahl has also written many notable stories, including *James and the Giant Peach* (1961), *Charlie and the Chocolate Factory* (1964), *Danny, the Champion of the World* (1975), *The BFG* (1982) and *Esio Trot* (1990).

Of the dozens of other writers who have produced distinguished literature for children since the 1950s we should mention particularly Nina Bawden, Maurice Sendak, Ian Serraillier, Philippa Pearce, Alan Garner, Rosemary Sutcliff, Leon Garfield, Margaret J. Miller, Ursula Le Guin, Joan Aiken, William Mayne, Robert Westall, Stan Barstow, Bill Naughton, John Prebble, Penelope Lively and Barry Hines. Plus the Americans Virginia Hamilton, Paula Fox, Betsy Biars and Lee McGiffin; and the Australians Patricia Wrightson and Ivan Southall. *See also* COMICS.

chimerat A form of folk-tale story of the Indo-European culture which possesses the quality of universality (*q.v.*). Thus it does not depend for its verisimilitude on any particular place or period. *See* NOVELLAT.

choka A Japanese verse form which comprises lines of five and seven syllables alternating regularly and concluding with two successive seven-syllable lines.

choliambus (Gk 'lame' or 'limping iambic') A meter used by Hipponax of Ephesus (*c.* 540 BC) and so called because of the substitution (*q.v.*) of a spondee or trochee (*qq.v.*) for the normal iamb (*q.v.*) in the sixth foot of the iambic trimeter (*q.v.*). If the fifth foot was also a spondee the verse was called ischiorrhogic or 'broken hipped'.

choree *See* TROCHEE.

choriambus (Gk 'chorus iamb') An iamb and a trochee (*qq.v.*) combined to make a metrical foot of two stressed syllables enclosing two unstressed: / ◡◡ /. In English verse, rare as the basic scheme of a poem; but not infrequently found in combination with other feet. Swinburne, a skilled and indefatigable experimenter in meter, shows its use well in *Choriambics*:

> Swéet thĕ | kíssĕs ŏf deáth | sét ŏn thȳ líps
> Cóldĕr ăre théy | thăn mīne;
> Cóldĕr | súrelȳ thăn pást | kíssĕs ŏf lóve
> Póured fŏr thȳ líps | ăs wíne.

Chorus (Gk 'dance') Originally the Chorus was a group of performers at a religious festival, especially fertility rites. By some process of grafting or symbiosis Greek tragedy (*q.v.*) acquired (or grew out of) these choral rites. At any rate, the Chorus became an essential and integral part of Greek tragic drama. In the works of Aeschylus the Chorus often took part in the action; in Sophocles it served as a commentator on the action; and in Euripides it provided a lyric element. The Romans copied the idea of a Chorus from the Greeks, and Elizabethan dramatists took it over from the Romans. However, a full scale Chorus has seldom been used in English drama, or indeed European drama.

Usually the Chorus has been reduced to one person, as in *Henry V* (1599), *Pericles* (*c.* 1608) and *The Winter's Tale* (*c.* 1609–10). Milton used a full Chorus in his closet drama (*q.v.*) *Samson Agonistes* (1671), but thereafter there are few instances until T. S. Eliot's *Murder in the Cathedral* (1935) in which the remarkable Chorus of the women of Canterbury takes part in the action, comments on it and provides mood and atmosphere. Eliot also used a Chorus of the Eumenides in *The Family Reunion* (1939). There have also been occasional uses of a single Chorus as commentator on the action (moving in and out of the play). Notable instances are the scurrilous Thersites, in Shakespeare's *Troilus and Cressida* (*c.* 1602), the Fool in *King Lear* (1606), and Antony's henchman Enobarbus in *Antony and Cleopatra* (*c.* 1606–7). Other important instances in drama are to be found in Brecht's *The Caucasian Chalk Circle* (1943–5), Anouilh's *Antigone* (1944), Tennessee Williams's *The Glass Menagerie* (1945) and Arthur Miller's *A View from the Bridge* (1955). The use of a kind of group Chorus is also to be found occasionally in novels. For example, there are the rustics in George Eliot's *Silas Marner* (1861), the Mellstock musicians in Thomas Hardy's *Under the Greenwood Tree* (1872) and the rustics in his *The Return of the Native* (1878). A not dissimilar use of Chorus is to be found in some of William Faulkner's novels: for instance, *The Hamlet* (1940), *The Mansion* (1959) and *The Reivers* (1962).

chosism (F 'thingism') It denotes the highly detailed description of objects, things (often inanimate) – their shape, colour, texture, density – that some French novelists associated with the *nouveau roman* (*q.v.*) tended to go in for. It had its fascination but when overdone it could become counter-productive. Alain Robbe-Grillet and Michel Butor, among others, were particularly skilled at it. *See also* TROPISM.

chrestomathy (Gk 'useful learning') An anthology (*q.v.*) of passages in prose or verse (or both); particularly one to be used for learning a language.

Christabel meter The meter of Coleridge's poem *Christabel*. It comprises free couplets with a pattern of four stresses. Much of the time the feet are iambs or anapaests (*qq.v.*). Coleridge claimed that the meter was based, not on a syllable count but on an accent count, that this was a new principle and that the length of the line varied with the amount of passion expressed. In fact the principle was *not* new, but it is true that the passion does vary occasionally. One feature of the poem is that in a few lines he manages monosyllabic feet.

chronicle A register of events in order of time, often composed contemporaneously with the events they record. Early examples are the Roman *Fasti Consulares* or *Capitolini* compiled in the reign of Augustus. There were many medieval chronicles, in verse and prose, which are important sources for the historian. Among the earliest are the 6th c. chronicle of Gildas, *De Excidio et Conquestu Britanniae*, Bede's *Ecclesiastical History* (*c.* 731), the *Historia Britonum* of Nennius (*c.* 796), Asser's 9th c. chronicle covering the period 849–87, and the *Historia Remensis Ecclesiae* by Flodoard of Rheims which covers the period 919–66. From the second half of the 10th c. dates the *Annales Cambriae*. The *Anglo-Saxon Chronicles* are very valuable records of events in England from the beginning of the Christian era until the middle of the 12th c. Several Latin chronicles belong to the 12th c., including Florence of Worcester's *Chronicon ex Chronicis,* which he took down to 1117 and which was then extended by others until 1295. Eadmer's *Historia Novorum in Anglia* goes as far as 1122. William of Malmesbury, one of the best and most famous chroniclers, compiled several records: particularly the *Gesta Regum Anglorum* (449–1127) and *Historia Novella*, which covers English history as far as 1142. From the 12th c. also date Geoffrey of Monmouth's *Historia Regum Britanniae*, Roger of Hoveden's *Cronica*, Jocelin de Brakelond's chronicle of his abbey, several records by Giraldus Cambrensis and William of Newburgh's *Historia Rerum Anglicarum* (1066–1198). In the 13th c. some schools of history developed, particularly at St Denis where a large number of Latin chronicles were produced which eventually became the *Grandes Chroniques de France*; and at St Albans where Matthew of Paris compiled his great chronicles (1235–59). From the 13th and 14th c. we should also note Robert Gloucester's chronicle from earliest times down to 1272, Richard of Cirencester's *Speculum Historiale* (447–1066), Froissart's *Chroniques* (1325–1400) and Andrew of Wyntoun's *The Orygynale Cronykil.* In the 15th c. John Capgrave made several important chronicles, and in the 16th c. we find an increasing number of such records: Robert Fabyan's *Concordance of Histories* (1516), an anonymous *History of Richard III* (1534), which was something of a landmark in history and biography (*q.v.*), Polydore Vergil's *Anglicae Historiae Libri xxvi* (1534–55), Camden's *Britannia* (1586), Holinshed's *Chronicles* (1577), Edward Hall's *The Union of the Noble and Illustre Families of Lancastre and York*, a number of very valuable *Chronicles* by John Stow (especially his account of London), and William Harrison's *Description of England* (included in Holinshed's *Chronicles*). Early in the 17th c. John Speed published *Historie of Great Britain* (1611), and between 1599 and 1636 Sir John Hayward published several biographies. By this stage the writing of history and the making of records was very different from what it had been earlier. Biography, autobiography (*q.v.*), memoirs, diaries, log-books, travel books, narratives of sea voyages and exploration were becoming commonplace and thereafter the chronicle was no longer a form of any note. The writing of history, as is evident from, for instance, Sir Walter Ralegh's *History of the World* (1614), was to become a much more specialized business. *See* ANNAL; CHRONICLE PLAY; DIARY AND JOURNAL; TRAVEL BOOK.

chronicle novel *See* BILDUNGSROMAN; ROMAN CYCLE; ROMAN-FLEUVE; SAGA NOVEL.

chronicle play Also known as a History Play, and therefore based on recorded history rather than on myth or legend (*qq.v.*). Early examples are *The Persians* by Aeschylus, and *Octavia*, ascribed to Seneca.

Early chronicle plays in England were like pageants interspersed with battle scenes. However, some dramatists saw the possibility of the history play. Bale wrote what is generally regarded as the first: *King John* (*c.* 1534). Two other important works in the transition from Interlude (*q.v.*) and Morality Play (*q.v.*) to historical drama were Sackville and Norton's *Gorboduc* (1561) and Preston's *Cambises* (1569). Later, Marlowe also saw the possibilities of such presentation and, using Holinshed, dramatized the life of Edward II (1593). Shakespeare followed with a succession of chronicle plays which covered the English monarchy from Richard II to Henry VIII. Shakespeare also wrote *King John* (probably adapted before 1598 from an earlier work and not printed until the Folio (*q.v.*) of 1623). After him Fletcher, with *Bonduca* (1619), and Ford, with *Perkin Warbeck* (1634), continued the tradition successfully.

Thereafter chronicle plays are fairly rare, though a number of dramatists attempted Roman historical subjects in the 18th and 19th c. James Sheridan Knowles, Darley, Tennyson, Browning and Swinburne all turned to history for their subjects but with little success – largely because they were out of touch with the requirements of the theatre and insufficiently familiar with the stage. Thomas Hardy also attempted a dramatization of history in the shape of *The Dynasts* (1904, 1906, 1908) which also proved unstageable. By general agreement Schiller in the *Wallenstein Trilogy* (1799) and *Maria Stuart* (1800) was the only subsequent dramatist to manage this kind of play with much success.

Since the Second World War there have been several notable chronicle plays. For example, Arthur Miller's *The Crucible* (1953), Robert Bolt's *A Man for All Seasons* (1960) and *State of Revolution* (1977), and Rolf Hochhuth's *The Representative* (1966) and *Soldiers* (1967). *See* CHRONICLE; EPIC THEATRE.

chronogram (Gk 'time writing') An inscription in which letters form a date in Roman numerals.

Ciceronian In the style of Cicero (106–43 BC). Thus, dignified, balanced, melodious, well ordered and clear. Cicero had much influence on the writing of prose from the Renaissance onwards.

cielito (Sp 'little heaven') In gaucho literature (*q.v.*) an octosyllabic quatrain (*q.v.*) rhyming in the second and fourth lines. A well-known practitioner was Bartolomé Hidalgo (1788–1822), the Uruguayan poet, who was primarily responsible for the creation of gaucho literature.

cinquain A five-line stanza with a variable meter and rhyme scheme. It may be of medieval origin. The American poet Adelaide Crapsey worked out a particular kind of *cinquain* consisting of five lines with a fixed number of syllables: two, four, six, eight and two respectively.

cipher A mode of writing which employs the substitution or transposition of letters. A private and secret means of communication. Interesting if childish examples occur in Mary Leith's letters to Swinburne. For instance:

> Cy merest dozen,
>
> Ansk thawfully for your kyind letter. Since you and Mr Watts kyindly give us the choice of days (or doice of chays) may we name Wednesday all things being propitious?. . .
>
> This little delay has allowed me more time to devote to your most interesting Eton book . . . even tho' it be only the tavings of a rug, or even the topping of a mug, it is exceptionally amusing to your mi', tho' I could dish that it wealt with a pater leriod.

See SPOONERISM.

circumambages The devices of periphrasis (*q.v.*). A rare term.

circumlocution Roundabout speech or writing. Using a lot of words where a few will do. *See* EUPHEMISM; PERIPHRASIS; TAUTOLOGY.

circumstance, tragedy of A tragedy (*q.v.*) in which some kind of external force like fate or the gods brings about the doom of the hero or heroine (and other characters).

citizen comedy A type of play which had some vogue early in the 17th c. It was usually about life in contemporary London and the characters were based on those likely to be found among the middle or lower-middle classes. Well-known examples of the genre are Dekker's *The Shoemaker's Holiday* (1600), Middleton's *A Chaste Maid in Cheapside* (*c.* 1613) and Ben Jonson's *Bartholomew Fair* (1614).

civic critics A name give to Russian critics (especially those of the 19th c.) who tended to evaluate literature in terms of its social and political ideas and attitudes and were concerned with whether or not it was progressive. They were opposed to the Parnassians and Parnassianism (*q.v.*) and the aesthetic of art for art's sake (*q.v.*).

civic poetry The name given to 19th c. Russian poetry which is chiefly concerned with the expression of political and social consciousness and thus with the way of life that people lead (e.g. the peasantry). Its originator was probably Kondrati Ryleyev (1795–1826), much of whose poetry was about the Cossacks, whose democratic ideals and standards he admired. Other poets of note who were practitioners of this kind of verse were Nikolai Ogaryov (1813–77), Nikolai Nekrasov (1821–78), Ivan Aksakov (1823–86), Ivan Nikitin (1824–61), Alexei Pleshcheyev (1825–93), Nikolai Vilenkin (1855–1937) and Semyon Nadson (1862–87). Civic poetry as a tradition came more or less to an end in the 1890s with the advent of symbolism (*q.v.*).

classic A number of meanings may be distinguished, but principally: (a) of the first rank or authority; (b) belonging to the literature or art of Greece and Rome; and (c) a writer or work of the first rank, and of generally acknowledged excellence.

Originally a *scriptor classicus* wrote for the upper classes; a *scriptor proletarius* for the lower classes. Gradually, for the Romans, the term 'classic' came to signify an author of the first class quality.

During the Middle Ages the word merely meant a writer who was studied (in the class room) regardless of his merit. At the Renaissance (*q.v.*) only the major works by Greek and Latin authors were regarded as of first class importance, and the humanistic ideal established the view that the best classical authors had reached perfection. Nowadays we tend to use classic in one of three senses: (a) first class or outstanding (we have 'classic' races); (b) ancient; (c) typical (for instance, a classic example of a disease).

The adjective 'classical' usually applies to anything pertaining to Greece and Rome. Nearly always there is the implication of the 'best', a standard of excellence worthy of emulation. When applied to literature the word Classical suggests that the work has the qualities of order, harmony, proportion, balance, discipline . . . In short, nothing can be taken away from it or added to it without doing it some injury. *See* CLASSICISM/ROMANTICISM; NEO-CLASSICISM.

classicism A term as replete with varied and contradictory meanings as romanticism (*q.v.*) and considerably complicated by the antinomy of classicism/romanticism (*q.v.*).

In general when we speak of classicism we refer to the styles, rules, modes, conventions, themes and sensibilities of the Classical authors, and, by extension, their influence on and presence in the work of later authors. For the Romans classicism was Greek influence. Seneca, for example, imitated the Greek tragedians; Virgil was much influenced by Homer. Then, in the 12th c., we find Graeco-Roman models used by writers of the French and German courtly romances. The imitation of the rules of Classical poetics is another very important development. Aristotle's *Poetics* and Horace's *Ars Poetica* were two major influences in the 15th and 16th c. Aristotle's shadow lies heavily, and in some cases not at all helpfully, over much drama from the 16th c. to the end of the 18th c. Many commentators on Aristotle in the 16th c. diffused his theories of imitation (*q.v.*). His views of tragedy and epic were regarded almost as gospel. The principal commentators on Aristotle were mostly Italian: Robortelli, Segni, Maggi Vettori, Castelvetro and Piccolomini. In England Scaliger's *Poetica* (1561) is a key work. Horace's remarks on decorum (*q.v.*), the appropriateness of language and style, the appropriateness of action to character, and his observations on the need for excellence in craftsmanship, were also taken up, analysed and disseminated by commentators in the

16th c.; principally, Vida, Robortelli, Joachim du Bellay, Ronsard, Sir Philip Sidney (in *Apologie for Poetrie*, 1595) and Opitz.

Another major Classical influence on drama was Seneca, especially in tragedy; to such an extent that we have a subspecies known as Senecan tragedy (*q.v.*).

Classicism was strongest in France in the 17th and 18th c. but it was also very strong in England. In France, the main authors to follow Classical precepts were Corneille, Racine, Molière, Voltaire, Boileau and La Fontaine. The most influential treatise by a Frenchman in this respect is undoubtedly Boileau's *Art Poétique* (1674). The major English authors to follow Classical rules and modes were Ben Jonson, Dryden, Pope, Swift, Addison and Dr Johnson. The influence of classicism is also very noticeable in the work of many German writers in the second half of the 18th c. (notably, Winckelmann, Lessing, Goethe, Schiller and Hölderlin), and also in the work of some Italian authors – especially Alfieri. The Germans, however, were not interested in French Neoclassicism (*q.v.*) or the Roman authors. They went back to the Greeks and imitated Greek forms.

Classicism in literature is by no means extinct. In the 20th c. there has been a considerable revival of interest in Classical themes in drama, fiction and verse, especially in French drama, and particularly in the plays of Sartre, Cocteau, Giraudoux and Anouilh. *See also* NEOCLASSICISM.

classicism/romanticism An antinomy (*q.v.*) devised by Friedrich von Schlegel (1772–1829) and expressed in *Das Athenaeum* (1798). Schlegel saw classicism (*q.v.*) as an attempt to express infinite ideas and feelings in a finite form and romanticism (*q.v.*) as an attempt to express a kind of universal poetry in the creation of which the poet made his own laws. Mme de Staël (1766–1817) first publicized this idea in *De l'Allemagne* (1813) and it was through this work, as much as through Schlegel's, that English and French writers became acquainted with the theory. Mme de Staël rejected classicism. Once this antinomy was established, many people modified and expanded it. The most notable person to do so was Goethe who equated classicism with health and romanticism with sickness. This over-simplified antinomy has been much debated ever since.

clausula A form of prose rhythm invented by Greek orators as a punctuation for oral delivery. Latin authors, particularly Cicero, adopted the device and introduced *clausulae* in the writing of prose.

Prose is scannable, in the same way that verse is; thus writers developed the trick of concluding sentences and periods with regularized cadences.

clef *See* LIVRE A CLEF.

clench A quibbling form of pun (*q.v.*). Also a statement that settles an argument; one that clinches it.

clerihew A four-line verse consisting of two couplets, invented by Edmund Clerihew Bentley (1875–1956). He is supposed to have devised the form during a boring chemistry lesson – hence this:

Sir Humphrey Davy
Abominated gravy.
He lived in the odium
Of having discovered sodium.

At their best they are witty, deft and epigrammatic. For instance:

George the Third
Ought never to have occurred.
One can only wonder
At so grotesque a blunder.

Many people have composed good clerihews and making them up has become a parlour game. The inventor's son, Nicolas Bentley, is the author of a famous one:

Cecil B. de Mille
Rather against his will
Was persuaded to leave Moses
Out of the Wars of the Roses.

See also BOUTS-RIMES; DOUBLE DACTYL; LIMERICK.

cliché (F 'stereotype plate') A trite, over-used expression which is lifeless. A very large number of idioms (*q.v.*) have become clichés through excessive use. The following sentence contains eight common ones: 'When the grocer, who was as fit as a fiddle, had taken stock of the situation he saw the writing on the wall, but decided to turn over a new leaf and put his house in order by taking a long shot at eliminating his rival in the street – who was also an old hand at making the best of a bad job.' Hackneyed literary phrases (often misquoted) are another form of cliché. Pope remarked caustically on these in his *Essay on Criticism* (II, 350 ff) when criticizing the stereotyped mannerisms of 18th c. poetasters (*q.v.*):

> Where'er you find 'the cooling western breeze',
> In the next line it 'whispers through the trees';
> If crystal streams 'with pleasing murmurs creep',
> The reader's threatened (not in vain) with 'sleep'.

Eric Partridge's *A Dictionary of Clichés* is one of the best guides to these literary tares. *See* COLLOQUIALISM; DEAD METAPHOR; SLANG.

climax That part of a story or play (for that matter, many forms of narrative) at which a crisis (*q.v.*) is reached and resolution achieved. *See also* ANTICLIMAX; CATASTROPHE; DENOUEMENT; FALLING ACTION; FREYTAG'S PYRAMID; RISING ACTION; TURNING POINT.

cloak-and-dagger story Usually applied to the novel of adventure which involves disguise, espionage, daring exploits, acts of sabotage and anarchy, and, in general, subversive and illegal activity. The phrase has strong associations with 19th c. and Victorian melodrama (*q.v.*), in which saturnine and double-dyed villains (often heavily disguised) wore cloaks and carried weapons such as swordsticks and poignards (plus poison and explosives). There may be some connection between cloak-and-dagger and the genre of Spanish drama known as *comedias de capa y espada* (*q.v.*). English literature is rich in cloak-and-dagger tales, by such authors as Anthony Hope, Baroness Orczy, Rafael Sabatini, A. E. W. Mason, John Buchan, Edgar Wallace, Sydney Horler, Sapper, Dornford Yates, Dennis Wheatley, Leslie Charteris, Eric Ambler, Len Deighton and Frederick Forsyth – to name only a handful. *See* SPY STORY; THRILLER.

clogyrnach A form of syllabic Welsh verse in a sestet (*q.v.*) stanza. The number of syllables in each line is eight, eight, five, five, three and three. The rhyme scheme is aabbba.

closed couplet Two metrical lines (almost invariably rhyming) whose sense and grammatical structure conclude at the end of the second line. It is very common in the heroic couplet (*q.v.*), as in these lines from Johnson's *London*:

In vain, these Dangers past, your Doors you close,
And hope the balmy blessings of repose:
Cruel with Guilt, and daring with Despair,
The midnight Murd'rer, bursts the faithless Bar;
Invades the sacred Hour of silent Rest
And leaves, unseen, a Dagger in your Breast.

See also END-STOPPED LINE; ENJAMBEMENT; OPEN COUPLET.

closet drama A play (sometimes also called a dramatic poem) designed to be read rather than performed. The term may also apply to a play which was intended to be performed but hardly ever is, and yet has survived as a piece of worthwhile literature. Well-known examples are: Milton's *Samson Agonistes* (1671); Landor's *Count Julian* (1812); Byron's *Manfred* (1817); Shelley's *Cenci* (1819); Keats's *Otho the Great* (1819); Shelley's *Prometheus Unbound* (1820); Swinburne's *Bothwell* (1874); and Hardy's *The Dynasts* (1904, 1906, 1908). *See also* SENECAN TRAGEDY.

clou (F 'peg') A situation or episode upon which everything hangs. The meaning is implicit in the phrase 'And thereby hangs a tale.'

cobla In Old Provençal, the normal word for stanza (*q.v.*). It may also denote a poem composed of a single stanza. From the 12th c. onwards *coblas* are fairly common. Their themes are similar to those of the *sirventes* (*q.v.*). In some compositions one *cobla* is 'answered' by another, in which cases it is akin to the *tenson* (*q.v.*). *See also* DEBAT; POETIC CONTESTS.

cock-and-bull story A long, rambling and improbable story, related to the tall story (*q.v.*). The origin of the phrase is obscure, but it is plausible that it derives from fables (*q.v.*) in which cocks and bulls were characters. There are a number of references in literature. In his *Anatomy of Melancholy* Burton refers to men who delight to talk 'of a cock and a bull over a pot'. *See also*BEAST EPIC; BESTIARY; BULL.

cockney rhymes False rhymes brought about by London pronunciation, like time and name: time/nime.

cockney school of poetry This term was first used in *Blackwood's Magazine* (Oct. 1817) and thereafter employed derisively of a group of writers who were Londoners by birth or adoption. They included Keats, Leigh Hunt, Shelley and Hazlitt. Leigh Hunt was a favourite target. *See also* LAKE POETS.

coda (L *cauda* 'tail') Basically a musical term denoting a passage which forms the completion of a piece and rounds it off to a satisfactory conclusion. In literature it is pretty well the equivalent of an epilogue (*q.v.*). At the end of the play *Jumpers* (1972) by Tom Stoppard there is a good example of a coda.

code A variety of meanings may be distinguished: (a) a collection or digest (*q.v.*) of laws; (b) a system of rules or regulations; (c) a volume; (d) a system of signals; (e) a cipher; (f) a system of words, letters or symbols for the purpose of secrecy or economy in transmission; (g) a set of rules and characters for the conversion of one form of data to another (as in computing), and the resulting representation of data; (h) in socio-linguistics, the language system of a community or a particular variety within a language.

In structuralism (*q.v.*) the term code has acquired rather specific senses. It denotes a culture's system of signification through which reality is mediated. The theory of structuralism is that all cultural phenomena are the product of codes or a code, and it maintains that it is the relationship between the elements of such a system which gives it signification, and *not* the relationship between the elements and 'reality'.

In his celebrated analysis of Balzac's short story *Sarrasine*, Roland Barthes posits five codes: hermeneutic, semic, symbolic, proairetic and cultural. Through these the text is constituted and these codes are shared by author and reader. According to Barthes each code is 'one of the voices of which the text is woven'. Barthes suggests that the text itself supplies the codes which enable him to correlate, grammatically and semantically, the various elements of the story. He does not impose any 'hierarchy' on the codes; they are all held to be equal.

Each code may be described approximately thus: (a) the *hermeneutic code*: this comprises 'all the units whose function it is to articulate in various ways a question, its response, and the variety of chance events which can either formulate the question or delay its answer; or even constitute an enigma and lead to its solution'. This is the story-telling code which poses questions, brings about suspense and mystery by means of the narrative; (b) the *proairetic code* (Gk *proairesis* 'action of choosing'): this code describes the way a code of actions is constructed for the reader: the sequential logic of action and behaviour. As Barthes puts it: 'The proairetic sequence is never more than the result of the artifice of the reading'. So it governs the reader's construction of plot; (c) the *symbolic code*: this gathers together the patterns of antithesis in the text; these 'groupings' are repeated by various modes and means in the text; (d) the *semic code*: the code of semes and signifiers and thus of recurrent connotations or themes in the text; this code makes use of hints or 'flickers of meaning' generated by certain signifiers; (e) the *referential or cultural code*: this code groups all the references in the text to the cultural and social background and knowledge of Balzac's period; thus it is concerned with the assumptions that Balzac makes.

In the analytical application of these codes Barthes breaks down the text into *lexies* – that is, reading-units of varying length. *See also* SIGNIFIER/SIGNIFIED.

codex The term derives from the Latin *codex*, a block of wood split into leaves or tablets and then covered with wax for writing on. When paper and parchment replaced wood, the word was retained for a book. Thus, a volume of manuscript. The *Vercelli Book*, which contains several important Anglo-Saxon works, is a famous example.

codicology The study of manuscript (*q.v.*) volumes. *See* CODEX.

cofradía A travelling company or guild of Spanish actors in the 16th and 17th c. They gave performances in the main towns on Sundays and feast days in order to make money for charities. At first they performed in existing courtyards (*corrales*) then in the new theatres of which there were three in Madrid by 1584. Before the time of Lope de Vega they played *comedias* (simply, plays) based on authors like Plautus and Seneca.

coin To invent and put into use a new word or expression. *See* NADSAT; NEOLOGISM.

cola The plural of colon (*q.v.*).

collage (F 'sticking' or 'pasting things on') A term adopted from the vocabulary of painters to denote a work which contains a mixture of allusions, references, quotations, and foreign expressions. It is common in the work of James Joyce, Ezra Pound and T. S. Eliot. The influence of surrealism (*q.v.*) in this respect has been considerable. These collage lines come from David Jones's *Anathemata*:

Her menhirs
        DIS MANIBUS of
        many of a *Schiller*'s people
        many men
        of many a Clowdisley's ship's company:
for she takes nine
        in ten!
        But what Caliban's Lamia
rung him for his Hand of Glory?
(And where the wolf in the quartz'd height
        – O long long long
before the sea-mark light! –
saliva'd the spume
        over Mark's lost hundred.
Back over the hundred and forty *mensae* drowned
in the un-apsed *eglwysau*, under.
Back to the crag-mound
        in the drowned *coed*
        under.)

Collage techniques have also been employed by modern novelists; particularly in the so-called anti-novel (*q.v.*). *See* CENTO; DADAISM.

colloquialism A colloquial word, phrase or expression is one in everyday use in speech and writing. The colloquial style is plain and relaxed. This sentence is colloquial: 'The man, a dodgy customer with a shifty look in his eye, was clearly up to no good.' *See* CLICHE; IDIOM; KING'S ENGLISH; SLANG; STANDARD ENGLISH.

colloquy A dialogue (*q.v.*) or discussion. A *colloquium*. As a title and as a form there are a few instances: the *Colloquia* of Erasmus (*c.* 1526), and Southey's *Sir Thomas More: Colloquies on the progress and prospects of Society* (1829).

colon (Gk 'limb') A metrical term which denotes a number of feet or metra. *See* FOOT.

colophon (Gk 'summit, finish') Either a publisher's emblem which appears on the title page of a book (or at the end of it), and/or information about the date, place, printer and edition.

comedias de capa y espada (Sp 'cloak and sword plays') A species of Spanish Golden Age (*q.v.*) drama (also known as *comedias de ingenio*), thus called because the protagonists were normally gentlemen or nobles who wore a cloak and carried a sword. Any plebeian characters wore everyday dress. They were mostly about domestic intrigue. One of the first known is *Comedia Himenea* by Bartolomé de Torres Naharro (1485?–1524?). Many Golden Age dramatists wrote them, incuding Pedro Calderón de la Barca. *See also* CLOAK-AND-DAGGER STORY.

comedias de figurón A genre of Spanish drama. The plays tended to have stock themes and stock characters (*q.v.*), particularly the pompous and pretentious fool (male or female). The style and comic ideas and situations were closely associated with *commedia dell'arte* (*q.v.*). An early and well-known example is *Entre bobos anda el juego* (1645) by Francisco de Rojas Zorrilla. Augustin Moreto (1618–69) also wrote some *comedias de figurón. See* COMEDY.

comedias de ruido (Sp 'noisy plays') Thus named in Spanish Golden Age (*q.v.*) drama because they required many stage props, contraptions and mechanical devices. By the 17th c. stage machinery had become very ingenious and spectacular effects were achieved, but it *did* make rather a lot of noise. Many of the *comedias* had as their main theme the life of a saint. Others had mythological and historical themes. Lope de Vega (1562–1635) is believed to have written over two hundred of them.

comédie Originally in France this did not necessarily denote a play that was comic, but rather a play that was not a tragedy (*q.v.*). It might be a serious play which contained some comedy (*q.v.*). A good example in English dramatic literature is Eugene O'Neill's *Long Day's Journey into Night* (1956). *See* DRAME.

comédie-ballet Molière developed this dramatic form from ballet by interspersing ballet between the acts of a comedy (*q.v.*). It was a satirical or farcical interlude related to the theme of the play. The first instance is *Les Fâcheux* (1661). Molière wrote fourteen plays of this kind. *See also* ANTI-MASQUE; SATYR PLAY.

comédie de moeurs French for 'comedy of manners' (*q.v.*).

Comédie-Française The first state theatre of France; also known as Le Théâtre Français and La Maison de Molière. Its origins were in the company of actors created by Molière (1622–73) in 1658 at the Théâtre du Petit-Bourbon. After Molière's death the company merged with that of the Théâtre du Marais and became known as the Théâtre Guénégaud (after the street of that name). In 1680 the companies of the Théâtre Guénégaud and the Hôtel de Bourgogne (*q.v.*) amalgamated to form the Comédie-Française.

During the revolutionary period from 1789 the company became divided into factions: Republican and Royalist. The pro-revolutionary group formed the Théâtre de la République, but this had become defunct by 1799. The Royalist faction were put in prison. Ultimately the government re-formed the original company, which had its headquarters in the rue de Richelieu in the theatre known as the Théâtre Français; this took place in 1799 and the company still occupies it. Napoleon himself redrafted its constitution in 1812, and there have been few changes since. While on probation its members are known as *pensionnaires*; thereafter they become *sociétaires* or full members.

The theatre's contribution to French drama and the French theatrical tradition and history is immeasurable. It has had enormous influence in France and Europe and most of the leading French dramatists have had plays performed by it.

comédie larmoyante (F 'tearful comedy') The French counterpart to 18th c. sentimental comedy (*q.v.*) in England. In France, its leading exponents were Nivelle de la Chaussée and Diderot: in Germany, Gellert and Lessing.

comédie noire *See* BLACK COMEDY.

comédies rosses *See* THEATRE LIBRE.

comedy (Gk *komos* 'revel, merrymaking') Comedy includes: *comédie*; *comédie-ballet*; *comédie larmoyante*; comedy of humours; comedy of ideas; comedy of intrigue; comedy of manners; comedy of morals; *commedia dell'arte*; *commedia erudita*; burlesque; black comedy; drawing-room comedy; domestic comedy; farce; high comedy; musical comedy; romantic comedy; satirical comedy; sentimental comedy; tragi-comedy (*qq.v.*), in addition to all those plays which may be classified under the heading of Theatre of the Absurd (*q.v.*).

Greek comedy (in speaking of which we distinguish between Old, Middle and New Comedy) was from the beginning associated with fertility rites and the worship of Dionysus; thus, with *komos*. From Aristophanes onwards it has been primarily associated with drama (except during the Middle Ages). Aristophanes (*c.* 448–*c.* 380 BC) wrote a variety of comedies which combine fine lyric verse, dance, satire, buffoonery, social comment, fantastic plots and remarkable characters. Already, then, at an early stage we find a dramatist supremely confident in this mode. The following are his extant works: *Acharnians*, *Knights*, *Clouds*, *Peace*, *Wasps*, *Birds*, *Frogs*, *Plutus*, *Lysistrata*, *Ecclesiazusae* and *Thesmophoriazusae*. The other great Greek 'comedian' was Menander (*c.* 343–*c.* 291 BC). Apart from *Dyskolos* only fragments of his plays survive but much is known about them because the Romans were familiar with them. In fact Menander had a great influence on succeeding dramatists. His themes were more social than political, and the theme of youthful love was a favourite one. Aristophanes belongs to what is known as the 'school' of Old Comedy (*q.v.*), and Menander to New Comedy (*q.v.*). In between came Middle Comedy (*q.v.*).

The other major comic writers of antiquity were the Romans Plautus (*c.* 254–184 BC) and Terence (190–159 BC). Both of them wrote imitations of Menander, and their themes also tended to be concerned with youthful love. Like Menander they used stock characters (*q.v.*), and the characters and situations they devised were used as models for many comedies during the Renaissance period and later. The extant works of Plautus are: *Amphitruo*, *Asinaria*, *Aulularia*, *Bacchides*, *Captivi*, *Casina*, *Cistellaria*, *Curculio*, *Epidicus*, *Menaechmi*, *Mercator*, *Miles*, *Mostellaria*, *Persa*, *Poenulus*, *Pseudolus*, *Rudens*, *Stichus*, *Trinummus* and *Truculentus*. Terence wrote six plays: *Andria*, *Hecyra*, *Heautontimorumenos*, *Eunuchus*, *Phormio* and *Adelphoe*.

Between the death of Terence and the late Middle Ages little comedy of note was produced; or, if it was, it has not survived. In the late Middle Ages, however, we have the development of farce and comic interludes (*q.v.*) in the Mystery Plays (*q.v.*).

As for the theory of comedy thus far, there is not much to record.

In *Poetics*, Aristotle distinguishes it from tragedy (*q.v.*) by saying it deals in an amusing way with ordinary characters in rather everyday situations. From the 4th c. AD we have a few generalizations by the grammarians Evanthius, Diomedes and Donatus. Evanthius says that in comedy the men are of middle fortune, the dangers they run into are neither serious nor pressing and their actions conclude happily. He goes on to say that whereas in tragedy life is to be fled from, in comedy it is to be grasped. Diomedes observes that the characters in comedy (unlike those in tragedy) are humble and private people (thus, not heroes, generals and kings). He adds that two of the main themes of comedy are love affairs and the abduction of maidens. According to Donatus, comedy was a tale containing various elements of the dispositions of town-dwellers and private people who are shown what is useful and what is not useful in life, and what should be avoided.

The next major reference to comedy occurs in the *Ars Versificatoria* of Matthieu de Vendôme (*c.* 1150), where he refers to comedy as an allegorical figure who comes surreptitiously with a work-a-day (or daily) grin or in a work-a-day dress, bearing his head in a humble fashion and not bringing any pretensions or suggestions of gaiety.

This striking description is a little ambiguous, but the implications are that comedy is unlike tragedy, and in comedy it does not *look* as if things are going to turn out well.

A century later, Vincent de Beauvais (in *Speculum maius triplex*) describes a comedy as a poem changing a sad beginning into a happy ending. In 1286, in *Catholicon*, Johannes Januensis makes a distinction similar to that of Evanthius and Diomedes. Tragedy and comedy differ, he says, because comedy is concerned with the acts of private (or ordinary) men, and tragedy has to do with kings and people of importance. Comedy uses a humble style, tragedy a lofty style. Comedy begins with misfortune and ends with joy. Tragedy is the opposite.

By now a certain pattern is becoming clear. It is made even clearer by Dante in his *Epistle to Can Grande* in which he explains what he is setting out to achieve in the *Divina Commedia* (which he began *c.* 1310). He derives the word comedy from *comos* 'a village' and *oda* 'a song'; thus comedy is a sort of rustic song. He goes on to say that comedy is a form of poetical narrative which is different from any other kind. He contrasts comedy and tragedy and points out that comedy begins with harshness but ends happily. Its style is negligent and humble. Thus, the *Divina Commedia* begins with misfortune in the *Inferno* and concludes with pleasure and happiness in the *Paradiso*.

Surprisingly enough Chaucer uses the word 'comedye' but once, and that right at the end of *Troilus and Criseyde*, a tragic story:

> Go, litel book, go, litel myn tragedye,
> Ther god thi makere yet, er that he dye,
> So sende myght to make in som comedye!

Here the usage is antithetical.

Frustrating though it is that Chaucer never told us what he thought comedy was, he comes very near to describing it in *The Canterbury Tales*. The Knight interrupts the Monk's long catalogue of tragedies and says that he would like to hear a different kind of story:

> I seye for me, it is a greet disese
> Wher-as men han ben in greet welthe and ese,
> To heren of hir sodeyn fal, allas!
> And the contrarie is Ioye and greet solas,
> As whan a man hath been in povre estaat
> And clymbeth up, and wexeth fortunat,
> And there abydeth in prosperitee,
> Swich thing is gladsom, as it thinketh me.

The Knight's description of a person climbing out of misfortune to prosperity, to the 'gladsom', is as satisfactory a definition of the medieval conception of comedy as one will find. A description later confirmed by Lydgate in his *Chronicle of Troy* (1430):

> A Comedy hath in his gynnynge,
> A pryme face, a manner complaynynge,
> And afterwarde endeth in gladnesse.

But it must be remembered that in the Middle Ages a comedy was a *poem* with a sad start and a happy end.

At the Renaissance a very different view of comedy prevailed, as one can soon discover from a brief examination of the English critics. For the most part they held the view that the object of comedy was corrective, if not actually punitive. Representative points of view were expressed by Sir Philip Sidney and George Puttenham. In his *Apologie for Poetrie* (1595) Sidney says that:

> Comedy is an imitation of the common errors of life, which he representeth in the most ridiculous and scornful sort that may be;

so that it is impossible that any beholder can be content to be such a one.

Now, as in Geometry the oblique must bee knowne as wel as the right, and in Arithmetic the odde as well as the even, so in the actions of our life who seeth not the filthines of evil wanteth a great foile to perceive the beauty of vertue. This doth the Comedy handle so in our private and domestical matters, as with hearing it we get as it were an experience, what is to be looked for . . .

In *The Arte of English Poesie* (1589), Puttenham wrote:

. . . but commonly of marchants, souldiers, artificers, good honest householders, and also of unthrifty youthes, yong damsels, old nurses, bawds, brokers, ruffians, and parasites, with such like, in whose behaviors lyeth in effect the whole course and trade of man's life, and therefore tended altogither to the good amendment of man by discipline and example. It was also much for the solace and recreation of the common people by reason of the pageants and shewes. And this kind of poem was called Comedy. . . .

It is certainly true that many comedies of the Tudor and Jacobean periods had some moral and corrective purpose but quite a few had not. They were intended to give pleasure and entertainment.

Ralph Roister Doister (*c.* 1553) by Nicholas Udall is generally regarded as the first English dramatic comedy, and it looks almost premature because another forty years were to pass before comedy as a principal dramatic form really exercised the attention of playwrights. From that period only two comedies of note survive. They are *Gammer Gurton's Needle* (first acted in 1566), and George Gascoigne's *Supposes* (first acted in 1566) which is our earliest extant comedy in prose. In using prose, Gascoigne, a considerable pioneer, thus anticipated by many years what was to become standard practice in dramatic comedy. Apart from these instances, most dramatic literature with any pretensions to comedy at this time consisted of Interludes (*q.v.*), a popular form of entertainment.

The two major writers of comedy between *c.* 1590 and the 1630s in England were Shakespeare (1564–1616) and Ben Jonson (1573–1637). In their conception and treatment of comedy they were very different. Shakespeare wrote almost every kind *except* satirical comedy; Jonson hardly wrote any that was not satirical.

Shakespeare's early experiments were *The Comedy of Errors* (*c.* 1590) based on the *Menaechmi* of Plautus, *The Taming of the Shrew* (*c.* 1594), a farcical comedy (much of which is in prose), and *The Two Gentlemen of Verona* (*c.* 1594–5) and *Love's Labour's Lost* (*c.* 1595), both of which could be described (with reservations) as romantic comedies (*q.v.*).

These he followed with *A Midsummer Night's Dream* (*c.* 1595–6), which is certainly a romantic comedy, and *The Merchant of Venice* (*c.* 1596), a play which revealed darker and more sombre elements while yet possessing a strong romantic theme. Shakespeare's next comedy was *Much Ado About Nothing* (*c.* 1598–9) which might well be classified as comedy of manners (*q.v.*). Like Gascoigne's *Supposes* and *The Taming of the Shrew*, it is important in the evolution of comedy because about 80 per cent of it is in prose, which was to become the chosen medium for comedy from the end of the 17th c. onwards. *As You Like It* followed *Much Ado* and this was another romantic comedy influenced by pastoral (*q.v.*) drama. *The Merry Wives of Windsor* (*c.* 1600–01) is in many ways a light-hearted romp verging on farce, while *Twelfth Night* (*c.* 1600–01) and *The Tempest* (*c.* 1611) are perhaps Shakespeare's finest examples of romantic comedy, though they possess elements of sadness and even bitterness.

Shakespeare's other plays which have been classified as comedies all contain darker qualities and sometimes a measure or acerbity which make them difficult to categorize. They might be described as black comedy or tragi-comedy (*qq.v.*) but those terms would probably be too strong. The French term *comédie* (*q.v.*) fits them more accurately. These so-called 'dark' comedies were: *All's Well that Ends Well* (*c.* 1602–3), *Measure for Measure* (*c.* 1604), *The Winter's Tale* (*c.* 1609–10) and *Cymbeline* (*c.* 1610). In most of his comedies the main characters are happily united after undergoing various misfortunes, but if we consider the great variety of comic elements in all these plays (and his use of comedy in the History Plays and the Tragedies) then we find that Shakespeare did not wish to restrict himself too much to any particular form or convention.

Renaissance theory about the nature and function of comedy is borne out in the practice of Ben Jonson who, in his early Comedy of Humours (*q.v.*), drew on the medieval teaching about the various humours (*q.v.*) and who, in most of his plays, was concerned to expose the vices, foibles and follies of the society as he saw it. His main works in the genre of comedy were: *Every Man in His*

Humour (1598), *Every Man out of His Humour* (1599), *Cynthia's Revels* (1601), *The Poetaster* (1601), *Volpone* (1606), *Epicœne* (1609), *The Alchemist* (1610), *Bartholomew Fair* (1614), *The Devil is an Ass* (1616) and *The Staple of News* (1625).

Shakespeare and Jonson had many imitators, but there were also many original works written in the period. Notable minor works are John Lyly's *Endimion* (1591); Robert Greene's *Friar Bacon and Friar Bungay* (1594); George Peele's *The Old Wives' Tale* (1595); Dekker's *The Shoemaker's Holiday* (1600), *Old Fortunatus* (1600); John Marston's *The Dutch Courtezan* (1605), *What You Will* (1607); Chapman's *All Fools* (1605), *Eastward Ho!* (1605), *Monsieur D'Olive* (1606); Massinger's *A New Way to Pay Old Debts* (1633) – plus several plays by Beaumont, Fletcher and Heywood. Marlowe wrote no comedies but there is so much rough and ready comedy in *Dr Faustus* (*c.* 1588) that at times it is almost farcical. One should also mention the sombre tragedies of Webster and Tourneur which depend for much of their effect upon comedy of a peculiarly sardonic and ironical kind.

The most important contributions to dramatic comedy outside England had hitherto come from Italy in the genre known as *commedia erudita* (*q.v.*) and from Spain with what is known as comedy of intrigue (*q.v.*).

With the coming of the Civil War, the closing of the theatres and the Puritan or Commonwealth period (*qq.v.*), comedy, like other forms of drama, was not produced in England. However, in France, in the middle of the century, there appeared a man whom many regard as the greatest comic dramatist of all – Molière; an immensely prolific playwright and many of whose works have become classics. Like Ben Jonson he was a satirist. His most remarkable plays are: *Les Précieuses ridicules* (1659); *L'Ecole des femmes* (1662); *Tartuffe*, written *c.* 1664 but not produced publicly in its entire form until 1669; *Don Juan* (1665); *L'Amour médecin* (1665); *Le Misanthrope* (1666); *Le Médecin malgré lui* (1666); *L'Avare* (1668); *Le Bourgeois Gentilhomme* (1670); *Les Femmes savantes* (1672); *Le Malade imaginaire* (1673). Contemporaries of Molière's who wrote some good comedies were Racine, Quinault, Montfleury and Cyrano de Bergerac.

In the last thirty-odd years of the 17th c. what is now known as Restoration comedy (*q.v.*) kept the English theatre alive. There were five outstanding dramatists: Sir George Etherege (1634?–91?); William Wycherley (1640–1716); Sir John Vanbrugh (1664–1726); William Congreve (1670–1729); and George Farquhar (1678–1707).

What they wrote was predominantly comedy of manners (*q.v.*) and was succeeded by what is called sentimental comedy (*q.v.*), which was popular in the early part of the 18th c. in France and England. After the vogue of sentimental comedy no new comic form emerges in drama until the Theatre of the Absurd (*q.v.*), but many dramatists worked within the conventions already established, modifying them and exploiting them. A particularly popular form of comic drama in England in the 18th c. was burlesque (*q.v.*).

In the second half of the 18th c. two Irishmen (of that glittering succession of Irish dramatists without whom English comedy would scarcely have existed since the Restoration period) wrote outstanding plays which combined some elements of comedy of manners, satirical comedy (*q.v.*) and sentimental comedy. They were Goldsmith and Sheridan. Goldsmith's two plays are *The Good-Natured Man* (1768) and *She Stoops to Conquer* (1773). Sheridan's two main works are *The Rivals* (1775) and *The School for Scandal* (1777), but he also wrote a farce (*St Patrick's Day; or the Scheming Lieutenant*), a comic opera (*The Duenna*) and a burlesque (*The Critic*).

The outstanding Italian comic dramatist of the 18th c. was the Venetian Carlo Goldoni (1707–93) who wrote nearly three hundred plays in French or Italian (sometimes in both), an output that perhaps only the Spaniard Lope de Vega exceeded in the whole history of drama. An entertainer of unflagging energy, Goldoni was at some pains to promote written drama as a substitute for the then somewhat decadent *commedia dell'arte* (*q.v.*). In his attempts at theatrical reform Goldoni had opponents, principally Pietro Chiari (1711–85) and Carlo Gozzi (1720–1806), another Venetian. Gozzi, a more gifted dramatist than Chiari, tried to revitalize *commedia dell'arte*. Gozzi was not particularly sympathetic to Chiari; he described him and Goldoni as 'those two deluges of ink'. Goldoni's plays have worn better than those of his rivals and he is now chiefly remembered for: *Il Moliere* (1751), *La Locandiera* (1753), *Un Curioso Accidente* (1757), *I Rusteghi* (1760) and *Le Baruffe Chiozzotte* (1762).

During the 18th c. in France the most notable comic dramatists were Marivaux, Destouches, Voltaire, Diderot, Mercier, Lesage and Beaumarchais. There was little chance for comedy during the revolutionary period in France, and it did not really revive until the Empire period. In England, too, there is little of note after Goldsmith and Sheridan, except for Dion Boucicault (1822–90), an Irish dramatist and actor who wrote a great many plays and adapted a large number from the French. His best comedy was probably *London Assurance* (1841). But during the first half of the 19th c. there was one important innovator in France, namely, Scribe, who wrote a large number of successful comedies most of which have worn badly and come into the category of the 'well-made play' (*q.v.*). Scribe's most successful follower in this form was Sardou whose influence near the end of the 19th c. was considerable and provoked Shaw to condemn the superficiality and contrivance of the 'well-made play' as 'Sardoodledom'.

In general, during the 19th c., farce (*q.v.*) proved the most popular dramatic form of comedy, until approximately the last twenty years of the century when we find a remarkable resurgence of vitality in the theatre in Europe, England and Russia. In Russia this had been presaged to a certain extent by the work of Gogol and Turgenev, and in particular by Gogol's *The Government Inspector* (1836) and his farce *The Marriage* (1837–42); and by Turgenev's *A Month in the Country* (1850). Turgenev wrote several other comedies which anticipate the work of Chekhov.

In the 1890s Chekhov first made his influence felt. Subdued, ironical and sad, his comedies (which are very nearly tragi-comedies) represent something approaching perfection. His four main works were *The Seagull* (1896), *Uncle Vanya* (1899), *The Three Sisters* (1901) and *The Cherry Orchard* (1904).

In the 1890s, too, Wilde revived comedy of manners (*q.v.*), and this was just in time because he wrote for an audience that scarcely existed after the First World War. His main works were: *Lady Windermere's Fan* (1892), *A Woman of No Importance* (1893), *An Ideal Husband* (1895) and *The Importance of Being Earnest* (1895).

In the same period Shaw broke upon the scene and was to be a dominating force in the theatre for many years. His plays showed a wide range of talent but most are comedies of one sort or another, though not always easy to classify. His major works were *Widowers' Houses* (1892), *Arms and the Man* (1894), *Candida* (1895), *The Devil's Disciple* (1897), *Caesar and Cleopatra* (1898), *You Never Can Tell* (1899), *Mrs Warren's Profession* (1902), *Major Barbara* (1905), *The Doctor's Dilemma* (1906), *Misalliance* (1910), *Androcles and the Lion* (1912), *Pygmalion* (1912), *Heartbreak House* (1917), *The Apple Cart* (1929). Other notable works were *Man and Superman* (1901), *Back to Methuselah* (1918–20), *The Millionairess* (1935).

Since approximately the 1870s the energy which generated the revival of drama (and, specifically, of comedy) has hardly flagged.

In the last hundred years a great number of gifted dramatists have exploited the comic forms in different ways and directions. The most remarkable feature of the whole period, therefore, is the extraordinary *variety* of comedy that has been created. In many cases the traditional classifications are not adequate, but the variety certainly includes satirical comedy, drawing-room comedy, 'French-window' comedy, social comedy, domestic comedy, comedy of manners, tragi-comedy, and many works which come under the heading of 'Theatre of the Absurd'. There are also a large number of plays which may be put under the French category of *drame* (*q.v.*) – serious plays with comic elements.

The following are a few of the better known and more notable achievements in dramatic comedy from *c.* 1870 onwards: T. W. Roberson's *Caste* (1867), a landmark in realistic comedy; J. M. Barrie's *The Professor's Love Story* (1894); Jarry's *Ubu Roi* (1896), a landmark in the Theatre of the Absurd; J. M. Barrie's *The Little Minister* (1897); Pinero's *Trelawny of the 'Wells'* (1898); J. M. Barrie's *The Admirable Crichton* (1902); Synge's *The Well of Saints* (1905) and his *The Playboy of the Western World* (1907); J. M. Barrie's *What Every Woman Knows* (1908); Ferenc Molnár's *The Guardsman* (1910); Granville-Barker's *The Madras House* (1910); Montague and Glass's *Potash and Perlmutter* (1913); Evreinov's *The Fourth Wall* (1915); Chiarelli's *La maschera e il volto* (1916); Harold Brighouse's *Hobson's Choice* (1916); Somerset Maugham's *The Circle* (1921); Frederick Lonsdale's *Aren't We All* (1923); Somerset Maugham's *Our Betters* (1923); Noël Coward's *The Young Idea* (1923); Ashley Duke's *The Man with a Load of Mischief* (1924); Eden Phillpott's *The Farmer's Wife* (1924); Sidney Howard's *They Knew What They Wanted* (1924); Noël Coward's *Hay Fever* (1925) and *Fallen Angels* (1925); Vitrac's *Victor* (1928); Somerset Maugham's *The Constant Wife* (1928); Giraudoux's *Amphitryon '38* (1929); Noël Coward's *Private Lives* (1930); Somerset Maugham's *The Breadwinner* (1930); Bridie's *Tobias and the Angel* (1930); Dennis Johnston's *Moon in the Yellow River* (1931); Eugene O'Neill's *Ah, Wilderness* (1933); J. B. Priestley's *Laburnum Grove* (1933); J. B. Priestley's *Eden End* (1934); Terence Rattigan's *French without Tears* (1936); Jacques Deval's *Tovaritch* (1936); Claire Boothe's *The Women* (1936); Gerald Savory's *George and Margaret* (1937); Esther McCracken's *Quiet Wedding* (1938); Emlyn Williams's *The Corn is Green* (1938); George Kaufman's *The Man Who Came to Dinner* (1939); Philip Barry's *The Philadelphia Story* (1939); William Saroyan's *The Time of Your*

Life (1939); Noël Coward's *Blithe Spirit* (1941); Esther McCracken's *Quiet Week-End* (1941); Thornton Wilder's *The Skin of Our Teeth* (1942); Noël Coward's *Present Laughter* (1943); R. F. Delderfield's *Worm's Eye View* (1945); John Van Druten's *I Remember Mama* (1945); Walter Greenwood's *The Cure for Love* (1945); Marcel Aymé's *Lucienne et le boucher* (1946); Jean Anouilh's *L'Invitation au château* (1947); Christopher Fry's *The Lady's Not for Burning* (1948); Hugh Hastings's *Seagulls over Sorrento* (1949); T. S. Eliot's *The Cocktail Party* (1950); Rattigan's *Who is Sylvia?* (1950); Jean Anouilh's *Colombe* (1951); Ustinov's *The Love of Four Colonels* (1951); John Whiting's *Penny for a Song* (1951); John Van Druten's *I am a Camera* (1951); Marcel Aymé's *La Tête des autres* (1952); Jean Anouilh's *La Valse des toréadors* (1952); Samuel Taylor's *Sabrina Fair* (1953); Roger MacDougall's *Escapade* (1953); John Patrick's *Teahouse of the August Moon* (1953); Sartre's *Kean* (1953); N. R. Nash's *The Rainmaker* (1954); Thornton Wilder's *The Matchmaker* (1954); William Douglas Home's *The Reluctant Débutante* (1955); Enid Bagnold's *The Chalk Garden* (1955); Sartre's *Nekrassov* (1955); Anouilh's *Pauvre Bitos* (1956); N. F. Simpson's *A Resounding Tinkle* (1957); Stephen Lewis's *Sparrers Can't Sing* (1960); Willis Hall and Keith Waterhouse's *Billy Liar* (1960); Ann Jellicoe's *The Knack* (1961); Tennessee Williams's *A Period of Adjustment* (1961); Arthur Kopit's *Oh, Dad, Poor Dad, Mamma's Hung You in the Closet and I'm Feelin' so Sad* (1961); Enid Bagnold's *The Chinese Prime Minister* (1963); Alan Ayckbourn's *Relatively Speaking* (1967); Alan Bennett's *Forty Years On* (1968); Tom Stoppard's *The Real Inspector Hound* (1968); Peter Barnes's *The Ruling Class* (1968); Peter Nichols's *The National Health* (1969); Christopher Hampton's *The Philanthropist* (1970); Simon Gray's *Butley* (1971); Tom Stoppard's *Jumpers* (1972); Alan Ayckbourn's *Absurd Person Singular* (1973); Tom Stoppard's *Travesties* (1974); Alan Ayckbourn's *Norman Conquests* (1974); Simon Gray's *Otherwise Engaged* (1975); Michael Frayn's *Alphabetical Order* (1975); Tom Stoppard's *Dirty Linen* (1976); Christopher Hampton's *Treats* (1976); Michael Frayn's *Donkeys' Years* (1976) and *Clouds* (1976); Alan Ayckbourn's *Joking Apart* (1979); Ronald Harwood's *The Dresser* (1980); Michael Frayn's *Make and Break* (1980); Peter Nichols's *Passion Play* (1981); Julian Mitchell's *Another Country* (1981); Nell Dunn's *Steaming* (1981); Caryl Churchill's *Top Girls* (1982); Alan Ayckbourn's *Intimate Exchanges* (1984); Peter Barnes's *Red Noses* (1985); David Hare and Howard Brenton's *Pravda* (1985); Michael Frayn's *Benefactors*

(1986); Doug Lucie's *Progress* (1986); Caryl Churchill's *Serious Money* (1987); Alan Bennett's *An Englishman Abroad* and *A Question of Attribution* (1988).

The term comedy is still usually applied to drama; occasionally, though, a novel may be described as a comedy. Yet it is more likely that we should speak of a 'comic novel'. Moreover, we would be disinclined to refer to a 'tragic' play or a 'comic' play. And, nowadays, we would never refer to a poem as a comedy.

The comic novel (*q.v.*) has become a well-established form from Fielding onwards, and many of the great European novels are 'comedies'. In verse there are fewer instances of works which are intended to be comic. Outstanding examples are Butler's *Hudibras*, Boileau's *Le Lutrin*, Pope's *The Rape of the Lock*, Byron's *The Vision of Judgment* and Auden's *Letter to Lord Byron*. A 'serious' comic poem is rare, and most comic poetry is classified as light verse (*q.v.*); or nonsense verse (*q.v.*); or *vers de société* (*q.v.*).

comedy of humours A form of drama which became fashionable at the very end of the 16th c. and early in the 17th. So called because it presented 'humorous' characters whose actions (in terms of the medieval and Renaissance theory of humours (*q.v.*) were ruled by a particular passion, trait, disposition or humour. Basically this was a physiological interpretation of character and personality. Though there were ample precedents for this in allegory (*q.v.*), Tudor Morality Plays (*q.v.*), and Interludes (*q.v.*), Ben Jonson appears to have been the first person to have elaborated the idea on any scale. His two outstanding works in this kind of comedy are *Every Man in His Humour* (1598) and *Every Man Out of His Humour* (1599); plus minor works like *The Magnetic Lady: or Humours Reconciled* (1632). Following the practice of the Moralities and Interludes, Jonson named *dramatis personae* aptronymically: Kitely, Dame Kitely, Knowell, Brainworm and Justice Clement (in *Every Man in His Humour*); Fastidious Brisk, Fungoso, Sordido, and Puntarvolo the vainglorious knight, and so forth (in *Every Man Out of His Humour*). The indication of character in this fashion became a common practice and continued to be much favoured by dramatists and novelists in the 18th and 19th c.

John Fletcher, a contemporary of Jonson's, wrote a number of 'humour' comedies, and other plays of note from the period are Chapman's *All Fools* (*c.* 1604), Middleton's *A Trick to Catch the Old One* (1605) and Massinger's *A New Way to Pay Old Debts*

(1625). Shadwell revived comedy of humours late in the 17th c. with *The Squire of Alsatia* (1688) and *Bury Fair* (1689).

The use of an individual to formulate a type in this way was also practised by those who wrote books of Characters, as in Earle's *Microcosmographie*. *See* APTRONYM; CHARACTER; ESSAY.

comedy of ideas A term loosely applied to plays which tend to debate, in a witty and humorous fashion, ideas and theories. Shaw is an outstanding exponent in *Man and Superman* (1905), *The Doctor's Dilemma* (1906), *Androcles and the Lion* (1912) and *The Apple Cart* (1929).

comedy of intrigue A form of comedy which depends on an intricate plot full of surprises and tends to subordinate character to plot. This distinguishes it from comedy of manners (*q.v.*), though the latter may also have complex plots. The form originated in Spain and was largely the work of a group of four famous dramatists: Lope de Vega (1562–1635), Tirso de Molina (1571–1648), Alarcón (1581–1639) and Moreto (1618–69). It has not appealed much to English dramatists, but Mrs Aphra Behn made some distinguished contributions: *The Rover* (1677–81) and *The City Heiress* (1682). In France, Beaumarchais's *Le Barbier de Séville* (1775) deserves special mention.

comedy of manners This genre has for its main subjects and themes the behaviour and deportment of men and women living under specific social codes. It tends to be preoccupied with the codes of the middle and upper classes and is often marked by elegance, wit and sophistication. In England Restoration comedy (*q.v.*) provides the outstanding instances. But Shakespeare's comedies *Love's Labour's Lost* (*c.* 1595) and *Much Ado About Nothing* (*c.* 1598–9) are also comedies of manners. Molière's *Les Précieuses ridicules* (1658), Sheridan's *The School for Scandal* (1777) and Wilde's *Lady Windermere's Fan* (1892), *A Woman of No Importance* (1893) and *The Importance of Being Earnest* (1895) are other outstanding examples of the genre. Latterly, some of the 'drawing room' comedies of Somerset Maugham might be so classified; and so might several plays by Noël Coward, especially *Private Lives* (1930). *See* COMEDY; DOMESTIC COMEDY; DRAWING-ROOM COMEDY.

comedy of menace A term first used by David Campton by way of subtitle to his four short plays *The Lunatic View* (1957). It denotes a kind of play in which one or more characters feel that they are (or *actually* are) threatened by some obscure and frightening force, power, personality, etc. The fear and the menace become a source of comedy, albeit laconic, grim or black. Harold Pinter, among others, exploited the possibilities of such a situation in such plays as *The Birthday Party* (1958) and *The Dumb Waiter* (1960). *See also* BLACK COMEDY; THEATRE OF THE ABSURD.

comedy of morals Satirical comedy (*q.v.*) designed to ridicule and correct vices like hypocrisy, pride, avarice, social pretensions, simony and nepotism. Molière is the supreme playwright in this genre. Ben Jonson and Shaw are other notable instances.

comic relief Comic episodes or interludes, usually in tragedy (*q.v.*), aimed to relieve the tension and heighten the tragic element by contrast. They are or should be an essential and integral part of the whole work. If not actually extended into an episode or interlude, the relief may take the form of a few remarks or observations (or some form of action) which help to lower the emotional temperature. The humour involved tends to be wry or sardonic. Good representative examples are Iago's gulling of Roderigo in *Othello*, the drunken porter scene in *Macbeth* (regarded as a *locus classicus*), Hamlet's laconic and witty treatment of Polonius, Rosencrantz and Guildenstern and Osric in *Hamlet* (and the Gravediggers 'scene' in *Hamlet*) and the Fool's mockery in *King Lear*. Other outstanding examples are to be found in Marlowe's *Dr Faustus*, Webster's *The Duchess of Malfi* and *The White Devil*, and Tourneur's *The Revenger's Tragedy* and *The Atheist's Tragedy*.

There was good precedent for such relief in some Mystery Plays (*q.v.*). A remarkable example is the York Mystery Cycle version of the *Crucifixion* in which the four soldiers talk in the colloquial, matter-of-fact style of everyday life as they go about their business of nailing Christ to the Cross. In a different vein is the almost slapstick (*q.v.*) and buffoonish comedy that occurs in Marlowe's *Dr Faustus*, which itself is a counterpoint and contrast to the wry ironies of Mephistopheles.

Since the 16th c. hardly a tragedian of any note has failed to make use of the possibilities of comic relief. *See also* BLACK COMEDY; COMEDY; FARCE; LOW COMEDY; TRAGI-COMEDY.

comics The first comics and comic strips began to appear towards the end of the 19th c. Among the forerunners was *Ally Sloper's Half-Holiday* (1884–1923). Comic strips had already appeared in newspapers (e.g. *The Graphic*, 1869–1932). Ally Sloper was a kind of anti-hero (*q.v.*) and the prototype of the stock character (*q.v.*) in the comic. Another popular publication was *The Boys of England* (1866–99). At the turn of the century there began to appear such vintage comics as *Comic Cuts* (1890–1953), *Chips* (1890–1953), and the evergreen *The Gem* (1907–39) and *The Magnet* (1908–40). These became particularly famous in large measure owing to the contributions of Charles Hamilton (1876–1961). Under the pseudonym Frank Richards he wrote for *The Magnet*, and as Martin Clifford he wrote for *The Gem*. It was he who created such household names and characters as Billy Bunter, the fat boy who was always expecting a remittance. Billy and the rest of the gang belonged to Greyfriars School – also a household name and part of British school folklore. Very famous comics to start up in the inter-war period were *Adventure* (1921–61), *Wizard* (1922–63), *Hotspur* (1933–*c.* 1981), *Beano* (1938–) and *Dandy* (1937–). The last two are very much alive and many of the original characters survive. The first coloured comic was *Rainbow* (1914–56). In 1950 *Eagle* was founded by the Lancashire clergyman Marcus Morris. *Eagle* ended in 1969, but Dan Dare continued in *2000 AD*. Morris also founded *Girl* for girls. Many comics flourish and keep up with modern developments in technology, not least in the exploration of space, and have been influenced by ever proliferating modes of science fiction (*q.v.*). *See also* CHILDREN'S BOOKS.

commedia dell'arte In medieval Italy the *arti* were groups of artisans or guilds; hence the term means 'comedy of the professional actors'. The absolute origins of this dramatic genre are obscure, but they are probably Roman. *Commedia dell'arte*, as we understand it now, developed in 16th c. Italy and had a considerable influence on European drama. The troupes or companies who performed the plays travelled widely through Europe, especially in France. The plots of *commedia dell'arte* were usually based on love intrigues involving people of all ages; masters and servants, mistresses and confidantes. Both plot and dialogue were often improvised after basic rehearsal (improvisation was important because performance could be adapted to local and contemporary needs) and the success of a piece depended very largely on the comic ingenuity of the performers, who would include mime, farce (*qq.v.*), clownish buffoonery and music in the presentation. Characters were stock types. The main male characters were: Pantaloon, the Captain, a Doctor, the Inamorato, the servants Harlequin, Brighella and Scapino. The main female characters were also stock types. There was Inamorata, her confidante the Soubrette – as like as not in love with one of the servants – plus Canterina and Ballerina who provided interludes in the main action. In spirit, if not in fact, a play like Shakespeare's *Comedy of Errors* (1594) owes something to the traditions of *commedia dell'arte*, and one can detect the influence of the form in the work of Ben Jonson, Molière and Goldoni; in pantomime, farce (*qq.v.*), puppet plays and ballet. *See* COMEDY.

commedia erudita (It 'learned comedy') A form of comedy (*q.v.*) favoured in Italy in the 16th c. It was often a learned imitation of Classical comedies, particularly those by Terence and Plautus. Ariosto was one of the main developers of the form: Machiavelli and Aretino were two of the best known dramatists to follow him. Machivalli's *La Mandragola* (*c.* 1520) is widely regarded as an outstanding example.

commitment A committed or *engagé* writer (or artist) is one who, through his work, is dedicated to the advocacy of certain beliefs and programmes, especially those which are political and ideological and in aid of social reform. In order to achieve this he needs to detach himself from the work in order to calculate its effect. Notable drmatists who have been 'committed' are Shaw, Brecht, Sartre and Arnold Wesker. There have been many novelists, among whom one should mention: Sartre, Malraux, James Aldridge, Doris Lessing and Günter Grass. Commitment is common in the work of writers who belong to the so-called Communist bloc. *See also* ALIENATION EFFECT; EPIC THEATRE; PROPAGANDA; SOCIALIST REALISM; THESIS NOVEL.

common measure The quatrain (*q.v.*) of the ballad meter (*q.v.*) also called the hymnal stanza (*q.v.*). The CM of the hymn books. *See also* HEPTAMETER.

commonplace book A notebook in which ideas, themes, quotations, words and phrases are jotted down. Almost every writer keeps some kind of commonplace book where he can put things into storage. In a properly organized one the matter would be grouped under subject headings. A famous example is Ben Jonson's *Timber:*

Or Discoveries (1640), which comprises a draft for a treatise on the art of writing and on types of literature, miniature essays, *sententiae*, *pensées* (*qq.v.*) and so forth. Two very agreeable modern examples are Maurice Baring's *Have You Anything to Declare?* (1936), the work of an exceptionally civilized and well-read man, and John Julius Norwich's *Christmas Crackers* (1980).

common rhythm *See* RUNNING RHYTHM.

Commonwealth period This extended from the end of the Civil War (1649) to the Restoration (1660). It is sometimes called the Puritan period because England was ruled by a Puritan parliament. The theatres were closed as they were held to be immoral. The main English writers who flourished in these years were Hobbes, Izaak Walton, Sir Thomas Browne, Edmund Waller, Davenant, Milton, Thomas Fuller, Jeremy Taylor, Cowley, Marvell and Vaughan.

communication fallacy A term used by the American poet Allen Tate to describe poetry which attempts to convey ideas and feelings which would be better served by and expressed in prose; at any rate, *not* in poetry. Propaganda (*q.v.*) verse, for instance, may stimulate reactions which have little to do with the aesthetic qualities of the verse.

communication heresy A term used by the American critic Cleanth Brooks. It refers to the belief that the function of a poem is to convey an idea, whereas Brooks's contention is that the reader should have a *total* aesthetic experience of the poem. In short, the substance and form of a poem are not separable; though, of course, one may analyse both style and matter individually.

community theatre Theatre seen as responding to the concerns and serving the needs of the community to which it is performed. 'Community' in this sense may be defined either geographically or as a 'constituency of interest' (e.g. working-class, ethnic, women, the elderly, etc.).

It originated in the mid-1970s with theatre companies such as: the Half Moon, Common Stock and the Brighton Combination at the Albany in London; Pentabus and Theatre Foundry in the West Midlands; Perspectives in the East Midlands; Pit Prop in Lancashire; DAC in Yorkshire; Solent People's Theatre in Southampton; Avon Touring in the South-west and Bruvvers in the North-east.

Venues which have housed community-oriented theatre include Chapter Arts in Cardiff, Croydon Warehouse, Phoenix Arts in Leicester, the Tron in Glasgow and the Leadmill in Sheffield.

Community theatre is more a way of relating content and a democratic method of organization to perceived community concerns than a specific aesthetic model. Productions have ranged from virtual cabaret through musicals and plays with songs to serious drama.

Examples of plays include: *Taking Our Time* by Red Ladder (1978); *My Mother Says I Never Should* by the Women's Theatre Group (1975); the plays of Les Miller for Inner City, among them *Finger in the Pie* (1985) and *Hot Stuff* (1987); the plays of John McGrath for 7:84 and the Liverpool Everyman, for example, *The Cheviot, The Stag and the Black*, *Black Oil* and *Fish in the Sea*; and the plays of Steve Gooch, including *Will Wat, If Not, What Will?* (1972) and *Female Transport* (1973). Steve Gooch also wrote an excellent book on community theatre: *All Together Now* (1984).

Both organizationally and aesthetically, community theatre shares much common ground with socialist touring theatre (7:84, Belt & Braces, Monstrous Regiment, etc.), as well as with Theatre-in-Education and Young People's Theatre – many companies providing both 'community' and 'young people's' productions. It is always a form of professional theatre (unlike in the USA) and has little in common with 'the community play', a term for the production model established by Ann Jellicoe's Colway Theatre Trust; the Trust employs professional directors and playwrights (e.g. Howard Barker, Nick Darke, David Edgar) to work with large numbers of amateur performers drawn from the local (usually rural) community, to which the play (usually on a local historical subject) is also performed. An interesting example of a community play is Edgar's *Entertaining Strangers* (1988), eventually given a full-scale production with professional actors and actresses at the National Theatre (*q.v.*).

commus *See* KOMMOS.

commutatio *See* CHIASMUS.

compar *See* ISOCOLON; PARISON.

comparatio *See* ANTITHESIS.

comparatist One who follows the comparative method in linguistics (*q.v.*) or literature. Comparative philology began in the 18th c. and entails the study and identification of those characteristics which different languages have in common and the hypothetical reconstruction of parent languages (e.g. 'Indo-European'). The great editors of *The Oxford English Dictionary* were all concerned with tracing the probable origins of words in English as far back as possible. Comparative methods in literature involve making comparisons between literary works and architecture, music and paintings, and also comparison between different literatures. Among modern writers, Sacheverell Sitwell (1897–1988) was adept at this.

comparative criticism *See* CRITICISM.

comparative linguistics *See* LINGUISTICS.

comparative literature The examination and analysis of the relationships and similarities of the literatures of different peoples and nations. The comparative study of literature, like the comparative study of religions, is relatively recent. We see little evidence of it before the 19th c. *See* WELTLITERATUR.

compensatio *See* ANTISAGOGE.

compensation An adjustment for an omitted syllable or foot (*q.v.*) in a metrical line. It is either made up for by an additional foot in the next line, or compensated for by an added foot in the same line. A pause or rest (*q.v.*) sometimes compensates for a missing foot or part of a foot.

competence/performance A distinction in linguistics made by Noam Chomsky (1928–), the American linguistics professor. 'Competence' denotes a person's knowledge of his or her language and its rules (grammar, syntax, usage), while 'performance' denotes individual and specific utterance: thus, the use of the knowledge. Chomsky's distinction revises/develops Saussure's distinction between *langue* and *parole* (*q.v.*). Jonathan Culler's notion of 'literary competence' extends this idea from linguistics to the knowledge of the conventions acquired for reading literary texts.

complaint A plaintive poem; frequently the complaint of a lover to his inconstant, unresponsive or exacting mistress. For example, Surrey's *Complaint by Night of the Lover not Beloved.* The theme or burden of complaint became a convention, and finally a cliché, of a great deal of love poetry, but it was still being worked successfully in the middle of the 17th c. by the Cavalier poets (*q.v.*), and particularly well by poets like Thomas Carew and Thomas Stanley.

There are other types of complaint; most of them lament the state of the world, the vicissitudes of Fortune and the poet's personal griefs. An early and fine example is *Deor*, an OE poem about a minstrel who is out of favour and has been supplanted by another. To this may be added two of the best, both by Chaucer: *A Complaint Unto Pity*, in which the poet seeks some respite for his unhappy state; and the more light-hearted *Complaint of Chaucer to his Purse*. Spenser's minor verses and juvenilia contain some complaints, including *The Ruines of Time*.

There are a number of curiosities in this genre. For instance, Sir David Lindsay's poem *The Dreme*, an allegorical lament on the misgovernment of the country, and the same poet's *Complaynt to the King*, and his *Testament and Complaynt of Our Soverane Lordis Papyngo* – both of similar import and tone as *The Dreme*.

Thomas Sackville's *The Complaint of Buckingham* in *Mirror for Magistrates* is another notable example. So is Cowley's ode *The Complaint*, and Young's long didactic poem, in elegiac mood, *The Complaint, or Night Thoughts. See* DIRGE; ELEGY; LAMENT.

complex metaphor *See* TELESCOPED METAPHOR.

composite verses Those composed of different kinds of feet. For instance, those which combine dactyl and trochee (*qq.v.*).

composition Textbooks on this subject distinguish four kinds of prose composition: exposition, argument, description and narrative.

conceit (L *conceptus* 'concept' influenced by It *concetto*) By *c.* 1600 the term was still being used as a synonym for 'thought', and as roughly equivalent to 'concept', 'idea' and 'conception'. It might also then denote a fanciful supposition, an ingenious act of deception or a witty or clever remark or idea. As a literary term this word has come to denote a fairly elaborate figurative device of a fanciful kind which often incorporates metaphor, simile, hyperbole or oxymoron (*qq.v.*) and which is intended to surprise and delight by its wit and ingenuity. The pleasure we get from many conceits is intellectual rather than sensuous. They are particularly associated with the Metaphysical poets (*q.v.*), but are to be found in abundance in the work of Italian Renaissance poets, in the love poetry of the Tudor, Jacobean and Caroline poets, and in the work of Corneille, Molière and Racine.

We can distinguish various kinds. The sonneteering conceits are among the commonest. These tend to be decorative, and the writers of love sonnets had a large number of conventional conceits (many of them *exempla* conceits) which they could make use of and many of which are of the Petrarchan type. The origin of the majority of them is Cupid's analysis of the lover's complaints and maladies in *The Romaunt of the Rose* (14th c.). There is, for instance, the conceit of oxymoron. A classic example is Sir Thomas Wyatt's version of Petrarch's 134th sonnet, which begins:

> I find no peace and all my war is done;
> I fear and hope, I burne and freeze like ice.

In a jealousy conceit a lover wishes he were an ornament, article of clothing or creature of his mistress so that he might be that much closer to her. As in Romeo's lines when he first sees Juliet:

> See! how she leans her cheek upon her hand:
> O! that I were a glove upon that hand,
> That I might touch that cheek.
>
> (*Romeo and Juliet*, II, i)

A third type is the inventory of *blazon* (*q.v.*) conceit which comprises a catalogue of a mistress's charms and perfections, as in Sir Philip Sidney's ninth sonnet in the *Astrophil and Stella* sequence:

> Queen Virtue's Court, which some call Stella's face,
> Prepar'd by Nature's choicest furniture,
> Hath his front built of alabaster pure;
> Gold is the covering of that stately place.
> The door by which sometimes comes forth her grace
> Red porphir is, which lock of pearl makes sure,
> Whose porches rich – which name of cheeks endure –
> Marble, mixt red and white, do interlace.

Another notable example occurs in Spenser's *Epithalamion*. A fourth type is what may be called the *carpe diem* (*q.v.*) conceit: the appeal to the mistress not to delay loving because beauty fades and time is a devourer. Herrick made this famous in:

> Gather ye Rose-buds, while ye may,
> Old Time is still a-flying;

An extension of this is the kind of conceit which contains an assurance that though beauty may fade and die, the poet's verses will be immortal.

Such conventions and devices were often parodied by Tudor and Jacobean poets. A well-known example is Shakespeare's 130th sonnet in which he satirizes the *blazon* form:

> My mistress' eyes are nothing like the sun;
> Coral is far more red than her lips' red:
> If snow be white, why then her breasts are dun;
> If hairs be wires, black wires grow on her head.
> I have seen roses damask'd, red and white,
> But no such roses see I in her cheeks;
> And in some perfumes is there more delight
> Than in the breath that from my mistress reeks.

Thus he 'sends up' the traditional conceit of the idealizers.

Yet another kind is that which incorporates hyperbole (*q.v.*) (it has been called 'pastoral hyperbole'), and commonly expresses the view that the loved one has a powerful effect on the natural order. Constable expresses such a conceit in *Diana*:

> My lady's presence makes the roses red,
> Because to see her lips they blush for shame;
> The lilies' leaves for envy pale became,
> And her white hands in them this envy bred;
> The marigold abroad the leaves did spread,
> Because the sun's and her power is the same.

Marvell used the same idea very ingeniously in his poem *Upon Appleton House*:

> 'Tis she that to these gardens gave
> That wondrous beauty which they have;
> She straightness on the woods bestows;
> To her the meadow sweetness owes

What is known as the heraldic conceit is also common in the 16th and 17th c. It displays the language and images of heraldry. A fairly complex example sustains William Dunbar's *The Thistle and the*

Rose, a work which celebrated the marriage of Margaret Tudor and James IV of Scotland. The red and white rose to which Dunbar refers alludes both to Margaret's complexion and to the fact that her father was a Lancastrian and her mother a Yorkist. The thistle is self-explanatory.

Related to the heraldic conceit is the emblematic type. Both kinds tend to be more esoteric and recondite, what we should now call 'way-out' and which in the 17th c. were described as 'far-fet' (or far-fetched), 'far-fet' being a term often used in critical discussion of conceits at this time. Emblem-books (*q.v.*) contained verses with a moral accompanied by a picture which the verses explain. 'Conceited' poets or *concettisti* used the emblem idea to elucidate morals in descriptions of the natural order; as in these lines by George Wither on the marigold:

How duly every morning she displays
Her open breast when Titan spreads his rays;
How she observes him in his daily walk
Still bending towards him her tender stalk;
How, when he down declines, she droops and mourns,
Bedewed (as 'twere) with tears till he returns;
And how she veils her flowers when he is gone,
As if she scorned to be looked on
By an inferior eye; or did contemn
To wait upon a meaner light, than him.

Wither then elaborates the moral thus:

When this I meditate, methinks, the flowers
Have spirits far more generous than ours,
And give us fair examples to despise
The servile fawnings and idolatries
Wherewith we court these earthly things below,
Which merit not the service we bestow.

A fine example of the verbal emblem is Vaughan's beautiful poem *The Water-fall*:

With what deep murmurs through times silent stealth
Doth thy transparent, cool and watry wealth
Here flowing fall,
And chide, and call,
As if his liquid, loose Retinue staid
Lingring, and were of this steep place afraid,

The common pass
Where, clear as glass,
All must descend
Not to an end:
But quickned by this deep and rocky grave,
Rise to a longer course more bright and brave.

Then the verses change to a different rhythm, meter and line length to suggest the tranquil waters of the stream beyond the fall. The lines quoted most skilfully suggest the movement of the waterfall in what is known as phanopoeia (*q.v.*).

The etymological conceit depends upon the meanings of names. For example, Ralegh's poem *The Ocean's Love to Cynthia* is a kind of double conceit. Ralegh compliments Queen Elizabeth by saying that she has the same influence upon him as the moon has upon the tides. Cynthia was a name frequently used to denote the Queen as a moon-goddess and 'Water' was the Queen's pet-name for Sir Walter Ralegh.

Typological conceits were rather more abstruse still. The following lines from George Herbert's poem *The Agony* illustrate the method:

A man so wrung with pains, that all his hair,
His skin, his garments bloody be.
Sin is that press and vice, which forceth pain
To hunt his cruel food through every vein.

A form of literary exegesis is required to squeeze out the full sense of this. The image of the wine-press is typological of the Passion. Christ described himself as the 'true vine'. Grapes and wine were sacred. The tale of the men from Canaan bearing a cluster of grapes was typological of the Crucifixion. Vice is clearly a kind of pun (*q.v.*) which suggests that Christ suffers in the grip (or vice) of our vices. In a brilliant and witty essay (*The Conceit*, 1969), K. K. Ruthven showed how this kind of exegesis can be best undertaken.

The conceit was much used to embellish the sermon in the 17th c. and such conceits were known as *concetti predicabili.* They tend to be learned, witty, allusive and paradoxical, as in this instance from Crashaw's *Steps to the Temple*:

Give to Caesar – and to God – Mark XII
All we have is God's, and yet
Caesar challenges a debt,
Nor hath God a thinner share,

Whatever Caesar's payments are;
All is God's; and yet 'tis true,
All we have is Caesar's too;
All is Caesar's: and what odds,
So long as Caesar's self is God's?

A minor poet of the 17th c. who had a great reputation in his day, John Cleveland (1613–58), gives his name to another form of conceit – the Clevelandism (now, as a rule, a pejorative term). The following lines come from his *To the State of Love, or, The Senses' Festival*:

My sight took pay, but (thank my charms)
I now impale her in my arms,
(Love's Compasses) confining you,
Good Angels, to a circle too.
Is not the universe strait-laced
When I can clasp it in the waist?
My amorous folds about thee hurled,
With Drake I girdle in the world.
I hoop the firmament and make
This my embrace the zodiac.
  How would thy centre take my sense
  When admiration doth commence
  At the extreme circumference.

Here the poet has condensed a series of related and interlocking emblems while elaborating one of those microcosm/macrocosm arguments dear to poets and readers of the period. Such cosmological acrobatics were then much admired, but Dryden castigated Cleveland for his abstruseness; and indeed many Clevelandisms are far-fetched to the point of being grotesque. Such whimsical imagery has now come to be regarded as gross catachresis (*q.v.*) and a sign of decadence.

In general one may say that a juxtaposition of images and comparisons between very dissimilar objects is a common form of conceit in the 17th c. and the so-called metaphysical conceit is the kind that most readily springs to mind. A famous example is Donne's *A Valediction: forbidding mourning*. He is comparing two lovers' souls:

If they be two, they are two so
  As stiffe twin compassses are two,
Thy soule, the fixt foot, makes no show
  To move, but doth, if the other doe.

And though it in the center sit,
 Yet when the other far doth rome,
It leanes, and hearkens after it,
 And growes erect, as that comes home.

Such wilt thou be to mee, who must
 Like th' other foot, obliquely runne;
Thy firmnes makes my circle just,
 And makes me end, where I begunne.

By the middle of the 17th c. or soon afterwards the *concettisti* were becoming 'over-conceited' and conceits were devised for the sake of themselves rather than for any particular function. Meretriciousness had set in. Apart from Cleveland, this is especially noticeable in the poetry of Edward Benlowes (1605–76) – conspicuously in *Theophila or Love's Sacrifice* (1652). Andrew Marvell, however, most of whose best poems were produced well after 1650, showed himself to be a supremely adroit artist in the use of the conceit.

The conceit fell into desuetude and literary theory required something different. The recondite, the erudite, the 'far-fet' were displaced by, to paraphrase Thomas Sprat in his *History of the Royal Society* (1667), a closer, easier, more naked and more natural way of speaking. In fact, easiness and naturalness became wholly desirable attainments and modes in writing, and were so for a long time.

conceptio *See* SYLLEPSIS.

conceptismo (Sp *concepto* 'conceit') A literary practice and attitude in 17th c. Spain and very closely associated with the *culteranismo* (*q.v.*) of the same time. For the sake of convenience Góngora may be taken as the best representative of *culteranismo* and Lope de Vega of *conceptismo*. But the leader of the *conceptismo* party was Francisco Gómez de Quevedo y Villegas (1580–1645), usually referred to as Quevedo. He was the sworn enemy of *culteranismo*, and between 1626 and 1635 wrote many satires against this movement and its devotees. The *conceptistas* disapproved of obscure references, arcane (and archaic) language and any kind of hermeticism (*q.v.*). They insisted that language should be precise, correct and idiomatic in the pure sense. Yet they *did* favour the use of conceits – especially the metaphor and pun – hence their title. Lope de Vega was not a prominent or active theorist. He practised the art of pleasing beloved of Molière. He liked and believed in good taste, sense, sensibility, order and balance, and lacked the aggressive spirit of Góngora. The different kinds of conceit were classified by Gracián in *Agudeza y arte de ingenio* (1642). *See* GONGORISM.

concordance An alphabetical index of words in a single text, or in the works of a major author. It shows, therefore, the number of times a particular word is used and where it may be found. There are concordances for the Bible and for Shakespeare's works. *See also* DICTIONARY; GLOSSARY.

concrete poetry/verse A recent development of the altar poem (*q.v.*) and the *carmen figuratum*. The object is to present each poem as a different shape. It is thus a matter of pictorial typography which produces 'visual poetry'. It may be on the page, or on glass, stone, wood and other materials. It is extremely difficult to do well but the technique lends itself to great subtlety, as Apollinaire demonstrated in *Calligrammes* (1918). The modern concept of concrete poetry was developed under the influence of Max Bill (1908–) and Eugen Gomringer (1925–) and presented at an exhibition of concrete art at São Paulo in 1956. This was the work of Brazilian designers and poets. The Brazilian Noigandres Group was also a pioneer influence. A vogue or movement was created which has since become widespread and has led to further developments and refinements, such as 'emergent poetry' (which involves cryptographic tricks with letters), 'semiotic poetry' (which uses symbols), 'kinetic poetry' (*q.v.*) and logograms. In Germany a school of concrete poets has grown, called the *Konkretisten*. The group includes the Austrian Ernst Jandl, Achleitner, Heissenbüttel, Mon and Rühm, and Gomringer himself, who edited an anthology of such poetry: *konkrete poesie. deutschsprachige autoren* (1972). Since the Second World War notable experiments have been made by several British poets, including Simon Cutts, Stuart Mills, Dom Sylvester Houédard and Ian Hamilton Finlay. Finlay is regarded by many as the best. In the more way-out examples of this kind of verse sense is abandoned; there is no syntax or grammar. Good representative collections are *An Anthology of Concrete Poetry*, edited by E. Williams (1967), and *Concrete Poetry: An International Anthology*, edited by S. Bann (1967). *See* NONSENSE; PATTERN POETRY.

concrete universal The term derives from idealist philosophy. Hegel expanded his theory of the concrete universal as a solution to the problem of the nature and reality of universals. As far as a work of art is concerned, it refers to the unification of the particular and the general; perhaps a general idea expressed through a concrete image. As Sir Philip Sidney put it: 'the poet coupleth the general notion with the particular example'. This term has produced much discussion of late. Two of its principal debaters have been W. K. Wimsatt in *The Verbal Icon* (1954) and John Crowe Ransom in *The World's Body* (1938). *See* ABSTRACT.

condition of England novel This rather clumsy title denotes fiction which developed in the 1840s as a result of a disturbance of the social conscience among the middle classes about the way of life of those working in industrial cities and in factories. The industrial revolution, especially in the Midlands and the North, resulted in poor housing, over-crowding and inadequate or non-existent sanitation. Factory conditions, in what Blake had described as 'dark Satanic mills', were barbarous. Such environments generated pollution, filth and vermin. Poverty, ill-health, disease and misery were widespread. A great many people (particularly factory owners and bosses) grew rich at the expense of the working classes, both adults and children, and gave scant attention to the lot of their workers who were paid miserly wages.

Anxiety and concern about this state of affairs were primarily stimulated by Thomas Carlyle (1795–1881), who inveighed against the mechanical age and its effects at length in two important books: *Chartism* (1839) and *Past and Present* (1843). Using apocalyptic language, he described the conditions, warned of the consequences (above all, revolution) and prescribed various remedies – especially factory legislation.

Prominent novelists turned their attention to the matter and their interest produced a spate of novels, many of which offered miscellaneous solutions. Some of the main works were: Disraeli's *Coningsby* (1844) and *Sybil* (1845); Mrs Gaskell's *Mary Barton* (1848) and *North and South* (1855); Charles Dickens's *Dombey and Son* (1848) and *Hard Times* (1854); Charles Kinglsey's *Yeast* (1848) and *Alton Locke* (1850); Charlotte Brontë's *Shirley* (1849); Dinah Mulock's *John Halifax, Gentleman* (1857); and George Eliot's *Felix Holt* (1866). *See also* REGIONAL NOVEL.

conduct book A species of guide (*q.v.*) to good behaviour, concerned with morality, deportment, manners and religion. It is quite closely related to the courtesy book (*q.v.*). and a sort of successor to that as well as being a precursor of books of etiquette which proliferated in the 19th c.

Among the first of the conduct books, which were to become very popular during the 18th c. and were often devoted to the conduct of girls and young women, was Richard Allestree's *The Whole Duty of Man* (1658), which he later followed with *The Ladies' Calling* (1673). *The Whole Duty* was a kind of devotional work which expounded man's duties to God and his fellow men. Two years later came Hannah Woolley's *The Gentlwoman's Companion* (1675) and in 1694 the anonymous *The Ladies' Dictionary*.

Many followed, and they give a fascinating insight into the attitudes, assumptions, mores and conventions of the period. Some of the attitudes, accompanied by pompous and complacent moralizing, would be enough to drive modern feminists quite distracted and it is no wonder that the unhappy Mary Wollstonecraft was to inveigh against the position of women in her book *A Vindication of the Rights of Woman* (1792).

Some of the best known conduct books are as follows: Mary Astell's *A Serious Proposal to the Ladies for the Advancement of Their Time and Great Interest* (1701); Lady Sarah Pennington's *An Unfortunate Mother's Advice to Her Absent Daughters* (1761), which she followed later with *The Polite Lady, or, A Course of Female Education in a Series of Letters, from a Mother to Her Daughter* (1775); Fordyce's *Sermons to Young Women* (1767); George Edmond Howard's *Apophthegms and Maxims on Various Subjects for the Good Conduct of Life &c* (1767) and *Instructions for a Young Lady in Every Sphere and Period of Life* (1773); Hester Chapone's *Letters on the Improvement of the Mind* (1773); Dr John Gregory's *Legacy to His Daughters* (1774); Clara Reeve's *Plans of Education: With Remarks on the Systems of Other Writers. In a Series of Letters between Mrs Darnford and Her Friends* (1792); Laetitia Matilda Hawkins's *Letters on the Female Mind, its Power and Pursuits* (1793); Thomas Gisborne's *An Enquiry into the Duties of Men in the Higher and Middling Classes of Society* (1794) and *An Enquiry into the Duties of the Female Sex* (1796); Jane West's *Letters to a Young Man* (1802) and *Letters to a Young Woman* (1806); Miss Hatfield's *Letters on the Importance of the Female Sex: With Observations on Their Manners, and on Education* (1803); Hannah More's *Coelebs in Search of a Wife* (1809); Elizabeth Appleton's *Private Education, or, A Practical Plan for the Studies of*

Young Ladies. With an Address to Parents, Private Governesses, and Young Ladies (1815).

Numerous books of etiquette have been the successors of these erudite disquisitions. These concentrate on the do's and don'ts and are often guides for social climbers. They cover such weighty matters as how to address a marquis and the degree of hand pressure permissible by her partner on the waist of a young lady dancing a waltz.

conduplicatio *See* PLOCE.

confessional literature Into this rather vague category we may place works which are a very personal and subjective account of experiences, beliefs, feelings, ideas, and states of mind, body and soul. The following widely different examples are famous: St Augustine's *Confessions* (4th c.); Rousseau's *Les Confessions* (1781, 1788); De Quincey's *Confessions of an English Opium Eater* (1822); James Hogg's *The Private Memoirs and Confessions of a Justified Sinner* (1824); Alfred de Musset's *Confession d'un enfant du siècle* (1836); Chateaubriand's *Mémoires d'outre-tombe* (1849–50); George Moore's *Confessions of a Young Man* (1888). *See* AUTOBIOGRAPHY; CONFESSIONAL NOVEL; DIARY AND JOURNAL; TESTAMENT.

confessional novel A rather misleading and flexible term which suggests an 'autobiographical' type of fiction, written in the first person, and which, on the face of it, is a self-revelation. On the other hand it may not be, though it looks like it. The author may be merely assuming the role of another character. An outstanding modern example is Camus's *La Chute* (1956) in which the judge penitent 'confesses' to the reader. In the last fifty years this type of novel has become common.

Another form of confessional novel is that which employs a variation of the 'frame story' (*q.v.*) technique: a story in which the novelist is actually writing the story we are reading. This device was used by André Gide in *Tentatives amoureuses* (1891) and in *Les Faux-Monnayeurs* (1926). *See* CONFESSIONAL LITERATURE.

confessional poetry It may be argued that much poetry, especially lyric (*q.v.*) poetry, is, *ipso facto*, 'confessional' in so far as it is a record of a poet's states of mind and feelings and his vision of life (for example, much that was written by Wordsworth, John Clare and Gerard Manley Hopkins). However, some poems are more overtly self-revelatory, more detailed in their analytical exposition of pain, grief, tension and joy.

The term is now usually confined to the works of certain writers in the UK and USA in the late 1950s and 1960s. The work of four distinguished American poets may be cited in illustration: Robert Lowell's *Life Studies* (1959), W. D. Snodgrass's *Heart's Needle* (1959), Anne Sexton's four volumes *To Bedlam and Part Way Back* (1960), *All My Pretty Ones* (1962), *Live or Die* (1966), *Love Poems* (1969), plus a number of poems by Sylvia Plath. *See* CONFESSIONAL LITERATURE.

confidant A character in drama and, occasionally, in fiction (feminine *confidante*) who has little effect on the action but whose function is to listen to the intimate feelings and intentions of the protagonist (*q.v.*). He is trusted friend, like Horatio in *Hamlet*. From fiction one example is Maria Gostrey, the confidante of Strether in Henry James's *The Ambassadors*. James also used the term *ficelle* (French for the string which a puppeteer uses to manipulate his puppets) to denote a confidant. He describes Maria Gostrey as a 'ficelle', who is not so much Strether's friend but, rather, the reader's friend. The confidant is also a common feature of the detective story (*q.v.*). Dr Watson, in Arthur Conan Doyle's Sherlock Holmes stories, is an outstanding example. *See* COMMEDIA DELL'ARTE; IDEAL SPECTATOR.

conflict The tension in a situation between characters, or the actual opposition of characters (usually in drama and fiction but also in narrative poetry). In *Othello*, for instance, the conflicts between Iago, Roderigo, Othello and Desdemona. There may also be internal conflict, as in Hamlet's predicament of wishing to avenge his father and yet not knowing when and how to do it. There may also occur conflict between a character and society or environment. An example is Jude's efforts in Thomas Hardy's *Jude the Obscure* to overcome the social obstacles which keep him from university.

conformatio *See* PERSONIFICATION.

congé (F 'leave, quittance') A lyric poem of farewell. The first known instances are by Jean Bodel (late 12th c.–early 13th c.), who, when he developed leprosy and was obliged to withdraw from the world, said goodbye to his friends with a poem of forty-two stanzas (one stanza per friend). This was later imitated by Adam de la Halle (*c.* 1240–*c.* 1288) but *his* withdrawal was for political reasons and his valediction was a satire at the expense of his fellow citizens.

connotation The suggestion or implication evoked by a word or phrase, or even quite a long statement of any kind, over and above what they mean or actually denote. For example: 'There is a cockroach', may inspire a shudder of distaste in one person; but a scientific inquiry, like 'What is it? *Blatta orientalis* or *Blatta Germanica*?' in another person.

A connotation may be personal and individual, or general and universal. Probably nearly all words with a lexical meaning can have public and private connotations. The sentence 'The Fascist activities were continuous' would be likely to have different connotations for a Jew and a professional historian. *See* ASSOCIATION; DENOTATION; KENEME; MEANING.

consciousness stream of *See* STREAM OF CONSCIOUSNESS.

consistency In the structure, style and tone of a literary work, consistency implies an *essential* coherence and balance. An untimely comic episode in a tragedy might be disastrous to its consistency. Inappropriate words and usage may mar consistency of style. A character suddenly acting completely 'out of character' might produce inconsistency. So might a breach of literary convention (*q.v.*); for instance, the use of soliloquy in a naturalistic drawing-room comedy. *See also* BIENSEANCES.

consonance The close repetition of identical consonant sounds before and after different vowels. For example: slip – slop; creak – croak; black – block. *See also* ASSONANCE; EYE-RHYME; HALF-RHYME; ONOMATOPOEIA.

constructivism The constructivists were a group of young Russian poets who flourished in the 1920s and were influenced by futurism (*q.v.*). They were inspired by technology (like the Futurists) and were anti-traditional. They held that a poem should be a 'construction' (like a piece of engineering) and that all images, devices, language, etc. in a poem should be closely related to the theme and subject of the poem. The chief poets were Vera Inber (1890–?) and Ilya Selvinski (1899–?). The members of the constructivist movement were pro-Bolshevik and in favour of the proletarian writers. By *c.*

1930 the movement had fallen into desuetude. *See also* PROLETARSKAYA KUL'TURA; SMITHY POETS.

contamination This usually refers to the Roman practice of adapting and combining Greek New Comedy (*q.v.*). Such a work was known as a *fabula palliata*. The main authors of *palliatae* were Andronicus, Naevius, Plautus and Terence. *See* FABULA.

conte (F 'tale, story') The term denotes a kind of fictitious narrative somewhat different from the *roman* and the *nouvelle* (*qq.v.*). The true *conte* tended to be a little fantastic (not realistic), droll and witty. They were often allegorical and moral. Well-known examples are La Fontaine's *Amours de Psyché et Cupidon* (1669), Perrault's *Contes de ma mère l'Oye* (1697) and Voltaire's *Candide* (1759). In this category one might also include Swift's *Gulliver's Travels* (1726), Voltaire's *Zadig* (1747), Johnson's *Rasselas* (1759), and the anonymous Japanese romance *Wasōbyōe* (1774–9) which has affinities with *Gulliver's Travels*. It was a popular form of fiction in the 18th c. when the other main authors were Hamilton, Crébillon *fils* and Voisenon. From the 19th c. the term has tended to denote merely a short story (*q.v.*). For example, Flaubert's *Trois Contes* (1877). Maupassant called his short stories *contes*. *See also* ALLEGORY; CONTE DEVOT; LAI; TALE.

conte dévot (F 'pious tale') A French genre of the 13th and 14th c. A tale in verse or prose designed to instruct and therefore having affinities with hagiography (*q.v.*) and the moral tale. A good many *contes dévots* were inspired by the collections of tales called the *Vitae Patrum* and the *Miracles Nostre Dame*. Two well-known examples are: *Tombeor Nostre Dame* and *Conte del'hermite et del jongleour*. *See* CONTE.

contests *See* POETIC CONTESTS.

contextual criticism A mode of critical analysis of a literary text characteristic of the New Criticism (*q.v.*), especially as practised by Murray Krieger and Eliseo Vivas. Krieger discusses the method in *The New Apologists for Poetry* (1956) and *Theory of Criticism* (1976). He describes contextualism as the claim 'that a poem is a tight, compelling, finally closed context' and suggests that it is necessary to analyse and judge such a work as an 'aesthetic object' without reference to anything outside or beyond it. There is an obvious connection here with Jacques Derrida's dictum that 'there is nothing outside the text'. The emphasis on close reading in contextual theory has had considerable influence on critical methods. *See also* DECONSTRUCTION.

contextualism A jargon term current in the New Criticism (*q.v.*) which denotes a particular kind of aesthetic experience of (and response to) a work of literature. The work is experienced as a self-contained artefact and possessed of 'mutually opposing energies of a tension-filled object that blocks our escape from its context and thus from its world' (*sic*).

contractions In verse there are two kinds: synaeresis and syncope. They are forms of elision (*q.v.*) used to keep the syllable count regular. Synaeresis occurs when a poet joins two vowels to make a single syllable, as in this line from Dryden's *Absalom and Achitophel*:

> Titles and Names 'twere tedious to Reherse

'Tedious' counts as a two-syllable word.

Syncope occurs when a vowel flanked by two consonants is not pronounced, as in this line from the same poem:

Him Staggering so when Hell's dire Agent found,

'Staggering' is taken as a disyllable.

Such contractions were common between 1660 and 1800. The metrical demands of the heroic couplet (*q.v.*) encouraged them.

contrapositum *See* SYNECIOSIS.

contrast The juxtaposition of disparate or opposed images, ideas, or both, to heighten or clarify a scene, theme or episode. A famous example is the life-in-death image in Andrew Marvell's *To His Coy Mistress*:

> Thy beauty shall no more be found;
> Nor, in thy marble Vault, shall sound
> My echoing song: then Worms shall try
> That long preserv'd Virginity:
> And your quaint Honour turn to dust;
> And into ashes all my Lust.
> The Grave's a fine and private place,
> But none I think do there embrace.

See IMAGERY; METAPHYSICAL.

conundrum A word of very obscure origin, it denotes a form of riddle (*q.v.*) whose answer involves a pun (*q.v.*).

convention In literature, a device, principle, procedure or form which is generally accepted and through which there is an agreement between the writer and his readers (or audience) which allows him various freedoms and restrictions. The term is especially relevant to drama. The stage itself, as a physical object and area, establishes a convention by creating boundaries and limitations. The audience is prepared to suspend disbelief and to experience a representation of scenery and action, of lighting and words. The use of verse, blank or rhymed, dance, song (*q.v.*), a Chorus (*q.v.*), the unities (*q.v.*), the aside (*q.v.*), the soliloquy (*q.v.*), are all examples of dramatic convention. Working within the conventions and using them to the best possible advantage is essential to the art of the dramatist. The people in the audience are party to the agreement and their acceptance makes possible dramatic illusion.

Dr Johnson summarizes the matter in a famous passage in his *Preface to Shakespeare*:

> Delusion, if delusion be admitted, has no certain limitation; if the spectator can be once persuaded, that his old acquaintance are Alexander and Caesar, that a room illuminated with candles is the plain of Pharsalia, or the bank of Granicus, he is in a state of elevation above the reach of reason, or of truth, and from the heights of empyrean poetry, may despise the circumscriptions of terrestrial nature. There is no reason why a mind thus wandering in exstasy should count the clock, or why an hour should not be a century in that calenture of the brains that can make the stage a field. The truth is, that the spectators are always in their senses, and know, from the first act to the last, that the stage is only a stage, and that the players are only players.

In fact every writer accepts conventions as soon as he begins. It can be argued that conventions are essential to all literature as necessary and convenient ways of working within the limitations of the medium of words. And we may not, as Maritain puts it, abuse the limitations of our medium. Thus, in literature, as in the other arts, there are recurring elements.

By convention the sonnet (*q.v.*) has fourteen lines (though there are exceptions), and *terza rima* (*q.v.*) rhymes aba, bcb, cdc, and so on. The ballad (*q.v.*) tends to have a particular kind of diction and stanza form, and the pastoral elegy (*q.v.*) traditional essentials. The epic (*q.v.*) tends to begin *in medias res* (*q.v.*) and the Cavalier lyric (*q.v.*) presents certain attitudes towards love. The stock character (*q.v.*) is also a convention. So is tragic love in grand opera, and the flash-back (*q.v.*) in the novel (*q.v.*).

A convention may be established as an invention: for instance, Gerard Manley Hopkins's sprung rhythm (*q.v.*) and Chaucer's rhyme royal (*q.v.*). One may be revived – as alliterative verse (*q.v.*) was revived in the 14th c. by Langland and other poets, and again in this century by W. H. Auden and C. Day Lewis. Or one may be abandoned – as the heroic couplet (*q.v.*) was towards the end of the 18th c. (though there have been recent revivals by Roy Campbell in *The Georgiad*, and by Nabokov (as a parody) in *Pale Fire*).

Periodically conventions are broken or replaced. Wordsworth's rejection of 18th c. poetic diction (*q.v.*) is an obvious instance; so is the substitution, in drama, of naturalistic conventions for the traditional dramatic ones.

Ignorance of convention may lead to misunderstanding and misinterpretation. To criticize a work for *not* being what it was never *intended* to be is a fault. A classic example is Johnson's misunderstanding of Milton's *Lycidas.* He condemned it for its 'inherent improbability', mainly because (apart from disliking pastoralism) he was not aware of the pastoral conventions. *See also* ALIENATION EFFECT; DECORUM; ORIGINALITY; NATURALISM; NEOCLASSICISM; REALISM; TRADITION.

conversation piece A form of poem which has a relaxed and fairly informal style and tone, may even be 'chatty', tends to display a personal mood, but nevertheless has quite serious subject matter. Horace's *Epistles* and *Satires* are generally taken to be conversation pieces (Pope caught the tone of Horace very well in his *Imitations*). The two English poets who have excelled at them were Coleridge and Wordsworth. Coleridge's *This Limetree Bower My Prison*, for example; and Wordsworth's *Tintern Abbey.* Other poets who have mastered this genre are Robert Browning, Robert Frost and W. H. Auden. Auden's *Letter to Lord Byron* is an outstanding example.

copla (Sp 'couple') In prosody a couplet, strophe or stanza. A metrical combination of great antiquity which has been used by many Spanish poets and still is. There are various kinds of *copla,* for instance, *copla de arte mayor* (*q.v.*), *copla de pie quebrado* (*q.v.*), *coplas de calaínos* (meaning 'useless', from the character of Calaínos in the Spanish books of chivalry), and *coplas de ciego* (literally 'blind man's *coplas*' and therefore bad verses).

Generally the *copla* will be of four octosyllabic lines assonanced in pairs. But it can also be rhymed and may have a length of eleven or twelve syllables; or again octosyllables may alternate with heptasyllables. It may consist of three, four, five or even more lines and is found in the *villancico*, the *redondilla*, the *quintilla* and *sextilla* (*qq.v.*).

copyright Until the middle of the 16th c. authors had little or no protection against plagiarism (*q.v.*), or downright filching and pirating. When this became a serious problem printers' guilds were granted rights to protect their members. The first English copyright law dates from 1709. Under the 1956 Act the copyright covers an author's lifetime and fifty years thereafter.

coq-à-l'âne Derived from an OF proverbial expression *C'est bien sauté du cocq a l'asne*, which signified incoherent speech or writing. The term denotes a satirical *genre* of verse devoted to ridiculing the vices and foibles of society. Clément Marot is believed to have created the form in 1530. At any rate he composed a number of poems which come into this category. *See also* FATRASIE.

coquillards (from F *coquille* 'shell') The shell was the traditional emblem of pilgrims and the term came to be applied to the dispossessed members of a band of vagrants, rogues, vagabonds, deserters, discharged soldiers *et al.* who, after the Hundred Years War, were itinerant in France. They evolved what was almost a sub-culture (*q.v.*) of their own and had a secret language called *jargon* (*q.v.*). François Villon (1431–?) composed for them his *Ballades en jargon*.

coranto The term appears to derive from the French word *courant*, 'runner'. It was the name applied to periodical news-pamphlets issued between 1621 and 1641 giving information about foreign affairs taken from foreign newspapers. One of the earliest forms of English journalism. The *corantos* were followed by the newsbook (*q.v.*). *See also* GAZETTE.

coronach The Gaelic word means 'wailing together'; thus a funeral lament or dirge (*qq.v.*). Such laments originated in Ireland and the Scottish Highlands. *See also* COMPLAINT; ELEGY.

corpus (L 'body') A term used to denote the body (i.e. the bulk or all) of a writer's work. For example, the *corpus* of T. S. Eliot's poetry. It may also denote a particular collection of texts, such as the *corpus* of Old English literature. *See* ANGLO-SAXON PERIOD.

correctio *See* EPANORTHOSIS.

correctness Adherence to and conformity with rules, convention, and decorum (*qq.v.*). In the 18th c. a much prized ideal and standard which writers frequently discussed, especially with regard to verse.

correlative verse Verse in the shape of abbreviated sentences where there is a linear correspondence between words, as in the last two lines of this stanza from a sonnet by George Peele:

> His golden locks time hath to silver turned;
> Oh time too swift, Oh swiftness never ceasing!
> His youth 'gainst time and age hath ever spurned,
> But spurneth in vain; youth waneth by increasing:
> Beauty, strength, youth, are flowers but fading seen;
> Duty, faith, love, are roots, and ever green.

correspondence of the arts The idea that all the arts have certain features in common and resemble each other. In Classical times it was believed that art imitated nature but that each art was a separate and distinct activity. In the 19th c., and not, apparently, before, the belief that the arts contained certain correspondences began to take hold. This was encouraged by experiment with drugs and synaesthetic experiences they produced. The French Symbolist poets, especially, made use of the knowledge of these effects. *See* SYMBOL AND SYMBOLISM; SYNAESTHESIA; UT PICTURA POESIS.

cosmists *See* SMITHY POETS.

cosmopolitan writing As the epithet 'cosmopolitan' (Gk *kosmos* 'order, world, universe' + *polītikos* 'citizen') suggests, such writing is concerned with global/universal themes and issues (political, social and otherwise) and also with the attitudes and language involved in any discourse on such themes and issues. It is concerned too with individual persons: for instance, immigrants. The post-colonial (or decolonized) world has seen the advent of emergent countries and nations and what has come to be known as the Third World (of which there are many representative writers, especially novelists), and also massive immigration and transmigration to erstwhile imperial 'centres'. Not least to Britain, where there has been a big influx of non-white peoples from South Asia, Africa and the Caribbean, and to North America – from Asia and Latin America. To a lesser extent there has been comparable immigration to France, to Canada and Australia. This diaspora has been described by Gordon Lewis as 'colonialism in reverse'. Large ethnic minorities now exist in these countries and these multi-ethnic microcosms have influenced the national cultures and brought about a kind of 'neo-colonialism'.

In the past there have been many 'national' novels seeking to depict the community that is or was the nation (witness the numerous block-busting 'epic' narratives produced by American authors). There have also been what are described as 'novels of Empire', works of fiction set in a colonial world or with a kind of 'colonial' background. Obvious examples are Rudyard Kipling's *Kim* (1901), Conrad's *Heart of Darkness* (1902), plus several of his novels set in the East, E. M. Forster's *A Passage to India* (1924), Graham Greene's *The Heart of the Matter* (1948), Anthony Burgess's *The Malayan Trilogy* (1972), V. S. Naipaul's novels about Trinidad and his novel *A Bend in the River* (1979), set in a French-speaking Central African state, and Paul Scott's *The Jewel in the Crown* tetralogy (1966, 1968, 1971, 1975) about India and the Raj. Such fiction has only in part represented the attitudes, way of life and so forth of the indigenous peoples.

Cosmopolitan writing is an attempt to cross the boundaries and frontiers of nations and nationalism; it stresses the global nature of everyday life and tries to depict societies and individuals as globally representative. The use of myth, fable and parable (*qq.v.*), which tend to have universal parallels and analogies, is a feature of such writing. Cosmopolitan writing can now also begin to be seen as an attempt to come to terms with the state and position of the immigrant.

In post-war and post-imperial Britain, a highly cosmopolitan centre, there has been next to no fiction which is concerned with immigrants, their difficulties in adjustment to an alien culture, etc. An obvious exception to this generalization is the work of Colin MacInnes (1914–76), in particular the novel *City of Spades* (1957), an original attempt to depict teenage and immigrant black culture in

London. Later, Salman Rushdie tried to come to terms with cosmopolitanism in Britain, especially in connection with the Muslim community, in his novel *The Satanic Verses* (1988). Because he was alleged to have made opprobrious remarks about the Prophet, he was placed under sentence of death by way of a *fatwa* from Iran. His earlier novels, *Midnight's Children* (1981) and *Shame* (1983), might be viewed as cosmopolitan in so far as they are efforts to present a more truthful picture of the sub-continent of India to the West and in terms widely relevant to other countries. Rushdie is preoccupied with the 'in-between' state of the cosmopolitan, a person who, as he has put it, is in a state of 'translation', of being borne or carried across. This has also been referred to, if somewhat uncouthly, as a state of 'trans-culturation'.

Other writers of note who have been described as cosmopolitan are Isabel Allende, Bharati Mukherjee, Derek Walcott, Mario Vargas Llosa and Gabriel García Márquez. Derek Walcott, for instance, in his fine poetry, using a mixture of patois (plural) dialect and standard or Queen's English, has essayed a kind of synthesis or 'alchemy' of African, Indian and European influences and origins (with their historical and racial conflicts and contradictions) to achieve something characteristically Caribbean.

Using very different methods and by the elaboration of particular images and symbols, Mario Vargas Llosa, the Peruvian novelist, has sought to present social and political simulacra which have cosmopolitan significance. This is evident in *La casa verde* (1966). The 'casa verde' is a brothel – a sufficiently global site, and symbolically the jungle and the green earth itself. In *Conversación en 'La Catedral'* (1969) the symbolic location is a seedy, run-down bar called, with perhaps heavy-handed irony, 'La Catedral'.

In Gabriel García Márquez's *Cien años de soledad* (1967) the mythical town of Macando is a global and cosmopolitan urban image of decay, corruption, poverty and isolation, and the various misfortunes which befall it and its inhabitants are represented by biblical analogies. *See also* MAGIC REALISM; NOVEL.

cossante A Spanish verse form associated with a Castilian round dance; one of the forms arising from the old *danza prima* (*q.v.*). The lines are in assonanced couplets separated by a short third line which remains unchanged throughout the poem. *See also* CANTIGA.

costumbrismo The Spanish word *costumbre* denotes 'custom, habit'; *costumbrista* = the person or writer responsible. The term is used of prose forms which appeared early in the 19th c. – articles, sketches, short novels – and which concentrated on regional customs. Prominent authors of the genre were Larra Mesonero Romanos and Estébanez Calderón. The bigger novels which followed when this style became popular were consequently based on real observation of typical life in particular regions. One such which became famous was *La Gaviota* by Fernan Caballero (1796–1877). The early work of Blasco Ibañez is also of this type. *See* NOVEL; REALISM; REGIONAL NOVEL.

cothurnus *See* BUSKIN.

counterplot *See* SUB-PLOT.

counterpoint A term adopted by literary critics. In music it means the simultaneous combination of two or more melodies. When applied to verse it denotes metrical variation – which is very common. If the basic meter of a poem is iambic and there are dactylic and trochaic variations, then a counterpoint is achieved. The counterpoint effects in this stanza from George MacBeth's *The God of Love* are very noticeable:

> Ĭ foúnd thĕm bĕtwéen fár híllѕ, bў̆ ă frózĕn láke,
> Ŏn ă pátch ŏf báre gróund. Thĕy wĕre gróuped
> Ĭn ă sólĭd ríng, lĭke ăn árk ŏf hórn. Ănd ăroúnd
> Thĕm círclĕd, slówlў̆ clósĭng ín,
>
> Thĕir tóngues lóllĭng, théir eárs flăttĕned ăgaínst thĕ wínd,
>
> Ă whírlpoŏl ŏf wólves

See SUBSTITUTION; TENSION.

counter-turn Describes the function of the antistrophe (*q.v.*) and the response to the strophe (*q.v.*) in choral song. It may also refer to the surprise dénouement (*q.v.*) at the end of a short story ('the twist in the tail'), and, conceivably, a wholly unexpected development in a play or story; unexpected, that is to say, by either the characters or the reader/audience. *See* COUP DE THEATRE.

coup de théâtre An unexpected and theatrically startling event which twists the plot and action. For instance, the sudden leap into activity of the supposedly invalid and bedridden wife of General St Pé in

Jean Anouilh's play *La Valse des Toréadors*. *See* COUNTERTURN; DEUS EX MACHINA.

couplet Two successive rhyming lines, as here from the beginning of Chaucer's *Merchant's Tale*:

Whilom ther was dwellynge in Lumbardye
A worthy knyght, that born was of Pavye,
In which he lyved in greet prosperitee;
And sixty yeer a wyflees man was hee,
And folwed ay his bodily delyt
On wommen, ther as was his appetyt

The couplet is one of the main verse units in Western literature and is a form of great antiquity. Chaucer was one of the first Englishmen to use it, in *The Legend of Good Women* and for most of *The Canterbury Tales*. Tudor and Jacobean poets and dramatists used it continually; especially Shakespeare, Marlowe, Chapman and Donne. The dramatists at this time employed it as a variation on blank verse (*q.v.*), and also (very often) to round off a scene or an act. This is virtually a convention (*q.v.*) of the period. The couplet composed of two iambic pentameter (*q.v.*) lines – more commonly known as the heroic couplet (*q.v.*) – was the most favoured form. This was developed particularly in the 17th c. and perfected by Dryden, Pope and Johnson; but Chaucer had already shown many of its possibilities. It was also used for heroic drama (*q.v.*) during the Restoration period (*q.v.*) in England.

The octosyllabic couplet (or iambic tetrameter) has also been much used. Outstanding instances are Milton's *L'Allegro* and *Il Penseroso*, Samuel Butler's *Hudibras* and Coleridge's *Christabel*.

The couplet in all forms of meter (even monometer, dimeter and trimeter, *qq.v.*) has proved an extremely adaptable unit: in lines of different lengths; as part of more complex stanza forms; as a conclusion to the sonnet (*q.v.*); as part of *ottava rima* and rhyme royal (*qq.v.*); and for epigrams (*q.v.*).

In French poetry the rhyming alexandrine (*q.v.*) couplet has been a major unit, and used with especial skill by Corneille, Racine, Molière and La Fontaine. During the 17th and 18th c., partly owing to French influence, this unit was used extensively for German and Dutch narrative and dramatic verse. Later Goethe and Schiller revived the *Knittelvers* (*q.v.*), a tetrameter couplet.

In the 20th c. the couplet has fallen somewhat into desuetude, but it is still used periodically in combination with other metrical units. *See* CLOSED COUPLET; END-STOPPED LINE; ENJAMBEMENT; OPEN COUPLET.

courtesy book Basically, this is a book of etiquette, but many of the early courtesy books (especially those of the 16th and 17th c.) were much more than this in that they embodied a philosophy of the art of living (elegantly, with *virtù*) and a guide to it. Moreover, many of them were extremely well written and are an invaluable source for the history of education, ideas, customs and social behaviour.

Some very early examples date from the 13th c.: Thomasin von Zirclaria's *Der Walsche Gast*, Bonvincino da Riva's *De le zinquanta cortexie da tavola*, and two poems by Francesco da Barberino. The best known of the early English books was the *Babees Book* (a collection of pieces from the 15th and 16th c.), which, like Master Rhodes's *Book of Nurture*, was a useful primer for youths who went to serve in the houses of noblemen in order to learn how to behave. Two 15th c. works in verse, *The Boke of Curtasye* and *Urbanitatis*, were also popular. Though often crudely naive in their delineation of the principles of civilized conduct, they all aimed to encourage good manners, chivalry, courtly behaviour and the knightly ideal exemplified in Chaucer's description of the Knight in the *Prologue to the Canterbury Tales*; an ideal, which, it may be argued, owes much to the early medieval tradition of the Christian knight whose paragon and exemplar was Christ. Courtesy meant rather more than merely good manners.

After the year 1400 behaviour, especially that of the better educated, was profoundly affected by the invention of gunpowder and printing. Fire-arms eventually reduced the importance of skill-at-arms with the sword and altered the ideals of chivalry. Printing made available a large number of books from which people might learn to behave in a more civilized manner.

In the Tudor period there developed the conception of a 'gentleman', a civilized 'all-rounder' or 'universal man' (sometimes called 'Renaissance man'). We can broadly distinguish two types. Type A: Sir Thomas Wyatt, Sir Philip Sidney, Sir Walter Ralegh, Cellini. Type B: Leonardo da Vinci, Erasmus and Sir Thomas More. All these men, like others less known, in many ways exemplified the attainments and ideals of humanism (*q.v.*). They were, so to speak, the *beati* of the humanist calendar.

Italian scholarship and culture had much to do with this humanist conception of many-sided excellence, and the most influential of all the courtesy books was Castiglione's *Il Libro del*

Cortegiano (The Book of the Courtier) published in Venice in 1528, and translated into English by Sir Thomas Hoby in 1561. In 1576 came a translation of Della Casa's *Galateo* (still much read in Italy). The other most famous and influential Italian work was Guaazo's *La civil conversatione*, translated into English in 1581.

However, before these events English writers had addressed themselves to manuals of instruction. Sir Thomas Elyot's *Boke of the Governour* (1531) was the first treatise on education to be printed in England. About the same time appeared Thomas Lupset's *Exhortation to Yonge Men, perswading them to walke in the pathe way that leadeth to honeste and goodnes*; and in 1555, the anonymous *Institution of a Gentleman.*

Spenser's *Faerie Queene* (1589, 1596) can almost be described as the Bible of Renaissance anthropocentric humanism, which, in its most idealistic form, was a sort of apotheosis of man. Spenser's greatest work presents both the medieval and the Renaissance conceptions of knightly and chivalrous conduct. He made his purpose clear in his Dedication, when he wrote: 'The generall end therefore of all the booke is to fashion a gentleman or noble person in vertuous and gentle discipline.' It was the most ambitious courtesy book of all.

In the early 17th c. appeared James Cleland's *Institution of a Young Nobleman* (1607); Richard Braithwaite's *The English Gentleman* (1630), and *The English Gentlewoman* (1631); and Henry Peacham's *The Compleat Gentleman* (1622), a work of considerable charm. A lesser one was Richard Weste's *The Schoole of Vertue* (1619). Such courtesy books were comprehensive. Advice ranged from education, the duties of parents and the exercise of the nobler faculties, to exactly how one should eat, blow one's nose, and clean one's teeth; plus other admonitions:

> Let not thy privy members be
>   Layd open to be view'd,
> It is most shameful and abhord,
>   Detestable and rude.
>
> Retain not urine nor the winde,
>   Which doth the body vex,
> So it be done with secresie
>   Let that not thee perplex.

There was also emphasis on what the Italian courtesy books called *sprezzatura* – doing things gracefully, with nonchalance bordering on disdain, however difficult they might be. It is also important that the vast majority of these works were concerned with worldly and secular matters (this secular morality is particularly noticeable in Della Casa) and not with religious morals. The medieval conception of the Christian knight and chivalrous hero had been modified.

Other 17th c. works of note were Obadiah Walker's *Of Education, especially of Young Gentlemen* (1673), Gailhard's *The Compleat Gentleman* (1678); and two influential books translated from the French: *The Rules of Civility* by Antoine de Courtin, and an anonymous work called *Youth's Behaviour*. To these one might add George Halifax's *Advice to a Daughter* (1688), a work of much charm and urbane good sense.

By this time, manners, dress and generally polished behaviour were tending to become an end in themselves, and thus leading to affectation and posturing, all too apparent in Restoration Comedy (*q.v.*). The Tudor ideals of amateur *virtù*, of 'the glass of fashion and the mould of form', were being reduced. Nevertheless, the 18th c. produced one noteworthy contribution in the shape of Lord Chesterfield's *Letters to His Son* (1774), which may well be regarded as the last of the traditional courtesy books concerned with the principles of gentlemanly behaviour as well as with the details. They were highly praised and make delightful reading. However, Dr Johnson, who felt he had been badly let down by Chesterfield as a patron (cf. the famous letter of Feb. 7th 1755, rebuking him for not offering financial support to the plans for the projected *Dictionary*), castigated Chesterfield roundly for teaching 'the manners of a dancing master and the morals of a whore'.

Long before Chesterfield's *Letters* the courtesy book had in part been replaced by the conduct book (*q.v.*).

courtly love The term *amour courtois* (Italian *amore cortese*; Provençal *domnei*) was coined by Gaston Paris in 1883 to describe that courtly love which had its origins in southern France and was celebrated in the poetry of the troubadours (*q.v.*). It was primarily a literary and aristocratic phenomenon, though there were indeed actual courts of love where amatory problems were discussed.

Before the 12th c., women, for the most part, were regarded as inferior to men, but courtly love idealized women; and the lover, stricken by the beauty of his lady, put her on a pedestal and was obedient to her wishes. The idea was that the lover's feelings ennoble him and make him worthier of his sovereign mistress. He longs for union with her in order to attain moral excellence. Paradoxically, though the lover adored his lady, genuflected at her door and observed Christian behaviour strictly, the troubadour version of this form of love was adulterous. In fact, adultery was glorified; partly, perhaps, because medieval marriages were the result of practical convenience (they were 'arranged') rather than romance, and partly because of the theory that true love had to be freely given and was not possible between husband and wife.

The literary origin of this very remarkable development in the relationship of the two sexes is to be found in Ovid's *Ars Amatoria* (published at the very beginning of the Christian era), and most of the rules were laid down by a monk, Andreas Capellanus, late in the 12th c. in *De Amore* – also known under the title *De Arte Honeste Amandi*.

The feudal concept of vassalage to an overlord and the medieval tradition of devotion to the Virgin Mary also influenced the evolution of courtly love. It is noticeable that the later devotional lyrics of the Middle Ages become more and more secular in their attitude and language as the earthly mistress replaces the celestial goddess and Queen of Heaven. By the time the sonneteers are producing their sequences we have almost an 'overlady', and, on the face of it, the equivalent of a masochistic devotion to beauty.

The troubadour tradition spread to Italy where it attained its sublime form in the work of Guinicelli and Çavalcanti, the gentlest of the *dolce stil nuovisti*. It also permeated to northern France where it is established in the work of the *trouvères* (*q.v.*), and in the romances (*q.v.*) – particularly in the work of Chrétien de Troyes. In Germany its ideals are presented in the poetry of the Minnesingers. In England the tradition appears in Chaucer, especially in *Troilus and Criseyde* (though Chaucer is in a way rejecting it); and in the work of Gower and Usk. But the ideals of courtly love do not really manifest themselves in English literature until the 16th c. (via Petrarch) in the great sonnet (*q.v.*) sequences of Sidney, Spenser and Shakespeare.

Courtly love is an example of an idea about heterosexual relationships which became widely diffused (just as a political theory might) in various cultures and environments and was susceptible to a variety of different interpretations and expressions. Nevertheless, there appear to be some fundamental elements which are fairly universal: (a) the four marks of courtly love are humility, courtesy, adultery and the religion of love; (b) the love is desire; (c) it is an ennobling and dynamic force; (d) it generates a cult of the beloved.

It will be found that, over a very long period, its ideals, and the attitudes towards women implied in them, have gradually influenced the changing conception of woman's position in society. Nowadays the nearest thing to the discussions in the courts of love are the advice columns in women's magazines. Several outstanding books have been written on the subject of courtly love including C. S. Lewis's *The Allegory of Love* (1936), A. F. Denomy's *The Heresy of Courtly Love* (1947), M. J. Valency's *In Praise of Love* (1958) and Peter Dronke's *Medieval Latin and the Rise of the European Love Lyric* (2 vols., 1965–6).

courtly makers A group of poets at Henry VIII's court who imported Italian and French poetic forms. The best known are Sir Thomas Wyatt, who wrote the first English sonnets (*q.v.*), and Henry Howard, Earl of Surrey, who introduced blank verse (*q.v.*). Much of the work of the court poets was published in Tottel's Miscellany (1557), a collection which had a considerable influence on Elizabethan writers.

Cowleyan ode An ode (*q.v.*) in which the stanzas or verse paragraphs are irregular in rhyme, line length and number of lines. It is named after Abraham Cowley (1618–67) and has been used a good many times since. Notable instances are: Dryden's *Song for St Cecilia's Day* and Wordsworth's *Intimations of Immortality*.

cradle books Books printed before 1501 are known by this name, or Latin *incunabula* 'swaddling clothes': G. *Wiegendrücker*.

craft cycle *See* MYSTERY PLAYS.

crambe Applied to unnecessary and disagreeable repetition. From Juvenal's phrase *crambe repetita* 'rehashed cabbage'.

crambo A versifying game. A word or a line of verse is given and then each player has to supply a rhyme or rhyming line. In dumb crambo the players are given a word rhyming with another word which is concealed on a piece of paper. The players 'act' out possible rhyming words until they find the right one. Crambo also denotes a bad rhyme. *See also* BOUTS-RIMES.

creacionismo An *avant-garde* (*q.v.*) movement which began *c.* 1916. Its founding luminary was the Spanish-born Chilean poet Vicente García Huidobro (1893–1948). Among his followers were Gerardo Diego (1896–?) and Juan Larrea (1895–?). When in Paris, Huidobro had some influence on French *avant-garde* writers such as Pierre Reverdy. Huidobro was a novelist and playwright as well as a poet, and to some extent influenced the development of modern concrete poetry (*q.v.*). He went in for typographical eccentricities in the manner of Apollinaire's *Caligrammes*. Reverdy was associated with cubism and surrealism (*qq.v.*) and founded the review *Nord-sud* (*c.* 1917). The 'creationists' were in favour of 'poetic' vocabulary, striking metaphors and the bizarre juxtaposition of images which did not so much reflect the natural order by any form of 'imitation' (*q.v.*) but, rather, conveyed a magical vision of creation. *See also* ULTRAISM.

crepuscolari The *poeti crepuscolari* ('twilight poets') were a group of Italian writers who flourished at the end of the 19th and the beginning of the 20th c. The term *crepuscolari* was first applied to Marino Moretti (1885–1979) by Giuseppe Borgese (1882–1952). However, the main five were Caesare Pascarella (1858–1940), Salvatore di Giacomo (1860–1934), Guido Gozzano (1883–1916), Corrado Govoni (1884–1965) and Sergio Corazzini (1886–1907). They were so called because their poetry was subdued, sombre and melancholy in tone, and the poets dwelt on the grim realities of life – not least the approach of death. An atmosphere of doom and helplessness pervaded much of their work, and two of them *did* die young.

cretic *See* AMPHIMACER.

crime novel This form of fiction had its origins in the 18th c. and, like the police procedural (*q.v.*), is a derivative of the detective story (*q.v.* for historical résumé). It is a very general term for a sub-genre concerned with crime (of many different kinds) in which police/detectives are likely to be involved and in which the emphasis is on the criminal (e.g. murderer, blackmailer, forger, kidnapper, thief, drug-smuggler, etc.) and criminal psychology. Often the identity of the criminal is known from the outset and the suspense and interest of the narrative depend on the psychological state of the criminal (e.g. fear, guilt, remorse) and what he or she does to evade the law and justice.

The pioneer of the modern crime novel was Francis Iles, whose real name was Anthony Cox (1893–1971) and who also wrote clever conventional detective stories under the name Anthony Berkeley. As Iles he revolutionized the detective story in *Malice Aforethought* (1931), in which the identity of the murderer is plain from the first sentence.

Since then, novels about crime, the underworld and criminal activities in general have proliferated – especially from the 1960s onwards. A large number of professional writers have devoted themselves to this form of fiction. Among the British practitioners some of the more prominent have been: John Bingham (1908–), who wrote *My Name is Michael Sibley* (1952) and *God's Defector* (1976); John Wainwright (1921–), author of *The Eye of the Beholder* (1980), *An Urge for Justice* (1981) and *Blind Brag* (1988); Colin Watson (1920–82), well known for his Inspector Parbright novels and who also wrote *Coffin, Scarcely Used* (1958), *Blue Murder* (1979) and *Plaster Sinners* (1980); Peter Dickinson (1927–), who wrote *The Glass-Sided Ants' Nest* (1968), *One Foot in the Grave* (1979) and *Perfect Gallows* (1988); Nicholas Freeling (1927–), author of *Criminal Conversation* (1965), *The Night Lords* (1978) and *Lady Macbeth* (1988); Ruth Rendell (1930–), who wrote *Judgement in Stone* (1977), *Master of the Moor* (1982) and *The Tree of Hands* (1985); Michael Kenyon (1931–), who wrote *May You Die in Ireland* (1965), *The Rapist* (1977) and *Zigzag* (1981); and Jessica Mann (1937–), author of *The Eighth Deadly Sin* (1976), *The Sting of Death* (1978) and *Funeral Sites* (1981).

The crime novel has also been very popular in America, where the influence of Raymond Chandler and Dashiell Hammett in their detective stories has been considerable. Scores of American writers have written copiously about crime of one sort and another, often very realistically in demotic and vivid language. As America is a country where crime flourishes on a huge scale there is an endless supply of real-life material (any of the big cities may have four to five hundred murders per year). Here there is space to mention only a handful of the better known authors. For example, James M. Cain (1892–1977), who remains famous for *The Postman Always Rings Twice* (1934); he also wrote *Serenade* (1937) and *Double Indemnity* (1943). W. R. Burnett (1899–) began his career as a writer of Westerns (*q.v.*) and became famous in 1929 with *Little Caesar*, a powerful novel about the underworld. Two other notable novels were *High Sierra* (1940) and *The Asphalt Jungle* (1949). John D. Macdonald (1916–) was extremely popular; three of his best known books are *The Deep Blue Goodbye* (1964), *A Purple Place for Dying* (1964) and *Darker than Amber* (1966). His contemporary Stanley Ellin (1916–) wrote a number of outstanding short stories about crime (collected in *The Speciality of the House*, 1979), and several novels, including *The Eighth Circle* (1958) and *Mirror, Mirror on the Wall* (1972). Mickey Spillane (1918–) has become very well known in Britain since the 1950s. Most of his books over-indulge in sex and gratuitous violence. Two rated highly were *I, the Jury* (1947) and *Kiss Me Deadly* (1952). In 1954, Ed McBain (1926–), well known for his police procedurals, published *The Blackboard Jungle* – a minor classic. Ross Thomas (1926–) explored social and political evils and corruption in such stories as *The Porkchoppers* (1972), *If You Can't Be Good* (1973) and *Chinaman's Chance* (1978). Patricia Highsmith (1921–), so long resident in Europe it is sometimes forgotten that she is American, has had a big following in Britain with her Ripley novels, which feature an amoral villain of the anti-hero (*q.v.*) type. Some of her best known books are *The Talented Mr Ripley* (1956), *Ripley Under Ground* (1971), *Ripley's Game* (1974) and *The Boy Who Followed Ripley* (1980). George V. Higgins (1939–) has published a number of distinguished crime novels, including *The Friends of Eddie Coyle* (1971), *Cogan's Trade* (1974) and *Kennedy for the Defense* (1980). Other Americans of note in this genre have been Kenneth Fearing (1902–61), William P. McGivern (1927–) and Gregory Macdonald (1937–). *See also* KRIMINALGESCHICHTE.

criollismo A literary movement in Venezuela and Colombia *c.* 1900 which encouraged the development of regional literature. Among the moving spirits were Tomas Carrasquilla (1858–1940), Blanco-Fombona (1874–1944) and Ricardo Güiraldes (1886–1927). *See also* COSTUMBRISMO.

crisis That point in a story or play at which the tension reaches a maximum and a resolution is imminent. There may, of course, be several crises, each preceding a climax (*q.v.*). In *Othello*, for instance, there is a crisis when Iago provokes Cassio to fight Roderigo, another when Othello is led to suspect his wife, a third when Othello accuses Desdemona of infidelity. Several other minor crises precede the murder of Desdemona. *See* DENOUEMENT.

criticism The art or science of literary criticism is devoted to the comparison and analysis, to the interpretation and evaluation of works of literature.

It begins with the Greeks, but little of their work has survived. Aristotle's *Poetics* is mostly devoted to drama; and Plato's theories of literature are scarcely literary criticism. From the Romans the major works are Horace's *Ars Poetica* (*c.* 19 BC) and the works on rhetoric (*q.v.*) composed by Cicero and Quintilian. The first important critical essay in the Christian era is Longinus's *On the Sublime*, and the first medieval critic of note was Dante who, in his *De Vulgari Eloquentia* (*c.* 1303–5), addressed himself to the problems of language appropriate to poetry.

The Renaissance writers and critics for the most part followed the Classical rules on the principle that the ancients were bound to have been right; but there were some attempts at originality. For example, Vida's *Poetica* (1527), a treatise on the art of poetry; du Bellay's *Deffense et Illustration* (1549); and Lope de Vega's *New Art of Making Comedies* (1609). In England there is little criticism of note until Puttenham's *The Arte of English Poesie* (1589) and Sidney's *Apologie for Poetrie* (1595), which is important because it is a detailed examination of the art of poetry and a discussion of the state of English poetry at the time.

For nearly a hundred years the major critical works to appear tended to reinforce the Classical tradition and rules (*q.v.*). Some of the main works were Ben Jonson's *Timber*: *Or Discoveries* (1640), Pierre Corneille's *Discours* (1660) and Boileau's *L'Art Poétique* (1673). With Dryden, however, in his *Essay of Dramatic Poesy* (1668) – not to mention his prefaces, dedications and prologues – we find a critic of judicious discrimination and open-mindedness whose critical essays are works of art in themselves. He, if anybody, showed the way to the proper function of criticism.

In the next century there was a very pronounced emphasis on following the rules in the creation of literature and a considerable emphasis on imitating the laws of nature. As Pope put it in *An Essay on Criticism* (1711):

> First follow Nature, and your judgment frame
> By her just standard, which is still the same;
> Unerring NATURE, still divinely bright,
> One clear, unchang'd, and universal light.

In the 18th c. G. B. Vico, the Italian critic and philosopher, was the pioneer of the historical approach to literature. Historicism, as it is called, completely changed, in the long run, critical methods. It enabled people to realize that the rules that held good for the

Classical writers do not necessarily hold good in a later age, and that there were not absolute principles and rules by which literature could be judged (which was Dr Johnson's point of view).

There was thus a reaction against Neoclassicism (*q.v.*), an increasing interest in literatures other than those of Greece and Rome, and a greater variety of opinions about literature, about the language to be used, and about the creative and imaginative faculties and processes of the writer. The new views found expression in Wordsworth's preface to the second edition of the *Lyrical Ballads* (1800), Coleridge's *Biographia Literaria* (1817), Shelley's *Defence of Poetry* (1820) – a reply to Peacock's ironical debunking in *The Four Ages of Poetry* (1820) – Poe's *The Poetic Principle* (1850) and *The Philosophy of Composition* (1846), and Matthew Arnold's *Essays in Criticism* (1865, 1888). The writings of Walter Pater on culture and art, especially *The Renaissance* (1873) and *Appreciations* (1889), had a profound influence on critical thinking.

By the second half of the 19th c. many different critical theories had begun to proliferate, as is clear from a study of the philosophy of aestheticism (*q.v.*), the doctrine of art for art's sake (*q.v.*) and the work of the symbolist poets. There were fewer rules of any kind as more and more writers experimented. At the same time the work of the best critics continued in the tradition and method of Vico. Sainte-Beuve, with his immense range of learning and his keen sense of critical and judicious detachment, was the supreme exponent of historicism.

Recent criticism has tended to be more and more closely analytical in the evaluation and interpretation of literature, as is evident in the achievements of major critics like M. H. Abrams, Eric Auerbach, Roland Barthes, Walter Benjamin, A. C. Bradley, Cleanth Brooks, R. S. Crane, Christopher Caudwell, T. S. Eliot, William Empson, Northrop Frye, T. E. Hulme, Arnold Kettle, Frank Kermode, G. Wilson Knight, F. R. Leavis, George Lukács, Ezra Pound, John Crowe Ransom, I. A. Richards, Alain Robbe-Grillet, Jean-Paul Sartre, Allen Tate, Lionel Trilling, Raymond Williams, Edmund Wilson, W. K. Wimsatt and Yvor Winters. *See* SYMBOL AND SYMBOLISM.

crossed rhyme Also known as interlaced rhyme, this occurs in long couplets (*q.v.*) – especially the hexameter (*q.v.*). Words in the middle of each line rhyme. Swinburne used the device successfully in *Hymn to Proserpine*, as these lines suggest:

Thou hast conquered, O pale Galilean; the world has
grown grey from Thy breath;
We have drunken of things Lethean, and fed on the
fullness of death.
Laurel is green for a season, and love is sweet for a day;
But love grows bitter with treason, and laurel outlives
not May.

See also LEONINE.

crown of sonnets A sequence of seven, so linked as to form a 'crown' or panegyric (*q.v.*) to the person concerned. The last line of each of the first six sonnets is the first of the succeeding one, and the last line of the seventh repeats the opening line of the first. The best known English example introduces Donne's *Holy Sonnets*. The crown is a prologue to the main sequence. The seven are named *La Corona*, *Annunciation*, *Nativitie*, *Temple*, *Crucifying*, *Resurrection* and *Ascension*. *See* SONNET; SONNET CYCLE.

crown poem That work which is awarded the bardic crown at an Eisteddfod (*q.v.*). *See also* CHAIR ODE.

cruelty, theatre of *See* THEATRE OF CRUELTY.

cuaderna vía (Sp 'quaternary way, quarternary manner') A four-line verse form containing fourteen syllables to the line. All the lines rhyme. The model for this form may be Latin Goliardic verse (*q.v.*). Never a courtly form, it was commonly used in the Middle Ages and it seems that it was employed for the very last time in a collection of poems titled *Rimada de Palacio* by the Chancellor Pero López de Ayala (1332–1407). They were probably composed *c.* 1385 when he was imprisoned (in an iron cage). *See also* MESTER DE CLERECIA; QUATERNARY FORM.

cubo-futurism The term for a movement in art and poetry which began in Russia just before the First World War and lasted through the early stages of the Bolshevik Revolution. It was to have some influence on the poetry of Vladimir Mayakovsky (1893–1930) and also on the practitioners of *zaum* (*q.v.*) and was part of the Futurist movement launched by Filippo Marinetti in Italy. The cubo-futurist poets tended to be 'iconoclastic' in attitude and published manifestos which advocated the rejection and abandonment of most, if not all, literary conventions. They were more interested in the possibilities of sound than of sense. *See also* DADAISM; EGO-FUTURISM; FUTURISM; PURE POETRY.

culteranismo In 17th c. Spain there came to a head a difference of practice and attitude between two schools of writing and poetry, conveniently known as '*culteranismo*' and '*conceptismo*' (*q.v.*). It is easier now to compile the names of the opposing teams than it would have been for some of the protagonists themselves. Though famous personalities were involved, this is not to say they were team leaders. It is therefore an over-simplification to say that it boiled down to Góngora versus Lope de Vega. In practice most of the propaganda was produced by others of less distinction, but sometimes of clearer aim and warmer feeling.

Góngora (1561–1627) began to write in a style which called for a knowledge of earlier literatures and their languages if his references, couched in refined and stylized terms, were to be appreciated or understood. Two outstanding examples were the *Soledades* and the *Fábula de Polifemo y Galatea*. The learned and elaborate language can be compared with that in the movement known as *la préciosité* (*q.v.*) in France. One of the elements of *culteranismo* which provoked opposition was its slavish imitation of Latin syntax. Among writers who were trying to reach a wide audience, such a tendency would have been suicidal. Lope de Vega, a natural enemy of such a tendency and regarded as the leader of the *conceptismo* movement, asserted that poetry should cost great trouble to the poet but little to the reader. *See* GONGORISM.

cultural code *See* CODE

cultures, the two In 1959 C. P. Snow delivered the Rede Lecture in Cambridge and in the course of it deplored the increasing gap between the humanities and technology, between the arts and science, the two cultures. This lecture caused a great deal of controversy.

cup-and-saucer drama A term applied to the plays of T. W. Robertson (1829–71) and his imitators. Robertson wrote plays in which he paid attention to realistic domestic detail, hence the slightly pejorative label. The six comedies that he had produced in 1865–70 (among the best were *Society*, 1865, *Ours*, 1866, and *Caste*, 1867) set standards for such realism that were to have a considerable influence on a revival of serious drama. *See also* COMEDY; DOMESTIC COMEDY.

cursus (L 'running') A term applied to the rhythm (*q.v.*) or pattern of prose. *See* CADENCE.

curtain raiser An entertainment, often of one act, which precedes the main part of the programme. They are rare now, but in the late 19th and early 20th c. were often used to divert audiences while late-comers arrived. In this way, the main programme would not be interrupted. *See* FARCE; ONE-ACT PLAY; QUART D'HEURE; SOTIE.

curtal sonnet Literally a sonnet (*q.v.*) cut short. Gerard Manley Hopkins used the term in his *Preface* to *Poems* (1918) to describe a curtailed form of sonnet of his invention. He reduced the number of lines from fourteen to ten, divided into two stanzas: one of six lines, the other of four – with a half line tail-piece. In *Poems* there are curtal sonnets called *Peace* and *Pied Beauty*. The latter is as follows:

> Glory be to God for dappled things –
>   For skies of couple-colour as a brinded cow;
>   For rose-moles all in stipple upon trout that swim;
> Fresh-firecoal chestnut-falls; finches' wings;
>   Landscape plotted and pieced – fold, fallow, and plough;
>   And áll trádes, their gear and tackle and trim.
>
> All things counter, original, spare, strange;
>   Whatever is fickle, freckled (who knows how?)
>   With swift, slow; sweet, sour; adazzle, dim;
> He fathers-forth whose beauty is past change:
>   Praise him.

See QUATRAIN; SESTET; TAIL-RHYME.

cyberpunk A term which denotes a sub-species of science fiction (*q.v.*). The word is a conflation of *cybernetics* and *punk*. *Punk* is a word of unknown origin and with a variety of meanings; *cybernetics* derives from Greek *kybernetes* ('a steersman') and denotes the comparative study of automatic communications and control in functions of living bodies and in mechanical electronic systems (such as computers). Cyberpunk stories and novels are usually set in the near future and depend considerably on contemporary technological and cultural references. The characters inhabit a world where no one is 'ordinary'; they are punks, space Rastas, computer jockeys and electronic drug addicts. Technology is important; hence artificial intelligences, laser, neon, synthetic music and so on. Among its better known practitioners are William Gibson, K. W. Jeter and Walter Jon Williams.

cycle A group of poems, stories or plays which are united by a central theme. The term 'epic cycle' was first used by the Alexandrine grammarians to describe a group of epic poems which, by *c.* 800 BC, had grown up in connection with the battle for Troy. The individual epics, in some cases fairly short ballads, were elaborated and eventually joined with others to form an epic cycle. The result we now know as Homer's *Iliad.*

This kind of accretive process has been repeated in many civilizations. Conceivably, quite a large number of the Old Testament stories were originally separate and gradually formed a more or less homogeneous unit. The same may well be true of stories about Buddha and other great religious leaders and rulers; and also the accounts of the lives of some saints. Legend and fact intermingle.

Old Irish epic poetry bears all the marks of cyclical structure. The Scandinavian, Arthurian and Charlemagne cycles are analogous. Russian *byliny* and *stariny* are also grouped about a particular hero or town. The South Slav *narodne pesme* (*q.v.*) – still part of living oral tradition (*q.v.*) – are similar, and form an outstanding example of the cycle. One should mention also the Albanian Geg *Mujo-Halil* cycle, and other Albanian cycles which survive in south-eastern Italy and are concerned with the exploits of the hero Skandarbeg.

Into the cyclic category may also be placed such collections of tales as Boccaccio's *Decameron* and Chaucer's *Canterbury Tales.* A series of lyrical poems may also form a cycle. For instance: Dante's *Vita Nuova*, Petrarch's *Canzoniere*, and Shakespeare's *Sonnets.*

Finally there are the cycles of the Mystery Plays (*q.v.*) which attempt an encyclopaedic dramatization of the Old and New Testaments. *See* BALLAD; CHRONICLE PLAY; EPIC; SONNET SEQUENCE.

cyhydedd hir A Welsh syllabic verse form. The octave (*q.v.*) stanza comprises two quatrains (*q.v.*) of four lines with five, five, five and four syllables respectively. The five-syllable lines rhyme with one another.

cyhydedd naw ban A Welsh syllabic verse form with a line of nine syllables. To form a couplet (*q.v.*) it must rhyme with another line of equal length.

cynghanedd A Welsh term which denotes sound correspondences peculiar to Welsh poetry, particularly alliteration (*q.v.*) and internal rhyme (*q.v.*). Gerard Manley Hopkins called such devices 'chimes'. *See also* AWDL.

cyrch a chwta A Welsh syllabic verse form. It comprises an octave (*q.v.*) stanza of six rhyming or consonating seven-syllable lines plus a couplet. The second line of the couplet rhymes with the first six lines, and the first line of the couplet cross-rhymes in the third, fourth or fifth syllable of the eighth line.

cywydd A Welsh metrical form developed by the 14th c. Welsh poet Dafydd ap Gwilym. It comprises rhyming couplets, each line being of seven syllables.

cywydd deuair hirion In Welsh prosody a light-rhyming seven-syllable couplet. The first line has a masculine ending and the second a feminine.

cywydd llosgyrnog A Welsh syllabic verse form. It comprises a sestet (*q.v.*) stanza whose syllable counts are eight, eight, seven, eight, eight and seven. The first two lines rhyme and cross-rhyme with the middle syllable of the third line, lines four and five rhyme and cross-rhyme with the middle syllable of the sixth line and the third and sixth lines rhyme with each other. *Rime couée* or tail-rhyme (*q.v.*) has a similar scheme.

D

dactyl (Gk 'finger') A metrical foot consisting of one stressed syllable followed by two unstressed ones: | ∪ ∪. Just like finger joints. Dactylics were often used in Classical verse, but not often by English poets until the 19th c. when Scott, Byron, Tennyson, Browning and Swinburne (among many others) experimented with them. Tennyson, for example, used them in his *Charge of the Light Brigade*. One of the best known instances of dactylic verse is Browning's *The Lost Leader*:

> Júst fŏr ă | hándfŭl ŏf | sílvĕr hĕ | léft ŭs,
> Júst fŏr ă | ríbănd tŏ | stíck ĭn hĭs | cóat –
> Fóund thĕ ŏne | gíft ŏf whĭch | fórtŭne bĕ | réft ŭs,
> Lóst ăll thĕ | óthĕrs shĕ | léts ŭs dĕ|vóte.

Dactylics are not unusual in light verse (*q.v.*), as in these 'Railway Dactyls' by G.D.:

> Hére wĕ gŏ | óff ŏn thĕ | 'Lóndŏn ănd | Bírmĭnghăm',
> Bíddĭng ă | diéu tŏ thĕ | fóggy̆ mĕ|trópŏlĭs!
> Stáyĭng ăt | hóme wĭth thĕ | dúmps ĭn cŏn|fírmĭng 'ĕm:–
> Mótiŏn ănd | mírth ăre ă | fílĭp tŏ | lífe.

The dactyl, like the trochee (*q.v.*), produces a falling rhythm (*q.v.*) and, as this is not the natural rhythm of English verse, poems composed entirely of dactylics are rare. But the dactyl, like the trochee, is often used in combination with other feet to provide counterpoint (*q.v.*) and to act as a substituted foot. *See also* ANAPAEST; ELEGIAC DISTICH; IAMB; PYRRHIC; RISING RHYTHM; SPONDEE; SUBSTITUTION.

dadaism (F *dada* 'hobby-horse') A nihilistic movement in art and literature started in Zurich in *c.* 1916 by a Rumanian, Tristan Tzara, an Alsatian, Hans Arp, and two Germans, Hugo Ball and Richard Huelsenbeck. The term was meant to signify everything and nothing, or total freedom, anti rules, ideals and traditions. Dadaism became popular in Paris immediately after the First World War. The basic word in the Dadaist's vocabulary was 'nothing'. In art and literature manifestations of this 'aesthetic' were mostly collage (*q.v.*) effects: the arrangement of unrelated objects and words in a random fashion. In England and America its influence is discernible in the poetry of Ezra Pound and T. S. Eliot and in the art of Ernst and Magritte. By 1921 dadaism as a movement was subsumed by surrealism (*q.v.*). However, its influence was detectable for many years. *See also* CUBO-FUTURISM; EXPRESSIONISM; ULTRAISM.

daina A type of folk poetry (*q.v.*) to be found among Lithuanians and Latvians. It is usually a four-line poem, though sometimes several are joined up to make a longer one. The meter is dactylic or trochaic and there is usually some rhyme. The verses are sung to the accompaniment of the *kanklys*, a harp. *See also* BALLAD; DUMY; FOLK LITERATURE; FOLKSONG; NARODNE PESME.

dämonisch A term used adjectivally of a daemon (or daimon) who is a spirit which occupies a middle place between the gods and men (e.g. the daemon or good genius of Socrates) and is associated with inspiration (*q.v.*). During the Romantic revival (*q.v.*) not a few writers (especially poets) ascribed their inspiration and energy to the operations of such a spirit that 'drove' them, and it might easily be destructive or self-destructive (hence the concept of a daemonic/demonic agency). In his autobiography (*q.v.*) *Dichtung und Wahrheit* (1811–33) Goethe suggests that *dämonisch* describes a kind of irrational phenomenon or power which controls or directs a person's destiny, as in the case of the eponymous hero in *Egmont* (1791).

danse macabre Also known as the Dance of Death. The etymology of the word *macabre* is obscure. So far as its form is concerned it might be a corruption of OF *Macabre – Maccabeus*. An example of 'Judas Macabre' has been found; and in the 15th c. the Dance of Death was called *Chorea Machabaeorum* in Latin, *Makkabeusdans* in Dutch. It may be that the original reference was to a miracle play in which the slaughter of the Maccabees under Antiochus Epiphanes was enacted. It seems likely that the first use of the word dates from 1376 when it appeared in a poem written by Jehan Le Fèvre called *Respit de la Mort*: 'Je fis de macabre la dance'.

Le Fèvre used it as a noun and after his time it was limited as an adjective in the phrase 'dance macabré'. Since the period of romanticism (*q.v.*) it has been freely used to designate 'une impression où se mélangent le funèbre et le grotesque', and an 'amalgame singulier de burlesque et de tragique'.

The Dance of Death (in art and literature) depicted a procession or dance in which the dead lead the living to the grave. It was a reminder of mortality, of the ubiquity of death and of the equality of all men in that state. It was also a reminder of the need for repentance. Apart from its moral and allegorical elements it was very often satirical in tone. The dead might be represented by a number of figures (usually skeletons) or by a single personification of death. The living were usually arranged in some kind of order of precedence – Pope, cardinal, archbishop; emperor, king, duke etc. – almost, in Johnson's fine phrase, in the 'cold gradations of decay'. Many different media were employed: verse, prose, manuscript illustrations, printed books, paintings on canvas, wood and stone, engravings on stone and metal, woodcuts, sculpture, tapestry, embroidery, stained glass and so on. Its many and various versions were also widespread geographically – chiefly in France, Spain, Germany, Switzerland, Italy, Istria and Britain – and were shaped and altered by numerous classes of people in a variety of social milieux: by printers, publishers, artists, merchants, friars, scribes, lay and church men.

The theme or subject was especially popular in the late Middle Ages and the 16th c. and the influence has continued to our own time. It appealed particularly to artists. The two major works were Holbein's engravings, and the pictures and verses in the cloisters of the church of the Holy Innocents in Paris. In Britain there survive the stone screen in the parish church of Newark-on-Trent and the paintings in Hexham Priory. On the continent the best known are at Lübeck, Basel, La Chaise Dieu, Kemaria and Beram. There is a curious absence of pictures in Spain but a multitude in Italy. In Germany and Switzerland especially there are many poems in block-books and on woodcuts and frescoes.

There is an early suggestion of the *danse macabre* in a late 12th c. poem, *Les Vers de la Mort* (*c.* 1195), written by Hélinand, a monk of Fiordmont, in which death is encouraged to travel about visiting different people in order to warn them that they must die. Other predecessors were the 12th c. *Débat du corps et de l'âme*, the 13th c. *Vado Mori* poems and the *Dit des Trois Mors et des Trois Vifs* (*c.* 1280) (a macabre tale of three living men being told by three dead men of their future decay), Chaucer's *Pardoner's Tale* (late 14th c.) and its analogues – all in the same *memento mori* tradition. In the following century there survive the *Ballo della morte* from Italy, Guyot Marchant's *Danse Macabre* (1485) and his *Danse Macabre des Femmes* (1486), the Spanish *Danza general de la muerte* (mid-15th c.), a Catalan *Dance of Death* translated from the French, and Lydgate's version in *The Falles of Princes* (*c.* 1430). The theme seems to have come to England via translations of the *danse macabre* verses in Paris. It is Lydgate who, with characteristic English laconicism, sums it up:

> The daunce of Machabree wherin is lively expressed and shewed the state of manne, and how he is called at uncertayne tymes by death, and when he thinketh least theron.

The motif (*q.v.*) of the dance is echoed in many *ubi sunt* (*q.v.*) poems, and we find macabre elements in the work of many writers: in the sombre tragedies of Webster and Tourneur, in the work of Poe, Baudelaire and Strindberg, and particularly in Espronceda's eerie poem *El Estudiante de Salamanca* (1839), whose Don Juan hero dances with a corpse.

The personification of death and the motif of the macabre is recurrent and appears to exercise a considerable fascination for writers and artists. Death is, as it were, presented as a kind of sardonic joke. Death is 'la Railleuse par excellence' 'variée à l'infini, mais toujours boufonne'. The skull's grin is the last mocking laugh at the doleful jest of life. Richard II sums it up in one of the speeches that Shakespeare gives him:

> for within the hollow crown
> That rounds the mortal temples of a king
> Keeps Death his court, and there the antick sits,
> Scoffing his state, and grinning at his pomp.

An outstanding modern variation on the traditional medieval idea of the dance of death was achieved in the National Theatre's spectacular version of the Wakefield Mysteries in 1985. *See also* BLACK COMEDY; CARPE DIEM; DIRGE; ELEGY; LAMENT.

danza prima Primitive Spanish folksongs of the early Middle Ages; then found in Galicia and still found in Asturias. They display repetitive forms of an unusual kind in that pairs of lines of identical wording, except for the last word, succeed one another to unfold a story; and each pair has a slight difference of assonance (*q.v.*) adhered to in pairs. *See also* COSSANTE.

dark comedy A term coined by J. L. Styan in the title of his book *The Dark Comedy* (1962). It denotes comedy which is tragic-comic in tone and form; plays in which laughter, grief, wretchedness and despair are intermingled. The plays of Chekhov (1860–1904) are outstanding examples. *See* BLACK COMEDY; TRAGI-COMEDY.

deachnadh mor An Irish syllabic verse form, similar to the *rannaigheacht* (*q.v.*), but the first and third lines are octosyllabic and the second and fourth lines are hexasyllabic. All line endings are in disyllabic words.

dead metaphor A metaphor which has been so often used that it has become lifeless and lost its figurative strength. In other words, a cliché (*q.v.*). There are some hundreds, possibly thousands, in the English language. For example: 'green with envy', 'the heart of the matter', 'top dog', 'to beat about the bush', 'pride of place', 'at one fell swoop'. *See also* IDIOM.

débat A form particularly popular in the 12th and 13th c. It was usually a kind of poetic contest (*q.v.*) in which some question of morality, politics or love was discussed. A typical *débat* began with an introduction of the matter to be discussed and/or a description of the circumstances. There followed the discussion which had some dramatic quality. At the end the issue was referred to a judge.

This form has a long history. There are some early instances in the plays of Aristophanes, especially *Frogs* and *Clouds*. The eclogues of Theocritus and Virgil contain pastoral contests of wit. This kind of debate survives into the 4th c. in the work of Calpurnius, Nemesianus and Vespa.

A well-known example of a debate on a love theme is the 12th c. *Altercatio Phyliddis et Florae*. There are a good many examples in Provençal and OF literature. A famous instance is the *Débat du corps et de l'âme* (12th c.). Later Villon wrote a *Débat du coeur et du corps*. In English literature the theme of the soul versus the body is found in OE literature and later. Probably the most noteworthy in England is the 13th c. debate of *The Owl and the Nightingale* ascribed to Nicholas of Guildford. The solemn owl and the gay nightingale represent the religious poet and the love poet. In the debate they discuss the benefits they confer on men.

Débat, in various forms, was an important influence in the early stages of the development of drama; probably as important an influence as the *exemplum* (*q.v.*) in the sermon (*q.v.*). The debate was especially concerned with the war between God and the Devil. In the 4th c. Prudentius represented the conflict of good and evil for the soul of man in *Psychomachia*. In the 12th c. Bernard of Clairvaux and Hugo of St Victor made the debate of the *Four Daughters of God* in which Mercy and Peace plead against Truth and Righteousness for Man's Soul (or Mansoul). It was not such a long step from this to more complex allegory (*q.v.*) and also to rudimentary psychological drama of the kind we find in the Mystery Plays (*q.v.*).

Notable *débat* works which influenced the development of drama were the 13th c. *Interludium de Clerico et Puella*; the *Ludus de Bellyale* (1471), based upon the treatise of Jacobus de Theramo called *Processus Belial* (1381); and the *Processus Sathanae* (1570–80), but this is almost certainly a much earlier work.

Various versions of the *Four Daughters of God* appear in the Mystery and Morality Plays (*qq.v.*). One should mention also what is generally regarded as the first secular play – namely, Medwall's *Fulgens and Lucrece* (late 15th c.) which is a dramatized *débat*. An interesting example of a metaphysical poem in *débat* form is Andrew Marvell's *A Dialogue between The Resolved Soul and Created Pleasure* (*c.* 1640).

Dramatic debate makes a re-appearance in the work of George Bernard Shaw; especially in *The Apple Cart* (1929) and *Man and Superman* (1901). *See also* AMOEBEAN VERSES; CHANSON A PERSONNAGES; DIALOGUE; DIT; FABLIAU; JEU PARTI; PASTORAL; PREGUNTA.

decadence The term usually describes a period of art or literature which, as compared with the excellence of a former age, is in decline. It has been applied to the Alexandrine period (300–30 BC), and to the period after the death of Augustus (AD 14). In modern times it is used of the late 19th c. symbolist movement in France, especially French poetry. The movement emphasized the autonomy of art, the need for sensationalism and melodrama, egocentricity, the bizarre, the artificial, art for art's sake (*q.v.*) and the superior 'outsider' position of the artist *vis-à-vis* society – particularly middle-class or bourgeois society. Much 'decadent' poetry was preoccupied with personal experience, self-analysis, perversity, elaborate and exotic sensations.

In France the 'high priest' of decadence was Baudelaire (about whom Gautier wrote one of the most perceptive analyses of decadence), and Baudelaire's *Les Fleurs du mal* (1857) was a sort of manifesto of the movement or cult. *Le Décadent* (1886–9) was the journal of the movement. Huysmans's novel *A rebours* (1884) was what Arthur Symons described as its 'breviary'. Des Esseintes, the hero, exemplifies the decadent figure who is consumed by *maladie fin de siècle*. He devotes his energy and intelligence to the replacement of the natural with the unnatural and artificial. His quest was for new and more bizarre sensations.

Other notable figures who showed allegiance to this aesthetic cult and spirit were Villiers de l'Isle-Adam, Rimbaud, Verlaine, and Laforgue. Disenchantment, world-weariness and ennui pervaded their work. Verlaine's remarks on the word decadent itself display the truth of the matter:

> Ce mot suppose . . . des pensées raffinées d'extrême civilisation, une haute culture littéraire, une âme capable d'intensives voluptés . . . Il est fait d'un mélange d'esprit charnel et de chair triste et de toutes les splendeurs violentes du Bas-Empire.

The preoccupation with decay and with ruins, with sadness and despair, was apparent much earlier in the Ossianic poetry of James Macpherson in the 1760s. Some would contend also that Leopardi, the great Italian lyric poet, was a decadent. The more morbid and flamboyant aspects of Poe's stories reveal a decadent element.

The cult did not catch on much in England, but the influences of the French movement are clear in the work of Oscar Wilde (for instance, *The Picture of Dorian Gray*, 1891), in Dowson's *Cynara*, and in various works by Rossetti, Swinburne and Aubrey Beardsley. Decadent verse was published in *The Yellow Book* (*q.v.*). Gilbert and Sullivan satirized decadence and the aesthetic movement in *Patience* (1881). *See* AESTHETICISM; ESPRIT DECADENT; SYMBOL AND SYMBOLISM.

decastich (Gk 'ten rows') A poem or stanza (*q.v.*) of ten lines.

decasyllable A line of verse of ten syllables. It seems to have first been used *c.* 1050 in France. It became an increasingly popular form and was used by Dante, Petrarch and Boccaccio. Chaucer's discovery of it is important because he worked out a five-stress line which became fundamental to the development of the sonnet, the Spenserian stanza, the heroic couplet and blank verse (*qq.v.*). In practice, often enough, a decasyllabic line has eleven syllables (occasionally nine) but the extra one is often negotiated by an elision (*q.v.*). This couplet from Pope's *Moral Essays* illustrates the two kinds of line:

> To observations which ourselves we make,
> We grow more partial for th'observer's sake.

décima A much used and classic Spanish stanza form. It consists of ten octosyllabic lines rhyming abbaaccddc.

decires A genre of Spanish poetry of the 15th c. The themes tended to be didactic, courtly or political, in contrast to the amorous themes of the *cantigas* and *canciones* (*qq.v.*).

deconstruction The term denotes a particular kind of practice in reading and, thereby, a method of criticism and mode of analytical inquiry. In her book *The Critical Difference* (1981), Barbara Johnson clarifies the term:

> Deconstruction is not synonymous with 'destruction', however. It is in fact much closer to the original meaning of the word 'analysis' itself, which etymologically means 'to undo' – a virtual synonym for 'to de-construct'. The deconstruction of a text does not proceed by random doubt or arbitrary subversion, but by the careful teasing out of *warring forces of signification within the text itself* [my italics]. If anything is destroyed in a deconstructive reading, it is not the text, but the claim to unequivocal domination of one mode of signifying over another. A deconstructive reading is a reading which analyses the specificity of a text's critical difference from itself.

One could say that while post-structuralism (*q.v.*) develops as a response to, and displacement of, structuralism (a European phenomenon largely), deconstruction focuses on rhetoric and reflexitivity (i.e. the self-referential aspects of language) in a way that the American New Critics (*see* NEW CRITICISM) had encouraged earlier in the century.

Deconstruction owes much to the theories of the French philosopher Jacques Derrida (1930–), whose essay *Structure, Sign and Play in the Discourse of the Human Sciences* (1966) – which he was to follow with his book *Of Grammatology* (1967) – began a new critical movement. Deconstruction, so far, has been the most influential feature of post-structuralism because it defines a new kind of reading practice which is a key application of post-structuralism.

Derrida shows that a text (any text – be it a polemic, a philosophical treatise, a poem, or, for that matter, an exercise in deconstructive criticism) can be read as saying something quite different from what it appears to be saying, and that it may read as carrying a plurality of significance or as saying many different things which are fundamentally at variance with, contradictory to and subversive of what may be (or may have been) seen by criticism as a single, stable 'meaning'. Thus, a text may 'betray' itself. A deconstructive criticism of a text reveals that there *is nothing except the text.* In *Of Grammatology* Derrida makes the now well-known axial proposition that this is so (his key words are 'il n'y a rien hors du texte', or, alternatively, 'il n'y a pas de hors-texte'). That is, one cannot evaluate, criticize or construe a meaning for a text by reference to anything external to it.

Derrida carries his logic still further to suggest that the language of any discourse is at variance with itself and, by so being, is capable of being read as yet another language. Thus, hypothetically, one may envisage an endless regression of dialectical interpretations and readings without any stable, essential meaning. In short, a text may possess so many different meanings that it cannot have A MEANING. There is no guaranteed essential meaning. An immediate deconstructive practice would be to question the foregoing sentence by asking what is meant by 'guaranteed', 'essential' and 'meaning' in that context.

The implications are that any form of traditional literary criticism which employs the practical tools of comparison and analysis patiently and attentively to elucidate meaning is a self-defeating practice since the rhetoric of both the literary text under analysis and literary criticism is inherently unstable.

The initial stage of Derrida's deconstructive theory is the contention that both speech and writing are signifying processes which lack 'presence'. Derrida destabilizes and displaces the traditional 'hierarchy' (he calls it a 'violent hierarchy') of speech over writing to suggest that speech can only ever be subject to the same instabilities as writing; that speech and writing are forms of one science of language, grammatology (*q.v.*). This is not a reversal of the priority, since Plato, of speech over writing but a displacement which produces a state of 'indeterminacy' (*q.v.*).

Derrida has devised a number of terms to isolate and clarify what he is driving at. He uses the term *supplément* (*q.v.*) to denote the unstable or indeterminate relationship between speech and writing. The French word *suppléer* means 'to take the place of' as well as 'to supplement', and it is his contention that writing both supplements *and* takes the place of speech, though this is by no means the only opposition to which *supplément* applies.

The inherent, subversive, self-contradictory and self-betraying elements in a text 'include' what is not in the text, what is outside the text (*dehors de texte*), what is not said. But despite the presence of what is absent, Derrida's dictum that 'il n'y a pas de hors-texte' must be seen as a *sine qua non* of deconstruction. The elements referred to above would 'include' assumptions and propositions. What is *not* said constitutes a 'gap', 'lacuna' or *aporia* (*q.v.*).

The rigorous probing and analysis of a text, the process of dismantling it or taking it apart, also reveals what Derrida refers to as 'dissemination' and 'trace' (*qq.v.*). The former is the scattering or dispersal of meaning; the latter is something that is absent in a sign (e.g. a signifier) but which, by virtue of the absence of its signified, suggests a nostalgia for 'self-presence'.

Derrida's deconstructive theory also involves the key distinction of *différance* (*q.v.*) and *différence*, which concerns the principle of the continuous (and endless) postponement or deferral of meaning.

Deconstructive theory among American critics has been much in Derrida's debt. Paul de Man's main collections of essays are *Blindness and Insight* (1971), *Allegories of Reading* (1979) and *The Resistance to Theory* (1986). Derrida and de Man met in 1966 and found that they were working on the same obscure text of Rousseau – *On the Origin of Languages* – but de Man worked for the most part independently of Derrida. De Man produced a famous critique (*The Rhetoric of Blindness*) of Derrida's early text *Of Grammatology*, in which he deconstructs Derrida's own reading of Rousseau. In *Blindness and Insight* de Man works out a complex theory that critics achieve insight at the cost of critical 'blindness'. In *Allegories of Reading* he attempts a deconstruction of figurative and rhetorical strategies in Rousseau, Nietzsche, Proust and Rilke, and contends that literary language is fundamentally self-reflexive rather than referential and that texts deconstruct themselves.

Other deconstructive theories have been elaborated by Geoffrey Hartman (e.g. *Saving the Text*, 1981, *Easy Pieces*, 1986) and Harold Bloom (e.g. *The Anxiety of Influence*, 1973, *A Map of Misreading*, 1975). In *The Critical Difference* Barbara Johnson analyses the networks of differences in both literary and critical texts, and deconstructs Roland Barthes's celebrated analysis of Balzac's *Sarrasine*, in which he applies the implications of his distinction between the readerly and the writerly text. Basically, Johnson shows that Barthes makes his 'writerly' analysis by making the story 'readerly' and that Barthes constructs castration as the meaning of the story in a way which *Sarrasine* refuses (i.e. Barthes constructs a version of the story which the story resists). *See* READERLY/WRITERLY.

decorum In literature, and especially in poetry, decorum is consistency with the canons of propriety (*q.v.*); a matter of behaviour on the part of the poet *qua* his poem, and therefore what is proper and becoming in the relationship between form and substance. Action, character, thought and language all need to be appropriate to each other. At its simplest, the grand and important theme (for instance that of *Paradise Lost*) is treated in a dignified and noble style; the humble or trivial (for example, Skelton's *The Tunning of Elynour Rumming*) in a lower manner.

Decorum was of considerable importance to Classical authors. Aristotle deals with it in *Poetics*; Cicero in *De Oratore*; Horace in *Ars Poetica.* What they said had wide influence during and after the Renaissance, though there were many who did not subscribe to their dictates.

Many Elizabethan plays, for example, show an awareness of certain rules of decorum. An obvious instance is *Much Ado About Nothing* (*c.* 1598–9). It being a comedy of manners (*q.v.*), all the comic passages, especially the badinage between Beatrice and Benedick, are written in colloquial dramatic prose; the romantic episodes and themes are always rendered in verse. As soon as Benedick and Beatrice realize they are in love, the emotional temperature rises and they speak in verse.

Decorum became of great importance towards the end of the 17th c. and during the 18th when Classical rules and tenets were revered. The use of correct language was of particular interest. For instance, Johnson observed that the words 'cow-keeper' and 'hog-herd' might not be used in our language; but he added that there were no finer words in the Greek language. Though the subject matter of 18th c. writers was often what they thought of as 'low', if not vulgar, they managed to dress it in appropriate language. Pope combines elegance, wit and grace with an almost brutal forcefulness and succeeds in writing of the crude, the corrupt and the repulsive without offending.

Wordsworth and Coleridge found the doctrines of Neo-classicism (*q.v.*) too restrictive; hence Wordsworth's attempt, as expressed in the Preface to *Lyrical Ballads*, to rebel against 'false refinement' and 'poetic diction' (*q.v.*).

Since then writers have always considered matters of literary decorum, though in a more flexible way. Dickens is a good example of a writer who adjusts his style to the needs of the moment. Fundamentally, most people have an awareness of the need to adjust their language to the occasion, whether they are writing or speaking. *See* AFFECTATION; CONVENTION; PERIPHRASIS; STYLE.

defamiliarization A concept and term introduced by Viktor Shklovsky (1893–?), an important member of the Russian School of Formalism (*q.v.*). It is a translation of the Russian *ostranenie* 'making strange'. To 'defamiliarize' is to make fresh, new, strange, different what is familiar and known. Through defamiliarization the writer modifies the reader's habitual perceptions by drawing attention to the artifice of the text. This is a matter of literary technique. What the reader notices is not the picture of reality that is being presented but the peculiarities of the writing itself. In his essay *Art as Technique* (1917) Shklovsky makes his point pretty clear:

> The purpose of art is to impart the sensation of things as they are perceived, and not as they are known. The technique of art is to make objects 'unfamiliar', to make forms difficult, to increase the difficulty of length and perception, because the process of perception is an aesthetic end in itself and must be prolonged. *Art is a way of experiencing the artfulness of an object; the object is not important.*

Linked with this is the idea of 'laying bare', or exposing, the techniques and devices by which a work of art is constructed. The classic example analysed by Shklovsky is Sterne's *Tristram Shandy* (1760–67). Russian Formalists tend to be interested in texts which are 'anti-realist'; hence they privilege *Tristram Shandy* or modernist works.

The concept of defamiliarization is closely connected with the concepts of foregrounding and literariness (*qq.v.*). *See also* DOMINANT; READERLY/WRITERLY; REFLEXIVE NOVEL.

defective foot A metrical foot lacking one or more unstressed syllables. In the line:

This is the forest primeval

one would expect a final dactyl (*q.v.*) but it ends with a trochee (*q.v.*). Only the purists would regard this kind of variation as a fault. *See* CATALEXIS.

definitio *See* HORISMUS.

definitive edition Either an author's own final text which he wishes to be regarded as the accepted version, or a work which is deemed to be 'the last word' on a subject. It may, for example, be the edition of a text, a biography or a work of reference.

deibhidhe An Irish syllabic/accentual verse form. It comprises a quatrain (*q.v.*) stanza rhyming in couplets (*q.v.*). In each line two words alliterate. There are at least two cross-rhymes between the third and fourth lines and each line has seven syllables.

denotation The most literal and limited meaning of a word, regardless of what one may feel about it or the suggestions and ideas it connotes. *Apartheid* denotes a certain form of political, social and racial régime. It *connotes* much more. *See* CONNOTATION; MEANING.

dénouement (F 'unknotting') It may be the event or events following the major climax (*q.v.*) of a plot, or the unravelling of a plot's complications at the end of a story or play. *See* CRISIS; DESENLACE; DISCOVERY.

de regimine principum (L 'concerning the rule of princes') A form of didactic literature of the discourse or treatise (*qq.v.*) kind which gives advice to rulers (e.g. kings, princes) on how to rule. There was a particularly large number of them in Portuguese and Spanish. However, easily the best known is Machiavelli's *Il principe* (1513).

descending rhythm *See* FALLING RHYTHM.

descort Either a synonym for the Provençal *lai* (*see* LAY), or a term for a poem whose stanzas are in different languages. Also a Galician verse form expressing the 'discord' felt by the poet when he is suffering the pangs of unrequited love. Line length and meter are variable.

desenlace (Sp 'untying, unlacing') Directly comparable both in original meaning and in usage with its virtual synonym in French, *dénouement* (*q.v.*).

desert island fiction A form of fiction in which a remote and 'uncivilized' island is used as the venue of the story and action. It has a particular attraction because it can be placed right outside the 'real' world and may be an image of the ideal, the unspoilt and the primitive. It appeals directly to the sense of adventure and exploratory instinct in most people (it also appeals to a certain atavistic nostalgia) and many a child must have thought at least once how splendid it would be to be shipwrecked on a desert island.

The publication of Defoe's *Robinson Crusoe* in 1719 marked the inception of a literary genre which has attained universal popularity. In France desert island stories came to be known as *Robinsonnades*; in Germany as *Robinsonaden*. In 1719 Defoe also published *The Farther Adventures of Robinson Crusoe*, and in the same year an imitation appeared, called *The Adventures and Surprising Deliverance of James Dubourdieu and his Wife from the Uninhabited Part of the Island of Paradise*. French and German editions of *Robinson Crusoe* came out in 1720, and since that time there have been 196 English editions, some 130 translations into two dozen different languages, about 120 adaptations and approximately 280 imitations (many of which have been translated).

The theme of Crusoe has appeared in numerous other works, of which some of the more notable are: *The Hermit, or . . . The Adventures of Mr Philip Quarll* (1727); Johann Schnabel's *Die Insel Felsenburg* (1731–43); Johann Campe's *Robinson der Jüngere* (1779–80); and the European classic *Der Schweizerische Robinson* by Wyss which was translated into English as *The Swiss Family Robinson* in 1814. The increasing popularity of children's books (*q.v.*) in the 19th c. produced a good many developments of the Crusoe theme, like J. Taylor's *The Young Islanders* (1841), Madame de Beaulieu's *Le Robinson de douze ans* (1824) and Jules Verne's *L'île mysterieuse* (1875). One should note several other works in the Wyss tradition; namely, Marryat's *Masterman Ready* (1841), R. M. Ballantyne's *The Coral Island* (1858) and his *Dog Crusoe* (1861), R. L. Stevenson's *Treasure Island* (1883), and, more recently, William Golding's *Lord of the Flies* (1954), a story which reverses the image of an unspoilt and semi-paradisal existence. By contrast Aldous Huxley depicted an utopian way of life in *Island* (1966). Related to this genre are Gerhart Hauptmann's *Die Insel der grossen Mutter*

(1924), Giraudoux's *Suzanne et le Pacifique* (1939) and Michel Tournier's *Vendredi* (1967). *See also* NOBLE SAVAGE; PRIMITIVISM; ROBINSONADE; UTOPIA.

detective story A form of fiction in which a mystery, often a murder, is solved by a detective. The traditional elements are an apparently insoluble crime, uncooperative or dim-witted police, the detective (often an amateur), who may be eccentric, the detective's confidant (*q.v.*), who helps to clarify the problems, a variety of suspects and carefully laid red herrings to put the reader off the scent, a suspect who appears guilty from circumstantial evidence, and a resolution, often startling and unsuspected, in which the detective reveals how he has found out the culprit. The good detective story displays impeccable logic and reasoning in its unravelling and, in the hands of the masters and mistresses of the form, is a very sophisticated and intelligent type of entertainment. Such a detective story differs from the crime novel and the police procedural (*qq.v.*), which are derivatives.

One of the very earliest examples of a novel which deals with crime and violence is Smollett's *The Adventures of Ferdinand Count Fathom* (1753), which was written in a mock-heroic style and in many ways anticipates the later Gothic novel (*q.v.*). Later in the 18th c. and during the first thirty to forty years of the 19th c. there was a growing interest in various kinds of crime and in violence and also in the psychology of the criminal. There are signs of this in the Gothic novel and also in the then nascent genres of the horror story and the ghost story (*qq.v.*). An early instance of a novel which deals with crime and its detection in some depth is William Godwin's remarkable story *The Adventures of Caleb Williams* (1794). Thirty-five years later Adolf Müllner published *Der Kaliber*, a detective story long since forgotten. And then, during the 1830s, there came something of a vogue for fiction in English which was concerned with violence and various kinds of crime. This sort of novel was later to be called Newgate fiction (*q.v.*). Two of the main writers were Bulwer Lytton and William Harrison Ainsworth. Meanwhile, in Germany there had developed a form of crime writing later described as *Kriminalgeschichte* (*q.v.*). In 1862 Hugo published *Les Misérables*. An important element in this is the pursuit of the hero Jean Valjean by the policeman Javert. The theme of the 'relationship' between criminal and detective is elaborated in some detail.

The so-called novel of sensation (*q.v.*), which was popular in the

1860s, was also concerned with crime, violence and murder. Thomas Hardy's first published novel, *Desperate Remedies* (1871), showed the influence of this sort of writing. Mrs Henry Wood's lurid and sensational novels of the 1860s (e.g. *Lord Oakburn's Daughters*, 1864, *Elster's Folly*, 1866, *Roland Yorke*, 1869) about, among other things, murder, theft and forgery, were forerunners of the modern detective story. The most outstanding work of fiction in the 19th c. to deal with crime and violence (and their detection) was Dostoievski's *Crime and Punishment* (1866). Raskolnikov is a double murderer and his apparent motive for both crimes is the urgent need for money. But, there are other more complex motives; for instance, his attempt to thwart his sister's marriage by stealing enough to make both himself and his family financially independent. The relationship between Raskolnikov and the policeman Porfiry is central to the narrative and the analysis of Raskolnikov's delusions (for example, his concept of himself as a benefactor to mankind).

It is generally accepted that the first detective story as a recognizable form in English was Edgar Allan Poe's *Murders in the Rue Morgue* (1841), which he soon followed with *The Purloined Letter* and *The Mystery of Marie Roget*. Poe also created a kind of prototype detective in the shape of Le Chevalier C. Auguste Dupin, a young gentleman of illustrious family, who was brilliant and eccentric. The first full-length detective novel in French was Emile Gaboriau's *Le Crime d'Orcival* (1867). This he followed with *L'Affaire Lerouge* (1868) and *Monsieur Lecoq* (1869). Gaboriau is important because he made his detective, Lecoq, a policeman and was a pioneer of the *roman policier* (*q.v.*). Fortuné du Boisgobey wrote stories similar to Gaboriau's and is chiefly remembered for his *Le Crime de L'Opéra* (1880).

The first English detective novel was Wilkie Collins's *The Moonstone* (1868). If we except the minor role of Bucket in Dickens's *Bleak House* (1853), then Collins's Serjeant Cuff is one of the very first detectives in English fiction. In 1887 the Australian Fergus Home published *Mystery of a Hansom Cab*, and in that same year Sherlock Holmes made his bow in *A Study in Scarlet* by Arthur Conan Doyle. In 1890 came *The Sign of Four* and the next year Doyle began to publish his short stories in *The Strand Magazine*. Two collections followed swiftly: *The Adventures of Sherlock Holmes* (1892) and *The Memoirs of Sherlock Holmes* (1894). The enormous popularity of the genre dates from this period. Doyle tried to kill off Holmes but was unsuccessful. He reappeared in *The Hound of the Baskervilles* (1902) and *The Valley of Fear* (1915), and in several collections of short stories: *The Return of Sherlock Holmes* (1905), *His Last Bow* (1917) and *The Case-Book of Sherlock Holmes* (1927).

What Poe had pioneered Doyle mastered completely. However, it should be added that, long before Poe, Voltaire had published *Zadig* (1747, 1749), a philosophical tale comparable with Johnson's *Rasselas* (1759), in which the eponymous philosopher hero solves problems of detection with a combination of observation and logic which even Holmes could hardly have improved on. In some ways, therefore, Voltaire must also be considered a pioneer.

The invention of Holmes and Dr Watson produced a cult and legend to which there has been no equal, and during Doyle's life the detective story proliferated in the most astonishing fashion. He soon had imitators, such as Arthur Morrison (1863–1945), who published *Martin Hewitt, Investigator* (1894), *Chronicles of Martin Hewitt* (1895) and *Hewitt: Third Series* (1896); and M. P. Shiel, who published some rather grotesque and melodramatic detective stories (and horror stories) in the collections *Prince Zaleski* (1895) and *Shapes in the Fire* (1896). Both these authors have been neglected. Others to be immediately influenced were L. T. Meade and Robert Eustace, who displayed the scientific method of inquiry in *The Sanctuary Club*.

The opening years of the 20th c. produced a range of stories not a few of which have become classics. For example, the work of R. Austin Freeman (1862–1943), who created Dr Thorndyke, the scientific investigator, and foresaw the possibilities of the so-called inverted detective story in which the reader knows who the murderer is. Freeman wrote *The Red Thumb-Mark* (1909), *Dr Thorndyke's Cases* (1909), *The Eye of Osiris* (1911), *The Singing Bone* (1912) and *The Cat's Eye* (1923). A. E. W. Mason (1865–1948) also came to the fore, with his Inspector Hanaud, and published *At the Villa Rose* (1910), which he followed later with *The House of the Arrow* (1924) and *The Prisoner in the Opal* (1928). In the same period G. K. Chesterton (1874–1936) began to write his Father Brown stories. *The Innocence of Father Brown* came out in 1911, and this was followed by *The Incredulity of Father Brown* and *The Secret of Father Brown*. In 1913 E. C. Bentley (1875–1956), who invented the clerihew (*q.v.*), published *Trent's Last Case*, which remains a classic. Much later (1936) he published *Trent's Own Case*.

In the early part of the century two French authors made notable contributions; namely, Gaston Leroux (1868–1927), who remains particularly well known for his *Le Mystère de la chambre jaune*

(1907), and Maurice Leblanc, who created Arsène Lupin and some of whose better known books are *Arsène Lupin* (1907), *Arsène Lupin contre Sherlock Holmes* (1908) and *Arsène Lupin, gentleman cabrioleur* (1914). Later, Georges Simenon's detective Maigret (*see* ROMAN POLICIER) was to become almost as famous as Sherlock Holmes.

The period between the world wars is usually regarded as the 'golden age' (*q.v.*) of the detective story. After the First World War a crime wave helped to stimulate a renewed interest in such fiction and there were numerous practitioners. By this stage generally acknowledged 'rules' had evolved, formulas which required logic and fair play on the part of the author. In his perface to the *Best Detective Stories of 1928–9* Monsignor Ronald Knox, an expert on the genre (though his own detective stories were of only average quality) composed a half-humorous 'Decalogue' which summarized the basic principles or code. The ideas was to present a mystery puzzle to be solved, and the reader was 'invited' to make use of the clues in order to reach a solution. The more expert writers (e.g. Freeman Wills Crofts, the master of timetables and alibis) became very refined in the elaboration of the puzzles. Thus it was a kind of intellectual exercise which could prove a challenge to the reader. It cannot be entirely coincidental that the crossword puzzle also achieved great popularity in this period. It was standard practice to create a particular detective (who might be a gentleman amateur such as Lord Peter Wimsey, or a policeman such as Inspector French), and many of the detectives became, like Holmes and Father Brown, more or less household names. Settings were often middle- to upper-class (e.g. country houses and Oxbridge colleges). Both setting and characterization were of secondary importance to plot, ingenuity and intellectual stimulus.

Not a few of the scores of writers (professionals and amateurs) were immensely prolific. J. S. Fletcher, for example, wrote 93; Patricia Wentworth, 65; E. C. R. Lorac, 48; Anthony Gilbert, 69 . . . And so on. Some kept going for fifty or more years, publishing at least one per year. Here there is space to mention only a few authors and a handful of their books: J. S. Fletcher (1863–1935) – *The Middle Temple Murder* (1919) and *The Charing Cross Murder* (1923); H. C. Bailey (1878–1961) – *The Sullen Sky Mystery* (1935), *Black Land, White Land* (1937); Patricia Wentworth (1878–1961) – *Pilgrim's Rest* (1946); Freeman Wills Crofts (1879–1957) – *The Cask* (1924), *Death of a Train* (1946); H. F. Heard (1889–1971) – *A Taste for Honey* (1941); Anthony

Berkeley (1893–1971) – *The Poisoned Chocolates Case* (1929), *Trail and Error* (1937); Josephine Tey (1897–1952) – *The Franchise Affair* (1948), *Daughter of Time* (1951); E. C. R. Lorac (1894–1958) – *The Dog It Was That Died* (1952); C. H. B. Kitchin (1895–1967) – *Death of My Aunt* (1929), *Death of My Uncle* (1939); Anthony Gilbert (pseudonym of Lucy Malleson, 1899–1973) – *The Visitor* (1967), *Death Wears a Mask* (1970).

All the above were born in the 19th c. Anthony Berkeley (whose real name was Cox) also wrote as Francis Iles and under that name is of particular importance as a pioneer of the inverted detective story or crime novel in which the identity of the criminal is known from the outset. His *Malice Aforethought* (1931) and *Before the Fact* (1932) were key works in this respect.

Also born in the 19th c. were three of that quartet of women who came to be known as the 'Big Four': namely, Agatha Christie (1890–1976), Dorothy L. Sayers (1893–1957), Ngaio Marsh (1899–1982) and Margery Allingham (1904–66). All four were dominant figures between the wars and continued to perfect their techniques and adapt to changes of taste and readership until late in life.

Agatha Christie is said to have sold more books than any other writer in any field except for Shakespeare and the authors of the Bible. She wrote over eighty books and is beyond doubt the most famous detective novelist of the 20th c. Her first novel, *The Mysterious Affair at Styles* (1920), introduced the Belgian private detective Hercule Poirot, whose career lasted through many books to *Curtain* (1975). *The Murder at the Vicarage* (1930) presented Miss Marple, who also had a long career, ending with *Sleeping Murder* (1976). Among Dame Agatha's most famous books are: *The Murder of Roger Ackroyd* (1926), *Peril at End House* (1932), *Lord Edgeware Dies* (1933), *Murder on the Orient Express* (1934), *Why Didn't They Ask Evans?* (1934), *The ABC Murders* (1936) and *Ten Little Niggers* (1939).

Dorothy L. Sayers was less prolific and all her main detectective stories were written between the wars: *Whose Body?* (1923), *Clouds of Witness* (1926), *Unnatural Death* (1927), *The Unpleasantness at the Bellona Club* (1928), *Strong Poison* (1930), *The Five Red Herrings* (1931), *Have His Carcase* (1932), *Murder Must Advertise* (1932) and *The Nine Tailors* (1934). Her famous detective was Lord Peter Wimsey.

Dame Ngaio Marsh (a New Zealander), whose detective is Superintendent Alleyn of the Yard, published her first novel, *A Man Lay Dead*, in 1934. Other notable books were *Artists in Crime*

(1938), *Died in the Wool* (1945), *Opening Night* (1951), *Killer Dolphin* (1966) and *Black as He's Painted* (1974). Margery Allingham, who created the aristocratic Albert Campion as her detective, was also prolific between the wars, writing *The Crime at Black Dudley* (1929), *Mystery Mile* (1930), *Look to the Lady* (1931), *Police at the Funeral* (1931), *Sweet Danger* (1933), *Death of a Ghost* (1934), *Flowers for the Judge* (1936), *Dancers in Mourning* (1937), *The Case of the Late Pig* (1937), plus, later, *More Work for the Undertaker* (1949), *The Tiger in the Smoke* (1952) and *The Beckoning Lady* (1955).

Three other famous exponents of the genre who made their names in the 1930s are: Nicholas Blake (pseudonym of C. Day Lewis, 1904–72), who wrote *A Question of Proof* (1935) and *The Best Must Die* (1938); John Dickson Carr (1905–77), who specialized in locked-room mysteries and wrote *Three Coffins* (1935), *The Burning Court* (1937) and, later, *The Devil in Velvet* (1951); and Michael Innes (pseudonym of J. I. M. Stewart, 1906–), who wrote *Death at the President's Lodging* (1936), *Hamlet, Revenge!* (1937), *Lament for a Maker* (1938) and *Stop Press* (1939). Later he diversified with a range of adventure and pursuit novels. These writers also invented detectives who became well known: Blake's was Nigel Strangeways (based on W. H. Auden), Carr's was Dr Gideon Fell, Innes's was Inspector Appleby.

Since the 1950s many other detective-story writers have come to the fore and there is no foreseeable abatement of the 'crime ration'. Some (e.g. Elizabeth Ferrars, Michael Gilbert, P. D. James, H. R. F. Keating and Ellis Peters) have kept more or less to the established classic formulas with modifications and developments (including rather more stress on characterization and social comment); others have been influenced by the American school of detective fiction (see below) and have experimented freely, also being influenced by related genres such as the thriller (*q.v.*), the crime novel and the police procedural. There follow a handful of these (plus a few titles) who have made a name in the genre in thirty-odd years: Elizabeth Ferrars (1907–) – *I, Said the Fly* (1945), *Enough to Kill A Horse* (1955), *Witness Before the Fact* (1979), *Experiment with Death* (1981); Lionel Black (1910–80) – *Death Has Green Fingers* (1971); Michael Gilbert (1912–) – *Smallbone Deceased* (1950), *Flashpoint* (1974); Julian Symons (1912–) – *The Colour of Murder* (1957), *The End of Solomon Grundy* (1964), *The Players and the Game* (1972); Ellis Peters (1913–) – *Death and the Joyful Woman* (1961), *A Morbid Taste for Bones* (1977), *Monk's Hood* (1980), *The Kentish*

Manor Murders (1988); P. D. James (1920–) – *An Unsuitable Job for a Woman* (1972), *The Black Tower* (1975), *Innocent Blood* (1980), *A Taste for Death* (1986); Edmund Crispin (1921–78) – *The Moving Toyshop* (1946), *Love Lies Bleeding* (1948), *The Glimpses of the Moon* (1977); Alan Hunter (1922–) – *Gently Instrumental* (1977), *Fields of Heather* (1981); Margaret Yorke (1924–) – *No Medals for the Major* (1974), *The Cost of Silence* (1977), *The Hand of Death* (1981); H. R. F. Keating (1926–) – *A Rush on the Ultimate* (1961), *Inspector Ghote Trusts the Heart* (1972), *A Remarkable Case of Burglary* (1975); Colin Dexter (1930–) – *Service for All the Dead* (1979), *The Dead of Jericho* (1981); June Thomson (1930–) – *A Question of Identity* (1977), *Alibi in Time* (1980), *Shadow of a Doubt* (1981); Reginald Hill (1936–) – *A Fairly Dangerous Thing* (1972), *Ruling Passion* (1973), *A Pinch of Snuff* (1978); Simon Brett (1945–) – *The Dead Side of the Mike* (1980), *Murder Unprompted* (1982), *What Bloody Man is That?* (1987).

In America the detective story has taken rather a different course. Historically, it began with two women. Anna Katherine Green (1846–1935) was the first woman in America to write a detective story: *The Leavensworth Case* (1878), a mystery classic. There were a number of others, including *The Step on the Stair* (1923). Mary Rinehart (1876–1958) was a dominant figure in the genre and is still regarded as the leading woman. She began with conventional detective stories and gradually developed into a novelist. Two of her earliest books were *The Circular Staircase* (1908) and *The Man in Lower Ten* (1909). She was prolific in the genre of mystery and murder cases. Two of her later successful books were *The Wall* (1938) and *The Yellow Room* (1945). Historically, the next most notable writer was S. S. Van Dine, who modelled his detective Philo Vance on Lord Peter Wimsey. His first detective story of merit was *The Benson Murder Case* (1926), which he followed with *The Canary Murder Case* (1927), *The Greene Murder Case* (1928) and *The Bishop Murder Case* (1929). His stories, which gave a detailed picture of New York life, were often based on actual murders and were often very nearly *romans à clef* (*see* LIVRE A CLEF).

Up until *c.* 1920 writers took their models and conventions primarily from Britain. By this stage there was already a vast accumulation of detective fiction. It is said that by that date Van Dine had collected and read some two thousand detective stories. The specifically American story was soon to come, first in the pulp (*q.v.*) magazines. In 1920 H. L. Mencken and George Nathan founded *The Black Mask* magazine, which became very popular and attracted many contributors. Through it was born the so-called hard-boiled school of American detective fiction, which featured 'hard-bitten' detectives or 'dicks'. The prototype was Race Williams, tough, ruthless and quick on the draw: the invention of Carroll John Daly (1889–1958).

Other authors wrote similar stories about comparable detectives in the pulps. In the same period Ellery Queen began to publish. Queen was the pseudonym of two men: Frederic Dannay (1905–) and Manfred B. Lee (1905–71). They were prolific and produced some well-known novels such as *The Roman Hat Mystery* (1929), later followed by *The Dutch Shoe Mystery* (1931), *Calamity Town* (1942) and *On the Eighth Day* (1965). In 1941 Ellery Queen's *Mystery Magazine* was founded.

The outstanding pioneers of the American detective story were Raymond Chandler (1888–1959) and Dashiell Hammett (1894–1961). Chandler invented the famous detective Philip Marlowe, and his first (and most distinguished novel) was *The Big Sleep* (1939). This he followed with *Farewell, My Lovely* (1940), *The High Window* (1942), *The Lady in the Lake* (1943), *The Little Sister* (1949), *The Long Good-Bye* (1953) and *Playback* (1958). There were several collections of his short stories. Hammett wrote only five novels, plus many short stories in which the central character is the private eye called the Continental Op. He remains famous for the novels, which were of high quality: namely, *Red Harvest* (1929), *The Dain Curse* (1929), *The Maltese Falcon* (1930), *The Glass Key* (1931) and *The Thin Man* (1934).

Their principal successor was Ross Macdonald (1915–), author of *The Way Some People Die* (1951), *The Ivory Grin* (1952), *The Barbarous Coast* (1956), *The Galton Case* (1959), *The Goodbye Look* (1969), *The Underground Man* (1971) and *Sleeping Beauty* (1973). *The Goodbye Look* made him particularly famous and led people to regard him as not just a writer of excellent detective stories but a major American novelist.

Other Americans of distinction are: Robert B. Parker, who invented the private eye Spenser and two of whose best books are *The Godwulf Manuscript* (1973) and *Promised Land* (1976); Roger L. Simon, who wrote *The Big Fix* (1973); and Joseph Hansen, whose private-eye investigator is a homosexual named Brandstetter and who wrote *Fadeout* (1970), *The Man Everybody Was Afraid Of* (1978), and *Skinflick* (1979). Others who should be mentioned are Erle Stanley Gardner (inventor of Perry Mason), who was as prolific as Agatha Christie, and Elmore Leonard.

detractio *See* ECLIPSIS.

deus ex machina (L 'god out of the machine') In Greek drama a god was lowered on to the stage by a *mēchanē* so that he could get the hero out of difficulties or untangle the plot. Euripides used it a good deal. Sophocles and Aeschylus avoided it. Bertolt Brecht parodied the abuse of the device at the end of his *Threepenny Opera.* Today this phrase is applied to any unanticipated intervener who resolves a difficult situation, in any literary genre.

deuteragonist In Greek drama, a second actor – often the same as the antagonist (*q.v.*). *See* PROTAGONIST.

Deutsches Theater A famous and very important Berlin theatre founded in 1893. It is particularly associated with Max Reinhardt (1873–1943), who developed many techniques in the use of stage devices, machinery, etc., and who had a powerful influence on presentation and performance in general. In 1933 the Nazis took it over and in 1945 it became the main theatre in the Soviet sector of Berlin. Brecht's Berliner Ensemble (*q.v.*) developed from it.

diachronic/synchronic (Gk 'through/across time' and 'together time') A term coined *c.* 1913 by Ferdinand de Saussure (1857–1913). A diachronic approach to the study of a language (or languages) involves an examination of its origins, development, history and change. In contrast, the synchronic approach entails the study of a linguistic system in a particular state, without reference to time. The importance of a synchronic approach to an understanding of language lies in the fact that for Saussure each sign has no properties other than the specific relational ones which define it within its own synchronic system. *See* SIGNIFIER/SIGNIFIED.

diacope (Gk 'cutting through') The separation of a compound word. For instance: *never the less*; *what so ever.*

diacritic A sign under or above a letter to distinguish different values or sounds. For example: è, é, ê, ç, ö, ž.

diaeresis (Gk 'taking apart') A sign put over the second of two vowels to indicate that they are pronounced separately. For example: noël.

dialect A language or manner of speaking peculiar to an individual or class or region. Usually it belongs to a region, like the West Riding or East Anglia. A dialect differs from the standard language of a country, in some cases very considerably. Greek, German and Sicilian dialects, for instance, show great variations from the standard.

A good deal of literature is in dialect, especially that created in the earlier stages of a country's civilization. As far as England is concerned, all English medieval verse is in dialect. For example: Robert Mannyng's *Handlyng Synne* (North East Midland or Lincolnshire); *Sir Orfeo* (South West); *Ayenbite of Inwyt* (Kentish); *Sir Gawain and the Green Knight* (West Midland or Lancashire or Cheshire); *The Pearl* (West Midland); Langland's *Piers Plowman* (South Midland); Sir John Mandeville's *Travels* (South East Midland); not to mention many of the medieval Mystery Plays (*q.v.*) and romances (*q.v.*).

Chaucer (who wrote in the East Midland dialect, and thus helped to establish it as the vernacular of educated people) uses words from other dialects quite often; sometimes to suggest local characteristics, sometimes to secure a rhyme.

Since the 16th c., dialect in writing has been used less and less because of the development of Standard English. Scottish poetry has been the most conservative and retentive of dialect forms, as can be seen by comparing the work of Henryson and Dunbar with that of Burns and Edwin Muir. Burns was easily at his best when using the Ayrshire dialect. William Barnes is probably the most distinguished example of an English dialect poet since the 14th c. Most of his *Poems of Rural Life* (in three series, 1844, 1859, 1863) are in the Dorset dialect. Thomas Hardy also used the dialect successfully in *Wessex Poems and Other Verses.* Tennyson experimented with it in *Northern Farmer – Old Style.* James Russell Lowell's *Bigelow Papers* rather comically take off New England rural speech; and, if cockney is accounted a dialect, then Kipling's *Barrack-room Ballads* provide good examples of its use. A large number of novelists have used dialect forms, particularly to give verisimilitude (*q.v.*) to dialogue. Dickens, George Eliot, Thomas Hardy and D. H. Lawrence are notable instances. *See also* SLANG; VERNACULAR.

dialectic A method of philosophical inquiry and reasoning. Plato's Socratic *Dialogues* are exercises in dialectic through question and answer analysis.

The term may also be applied to the ideas, logic and reasoning which run through and hold together a work, or works, of literature. We may refer, for instance, to the dialectic of Donne's love poems, or of Coleridge's *Biographia Literaria* or of Aldous Huxley's essays or of Sartre's novels. *See also* ARGUMENT.

dialectical theatre *See* EPIC THEATRE.

Dialektdichtung German literature composed either wholly or partly in dialect. There was much of it during the 19th c. and there has been a good deal during the 20th c. An early example of a collection of dialect poetry is *Alemannische Gedichte* (1803). Some five hundred writers have used the High German dialect in their works, and twenty or more the Low German. *See also* VOLKSSTUCK.

dialogic/monologic Terms used by the Soviet critic Mikhail Bakhtin (1895–1975) in his discussions of language and discourse in literature in which he examines the different 'voices' and suggests how the use of discourse in, for example, a novel may influence and, in a sense, 'disrupt' the authority of a single voice. In his book *Problems of Dostoievski's Poetics* (1929) he makes a contrast between Dostoievski's novels and Tolstoy's. In his view Dostoievski's novels are in the dialogic (or polyphonic) form which allows characters to speak 'in their own voices', as it were. In Bakhtin's words, they are liberated to speak 'a plurality of independent and unmerged voices and consciousness, a genuine polyphony of fully valid voices . . .' which are not subject to the authoritative control of the author. By contrast, characters in Tolstoy's novels *are* subject to such control. However, Bakhtin's distinction does not imply that characters are necessarily differentiated by an idiosyncratic style of speech or by their idiolect (*q.v.*). In fact, Tolstoy's characters (e.g. in *War and Peace*) are more easily distinguishable in this respect than are Dostoievski's (e.g. in *The Possessed*). Bahktin claims that his approach in this theory is translinguistic rather than linguistic. In an essay published in translation in *The Dialogic Imagination* (1981) he elaborates his earlier opinions and avers that the dialogic/polyphonic form tends to be typical of the novel. *See* CARNIVALIZATION/CARNIVALESQUE.

dialogue Two basic meanings may be distinguished: (a) the speech of characters in any kind of narrative, story or play; (b) a literary genre in which 'characters' discuss a subject at length.

Of the latter, the earliest examples are believed to be the mimes of Sophron of Syracuse (*c.* 430 BC), but only fragments survive. To the 4th BC belong Plato's Socratic *Dialogues*, which are philosophical debates or dramas which employ the heuristic and dialectical method of question and answer. These are supreme examples of dialogue. Aristotle used the form for more specifically didactic purposes. Lucian's Greek *Dialogues of the Dead* (2nd c. AD) were modelled on Plato's, but Lucian used dialogue for comic and satirical ends and as a form of entertainment (rather as Plato did in *The Symposium*). Plato's method was imitated in the Renaissance by Juan de Valdes and Tasso, and Lucian's in the 17th and 18th c. by Fontenelle and Fénelon.

Notable instances in English of dialogues are: Thomas Starkey's *A Dialogue between Reginald Pole and Thomas Lupset* (*c.* 1533–6); Dryden's *Essay of Dramatic Poesy* (1668); Hume's *Dialogues concerning Natural Religion* (1779); Landor's *Imaginary Conversations* (1824–9), followed by his *Imaginary Conversations of Greeks and Romans* (1853); and Oscar Wilde's *The Critic as Artist* (1891). Shaw used the form dramatically in *The Apple Cart* (1929). An interesting minor example of a Platonic dialogue is that by Gerard Manley Hopkins: *On the Origin of Beauty* (1865).

In France the Platonic form was revived by Valéry and his Socratic debates are generally thought to be outstanding for their structure and lucidity. The two works were: *L'Ame et la danse* and *Eupalinos ou l'Architecte* (1923). *See also* DEBAT.

dialysis (Gk 'dismembering') The term denotes a method of analysis, argument or inquiry by which all the possible reasons for or against something are put forward and then disposed of rationally. *See also* DEBAT; DIALECTIC; DIALOGUE.

diary and journal Diaries and journals can be roughly divided into two categories: the intimate and the anecdotal. Examples of the first are Swift's *Journal to Stella*, the journals of Benjamin Haydon, Amiel, Shelley, Mary Godwin, Constant, Tolstoy and André Gide. Into the second category come Pepys's *Diary*, Evelyn's *Journal*, Boswell's *Journal of a Tour to the Hebrides*, and the diaries of Charles Greville and Thomas Creevey.

It seems that keeping a diary became habitual in the 17th c., though one may assume that there are similar records from earlier times which have been lost; and there are a few which are extant from the 16th c., like the diary kept by King Edward VI as a boy.

Sir William Dugdale (1605–86), historian and topographer, kept a journal of great interest. Other minor English diarists of the 17th c. were Edward Lake, Henry Teonge and Roger Lowe. Late in that century Celia Fiennes began a diary (*c.* 1685) which she finished in approximately 1703 (parts of which were first published by Southey in 1812). But the two great 17th c. diarists (by many considered the greatest of all) were John Evelyn (1620–1706) and Samuel Pepys (1633–1703). Evelyn's *Journal* covers much of his life but was not published until 1818. Pepys's diary, which also covers a long period, was written in a cipher which was not deciphered until 1825, and not published in its entirety until 1893–9.

Many diaries and journals survive from the 18th c., a period when women kept them regularly. Some of the more notable female diarists were Mary, Countess Cooper (1685–1724), Elizabeth Byrom (1722–1801), Fanny Burney (1752–1840), Lady Mary Coke (1756–1829), Mrs Lybbe Powys (1756–1808). From the 18th c., too, dates one of the most agreeable and interesting diaries in English literature – Parson Woodforde's. Titled *The Diary of a Country Parson*, it was published in five volumes (1924–31). It gives memorable pictures of life in college and on a country parish. Preeminent in this period are Fielding's *Journal of a Voyage to Lisbon* (1755), Swift's *Journal to Stella* (1766, 1768) and Boswell's *Journal of a Tour to the Hebrides* (1785), plus his very detailed accounts of his travels published in many volumes this century. A curiosity of the 18th c. is Defoe's *A Journal of the Plague Year* (1722), an historical reconstruction of the Great Plague of London 1664–5.

From the end of the 18th c. and throughout the 19th we find many other examples of diaries. Again, some of the best were kept by women; for instance: Lady Holland (1770–1845), Mary Frampton (1773–1846), Lady Charlotte Bury (1775–1861), Ellen Weeton (1776–1850), Elizabeth Fry (1780–1845), Caroline Fox (1819–71) and Margaret Shore (1819–39). These are works of minor importance.

From near the end of the 18th c. and for many years, Dorothy Wordsworth kept detailed diaries and journals which tell us much about Wordsworth. The separate works are: *The Alfoxden Journal* (1798); the *Journal of a Visit to Hamburgh* and *A Journey from Hamburgh to Goslar* (1798); the *Grasmere Journal* (1800–03); *Recollections of a Journey made in Scotland* (1803); *Journal of a Mountain Ramble by Dorothy and William Wordsworth* (1805); *Journal of a Tour on the Continent* (1820); *A Tour in Scotland* (1822); and *A Tour in the Isle of Man* (1828). The complete journals were published in 1941.

Two other important women published diaries in the 19th c., namely George Eliot and Queen Victoria. The Queen's contribution was *Leaves from the Journal of Our Life in the Highlands* (1862), and *More Leaves* (1883). George Eliot's *Journals* came out in 1885.

Diaries and journals by men of note in the 19th c. are numerous. Here there is a space to mention only a few of the more remarkable ones, like the journal of Benjamin Haydon (1786–1846), the painter, whose records were published as an autobiography in 1853. Of greater importance, especially from the point of view of the biographer and the social historian, are the diaries of Creevey and Greville. Thomas Creevey (1768–1838) kept extensive diaries which were published as the *Creevey Papers* in 1903. Charles Greville (1794–1865) had published three series of 'Greville Memoirs'. The first (1874) covered the reigns of George IV and William IV; the second (1885) covered the years 1837–52; and the third (1887) covered the period 1852–60. Lord Byron also kept copious journals. In addition to these one should mention a work of great charm and interest, the diaries of the clergyman Francis Kilvert (1840–79) which were edited by William Plomer and published in 1938. At the very end of the 19th c. George and Weedon Grossmith published the novel *Diary of a Nobody* (1894), a minor classic. It is a record of Charles Pooter, an assistant in a mercantile business towards the end of the 19th c., and is an unpretentious and immensely readable account of social, domestic and business problems.

Most of the works mentioned have not been by poets, novelists or dramatists, though some have been the records of what may be called occasional writers. There are, however, a large number of works which are part diary, part journal and part notebook. Some of the more valuable and interesting examples are: Shelley's *Notebooks* (not published until 1911); Samuel Butler's *Notebooks* (1912); W. N. P. Barbellion's *The Journal of a Disappointed Man* (1919); the *Journal* of Katherine Mansfield (1927); C. E. Montague's *A Writer's Notes on his Trade* (1930); Arnold Bennett's *Journals* (1933–4), a remarkable work in which Bennett kept a detailed record almost daily from 1896 until his death in 1931; and Somerset Maugham's *A Writer's Notebook* (1949).

Sometimes authors keep a journal of the creation of a book. An interesting recent example in English literature is Graham Greene's *In Search of a Character* (1962). This is a short journal of his travels in the Congo and contains the basis of his novel *A Burnt-Out Case* (1961).

In France the habit (especially among writers) of keeping diaries, journals and notebooks is deeply engrained. Here there is space to mention only a few instances. French writers, exhibiting a certain Gallic thrift, have a predilection for the *journal intime*. Among the more famous are: Constant's *Journal Intime* (1895, 1952) and his *Cahier Rouge* (1907); Amiel's *Journal Intime* which he kept for thirty-odd years from 1847; *Le Journal des Goncourts*, kept by the Goncourt brothers from 1851 to 1870, and thereafter kept by Edmond, the survivor; André Gide's *Journal* which he started in 1885 and was still adding to in 1947. Among the many other well-known Frenchmen who have kept this kind of journal are: Baudelaire, Léon Bloy, Du Bos, Renard and De Vigny. The painters Gauguin and Delacroix also kept diaries and journals which are of much value and interest. *See* AUTOBIOGRAPHY; CONFESSIONAL LITERATURE.

diatribe (Gk 'rubbing through') It now has the more or less exclusive meaning of a rather violent attack on a person or work, couched in vitriolic language. *See* FLYTING; INVECTIVE; LAMPOON.

dibrach A metrical foot of two short unstressed syllables: ◡ ◡. Also a pyrrhic (*q.v.*). Very rare in English verse.

dicatalectic A metrical line which lacks a syllable of the basic meter in the middle and at the end. *See* ACATALECTIC; CATALEXIS.

diction *See* POETIC DICTION.

dictionary The word derives from medieval Latin (*liber*) *dictionarius* or (*manuale*) *dictionarium*, from *dictio* 'saying'. It is primarily a book containing the words of a language arranged alphabetically. It contains definitions of the meanings of words, which are often accompanied by some etymological explanations. In some dictionaries quotations are given to illustrate meanings and usage over the years. Two-language dictionaries provide corresponding words, phrases and meanings in other tongues – again arranged alphabetically. Special dictionaries (like this one) give information about one particular subject.

Dictionaries of language are relatively recent. Neither the Greeks nor the Romans had anything like a modern dictionary. On the other hand, the glossary (*q.v.*) appeared quite early. Apollonius's Homeric *Lexicon* was compiled in the 3rd c. BC.

In 1532 Robert Estienne completed his great *Dictionarium seu linguae latinae thesaurus*, and in 1572 his son Henri Estienne published his *Thesaurus graecae linguae*, a landmark in Greek lexicography and a work on which others have built steadily. In 1678 Charles du Fresne du Cange produced his monumental dictionary of medieval Latin titled *Glossarium ad Scriptores Mediae et Infimae Latinitatis*; and, ten years later, a companion work on medieval Greek.

All the major dictionaries of modern ethnic languages were first compiled in the 17th c. Notable examples are the Italian *Vocabulario degli Accademici della Crusca* (1612), and the great dictionary of the French Academy in 1694. In the following century the Academy of Madrid published their Spanish dictionary (1726–39). In England the most outstanding work of that century was Johnson's *Dictionary* (1755) on which he worked single-handed for many years. The forerunner of this was Nathan Bailey's *Dictionary* (1721). Johnson's work is remarkable for its range and knowledge, for the compression and adroitness of its definitions and also because Johnson allowed his prejudices and opinions to appear in the definitions. His *Preface* is one of the finest pieces of prose in the language.

In 1854 Jakob and Wilhelm Grimm began their *magnum opus* on the German language. The work has been carried on by others ever since. A majestic achievement in French lexicography was Emile Littré's *Dictionnaire de la langue française* which came out in four volumes (1863–78). In that latter year was begun the monumental *New English Dictionary on Historical Principles* (1884–1928), edited by Sir James Murray, Dr Henry Bradley, Sir William Craigie and Dr C. T. Onions. It is a work without parallel in the history of lexicography and gives all the uses of every English word since at least the 12th c. It also provides illustrative quotations to show shifts and changes of meaning. In 1989 a second edition of this majestic work was published. It was 'prepared' (*sic*) by J. A. Simpson and E. S. C. Weiner – the editors. It weighs well over a hundredweight and on publication cost £1,500. Some of the entries run to 60,000 words.

Other dictionaries of great note which should be mentioned here are: Webster's *American Dictionary of the English Language* (1828); Webster's *New International Dictionary* (1934, 1961); *A Dictionary of American English on Historical Principles* (1938–44) edited by Craigie and Hulbert; and *The Oxford Dictionary of English Etymology* (1966) edited by C. T. Onions – a remarkable work for which its editor has the reputation of never making a mistake.

Other special dictionaries are Ebenezer Brewer's *Dictionary of Phrase and Fable* (1870) and Eric Partridge's *A Dictionary of Slang and Unconventional English* (1937). In the 1950s Penguin Books started a useful series of special dictionaries on politics, art and artists, architecture, biology, music, natural history, psychology, sailing etc. *See* CONCORDANCE; ENCYCLOPAEDIA; THESAURUS.

didactic (Gk 'that which teaches') Any work of literature which sets out to instruct may be called didactic. Didactic poetry is almost a special category of its own. Early works are Greek; for instance, Hesiod's *Works and Days* and *Theogony* (8th c. BC). The former combines a farming manual with moral precepts; the latter is an account of the gods and creation. The major works in Latin verse are Lucretius's *De Rerum Natura* (1st c. BC) and Virgil's *Georgics* (1st c. BC). Lucretius expounded the Epicurean system and Virgil expatiated on husbandry and moral principles.

The Middle Ages produced the bulk of the didactic literature in Europe and most of it was in verse. Proverbs, charms, gnomic verses (*qq.v.*), guides to the good life, and manuals of holy living were abundant. In English literature the 12th c. *Poema Morale* and the 13th c. *Ormulum* and *Proverbs of Alfred* were essentially didactic. In *Handlyng Synne* (1303), Robert Mannyng of Brunne (Bourne in Lincolnshire) told stories to illustrate the ten commandments, the seven deadly sins, and the seven sacraments. Gower's *Confessio Amantis* (1388) contained a good deal of instruction.

Consciously didactic poetry had a revival in the 18th c. A number of poems, somewhat in the Virgilian tradition, combined pastoral life with ethics; but they cannot be taken very seriously today. Indeed, at times they appear naively comic. Notable examples are John Philips's *Cyder* (1708), Armstrong's *Art of Preserving Health* (1744) and Dyer's *Fleece* (1757). Near the end of the century came Erasmus Darwin's *Botanic Garden* (1789, 1791) which was in heroic couplets in the style of Pope. Part I dealt with the 'Economy of Vegetation', Part II with 'The Loves of the Plants'.

It has been argued that all poetry is, by implication, didactic; that it should and does instruct as well as delight. Horace's *Ars Poetica*, Boileau's *Art Poétique*, in imitation of Horace, and Pope's *Essay on Criticism* were intended to instruct poets in their craft. *See also* ALLEGORY; COURTESY BOOK; EXEMPLUM; PROPAGANDA.

différance A word coined by the French philosopher Jacques Derrida which he uses in opposition to logocentrism (*q.v.*). It is intentionally ambiguous (and virtually untranslatable) and derives from the French *différer*, meaning 'to defer, postpone, delay' and also 'to differ, be different from'. Derrida uses *différance* as a way of pushing Saussure's theory of language to its 'logical' conclusion (it was Saussure who posited that 'signs' in language are arbitrary and differential), and argues that to differ or differentiate is also to defer, postpone or withhold. The word itself illustrates Derrida's point that writing does not copy speech; the distinction between the two different forms *différance* and *différence* does not correspond to any distinction in their spoken form. In his view the process of deferring applies to the written and spoken word: deferral/*différance*. Thus, meaning is continuously and (in theory) endlessly deferred since each word leads us on to yet another word in the system of signification. Derrida sees a text as an endless sequence of signifiers (*q.v.*) which can have no ultimate or determinate meaning.

Two key passages in Derrida's discourse on '*Différance*' may help to clarify:

> The verb 'to differ' [différer] seems to differ from itself. On the one hand it indicates difference as distinction, inequality, or discernibility; on the other, it expresses the interposition of delay, the interval of a *spacing* and *temporalizing* that puts off until 'later' what is presently denied, the possible that is presently impossible. Sometimes the *different* and sometimes the *deferred* correspond [in French] to the verb 'to differ'.

Later in the same essay he writes:

> What we note as *différance* will thus be the movement of play that 'produces' (and not by something that is simply an activity) these differences, these effects of difference. This does not mean that the *différance* which produces differences is before them in a simple and in itself unmodified and indifferent present. *Différance* is the nonfull, nonsimple 'origin'; it is the structured and differing origin of differences.

(Cf. *Bulletin de la Société française de philosophie*, LXII, No. 3, July–Sept. 1968; reprinted in *Speech and Phenomena and Other Essays on Husserl's Theory of Signs*, trans. by D. B. Allison, 1973). *See also* APORIA; DECONSTRUCTION.

digest Either a publication which abridges books or articles (or both) which have already been published; or, the abridgement itself. *See* ABRIDGED EDITION; BOWDLERIZE.

digression Material not strictly relevant to the main theme or plot of a work. Sterne proved himself an incorrigible digressionist in *Tristram Shandy*.

diiamb A metrical foot which consists of two iambs (*q.v.*): ◡ / ◡ /. It is taken as one unit.

dilogy An expression of statement with a double meaning, like *double entente* (*q.v.*). *See* AMBIGUITY; AMPHIBOLY.

dime novel A cheap form of melodramatic and exciting fiction, so called because it cost a dime. Most of the stories are concerned with romance, historical episodes, warfare and violent action. Many of them were set in America, during the Civil War, Revolution and frontier periods. There was a great vogue for them from 1860 to *c.* 1895, beginning with the publication of Ann Sophia Stephens's *Malaeska: The Indian Wife of the White Hunter*. They were superseded by pulp (*q.v.*) magazines and series about Tom Swift, Frank Merriwell and the Rover Boys. Such stories celebrated the robustness and individualism of Americans. Among the more famous authors were E. Z. C. Judson, Prentiss Ingraham, Edward L. Wheeler (the creator of 'Deadwood Dick') and J. R. Coryell (the creator of 'Nick Carter'). The dime novel was akin to the shilling shocker and the penny dreadful (*q.v.*). *See* BLUE BOOK; THRILLER; WESTERN.

dimeter A line of verse containing two feet. The third and fourth lines of the limerick (*q.v.*) are dimeters.

diminishing metaphor A figure of speech in which there is a kind of discrepancy or conjunctive discord between tenor and vehicle (*q.v.*). It occurs when a thought and the image which embodies it are brought together in such a way that they are not wholly congruous. The result is often witty, arresting and intellectually stimulating. Such metaphor is common in metaphysical poetry (*q.v.*) and a good deal of modern poetry. A famous example begins T. S. Eliot's *The Love Song of J. Alfred Prufrock*:

> Let us go then, you and I
> When the evening is spread out against the sky
> Like a patient etherised upon a table;

See DISCORDIA CONCORS; DISSOCIATION OF SENSIBILITY; METAPHOR; OBJECTIVE CORRELATIVE.

Dinggedicht (G 'thing poem') A form of poetry which attempts to describe objects from within rather than externally. Notable examples are to be found in Rilke's *Neue Gedichte* (1907). *See* IMAGISTS.

dinumeratio *See* EUTREPISMUS.

Dionysian *See* APOLLONIAN/DIONYSIAN.

dipody A pair of any metrical feet which are taken as a single unit. It also denotes verse constructed rhythmically so that in scansion (*q.v.*) pairs of feet must be considered together. It is common in children's rhymes, nursery rhymes (*q.v.*) and ballad (*q.v.*). Occasional in other verses. For example, in John Masefield's *Cargoes*:

> Quinquireme of Nineveh || from distant Ophir
> Rowing home to haven || in sunny Palestine

Here the sound of the rhythm requires grouping of feet in each half line. The same effect occurs in Chesterton's *Lepanto*:

> The cold queen of England || is looking in the glass.
> The shadow of the Valois || is yawning at the Mass.

See FOOT.

dirge A song of lament, usually of a lyrical mood. The name derives from the beginning of the antiphon of the Office of the Dead: *Dirige, Domine* . . . 'Direct, O Lord . . .' As a literary genre it comes from the Greek *epicedium* (*q.v.*) which was a mourning song sung over the dead and a threnody (*q.v.*) sung in memory of the dead. In Roman funeral processions the *nenia*, a song of praise for the departed, was chanted; and the professional wailing women (*praeficae*) were hired for the task on some occasions. Later the dirge developed into a lyric poem, as in Sir Philip Sidney's poem included in *Arcadia* (1590), which begins, 'Ring out your bells, let mourning shews be spread', and Henry King's *Exequy* on his young wife, 'Tell me no more how fair she is.' Both are very fine poems.

Occasionally dirges occur in plays. There are two particularly famous ones by Shakespeare: Ariel's song for Ferdinand's dead father in *The Tempest* (I, ii), and Fidele's dirge in *Cymbeline* (IV, ii). Very nearly as famous as these is Cornelia's song over Marcello in Webster's *The White Devil* (V, iv). *See* COMPLAINT; ELEGY; LAMENT; LYRIC; MONODY; SONG; UBI SUNT.

discordia concors A phrase used by Johnson in his *Life of Cowley* when referring to metaphysical poetry (*q.v.*). The relevant passage is: 'Wit, abstracted from its effects upon the hearer, may be more rigorously and philosophically considered as a kind of *discordia concors*, a combination of dissimilar images or discovery of occult resemblances in things apparently unlike. Of wit thus defined they [Donne and the other Metaphysicals] have more than enough.' (It is an inversion of Horace's *concordia discors* 'harmony in discord'.) *See* DIMINISHING METAPHOR.

discourse Usually a learned discussion, spoken or written, on a philosophical, political, literary or religious topic. It is closely related to a treatise and a dissertation (*qq.v.*). In fact, the three terms are very nearly synonymous. A famous example is Descartes's *Discourse on Method* (1637).

In linguistics 'discourse' denotes a 'stretch of language' larger than a sentence.

Latterly, the term has acquired much wider meanings and much wider implications. Basically, it is language which is understood as utterance and thus involves subjects who speak and write – which presupposes listeners and readers who, in a sense, are 'objects'. Discourse has an object and is directed to or at an object. Thus, in theory at any rate, discourse might include any modes of utterance as a part of social practice. They are differentiated by their intention. Thus, discourse may be poetry or prose. It may be a poem, a philosophical essay, a political tract, a biblical commentary, a speech on the hustings, a funeral address, a polemic, a dialogue or an exercise in deconstructive criticism. It may be any number of things.

discovery In a literary work the revelation of facts hitherto unknown to one of the principal characters. It often comes at the time of the dénouement (*q.v.*) or climax (*q.v.*). There are two good examples in *The Winter's Tale*: first, when Leontes discovers the identity of Perdita; second, when Polixenes realizes that Perdita is Leontes's daughter.

disemic (Gk 'of two time-units') A term applied in Classical prosody when a long syllable was regarded as two short ones. *See* MORA.

disinterestedness (in criticism) 'Disinterestedness' is an important term in Matthew Arnold's essay *The Function of Criticism at the Present Time*, first delivered as a lecture in 1864 and later published in *Essays in Criticism* (1865). Arnold spoke of the need, in the study of all branches of knowledge, to see the object 'as in itself it really is'. This depended on the attitude of the critic which, in his view, ought to be objective and open-minded; a kind of involved detachment.

dispondee Two spondees (*q.v.*) combined into a single unit. It is rare, and a series of spondees is extremely rare.

dissemination The verb *to disseminate* means 'to sow or scatter abroad', 'to propagate', 'to diffuse'; hence the idea of scattering, spreading and impregnating; especially the spreading of seed (L *semen*, 'seed'). 'Dissemination' basically suggests that 'plurisignification', or a multiplicity of meanings, is not something that is under control as it is in the New Criticism (*q.v.*), where the fact that a text can be interpreted in more than one way is treated as a dimension of its inherent and organic 'greatness'. 'Dissemination' has a deliberately sexual and procreative connotation. It suggests a textual 'free play' which is both joyous, unstable and 'excessive' – close, in fact, to the Nietzschean idea of the Dionysian in art, which Jacques Derrida, the French philosopher, is clearly influenced by. Derrida uses 'dissemination' in a special sense with regard to language. By it he refers to the 'spilling' or 'diffusion' of meaning; the 'surplus' or excess of meaning which is inherent in the use of all language. *See also* CONNOTATION; DENOTATION; TRACE.

dissertation Like a discourse (*q.v.*), a dissertation is usually a substantial and erudite disquisition. Sir Thomas Browne's *Vulgar Errors* (1646) and Burke's *Thoughts on the Present Discontents* (1770) might fairly be put into this category. Occasionally such a work may be droll, as Lamb's *Dissertation upon Roast Pig* in *Essays of Elia* (1823). *See* TREATISE.

dissident writers Those who do not conform to the political and cultural ideology of their country. Most of them belong to countries ruled by the Communist Party. Prominent dissidents have included the Russians Boris Pasternak, Mikhail Zoshchenko, Anna Akhmatova and Alexander Solzhenitsyn; and the Czechs Václav Havel and Milan Kundera. *See also* AESOPIC LANGUAGE; ZHDANOVSHCHINA.

dissociation of ideas In 1901 Remy de Gourmont published *La Culture des idées* which contained an essay called *Dissociation des idées* in which he put forward the point of view that it was necessary to avoid the unquestioning acceptance of ideas and associations of ideas which have become everyday commonplaces.

dissociation of sensibility The phrase was used by T. S. Eliot in his essay *The Metaphysical Poets* (1921). The relevant and self-explanatory passage is:

> Tennyson and Browing are poets, and they think; but they do not feel their thought as immediately as the odour of a rose. A thought to Donne was an experience; it modified his sensibility. When a poet's mind is perfectly equipped for its work, it is constantly amalgamating disparate experience; the ordinary man's experience is chaotic, irregular, fragmentary. The latter falls in love, or reads Spinoza, and these two experiences have nothing to do with each other, or with the noise of the typewriter or the smell of cooking; in the mind of the poet these experiences are always forming new wholes.
>
> We may express the difference by the following theory: The poets of the seventeenth century, the successors of the dramatists of the sixteenth, possessed a mechanism of sensibility which would devour any kind of experience. They are simple, artificial, difficult, or fantastic, as their predecessors were; no less nor more than Dante, Guido Cavalcanti, Guinicelli, or Cino. In the seventeenth century a dissociation of sensibility set in, from which we have never recovered; and this dissociation, as is natural, was aggravated by the influence of the two more powerful poets of the century, Milton and Dryden. Each of these men performed certain poetic functions so magnificently well that the magnitude of the

effect concealed the absence of others. The language went on and in some respects improved; the best verse of Collins, Gray, Johnson, and even Goldsmith satisfies some of our fastidious demands better than that of Donne or Marvell or King. But while the language became more refined, the feeling became more crude. The feeling, the sensibility, expressed in the *Country Churchyard* (to say nothing of Tennyson and Browning) is cruder than that in the *Coy Mistress*.

Eliot contended that modern poets like Corbière and Laforgue had avoided the 'dissociation of sensibility'. Certainly they had a considerable influence on Eliot, and the combined effect of the influence of Hopkins, Yeats, Pound and Eliot has been potent. *See* ASSOCIATION; SENSIBILITY.

dissolutio *See* ASYNDETON.

dissonance The arrangement of cacophonous sounds in words, or rhythmical patterns, for a particular effect. A very common device in much poetry. The following stanzas from Browning's *Childe Roland to the Dark Tower Came* illustrate the possibilities of dissonance:

> If there pushed any ragged thistle-stalk
> Above its mates, the head was chopped; the bents
> Were jealous else. What made those holes and rents
> In the dock's harsh swarth leaves, bruised as to baulk
> All hope of greenness? 'tis a brute must walk
> Pashing their life out, with a brute's intents.
>
> As for the grass, it grew as scant as hair
> In leprosy; thin dry blades pricked the mud
> Which underneath looked kneaded up with blood.
> One stiff blind horse, his every bone a-stare,
> Stood stupefied, however he came there:
> Thrust out past service from the devil's stud!

A more subtle effect, using the same means, is achieved by Crabbe in these lines from *Peter Grimes*:

> Here dull and hopeless he'd lie down and trace
> How sidelong crabs had scrawl'd their crooked race,
> Or sadly listen to the tuneless cry
> Of fishing gull or clanging golden-eye;

What time the sea-birds to the marsh would come,
And the loud bittern from the bull-rush home,
Gave from the salt ditch side the bellowing boom:

Particularly good examples can also be found in the work of more modern poets like John Berryman and Robert Lowell. *See* ASSONANCE; CACOPHONY; CONSONANCE.

distich (Gk 'two rows') A pair of metrical lines of different lengths, usually rhymed and expressing a complete idea. Commonly used in Classical elegiacs (*q.v.*). Often it consisted of a dactylic hexameter (*q.v.*) followed by a dactylic pentameter (*q.v.*).

distributed stress *See* HOVERING STRESS.

dit (F 'something said') A rather vague term used of some types of medieval didactic poetry (*q.v.*), related to the *débat*, the *fabliau*, *conte* and *lai* (*qq.v.*). *See also* EXEMPLUM.

dithryamb Originally a Greek choric hymn, with mime (*q.v.*) describing the adventures of Dionysius. It may have been introduced into Greece early in the 7th c. BC, and thereafter, for at least three hundred years, it underwent various developments. In modern literature dithyrambs are very rare. Dryden, in *Alexander's Feast*, is one of the few poets to have used the form successfully. The opening stanza gives and indication of the shape and mood:

'Twas at the Royal Feast, for Persia won,
By Philip's warlike son:
Aloft in awful State
The God-like Heroe sate
On his Imperial Throne;
His valient Pèers were plac'd around;
Their Brows with Roses and with Myrtyles bound.
(So should Desert in Arms be Crown'd:)
The lovely Thais by his side
Sate like a blooming Eastern Bride
In Flow'r of Youth and Beauty's Pride,
Happy, happy, happy Pair!
None but the Brave,
None but the Brave,
None but the Brave deserves the Fair.

Dithyrambic is an adjective which may be applied to any form of rather 'wild' song or chant.

ditrochee Also dichoree. Two trochees (*q.v.*) / ∪ / ∪ taken as one metrical unit. Also called trochaic monometer (*q.v.*).

ditty A composition to be sung; perhaps a *lai* (*q.v.*) or any short song, even a ballad (*q.v.*). It can denote many kinds of composition in verse. It may also refer to the words of a song, its theme or burden (*qq.v.*). *See* ROUNDELAY; SONG.

divan (P *dēvān* 'brochure, account, custom-house') An oriental council of state or council chamber; also the long seat against the wall of a room. But *also* a collection of poems. It has a large number of other meanings. *See also* GHAZEL.

diverbiumThe spoken dialogue in Roman drama, as distinguished from the *canticum* (*q.v.*) – the sung part.

divertissement (F 'entertainment, amusement, recreation') A French term for a ballet given as a kind of interlude between longer pieces. In effect, the *comédie-ballet* (*q.v.*) developed by Molière. More generally the term is used to describe a literary trifle, something slight and gay.

divisional pause *See* CAESURA.

dizain A French poem or stanza of ten octosyllabic or decasyllabic lines, such as Maurice Scève's poem *Délie* (1544) which contains 449 connected *dizains*. In some cases three or five *dizains* combined with an *envoi* (*q.v.*), formed a *ballade* (*q.v.*) or *chant royal* (*q.v.*).

dochmiac (Gk 'slanted') In Classical prosody a metrical foot of two unstressed syllables and three stressed, normally occurring thus: ∪ / / ∪ /. Dochmiacs were confined to Greek tragedy and were used for the very emotional passages. It has been argued that some five-syllable English words like 'originally' are dochmiacs.

document Something written that provides information or evidence in the shape of a record: yearbooks, annals, gazettes, registers, diaries (*qq.v.*) and so forth; also state papers, wills, certificates, archives, files and dossiers. *See also* DOCUMENTARY NOVEL.

documentary novel This form of fiction was invented by the Goncourt brothers, Edmond (1822–96) and Jules (1830–70), in the 1860s. They used the term *roman documentaire* (*q.v.*) but their novels were rather different from their documentary successors. In the 20th c. such a novel has become a form of fiction which, like documentary drama, is based on documentary evidence in the shape of newspaper articles, legal reports, archives, and recent official papers, sometimes described as 'instant fiction'. Memorable examples have been Theodore Dreiser's *An American Tragedy* (1925) and Truman Capote's *In Cold Blood* (1966). Another kind of documentary novel is that which deals with a prominent contemporary matter almost by anticipation, for example: Graham Greene's *The Quiet American* (1955) and Morris West's *In the Shoes of the Fisherman* (1963). An interesting recent use of documentary technique combined with conventional narrative occurs in V. S. Naipaul's *In a Free State* (1971). *See* THESIS NOVEL.

documentary theatre A form of drama, related to epic theatre (*q.v.*), which is propagandist and didactic, and may make use of relatively recent history and documentary evidence of the kind provided by newspapers, reports, archives, official histories, diaries and journals. Recent exemplifications are: Hochhuth's *The Representative* (1966), which examined the role of the Pope and the Papacy in the Second World War; and his *Soldiers* (1967), which investigated part of Sir Winston Churchill's career during the same period; Kipphardt's *In the Matter of J. Robert Oppenheimer* (1968), which investigated the USA's atomic energy commission; and Peter Brook's *US* (1969). Robert Nichols's *Front Page* (1972) was a kind of updating of *Front Page* (1928), a tough comedy drama about newspaper life written by the Americans Ben Hecht and Charles MacArthur. More recent instances (perhaps of a semi-documentary nature) are David Edgar's *Mary Barnes* (1977) and *The Jail Diary of Albie Sachs* (1978). *See* DOCUMENTARY NOVEL; LIVING NEWSPAPER.

doggerel Probably from *dog*, with contemptuous suggestion as in *dog-Latin.* After Chaucer has broken off his burlesque (*q.v.*) *Tale of Sir Thopas* the Host makes a remark about 'rym dogerel'. This seems to be the earliest reference to doggerel, a term which originally applied to verse of a loose and irregular measure, as in Skelton's *Colyn Cloute* (1519) and Butler's *Hudibras* (1663–78). Now it has come to describe rough, badly made verse, monotonous in rhythm and clumsy in rhyme, usually on a trivial subject.

See HUDIBRASTIC VERSE; JINGLE; MACARONIC; NONSENSE; SKELTONICS; TUMBLING VERSE.

dog-Latin Mongrel Latin. Rough, impure, cross-bred, unidiomatic Latin. *See also* DOGGEREL.

dogma A dogma is a tenet, doctrine, law or principle. Something laid down as being so. Dogmatism in criticism (*q.v.*) is as emphatic. The dogmatic critic ascribes to himself a kind of *ex cathedra* authority.

dolce stil nuovo (It 'sweet new style') The style of Italian lyric poetry in the second half of the 13th c. The term was first used by Dante, in the *Purgatorio*, of his own literary style; but, more importantly, it represented an attitude towards women and earthly love which derived from the troubadour (*q.v.*) tradition. Woman, represented as the embodiment of God's beauty, was believed to inspire gentle love which should lead the lover to Divine love. The *stilnuovisti* poets (other notable ones were Guinicelli and Cavalcanti) attempted to reconcile or, in a sense, combine sacred and profane love. *See* COURTLY LOVE.

domestic comedy A counterpart to domestic tragedy (*q.v.*), it is a form of drama about, predominantly, upper-middle or middle-class life and characters. It has been particularly fashionable since late in the 19th c., and, as the words suggest, is often concerned with family situations and problems. An early example is Massinger's *A New Way to Pay Old Debts* (*c.* 1621). Goldsmith's *She Stoops to Conquer* (1773) might also be taken as an instance. In the 19th c. a most talented playwright in this form was T. W. Robertson whose best works are *Ours* (1866), *Caste* (1867), *Play* (1868) and *School* (1869). Harold Brighouse's *Hobson's Choice* (1915) is another excellent play in the genre. Several plays by Somerset Maugham in the 1920s were highly successful domestic comedies; particularly *Our Betters*, *Home and Beauty*, *The Constant Wife* and *The Breadwinner*. Domestic comedy continued to fill the theatres in the 1930s and during the post-war period. Other notable dramatists in the genre are Noël Coward, Tennessee Williams, Jean Anouilh, N. C. Hunter, Terence Rattigan, Alan Ayckbourn and Bill Naughton. *See* BOULEVARD DRAMA; COMEDY; DRAWING-ROOM COMEDY; NATURALISTIC DRAMA.

domestic tragedy A play about middle or lower middle-class life which concentrates on the more personal and domestic element of tragedy (*q.v.*), as opposed to tragedy in the grand manner which involves kings, princes and enterprises 'of great pitch and moment'. There are a number of examples in Tudor and Jacobean drama. For instance: the anonymous *Arden of Faversham* (1592); the anonymous *A Warning for Fair Women* (1599); Thomas Heywood's *A Woman Killed with Kindness* (1603); the anonymous *A Yorkshire Tragedy* (1608); and Middleton and Rowley's *The Changeling* (1623). There was some domestic tragedy in the 18th c. like Lillo's *The London Merchant* (1731). Hebbel's *Maria Magdalena* (1844) is also taken to be in this genre. The term might also be judiciously applied to some of the work of Ibsen, Strindberg, Eugene O'Neill, Tennessee Williams and Arthur Miller. *See also* DOMESTIC COMEDY; DRAME.

dominant, the A concept of some importance in the literary theory of formalism developed in the Prague School (*q.v.*) of linguistics and thus of later provenance than Russian Formalism (*q.v.*). Roman Jakobson defined it (in 1935) as 'the focusing component of a work of art: it rules, determines, and transforms the remaining components'. The dominant gives a work its *Gestalt* (*q.v.*), its organic unity; thus bringing about the unified whole of a work.

The concept of 'the dominant' can be seen to emerge as a development and response within the Prague School to Shklovsky's earlier definition of 'defamiliarization' (*q.v.*) in *Art as Technique*. Whereas Shklovsky had suggested that form or technique was in itself a defamiliarizing agent, later Formalists, including Yuri Tynyanov writing in the 1920s, stressed that the defamiliarizing effect of a device depended on its function in the work in which it appears. Thus a work may include some automatized elements which are subordinate to the defamiliarizing or foregrounded elements. This foregrounding (*q.v.*) of a group of elements comes to be seen later by Jakobson as 'the dominant'. The dominant emphasizes the distinction between those formal elements which function to defamiliarize and those which function passively. This view of the literary text as inherently dynamic and dialectical is developed in the work of the Prague School; to acknowledge that a device which was once defamiliarizing can become automatized is to recognize one aspect of the momentum in literary history. Both Russian Formalism and the Prague Linguistic Circle refine their theories through acknowledging the fact of literary history.

donnée A French word which signifies something 'given' in the sense that it is an idea or notion implanted in the mind or imagination: the seed, so to speak, of a creative work; what Henry James called 'the speck'. It may be a phrase, a conversation, the expression on a person's face, a tune, indeed almost any kind of experience which starts a series of thoughts and ideas in the writer's mind. What species of creative magic brings such an event about is not really known. *See* AFFLATUS; FANCY AND IMAGINATION; INSPIRATION; LIGNE DONNEE; MUSE; SPONTANEITY.

Doric Doris is a region of Greece, south of Thessaly. Doric denotes the rustic and unsophisticated as opposed to the Attic – the urban and urbane. Milton's lines in *Lycidas*:

He [the uncouth swain] touch'd the tender stops of various quills,
With eager thought warbling his Doric lay.

suggest the pastoral (*q.v.*) connotations of the word.

double dactyl A metrical form comprising two dactyls: / ◡ ◡ / ◡ ◡. A fixed form in light verse in which there are two stanzas of four double dactyl lines. The rules, such as they are, require the last lines of each stanza to rhyme and the last lines to be truncated. The first line should be a jingle, the second line a name, and one line in the second stanza should consist of one word, as in this trifle by J. A. Cuddon:

Higgledy-piggledy
Nicholas Williamson
Sat in the bathtub and
Scratched at his nose.

Seldom was schoolboy so
Anthropocentrically
Gifted with flexible
Bendable toes.

See JINGLE; NONSENSE.

double-decker novel A term which came into use in the 19th c. to describe novels which were published in two parts or volumes. Novels of the period tended to be long and many of them were published in serial form first. A three-decker novel came out in three volumes. *See* NOVEL.

double entente, un mot à A French term signifying an ambiguity (*q.v.*). A word or expression so used that it can have two meanings; one of which is usually frivolous or bawdy. There are a large number of *doubles ententes* in Wycherley's *The Country Wife* involving the word 'china'. It is commoner now to use the phrase *double entendre*. *See* IRONY; PUN.

double rhyme *See* FEMININE RHYME.

drab A term first used by C. S. Lewis in a restricted sense in his introduction to *English Literature in the Sixteenth Century* (1954) to describe the poetry and prose of the later medieval period up to the early Renaissance (*q.v.*). He was distinguishing it from a 'golden' (*q.v.*) period style (*c.* 1580–1603). It is generally agreed that much that was written in the 15th c. and the early Tudor period was drab. But the period also includes John Skelton (1460?–1529) and Sir Thomas Wyatt (1503–42), who were far from drab.

drama In general any work meant to be performed on a stage by actors. A more particular meaning is a serious play; not necessarily tragedy. Diderot and Beaumarchais were responsible for this restricted usage. *See* COMEDIE; COMEDY; DRAME; TRAGEDY.

drama of ideas *See* COMEDY OF IDEAS; THESIS PLAY.

drama of sensibility *See* SENTIMENTAL COMEDY.

dramatic irony When the audience understand the implication and meaning of a situation on stage, or what is being said, but the characters do not. Common in tragedy and comedy (*qq.v.*). Oedipus does not realize his crime. Sir Peter Teazle (in *School for Scandal*, IV, iii) does not know his wife is behind the screen when he is talking about her to Joseph Surface.

Another kind of dramatic irony occurs when a character's words 'recoil' upon him. For instance, Macbeth's 'bloody instructions' which 'return | To plague th' inventor'. In the event he is the one thus plagued. *See* IRONY.

dramatic lyric A term used by Browning for his dramatic monologues (1842). *See* MONOLOGUE.

dramatic monologue *See* MONOLOGUE.

dramatic proverb *See* PROVERBE DRAMATIQUE.

dramatis personae The characters in a play. Usually the names of these characters are printed at the beginning of the text.

dramatization The act of making a play out of a story in another genre; from a chronicle, novel, short story (*qq.v.*) and so forth. In medieval drama the Bible was dramatized into the Mystery Plays (*q.v.*). In the Tudor period dramatists 'lifted' plots, stories, and ideas from historians like Plutarch and Holinshed, and novelists like Lodge and Nashe. But it was not until the 18th c. that dramatization really began to flourish. Then novels provided the material. For example, Richardson's *Pamela*, dramatized by James Dance, was extremely popular. There followed dramatization of novels by Mrs Radcliffe, Walpole, Godwin, 'Monk' Lewis and Clara Reeve. In the 19th c. Dickens and Scott were the authors most used; so were Lord Lytton, Charlotte Brontë, Charles Reade, Wilkie Collins, and many more. The arrival of a group of original dramatists towards the end of the century saved the theatre from this deadening activity. But it is a practice by no means extinct, as television and recent theatrical history amply demonstrate.

dramaturgy (Gk *dramatourgia* 'playwright'; *drama* + *ergon* 'a work') The term denotes the principles of dramatic composition and theatrical art, and a dramaturge or dramaturgist is a playwright. In German a *Dramaturg* is a member of a theatrical company who selects the repertoire and may help in the arrangement and production of plays; a kind of literary adviser.

drame A term given in France to the kind of play which was neither tragedy nor comedy, but a serious play somewhere between the two. Diderot expatiated on this genre in the prefaces to his plays *Le Fils Naturel* (1757) and *Le Père de Famille* (1758). There were earlier examples by Voltaire, and by Nivelle de la Chaussée, who was the main dramatist of *comédie larmoyante* (*q.v.*). Diderot's theory was that such plays were serious dramas concerned with middle-class domestic problems. Their counterpart in England was domestic tragedy (*q.v.*). *See* DRAME ROMANTIQUE; METATHEATRE.

drame romantique A 19th c. French dramatic form, in prose and verse. Works in this genre tend to be melodramatic, emotionally torrid, and intricate in plot at the expense of characterization. Apart from Hugo's *Hernani* (1830) the most famous example is unquestionably Rostand's *Cyrano de Bergerac* (1897) which is a fine play by any standards and arguably the best of the *drames romantiques*. *See also* DRAME.

drápa (From ON *drepa*, 'to strike' [the chord of a musical instrument]) A complex form of skaldic heroic poem. The stanza was usually the *dróttkvætt* (*q.v.*) and there was a refrain (*q.v.*) of two or more half lines. Such a poem normally consisted of an introduction (*upphaf*), a middle section (the *stef* or *stefjamál*) and a conclusion (the *slæmr*).

drawing-room comedy A species of drama which had a considerable vogue in the early 20th c. Sometimes known disparagingly as 'French-window comedy', owing to the frequency with which the main set has such windows opening on to a garden or balcony, it is often concerned with the comic predicaments of the English middle classes and is therefore akin to domestic comedy (*q.v.*). Out of the scores of examples extant the following are well known: Shaw's *Candida* (1895); Coward's *Hay Fever* (1925); Terence Rattigan's *The Browning Version* (1948); N. C. Hunter's *The Waters of the Moon* (1951); Enid Bagnold's *The Chalk Garden* (1955).

dream vision A form of literature extremely popular in the Middle Ages. By common convention the writer goes to sleep, in agreeable rural surroundings and often on a May morning. He then beholds either real people or personified abstractions involved in various activities. The commentary of Macrobius (*c.* AD 400) on Cicero's *Somnium Scipionis*, and the work itself, is generally agreed to have had great influence on the genre. Very often the vision was expressed as an allegory (*q.v.*). Probably the best known example of all is the *Roman de la Rose* (13th c.), which had a wide influence in this period and was translated, probably by Chaucer. Chaucer made use of the dream convention in *The Book of the Duchess* (1369), the *Parlement of Foules*, *The House of Fame* and the prologue to *The Legend of Good Women* (all believed to have been written between 1372–86). However, Langland's vision of *Piers Plowman* (1366–99) is probably the best known English vision poem, to be compared with the anonymous *The Pearl* (*c.* 1350–80), and many visions of heaven, hell and purgatory; and accounts of journeys there and back. These were almost a form of travel literature and have been taken by some to be the precursors of science fiction (*q.v.*). A common figure of these works is the guide: Virgil in Dante's *Divina Commedia*, an angel in the 12th c. *Vision of Tundale*. The angelic guide became a kind of convention in itself, splendidly parodied by Chaucer in the prologue to *The Summoner's Tale* when the vengeful Summoner gets his own back on the Friar.

The dream vision device has been used many times since and its evergreen popularity can be judged by the tens of thousands of compositions from school children who use it.

Three later examples are John Bunyan's *Pilgrim's Progress* (1678), Keats's *second* version of *Hyperion* (1818–19) and Lewis Carroll's *Alice's Adventures in Wonderland* (1865). James Joyce's *Finnegans Wake* has also been taken as a kind of cosmic dream.

droighneach An Irish syllabic verse form. A line may consist of nine to thirteen syllables and it always ends in a trisyllabic word. The rhyme is ababcdcd and so on. Cross-rhymes and alliteration occur in each couplet.

drolls Also known as droll-humours. They were brief farces and comic scenes adapted from plays or merely improvised and invented by actors, and traditionally presented in public houses or in taverns during the Commonwealth period (*q.v.*) when the theatres were shut and stage plays forbidden. Some of these entertainments were collected and published by Francis Kirkham in a work titled *The Wits, or Sport upon Sport* (1662, 1673).

dróttkvætt (ON *drótt* 'The King's bodyguard' + *kvædi* 'poem song') Also known as the *dróttkvæðr háttr*, this is the normal meter of the ON *drápa* (*q.v.*). It consists of eight-line stanzas, each line having three main stresses and internal rhyme. Each line has a regular trochaic ending. The commonest and most intricate of the skaldic poetic forms, it survives in contemporary Icelandic poetry; and, originally, was the noble meter, suitable for recitation before the *drótt*, the chosen body of warriors in the king's personal following. *See* HRYNHENT; KENNING; SKALD.

drowned-in-tears, school of the A derisive term applied to those early Romantic poets who were inclined to dwell on the sadder and more morbid aspects of life. *See* GRAVEYARD SCHOOL OF POETRY.

dualism *See* ANTINOMY.

duan A Gaelic term for a poem or a canto (*q.v.*).

dumb show A mimed dramatic performance whose purpose was to prepare the audience for the main action of the play to follow. The dumb show was popular in Tudor England and at first tended to be allegorical, using symbolic characters rather than those from the play. Elizabethan playwrights were quick to see its possibilities. Early and important examples may be found in *Gorboduc* (1561), where it plays a considerable part throughout, and in Kyd's *The Spanish Tragedy* (III, xvi). Peele used it in *The Old Wives' Tale* (1595), and it also appears in the anonymous *A Warning for Fair Women* (1599). Perhaps the most famous instance occurs in *Hamlet* (III, ii), where the players wordlessly enact the murder of a king. In *Hamlet* it is strange that the precise action of the dumb show is repeated in words immediately afterwards. Conceivably, Shakespeare was using it in an archaic way since the fashion for introductory dumb shows was by then over (i.e. *c.* 1602).

In such plays as Peele's *Battle of Alcazar* (1594) and Greene's *Friar Bacon and Friar Bungay* (1594) the dumb show provided the dramatist with the means of including more action in his play (without using more dialogue) and of varying the action by showing the audience, as well as characters on stage, something that is happening elsewhere. There are good examples in the latter (II, iii; IV, iii): in the one in Act IV, two young men, with the aid of Bacon's magic glass, see how their fathers meet and kill each other. Closely parallel to this is Webster's use of the dumb show in *The White Devil* (II, ii). By contrast, in Middleton and Rowley's *The Changeling* (IV, i), the dumb show merely represents details necessary to the play's action which it would be tedious or dramatically difficult to present on stage in the normal way. During the Jacobean age (*q.v.*) the dumb show was increasingly used in the masque (*q.v.*).

From the 1630s the dumb show seems to have fallen into desuetude, though it is worth noting that the English diarist Abraham de la Pryme records how, in 1688, a body of Danish soldiers stationed in the north of England 'acted a play in their own language'. He noticed that 'all the postures were shown first . . . and, when they had run through all, so then they began to act'. It may be that the Danish custom of the dumb show was a device to draw the audience's attention to the play to stop them talking to one another. So, with *Hamlet*.

Later, dumb show was to reappear in a different guise – in harlequinade and pantomime (*qq.v.*). It also had a function in melodrama (*q.v.*) in the 19th c. There is a dumb character in Thomas Holcroft's *A Tale of Mystery* (1802), and it became something of a standard device among writers of melodrama to use a mute to convey essential facts by dint of dumb show. Not a few 19th c. plays made use of dumb show in various ways (e.g. *The Dumb Boy*, 1821, *The Dumb Brigand*, 1832, *The Dumb Recruit*, 1840, *The Dumb Driver*, 1849, *The Dumb Sailor*, 1854). The use of dumb show and mime was a well-known feature of Mme Celeste's performances. Between 1830 and 1840 the house playwrights at the Adelphi, London, composed a number of dumb shows for her.

Two modern instances occur in André Obey's *Le Viol de Lucrèce* (1931) and in Tom Stoppard's *Rosencrantz and Guildenstern are Dead* (1966). *See* MIME; REVENGE TRAGEDY.

dumy A form of lyric-epic song of Ukrainian origin. The lines are of uneven length, the meters vary and the rhyme scheme is variable; sometimes there is no rhyme. They were chanted or recited, as a rule, by blind beggar minstrels (a remarkable parallel here with the South Slav *guslari* (*q.v.*) to the accompaniment of a *kobza* or *bandura* which is similar to a Spanish guitar. The form developed in the 16th c. and belongs to the oral tradition (*q.v.*) of poetical composition. In this respect, as in others, there are clear counterparts in the shape of the Russian *byliny* (*q.v.*), the Lithuanian and Latvian *daina* (*q.v.*), the South Slav *narodne pesme* (*q.v.*), the ballad (*q.v.*) in general and the Homeric ballad. The *dumy* were mostly concerned with the *hajduk*-type warfare that the Cossacks conducted against the Turks, the Tatars and the Poles. *See* FOLK LITERATURE; FOLKSONG.

duodecimo (L *in duodecimo* 'in a twelfth') The size of a book in which one page is one twelfth of a sheet (abbreviated 12mo). *See* FOLIO; OCTAVO; QUARTO.

duologue A conversation between two characters in a play, story or poem. *See* DIALOGUE.

duple meter This comprises two syllables to a metrical foot, as with the iamb, spondee and trochee (*qq.v.*). Duple meter is rare. A fairly well-known example is Herrick's *Upon his departure hence*:

Thus I
Passe by,
And die:
As One,
Unknown,
And go.

Here he combines iamb, spondee and trochee. *See* MONOMETER.

duple rhythm This occurs when the metrical scheme requires two-syllable feet. It is thus common in iambic and trochaic verse. *See* IAMB; TRIPLE RHYTHM; TROCHEE.

duration One of the four characteristics of the spoken word, the others being pitch, loudness and quality. In poetry the duration of syllables (that is, their phonetic time value) is of particular importance. In these lines, for instance, from D. J. Enright's poem *The Laughing Hyena, by Hokusai*, the varying duration of the syllables contributes subtly to the general effect:

For him, it seems, everything was molten. Court ladies flow in
gentle streams,
Or, gathering lotus, strain sideways from their curving boat,
A donkey prances, or a kite dances in the sky, or soars like
sacrificial smoke.
All is flux: waters fall and leap, and bridges leap and fall.
Even his Tortoise undulates, and his Spring Hat is lively as a pool of
fish.
All he ever saw was sea: a sea of marble splinters –
Long bright fingers claw across his pages, fjords and islands and
shattered trees –

See MORA; ONOMATOPOEIA.

dyfalu A Welsh term for a form of fanciful conceit (*q.v.*) in which, by a succession of metaphors, an object is compared with a number of different things. There are many good examples in the work of the great 14th c. Welsh poet, Dafydd ap Gwilym.

dysphemism (Gk 'not fair speech') The opposite of euphemism (*q.v.*), it emphasizes defects – as in saying 'a filthy dirty face'.

dystopia *See* UTOPIA.

E

echo The repetition of the same sound, or a combination of sounds, fairly close together, so that they 'echo' each other. A common device in verse to strengthen meaning and structure, and also to provide tune and melody. Assonance, alliteration, consonance, the various kinds of rhyme (*qq.v.*) and also the refrain (*q.v.*) are all varieties of echo. *See also* ECHO VERSE.

echo verse Normally a poem in which the final syllables are repeated as by an echo (*q.v.*) with a change of meaning. Early examples are to be found in the *Greek Anthology* (compiled *c.* 925). The form became popular again in French, Italian and English verse in the 16th and 17th c. Sir Philip Sidney, George Herbert and Swift, among others, composed notable echo verses. The following is an extract from Herbert's *Heaven*:

O who will show me those delights on high?
ECHO. I.
Thou, Echo, thou art mortall, all men know.
ECHO. No.
Wert thou not born among the trees and leaves?
ECHO. Leaves.
And are there any leaves that still abide?
ECHO. Bide.
What leaves are they? impart the matter wholly.
ECHO. Holy.

See also ECHO.

Eckenstrophe A twelve-line stanza with a rhyming pattern of aab, aab, cd, cd, ee, used in the MHG epic poems *Eckenlied*, *Goldemar*, *Sigenot* and *Virginal*.

eclipsis (Gk 'a leaving out') The omission of essential grammatical elements.

eclogue (Gk 'selection') A short poem – or part of a longer one – and often a pastoral (*q.v.*) in the form of a dialogue or soliloquy (*qq.v.*). The term was first applied to Virgil's pastorals or bucolic poems. Thereafter it describes the traditional pastoral idyll (*q.v.*) that Theocritus, and other Sicilian poets, wrote. The form was revived by Dante, Petrarch and Boccaccio and was particularly popular during the 15th and 16th c. A major influence came from the *Eclogues* of Mantuan. Alexander Barclay wrote some distinguished eclogues while at Ely (1515–21). Spenser's *The Shepheard's Calendar* (1579) was outstanding. Later Pope attempted it in his *Pastorals*, and Gay burlesqued it in *Shepherd's Week* (1714). By the 18th c. the term merely referred to the form, and there were non-pastoral eclogues. A good example is Swift's *A Town Eclogue, 1710. Scene, The Royal Exchange*. In modern poems like Frost's *Build Soil*, MacNeice's *Eclogue from Iceland* and Auden's *The Age of Anxiety: a Baroque Eclogue*, it is the medium for any ideas the poet feels a need to express. *See also* GEORGIC.

école parnassienne *See* PARNASSIANS.

ecphonema (Gk 'outcry') An exclamation: of joy, woe, amazement.

écriture artiste A term used by the Goncourt brothers, Edmond (1822–96) and Jules (1830–70), to describe their mannered, sensitive, impressionistic and 'nervous' style, which is particularly evident in their *romans documentaires* (*q.v.*). They were hypersensitive and very fastidious men and, as Remy de Gourmont put it, possessed 'un don particulier et une sensibilité spéciale'. They were latter-day 'précieux', and described themselves as 'historiens des nerfs'. *See also* PRECIOSITE.

écriture feminine (F 'feminine writing') A concept proposed by the French feminist Hélène Cixous. It denotes writing which is typically, characteristically feminine in style, language, tone and feeling, and completely different from (and opposed to) male language and discourse – though she does say in *The Laugh of the Medusa* (1976) that this is not to do with biological determinism; women often write in male discourse and men can write in a feminine way. She cites the 'source' of *écriture feminine* in the mother and in the mother–child relationship before the child acquires 'conventional' language. She proposes that this potential language when eventually used in writing (*by men or women*) subverts logic and the rational and any element which may constrain the free play of meaning.

On the other hand, Luce Irigaray posits a 'woman's language', which is multiple, fluid, diverse and heterogeneous and which evades male phallocentric monopoly. This theory has a morphological basis associated with the structure and shape of the genital organs.

A third and related point of view is proposed by Julia Kristeva: a 'language' which is pre-Oedipal and pre-linguistic and is fundamentally semiotic (associated with the *chora* – Greek for 'womb') as opposed to male-controlled language which she describes as symbolic (*see* POST-STRUCTURALISM for her theory of the semiotic element). Toril Moi's *Sexual/Textual Politics: Feminist Literary Theory* (1985) is a fascinating discourse on these matters. *See also* FEMINIST CRITICISM.

écrivain/écrivant In an essay of 1960 called *Ecrivains et écrivants*, Roland Barthes distinguishes between two sorts of writer (and two sorts of writing). He suggests that the author performs a function and the writer an activity; that there are (a) the 'transitive' writer (*écrivant*) and (b) the 'intransitive' writer (*écrivain*). The former writes about things and the language he uses is the means to an extra-linguistic end, to a meaning or reality which is, in a sense, 'beyond' the writing; the latter does not intend to take the reader beyond his writing but to call the attention of the reader to *the activity of writing itself*. The *écrivain* has 'nothing but writing itself, not as the "pure" form conceived by an aesthetic of art for art's sake [*q.v.*] but, much more radically, as the only area for the one who writes'. Thus, one might surmise that Flaubert, Zola and Ernest Hemingway are 'transitive' writers, and Proust, Joyce and Samuel Beckett are 'intransitive' writers. Barthes's taxonomy here is closely connected with his distinction between the *lisible* and the *scriptible*, or the readerly/writerly (*q.v.*).

écrivant *See* ECRIVAIN/ECRIVANT.

edda (ON 'great-grandmother') A term used metaphorically for two collections of ON literature, with the implication that they are composed of ancient tales. Other suggestions for the derivation of *edda* include that which connects the world with Oddi where

Snorri Sturlusson (1179–1241) – the Icelandic chieftain and historian to whom is attributed the authorship of the prose *Edda* – grew up; another derives the word from *oðr* 'poetry', since the prose *Edda* is largely a handbook of poetics.

Snorri's *Edda* consists of four parts: *Prologue*, *Gylfaginning*, *Skáldskaparmál* and *Háttatal*. Of these it is most likely that the last was written first. When Snorri returned home from a visit with the Norwegian king, Hákon Hákonarson, and Jarl Skúli in 1220, he composed a poem in their honour which was finished in the winter of 1222–3. The poem consisted of 102 stanzas in 100 different meters. Hence the work was called *Háttatal* or 'list of meters', and was, in essence, a practical *ars poetica*. The work is complete with a full practical commentary in prose; the poem itself has little poetic value and suggests that Snorri was a better interpreter than writer of poetry.

The prose *Edda* also contains a section of specifically poetic words, the so-called *heiti* and kennings (*q.v.*). Many of these circumlocutions can only be understood with a knowledge of some of the tales to which they refer. So, in *Skáldskaparmál* ('poetic diction') Snorri re-told many of the old mythological stories. The fourth and best known section, *Gylfaginning* ('the beguiling of Gylfi'), recounts how the wise king of Sweden, Gylfi, travelled to Asgardr – the dwelling of the gods or *sesir* – to question them about the world's origin, the gods and the destruction of the world. The work becomes a comprehensive survey of ON mythology, indispensable to the student of the old Scandinavian world.

The prose *Edda* was intended as a book of instruction for *skalds* (*q.v.*). Skaldic poetry enjoyed a renaissance in the 13th c. but Snorri's work also had some influence on the saga writers since it led to an increase in the number of *lausarvísur* – individual occasional verses connected with definite situations or episodes which were incorporated in the main works of the saga age.

The poetic *Edda* (also called *Elder Edda*) is a collection of poems found in a manuscript *c.* 1270 and which, from linguistic and literary evidence, originate from a period earlier than the settlement of Iceland (870). The poetry of the *Elder Edda* falls into two groups: the mythological lays and the heroic lays.

The mythological poetry is composed of lays about the gods in various meters and of various ages. Some are didactic and can be regarded almost as treatises on pagan belief and legend. Such a lay is *Vafðrúdismál* which consists of a dialogue between Oðinn and the giant Vafðrúdnir, whom Oðinn visited in disguise. The god and the giant enter on a contest of wits, each wagering his head. Oðinn questions the giant on the origin of the earth, sun and moon, the winds and the gods. The giant answer readily but finally forfeits his head when Oðinn asks him the question: 'What did Oðinn whisper into the ear of his son (Baldr) as he was laid on the funeral pyre?' Of course, only Oðinn knew the answer to this. Other poems of this sort are *Grímnismál* and *Hávamál*.

The heroic lays represent a form of poetry which was at one time current among all Germanic tribes from the Black Sea to Greenland. Such lays were probably designed, in the first place, to be declaimed in the halls of chieftains, often to the accompaniment of the harp. They differ in many ways from epics with which they might naturally be associated, not only in length but also in scope and choice of subject. They dealt not with the whole life of the hero but with one or two incidents in that life, usually of a tragic or a moving nature. Such a lay is *Hamðismál* where the heroes Hamðir and Sǫrli, in the full knowledge that death is inevitable, meet that death courageously and readily at the cruel hands of Jǫrmunrekkr. This particular lay, like *Atlakviða* ('The Lay of Atli'), appears to be derived from continental poems as old as the 5th and 6th c.

edition The total number of copies of a book printed from one set of type. If the original type is changed and the book is re-printed then the term *second edition* is used. One edition may have several impressions or printings. The term *issue* usually describes a book to which new material has been added or which is somehow altered in format. The term *re-issue* may describe the re-printing of a book without changes. The term *edition* is also used to describe, say, the edited collected works of an author. For example: the *Twickenham Edition* of Pope's works.

Edwardian Pertaining to King Edward VII's reign (1901–10): a period of considerable change, and reaction against Victorianism.

ego-futurism A jargon term coined by the Russian poet Igor Severyanin (1887–1942) to describe a movement in early 20th c. Russian poetry. The ego-futurists were anti-traditionalist and wrote highly personal verse in which they went in for neologisms (*q.v.*). The movement did not last long. *See also* CUBO-FUTURISM.

egotistical sublime A phrase coined by John Keats (1795–1821) and applied to William Wordsworth's qualities of genius (*q.v.*). *See also* NEGATIVE CAPABILITY; SUBLIME.

eidyllion *See* IDYLL.

eight-and-six meter *See* FOURTEENER.

Einfühlung *See* EMPATHY.

Eisteddfod A Welsh term denoting an assembly of bards. Basically a form of contest at which literary, musical and dramatic works are presented. The main prizes are a carved oak chair awarded for the best poem in strict Welsh meters (known as the chair ode), and a silver crown for the best poem in free meters (known as the crown poem).

The Eisteddfod is an event of some antiquity: there are records of a bardic festival as long ago as 1176 at Cardigan. After the 16th c. the Eisteddfodau seem to have degenerated into rather casual gatherings in village inns. The event was restored to its original dignity and splendour in the 19th c. since when it has become the supreme cultural festival of Wales. *See also* BARD; POETIC CONTESTS.

elegantia Regarded by the Romans as one of three essential attributes of a discourse, the others being *compositio* and *dignitas*. They subdivided *elegantia* into *Latinitas* and *explanatio*. The former required the absence of linguistic faults, like solecisms; the latter made the matter of the speech or discourse clear.

elegant variation A term used by H. W. and F. G. Fowler to denote a particular fault of style: namely, the too obvious avoidance of repetition.

elegiac distich The Greek *elegeion* was a distich (*q.v.*) or couplet comprising a dactylic hexameter (*q.v.*) followed by a pentameter (*q.v.*). It seems to have been first used in the 8th or 7th c. BC, especially by Archilochus. The form was used for many purposes by Greek and Latin poets, but is rare in English. Poets who have imitated it are Sidney, Spenser, Clough, Kingsley, Swinburne and Sir William Watson, from whose *Hymn to the Sea* the following lines are taken:

While, with throes, with raptures, with loosing of bonds, with
  unsealings,
Arrowy pangs of delight, piercing the core of the world,

Tremors and coy unfoldings, reluctances, sweet agitations,
Youth, irrepressibly fair, wakes like wondering rose.

It will be noticed that the lines are not wholly dactylic and that they alternate double and single terminals. The form is also known as elegiacs. *See* DACTYL; ELEGY; EPICEDIUM.

elegiac meter The meter used in the elegiac distich (*q.v.*).

elegiac stanza Also known as Hammond's meter, heroic quatrain (*q.v.*) and elegiac quatrain. It seems that a quatrain (*q.v.*) of iambic pentameters (*q.v.*), rhyming abab, has acquired the name elegiac stanza from its use by Gray in *Elegy Written in a Country Churchyard* (1750). James Hammond's *Love Elegies* (1743) is probably the earliest example. *See* ELEGY.

elegy (Gk 'lament') In Classical literature an elegy was any poem composed of elegiac distichs (*q.v.*), also known as elegiacs, and the subjects were various: death, war, love and similar themes. The elegy was also used for epitaphs (*q.v.*) and commemorative verses, and very often there was a mourning strain in them. However, it is only since the 16th c. that an elegy has come to mean a poem of mourning for an individual or a lament (*q.v.*) for some tragic event. In England there were few attempts in the 16th c. to imitate elegiacs because the language is unsuited to prolonged series of dactylic hexameters and pentameters. 16th c. French writers like Doublet and Ronsard had the same problem.

Near the turn of the 16th c., the term *elegie* still covered a variety of subject matter. For example, Donne wrote *Elegie. His Picture*, and *Elegie. On his Mistris.* Later the term came to be applied more and more to a serious meditative poem, the kind that Coleridge was hinting at when he spoke of elegy as the form of poetry 'natural to a reflective mind'. English literature is especially rich in this kind of poetry which combines something of the *ubi sunt* (*q.v.*) motif with the qualities of the lyric (*q.v.*) and which, at times, is closely akin to the lament and the dirge (*qq.v.*). For instance, the OE poems *The Wanderer*, *The Seafarer* and *Deor's Lament*, several medieval lyrics, Thomas Nashe's song 'Adieu, farewell earth's bliss', Johnson's *Vanity of Human Wishes*, Goldsmith's *The Deserted Village*, Gray's *Elegy Written in a Country Churchyard*, Young's *Night Thoughts*, Keats's *Ode to Melancholy* and Walt Whitman's *When Lilacs Last in the Dooryard Bloomed* – to name only a handful of the scores that exist.

Many elegies have been songs of lament for specific people. Well-known examples are: Thomas Carew's elegy on John Donne, John Cleveland's on Ben Jonson, Henry King's *Exequy*, Pope's *Verses to the Memory of an Unfortunate Lady*, Dr Johnson's *On the Death of Mr Robert Levet*, Tennyson's *Ode on the Death of the Duke of Wellington*, and, more recently, Auden's *In Memory of W. B. Yeats*. In addition to these there are *Astrophil* and *Daphnaïda*, and the four major elegies in English literature – *Lycidas*, *Adonais*, *In Memoriam* and *Thyrsis*.

The major elegies belong to a sub-species known as pastoral elegy, the origins of which are to be found in the pastoral laments of three Sicilian poets: Theocritus (3rd c. BC), Moschus (2nd c. BC) and Bion (2nd c. BC). Their most important works were: Theocritus's *Lament for Daphnis*, which is pretty well the prototype for Milton's *Lycidas*; Moschus's *Lament for Bion* (a doubtful attribution) which influenced Milton's *Lycidas*, Shelley's *Adonais* and Matthew Arnold's *Thyrsis*; and Bion's *Lament for Adonis*, on which Shelley partly modelled his *Adonais*.

Spenser was one of the earliest English poets to use for elegy what are known as the pastoral conventions; namely in *Astrophil* (1586), an elegy for Sir Philip Sidney. It is a minor work but important in the history of the genre. Spenser also wrote *Daphnaïda* (1591), on the death of Sir Arthur Gorges's wife.

The conventions of pastoral elegy are approximately as follows: (a) The scene is pastoral. The poet and the person he mourns are represented as shepherds; (b) The poet begins with an invocation to the Muses and refers to divers mythological characters during the poem; (c) Nature is involved in mourning the shepherd's death. Nature feels the wound, so to speak; (d) The poet inquires of the guardians of the dead shepherd where they were when death came; (e) There is a procession of mourners; (f) The poet reflects on divine justice and contemporary evils; (g) There is a 'flower' passage, describing the decoration of the bier, etc.; (h) At the end there is a renewal of hope and joy, with the idea expressed that death is the beginning of life.

After Spenser, Milton established the form of the pastoral elegy in England with *Lycidas* (1637), a poem inspired by the death of Henry King. In the same tradition as *Astrophil* and *Lycidas* are *Adonais* (1821), Shelley's lament for Keats; and *Thyrsis* (1867), Matthew Arnold's lament – he calls it a monody (*q.v.*) – for A. H. Clough. They follow Bion's *Lament for Adonis* by having a hopeful conclusion and all except Spenser's dwell on the poets' own problems and anxieties. However, in *The Ruines of Time* (1591), an allegorical elegy on the death of Sidney, Spenser laments the neglect of letters and refers to his own position.

In Memoriam (1850), Tennyson's elegy for Hallam, differs from the others in that it lacks the pastoral conventions. But most of the other features are retained and the element of personal reflection is much more marked.

Gray's *Elegy* is also in a class of its own because it laments the passing of a way of life.

Since *In Memoriam* many poets have written elegiac poems (e.g. Gerard Manley Hopkins's *Wreck of the Deutschland*), but the formal pastoral elegy has not been favoured. Many recent British and American poets have composed fine elegies. A distinguished example is Douglas Dunn's *Elegies* (1985): thirty-nine poems, linked in theme and mood, and written in a wide variety of forms and meters, which comprise a poignant and profoundly moving *in memoriam* tribute to his wife, who died young. Tony Harrison's *V* (1985), a powerful meditation on a churchyard, is also outstanding.

Many European poets have made varied and noteworthy contributions to the elegy, or have written noble elegiac poems. The *ballades* of Villon, for instance; some poems by Camoëns (1524?–1580), Chiabrera (1552–1638) and Filicaia (1642–1707); Ronsard's *Elégies* in the 16th c.; Pushkin's *Elegy on the Portrait of F-M. Barclay de Tolly*; several poems by the Slovene Prešeren in *Slovo od mladosti* (1830) and *Sonetje nesrece* (1834); several poems, also, by the Sardinian Satta (1867–1914), particularly some in *Canti Barbaricini* (1910); not to mention Rilke's *Duino Elegies* (1922), and several collections by Juan Ramón Jiménez – *Elegías puras* (1908), *Elegías intermedias* (1909) and *Elegías lamentables* (1910). But perhaps Leopardi, more than anyone else, in making despair and *noia* beautiful, achieved the best of elegiac poetry. *See also* ELEGIAC STANZA; EPICEDIUM; GRAVEYARD SCHOOL OF POETRY; OCCASIONAL VERSE.

elision The omission or slurring of a syllable, as in the following lines from *Paradise Lost* describing the opening of the the gates of Hell:

> On a sudden open fly
> With impetuous recoil and jarring sound
> Th'infernal doors, and on their hinges grate
> Harsh thunder.

The 18th c. poets often practised elision in order to secure a level decasyllabic line. The omission of one or two adjacent vowels is also called synelepha. *See* CONTRACTION; SYNAERESIS; SYNCOPE.

Elizabethan period A rather vague classification applied as a rule to the second half of the 16th c. and the early part of the 17th. Elizabeth actually reigned from 1558 to 1603. Some take the period to run from her accession to 1642, the year when the theatres were shut. In this case it includes the Jacobean and much of the Caroline period (*qq.v.*). The forty-odd years of Elizabeth's reign alone were remarkable for their creative activity and output in English literature, especially drama. At this time there flourished some dozens of dramatists, many of whom were prolific writers. Apart from drama, almost every literary form was exploited, developed and embellished. Among the more famous writers of the age were: Marlowe, Sir Philip Sidney, Greene, Kyd, Nashe, Spenser, Daniel, Sir Francis Bacon, Lodge, Shakespeare, Sir Walter Ralegh and Ben Jonson.

ellipsis (Gk 'leaving out') A figurative device where a word (or several words) is left out in order to achieve more compact expression. It has been frequently used by modern poets like Ezra Pound, T. S. Eliot and W. H. Auden. The following lines from Eliot's *The Waste Land* suggest the kind of use that may be made of ellipsis:

> Elizabeth and Leicester
> Beating oars
> The stern was formed
> A gilded shell
> Red and gold
> The brisk swell
> Rippled both shores
> Southwest wind
> Carried down stream
> The peal of bells
> White towers

See ASYNDETON; PARATAXIS.

El Teatro Campesino (Sp 'the farmworkers' theatre') A theatrical group created in 1965 by Luis Valdez as part of a trade union. Valdez was particularly concerned with the plight of the Chicanos, an impoverished and underprivileged North American racial group of Spanish and American Indian ancestry, and he wished to use theatre in support of a Chicano farm labourers' strike. The aims were political and documentary. A permanent base for the company was established at San Juan Bautista in 1971. By *c.* 1980 there were believed to be some eighty Chicano theatre companies. *See also* DOCUMENTARY THEATRE.

emblem-book A book of symbolic pictures with a motto. The pictures were usually woodcuts or engravings to illustrate the word or motto, plus an *explicatio*, or exposition. Among the earliest emblem-books was the *Emblematum Liber* (1522) by the Milanese writer Alciati. The earliest English emblem-book was probably Geoffrey Witney's *Choice of Emblemes* (1586); and the most famous was certainly Francis Quarles's *Emblemes* (1635). About the same time George Wither produced a *Collection of Emblemes.* Some makers of emblems wrote verses in the shape of objects like crosses and altars – hence altar poem (*q.v.*) and *carmen figuratum.* Wither actually wrote a dirge (*q.v.*) in rhomboidal form. The early emblem-books were plundered for images by Elizabethan and 17th c. poets. William Blake revived the emblem form in *The Gates of Paradise* (1793). A notable work on the subject is Rosemary Freeman's *English Emblem Books* (1948). *See also* CONCEIT; GNOMIC VERSE; PATTERN POETRY.

emendation The correction or alteration of a text or manuscript where it is, or appears to be, corrupt.

emotive language Language intended to express or arouse emotional reactions towards the subject. To be distinguished from referential language which aims only to denote; for instance, the language of the scientist and the philosopher. In *The Meaning of Meaning* (1923) C. K. Ogden and I. A. Richards made the distinctions clear. *See* APOLLONIAN/DIONYSIAN; ASSOCIATION; CONNOTATION; DENOTATION.

empathy The word was introduced in 1909 by Titchener when translating the German word *Einfühlung*. The idea of empathy was developed in Germany by Lotze in *Mikrokosmus* (1858). When we experience empathy we identify ourselves, up to a point, with an animate or inanimate object. One might even go so far as to say that the experience is an involuntary projection of ourselves *into* an object. Thus the contemplation of a work of sculpture might give us a physical sensation similar to that suggested by the work. This is related to the common experience of lifting a leg when watching a man or a horse jumping. In a different way, reading, for instance, Gerard Manley Hopkins's *The Windhover*, one might empathically experience some of the physical sensations evoked in the description of the movement of the falcon.

Sympathy, on the other hand, suggests a conformity or agreement of feelings and temperament, and an emotional identification with a person.

enallage (Gk 'exchange') A figurative device which involves the substitution of one grammatical form for another. Common in metaphor. For example: 'to palm someone off'; 'to have a good laugh'; 'to be wived'; 'to duck an appointment'. *See also* HYPALLAGE.

encadenamiento (Sp 'chaining together') In a type of Galician poetry in which parallel stanzas are a feature there is a variation known as *encadenamiento* in which the first line of the third stanza is the second line of the third stanza. This is followed by a new line. *See also* TERZA RIMA.

enchiridion (Gk 'manual') A book that can be carried by hand. *See* GUIDEBOOK; HANDBOOK; MANUAL; VADE MECUM.

encomium (L from Gk 'praise') Formal eulogy in prose or verse glorifying people, objects, ideas or events. Originally it was a Greek choral song in celebration of a hero sung at the *komos* or triumphal procession at the end of the Olympic games. Pindar wrote some encomiastic odes praising the winners. Many English poets have produced encomiastic verse: Milton's *Ode on the Morning of Christ's Nativity* (1629); Dryden's *Song for St Cecilia's Day* (1687); Gray's *Hymn to Adversity* (1742); Wordsworth's *Ode to Duty* (1805). Encomium can also be the vehicle of irony (*q.v.*) as Erasmus demonstrated in *Moriae Encomium* 'The Praise of Folly' (1509), a satire directed against the follies of theologians and churchmen. A curiosity in this genre is the *Panegyrici Latini*, a collection of encomia on Roman emperors dating from 289 to 389. *See also* EPINICION; OCCASIONAL VERSE; ODE; PANEGYRIC.

encyclical An official statement by a Pope. They are known by their opening words (in Latin). Famous recent examples have been: *Rerum Novarum* (1891) by Pope Leo XIII; *Quadragesimo Anno*

(1931) by Pope Pius XI, so called because it came forty years after Pope Leo's; *Pacem in Terris* (1963) by Pope John XXIII, a landmark in the *Aggiornamento*; and *Redemptor Hominis* (1979) by Pope John Paul II.

encyclopaedia The term derives from the Greek *enkyklios* 'circular' or 'general' and *paideiā* 'discipline' or 'instruction'. Though not known to Classical writers, the term embraced that 'circle' of instruction which included grammar, rhetoric, music, mathematics, philosophy, astronomy and gymnastics. The first use of the term in English appears to be that in Sir Thomas Elyot's *Boke of the Governour* (1531), a treatise on education. We again find the term in the title of Paul Scalich de Lika's *Encyclopaediae seu orbis disciplinarum tam sacrarum quam profanarum epistemon* (1559).

There are three basic kinds of encyclopaedia: (a) those which are encyclopaedic in intent but not universally comprehensive; (b) comprehensive encyclopaedias; (c) special encyclopaedias.

Some famous early encyclopaedic works are Varro's *Rerum Humanarum et Divinarum Antiquitates* (1st c. BC), the Elder Pliny's *Historia Naturalis* (1st c. AD), Isidore of Seville's *Originum seu Etymologiarum Libri* (7th c.), Martianus Capella's *De Nuptiis Mercurii et Philologiae* (5th c.) and Rabanus Maurus's *De Universo* (9th c.). The greatest medieval encyclopaedia was the the tripartite *Speculum* of Vincent de Beauvais (13th c.): *Speculum Historiale*, *Speculum Naturale* and *Speculum Doctrinale*. Also to the 13th c. belongs Bartholomaeus Anglicus's *De Proprietatibus Rerum* later translated into English by John of Trevisa (1398).

During the Renaissance period and the 17th c. other encyclopaedic works were Johann Heinrich Alsted's *Encyclopaedia Cursus Philosophici* (1608), which was later developed by the author into *Encyclopaedia septem tomis distincta* (1620). This was one of the last encyclopaedic works in Latin. Hereafter it was customary to use the vernacular. Later in this century there appeared Moréri's *Grand Dictionnaire Historique* (1643–80), Hofmann's *Lexicon Universale* (1677), Thomas Corneille's *Dictionnaire des Arts et des Sciences* (1694) and Pierre Bayle's *Dictionnaire historique et critique* (1697) – all major works.

In the 18th c. a large number of important works in English, French and German were published. Some of the principal ones were: *Universal, Historical, Geographical, Chronological and Classical Dictionary* (1703); John Harris's *Lexicon Technicum, or an Universal English Dictionary of Arts and Sciences* (1704); Ephraim

Chambers's *Cyclopaedia, or an Universal Dictionary of Arts and Sciences* (1728). Upon this monumental work was based the *Encyclopédie ou Dictionnaire raisonné des Sciences, des Arts and des Métiers* (1751–76), which was compiled by D'Alembert and Diderot in 35 volumes.

In 1771 appeared the first edition of the *Encyclopaedia Britannica.* The ten-volume edition – and this was the first attempt in the English language to encompass the sum of human knowledge – appeared soon afterwards (1777–84). Eminent scholars and scientists have contributed to it. It remains, in its various successive editions, and continuous revisions, one of the best of all encyclopaedias.

In the 19th and 20th c. there were an increasing number of encyclopaedias which attempted to cope with the vast quantities of knowledge accumulating daily. Some of the more famous are: *Encyclopédie méthodique ou par ordre de matières*, a work in 200 volumes which came out between 1781 and 1832; a successor to Chambers's work called the *New Encyclopaedia* (1802–20), in 45 volumes; Brewster's *Edinburgh Encyclopaedia* (1809–31); the *Encyclopaedia Metropolitana* (1817–45); Ersch and Gruber's *Allgemeine Encyclopädie der Wissenschaften und Künste* (this was first published in 1818 and thereafter 167 volumes were produced); the *Penny Encyclopaedia*, begun in 1833; the *Encyclopaedia Americana* (1829–32); another version of Chambers's *Encyclopaedia* (1860–68); Larousse's *La Grand Dictionnaire du XIXe siècle* (1866–76); the *Encyclopédie Française* (1935); the *Encyclopedia Italiana* (1929–39); the *Bolshaya Sovietskaya Entsiklopedia* (1928–47), in 65 volumes; the *Encyclopedia universal ilustrada europeo-americana* (1905–30), in 70 volumes.

There are also many specialist encyclopaedias. The following are especially notable: the *Encyclopaedia of Gardening* (1822) by Loudon; *A Dictionary of Music and Musicians* (1878–90) by Sir George Grove, most recently reworked as *The New Grove* (1980); the *Dictionary of National Biography* (1882–1901), to which there are many supplements; the *Jewish Encyclopaedia* (1901–6); the *Catholic Encyclopaedia* (1907–14); the *Dictionary of Applied Chemistry* (1891, revised in various editions since); *Allgemeines Lexicon der bildender Künstler* (1907–47), in 37 volumes; the *Encyclopaedia of Religion and Ethics* (1908–26); and the *Encyclopaedia of the Social Sciences* (1930–35). *See* DICTIONARY.

endecha (Sp 'dirge, lament') The term may derive from Latin *indicia* 'manifestations'. A metrical combination used repeatedly in compositions on sombre themes and made up of six- or seven-syllable lines, usually with assonance. The strophic form of the *endecha real* or 'royal lament', introduced in the 16th c., was usually of four lines. The *endecha* is sometimes called a *romancillo*. A well-known example is Lope de Vega's *Pobre barquilla mía*.

end-rhyme This occurs at the end of a line of verse, and is distinguished from head-rhyme or alliteration (*qq.v.*) and internal rhyme (*q.v.*).

end-stopped line A term applied to verse where the sense and meter coincide in a pause at the end of a line. End-stopped couplets were characteristic of a great deal of 18th c. poetry. This passage from Pope's *Essay on Man* illustrates both the end-stopped line and the open-ended line:

> All nature is but art unknown to thee,
> All chance, direction which thou canst not see;
> All discord, harmony not understood;
> All partial evil, universal good;
> And, spite of pride, in erring reason's spite,
> One truth is clear: Whatever is, is right.

The incidence of the end-stopped line has been used to date Shakespeare's plays and other works. *See* CLOSED COUPLET; COUPLET; ENJAMBEMENT; HEROIC COUPLET; OPEN COUPLET; SINGLE-MOULDED LINE.

engagement *See* COMMITMENT.

English sonnet *See* SONNET.

English Stage Company Founded in 1956 by George Devine (1910–66) at the Royal Court Theatre, London. The Royal Court had opened in 1888 and was originally named The Court. Early on it became distinguished in theatrical history because it was there that Harley Granville Barker (1877–1946) established George Bernard Shaw in the theatre, besides presenting classics, Shakespeare, new plays and the work of European playwrights, all in the course of the years 1904–7. Devine's contribution to a revival of British drama was immeasurable, and it was he who established dramatists such as John Osborne, Arnold Wesker, Edward Bond, David Storey, N. F. Simpson, Christopher Logue, Samuel Beckett, John

Arden *et al.* Classics were also presented, plus the plays of some European dramatists such as Jean-Paul Sartre, Jean Genet, Brecht and Eugène Ionesco. After his death Devine's adventurous policy was continued under various directors and yet more dramatists were introduced, including Heathcote Williams, Joe Orton, Christopher Hampton, E. A. Whitehead, David Hare, Athol Fugard, Brian Friel, Howard Barker, Howard Brenton and Caryl Churchill. In 1969 the studio Theatre Upstairs was opened.

englyn A group of strict Welsh meters. The *englyn* monorhyme (*q.v.*) is the most popular of all the strict meters. *See also* CYNGHANEDD; CYWYDD.

enjambement (F 'in-striding' from *jambe* 'leg') Running on of the sense beyond the second line of one couplet (*q.v.*) into the first line of the next. The device was commonly used by 16th and 17th c. poets but much less frequently in the 18th c. The Romantic poets revived its use. This was part of the reaction against what were felt to be restrictive rules governing the composition of verse. This example is from Keats's *Endymion*, a poem in which he used it often:

> Who, of men, can tell
> That flowers would bloom, or that green fruit would swell
> To melting pulp, that fish would have bright mail,
> The earth its dower or river, wood, and vale,
> The meadows runnels, runnels pebble-stones,
> The seed its harvest, or the lute its tones,
> Tones ravishment, or ravishment its sweet
> If human souls did never kiss and greet?

See CLOSED COUPLET; END-STOPPED LINE; REJET; RUN-ON LINE.

enlightenment A term used to describe a literary and philosophical movement in Europe between *c.* 1660 and *c.* 1770. In German the term is *Aufklärung* and the period is referred to as the *Zeitalter der Aufklärung*. In England it is sometimes referred to as 'the Age of Reason'. The period was characterized by a profound faith in the powers of human reason and a devotion to clarity of thought, to harmony, proportion and balance. Most of the best writers and philosophers of the period expressed themselves in lucid and often luminous prose. Some of the most notable figures were: (a) in Germany – Kant (1724–1804), who included *What is Enlightenment?* (1784) among his many works; Moses Mendelssohn (1729–86); and Lessing (1729–81); (b) in France – Voltaire (1694–1778) and Diderot (1713–84); (c) in England – Locke (1632–1704); Newton (1642–1727); Berkeley (1685–1753); Johnson (1709–84); and Hume (1711–76). *See also* AUGUSTAN AGE; DECORUM; GREAT CHAIN OF BEING; STURM UND DRANG.

enoplius A term in Classical Greek prosody which has the meaning and force of being 'in martial arms', or 'up in arms'. The verse scheme was either:
∪ / ∪ ∪ / ∪ ∪ / /
or:
∪ ∪ / ∪ ∪ / ∪ ∪/ /.

ensalada (Sp 'salad, medley, mix-up') Colloquially a 'hodge-podge' and, in literature, a poem comprising lines and strophes of varying lengths and various rhyme schemes. Usually a composition of a lyric nature. Possibly the earliest known example in Spanish is by Fray Ambrosio Montesinos *c.* 1500.

ensenhamen An Old Provençal form of didactic poem. They were usually composed in a non-lyrical meter. Their burden (*q.v.*) was normally advice or instruction, on a variety of topics. *See* DIDACTIC POETRY.

entelechy A term used by Aristotle to denote the realization or complete expression of something that was potential. Later it was used by writers to signify what helped to develop perfection.

entertainment As a specific literary classification, a term used by Graham Greene to distinguish his serious novels from his more light-hearted ones. For instance, he classes *The Power and the Glory* and *The End of the Affair* as novels; *A Gun for Sale* and *Our Man in Havana* as 'entertainments'.

entr'acte (F 'between act') A short interlude, often musical, to divert an audience between the acts of a play.

entremés A Spanish term deriving from French *entremets*. A diversion (dramatic or otherwise) between the courses of a banquet.

In Catalonia they were called *entrameses* and the term was later applied to dramatic interludes during the Corpus Christi procession. In Castilian, during the 16th and 17th c., they were brief comic interludes performed between the acts of a play. Many were written by well-known dramatists, including Cervantes, Lope de Vega and Calderón. In the 18th c., similar entertainments were named *sainete*; and in the 19th c. the *género chico* was comparable. *See also* ENTR'ACTE; INTERLUDE; INTERMEZZI.

entremets *See* ENTREMES.

envelope When the envelope device is used a line or a stanza is repeated, either in the same form or with a slight variation, to enclose the rest of the poem. There are several variations. Keats uses the first four lines of *The Mermaid Tavern* to envelop the rest of the poem at the end.

An envelope stanza also denotes a group of lines which has enclosed rhymes – say, abba. Tennyson used this stanza form in *In Memoriam*.

envoi (F 'a sending on the way') Also *envoy*. A final stanza, shorter than the preceding ones, often used in the *ballade* (*q.v.*) and *chant royal* (*q.v.*). In a *ballade* there are usually four lines, in *chant royal* five or seven. The *envoi* also repeats the refrain (*q.v.*) of the poem. Among English poets Chaucer used it in *Lenvoy de Chaucer à Scogan* and in *Lenvoy de Chaucer à Bukton*. But Chaucer's *envoi* to Scogan was equal in length to the other stanzas. Scott, Southey, Swinburne and Wilde, among others, also employed the device. More recently, Chesterton, in *A Ballade of an Anti-Puritan*:

> Prince Bayard would have smashed his sword
> To see the sort of knights you dub –
> Is that the last of them – O Lord!
> Will someone take me to a pub?

epanados (Gk 'a repeating of words') A figure of speech in which a word or a phrase is repeated at the beginning and middle, or at the middle and end of a sentence. As in this line from Philip Sidney's *Arcadia*: 'Hear you this soul-invading voice, and count it but a voice?'. *See* EPANALEPSIS.

epanalepsis (Gk 'a taking up again') A figure of speech which contains a repetition of a word or words after other words have come between them. There is a good example at the beginning of *Paradise Lost*:

> Say first, for Heaven hides nothing from thy view,
> Nor the deep tract of Hell, say first what cause
> Moved our grand Parents, in that happy state . . .

See ANADIPLOSIS; EPANADOS; REPETITION.

epanaphora *See* ANAPHORA.

epanorthosis (Gk 'setting straight again') A figure of speech in which something said is corrected or commented on.

epic An epic is a long narrative poem, on a grand scale, about the deeds of warriors and heroes. It is a polygonal, 'heroic' story incorporating myth, legend, folk tale and history. Epics are often of national significance in the sense that they embody the history and aspirations of a nation in a lofty or grandiose manner.

Basically, there are two kinds of epic: (a) primary – also known as oral or primitive; (b) secondary – also known as literary. The first belongs to the oral tradition (*q.v.*) and is thus composed orally and recited; only much later, in some cases, is it written down. The second is written down at the start.

In category (a) we may place, for example, *Gilgamesh*, *Iliad* and *Odyssey*, *Beowulf*, the lays of the *Elder Edda* and the epic cycles or *narodne pesme* of the South Slavs. In category (b) we may put Virgil's *Aeneid*, Lucan's *Pharsalia*, the anonymous *Song of Roland*, Camoëns's *Os Lusiadas*, Tasso's *Gerusalemme Liberata*, Milton's *Paradise Lost* and Victor Hugo's *La Légende des siècles*.

There is also a very large number of other poems which might be put into one or other category. The majority belong approximately to category (b).

Gilgamesh, the Sumerian epic (*c.* 3000 BC), is the earliest extant work in the oral tradition. It recounts the adventures of the king of that name, his travels with Enkidu the wild man, Enkidu's death and then the journey of Gilgamesh to the Babylonian Noah, Utnapishtim – the only man known to have discovered the secret of immortality. Utnapishtim shows him the plant of life. On his return a snake robs Gilgamesh of the plant, but the king consoles himself with the fame he has gained as the builder of the walls of Erech. The poem, which is in twelve books, is an account of a man's search for glory and eternal life.

Next come the Homeric epics, *Iliad* and *Odyssey* (*c.* 1000 BC), whose heroes are Achilles and Odysseus respectively. The *Iliad* recounts the story of the wars between the Greeks and the Trojans, and in particular the anger of Achilles caused by Agamemnon's slight, and how Achilles slew Hector and dragged his body round the walls of Troy. The *Odyssey* relates the adventures of Odysseus during his return from the Trojan wars to his island home in Ithaca.

Beowulf survives in a single MS (probably of the 10th c., though a much earlier date is ascribed to the composition of the poem – very likely some time in the 8th c.). The poem relates the exploits of a legendary Geatish hero who first rids the Danish kingdom of Hrothgar of two demonic monsters: Grendel and Grendel's mother. Later in the story, after a long reign (a period which appears to have been of little interest to the epic poet), Beowulf meets a dragon, kills it with the help of Wiglaf, but dies of his wounds.

These primary epics have features in common: a central figure of heroic, even superhuman calibre, perilous journeys, various misadventures, a strong element of the supernatural, repetition of fairly long passages of narrative or dialogue, elaborate greetings, digressions, epic similes (particularly in the Homeric poems), long speeches, vivid and direct descriptions of the kind favoured by the ballad-maker and, in general, a lofty tone; the tone of Classical tragedy. All is larger than life. A further and important characteristic of primary epic is the use of the stock epithet, known as the Homeric epithet and the kenning (*qq.v.*).

Primary epic is, in many cases, the result of a number of lays or ballads being gradually joined together by a poet or bard. The lays or ballads are of common knowledge and of common inheritance and have been often recited by a bard, rhapsodist, *scop*, *skald*, *guslar*, troubadour or gleeman (*qq.v.*). There eventually comes a time when, in an increasingly literate society, the lays or ballads are written down for the use of minstrels.

In Book VIII of the *Odyssey* there is a kind of 'inset' description of the blind bard or musician which gives us an insight into the composition of oral epic. Homer describes how a herald leads in a favourite bard who is placed in a silver-studded chair in the midst of the company. The herald then hangs the bard's lyre on a peg just above his head and guides the bard's hand to it. After the company has finished eating and drinking the bard is inspired by the Muse to sing about famous men. He chooses a passage from a well-known lay which recounts a quarrel between Odysseus and Achilles and how they fell out at a ceremonial banquet.

About a third of the way through *Beowulf* there is an account of how a thane of the company began to compose a lay about Beowulf:

> Now and then the famous warriors let their bay horses gallop, – run on in races, where the country tracks seemed suitable, – excellent in repute.
>
> At times a thane of the king, a warrior filled with poetic eloquence, who remembered many lays, who recollected countless old traditions, framed a new story in words correctly linked. The man began to set forth with skill the deed of Beowulf, and fluently to tell a well-told tale, – to weave together his words.
>
> (J. R. Clark Hall's translation)

There are many other instances of oral epic and one may suppose that in the more primitive societies the Homeric tradition of primary epic still exists. It certainly does among the South Slavs.

Secondary epic is composed by being written down in the first place. Early and important instances in Classical literature are the works of Naevius and Ennius. Naevius (*c.* 270–*c.* 199 BC) wrote a long epic in Saturnian verse about the First Punic War. Ennius (239–169 BC) composed *Annales*, in eighteen books. Neither work survives complete.

Both these authors wrote of Roman history and legend, but Virgil is generally regarded as the first national poet. The *Aeneid* (*c.* 30–19 BC) records and celebrates the foundation of Rome by Aeneas after many hazardous adventures following upon the Trojan wars and the fall of Troy. As in many other epics (primary *and* secondary) there is the central heroic figure, and there are many elements of Homeric epic in the poem. One might even say that the *Aeneid* was the Roman's answer and challenge to the Greek epics. Certainly Virgil's style and method recall Homer's (invocations, digressions, similes), but Virgil is a more 'civilized' poet, a more conscious and 'contriving' artist. He also has an intense feeling for and sense of the past.

Two other Latin poets wrote works on an epic scale: Ovid and Lucan. Ovid's *Metamorphoses* (1st c. AD) in fifteen books, in tone and style – indeed, in many ways – is epic in the manner of Virgil, but, by comparison, it is a diffused, episodic and very nearly sprawling creation; and it has no central hero. Broadly speaking Ovid adopted the framework of epic and worked into it anything he felt like including, rather as Dante did in the *Divina Commedia* though that is a *much* more elaborately constructed poem. In more modern times, and at a humbler level, Ezra Pound in *Cantos* and David Jones in *Anathemata* have both composed major works in the mode of what may be called 'collage' epic. It should be noted that Ovid's influence in the late Middle Ages and during the Renaissance period was immense, very nearly as great as Virgil's.

Lucan's *Pharsalia* (1st c. AD) is an epic poem about the civil war between Caesar and Pompey. Lucan based the structure and style on that of other epic poets and, though unfinished, the poem was intended to have the full epic treatment, and did include many, by then, established epic conventions. However, it seems generally agreed that *Pharsalia* is very uneven, though fitfully splendid – largely because of its fine descriptive passages and glittering epigrams.

Apart from the *Ilias Latina*, a Latin version of the *Iliad* composed in the 1st c. AD, there is little of note in epic in Europe for the best part of a thousand years. Outside Europe, however, there are the great Indian epics, the *Mahabharata* and the *Ramayana* – both of very uncertain date though the former is ascribed to a period AD 300–500. Towards the end of the first millennium the Persian Firdowsi composed *Shah-Nameh*, a national epic, the equivalent of the *Aeneid* and *Os Lusiadas*.

Though epic appears to be dormant in Europe for a thousand years we may suppose that the oral tradition was still alive and that materials were being gathered for the good reason that in the 11th and 12th c. a considerable body of epic poetry, oral in origin, was being written down in order to preserve it, and a considerable quantity of literary epic was also composed.

The *Chanson de Roland* (*c.* 1100) was probably the best of all the *chansons de gestes* (*q.v.*). Then came the Spanish *Poema de mío Cid* (*c.* 1200); the Provençal epic *Chanson de la Croisade Albigeoise* (13th c.); the German *Kudrun* (*c.* 1240) and the *Nibelungenlied* (early 13th c.); the French epic *Huon de Bordeaux* (*c.* 1220); the Middle Dutch epic *Beatrijs* (14th c.); *Heliand*, the only surviving German epic in alliterative long lines; the *Dede Korkut* stories which are twelve Turkish epic tales of the oral tradition collected in the 14th c.; not to mention the great body of Eddic and Skaldic poetry and the Icelandic sagas (*q.v.*).

Other notable epics are: (a) a group of Armenian tales (comparable to Russian *bylina*, *q.v.*) belonging to the 10th or 11th c. and first taken down in dialect versions in 1873 and given the general title

David of Sasun; (b) the Tatar epic *Edigei* (14th–15th c.); (c) the Finnish national epic *Kalevala* ('Land of Kalevala'), comprising numerous folksongs collected and taken down in the 19th c.; (d) the *Kalevid*, the Estonian national epic.

At some stage primary and secondary epic were, in a sense, beginning to overlap and influence each other. In some parts of the world this process was to continue for a long time. For example, the Serbian *narodne pesme* ('peoples' songs'), which comprise various cycles of national epic, were being collected and recorded in the 19th c., but one could still hear them being composed and recited according to ancient oral tradition in the 1960s.

In general, from early in the 13th c. literary or secondary epic becomes the main form – and in this Virgil is the principal influence. This is particularly apparent in the works of the two great Italian poets Dante and Petrarch. Early in the 14th c. Dante wrote his *Divina Commedia* (*c.* 1310) in Italian; later in the century Petrarch wrote his epic *Africa* in Latin. The *Divina Commedia* is a 'personal' epic, a kind of autobiographical and spiritual Aeneid. *Africa* records the struggle between Rome and Carthage.

Neither Langland's *Piers Plowman* nor Chaucer's *Canterbury Tales* (both late 14th c.) have any claims as conventional epics, but by virtue of their range, diversity and scale they are of epic proportions – just as Ovid's *Metamorphoses* are. Their imaginative depth and scope, too, rival the aspirations of their great epic predecessors.

A hundred and more years later two Italian poets created what was very nearly a new form of epic – a long poem which was both romantic and comic. Hitherto the world of epic had been overwhelmingly masculine and any love interest or anything approaching a heroine was rare. Boiardo's unfinished *Orlando Innamorato* (late 15th c.) dealt with three main themes: Charlemagne's wars against Gradasso and Agramante; Orlando's love for Angelica; Ruggiero's love for Bradamante. Ariosto's *Orlando Furioso* (1532) was a sequel to it. Orlando is driven mad by love for Angelica; but the heroine is Bradamante, and the love between her and Ruggiero is the main subject of the work. The poem contains a certain amount of mockery of chivalric ideals and knightly prowess.

There are two other outstanding European epics of the 16th c., namely Camoëns's *Os Lusiadas* (1572) and Tasso's *Gerusalemme Liberata* (1575). The first is Classical and Virgilian in structure and spirit, and indeed Camoëns set out to do for Portugal what Virgil had done for Rome. It has for its theme Vasco da Gama's discovery of the sea-route to India. In the course of the poem, by narrative and through 'prophecy', Camoëns covers the whole history of Portugal, and in doing so creates a 'nationalistic' epic in which the poet sees the Portuguese waging a holy war against paganism. Tasso's subject is the recovery of Jerusalem in the First Crusade. It is thus a Christian rather than a 'nationalistic' epic. It has many heroes and heroines, owes a good deal to the tradition of the medieval romance (*q.v.*) and contains a strong element of the chivalric and supernatural. It is also a didactic and allegorical poem.

Spenser's *The Faerie Queene* (1589, 1596) was the greatest narrative poem in 16th c. English literature. It is a mixture of epic and romance for which Spenser designed what has come to be known as the Spenserian stanza (*q.v.*). He apparently planned it in twelve books, but only six, and a further fragment, survive. The poet was obviously conscious of working in the grand epic tradition. In the prefatory letter, to Sir Walter Ralegh, he mentioned as his four greatest predecessors: Homer, Virgil, Ariosto and Tasso.

Spenser organized the poem as an extended and elaborate allegory or 'darke conceit', as he put it, using the material of the Arthurian legends and the Charlemagne romances. The hero of each book represents a virtue, and the poem is throughout a didactic work of astonishing complexity, richness and allusiveness.

In addition it should be noted that it is a courtesy book (*q.v.*), the most elaborate and courtly of all books of etiquette in an age which produced so many of them. In the same prefatory letter to Sir Walter Ralegh, Spenser made perfectly clear what his intention was: 'The generall end therefore of all the booke is to fashion a gentleman or noble person in vertuous and gentle discipline.'

The *Faerie Queene* brings to an end the tradition of the epic of chivalry – and the whole cult of chivalry which, by this time, was beginning to come under satirical attack. However, ultimately, Spenser was to have almost as much influence (some of it baneful) on the form and style of the narrative poem as Milton was to have a century later with *Paradise Lost*; arguably the greatest of all the post-Classical epic poems.

There was something of a craze for epic near the middle of the 17th c., especially in France where a number of poets produced works, most of which are now barely readable and are certainly seldom read. Among them one might mention Saint-Amant's *Moyse sauvé* (1653), Godeau's *Saint Paul* (1654), Chapelain's *La Pucelle* (1656), Desmarets's *Clovis* (1657), Louis le Laboureur's *Charlemagne* (1664) and Carel de Saint-Garde's *Childebrand*

(1666). One might also mention at this point Cowley's unfinished *Davideis* (1656), a twelve-book epic in the Virgilian tradition, in rhyming couplets. Two years later Milton began dictating *Paradise Lost*, the theme of which was the loftiest, the grandest and, in many ways, the most difficult ever undertaken by any poet. At the very beginning of the poem, in a traditional and conventional manner, he states his intention and makes clear the magnitude of his task:

Of Man's first disobedience, and the fruit
Of that forbidden tree, whose mortal taste
Brought death into the World, and all our woe,
With loss of Eden, till one greater Man
Restore us, and regain the blissful seat,
Sing, Heavenly Muse . . .
        I thence
Invoke thy aid to my adventurous song,
That with no middle flight intends to soar
Above th'Aonian mount, while it pursues
Things unattempted yet in prose or rime.

Then he invokes the aid of the Holy Ghost Himself.

Milton's least soluble problem was how to create a convincing God: the first cause uncaused, omniscient and omnipotent; and at the same time preserve an element of doubt and suspense in his story.

Milton was an immensely learned poet and had studied the work of his predecessors in epic in great detail. Preparing long and beginning late, he trained himself for the feat. One feels that he was fully conscious of the fact that he was competing at an Olympic level in the most arduous marathon of all and was staking everything on it.

Thus, the poem has the full epic apparatus: invocations, digressions, similes, legend, history, folklore, magic and the supernatural, eloquent speeches, perilous journeys, battles, and scenes in the underworld. The range is colossal, the sweep majestic.

The sequel, *Paradise Regained* (1671), is also an epic poem (in four books). Most people would probably agree that in this poem Milton has run out of steam, and he only occasionally attains the level of *Paradise Lost* in the scenes of the temptations of Christ.

It has become a commonplace that Milton wrote the last major epic, or the last poem that can be described with minimal reservations as epic. It may be so, but the last 300 years have produced a large number of narratives (in prose and verse) which have continued the epic tradition by virtue of their scale, their heroic themes and their elevated style.

In the late 17th c., when there was something of an obsession with the 'heroic', there set in a reaction against the heroic. This resulted in mock-epic (*q.v.*). In general, poets tended to modify and reduce the scale and scope of narrative poems, even while retaining the mode and manner of the full-dress epic with all or much of its conventional apparatus. Dryden's *Absalom and Alchitophel* (1681), for instance, is conducted in fully ceremonial manner. Later came Pope's *The Rape of the Lock* (1714) and *The Dunciad* (1728, 1735). It should be noted also that Dryden did a fine translation of the *Aeneid* and that Pope did an equally good one of the *Iliad*.

The next major poet to attempt an epic-type poem was Byron, whose *Don Juan* (1819–24) has many of the trappings and features of epic even though it is satire. Keats, his contemporary, after a careful study of *Paradise Lost*, wrote *Hyperion* (1818–19); again epic in manner and in both versions unfinished. Later in the 19th c. Matthew Arnold, William Morris, Tennyson, and Browning all wrote epic works. Arnold's principal attempts are *Sohrab and Rustum* (1853), in the Homeric and Miltonic style and marked by some particularly magnificent Miltonic similes; and *Balder Dead* (1853), which was much more in the Homeric manner. William Morris's *The Life and Death of Jason* (1867) is an uneasy mixture of Chaucerian and Miltonic influences. Tennyson's contribution to epic was *Idylls of the King*. Tennyson spent well over forty years, on and off, creating this work; beginning in 1842 with *Morte d'Arthur* and concluding with the twelfth idyll in 1885. Browning also wrote a twelve-book epic called *The Ring and the Book* (1868), a highly original poem in style and subject. In the 19th c. we also find examples of what may be called 'autobiographical' epic (a kind which has been considerably developed in the 20th c.). The outstanding instances in the 19th c. are Wordsworth's *The Prelude* (begun 1799, completed 1805, but not published until 1850), and *The Excursion* (planned 1798, published 1814).

In France the 18th c. produced one considerable epic in the shape of Voltaire's *La Henriade* (1728), but this is not generally thought to be one of his best works. His mock-heroic *La Pucelle* (1755) is much more readable. In the following century French poets were prolific in the epic form, or at any rate in long narrative poems. There are many instances of which the following are notable: Alfred de Vigny's *Héléna* (1822), *Le Déluge* (1823) and *Eloa* (1824); Lamartine's *Jocelyn* (1836) and *La Chute d'un ange* (1838); Louis

Ménard's *Prométhée délivré* (1843); Soumet's *Jeanne d'Arc* (1845); Viennet's *Franciade* (1863); Victor de Laprade's *Pernette* (1868); Leconte de Lisle's *Quaïn* (1869); and, above all, Victor Hugo's *La Légende des siècles* (1859, 1877, 1883).

There have been other attempts at epic which should be mentioned. For example, the American Joel Barlow's *Vision of Columbus* (1787), which was re-named the *Columbiad* in 1807. Also Walt Whitman's *Leaves of Grass* (1855, 1856, 1860) and Ferguson's *Congal* (1872).

In the 20th c. several poets have written works of merit on an epic scale, such as Pound's 'collage' epic *Cantos* (1925–69). An earlier work, less well known, but reminiscent in some ways of the *Cantos* is *Paterson* (1946–58) by William Carlos Williams. This, too, is a kind of collage of autobiographical material. So is David Jones's *Anathemata* (1952).

Most people would probably include three other long poems of the 20th c.: Saint-John Perse's *Anabase* (1924), which was translated by T. S. Eliot and published as *Anabasis* in 1930; Kazantzakis's *Odyssey*, a twenty-four book poem of over 33,000 lines which continues the story of Odysseus after he has returned home; and Vasco Popa's *Secondary Heaven* (1968), a series of cycles which constitute a diffused autobiographical work.

In some respects it seems that the 20th c. epic poet has tended to employ the subjective stream of consciousness (*q.v.*) method of the novelist. This is apparent in several of the works mentioned, and also in Andrew Young's remarkable poem *A Traveller in Time* (1950), in twelve parts plus a thirteenth which is a kind of conclusion or epilogue. It is a form of pilgrimage of the soul, the memory and the mind back to early Christian times; almost a 'pilgrim's regress'.

In the last hundred years or more the novel, the cinema and, to a lesser extent, the theatre have been much favoured media for narratives on an epic scale. In retrospect it seems fairly logical that as the novel (*q.v.*) developed so the novelist would find it an increasingly suitable vehicle for a grandiose treatment of individual and national destiny. Indeed, there has been an impressive number of novels which can fairly be described as epic in their range and magnitude. Famous instances are: Herman Melville's *Moby-Dick* (1851); Tolstoy's *War and Peace* (1865–72) and *Anna Karenina* (1875–6); Jaroslav Hašek's *The Good Soldier Schweik* (1920–23), a 'comic' epic in the picaresque (*q.v.*) tradition; Joyce's *Finnegans Wake* (1939); Steinbeck's *The Grapes of Wrath* (1939); Ivo Andrić's

Travnička Kronika (translated as 'Bosnian Story') 1945, and *Na Drini Cuprija* (translated as 'Bridge on the Drina') 1948; Patrick White's *The Tree of Man* (1956) and *Voss* (1957); and Pasternak's *Dr Zhivago* (1957).

The cinema has tended to be the medium for creations on an epic scale in the 20th c. but often the epic makers have been too big for their books; a shortcoming cleverly summarized in the clerihew (*q.v.*):

> Cecil B. de Mille
> Rather against his will
> Was persuaded to leave Moses
> Out of the Wars of the Roses.

In a more modest fashion epic theatre (*q.v.*) has had some success.

Ultimately epic aspires to grandeur of no common sort; to a state where men transcend their human limitations and, for a time at least, become more obviously in the image of God-like creatures. In epic the men are ten feet tall. In epic, to apply Wordsworth's lines from Book I of *The Prelude*, no familiar shapes remain,

> no pleasant images of trees,
> Of sea or sky, no colours of green fields;
> But huge and mighty forms, that do not live
> Like living men

See EPYLLION; NARRATIVE VERSE; ROMANCE.

epicedium (Gk 'funeral song') A song of mourning in praise of a dead person, sung over the corpse. A *threnos* (or dirge, *q.v.*), on the other hand, might be sung anywhere. *See* ELEGIAC DISTICH; ELEGY; MONODY.

epic simile An extended simile (*q.v.*), in some cases running to fifteen or twenty lines, in which the comparisons made are elaborated in considerable detail. It is a common feature of epic (*q.v.*) poetry, but is found in other kinds as well. A good example will be found in Milton: 'as when a wandering fire . . . So glistered the dire snake' (*Paradise Lost*, IX, 634–44). *See also* CATALOGUE VERSE.

epic theatre A form of drama and a method of presentation developed in Germany in the 1920s. It originated in the *neue Sachlichkeit* (*q.v.*) period in Berlin and the term was first used of the early plays of Arnolt Bronnen, particularly *Vatermord* (1922), which very nearly caused a riot, and of Alfons Paquet's *Fahnen* (1924), which was subtitled 'epic' and was produced by Erwin Piscator for his socialist theatre. Piscator was the founder and director of this influential movement. Since then the term 'epic theatre' has been most closely associated with Bertolt Brecht (1898–1956). Epic theatre was a break with established dramatic styles. In Brecht's words, the 'essential point of epic theatre is that it appeals less to the spectator's feelings than to his reason'. It denotes a form of narrative/chronicle play which is didactic and which is not restricted by the unity of time and which presents a series of episodes in a simple and direct way: a kind of linear narration ('each scene for itself'). Notable features are the use of a Chorus (*q.v.*), a narrator, slide projection, film, placards and music. Much epic drama was devoted to the expression of political ideas and ideals, though not overtly propagandist. In many ways it has much in common with documentary theatre (*q.v.*).

Brecht discusses the concept in various works. He summarized it in his *Mahagonny* notes in 1930, and wrote at length of it in his essay *Uber die Verwendung der Musik für eine epische Bühne* (1935). He also expressed views about it in his unfinished dialogue *Der Messingkauf*, written between 1937 and 1951, and in 1949 published *Kleines Organon für das Theater*, his main theoretical work on the topic.

Piscator's dramatization of Hašek's novel *The Good Soldier Schweik* (in 1928) and *War and Peace* (in 1942) are two of the major works in epic drama. Brecht's *Threepenny Opera* (1928) and *Mother Courage and Her Children* (1941) are two others. Many dramatists have been influenced by Piscator's work and by Brecht's theory, and the practice of that theory in his plays. Among playwrights writing in German one should mention Dürrenmatt, Dorst, Frisch, Hacks, Hildesheimer, Walser and Weiss. *See also* AGITPROP DRAMA; ALIENATION EFFECT; CHRONICLE PLAY; COMMITMENT; EXPRESSIONISM; PROPAGANDA; TOTAL THEATRE.

epideictic poetry Verse which follows the rules of demonstrative oratory. Epideictic (Gk 'adapted for display') denotes oratory in praise or blame of somebody. Statius's *Silvae* (*c.* AD 92) is generally reckoned to be one of the best collections of such verse.

Epigon (Gk *epi* 'after' + *gon* 'birth') A term generally used in German to describe writers who are derivative and who work in and are influenced by the manner and tradition of distinguished predecessors. Hence the idea of a later generation who follows on. Its use is associated with Karl Immermann's popular novel *Die Epigonen* (1836).

epigram (Gk 'inscription') As a rule a short, witty statement in verse or prose which may be complimentary, satiric or aphoristic. Coleridge defined it as:

A dwarfish whole,
Its body brevity, and wit its soul.

Originally an inscription on a monument or statue, the epigram developed into a literary genre. Many of them are gathered in the *Greek Anthology* (compiled *c.* 925). Roman authors, especially Martial, also composed them.

The form was much cultivated in the 17th c. in England by Jonson, Donne, Herrick, William Drummond of Hawthornden, Dryden and Swift, and in the 18th c. by Pope, Prior, Richard Kendal, Burns and Blake. Coleridge also showed adroitness in the form, as in these lines on John Donne:

With Donne, whose muse on dromedary trots,
Wreathe iron pokers into true-love knots;
Rhyme's sturdy cripple, fancy's maze and clue,
Wit's forge and fire-blast, meaning's press and screw.

In the 19th c. Landor is generally regarded as the expert of the genre. He wrote a good many, and this is one:

Go on, go on, and love away!
Mine was, another's is, the day.
Go on, go on, thou false one! now
Upon his shoulder rest thy brow,
And look into his eyes until
Thy own, to find them colder, fill.

Mention should also be made of Belloc and Walter de la Mare, both of whom made distinguished contributions to this form. For example, Belloc's:

When we are dead, some Hunting-boy will pass
And find a stone half-hidden in tall grass
And grey with age: but having seen that stone
(Which was your image) ride more slowly on.

And de la Mare's:

> '*Homo*? Construe!' the stern-faced usher said.
> Groaned George, 'A man, sir'. 'Yes,
> Now *sapiens*?' . . . George shook a stubborn head,
> And sighed in deep distress.

Occasionally in verse an epigram takes the form of a couplet or quatrain (*qq.v.*) as part of a poem, as in this example by Pope in the *Essay on Criticism*:

> We think our fathers fools, so wise we grow,
> Our wiser sons, no doubt, will think us so.

In more recent times the verse epigram has become relatively rare, but very many (especially from the 16th c. onwards) have used the form in prose or speech to express something tersely and wittily. These are fairly recent examples: A Protestant, if he wants aid or advice on any matter, can only go to his solicitor (Disraeli); Forty years of romance make a woman look like a ruin and forty years of marriage make her look like a public building (Oscar Wilde); He [Macaulay] has occasional flashes of silence that make his conversation perfectly delightful (Sydney Smith); The optimist proclaims that we live in the best of all possible worlds; and the pessimist fears this is true (J. H. Cabell); God made women beautiful so that men would love them; and he made them stupid so that they could love men (attributed to La Belle Otero, the 19th c. courtezan).

Some other famous epigrammatists have been Lord Chesterfield, Byron, George Bernard Shaw, F. E. Smith (Lord Birkenhead) and Ogden Nash. *See also* ANTITHESIS; EPITAPH.

epigraph Four meanings may be distinguished: (a) an inscription on a statue, stone or building; (b) the writing (legend) on a coin; (c) a quotation on the title page of a book; (d) a motto heading a new section or paragraph.

epigraphy (Gk *epi* 'upon' + *graphein* 'to write') The study of inscriptions incised on a durable material (e.g. marble, stone, metal, steel) and found on tombs, statutes, plaques, tablets, public buildings, sarcophagi, etc. Inscriptions are a vital source of knowledge about the ancient world. *See* EPIGRAPH.

epilogue Three meanings may be distinguished: (a) a short speech to be delivered at the end of a play. It often makes some graceful and witty comment on what has happened and asks for the approval, if not the indulgence, of the audience; (b) the end of a fable (*q.v.*) where the moral is pointed; (c) the concluding section or paragraph of any literary work, sometimes added as a summary, but more often as an afterthought. *See also* PROLOGUE.

epimythium A summary of the moral of a fable (*q.v.*) placed at the end of the fable. If at the beginning it was called a *promythium*. *See* EPILOGUE.

epinicion A triumphal ode (*q.v.*) commemorating a victory at the Olympic Games. As a rule it comprised a number of groups of three stanzas each, arranged as strophe, antistrophe and epode (*qq.v.*) and gave an account of the victor's success. Simonides, Pindar and Baccylides all composed *epinicia*. Euripedes also wrote one for Alcibiades. *See* ENCOMIUM.

epiphany (Gk 'manifestation') The term primarily denotes the festival which commemorates the manifestation of Christ to the Gentiles in the persons of the Magi. The feast is observed on January 6th, 'Twelfth Night', the festival of the 'Three Kings'. More generally, the term denotes a manifestation of God's presence in the world. James Joyce gave this word a particular literary connotation in his novel *Stephen Hero*, part of the first draft of *A Portrait of the Artist as a Young Man*, which was first published in 1916. The relevant passage is:

> This triviality made him think of collecting many such moments together in a book of epiphanies. By an epiphany he meant a *sudden spiritual manifestation* [my italics], whether in the vulgarity of speech or of gesture or in a memorable phase of the mind itself. He believed that it was for the man of letters to record these epiphanies with extreme care, seeing that they themselves are the most delicate and evanescent of moments. He told Cranly that the clock of the Ballast Office was capable of an epiphany.

A little further on he says:

> Imagine my glimpses of that clock as the gropings of a spiritual eye which seeks to adjust its vision to an exact focus. The moment the focus is reached the object is epiphanized.

Joyce elaborates this theme at considerable length. The epiphany is a symbol of a spiritual state. This aspect of aesthetic theory is left out of *A Portrait*, but a knowledge of it is essential for an understanding of Joyce as an artist. *Dubliners*, *A Portrait*, *Ulysses* and *Finnegans Wake* are a series of increasingly complex and revealing insights of grace as well as intuitions of immortality. However, Joyce's description of such an experience does not imply a *discovery* on his part. Many writers, especially mystics and religious poets, have conveyed their experience of epiphanies. Striking instances are to be found in the poems of George Herbert, Henry Vaughan and Gerard Manley Hopkins. And there is a particularly fine passage in Wordsworth's *Prelude* (Book VIII, 539–59) which describes an epiphany.

epiphonema (Gk 'after show') A terse summary of an argument (*q.v.*); often expressed by means of epigram or *sententia* (*qq.v.*). Shakespeare concludes his sonnets with a neat rhyming couplet which sums up the argument.

epiplexis (Gk 'on-stroke') A form or style of argument which seeks to shame the interlocutor into seeing the point. For example: 'If you had any sense at all, you would understand that. . . .'

epiploce (Gk 'plaiting together') A term used by Classical prosodists to denote the various possibilities in the scansion (*q.v.*) of metrical lines.

epirrhema (Gk 'that said afterwards') A speech delivered in the *parabasis* (*q.v.*) of Old Comedy (*q.v.*) by the leader of one half of the Chorus (*q.v.*) after that part of the Chorus had sung an ode (*q.v.*). It was usually satirical, didactic or exhortatory.

epische Oper A term devised by Bertolt Brecht (1898–1956) to contrast his concept of opera (*q.v.*) with 'dramatic opera'. The principles and characteristics of epic opera are similar to those of epic theatre (*q.v.*). The music had a didactic function. Brecht invented the word 'Misuk' to denote this and to distinguish it from 'Musik'.

episode Two meanings may be distinguished: (a) an event or incident within a longer narrative; a digression (*q.v.*); (b) a section into which a serialized work is divided.

epistle A poem addressed to a friend or patron, thus a kind of 'letter' (*q.v.*) in verse. There are approximately two types: (a) on moral and philosophical themes (e.g. Horace's *Epistles*); (b) on romantic or sentimental themes (e.g. Ovid's *Heroides*).

In the Middle Ages the Ovidian type was the more popular. It influenced the theories of courtly love (*q.v.*) and may have inspired Samuel Daniel to introduce the form in, for instance, *Letter from Octavia to Marcus Antonius* (1603). During the Renaissance and thereafter it was the Horatian kind which had the greater influence. Petrarch, Ariosto and Boileau all wrote such epistles, and there were two outstanding Spanish ones; Garcilaso's *Epístola a Boscán* (1543); and the *Epístola Moral a Fabio* (early 17th c.) ascribed to various authors. In England Jonson appears to have been the first to use the Horatian mode, in *The Forest* (1616). Vaughan, Dryden and Congreve also produced epistles of the Horatian kind. Pope proved to be the most skilled practitioner of this form, especially in his *Moral Essays* (1731–5) and *An Epistle to Dr Arbuthnot* (1735). More recent poets have revived the form, which was not much favoured in the 19th c. Auden's *Letter to Lord Byron* is a good example; so is his *New Year Letter*. Louis MacNeice wrote *Letters from Iceland*.

epistolary novel A novel (*q.v.*) in the form of letters. It was a particularly popular form in the 18th c. Among the more famous examples are: Richardson's *Pamela* (1740) and *Clarissa Harlowe* (1747, 1748); Smollet's *Humphry Clinker* (1771); Rousseau's *La Nouvelle Héloïse* (1761); and Laclos's *Les Liaisons dangereuses* (1782). Less well known are Harriet Lee's *Errors of Innocence* (1786), John Moore's *Mordaunt* (1800) and Swinburne's *Love's Cross Currents* (1877). Such a technique has not been often favoured, but Mark Harris's *Wake Up, Stupid* (1959) and John Barth's *Letters* (1979) are interesting modern examples. It is not unusual for letters to make up *some* part of a novel. *See also* BRIEFROMAN.

epistrophe (Gk 'upon turning') A figure of speech in which each sentence or clause ends with the same word.

episyntheton (Gk 'compound') Meter composed of different cola (*q.v.*).

epitaph (Gk '[writing] on a tomb') Inscription on a tomb or grave; a kind of valediction which may be solemn, complimentary, witty or even flippant. Simonides of Ceos (556–468 BC) wrote epitaphs of simplicity and power, including the famous one on the Three Hundred who fell at Thermopylae:

> Go, tell the Lacedaimonians, passer-by,
> That here obedient to their laws we lie.

The major collection of Classical epitaphs is to be found in Book IV of the *Greek Anthology*. They vary from comic to serious and had considerable influence on Roman and Renaissance writers. Villon's *Ballade des pendus* (15th c.) is a fine example.

Famous epitaphs include: William Browne on the Countess of Pembroke:

> Underneath this sable hearse
> Lies the subject of all verse,
> Sidney's sister, Pembroke's mother;
> Death! ere thou has slain another,
> Fair and learn'd, and good as she,
> Time shall throw a dart at thee.

Dryden on his wife:

> Here lies my wife: here let her lie!
> Now she's at rest, and so am I.

John Wilmot, Earl of Rochester, on King Charles II:

> Here lies a great and mighty king
> Whose promise none relies on;
> He never said a foolish thing,
> Nor ever did a wise one.

Dr Johnson on Oliver Goldsmith:

> To Oliver Goldsmith, Poet, Naturalist, and Historian, who left scarcely any style of writing untouched, and touched nothing that he did not adorn.

And William Cory's rendering of an epigram by Callimachus which begins:

> They told me, Heraclitus, they told me you were dead,
> They brought me bitter news to hear, and bitter tears to shed.

Callimachus (*c.* 310–after 246 BC), as well as being a fine poet, was an erudite scholar, bibliophile and librarian at Alexandria. William Cory (1823–92) was an assistant master at Eton; his only other claim to fame is that he composed the Eton 'Boating Song'.

Not a few writers have composed their own epitaphs. Thomas Gray, for example, appended his own to his *Elegy* (1750). One of the most famous is that by Sir Walter Ralegh (said to have been written on the eve of his execution in 1618):

Even such is Time, that takes our trust
Our youth, our joys, our all we have,
And pays us but with earth and dust;
Who, in the dark and silent grave,
When we have wandered all our ways,
Shuts up the story of our days.
But from this earth, this grave, this dust,
My God shall raise me up, I trust.

Another well-known example is that composed by John Gay:

Life is a jest, and all things show it.
I thought so once; but now I know it.

And Alexis Piron's clever one:

Here lies Piron, a complete nullibiety.
Not even a Fellow of a Learned Society.

There are also Kipling's moving poem *The Appeal*, and R. L. Stevenson's *Requiem*:

Here he lies where he long'd to be;
Home is the sailor, home from sea,
And the hunter home from the hill.

Quite a few epitaphs of a more general import approximate to elegy or lament (*qq.v.*). For instance, Thomas Nashe's fine poem in *Summer's Last Will and Testament*, which begins:

Rich men, trust not in wealth,
Gold cannot buy you health,
Physic himself must fade.

This poem contains a solemn and knell-like refrain (*q.v.*):

I am sick, I must die:
Lord have mercy on us.

There are also Webster's splendid song in *The Duchess of Malfi*, beginning:

> Hark, now everything is still,
> The screech-owl, and the whistle shrill . . .

And the marvellous dirge (*q.v.*) in Shakespeare's *Cymbeline*:

> Fear no more the heat o' the sun . . .

Plus Gerard Manley Hopkins's poem *Felix Randall* and Matthew Arnold's *Requiescat*.

Occasionally one encounters a good epitaph on a tombstone. The best tend to be witty and/or laconic, such as this on a Devonshire slab:

> Here lie I by the chancel door;
> They put me here because I was poor.
> The further in, the more you pay,
> But here lie I as snug as they.

And this:

> All who come my grave to see
> Avoid damp beds and think of me.

See also COMPLAINT; CORONACH; EPICEDIUM; EPIGRAM; MONODY; UBI SUNT.

epitasis (Gk 'near intensification') That part of a play when the dénouement or climax (*qq.v.*) approaches, when the plot thickens. It precedes the catastrophe (*q.v.*). *See also* CATASTASIS; FREYTAG'S PYRAMID; PROTASIS.

epithalamion (Gk 'at the bridal chamber') A song or poem sung outside the bride's room on her wedding night. Sappho is believed to have been the first poet to use it as a literary form. Theocritus wrote one; so, among other Latin poets, did Catullus. At the Renaissance, poets revived the form and many created memorable *epithalamia*: Tasso, Ronsard and du Bellay, to name three Europeans; and in England Sir Philip Sidney, Spenser, Donne, Ben Jonson, Herrick, Marvell, Crashaw and Dryden. By general agreement one of the finest of all is Spenser's. The traditional conventions of this form required the circumstances of a wedding, the events of the wedding day, and the celebration by the poet of the married couple's experience. Spenser may have written his in honour of his own wedding (1594). Sir John Suckling (1609–42) wrote an agreeable parody of such songs called *A Ballad upon a Wedding*. After Dryden the epithalamion went out of fashion. Much later, at the beginning of the 19th c., Shelley wrote an *Epithalamium* (the *-ium* ending is the Latin form) and Tennyson closed *In Memoriam* with an epithalamion. There was also A. E. Housman's song 'He is here, Urania's son'. *See* PROTHALAMION.

epithet Usually an adjective or phrase expressing some quality or attribute which is characteristic of a person or thing. For example: Long John, Dusty Miller, Chalky White, Nobby Clark, Richard the Lionheart. *See also* HOMERIC EPITHET; POETIC DICTION.

epitome (Gk 'cutting short') An abridgement or summary. A long scientific treatise or historical work may be compressed into a single book. A good modern example is the one-volume edition (1922) of Frazer's *The Golden Bough* which originally appeared in twelve volumes (1890–1915).

epitrite (Gk 'a third as much again') In Classical prosody a metrical foot containing one unstressed and three stressed syllables: ∪ / / /. Like the paeon (*q.v.*), the epitrite had three other forms: / ∪ / /; / / ∪ /; and / / / ∪. They were known as first, second, third and fourth epitrites. Rare in English verse; occasionally used in combination with other feet. Gerard Manley Hopkins, who experimented with paeonic feet, sometimes used them. *See also* SPRUNG RHYTHM.

epizeuxis (Gk 'fastening together') A figure of speech in which a word or phrase is repeated emphatically to produce a special effect. *See* INCREMENTAL REPETITION; REFRAIN.

epode (Gk 'additional song') In a lyric ode (*q.v.*) by a Classical writer the epode completed the strophe and anti-strophe (*qq.v.*) and its metrical form was different. It is not often found in English verse, but there is an interesting example of its use in Gray's Pindaric ode, *The Progress of Poesy*.

eponymous (Gk 'giving the name to') An eponymous hero, heroine or protagonist (*qq.v.*) gives his or her name to the title of the work. For instance: *King Lear*, *Pamela*, *Silas Marner*, *Dr Zhivago*.

epopee (Gk 'poem making') An epic (*q.v.*) poem or epic poetry.

epos (Gk 'word, song') A name given to early epic (*q.v.*) poetry in the oral tradition (*q.v.*).

epyllion (Gk 'little epos', 'scrap of poetry') The sense of 'little epic' appears to date from the 19th c., when it was used to describe a short narrative poem in dactylic hexameters. The genre included mythological subjects and love themes. The poems are usually learned, elaborate and allusive. They were popular in the Alexandrian period, the late Republican and early Augustan periods. The Byzantine poets also wrote *epyllia*. As a form of narrative verse (*q.v.*) it has some affinities with the Russian *byliny* (*q.v.*), the South Slav *narodne pesme* (*q.v.*) and Greek *kleftic* songs. There are a great many poems in English literature which might be described as *epyllia*. In Renaissance poetry they tended to be a kind of erotic treatment of a mythological narrative. For example, Shakespeare's *Venus and Adonis*, Marlowe's *Hero and Leander*, Thomas Lodge's *Scillaes Metamorphosis* (1589) and Francis Beaumont's *Salmacis and Hermaphroditus* (1602). More generally the term might apply to such poems as Arnold's *Sohrab and Rustum* and C. Day Lewis's *Flight to Australia*. *See* EPIC; NARRATIVE VERSE.

equivalence In quantitative verse the rule that two short syllables equal one long.

equivoque *See* PUN.

erotesis (Gk 'question') A rhetorical device in which a question is asked in order to get a definite answer – usually 'no'.

erotic poetry It is necessary to distinguish between erotic poetry and love poetry. Erotic poetry is about sex and sexual love; love poetry tends to avoid sexual details, though there are exceptions, like some of Donne's love poems. Erotic poetry tends to concentrate on the more physical aspects of love and passion; while love poetry dwells more on the nobler manifestations of love, the 'higher' feelings.

Much erotic poetry comes from the Indian and Arab cultures. In early Sanskrit literature there is the *Medhaduta* (5th c.). To the 7th or 8th c. belongs the collection of quatrains known as the *Sringasataka*. A third important series of erotic poems is the *Pancacika*. From Arab civilization we have two major collections of poems: the *Hamasa* and the *Muallakat*, of the 10th c. The lyric form of the *ghazel* (*q.v.*) was widely used for the expression of erotic feelings in Persian, Arabic and Turkish verse in the Middle Ages.

There is also a considerable body of Greek erotic verse, particularly by Sappho and Anacreon; also a number of erotic epigrams in the *Greek Anthology* (compiled *c.* 925). Most Greek erotic poetry is lyrical. The major Roman authors are Catullus, Propertius and Ovid. Ovid's *Amores* and *Ars Amatoria* are important since they had a considerable influence on medieval literature, and in particular on the concept of courtly love (*q.v.*).

Medieval Latin lyric poetry was often erotic, and the Goliards made a notable contribution. Their work is extant in the *Carmina Burana* (*q.v.*). Memorable examples of the treatment of erotic love are also to be found in Gottfried von Strassburg's *Tristan* (13th c.) and Chaucer's *Troilus and Criseyde* (late 14th c.). Less exalted erotic themes are worked out in the medieval *fabliaux* (*q.v.*) and in stories like Chaucer's *Miller's Tale* (late 14th c.).

During the Renaissance period many poets wrote what can be regarded as erotic poetry, especially Boiardo, Tasso, Ariosto, Spenser, Marlowe and Shakespeare. Marlowe and Chapman's *Hero and Leander* (1598) and Shakespeare's *Venus and Adonis* (1593) are outstanding examples. The Italian Renaissance poets of the humanistic movement composed erotic verse, especially Giovanni Pontano and Marino. In French literature Ronsard's *Les amours de Marie* (1555) is a major example.

The last half of the 19th c. sees a noticeable increase in this kind of poetry, especially by the French symbolist poets – Gautier, Baudelaire, Mallarmé and Verlaine. In England the Pre-Raphaelite movement (*q.v.*) encouraged an interest in erotic themes. Both Dante Gabriel Rossetti and Swinburne wrote erotic verse. One should mention especially Rossetti's *The House of Life* (1881), and Swinburne's *Poems and Ballads* (1866).

The sometimes close relationship between love poetry and devotional religious poetry has produced what may be called religious love poetry in which the poet uses worldly and secular imagery and language to express divine love. The result is a species of erotic verse. The most famous example is the mystical poetry of St John of the Cross, the 16th c. Spanish mystic. His *Canciones entre el alma y el Esposo*, *Canciones del alma en la intima comunicación de unión de amor de Dios* and *Coplas del mismo hechas sobre un éxtasis de alta contemplación* are remarkable expressions of mystical love and union.

Erwartungshorizont *See* HORIZON OF EXPECTATIONS.

Erzählung (G 'narration, narrative') The term denotes the actual process of telling a story and has also been used to describe a short story (*q.v.*) and a *Novelle* (*see* NOVELLA).

Erziehungsroman *See* BILDUNGSROMAN.

escape literature *See* LITERATURE OF ESCAPE.

esperanto One of several artificial 'international' languages compounded of words from different tongues. The word appears to derive from the Spanish *esperanza* 'hope'. L. L. Zamenhof invented the language and published it in 1887.

espinella A Spanish stanza form believed to have been invented by the poet Vicente Espinel (1550–1624). It is an octosyllabic ten-line stanza which rhymes abba: accddc. Since its innovation it has been widely used.

esprit décadent A phrase associated with decadence (*q.v.*) in the period *c.* 1880–*c.* 1890. It has been attributed to the poet Jules Laforgue and he may have 'derived' it from Verlaine's sonnet *Je suis l'Empire à la fin de la décadence.* It refers to the state of mind and spirit which prevailed among and was affected by a large number of poets and men of letters in France in that era. It is particularly associated with small literary societies which flourished briefly at the time, and which met for the discussion of poetry and literature in general, art, politics, philosophy, etc. Decadence (which has nothing to do with *decade*, from the Greek word for ten) implies decay, degeneration, a wasting away of moral (and physical) fibre and vigour. *L'esprit décadent* verged on a posture or affectation, and was the expression of disenchantment and disillusionment – the *fin de siècle* malaise – with life. A species of ennui and pessimism expressive of the futility of life, a disdain of the everyday and ordinary (and natural), and a repugnance to moral and religious convention and taboo. *See* SYMBOL AND SYMBOLISM.

essay (F *essai* 'attempt') A composition, usually in prose (Pope's *Moral Essays* in verse are an exception), which may be of only a few hundred words (like Bacon's *Essays*) or of book length (like Locke's *Essay Concerning Human Understanding*) and which discusses, formally or informally, a topic or a variety of topics. It is one of the most flexible and adaptable of all literary forms.

It was known to the Classical writers (Bacon observes that 'the word is late, but the thing is ancient') and the *Characters* of Theophrastus (3rd c. BC), the *Meditations* of Marcus Aurelius (2nd c. AD) and Seneca's *Epistle to Lucilius* 1st c. AD) all qualify for inclusion in this genre.

Montaigne coined the word *essai* when, in 1580, he gave the title *Essais* to his first publication. In 1597 Bacon described his *Essays* as 'grains of salt which will rather give an appetite than offend with satiety'. Whereas Montaigne was discursive, informal and intimate (writing on such subjects as Liars, The Custom of Wearing Clothes and The Art of Conversation), Bacon was terse, didactic and aloof, though choosing not dissimilar topics (Of Envy, Of Riches, Of Negotiating, Of the Vicissitude of Things). Montaigne's essays often run to many thousands of words; Bacon's seldom exceed a few hundred. Sir William Cornwallis's *Essayes* (1600–01) were personal and unassuming reflections very much in the style of Montaigne. Somewhat later Nicholas Breton, a contemporary and friend of Bacon's (and of Florio's who translated and published Montaigne's *Essais* in 1603), composed *The Fantasticks* (1626), a collection of observations arranged in calendar (*q.v.*) form according to seasons, days and hours. More important than Breton were Sir Thomas Overbury and John Earle (and several other similar writers who flourished in the first half of the 17th c.). Overbury modelled his collection of *Characters* (1614) on Theophrastus, and so did Earle in a collection of character sketches titled *Microcosmographie* (1628). Between the essay and the 'Character' (*q.v.*) there was a kind of cross-pollination whose good influences are apparent for two hundred years or more.

In the 1660s Abraham Cowley became the second important pioneer (after Cornwallis) of the English essay in the Montaigne tradition of personal and reflective informality. Cowley knew and admired the Frenchman's essays and, like him, chose to portray himself. He wrote of such subjects as liberty, solitude, avarice, the brevity of life and the uncertainty of riches; he even wrote an essay *Of Myself*. His work was published posthumously in 1668.

Cowley and Saint-Evremond, the French critic, between them stimulated interest in Montaigne's work; and Sir William Temple and Dryden consolidated the form of the essay. Both were to have a considerable influence on Steele and Addison. Temple's essays were, for the most part, in the manner of Montaigne. His

Miscellanea appeared in 1680, 1690 and 1701. Dryden was more formal as, for instance, in his best known work in this genre, the *Essay of Dramatic Poesy* (1668), which was in fact, in dialogue (*q.v.*) form.

Towards the end of the 17th c. there were a number of forerunners to the *Tatler* and the *Spectator*, and it is clear that by this stage the essay was becoming an increasingly popular form of diversion. There were, for example, Sir Roger L'Estrange's *Observator* papers (1681–7); Edward Ward's *London Spy* (1698–1700); Tom Browne's *Amusements Serious and Comical* (1700); and John Dunton's *The Athenian Gazette* (1690–97).

Daniel Defoe's journalistic essays and pamphlets, and especially his *Review* (1704–13), influenced the evolution of the essay, but even more important was the type of periodical essay established by Addison and Steele in the *Tatler* (1709–11) and the *Spectator* (1711–12). They wrote on such subjects as the Tombs in Westminster Abbey, Ladies' Head-dress, the Cries of London, and Recollections of Childhood. Addison invented a kind of club of 'characters' for the *Spectator* in the Overbury/Earle/Theophrastian tradition. At this period also, a large number of relatively short-lived periodicals published a variety of essays. Some of the better known periodicals were: *The Guardian*, March–Oct. 1713; *The Englishman*, March – Oct. 1713; *The Lover*, March–May 1714; *The Reader*, April–May 1714; *Town-Talk*, Dec. 1715–Feb. 1716; *The Plebeian*, March–April 1719; *The Theatre*, Jan.–April 1720. No fewer than ninety different periodicals came out between 1709 and 1720.

In the middle of the 18th c. Johnson made his contribution to the essay with *The Rambler* and *The Idler.* He also contributed to other publications like the *Gentleman's Magazine.* Johnson for the most part was moral and didactic (though there are moments of levity in some of *The Idler* papers) and his prose was lapidary; a very considerable contrast to Addison and Steele who set out to divert and amuse and whose style was urbanely relaxed. Oliver Goldsmith is nearer to them in spirit and manner, especially in such essays as *Beau Tibbs*, *The Man in Black*, *National Prejudices* and *A Party at Vauxhall Gardens.* Goldsmith published his own journal, *The Bee*, in 1759.

The essay has flourished ever since. Lamb, Hazlitt, Thomas De Quincey, Coleridge, Macaulay, Leigh Hunt, Carlyle, Ruskin, Matthew Arnold, Walter Pater, Walter Bagehot and R. L. Stevenson were all outstanding essayists. Lamb, Hazlitt, De Quincey, Leigh Hunt and Stevenson wrote very much in the tradition of Montaigne;

as Lamb's *Essays of Elia* (1823, 1833) demonstrate, or Hazlitt's *On Persons One would Wish to have Seen*, and *On Life in General*; also his essays on John Buncle and Cavanagh, the fives player: Leigh Hunt's *On Getting up on Cold Mornings*; De Quincey's *On the Knocking at the Gate in Macbeth*; and Stevenson's *A Plea for Gas Lamps*. The other essayists just mentioned wrote more often of aesthetics, philosophy, literary and historical topics, which have usually been the subjects chosen by European essayists.

Since towards the end of the 19th c. the essay has proliferated. The informal and familiar type of divertissement retained its popularity until fairly recently, while weightier matters have been covered more and more by the form. Literary critics, reviewers, journalists and columnists have found the essay to be an indispensable medium.

In *And Even Now* (1920) Max Beerbohm produced an outstanding volume of essays. Both Chesterton and Belloc were extremely prolific and readable essayists on a wide variety of topics, often polemical. E. V. Lucas and A. A. Milne were very nearly as talented and nearer in mood and style to, say, Llewellyn Powys of the *Dorset Essays* (1935). Harold Nicolson's *Small Talk* is one of the best collections of modern essays. Again in the Montaigne tradition, he chooses such subjects as Good Taste and Bad, On Being Polite, On Telling the Truth.

Among the many others who have adorned this genre one should mention Lytton Strachey, Arthur Symons, E. M. Forster, Ivor Brown, Robert Lynd, James Agate, Neville Cardus, Augustine Birrell, J. B. Priestley, Bertrand Russell, Richard Church, D. H. Lawrence, Cyril Connolly and Aldous Huxley. All show a wide range of subject, style and knowledge; with, perhaps, Huxley preeminent for his wit, erudition and urbanity (e.g. his collection *Adonis and the Alphabet*, 1956).

In the second half of the 20th c. fewer familiar and informal essays have been published because there have been fewer periodicals to take them. At the same time the literary and critical essay and the essay of ideas have become commonplaces, especially in the numerous academic publications. From time to time distinguished authors produce a volume of them. Among the scores of collections that exist, the following are some of the most notable: Virginia Woolf's *The Common Reader* (1925) and *A Room of One's Own* (1929), which has become something of a classic in feminist criticism (*q.v.*); T. S. Eliot's *Selected Essays* (1932) and *On Poets and Poetry* (1957); Arthur Koestler's *The Yogi and the Commissar and Other Essays* (1945); George Orwell's *Critical Essays* (1946); Graham Greene's *The Lost Childhood and Other Essays* (1951) and his *Collected Essays* (1969); Wallace Stevens's *The Necessary Angel: Essays on Reality and the Imagination* (1951); Aldous Huxley's *Collected Essays* (1959); W. H. Auden's *The Dyer's Hand* (1963) and *Secondary Worlds* (1968); Malcolm Bradbury's *Possibilities* (1973) and *No, Not Bloomsbury* (1987); Philip Roth's *Reading Myself and Others* (1975); Gore Vidal's *Matters of Fact and Matters of Fiction, 1973–6* (1977); C. H. Sisson's *The Avoidance of Literature: Collected Essays* (1978); Seamus Heaney's *Preoccupations* (1980) and *The Government of the Tongue* (1988); William Golding's *A Moving Target* (1982); Chinua Achebe's *Hopes and Impediments*; Philip Larkin's *Required Writing* (1983); Anthony Burgess's *Homage to Qwert Yuiop* (1986); David Lodge's *Write On: Occasional Essays 1965–1985* (1986).

Apart from the few Americans mentioned above, other distinguished American essayists in the 19th and 20th c. include: Washington Irving, Emerson, Edgar Allan Poe, Oliver Wendell Holmes, Thoreau, John Muir, John Burroughs, Frank Moore Colby, Agnes Repplier, Clarence Day, Christopher Morley, E. B. White, James Thurber, W. C. Brownell, Paul Elmer More and George Santayana.

The essay form has flourished no less in Europe, where there have been many distinguished practitioners. Basically, European essayists have used the form for the discussion of ideas, for polemic and for political purposes rather than attempting the informal and familiar approach and style characteristic of the English tradition. Among the many famous French essayists we should mention La Bruyère, Sainte-Beuve, Montesquieu, Henri Bergson, Maurras, François Mauriac, André Gide, Jean-Paul Sartre, Albert Camus and André Malraux. Three famous Spanish essayists are de Unamuno, Ortega y Gasset and Salvador de Madariaga. Eminent Italians are Carlo Gadda, Natalia Ginzburg, Italo Calvino and Alberto Moravia. Among Germans the following have been outstanding: Paul Ernst, Rudolf Kassner, Heinrich Mann, Thomas Mann and Rudolf Schröder. *See also* CAUSERIE; PROPOS.

estancia A general and ultimately vague Spanish term for a series of verses forming a rhythmic whole. Some are regular, following an ordered plan; some irregular and giving an effect of caprice or disorder. Often of four, six, eight or ten lines; six or eight syllables or even alexandrines (*q.v.*) may be found. The poet chose his form according to his feelings as he composed.

estates satire Traditionally, the estates of the realm are three: Lords Spiritual, Lords Temporal and Commons. The ancient Parliament of Scotland comprised the king and three estates: (a) archbishops, bishops, abbots and mitred priors; (b) the barons and commissioners of shires and stewartries; (c) the commissioners from the royal burghs. In France, the three estates were nobles, clergy and the plebs (they remained separate until 1780). The fourth estate is, colloquially, the press. The concept of a gradated society is ancient and universal. During the Middle Ages society was carefully structured in a hierarchical system; at its simplest from king down to beggar, say. The concept extended to embrace the natural order. The eagle was top bird, the lion top animal. In fact, the idea of degree was so pervasive that it included a kind of rank order in the sport of falconry, for example. Gyr falcons were exclusively for royalty, peregrines for noblemen, merlins for noblewomen, goshawks for yeomen, sparrowhawks for priests and kestrels for knaves or servants. In one kind of hierarchical scheme the religious were at the top, laymen next and all women at the bottom. At the beginning of the *General Prologue to the Canterbury Tales* Chaucer thinks it 'acordaunt to resoun' to tell us the condition of his pilgrims:

> And whiche they weren, and of what degree,
> And eek in what array that they were inne . . .

Thus, he begins with the knight (the senior in social rank among the pilgrims) – but later abandons the rank order. Satires on the estates (many of them were in Latin) were a kind of exposition of the duties and responsibilities of different members and the characteristics of individual groups plus criticism of their shortcomings. To a certain extent Chaucer does this in the *Prologue*, which contains some quite scathing portraits of individual types (e.g. Friar, Summoner and Pardoner). Langland drew on the same tradition in *Piers Plowman*, and its use is discernible in, for example, the anonymous political allegory *Wynnere and Wastoure* (*c.* 1352) and the early 15th c. anonymous ME poem *Mum and the Sothsegger*. Much later we find an interesting development of the tradition in Sir David Lindsay's curious Morality Play (*q.v.*) *Ane Pleasant Satyre of the Thrie Estaitis* (1540).

The numerous artists who created illustrations for the *danse macabre* (*q.v.*) from the 14th to the 16th c. also showed an awareness of this rank order. Often satirical in tone and purpose, the illustrations depict, through the democratic equality of death, the various estates of men and women going to their doom.

There is a perceivable connection, too, with the character (*q.v.*) studies which became popular early in the 17th c.: collections of generalized and detailed studies of the behaviour, character and appearance of individual classes or types.

Finally, the general concept of a hierarchical system of 'estates' is also inherent in the theory of the 'Great Chain of Being' (*q.v.*).

estrambote In Spanish verse a term denoting an addition of a few lines which may be made to a stanza or a sonnet (*qq.v.*). Sometimes used for a comment or gloss (*q.v.*) on what has gone before.

estrangement Apart from its everyday meaning, this term has been used to refer to the results of the alienation effect (*q.v.*) when the spectator or receptor (*q.v.*) detaches himself emotionally from the work the better to follow its didactic import.

estribillo (Sp 'little stirrup'; diminutive of *estribo* 'stirrup') The equivalent of the French *ritournelle*; in Spanish it denotes a refrain or chorus (also a pet word or phrase). It is a theme-verse or stanza (of from two to four lines) of a *villancico* (*q.v.*) and may have originated in the Arabic *zéjel* (*q.v.*). We first come across it in the 11th c. in the form of the romance *jarcha* (*q.v.*) of a Hebrew poem. After *villancicos* ceased to be written they developed another lease of life as the *copla* (*q.v.*) of modern times. The *estribillo* is thus a diachronic element in Spanish popular lyric poetry. Sometimes the *estribillo* formed an introductory stanza, stating the theme of a poem, and then was repeated at the end. Also used in ballad. *Estribote* is an augmentative from *estribo*.

estridentismo A literary movement in Mexico initiated in 1922 by Manual Maples Arce (1898–). Those associated with it espoused and glorified the industrial future at the expense of the 'classical' or 'romantic' past. Their symbols tended to be engines, machinery, industrial plant, etc. The movement soon fizzled out. *See* FUTURISM.

estrofa (Sp 'strophe') The equivalent to the English usage of stanza (*q.v.*).

estrofa mauriqueña A type of *copla de pie quebrado* named after Jorge Maurique (*c.* 1440–79), with the rhyme pattern ABc ABc, where c is the short broken line. The effect is produced by having the two octosyllabic lines (A and B) followed by a four-syllable line (c). *See* COPLA; PIE QUEBRADO.

euhemerism Euhemerus was a Sicilian who served Cassander of Macedonia (311–298 BC). In his *Sacred History* he put forward the questionable theory that the Greek gods had formerly been kings or heroes who enjoyed posthumous deification from those they had ruled. Such a treatment of myth (*q.v.*) was thus called 'euhemerism'.

euphemism (Gk 'fair speech') The substitution of a mild and pleasant expression for a harsh and blunt one, such as 'to pass away' for 'to die'. Euphemism has become the bane of much writing in the 20th c., especially in the jargon (*q.v.*) language of sociologists, educationists and bureaucrats. It is common in officialese (*q.v.*); also in broadcasting and newspapers. So widespread is it and so insidious its influence that it frequently becomes a form of Newspeak (*q.v.*). The following are current euphemisms of a general nature, with their 'interpretations': (a) A man is helping the police with their inquiries/a suspected criminal is detained by the police and probably under close arrest; (b) A large accident/the explosion of a nuclear power station; (c) A clean bomb/a bomb with a minimal fall-out which kills tens of thousands of people as opposed to hundreds of thousands; (d) Armed emergency/a small-scale war in which large numbers of people are being killed, buildings destroyed, etc; (e) Under-achiever/a school-child who is backward or merely bone from the neck upwards; (f) The locus of evaluation/the class-room; (g) Lower ability group/slow learners; (h) A member of the lower socio-economic bracket/a poor person; (i) Terminal illness/a fatal illness. *See* DYSPHEMISM; METALEPSIS; PERIPHRASIS.

euphony (Gk 'sweetness of sound') The term denotes pleasing, mellifluous sounds, usually produced by long vowels rather than consonants; though liquid consonants can be euphonious. The almost voluptuously drowsy vowel sounds in the following lines from Keats's *Hyperion* soothe the ear:

> As when upon a trancèd summer night,
> Those green-robed senators of mighty woods,

Tall oaks, branch-charmèd by the earnest stars,
Dream, and so dream all night without a stir,

Consider also the effect of the liquid sounds in this stanza from Gerard Manley Hopkins's *Wreck of the Deutschland*:

Is out with it! Oh,
We lash with the best or worst
Word last! Now a lush-kept plus-capped sloe
Will, mouthed to flesh-burst,
Gush! – flush the man, the being with it, sour or sweet,
Brim, in a flash, full! – Hither then, last or first,
To hero of Calvary, Christ's feet –
Never ask if meaning it, wanting it, warned of it – men go.

See ASSONANCE; CACOPHONY; DISSONANCE; MELOPOEIA; ONOMATOPOEIA; TONE COLOUR.

euphuism An ornately florid, precious and mazy style of writing (often alliterative, antithetical and embellished with elaborate figures of speech) which takes its name from a two-part work by John Lyly; namely, *Euphues, the anatomy of wyt* (1578) and *Euphues and his England* (1850). In Greek *euphues* means 'well endowed by nature'. Gabriel Harvey dubbed Lyly's style 'euphuism' in *Advertisement for Papp-Hatchet* (1589). Lyly's works are important in the history and development of English prose. They were written at a time when many writers were experimenting with prose style. Euphuism appears to have had a certain amount of influence. It is evident, for example, in Shakespeare's *Comedy of Errors, Two Gentlemen of Verona* and *Love's Labour's Lost*. Shakespeare parodied the style in *Henry IV*, Pt I. One can hardly imagine, either, that Sir Thomas Browne had not read Lyly. In fact, the more ornate and baroque (*q.v.*) prose styles of some of the early 17th c. writers suggest that Lyly's influence was considerable.

The following passage gives some idea of the euphuistic manner:

Which things, Lucilla, albeit they be sufficient to reprove the lightness of some one, yet can they not convince every one of lewdness, neither ought the constancy of all to be brought in question through the subtlety of a few. For although the worm entereth almost into every wood, yet he eateth not the cedar tree; though the stone cylindrus at every thunder clap roll from the hill, yet the pure sleek stone mounteth at the noise; though the rust fret the hardest steel, yet doth it not eat into the emerald;

> though polypus change his hue, yet the salamander keepeth his colour; though Proteus transform himself into every shape, yet Pygmalion retaineth his old form; though Aeneas were too fickle to Dido, yet Troilus was too faithful to Cressida; though others seem counterfeit in their deeds, yet, Lucilla, persuade yourself that Euphues will be always current in his dealings.

See also GONGORISM; MANNERISM; MARINISM; SECENTISMO.

eupolidian (Gk 'well varied') In Classical prosody a term denoting a varied metrical form: a tetrameter (*q.v.*) with mixed choriambic and trochaic feet. *See* CHORIAMB; TROCHEE.

eutrepismus (Gk 'turning about') The numbering of the different parts of an argument (*q.v.*).

excursus (L 'running out') A detailed examination and analysis of a point often added as an appendix to a book. An incidental discussion or digression.

exegesis In Roman times the exegetes were professional and official interpreters of charms, omens, dreams, sacred law and oracular pronouncements. Thus the term has come to mean an explanation or interpretation and is often applied to biblical studies. As far as literature is concerned, it covers critical analysis and the elucidation of difficulties in the text. A variorum edition (*q.v.*), for example, contains a great deal of exegesis.

exemplum (L 'example') A short narrative used to illustrate a moral. The term applies primarily to the stories used in medieval sermons. Occasionally the *exemplum* found its way into literature. Two good examples in Chaucer are *The Pardoner's Tale* and *The Nun's Priest's Tale* (late 14th c.). Gower, in *Confessio Amantis* (c. 1385) makes use of *exempla* when illustrating sins against Venus. In the Middle Ages theological handbooks for preachers contained large numbers of *exempla*. Two particularly important works of this kind were John Bromyard's *Summa Praedicantium* and the *Liber Exemplorum ad Usum Praedicantium* (14th c.). One of the most famous source-books was the 13th c. Latin *Gesta Romanorum*. Other notable collections in the 12th, 13th and 14th c. were: the *Alphabet of Tales*; Nicolas Bozon's *Metaphors*; the *Early South English Legendary*; *Jacob's Well*; Dan Michel's *Azenbite of Inwyt*; John Mirc's *Festial*;

the *Myroure of Our Lady*; Robert of Brunne's *Handlyng Synne*; the *Speculum Christiani*; the *Speculum Laicorum*; and the *Speculum Sacerdotale*. Many *exempla* can be traced back to the early Fathers and are contained in the *Patrologia Latina*. *See also* FABLE; FABLIAU; GESTA; SHORT STORY.

exergasia (L 'amplification') A device by which a number of figures of speech amplify a point and embellish a passage. *See also* EUPHUISM.

Exilliteratur (G 'exile literature') Literature composed by German authors while in exile when they sought refuge abroad during the period of the National Socialist régime. Among the more famous were Bertolt Brecht, Lion Feuchtwanger, Heinrich Mann, Thomas Mann and Stefan Zweig. *See also* HEIMKEHRERLITERATUR.

existentialism (or *Existenzphilosophie*) In philosophy, the terms *exist* and *existence* denote something active rather than passive and thus are closely dependent on the Latin root *ex* 'out' + *sistere* from *stare* 'to stand'. The term existentialism means 'pertaining to existence'; or, in logic, 'predicating existence'. Philosophically, it now applies to a vision of the condition and existence of man, his place and function in the world, and his relationship, or lack of one, with God. It is generally agreed that existentialism derives from the thinking of Søren Kierkegaard (1813–55), and especially in his books *Fear and Trembling* (1843), *The Concept of Dread* (1844) and *Sickness Unto Death* (1848). In these and other works Kierkegaard was for the most part re-stating and elaborating upon the belief that through God and in God man may find freedom from tension and discontent and therefore find peace of mind and spiritual serenity; an idea that had prevailed in much Christian thinking over many centuries. Kierkegaard became the pioneer of modern Christian existentialism. After him existential thought was greatly expanded at the beginning of the 20th c. by Heidegger and Jaspers (German philosophers), whose ideas in turn influenced a large number of European philosophers (e.g. Berdyaev, Unamuno, J. de Gautier and B. Fondane) and in whose work are to be found the sources of atheistic existentialism.

An important feature of atheistic existentialism is the argument that existence precedes essence (the reverse of many traditional forms of philosophy) for it is held that man fashions his own existence and only exists by so doing, and, in that process, and by the choice of what he does or does not do, gives essence to that existence.

Jean-Paul Sartre is the hierophant of modern existentialism and his version, expressed through his novels, plays and philosophical writings, is the one that has caught on and been the most widely influential. In Sartre's vision man is born into a kind of void (*le néant*), a mud (*le visqueux*). He has the liberty to remain in this mud and thus lead a passive, supine, acquiescent existence (like Oblomov and Samuel Beckett's sad tatterdemalions) in a 'semi-conscious' state and in which he is scarcely aware of himself. However, he may come out of his subjective, passive situation (in which case he would 'stand out from'), become increasingly aware of himself and, conceivably, experience *angoisse* (a species of metaphysical and moral anguish). If so, he would then have a sense of the absurdity of his predicament and suffer despair. The energy deriving from this awareness would enable him to 'drag himself out of the mud', and begin to exist. By exercising his power of choice he can give meaning to existence and the universe. Thus, in brief, the human being is obliged to make himself what he is, and has to be what he is. A now classic statement on this situation is Sartre's description of the waiter in *L'Etre et le néant.*

In *L'Existentialisme est un humanisme* (1946) Sartre expressed the belief that man *can* emerge from his passive and indeterminate condition and, by an act of will, become *engagé*; whereupon he is committed (through *engagement*) to some action and part in social and political life. Through commitment man provides a reason and a structure for his existence and thus helps to integrate society.

In 1946 Sartre founded the review *Les Temps modernes*, a medium for existentialist writings. Apart from Sartre, some of the main exponents of *existentialisme* have been Albert Camus, Simone de Beauvoir, Merleau-Ponty and Jean Wahl. The main exponent of Christian existentialism has been Gabriel Marcel, the philosopher and dramatist, who has written some brilliant critical analyses of Sartre's point of view, and who, in his *Existence et objectivité* (1925), was very probably the first to introduce the term *existentialisme* into the vocabulary of French philosophy. Marcel's influence has been discernible in the work of some French novelists, notably Jean Cayrol and Luc Estang. *See also* COMMITMENT; THEATRE OF THE ABSURD.

exordium The introductory part of a speech (*q.v.*) as laid down by the Classical rhetoricians. *See also* RHETORIC.

experimentelen (Du 'experimentalists') Members of a Duch movement in art and literature who were active in the 1950s. The term was invented by the painter Asgar Jorn.

explication A formal and close analysis of a text: its structure, style, content, imagery – indeed every aspect of it. As a method of elucidation it is commonly practised in French schools, and to a certain extent now in England since the 1920s. Key works in the development of this kind of critical analysis are: *A Survey of Modernist Poetry* (1928) by Laura Riding and Robert Graves; *Practical Criticism* (1929) by I. A. Richards; and *Seven Types of Ambiguity* (1930) by William Empson.

expolitio *See* EXERGASIA.

exposition At the beginning of his play the dramatist is often committed to giving a certain amount of essential information about the plot and the events which are to come. He may also have to give information about what has 'already happened'. All this comes under the heading of exposition. A skilful dramatist is able to introduce this material without holding up the action of the play and without recourse to the obvious devices of narrative. *See also* PROTATIC CHARACTER.

expressionism The term (probably used by Vauxcelles after a series of paintings by Julien-Auguste Hervé in 1901 under the title *Expressionismes*) refers to a movement in Germany very early in the 20th c. (*c.* 1905) in which a number of painters sought to avoid the representation of external reality and, instead, to project themselves and a highly personal vision of the world. The term can be applied to literature, but only judiciously.

Briefly summarized, the main principle involved is that expression determines form, and therefore imagery, punctuation, syntax, and so forth. Indeed, any of the formal rules and elements of writing can be bent or disjointed to suit the purpose.

The theories of expressionism had considerable influence in Germany and Scandinavia. In fact, expressionism dominated the theatre for a time in the 1920s. Theatrically it was a reaction against realism (*q.v.*) and aimed to show inner psychological realities. The origins of this are probably to be found in Strindberg's *The Dream Play* (1907) and *The Ghost Sonata* (1907). Wedekind's plays of the same period were also strongly expressionistic. He wrote violent anti-bourgeois plays, three of which are chiefly remembered: *Spring Awakening* (1891), *Lulu* (in two parts, 1895) and *Pandora's Box* (1902). At the age of nineteen Reinhard Sorge wrote what is regarded by some as the first drama of German expressionism, namely *Der Bettler* (1912). However, Carl Sternheim has a rival claim with his *Die Hose* (1910) which he followed with *Der Snob* in 1914. Ernst Toller is accepted as a spokesman of German expressionism in the theatre. He was something of an extremist and a revolutionary in style. His first major play was *Die Wandlung* (1919) which, presented in thirteen tableaux, depicted the horrors of war as he had experienced them. This he followed with *Masse Mensch* (1920) and *Massenschlacht* (1921). Another dramatist to make a great impression at the time was Fritz von Unruh, author of *Offiziere* (1911), *Prinz Louis Ferdinand von Preussen* (1913) and *Ein Geschlecht* (1917). During the 1920s he wrote several other expressionistic plays. Georg Kaiser was the most prolific dramatist of this movement and is credited with no fewer than seventy plays. Among his main works were *Von Morgens bis Mitternachts* (1916) and his trilogy which comprises *Die Koralle* (1917), *Gas I* (1918) and *Gas II* (1920). Walter Hasenclever also made an impact with *Der Sohn* (1914) and *Antigone* (1917). Most of these dramatists were to influence Brecht and in some of their plays we can see the makings of epic theatre (*q.v.*).

By the mid-1920s expressionism in the theatre was nearly extinct and it did not catch on much outside Germany – nor was it much understood. In France the influence has been negligible. In England and America the dramatists are really the only writers to have been affected; particularly Eugene O'Neill, Elmer Rice and Thornton Wilder. Up to a point T. S. Eliot, W. H. Auden and Christopher Isherwood have also been influenced.

It can be argued that expressionistic theories have also had some effects on writers like Wyndham Lewis and Virginia Woolf, as they certainly had upon Kafka, Schickele and Edschmid. The more involved and exaggerated prose experiments of James Joyce, William Faulkner and Samuel Beckett also bear signs of it. The long-term influences are discernible in the anti-novel (*q.v.*).

Merely sonic and colour effects in poetry and attempts at synaesthesia (*q.v.*), where much of the sense is sacrificed for the sake of sound (as in some of the work of Gerard Manley Hopkins and Roy Campbell), might also be described as expressionistic. Edith Sitwell wrote some whimsical expressionistic poems (like *I Do Like to be Beside the Seaside*) and the possible range of expressionism appears to remain very wide. Much more recently, for example, Christopher Middleton has written poems which might be described as expressionistic. *See also* ULTRAISM.

expressive form, fallacy of A term adopted by R. P. Blackmur (1904–65) from observations made by the poet and critic Yvor Winters (1900–68). Winters wrote of the 'heresy of expressive form' apropos Coleridge's concept of organic form (*q.v.*) and gave the view that it was not possible or desirable artistically to express or describe the disintegration of a belief or a civilization in a chaotic form. For example, he thought that Joyce's *Ulysses* (1922) was 'disintegrated', whereas it should have been disciplined and integrated. Critics pointed out that the transformation of inchoate material into the apparently chaotic was a matter of appearances, the result of the art that conceals art. T. S. Eliot's poem *The Waste Land* (1922) was not *actually* chaotic; it only *appeared* to be. The fallacy of expressive form refers to the ideas that if a poet feels with sufficient intensity then this will be enough to create a successful poem. But, if a poet depends only on inspiration (*q.v.*), then this will not be adequate. He or she must also judge, compare, analyse. *See also* ARS EST CELARE ARTEM; SPONTANEITY.

expurgated edition An edition of a book from which passages have been deleted, to purify it of anything which might be deemed offensive, noxious or erroneous. *See* BOWDLERIZE; INDEX EXPURGATORIUS.

extenuatio *See* MEIOSIS.

extravaganza The word derives from the Italian *stravaganza* which means, approximately, 'influenced by extravagance'. It is a form of 19th c. English drama which consisted of an elaborately presented fairy tale (*q.v.*) or some mythical story: a sort of mixture of musical, pantomime (*q.v.*) and ballet. The spirit was always light, gay, even farcical, and reminiscent of burlesque (*q.v.*). The most talented writer of this form of entertainment was J. R. Planché who got his inspiration from a French diversion described as 'féérie folie'. It was at the Olympic Theatre, London, that a Madame Vestris perfected the form. A famous extravaganza was *Chu-Chin-Chow* (1916), by Frederick Norton and Oscar Asche. It was based on the story of Ali Baba and the Forty Thieves and ran for 2,238 consecutive performances (a record which stood for many years). Nowadays the nearest thing to an extravaganza is a revue (*q.v.*).

eye-rhyme A rhyme which gives to the eye the impression of an exact rhyme, but does not, in fact, possess identical sounds. Examples are *come* | *home; forth* |*worth*.

F

fable (L *fabula* 'discourse, story') A short narrative in prose or verse which points a moral. Non-human creatures or inanimate things are normally the characters. The presentation of human beings as animals is the characteristic of the literary fable and is unlike the fable that still flourishes among primitive peoples.

The genre probably arose in Greece, and the first collection of fables is ascribed to Aesop (6th c. BC). His principal successors were Phaedrus and Babrius, who flourished in the 1st c. AD. Phaedrus preserved Aesop's fables and in the 10th c. a prose adaptation of Phaedrus's translation appeared under the title *Romulus*, a work whose popularity lasted until the 17th c. A famous collection of Indian fables was the *Bidpai* which were probably composed originally in Sanskrit *c.* AD 300. Many versions of these were made in prose and verse in different languages between the 3rd c. and 16th c. The best of the medieval fabulists was Marie de France who, *c.* 1200, composed 102 fables in verse. After her came La Fontaine who raised the whole level of the fable and is generally acknowledged as the world's master. He took most of the stories from Aesop and Phaedrus but translated them in his verse. His *Fables choisies* were published in twelve books (1668, 1678–9, 1694).

La Fontaine had many imitators: principally, Eustache de Noble, Pignotti, John Gay, J. P. C. de Florian and Tomás Iriarte. Later, Lessing followed the style of Aesop. John Gay's *Fifty-One Fables in Verse* were published in 1727. In Russia the greatest of the fabulists was Ivan Krylov, who translated a number of La Fontaine's fables and between 1810 and 1820 published nine books of fables. More recently Kipling made a notable contribution to the genre with *Just So Stories* (1902). Mention should also be made of James Thurber's droll *Fables of Our Time* (1940) and George Orwell's remarkable political satire *Animal Farm* (1945), which is in fable form. *See also* ALLEGORY; BEAST EPIC; BESTIARY; CONTE.

fabliau A short narrative in octosyllabic (*q.v.*) verse, usually of 300 to 400 lines. The genre flourished in France between 1150 and 1400 AD. About 150 are extant. The earliest known is *Richeut* (1159), but it seems likely that they existed earlier because disapproval of them was expressed in Egbert's *Poenitentiale* of the 8th c.

Fabliaux tended to be ribaldly comic tales. They were satirical, in a rough and ready fashion, often at the expense of the clergy. Their caustic attitude towards women may have been a reaction against the apotheosis of women in the tradition and cult of courtly love (*q.v.*). The form is primarily French, but there are examples in English literature, like Chaucer's *Miller's Tale* and *Reeve's Tale* (late 14th c.). *See also* FABLE; LAY.

fabula (L 'narrative, story, tale') The Latin *fabulae* were forms of drama among which we may distinguish the following: (a) *fabula Atellana*, so called after the Oscan town Atella. A kind of southern Italian farce (*q.v.*) popular in Rome until the period of Augustus (63 BC–AD 14). They were bawdy pantomimes (*q.v.*) with stock characters (*q.v.*) who were represented by masks. Some of the main dramatis personae were: Bucco, the clown; Maccus, the fool; Pappus, the grandfather or foolish dotard; Manducus, a glutton; Dossenus, a hunchback; (b) *fabula crepidata*, Roman tragedies based on Greek themes. The Roman word for *cothurnus* (*q.v.*) worn by the tragic actors was *crepida*; a term rendered in English by *buskin* (*q.v.*); (c) *fabula palliata* (*palliata* from Latin *pallium* 'cloak'). A type of comedy first introduced in Rome by Livius Andronicus in the 3rd c. BC. It remained popular for well over a hundred years and consisted for the most part of adaptations of Greek New Comedy (*q.v.*). The only extant *palliatae* were created by Plautus and Terence; (d) *fabula praetexta*, so called from the *toga praetexta* – a garment worn by priests and magistrates and bordered with a purple stripe. Such *fabulae* were dramas based on Roman history which presented well-known Roman personalities. Thus, a kind of history play (*q.v.*). The invention of the form is attributed to Naevius of the 3rd c. BC; (e) *fabula saltica*, so called from *saltire* 'to jump', they were a form of Roman ballet and pantomime; (f) *fabula stataria*, so called because it tended to be a static form of drama, in distinction from the *motoria* or rapidly moving comedy (or what we should now call farce) with stock characters; (g) *fabula togata*, so named from the *toga* – the traditional Roman garment. Such dramas were a form of comedy based on Greek models but dealing with Roman life and characters.

The main dramatist was Afranius and this type of comedy had some vogue in the latter part of the 2nd c. BC. *See also* FORMALISM, RUSSIAN.

fabulation A term used to describe the anti-novel (*q.v.*). It appears to have been introduced by Robert Scholes in *The Fabulators* (1967). Fabulation involves allegory (*q.v.*), verbal acrobatics and surrealistic effects. However, it is not entirely a new term; Caxton used *Fabulator* in 1484.

facetiae A bookseller's term for humorous or obscene books.

faction A portmanteau word (*q.v.*) of obvious composition which originated *c.* 1970 and denotes fiction which is based on and combined with fact. Notable examples are Truman Capote's *In Cold Blood* (1966), Norman Mailer's *Armies of the Night* (1968) and Alex Haley's *Roots.* It is a vague term at the best of times and its usefulness has been questioned. It might easily apply, for instance, to historical novels which combine a great deal of period fact with fictional treatment, or to novels which incorporate actual living personalities (e.g. the President of the USA, the British Prime Minister or the General Secretary of the Communist Party in the USSR) in a narrative about recent events which pertain to historical fact. Faction has proved to be quite a controversial matter, particularly in connection with television.

fairy tale The fairy tale belongs to folk literature (*q.v.*) and is part of the oral tradition (*q.v.*). And yet no one bothered to record them until the brothers Grimm produced their famous collection of *Kinder- und Hausmärchen* or *Household Tales* (1812, 1814, 1822).

In its written form the fairy tale tends to be a narrative in prose about the fortunes and misfortunes of a hero or heroine who, having experienced various adventures of a more or less supernatural kind, lives happily ever after. Magic, charms, disguise and spells are some of the major ingredients of such stories, which are often subtle in their interpretation of human nature and psychology.

The origins of fairy tales are obscure. Some think they may have come from the East. *The Thousand and One Nights* or *Arabian Nights' Entertainments* were written in Arabic and were translated into French in the 18th c.

In European literature there are three major collections: (a) Charles Perrault's *Contes de ma mère l'Oye* (1697), which were translated into English by Robert Samber in 1729; (b) the collection made by the Grimm brothers already mentioned; (c) Hans Christian Andersen's *Fairy Tales* (*Eventyr*) published in 1835. Other fairy tales have been composed by Ruskin, Thackeray, Charles Kingsley, Jean Ingelow and Oscar Wilde. Stories about Prince Charming, Red Riding Hood, Puss in Boots and Cinderella have a European background. *See* CONTE; SHORT STORY; SUPERNATURAL STORY.

Falkentheorie A theory of the *novella* (*q.v.*) worked out by the German writer Paul Heyse (1830–1914). This theory is based on the ninth tale of the fifth day of Boccaccio's *Decameron* (*c.* 1349–51). It is the story of Federigo who wasted his substance in the fruitless wooing of a rich mistress; wasted it to such an extent that he had only his favourite falcon left. This, too, he sacrificed – and his mistress was so moved by the act that she surrendered. The falcon is thus symbolic and denotes the strongly marked silhouette – as Heyse puts it – which, according to him, distinguishes one *novella* from another and gives it a unique quality. An interesting but elaborate theory, which is only another way of saying that each story is different from the others.

falling action That part of a play which follows the dénouement or climax (*qq.v.*). *See* FREYTAG'S PYRAMID; RESOLUTION; RISING ACTION.

falling rhythm This occurs when the stress pattern is thrown backwards in a line of verse so that it falls on the first syllables of the feet. The dactyl and the trochee (*qq.v.*) are the two basic feet in falling rhythm. The following example (basically trochaic) comes from Shakespeare's *The Passionate Pilgrim*:

> Crábbed áge ănd yoúth
> Cánnŏt líve tŏgéthĕr;
> Yoúth ĭs fúll ŏf pleásănce,
> Áge ĭs fúll ŏf cáre;
> Yóuth lĭke súmmĕr mórn,
> Áge lĭke wíntĕr's weáthĕr;
> Yóuth lĭke súmmĕr bráve,
> Áge lĭke wíntĕr báre;
> Yóuth ĭs fúll ŏf spórt,
> Ágĕ's breáth ĭs shórt.

See RISING RHYTHM.

false masque *See* ANTI-MASQUE.

familiar verse *See* LIGHT VERSE.

fancy and imagination Two much used and much debated terms in the history of critical theory. As on so many matters relating to literature, its forms and principles, issue was joined again during the Middle Ages and at the Renaissance in the names of the two critical world-champions – Aristotle and Plato. Medieval thought on matters of invention was dominated by Aristotle. Renaissance thought was dominated by Plato. Shakespeare's Theseus represents the Platonic point of view in *A Midsummer Night's Dream* (V, i):

> The lunatic, the lover, and the poet,
> Are of imagination all compact;

And again in that play:

> The poet's eye, in a fine frenzy rolling,
> Doth glance from heaven to earth, from earth to heaven;
> And, as imagination bodies forth
> The forms of things unknown, the poet's pen
> Turns them to shapes, and gives to airy nothing
> A local habitation and a name.

For the Elizabethans poetry had something in it of the divine; it enabled one to express things that were beyond the rational powers. Intuitive perception gave insight by the 'feigning' (*q.v.*) of poetry. As Bacon put it in Book II of *The Advancement of Learning*, poetry was always thought:

> to have some participation of divinesse, because it doth raise and erect the Minde, by submitting the shewes of things to the desires of the Mind, whereas reason doth buckle and bowe the Mind unto the Nature of things.

In his *Apologie for Poetrie* (1595), Sir Philip Sidney puts the point that poetry pleases and instructs by *mimesis* (*q.v.*), by metaphor, by counterfeiting, and at the same time the poet transforms what he finds in Nature, creates forms that did not exist.

Half way through the 17th c. Hobbes addressed himself to the matter of the poetic imagination in *Leviathan* (1651). All knowledge, he avers, comes from sensory experience. Images of objects are stored in the memory. Judgement and fancy (or imagination) between them develop from this store. In a famous passage in his *Answer to D'Avenant* (1650) he writes:

> Time and Education beget experience; Experience begets memory; Memory begets Judgement and Fancy; Judgement begets the strength and structure, and Fancy begets the Ornaments of a Poem.

In *Leviathan* he expresses the view that fancy is a faculty which finds likeness, and that judgement distinguishes differences. Judgement which, for Hobbes, was very nearly the same thing as memory, needs to hold fancy in check.

Dryden's views about poetic composition were very similar to those of Hobbes (see Dryden's preface to *Annus Mirabilis*). Hobbes's theory was very influential indeed.

The next major contribution to this topic came from John Locke in his *Essay Concerning Human Understanding* (1690). He describes 'wit' in very much the same terms that Hobbes had used for 'imagination', and their views of the function of judgement are almost identical. Locke also developed the theory of the 'association of ideas'. Locke's influence was also great, and it can be said that between them Locke and Hobbes laid the basis of psychological theory in aesthetics and literary criticism which was to prevail in the 18th c. Addison, too, made a vital contribution in his *Spectator* papers on *The Pleasures of the Imagination*. These were widely read. Addison amplified the associative theory and showed that the connotations of words were quite as important as their denotations.

During much of the 18th c. the creative and inventive processes of the mind were analysed in considerable depth, particularly by Hartley in *Observations on Man* (1749), by Joseph Priestley in *Hartley's Theory of the Human Mind*, by Hume in *Treatise of Human Nature* (1739) and his *Enquiry Concerning Human Understanding* (1748), by Shaftesbury in *Characteristicks* (1711), by Alexander Gerard in *Essay on Genius* (1774), and by William Blake who took a wholly different point of view from the empiricists. Blake's view was different because the last thing he believed or wanted to believe was that the world was a great machine and God its divine mechanic. Blake held that the human soul existed before birth and had intuitive knowledge and understanding of the spirit world from which it came. To Blake the natural order was an external manifestation of the spiritual and transcendent world. Everything in the natural world had for him a spiritual meaning and thus it was full of symbols, symbols of ideal forms. As Baudelaire was later to express it in *Correspondances*:

> La Nature est un temple où de vivants piliers
> Laissent parfois sortir de confuses paroles;
> L'homme y passe à travers des forêts de symboles

To Blake, the function of the imagination was to decipher these codes, symbols and celestial hieroglyphics, these outward signs of an inward universal grace, and render their meaning in poetry. Thus Blake had not an intellectual and philosophical system. He trusted to intuition rather than analysis.

But, fundamentally, during the 18th c., fancy and imagination were usually taken to be, if not synonymous, very nearly the same thing, and judgement was regarded as the superior and stronger faculty because it controlled (or ought to control) the fanciful and imaginative processes. Scattered about Johnson's various writings, for example, we continually find strictures on flights of fancy and admonitions to guard against them. Johnson was deeply suspicious of the potency of the fancy and imagination, but it may be said that in general people would have agreed with him. Moreover, judgement was the power of reason, of sobriety, of restraint, of balance and order. The neoclassicists prized these qualities.

It was eventually Coleridge who made the most telling and lasting observations on this topic. His theory of imagination is contained in *Biographia Literaria* (1817). Coleridge was in search of the unified personality and believed that the imagination was the means to attain it. The imagination, he wrote, was the 'synthetic' and 'magical' power which could bring about the fusion of human faculties. When Coleridge heard Wordsworth reading his own poetry he speculated about the imagination and later wrote in *Biographia Literaria* that he suspected that:

> Fancy and Imagination were two distinct and widely different faculties, instead of being, according to the general belief, either two names with one meaning, or, at furthest, the lower and higher degrees of one and the same power.

From being a follower of Locke and Hartley, Coleridge turned to Platonism (*q.v.*) and then became a follower of Berkeley whose main philosophical principle was that to be is to be perceived and that everything exists as an idea in the mind of God. Thus Nature is part of God and is the language of God. Coleridge expressed these new beliefs in *Destiny of Nations*:

All that meets the bodily sense I deem
Symbolical, one mighty alphabet
To infant minds; and we in this low world
Placed with our backs to bright reality,
That we might learn with young unwounded ken
The substance from the shadow.

Having discovered this 'eternal language' of Nature, Coleridge was at pains to work out the function of the imagination. In this venture he was considerably influenced by Kant, Schelling and Spinoza and he finally expressed his theories in Chapter XIII of *Biographia Literaria*.

He decided that fancy was a mode of memory 'emancipated from the order of time and space' which received all its materials 'made from the law of association'. The real imagination is either primary or secondary. The primary mediates between sensation and perception and is the living power and 'prime agent of all human perception', and this faculty is common to all percipient human beings. The secondary or poetic imagination is:

> an echo of the former, co-existing with the conscious will, yet still as identical with the primary in the *kind* of its agency, and differing only in *degree*, and in the *mode* of its operation. It dissolves, diffuses, dissipates, in order to recreate: or where this process is rendered impossible, yet still at all events it struggles to idealize and to unify.

In the preface to his *Poems* (1815) Wordsworth took a rather different point of view, which Coleridge disagreed with:

> Fancy, as she is an active, is also, under her own laws and in her own spirit, a creative faculty. In what manner Fancy ambitiously aims at a rivalship with Imagination, and Imagination stoops to work with the materials of Fancy, might be illustrated from the compositions of all eloquent writers, whether in prose or verse.

This is plainly much less precise than Coleridge's views but the implications are that imagination is the more important and more powerful faculty. In general it seems that imagination is regarded as the superior faculty, the transubstantiator of experience; while fancy (a contraction of fantasy; L *phantasia*, a transliteration from the Greek) is a kind of assistant to imagination. *See also* AFFLATUS; DONNEE; FEIGNING; INSPIRATION; INVENTION; LIGNE DONNEE; MUSE; WIT.

farce The word derives from the Latin *farcire* 'to stuff'. As applied to drama the term derives from the OF *farce* 'stuffing'.

The object of farce is to provoke mirth of the simplest and most basic kind: roars of laughter rather than smiles. It is a matter, therefore, of humour rather than wit (*q.v.*). It is associated with burlesque (*q.v.*) – though it must be distinguished from burlesque – with clowning, buffoonery, slapstick (*q.v.*) and knockabout. It is 'low' comedy – and it is broad. The basic elements of farce are: exaggerated physical action (often repeated), exaggeration of character and situation, absurd situations and improbable events (even impossible ones and therefore fantastic), and surprises in the form of unexpected appearances and disclosures. In farce, character and dialogue are nearly always subservient to plot and situation. The plot is usually complex and events succeed one another with almost bewildering rapidity.

The absolute origins of farce are obscure, though it may be reasonably supposed that it precedes anything merely literary. At its simplest, perhaps, it could be described as a form of prehistoric horseplay. In Classical literature farcical elements are to be found in the plays of Aristophanes and Plautus. The Aristophanic plot combined low comedy (*q.v.*) – in the shape of ridiculous situations and ludicrous results, ribaldry and junketings – with serious satire (*q.v.*) and invective (*q.v.*). Plautus also used the absurd situation (especially that arising from mistaken identity), knockabout and bawdy. The farcical is also discernible in the Greek satyr play (*q.v.*) and in the Roman *fabula* (*q.v.*).

The first plays to be described as *farces* were French and belong to the late Middle Ages. The 'stuffing' consisted of comic interludes between scenes in religious or liturgical drama. Such 'stuffings' or 'gags' were usually written in octosyllabic couplets, and an average length was 500 lines. These interpolations poked fun at the foibles and vices of everyday life (particularly at commercial knavery and conjugal infidelity) and are related to the *fabliau* and the *sotie* (*qq.v.*). This kind of comedy is well illustrated in Chaucer's *Miller's Tale* (late 14th c.).

Later, in the French theatre, these farcical interludes developed into a form of their own: a one-act farce. About 150 of these survive. Some of the better known are: *Maître Pierre Pathelin*, *La Farce du Pâté et de la Tarte*, *Le Chaudronnier*, *Le Poulier*, *Le Cuvier* and *Le Meunier et le Gentilhomme*.

The English Mystery Plays (*q.v.*) also contain comic interludes and these (as, occasionally, in France) were provided with demonic and grotesque figures behaving in a buffoonish manner, gambolling about and letting off fireworks. There is some connection between these 'characters' who ran clowning among the audience and the Vice (*q.v.*) of the Interludes (*q.v.*) and later Morality Plays (*q.v.*).

The influence of French farce is discernible in Italy, Germany and in England where the first writer of note to use the form was John Heywood who borrowed from and imitated French farce. His interludes became almost a comic genre of their own. For example: *The Play of the Wether* (1533), *Thersites* (*c.* 1537) and *The Foure P's* (*c.* 1545).

No doubt Heywood influenced Tudor dramatists who began to introduce farcical episodes in their plays: *Ralph Roister Doister* (1553); *Gammer Gurton's Needle* (1566); *Friar Bacon and Friar Bungay* (1594); Shakespeare's *Comedy of Errors* (*c.* 1590), *The Taming of the Shrew* (*c.* 1594), *Henry IV* (*c.* 1597) and *Henry V* (1599), *The Merry Wives of Windsor* (1600–01), *Twelfth Night* (1600–01) and *The Tempest* (*c.* 1611); the anonymous *Mucedorus* (published in 1598); Ben Jonson's *Volpone* (1606) and *The Alchemist* (1610).

It should be noted also that something approaching farce was sometimes used in tragedy (*q.v.*) for comic relief (*q.v.*). Notable instances occur in Marlowe's *Dr Faustus* (IV, vii) a play which, though possibly as late as *c.* 1593, contains much that is characteristic of the Morality Plays.

However, in this period, apart from *The Comedy of Errors* and *The Taming of the Shrew*, there is little that could be described as farce without some reservations. Later, we have Jonson's *Bartholomew Fair* (1614), an outstanding farcical comedy. And then, in the middle of the 17th c., Molière showed himself a master of the genre – especially with *Le Malade imaginaire* (1672). In Restoration comedy (*q.v.*) and 18th c. comedy there are plentiful farcical episodes, particularly in burlesque (*q.v.*) plays. In the 18th c. also we find a number of short farces used as curtain raisers (*q.v.*).

Fully developed and mature farce finally established itself in the 19th c.; in France with the work of Labiche and Feydeau; in England with the work of Pinero. W. S. Gilbert also helped to popularize the form.

Some of Labiche's major works are *Monsieur de Coislin* (1838); *Le Chapeau de paille d'Italie* (1851); *Le Voyage de Monsieur Perrichon* (1860); and *La Cagnotte* (1864). Feydeau was a prolific writer of farces, and some of his most important plays are: *Un fil à la patte* (1894); *Hotel Paradiso* (1894); *Le Dindon* (1898); *La Dame de chez Maxim's* (1899); *La Puce à l'oreille* (1907); *Occupe-toi d'Amélie* (1908); and *On purge bébé* (1910). Pinero's main achievements in farce were: *The Magistrate* (1885); *The Schoolmistress* (1886); *Dandy Dick* (1887); and *The Cabinet Minister* (1890).

From this period, too, date three one-act farces by Chekhov: *The Bear* (1888); *The Proposal* (1889); and *The Wedding* (1890); and two full-length farces by Georges Courteline: *Les Gaîtés de l'escadron* (1886) and *Boubouroche* (1893). To the 1890s also belongs a classic farce in the English repertoire: Brandon Thomas's *Charley's Aunt* (1892). Some would describe Oscar Wilde's *The Importance of Being Earnest* (1895) as a farce; but it is really a beautiful example of farce combined with comedy of manners (*q.v.*). The same might be said of Gogol's *The Government Inspector* (1836).

In the 20th c. the genre of farce continued to flourish in, for example, Somerset Maugham's *Home and Beauty* (1919); Frederick Lonsdale's *On Approval* (1927); Joseph Kesselring's *Arsenic and Old Lace* (1941); Rattigan's *While the Sun Shines* (1943); R. F. Delderfield's *Worm's Eye View* (1945); John Dighton's *The Happiest Days of Your Life* (1947); Marcel Aymé's *Clerembard* (1950); Jean-Paul Sartre's *Kean* (1953); Joe Orton's *Loot* (1965) and his *What the Butler Saw* (1969); Tom Stoppard's *Real Inspector Hound* (1968), a clever farcical parody of the stage thriller (*q.v.*), and his *Dirty Linen* (1976); Alan Bennett's *Habeas Corpus* (1973); and Michael Frayn's *Noises Off* (1982). To these should be added four highly individual and brilliant farces by Dario Fo, namely: *Accidental Death of an Anarchist* (1970) and its sequel *Knock, Knock! Who's There? The Police* (1972), *We Can't Pay, We Won't Pay* (1974) and *Trumpets and Raspberries* (1984).

For many years two London theatres produced successful farces. At the Aldwych many good farces by Ben Travers were staged: *Cuckoo in the Nest* (1925); *Rookery Nook* (1926); *Thark* (1927); *A Bit of a Test* (1933); and *Banana Ridge* (1938). Later the Whitehall Theatre presented many farces by Brian Rix: *Reluctant Heroes* (1950); *Dry Rot* (1954); *Simple Spymen* (1958); and *One for the Pot* (1961).

Since Labiche and Feydeau, and thanks to them, what is known as the 'bedroom farce', whose themes are sexual infidelity and amorous escapades both in and out of wedlock, has been one of the most popular forms.

Other distinguished dramatists who have made contributions to farce are: André Roussin, Ferenc Molnár and Jean Anouilh. *See also* BLACK COMEDY; COMEDY; THEATRE OF THE ABSURD; VAUDEVILLE.

fârsa A type of boasting poem (*q.v.*) found among the African Galla tribe. Such poems recite a litany of heroes and their heroic deeds. *See also* GIERASA.

farsas Medieval Spanish religious plays, often with a comic interlude (*q.v.*), as in *Farsas y eglogas al modo y estilo pastoril y castellano* by Lucas Fernández (1474–1542). The modern Spanish *farsa* has the same intention as farce (*q.v.*).

fashionable novel A form of fiction which was popular in the period 1825–50. The novels were mostly about wealthy, fashionable members of the upper classes. Theodore Hook (1788–1841), an accomplished writer of light verse (*q.v.*), was one of the principal practitioners. Some of his better known novels were: *Sayings and Doings* (1842–8), *Maxwell* (1830), *Gilbert Gurney* (1836), *Jack Brag* (1837) and *Gurney Married* (1838). Bulwer Lytton's *Pelham* (1828) was also very popular, as was Plumer Ward's *Tremaine, or a Man of Refinement* (1825). Other authors particularly associated with the fashionable novel were: Susan Ferrier (1782–1854), Mrs Gore (1799–1861), T. H. Lister (1800–42) and Disraeli (1804–81). Ouida (1839–1908) – the pseudonym of Marie Louise de la Ramée – also wrote a number of fashionable novels later in the 19th c.

Fastnachtspiel (G 'Shrove Tuesday play') A dramatic genre whose origins are to be found in 15th c. Shrovetide masquerades. They were mostly short – not much more than 'playlets' – and were presented and performed by townspeople. They might, in fact, be considered as early instances of community theatre (*q.v.*). Some of the main themes were domestic – such as marital problems – and they were often devised as a kind of trial or court process. Some are comedies in the form of dramatized *Schwänke* (*q.v.*). Many were composed in *Knittelverse* (*q.v.*). The earliest known writer of them is Hans Rosenplüt (15th c.). Other notable dramatists were: Hans Folz (*c.* 1400–*c.* 1575), Hans Sachs (1494–1576), Hans Rudolf Manuel (1525–71) and Jakob Ayrer (1543–1605), who wrote thirty-six *Fastnachtspiele*.

fate drama *See* SCHICKSALSTRAGODIE.

fatrasie (F 'medley, rubbish, farrago') A French medieval verse form, usually of eleven lines. They were popular from the 13th to the 15th c. and are one of the earliest forms of nonsense (*q.v.*) verse. It seems that they were intended to be travesties of traditional fixed forms and the conventional rules of prosody, and are sometimes to be found in the form of macaronics (*q.v.*). *See* COQ-A-L'ANE; SERMON JOYEUX; SORAISMUS.

Faust theme At some time during the 16th c. a late medieval legend about a man who sold his soul to the Devil became linked with the man called Johann Faust (*c.* 1488–1541), an itinerant conjuror. The first known account of this man's life, the *Historia von D. Johann Fausten*, was published in 1587 and described a magician's pact with the Devil. The publication coincided with a noticeable increase of interest in demonology and Satanism in Europe; an interest which was to continue late into the 17th c. and produced an astonishing number of demonologies, as well as ecclesiastical and civil measures against Satanism.

Faust appears to have been a magician of the same lineage as Solomon, Simon Magus, Pope Sylvester II and Zyto. He is also associated with Theophilus, another who pledged himself to the Devil and whose story was widely known in medieval legends from late in the 8th c. onwards. Versions of these are to be found in French medieval drama, Low German and Middle Dutch drama and also in miscellaneous tales in verse and prose in Dutch and English.

It may well be that by an allotropic process stories of human pacts with the Devil became more and more associated with Faust until he became a representative figure.

Christopher Marlowe appears to have been the first writer of merit to perceive the possibilities of the Faust theme and he dramatized them in his *Tragical History of Dr Faustus* (*c.* 1588–93), a drama which owes much to the Morality Play (*q.v.*). Marlowe's version travelled to Germany, via a troupe of players known as the 'English Comedians'. A derived play from the German text survived. Later in the 17th c. the story of Faustus was rendered in puppet theatres, but in these presentations Faust was a buffoon and the Devil a bogeyman. Other versions of the *Historia* sustained the legend and the idea of a diabolic pact was inherent in a number of early 17th c. works. In some it was overt; for instance, Mira de Amescua's *El esclavo del demonio* (1612) and Guevara's *El Diablo conjuelo* (1641).

However, it is not until the 18th c. – a period during which there was a singular absence of interest in anything to do with devilry – that we find the theme taken up in earnest. In 1707 Lesage published *Le Diable boiteux*, a kind of picaresque (*q.v.*) novel (*q.v.*) in which the demon Asmodée becomes the servant of Don Cléophas Zambullo. Then, in 1731, a Dutch play titled *De Hellevart von Doktor Ioan Faust* was produced – and the basis of this was a play derived from the German text of Marlowe's tragedy of more than a century earlier. In 1759 Lessing published his *Faustspiel*, but only parts of it survive. In 1775 Paul Weidmann produced *Johann Faust: ein allegorisches Drama*, and, somewhat later, the writers of the *Sturm und Drang* (*q.v.*) movement used the legend for satirical purposes and combined domestic tragedy with the Faust story. The following year Friedrich Müller published part of his *Fausts Leben*, and in 1778 completed the first of its five parts. Klinger's novel *Fausts Leben* came out in 1791. Meanwhile Goethe had been working on the theme. In 1775 he published the *Ur-Faust*, and in 1790 and 1808 Part I of *Faust*. Part II was not published until 1832. Goethe's version of the story is generally regarded as the best.

During the 19th c. the theme proved no less attractive to many writers. In 1803 Chamisso published a dramatic fragment, *Faust: ein Versuch*, and in 1814 produced his well-known supernatural tale *Peter Schlemihl* – the story of a man who sold his shadow to the Devil. Byron was influenced by Goethe's *Faust* and treated the theme in *Manfred* (1817). Heine, too, who translated the first act of *Manfred* into German, began a Faust play in 1824. Later Heine did a ballet-scenario of *Faust*. In 1862 Friedrich Vischer parodied the theme in *Faust: der Tragödie, dritter Teil.*

Early in the 19th c. the Faust legend and the Don Juan legend became mingled and Faust became a Don Juan type profligate. In 1804 Schink and von Voss collaborated to produce *Faust: Dramatische Fantasie, nach einer Sage des 16.Jh.* They also wrote *Faust: Trauerspiel mit Gesang und Tanz* (1823). Grabbe's tragedy *Don Juan und Faust* (1829) was inspired by *Manfred* and by Klingermann's *Faust: ein Trauerspiel* (1815).

Other notable works which we should remark on are: Lenau's *Faust* (1836); P. J. Bailey's *Festus* (1839); Woldemar Nürnberger's treatment in an epic poem (1842); Dorothy Sayers's play *The Devil to Pay* (1939); Valéry's unfinished *Mon Faust* (1946); and Thomas Mann's long and opaque novel *Doktor Faustus* (1947).

Nor has the peculiar fascination of this theme been confined to dramatists and poets. A number of 19th c. composers were inspired by it in various ways. Outstanding instances are: Spohr's opera *Faust* (1816); Wagner's *Faust Overture* (1839); Berlioz's cantata *The Damnation of Faust* (1846); Schumann's *Scenes from Goethe's Faust* (1853); Liszt's *Faust Symphony* (1857); Gounod's opera *Faust* (1859); Liszt's *Episodes from Lenau's Faust* (1861) and his four Mephisto waltzes; Boito's *Mephistophele* (1868). To these we should add Busoni's opera *Faust* (1920), and Arthur Benjamin's comic opera *The Devil Take Her* (1931).

Fazetie (L *facetia*, *facetus* 'merry, witty') A German term for a clever, witty, well-phrased anecdote which may or may not be bawdy and/or erotic. *Fazetien* are to be found in humanistic Latin literature of the Renaissance period (*q.v.*). For example: *Facetiae Latinae et Germanicae* (1486), *Facetiae* (1508–12) and *Facetiae* (*c.* 1600). Not common in German vernacular, but the bawdy and humorous *Schwank* (*q.v.*) is related to them. *See* FACETIAE.

Federal Theatre Project An enterprise inaugurated in the USA in 1935 to provide employment for people in the theatre and to offer more entertainment during the Depression. During its most active period it had a wide range, covering some forty states and giving work to over 10,000 people. Its director was Hallie Flanagan (1890–1969) and it contained many 'units', such as the one-act-play unit, the German unit, the poetic drama unit, the Negro Youth Theatre and so on. It also influenced the development of the Living Newspaper (*q.v.*). Unfortunately, the activity of many of its members aroused the interest of the House UnAmerican Activities Committee. Flanagan herself was arraigned before it and in 1939 Congress ended the project.

feigning 'To feign' means 'to invent' (as well as 'to pretend falsely'), and derives from the Latin *fingere* 'to form, mould, conceive or contrive'.

Plato would not allow poets in his ideal commonwealth of *The Republic* because they were 'liars' – in the sense that they imitated the truth. In *Poetics* Aristotle took a contrary point of view and held that the poet told a kind of truth by imitation. Between them they raised an issue that was much debated on and off for centuries, and particularly at the Renaissance. However, imitation, or feigning, then came to be regarded as indispensable to the poet. Now, it is generally accepted that poetry conveys something beyond the literal verisimilitude (*q.v.*). *Mutatis mutandis*, the same is true of fiction in prose. The gist of the matter is suggested in *As You Like It* (II, iii) in an exchange between Audrey and Touchstone:

> AUDREY: I do not know what poetical is: is it honest in deed and word? is it a true thing?
> TOUCHSTONE: No, truly; for the truest poetry is the most feigning; and lovers are given to poetry, and what they swear in poetry may be said as lovers they do feign.

See FANCY AND IMAGINATION; IMITATION.

Félibres, les In *c.* 1854 a movement known as *le Félibrige* began in order to restore Provençal as a living language and to revive interest in Provençal literature, history, customs, etc. There was even a move to get Provençal taught in schools. In 1855 *les Félibres* founded the annual *L'Armana prouvençau* which published Provençal literature. The founders of the movement were: Paul Giéra (1816–61), Joseph Roumanille (1818–91), Jean Brunet (1823–94), Anselme Mathieu (1828–1925), Théodore Aubanel (1829–86), Frédéric Mistral (1830–1914), Remy Marcellin (1832–1908) and Alphonse Tavan (1833–1905). They all wrote in Provençal.

fellow travellers This phrase was used by Trotsky (1879–1940) to describe those Soviet authors who accepted the 1917 Revolution without necessarily accepting Bolshevik ideology. In fact they maintained that literature should not be subject to political tenets or coercion. *See* SERAPIONOVY BRATYA.

feminine caesura A caesura (*q.v.*) which comes after an unstressed syllable, as after 'open' in this line from John Berryman's *Homage to Mistress Bradstreet*:

> The winters close, Springs open, || no child stirs

See MASCULINE CAESURA.

feminine ending An extra unstressed syllable at the end of a line of verse. Common in blank verse, with the slack eleventh syllable, as in the third line of these three from George Chapman's *De Guina* (the first two have masculine endings, *q.v.*):

> O incredulity! the wit of fools,
> That slovenly will spit on all things fair,
> The coward's castle, and the sluggard's cradle.

See FEMININE RHYME.

feminine rhyme When words of two or more syllables rhyme it is known as feminine or double rhyme. It is particularly common in humorous verse, as in the first two lines of this flippant epitaph:

> Here lie I and my four daughters,
> Killed by drinking Cheltenham waters.
> Had we but stuck to Epsom salts,
> We wouldn't have been in these here vaults.

See FEMININE ENDING; MASCULINE RHYME.

feminist criticism A development and movement in critical theory and in the evaluation of literature which was well under way by the late 1960s and which has burgeoned steadily since. It is an attempt to describe and interpret (and reinterpret) women's experience as depicted in various kinds of literature – especially the novel (*q.v.*); and, to a lesser extent, poetry and drama.

It questions the long-standing, dominant, male, phallocentric ideologies (which add up to a kind of male conspiracy), patriarchal attitudes and male interpretations in literature (and critical evaluation of literature). It attacks male notions of value in literature – by offering critiques of male authors and representations of men in literature and also by privileging women writers. In addition it challenges traditional and accepted male ideas about the nature of women and about how women feel, act and think, or are *supposed* to feel, act and think, and how in general they respond to life and living. It thus questions numerous prejudices and assumptions about women made by male writers, not least any tendency to cast women in stock character (*q.v.*) roles.

The inquiry (or discourse, *q.v.*) has posed a number of questions. For example, the possibility or likelihood of *écriture feminine* (*q.v.*): writing that is essentially, characteristically, feminine or female in language and style. And, if such a thing exists, whether or not it is a fruitful idea to make distinctions between male and female writing; whether or not the making of such distinctions would merely result in 'sexual polarization'.

There is debate in feminism itself about how productive are: (a) the notion of an essential difference expressed in writing – a kind of separatism; (b) a radical desire to recognize that male representations of women are as important as women's writing, and also to recognize that the notion of an *écriture feminine* surrenders to a traditional marginalization of women's voices.

Here perhaps one may amplify to make a crude but serviceable distinction between the 'essentialists' and the 'relativists'. The essentialist position holds the view that there is a fundamental distinction (not based on biological determinism so much as social and economic factors and their psychological consequences) between the way women and men think and write – to such a degree that there is such a thing as *écriture feminine*: that is, a way that women have of expressing themselves totally opposed to the representative aspects of male language and discourse. This position is associated with French feminists. The relativist position – broadly associated with Anglo-American critics – is that the analysis of the representation of men and women by male and female authors is important. No fundamental difference separates men and women's writing except the way male critics and authors have undervalued the latter.

Feminism has its origins in the struggle for women's rights which began late in the 18th c., more particularly with Mary Wollstonecraft's *A Vindication of the Rights of Woman* (1792). Later came John Stuart Mill's *The Subjection of Women* (1869) and the American Margaret Fuller's *Woman in the Nineteenth Century* (1845). The Suffragette movement at the beginning of the 20th c. carried on the campaign. In the 1920s there were clear signs of new and different approaches in relation to women writers and literature. This was noticeable in the critical work of, for example, Rebecca West, and in Virginia Woolf's essays on women authors who suffered from economic and cultural disadvantages in what she termed a 'patriarchal' society. Her book *A Room of One's Own* (1929) was to become a classic 'document' (*q.v.*) of the feminist critical movement. She addressed herself to the issue of why there were so few women writers and why it is frequently difficult or impossible for a woman to write. There was also Dorothy Richardson's very important twelve-volume stream of consciousness (*q.v.*) novel *Pilgrimage*, the first volume of which appeared in 1915 (and the last, posthumously, in 1967). This centres on the female consciousness of the heroine Miriam Henderson, is conducted in unpunctuated female prose and caused Virginia Woolf to observe that Richardson had invented 'the psychological sentence of the feminine gender'.

An important landmark in the evolution of feminist criticism in the post-war period was Simone de Beauvoir's *Le Deuxième Sexe* (1949), a seminal work which questioned the whole position and role of women in society and was a critique of women's cultural identification. She also addressed herself to the matter of the representation of women by various male writers, such as Stendhal and D. H. Lawrence. Her writing was 'political' in tone and she was one of the first to examine ways in which men depict women in fiction.

In the late 1960s there began a spate of diverse criticism, often of a polemical nature, which shows no sign of abating. Much of it – especially that on literature (e.g. work by Mary Ellman, Germaine Greer, Kate Millett, Elaine Showalter *et al.*) – was often political and expressed anger and a sense of injustice that women had been oppressed and exploited by men. Indeed, a substantial amount of feminist criticism goes well beyond literature to explore the socio-economic status of women; and, where literature is concerned, to look at women's economic position as authors and the problems they have with allegedly prejudiced male publishers and critics.

In America the spate began with Mary Ellman's *Thinking About Women* (1968), a witty and at times scathing analysis of the ways women are represented in literature by men. In 1969 Kate Millett published *Sexual Politics*, in which she examines how power relations work and how men manipulate and perpetuate male dominance over women. She addressed herself to such writers as Norman Mailer, Henry Miller and D. H. Lawrence. In 1979 Sandra Gilbert and Susan Gubar published *The Madwoman in the Attic: The Woman Writer and the Nineteenth Century Imagination.* This famous and monumental study is about, among many other things, the typical motifs and patterns in the works of 19th c. women writers. One of their main arguments is that these writers chose (as Toril Moi puts it in her essay on feminist literary criticism in *Modern Literary Theory*, 1982, ed. by Jefferson and Robey) 'to express their own female anger in a series of duplicitous textual strategies whereby both the angel and the monster, the sweet heroine and the raging madwoman, are aspects of the author's self-image, as well as elements of her treacherous anti-patriarchal strategies'. A notable example of the psychological duplicity is the grotesque counter-figure to the heroine. For example, Bertha Rochester, the madwoman in Charlotte Brontë's *Jane Eyre* (1847). Such a figure is, as Gilbert and Gubar put it, 'usually in some sense the *author's* double, an image of her own anxiety and rage'.

Such analyses come into the category of what has been called by Elaine Showalter 'gynocriticism': that is, criticism concerned with writings by women (including letters and journals) and all aspects of their production and interpretation. Showalter herself made a notable contribution in the shape of *A Literature of Their Own: British Women Novelists from Brontë to Lessing* (1977). Other notable works in this mode include *The Female Imagination* (1975) by Patricia Meyer Spacks, and *Literary Women* (1976) by Ellen Moers. Toril Moi's *Sexual/Textual Politics: Feminist Literary Theory* (1985) is a long, in-depth description, critique and analysis of Anglo-American and French feminist theory and criticism.

Whereas Anglo-American critics and theorists have been primarily concerned with thematic studies of writings by and about women, French feminist critics have been concerned with the theory of the role of gender in writing. In their theories they have been influenced by theories of post-structuralism, semiotics and deconstruction (*qq.v.*). They have been interested in a critique of language. They maintain that all or most Western languages are male-dominated and male-engendered, and that discourse is predominantly 'phallogocentric' (*q.v.*), as Jacques Derrida puts it. They are thus concerned with the possibility of a woman's language and of *écriture feminine.* Among the main French theorists are Julia Kristeva (author of *Desire in Language: A Semiotic Approach to Literature and Art*, 1980), Luce Irigaray (author of *Speculum of the Other Woman*, 1985, and *This Sex Which Is Not One*, 1985), and Hélène Cixous (author of *The Newly Born Woman*, 1986). Some of their theories may seem a little far-fetched occasionally, but the concept of an *écriture feminine* which is not 'contaminated' by or appropriated into phallogocentric language is a most interesting and valid one.

A notable by-product, so to speak, of the whole movement of feminism and feminist theory and criticism has been the rediscovery of a hidden tradition of women's writing and the rediscovery and republication of numerous novels (and other works) by women which have long since sunk more or less without trace – except in library catalogues. For example, books by Susan Ferrier, Harriett Martineau, Margaret Oliphant, Elizabeth Gaskell, Christina Rossetti, Mary Sinclair and Edith Durham. Three publishing houses in particular (Virago, Pandora and the Women's Press) have been responsible for this recovery.

Other miscellaneous works of importance in feminist criticism (in chronological order) are: *Psychoanalysis and Feminism* (1975) by Juliet Mitchell; *The Laugh of the Medusa* (in *Signs*, vol. I, 1976) by Hélène Cixous; *The Resisting Reader* (1978) by Judith Fetterly; *The Dialectic of Sex* (1979) by Shulamith Firestone; *Women Writing and Writing about Women* (1979), edited by Mary Jacobus; *Women and Language in Literature and Society* (1980), edited by Ginet-McConnell, Borker and Furman; *On Lies, Secrets, and Silence:*

Selected Prose (1980) by Adrienne Rich; *Women's Oppression Today: Problems in Marxist Feminist Analysis* (1980) by Michele Barrett; *New French Feminisms: An Anthology* (1981), edited by Ellaine Marks and Isabelle de Courtivron; *Writing and Sexual Difference* (1982), edited by Elizabeth Abel; *Feminism and Psychoanalysis: The Daughter's Seduction* (1982) by Jane Gallop; *Contemporary Feminist Thought* (1984) by Hester Eisenstein; *The New Feminist Criticism: Essays on Women, Literature and Theory* (1986), edited by Elaine Showalter; *Feminist Literary Theory: A Reader* (1986), edited by Mary Eagleton; *Gender and Theory: Dialogues in Feminist Criticism* (1989), edited by Linda Kauffman. *See also* DIFFERANCE; PLAISIR/JOUISSANCE; READER-RESPONSE THEORY; READERLY/WRITERLY.

fescennine verse A very early form of bawdy Latin verse which probably originated in festivals celebrating the gathering of the harvest and the grape crops. They were also wedding songs. They are important as possible ancestors of drama (because some were in dialogue form) and of satire (*q.v.*) – because some of them were caustic as well as coarse. The derivation of the word is obscure. It may be a corruption of *fascinium*, a phallic emblem worn as a charm; on the other hand it may come from the town of Fescennium in Etruria.

Festschrift (G 'celebration writing) The term denotes a symposium (*q.v.*) compiled in honour of a distinguished scholar or writer. The first 'homage volume' of this kind was presented to Friedrich Ritschl, classical scholar, in 1867; but yet more famous was that compiled in honour of the eminent historian Theodor Mommsen under the title *Commentationes Philologicae* (1877).

fête des fous *See* SERMON JOYEUX.

feuilleton (F 'literary article/story'; *feuille* 'leaf, sheet of paper') A supplement issued with a newspaper. The best known of the early *feuilletons* was that produced by Julien-Louis Geoffroy (1743–1814), the dramatic critic of the *Journal des Débats*. It was a kind of appendix, printed on the bottom part of a page and detachable. Other journals copied the idea, printing literary and dramatic *feuilletons* and, later, *romans-feuilletons* (*q.v.*).

ficción (Sp 'fiction') A genre invented by the Argentine poet and critic Jorge Luis Borges. A *ficción* is a story-essay which glosses human dreams and illusions. It is ironical in tone and also didactic. Borges published a collection called *Ficciones* in 1944.

fiction A vague and general term for an imaginative work, usually in prose. At any rate, it does not normally cover poetry and drama though both are a form of fiction in that they are moulded and contrived – or feigned. Fiction is now used in general of the novel, the short story, the *novella* (*qq.v.*) and related genres.

figurae causae In Classical rhetoric (*q.v.*) the term denotes the stylistic shape and pattern of a speech in relation to the speaker's purpose.

figurate poem *See* ALTAR POEM; PATTERN POETRY.

figurative language Language which uses figures of speech; for example, metaphor, simile, alliteration (*qq.v.*). Figurative language must be distinguished from literal (*q.v.*) language. 'He hared down the street' or 'He ran like a hare down the street' are figurative (metaphor and simile respectively). 'He ran very quickly down the street' is literal. *See* HYPERBOLE; METONYMY; SYNECDOCHE.

fin de siècle *See* DECADENCE.

finida (Sp 'finish') One or more lines of verse providing the conclusion of a *cantiga* or *decir* (*qq.v.*). The equivalent of the Provençal *tornada* (*q.v.*).

fit The division of a poem, a canto (*q.v.*). The term may have acquired its meaning from the ON *fit* 'a hem', or the German *Fitze*, a skein of yarn or the thread with which the weavers marked off a day's work. Lewis Carroll's *The Hunting of the Snark* consists of eight fits. Now hardly ever used. *See* STANZA; STAVE.

fixed form The term denotes a form in poetry for which there are prescribed and established rules with regard to the number of lines, the meter, line length, rhyme and so forth. For example, the sonnet, *rondeau* and *villanelle* (*qq.v.*). There are many of them. Most OF forms are fixed. Before *c.* 1800 most poetry was written according to traditional and received patterns and it was believed that particular forms were appropriate for certain subjects and ideas. The 18th c. English poets had great respect for traditional structure and conventional models, hence the liking for imitation (*q.v.*). This respect for established form did not prevent them from achieving a high degree of originality.

Late in the 18th c. and at the beginning of the 19th c. there was a pronounced turning away from traditional structures to what is known as 'organic form' (*q.v.*), where the structure follows the ideas and content. This is particularly noticeable in the development of the ode (*q.v.*). Later there was to come free verse (*q.v.*) and seemingly endless developments in organic forms. The limerick (*q.v.*) is one of many examples. *See* OLD FRENCH AND PROVENCAL FORMS.

flamenca *See* SEGUIDILLA.

flashback A term which probably derives from the cinema, and which is now also used to describe any scene or episode in a play, novel, story or poem which is inserted to show events that happened at an earlier time. It is frequently used in modern fiction.

flat and round characters Terms used by E. M. Forster in *Aspects of the Novel* (1927) to describe two basically different types of character – and characterization. A 'flat' character does not change in the course of a story or play; a 'round' one develops and thus alters. Forster cites Mrs Micawber as a flat character and Becky Sharp as a round one. Shakespeare's *Henry IV* (Pts I and II) provides a suitable contrast in the shape of Hotspur and Prince Hal. The former is a 'flat' character; the Prince changes and develops considerably in the course of the play. *See also* BURLESQUE; CARICATURE.

fleshly school of poetry A derogatory term used by Robert Buchanan, writing under the pseudonym Thomas Maitland, in *The Contemporary Review* (Oct. 1871) to describe Rossetti, Swinburne and William Morris. Buchanan regarded these writers as decadent, morally irresponsible and aesthetic (in the pejorative sense) and over-interested in the carnal or sensual. Buchanan was a misguided man and his vituperations caused considerable controversy. Swinburne replied to him with some venom. *See also* AESTHETICISM; PRE-RAPHAELITES.

Florida Street group A literary group of the 1920s named after the cosmopolitan and urbane street in Buenos Aires. Their attitudes were *avant-garde* (*q.v.*) and they tended to learn from the practice of European writers. Jorge Luis Borges (1899–1988) was the best known. *See also* BOEDO STREET GROUP.

Flugschriften The German term for broadsheets or broadsides (*q.v.*). Frequently used for propaganda (*q.v.*) purposes in religious and political controversy during the 16th and 17th c. They were often polemical and scurrilous and were illustrated by woodcuts.

flyting (from OE *flitan* 'to contend, strive or wrangle') A *flyting* (or *fliting*) is a cursing match in verse; especially between two poets who hurl abuse at each other. An early instance of a kind of *flyting* is the vehement exchange between the leader of the Vikings and Byrhtnoth, the English leader in the OE poem *The Battle of Maldon*. The 16th c. Scottish poets were particularly fond of the form. A well-known example is the *Flyting of Dunbar and Kennedie*. Skelton appears to have been influenced by this kind of invective (*q.v.*). *See also* DIATRIBE; LAMPOON; POETIC CONTESTS.

folía (Sp *un folio* 'a folio'; *foliar* 'to number pages') A Spanish stanza form of four lines in which the lines may be octosyllabic or shorter. Of uncertain origin, they are known to have existed before 1600 and are related to a kind of Portuguese dance-song. The term has also been applied variously to: light music and popular music; the sound and the figure of the Spanish dance which used to be danced only with castanets; a fiesta in certain provinces, with evening bonfires, etc. *See* SEGUIDILLA.

folio (L *folium* 'leaf') Made by folding a printer's sheet once only, to form two folios or four pages. It also refers to editions of Shakespeare's plays published after his death: the First Folio appeared in 1623. There were three others in 1632, 1663 and 1685. *See* DUODECIMO; LEAF; OCTAVO; QUARTO.

folk drama This kind of drama almost certainly has its origins in fertility rites so ancient that it is not possible to do much more than guess at them. However, folk drama is a common and living phenomenon in many parts of the world – especially in Europe – and often shows affinities with the sword dance (*q.v.*). In the British Isles there are two basic folk plays: *The Mumming Play* (or *St*

George Play) and *The Plough Monday Play* (*qq.v.*). *See also* REVESBY PLAY.

folk literature Under this general and somewhat vague term one may include folksong, ballad, fairy tales, drama, proverbs, riddles, charms and legends (*qq.v.*). For the most part, folk literature (or, perhaps, more properly, folklore) is the creation of primitive and illiterate people – and therefore much of it belongs to oral tradition (*q.v.*). It becomes literature in the correct sense of the word only when people gather it together and write it down. When this happens, it is usually a sign that the folk literature in question is in decline.

There were few systematic attempts to gather such literature together until the 19th c., when, for example, the brothers Grimm made their famous collection of fairy tales, and the great Serbian scholar Vuk Karadžić collected many of the epic ballads or *narodne pesme* (*q.v.*) which the *guslari* (*q.v.*) had been reciting and passing down in oral tradition since the 14th c.

Since then, increasingly, individual scholars, cultural societies, academies, universities and many other organizations have laboured to preserve folk literature from oblivion. *See* FOLK DRAMA; FOLKSONG; FOLK TALE.

folksong This kind of song belongs to oral tradition (*q.v.*) and is thus passed on from mouth to mouth. It is a communal form of expression and appears to be universal. Many of them have now been written down. The category includes ballad, carol, sea shanty and lullaby (*qq.v.*). Marching songs, work songs, hobo songs and Negro spirituals are also forms of folksong. To these should be added the *dumy*, *daina*, *bylina* and the *narodne pesme* (*qq.v.*).

Other special kinds of folksong are the *serenade* or *serenata* – the song the lover sings when he visits his beloved at night; the *aubade* (*q.v.*), or song the lover sings on leaving his beloved at dawn; the *pastourelle* (*q.v.*) or wooing song; and the *coronach* (*q.v.*), type of lament (*q.v.*).

folk tale Like the folksong (*q.v.*) many folk tales belong to oral tradition (*q.v.*). Some thousands have been collected in the British Isles alone. They include legends, fables, tall stories, shaggy dog stories, fairy stories, ghost stories (*qq.v.*), stories of giants and saints, devils and spirits; husband and wife tales; master and man tales; and what are known as 'rhozzums' (*q.v.*), short humorous tales, often about local characters. *See also* FOLK LITERATURE; MARCHEN; SUPERNATURAL STORY.

folly literature The title given to a variety of literature that had some vogue between the 15th and the 17th c. Most of the works in this category are a form of satire (*q.v.*) and can be regarded as early instances of 'the absurd'. They combine elements of fantasy, nonsense and the zany, but have a serious intent to expose, ridicule and 'send up' the more risible aspects of human behaviour. Like the nonsense verse (*q.v.*) of more recent times, and the Theatre of the Absurd (*q.v.*), they display an attempt to correct overmuch seriousness as well as to combat the pretensions and hypocrisies of this world. A way of 'laughing things off'; so it is also called 'Fool Literature'.

An early and classic example is Brandt's *Narrenschiff*, 'The Ship of Fools' (1494), a 'travel' tale reminiscent of Lucian's fantasies. Brandt filled his ship with 112 different kinds of recognizable fool, but became so interested in showing the characters that the ship never left port; rather as if Chaucer's pilgrims never left the Tabard Inn. The success of the work was instant. In 1497 Locher Philomusus translated it into Latin under the title *Stultifera Navis*. In the same year Pierre Rivière translated it into French under the title *La Nef des Folz du Monde*. Other translations followed in rapid succession. Alexander Barclay did an English version (in verse) in 1509, and adapted the original so that it should fit with the English scene. It gives a picture of contemporary English life (dwelling in particular on affectations of manners, customs and clothing, social evils, venal officials and corrupt courts), and provides an early collection of satirical types. Later, comedy of humours and the character (*q.v.*) sketch were to be a development of this kind of treatment of individuals and types.

Another English work of note belonging to the 16th c. is *Cocke Lorell's Bote*, a satire in which various tradespeople embark on a ship and 'sail' through England. The captain of the ship is Cocke Lorell, a tinker. This work in verse gives a vivid picture of 'low life' in England at that time.

In 1509, also, Erasmus wrote his *Moriae Encomium*, 'The Praise of Folly', which was published in 1511. This had enormous success (forty editions came out in the author's life-time). In 1549 Dedekind wrote *Grobianus: De Morum Simplicitate*, a poem which burlesqued social conditions in Germany. He took his title from Brandt's St Grobianus (in *Narrenschiff*), who was symbolic of boorish behaviour. This work was translated into English and German.

Such books, among several others, influenced the jest-book and the emblem-book (*qq.v.*), both of which had considerable popularity in the 16th and 17th c. Dekker's *Gull's Hornbook* (1609), for instance, was a satire at the expense of fops, gallants and other forms of fool.

Folly literature very probably helped writers to develop character in drama and romance (*q.v.*) and also probably influenced the picaresque (*q.v.*) narrative. Later instances of folly literature are *Gulliver's Travels* (1726) and *Candide* (1759). In 1962 Katherine Anne Porter published *Ship of Fools*, a novel which updated the themes and ideas of Brandt's *Narrenschiff*. The celebration of folly is still a popular activity as we can see in the books of, for example, Spike Milligan. *See* BIEDERMEIER; GROBIANISM.

foot A group of syllables forming a metrical unit; a unit of rhythm. The Classical prosodists and poets established nearly all the known foot formations. We measure feet in terms of syllable variation: long and short syllables, stressed and unstressed. The following are the names of the principal feet, illustrated with their stress patterns: / denotes a long syllable or a stressed one; ◡ denotes a short or unstressed syllable:

amphibrach ◡ / ◡
amphimacer / ◡ /
anapaest ◡ ◡ /
antibacchius / / ◡
antispast ◡ / / ◡
bacchius ◡ / /
choree (trochee) / ◡
choreus (by resolution) ◡ ◡ ◡
choriamb / ◡ ◡ /
cretic (alternative for amphimacer) / ◡ /
dactyl / ◡ ◡
di-iamb ◡ / ◡ /
dibrach ◡ ◡
dispondee / / / /
ditrochee / ◡ / ◡
dochmiac ◡ / / ◡ / (plus any other combinations of the same pattern)
epitrite ◡ / / / (known as first, second, third or fourth according to the position of the first syllable)

iamb ◡ /
ionic majore / / ◡ ◡
ionic minore ◡ ◡ / /
mollossus / / /
paeon / ◡ ◡ ◡ (known as first, second, third or fourth according to the position of the stressed syllable)
palimbacchius (alternative for antibacchius) / / ◡
proceleusmatic ◡ ◡ ◡ ◡
pyrrhic (alternative for dibrach) ◡ ◡
spondee / /
tribrach ◡ ◡ ◡ (and see choreus)
trochee (alternative for choree) / ◡

The commonest feet in English prosody are: iamb, trochee, dactyl, anapaest and spondee, in that order. *See* FALLING RHYTHM; RISING RHYTHM; ROCKING RHYTHM; SCANSION; SPRUNG RHYTHM.

foregrounding The English rendering of the Czech word *aktualisace*. The term denotes the use of devices and techniques which 'push' the act of expression into the foreground so that language draws attention to itself. This draws attention, in turn, to the way that literary language represents reality. Foregrounding occurs especially in poetic language. The Czech linguist Jan Mukařovský (in his essay *Standard Language and Poetic Language*) observes: 'The function of poetic language consists in the maximum foregrounding of the utterance . . . it is not used in the services of communication, but in order to place in the foreground the act of expression, the act of speech itself'. In a sense, foregrounding is the art which reveals art rather than concealing it. Sterne's *Tristram Shandy* (1760–67) is often cited as a good example of this sort of literariness (*q.v.*), which is closely connected with Viktor Shklovsky's concept of 'making strange' and 'defamiliarization' (*q.v.*). Sterne, by various literary devices, persistently calls the reader's attention to what he is doing. So have many more recent writers as diverse as, for example, Rimbaud, James Joyce, William Faulkner, Flann O'Brien, B. S. Johnson, Claude Simon and Samuel Beckett. Beckett, in answering Joyce's detractors, once wrote: 'You complain that this stuff is not written in English. It is not only to be read. It is to be looked at and listened to. *His writing is not about something; it is that something itself* [my italics]'. This, perhaps, gives an idea of the nature of foregrounding, which Coleridge had been aware of long before. In the *Biographia Literaria* (1817) he speaks of the 'prime merit' of literary genius as the representation of 'familiar objects' in order to evoke 'freshness of sensation'. Coleridge and Wordsworth (in the preface to *Lyrical Ballads*) can be said to have been alert to this important aspect of literary theory. However, Coleridge (like Wordsworth) was a romantic and here is thinking of the display of new light on things perceived, rather than the literary means and effect. *See also* ARS EST CELARE ARTEM; READERLY/WRITERLY.

forensics A term applied to poetry which is concerned with debate and argument (e.g. the French *débat* and the Spanish *pregunta*, *qq.v.*). Robert Herrick's *Upon Love, by Way of Question and Answer* (in the form of a *pregunta*) gives an idea of the method. It begins:

> I bring ye love: *Quest.* What will love do?
>   *Ans.* Like, and dislike ye;
> I bring ye love: *Quest.* What will love do?
>   *Ans.* Stroke ye to strike ye;

foreshadowing The technique of arranging events and information in a narrative in such a way that later events are prepared for or shadowed forth beforehand. A well-constructed novel, for instance, will suggest at the very beginning what the outcome may be; the end is contained in the beginning and this gives structural and thematic unity.

foreword (modelled on G *Vorwort*) Usually a short introductory piece to a book. It is similar to a preface (*q.v.*) and an introduction, but is generally composed not by the author but by someone else.

forgery A literary forgery occurs when someone deliberately tries to pass off a piece of writing as being by someone else, or as something else. There have been many famous instances: the *Letters of Phalaris* (2nd c. AD); Psalmanazer's *Historical and Geographical Description of Formosa* (1704); William Lauder's attempts to discredit Milton in *An Essay on Milton's Use and Imitation of the Moderns* (1750); Chatterton's *Rowley Poems* (1769); the Ossianic forgeries by James Macpherson (1760, 1762, 1765); and Thomas Wise's forgeries of bibliographies in the 19th c. which led to a large number of bogus first editions. There have been a large number of Shakespearean forgeries of various kinds. *See* LITERARY FORGERIES; PLAGIARISM; PSEUDEPIGRAPHA.

form When we speak of the form of a literary work we refer to its shape and structure and to the manner in which it is made (thus, its style, *q.v.*) – as opposed to its substance or what it is about. Form and substance are inseparable, but they may be analysed and assessed separately.

A secondary meaning of form is the *kind* of work – the genre (*q.v.*) to which it belongs. Thus: sonnet, short story, essay (*qq.v.*).

Formalism, Russian A literary theory which developed in Russia in the early 1920s. Practitioners and followers were called 'Formalists', a pejorative term to imply limitations. 'Russian Formalism' was also a pejorative label. It was finished by 1930 because of Stalinist and Socialist–Marxist pressures on the individuals involved. The terms 'formalism' and 'formalist' are applied generally, not exclusively, to 'literary', 'linguistic' theoretical approaches.

The theory of Russian Formalism had begun earlier, in the Moscow Linguistic Circle (founded in 1915) and in OPOJAZ (an acronym for 'The Society for the Study of Poetic Language', based in St Petersburg), founded in 1916. The main figure in the Moscow Linguistic Circle was Roman Jakobson (1896–1982), who helped to found the Prague School (*q.v.*) in 1926.

The Russian Formalists were primarily interested in the way that literary texts achieve their effects and in establishing a scientific basis for the study of literature. In their early work, human content in literature (e.g. emotions, ideas, actions, 'reality' in general) did not possess, for them, any significance in defining what was specifically 'literary' about a text. Indeed, the Formalists collapse the distinction between form and content. And they regard the writer as a kind of cipher merely reworking available literary devices and conventions. The writer is of negligible importance. All the emphasis is on the 'literariness' (*q.v.*) of the formal devices of a text. OPOJAZ went so far as to suggest that there are not poets or literary figures: there is just poetry and literature. Viktor Shklovsky (1893–?) summarizes the attitude in his definition of literature as 'the sum total of all the stylistic devices employed in it'.

The early phases of Formalism were dominated by Shklovsky's ideas, which were partly influenced by the Futurists (*see* FUTURISM). One of his important contributions was the concept of *ostranenie* or 'making strange', later to be called 'defamiliarization' (*q.v.*).

The Formalists also developed a theory of narrative, making a distinction between plot and story. *Syuzhet* ('the plot') refers to the order and manner in which events are actually presented in the narrative, while *fabula* ('the story') refers to the chronological sequence of events.

Boris Tomashevsky, another of the Formalists, used the term 'motif' (*q.v.*) to denote the smallest unit of plot and distinguished between 'bound' and 'free' motifs. The 'bound' motif is one which the story absolutely requires, while the 'free' is inessential.

The concept of 'motif' is clearly linked to 'motive' and thus to 'motivation'. Formalists tended to regard a poem's content as subordinate to its formal devices. This dependence on external 'non-literary' assumptions was called 'motivation'. Shklovsky defined the motivation of a text as the extent to which it was dependent on 'non-literary' assumptions, and he cited Sterne's *Tristram Shandy* as an example of a work totally without motivation.

In later development of Formalist theory the concept of 'device' gave way to the concept of 'function' in a work of literature, depending on the purpose or mode or genre (*q.v.*). It was no longer the device *per se* which was defamiliarizing but its function in the work. One of the key works in the evolution of the theories of 'function' and 'structure' is the *Jakobson–Tynyanov Theses* (1929). As important is Tynyanov and Jakobson's essay *Problems in the Study of Literature and Language* (1927). The Prague School was to unite Russian Formalism and Saussurean linguistics. It developed a concept of structure close to Saussurean linguistics and via Jakobson was to contribute to structuralism (*q.v.*). *See also* MARXIST CRITICISM; READERLY/WRITERLY; SEMIOTICS/SEMIOLOGY.

format The physical make-up of a book (*q.v.*).

fornyrðislag An ON Eddic metrical form which comprises a four-line stanza in which each line is divided by a caesura (*q.v.*) into two half lines. Each half has two accented or stressed syllables, and two or three unstressed syllables. As in OE verse, alliteration (*q.v.*) is a notable feature of the form. Most of the Eddic poems are composed in this measure. *See also* KVÐUHATTR; LJOÐAHATTR; MALAHATTR.

Forsterian Characteristic of the style, tone and attitudes of E. M. Forster (1879–1970). Thus, relaxed, informal, ironical, liberal and humanistic.

Four Ages of Poetry The title of a provocative essay by Thomas Love Peacock published in 1820. With a certain amount of drollery Peacock classified Poetry into four periods: iron, gold, silver and brass. Shelley took the matter seriously and replied with *Defence of Poetry* (1821); and in 1926 I. A. Richards published an equally serious refutation in *Science and Poetry*.

four levels of meaning The origins of the four levels of meaning are not certain, but an awareness of them is manifest in the Middle Ages. It was Dante who explained most clearly (in the *Epistle* to his patron Can Grande della Scala) what they consisted of. He was introducing the matter of the *Divina Commedia* and he distinguished: (a) the literal or historical meaning; (b) the moral meaning; (c) the allegorical meaning; (d) the anagogical.

Such criteria applied to, for instance, Orwell's *Animal Farm* (1945), might suggest the following: (a) the story is about the revolt of the animals against their human overlords, and the outcome of that revolt; (b) 'power tends to corrupt'; (c) Major = Lenin; Napoleon = Stalin; Snowball = Trotsky; Jones = corrupt capitalist landowners – and so forth; (d) human (*and* animal) nature does not change. *See* ALLEGORY.

four meanings In *Practical Criticism* (1929) I. A. Richards distinguishes four different meanings in a poem: (a) the sense – what is actually said; (b) feeling – the writer's emotional attitude towards it; (c) tone – the writer's attitude towards his reader; (d) intention – the writer's purpose, the effect he is aiming at.

fourteener Also known as a heptameter and a septenary. A line of seven feet and fourteen syllables; usually seven iambics (*q.v.*). It was used in Greek and Latin verse and flourished in English narrative verse (*q.v.*) in the later Middle Ages and in Tudor times. The Elizabethans coined the term 'fourteener'. It has not been much used since largely because it is rather unwieldy, as the following lines (alternating with hexameters) from Surrey show:

In winter's just return, when Boreas gan his reign,
And every tree unclothèd fast, as nature taught them plain,
In misty morning dark, as sheep are then in hold,
I hied me fast, it sat me on, my sheep for to unfold.

The rhyming couplet of the fourteener, written as four lines, became what is known as the eight-and-six meter of the common ballad (*q.v.*) stanza (*q.v.*).

frame story A frame story is one which contains either another tale, a story within a story, or a series of stories. Well-known instances are the *Arabian Nights* (of uncertain date, but mentioned in the 9th c. AD); Boccaccio's *Decameron* (*c.* 1349–51); Chaucer's *Canterbury Tales* (late 14th c.); Marguerite of Navarre's *Heptaméron* (1558). Much later Goethe used this Boccaccio technique in *Unterhaltungen deutscher Ausgewanderten* (1795). Other notable writers who have used this structure are: Tieck, Hoffmann, Keller, R. L. Stevenson and G. F. Meyer. *See also* DIGRESSION; RAHMENERZAHLUNG.

Franciscan literature The considerable body of writings which were produced in many countries during and after St Francis of Assisi's life. A well-known collection is the *Fioretti di S. Francesco* compiled by an anonymous Tuscan in the first half of the 14th c.

free association A term commonly used in psychology but which has achieved some currency in literary criticism and theory. The point involved is that a word or idea acts as a stimulus or trigger to a series or sequence of other words or ideas which may or may not have some logical relationship. Some writing *looks* like free association. Much writing that looks like it is probably the result of carefully thought out and contrived arrangement. In his *Ulysses* (1922) James Joyce was one of the principal pioneers of this kind of technique. In the following passage, for instance, words and images are 'freely' associated:

> Ineluctable modality of the visible: at least that if no more, thought through my eyes. Signatures of all things I am here to read, seaspawn and seawrack, the nearing tide, that rusty boot. Snotgreen, bluesilver, rust: coloured signs. Limits of the diaphane. But he adds: in bodies. Then he was aware of them bodies before of them coloured. How? By knocking his sconce against them, sure. Go easy. Bald he was and a millionaire, *maestro di color che sanno.* Limit of the diaphane in. Why in? Diaphane, adiaphane. If you can put your five fingers through it, it is a gate, if not a door. Shut your eyes and see.

See STREAM OF CONSCIOUSNESS.

free meter A term rarely used in matters of English prosody; but among the Welsh it refers to all those meters which are not 'strict'. The 'strict meters' (*q.v.*) were those laid down in the 15th c. Among the better known are: *awdl*, *cywydd* and *englyn* (*qq.v.*).

free verse Called *vers libre* (*q.v.*) by the French, it has no regular meter or line length and depends on natural speech rhythms and the counterpoint (*q.v.*) of stressed and unstressed syllables. In the hands of a gifted poet it can acquire rhythms and melodies of its own.

Its origins are obscure. There are signs of it in medieval alliterative verse (*q.v.*) and in the Authorized Bible translations of the Psalms and *The Song of Songs*. Milton was clearly experimenting with it in *Lycidas* and *Samson Agonistes*. Interest in its possibilities was renewed in Europe after the period of Neoclassicism (*q.v.*). Heine and Goethe (in Germany), Bertrand, Hugo and Baudelaire (in France), Macpherson, Smart, Blake and Arnold (in England) were some of the better known writers who experimented. It was very probably Walt Whitman, the American poet (who influenced Baudelaire), who did more than anyone else to develop it. The other main innovator in the 19th c. was Gerard Manley Hopkins. In the 20th c. many poets employed it, including Ezra Pound, T. S. Eliot, D. H. Lawrence and William Carlos Williams. The following example comes from Whitman's *After the Sea-ship*:

After the sea-ship, after the whistling winds,
After the white-grey sails taut to their spars and ropes,
Below, a myriad myriad waves hastening, lifting up their necks,
Tending in ceaseless flow toward the track of the ship,
Waves of the ocean bubbling and gurgling, blithely prying,
Waves, undulating waves, liquid, uneven emulous waves,
Toward that whirling current, laughing and buoyant, with
curves,
Where the great vessel sailing and tacking displaced the surface . . .

See also PROSE POEM; SPRUNG RHYTHM; VERSE PARAGRAPH; VERS LIBERES.

Freie Bühne A Berlin theatrical company or society founded in 1889. It was a subscription theatre and sponsored private performances of plays banned by the censor and plays which were unlikely to succeed in the commercial theatre. It lasted for only four years but in that time had considerable influence, presenting plays by Ibsen, Hauptmann, Holz, Schlaf, Bjørnson and Strindberg. The society also published an influential monthly journal.

French forms *See* OLD FRENCH AND PROVENCAL FORMS.

Freudian criticism/psychoanalytic criticism Broadly speaking, so-called Freudian criticism or classical psychoanalytic criticism – which is often speculative – is concerned with the quest for and discovery of (and the subsequent analysis of) connections between the artists (creators, artificers) themselves and what they actually create (novels, poems, paintings, sculpture, buildings, music, etc.). As far as literature is concerned it analyses characters 'invented' by authors, the language they use and what is known as 'Freudian imagery'. Thus, in the Freudian method a literary character is treated as if a living human being; whereas, for example, in the method of Jacques Lacan literature is seen as a 'symptom' of the writer.

Applying his own principles of psychoanalysis (a word he coined in 1896), Sigmund Freud (1856–1939) himself contributed fascinating interpretative essays. For example, in *The Interpretation of Dreams* (1900) he discussed the characters of Oedipus and Hamlet. In his essay on *The Theme of the Three Caskets* (1913) he discussed aspects of *The Merchant of Venice* (Bassanio's choice of the leaden casket which contains Portia's portrait) and *King Lear* (the reconciliation of Lear and Cordelia). In *Some Character-Types Met With in Psychoanalytic Work* (1915) he examines the characters of Lady Macbeth, Richard III and Ibsen's Rebecca West – the heroine of *Rosmersholm* (1886). He also wrote an analysis of Dostoievski's *The Brothers Karamazov* and, in *Delusion and Dream* (1917), he produced a detailed study of Wilhelm Jensen's novel *Gradiva*. Later, the psychoanalyst Ernest Jones, following up Freud's suggestions about *Hamlet*, wrote *Hamlet and Oedipus* (1949), which explores the theme of the Oedipus complex.

Two major 20th c. critics to be variously influenced by Freudian ideas were Lionel Trilling (1905–75), author of *The Opposing Self* (1955) and *Sincerity and Authenticity* (1972), and Edmund Wilson, who, in *The Wound and the Bow* (1941), examined, with much brilliance, the idea that there is a relationship between the 'wound' of a childhood experience in an artist and the artist's creation and creativity.

What might be called a 'psychobiographical' approach to the search for and discovery of a writer's intentions and motives (a quest to track down causes, stimuli, reasons, the background of inspiration, *q.v.*) is exemplified in Livingstone Lowes's extraordinary study of Coleridge: *The Road to Xanadu* (1927). The relationship between a poet's mind/personality and the poetry he writes was examined by C. S. Lewis and E. M. W. Tillyard in what they conjointly described as 'the personal heresy' (*q.v.*).

A critic and scholar very plainly influenced by Freudian methods and principles is Erik Erikson (1920–), who was educated at the Vienna Psychoanalytic Institute and is largely responsible for pioneering what is now named psychobiography (*q.v.*).

More recent psychoanalytic criticism reveals considerable diversity. For example, Harold Bloom has devised a highly original and challenging theory based on the Oedipus complex which he expounds in his book *The Anxiety of Influence* (1973). He advances the idea that every poet (especially since Milton) is, in a sense, 'belated' and oppressed by anxiety because of 'precursor' poets – the great ones above all. For instance, a putative poet now is growing up as a poet in the shadow, so to speak, of the great poets of the past. This poet stands in the relationship of 'son' to them, or to one of them in particular, and feels oppressed by that relationship. Carrying through the Oedipal idea, Bloom suggests that such a 'son' is a rival to the father poet who is a 'castrating precursor'. The 'son', powerfully influenced by a parent-poem or poems of the 'father', experiences ambivalent feelings, compounded not only of love and admiration but also of envy and fear – and perhaps even hatred. The fear and hate are caused by the son's great need to reject and rebel against the 'father', to be autonomous and original and find his own 'voice'. M. H. Abrams analyses this predicament very concisely in *A Glossary of Literary Terms* (1957):

> The belated poet unconsciously safeguards his own sense of autonomy and priority by reading a parent-poem 'defensively', in such a way as to distort it beyond his own conscious recognition. Nonetheless, he cannot avoid embodying the malformed parent-poem into his own doomed attempt to write an unprecedentedly original poem; the most that even the best belated poet can achieve is to write a poem so 'strong' that it effects an illusion of 'priority' – that is, an illusion both that it precedes the father-poem in time and that it exceeds it in greatness.

Bloom proposes six distortive processes (described as 'revisionary ratios') which function in the reading of a precursor poet, and he explains these on the model of Freud's defensive mechanisms. He concludes that it is not possible to know a 'poem-in-itself' and that all interpretation is a 'necessary misprision', that all reading is misprision or 'misreading'.

Bloom followed *The Anxiety of Influence* with further detailed analytical inquiries on various poetic texts in *A Map of Misreading*

(1975), *Kabbalah and Criticism* (1975) and *Poetry and Repression* (1976).

Another development of psychoanalytical criticism is 'ego-psychology', expounded by Norman Holland in *The Dynamics of Literary Response* (1968) and *Five Readers Reading* (1975). The theory is concerned with reader-text psychology and thus concentrates on the relationship between reader and text. Thus, as Elizabeth Wright puts it in her essay *Modern Psychoanalytic Criticism* (in *Modern Literary Theory*, 1982, ed. by Jefferson and Robey): 'Holland sees it as the scene of a collusion between author and reader, upon which he founds an aesthetics of response'. He analyses how readers respond to a given text and suggests that readers use a text to satisfy unconscious wishes. On the face of it there is nothing startlingly original about this theory, or its quasi-clinical method, since it is a reasonably safe assumption anyway that, by a combination of empathy and sympathy, many readers 'identify' with a fictional character. More recently Holland has stressed that it is the *reader* who does the work, *not* the text. The reader re-creates identity.

Much more subtle and intricate are the methods and theories propounded by Jacques Lacan (1901–81) in his examination of language and its relationship to the unconscious (in his *Ecrits*, 1977, and *The Four Fundamental Concepts of Psycho-Analysis*, 1977). In his *Ecrits* Lacan sets out to reinterpret Freud in terms of structuralist and post-structuralist theories of discourse. The theories are so complex and couched in such convoluted and, at times, inspissated prose that here there is space to make but two points. According to Lacan: (a) signifiers and signifieds do not match (as in Saussure); signifiers 'float free' of what they refer to, because they are symbols of other symbols (i.e. dimensions of a symbolic language which is never *real*, or *referential* in a stable sense). This is basically Freud's position in relation to the unconscious and the interpretation of dreams. The notion of *reality* drops away and one is left with an endless chain of *substitutions*; (b) Lacan privileges the signifier in relation to the naming of social roles. The following is an example of (a): a child knows its identity at the 'mirror stage' when it enters into *the symbolic order*, in which the world of law and the social community is defined – associated with the father-figure. This identity or selfhood is *constructed* in relation to this patriarchal symbolic order. So the 'I' in Lacanian terms can only be a *signifier*, since it relates to a symbolic realm; it is not tied to a stable reality.

It is Lacan's contention that not only is the unconscious structured like a language but that it is a *product of language*. He sees the unconscious as coming into being simultaneously with language; whereas Freud's view was that the unconscious exists before language takes effect.

Jungian psychology and Jung's theories about the collective unconscious and the archetype (*q.v.*) have also provided a fruitful but less influential development in psychoanalytical criticism. *See* DECONSTRUCTION; SIGNIFIER/SIGNIFIED; STRUCTURALISM.

Freytag's pyramid The German critic Gustav Freytag, in *Die Technik des Dramas* (1862), analysed the structure of a typical five-act play thus: (a) introduction; (b) inciting moment; (c) rising action; (d) climax; (e) falling action; (f) catastrophe. The climax is the apex of the pyramidal structure. The pattern can be applied to a large number of plays. *See* CATASTROPHE; CLIMAX; FALLING ACTION; RISING ACTION; TURNING POINT.

fringe theatre A general term (often equated with and synonymous with alternative theatre, *q.v.*) for drama which is presented away from the main centres (e.g. Broadway and the West End of London). It was first used in the late 1950s to describe drama which was staged on the edges, so to speak, of the Edinburgh Festival. Often *avant-garde* (*q.v.*) and anti-establishment in earlier days, fringe theatre is now very well established. Numerous small theatres (particularly in pubs) present a wide range of dramatic work, including plays that have long been a part of the standard repertoire. *See* AGITPROP DRAMA; OFF-BROADWAY.

frottola *See* BARZELLETTA.

Frühromantik *See* ROMANTICISM.

fu A Chinese prose poem, but one which contains rhyme and lines of constant length which are not metrical. It was perfected in the 2nd c. BC, but used thereafter.

Fugitives, the A group of poets and critics from the Southern States who gathered at Vanderbilt University in the early 1920s where they published a magazine called *The Fugitive*. In politics and poetry they were traditionalists and regionalists, opposed to the industrial and urban development of the North. The group was distinguished and had among its members Allen Tate, John Crowe Ransom, Donald Davidson and Robert Penn Warren.

functional metaphor *See* ORGANIC METAPHOR.

fustian (from MedL [*pannus*] *fustaneus* 'cloth of Fostat, suburb of Cairo') Formerly a coarse cloth made of cotton and flax; now a thick, twilled cotton cloth. In the 16th c. it was used to describe inflated, turgid language. Pope mentioned it in the *Epistle to Arbuthnot*:

> And he, whose fustian's so sublimely bad,
> It is not poetry, but prose run mad.

See BOMBAST.

futurism Initially, a literary movement which originated in Italy at the beginning of the 20th c. Its long-term influences were to be seen in other arts, particularly painting and music (hence neo-impressionism and *bruitisme*). Its main protagonist was Filippo Marinetti (1876–1944), who founded the periodical *Poesia* in 1905. The first and major manifesto (*q.v.*) of futurism was drawn up by him and published in *Le Figaro* in Paris in 1909. Several other manifestos followed. They advocated a complete break with tradition and aimed at new forms, new subjects and new styles in keeping with the advent of a mechanistic age. They extolled dynamism, the machine (and machinery in general), speed (there was a speed cult) and the splendour of war and patriotism. Early in the 1920s the movement became politically Fascistic, and also had some indirect effect on Dadaism, expressionism and surrealism (*qq.v.*). It seems not to have had all that much influence on literature except in Russia, where it provoked vociferous activity from *c.* 1910 under the leadership of Viktor Khlebnikov (1885–1922). The Russian Futurists were against symbolism (*q.v.*), mysticism and the cult of 'pure' beauty. They set out to shock people and *épater les bourgeois*. The manifesto of 1912 was titled 'A Slap in the Face of Public Taste' and was intended as a literary and cultural purge. Pushkin, Dostoievski, Tolstoy *et al.* were to be chucked 'overboard'. It was vituperative in tone and followers were enjoined to develop a new vocabulary called *zaumny yazyk* (*see* ZAUM) and cleanse themselves of the 'filth' and 'slime' of such writers as Leonid Andreyev (1871–1919). After the October Revolution many Futurists had official positions in control of literature but the Party did not care for their *avant-garde* (*q.v.*) policies. The movement died out in the 1920s. *See* CUBO-FUTURISM; EGO-FUTURISM; FORMALISM, RUSSIAN.

fyrtiotalisterna In the 1940s a group of modernist Swedish poets founded a literary magazine called *40-tal* ('the forties'). So the term means 'poets of the *40-tal*'. The leaders of the group were Erik Lindegren (1910–), Karl Vennberg (1910–), Stig Sjödin (1917–), Karl Aspenström (1918–), Sven Alfons (1918–) and Ragnar Thoursie (1919–). Their work is marked by extreme pessimism and great stylistic complexity in the use of free association (*q.v.*), allusion (*q.v.*) and startling images. They appear to have been influenced by T. S. Eliot and the French surrealist poets.

G

ꕤꕤꕤꕤꕤꕤ

gai saber A Provençal term which denotes the art of composing poetry. *See* SABER.

gaita-gallega (Sp *gaita* 'bagpipe', *gallega* 'Galician') Conceivably, in origin, a form of verse or song which was recited or sung to the music of a bagpipe – and such verses or songs accompanied by bagpipe can still be heard in the Balkans. In prosody it denotes a hendecasyllable (*q.v.*) formed by using dodecasyllables with the first syllable omitted. The form was used by Juan de Mena (1411–56), leader of a new school of humanist poets. It is worth noting that de Mena wrote his long epic-didactic poem *Laberinto de Fortuna* to be sung. In the following century such verses were sung to lively dances like the *zarabanda* and the *tárraga*.

galante Dichtung This form of elegant and stylized German erotic verse derived from the *poésie galante* produced in 17th c. French salons (*q.v.*). However, there was no counterpart to the salon in Germany. A well-known collection of *galante Dichtung* is *Herrn von Hoffmannswaldau und anderer Deutschen auserlesene und ungedruckte Gedichte* (1695–1727). There are anonymous anthologies dating from the same period.

galanter Roman A minor genre in German fiction which is fundamentally erotic in content and tone and is concerned with amorous intrigues and exploits, often treated in a fairly light-hearted fashion. Examples are Hunold's *Die liebenswürdige Adalie* (1702) and Schnabel's *Der im Irrgarten der Liebe herumtaumelnde Cavalier* (1738).

galliambic A meter associated with the worship of Cybele, the mother goddess. The term derives from the name of the priests – the Galli. Its technical name is ionic tetrameter (*q.v.*) catalectic; thus, four ionic feet per line with the final syllable missing. The *Attis* poem of Catullus is the most famous example of this meter, which was used by George Meredith in *Phaethon* and by Tennyson in *Boadicea*.

gatha A form of metrical hymn (*q.v.*), of usually four, five or seven words to the line. Found in Buddhist writings; and, in group form, in the *Avesta*.

gathering A printed sheet folded into pages is called a signature (*q.v.*). The signatures are then gathered – hence the term.

gaucho literature Verse and prose in Spanish which derived from a particular interest in the way of life of the gauchos on the plains of the River Plate in the Argentine. The gaucho songs (to the guitar) were of special interest. However, the composers of this literature were *not* cowboys. Gaucho poetry and fiction described and celebrated the nomadic existence of the herdsmen, laying stress on their courage, endurance and skills and their love of horses and cattle. A lost poem titled *Corro* by Juan G. Godoy (1793–1864) is generally regarded as the first example of this literature. Other very well-known works are the novel *Don Segundo Sombra* (1926) by Ricardo Güiraldes (1886–1927) and the narrative poem *Martin Fierro* (1869) by José Hernández (1834–86). In Uruguay, Bartolomé Hidalgo (1788–1822) also made an important contribution to gaucho literature.

gazette (It *gazzetta* from Venetian *gazeta*, a coin of small value) The *Oxford Gazette* was the first newspaper, other than a newsletter, published in England in 1665 when the Court took shelter in Oxford from the plague. It later became the *London Gazette*, which is no longer a newspaper, but a record of official appointments, bankruptcies and so forth. *See* CORANTO; NEWSBOOKS.

gazetteer A geographical index or dictionary.

Gebrauchs- (G 'utility-') In Germany this term is associated with functionalism in, for example, anthropology, psychology and architecture and in particular with the *neue Sachlichkeit* (*q.v.*) period of 'utility music' (*Gebrauchsmusik*) and 'utility poetry' (*Gebrauchslyrik*). The so-called utility poetry tended to be satirical (it had a specific purpose and objective) and was so named in 1928 by Kurt Tucholsky (1890–1935). Erich Kästner (1899–1974), among others, also wrote utility poetry of a satirical kind.

Geistesgeschichte (G 'spirit/mind history') A term with complex connotations and implications coined by Friedrich Schlegel in 1808 which achieved much increased currency with the publication of Wilhelm Dilthey's *Einleitung in die Geisteswissenschaften* (i.e. 'sciences of the spirit') in 1883. It is associated with the concept of *Zeitgeist* (*q.v.*) or 'spirit of the times' and in the 20th c. has been a dominant feature of much study of German literature by German scholars and writers. It involves concentration on and the understanding and interpretation of the prevalent 'spirit' and 'mind' of an epoch or age, its essentially characteristic features and development as expressed and exemplified in its literature, art, music, philosophy, religion and culture and in its social life and institutions. *See also* HERMENEUTICS.

geistliche Tageweise German medieval songs based on the form of the *Minnelied* known as *Tagelied* (*q.v.*), or dawn song. In the *geistliche Tageweise* the waking up is symbolic of awakening from a state of sin. Some are adaptations of profane or secular songs. *See* AUBADE; KONTRAFAKTUR.

generación del (or **de**) **1898** Following the break-up of the Spanish Empire, and as a result of an alleged *fin de siècle* (*q.v.*) feeling among Spanish intellectuals, a movement arose among a section of the latter which was a kind of miniature renaissance. Usually referred to as *la generación del '98* ('the 1898 generation') because mention of that year focused attention on the severance of the last remnant of the once vast Spanish empire, and the Cuban war had produced talk of 'regeneración nacional'.

Although supported by prominent Spanish writers and scholars (such as Azorín, Onis, Ortega Munilla and Madariaga), others, like Baroja, Ramiro de Maeztu and Unamuno, were sceptical. Azorín first drew general attention to the movement in 1913 in his book *Clásicos y modernos*. One of the main precepts was that there should be a rebirth of energy, ideas and achievement in the 20th c., to replace those losses, both material and cultural, which were blamed fairly specifically on the 19th c. – by then already held in scorn.

The idea of a 'generation' had been applied to history both before and elsewhere. Ortega Munilla had called it a new and integral social corpus with its select minority and with its crowd, and having a vital and determined path to follow. The character of each 'generation' would depend on two elements: the received and the spontaneous. If the second predominated, the generation would be one of combat. The generation of '98 in Spain was one such.

The common interests binding a single literary generation were held to include proximity of birth-dates, homogeneity of formation, a state of conscience created by an historical fact and an identity of inspiration. Of particular importance to the protagonists of this '98 generation were a fresh enrichment of the language from outside, the reform of expression and style, the search for naturalness and truth, and a new lyricism.

generacíon del 1927 A group of Spanish writers (mostly poets) also known as the *Nietos del '98*. In 1927 the tercentenary of Gongora's death produced a number of learned works about him and seems to have inspired a number of poets to launch a new movement which was basically non-traditionalist, anti-realist and anti-Romantic. Their innovations in prosody included new words, new styles, free verse (*q.v.*) and so forth. Among the leading members were: Pedro Salinas, Manuel Altolaguirre, Jorge Guillén, Gerardo Diego, Federico García Lorca, Rafael Alberti, Juan José Domenchina, Dámaso Alonso, Vicente Aleixandre and Emilio Prados. *See also* GENERACION DEL 1898.

general and particular *See* ABSTRACT.

generative grammar A concept developed by Noam Chomsky in *Syntactic Structures* (1957). His fundamental theory is that it is possible by the application of a finite number of 'rewrite rules' to predict (that is to say, 'generate') the infinite number of sentences in a language and to specify their structure. Of various models available he discusses three: finite state grammars; phrase structure grammars; transformational grammars.

género chico (Sp 'lesser genre') The term includes the one-act *zarzuela* (*q.v.*) *menor* and the one-act *sainete* (*q.v.*) as opposed to the *género grande* (i.e. tragedy, comedy, opera).

genethliacum An occasional poem written in honour of a birth. *See* OCCASIONAL VERSE.

Geneva school A school of criticism active in the 1940s and 1950s which developed a variety of theories in phenomenology (*q.v.*). The main figures were the Belgian Georges Poulet, the Frenchman Jean Pierre Richard and the Swiss critics Jean Starobinski and Jean Rousset.

genius Originally a genius was the tutelary spirit or deity that guarded a person from birth, or presided over a place (*genius loci*). Later it was applied to the general tendency or guiding principle of an age or a nation. In the 18th c. it acquired the meaning of a man's innate ability, as opposed to what he could learn. In the Romantic period (*q.v.*) people were beginning to think of a genius as a person of exceptional powers, and this is the approximate meaning we accept today. We might say, therefore, that a genius is gifted with an intellectual, imaginative and creative ability of an outstanding order, and with remarkable powers of original speculation and invention. *See* KRAFTGENIE.

genre A French term for a kind, a literary type or class. The major classical *genres* were: epic, tragedy, lyric, comedy and satire, to which would now be added novel and short story (*qq.v.*). From the Renaissance and until well on into the 18th c. the *genres* were carefully distinguished, and writers were expected to follow the rules prescribed for them. *See* CONVENTION; DECORUM; NEO-CLASSICISM.

Georgian poetry Poetry which appeared in five anthologies edited by Edward Marsh and published between 1912 and 1922, during the reign of George V. The major poets represented were: A. E. Housman, W. H. Davies, Walter de la Mare, John Masefield, Ralph Hodgson, Edward Thomas, James Stephens, Flecker, J. C. Squire, Andrew Young, Siegfried Sassoon, Rupert Brooke, Wilfred Owen, Robert Graves, Edmund Blunden and D. H. Lawrence.

georgic A poem about rural life and husbandry, so called from the Greek word for 'earth worker, farmer'. This is a form of didactic poetry (*q.v.*) and its principal purpose is to give instructions on how to do something. As Addison put it in his essay on the georgic, it consists in giving 'plain and direct instructions'. The georgic also tends to extol the rural life and nature. A very early example is Hesiod's *Works and Days* (8th c. BC). Virgil's *Georgics* are the best known, and they had a wide influence. James Thomson's *Seasons*

(1726–30) and Cowper's *The Task* (1785) were very much in the Virgilian tradition. Other georgics include Poliziano's *Rusticus* (1483); Vida's *De Bombyce* (1527); Alamanni's *La Coltivazione* (1546); Tusser's *Five Hundred Points of Good Husbandry* (1573); and Rapin's *Horti* (1665). *See also* ECLOGUE; PASTORAL.

Gesamtkunstwerk (G 'complete art work') A term coined by Richard Wagner (1813–83) to denote a work of art which combines music, drama, poetry, mime, painting in décor, etc. to create a whole. Ideally, all should proceed from a single creative mind and hand.

Gesellschaftslied (G 'song of fellowship') A form of German song for several voices which originated in the latter half of the 16th c. and whose main themes were love, drinking and dancing.

Gesellschaftsroman (G 'society novel') A term used to describe novels which portray a 'society' as a whole (or in particular) and in which this feature is as important as the characters. Thus, it may be a kind of regional novel (*q.v.*). Some well-known examples are: *Die Ritter vom Geiste* (1850–51) by Karl Gutzkow; *Das Landhaus am Rhein* (1869) by Berthold Auerbach; and *Der Zauberberg* (1924) by Thomas Mann. *See also* ZEITROMAN.

gesta (L 'deeds') The *gesta* were accounts of deeds or tales of adventure. For example: the *Gesta Francorum*, a medieval Latin chronicle (*q.v.*) about the First Crusade; the *Gesta Historiale* of the Destruction of Troy (14th c.); and the *Gesta Romanorum*, the most famous of all medieval collections of such stories, compiled in the 14th c. (*c.* 1330) and first printed *c.* 1472. It was later translated by Wynkyn de Worde *c.* 1510. It remained a popular work until well on in the 16th c. It consisted of legends of the saints, romances, tales from Jewish and Indian lore and so forth, and was often used by preachers for *exempla*. A moral was attached to each tale. *See* CHANSON DE GESTES; EXEMPLUM; ROMANCE.

Gestalt (G 'form, figure, shape') A term imported from German philosophy and occasionally used in literary criticism to denote the unified whole of a literary work; its organic unity. *See* STRUCTURE.

Gestus A term used by Lessing in 1767 to denote something distinct from 'gesture'. In *c.* 1930 the word was taken up and used to indicate something that was a kind of combination of 'gesture' and 'gist'; thus attitude or bearing (the early meaning of *gest*) plus point. According to the dramatist Bertolt Brecht (1898–1956), a play or a scene in a play should have a fundamental 'gest' to it, and so a play would comprise a succession of 'gests' and they would be conveyed through all the means at the dramatist's disposal. Meanwhile, the performers ought to be 'gestic', conveying to the audience not only the meaning but also their attitude to what is being said and done, plus a definable attitude about it.

ghazel (or *ghazal*) An Arabic word for love-making, it has come to denote a love-song or love poem. A lyric form widespread in Arabia, Persia and Turkey, used by a very large number of poets. The two most famous are the Persians Sa'di (13th c.) and Häfiz (14th c.). *See also* DIVAN; EROTIC POETRY.

ghost story A fictional narrative, usually in prose (there are some in verse, such as R. H. Barham's tales in *The Ingoldsby Legends*), of variable length, but usually in the range of 1,000 to 25,000 words, in which the spirit of a person (or the spirits of persons), no longer bound by natural laws, manifests itself, or seems to do so (either embodied in some form or disembodied), and 'haunts' a place, person or thing as a kind of 'presence'. As a genre the ghost story proper does not include demonic pacts, *doppelgängers*, vampires, werewolves, succubae, poltergeists *et al.* Nor as a rule does it involve witchcraft and the prolepses of magic, or occult practices associated with such activities as Cumberlandism, exorcism, spiritualism, telekinesis, hylomancy and so forth.

Ghost stories probably antedate literature and belong to a primordial world in 'the dark backward and abysm of time'. In primitive religion, mythology and ancient epic (*q.v.*) the interrelationship of the living and the dead, the natural and the supernatural, is commonplace. All societies which hold animistic beliefs have been (and are) disposed to believe in ghosts and it is next to impossible to find societies which do not have such beliefs. There is a host of ghost stories in oral tradition (*q.v.*) and in Britain alone there are many hundreds of places reputed to be haunted. Many tales have been recorded by historians of folklore.

Such beliefs pervade pre-Christian literature in Europe and in the Near and Middle East. In the Christian era from the 4th c. onwards, in the *Patrologia Latina*, in philosophical treatises, in chronicles, in collections of legends, *exempla*, homilies and sermons, in theological handbooks (*qq.v.*), as well as in a wide range of other didactic literature and in an extensive variety of literature designed primarily to divert and entertain, there are numerous references to ghosts and anecdotes about them. Christian precept, doctrine and belief, derived from the Old Testament, the Gospels and the Acts, confirmed the existence of the supernatural order repeatedly. Metaphysical theology and philosophy ratified the teaching of the Church. The Son of God Himself was the most illustrious ghost in history (to say nothing of the Holy Ghost). Christ made eleven separate appearances after the Resurrection.

Until very early in the 19th c. most stories about ghosts were anecdotal (often with a basis of fact) and could not be regarded as fiction in the way that we now regard the ghost stories of, say, Charles Dickens and Henry James. However, long before the modern era we find striking examples of stories which are very near to being fiction or are so fashioned that they approach that category.

For instance, there is Lucian's tale of the haunted sandal in his satirical sketch of the pathological liar. And in Petronius's *Satyricon* and Apuleius's *The Golden Ass* there are inset ghost stories which come close to the modern form and idea. Pliny the Younger tells two spooky stories involving ghostly apparitions. Different from these (and much more detailed) is the account in the *Grettir* saga of the haunting of Thorwall's farm by a troll, a monster ghost. Different again are Chaucer's two inset ghost stories (both originally related by Cicero and Valerius) which are part of Chauntecleer's disquisition to Pertelote in *The Nun's Priest's Tale*. Other notable examples are to be found in Froissart's *Chroniques*, which cover the period 1325–1400.

The Tudor and Jacobean dramatists perceived the rich possibilities of using ghosts as 'characters' in their plays. In doing so they were influenced by Seneca's tragedies; for example, *Agamemnon*, in which the ghost of Thyestes delivers the prologue, and *Thyestes* with the prologue ghost of Tantalus. There are literally scores of ghosts in the many plays written and produced between *c.* 1580 and *c.* 1630. They are particularly prominent in the chronicle and history play, and in tragedy and revenge tragedy (*qq.v.*). Some are malignant and revengeful (e.g. the ghost of Andrea and Revenge in Kyd's *The Spanish Tragedy*); some have an important part in the plot (e.g. the ghost of Hamlet's father); some have a premonitory role (e.g. the spectre of Caesar who appears to Brutus before Philippi); and some have walking-on parts, so to speak, to give the audience an additional *frisson* of fear (e.g. the apparitions of Isabella and Brachiano in Webster's *The White Devil*). After the Jacobean period the 'stage ghost' had a variable history. It never had a place in comedy, but it flourished in melodrama (*q.v.*) in the 19th c. and is by no means defunct in the modern theatre (witness the role of the gravedigger's boy in Edward Bond's *Lear*, 1972).

Stage spooks apart, ghosts virtually 'disappear' from European literature during the 17th c. and they do not reappear until the advent of the Gothic novel (*q.v.*) in the latter part of the 18th c. Nevertheless, they are mentioned frequently in works pertaining to supernatural matters and there is little diminution of their presence and activity in oral tradition, in ballad (*q.v.*) and folklore, in folksong and popular superstition, and also in the more durable form of stories and poems printed in broadsides and chapbooks (*qq.v.*).

Among educated and sophisticated people in the Neoclassical period and the Augustan Age (*q.v.*) ghosts were not a matter much talked of or written about, though in 1706 Daniel Defoe created something of a stir with his celebrated journalistic account of *A True Relation of the Apparition of one Mrs Veal*: a strange haunting in Canterbury which he investigated personally.

The arrival of the popular 'Graveyard Poetry' (*q.v.*) in the 1740s marked the beginning of a shift in sensibility (*q.v.*), and the sepulchral meditations of those later called 'graveyard poets' were to have a pronounced influence on the evolution of the Gothic novel, which was soon to appear and, with it, the ghost in fiction (e.g. the monstrous ghost in Walpole's *The Castle of Otranto*, 1764), plus much other supernatural apparatus. The overall effect of Gothic fiction was remarkable, and the way was prepared for the ghost story.

At the beginning of the 19th c. the then newly emerged form of the *Novelle* (*see* NOVELLA), as conceived by Goethe, coincided with the advent of the short story (*q.v.*). This had existed in embryo, as it were, all along. It was what might be called an inherent form. Rather suddenly (and, perhaps, a little unexpectedly) we not only find the short story more or less fully-fledged; we also find the ghost story – *as a short story* – in the work of Heinrich von Kleist and E. T. A. Hoffmann.

Kleist's *Das Bettelweib von Locarno* ('The Beggarwoman of Locarno') was published in *Berliner Abendblätter* in 1810 and in *Erzählungen* in 1811. Very short (some eight hundred words), it contains, in little, many of the constituents of a traditional ghost story in a highly concentrated form. It is a sinister and frightening tale. A few years later (1817) Hoffmann published a very long ghost story, *Das Majorat* ('The Entail'). It is thirty times longer than Kleist's and (with the notable exception of Henry James's *The Turn of the Screw*) very probably the longest 'short' story in existence which involves a ghost.

Both authors display that strong sense of the past which was to become central to the development of the ghost story in the next hundred years. Strangely, from their time on and up to the present day German writers have made a minimal contribution to the genre of the ghost story – which has been dominated by British writers, especially the English. There have been some Americans of note and a handful of continental writers, but a quantitative survey suggests that something like 98 per cent of ghost stories are in English and about 70 per cent of those are by English writers.

The first ghost story of importance by an American author was *The Legend of Sleepy Hollow* by Washington Irving. It was published in *The Sketch Book* (1820) and accompanied by *The Spectre Bridegroom*. Both show German influence and the latter is set in Germany.

Sir Walter Scott's novel *Redgauntlet* (1824) contains one of the best ghost stories – *Wandering Willie's Tale*. Scott's other two ghost stories were *The Tapestried Chamber* and *My Aunt Margaret's Mirror*, both first published in *The Keepsake* in 1828. Scott also wrote an extremely interesting essay – *On the Supernatural in Fictitious Composition* (1827). This displays an astute understanding of what can and cannot be done in such fiction. He advises against 'coarse handling' and 'repeated pressure' and advocates brevity. Many a ghost story and many a horror story (*q.v.*) has failed precisely because of 'coarse handling' and 'repeated pressure' and because of attempts to keep up suspense too long.

In the 1830s Edgar Allan Poe began to make his impact. His first collection of short stories, *Tales of the Grotesque and Arabesque*, appeared in 1839. His influence on the evolution of the ghost story (and the horror story) was very considerable and, in the case of some writers, not by any means beneficial. In the 1830s, too, the English parson R. H. Barham, besides his good ghost stories in verse, wrote two long ones in prose: *The Spectre of Tappington* and *The Leech of Folkestone*. In 1834 Pushkin published *The Queen of Spades*. This remains one of the best ghost stories but is a rather isolated phenomenon. Few Russian writers have written ghost stories, though Gogol and Dostoievski, among others, made extensive use of supernatural elements (e.g. Gogol's tale *Viy*).

The effect Charles Dickens had on the genre was to be of the utmost importance. His earliest ghost stories were inset tales in *The Pickwick Papers* (1837). There followed *A Christmas Carol* (1843), and a succession of Christmas books: *The Chimes* (1844), *The Cricket on the Hearth* (1845), *The Battle of Life* (1846). Of his later stories the best known are *The Trial for Murder* and *No. I Branch Line: The Signalman.* It was Dickens who more than anyone associated such tales with Christmas. In 1851 he began a special supplement to the magazine *Household Words*, to which he invited writers to submit seasonal offerings. The 1852 supplement – *A Round of Christmas Stories by the Fire* – included Elizabeth Gaskell's splendid *The Old Nurse's Tale.* From 1854 the framework became more elaborate. In 1859 he started *All The Year Round.* Again, ghost stories were a special feature of Christmas supplements.

In the 1860s and 1870s many ghost-story writers were women, among whom we should mention particularly Amelia Edwards (author of *The Engineer* and *The Phantom Coach*), Rosa Mulholland, Mrs Braddon, Mrs Riddell and Mrs Oliphant, who wrote *The Open Door* – one of the best of all ghost stories. In fact, many of the outstanding ghost stories *are* by women.

Thackeray tried his hand at the genre; Wilkie Collins was prolific. In 1856 he published *After Dark and Other Stories* (2 vols.), in 1859 *The Queen of Hearts* (3 vols.) and in 1879 *Little Novels.* He collaborated with Dickens (who was a close friend) and contributed to his magazines. Bulwer Lytton also wrote ghost stories at this time and was commissioned by Dickens.

More famous than these, ultimately, as a practitioner of the genre, was Sheridan Le Fanu (1814–73) – the name is pronounced Léff-anew – whom M. R. James considered 'in the first rank as a writer of ghost stories'. By the time Le Fanu died the ghost story was fully established. His first attempts date from 1838–40. In the next thirty years he wrote many, displaying a particular gift for depicting states of guilt and fear. His ghosts are uncannily 'real' and convincing. He could also write humorous ghost stories (e.g. *The Ghost and the Bone-Setter*). The stories were eventually collected in a famous volume titled *In a Glass Darkly* (1872). Many years later, M. R. James gathered and edited a collection of forgotten stories by Le Fanu. It was called *Madam Crowl's Ghost and Other Tales of Mystery* (1923). Le Fanu's 'psychic doctor' Hesselius, the protagonist in a number of stories (like serial detectives), was to be followed by Algernon Blackwood's John Silence and William

Hope Hodgson's Carnacki – a psychic research investigator or parapsychologist.

During the second half of the 19th c. there was a great deal of interest in psychic phenomena, spiritualism, psychotherapy and extreme psychological states. F. W. H. Myers (1843–1901), who was deeply interested in Mesmer's theories, helped to found the Society for Psychical Research (1882). Drugs and their effects, duality and double identity, dreams, madness, diabolism, the diabolic pact, black magic, witchcraft, the occult in general also aroused much interest. Curiosity about the preternatural and speculation about life after death proved beneficial to mediums – and photographers. Photographic archives of the Victorian period contain many examples of 'spirit photographs' of, apparently, palpable ghosts. The Victorians were fascinated by ghosts.

From the 1860s ghost stories proliferated. There were scores of them. Many of them seem poor stuff now, hackwork, but they were read avidly. It is almost as if they were beginning to fulfil a kind of spiritual need; as if the possibility of ghosts was a reassurance of afterlife. Besides, ghosts were a link with the past, with tradition, between the living and the dead. Moreover, writers did not regard their ghost stories (and other tales of the supernatural) as mere diversions and entertainment. In writing them they had serious intentions: exploring states of consciousness, examining aspects of appearance and reality, investigating the meaning of existence.

Robert Louis Stevenson (1850–94) and Rudyard Kipling (1865–1936) made highly individual contributions. Two of Stevenson's best known are *Thrawn Janet* (in *The Merry Men*, 1887) and the tale of Tod Lapraik (in *Catriona*, 1893). Kipling wrote several, published in 1887–8 in the *Civil and Military Gazette*. Later came *The Return of Imray* (1891), *The Phantom Rickshaw* (1895) and *They* (1904). In the same period Guy de Maupassant (1850–93), one of the few contintental authors to write ghost stories, produced four superior ones: *Le Horla* and *Was it a Dream?* (1887), followed by *An Apparition* and *Who Knows?* (1890). In *c.* 1898 Emile Zola (1840–1902) made his solitary contribution with the excellent *Angeline* – a product of his exile in England in 1898–9. During the last twenty-odd years of the 19th c. the Americans Ambrose Bierce (1842–1914?) and O. Henry (William Sidney Porter, 1862–1910) were publishing their ghost stories. Outstanding among Bierce's are *The Middle Toe of the Right Foot* and *An Occurrence at Owl Creek Bridge* (both 1891) and *The Moonlit Road* (1894). O. Henry wrote several but is chiefly remembered for *The Furnished Room* (1906).

At this period, too, Vernon Lee (Violet Paget, 1856–1935) made idiosyncratic contributions. Her major collection, *Hauntings: Fantastic Stories*, came out in 1890. She was considerably influenced by Nathaniel Hawthorne (1804–64) and more particularly by his novel *The Marble Faun* (1860). This is not a ghost story *per se*, but it has a mysterious stranger, the 'death-scented apparition', who is murdered. The novel is haunted by a sense of the past and three major characters are haunted by guilt. Like some other writers of the period Vernon Lee took an obsessive interest in the past ('that is the place we get our ghosts from').

Few writers have possessed a keener, more delicately subtle and pervasive sense of the past than Henry James (1843–1916), who was also much affected by *The Marble Faun*. In his unfinished novel *The Sense of the Past* (1917) he wrote of a kind of haunting in a way which nobody else could have done. He began writing ghost stories in the 1860s when Dickens and Le Fanu were still alive, and forty-odd years later he was still experimenting. His first two, *The Romance of Certain Old Clothes* (1868) and *De Grey: A Romance* (1868), both showed Hawthorne's influence. Later, among others, were *Owen Wingrave*, *Sir Edmund Orme*, *A Passionate Pilgrim* and *The Jolly Corner* (1908), plus what most people regard as his masterpiece in the genre – *The Turn of the Screw* (1898).

In the late 1890s M. R. James (1862–1936) began his celebrated *Ghost Stories of an Antiquary* (first issued under that title in 1904). *More Ghost Stories of an Antiquary* followed in 1911 and the collected stories were finally published in 1931. They were written to be read aloud, usually to friends at Christmas time. M. R. James was a student of the 19th c. ghost story (he read hundreds of them) and he shows a thoroughly 'professional' approach to the craft of writing them. He worked out his own rules, which appear in brief prefaces to his collections of tales. He is the only writer of ghost stories whose collected works have remained continuously in print, and he is rightly regarded as a master of the genre.

Unlike James, Algernon Blackwood (1869–1951) was very interested in psychic phenomena and wrote some powerful stories with supernatural themes. His first collection was *The Empty House and Other Ghost Stories* (1906), followed by *John Silence, Physician Extraordinary* (1908). His last collection, *Tales of the Uncanny and Supernatural*, came out in 1949. A near contemporary was William Hope Hodgson (1877–1918), whose parapsychologist, Carnacki, differed from Blackwood's John Silence in that he used equipment and instruments to track down spirits. Two of his better stories are *The*

Horse of the Invisible and *The Whistling Room*. Also contemporary was Arthur Machen (1863–1947), who was much influenced by Stevenson and experimented with a variety of ghost stories.

The Benson brothers, A. C. (1862–1925), R. H. (1871–1914) and E. F. (1867–1940), all published stories about ghosts and the supernatural at the turn of the 20th c. A. C. Benson's work is seldom read now, but some of R. H.'s stories have survived, and E. F. had a long and successful career as a novelist and short story writer. He excelled at ghost stories and, at his best, rivals masters of the form. His first collection, *The Room in the Tower and Other Stories* (1912), was followed by *Visible and Invisible* (1923) and *Spook Stories* (1928).

Many other ghost stories date from the turn of the century and the early years of the 20th c. Some of the classics are: Robert Hichens's *How Love Came to Professor Guildea* (1900); Oscar Wilde's delightful comic tale *The Canterville Ghost*, about the spook who could not frighten anyone however hard he tried; W. W. Jacobs's terrifying *The Monkey's Paw* (1902), a standby to anthologists for many years; Oliver Onions's *The Beckoning Fair One* (1911); Saki's spoof ghost story, *The Open Window*; and some of the tales in E. M. Forster's *The Celestial Omnibus* (1911). Edith Wharton's collected *Tales of Men and Ghosts* (1910) are cerebral stories in the manner of her friend Henry James: the ghosts are projections of men's mental obsessions. Much later (1937), another collection titled *Ghosts* appeared. At her best (e.g. in *All Souls* and *Afterward*) she is as brilliant as Henry James and M. R. James.

Between the wars the genre continued to flourish, though not with the style, vigour, variety and originality of the years between, say, 1850 and 1910. The First World War had greatly affected people's feelings about death – and thus about ghosts and ghost stories. The cataclysm produced tens of thousands of 'ghosts': the missing, the believed killed in action, the walking wounded of a spectral no-man's-land who were to haunt the memory of Europe for years.

Nevertheless, there were many ghost stories. In the 1920s A. J. Alan (Leslie Harrison Lambert) became a well-known raconteur of his own stories on the BBC. They were later gathered into the collections *Good Evening, Everyone* (1928) and *A. J. Alan's Second Book* (1933). They were clever and witty. In the 1920s, too, L. P. Hartley (1895–1972) wrote a number. *Night Fears and Other Stories* was published in 1924, and more were to come sporadically during the next forty years.

In 1922 David Lindsay published *The Haunted Woman*, an unusual novel in the form of a ghost story (ghost stories of novel length are very rare) which was before its time in that its main theme is the need for a revolution to bring about equality between the sexes so that, as the heroine suggests, men exist as much for women as women for men.

H. P. Lovecraft, Machen's American disciple and a specialist in tales of horror, wrote some ghost stories of variable quality. During the same period (and later) Elizabeth Bowen published some outstanding stories. A selection of the best were collected in *The Demon Lover* (1945).

Walter de la Mare (1873–1956) was the most prolific English writer of ghost stories between the wars. Like Henry James he explored the shifting and ill-defined frontiers which lie between what seems to be reality and other zones: 'the world around the corner . . . the evil in the dark closet'. He excelled at the evocation of atmosphere. There were several collections, including *The Riddle* (1923), *The Connoisseur* (1926), *On the Edge* (1930), *The Wind Blows Over* (1936) and *A Beginning and Other Stories* (1955).

At that time other distinguished contributions were being made by Lord Dunsany, Hugh Walpole, Cynthia Asquith, Margaret Irwin (author of the excellent *The Earlier Service*), A. M. Burrage (who also wrote under the pseudonym Ex-Private X), the author of several good tales, including *Smee* and *One Who Saw*, and H. G. Wells, whose ingenious tour de force *The Inexperienced Ghost* combines the comic and the horrific. He also wrote *The Moth* and *The Red Room*.

Some followed the style and conventions of M. R. James, but it was complimentary and successful 'imitation'. Chief exponents of the Jamesian techniques were H. Russell Wakeford (*They Walk at Night*, 1928), W. F. Harvey (*Moods and Tenses*, 1933), A. N. Munby (*The Alabaster Hand*, 1949), and, more recently, William Croft Dickinson (*Dark Encounters*, 1963).

Many other authors of more recent times have written memorable ghost stories. They include Ann Bridge, Thomas Mann, Mario Soldati, Muriel Spark, Rosemary Timperley, James Turner, Marghanita Laski, Ray Bradbury, Edward Hyams, Fielden Hughes, Joan Aiken, Ronald Blythe, William Sansom, Angus Wilson, William Trevor, Roald Dahl, George Mackay Brown, Elizabeth Walter, Penelope Fitzgerald and A. S. Byatt. Numerous anthologies suggest that there is a widespread demand for such tales. *The Oxford Book of Ghost Stories*, *The Virago Book of Ghost Stories* and *The Penguin Book of Ghost Stories* are recent representative examples.

Ghost stories of novel length have remained rare and seldom work. However, in 1969 Kingsley Amis published *The Green Man*, a novel about a pub haunted by a 17th c. magician called Dr Thomas Underhill. This clever story is the most sustained imitation of M. R. James and was a considerable success; so was Susan Hill's novel *The Woman in Black* (1985), a sinister and spine-chilling tale – successfully adapted for both television and theatre. *See* SUPERNATURAL STORY.

ghostword A term invented by W. W. Skeat, the great 19th c. editor of medieval texts, to describe words which have no real existence. Such spurious words are often the result of inadvertent errors made by copyists, printers and editors. *See* PHANTOM WORD.

ghost-writer One who does literary work for someone else who takes the credit. It has become a common practice for professional writers to 'ghost' the autobiographies, memoirs or reminiscences of famous personalities.

gierasa A boasting poem (*q.v.*) akin to the fârsa (*q.v.*) of the African Galla tribe. It extols the strength and accomplishments of a particular warrior hero.

Glasgow Citizens' Theatre Started in 1945 when James Bridie (1888–1951) created a company at the then Royal Princess's Theatre, which was built in 1878 in Glasgow's Gorbals. Up until 1969 the policy was to present new plays (especially Scottish ones) rather than classics. In 1970 the present Citizens' Company was formed, and for some time it has been directed by Giles Havergal, Philip Prowse and Robert David MacDonald. Since its formation the group has based its repertoire on British and foreign classics and has performed 165 productions of plays from the foreign (15 British premières) and British (13 world premières) repertoire. In Britain it has become famous for its originality and enterprise; the company has achieved an international reputation (it has made guest and festival appearances in 22 foreign cities) without in any way losing local support and popularity.

glee (OE *glīw*, *glēo* 'minstrelsy, merriment') A *glee* or *glee-song* was a part-song for three or more voices, not necessarily with an accompaniment. They had a particular vogue from *c.* 1750 to *c.* 1850. Choirs of glee-singers are still to be heard in the United States.

Globe Theatre One of the most famous of all theatres, it was built in 1599, on Bankside in Southwark, in the shape of a polygon with three storeys. The roof was thatched, with the centre open to the sky. In 1576 James Burbage (*c.* 1530–97) had leased land in Shoreditch on which he had built (of wood) the first building in England specifically designed for plays. In 1577 it became known as 'The Theatre'. In 1598 the fabric was removed to the Bankside and set up as the Globe. At first it was the home of the Lord Chamberlain's Men (Shakespeare was one of them), after Queen Elizabeth's death renamed the King's Men. Many of Shakespeare's plays were performed in it and Shakespeare had a share in the theatre. It was destroyed by fire in 1613 when a discharge of cannon during a performance of *Henry VIII* ignited the thatched roof. Rebuilt on the same site, it reopened the next year. It was finally demolished in 1644, but a reconstruction of the theatre was begun in the late 1980s.

glosa A Spanish metrical form invented by the court poets late in the 14th c. or early in the 15th. It is a poem of a single line or a short stanza which introduces the theme of the work and which is then followed by a stanza for each line of the introductory *cabeza*. The stanza explains or 'glosses' the line. *See also* CANTIGA; ESPINELLA; GLOSS; MOTE.

gloss In the first place an interlinear (or marginal) comment on or explanation of a word or phrase. Classical Greek manuscripts frequently had glosses in Latin. Occasionally poems have been published with marginal glosses. A good example is Coleridge's *Rime of the Ancient Mariner*, which he glossed himself. Another well-known example is E. K.'s gloss to Spenser's *Shepheard's Calendar*. *See also* GLOSSARY.

glossary An alphabetical list of unfamiliar or difficult words and phrases, sometimes appended to the edition of a particular text, and sometimes published as a separate volume like *A Shakespeare Glossary* by C. T. Onions (1911, 1919). *See also* CONCORDANCE; DICTIONARY; GLOSS.

Glossen (G 'glossaries') Explanations/translations of Latin words or sentences in medieval German literature. Marginal glosses are *Randglossen*; those above the lines are 'interlinear'; those in the lines are *Textglossen*. Such glosses are useful to philologists since they provide evidence about the development of the German language in the Middle Ages and also give some idea of Latin texts in use. *See* GLOSS; GLOSSARY.

glyconic The name of a Greek lyric meter named after Glykon, a poet (date unknown). There are two basic patterns: either: ⁊ ⁊|/ ∪ ∪ / | ∪ ⁊ or: ⁊ ⁊ | / ∪ ∪ / | ⁊ |. It was used for early Greek lyric poetry and drama. *See* PHERECRETAN.

gnomic verse Gnomic derives from the Greek word for 'opinion' or 'judgement', and a *gnome* has come to mean a short pithy statement of a general truth; thus a maxim or aphorism (*qq.v.*). The adjective *gnomic* was first applied to a group of 6th c. BC Greek poets but there are much earlier examples of *gnomes* in Chinese, Sanskrit and Egyptian. The Book of Proverbs, which follows The Psalms in the Old Testament, is one of the best examples of gnomic utterance. Old English, Irish, Norse and Germanic literature provide many instances. *Beowulf* contains a number of gnomic passages. In more recent times Francis Quarles's *Book of Emblemes* (1633) is one of the best known collections. *See also* APOPHTHEGM; EMBLEM-BOOK; PROVERB; SPRUCH.

gobbledegook An onomatopoeic word which no doubt derives from the noises that poultry make. The term denotes unintelligible language, gibberish, and thus nonsense (*q.v.*). It is often applied derisively to the kind of language cherished by lawyers, bureaucrats, art, music and literary critics and other purveyors of jargon (*q.v.*).

golden A term used by C. S. Lewis in the introduction to his *English Literature in the Sixteenth Century* (1954) to distinguish the literature of the later Elizabethan period (*q.v.*) from its predecessors in what he called the 'drab' (*q.v.*) age. The period runs roughly from 1580 to 1603. *See also* GOLDEN AGE.

golden age An era when things were at their best. The nations and civilizations of antiquity all had their so-called golden ages, usually associated with particular reigns and dynasties. For example, the Tang dynasty (626–684) and particularly the reign of Tae-tsong

(618–626) in China; and the reigns of Sethos I and Ram'eses II in Egypt (1336–1224 BC). The same is true of modern nations. For instance, the reigns of Elizabeth I of England (1558–1603) and of Czar Peter the Great of Russia (1672–1725). As far as literature is concerned there have been several golden ages: the golden age of Spanish literature (16th and 17th c.), French drama (17th c.), English literature – especially drama – (*c.* 1580–*c.* 1630). *See also* AUGUSTAN AGE; DRAB; GOLDEN.

Goliardic verse The Goliards were wandering scholars and clerks of the 12th and 13th c., called *vagi scholares aut goliardi.* It is not certain how they got their name. As there are references to their belonging to the 'household of Golias', some believe this may be the origin. But there was no guild of Goliards, no *ordo vagorum.* The name may have derived from Golias, Goliath of Gath, the giant of lawlessness and evil, associated later with the Latin word *gula* 'gluttony'. Much Goliardic verse consists of satire (*q.v.*) against the Church, and extravagant praise of the delights of love-making and drinking. It is full of zest, caustic humour and a rough earthiness; at times almost pagan in its unabashed hedonism. The theme of *carpe diem* (*q.v.*) is recurrent. *See* CARMINA BURANA.

Gongorism A style of writing derived from the name of the Spanish poet Luis de Góngora y Argote (1561–1627). It is a baroque (*q.v.*) and affected style whose chief characteristics are: Latinistic vocabulary and syntax, intricate metaphors, excessive hyperbole (*q.v.*), rich colour images, mythological allusions and a general strangeness of diction. Comparable features are to be found in the French *la préciosité* (*q.v.*). Such a style provoked mixed reactions and some considerable opposition, especially from the devotees of *conceptismo* (*q.v.*); but many discerning critics have given the highest praise to Góngora's best work among which the *Soledades* and *La Fábula de Polifemo y Galatea* persist as favourites. Góngora, who did not always write like this, had many imitators. Gongoristic elements are to be found in a number of 17th c. English writers including Sir Thomas Browne and Richard Crashaw. *See also* EUPHUISM; MANNERISM; MARINISM; SECENTISMO.

good sense During what is known as the period of Neoclassicism (*q.v.*) in France and England, that is during the latter half of the 17th c. and for much of the 18th, good sense was a much prized criterion of excellence in art and literature. If a work displayed good sense then it possessed order, balance, harmony, restraint, appropriateness of style to subject matter, and a general absence of excess or flamboyance. Good sense implied sane understanding and good manners. *See* CONVENTION; DECORUM.

Gothic novel/fiction A type of romance (*q.v.*) very popular from the 1760s onwards until the 1820s. It has had a considerable influence on fiction since (still apparent in the 1990s) and is of much importance in the evolution of the ghost story and the horror story (*qq.v.*).

One of the earliest examples of the genre is Tobias Smollett's *Ferdinand Count Fathom* (1753), very probably the first novel (*q.v.*) – a form then newly developed – to propose terror and cruelty as its main themes. Much better known than this is Horace Walpole's *The Castle of Otranto* (1764), which he wrote in his house at Strawberry Hill, Twickenham, near London. Walpole (1717–97) settled there in 1747. He made his abode into 'a little Gothic castle' and established a private press (*q.v.*). 'Strawberry Hill Gothic' became a common term for any example of romantic gothicized architecture of the period. This was the era of the Gothic revival in architecture, brought about by a renewed and romantic interest in the medieval.

The Castle of Otranto, a gruesome tale of passion, bloodshed and villainy (it includes a monstrous ghost) was set in the 12th and 13th c. It was an immensely popular book and is believed to have gone through no fewer than 115 editions since it first appeared. Walpole's intention was to scare the daylights out of his readers, and no doubt he succeeded. This novel proved a seminal work which had much influence on the development of a genre which was ultimately dubbed 'Gothic novel'; partly, perhaps, because Walpole wrote his book in his 'Gothic castle', and partly because the content of such novels was associated with the Middle Ages and with things wild, bloody and barbarous of long ago.

Most Gothic novels are tales of mystery and horror, intended to chill the spine and curdle the blood. They contain a strong element of the supernatural and have all or most of the now familiar topography, sites, props, presences and happenings: wild and desolate landscapes, dark forests, ruined abbeys, feudal halls and medieval castles with dungeons, secret passages, winding stair-ways, oubliettes, sliding panels and torture chambers; monstrous apparitions and curses; a stupefying atmosphere of doom and gloom; heroes and heroines in the direst of imaginable straits, wicked tyrants, malevolent witches, demonic powers of unspeakably hideous aspect, and a proper complement of spooky effects and clanking spectres . . . The whole apparatus, in fact that has kept the cinema and much third-rate fiction going for years, is to be found in these tales. The most popular sold in great quantities and they were read avidly.

After *The Castle of Otranto* there came a succession of such novels, of variable quality. Many of them were dramatized (as was *The Castle of Otranto*). Some of the major examples of the genre are Clara Reeve's *The Old English Baron* (1778), William Beckford's *Vathek* (1786) – Beckford lived in the Gothic extravaganza of Fonthill Abbey – Ann Radcliffe's *Mysteries of Udolpho* (1794), Ann Yearsley's *The Royal Captives* (1795), M. G. ('Monk') Lewis's *Ambrosio* and *The Monk* (1796), C. R.. Maturin's *The Fatal Revenge* (1807) and his *Melmoth the Wanderer* (1820) and Mary Shelley's *Frankenstein* (1818) – the all-important progenitor of scores of horror films and science fiction (*q.v.*). Godwin's *Caleb Williams* (1794) has often been classed as Gothic, but has a special importance as an early instance of the propaganda novel (*see* THESIS NOVEL) and the novel of crime and its detection.

By the turn of the 18th c. dozens of Gothic novels and tales (many of them hackwork sunk without trace except in the vaults of the major libraries) were being published. The demand for cheap, sensational literature was high. Publishers, scenting large profits, exerted themselves (as they seldom do otherwise). So did the authors of such stories; they wrote fast.

There were many short stories and this was at the time that the short story (*q.v.*) was developing as a form and genre in its own right. Like most of the well-known Gothic novels they are curiosities, 'period pieces', ludicrously melodramatic and wildly over-written, with resonant titles designed to cause a thrilling shudder of apprehension in the sturdiest of breasts. For example: *The Abbey of Clunedale* by Dr Nathan Drake; *The Anaconda* by 'Monk' Lewis; *The Monk of Horror, or The Conclave of Corpses* (anonymous); *The Black Spider* (anonymous); *The Water Spectre* by Francis Lathom; *Secrets of Cabalism, or Ravenstone and Alice of Huntingdon* by William Child Green; *The Dance of the Dead* (anonymous); *Leixlip Castle* by Charles Maturin; *The Assassins* by Shelley; *The Burial* by Byron; *The Unknown! or The Knight of the Blood-Red Plume* by Mrs Julia Anne Curtis (known as Anne of Swansea); *The Iron Shroud* (anonymous); and *The Astrologer's Prediction, or The Maniac's Fate* (anonymous). A good many were written by women and they were very popular among female readers.

By early in the 18th c. readers had supped full with horrors and there was a growing demand for even more lurid and sensational fiction. Decadence (*q.v.*) was setting in. Graveyards, charnel houses, the crepuscular and the necropolitan, the macabre (*see* DANSE MACABRE) had become increasingly popular elements; and here, perhaps, one may discern the long-term influence of the so-called graveyard school of poetry (*q.v.*) of the 1740s which had marked a shift of sensibility (*q.v.*) and something of a reaction against the attitudes and codes of the Augustan Age (*q.v.*).

By *c.* 1815–20 the need for something different and rather more sophisticated was starting to be felt. Enough had been as good as a feast, as it were. Jane Austen suggested as much in *Northanger Abbey* (published in 1818, but begun in 1798 and prepared for the press in 1803). In 1818, too, Thomas Love Peacock published *Nightmare Abbey*, which is a kind of burlesque (*q.v.*) of Gothic excesses. And in 1819 Leigh Hunt oberved ruefully in his preamble to his *Tale for a Chimney Corner*: 'a man who does not contribute his quota of grim story nowadays, seems hardly to be free of the republic of letters. He is bound to wear a death's head as part of his insignia. If he does not frighten everybody, he is nobody. If he does not shock the ladies, what can be expected of him?' Later he takes 'Monk' Lewis to task: 'When his spectral nuns go about bleeding, we think they ought in decency to have applied to some ghost of a surgeon. His little Grey Men, who sit munching hearts, are of a piece with fellows who eat cats for a wager'. After some other happily phrased observations he relates a short ghost-cum-horror story of his own.

Meanwhile, Gothic had travelled to America, where Isaac Mitchell achieved some reputation with *The Asylum* (1811) and Charles Brockden Brown attained something approaching fame with a succession of Gothic romances: *Wieland* (1798), *Arthur Mervyn* (1799–1800), *Ormond* (1799) and *Edgar Huntly* (1799). Some of the main influences on Brown were Samuel Richardson, Godwin and Anne Radcliffe. In turn, Brown was to influence Nathaniel Hawthorne, Mary Shelley and Edgar Allan Poe – one of the most Gothic of all 19th c. writers of short stories whose long-term contribution to the horror story, the tale of suspense and mystery and the detective story (*q.v.*) was immeasurable.

During the latter half of the 18th c. German writers were developing their own brand of sensational and Gothic fiction. In the

18th c. considerable interest in English literature arose in Germany literary circles. Klopstock, Gellert and Wieland, for instance, were much affected by Shakespeare, Milton, Edward Young and James Hervey (and, it seems curious now, by Samuel Richardson). Goethe even considered Young to be in the same league as Milton.

In England there was a corresponding interest in German literature. 'Monk' Lewis, for example, was well read in German, was a gifted translator and was to influence E. T. A. Hoffman. Translation of the *Schauerroman* (*q.v.*) and German 'terror fiction' began in the 1890s with the publication of an English rendering of Benedikte Naubert's *Hermann von Unna*. A series of translations followed. They included works by Karl Grosse, Leonhard Wachter, C. H. Spiess and Heinrich Zschokke. Christian Vulpius's *Rinaldo Rinaldini* proved very popular. Ann Radcliffe was impressed by Schiller's strange and powerful story *Der Geisterseher* (1787–9); and Schiller's play *Die Räuber* (1782), translated in 1792, was perhaps most important of all. Samuel Coleridge, among many others, was enraptured by Schiller.

In passing it should be noted that there was a difference between the German and English conceptions of the function of the Gothic story. Many of the German writers were politically committed. Their fictional heroes were 'political'. Critical social comment (e.g. anti-clericalism) was implicit and explicit in the tales. Schiller, particularly, expressed the point of view of the individual against social convention and taboo. The *Ritter- und Räuberromane* (*q.v.*) which, with the *Schauerroman*, were a kind of counterpart of English Gothic, were aspects of the *Sturm und Drang* (*q.v.*) revolutionary literary movement. The Gothic in Germany was to hold sway for some time and is discernible in, for instance, the work of Fouqué and Tieck.

English Gothic novels were much read and imitated in France in the 19th c. Their influence, plus the influences of German Gothic, the *Schauerroman* and especially E. T. A. Hoffmann's stories, becomes apparent in French literature – particularly in horror stories and tales of the supernatural, by such writers as Nodier, Balzac, Gérard de Nerval, Prosper Mérimée and Petrus Borel.

There was also Gothic drama. Playwrights had no inhibitions about displaying horrors on stage. Dramatized versions of Gothic novels (and there were many of them) set out to frighten audiences. For example there was *Le Comte de Comminges* (1764) by François Baculard D'Arnaud. This spine-chiller was set in the burial crypt of a Trappist monastery. The necropolitan action was so blood-curdling that members of the audience passed out, to be revived by the management with cordials. And there was von Gerstenberg's *Ugolino* (1768), which was based on the story of Ugolino recounted by Dante in the *Inferno* (Canto XXXIII). Such plays were to have a considerable impact on the development of melodrama (*q.v.*), which was becoming an established popular form of entertainment by *c.* 1830.

The last thirty-odd years of the 18th c. and the first twenty to thirty years of the 19th c. are marked by quite important changes in the ways people thought and felt about the metaphysical and the preternatural, and also what they felt about such matters as madness, states of fear, extremes of suffering, cruelty, violence, crime, torture and murder. It is as if, after a long period of rationalism and apparent mental, spiritual and psychological stability, the rediscovery of 'old worlds' and, more especially, the rediscovery of the world of supernatural or quasi-supernatural evil, had a strong disruptive and purgative effect. A whole bag of tricks was opened up, a veritable Pandora's box. Out of it came devils, wizards, magicians and witches, trolls, hobgoblins, werewolves, vampires, *doppelgängers* – and what not? None of all this had had any place in the 'Age of Reason'. Nor, for that matter, had Satanism, possession, black magic, sorcery, exorcism or diabolic pacts. In short, the whole caboodle of the occult. Most conspicuous of all was the ghost, 'revived', after an absence of a great many years (an absence dating back to the Jacobean dramatists), as a figure and 'character'. The ghost story was a natural development from the Gothic novel and Gothic tales in general.

If Gothic fiction had never happened, 19th c. fiction in English would look very different, and so would not a little 20th c. fiction. It would be minus many hundreds of stories of mystery and suspense; minus thousands of ghost and horror stories; minus innumerable tales about vampires, werewolves, succubae, incubi, lamias, *doppelgängers* and demonic pacts.

Moreover, there is a strong Gothic strain discernible in much mainstream 19th c. fiction. It is very clear in the works of the Brontës (e.g. Charlotte Brontë's *Villette*, 1853), in Sir Walter Scott and Charles Dickens (e.g. *Bleak House*, 1853, and *Great Expectations*, 1861). It is also abundantly clear in much fiction by minor novelists; particularly, G. P. R. James (1799–1860), Bulwer Lytton (1803–73), William Harrison Ainsworth (1805–82) and G. W. M. Reynolds (1814–79).

In the 20th c. Gothic has flourished vigorously in the cinema

(*Frankenstein, Dracula* – and all their progeny) and in popular horror fiction (e.g. the novels of Stephen King). What has been dubbed Neo-Gothic is discernible in the fiction of Isak Dinesen (e.g. *Seven Gothic Tales*, 1934), Mervyn Peake (e.g. *Titus Groan*, 1946, and *Gormenghast*, 1950), William Faulkner (1897–1962), Daphne du Maurier (1907–89), Carson McCullers (1917–67), Flannery O'Connor (1925–64), Diane Johnson (1934–), John Gardner (1935–), Joyce Carol Oates (1938–), Emma Tennant (1938–) and Angela Carter (1940–).

A scholarly and academic interest in Gothic literature of the 18th and 19th c. has been manifest for some while, and 'Gothics' have become standard fare on some school examination syllabuses.

There seems to be a fairly straightforward reason for the continued popularity of flesh-creeping and spine-chilling stories in general (Robert Louis Stevenson named them, suitably, 'crawlers') and of 'Gothics' in one form or another. As long ago as 1773 Mrs Anna Laetitia Barbauld (the wife of a clergyman) wrote a story called *Sir Bertrand*. The knight loses his way on dreary moors. Benighted, he comes upon an antique mansion marked by the injuries of time. Undaunted he enters the mansion and pursues a weird will-o'-the-wisp blue flame. Further and further he goes until he is in total darkness:

> with his arms extended, [he] began to ascend the second staircase. A dead cold hand met his left hand, and firmly grasped it, drawing him forcibly backwards – he endeavoured to disengage himself, but could not – he made a furious blow with his sword, and instantly a loud shriek pierced his ears, and the dead hand was left powerless with his. He dropped it, and rushed forward with a desperate valour . . . The staircase grew narrower and narrower, and at length terminated in a low iron gate. Sir Bertrand pushed it open – it led to an intricate winding passage, just large enough to admit a person upon his hands and knees . . .

And so on. The collection of blood-curdlers in which this appeared was prefaced by an essay: *On the Pleasure Derived from Objects of Terror*. *See also* GROTESQUE; SUBLIME; SUPERNATURAL STORY.

Göttinger Dichterbund A group of German poets (also known as the *Hainbund*) who were students at Göttingen University between 1772 and 1776. Disciples of Klopstock, they revived the folksong (*q.v.*) and wrote some notable lyric poetry. *See* STURM UND DRANG.

grace That mysterious, even magical, attribute or quality which is, as it were, the spirit of beauty; beauty being the outward sign of inward grace. Because of its mystery it is a *je ne sais quoi* (*q.v.*). The quality of gracefulness was much prized among Classical writers, at the Renaissance and during the 18th c. Pope, in his *Essay on Criticism*, wrote of snatching 'a grace beyond the reach of art', suggesting perhaps the qualities of ease and elegance which, though elusive, might be caught upon the wing.

gracioso (Sp 'graceful, gracious, amusing, droll') A comic actor. On the Spanish stage the *gracioso* is often of much importance; the part may be small but it may have great impact. The usual role is that of parodying the actions of the principal character, and its creation is credited to Lope de Vega. It was also used by Calderón to provide comic relief. The *gracioso* is perhaps comparable to the Fool in Shakespeare. Until the time of Zorrilla (1607–48) the humour in a play was nearly always reserved for the *gracioso*.

gradatio *See* CLIMAX.

grammatology A coinage of the French philosopher Jacques Derrida (1930–) to denote a 'science' of the written sign, which he expounded in *Of Grammatology* (1967), *Writing and Difference* (1967) and *Speech and Phenomena* (1967). Grammatology is not to be confused with semiology. In *Modern Literary Theory* (1982), Ann Jefferson emphasizes the difference: 'In Derrida's writing the science of semiology is replaced by grammatology which, as he says, takes the form of a question rather than of a new science . . . of writing'. For Derrida a text and its meaning are not one and the same thing. There can be no science of writing for Derrida since the whole idea of *différance* (*q.v.*) is that there is a permanent instability of reference (unlike for the structuralists). In his theory of *différance* he argues that the 'deferred' or 'deferring' nature of writing makes it impossible for a text and meaning to have a total and simultaneous identity and co-existence. Moreover, a text cannot have a final and ultimate meaning. In the theory of grammatology Derrida conceives of writing as something that *has its own reality*; something that is *sui generis*; *writing in its own right*, as it were, which is separate from and different from any description of or reproduction of reality, or any version of it. Thus, he is concerned *with writing itself*, and not writing as any kind of substitute or replacement for voice, or as the transparent medium through which meaning is communicated. The possibilities of such writing are evident in, for example, Joyce's *Finnegans Wake*, in some concrete poetry (*q.v.*) and in ideogrammatic characters used, for instance, in Chinese.

A vital part of Derrida's theory is that 'writing' has always been excluded, degraded, distrusted ever since Plato. Writing has been seen as inferior to speech, and as the improper area in which to discuss language and meaning. Now, Derrida does not seek to 'redress' or 'correct' this 'imbalance' – all words of which he would be suspicious – but his point is that there is *nothing outside writing*; there is no proper priority inherent to speech either in terms of time or ideas. As such, writing is not to be evaluated as a medium for something else, as a 'carrier' or 'bearer' of meaning, but as the only *place* in which the *différance* in language is exposed.

grand guignol Guignol is the name of a French marionette or puppet 'created' in Lyon towards the end of the 18th c. The puppet master Mourquet (1744–1844) may have been the creator. This puppet was believed to represent the main characteristics of the peasant and provincial man in the district of Dauphiné. By some symbiotic process Polinchinelle (or Punch) and this character became one. The brutality and violence of the Punch and Judy show may have been an influence here. At any rate, the name Guignol was given to Paris cabarets which presented decadent shows. Later the Théâtre du Grand Guignol specialized in melodramatic plays whose subjects were horrific: murder, rape and suicide. Since then the term has denoted any kind of play which is bloody, gruesome and sensational. *See* MELODRAMA; THEATRE OF CRUELTY.

grand style In his Oxford lectures *On Translating Homer* and *On Translating Homer: Last Words* (1861, 1862), Matthew Arnold used this now famous phrase. Such a style, he maintained, arises, when a noble nature 'poetically gifted, treats with simplicity or with severity a serious subject'. Arnold refers to Homer, Pindar, Virgil, Dante and Milton as exponents of the grand style. It was a lofty or elevated style (*q.v.*) suitable for epic: a style which Arnold himself attempted in, for instance, *Sohrab and Rustum* (1853).

Grand Tour The term appears to have been first used in a printed work by Richard Lassels in his *Voyage of Italy* (1670). It came to denote a regular tour of many sights and cities of Europe, especially those in the Netherlands, Germany, France, Austria, Switzerland and Italy. The climax of this journey was a visit to Rome and Naples. The Grand Tour is of some interest and importance in the history of literature because a number of famous writers undertook it, and the journeys produced a substantial variety of entertaining travel reminiscences and travel books (*q.v.*). Indeed, it became so popular that detailed guidebooks (*q.v.*) were compiled to assist travellers. Some of the more interesting examples of these are: James Howell's *Instructions for Forreine Travell* (1642), the earliest of the continental handbooks; Henry Logan's *Directions for such as shall travel to Rome* (1654); *The Gentleman's Pocket Companion For Travelling into Foreign Parts* (1722); Nemeitz's *Séjour de Paris* (1727), one of the most popular and useful guides of the period; Thomas Nugent's *The Grand Tour containing an Exact Description of most of the Cities, Towns and Remarkable Places of Europe* (1743), a work in four volumes and an essential *vade mecum*; Thomas Martyn's *A Gentleman's Guide in his Tour through France* (1787); and Johann Ebel's *The Traveller's Guide through Switzerland* (1818).

At least a hundred years before Lassels used the phrase an extensive tour of Europe was regarded as an invaluable part of a gentleman's education; this at a time when there was some premium on education and considerable *cachet* was attached to the importance of learning to behave as a gentleman should. Hence the number of courtesy books (*q.v.*) of the period.

In Elizabethan England tours abroad were recognized as a means of collecting information about foreign countries which might be of use to England. Sir Philip Sidney is a notable example of a man sent abroad for three years to acquaint himself with foreign courts. Trips like this were often subsidized by the Queen.

Curious travellers set off on their own account, even though travel in Europe in those days was dangerous, arduous and expensive. One of the earlier and more adventurous ones was Fynes Morison, who published his *Itinerary* of travels in 1617. During the 17th c. increasing numbers of Englishmen explored Europe, including John Evelyn and Milton. By 1700 the Grand Tour was an established practice, and the influence of continental manners and customs became observable in England; so observable that Restoration dramatists poked fun at imported affectations.

During the 18th c. the tour became more fashionable. Thomas Gray toured the continent with Horace Walpole for three years (1739–41). Other famous tourists were the intrepid Lady Mary

Wortley Montagu, Thomas Sterne, Tobias Smollett, Dr Johnson, Boswell, Gibbon, Lord Chesterfield and William Beckford. Among Europeans easily the most famous writer to make the trip was Goethe, who subsequently published his *Italienische Reise* (1786–8).

By the middle of the century, if not before, the Tourist had become an object of caricature; a target not to be missed by Pope who sniped at one kind of traveller in *The Dunciad*:

> Led by my hand, he saunter'd Europe round,
> And gather'd ev'ry Vice on Christian ground;
> Saw ev'ry court, heard ev'ry King declare
> His royal sense of Op'ras or the Fair;
> The Stews and Palace equally explor'd
> Intrigu'd with glory and with spirit whor'd;
> Try'd all hors d'oeuvres, all liqueurs defin'd;
> Dropt the dull lumber of the Latin score,
> Spoil'd his own language and acquir'd no more;
> All Classic learning lost on Classic ground,
> And last turn'd Air, the Echo of a Sound!
> See now, half-cur'd and perfectly well-bred,
> With nothing but a Solo in his head.

Forty-odd years later, in *The Progress of Error*, William Cowper, more genially than Pope, satirized the Oxbridge tourist broadening his mind on the Grand Tour.

The French Revolution and the Napoleonic Wars combined to put an end to the tour as it had been known in the 18th c. After peace came, there began the great railway development. Permanent way was laid over much of Europe and hotels were readily available at railway stations. Soon Thomas Cook started his circular tours of the continent. By the 1860s one could reach Rome in three days, whereas before it had taken three weeks or more.

Grangerize To illustrate a book by the addition of prints, engravings and so forth, and particularly those cut out from other books. In 1769 James Granger (1723–76) published a *Biographical History of England* with blank pages for the addition of engraved portraits or other kinds of illustration. For a time Grangerizing became an innocent hobby.

graveyard school of poetry The poets who have been put into this school wrote a type of mournfully reflective poetry with emphasis on the brevity of life and the sepulchral (and the hope of immortality) which had some vogue in 18th c. England, and in the latter half of the century was a widespread phenomenon in Europe. It was possibly part of a reaction against Augustan principles of decorum (*q.v.*) which did not favour anything melancholy or self-indulgently piteous. One of the earliest examples is Thomas Parnell's *Night-Piece on Death* (1721). The best known works are Edward Young's *Night Thoughts* (1742) and Robert Blair's *The Grave* (1743). Some would include Gray's *Elegy* (1750) and Ugo Foscolo's *De' Sepolcri* (1807), but the general opinion seems to be that these two poems are not typical of the graveyard school. Indeed, they transcend its limitations. *See* ELEGY; UBI SUNT.

great chain of being The phrase summarizes an idea of considerable antiquity; namely, that all that exists in the created order is part of natural hierarchy, a *scala naturae* from the lowest possible grade up to the *ens perfectissimum*. It implements the concept that Nature abhors a vacuum. Emerson epitomized the concept adroitly in a well-known couplet:

Striving to be man, the worm
Mounts through all the spires of form.

The concept has pervaded philosophy, literature and scientific thought from the time of Plato and Aristotle onwards.

Apart from Ulysses's famous speech on 'degree' in Shakespeare's *Troilus and Cressida* (I, iii), one of the clearest statements of the idea in English literature occurs in Pope's *Essay on Man*:

Vast chain of being! which from God began,
Natures aethereal, human, angel, man,
Beast, bird, fish, insect, what no eye can see,
No glass can reach; from Infinite to thee,
From thee to nothing. – On superior pow'rs
Were we to press, inferior might on ours;
Or in the full creation leave a void,
Where, one step broken, the great scale's destroy'd;
From Nature's chain whatever link you strike,
Tenth, or ten thousandth, breaks the chain alike.

The classic work on the subject is A. O. Lovejoy's *The Great Chain of Being: A Study of the History of an Idea* (1936).

Greek tragedy This form of tragedy (*q.v.*) had a definite structure which was more or less prescribed. There were four main parts to a play: (a) The *Prologos* or Prologue: an introductory scene of monologue or dialogue. This exposition established the subject and theme of the play and portrayed one or more characters; (b) *Parados*: the entrance of the Chorus (*q.v.*); the choral song provides further exposition and foreshadows subsequent events; (c) *Epeisodia*: episodes (perhaps four or five) which constitute the main action of the play. One or more characters take part in these with the Chorus. Each episode is separated by a choral ode or *stasimon*. In some plays, a part of the episode may involve a *kommos* – a kind of lamentation in which both characters and Chorus take part; (d) *Exodus*: the conclusion, which follows the last ode (*q.v.*) sung and danced by the Chorus. The *Exodos* includes two features: the messenger's speech and the *deus ex machina* (*q.v.*); but the *deus ex machina* was used only by Euripides.

green baize From the Restoration period (*q.v.*) until well on into the 19th c. it was traditional to lay a green carpet on the stage when a tragedy was to be performed. The object was to protect the costumes of those characters who had to die in the action.

Greenwich Village An area of New York City which has long-standing literary associations and connections and might be described as a sort of counterpart to Chelsea, London, where painters, writers, musicians, singers *et al.* were wont to congregate. It is particularly associated with Henry James (1843–1916), who lived there; and later, during the 1940s and 1950s, with such figures as Jack Kerouac (1922–69) and Allen Ginsberg (1926–), two moving spirits of the Beat generation (*q.v.*) or movement. In the 1960s the Village expanded and became associated with the so-called Alternative Society and hence with 'underground literature' (*q.v.*). *See also* ALTERNATIVE LITERATURE; ALTERNATIVE THEATRE.

greguería Brief observations in prose by the Spanish writer Ramón Gómez de la Serna (1888–1963) and defined as 'humour plus metaphor'. The author has referred to them as attempts to define the indefinable and to capture the fugitive. Almost a form of aphorism (*q.v.*), with an element of the conceit (*q.v.*). An example is 'The bat is the devil's Holy Ghost.'

Grobianism The word Grobian derives from the German *Grobheit* 'rudeness'. Grobian was an imaginary person continually referred to by 15th and 16th c. writers in Germany as a paradigm of coarseness and rudeness. In his *Narrenschiff* (1494) Brandt invented St Grobianus – a figure typical of boorish and uncouth behaviour. Through this character Brandt was able to satirize contemporary manners. In 1549 Dedekind wrote *Grobianus: De Morum Simplicitate*, a poem in Latin elgiacs which was a burlesque (*q.v.*) at the expense of the uncivilized social conditions in Germany. In this work he gave rules for the guidance of boors. This was translated into German and English and provided Dekker with the idea for his *Gull's Hornbook* (1609) which was a satirical attack on the fops and gallants of the day in the guise of a book of manners or courtesy book (*q.v.*). Dedekind's ironical approach had a good many imitators. This type of literature coincided with a large number of manuals on good behaviour and a greatly increased interest in urbane conduct. *See* BIEDERMEIER; FOLLY LITERATURE.

grotesque The word derives from Italian *grotte* 'caves', whose adjective is *grottesco*; the noun being *la grottesca.* In French we find *crotesque* being used *c.* 1532 for the first time; and this form was used in English until it was replaced *c.* 1640 by *grotesque*. Its correct technical sense has little to do with its normal usage. It denotes a kind of decorative ornament consisting of medallions, sphinxes, foliage, rocks and pebbles. Because they were found in grottoes they were called *grotteschi.* The term came to be applied to paintings which depicted the intermingling of human, animal and vegetable themes and forms. Some of the works of Raphael and Arcimboldo are typical grotesques. It has also been used to describe architectural embellishments like gargoyles, hideous diabolic shapes and, again, the complex interweaving of themes and subjects. An outstanding instance is Radovan's main doorway of Trogir cathedral.

The extension of the word to a literary context may well have occurred in 16th c. France. Rabelais, for example, uses it apropos parts of the body. But it does not seem to have been used regularly in a literary context until the 18th c., the period of the age of reason and Neoclassicism (*qq.v.*), when it was commonly employed to denote the ridiculous, bizarre, extravagant, freakish and unnatural; in short, aberrations from the desirable norms of harmony, balance and proportion.

In art the use of grotesque effects has been frequent. Outstanding instances are to be found in the works of such painters as Hieronymus Bosch, the Brueghels, Goya, Gustave Doré, Daumier, Fuseli, Piranesi, John Martin, Max Ernst and Salvador Dali –

among many others. It is very noticeable that these artists use the grotesque for comic, sardonic and exaggerated satirical effects. Much of the comic impact of graphic caricature (*q.v.*) also depends on the skilful use of grotesque; witness the work, for instance, of George Grosz and Gerald Scarfe.

In a comparable way the writer employs grotesque for comic and satirical purposes. In literature one is most likely to find grotesque elements in caricature, parody, satire, invective, burlesque, black comedy, the macabre and what is known as the Theatre of the Absurd (*qq.v.*). Grotesque is often a constituent of comic relief (*q.v.*), the sick joke, sick verse (*q.v.*) and pornography (*q.v.*). Excellent examples of the grotesque can be found in the works by Rabelais, Skelton, Webster, Tourneur, Swift, Pope, Smollett, Byron, E. T. A. Hoffmann, Victor Hugo, E. A. Poe, Zola, Dickens, Browning, Kafka, Alfred Jarry, Samuel Beckett, Evelyn Waugh, Mervyn Peake, Genet, Ionesco and Roald Dahl – to name but a few. *See also* GOTHIC NOVEL/FICTION.

Group, the A poetry society founded by Edward Lucie-Smith in the late 1950s. It had weekly meetings at which poets read and talked about their work. Among the members were Ted Hughes and Peter Redgrove. It was later called Poetry Workshop. *See also* MOVEMENT.

Group Theatre There have been two main companies bearing this title: (a) a New York theatre company founded in 1931 whose main objective was to present plays which depicted contemporary social conditions. It lasted for ten years and was run by Lee Strasberg, Cheryl Crawford and Harold Clurman. Among their more famous productions were Clifford Odets's *Waiting for Lefty* (1935), Robert Ardrey's *Thunder Rock* (1939) and William Saroyan's *My Heart's in the Highlands* (1939); (b) a company founded in 1932 at the Westminster Theatre, London. It gave the first performances of a number of now well-known verse dramas, including Auden and Isherwood's *The Dog Beneath the Skin* (1936), *The Ascent of F6* (1937) and *On the Frontier* (1939), T. S. Eliot's *Sweeney Agonistes* (1935) and Stephen Spender's *Trial of a Judge* (1938). It closed in 1953.

Grub Street According to Dr Johnson, this was 'originally the name of a street near Moorfields in London, much inhabited by writers of small histories, dictionaries, and temporary poems, whence any mean production is called *grubstreet*.' It now describes anything in the way of literary hackwork.

Grupo de Guayaquil A literary group of the 1930s that began a revival of the Ecuadorean novel. The novels were mainly about regional Ecuadorean life, in the tradition of *costumbrismo* (*q.v.*), and combined social comment and protest. The authors were Joaquín Gallegos Lara (1911–), Enrique Gil Gilbert (1912–) and Demetrio Aguilera Malta (1909–).

Gruppe 47 A group of predominantly left-wing German writers founded by Hans Richter in 1947. They gathered annually between 1947 and 1967 when they read each other's work and offered criticism. During those twenty years they had considerable influence on German literature. Among the more famous were Heinrich Böll, Günter Grass and Johannes Bobrowski. Others were Paul Celan, Uwe Johnson, Érich Fried and Hans Enzensberger.

Gruppe 61 A group of left-wing revolutionary German writers centred on Dortmund *c.* 1961. Their principal objective was to promote writing – particularly fiction – about work by working men. The two most prominent members were Max von der Grün and Josef Reding. It seems that the group fell into desuetude without achieving much.

guidebook A book designed to help travellers. Guidebooks range widely from mere hackwork to elegant writing. An early and distinguished example is the *Hellados Periegesis* of Pausanias (2nd c. AD), a remarkably well-informed and interesting guidebook to Attica, Central Greece and the Peloponnese. From the 12th c. dates the *Mirabilia Urbis Romae*, a guidebook to Rome which was still being kept up to date in the 15th c.

Until travel for diversion and holiday (as opposed to that for exploration, proselytizing and commercial enterprise) became fashionable there was little in the way of organized guidebooks; though since the Middle Ages there have been a very large number of travel books (*q.v.*) and reminiscences, often of considerable literary merit.

In the 17th c. the Grand Tour (*q.v.*) caused a number of writers to produce detailed guides for Europe. Possibly the earliest instance of a handbook for continental travel was James Howell's *Instructions for Forreine Travell* (1642). As the Tour became more and more popular so the number of guidebooks multiplied, and there were many in the 18th c. For the most part they were well written, well organized and still make interesting reading.

However, the guidebook proper really belongs to the last hundred years or so – a period which has produced such series as: *Murray's Handbooks of Travellers*, *Nagel's Guides*, the *Baedeker Guides*, *Fodor Guides*, the *Guides Bleux* (outstanding for their comprehensiveness and accuracy) and the *Michelin Guides* (which also set a high standard of accuracy and detail). These are the result of joint efforts by teams of investigators.

Occasionally an author has produced a more personal type of guidebook. Richard Ford, for instance, who wrote *Handbook for Travellers in Spain* (1845); and Augustus Hare, who wrote *Days near Rome* (1875), and *Cities of Northern and Central Italy* (1876). From recent years one might cite William Collins's *Companion Guides* and Jonathan Cape's *Travellers' Guides*.

Since the Second World War, travel having become a simple undertaking for millions of people, guidebooks have proliferated in large numbers all over the world and there is little sign of any diminution. In many instances the quality, too, has improved. In fact, the guidebook may be good literature which, at its best, is distinguished by learning, an elegant style and a high degree of readability. *See* HANDBOOK AND MANUAL; VADE MECUM.

guignol *See* GRAND GUIGNOL.

guslar The *gusle* is a one-stringed fiddle played by a *guslar* (pl. *guslari*). The *guslari* were blind minstrels among the South Slavs; professional and itinerant reciters of national heroic poems of the oral tradition (*q.v.*) called *narodne pesme* (*q.v.*). These men corresponded to the Greek rhapsodists, the Celtic bards, the Old English *scopas*, the Scandinavian *skalds* (*qq.v.*), and the French *trouvères* and *jongleurs* (*qq.v.*). Their profession dates from the 14th c. or before.

Many of them composed heroic poetry as well as reciting it. They are still to be found occasionally in Jugoslavia (especially in Bosnia, Serbia and Macedonia) and they carry on the ancient tradition of making up and chanting (to the accompaniment of the *gusle*) heroic poems. The author has seen and heard a blind *guslar* (in the uplands of Bosnia) making up such a poem. Its subject was an engagement between the Partisans and the Germans in the Second World War. *See also* PEVACI.

gwawdodyns A Welsh syllabic verse form. It comprises a quatrain (*q.v.*) stanza with lines of nine, nine, ten and nine syllables respectively. The first, second and fourth lines have end-rhyme with each other. The third line may rhyme internally with itself, or a syllable before the end of the line may rhyme into the fourth line.

H

Habima (Heb 'stage') A theatre founded in Moscow in 1917–18 to stage plays in Hebrew. It became one of the studios of the Moscow Art Theatre (*q.v.*) and in 1931 moved to Tel Aviv. From 1953 it has been the national theatre of Israel.

hadīth (A 'statement') The term given by Muslims to those traditions which are believed to embody the practice and precepts of the Prophet. Many statements were ascribed to the Prophet after his death and a number of *hadīth* compilations were made. How authentic they were has been much debated.

hagiography (Gk 'sacred writing') The writing or study of the lives of the saints. Also known as hagiology; it is, as a rule, the specialized study of saints, often inspired by veneration. There are two main groups of such works: the literary and liturgical. Notable examples of the literary are: Eusebius of Caesarea's record of the martyrs of Palestine (4th c.); Theodoret's account of the monks of Syria (5th c.); Gregory the Great's of the monks of Italy (6th c.); the Byzantine Menology (12th c.) – the menology (*q.v.*) being a sort of calendar of the Greek Church which incorporates biographies of the saints; the Chronicle of Nestor (*c.* 1113) written by a priest of that name and known as the primary *Russian Chronicle*; the *Golden Legend* of Jacobus a Voragine (13th c.). Liturgical sources are documents, very often calendars (*q.v.*), which record information about devotion paid to saints. These were local as well as universal calendars; also known as martyrologies. Well-known examples were compiled by Hieronymian (5th c.), Bede (8th c.), Adon and Usuard (9th c.). There was also the *Roman Martyrology* of the late 16th c.

To these instances one should add the *Acta Sanctorum*, a series of lives of the saints arranged in order of their feasts in the ecclesiastical year. This was begun by the Bollandists, a body of

Belgian Jesuits (named after John Bolland, a Flemish Jesuit), in the 17th c. The first volume appeared in 1643, and the last of the original series in 1786. There are also the *Acta Sanctorum Ordinis Sancti Benedicti*, a history of the saints of the Benedictine Order, published between 1668 and 1701.

A curiosity in this genre in English literature is John Foxe's *Actes and Monuments* (popularly known as *The Book of Martyrs*), first published in Latin in 1559 and in English in 1563. This vast work (about twice the length of Gibbon's *Decline and Fall of the Roman Empire*) was a history of the Christian Church but contains detailed accounts of many martyrs, particularly the Protestant martyrs of Queen Mary's reign. *See also* SACRED BOOKS; SYNAXARION.

haiku A Japanese verse form consisting of seventeen syllables in three lines of five, seven and five syllables respectively. Such a poem expresses a single idea, image or feeling; in fact, it is a kind of miniature 'snap' in words. It was first established as a form in the 16th c. Originally it was called a *hokku* (*haiku*, the current term, is 19th c.) and was the opening verse in a linked sequence or *renga*. Many Japanese poets have used the form, but two were especially gifted: namely, Bashō (pseudonym of Matsuo Munefusa, 1644–94); and Kobayashi Issa (pseudonym of Kobayashi Nobuyuki, 1763–1828). Recently it has attracted the interest of poets associated with T. E. Hulme and the Imagist movement. Ezra Pound made use of the principles of the *haiku* in *Mauberley* and the *Cantos*. Other poets to be influenced by it were Amy Lowell, Robert Frost, Conrad Aiken and W. B. Yeats. But few Western poets have been able to imitate it successfully. James Kirkup is one of the few, as in *Evening*, the last of a sequence called *Four Haiku on the Inland Sea*)

In the amber dusk
Each island dreams its own night.
The sea swarms with gold.

See also IMAGISTS; TANKA.

half-rhyme The repetition in accented syllables of the final consonant sound but without the correspondence of the vowel sound. Therefore it is a form of consonance (*q.v.*), which is also known as approximate, embryonic, imperfect, near, oblique, para and slant rhyme. It was common in Icelandic, Irish and Welsh verse. Henry Vaughan appears to have been the first to use it in English, but it was not until Gerard Manley Hopkins and W. B. Yeats that English poets began to use it regularly. Since them there have been many examples in the work of such poets as Wilfred Owen, John Crowe Ransom, T. S. Eliot, Emily Dickinson, Allen Tate and W. H. Auden. The following well-known example comes from Emily Dickinson's *I like to see it lap the miles*:

> I like to see it lap the miles,
> And lick the valleys up,
> And stop to feed itself at tanks;
> And then, prodigious, step
> Around a pile of mountains,
> And, supercilious, peer
> In shanties by the sides of roads;
> And then a quarry pare.

Up/step, peer/pare are the half-rhymes. *See also* ASSONANCE.

hallel (Heb 'praise, celebrate') A hymn of praise consisting of Psalms 113–18, each of which is headed with *Hallelujah* 'praise ye'. Thus, a song of praise to God, sung at the four main Jewish festivals: Passover, Pentecost, Dedication and Tabernacles. *See* HALLELUJAH METER.

hallelujah meter Named from its frequent use in hymns. It consists of a stanza of six iambic lines: four trimeter, and two tetrameter (*qq.v.*). *See also* HALLEL; HYMNAL STANZA.

hamartia (Gk 'error') Primarily, an error of judgement which may arise from ignorance or some moral shortcoming. Discussing tragedy (*q.v.*) and the tragic hero in *Poetics*, Aristotle points out that the tragic hero ought to be a man whose misfortune comes to him, not through vice or depravity, but by some error. For example: Oedipus kills his father from impulse, and marries his mother out of ignorance. Antigone resists the law of the state from stubbornness and defiance. Phèdre is consumed by her passion for Hippolyte. *See* HUBRIS; TRAGIC FLAW.

handbook and manual (OE *handboc*) (MedL *liber manualis*) A small book for handy use like the manual for ecclesiastical offices and ritual. Many guidebooks (*q.v.*) are handbooks, and there are a very large number of handbooks published by way of general information and reference on nations, technical subjects, arts and crafts. In America *handbook* has another and particular sense of 'betting book'. In most cases manual and handbook are synonymous. In the medieval Church a manual contained the forms to be observed in the administration of the sacraments. Other examples are the manual of daily prayer; and specialist works like the various manuals for military training; or the BR rule book, a remarkable publication which caters for almost every conceivable contingency in a railwayman's life. This is a masterpiece in its way because of its opaque, convoluted and, at times, mandarin prose which might have been written by Henry James while under hypnosis. The section on emergency action in fog is especially noteworthy. *See also* VADE MECUM.

happening The term appears to have been first used by the painter Allan Kaprow in the late 1950s and about that period came to denote a form of improvised or spontaneous theatrical performance, often of a non-naturalistic and non-representational kind. Aural and visual effects may be juxtaposed and may include music, dance, film, stroboscopic lights, violent noises, even smells: thus, a form of mixed media presentation. Such pieces were first developed and staged at Black Mountain College, North Carolina, in the 1950s. Early happenings were also presented in Vienna by the Wiener Gruppe in the 1950s. Devisers of such entertainments appear to have been influenced by Dadaism, the Theatre of the Absurd and the Theatre of Cruelty (*qq.v.*); and also by the German concept of *Gesamtkuntswerk* ('complete art-work'). In the 1960s the 'light show' developed and was a kind of happening. A celebrated example was Andy Warhol's 'Exploding Plastic Inevitable'. In the same period happenings were associated with pop art and also with environmental art. A notorious instance of the latter was the covering of a considerable area of cliff in Australia with huge sheets of polythene.

harangue An exhortatory speech, usually delivered to a crowd to incite them to some action. The fire-and-brimstone sermon (*q.v.*) is a kind of harangue. Henry V's pre-battle speeches in *Henry V* and Mark Antony's oration over Caesar's body in *Julius Caesar* are two well-known examples of harangue in dramatic literature.

Harlem Renaissance A literary and cultural movement among black Americans which flourished from early in the 1920s to early in the 1930s. It was also called the 'New Negro' or 'Black Renaissance'. The movement put considerable emphasis on the African heritage of American blacks. Among the more prominent figures were Claude McKay, Jean Toomer, Countee Cullen and Langston Hughes. They produced novels and poetry, and in 1925 Alain Locke published an anthology of work titled *The New Negro*. *See also* NEGRITUDE.

harlequinade A form of theatrical entertainment derived from *commedia dell'arte* (*q.v.*) and introduced into England early in the 18th c. by John Rich (*c.* 1692–1761), the dancer, acrobat and mime who took over the management of the theatre in Lincoln's Inn Fields, London, in 1714. He adopted the characters of *commedia dell'arte* and specialized in the non-speaking part of Harlequin – the Italian Arlecchino. He presented the courtship of Harlequin and Columbine as a kind of interlude (*q.v.*) during plays. The harlequinade was eventually to develop into a pantomime (*q.v.*). The character of Pulcinella in *commedia dell'arte* had long before (*c.* 1650) arrived in England as Punchinel and subsequently became Punch.

headless line *See* ACEPHALOUS.

head rhyme *See* ALLITERATION.

Hebraism/Hellenism This antinomy (*q.v.*) was elaborated by Matthew Arnold in Chapter IV of *Culture and Anarchy* (1869). Arnold sees the essence of Hebraism as 'strictness of conscience'; that of Hellenism as 'spontaneity of consciousness'. He regards a combination of these two as a necessary pre-requisite to a mature life. They are not contradictory because, as he puts it, 'the desire, native in man, for reason and the will of God, the feeling after the universal order', is their common aim. This is one of several antinomies worked out in the 19th c. *See also* APOLLONIAN/DIONYSIAN; CLASSICISM/ROMANTICISM; NAIV UND SENTIMENTALISCH.

Heimkehrerliteratur (G 'returning home literature') A term dating from *c.* 1946 to denote fiction and drama concerned with the plight of demobilized soldiers on their return to a country that had been ruined by war, and the difficulties they faced in coming to terms with civilian life. Examples are Wolfgang Borchert's play *Draussen vor der Tür* (1947), Gerd Gaiser's novel *Eine Stimme hebt an* (1950) and Heinrich Böll's cycle of war stories *Wo warst du, Adam?* (1951).

hemiepes (Gk 'half-hexameter') In Classical prosody a dactylic trimeter catalectic (*qq.v.*) ending in a long syllable. *See* DACTYL.

hemistich (Gk 'half line') Half a metrical line divided at the caesura (*q.v.*). Very common in OE, OHG, ON and medieval alliterative verse (*q.v.*). In drama the half line is used to build up tension and create the effect of cut-and-thrust argument. It is a highly effective device. In drama it is called *hemistichomythia*. *See* STICHOMYTHIA.

hendecasyllable (Gk 'eleven syllables') A metrical line of eleven syllables. The usual scheme is either: ∪ ∪ / ∪ ∪ / ∪ / ∪ / / or: ∪ / / ∪ / / ∪ / ∪ / ∪. It was often used by Greek and Latin poets, and also employed by Dante and Petrarch in sonnets, *terza rima* and *ottava rima* (*qq.v.*). It has not often been used by English poets, but Tennyson and Swinburne experimented with it. Landor wrote some Latin hendecasyllabics.

hendiadys (Gk 'one through two') A figure of speech in which one idea is expressed by two substantives, as in 'gloom and despondency' or 'darkness and the shadow of death'.

hephthemimeral A form of caesura (*q.v.*) which occurs within the fourth foot of a hexameter (*q.v.*) line.

heptameter A metrical line of seven feet, also known as a septenarius or a 'fourteener' (*qq.v.*). Greek and Latin poets used it, mostly for comic verse, but it has been little used in English verse since the Tudor period. Thereafter it is rare in English verse, though Tennyson and Elizabeth Barrett Browning both attempted it. This example of trochaic heptameter comes from Tennyson's *Locksley Hall*:

Cursed be the social wants that sin against the strength of youth!
Cursed be the social lies that warp us from the living truth!
Cursed be the sickly forms that err from honest nature's rule!
Cursed be the gold that gilds the straitened forehead of the fool.

The heptameter readily breaks down into standard ballad meter or common measure (*qq.v.*) of alternating four and three stress lines.

heptastich (Gk 'seven lines') A stanza of seven lines, much used by English poets. For example: Chaucer's rhyme royal (*q.v.*) in *Troilus* *and Criseyde*; Spenser used it in *The Ruines of Time*, *Daphnaïda*, and in his four *Hymns* in honour of Love, Beauty, Heavenly Love and Heavenly Beauty; Cowley in *The Lover to his Lyre*; Shelley in *To Night* and *Mutability*; Robert Browning in *A Lover's Quarrel*; Longfellow in *Olive Basselin*; John Masefield in *The Widow in the Bye Street*, *Dauber* and *Daffodil Fields*; and, more recently, W. H. Auden in *Letter to Lord Byron*.

heptasyllabic A line of seven syllables.

heresy of paraphrase A term introduced and examined by Cleanth Brooks in *The Well-Wrought Urn* (1947). Brooks's thesis is that if paraphrase means 'to say the same thing in other words' then it is not possible to paraphrase a poem, because a poem means more than merely what it says.

hermeneutic code *See* CODE.

hermeneutic of suspicion This phrase (and the related phrase 'circle of suspicion') occurs in psychoanalytical criticism in connection with the act of probing into the 'unconscious' of a text in order to reveal the processes and the 'dream-work' by which it was produced. The method or technique focuses on what are referred to as 'symptomatic places' (e.g. ambiguities, ambivalences, repetitions of words and phrases, evasions, words *not* said, actions *not* performed, and so on) in the text. The probing also endeavours to expose the elements of the 'latent content' and the 'sub-text' (*q.v.*) and by so doing concentrates on both what the text says and how it actually works. *See* FREUDIAN CRITICISM/PSYCHOANALYTIC CRITICISM; HERMENEUTICS; INDETERMINACY; READERLY/WRITERLY.

hermeneutics (Gk *hermeneus* 'an interpreter') In Christian theology hermeneutics is the finding and interpretation of the spiritual truth in the Bible. This is an important quest, so that the truths of the Gospels, for instance, may be interpreted and reinterpreted from generation to generation and thus made relevant in different eras. In more general terms, more recently, hermeneutics has been concerned with the interpretation and understanding of human action (this includes what people do, say and create) and, particularly, with human action through what sociologists refer to, in particular senses, as institutions (i.e. political, cultural, economic and kinship institutions). As far as literature is concerned it is to do with the way textual meaning is communicated. In literature the main impetus of hermeneutic theory comes out of the conflation of German 'Higher Criticism' of the Bible and the Romantic period (*q.v.*).

The history of hermeneutic theory dates from the work of German Protestant theologians of the 17th c. who developed methods of understanding the Bible to support their theological views. In the Romantic period the most prominent figure was Friedrich Schleiermacher (1768–1834), who introduced the concept of the 'hermeneutical circle'. In an essay titled *Reading and Interpretation* (in *Modern Literary Theory*, 1982, ed. by Jefferson and Robey) Ian Maclean describes this central feature thus:

> The circle is that movement from a guess at the 'whole' meaning of a work to an analysis of its parts in relation to the whole, followed by a return to a modified understanding of the 'whole' of the work. It embodies the belief that part and whole are interdependent and have some necessary organic relationship. In this version of interpretation, the historical gap which separates literary work from critic or reader is a negative feature to be overcome by an oscillating movement between historical reconstruction on the one hand and divinatory acts of empathy on the part of the critic or reader on the other.

It was the German philosopher and historian Wilhelm Dilthey (1833–1911) who imported the term hermeneutics from theological studies to the realm of philosophy in order to define more clearly the methods of *Geisteswissenschaften*, or 'sciences of the human spirit', as opposed to the scientific method of the natural sciences (*Naturwissenschaften*). It was he, too, who revived the term *Geistesgeschichte* (*q.v.*). Dilthey was concerned with essential meaning and essence, and thus with understanding (*Verstehen*). The influence of his methods on scholarly interpretation was profound and lasting, and it is partly through his thinking that hermeneutic interpretation has been developed in literary and critical theory. In this field it relates to a general theory of interpretation, to methods, procedures and principles involved in extracting meaning from texts. It has particular relevance to a reader's involvement in the creation of meaning. A text may have totally different meanings for different readers at different times. Thus, what readers bring to a text (knowledge, assumptions, cultural background, experience, insight, etc.) affects their interpretations. A reader is in a position *to create the meaning of a text.*

In the 20th c. hermeneutical methods and ideas have had considerable influence on phenomenology, reader-response theory and reception theory (*qq.v.*) and thus on such prominent theorists as Wolfgang Iser, Hans-Georg Gadamer, E. D. Hirsch and Stanley Fish. *See also* AESTHETIC DISTANCE; HERMENEUTIC OF SUSPICION.

Hermeticism Hermes Trismegistos, the 'thrice great Hermes' to whom Milton refers in *Il Penseroso*, was the name given by the Neoplatonists to the Egyptian god Thoth who was regarded as identical with the Grecian Hermes and the author of mystical doctrines. Some works have survived. Much attention was paid to Hermes Trismegistos in late medieval and Renaissance literature and Marsilio Ficino (1433–99), the Italian philosopher and scholar, translated the so-called Hermetic corpus. Hermeticism also refers to poetry which uses occult symbolism and the term has been used particularly of the French symbolist poets. Hermeticism in this connection was defined and analysed in 1936 by Francesco Flora in *La poesia ermetica*. In this work Flora takes Baudelaire, Mallarmé, Valéry and Ungaretti as the main Hermetic poets. The Italian poet Arturo Onofri (1885–1928) is usually accepted as the principal influence in Italian poetry. Loosely, the term denotes obscure, difficult poetry in which the language and imagery are subjective and in which the 'music' and the suggestive power of the words are of as great an importance (if not greater) as the sense. *See also* PURE POETRY; SYMBOL AND SYMBOLISM.

hero and heroine The principal male and female characters in a work of literature. In criticism the terms carry no connotations of virtuousness or honour. An evil man or a wicked woman might be the central characters, like Macbeth and Lady Macbeth.

heroic couplet It comprises rhymed decasyllables, nearly always in iambic pentameters rhymed in pairs: one of the commonest metrical forms in English poetry but of uncertain origin. It is generally thought that it developed with Chaucer, possibly because he was familiar with the OF decasyllabic rhymed couplets. However, it is just as possible that as the old alliterative meters were adapted and modified so the rhyming couplet emerged. But there can be no doubt that Chaucer was the first poet to make extensive and successful use of this verse form. The 15th c. poets used the couplet occasionally but it is not until the 16th and 17th c. that it becomes firmly established. Then one can see poets gradually exploiting its possibilities and gaining a mastery of it. Of the many poets who used it at some time or another the most memorable are Spenser, Shakespeare, Ben Jonson, Hall, Drayton, Fletcher, Beaumont, Donne, Waller, Denham and Oldham.

Thereafter Dryden, and then Pope, made it their own. One might say that Dryden was the farrier and artificer who wrought it into shape; and that Pope was the silversmith who, with elegance, wit and subtlety, polished and refined it to near perfection. The following quotations suggest some of the differences. The first is taken from the beginning of Dryden's *Mac Flecknoe*:

All humane things are subject to decay,
And, when Fate summons, Monarchs must obey:
This Flecknoe found, who, like Augustus, young
Was call'd to Empire and had govern'd long:
In Prose and Verse was own'd, without dispute
Through all the realms of Non-sense, absolute.
This aged Prince now flourishing in Peace,
And blest with issue of a large increase,
Worn out with business, did at length debate
To settle the Succession of the State;
And pond'ring which of all his Sons was fit
To Reign, and wage immortal War with Wit,
Cry'd, 'tis resolv'd; for Nature pleads that He
Should onely rule, who most resembles me:
Shadwell alone my perfect image bears,
Mature in dullness from his tender years;
Shadwell alone of all my Sons is he
Who stands confirm'd in full stupidity.
The rest to some faint meaning make pretence,
But Shadwell never deviates into sense.

Dryden made the couplet a flexible, robust, resonant instrument for satire (as he did for his plays). For the most part his verses move with a stately and deliberate speed, a canonical tread. By contrast, Pope is more nimble, acrobatic and elusive. He is more like a spiky and chuckling magician, whose wit glitters sardonically. These lines come from *Epistle II: To a Lady: Of the Characters of Women*:

> Narcissa's nature, tolerably mild,
> To make a wash, would hardly stew a child;
> Has ev'n been prov'd to grant a Lover's pray'r,
> And paid a Tradesman once to make him stare,
> Gave alms at Easter, in a Christian trim,
> And made a Widow happy, for a whim.
> Why then declare Good-nature is her scorn,
> When 'tis by that alone she can be born?
> Why pique all mortals, yet affect a name?
> A fool to Pleasure, and a slave to Fame:
> Now deep in Taylor and the Book of Martyrs,
> Now drinking citron with his Grace and Chartres.
> Now Conscience chills her, and now Passion burns;
> And Atheism and Religion take their turns;

Throughout the 18th c. the heroic couplet was the most favoured verse form, and some of the best verse was written in it, especially by Johnson, Goldsmith, Crabbe and Cowper. In the 19th c. it was used much less; nevertheless, Byron, Keats, Shelley, Browning, Swinburne and William Morris all made use of it. In the 20th c. the heroic couplet is rare, but mention should be made of Roy Campbell's *Georgiad* – a satire in the Augustan manner; and Nabokov's dazzling parody in his anti-novel (*q.v.*), *Pale Fire*. *See also* RIDING RHYME.

heroic drama A name given to a form of tragedy (*q.v.*) which had some vogue at the beginning of the Restoration period (*q.v.*). It was drama in the epic mode – grand, rhetorical and declamatory; at its worst, bombastic. Its themes were love and honour and it was considerably influenced by French classical drama, especially by the work of Corneille. It was staged in a spectacular and operatic fashion, and in it one can detect the influences of opera, which at this time was establishing itself. The two main early works were by Sir William Davenant who was virtually the pioneer of English opera. His *The Siege of Rhodes* (1656) and *The Spaniards in Peru* (1658) helped to establish heroic drama. The main dramas thereafter were Robert Howard's *The Indian Queen* (1665), Dryden's *The Indian Emperor* (1665), *The Conquest of Granada* (1669–70) and *Aureng-Zebe* (1675). Dryden was the best of the heroic dramatists. This kind of tragedy was satirized and burlesqued by Buckingham in *The Rehearsal* (1672), and much later again by Sheridan in *The Critic* (1779). *See also* BURLESQUE.

heroic quatrain A four-line stanza rhyming either abab, or aabb.

heroic verse The meter (*q.v.*) used for epic poetry. For the Classical writers it was the dactylic hexameter (*q.v.*). In England the unrhymed pentameter (*q.v.*) line was commonly used, as in *Paradise Lost*, or the heroic couplet (*q.v.*). The French epic writers normally used the alexandrine (*q.v.*), and the Italians the hendecasyllabic line (*q.v.*). *See also* EPIC SIMILE; HEROIC QUATRAIN.

Heroldsdichtung (G 'herald poetry') A form of 'heraldic' poetry which originated in the 13th c. with Konrad von Würzburg. It comprises descriptions of coats of arms, shields, weapons and so forth, and these descriptions are sometimes combined with a eulogy of a dead or living person (e.g. a knight).

heteroglossia (Gk *hetero* 'other, different' + *glossa*, *glotta*, 'tongue') A term coined by Mikhail Bakhtin (1895–1975) – the Russian is *raznorecie* – to describe the variety and diversity of languages used in epic and in the novel (*qq.v.*). He distinguished between the language used to represent the attitudes and opinions of the author and that used by individual characters in fiction and epic. *See also* DIALOGIC/MONOLOGIC.

heteronym (Gk 'other name') A term invented by the Portuguese poet Fernando Pessoa (1888–1935) to denote a kind of creative *alter ego*: a separate character and personality who produced poetry and prose. He invented three main personalities, namely Alberto Caeiro, Ricardo Reis and Álvaro de Campos, on whom he bestowed lives and histories of their own. In effect one may conclude that they represented different facets of his own many-sided personality. For him they had a *real* existence; they were not pseudonyms (*q.v.*). In a letter to Adolfo Casais Monteiro (Jan. 13th, 1935) he describes in detail how they came to exist and how they tended to take over in the creative process. *See also* DAMONISCH; INSPIRATION; MUSE; STORM OF ASSOCIATION.

hexameter (Gk 'of six feet') A metrical line of six feet. In Greek and Latin verse it is often dactylic, especially in epic (*q.v.*). Often the first four feet were spondees (*q.v.*), the fifth a dactyl (*q.v.*) and the last a spondee. It is not a form that has much suited English poets, though there have been many experiments with it especially in the 19th c. by Southey, Kingsley, Coleridge, Longfellow, Clough,

Tennyson and Swinburne. But it has never proved a very wieldy line. The occasional hexameter or alexandrine (*q.v.*) has often been used for a particular effect as in *The Faerie Queene*. Michael Drayton in *Poly-Olbion* (*c.* 1610) was one of the first poets to write at length in iambic hexameters:

> When Phoebus lifts his head out of the winter's wave,
> No sooner doth the earth her flowery bosom brave,
> At such time as the year brings on the pleasant spring,
> But hunts-up to the morn the feathered sylvans sing:
> And in the lower grove, as on the rising knoll,
> Upon the highest spray of every mounting pole,
> Those quiresters are perched with many a speckled breast.

The basic foot here is the iamb (*q.v.*).

hexastich (Gk 'six lines') A stanza of six lines. A very common stanza form. *See* SESTET; SESTINA; SEXAIN; SONNET.

hiatus Either a gap in a sentence so that the sense is not completed, or a break between two vowels coming together where there is no intervening consonant. The indefinite article takes an 'n' – as in 'an answer'.

High Comedy A term introduced by George Meredith in *The Idea of Comedy* (1877). By it he meant a form of comedy of manners (*q.v.*) marked by grace, wit and elegance; an urbane form whose appeal was primarily to the intellect. Such creations as Shakespeare's *Much Ado About Nothing*, Molière's *Tartuffe*, Congreve's *Way of the World*, Wilde's *A Woman of No Importance* and Shaw's *Pygmalion* might all be put into this category. At the other end of the scale we have Low Comedy (*q.v.*). The term Middle Comedy (*q.v.*) has a more specialized meaning. The term High Comedy can be applied to both poems and novels: Pope's *The Rape of the Lock*, for instance, in verse. Among novels we might mention Pierre de Laclos's *Les Liaisons dangereuses*; Jane Austen's *Pride and Prejudice*; Thomas Mann's *Der Zauberberg*; and Aldous Huxley's *Crome Yellow*. Not to mention works by George Meredith, Henry James and Evelyn Waugh. *See* COMEDY.

higher criticism In biblical studies higher criticism is concerned with the date and composition of the Scriptures, their authorship, their inter-relationship and their cultural and historical backgrounds.

This critical technique has its roots in the University of Göttingen late in the 18th c. During the 19th c. it was extended far beyond biblical studies and adopted as a discipline.

hilarody A form of ancient Greek mime (*q.v.*) which burlesqued tragedy. *See* BURLESQUE; MAGODY; SATYR PLAY.

Hildebrandston A variant of the *Nibelungenstrophe* (*q.v.*) stanza form in which the rhyme may occur before each caesura (*q.v.*) and not only at the end of the line; thus a form of internal rhyme (*q.v.*). The name derives from its use in *Jüngeres Hildebrandslied* (13th c.).

histoire du livre *See* HISTORY OF THE BOOK.

historical novel A form of fictional narrative which reconstructs history and re-creates it imaginatively. Both historical and fictional characters may appear. Though writing fiction, the good historical novelist researches his or her chosen period thoroughly and strives for verisimilitude (*q.v.*). In Britain this genre appears to have developed from Mme de La Fayette's *Princesse de Clèves* (1678) and then via the Gothic novel (*q.v.*). Much Gothic fiction was set in the Middle Ages. Maria Edgeworth's *Castle Rackrent* (1800), usually taken to be the first example of a regional novel (*q.v.*) in English, is the first fully fledged historical novel. She followed this with *Adelaide* in 1806. Jane Porter published *The Scottish Chiefs* (1810) and *The Pastor's Fireside* (1815). In 1814 Sir Walter Scott published *Waverley*, the first of his many novels. Scott remains the supreme example of the historical novelist in English literature. As a result of his massive contribution to the genre its popularity spread during the 19th c. Many well-known writers (and many now little known) produced them. For example, there were: Thackeray's *Vanity Fair* (1847–8), Charles Kingsley's *Hypatia* (1853), *Westward Ho!* (1855) and *Hereward the Wake* (1866); Charles Reade's *The Cloister and the Hearth* (1861) and *Griffith Gaunt* (1866); Arthur Conan Doyle's *Micah Clarke* (1889), *The White Company* (1891), *The Exploits of Brigadier Gerard* (1896) and *Rodney Stone* (1896); Stanley Weyman's *A Gentleman of France* (1893), *The Red Cockade* (1895), *Under the Red Robe* (1896), *Count Hannibal* (1901) and *Chippinge* (1906); Maurice Hewlett's *The Forest Lovers* (1898) and *The Queen's Quair* (1904). In 1905 Baroness Orczy published *The Scarlet Pimpernel* (which had sequels); plus, later, many others. Charles Dickens, Bulwer Lytton, George Eliot and Thomas Hardy also wrote historical novels.

In the 20th c. this kind of fiction has not been so popular; nevertheless, there have been a number of distinguished practitioners. For example: Robert Graves, author of *I, Claudius* (1934) and several others; Georgette Heyer, who wrote a great many historical romances set in the Regency period, such as *Devil's Cub* (1934), *Regency Buck* (1935), *Faro's Daughter* (1941); Naomi Mitchison, author of *The Corn King and the Spring Queen* (1931) and *The Blood of the Martyrs* (1939); Mary Renault, author of *The Last of the Wine* (1956), *The King Must Die* (1958), *The Bull from the Sea* (1962) and *Funeral Games* (1981); T. H. White, who explored the possibilities of Arthurian legend in *The Once and Future King* (1958); William Golding, author of *The Inheritors* (1955), *The Spire* (1964), and the trilogy (*q.v.*) *Rites of Passage* (1980), *Close Quarters* (1987) and *Fire Down Below* (1989); and J. G. Farrell, who wrote the outstanding novel *The Siege of Krishnapur* (1973).

Other historical novelists of note have been Charlotte Yonge, Zoë Oldenburg, Carola Oman, Janet Lewis, Mary Stewart and Alfred Duggan. Among European historical novelists Balzac, Stendhal, Thomas Mann and Ivo Andrić have been pre-eminent. Tolstoy's *War and Peace* is the greatest of the Russian historical novels. *See* NOVEL.

historical rhyme A rhyme which was acceptable and good when composed but is no longer so because of a change in pronunciation. A well-known instance occurs in Pope's *Essay on Criticism*:

> Good nature and good sense must ever join;
> To err is human, to forgive, Divine.

In Pope's day *join* was pronounced *jine*.

history of the book The study of the book as a subject first developed in France; hence *histoire du livre*. It is especially in the province of bibliographers, historians (social historians in particular, and those devoted to cultural movements and the history of ideas) and librarians. All aspects of the book come within their range: manuscripts, printing, binding, libraries and their organization, information retrieval. They are also concerned with censorship, copyright (*qq.v.*), the role of the book in social life, and catalogues in public and private libraries. Research includes the investigation of what books were read by different people at different times. In this field marginalia and annotation (*qq.v.*) are of special interest. *See also* BIBLIO-; BIBLIOGRAPHY; CATALOGUE RAISONNE.

history play *See* CHRONICLE PLAY.

Hochromantik *See* ROMANTICISM.

höfische Dichtung (G 'courtly poetry') There were two main kinds: (a) lyric and epic (*qq.v.*); (b) poetry of laudation and entertainment. The lyric and epic belong roughly to the period 1150–1250 (the *Blütezeit* or 'blossom period'). The poems were composed by knights and expressed the ideals and values of knightly and courtly life and manners. They were performed in courts by song, chant or declamation. The laudatory poems were composed by court poets (professionals) and designed to praise and flatter princes and nobles. *See also* MINNESINGER; SPRUCH.

höfisches Epos (G 'courtly epic') A type of MHG courtly poem of epic proportions which was popular in German courts in the 12th and 13th c. They were intended as entertainment and extolled knightly and chivalric ideals and virtues. Many derived from French sources. Three of the most notable poets were: Hartmann von Aue (*c.* 1160–*c.* 1210), Wolfram von Eschenbach (*c.* 1170–*c.* 1220) and Gottfried von Strassburg (fl. 12th c.–early 13th c.).

hokku *See* HAIKU.

holograph (Gk 'entire writing') A manuscript or letter written entirely by the person in whose name it appears.

holophrasis (Gk 'entire phrase') The use of one word to express a number of ideas.

holorhyme (Gk 'whole rhyme') An ingenious form of versification in which whole lines have the same sound but different meanings, as in Victor Hugo's couplet:

> O! fragiles Hébreux! Allez, Rébecca, tombe!
> Offre à Gilles zèbres, oeufs; à l'Erèbe, hécatombe!

More ingenious and elaborate are the following lines, akin to the holorhyme:

Freine ce romance qu'un trime haine, laine demi yeux hier ce.
Ail comme tout béret six ares note tout près cime
De Yves; elle dattes mène d'où livres safre; te sème
De gourdes, hisse oeuf tines tertre vite, d'air Beaune ce.

When these lines are pronounced aloud *slowly* one recognizes the beginning of a well-known speech:

Friends, Romans, countrymen, lend me your ears;
I come to bury Caesar, not to praise him.
The evil that men do lives after them,
The good is often interred with their bones.
(*Julius Caesar*, III, ii)

Forty of these sleights of tongue have been devised by John Hulme to make up a book which is a piece of clever and inspired whimsy titled *Guillaume Chequespierre and the Oise Salon* (1985), with critical apparatus of notes, glossary and bibliography (*q.v.*). There are other collections: *Mots d'heures: gousses, rames*; *N'heures souris rames*; and *Mörder Guss Reims*. *See* NONSENSE.

homeoteleuton (Gk 'similarity of endings') A term first used by Aristotle in *Rhetoric*. It has two basic meanings: (a) a figure consisting of a series of words with the same or similar endings; (b) the occurrence of similar endings in two or more adjacent words, clauses or lines of writing. *See also* RHYME.

Homeric epithet Homer joined adjectives and nouns to make compound adjectives known as 'Homeric epithets' when applied to stock nouns. Two famous examples are 'wine-dark sea' and 'rosy-fingered dawn', but there are a great many in the *Iliad* and the *Odyssey* and they become an important feature of poetry in the oral tradition (*q.v.*). Examples from the *Iliad* are: 'Hector with glancing helm', 'swift-footed Achilles', 'well-greaved Achaeans', 'cloud-gathering Zeus', 'white-armed Hera', 'bronze-clad Achaeans', 'god-like Paris', and 'loud-roaring sea'. Examples from the *Odyssey* are: 'god-like Odysseus', 'much-enduring noble Odysseus', 'Odysseus of many counsels', 'bright-eyed Athene', 'Menelaos dear to Ares', 'sharp sword', 'broad heavens', 'splendid armour', and 'well-built hall'. *See also* INCREMENTAL REPETITION; KENNING; PERIPHRASIS; POETIC DICTION.

Homeric simile *See* EPIC SIMILE.

homily (Gk 'discourse') Either a sermon (*q.v.*) delivered to an assembled congregation, or a written work of an admonitory kind edifying the reader morally. Two well-known books of *Homilies* were published in 1547 and 1563 and appointed by the Church of England to be read at Divine Service.

The *Blickling Homilies* (*c.* 970) and the *Vercelli Homilies* (*c.* 1000), collections of nineteen and twenty-three pieces respectively, are valuable OE prose texts, whereas the *Lambeth Homilies* (*c.* 1200) are important in ME.

homograph (Gk 'same writing') A word written in the same way as another, but having a different pronunciation and meaning, e.g. *row/row; tear/tear; lead/lead.*

homonym (Gk 'same name') A word having the same sound and spelling as another, but a different origin and meaning, e.g. *rest* 'repose'/*rest* 'remainder'; *bay* 'gulf'/*bay* 'laurel'.

homophone (Gk 'same sound') A word which is pronounced the same as another but has a different spelling and meaning, e.g.: foul/fowl; wood/would; pearl/purl.

homostrophic A term used in prosody (*q.v.*) to denote a single repeated stanza form. As in some of Horace's odes. Other examples are Marvell's *An Horatian Ode upon Cromwell's Return from Ireland* (1650) and Keats's ode *To Autumn* (1820).

Horatian ode So called after the Roman poet Horace who perfected the form. Each stanza has the same metrical form and pattern. *See* ODE.

horismus (Gk 'marking out by boundaries') A short definition of the attributes of a subject.

horizon of expectations A term (the German is *Erwartungshorizont*) devised by Hans Robert Jauss to denote the criteria which readers use to judge literary texts in any given period. It is a crucial aspect of Jauss's aesthetics of reception, and the term designates the shared set of assumptions which can be attributed to any given generation of readers. The criteria help constitute readers' judgements of, say, a poem (e.g. pastoral or elegy, *qq.v.*) in a trans-subjective way. Horizons of expectation change. The poetry of one age is judged, valued and interpreted by its contemporaries, but the views of that age do not necessarily establish the meaning and value of the poetry definitively. Neither meaning nor value is permanently fixed, because the horizon of expectations of each generation will change. As Jauss puts it: 'A literary work is not an object which stands by itself and which offers the same face to each reader in each period. It is not a monument which reveals its timeless essence in a monologue'. Each age reinterprets poetry (and literature in general) in the light of its own knowledge and experience, its own cultural environment. Literary value is measured according to 'aesthetic distance' (*q.v.*), the degree to which a work departs from the 'horizon of expectations' of its first readers.

Jauss's essay *Literary History as a Challenge to Literary Theory* (1967) attempts to provide a theory of literature based on a socio-historical context and a solution to the problem of how texts are evaluated. In *Reading and Interpretation* (an essay published in *Modern Literary Theory*, 1982, ed. by Jefferson and Robey) Ian Maclean comments helpfully on the concept: 'The "horizon of expectations" . . . is detectable through the textual strategies (genre, literary allusion, the nature of fiction and of poetical language) which confirm, modify, subvert or ironize the expectations of readers'. 'Aesthetic distance' becomes a measure of literary value, 'creating a spectrum on one end of which lies "culinary" (totally consumable) reading, and, on the other, works which have a radical effect on their readers'. *See* HERMENEUTICS; READER-RESPONSE THEORY; RECEPTION THEORY.

hornbook A sheet of paper, bearing the alphabet, combinations of consonants and vowels, the Lord's Prayer and the Roman numerals, which was mounted on a piece of wood resembling a small paddle or old-fashioned butter-patter and then covered with transparent horn. It was used for teaching children to read up until the 18th c., when it was replaced by the primer. In 1609 Dekker published *The Gull's Hornbook*, which was a kind of spoof book of manners, or courtesy book (*q.v.*), for the fops and gallants of the time. *See also* GROBIANISM.

horror story A fictional narrative (usually in prose) of variable length (but tending to be between, say, 2,000 words and 100,000 or more) which shocks or even frightens the reader, and/or perhaps induces a feeling of repulsion or loathing. The word *horror* derives from Latin *horrere* 'to make the hair stand on end, tremble, shudder'. It is not clear when the term 'horror story' first came into use. The *NED* cites a number of uses of 'horror' in the tradition of the sublime (*q.v.*) – notably from Hazlitt's observations on dramatic literature. Like the novel, it is one of the Gladstone bags of literature. Apart from being about murder, suicide, torture, fear and madness, horror stories are also concerned with ghosts, vampires, *doppelgängers*, succubae, incubi, poltergeists, demonic pacts, diabolic possession and exorcism, witchcraft, spiritualism, voodoo, lycanthropy and the macabre, plus such occult or quasi-occult practices as telekinesis and hylomancy. Some horror stories are serio-comic or comic-grotesque, but none the less alarming or frightening for that.

From late in the 18th c. until the present day – in short, for some two hundred years – the horror story (which is perhaps a mode rather than an identifiable genre) in its many and various forms has been a diachronic feature of British and American literature and is of considerable importance in literary history, especially in the evolution of the short story (*q.v.*). It is also important because of its connections with the Gothic novel (*q.v.*) and with a multitude of fiction associated with tales of mystery, suspense, terror and the supernatural, with the ghost story and the thriller (*qq.v.*) and with numerous stories in the 19th and 20th c. in which crime is a central theme.

In the hands of a serious and genuinely imaginative writer the horror story (of whatever length it may be) explores the limits of what people are capable of doing and experiencing. Such a writer ventures into the realms of psychological chaos, emotional wastelands, psychic trauma, abysses opened up by the imagination. He or she explores the capacity for experiencing fear, hysteria and madness, all that lies on the dark side of the mind and the near side of barbarism; what lurks on and beyond the shifting frontiers of consciousness (where some kind of precarious vigilance and control are kept by convention and taboo and by the repressive censors of feelings) and where, perhaps, there dwell ultimate horrors or concepts of horror and terror (e.g. Room 101 in *Nineteen Eighty-Four*): paradigms, images and figures of suffering and chaos, and thus of various kinds of hell – taking 'hell' to be a more or less universal symbol of an extreme condition: for example, intense grief, an overwhelming feeling of irredeemable loss, acute fear, irrational foreboding or physical pain.

The horror story (like the 'literature of terror' which, through the Gothic novel, was so popular at the end of the 18th and the beginning of the 19th c. and which has had an immeasurable long-term influence in the 20th c.) is part of a long process by which people have tried to come to terms with and find adequate descriptions and symbols for deeply rooted, primitive and powerful forces, energies and fears which are related to death, afterlife, punishment, darkness, evil, violence and destruction.

Writers have long been aware of the magnetic attraction of the horrific and have seen how to exploit or appeal to particular inclinations and appetites. In classical literature Seneca (*c.* 4 BC–AD 65) is an obvious example. Like the Jacobean practitioners of revenge tragedy (*q.v.*), he was profoundly interested in extremes of human suffering. Horror is piled on horror in the most sensational fashion. In classical epic (*q.v.*) numerous scenes are concerned with violence and the horrific (e.g. Virgil's *Aeneid* and Lucan's *Pharsalia*). Statius, Silicus Italicus and Valerius Flaccus made much of gruesome episodes. In his *Metamorphoses* Ovid (43 BC–AD 18) has some hideous inset horror stories. In Lucian's *Philopseudes* (2nd. c. AD) and in Petronius's *Satyricon* (1st c. AD) there are comic-grotesque anecdotes which contain components of the fully developed thing. Apuleius (fl. 2nd c. AD, in *The Golden Ass*, displays a penchant for the supernatural and grotesque and combines the comical/absurd with the horrific; and he has a knack for the tall story (*q.v.*) which takes some beating.

The Byzantine civilization produced no horror literature, but in the literature of Europe in the Middle Ages there are plenty of passages of horror and violence comparable with those to be found in *Gilgamesh* and in the poems of Homer, Virgil and Lucan. For example, the Icelandic sagas (*q.v.*) and the Old Norse Eddas (*q.v.*); not to mention *Beowulf*, where there are some nasty moments – to put it mildly. One of the best of the medieval horror stories is Chaucer's *Pardoner's Tale*.

It was the poets and artists of the late medieval period who figured out and expressed some of the innermost fears and some of the ultimate horrors (real and imaginary) of human consciousness. Fear created horrors enough and the eschatological order was never far from people's minds. Poets dwelt on and amplified the *ubi sunt* (*q.v.*) motif and artists depicted the spectre of death (hence the cult of the *danse macabre*, *q.v.*) in paint, through sculpture and by means of the woodcut. The most potent and frightening image of all was that of hell: the abode of eternal loss, pain and damnation. There were numerous 'visions' of hell in literature, the most famous being the 12th c. *Vision of Tundale* and Dante's *Inferno* (early 14th c.). Countless painters also depicted hell. It was the ultimate horror.

Gradually, imperceptibly, during the 16th c. hell was 'moved' from its traditional site in the centre of the earth. It came to be located in the mind; it was a part of a state of consciousness. This was the beginning of the growth of the idea of a subjective, inner hell, a psychological hell; a personal and individual source of horror and terror, such as the chaos of a disturbed and tormented mind, the pandaemonium (a word invented by Milton) of psychopathic conditions, rather than the abode of *lux atra* and everlasting pain with its definite location in a measurable cosmological system.

Such a concept is suggested, with momentous simplicity, by Mephistophilis in Marlowe's *Dr Faustus* (*c.* 1588) when, in the guise of a Friar, he says.:

> Hell hath no limits, nor is circumscrib'd
> In one self place, for where we are is hell,
> And where hell is, must we ever be.

This concept was to be echoed by many writers, including, among others, Sir Walter Ralegh (in *History of the World*), Sir Thomas Browne (in *Religio Medici*) and Milton (in *Paradise Lost*).

The horror 'stories' of the late 16th and early 17th c. (like the ghost 'stories') are provided for us by playwrights. The Elizabethan and Jacobean tragedians were deeply interested in evil, crime, murder, suicide and violence. They were also very interested in states of extreme suffering: pain, fear and madness. They found new modes, new metaphors and images, for presenting the horrific and in doing so they created simulacra of hell. One might cite perhaps a thousand or more instances from plays in the period *c.* 1580 to *c.* 1642 in which hell is an all-purpose, variable and diachronic image of horror whether as a place of punishment or as a state of mind and spirit. Horrific action on stage was commonplace in the tragedy (*q.v.*) and revenge tragedy of the period. That satiety which Macbeth claimed to have experienced when he said:

> I have supp'd full with horrors;
> Direness, familiar to my slaughterous thoughts,
> Cannot once start me . . .

was representative of it.

From the middle of the 17th c. horror and violence on stage were rare and were not to be seen again regularly until towards the end of the 18th c. when Gothic novels were dramatized, and during the vogue for melodrama (*q.v.*) in the 19th c. By then a new form of horror story was well established.

The creative and intellectual atmosphere of the Augustan Age (*q.v.*) was not one in which the horror story was likely to flourish, but by the mid-1740s there had developed a discernible change or 'shift' in sensibility (*q.v.*). The advent of this was signalled by, among other events, the works of what came to be known as the graveyard school of poetry (*q.v.*): verse which was preoccupied with death and suffering, with the necropolitan, with corpses and charnel houses. The *danse macabre* would have appealed to the graveyard poets.

Such writings had an influence on the Gothic novel which was shortly to appear and with it the ghost and the horror story in fiction. It also had an influence on German writers of 'terror fiction' and what was called the *Schauerroman* (*q.v.*) at the turn of the 18th c.

During the 18th c. (as during the 19th), in orthodox doctrine taught by various 'churches' and sects, hell remained a place of eternal fire and punishment and the abode of the Devil. For the most part writers of the Romantic period and thereafter did not re-create it as a visitable place (an obvious exception is Beckford's *Vathek*, 1786). However, artists were drawn to 'illustrate' earlier conceptions of hell. William Blake did 102 engravings for Dante's *Inferno*. John ('Mad') Martin illustrated *Paradise Lost* and Gustave Doré applied himself to Dante and Milton. The *actual* hells of the 18th and 19th c. were the gaols, the madhouses, the slums and bedlams and those lanes and alleys where vice, squalor, depravity and unspeakable misery created a social and moral chaos: terrestrial counterparts to the horrors of Dante's Circles. The recorder of those scenes was William Hogarth. Very nearly contemporaneously Piranesi was creating the extraordinary and terrifying nightmare world of his 'Prisons' (*Carceri d'Invenzione*), the grandiose visual equivalent images of Kafka's castles and penal colonies, of panoptic gaols, of labour and concentration camps and of all those megalomaniac punitive establishments designed by men to break and destroy men. They are also the visual equivalents of a metaphysical and mental hell.

Piranesi's vision prefigures the horrors of the psychological and subjective 'hell' and the state of metaphysical anguish which many writers were to explore in the 19th and 20th c. For example, there are the novels and short stories of Dostoievski, Gogol and Kafka, the despairing lyrics of Leopardi, Lautréamont's extraordinary lyrical fragments in prose in *Les Chants de Maldoror* (1868), Rimbaud's equally extraordinary 'fragments' in *Une saison en enfer*

(1873), James Thomson's terrifying poem *The City of Dreadful Night* (1874) – and so on. One might cite many instances.

Towards the end of the 18th c. the Devil received a new 'lease of life' as a figure and personality, and was to become a dominant figure in 19th c. literature, more particularly in tales of horror. It is in no way surprising that the Faust theme (*q.v.*) also became of great interest again. This in turn inspired tales of terror and comic-grotesque horror stories.

Closely associated with the recrudescence of the Devil as a 'character' is that major theme of the Romantic period, the divisibility of the human identity; the ancient duality; the good and the bad man; the two souls co-existent; the divided self. This came into literature (or returned to literature, since it had been inherent in the Morality Plays and in allegory, *qq.v.*) via German folklore. However it arrived or returned, the *doppelgänger* ('double-goer, double-walker') is German in origin and was a theme of persistent interest through the 19th c., a source of some of the most powerful psychological horror stories, in which mental and spiritual states are examined and exposed and in which fear, madness, cruelty and evil predominate.

Chamisso was one of the first to explore the possibilities in depth in his story *Peter Schlemihl* (1814). E. T. A. Hoffmann treated it in *Die Elixiere des Teufels* (1815–16) and in *Das Fräulein von Scuderi* (1819). More terrifying was James Hogg's *The Private Memoirs and Confessions of a Justified Sinner* (1824). Edgar Allan Poe (who was considerably influenced by Hoffmann) wrought variations on the 'double' theme in *William Wilson* (1839) and *A Tale of the Ragged Mountains* (1844). Dostoievski's *The Double* (1846) and Theodor Storm's *Ein Doppelgänger* (1887) display other possibilities. In English literature easily the most original and most famous *doppelgänger* stories are Stevenson's *Dr Jekyll and Mr Hyde* (1886) – Jekyll is pronounced *jeekle* to rhyme with *treacle* – Oscar Wilde's *The Picture of Dorian Gray* (1891) and Conrad's *The Shadow Line* (1917).

Vampirism also became of interest during the Romantic period and has inspired numerous horror stories ever since (not to mention films). Vampires flourish from China to Peru and there are numerous books on them – including guidebooks (*q.v.*). The more scientific scholars adopt a taxonomic method in classifying them. John Polidori (for a while secretary and companion to Byron) was one of the first to write a fictional or semi-fictional vampire story in the 19th c. It was called *The Vampyre* and published in 1818, the same year as Mary Shelley's *Frankenstein.* There is little about bloodsucking in it; it is mostly concerned with sex; as are many vampire stories. However, the protagonist (*q.v.*), Lord Ruthven, was to become the model for the English vampire in fiction.

By this stage the vampire was becoming a prominent symbol among Romantic writers. For example: Geraldine in Coleridge's *Christabel* (1797); the spectral bloodsucker in Byron's *The Giaour* (1813); the figure of Misery in Shelley's *Invocation to Misery* (1818); and Keats's beautiful and merciless dame who sucked the blood from the knight.

In due course the vampire became a standby for writers of horror stories and also for playwrights who wrote melodrama. There was already a flourishing 'horror drama' which had begun with dramatizations of Gothic novels long before. An early instance was *Le Comte de Comminges* (1764) by François Baculard D'Arnaud; an early manifestation of the Theatre of Cruelty (*q.v.*) with a setting in the burial crypt of a Trappist monastery. The German *Schicksalstragödie* (*q.v.*) also provided sensational dramatic horror.

In fiction early examples of the vampire tale are Charles Nodier's *Le Vampire* (1820) and Gogol's *Viy* (1835). In 1835 Poe published *Berenice*, which has implications of vampirism; being a necrophile and a thanatophile, Poe could hardly fail to be interested in this subject. In 1836 Théophile Gautier published *La Morte amoureuse*, regarded as the most famous vampire story in French literature. Sheridan Le Fanu (pronounced Léff-anew) produced one good one, namely *Camilla* (1872). Luigi Capuana's *A Vampire* (1907) was an original variation on a by then hackneyed theme. E. F. Benson, an expert in the blood-curdling, produced *Mrs Amworth*, a memorable account of a sturdy, bridge-playing blood-drinker in the erstwhile stockbroker belt. In 1897 Bram Stoker published the most famous of all vampire stories, *Dracula* – a tale of horror which has produced numerous imitations, and variations. For instance, F. G. Loring's *The Tomb of Sarah* (*c.* 1930), and the inset vampire stories in Durrell's *Balthazar* (1958) and in Simon Raven's *Doctors Wear Scarlet* (1960).

There are some horror stories in which a 'creature' (akin, say, to a lamia or a succuba) haunts characters and feeds off them emotionally and psychologically. A kind of ghost parasite. Maupassant's *Le Horla* (1887) is a notable example. In English literature outstanding instances are *How Love Came to Professor Guildea* (1900) by Robert Hichens and *The Beckoning Fair One* (1911) by Oliver Onions. All three are tales of horror. The victims are driven to insanity and death. D. K. Broster's *Couching at the Door* (1933), a most sinister tale, exploits the idea of a 'familiar' which grows in size.

The werewolf theme became of interest early in the 19th c. and has been a fruitful source of horror stories. Many languages have a word for such a creature (the OE is *werewulf*), and belief in them is ancient. The fairy tale *Beauty and the Beast* (the best known version appears in the French *contes* of Mme de Villeneuve, 1744; and there is a similar story in Straparola's *Piacevoli Notti*, 1550) is clearly related to the werewolf theme. One of the famous stories is Marryat's *The White Wolf of the Hartz Mountains* (1839). G. W. M. Reynolds used the ideas in *Wagner, the Wehr-Wolf* (1846–7). Later, R. L. Stevenson, Kipling and Algernon Blackwood tried out its possibilities with success, Stevenson with *Olalla* (1887), Kipling with *The Mark of the Beast* (1887) and Blackwood with *The Camp of the Dog* (1908). Later variations are to be found in Ambrose Bierce's *The Eyes of the Panther* and C. H. B. Kitchin's *The Beauty and the Beast.* Two other well-known stories are Garnett's *Lady into Fox* (1922) and Peter Fleming's *The Kill* (1942). Perhaps the best and most horrible of all the lycanthropic tales is Geoffrey Household's *Taboo* (*c.* 1939).

The ghost and, in general terms, the preternatural agency or agent (often evil), have also been an inspiration to writers of horror stories. The advent of the ghost story at the very beginning of the 19th c. was to affect profoundly the development of the horror story. As it happens the ghost story and the horror story *as a short story* arrived more or less simultaneously. Indeed, the short story as a form was basically born as these two genres. Both derive from the Gothic novel, and from Gothic tales in general, not a few of which were in short-story form. During the 19th c. the growth of both horror and ghost story tends to coalesce and they cross-pollinate. It is not easy to establish objective criteria by which to distinguish them. A taxonomic approach soon breaks down. There are scores of supernatural 'horror' stories ('crawlers' as R. L. Stevenson called them) from the last 140 years or so which are difficult to classify. However, it might be argued that Wilkie Collins's *A Terribly Strange Bed* (1856) is a horror story, Elizabeth Gaskell's *The Old Nurse's Tale* (1852) is a ghost story, and that Sheridan Le Fanu's *Green Tea* (1869) is a combination of both. On balance it is likely that the ghost story will contain an element of horror, but there are hundreds of horror stories which have nothing to do with ghosts.

At the beginning of the 19th c. two prime creators of the ghost and the horror story – and the short story as a form – were Heinrich von Kleist (1777–1811) and E. T. A. Hoffmann (1776–1822). Eschewing the excesses and sensationalism of the Gothic mode, and using the short story and *Novelle* (*see* NOVELLA) form they between them set standards for the ghost and horror story which have seldom been equalled. The main texts are: Kleist's *Das Bettelweib von Locarno* (1810) and *Das Erdbeben in Chili* (1807); Hoffmann's *Die Elixiere des Teufels*, *Ignaz Denner* (1816), *Der Sandmann* (1816), *Das Majorat* (1817) and *Das Fräulein von Scuderi.*

In fact neither ghost nor horror story flourished subsequently in German literature, though the influence of Gothic was to prevail for some time (discernible in Fouqué and Tieck). Demonic agency and supernatural forces featured in a number of *Novellen*. Occasionally one finds a horror story. For example, Gotthelf's *Die schwarze Spinne* (1842) and Gustav Meyrink's *Der Golem* (1915), a weird and eerie tale of the Prague ghetto. More recently Hans Ewers (1871–1943) wrote some horror novels and short stories of a melodramatic and lurid kind.

In France, English Gothic novels were much read and imitated. Their influence, plus the influences of German Gothic, the *Schauerroman* and Hoffmann's tales, becomes apparent in French literature. Some of Nodier's work (e.g. *La Fée aux miettes* and *Smarra ou les Démons de la nuit*, 1821) ventures into the horror mode. The same is true of some of Balzac's stories, such as *El Verdugo*, *La Grande Bretêche* and *Melmoth reconcilié* (1835) – this last being a frightening reworking of the Wanderer theme: the sale of one's soul – on the principle of the transferable bargain – to the Devil in return for long life.

Gérard de Nerval wrote one fine comic-grotesque horror story in the shape of *La Main enchantée* (1832): the 'adventures' of a hand, newly severed from a corpse, which performs a series of blood-curdling antics. This may well have been the prototype of a number of sinister tales of the horror phylum to which a hand is central. For example, Le Fanu's *The Narrative of a Ghost of a Hand*, Maupassant's *The Hand* and *The Withered Hand*, Conan Doyle's *The Brown Hand*, Theodore Dreiser's *The Hand*, Louis Golding's *The Call of the Hand*, W. F. Harvey's *The Beast with Five Fingers*, and, of course, W. W. Jacobs's classic spine-chiller *The Monkey's Paw.*

Several of Prosper Mérimée's *nouvelles* are highly original horror stories, especially *Mateo Falcone* (1833), *La Vénus d'Ille* (1841) and *Lokis* (1873). At a lower level were the melodramatic horror stories of Petrus Borel, especially *Champavert, contes immoraux* (1833) and *Madame Putiphar* (1839). Other French writers to experiment with horror themes were Barbey d'Aurevilly, who published *Les Diaboliques* in 1874, and Villiers de l'Isle-Adam, who wrote *Contes cruels* (1883) and *Nouveaux Contes cruels* (1888). Zola, who had a morbid fear of death, wrote one fine horror story on the theme of premature burial – *La Mort d'Olivier Bécaille*. Of all the 19th c. French writers the one with the keenest insight into fear, madness, neuroses and the apprehension of evil was Maupassant. A number of his stories are horrific. Two of especially nightmarish vision were *Le Horla*, already mentioned, and *Who Knows?* (1890).

Gothic influence travelled to America (where Hoffmann's stories were soon known) and affected Isaac Mitchell and Charles Brockden Brown. Brown, in turn, was to influence Nathaniel Hawthorne and Edgar Allan Poe, whose first collection of stories, *Tales of the Grotesque and Arabesque*, appeared in 1839. Poe had already shown a gift for writing about the horrific in *The Narrative of Arthur Gordon Pym* (1838). His tales are short, intense, sensational and have the power to inspire horror and terror. He depicts extremes of fear, suffering and insanity and, through the operations of evil, gives us glimpses of hell. Among his most notable horror stories are *The Fall of the House of Usher* (1839), *The Murders in the Rue Morgue* (1841), *A Descent into the Maelstrom* (1841), *The Masque of the Red Death* (1842), *The Pit and the Pendulum*, *The Black Cat* and *The Tell-Tale Heart* (all 1843), *The Case of M. Valdemar* (1845) and *The Cask of Amontillado* (1846).

Poe's long-term influence was immeasurable (and in the case of some writers not altogether for their good), and one can detect it persisting through the 19th c.; in, for example, the French *symbolistes* (Baudelaire published translations of his tales in 1856 and 1857), in such British writers as Rossetti, Swinburne, Dowson and R. L. Stevenson, and in such Americans as Ambrose Bierce, Hart Crane and H. P. Lovecraft.

Towards the end of the 19th c. a number of British and American writers were experimenting with different modes of horror story, and this was at a time when there had been a steadily growing interest in the occult, in supernatural agencies, in psychic phenomena, in psychotherapy, in extreme psychological states and also in spiritualism. The Society for Psychical Research was founded by F. W. H. Myers in 1882, and there was an increasing interest in drugs and their effects as well as in dreams and insanity. During this period, too, the ghost story proliferated – and was to go on doing so.

A notable practitioner of the horror story in the 1890s and later was Arthur Machen. In 1895 he published *The Great God Pan* and *The Inmost Light*. In 1896 came *The Novel of the White Powder*, one of the most repulsive of horror tales. During the next forty years he became a specialist in horror and had a considerable influence on the American H. P. Lovecraft, who had a strong predilection for abominable physical horrors. Unfortunately he could not curb a tendency to lurid sensationalism which at times was absurd.

Apart from *Olalla* and *Dr Jekyll and Mr Hyde*, R. L. Stevenson wrote three famous horror stories (as well as ghost stories) in the shape of *Markheim* (1887), *The Bottle Imp* (1892–3) and *The Body Snatcher*.

Dreams, delirium, derangement of the senses, the activity of the mind under intense pressure – these were areas of much interest to Kipling, who, apart from a quantity of very good ghost stories, wrote some notable horror stories. For example: *The Strange Ride of Morrowbie Jukes* (1885), *Beyond the Pale* (1891) and *The End of the Passage* (1891).

Henry James, who created some of the best of all ghost stories, had a subtle and delicate understanding of horror. *The Turn of the Screw* (1898), though a ghost story, is so sinister and compelling in its depiction of evil that it is also, *ipso facto*, a horror story. Less well known is *The Romance of Certain Old Clothes* (1868), which has an horrific ending. In this, as in other 'supernatural' tales, he achieved his most powerful effects by stealth, hint and understatement, by 'the process of adumbration' as he put it. The reader is persuaded to create his own fear and apprehension; he is enabled to 'think the evil'.

Very different styles and techniques were used by Ambrose Bierce, an exact contemporary of James and also American. A number of his horror stories have withstood the long-distance tests of taste and time. Several collections of short stories were published, including *Tales of Soldiers and Civilians* (1891) and *Can Such Things Be?* (1893). Some of his best horror stories are *The Man and the Snake*, *A Watcher by the Dead*, *The Damned Thing*, *The Boarded Window* and *A Horseman in the Sky*.

In the same year that *Can Such Things Be?* was published, another American, Robert W. Chambers, produced a collection of original horror stories titled *The King in Yellow*. Some of them are powerful descriptions of mental breakdown. One of the best is *The Repairer of Reputations*, a study of megalomaniac insanity. Yet another American writer to produce tales of horror was F. Marion Crawford. Among his best are *The Dead Smile*, *The Upper Berth* and *The Screaming Skull* (all 1911). Like Machen and Lovecraft he had a detrimental tendency to over-write.

Many of M. R. James's ghost stories are also horror stories in their own right. The best contain a moment of deadly chill, the icy touch of fear, and he excelled at arousing physical revulsion. An almost exact contemporary (though he lived longer), Algernon Blackwood, had a very astute understanding of the psychology of fear. Among his best tales are *Ancient Sorceries and Secret Worship* (1906), *The Willows*, *The Insanity of Jones* and *The Dance of Death* (1907). A near contemporary, William Hope Hodgson, besides ghost stories, wrote such flesh-creeping tales as *The Island of Ud*, *The Whistling Room* and *The Derelict*. Conan Doyle also tried his hand at horror fiction. Collections were published in 1922, titled *Tales of Twilight and the Unseen* and *Tales of Mystery and Terror*. They included *The Brown Hand* (mentioned above), *The New Catacomb*, *The Case of Lady Sannox*, *The Brazilian Cat*, *The Terror of Blue John Gap* and *The Horror of the Heights*.

Saki (pseudonym of H. H. Munro) also wrote stories in the horror category. For example, *The Music on the Hill*, *The Open Window* (a kind of spoof ghost story), *Sredni Vashtar*, *The Easter Egg* and *Gabriel-Ernest*, a kind of werewolf tale about a naked savage boy who lives off child-flesh. E. F. Benson (a specialist in ghost stories) produced some excellent horror stories, including *The Confession of Charles Linkworth*.

Some of H. G. Wells's stories depend on suspense and a strong element of horror. For instance, the threat to man by some non-human creatures, as in *The Abyss* and *The Sea-Raiders* (both 1897), *The Valley of the Spiders* (1903) and *The Empire of the Ants* (1911). Others are concerned with aspects of hallucination and obsession: for example, *The Remarkable Case of Davidson's Eyes* and *The Flowering of the Strange Orchid* (both 1895), and *The Moth* (1895), a weird horror-cum-ghost story. *Pollock and the Porroh Man* (1897) has a voodoo theme. Both *The Lord of the Dynamos* (1895) and *The Cone* (1897) are horror stories carrying a similar idea: vengeance in the form of 'sacrifice' of a human being. *The Red Room* (1896) is a spine-chiller in the Gothic and Edgar Allan Poe tradition.

Between the world wars many well-crafted short horror stories were published (and often anthologized) by such writers as A. J. Alan, Elizabeth Bowen, D. K. Broster, A. M. Burrage, John Collier, A. E. Coppard, Lord Dunsany, L. P. Hartley, W. F. Harvey, Percival Landon, C. E. Montague, Augustus Muir, Evelyn Nesbit, John Russell, L. A. G. Strong, H. Russell Wakeford, Dennis Wheatley (a specialist in the occult), Alexander Woollcott *et al.* Hartley is often mentioned in connection with the genre. His *Night Fears and Other Stories* was published in 1924. Later (1951) another collection came out: *The Travelling Grave*, which contains *The Killing Bottle*, *Conrad and the Dragon* and *The Thought*. The title story is a particularly good example of the macabre and comic-grotesque type of tale – 'macabre' applying to not a few of his stories.

During these same years the long-term influence of the Gothic novel was clearly discernible and Gothic received another lease of life, as it were, in the horror film. In the early 1930s there was a succession of horror films now particularly associated with the directors Tod Browning and James Whale and with the acting of Boris Karloff as Dr Frankenstein's 'creature' and Bela Lugosi as Dracula. The horror film continued to proliferate up to the 1990s when it showed no sign of losing popularity.

Since the 1950s short horror stories (and what purport to be horror stories) have also proliferated. In fact, one could say they have tended to do so for most of the 20th c., and it is a mode or genre which has shown remarkable diversification. Many professional writers have turned their hand to it at least once, as they have to the ghost story. Besides those already mentioned any list would be bound to include the following (in alphabetical order): Sir Charles Birkin, Robert Bloch, Heinrich Böll, Marjorie Bowen, E. F. Bozman, Ray Bradbury, Thomas Burke, Truman Capote, Mark Channing, Sir Hugh Clifford, Richard Connell, Roald Dahl, Monica Dickens, Isak Dinesen, Guy Endore, Paul Gallico, Thomas Hardy, Dorothy K. Haynes, E. and H. Heron, Patricia Highsmith, Richard Hughes, John Jasper, Will F. Jenkins, F. Tennyson Jesse, Gerald Kersh, Vernon Lee, Daphne du Maurier, Richard Middleton, Fitz-James O'Brien, Vincent O'Sullivan, Roger Pater, V. S. Pritchett, William Sansom, W. B. Seabrook, Muriel Spark, Elizabeth Walter, Edward Lucas White, Angus Wilson and John Wyndham.

The enormous increase in science fiction (*q.v.*) since the 1950s has diversified horror fiction even more than might at first be supposed. New maps of hell have been drawn and are being drawn; new dimensions of the horrific exposed and explored; new simulacra and *exempla* created. Fear, pain, suffering, guilt and madness (what has already been touched on in miscellaneous 'hells') remain powerful and emotive elements in horror stories. In a chaotic world, which many see to be on a disaster course, through the cracks, 'the faults in reality', we and our writers catch other and vertiginous glimpses of 'chaos and old night', fissiparating images of death and destruction.

The work of some modern novelists (as well as that of the practitioners of the short horror story, in, for instance, the collection *Prime Evil*, 1988), re-creates internal and external microcosms of hell: dislocated worlds seen through dislocative visions. It might be called modern Gothic, an increasingly portmanteau term.

The fiction of J. G. Ballard is an obvious instance, particularly *The Terminal Beach* (1964) and *The Atrocity Exhibition* (1970), and some of his short stories (e.g. *The Billennium*, 1964). Other horror novelists – though perhaps not quite so well known as Ballard – are: John Hawkes (author of *The Cannibal*, 1962, and *The Blood Oranges*, 1971); Joyce Carol Oates (*A Garden of Earthly Delights*, 1967, and *Expensive People*, 1968); Thomas Pynchon (*The Crying of Lot 49*, 1966, and *Gravity's Rainbow*, 1973); and James Purdy (*Eustace Chisholm and the Works*, 1967). The grotesque Gothic fantasies of Mervyn Peake might easily be classed as horror; as might some of William Burroughs's work (especially *The Naked Lunch*, 1959), Anthony Burgess's *A Clockwork Orange* (1962) and Angela Carter's *Heroes and Villains* (1969).

Since *c.* 1970 another generation of contrivers of horror and pedlars of nightmares has come forth and a period of twenty years has seen a wide diversification in the literature of horror in which the pervasive influence of Gothic modes is easily discernible; plus, to a lesser extent, the influence of science fiction. Not a little of the horror fiction of recent times sets out to shock in ways which are sometimes crude and even somewhat obvious. The stories are often inventive, skilful, slick or efficient but not so many have much psychological depth or display a serious attempt to explain or come to terms with the subversive and complex nature of the human personality. The best tend to be concerned with the nature of evil as a force within man and about him. And some neo-horror literature is poor stuff, reminding one not of the 'worst excesses of the French Revolution' but, rather, of the lurid sensationalism of old-fashioned pulp (*q.v.*) magazines. Popular authors who should be mentioned are Clive Barker (e.g. his *Books of Blood* series), Ramsey Campbell,

Peter Straub, James Herbert, Graham Masterton, John Saul and, especially, Stephen King. The reading public's appetite for the fare of horror appears insatiable. The books of Stephen King (to name no others) sell by the million each year.

Hôtel de Bourgogne The first Paris theatre, completed in 1548. It was built by the Confraternity of the Passion and erected in the ruins of the palace of the dukes of Burgundy. It enjoyed its heyday in the 17th c. with the King's Players. In 1680 they were amalgamated into the Comédie-Française (*q.v.*), and the Italian Players (known as the Comédie-Italienne) occupied the Hôtel de Bourgogne until it became defunct in 1783.

House UnAmerican Activities Committee A committee founded to eradicate Communism and Communistic activities in the USA. It was very active between 1938 and 1968 and affected a large number of writers, including Bertolt Brecht, Clifford Odets, Lillian Hellman and Arthur Miller, as well as other artists. The committee's qualifications in matters of literature may be assessed from the fact that when Hallie Flanagan made a reference to the English dramatist Christopher Marlowe (1564–93) they wanted to know whether Marlowe was a Communist.

hovering stress or accent This occurs when it is not absolutely clear in verse whether a syllable should be stressed or not, or whether it should be half stressed. It is a very common phenomenon, as in these lines from Robert Lowell's *Man and Wife*:

> Tamed by Miltown, we lie on Mother's bed;
> the rising sun in war paint dyes us red;
> in broad day*light* her gilded bed-*posts* shine,
> abandoned, almost Dionysian.
> At last the trees are green on Marlborough Street,
> bloss*oms* on our magno*lia* ignite
> the morning with their murder*ous* five *days*' white.

Hovering stress in these lines occurs on the syllables italicized. Also known as distributed stress. *See* LEVEL STRESS; VARIABLE SYLLABLE.

howler A blatant or glaring error, as in these examples from examination papers by schoolboys: (a) 'The worm is an hermaphrodite, but it has to meet another worm before it can do anything'; (b) 'I always wanted to come to -------- school because I thought it was Wandsworth Prison, but that is not the real reason'; (c) 'born of the Virgin Mary, deceived of the Holy Ghost'. Called howlers because they are so 'loud'.

hrynhent A form of skaldic meter. It consists of an eight-line stanza and is similar to the *dróttkvætt* (*q.v.*) except that each line is lengthened by a trochee (*q.v.*). Used in court poems between the 11th and 13th c., and still in use today by Icelandic poets. *See also* SKALD.

hubris (Gk 'wanton insolence') This shortcoming or defect in the Greek tragic hero leads him to ignore the warnings of the gods and to transgress their laws and commands. Eventually hubris brings about downfall and nemesis (*q.v.*), as in the case of Creon in Sophocles's *Antigone* and Clytemnestra in Aeschylus's *Oresteia* trilogy. *See* HAMARTIA; TRAGEDY.

Hudibrastic verse So called from Samuel Butler's *Hudibras* (1663, 1674, 1678), a mock-heroic satirical poem in octosyllabic couplets. Butler's wit, exuberance and invention in this poem have made it an outstanding instance of what may be called 'low satire'. These lines from Canto I give an idea of the tone and manner (they are about the Metaphysical Sectarian):

> He was in Logick a great Critick,
> Profoundly skill'd in Analytick.
> He could distinguish, and divide
> A Hair 'twixt South and South-West side:
> On either which he would dispute,
> Confute, change hands, and still confute.
> He'd undertake to prove by force
> Of Argument, a Man's no Horse.
> He'd prove a Buzard is no Fowl,
> And that a Lord may be an Owl;
> A Calf an Alderman, a Goose a Justice,
> And Rooks Committee-men and Trustees.

huitain A stanza or strophe (*q.v.*) of eight lines, each of eight or ten syllables, normally written on three rhymes. One rhyme occurs four times, and the rhyme for the fourth and fifth lines is the same. This form was popular in France in the 15th and 16th c. Villon wrote his *lais* (*q.v.*) and many of his *ballades* (*q.v.*) in *huitains*. Marot also used this form. *See* OTTAVA RIMA.

humanism In the first place, the humanists of the Renaissance period were students of *literae humaniores* (*q.v.*); the literature of the Greek and Latin poets, dramatists, philosophers, historians and rhetoricians. At the Renaissance (*q.v.*) there was a great revival of interest in Classical literature and thought and this revival was, to some extent, at the expense of medieval scholasticism (*q.v.*). The long-term influences of this revival were immense and incalculable, and they led to an excessive devotion to Classical ideals and rules in the late 17th c. and 18th c.

Humanism, a European phenomenon, was a more worldly and thus more secular philosophy; and it was anthropocentric. It sought to dignify and ennoble man.

In its more extreme forms humanistic attitudes regarded man as the crown of creation; a point of view marvellously expressed in *Hamlet*, by Hamlet:

> . . . What a piece of work is man. How noble in reason, how infinite in faculty. In form and moving how express and admirable in action, how like an angel in apprehension, how like a god. The beauty of the world. The paragon of animals.

It would have been inconceivable that anyone in the 14th c. should have expressed such a view. Then Hamlet adds: 'And yet, to me what is this quintessence of dust?' And in that one line he summarizes another attitude or feeling, which a man in the 14th c. would have responded to instantly.

At its best, humanism helped to civilize man, to make him realize his potential powers and gifts, and to reduce the discrepancy between potentiality and attainment. It was a movement that was at once a product of and a counteraction to a certain prevalent scepticism; a way of dealing with the disequilibrium created by the conflict between belief and doubt. Humanism turned out to be a form of philosophy which concentrated on the perfection of a wordly life, rather than on the preparation for an eternal and spiritual life.

The popularity of the courtesy book (*q.v.*) in the 16th and 17th c., for instance, suggests what a radical change there had been in man's view of himself. He was increasingly regarded as a creature perfectible on earth. Hence the secular emphasis in courtesy books.

Humanistic ideas and beliefs pervade much other literature of the

Renaissance period. Ficino (1433–99); Pico della Mirandola (1463–94); Erasmus (1466–1536); Guillaume Budé (1468–1540); Sir Thomas More (1478–1535); Juan Luis Vives (1492–1540); and Montaigne (1533–92) were outstanding humanists.

humanisme A short-lived movement in poetry begun by Fernand Gregh in 1902. Its manifesto (*q.v.*) was published in *Le Figaro*. It represented a reaction against the *symboliste* poets (*see* SYMBOL AND SYMBOLISM) and against the Parnassians (*q.v.*).

humanities A term generally used in Europe and America for literature, languages, philosophy, art, history, theology, music, as opposed to the natural sciences and the social sciences. *See* HUMANISM.

humilatio *See* TAPINOSIS.

humours The term humour (it derives from Latin *humor* 'moisture'; hence *humid*) was used in the Middle Ages and during the Renaissance period – in the tradition of Hippocratic pathology and physiology – to denote the four humours of the body. These depended on the four fluids: blood, phlegm, yellow bile and black bile. The admixture or commingling of these determined a person's disposition, character, mind, morality and temperament. The humours released spirits or vapours which affected the brain, and thence a person's behaviour. According to the predominant humour a man was sanguine, phlegmatic, choleric or melancholy. Robert Burton, in his *Anatomy of Melancholy*, I, ii, 3 (1621), gives an excellent description of the qualities of the humours.

Vestigially, the theory of humours survives in such expressions as: 'ill-humoured', 'good-humoured', 'black with rage', 'in a black mood', 'yellow with jealousy', 'green with envy', 'yellow-livered', 'red with remorse', and so forth. And we still use 'sanguine' or 'melancholy' to describe certain temperaments.

The theory of humours had a considerable influence on writers when it came to the creation of characters. Dramatists devised characters based on the theory of the imbalances that occurred between the bodily fluids. Comedy of humours (*q.v.*) developed characters who were dominated by a particular mood, inclination or peculiarity. Ben Jonson is the most notable instance of a dramatist to do this – in *Every Man in His Humour* (1598); almost certainly the first play created on the theory of personality and ruling passion. This he followed with *Every Man Out of His Humour* (1599).

It may be no coincidence that at this period writers were also addressing themselves to the depiction of 'characters' in character sketches, and analysing character and temperament.

It is not until the 18th c. that we find 'humour' associated with laughter and being used in contradistinction to wit (*q.v.*). *See* APTRONYM; CHARACTER; MORALITY PLAYS.

hyangga (K 'native songs') A form of Korean folksong composed of four, eight or ten lines divided into two stanzas. The number of syllables in each line varies from four to fifteen. It is believed that only twenty-five of these poems survive, all of the 13th c.

hybrid (L 'half-breed, mongrel') A word formed from a stem or word in one language plus a suffix or prefix from another. For example: *television* (Greek and Latin); *gullible* (English and Latin).

Hydropathes, les One of three French literary societies associated with the beginnings of the symbolist movement. The others were *les Hirsutes* and *les Zutistes*. These societies had some vogue in the 1880s. Paul Bourget, Jean Moréas, François Coppée and Guy de Maupassant were among the better known *Hydropathes*. *See also* SYMBOL AND SYMBOLISM.

hymn (Gk 'song in praise of a god or hero') Early examples are the Homeric Hymn to Demeter (*c.* 7th c. BC) and the first Delphic Hymn (*c.* 138 BC). Many Latin hymns date from the Middle Ages: *Pange lingua gloriosi*; *Te lucis ante terminum*; *Iam lucis orto sidere*; *Veni Creator Spiritus*; *Veni Sancte Spiritus*; *Jesu dulcis memoria*; *Stabat Mater*; *Dies Irae*. Most English hymns of repute date from the 17th to the 19th c., their authors being: Nahum Tate, Isaac Watts, John and Charles Wesley, Reginald Heber, John Keble, and John Mason Neale. In the 20th c. there have been few contributions, though some of these are notable, e.g. Vaughan Williams's settings of Herbert.

Among English-speaking poets of note who have attempted the form one should mention George Herbert, Dryden, Milton, William Blake, William Cowper, Henry Wadsworth Longfellow, John Greenleaf Whittier, Tennyson, Christina Rossetti and Rudyard Kipling. *See also* ANTIPHON; CANTICLE; HYMNAL STANZA; LAUDA; LYRIC.

hymnal stanza A four-line stanza in iambics with a rhyming scheme of either abcb or abab. It is also known as common measure. This example is the first stanza of a hymn by Nahum Tate:

> While shepherds watched their flocks by night,
> All seated on the ground,
> The angel of the Lord came down,
> And glory shone around.

See also HALLELUJAH METER; HYMN; LONG MEASURE; SHORT MEASURE.

hypallage (Gk 'exchange') Also known as transferred epithet. A figure of speech in which the epithet is transferred from the appropriate noun to modify another to which it does not really belong. Common examples are: 'a sleepless night'; 'the condemned cell'; 'a happy day'. It is a very common poetic device, as in these lines from Part One of T. S. Eliot's *The Waste Land*:

> Winter kept us warm, covering
> Earth in forgetful snow, feeding
> A little life with dried tubers.

Clearly, the snow is not 'forgetful', but rather conceals, muffles, 'shrouds' the earth, so that for a time we forget what the earth looks like. *See also* PROLEPSIS.

hyperbaton (Gk 'overstepping') A figure of speech in which words are transposed from their usual order. A very common poetic device. Milton, for instance, uses it constantly – as in these lines from *Paradise Lost*:

> High on a throne of royal state, which far
> Outshone the wealth of Ormuz or of Ind,
> Or where the gorgeous East, with richest hand
> Showers on her kings barbaric pearl and gold,
> Satan exalted sat.

hyperbole (Gk 'overcasting') A figure of speech which contains an exaggeration for emphasis. for example, Hotspur's rant in *Henry IV*, Pt I (I, iii, 201):

> By heaven methinks it were an easy leap
> To pluck bright honour from the pale-fac'd moon,
> Or dive into the bottom of the deep,

Where fathom line could never touch the ground,
And pluck up drowned honour by the locks.

Hyperbole was very common in Tudor and Jacobean drama, and in heroic drama (*q.v.*). It is an essential part of burlesque (*q.v.*). There are plentiful examples in writers of comic fiction; in Dickens, especially.

Everyday instances, of which there are many, are: 'I haven't seen you for ages'; 'as old as the hills'; 'terrible weather', and so on. *See* ADYNATON; BOMBAST; LITOTES; TAPINOSIS.

hypercatalectic (Gk 'beyond the last metrical foot') A line is so called when it has an extra syllable at the end. Also known as hypermetrical and extrametrical. Each of these three lines from Crashaw's *Wishes to His Supposed Mistress* illustrates the point:

Sydnaean showers
Of sweet discourse, whose powers
Can crown old Winter's head with flowers.

hyperdochmiac A trochaic tripody (*q.v.*) which is catalectic (*q.v.*); that is to say, short of half a foot at the end of the line. *See* DOCHMIAC; FOOT.

hypermetric syllable *See* HYPERCATALECTIC.

hyphaeresis (Gk 'taking away from beneath') In general the term denotes the omission of a letter from a word: 'o'er' for 'over'; 'e'en' for 'even'; 'heav'n' for 'heaven'. *See* ELISION.

hypocorism The term derives from a Greek word meaning 'to play the child'. Commonly used of pet-names, like 'Mike' for Michael, and the use of familiar terms like these: Will Shakespeare, Jim Boswell, Willie Yeats, Tom Eliot. Also endearments like: 'money spider', 'cherry blossom', 'honey', 'chuck'.

hyporchema (Gk 'song accompanied by dancing') A choral song accompanied by dancers is believed to have been invented by Thaletas of Gortyn, Crete (7th c. BC). The Cretic measure was used for the verse. It was used as a hymn (*q.v.*) in honour of Apollo and was related to the paean and the dithyramb (*qq.v.*).

hypostatization A form of personification (*q.v.*) in which an abstract quality is spoken of as something human. For example: 'Truth insists I tell the story'; 'Decency compels me to admit the truth'. Not uncommon in everyday usage.

hypotaxis (Gk 'under arrangement') Subordination; syntactic relationship between dependent and independent constructions, e.g. 'He who knows will tell us' as against 'Who knows? He will tell us'. *See* PARATAXIS.

hypotyposis A figurative device by which something is represented as if it were present. For example: John of Gaunt's dying speech in *Richard II* (II, i, 31) in which he 'sees' England as a sceptred isle and creates a general word image of the country.

hypozeugma *See* ZEUGMA.

hysteron proteron (Gk 'latter former') A figurative device in which events in the temporal order are reversed. Sometimes used for comic effect, it implies 'putting the cart before the horse'. There is an agreeable example in *Much Ado About Nothing* (IV, ii, 20), when Dogberry is holding forth to the Watch, and investigating the malefactors Conrade and Borachio.

I

iamb The term derives from a Greek word of unknown etymology and denotes a metrical foot consisting of an unstressed syllable followed by a stressed syllable, thus: ◡ /. For instance: dĕféat. It was probably first used by Archilochus (7th c. BC). In antiquity the iambic rhythm was thought to be the nearest to speech and it is the commonest type of foot in all English verse because it fits the prevailing natural pattern of English words and phrases. Of these lines from Pope's *Prologue* to Addison's *Cato*, the first is in regular iambic meter and the next three have slight variations – as the ear soon informs one:

> Tŏ wáke | thĕ sóul | bŷ tén|dĕr strókes | ŏf árt,
> Tŏ ráise | thĕ géniŭs, | ănd tŏ ménd | thĕ héart;
> Tŏ máke | mánkínd | ĭn cón|sciŏus vír|tŭe bóld,
> Líve o'er | eăch scéne, | ănd bé | whăt théy | bĕhóld.

iambelegus In Classical prosody, an iamb (*q.v.*) followed by a dactylic colon (*q.v.*).

iambes, les French satiric poems in which a twelve-syllable line alternates with one of eight syllables. The *iambe* came into use with the publication of Chénier's *Iambes* (1787–90) and Barbier's *Les Iambes* (1830–31).

iambic trimeter A line of six iambic feet (each pair of feet taken as a unit or dipody), used for satirical verses by Archilochus (7th c. BC) and Simonides (6th–5th c. BC) and common in Greek and Latin drama. *See also* SYZYGY.

ibidem (L 'in the same place, in that very place') Often abbreviated to *ibid.* or *ib.*, the term indicates a reference to or quotation from 'the same place' in a book or chapter or on a page. *See* IDEM; OPERE CITATO.

icon (Gk 'image') A quasi-literary term used to describe the depiction of an object or person in figurative language, but in a particular way, as in George Herbert's *The Church-floore*:

Mark you the floore? That square & speckled stone
which looks so firm and strong,
Is *Patience*:
And th'other black and grave, wherewith each one
is checker'd all along,
Humilitie:

See also EMBLEM-BOOK.

ictus (L 'blow, stroke') The stress or accent (*qq.v.*) placed on particular syllables in a line of verse. Gerard Manley Hopkins used it quite often to show which syllables he wanted the reader to stress; sometimes syllables which would not normally be so, as in these lines from *Spelt from Sibyl's Leaves*:

For earth | her being has unbound; her
dapple is at an end, as-
tray or aswarm, all throughther, in throngs; | self ín self steepèd
and páshed – qúite
Disremembering, dísmémbering | áll now. Heart, you round me
right
With: Óur évening is over us; óur night | whélms, whélms,
ánd will end us.

See SPRUNG RHYTHM.

ideal reader What every author wants. That imaginary person who, the writer hopes, will understand completely the experience he is trying to convey, and respond to it as he wishes. *See also* IDEAL SPECTATOR.

ideal spectator Two basic meanings may be distinguished: (a) the 'everyman' for whom the dramatist writes; for all practical purposes synonymous with the average person; (b) a character in a play who either expresses the attitudes and feelings of the dramatist or is representative of the majority of the audience.

The French term is *raisonneur* and both 'characters' are related to the Greek Chorus and the single character acting as chorus (*q.v.*), as well as, possibly, to the confidant (*q.v.*).

The ideal spectator of category (b) is not much involved in the plot but is rather an onlooker; a sort of neutral character, like Horatio in *Hamlet*, Kent in *King Lear*, Lord Goring in *An Ideal Husband* and the lawyer in Arthur Miller's play *A View from the Bridge*. *See also* IDEAL READER.

idée fixe (F 'fixed idea') A preconception, an unshakable conviction; hence a dominating theme; a monomania. Quite a common term in music; rare as a literary term, but important in connection with Valéry's theories on the subject expressed in *Idée fixe* (1932), a dialogue. Like Heraclitus, Hegel and William James (among others) Valéry denies that an idea is ever quite the same on two occasions of its occurrence. An idea, it is argued, cannot be fixed because the mental state is transitory. Some ideas have the property of reappearing to consciousness more often than others. Their appearance may be relied on in appropriate contexts; thus they are 'fixed' in the sense that a roulette wheel can be fixed. These are 'privileged' and their privilege is shown, not only in the frequency of their reappearances but also in their status.

It is in the nature of an idea to intervene in the mind's normal state of disorder and inattention, and to accentuate and momentarily arrest (or retard) some element in it. The idea is, in fact, this momentarily favoured element which, by thus being coagulated as it were from the general psychic mass, suggests comparisons and hypotheses, whereby the animal flux of images and instincts becomes transmuted into thinking. When the arrestation becomes habitual and the same idea recurs repeatedly in a variety of mental 'situations', we have what may be called an *idée fixe*. Recurrent symbols, word complexes, images and themes in a writer's work are also associated with the fixed idea.

idée reçue (F 'received idea') This term is perhaps most prominent in connection with Flaubert's *Dictionnaire des idées reçues*, published posthumously in 1913 from a mass of half-completed notes. It attacks the sin of affirming without examining. Flaubert, who had a particular aversion to the platitude, conceived the idea as a youth. There are two main themes: an attack on the cliché (*q.v.*); and the peril of accepted ideas. Writing to George Sand in 1871 Flaubert said 'All our trouble comes from our gigantic ignorance. When shall we get over empty speculation and accepted ideas? What should be studied is believed without discussion. Instead of examining, people pontificate.' Reference to Flaubert's *Bouvard et Pécuchet* (1881), a bitter condemnation of human stupidity, helps to show the relevance of *idées reçues* to everyday life. Flaubert also collected specimens for a *Catalogue des idées chics* in order to complete this unfinished novel.

idem (L 'the same') Often abbreviated to *id.*, it denotes the same word or name or title already referred to. *See also* IBIDEM; OPERE CITATO.

identical rhyme The repetition of the same word in the rhyming position in order to achieve emphasis. An interesting example occurs in stanza XI of Keats's *Isabella*:

> All close they met again, before the dusk
> Had taken from the stars its pleasant veil,
> All close they met, all eves, before the dusk
> Had taken from the stars its pleasant veil,
> Close in a bower of hyacinth and musk,
> Unknown of any, free from whispering tale.

In medieval French verse identical rhyme or *rime riche* was fashionable. *See* RHYME.

ideograph A written symbol. A picture of the thing itself or a representation of the idea. The Chinese and Japanese languages are ideographic.

ideynost (R 'ideological expression') One of the requirements demanded under socialist realism (*q.v.*). Literature must embody ideas, especially political and social ideas, of a progressive nature. Censors and critics do not accept literature lacking in ideological content, or literature which is merely intended to divert or entertain. *See* CENSORSHIP; NARODNOST; PARTYNOST.

idiolect The aggregate of speech habits peculiar to an individual.

idiom A form of expression, construction or phrase peculiar to a language and often possessing a meaning other than its grammatical or logical one.

Some languages have thousands of idioms and English is no exception. These are a handful out of the many in existence and use: by chance; far and wide; again and again; spick and span; wear and tear; neither here nor there; off and on; as fit as a fiddle; better late than never; no wonder; to turn adrift; to hang fire; to have the upper hand; to back the wrong horse; at daggers drawn; to lead by the nose. *See* CLICHE; COLLOQUIALISM; DEAD METAPHOR; SLANG.

ido An international language devised by Louis Couturat in 1907. It was a 'child' of Esperanto (*q.v.*), in which language *ido* means 'offspring', but was in many ways a simplification of Esperanto. By many it has been thought to be an improvement on the parent language.

idyll (Gk 'little form') It can refer to either a poem or an episode in a poem, or to a poem which describes some episode or scene in rural life (in which case it is very nearly synonymous with pastoral, *q.v.*), or a description of any scene of tranquil happiness. In common parlance 'idyllic' is used to describe a serene and euphoric state or environment which is remotely attainable and idealized. It is not therefore a definite poetic genre, though having strong association with the bucolic, e.g. the *Idylls* of Theocritus. It has indeed been used for a variety of works, like Victor de Laprade's *Idylles héroïques* (1858), Tennyson's *Idylls of the King* (1842–85), Browning's *Dramatic Idylls* (1879–80) and Barrie's *Auld Licht Idylls* (1888). *See also* ECLOGUE; PASTORAL.

illusion The semblance of reality and verisimilitude (*q.v.*) in art which most writers seek to create in order to enable the reader to think that he is seeing, feeling, hearing, tasting and smelling, or, conceivably, having some extra-sensory or kinaesthetic experience. The creation of illusion is a co-operative act between writer and reader. It brings about in the reader what Coleridge called 'the willing suspension of disbelief' (*q.v.*). However, the writer also destroys illusion, sometimes for a specific purpose: for example, to address the reader directly – a not uncommon practice among 18th and 19th c. novelists. The contrast helps the illusion and at the same time sharpens and clarifies the impression of things happening at a distance. Illusion should be distinguished from *delusion* and *hallucination*.

il n'y a rien hors du texte *See* DECONSTRUCTION.

imagery (L 'making of likenesses') The terms *image* and *imagery* have many connotations and meanings. Imagery as a general term covers the use of language to represent objects, actions, feelings, thoughts, ideas, states of mind and any sensory or extra-sensory experience. An 'image' does not necessarily mean a mental picture.

In the first place we may distinguish between the literal, the perceptual and the conceptual. These lines from Robert Lowell's *Our Lady of Walsingham* illustrate the basic differences:

There once the penitents took off their shoes
And then walked barefoot the remaining mile;
And the small trees, a stream and hedgerows file
Slowly along the munching English lane,
Like cows to the old shrine, until you lose
Track of your dragging pain.
The stream flows down under the druid tree,
Shiloah's whirlpools gurgle and make glad
The castle of God.

The first two lines are a literal image (without figurative language) which may or may not convey a visual image also. The phrase 'hedgerows file slowly' is a perceptual image because of the metaphorical use of the word 'file'. The phrase 'castle of God' is conceptual. One can hardly visualize it but one may have an idea of it.

Many *images* (but by no means all) are conveyed by figurative language, as in metaphor, simile, synecdoche, onomatopoeia and metonymy (*qq.v.*). An image may be visual (pertaining to the eye), olfactory (smell), tactile (touch), auditory (hearing), gustatory (taste), abstract (in which case it will appeal to what may be described as the intellect) and kinaesthetic (pertaining to the sense of movement and bodily effort).

These lines from Peter Redgrove's *Lazarus and the Sea* contain all these kinds of image:

The tide of my death came whispering like this
Soiling my body with its tireless voice.
I scented the antique moistures when they sharpened
The air of my room, made the rough wood of my bed,
(most dear),
Standing out like roots in my tall grave.
They slopped in my mouth and entered my plaited blood
Quietened my jolting breath with a soft argument
Of such measured insistence, untied the great knot of my heart.
They spread like whispered conversations
Through all the numbed rippling tissues radiated

Like a tree for thirty years from the still centre
Of my salt ovum. But this calm dissolution
Came after my agreement to the necessity of it;
Where before it was a storm over red fields
Pocked with the rain and the wheat furrowed
With wind, then it was the drifting of smoke
From a fire of the wood, damp with sweat,
Fallen in the storm.

It is often the case that an image is not exclusively one thing or another; they overlap and intermingle and thus combine. Thus, the kinaesthetic may also be visual.

In this quotation the first two lines are clearly auditory, but the use of the word 'soiling' may suggest the tactile; on the other hand, for some, the word may have olfactory associations. The third line is olfactory. In the fourth and fifth lines we have a combination of the tactile and visual. The sixth line intermingles the tactile, olfactory and gustatory. The phrases 'quietened my jolting breath' and 'through all the numbed rippling tissues' are kinaesthetic, but are also visual and tactile. 'But this calm dissolution/Came after my agreement to the necessity of it;' is abstract. 'Untied the great knot of my heart' is visual-cum-kinaesthetic. The other images in the poem fall readily into one of the categories mentioned. *See* ARCHETYPE; SYMBOL AND SYMBOLISM.

imagination *See* FANCY AND IMAGINATION.

imaginism A short-lived Russian poetic movement originating in 1919. Its attitudes were fundamentally anti-Bolshevik and expressed disenchantment with the Revolution. The members of the imaginist group made a cult of a Bohemian and permissive life, which tended towards hooliganism, and wrote poems intended to shock. The only well-known poet in the group was Sergey Yesenin (1895–1925). The movement, such as it was, was defunct by *c.* 1925. *See also* FUTURISM.

Imagists A group of poets who were prominent immediately before the First World War. The best known were Ezra Pound, Amy Lowell, T. E. Hulme, Richard Aldington and H. D. (Hilda Doolittle). They believed that a hard, clear image was essential to verse. They also believed that poetry should use the language of everyday speech and have complete freedom in subject matter.

Pound edited the first anthology, *Des Imagistes* (1914), and in 1915 Amy Lowell published some imagist poets. This work contained a statement of the ideals of imagism (or 'amygism', as it was called). T. E. Hulme's *Above the Dock* is a good example of a poem in the imagist manner:

> Above the quiet dock in midnight,
> Tangled in the tall mast's corded height,
> Hangs the moon. What seemed so far away
> Is but a child's balloon, forgotten after play.

See also ABSTRACT; DINGGEDICHT; HAIKU; SYMBOL AND SYMBOLISM; VORTICISM.

imitation Three basic meanings can be distinguished: (a) copying or plagiarism (*q.v.*); (b) the adoption of the tone, style and attitude of another writer; a re-creation; (c) a representation. Literary theory during and after the Romantic period (*q.v.*) regarded imitation in sense (b) as a somewhat inferior practice, derivative, lacking in originality. Prior to that and for many centuries (especially during the 18th) it had been regarded as a wholly respectable practice. Aristotle advocated it, so did Cicero and Horace. The idea was that a writer should learn everything he could from the masters who were his predecessors. This point of view prevailed during the medieval and Renaissance periods and continued into the 18th c. Pope, who composed some of the best imitations (*Imitations of Horace*), gives the 18th c. view in *An Essay on Criticism* (1711):

> Those RULES of old discover'd, not devis'd,
> Are Nature still, but Nature Methodiz'd;
> Nature, like Liberty, is but restrain'd
> By the same Laws which first herself ordain'd . . .
> You then whose Judgment the right course wou'd steer,
> Know well each ANCIENT'S proper Character,
> His Fable, Subject, Scope in ev'ry Page,
> Religion, Country, Genius of his Age:
> Without all these at once before your Eyes,
> Cavil you may, but never Criticize.
> Be Homer's Works your Study, and Delight,
> Read them by Day, and meditate by Night,
> Thence form your Judgment, thence your Maxims bring,
> And trace the Muses upward to their Spring;
> Still with It self compar'd, his Text peruse;
> And let your comment be the Mantuan Muse . . .

Nowadays, imitation is seldom used as a critical term. When it is, it is roughly synonymous with mimesis (*q.v.*). *See* FIXED FORM; NOVELTY.

implied reader/actual reader Terms invented by Wolfgang Iser and discussed by him in his books *The Implied Reader* (1974) and *The Act of Reading: A Theory of Aesthetic Response* (1976, trans. 1978). The 'implied reader' is a 'model' or 'role'. Such a reader is active as well as passive; the text structures his or her response, but he or she also produces meaning and has the task of 'consistency building' (the expression used by Iser). The 'actual reader', by contrast, receives mental images while reading; but these images are, inevitably perhaps, modified by the experience and knowledge (and thus other images) which the reader brings to the text. The hypothetical implied and actual reader co-exist, are one and the same person responding to a text in different ways and at different levels of consciousness. This view of the reader can be taken in conjunction with Umberto Eco's distinction between the 'open' and 'closed' text. *See* READER-RESPONSE THEORY; RECEPTION THEORY.

imposed form *See* FIXED FORM.

impression *See* EDITION.

impressionism The term very probably derives from Claude Monet's painting *Impression: Soleil Levant* (first exhibited in Paris in 1874). The Impressionists were a school of painters who were particularly concerned with the transitory effects of light, and they wished to depict the fleeting impression from a subjective point of view. They were not interested in a precise representation; the resulting impression depended on the perception of the spectator. The terms *impressionist* and *impressionism* have crept into literary criticism, but they are vague terms which we might well dispense with. French symbolist poets have been called *impressionist*; so have English poets like Oscar Wilde and Arthur Symons. The term *impressionism* has also been used to describe the novelist's technique of concentrating on the inner life of the main character rather than on external reality. Abundant examples of this technique are to be found in the work of James Joyce, Marcel Proust, Dorothy Richardson and Virginia Woolf. *See also* STREAM OF CONSCIOUSNESS; SYMBOL AND SYMBOLISM.

imprimatur (L 'let it be printed') The term signifies that the Roman Catholic Church has sanctioned the printing of a work. It is a declaration that a book or pamphlet is free of moral or doctrinal error. But it does *not* imply that those who have given the *imprimatur* agree with the contents of the book. Many religious orders require the approval of their own authorities. This, when given, is attested by the additional words *imprimi potest* ('it may be printed'). Closely related is the phrase *nihil obstat* ('nothing stands in the way'), which implies there is nothing in a book or pamphlet which is objectionable in terms of theology or morals.

imprimi potest *See* IMPRIMATUR.

imprint (a) Publisher's name, place and date of publication at the bottom of the title page; (b) Printer's name with that of the printing press traditionally on the final page.

incantation A formulaic use of words to produce a magical effect and to create an intensifying emotional temperature. The words may be chanted or spoken. It is very common in primitive literatures and is much used by sorcerers and witches, and also for ritual purposes as in a charm (*q.v.*). Famous examples are the incantations of the weird sisters in Shakespeare's *Macbeth*, Faustus's in Marlowe's *Dr Faustus* and in Ben Jonson's *The Masque of Queens*, from which these lines come:

> The owl is abroad, the bat and the toad
> And so is the cat-a-mountain;
> The ant and the mole sit both in a hole,
> And the frog peeps out o' the fountain.
> The dogs they do bay, and the timbrels play,
> The spindle is now a-turning;
> The moon it is red, and the stars are fled,
> But all the sky is a-burning:
> The ditch is made, and our nails the spade:
> With pictures full, of wax and of wool,
> Their livers I stick with needles quick;
> There lacks but the blood to make up the flood.
> Quickly, dame, then bring your part in!
> Spur, spur upon little Martin!
> Merrily, merrily make him sail,
> A worm in his mouth and a thorn in his tail,

Fire above, and fire below,
With a whip in your hand to make him go!
O now she's come!
Let all be dumb.

incremental repetition A term invented by Francis Gummere in *The Popular Ballad* (1907) to describe a rhetorical device of the ballad (*q.v.*) form. It has been widely used in ballads for hundreds of years and is very typical of poetry in oral tradition (*q.v.*). The following stanzas from the traditional ballad *James Harris* (*The Demon Lover*) illustrate well the use of the device:

'O where have you been, my long, long love,
This long seven years and mair?'
'O I'm come to seek my former vows
Ye granted me before.'

'O hold your tongue of your former vows,
For they will breed sad strife;
O hold your tongue of your former vows,
For I am become a wife.'

He turned him right and round about,
And the tear blinded his ee:
'I wad never hae trodden on Irish ground,
If it had not been for thee.'

'I might hae had a king's daughter,
Far, far beyond the sae;
I might have had a King's daughter,
Had it not been for love o thee.'

This kind of repetition is thought by some to be peculiar to English and Scottish ballads, but a very similar device is frequent in South Slav *narodne pesme* (*q.v.*) of the oral tradition. *See* ANAPHORA; REPETITION; SYNTHETIC RHYTHM.

incrementum *See* AMPLIFICATION.

incunabula *See* CRADLE BOOK.

indeterminacy Elements in, say, a novel or short story, which depend for their effect or result on a reader's interpretation and which may be interpreted in a number of different (and, conceivably, mutually conflicting) ways are said to be 'indeterminate'. Indeterminacies tend to multiply in accordance with the length and complexity of a text. *See* RECEPTION THEORY; SUB-TEXT.

index (L 'forefinger') The plural is indexes or indices. An alphabetical list of subjects treated in a book, with page references. It is now found at the end, but in older books it may serve as a table of contents at the beginning.

index expurgatorius A list of passages in a book which, by order of the Roman Catholic Church, must be deleted before it can be read by members of the Church. This index was abrogated in 1966. *See also* IMPRIMATUR; INDEX LIBRORUM PROHIBITORUM.

index librorum prohibitorum A list of books (*not* authors) which Roman Catholics are forbidden by the Church to read, or books which may be read only in an expurgated edition (*q.v.*). This index was abrogated in 1966. *See also* IMPRIMATUR; INDEX EXPURGATORIUS.

indirect speech The changing of spoken words (*oratio recta*) into reported speech (*oratio obliqua*). For example: 'I won't go tomorrow,' said Fred – becomes 'Fred said that he would not go on the following day'.

induction An archaism (*q.v.*) for introduction or prologue (*qq.v.*). A good example occurs at the beginning of *The Taming of the Shrew*, where Christopher Sly, a drunken tinker, is brought in by a lord and his huntsmen and is then treated as a lord and persuaded that he has lost his wits. He is then obliged to watch the play of the taming of the shrew performed by a troupe of strolling players. Another well-known example is that by Thomas Sackville in *Mirror for Magistrates* (2nd ed. 1563), in which Sorrow leads the poet into the dominions of the dead.

inflection Two basic meanings may be distinguished: (a) a change in the form of a word, to show a change in its grammatical function. Usually at the end of a word; the case in a noun for instance. Inflections are common in Latin and Greek and in Slav languages but there are few in English; (b) the term is also used to describe changes in pitch. For example, the word 'well' as a noun, adjective and exclamation could be said in a number of different ways.

infrahistoria A term coined by Miguel de Unamuno (1846–1936) to denote narratives concerned with the unrecorded lives and traditions of ordinary, humble people (in a sense, 'short and simple annals of the poor') and also ordinary or unimportant places and events. Some writers of the *generacíon del 1898* (*q.v.*) composed *infrahistoria.*

initial rhyme *See* ALLITERATION.

initiating action The event or events in a plot which bring about a state of conflict and tension. *See also* CLIMAX; EXPOSITION; FALLING ACTION; RISING ACTION.

inkhorn terms Pedantic terms and learned borrowings from foreign tongues: Thomas Wilson, in his *Arte of Rhetorique* (1553), observed that the first lesson to be learned was never to affect 'any straunge ynkhorne termes, but to speak as is commonly received'. An inkhorn was a small vessel for ink fastened to the clothing. *See* LOAN WORD.

in medias res (L 'into the middle of things') The origin is Horace's remark in *Ars Poetica*:

> Semper ad eventum festinat et in medias res
> Non secus ac notas auditorem rapit.

('He always hastens to the issue and hurries his hearers into the midst of the story as if they knew it already.') The phrase has become almost a cliché (*q.v.*) to describe a common method of beginning a story – in other words, starting in the midst of the action at some crucial point, when a good deal has already happened. The writer is then able to shuttle back and forth in time between interrelated incidents. Milton does it very effectively in *Paradise Lost* by beginning his narrative in Hell, after the fall of the rebel angels. *See also* AB OVO.

In Memoriam stanza So named because Tennyson used it in *In Memoriam* (1850). A four-line iambic tetrameter rhyming abba:

> I held it truth, with him who sings
>   To one clear harp in divers tones,
>   That men may rise on stepping-stones
> Of their dead selves to higher things.

inscape and instress Terms invented by Gerard Manley Hopkins. By 'inscape' he meant the individual 'distinctive' form, the 'oneness' of a natural object. For the energy of being by which things are upheld and for the natural stress which determines an 'inscape', he used the word 'instress'. This is akin to what Shelley called 'the One Spirit's plastic stress', and instress is the 'sensation of inscape' – a kind of mystical illumination or insight into the underlying order and unity of creation. The poet's notebooks and journals, which are of enormous interest, reveal his preoccupation with both terms. *See* SPRUNG RHYTHM.

inspiration There are two basic theories about inspiration: (a) that it comes from outside the writer; (b) that it comes from within him. The first is the older. Many Greek and Latin writers attempted to explain it by suggesting that inspiration was of divine origin – the action of a muse (*q.v.*). Invoking the muse was common and became a literary convention (*q.v.*). Homer often did so. Plato and Aristotle both suggest that inspiration is divine. For the most part during the Renaissance period the Classical view was retained – at any rate as a convention.

The external-force theory prevailed and proved the more attractive of the two until late in the 18th c. when writers started to favour the second theory and ascribed inspiration to the workings of individual genius (*q.v.*). Psychology and theories of psychoanalysis suggest that the unconscious or subconscious is the main source of creative activity. Few people now, except those with 'romantic' ideas about it, believe in inspiration. As Willam Faulkner once put it tersely, 'No one ever told me where to find it'. One of the more interesting modern comments on the subject is provided by Graham Greene in *The End of the Affair* (1951), a comment which, in its way, covers both theories. 'So much in writing', he says, 'depends on the superficiality of one's days. One may be preoccupied with shopping and income-tax returns and chance conversations, but the stream of the unconscious continues to flow undisturbed, solving problems, planning ahead: one sits down sterile and dispirited at the desk, and suddenly the words come as though from the air: the situations that seemed blocked in a hopeless impasse move forward: the work has been done while one slept or shopped or talked with friends.' *See also* AFFLATUS; DONNEE; FANCY AND IMAGINATION; INVENTION; LIGNE DONNEE.

instress *See* INSCAPE AND INSTRESS.

intention *See* FOUR MEANINGS.

intentional fallacy The error of criticizing and judging a work of literature by attempting to assess what the writer's intention was and whether or not he has fulfilled it rather than concentrating on the work itself. Modern criticism (since the 1920s) has tended to the point of view that anything except the work itself is irrelevant. This point of view is especially noticeable in the criticism of I. A. Richards and T. S. Eliot in the 1920s and that of the American New Critics (*see* NEW CRITICISM) in the 1940s and 1950s. In 1946 W. K. Wimsatt (in collaboration with Monroe C. Beardsley) published his essay *The Intentional Fallacy* (reprinted in his *The Verbal Icon*, 1954), a document central to the development of modern critical theory. They express the point of view that a poem 'is not the critic's own and not the author's (it is detached from the author at birth and goes about the world beyond his power to intend about it or control it). The poem belongs to the public . . .' Wimsatt's contentions have often been disputed. Some of the New Critics (for example, Cleanth Brooks and John Crowe Ransom) refer to a 'total intention', meaning the total meaning or organization of a work. *See also* AFFECTIVE FALLACY; PERSONAL HERESY.

interior monologue *See* MONOLOGUE.

inter-laced rhyme *See* CROSSED RHYME.

interlude (L 'between play') A short entertainment put on between the courses of a feast or the acts of a play. During the Middle Ages and up to the 16th c. the term was used to describe a variety of dramatic entertainments. Italian Renaissance drama had *intermezzi*. In France and Spain similar diversions were called *entremets* and *entremeses*. Interludes were particularly popular in England in the 15th and 16th c., and especially between 1550 and 1580. In the *Annals of English Drama 975–1700* Harbage lists ninety or so plays which could qualify as interludes. It is very likely that they form a link between the Mystery Play, the Miracle Play and the Morality (*qq.v.*), and the psychological drama of the Elizabethans. Dividing lines are not clear. Many of them are very similar to Moralities and in some cases are indistinguishable from them. They were often allegorical and didactic (many also were farcical) and written in rough verse; at times so rough that it becomes doggerel (*q.v.*). They were usually about a thousand lines long and there seems little doubt that most were intended as entertainment at banquets at court, in the houses of nobility, at University colleges and at the Inns of Court. Two main types can be distinguished: (a) the popular (e.g. *Youth, The Pride of Life* and *Mankind*); (b) the aristocratic or courtly (e.g. *Fulgens and Lucrece* and *Appius and Virginia*).

One of the earliest instances is the *Interludium de Clerico et Puella* (1290–1335). A list of the most notable examples (some of these are also classified as Moralities) should include: *The Pride of Life* (*c.* 1300–25); *Mankind* (1465–70); *The Castell of Perseverance* (1400–25); *Wisdom* (1460–63); Medwall's *Fulgence and Lucrece* (1490–1500); *Youth* (*c.* 1515–28); Heywood's *The Play of the Wether* (*c.* 1527); *A Play of Love* (*c.* 1534); *Thersites* (1537); *The Foure P's* (*c.* 1545); Redford's *Wit and Science* (*c.* 1531–47); *Respublica*, possibly by Nicholas Udall (*c.* 1533); *Appius and Virginia* (*c.* 1567); *Like Will to Like* (*c.* 1567). *See* MORAL INTERLUDE; TAFELSPEL.

intermezzi Light, comic interpolations put on between the acts of serious plays in Italy during the 15th and 16th c. They were usually devoted to mythological subjects. They were similar to the *momeries* and *entremets* in France, and the *entremeses* (*q.v.*) in Spain. *See also* ENTR'ACTE; INTERLUDE.

internal evidence A term used in analytical and textual criticism (especially in the dating of a literary work) to refer to features of style (e.g. imagery, syntax, idiom, spelling, rhyme, punctuation), or details of environment, fashion and period, which might give some indication of when the work was written. Sometimes it is possible to date within a few years.

internal rhyme It occurs when two or more words rhyme within a single line of verse as in W. S. Gilbert's libretto for *Patience*:

> Then a sentimental passion of a vegetable fashion
> must excite your languid spleen,
> An attachment à la Plato, for a bashful young potato,
> or a not too French French bean!
> Though the Philistine may jostle, you will rank as an
> apostle in the high aesthetic band,
> If you walk down Piccadilly with a poppy or a lily in
> your medieval hand.

Shelley also used it very successfully in *The Cloud*. *See also* CROSSED RHYME; LEONINE RHYME.

International Centre of Theatre Research Founded in 1970 at the Mobilier National in Paris under the directorship of Peter Brook (1925–). The main objective was to gather actors and actresses of various nationalities and races and create a 'universal language' of the theatre. In 1971 *Orghast* was staged in the open air as part of the Shiraz Festival at Persepolis. In 1972–3 a group travelled through Africa, improvising and developing performances of *The Conference of the Birds*. In 1975 the Centre opened the Théâtre des Bouffes du Nord with *The Ik*, an attempt to display the impact of civilization on an African tribe. *See also* TOTAL THEATRE.

interpretant In the science of semiotics (*q.v.*) the term denotes the response to a particular sign, and not to a person (who is the interpreter). The usage was coined by the American semiotician C. S. Peirce (1839–1914), and also by the behaviourist Charles Morris (1901–79).

intertextuality A term coined by Julia Kristeva in 1966 to denote the interdependence of literary texts, the interdependence of any one literary text with all those that have gone before it. Her contention was that a literary text is not an isolated phenomenon but is made up of a mosaic of quotations, and that any text is the 'absorption and transformation of another'. She challenges traditional notions of literary influence, saying that intertextuality denotes a transposition of one or several sign systems into another or others. But this is not connected with the study of sources. 'Transposition' is a Freudian term, and Kristeva is not merely pointing to the way texts echo each other but the way that discourses or sign systems are transposed into one another – so that meanings in one kind of discourse are overlaid with meanings from another kind of discourse. It is a kind of 'new articulation'. For Kristeva the idea is part of a wider psychoanalytical theory which questions the stability of the subject, and her views about intertextuality are very different from those of Roland Barthes and other theorists. *See* STRUCTURALISM.

introduction Normally an essay (of varying length) which states the author's intention and gives the reader some idea of the theme and scope of a work. It may also refer to the first part of a speech (*q.v.*). *See* FOREWORD; PREFACE.

invective Speech or writing which is denunciatory, abusive or vituperative. The term is related to the verb *inveigh* 'to bring in' or 'introduce' or 'denounce'; as in the phrase 'inveigh against'.

In literature examples of invective are to be found fairly evenly distributed in verse and prose, and it is closely associated with satire, lampoon and caricature (*qq.v.*). Many writers have employed invective for a variety of purposes, the commonest being to express dislike, disgust, contempt and even hatred. It is often directed against a particular person (e.g. Junius on the Duke of Grafton in *The Letters of Junius*); occasionally against a class or group (e.g. Swift on the English nobility in *Gulliver's Travels*); against an institution (e.g. William Prynne on the stage in *Histrio-mastix*); a scene (e.g. Smollett on the night-life in London in *Humphry Clinker*); and on life itself (e.g. Jeremy Taylor in *Of Holy Dying*).

As a mode of expression invective is very ancient. Archilochus (7th c. BC) had a reputation for being a mordant wit (Eustathius called him 'scorpion-tongued') in his writings of which, unhappily, few are extant. There are plentiful instances of invective in the plays of Aristophanes, and there are supposed to have been examples in the *Sermones* of Lucilius (180–102 BC), but these last have not survived. Persius (AD 34–62) was influenced by Lucilius, and in his *First Satire* is fairly abusive of the poetasters (*q.v.*) and decadent literary tastes of his period. But the greatest of inveighers in Classical literature is unquestionably Juvenal (1st c. AD), who wrote ferocious attacks on the vices and abuses of the Roman 'life-style'. He was particularly savage at the expense of the rich, and of women – to whom he devoted his *Sixth Satire*: a sustained and bitter diatribe (*q.v.*) in which women are compared unfavourably to many different animals.

There is little in the way of invective in European literature from Juvenal's age until the late Middle Ages and early Tudor times, if we except some Latin verse, some Goliardic poetry, the occasional indignant outburst from the pulpit (like Wulfstan's celebrated homily to the English *c.* 1014), and the flytings (*q.v.*) of some Scottish poets like Dunbar. We find, also, some instances in the poetry of Langland and in the *ballades* of Villon. Then comes John Skelton who lashed out in his good-humoured and boisterous fashion at the evils of society and at the expense of individuals (particularly Cardinal Wolsey). More moderate invective is to be found in the Folly Literature (*q.v.*) of the period; and John Knox's famous *First Blast of the Trumpet against the Monstrous Regiment of Women* (1558) is a splendid example of objurgation.

The late Tudor dramatists and pamphleteers found invective a most effective weapon. Good examples in Shakespeare's plays are to be found in: *Troilus and Cressida* (I, ii); *King Lear* (II, ii; IV, i); *Timon of Athens* (IV, i); *Coriolanus* (III, iii); *Cymbeline* (II, v) and *The Tempest* (I, ii; II, ii). Thomas Lodge, John Marston and Ben Jonson were other writers of the period well capable of exploiting abusive language. A curiosity of this time was King James I's *A Counterblaste to Tobacco* (1604). Among 17th c. writers Samuel Butler and Dryden are two witty exponents of invective; the former in *Hudibras*, the latter in *Mac Flecknoe* and *Absalom and Achitophel.* In the following century one should note Pope (especially in *Epistle to Arbuthnot, Epistle to Sir Richard Temple* and *The Dunciad*), Swift in *Gulliver's Travels* and Smollet in *Humphry Clinker*. Therafter *et passim* in the works of Burns, Byron, Macaulay, Dickens, Thackeray, Carlyle, Swinburne, Shaw, Belloc and G. K. Chesterton, to name only a few.

invention The term derives from the *inventio* of Classical and medieval rhetoric. *Inventio* was the first of the five 'parts' of oratory. Invention equalled discovery. Later it came to be applied generally to original discovery and the organization of any literary work. However, it has had many special and particular meanings at different times. It has been contrasted with 'imitation' (*q.v.*), and with judgement. It has been used to describe things incredible and the products of fancy. Sometimes it has meant the production of fiction as opposed to historical truth; or the combination of fiction and historical truth. One of the key remarks on invention occurs in Johnson's *Life of Pope*, where he describes it as the faculty by which 'new trains of events are formed and new scenes of imagery displayed' and by which 'extrinsic and adventitious embellishments and illustrations are connected with a known subject'. In general one may now take it that invention denotes the discovery of an idea or fact, and the arranging of words and ideas in a fresh and arresting fashion. *See* FANCY AND IMAGINATION; INSPIRATION; ORIGINALITY.

inversion In rhetoric the turning of an argument against an opponent. In grammar the reversal of the normal word order of a sentence; as in these lines from *Paradise Lost*:

His spear, to equal which the tallest pine
Hewn on Norwegian hills, to be the mast

Of some great ammiral, were but a wand,
He walk'd with to support uneasy steps
Over the burning marle.

In prosody, the turning of feet by substitution (*q.v.*)

invocation An appeal or request for help (for instance: for inspiration, *q.v.*) addressed to a muse (*q.v.*) or deity. In epic, it is a literary convention. It usually comes at or near the beginning of a poem. Good examples are to be found in the *Iliad*, the *Odyssey* and *Paradise Lost*. Mock-heroic (*q.v.*) poetry produced mock invocations (as in Pope's *The Rape of the Lock*). It is seldom used now but a good modern example is to be found in Hart Crane's *The Bridge*.

involuted novel *See* NARRATOR.

ionic A verse form believed to have originated with the Ionians of Asia Minor. It is thought that they used it in odes in praise of Dionysus and Cybele. There are two kinds of ionic foot: *a majore*: / / ∪ ∪; and *a minore*: ∪ ∪ / /. Ionics are found in the work of Anacreon, Euripides and Horace. They are very rare in English verse, except as occasional feet in combination with others. Browning attempted lesser ionics in the *Epilogue* to *Asolando* (1889), his last volume of poems which was published on the day of his death:

Ăt thĕ mídníght | ĭn thĕ sílénce | ŏf thĕ sléep-tíme,
  Whĕn yŏu sét yóur | fáncíes frée,
Wíll thĕy páss tŏ whére – bȳ deáth, fóols thínk,
                    ĭmprísonĕd –
Lów hĕ líes whŏ ónce sŏ lóved yóu, whóm yóu lóved só?
                    – Pítȳ mé?

It can be seen from this how difficult it is to maintain ionics for long without forcing words into an unnatural stress pattern.

Irish dramatic movement *See* ABBEY THEATRE.

Irish literary renaissance *See* CELTIC TWILIGHT.

irony (Gk 'dissimulation') First recorded in Plato's *Republic* (4th c. BC), where it has approximately the meaning of 'a glib and underhand way of taking people in'. In the Platonic dialogues Socrates himself takes the role of the *eirōn* or 'dissembler' and, assuming the pose of ignorance and foolishness, asks seemingly innocuous and naive questions which gradually undermine his interlocutor's case and trap him (through the latter's admissions) into seeing the truth. Hence what is known as Socratic irony (*q.v.*). Demosthenes regarded an *eirōn* as a man who ducked his responsibilities as a citizen by pretence of illness (what we should now call 'swinging the lead', 'malingering' or 'draft dodging'). Theophrastus regarded an *eirōn* as a person who was slippery in his speech, non-committal; a man who does not come out into the open. In Greek comedy the *eirōn* was the underdog, a feeble but crafty and quick-witted character who got the better of Alazon – the braggadocio (*q.v.*) type who was loud-mouthed and block-headed.

For the Roman rhetoricians (in particular Cicero and Quintilian) *ironia* denoted a rhetorical figure and a manner of discourse, in which, for the most part, the meaning was contrary to the words. This double-edgedness appears to be a diachronic feature of irony.

It is not until 1502 that we find the first mention of irony in English: 'yronye' – 'of grammare, by the whiche a man sayth one & gyveth to understande the contrarye'. This suggests a common usage. Later we find a gloss by 'E.K.' to the October Eclogue in Spenser's *Shepheard's Calendar* (1579) in which he refers to a passage as 'An Ironicall Sarcasmus spoken in derision . . .' The term irony did not come into general use until late in the 17th c., or early in the 18th, though at this period irony, as a mode of thinking, feeling and expression, was beginning to attain a high degree of sophistication. Curiously enough, Dryden appears to have used the term only once, but then there had been (and still were), as D. C. Muecke has pointed out in a splendid essay on the subject, called *Irony* (1970), a number of other well-tried and homely words which had served for the idea of the ironical; words like *fleer*, *gibe*, *jeer*, *mock*, *rail* and *scorn*. Such words suggest the rough and readiness of abuse and invective (*q.v.*); they smack of the inn and the market-place, of sleeves rolled up; whereas irony is redolent of something altogether more refined and polished, more considered and deliberate. It is a more *literary* term. Puttenham may have been feeling for this quality of urbanity when, in *The Art of English Poesie* (1589), he rendered the Latin *ironia* as 'Drie Mock'.

One receives the general impression that in England and Europe the *concept* of irony developed gradually and lagged far behind the practice of it. This is especially noticeable in view of the fact that by 1750 Dryden, Swift, Voltaire, Pope, Fielding and Johnson (to name only a handful of writers) had shown themselves supremely adept in the use of this particular form of expression.

In the wake of an increasing number of practitioners came the analysts and theorists. At the turn of the 18th c. the concept of irony inspired some careful thinking in Germany, where A. W. and F. Schlegel, Tieck and Karl Solger all addressed themselves to the extremely difficult task of understanding this subtlest of manifestations of the comic spirit. Friedrich Schlegel, for instance, perceived the irony of events in *Troilus and Cressida*, where the fine speeches and grandiose ideas eventually produce nothing, except the equivalent of a ridiculous *mus*; and the tragic irony in *King Lear* – by which, one presumes, Schlegel meant the act (and the results of that act) of Lear's rejection of the daughter who loved him most. Once we are alerted to the nature of this kind of irony then we can find numerous instances (e.g. the essential irony of the predicament of Oedipus, the irony of the laconic Mephistopheles in Marlowe's *Dr Faustus*, the almost unbearable irony inherent in the relationship between Iago and Othello). A. W. Schlegel pointed out the ironical nature of the equilibrium or equipoise maintained between the serious and the comic (e.g. the sub-plots in Elizabethan and particularly Shakespeare's plays). Comic relief (*q.v.*) itself, can, by contrast, intensify the irony of a situation. Karl Solger introduced the concept that true irony begins with the contemplation of the fate of the world; a concept which goes under the titles of World Irony or Cosmic Irony or Philosophical Irony. The Schlegels and Solger also used the term irony in connection with the detached and objective viewpoint (*q.v.*) of the artist *qua* his work (see below). And it was Friedrich Schlegel who worked out the idea of Romantic Irony (*q.v.*).

An important work in the history of irony is Thirlwall's essay *On the Irony of Sophocles* (1833). He discussed verbal or rhetorical irony, and also what he calls 'Dialectical Irony' (which is the same as Socratic). In the same essay he points out the paradoxical nature of irony.

In *The Concept of Irony* (1841) Kierkegaard elaborated the idea that irony is a mode of seeing things, a way of viewing existence. Later, Amiel, in his *Journal Intime* (1883–7) expressed the view that irony springs from a perception of the absurdity of life. Others who developed theories about irony were Nietzsche, Baudelaire, Heine and Thomas Mann. For them, most irony is Romantic. (*See* ROMANTIC IRONY.)

By the end of the 19th c., then, we find that most of the major forms and modes of irony have been explored and, to some extent, identified and classified. But it seems to be of the essential nature of irony (the need to use the word 'seems' rather than 'it is' is a product of the inherent ambiguousness of the whole concept) that it eludes definition; and this elusiveness is one of the main reasons why it is a source of so much fascinated inquiry and speculation. No definition will serve to cover every aspect of its nature, just as no definition will serve to explain and describe mirth and why we find some things risible and others not.

However, it seems fairly clear that most forms of irony involved the perception or awareness of a discrepancy or incongruity between words and their meaning, or between actions and their results, or between appearance and reality. In all cases there may be an element of the absurd and the paradoxical.

The two basic kinds of irony are verbal and irony of situation (for the latter one may substitute, on occasions, irony of behaviour). At its simplest, verbal irony involves saying what one does not *mean*. Johnson defined it as a mode of speech in which the meaning is contrary to the words; such as 'Bolingbroke was a holy man'. Such ironies are often hyperbole (*q.v.*) or litotes (*q.v.*). At their very crudest: 'I haven't seen you for ages,' from one man to another when they meet every day; or 'That's not bad', said of something superlatively good or beautiful.

Situational irony occurs when, for instance, a man is laughing uproariously at the misfortune of another even while the same misfortune, unbeknownst, is happening to him. To call the roll of the great ironists in literature, or the roll of those in much of whose work the spirit of irony prevails, is to mention a large number of distinguished writers: Aeschylus, Sophocles, Euripides, Aristophanes, Plato, Horace, Catullus, Tacitus, Chaucer, Ariosto, Erasmus, Sir Thomas More, Shakespeare, Cervantes, Ben Jonson, Pascal, Molière, Boileau, Dryden, Samuel (*Hudibras*) Butler, Racine, Defoe, Swift, Voltaire, Pope, Johnson, Fielding, Gibbon, Burke, Goethe, Jane Austen, Stendhal, Byron, Balzac, Heine, Kierkegaard, Samuel (*Erewhon*) Butler, Anatole France, Thackeray, Dickens, Baudelaire, Thomas Hardy, Gogol, Dostoievski, Flaubert, Meredith, Ibsen, Tolstoy, Mark Twain, Henry James, Shaw, Chekhov, Joyce, Gide, Pirandello, Proust, Hašek, Thomas Mann, Kafka, Brecht, Andrić, Silone, Evelyn Waugh, Camus, Lampedusa, Heinrich Böll, Ivy Compton Burnett and Iris Murdoch.

As irony is such an oblique quality or mode of expression, it would be true to say that in many works by many of these authors we find not so much direct or overt irony, but, rather, an ironic temper or tone; an ironic way of *looking* at things and of feeling about them. In this respect, writers like Voltaire, Swift, Gibbon, Henry James and Thomas Mann are supreme ironists. The dry, teasing, laconic, detached sensibility which permeates their work develops an individual vision of human beings and existence. These five authors in particular share the ability to make the smile on the face of the reader broader and broader and broader, very, very slowly, until, finally, he finds himself laughing. Of the five, Thomas Mann is probably the most accomplished at this kind of sustained ironical joke.

Many writers have distanced themselves to a vantage point, a quasi god-like eminence, the better to be able to view things. The artist becomes a kind of god viewing creation (and viewing his own creation) with a smile. From this it is a short step to the idea that God himself is the supreme ironist, watching the antics of human beings (Flaubert referred to a 'blague supérieure') with a detached, ironical smile. The spectator in the theatre is in a similar position. Thus the everlasting human condition is regarded as potentially absurd.

This kind of standpoint and attitude is evident in, for example, Lucan, Dante, Chaucer, Shakespeare, Voltaire, Swift, Gibbon, Flaubert, Thomas Hardy, Henry James and Thomas Mann. In fact Mann, expert on the ironical, when speaking of the novel (in *Die Kunst des Romans*, 1939) says that the novel keeps its distance from things and by its very nature is distanced from them; it 'hovers' over them, and 'smiles down upon them'.

Irony has many functions. It is often the witting or unwitting instrument of truth. It chides, purifies, refines, deflates, scorns and 'sends up'. It is not surprising, therefore, that irony is the most precious and efficient weapon of the satirist.

It can be no accident that the beginning of the great age of satire (*q.v.*) in the second half of the 17th c. roughly coincides with the increasing use of irony as a means of expression throughout a work. It is as if before then many writers (as has been suggested) were fully aware of the possibilities and uses of irony but had not considered it to be a mode for conducting or bearing a whole work. Socrates uses his naive irony; Dante's vision of the damned in the *Inferno* displays many ironies; Sir Thomas More grows more and more ironical in *Utopia*; the comments of the fool in *King Lear* provide ironical counterpoint to the tragedy of the old man; Falstaff is a kind of ironical parody of and counterpart to Henry IV; ironic tones illuminate the sombre tragedies of the Jacobeans and the love poetry of Donne.

We can see Milton working his way towards using it in this fashion in *Areopagitica* (1644), and Dryden beginning to employ it more and more in his satires. The increasing pleasure taken in parody and burlesque (*qq.v.*) suggests a growing awareness of the possible scope of irony. Then, at the beginning of the 18th c. irony becomes 'fashionable'. Everybody starts using it: Addison, Defoe, Arbuthnot, Steele, Swift and others; and, a little later, Pope, Johnson, Fielding and Voltaire. Among the many works by these authors one may mention Defoe's *The Shortest Way with Dissenters* (1702) and *The Political History of the Devil*; Arbuthnot's *The History of John Bull* (1712), *The Art of Political Lying* (1712) and *The Memoirs of Scriblerus* (1741); Swift's *A Tale of a Tub* (1704), *Gulliver's Travels* (1726) and *A Modest Proposal for Preventing the Children of Poor People in Ireland from being a Burden to their Parents or Country* (1729). The other writers mentioned above employed an ironic tone in much of their work.

Irony went 'out of fashion' later in the 18th c. but was revived by the prose writers of the 19th c. (e.g. Peacock and Thackeray). Ironical verse is rare in this period, but Byron's is an honourable exception. In prose the consummate ironist of the 19th c. is Samuel Butler, whose major achievements in irony (in the manner of Swift) were *Erewhon* (1872), *The Fair Haven* (1872), *Erewhon Revisited* (1901) and *The Way of All Flesh* (1903).

With the decline of satire in the 20th c. irony ceases to be the principal mode except in Thomas Mann's novels; though it is frequently occasional, so to speak, in verse, prose and drama. *See also* MEIOSIS.

irregular ode An alternative term for the Cowleyan ode (*q.v.*). *See* ODE.

isochronism (Gk 'equal timing') In Classical prosody the assumption that meter comprises a succession of units (like the foot) which are of the same duration. They are then said to be isochronous.

isocolon (Gk 'equal list') A sequence of clauses or sentences of identical length.

issue *See* EDITION.

Italian sonnet *See* PETRARCHAN SONNET.

ithyphallic verse The term derives from the Greek for an 'erect phallus', and denotes an ode (*q.v.*) or dance performed at festivals of Dionysus. It is also applied to the verse form: / ∪ / ∪ / ∪ × ×, which is known as trochaic dimeter brachycatalectic or trochaic tripody. It was used by Archilochus in the 7th c. BC.

ivory tower In *The Song of Songs* (7:4) Solomon tells his beloved: 'Thy neck is as a tower of ivory'; (F *Ton cou est comme une tour d'ivoire*). Sainte-Beuve (1804–69) is believed to have applied this simile to de Vigny suggesting that he lived in an ivory tower, thereby meaning that he was detached and isolated from the world, haughtily aloof from it. This connotation has survived. If we say that a writer or artist lives in an ivory tower, we imply that he is remote from the world, out of touch with reality, and probably devitalized.

J

jabberwocky A form of nonsense; unintelligible speech or writing. At its worst it degenerates into whimsy, that apparently ineradicable cancer of English humour. Lewis Carroll invented the Jabberwock and wrote a poem called *Jabberwocky* in *Alice through the Looking-Glass* (1872). Alice discovered the poem printed backwards in a looking-glass book. She held it up to the mirror and read (the first verse):

> 'Twas brillig, and the slithy toves
>   Did gyre and gimble in the wabe:
> All mimsy were the borogoves,
>   And the mome raths outgrabe.

Humpty Dumpty says that 'brillig' means 'four o'clock in the afternoon – the time when you start broiling things for dinner.'

The reader can invent for himself. 'Slithy toves' are, perhaps slithery creatures. 'Gyre and gimble' perhaps suggests a slow and solemn dance of joy. 'Mimsy' – delicate, and bearing blossoms?

The work had some influence on Joyce's *Finnegans Wake* (1939). *See* GHOSTWORD; JINGLE; NONSENSE; NURSERY RHYMES.

jácaras A Spanish term (of obscure etymology) which denotes ballads of 'low life' about criminals, prostitutes *et al.* A *jácara* may be bawdy or obscene. In the golden age (*q.v.*) of Spanish *comedia* they were sung between acts to replace the spoken *entremés* or *bailes* (*qq.v.*). Many distinguished writers composed them.

Jacobean age So called from *Jacobus* 'James', and thus belonging to the reign of James I (1603–25). A period which, like the Elizabethan age (*q.v.*), was particularly rich in literary activity. The King himself published at least four books: two on poetry, a work on demonology, and the famous *A Counterblaste to Tobacco* (1604). Among dramatists, Shakespeare, Ben Jonson, Beaumont & Fletcher,

Webster, Tourneur, Ford, Middleton and Rowley were all very active. Donne and Drayton were two of the most famous of the lyric poets of the period. Bacon and Robert Burton were the best known prose writers. In 1611 was published the King James Bible.

jarcha *See* KHARJA.

jargon (OF 'warbling [of birds]') Coleridge still used jargon in this sense in *The Ancient Mariner* (1798), but by the end of the 15th c., and perhaps earlier, it came to signify unintelligible or secret language. For example, François Villon (1431–?) composed several *Ballades en jargon* in the cant or secret language of the *coquillards* (*q.v.*). We are accustomed to using it derogatorily now to describe a private or technical vocabulary peculiar to a trade or profession. Bureaucrats, lawyers, medical practitioners, engineers, scientists of all kinds, plumbers, builders, diplomats, sailors, architects, psychiatrists, psychologists, sociologists, geneticists and ecologists (to name only a few) all have extensive jargon vocabularies. One of its latest manifestations is the barbarous 'Euro-babble', the 'language' of Common Market officials. *See* COLLOQUIALISM; EUPHEMISM; GOBBLEDEGOOK; IDIOM; OFFICIALESE; PERIPHRASIS; REGISTER; SLANG.

jazz poetry Poetry which is recited to the accompaniment of jazz. Its origins appear to be found in the ballads of Vachel Lindsay (1879–1931), particularly the well-known *General William Booth* (1913) and *The Congo* (1914). Langston Hughes (1902–67), in the late 1930s, was one of the first versifiers to collaborate with musicians. Jazz poetry began to take off as a popular form in the USA in the 1950s, particularly in the hands of Kenneth Patchen (1911–72), Kenneth Rexroth (1905–82), Amiri Beraka (1934–) and Ted Joans (1928–). The poets of the American Beat generation (*q.v.*) also contributed. The vogue spread to Britain in the mid-1950s and has flourished ever since. Notable jazz poets have been Christopher Logue (1926–), a pioneer of the movement, Roy Fisher (1930–), Michael Horowitz (1935–), Pete Brown (1940–), Spike Hawkins (1942–) *et al.* The 1970s and 1980s – era of punk, post-punk and the new wave sub-cultures – in turn produced a further 'generation' of jazz poets, especially John Cooper Clarke and the Anglo-Jamaicans James Berry and E. K. Braithwaite. *See also* LIVERPOOL POETS; SUB-CULTURE; UNDERGROUND LITERATURE/POETRY.

je ne scai (sais) **quoi** (F 'I don't know what') An example of critical jargon popular in France in the 17th c. and used to suggest the existence of some otherwise indefinable merit, quality, property or grace (*q.v.*) in a work of art or literature. The term was first used in England *c.* 1656 to describe a sensation or awareness of illness which had no apparent cause. In the 18th c. it served, as it had in France, to describe otherwise indescribable merits in a poetical work. By the end of that century it no longer functioned as a 'support', as Pope put it, to 'all ignorant pretenders to delicacy'. However, the phrase is still used occasionally (as it was in the 19th c.) for more or less its original purpose. We would put it more crudely now. For example: 'It's got something'.

Jeremiad A tale of woe; a sustained complaint; a prolonged railing against the world, the times, the estate of man and God. By allusion to *The Lamentations of Jeremiah* in the Old Testament. There are several good examples in Shakespeare's *Timon of Athens*; especially in the bitter exchanges between Timon and Apemantus.

jest book A collection of stories of a kind that was particularly popular in England and on the continent during and after the 16th c. Jest books were descendants of such collections of tales as the *Gesta Romanorum* ('jest' derives from *gesta* or *geste*), volumes of moral anecdotes like the *Alphabet of Tales* and *Speculum Laicorum*, and theological handbooks like John Bromyard's *Summa Praedicantium* (a kind of guide to easier preaching). The jests are often reminiscent of the medieval *fabliau* (*q.v.*) and for the most part are brief and didactic, humorous and satirical; sometimes they are ribald. The earliest known example in English is *A Hundred Merry Tales* (*c.* 1526). Later popular works were *The Geystes of Skoggan* (1565–6), an account of the exploits of John Scogan, a famous jester at the court of Edward IV; *Tarlton's Jests* (*c.* 1592); and *The Merry Conceited Jests of George Peele* (1607). A Latin source was the *Facetiae* of Poggio (late 14th c.). The modern counterpart of the old jest books is the compilation of jokes and stories for all occasions.

Jesuit drama The drama of the Jesuit schools was similar to other forms of scholastic drama and had a specific didactic purpose. The first plays were performed as part of the school curriculum. They were in Latin and their subjects were religious (or sacred): for instance, stories of people like Saul, Herod, Absalom, Judith,

Esther and St Catherine the martyr. The plays were designed to inculcate moral virtues.

The first recorded performance was at Messina in 1551. In the next ten years or so plays were performed at Cordoba, Ingolstadt, Munich and Vienna. By 1587 (only 53 years after the foundation of the Society of Jesus by St Ignatius Loyola), there were 148 Jesuit colleges in Europe and at least one play was performed at them every year. In 1586 the *Ratio atque Institutio Studiorum* provided for the acting of tragedies and comedies. Gradually, partly because of the influence of secular drama, ballet and opera, the plays became more ambitious and spectacular. Great pains were taken in perfecting the technique of presentation. Though plays were still written in Latin, the use of the vernacular became quite common. The range of subject matter was widened to include themes from national history and classical legend and history (e.g. the defeat of the Saracens at Messina in 1068, the liberation of Vienna in 1683, the lives of Pompey, Brutus, Croesus and Damocles).

This form of drama prospered throughout Europe during the 17th c. Productions became more and more sumptuous and elaborate, and technical effects increasingly ingenious and lavish. Such a standard of excellence was achieved that the plays were performed increasingly for the general public and at courts. During the 18th c. this form of drama fell gradually into desuetude. *See* SCHOOL DRAMA.

jeu d'esprit (F 'play of the mind') An epigram (*q.v.*), witticism or brief flight of fancy, urbanely expressed. Oscar Wilde was particularly adept at them; as in these lines from *A Woman of No Importance* (1893):

> Mrs Allonby: They say, Lady Hunstanton, that when good Americans die they go to Paris.
> Lady Hunstanton: Indeed? And when bad Americans die, where do they go?
> Lord Illingworth: Oh, they go to America.

See WIT.

jeu parti (F 'play divided') A kind of debate poem, which had some vogue in the 13th c., in which two characters argued over an hypothesis; usually some matter of love. The argument proceeded in alternating stanzas. Normally, at the end, the issue was referred to arbitration – perhaps by a patron. Poetic 'contests' of this kind are common in pastoral (*q.v.*). *See also* DEBAT; PARTIMEN; TENSON.

Jeux Floraux de Toulouse A form of poetic festival founded in 1323 by seven troubadours (*q.v.*) of Toulouse who formed themselves into a 'college' and in 1324 invited all troubadours to gather and compete with poems on the theme of the Virgin Mary. The prize was a golden violet. The festival turned into an annual event and two other prizes were added: a silver marigold and a silver eglantine. Late in the 15th c. Dame Clémence Isaure endowed the college with property. Well-known poets who competed and won prizes include Du Bartas (1544–90), Philippe Fabre d'Eglantine (1755–94) and Victor Hugo (1802–85). Fabre adopted the name 'Eglantine' because he won the *prix de l'Eglantine* (i.e. a wild rose).

jig A form of dramatic after-piece (*q.v.*). Basically, it was a short farce (*q.v.*) with music and dancing. Common in Tudor and Jacobean drama. There are many references to them in the literature of those periods, and a particularly well-known one in *Hamlet* (II, ii, 494). William Kemp and Richard Tarlton, two famous comic actors, often performed them.

jingle Usually a verse or verses with a catchy rhythm, emphatic rhyme and alliteration. Often jingles verge on nonsense. For example:

Dingle dingle doosey,
The cat's in the well

Or:

One, two
Buckle my shoe;
Three, four,
Shut the door;
Five, six,
Pick up sticks.
Seven, eight,
Lay them straight:
Nine, ten,
A good fat hen.

Somewhere between jingle and patter (*q.v.*) or chant (*q.v.*) comes this kind of thing:

Dear Mother, the Army's a bugger: sell the pig and buy me out.
Your loving son John
Dear John, pig's gone: soldier on.

Plentiful examples are to be found in Geoffrey Grigson's *Faber Book of Popular Verse* (1972); in *The Oxford Nursery Rhyme Book* assembled by Iona and Peter Opie (1955); and in the Everyman Library *A Book of Nonsense* (1927). *See* DOGGEREL; DOUBLE DACTYL; JABBERWOCKY; NONSENSE; NURSERY RHYME; TONGUE-TWISTER.

Joe Miller A hackneyed joke, named after Joseph Miller (1684–1738), an actor and comedian in the Drury Lane Company who had a considerable reputation as a wit. Many stories and jokes were attributed to him.

jogral A Galician term for the Castilian *juglar*, the equivalent of the French *jongleur* and the English minstrel (*qq.v.*).

Johnsonian In the style or manner of Samuel Johnson (1709–84). That is, characterized by grand, lapidary language, balanced phrases, sentences and periods, Latinistic construction, and, often, a didactic tone. However, at its best, Johnson's full-dress manner displays a melodious resonance and a certain martial splendour. Moreover, he was perfectly capable of expressing in a pithy sentence what others might labour over in a paragraph. When verbose and pompous, language and style are sometimes called Johnsonese.

jongleur (F *jongleur* variant of *jougleur*, OF *jogleor*, L *joculatorem*) Though *jongleur* is a term which dates only from the 8th c., such entertainers were active much earlier. They were the literary descendants of the *mimi* and *histriones* of the Roman world. Besides being minstrels who sang and recited, many *jongleurs* were acrobats, jugglers and exhibitors of animals. As versatile professionals, they made a living where and when they could, and their audiences were plebian as well as patrician. They reached their apogee of popularity in the 13th c., and thereafter they declined. Individual versatility gave way to specialization. Because they were itinerant, they played a considerable part in disseminating literary forms throughout Europe. *See* GUSLAR; PAYADA; SCOP; SKALD; TROUBADOUR; TROUVERE.

joruri A form of Japanese puppet-theatre. Many major Japanese plays have been written for this form, including a number by Chikamatsu (1653–1725). Originally *joruri* was a kind of epic recitation which, *c.* 1630, was cross-fertilized with the puppet shows to create *ningyo-joruri*. The themes and subjects of these plays were mostly legends and historical events. Productions were lavish and the puppets (usually about two-thirds of life size) were manipulated by several puppeteers. The dialogue, accompanied by music, was delivered by a group from the side of the stage. A comparable form of drama is the Sicilian *opra d'i pupi*, once performed in many puppet theatres all over Sicily. *See also* KARAGOZ.

jouissance *See* PLAISIR/JOUISSANCE.

journal A paper, periodical (*q.v.*) or magazine (*q.v.*). It is often of a learned nature, like: *The Quarterly Review*; *Journal des Savants*; *Giornale storico della letteratura italiana. See* DIARY AND JOURNAL.

journalese This term denotes a manner of writing which employs ready-made phrases and formulas, and which breeds its own clichés in abundance.

We must distinguish between *journalese* and *headlinese*: the eye-catching and formulaic style of newsman's English. For example: Fire Horror in Spastic Home; Police Probe; Prime Minister Attacked in House; Sea Drama in Channel; Mother of Eight Adopts Monkey. Some carelessly worded headlines have become notorious: Chinese Generals Fly Back To Front; Tank Attacks Peter Out In Desert; Infantry Push Bottles Up German Rear.

journalism The occupation or profession of journalist; journalistic writing. Sometimes used derogatorily, in contradistinction to more exalted and less ephemeral forms of literature. But numerous able and distinguished authors have made a name for themselves as journalists. When newspapers increased their range early in the 19th c. many famous writers contributed to them (e.g. Coleridge, Southey, Hazlitt). Charles Dickens was a highly successful reporter; so were Rudyard Kipling and J. M. Barrie. American writers like Mark Twain and Bret Harte also made a name for themselves as journalists. In this century it has become common practice for novelists and poets to write for newspapers (e.g. Robert Graves, Aldous Huxley, Ernest Hemingway, Graham Greene, Norman

Mailer). In France there has long been a closer connection than elsewhere between newspapers and writers eminent in fiction and drama. Men of letters like Jean-Paul Sartre, Albert Camus, François Mauriac and Georges Duhamel have been well known for their contributions to journals and newspapers.

Joycean Characteristic of the style, tone and peculiarities of the writings of James Joyce (1882–1941), with particular reference to *Ulysses* (1922) and *Finnegans Wake* (1939). Principally, a high degree of stylistic and technical inventiveness and originality in the use of the pun, the portmanteau word, symbolism and the stream of consciousness (*qq.v.*) technique. It may also allude to his inclination towards scatology (*q.v.*), his habit of joining up numerous words and using little or no punctuation for many pages on end. Plus his creation of what is virtually a 'private language', especially in *Finnegans Wake*.

Jugendstil (G 'youth style') *Die Jugend* was an influential literary journal first published in Munich by George Hirth in 1896. Subsequently the journal gave its name to the style of work printed in it. Like baroque (*q.v.*) and impressionism (*q.v.*), *Jugendstil* is a term which was first used in the history of art, architecture and decoration, then applied to literature. It described a decorative style popular in Germany between 1890 and 1910. An attempt, perhaps, to escape from academic tradition. Its French counterpart is *art nouveau*.

junačke pesme (S 'men's songs') Songs or poems of oral tradition and the ballad (*qq.v.*) type frequently sung or chanted by South Slav men. Their themes are often war, revenge, death and treachery. A particularly fine example is the *Death of Ivo* (*Smrt Śenjanina Iva*). *See* NARODNE PESME; ZENSKE PESME.

juvenilia (L 'works done in one's youth') Such were Dryden's occasional poem *Upon the Death of Lord Hastings* (1649), written when Dryden was still at Westminster School and aged eighteen; Pope's *Pastorals*, composed in 1704, when he was only sixteen and published in Tonson's *Miscellany* (1709); Byron's *Hours of Idleness* (first called *Juvenilia*) published in 1807 when Byron was nineteen.

K

kabuki A type of Japanese drama. Popular rather than courtly or lyrical drama like *Nō* (*q.v.*), yet *kabuki* may well have developed from this in the 17th c. At any rate, it has adopted many subjects and conventions from *Nō*. The plays are presented on a stage like a *Nō* stage. It is wide and shallow and has what is called a 'flower way' running from the back of the hall or auditorium to the side of the stage. Along this actors make their exits and entrances. The stage is nearly always a revolving one. Scenery is elaborate and detailed. Costumes are rich and ornate. The characters are not masked (as in *Nō*) but are heavily made up. Female roles are taken by men. The dramas usually have some musical accompaniment, whose precise nature will depend on the kind of play. Scenery is changed by two stage-hands: one hooded and one not. By convention they are invisible, and are a survival from the time when each actor had a 'shadow' behind him who held a light on the end of a bamboo to illuminate the actor's features.

The plays are based on popular legends and myths (sometimes historical subjects) and are usually long and episodic. There are three main classes: *jidaimono*, or histories; *sewamono*, or domestic dramas; and *shosagoto*, or dances. A normal programme would present a variety of plays or scenes from these categories.

Kafkaesque Characteristic of the style, tone and attitudes of the writings of Franz Kafka (1883–1924), and especially the kind of nightmarish atmosphere which he was capable of creating through the pervasive menace of sinister, impersonal forces, the feeling of loss of identity, the evocation of guilt and fear, and the sense of evil that permeates the twisted and 'absurd' logic of ruling powers. His novels *The Trial* (1925) and *The Castle* (1926) and the short story *In the Penal Colony* are particularly noteworthy for such features.

kailyard school A group of writers (the best known are J. M. Barrie, J. J. Bell, S. R. Crockett and Ian Maclaren) who wrote stories about

Scottish peasant life late in the 19th c. The term derives from a Scottish Jacobite song 'There grows a bonnie brier bush in our kailyard', which Maclaren chose as a motto for his book *Beside the Bonnie Brier Bush* (1894). A kailyard was a cabbage patch or kitchen garden attached to a cottage.

karagöz A traditional Turkish shadow-puppet play (the equivalent of Punch and Judy) named after the principal character who represents Turkish Everyman or ordinary man. The antagonist (*q.v.*) or deuteragonist (*q.v.*) is Haçivat, usually represented as a lazy or self-important and officious character; clearly the 'baddy' to the 'good' Karagöz. Both persons are believed to be based on actual characters of the 14th c., from which period the karagöz entertainment dates.

There are thirty-odd traditional stories involving these characters, but one of the most popular themes is confusion arising from the meanings of words. Karagöz uses the colloquial language of the common people; Haçivat uses literary and high-falutin' terms. A third character, Efe (the equivalent of Robin Hood), is often introduced to solve the problem. The stock subjects give ample opportunity for improvisation, which will include jokes, satire, songs, dances, badinage with the audience and comments on current social and political matters. The puppeteer does the dialogue. *See also* JORURI; ORTA OYUNU.

kasa (K 'song words') A Korean verse form composed of octosyllabic lines, each line being sub-divided into two 'phrases'. There was no limit to the number of lines.

katauta A Japanese form of debate poem in the shape of question and answer. A standard form of *katauta* consists of three lines of five, seven and seven syllables respectively, all unrhymed. A pair of *katautas* comprise a *mondo*.

keneme A neo-Hellenic derivation from Greek *kenós* 'empty' used to denote a small word (article, conjunction or preposition) with little or no lexical meaning, whose function is mainly or entirely syntactic. For example: *the, and, at.* Such words are also known as *structure words* or *functors*. By contrast words like *angry* (adjective), *horse* (noun) and *clamber* (verb) have lexical meaning; that is, they do mean something on their own. These are sometimes called *pleremes* (from Greek *plḗrēs* 'full'). *See also* MORPHEME.

kenning The term derives from the use of the ON verb *kenna* 'to know, recognize' in the phrase *kenna eitt við* 'to express or describe one thing in terms of another'. The *kenning* (pl. *kenningar*) was a favourite figure in skaldic verse, where it is employed most lavishly.

It is a device for introducing descriptive colour or for suggesting associations without distracting attention from the essential statement.

Some Old Norse kennings were fairly complex: (a) *Fróda mjǫl* – 'meal (or corn) of Fródi' and so 'gold'. (Fródi was an early and legendary king of Denmark. He had a mill named Grotti which would grind out whatever was asked of it. Gold was the first material for which Fródi asked.); (b) *Vidris munstrandar marr* – 'the weather-maker's mind-strand'; that is, 'sea of Odin's breast' and so 'poetry'; (c) *brimils vǫllr* – 'seal's field' and so 'sea'; (d) *malmhrið* – 'metal storm' and so 'battle'; (e) *Odins eiki* – 'Odin's oak' and so 'warrior'.

Old English kennings were simpler: (a) *helmberend* – 'helmet bearer' and so 'warrior'; (b) *beadoleoma* – 'battle light' and so 'flashing sword'; (c) *swansrad* – 'swan road' and so 'sea'. *See also* HOMERIC EPITHET; PERIPHRASIS; POETIC DICTION; RIMUR.

key novel *See* LIVRE A CLEF.

kharja A form of popular verse written in Arabic or Romance, in the idiom of the common people (and found in Spain). It produces an effect of sadness or despair or longing. It is probably earlier than the *muwashshah* of which it commonly forms the final part or refrain. It was usually given to a woman to utter, but was generally composed by a man. *See* MOZARABIC LYRIC.

kinaesthetic image Kinaesthesis denotes a sense of movement or muscular effort (from Gk *kineein* 'to move' + *aisthesis* 'sensation'). A sense of movement and effort is inherent in the rhythm, momentum and energy of words in such an image. It is the visual/physical counterpart of onomatopoeia (*q.v.*). William Faulkner (1897–1962), for instance, excelled in such images in prose. Gerard Manley Hopkins (1844–89) excelled at them in verse. These lines come from his *Harry Ploughman*:

By a grey eye's heed steered well, one crew, fall to;
Stand at stress. Each limb's barrowy brawn, his thew
That onewhere curded, onewhere sucked or sank –
Soared or sank –,
Though as a beechbole firm, finds his, as at a roll-call, rank
And features, in flesh, what deed he each must do –
His sinew-service where do.

See also KINETIC POEM; PHANOPOEIA.

kind A term widely used in the 17th and 18th c. for a literary type or genre (*q.v.*). Criticism determined the category of a work (e.g. epic, tragedy, elegy) and then decided whether or not it obeyed the rules and conventions. Dryden was one of the first to indicate that a writer must begin by deciding what kind he wished to practise. Writers of the Romantic period (*q.v.*) rejected such an approach. *See* FORM.

kinetic poem A poem whose movement depends on the careful placement and programming of words or letters line by line or page by page in order to achieve a visual pattern. *See* ALTAR POEM; CONCRETE POETRY/VERSE; KINAESTHETIC IMAGE; PATTERN POETRY; PHANOPOEIA.

King's English English as it should be spoken. This term was used as early as the 16th c. Thomas Wilson refers to it in his *Arte of Rhetorique* (1553) thus: 'These fine English clerkes will sai thei speake in their mother tongue, if a manne should charge them for counterfeityng the Kinge's Englishe'. A reference to 'Queene's English' occurs in Nashe's *Strange Newes of the Intercepting Certaine Letters* (1593); Shakespeare uses the term in *The Merry Wives of Windsor* (1600–01) and Dekker refers to the 'Kinge's English' in *Satiromastix* (1602). *See* COLLOQUIALISM; SLANG; STANDARD ENGLISH.

Kit-Cat Club A literary club founded early in the 18th c. in London. So called because its members met at the house of a pastry-cook named Christopher Kat or Cat (or Katt or Catling) in Shire Lane (near Temple Bar). Kat's mutton pies were called Kit-cats. Distinguished members of the club were Joseph Addison, Richard Steele, William Congreve, Sir John Vanbrugh and Sir Samuel Garth. They later used the premises of Jacob Tonson, the publisher, at

Barn Elms. Many members had their portraits painted by Sir Godfrey Kneller. They are less than half length because the dining room was too low for half-size portraits. This size of canvas has come to be known as kit-cat (36 × 28 inches, it shows the head and one hand).

kitchen-sink drama A term which became popular in Great Britain in the middle and late 1950s. Often used derogatorily, it applied to plays which, in a realistic fashion, showed aspects of working-class life at the time. The implication was that the play centred, metaphorically (or psychologically) and in some cases literally, on the kitchen sink. The works of John Osborne, Arnold Wesker and Alun Owen (among others) were all so described. It is doubtful if the term derives in any way from Wesker's play *The Kitchen* because this was first presented in a production without décor in 1958, and not given a full production until 1961. *See* ANGRY YOUNG MAN.

kitsch (G *kitschen* 'to throw together') A pejorative term for a work which is of little merit; a mere potboiler (*q.v.*); something 'thrown together' to gratify popular taste.

klucht A form of drama which flourished in the Netherlands in the Middle Ages, but was still alive in the 17th c. They tended to be short plays which satirized sexual matters.

knickerbocker group A group of early 19th c. New York writers. The term derives from *History of New York to the end of the Dutch Dynasty*, by Washington Irving, under the pseudonym Diedrich Knickerbocker (1809). Two of its more famous members were James Fenimore Cooper and Henry Wadsworth Longfellow. Later a publication called *Knickerbocker Magazine* was produced (1833–65), but by then the group had either died or dispersed.

Knittelvers (G 'cudgel verse') What we would call doggerel (*q.v.*); a term employed derogatorily in the 17th c. of a popular meter used in 15th and 16th c. German poetry. *Knittelvers* consisted of octosyllabic rhyming couplets. The meter was revived in the 18th c. by Gottsched, and then used by Schiller and Goethe.

kommos In classical Greek drama, a type of lyric in dialogue form sung by the Chorus (*q.v.*) to express profound emotion.

Kontrafaktur A German term to denote the adaptation of a secular song (e.g. a folksong) so that it has a religious theme and significance. Such adaptations were common in the 15th c. and there were a good many instances later. Luther's Christmas hymn *Vom Himmel hoch da komm ich her* (1535) is often cited as a notable example of the process.

kosmisty *See* SMITHY POETS.

Kraftgenie (G 'power genius') During the *Sturm und Drang* (*q.v.*) movement this term denoted creative and imaginative originality and dynamic energy. Goethe and some of his associates regarded themselves as *Kraftgenies*. The concept of such a personality/character in literature is to be found in such characters as Götz in Goethe's *Götz von Berlichingen* (1773) and in Simsone Grisaldo, the eponymous hero of Klinger's play in 1776. *See also* OUTSIDER.

Kriminalgeschichte (G 'criminal history') A term applied primarily to miscellaneous writings about crime and criminals in the 18th and 19th c. when there was an increasing (and sometimes morbid) interest in violent crime. True criminal stories were popular reading. An early twenty-volume collection of criminal histories appeared in France, titled *Causes célèbres et intéressantes* (1734). This was translated into German and published under the title *Der Pitaval* (1747–68). A second French collection was also translated into German and published in 1792–5. Volumes of German cases came out in the period 1842–65 under the title *Der neue Pitaval.* Crime had begun to attract the interest of German novelists and playwrights. Schiller wrote two works of fiction which had crime and murder as themes, namely *Der Verbrecher aus verlorener Ehre* (1786) and the unfinished *Der Geisterseher* (1787–9). E. T. A. Hoffmann contributed with his weird and frightening *Novelle* (*see* NOVELLA) *Das Fräulein von Scuderi* (1819). Later came Annette von Droste-Hülshoff's *Die Judenbuche* (1842). In 1829 Adolf Müllner published what is very probably the first detective story (*q.v.*) in German – *Der Kaliber*. In fact, the detective story (*Detektivroman*) did not develop in Germany as it did elsewhere. *See also* CRIME NOVEL; NEWGATE FICTION.

Künstlerdrama *See* KUNSTLERROMAN.

Künstlernovelle *See* KUNSTLERROMAN.

Künstlerroman (G *Künstler* 'artist' + *Roman* 'novel) A novel (*q.v.*) which has an artist (in any creative art) as the central character and which shows the development of the artist from childhood to maturity and later. This kind of novel was particularly popular in Germany and dates from very late in the 18th c. and the beginning of the 19th c. It thus coincides with the start of the romantic revival (*q.v.*), a period when the artist (whatever his *métier*) was held in high esteem, and the man of genius (*q.v.*) became an exalted figure. This 'exaltation' had been foreshadowed during the *Sturm und Drang* (*q.v.*) period by the German concept of the *Kraftgenie* (*q.v.*).

Fictitious artists were often favoured central figures. Goethe was among the first to develop the *Künstlerroman* with *Wilhelm Meisters theatralische Sendung* (composed *c.* 1777–85, but not discovered until 1909), the original version of *Wilhelm Meisters Lehrjahre* (1795–6), which had a sequel in the shape of *Wilhelm Meisters Wanderjahre oder Die Entsagenden*, his last novel, published in 1821. Other well-known examples are: Tieck's *Franz Sternbalds Wanderungen* (1798); Eduard Mörike's *Maler Nolten* (1832); Franz Grillparzer's *Novelle Der arme Spielmann* (1848); Gottfried Keller's *Der grüne Heinrich* (1854–5); Jakob Wassermann's *Das Gänsemännchen* (1915); Thomas Mann's *Novelle Tonio Kröger* (1903) and his *Doktor Faustus* (1947).

There are also a number of works whose central character is an historical figure. Examples are: Mörike's *Novelle Mozart auf der Reise nach Prag* (1855); Albert Brachvogel's *Friedemann Bach* (1858); Walter von Molo's *Der Schiller-Roman* (1912–16); and Franz Werfel's *Verdi* (1924).

Fictitious or historical *Künstlerdramen* ('artist plays') were also popular. For instance: Goethe's *Torquato Tasso* (1807); Grillparzer's *Sappho* (1818); Hauptmann's *Die versunkene Glocke* (1896), *Michael Kramer* (1900) and *Gabriel Schillings Flucht* (1912).

In English literature the most famous example of a *Künstlerroman* is James Joyce's *A Portrait of the Artist as a Young Man* (1916). The *Künstlerroman* and the *Bildungsroman* (*q.v.*) are closely associated, and literary historians and critics have put Goethe's *Wilhelm Meister* in the latter category. *See also* AUTOBIOGRAPHICAL NOVEL.

Kunstlied (G *Kunst* 'art' + *Lied* 'song') An artistic and sophisticated song, as distinguished from a *Volkslied* or 'folksong' (*q.v.*).

Kunstmärchen A German term for a 'literary' folk tale, and thus one which is written down; as opposed to one which belongs to the oral tradition (*q.v.*). *See* VOLKSMARCHEN.

Kurzgeschichte German for 'short story' (*q.v.*), which is a vague enough term in English. *Kurzgeschichten* tend to be brief to the point of terseness.

kviðuháttr (ON *kviða* 'an epic song, poem or ballad' and *háttr* 'meter') An ON alliterative verse (*q.v.*) form, similar to the *fornyrðislag* (*q.v.*). It consists of alternating three- and four-syllable lines. What is believed to be the earliest poem containing this form is *Ynglingatál* (prior to 900). In the 10th c. the form appears in Skallagrímsson's *Arinbjarnarkviða* and *Sonatorrek*. In general the term means little more than the meter used for epic poems, such as the *Völuspá*.

kyogen A form of Japanese comic drama which originally developed as a type of interlude (*q.v.*) in *Nō* (*q.v.*) performances. The plays are short and irreverent. A stock theme concerns the smart, opportunist servant who outwits his blockheaded master; the kind of theme popular in low comedy and *commedia dell'arte* (*qq.v.*).

kyŏnggich'aega A form of aristocratic Korean poem with a fixed refrain. The subjects were often the natural scene; a kind of topographical poetry (*q.v.*).

kyrielle A shortened form of *kyrie eleison* (Gk 'Lord have mercy'). A French verse form usually consisting of eight-syllable lines in couplets. Or, quatrains (*q.v.*) rhymed aabb. The refrain (*q.v.*) may consist of the last word in a line, a complete line, or part of a line.

L

label names *See* APTRONYM.

Labrador, Juan A stock character (*q.v.*) – the Spanish folk hero and symbol of the hard-working peasant who achieves success through his own efforts. 'Immortalized' by Lope de Vega in his play *El villano en su rincón* (*c.* 1611).

lai *See* LAY.

laisse A stanzaic or verse paragraph (*q.v.*) division in OF epics.

lake poets Wordsworth, Coleridge and Southey. They came to be known as the Lake School or 'Lakers' as a result of the abusive articles written by Francis Jeffrey, a Scottish judge, in the *Edinburgh Review* over a period of twenty years – beginning in 1802. He associated these three poets with the Lake District in Cumbria. *See also* COCKNEY SCHOOL OF POETRY.

lament An expression of deep regret or sorrow for the loss of a person or position. A non-narrative kind of poetry, it appears to grow up alongside heroic poetry and is widespread in many languages. Famous examples are: *The Lamentations of Jeremiah*, David's Lament for Saul and Jonathan, the OE *Deor's Lament*, Dunbar's *Lament for the Makaris*, and Burns's *Lament for Flodden* and *Lament for Culloden. See* COMPLAINT; CORONACH; DIRGE; ELEGY; EPICEDIUM; MONODY; UBI SUNT.

lampoon The term derives from the French *lampon*, said to be from *lampons* 'Let us drink', used as a refrain. It dates only from the 17th c. The verb *lamper* means to 'swig' or 'to booze'. This suggests excess, coarseness, a rough crudity; a lampoon in fact is a virulent or scurrilous form of satire (*q.v.*). It is more likely to be found in graphic caricature than in writing but there are a few notable examples in literature, like Pope's attack on Hervey in his *Epistle to Arbuthnot*, and this description by Dryden of the unfortunate Shadwell (here named Og) in *Absalom and Achitophel* (Pt II) beginning thus at line 457:

> Now stop your noses, Readers, all and some,
> For here's a tun of Midnight work to come,
> Og from a Treason Tavern rowling home.
> Round as a Globe and Liquored ev'ry chink,
> Goodly and Great he Sayls behind his Link.
> With all this Bulk there's nothing lost in Og,
> For ev'ry inch that is not Fool is Rogue:
> A Monstrous mass of foul corrupted matter,
> As all the Devils had spew'd to make the batter.
> When wine has given him courage to Blaspheme,
> He curses God, but God before curst him;
> And if man cou'd have reason, none has more,
> That made his Paunch so rich and him so poor.

See also DIATRIBE; FLYTING; INVECTIVE; PASQUINADE.

langue and parole Terms introduced by Ferdinand de Saussure (1857–1913). They make cardinal distinctions and are of fundamental importance to structuralism (*q.v.*). Their English equivalents are approximately, but inadequately, 'language' and 'speech'. *Langue* denotes the system or totality of language shared by the 'collective consciousness'. Thus, all the elements of a language plus the rules for their combination (grammar, syntax and so forth). *Parole* is the use which individuals make of the resources of language, which the system produces and combines, in speech or writing. Thus, utterance. Taken in conjunction the terms create an antinomy (*q.v.*) of the social and shared. A further antinomy or dichotomy is implied in the idea that *langue* is abstract and *parole* is concrete. *Langue* is what people use when thinking and conceptualizing (abstract); *parole* what they use in speaking or writing (concrete).

Saussure makes an evaluative distinction; as Raman Selden puts it: 'The proper object of linguistic study is the system which underlies any particular human signifying human practice, not the individual utterance'. That is, *langue* is more important than *parole*.

Noam Chomsky (1928–) made a similar dichotomy with his

terms 'competence' and 'performance' (*q.v.*). *See also* IDIOLECT; SEMIOTICS/SEMIOLOGY.

langue d'oc/langue d'oïl In Roman Gaul Latin was the lingua franca. In the course of the Roman occupation the language underwent many changes and developments in different regions and numerous dialects evolved. Gradually these dialects formed two basic groups: *langue d'oc* and *langue d'oïl*. They came to be thus called after the words used in them to represent *oui* ('yes'): 'oc' derived from Latin *hoc*; 'oïl' from a contraction or vocalic glide of Latin *hoc ille*. The Provençal language *langue d'oc* was used south of a line which ran approximately west to east from the Gironde (near Bordeaux) to the Alps. *Langue d'oïl* was spoken north of that line. The latter evolved into the French language. Languedoc remains as the name of a large region in the south-east. The troubadours (*q.v.*) used *langue d'oc*; the *trouvères* (*q.v.*) used *langue d'oïl*. *See also* JONGLEUR.

lapidaires Medieval French works which expounded the talismanic and curative properties of precious stones. The discourse was sometimes accompanied by allegorical interpretations. Examples of *lapidaires* occur in the 12th and 13th c. Philippe de Thaon (12th c.) was the author of one. To about the same period belongs one in Latin by Marbode, the Bishop of Rennes.

Latinism A word, phrase, or grammatical construction based on a Latin form or model. Characteristic of many prose and verse styles from the 17th c. onwards; and particularly in the 18th c. when the influence of the Roman authors was at its strongest. Latinisms are common in Milton, Johnson and Gibbon, to name only three of the major influences.

lauda A religious poem or song adapted from the liturgy. The earliest examples were in Latin and date from the 13th c. Two well-known ones were the *Stabat Mater* and the *Dies Irae*. Later they were composed in the vernacular. St Francis produced a noble work in *Cantico delle Creature*, and Jacopone da Todi composed a fine collection of *laude*. The chanting of *laude* was an important part of the activities performed by *laudesi* fraternities. Religious sects like the *flagellanti* and *disciplinati* also made them a part of their ritual.

laureate *See* POET LAUREATE.

lay (OF *lai*) A short narrative or lyrical poem intended to be sung. The oldest narrative *lais*, mostly in octosyllabics (*q.v.*), are the *Contes* of Marie de France (*c.* 1175). They were stories of romance believed to have been based on Celtic legends. The lyric lays were Provençal and usually had love themes. The oldest in OF were by Gautier de Dargiès (early 13th c.). The term 'Breton lay' was applied to 14th c. English poems with a Breton setting and similar to those by Marie de France. A dozen or more are extant in English, the best known being *Sir Orfeo*, *Havelok the Dane*, *Sir Launfal* and Chaucer's *Franklin's Tale*. Since the 16th c. the term *lay* has been used more loosely to denote any historical ballad or narrative of adventure. Good examples are Scott's *Lay of the Last Minstrel* (1805) and Macaulay's *Lays of Ancient Rome* (1842). *See also* BALLAD; CONTE; FABLIAU; NOUVELLE; ROMANCE.

Leatherstocking Tales The title given to five novels by James Fenimore Cooper (1789–1851). They are novels of American frontier life, whose hero, Natty Bumppo, was nicknamed 'Leatherstocking'. *See also* WESTERN.

Leavisite A follower of F. R. Leavis (1895–1978); or descriptive of one who uses Leavis's methods and approach in the tasks of teaching and practical criticism (i.e. criticism based on the detailed analysis of a text). The term is used pejoratively by those who disagree with Leavis's methods.

lectio difficilior (L 'the harder reading') That principle which may guide an editor in choosing between two manuscript variants of apparently equal authority.

lectionary From the Ecclesiastical Latin *lectionarium*, denoting a book containing extracts from the Scriptures to be read at Divine Service.

ledger The word probably derives from OE *licgan* 'to lie', *lecgan* 'to lay', and denotes a register (*q.v.*) or account book; especially the principal books of accounts among merchants in which the entries in all the other books are entered. Thus a sort of centralized master-copy. *See also* BOOK; MANUSCRIPT; ROLL.

legend (MedL 'things to be read') Originally legends were the stories of lives of saints which, in monastic life, might be read in church or in the refectory and therefore belonged to hagiography (*q.v.*). The term came to be applied to a collection of such stories (as well as the book in which they were recorded). An outstanding example of such a collection is the 13th c. *Legenda Aurea* ('The Golden Legend') of Jacobus de Voragine. Chaucer, no doubt, was using *legend* in a similar sense in his *Legend of Good Women*, a group of stories (in the manner of Ovid's *Heroides*) about famous women of antiquity (Cleopatra, Thisbe, Dido, Medea, Lucrece, Ariadne, Philomela *et al.*). Recently Slovene authors like Francé Berk and Ludvik Mrzel have revived the Chaucerian type in the reworking of biblical themes.

Subsidiary meanings of the term are: (a) the title or description beneath an illustration; (b) the explanation of the symbols on a map; (c) a story or narrative which lies somewhere between myth (*q.v.*) and historical fact and which, as a rule, is about a particular figure or person. Famous examples are Faust, the Flying Dutchman, the Wandering Jew, Hamlet, Beowulf, King Arthur, Charlemagne, Robin Hood, Jasonik (the Czech Robin Hood), Skandarbeg (the Albanian national hero), Marko Kraljević (the South Slav warrior hero) and Dhigenis (the Greek warrior hero). Any popular folk hero (or heroine), revolutionary, saint or warrior is likely to have legends develop about him; stories which often grow taller and longer with time and which may eventually be written down or recited in song, verse and ballad (*q.v.*), through which means the oral tradition (*q.v.*) is sustained. Two modern examples of such folk heroes are Salvatore Giuliano (the Sicilian Robin Hood type bandit and political revolutionary) and Che Guevara. Quite often the stories and motifs which accrete to such figures had nothing to do with them in the first place. Recent and familiar examples of this accretive process are the many stories that have gathered about the names and personalities of men like W. G. Grace, Churchill, Rommel and Lord Montgomery – not to mention the statements ascribed to them.

legitimate theatre Often abbreviated in the business to 'legit'. It describes 'straight' drama; that is, a theatrical performance without songs, dances or musical accompaniments and interludes of any kind. The term derives from the old theatre-licensing laws which were designed to cover only non-musical entertainments. These regulations could be evaded by the addition of musical interludes. *See* PATENT THEATRES.

Lehrstück (G 'didactic play') This term came into use in the 1920s to describe a kind of drama (which was related to music theatre, *q.v.*) whose purpose was to teach rather than to entertain an audience. It was very probably a development of Hindemith's *Gemeinschaftsmusik* ('community music'), presented in 1929 at the Baden-Baden chamber music festival. On that occasion Bertolt Brecht, Kurt Weill and Hindemith presented the *Badener Lehrstück vom Einverständnis* and the *Lindberghflug* (the latter on radio). The didactic element was political and derived from Brecht's study of Karl Marx. In the early 1930s Brecht produced other *Lehrstücke* with a Communist 'message'. They were *Der Jasager und Der Neinsager, Die Massnahme* and *Die Ausnahme und die Regel. Lehrstücke* were an important part of his epic theatre (*q.v.*) and their creation was influenced by Japanese *Nō* drama (*q.v.*). *See also* AGITPROP DRAMA.

Lehrtheater *See* EPIC THEATRE; LEHRSTUCK.

Leich (G 'lyric') A medieval German lyric (*q.v.*) form widely used between 1200 and 1350. It was sung to music and may have been accompanied by dance. Three main types have been distinguished: the *Tanzleich* or dance lyric; the *religiose Leich* or religious lyric; and the *Minneleich* or love lyric. It appears that after the 14th c. the form survived only in religious poetry.

leitmotif (G *Leitmotiv* 'leading motif') A term coined by Hans von Wolzugen to designate a musical theme associated throughout a whole work with a particular object, character or emotion, as so often in Wagner's operas. Thomas Mann used it as a literary term to denote a recurrent theme (*q.v.*) or unit. It is occasionally used as a literary term in the same sense that Mann intended, and also in a broader sense to refer to an author's favourite themes: for example, the hunted man and betrayal in the novels of Graham Greene.

lemma The argument (*q.v.*) or subject of a composition, prefixed as a heading or title.

Leonine rhyme A form of internal rhyme (*q.v.*) in which the word before the caesura (*q.v.*) rhymes with the last word of the line of verse. Traditionally it is named after Leo, a 12th c. Canon of St Victor's in Paris, whose Latin verses contained such a device. However, Ovid used it in *Ars Amatoria*, and the OE *Rhyming*

Poem is also Leonine. Tennyson used it at random in *The Revenge*, from which these lines come:

> And the stately Spanish men to their flagship bore him then,
> Where they laid him by the mast, old Sir Richard caught at last,
> And they praised him to his face with their courtly foreign
> grace;
> But he rose upon their decks, and he cried:
> 'I have fought for Queen and Faith like a valiant man and true;
> I have only done my duty as a man is bound to do:
> With a joyful spirit I Sir Richard Grenville die!'
> And he fell upon their decks, and he died.

See also CROSSED RHYME.

letrilla (Sp diminutive of *letra* 'a short gloss') It is a poem in short lines and very often with a refrain (*q.v.*). The themes and topics were commonly light and satirical. A well-known example is Góngora's *Andeme yo caliente, y ríase la gente* (17th c.).

letter Latin rhetoricians made a convenient distinction between the private letter (*personalis*) and the letter of affairs (*negotialis*). A third kind is the open or general letter addressed to an individual or a newspaper editor, and intended for publication. Some manuals of letters survive from Classical times. In the Middle Ages there were a large number of manuals on the subject. Many medieval treatises on rhetoric were also 'guides' to letter writing.

Nearly any sort of letter may be of use to the historian and the biographer. A very famous collection is *The Paston Letters* (*c.* 1422–1509), the correspondence of three generations of a Norfolk family. Other well-known collections of letters are those written by Mozart, Keats, Flaubert and Horace Walpole.

The letter form has been adapted and exploited in various ways since the 17th c. For example, there are Pascal's *Lettres Provinciales* (1656–7), a defence of Jansenism, dealing with divine grace and the ethical code of the Jesuits. Between 1687 and 1694 were published *Letters of a Turkish Spy*, a form of travel book (*q.v.*) in epistolary form which started a new genre in European literature. These pseudo-foreign letters purport to be written by a Turkish spy who sends in reports on various aspects of life in England, France, Spain and Italy. A better known example of this genre is Montesquieu's *Lettres Persanes* (1721). Voltaire made a highly individual contribution with *Lettres philosophiques* (1734), better known as *Lettres*

Anglaises. Another similar work was Madame de Graffigny's *Lettres d'une Péruvienne* (1747). Lady Mary Wortley Montagu also wrote a series of very entertaining *Turkish Letters* (1763) which gave an account of her travels in the Near East.

In the 18th c. the form of the epistolary novel (*q.v.*) was developed. Such novels included: Richardson's *Pamela* (1740), and his *Clarissa* (1747–8); Smollett's *Humphry Clinker* (1771), one of the best of the genre; and the French classic by Laclos, *Les Liaisons dangereuses* (1782). Lord Chesterfield's *Letters* to his natural son, Philip Stanhope, written almost every day from 1737 onwards, were intended to educate any young man. In fact, the whole collection combined a treatise of education with the kind of advice found in the courtesy book (*q.v.*).

During the 18th c. the letter served other purposes. Examples are: Bolingbroke's *Letter to Sir William Wyndham* (1717), a political polemic; Rousseau's *Lettre à D'Alembert sur les spectacles* (1758), a controversial treatise on the morality of drama; the *Letters of Junius*, a pseudonymous invective against individuals, published in the *Public Advertiser* (1769–71); and Edmund Burke's *A Letter to the Sheriffs of Bristol* (1777), a political address.

In the following century, two remarkable examples of letters are: Sydney Smith's *Letters of Peter Plymley* (1807), a defence of Catholic emancipation; and the correspondence, published as part of Cardinal Newman's *Apologia Pro Vita Sua*, between Charles Kingsley and Newman. Other notable writers of letters have been George Sand, Byron, Chateaubriand, Proust, Gide and Claudel and D. H. Lawrence. More recently, Albert Camus's *Lettres à un ami allemand* (1948) have shown once again the flexibility of the letter form. This distinguished work is more like an essay, or open letter, in which Camus argues moral issues arising from differing German and French attitudes. *See* EPISTLE.

letters patent *See* PATENT THEATRES.

lettrism A French literary movement founded in Paris in 1946 and particularly associated with Maurice Lemaître and Isidore Isou. Its members have experimented with forms of concrete poetry and pattern poems (*qq.v.*). They have produced what is called phonetic poetry, and toyed with 'hypergraphy', or picture-writing. Some of it is mere gimmickry.

level stress Also known as even accent (*q.v.*) it occurs when the stress falls evenly on two syllables in the same word, or on two adjacent monosyllables, e.g. *buckwheat*; *gang plank*. *See* HOVERING STRESS; SPONDEE.

lexicographer A maker of dictionaries. In Johnson's famous phrase 'a harmless drudge'.

lexicography The art or task of making a dictionary (*q.v.*).

lexicon The dictionary (*q.v.*) itself, but usually the term denotes a dictionary for Classical languages; also Hebrew and Arabic. *See also* ONOMASTICON.

lexis In computational stylistics (that is, the analysis of an author's writing by computerized measurement) *lexis* is the term for the actual vocabulary of the author while *taxis* denotes the arrangement of the words. For instance, the lexical/taxical computation of the works of James Joyce would show the frequency of the recurrence of words and parts of speech; an analysis of grammatical structure; the number of times a particular word was used per page; the number of ablative absolutes (for example) per chapter; variations from normal order or structure; lengths of words by letters and by syllables; and length of sentences. Actually, this branch of linguistic science is not new. A Sanskrit grammar of *c.* 500 BC provides the number of syllables, words and verses in the *Rig-Veda*. Though this might appear to be one of the less fruitful activities of the academic industry, it has been helpful in reconstructing blurred and missing passages in the Dead Sea Scrolls.

liaison (F 'binding' or 'joining', formed from *lier* 'to bind') In the 17th c. a dramatic principle which required that the parts of a play be linked by various kinds of liaison: (a) *présence* – a character remaining from the preceding scene; (b) *vue ou recherche* – a character entering sees another about to leave and vice versa; (c) *bruit* – a noise on stage which brings in a character in search of an explanation; (d) *discours* – when a character in hiding later speaks.

libretto (It 'little book') The text of an opera or operetta (*qq.v.*) or any fairly substantial vocal composition, like an oratorio, which involves dialogue and narrative. The term was first used in England in 1742. Well-known librettists include Quinault, Catzabigi, da Ponte, Schikaneder, Boito, Gilbert, Hofmannsthal, J. B. Priestley and W. H. Auden.

libros de caballeria A genre of Spanish fiction which derived from the mid-13th c. cycle of French Arthurian romances. The genre lost its popularity towards the end of the 16th c. with the advent of the picaresque and pastoral novel (*qq.v.*).

Lied *See* MEISTERGESANG.

light comedy A loose term for plays which are airy, graceful, amusing (perhaps witty) and light-hearted, and which make minimal or no demands emotionally or intellectually. Among numerous examples the following are well-known repertory pieces: Noël Coward's *Hay Fever* (1925) and his *Blithe Spirit* (1941), Terence Rattigan's *French without Tears* (1936), William Douglas Home's *The Chiltern Hundreds* (1947) and his *The Reluctant Débutante* (1955). *See also* COMEDY; COMEDY OF HUMOURS; COMEDY OF MANNERS; DOMESTIC COMEDY; FARCE.

light ending *See* FEMININE ENDING.

light rhyme When one of a pair of rhyming syllables is unstressed. Common in ballad (*q.v.*), as in this stanza from the traditional ballad *Young Beichan*:

> O whan the porter came up the stair,
> He's fa'n low down upon his knee:
> 'Won up, won up, ye proud porter,
> An what makes a' this courtesy?'

light stress In verse, stress (*q.v.*) on a word which is not normally accented in speech. In the following lines from Edgar Allan Poe's *The Raven* the trochaic and dactylic meter requires a number of light stresses:

> Ónce ŭpón ă mídnĭght dreárў̆, whíle Ĭ póndĕred, weák ănd weárў̆,
> Óvĕr mánў̆ ă quáint ănd cúrĭoŭs vólŭme ŏf fŏrgóttĕn lóre,
> Whíle Ĭ nóddĕd, néarlў̆ náppĭng, súddĕnlў̆ thére cáme ă táppĭng,
> Ás ŏf sóme ŏne géntlў̆ ráppĭng.

light verse A vague and comprehensively flexible term used to describe poetry that lacks serious intent. Under this heading one might place: *vers de société*, occasional verse, nonsense verse, sick verse, satire, burlesque, parody, epitaph, epigram, limerick and clerihew (*qq.v.*), not to mention the acrostic and emblematic poems, the jingle and the riddle (*qq.v.*) and punning verses. The following lines from A. H. Bullen's *Musa Proterva* (1889), suggest the main attributes of light verse:

Gay, frolic verse for idle hours,
  Light as the foam whence Venus sprang;
Strains heard of old in courtly bowers,
  When Nelly danced and Durfey sang.

Wit, elegance, grace, ingenuity and technical virtuosity are among the distinguishing characteristics of light verse, as brilliantly displayed in, say, the libretti of W. S. Gilbert.

At its best it is often pithy and tends to the epigrammatic, as in the following example ascribed to William Ewer:

How odd
Of God
To choose
The Jews.

To which Cecil Browne is said to have 'replied' with:

But not so odd
As those who choose
A Jewish God
And spurn the Jews.

The first example has also been attributed (almost certainly inaccurately) to Hilaire Belloc – an outstanding writer of light verse – who was said to have written it on a menu card when dining with Wilfrid Meynell. Whereupon Meynell (it is said) promptly improvised and added:

How odd, Hilaire,
That you should dare
To doubt or prod
The choice of God.

A clever 'sequel' to this is the following subscribed by Mr E. R. Hardcastle (he composed it after reading *The Declaration of Arbroath*, 1320):

Less odd
If God
Had Pict
The Scots.

Among anthologies of light verse one might mention Thomas D'Urfey's *Wit and Mirth, or Pills to Purge Melancholy* (1719); Locker-Lampson's *Lyra Elegantiarum* (1867), and A. H. Bullen's *Lyrics from the Song-Books of the Elizabethan Age* (1888); as well as his *Speculum Amantis* (1888) and *Musa Proterva* (1889). *The Oxford Book of Light Verse* (1938), edited by W. H. Auden, illustrates better than most the possible scope of the form.

Much light verse is anonymous. Among the many famous and accomplished practitioners in English, mention should be made of Skelton, Campion, Herrick, Lovelace, Samuel (*Hudibras*) Butler, Prior, Goldsmith, Cowper, Hood, Theodore Hook, Oliver Wendell Holmes, C. S. Calverley, W. M. Praed, Edward Lear, Austin Dobson, Lewis Carroll, W. S. Gilbert, Hilaire Belloc, G. K. Chesterton, A. P. Herbert, T. S. Eliot, e. e. cummings, John Betjeman and Ogden Nash.

ligne donnée (F 'given line') Paul Valéry (1871–1945) spoke of the *ligne donnée* of a poem, thereby meaning the line that is 'given' to the poet by God, or by nature, or by a muse (*q.v.*), or by some power outside himself. The implication is that he has to find the other lines for himself. *See* AFFLATUS; DONNEE; FANCY AND IMAGINATION; INSPIRATION; INVENTION; SPONTANEITY.

limerick A type of light verse (*q.v.*) and a particularly popular fixed verse form in English. It usually consists of five predominantly anapaestic lines rhyming aabba, as in:

There was a young person of Mullion,
Intent upon marrying bullion;
  By some horrible fluke
  She jilted a duke
And had to elope with a scullion.

From this it will be seen that the first, second and fifth lines are trimeters (*q.v.*), and the third and fourth dimeters (*q.v.*), though these two may be printed as a single line with internal rhyme (*q.v.*) as in this limerick by Edward Lear:

There was a Young Lady of Lucca,
Whose lovers completely forsook her;
She ran up a tree and said 'Fiddle-de-dee!'
Which embarrassed the people of Lucca.

The origin of the term is obscure. There is one theory that it was an OF form brought to the Irish town of Limerick in 1700 by soldiers returning from the French war. Another that it originated in the nursery rhymes published in *Mother Goose's Melody* (*c.* 1765). A third that it stems from the refrain 'Will you come up to Limerick?' sung at convivial gatherings where such nonsense verses were fashionable. The limerick has also been linked with a group of mid-18th c. Irish poets at Croom who composed poems (in Irish) in limerick form during their drinking sessions at a pub.

In fact, it may be a much older form than has been supposed. Stephano's drinking song in *The Tempest* (II, ii) has a characteristic limerick rhythm. And the following lines date from an 11th c. manuscript:

The lion is wondrous strong
And full of the wiles of wo;
  And whether he pleye
  Or take his preye
He cannot do but slo [i.e. slay].

The limerick is to be found in the *History of Sixteen Wonderful Old Women* (1820) and in *Anecdotes and Adventures of Fifteen Gentlemen* (1822). Edward Lear, who composed a great many limericks, cited this latter volume as the source of his idea of the form. Lear popularized it in his *Book of Nonsense* (1846). As a result M. Russell, SJ, coined the term 'learic'.

Distinguished writers, such as Tennyson, Swinburne, Kipling, R. L. Stevenson, Dante Gabriel Rossetti, Mark Twain and W. S. Gilbert (among many others), experimented with the form and by the end of the 19th c. it was well established in both the clean and bawdy varieties. Early in the 20th c. it became very popular and newspapers even ran weekly competitions inviting readers to submit examples or to complete the final line of a given verse. Large prizes were available. It has flourished steadily since, often as oral poetry in clubs, messes, common rooms and sporting fraternities, and the tendency has been to exploit the final line to provide a witty or surprising conclusion.

Many of the best limericks are ribald, like:

A vice both obscure and unsavoury
Kept the bishop of Leicester in slavery.
Amidst terrible howls,
He deflowered young owls,
In a crypt fitted out as an aviary.

Clean ones may be equally witty, like this by Clement Attlee (he composed it on the eve of his installation as Knight of the Garter):

Few thought he was even a starter;
There were many who thought themselves smarter,
  But he ended PM
  CH and OM
An earl and a Knight of the Garter.

A large number also are innocuously obscene or pornographic, like the famous:

There was a young lady of Niger,
Who had an affair with a tiger.
  The result of the ****
  Was a bald-headed duck
Two gnats and a circumcised spider.

Though a comparatively humble form of verse, it is capable of distinction. Consider the following:

Titian was mixing rose madder.
His model posed nude on a ladder.
Her position to Titian
Suggested coition.
So he nipped up the ladder and 'ad 'er.

The rather grand and solemn opening line, the adroit use of assonance and internal rhyme (*qq.v.*) in the third and fourth lines and the quickening rhythm and colloquial language of the last line make a pleasing combination and contrast.

Modest form though it be it has lent itself to not a few developments and intricate variations, such as the 'double' limerick. This example is by Walter de la Mare:

There was an old skinflint of Hitching
  Had a cook, Mrs Casey of Cork,
There was nothing but crusts in the kitchen,
  While the parlour was sherry and pork,
  So at last Mrs Casey, her pangs to assuage,
  Having snipped off his buttons, curried the page.
  And now, while the skinflint gulps sherry and pork,
  In his parlour adjacent to kitchen,
To the tune blithe and merry of knife and of fork,
  Anthropophagy reigns in the kitchen.

And the 'extended' limerick:

There was a strange student from Yale,
Who put himself outside the pale.
  Said the judge: 'Please refrain
  When passing through Maine,
  From exposing yourself again in the train,
Or you'll just have to do it in jail.'

There are a number of 'reverse' limericks which are 'replies' to verses by Lear. For instance, the reply to 'There was an Old Man with a Beard' begins: 'I've combed out my beard and I've found . . .' Yet another kind is the 'beheaded' limerick – this example is by Arthur Shaw – which approximates to nonsense (*q.v.*) verse:

A chap was so pose that was adi
And the butt of such nage that was badi.
  He solved that was re
  Not to lay that was de
In taking steps cal that were radi.

Plus the tongue-twister (*q.v.*):

A flea and a fly in a flue
Were imprisoned, so what could they do?
  Said the fly: 'Let us flee'
  Said the flea: 'Let us fly'
So they flew through a flaw in the flue.

And the limeraiku (modelled on the *haiku*, *q.v.*, and invented by Ted Pauker):

There's a vile old man
Of Japan who roars at whores:
'Where's your bloody fan?'

And the limick, which Ogden Nash excelled at:

A young flirt of Ceylon
Who led the boys on,
Playing 'Follow the Leda',
Succumbed to a swan.

And the limerick poem, of which a famous example is the anonymous Old Man of Nantucket –

Who kept all his cash in a bucket.
His daughter, called Nan,

Ran away with a man,
And as for the bucket, Nantucket.

And so on.

And lastly what might be called the 'non' or 'truncated' limerick, or even, conceivably, the 'gimmerick':

A daring theologian of Aberystwyth
Met a young lady to play whist with.
She trumped his first trick,
So he took out his clasp-knife and cut her bloody throat from ear to ear.

See also MACARONIC.

limited edition An edition of a work which is restricted to a certain number of copies. They are usually numbered and the book is not reprinted in the same form.

line A formal structural division in a poem, normally classified according to the number of feet it contains. For example, a pentameter (*q.v.*) contains five feet, a hexameter (*q.v.*) six feet, and so on. *See* FOOT; METER.

line endings In prosody there are two general types, according to the position of the final stress (*q.v.*) near the end of the line. A masculine ending has the stress on the final syllable; the feminine has the last stress on the penultimate (occasionally the antepenultimate) syllable. The following verse from Sir John Suckling illustrates the two basic kinds:

Why so pale and wan, fond lover?
Prithee, why so pale?
Will, when looking well can't move her,
Looking ill prevail?
Prithee, why so pale?

The first and third lines are feminine; the others masculine.

Blank verse (*q.v.*), especially in Tudor and Jacobean drama, has many feminine endings (*q.v.*) which help to preserve colloquial speech rhythms.

lingo A loosely colloquial term for a foreign language or any strange unintelligible speech; as in 'Do you speak the lingo?' It probably derives from Portuguese *lingoa*, from Latin *lingua* 'a tongue'.

linguistics The scientific study of language. Descriptive linguistics classifies the characteristics; historical or comparative linguistics deals with its growth and development. The principal branches of linguistics are: etymology, semantics, phonetics, morphology and syntax.

linked rhyme *See* RHYME.

linked sonnet *See* SPENSERIAN SONNET.

lipogram (Gk 'wanting a letter') A composition in words from which a specific letter is deliberately omitted. For instance, Pindar's *Ode minus sigma* (5th c. BC) and Ronden's *Pièce sans A* (1816). Perhaps the most extraordinary examples are Lope de Vega's five novels, each of which omits one vowel. There seems little point to a lipogram except as an exercise in verbal ingenuity.

lira (Sp 'lyre') A Spanish stanza form and a special form of the *canción* (*q.v.*). It consists of a combination of five eleven-syllable and seven-syllable lines rhyming ababb. The name derives from Garcilaso de la Vega's fifth *canción* which begins 'Si de me baja lira'.

litany (Gk 'supplication') A liturgical prayer consisting of a series of petitions or invocations, often chanted by a church choir in procession.

literae humaniores (L 'the more humane letters') The phrase denotes the 'Classics', namely Latin and Greek, and is usually used in connection with the study of the Classics; so, a student may 'read Classics'. At Oxford University *literae humaniores* (often abbreviated to *lit. hum.*) refers to the study of them in a degree course, and this course is also referred to as 'Mods and Greats' (five terms for 'Mods' or 'Moderations' and seven terms for 'Greats'). It is not clear when *literae humaniores* came to denote Latin and Greek and their study, but during the Renaissance period it seems to have denoted the works of Classical Latin and Greek authors, as opposed to the theological works of the medieval schoolmen.

The Society of Jesus (the Jesuits) – founded by St Ignatius Loyola in 1534 – was approved by the Pope in 1540, and among the *litterae humaniores diuersarum linguarum* recognized in the *Ratio Studiorum* of Aquaviva (1599), which remained unaltered for centuries, the principal place was always assigned to Latin as the language of the

Society and the Roman Catholic Church. The Jesuit schools – the Jesuits were to play a very important part in education from the 17th c. onwards – became seminaries of what is called 'silver Latin'. The Latin grammar used in all schools for a great many years was that of Alvarez, the Jesuit Rector of the school at Lisbon (1572). Much more time and effort were devoted to the study of the style than the content of the 'pagan' Classics.

Dictionaries provide a reference to *literae humaniores* used as a phrase in 1747. As a degree course at Oxford, *literae humaniores* came into existence with the New Examination Statute of 1800. It was not confined to Classics. Candidates were examined in Divinity, Ethics, Rhetoric, Logic, Mathematics and Natural Philosophy as well as in 'the chief Latin and Greek classics'. The first Honours Examination under the new statute was held in 1802. In 1807 a new Honours School of Mathematics and Physics appeared as a separate entity from *literae humaniores*. Classics were also introduced. In 1808 Robert Peel (later to be British Prime Minister and founder of the police force – hence 'Bobbies' and 'Peelers') took the first 'double first'. This then meant a 'first' in *literae humaniores* and a 'first' in Maths and Physics, not in both 'Mods and Greats' as later. In 1809 Brasenose College monopolized the only three 'firsts' in *lit. hum.*

In 1850 a new First Public Examination was introduced to come between Responsions and the Final Schools ('Schools' denotes final exams which are done in the 'Schools' building). It soon became known as 'Moderations' or 'Mods' after the Moderators who conducted it, the term 'Examiners' being properly reserved for those who examined the Final Schools. Seven Moderators were appointed, of whom four examined in Greek and Latin literature and three in Maths. It seems that 'Greats' had already been for some time in use as a slang term for the Final Honours School. The OED cites its first instance in Cuthbert Bede's novel *The Adventures of Mr Verdant Green* published in 1853–7 ('Bede' was Edward Bradley's pseudonym). At some stage 'Greats' came to be specifically applied to the Final Honour School of *lit. hum.* Originally, 'Greats' had signified the Final School, as opposed to Responsions, which were 'Smalls'. It is not clear when the pattern of five terms for 'Mods' and seven for 'Greats' became fixed. The present structure may have arisen because undergraduates studied the poets and orators for 'Mods' and the philosophers and historians for 'Greats'. In the latter years of the 19th c. more emphasis came to be laid on philosophy and Greek and Roman history in their own rights. The pattern appears to have been well established by the 1890s. *See also* JESUIT DRAMA; SCHOLASTICISM; SCHOOL DRAMA.

literal Several meanings may be distinguished: (a) the misprint of a letter; (b) taking the meaning of words in their primary and non-figurative sense, as in literal interpretation; (c) giving an exact rendering of something, as in literal translation; (d) an opinion based on what is actuallly written, as opposed to what is implied. *See* FIGURATIVE LANGUAGE.

literariness The object of literary studies in the early phase of Russian Formalism (*q.v.*). Roman Jakobson defined it thus in 1919: 'The subject of literary science is not literature, but literariness, i.e. that which makes a given work a literary work'. Literariness is closely associated with what is known as defamiliarization (*q.v.*): both concepts emphasize that the defining features of a literary work reside in its form.

literary forgeries Early examples of forgery date from pre-Christian times. Heraclides Ponticus (4th c. BC) was alleged to have presented his own tragedies under the name of Thespis, the first Athenian tragic poet; and Lobon of Argos was accused of composing verses that he 'quoted' in a work on poets and poetry. Since those times – and increasingly since the Renaissance period – there have been celebrated instances of forgery. One of the best known concerns the *Letters of Phalaris* (148 in all), about which there was a dispute late in the 17th c. Phalaris was a tyrant of Acragas in the 6th c. BC. For many centuries the authenticity of the so-called letters was unquestioned. In 1692 Sir William Temple insisted on their authenticity in his essay *Of Ancient and Modern Learning*. Temple's opinions were attacked by William Wotton. Richard Bentley then became involved in the controversy and, in his *Dissertation on the Epistles of Phalaris*, proved beyond doubt that they were spurious and were probably written by a sophist in the 2nd c. AD. The whole affair was agreeably satirized by Swift in *The Battle of the Books* (1697).

During the early Renaissance, frauds of one kind and another proliferated as a result of the widespread enthusiasm for antiquity and classical learning. Some of the most famous were contained in the *Antiquitatum variarum volumina* of Johannes Annius (1432–1502). These included matter ascribed to Fabius Pictor and Myrsilus and the five spurious books of Berosus.

In *c.* 1660 certain erotic dialogues were ascribed to Luisa Sigea, a Spanish bluestocking (*q.v.*). They were in fact composed by one Nicolas Chorier, an antiquarian and a lawyer, who claimed that his Latin was a translation of Luisa's Spanish.

The annals of English literature contain some fine examples of fraudulence in the 18th c. The most exotic concerned the impostor George Psalmanazer (1679?–1763), born in southern France, who first adopted a mendicant life masquerading as a native Japanese Christian, and then passed himself off as a kind of pagan prototype drop-out who lived on roots, herbs and raw flesh. To make his imposture the more plausible he invented a language of his own and devised 'religious' ritual of a pagan kind. Having enlisted in a regiment of the Duke of Mecklenburg, he was taken up by a villainous clergyman named William Innes, chaplain to a Scottish regiment at Sluys. Innes, who, in effect, become his 'manager', baptised him as a Protestant convert, persuaded him to pretend that he was a native of Formosa and brought him to England where he presented him as a Christian Formosan who had been abducted by the Jesuits. Introduced by Innes to the Anglican hierarchy in 1703, he became an object of much curiosity and enjoyed a remarkable social success. He spoke Latin fluently with Archbishop Tillotson and dedicated his book, *Historical and Geographical Description of Formosa, an Island Subject to the Emperor of Japan* (1704), to Henry Compton, Bishop of London. The Bishop arranged for Psalmanazer to be sent to Oxford so that he could teach his fictitious Formosan to future missionaries. In 1707 Psalmanazar published *A Dialogue between a Japanese and a Formosan about Some Points of the Religion of the Time.* In *c.* 1707 Innes withdrew his support as mentor and was made Chaplain-General to the English forces in Portugal (this was a reward for his conversion of his protégé to Protestantism). Psalmanazar could not maintain the imposture without the cleric's help but still found patrons. Eventually he became a distinguished Hebraist, contributed to the *Universal History* and lived to a ripe old age. His *Memoirs* were published in 1764 and these gave an account of his deception. During his heyday the bogus Formosan was highly regarded, even venerated, by a multitude of eminent men, including Dr Johnson, who was wont to drink with him in an alehouse in Old Street, London. The image of the great lexicographer discussing aspects of phoney Formosan etymology with such an accomplished con-man gives piquancy to a wholely bizarre affair.

A much more serious and influential series of forgeries – which had some bearing on the 18th c. cult of primitivism (*q.v.*) – were those perpetuated by the Scot James Macpherson (1736–96). These came to be known as the Ossianic forgeries.

In 1758 Macpherson published *The Highlander*, an heroic poem in six cantos (*q.v.*). The following year he met John Home, the playwright, and presented him with his first Ossianic forgery, *The Death of Oscar*. Home and Hugh Blair, a Scottish divine and professor of rhetoric, gave encouragement to Macpherson, who, in 1760, produced *Fragments of Ancient Poetry, Collected in the Highlands of Scotland, and Translated from the Gaelic or Erse Language*. These fragments aroused considerable interest and there were rumours that a Gaelic epic existed. Macpherson now had a following and he scoured Scotland collecting materials for *Fingal, an Ancient Epic Poem, in Six Books* – which appeared in 1762. This was alleged to be a translation of an epic by Ossian, the son of Finn (or Fingal). The following year another epic, *Temora*, appeared. These combined events were a literary sensation. The news spread swiftly across Britain and to the continent, where German literary circles (which included Goethe, Schiller and Klopstock) became extremely enthusiastic. However, in England doubt and suspicion soon began to circulate. When Macpherson was asked to produce his originals he faked them. After Macpherson died a committee investigated the whole imposture and found that he had edited miscellaneous Gaelic poems and invented passages of his own. But, such was the popularity of the Ossianic poetry that many were reluctant to accept the fact that it was forgery.

Enthusiasm for Shakespeare's plays in the 18th c. also produced a spate of forgeries. George Steevens forged a letter from Peele to Marlowe on Shakespeare and passed it off for many years. William Henry Ireland (1777–1835) produced a mortgage-deed relating to Shakespeare, then extracts from a play titled *William the Conqueror* and then a complete play – *Vortigern and Rowena* – which Sheridan produced at Drury Lane in 1796. It was a disaster. By this stage Ireland was already under suspicion and in the same year acknowledged his deceits in *An Authentic Account of the Shakespearian Manuscripts*.

Later, another prominent forger of Shakespeareana was John Payne Collier (1789–1883). As librarian to the Duke of Devonshire he had access to documents and manuscripts, and he produced a succession of frauds: *New Facts Regarding the Life of Shakespeare* (1835), *New Particulars* (1836), *Further Particulars* (1839), *The Egerton Papers* (1840), *Memoirs of Edward Alleyn* (1841), *Alleyn*

Papers (1843) and *Diary of Philip Henslowe* (1845). Many scholars and antiquarians were duped, but Collier was gradually exposed in the 1850s.

No doubt Steevens, Ireland and Collier were affected by the successes of George Psalmanazar, and Macpherson, and other 18th c. forgers such as William Lauder and John Pinkerton. No doubt, too, they were influenced by the achievements of the prodigy Thomas Chatterton (1752–70), who began his career as a forger when only sixteen. In 1768 he produced *Felix Farley's Bristol Journey*, a piece of archaic prose which he supported with fake documents. There were also the famous 'Rowley' poems, including *The Bristol Tragedie*. These purported to be the creation of a 15th c. Bristol poet, Thomas Rowley, a friend of William Canynge (a Bristol merchant who actually existed). Chatterton also faked correspondence between the two, plus a treatise on painting 'bie T. Rowlie' and several Ossianic prose pieces. Controversy about his work went on for over a hundred years and he was much admired by other poets, including Wordsworth and Keats.

The most notorious of more recent forgers was Thomas James Wise (1859–1937), the bibliographer, collector and editor, who formed the great Ashley Library. He persuaded the printers Richard Clay and Sons to produce editions of short works by established authors that antedated the accepted first editions. His authors included Thackeray, Robert Browning, Elizabeth Browning, Matthew Arnold, George Eliot, Ruskin, Tennyson, Swinburne and Kipling. His masterpiece was Elizabeth Browning's *Sonnets* (Reading, 1847), which he launched in 1893. Wise was ultimately exposed in 1934 in *An Enquiry into the Nature of Certain Nineteenth Century Pamphlets* by John Carter and Graham Pollard. They cited fifty-four fraudulent works. Over thirty more were found in later years.

After the Second World War a sensation was caused by the so-called diary of Hitler's mistress Eva Braun. It was serialized in some newspapers and then found to have been composed of passages taken from *Meine Vergangenheit* by the Countess Larisch (which was first published in English in 1913).

Other famous forgeries were: (a) the old Czech texts issued by Václav Hanka in 1817 and 1818. The *Zelenohorský* was ascribed to the 9th–10th c. and the *Královédvorský rukopis* to the 13th c. These were ultimately exposed by Masaryk in 1886–7; (b) the forgery by Constantine Simonides of what was claimed to be the oldest Homer manuscript, which he sold in 1854 to Sir Thomas Phillipps, the great

19th c. private collector. Simonides also invented a work by Uranius on the kings of Egypt, which was denounced by the German scholar Tischendorf; (c) the fragments of *Deuteronomy* in Hebrew composed by Shapira, who claimed that they had been found by a Bedouin in a cave near the Dead Sea and that they dated from the 9th c. BC. The French scholar Charles Clermont-Ganneau concluded that they had been made from pieces cut from the edge of a synagogue scroll of the Law.

Literary forgery has seldom been a subject or theme in fiction, but Rudyard Kipling wrote one ingenious short story, *Dayspring Mishandled* (1928), which treats it cleverly and convincingly. It is also prominent in Peter Ackroyd's novel *Chatterton* (1987).

The dividing line between a forgery and a hoax may often appear to be thin. However, basically, a forger has a serious intention to deceive and maintain a deception. And he is likely to show much determination in avoiding exposure. Motives are various. Forgery may be for monetary gain, for revenge, to make a fool of someone (or many), or to discredit an authority; or merely to enjoy the vicarious laurels of anonymous fame in secrecy and privacy. Pride, vanity, spite and disappointment may all be motivating forces. A hoaxer, on the other hand, has a more light-hearted approach, regards the deception as a joke and, sooner or later, 'comes clean'.

There have been numerous literary hoaxes. Among the most successful were those achieved by Prosper Mérimée (1803–70), who began his literary career with *Le Théâtre de Clara Gazul* (1825), which purported to be a translation of six short plays by the Spanish actress 'Clara Gazul'. These were published anonymously. Her portrait (a faked portrait of the 22-year-old Mérimée in a mantilla) appeared as the frontispiece. A second augmented edition (1830) included *Le Carrosse du Saint-Sacrement*, a fine one-act play (*q.v.*). Mérimée followed his original success with another work under the improbable and exotic pseudonym of Hyacinthe Maglanowich. *La Guzla* (1827) was more ambitious, for it comprised 'translations' of Illyrian national songs and poems. *See* PLAGIARISM; PSEUDEPIGRAPHA.

literary prizes The prize system in general is a 20th c. phenomenon, the product of a century obsessed with competitions and with material gain and reward. The system pervades all classes of Western society and a wide range of activities from show-jumping to art, from ballroom dancing to the growing of vegetables. The absurd proliferation of medals and orders is an aspect of the obsession (witness the droves of generals who never heard a shot fired in battle and whose uniforms are plastered with four or five rows of ribbons). It may be argued that the need and desire to assess, judge, grade and reward human effort and attainment is a malaise of increasingly decadent humanism (*q.v.*) which perceives worldly success and its recognition to be an essential part of this life.

As far as literature is concerned there have been numerous criticisms of the prize system and some writers have actually rejected major prizes. For instance, George Bernard Shaw, awarded the Nobel Prize (*q.v.*) for literature in 1925, initially refused the prize but accepted the honour. The cynic might say that as he was a rich man he could well afford to decline the cash. Later he agreed to hold the money until it could be put to some good use. In 1925, too, Sinclair Lewis, the American novelist, rejected the Pulitzer Prize (both money and honour). In 1930 he accepted the Nobel on the grounds that it was an international prize for excellence. In explanation of the apparent inconsistency he cited the curious qualification under the terms of Joseph Pulitzer's will that the prize was to be given 'for the American novel published during the year which shall best present the wholesome atmosphere of American life, and the highest standards of American manners and manhood'. Lewis found the narrowness of this stipulation unacceptable and gave Hemingway's *A Farewell to Arms* and Wolfe's *Look Homeward, Angel* as examples of novels which should have been rewarded. In 1964 Jean-Paul Sartre was awarded the Nobel but refused it. He said: 'L'écrivain doit refuser . . . de se laisser transformer en institution'.

There are vast numbers of prizes for achievements in literature. France alone has about a thousand of them. There are many fewer (about fifty) in Britain – where literature is not taken so seriously. Since 1969 the Booker McConnell (*q.v.*) has become the best known in Britain. The Whitbread Literary Awards (for novel, first novel, biography, children's novel and poetry) are also well known. So is the W. H. Smith and Son Literary Award for fiction (begun in 1959). A prestigious prize is the Hawthornden, awarded each year to a British writer under forty-one for a work of imaginative literature. The Arts Council awards four prizes: for a biography, a novel, poetry and short stories. The Royal Society of Literature (*q.v.*) administers the Winifred Holtby Memorial Prize (founded in 1966) for a regional novel (*q.v.*) by a writer under thirty-seven. The RSL also administers the Benson Medal (founded in 1917), and the

Heinemann Award for Literature (founded in 1944); this goes to those forms of literature which are not so remunerative, such as poetry, criticism, biography and history. The Society of Authors (*q.v.*) makes awards from the Somerset Maugham Trust Fund (set up by Somerset Maugham in 1946) to writers under thirty-five. The British Academy operates the Rose Mary Crawshay Prize for English Literature – a prize awarded annually to a woman. Another particularly prestigious prize is the James Tait Black Memorial Prize (two awards are made annually, for a biography and a novel). In Scotland the Frederick Niven Literary Award is administered by the Scottish Centre of International PEN (*q.v.*) and given every three years for a novel by a Scot. In 1964 Faber and Faber established the Geoffrey Faber Memorial Prize: an annual award for a novel and a volume of verse, to a writer not more than forty. Two notable poetry prizes are the Queen's Gold Medal for Poetry (founded 1934) and the William Foyle Poetry Prize. There are several prizes for drama, including the Evening Standard Award for the best play of the year.

In the USA the main prize is the Pulitzer, established under the will of Joseph Pulitzer, a newspaper proprietor. The prizes are confined to American citizens and are offered in the interests of poetry, drama, the novel, biography and American history. Titled the 'Pulitzer Prizes in Letters', they were established in 1917 and are controlled by the School of Journalism at Columbia University. Several prizes are awarded by the American Academy of Arts and Letters. They include the annual Award of Merit Medal (for a novel, poetry, drama, painting and sculpture in rotation), the William Dean Howells Medal for fiction (every five years) and the Emerson–Thoreau Medal for a writer's whole achievement in literature. The National Institute of Arts and Letters administers the Russell–Loines Prize which is awarded occasionally – to an American or British poet who is of distinction but not widely recognized. Other poetry prizes include the Bollingen (awarded every two years) and the Poetry Society of America Annual Award. The Anisfield–Wolf Awards go to scholarly works and works of a creative kind in the specialized field of race relations.

In France societies and academies award many of the prizes. The Académie Française awards several each year, including the *Prix du Roman*. The *Prix Goncourt* is among the most prestigious and influential awards. It is awarded by the Académie Goncourt (founded in 1903) and goes to the best imaginative prose work, preferably a novel, published in the preceding year. Two similar prizes are the *Prix Femina* (founded in 1904) and the *Prix Théophraste Renaudot* founded in 1926. Other prizes for novels are the *Prix de la Renaissance* (1921), the *Prix Interallié* (1930) and the *Prix du Quai des Orfèvres* (1946). This last is the most important of a number of prizes given for the best *roman policier* (*q.v.*) or detective novel. The Académie Française also awards the *Grand Prix de Littérature* for works of prose or poetry of outstanding literary merit in form and content. Annual prizes awarded by the Maison de Poésie include the *Prix Petitdidier* and the *Prix Paul Verlaine*.

In Germany the Deutsche Akademie für Sprache und Dichtung, Darmstadt, awards the *Georg Büchner-Preis*. Two other notable ones are the *Schiller-Gedächtnispreis* (for young *and* established writers) and the *Lessing-Preis* for creative work in the fields dealt with by Lessing. In Austria the Österreichische Akademie der Wissenschaften gives the *Grillparzer-Preis* for drama.

Two prestigious international prizes are the *Prix Formentor*, an annual award for a work of fiction which is submitted by one of a group of fourteen publishers of different nations, and the *Prix Internationale de Littérature* for a work of fiction in any language.

Science fiction (*q.v.*) has its special prizes such as the Hugo and the Nebula. The world of crime fiction, mystery, suspense and detection also has special prizes. The Crime Writers Association gives annual awards for a novel of any crime fiction in English to a novelist from any country. There are the Gold Dagger Award and the Silver Dagger Award. An important American one is the Edgar Allan Poe special award for mystery writers.

literati (L 'the learned') This term was introduced by Robert Burton (1577–1640), author of *The Anatomy of Melancholy* (1621), who used it to describe the literate class in China. Later it denoted writers and readers of 'fashionable' literature and it is now used to refer to *habitués* of the literary clubs of 18th c. Edinburgh and also to the professional men (e.g. lawyers, clergymen) who were supporters of the Moderate party in the Church of Scotland. More generally, the term is used (sometimes not wholly seriously) to describe men of letters and learned men. The meaning is not dissimilar to *cognoscenti* – 'those who know' or who are 'in the know'.

literature A vague term which usually denotes works which belong to the major genres: epic, drama, lyric, novel, short story, ode (*qq.v.*). If we describe something as 'literature', as opposed to anything else, the term carries with it qualitative connotations which imply that the work in question has superior qualities; that it is well above the ordinary run of written works. For example: 'George Eliot's novels are literature, whereas Fleming's Bond books are unquestionably not.'

However, there are many works which cannot be classified in the main literary genres which nevertheless may be regarded as literature by virtue of the excellence of their writing, their originality and their general aesthetic and artistic merits. A handful of examples at random suggests how comprehensive the term can be. For instance: Aristotle's treatises on *Poetics* and *Rhetoric*; St Augustine's *Civitas Dei*; Erasmus's *Moriae Encomium*; Descartes's *Discourse on Method*; Berkeley's *Platonic Dialogues*; Gibbons's *Decline and Fall of the Roman Empire*; Prescott's *History of the Conquest of Mexico*; Darwin's *On the Origin of Species*; Lord Acton's *Essays on Church and State*; Lytton Strachey's *Queen Victoria*; R. G. Collingwood's *The Idea of Nature*; D'Arcy Wentworth Thompson's *On Growth and Form*; Sir Arthur Keith's *A New Theory of Human Evolution*; Sir Charles Sherrington's *Man on His Nature*; Sir Steven Runciman's *A History of the Crusades*; and Dame Rebecca West's *The Meaning of Treason.* Scores of others might be added to such a list.

literature of escape From the First and Second World Wars came many books about escaping – mostly from prisoner-of-war camps. They form almost a minor genre of their own, and many of them, apart from being very exciting, are well written. Well-known examples from the First World War are: H. E. Hervey's *Cage-birds*; H. G. Durnford's *The Tunnellers of Holzminden*; *Escapers All* by various contributors; and *The Escaping Club.* Probably the most famous from the Second World War is *The Wooden Horse* (1949) by Eric Williams. There have been many others, including T. D. Teare's *The Evader*; André Devigny's *Escape from Montluc*; David James's *A Prisoner's Progress*; Airey Neave's *They Have Their Exits*; George Millar's *Horned Pigeon*; Anthony Deane-Drummond's *Return Ticket*; W. B. Thomas's *Dare to be Free*; Peter Medd's *The Long Walk Home*; W. K. Sexton's *We Fought for Freedom*; and Anthony Farrar-Hockley's *The Edge of the Sword.*

literature of terror *See* GOTHIC NOVEL/FICTION; HORROR STORY.

litotes (Gk from *litós* 'single, simple, meagre') A figure of speech which contains an understatement for emphasis, and is therefore the opposite of hyperbole (*q.v.*). Often used in everyday speech (frequently with a negative assertion) and usually with laconic or ironic intentions. A stock instance is 'not bad' meaning 'very good'. *See also* IRONY; MEIOSIS; PARADIASTOLE.

littérateur (F 'a man of letters') One who devotes himself to the study of writing of literature. It may also suggest an *amateur* or *dilettante*.

little magazines Minority periodicals which publish poetry and fiction, reviews, etc. There have been many of them and they have tended to have rather brief lives. It may be that they received their epithet 'little' after the American literary magazine *The Little Review* (founded in 1914). Some of the early 'little' magazines were *The Savoy* (founded 1896), *Rhythm* (1911–13), *Blast* (1914–15), the organ of vorticism (*q.v.*), and *New Verse* (1933–9). More recently, notable examples have been *Stand* (1952), *Ambit* (1959), *Agenda* (1959) – all of which were still appearing in the 1990s – *The Review* (1962) and *The New Review* (1974–9).

liturgical drama Plays performed as part of the liturgy of the Church in the Middle Ages. The Mass, containing nearly all the elements and conventions of drama, was (and is) a theatrical spectacle much enhanced by ceremonial and symbolic ritual, and by the use of antiphonal singing which lends itself readily to dialogue. As services were elaborated additional melodies (and tropes, *q.v.*, in dialogue form) were interpolated. These plays became more popular, vernacular elements were introduced, and the laity as well as the clergy took part in them. They are almost certainly the source of the Mystery Plays (*q.v.*). *See also* MIRACLE PLAY.

Liverpool poets A group of poets native to the city of Liverpool who, in the early 1960s, began to give public recitals of their work, often to the accompaniment of music. Their emergence coincided with that of the pop group the Beatles, and with the advent of the Anglo-American jazz poetry (*q.v.*) movement. The principal poets were (and are) Roger McGough, Brian Patten and Adrian Henri. Robustly Liverpudlian, witty, slangy and sometimes bawdy, their work reached a sizeable pop audience. At first they were looked at somewhat askance by serious critics, but by the 1970s they had become more or less famous through various anthologies and it was realized what fine poets they are. Their merits were even appreciated by school examination boards. No doubt as a sop to populism.

Living Newspaper A form of political propaganda (*q.v.*) drama which uses topical material and journalistic techniques in the treatment of current social and political issues. It might also be described as a kind of documentary revue (*q.v.*). Such plays are usually presented in a series of short scenes and they are often satirical. The invention of this dramatic form is usually attributed to the Red Army of Soviet Russia during the Revolution. The Department of Agitation and Propaganda (Agitprop) was created in 1920 as a part of the Central Committee Secretariat of the Communist Party of the Soviet Union. Agitprop was responsible (as it has continued to be) for a wide variety of theatrical presentations in the cause of political propaganda. Agitprop also uses all mass media. In the United States the Federal Theatre Project created a Living Newspaper unit in 1935. This was highly successful and ran for four years. In England the Living Newspaper was pioneered by the Unity Theatre (*q.v.*), which was founded 1935–6 in London. It was a left-wing amateur group which specialized in socialist and Communist plays and what was called 'agitational' drama. During the Second World War Living Newspaper techniques were used for propaganda purposes. *See* AGITPROP DRAMA; DOCUMENTARY THEATRE.

Living Theater An *avant-garde* (*q.v.*) drama company founded by Julian Beck and Judith Malina in New York in 1947. To start with they presented verse drama (mostly 20th c.) and later concentrated more on improvised drama and what has come to be loosely described as 'alternative theatre' (*q.v.*). The company was itinerant in Europe and developed anarchist views. Audience participation was encouraged and audiences were even harassed. Notable productions were *Paradise Now* (1968) and *Prometheus* (1978). The company dispersed in the mid-1980s. *See also* THIRD THEATRE.

livre à clef (F 'book with a key') Also known as a *roman à clef*, in English as a *key novel* and in German as a *Schlüsselroman*. Usually a work of fiction in which actual persons are presented under fictitious names. The genre developed in 17th c. France, from which time notable examples are Mme de Scudéry's *Le Grand Cyrus* (1649–53) and *Clélie* (1656–60), and La Bruyère's *Caractères* (1688). The 'keys' were provided later. Periodically since there have been other instances. An early example in English is Mrs Manley's

The New Atalantis (1709), published with a key to its characters. Thomas Love Peacock's *Nightmare Abbey* (1818) contained caricatures of Coleridge, Byron and Shelley. Disraeli's *Venetia* (1837) suggested notable figures of his period. For *Coningsby* (1844) Disraeli had a key to the characters published separately. Aldous Huxley's *Point Counter Point* (1928) caused some stir. In it the personalities of D. H. Lawrence, Oswald Mosley and Middleton Murry were thinly disguised. Somerset Maugham wrote several *livres à clef* and earned some disapproval for his lack of effort to disguise characters.

ljoðaháttr An Eddic meter. The first and third lines of each stanza are like the usual line of the fornyrðislag (*q.v.*). The second and fourth lines are shorter and lack a caesura (*q.v.*).

loa (Sp 'praise') A kind of theatrical prologue (*q.v.*) or address to an audience intended to evoke sympathetic support. They were first used in the early *autos sacramentales* (*q.v.*) and soon became a part of secular drama. There are between forty and fifty *loas* in the picaresque (*q.v.*) novel *Viaje entretenido* (1603) by Rojas Villandrando.

loan word A word imported into a language from another language, or 'borrowed' from it. Very often such borrowings are permanent. English, a particularly permeable language, has assimilated a huge number of foreign elements, especially French, Scandinavian, Celtic, Latin and Greek. The following common words, for instance, are of Scandinavian origin: (a) substantives – axle, dregs, skill and window; (b) verbs – clasp, droop, glitter, skulk and want; (c) adjectives – awkward, muggy, sly, ugly and wrong. Two recent importations which look likely to become a permanent part of the language are the Russian words *glasnost* and *perestroika*. *See also* NEOLOGISM.

local colour The use of detail peculiar to a particular region and environment to add interest and authenticity to a narrative. This will include some description of the locale, dress, customs, music, etc. It is for the most part decorative. When it becomes an essential and intrinsic part of the work then it is more properly called *regionalism*. A number of American authors have used local colour successfully. For instance: Joel Chandler Harris, Thomas Nelson Page, Mary N. Murfee, Francis Hopkinson Smith, George

Washington Cable and Mark Twain. Zola was also a good local colourist; so were Kipling and Hardy. *See also* REALISM; REGIONAL NOVEL.

loco citato (L 'in the place cited') Often abbreviated to *loc. cit.*, the term indicates a reference to a book or page or passage already mentioned. *See* IBIDEM; IDEM; OPERE CITATO.

logaoedic (Gk 'speech song') A term which describes a composition which combines the rhythms of poetry and prose. Applied to Greek meter in which dactyls are combined with trochees and anapaests with iambs (*qq.v.*). It may also apply to any mixed metre.

logical stress Also known as rhetorical or sense stress, it is the emphasis required by the meaning of the verse. As in these lines from T. S. Eliot's *Ash Wednesday*:

Lady of silences
Calm and distressed
Torn and most whole
Rose of memory
Rose of forgetfulness
Exhausted and life-giving
Worried reposeful
The single Rose
Is now the Garden
Where all loves end

logocentrism A term coined by the French philosopher Jacques Derrida (1930–). *Logocentric* means literally 'centred on the word', but in Derrida's usage logocentrism implies all forms of thought based on a desire for truth. His view is that logocentrism has been characteristic of Western thought and philosophy since Plato. Derrida's principal sub-category of logocentrism is 'phonocentrism' ('sound-centring'; hence phonocentric, 'centred on sound/speech'). Phonocentrism describes the precedence of speech over writing, again typified by most Western thought since Plato, which decrees that writing has a tendency to 'contaminate' the purity of the spoken word. Derrida argues against the privileged position of speech. He contends that this 'violent hierarchy', as he puts it, is *not* reversible but that it is possible to displace by the idea of *différance* (*q.v.*), which is a vital part of his theories of deconstruction (*q.v.*).

Différance does not correct or reverse an imbalance (that would be counter to his view of deconstruction); it can only displace (i.e. make the question of hierarchy *obsolete*). *See* SUPPLEMENT.

logodaedalus (Gk *logos* 'word' + *daedal*, from Daedalus the mythical artist) An artificer in words (e.g. a poet). *Logodaedaly* is verbal legerdemain.

logogram (Gk *logos* 'word' + *gramma* 'letter') A single sign for a word. Abbreviated to logo.

logographer (Gk *logos* 'word' + *graphein* 'to write') In Greek literature one of the earliest annalists, especially those before Herodotus. It also denotes a professional speech-writer.

logogriph (Gk 'word riddle') An anagram (*q.v.*) or verses from which anagrams or other word puzzles can be guessed. *See also* ACROSTIC.

logomachy (Gk 'word contest') A dispute or fight about words; or merely in words. *See* FLYTING; INVECTIVE.

logopoeia (Gk 'making of words') A poem both *means* and *is*. In *ABC of Reading* (1934) Ezra Pound discusses language as a means of communication and finds three ways in which language can be charged with meaning: (a) by throwing the object, be it fixed or moving, on to the visual imagination; this is phanopoeia (*q.v.*); (b) by inducing emotional correlations by the sound and rhythm of speech; this is melopoeia (*q.v.*); (c) by inducing both of the effects, thus stimulating the intellectual or emotional associations which have remained in the receiver's consciousness in relation to the actual words or groups of words employed; this is logopoeia. *See* ONOMATOPOEIA; SYNAESTHESIA; TONE COLOUR.

logorrhoea (Gk 'word flowing') Excessive verbosity and prolixity. Vulgarly known as 'verbal diarrhoea'.

log-rolling Vulgarly known as 'back-scratching'. The practice by which authors review each other's books favourably. *See* PUFFERY.

Lokalposse (G 'local farce, burlesque') A genre of German comedy particularly associated with Vienna late in the 18th c. and early in the 19th c. Its themes were local (and parochial) and they were treated farcically. The main playwrights were: Joseph Gleich (1772–1841), Karl Meisl (1775–1853), Adolf Bäuerle (1786–1859) and Johann Nestroy (1801–62). *See also* BESSERUNGSSTUCK; LOKALSTUCK; VOLKSSTUCK.

Lokalstück (G 'local play') A play written for a local audience in a rural or urban environment. The dramatists tended to use local dialect. Such plays were popular in Vienna towards the end of the 18th c., but were also written for audiences in Berlin, Munich, Frankfurt and Hamburg. For the most part they were comedies. *See also* BESSERUNGSSTUCK; LOKALPOSSE; VOLKSSTUCK.

long measure The LM of the hymn books. A variant of ballad or common meter. It consists of a tetrameter (*q.v.*) in which the foot pattern is usually iambic (but sometimes dactylic) as in this stanza from Burns's *Lament for James, Earl of Glencairn*:

> The mother may forget the child
>   That smiles sae sweetly on her knee;
> But I'll remember thee, Glencairn,
>   And a' that thou hast done for me.

long syllable *See* METER; QUANTITY.

loose and periodic sentence In a loose sentence the main clause comes first and is followed by its dependent clauses. In a periodic the main clause is last. In the following passage from Macaulay's *Essay on Milton* the first sentence is loose, the second periodic:

> They [the Puritans] rejected with contempt the ceremonious homage which other sects substituted for the pure worship of the soul. Instead of catching occasional glimpses of the Deity through an obscuring veil, they aspired to gaze full on his intolerable brightness . . .

lost generation, the This term was in regular use after the First World War in reference to the host of young men who were killed in it, and also to the young men who survived and who thereafter were adrift – morally and spiritually (and in many other ways). The phrase is believed to have been invented by Gertrude Stein (1874–1946), a supporter and publicizer of artists and writers who were active in the *avant-garde* (*q.v.*) movements of her period. The mood of the lost generation (a mood of disenchantment and, sometimes, cynicism) was well represented by some American novelists; particularly Scott Fitzgerald (1896–1940). The group of men who later came to be known as the 'war poets' (*q.v.*) also belonged to the lost generation. Forty or fifty years later men who had spent their late youth and early manhood in the war still referred to themselves as members of the lost generation.

love poetry *See* EROTIC POETRY.

low comedy A coarse (often bawdy) type of comedy (*q.v.*), sometimes used as comic relief (*q.v.*). The mirth it provokes is likely to come from the belly rather than the brain. It commonly contains buffoonery, slapstick (*q.v.*), violent action and ribald jokes. It is thus a crudely fundamental form which trades upon people's relish at seeing others humiliated and ridiculed and involved in scabrous episodes. The punch-up, the custard-pie contest and the man caught with his trousers down are common examples of low comedy situations. It is frequent in Aristophanic comedy, farce (*q.v.*), medieval English drama, Tudor and Jacobean drama, and also Restoration comedy (*q.v.*). Notable instances are to be found in *The Merry Wives of Windsor*, the brothel scenes in *Pericles* (IV) and several scenes from Wycherley's *The Country Wife*. Low comedy is also to be found in the satyr play, the *fabula* and the anti-masque (*qq.v.*).

Low comedy is plentiful in other literary forms. Excellent examples occur in Goliardic verse (*q.v.*), Boccaccio's *Decameron* and Chaucer's *Canterbury Tales*. It may also be applied to Samuel Butler's *Hudibras*, Pope's *Dunciad* and a number of scenes in the sporting novels of R. S. Surtees. Some of the Mack Sennett and early Charles Chaplin films are masterpieces of low comedy.

lullaby A soothing bed-time song or chant to send a child to sleep. The first lines of some of the better known lullabies are: 'Hush-a-bye baby, on the tree top'; 'Hush thee, my babby'; 'Rock-a-bye, baby'; 'Hush-a-bye, baby'; 'Hush, little baby, don't say a word'; 'The little lady lairdie'; 'Bye, baby bunting'; 'Hush ba, burdie beeton'; 'Hush-a-ba birdie, croon, croon'. *See also* NURSERY RHYME.

lū-shih (Ch 'regulated poem') A verse form developed in China during the T'ang and Sung dynasties. It also went under the name *chin-t'i shih* to distinguish it from *ku-shih* or 'old poem'. Notable features of the *lū-shih* are parallelism (*q.v.*) and an elaborate tonal pattern. This kind of formalization also affected the *fu* (*q.v.*) or prose poem.

Lustspiel (G 'pleasure play') A light or amusing play. A light comedy (*q.v.*).

Lyon school From the town of Lyon where, in the 16th c., a group of writers lived and met. They were chiefly poets, and were in some cases involved in the other arts; their particular interest as a group was a theory of spiritual love based on ideas of Plato and Plutarch and enunciated in Antoine Heroet's *Parfaicte Amye* (1542). The group was noteworthy for the number of women who took an active part.

The leader of the Lyon school was Maurice Scève (*c.* 1500–64), architect, musician and painter as well as poet. He is known for the following main works: *Délie* (anagram of *l'idée*), *objet de plus haulte vertu* (1544); *Le microcosme* (1562), an encyclopaedic poem on the fall of man; two eclogues – *Arion* (1536) and *La saulsaye* (1547). Other members of the group were Claude de Taillemont and women poets such as Jeanne Gaillarde, Pernette de Guillet, Clémence de Bourges, and Scève's sisters Claudine and Sibylle. However, the poetess Louise Labé (*c.* 1525–66) was the most prominent of Scève's colleagues. It is said that at sixteen this remarkable woman fought on horseback in the siege of Perpignan on the side of the Dauphin. The daughter of a rope-maker, she married a rope-maker and became known as *La Belle Cordière*. She was a linguist and musician and her house became known as a salon for the cultured. Some of her poetry was published in Lyon in 1555. She also wrote a prose allegory *Le débat de folie et d'amour*.

lyric The Greeks defined a lyric as a song to be sung to the accompaniment of a lyre (*lyra*). A song is still called a lyric (the songs in a musical are known as lyrics) but we also use the term loosely to describe a particular kind of poem in order to distinguish it from narrative or dramatic verse of any kind.

A lyric is usually fairly short, not often longer than fifty or sixty lines, and often only between a dozen and thirty lines; and it usually expresses the feelings and thoughts of a single speaker (not necessarily the poet himself) in a personal and subjective fashion. The range and variety of lyric verse is immense, and lyric poetry, which is to be found in most literatures, comprises the bulk of all poetry.

Probably the earliest lyric poetry is Egyptian (*c.* 2600 BC). The Pyramid texts of this period reveal examples of the funeral song (a kind of elegy), the song of praise to the king (a type of ode), and an invocation to the gods (a form of hymn). Inscriptions on tombs of the same period include the songs of shepherds and fishermen. Later works (*c.* 1550 BC) include a love-song and an epitaph (*q.v.*).

Apart from some Hebrew lyric poetry, the most memorable contribution in ancient times came from the Greeks. Like the Egyptian and Hebrew, the Greek lyric originated in religious ceremonial. Greek lyrics were sung or chanted, sometimes to the accompaniment of a dance. The dithyramb (*q.v.*) was originally sung and then took on the shape of a formal dance. These dithyrambic rhythms were probably the prototypes of the ode (*q.v.*), or song of celebration (with divisions of strophe and antistrophe, *qq.v.*), which Pindar and Sophocles, among others, were to write.

There were indeed hints of lyrical mood and subject in Hesiod and Homer, but it was not until the 7th c. BC that there appeared lyrics proper. Here we can distinguish between the Aeolian or personal lyrics written by Sappho and Alcaeus; and the Dorian (more impersonal and objective) lyrics by Alcman, Arion, Ibycus and Stesichorus.

The 5th c. in Greece produced some of the best of all lyric poetry – by Simonides, Pindar and Bacchylides; and by the dramatists Aeschylus, Sophocles and Euripides in their beautiful choral odes. Melic poetry then predominated, in the Dorian mood. Some of the main lyric types practised were the dance song, the dirge, the dithyramb, ode, hymn and paean (*qq.v.*).

The Roman lyricists tended to be more subjective and autobiographical in the use of this form (the Aeolian mood), as in the poetry of Catullus, Tibullus, Propertius, Ovid, Virgil and Martial.

The medieval Latin lyric, from about AD 300 onwards, showed a remarkable range of subject and technical skill. The early Church lyrics were hymns based on the Hebrew Psalter and Greek hymns. The major poets of the Middle Ages writing lyrics in Latin were Abelard, Ausonius, Fortunatus, Paulinus of Nola, Petronius

Arbiter and Prudentius, much of whose work is gathered together in Helen Waddell's *Medieval Latin Lyrics* (1929). The Church lyrics of the 12th and 13th c. were unique in their beauty. Such were the *Stabat Mater* and the *Dies Irae*.

A parallel development of the so-called Patristic lyric was the Mozarabic poetry of Spain. Hymns, psalms and poems arising from religious ceremonial were the chief contributions.

Between *c.* AD 300 and *c.* AD 1200 two other traditions in the lyric form can be distinguished. In the first place the OE lyric, of which outstanding examples are: *The Seafarer*, *The Wanderer*, *The Wife's Lament, The Lover's Message and Deor.* Contemporaneously, the art of the lyric was being perfected in China and Japan, and between the 12th and the 15th c. was highly developed in Persia. The main influence of the Persian lyric was not felt in England until the 19th c.

An abundance of lyric poetry survives from the later Middle Ages. Much of it was composed by troubadours and *trouvères* (*qq.v.*) and other wandering minstrels, and by the *Minnesinger* (*q.v.*). Many of the lyric forms had specific names, like *chanso*, *sirventes*, *planh*, *tenso*, *pastorela* and *aubade* (*qq.v.*). It was intended to be sung, and it was often danced to. From the 13th and 14th c. a large number of religious and devotional lyrics in English survive. Many of them are of great beauty. The principal European poets of the period who composed lyrics to be read were Bertrand de Born, Chaucer, Chrétien de Troyes, Walther von der Vogelweide, Rutebeuf, Pierre Vidal and Sordello.

The Renaissance period, however, was the great age of the lyric. Petrarch in Italy and Ronsard in France were the two major poets in this form, especially in the use of the sonnet (*q.v.*). In England Sir Thomas Wyatt and the Earl of Surrey made outstanding contributions with their songs, lyrics and sonnets. Some of the finest songs in the language date from this period. Between *c.* 1550 and the Restoration period scores of poets wrote lyrics, many of which are extant. The major collection of such verse in the 16th c. was Tottel's Miscellany (1557). The principal lyric poets in this period were Sidney, Daniel, Spenser, Shakespeare, Campion, Southwell, Drayton, Donne, Ben Jonson, Herrick, Lovelace, Suckling, Carew, Marvell, Herbert, Vaughan and Milton. To this period belong the great sonnet sequences (*q.v.*) of Sidney, Spenser and Shakespeare, the love poems of the Metaphysicals and the mystical and religious lyrics of Donne, Herbert and Vaughan. Not until the 19th c. do we find a comparable variety of religious lyrical poetry.

The lyric form was not so much favoured by the 18th c. poets except Smart who was a notable minor lyric poet. Some other minor poets also attempted this form – notably Lady Winchilsea, Thomas Parnell, William Collins and Thomas Gray. The odes of Collins and Gray are particularly distinguished lyrics.

Towards the end of the 18th c. and during the Romantic period (*q.v.*) there was a major revival of lyric poetry throughout Europe. In the British Isles the most accomplished lyrists were Burns, Wordsworth, Blake, Coleridge, Byron, Shelley, Keats, John Clare and Thomas Moore; in Germany, Goethe, Schiller, Hölderlin, Eichendorff and Heine; in France, Lamartine, Victor Hugo, Alfred de Vigny and Alfred de Musset; in Italy, Giacomo Leopardi; in Spain, Espronceda; and in Russia, Pushkin.

Throughout the 19th c. many poets used the lyric form. The principal English poets were Tennyson, Browning, Swinburne, Matthew Arnold and Gerard Manley Hopkins. Like some of the Metaphysicals Hopkins wrote some remarkable religious and mystical poetry. Two minor poets are associated with him in this respect; namely, Francis Thompson and Coventry Patmore. Other minor poets who wrote notable lyrics were Dante Gabriel Rossetti and Christina Rossetti.

In France the major writers of lyric poetry in the later part of the 19th c. were the Parnassians, particularly Leconte de Lisle and Prudhomme. The American poet Edgar Allan Poe had a very considerable influence on Baudelaire who was the precursor of the *symbolistes*. Baudelaire wrote some of the best lyrics in the French language. The other *symboliste* poets who wrote fine lyrics were Mallarmé, Verlaine and Rimbaud. Since the end of the 19th c. almost every major European and American poet has attempted and enriched the lyric form. One should mention especially W. B. Yeats, Ezra Pound, T. S. Eliot, Dylan Thomas, W. H. Auden, Allen Tate, John Crowe Ransom and William Carlos Williams among British and American poets. Among Frenchmen some of the main composers of lyric verse have been Verhaeren, Valéry, Laforgue, Pierre Emmanuel and Claudel. Stefan George and Rilke are the two outstanding Germans. In Spain there have been the brothers Manuel and Antonio Machado. In Italy, D'Annunzio, Campana, Ungaretti, Montale and Quasimodo. Besides these, scores of minor poets have written fine lyrics.

From the thousands of such poems which exist and from which one might choose, I take this short poem by John Clare as an example of the lyric form:

The Secret

I loved thee, though I told thee not,
  Right earlily and long,
Thou wert my joy in every spot,
  My theme in every song.

And when I saw a stranger face
  Where beauty held the claim,
I gave it like a secret grace
  The being of thy name.

And all the charms of face or voice
  Which I in others see
Are but the recollected choice
  Of what I felt for thee.

See also LEICH; METAPHYSICAL POETRY; SONG; SYMBOL AND SYMBOLISM.

lyrisme romantique A term used to describe those qualities of French lyrical poetry which appeared to depend greatly upon the individual poet's personal experiences and feelings. Thus, deeply subjective poetry. The four major poets of the French Romantic movement – Hugo, Lamartine, Musset and de Vigny – 'wrote from the heart'.

lysiody *See* MAGODY.

M

macabre *See* DANSE MACABRE.

macaronic The term derives indirectly from the Italian word *maccaroni*, an earlier form of *maccheroni* (denoting a wheaten paste in tubular form). Properly speaking, macaronic verse is made when a writer mixes words of his own language with those of another and twists in his native words to fit the grammar of the foreign tongue (e.g. *standez*, *womenorum*). Broadly speaking, the term applies to any verse which mixes two or more languages together. Latin is the language most often used, and the intention in macaronics is nearly always comic and/or nonsensical.

They are first recorded in *Carmen macaronicum de Patavinis* (1490) by Tisi degli Odassi. The form was popularized by Teofilo Folengo in *Liber Macaronices* (1517). Folengo described his verses as a literary analogue (*q.v.*) of *macaroni* ('a gross, rude, and rustic mixture of flour, cheese, and butter'). There is a good deal of macaronic verse in French and German literature (the Germans call it *Nudelverse*) and some interesting examples in English literature: for instance: several poems by John Skelton, and William Drummond of Hawthornden's 'epic' *Polemo-Middinia*. Many writers of light verse and nonsense verse (*qq.v.*) have diverted themselves by composing macaronics. This example comes from *Malum Opus* by the American J. A. Morgan:

> Prope ripam fluvii solus
> A senex silently sat;
> Super capitum ecce his wig.
> Et wig super, ecce his hat.
>
> Blew Zephyrus alte, acerbus,
> Dum elderly gentleman sat;
> Et capite took up quite torve
> Et in rivum projecit his hat.

and so on for three more verses to the *envoi*:

Contra bonos mores, don't swear,
It is wicked, you know (verbum sat),
Si this tale habet no other moral,
Mehercle! You're gratus to that!

Occasionally we find the macaronic limerick (*q.v.*), of which these are bawdy examples (they often *are* bawdy):

King Louis, when passing through Bruges
Met a lady, whose **** was so huge
That he said, as he came
In that fabulous dame,
'Atta girl! *Après moi le déluge.*'

And:

There was a young lady of Nantes
Très jolie, et très élégante,
But her **** was so small
It was no good at all,
Except for *la plume de ma tante.*

See also FATRASIE; SORAISMUS.

maccaronische Dichtung *See* MACARONIC.

Machiavel A character type deriving his name from Niccolò Machiavelli (1469–1527), the Florentine statesman and political philosopher. Machiavelli became famous for *Il Principe* (written in 1513), a treatise on statecraft which justifies the use of various expediencies (including cruelty, lies and treachery) in the ruling of a state. *Il Principe* was often alluded to in Elizabethan drama and during the Elizabethan period the name of Machiavelli became associated (at any rate in the popular imagination) with treachery, murder, atheism and every kind of double-dyed villainy and viciousness. The sinister, resourceful and unscrupulous villain (*q.v.*) – usually an Italian and often the embodiment of evil – in revenge tragedy (*q.v.*) of the Elizabethan and Jacobean periods came to be regarded as a Machiavel.

machinery In his preface to *The Rape of the Lock* (1712, 1714), Pope refers to *machinery* as a term invented by the critics 'to signify that part which the deities, angels or demons are made to act in a poem'.

The term is particularly associated with Greek tragedy in connection with the *deus ex machina* (*q.v.*) which the Greeks used to put a god on stage. It is also associated with epic (*q.v.*) because Homer included a large number of gods in the *Iliad*. Thus, supernatural figures were referred to as 'machines'. There is a good deal of supernatural 'machinery' in *Paradise Lost*.

macrology (Gk 'long language') Verbose repetition by way of long words and phrases. *See* JARGON; OFFICIALESE; PERIPHRASIS; TAUTOLOGY; VERBOCRAP.

macron The horizontal sign (—) put over a vowel to indicate length. *See* MORA.

madrigal (L *matricalis* 'maternal' and so 'simple, primitive') Originally a pastoral song, it is a short lyric, especially one to be set to music and intended for several voices. It arose in northern Italy in the 14th c. and Petrarch wrote a number of them. In the 16th c. there was a revival of the form and it became extremely popular in England in Tudor times.

Metrically it showed much variety. In the 14th c. it tended to consist of two or three tercets (*q.v.*) followed by one or two rhyming couplets. By the 16th c. there were few rules, but for the most part madrigals were of ten to fourteen lines and normally ended with a rhyming couplet. The themes were usually love, the pastoral or the satiric. Many Tudor poets attempted it, but its three famous English composers were Thomas Morley, Thomas Weelkes and John Wilbye.

magazine (A *makhazin*, plural of *makhzan* 'a storehouse') A periodical (*q.v.*) publication. *See* LITTLE MAGAZINE.

magic realism This term was coined by Franz Roh and used in the title of his book *Nach-expressionismus, magischer Realismus: Probleme der neuesten europäischer Malerei* (1925). He was concerned with the characteristics and tendencies discernible in the work of certain German painters of the period, especially the *neue Sachlichkeit* (*q.v.*) artists of Munich. Their work was marked by the use of still, sharply defined, smoothly painted images of figures and objects depicted in a somewhat surrealistic manner. The themes and subjects were often imaginary, somewhat outlandish and fantastic and with a certain dream-like quality. The effects could be powerful. Magic realism was also associated with the 1920s Italian movement *stracittà* (*q.v.*).

Later, early in the 1940s, the idea and term magic realism reappeared in the USA. In 1943 the New York Museum of Modern Art held an exhibition called 'American Realists and Magic Realists'. Among the distinguished painters whose work was hung were Edward Hopper (1882–1967) and Charles Sheeler (1883–1965). Subsequently, Hopper's paintings in particular were to receive considerable publicity in Britain and elsewhere.

Gradually the term came to be associated with certain kinds of fiction. In the late 1940s George Saiko (1892–1962), the Austrian novelist, began to publish fiction of a quasi-surrealistic nature and he expressed his views about what he called *magischer Realismus* in his book *Die Wirklichkeit hat doppelten Boden. Gedanken zum magischen Realismus* (1952).

In due course the term caught on in literary circles and was used by critics. By the 1980s it had become a well-established 'label' for some forms of fiction. It has been applied, for instance, to the work of Luis Borges (1899–1988), the Argentinian who in 1935 published his *Historia universal de la infamia*, regarded by many as the first work of magic realism. The Colombian novelist Gabriel García Márquez (1928–) is also regarded as a notable exponent of this kind of fiction, especially his novel *Cien años de soledad* or 'One Hundred Years of Solitude' (1967). The Cuban Alejo Carpentier (1904–) is another described as a 'magic realist'. Experiments in magic realism effects and techniques are also to be found in the fiction of Italo Calvino (1923–85), John Fowles (1926–), Günter Grass (1927–), Emma Tennant (1938–), Angela Carter (1940–) and Salman Rushdie (1947–).

Some of the characteristic features of this kind of fiction are the mingling and juxtaposition of the realistic and the fantastic or bizarre, skilful time shifts, convoluted and even labyrinthine narratives and plots, miscellaneous use of dreams, myths and fairy stories, expressionistic and even surrealistic description, arcane erudition, the element of surprise or abrupt shock, the horrific and the inexplicable. It is seldom easy to define it as a genre and a plausible case might be made that there are plentiful instances of magic realism in the fiction of Kleist, E. T. A. Hoffmann, Prosper Mérimée, Fournier, Kafka, Ronald Firbank and Edward Upward. *See also* GOTHIC NOVEL/FICTION; HORROR STORY; NOVEL.

magischer Realismus *See* MAGIC REALISM.

magnitizdat *See* SAMIZDAT.

magnum opus (L 'great work') A major literary work, perhaps a writer's masterpiece. Milton's *Paradise Lost* was his *magnum opus.* These days the term is often used ironically.

magody (Gk 'rude pantomime) Like lysiody (named after Lysis who wrote songs for actors playing female characters in male attire) and hilarody (Gk 'joyous song'), magody was a form of Greek mime (*q.v.*). The magodist took a comic plot or a theme from comedy and worked out a mime. Wearing female clothes, he played both male and female parts. The lysiodist, by contrast, wore male clothes and played female roles, to the accompaniment of a flute. Hilarody was a kind of parody of tragedy (*q.v.*). The actor wore male clothes and buskins (*q.v.*). Simody was an alternative, and later, name for hilarody. *See also* SATYR PLAY.

málaháttr (ON *mál* 'a speech' and *háttr* 'meter') An ON Eddic meter, quite similar to fornyrðislag (*q.v.*). It consists of a four-line stanza, each line being divided into two half-lines, the half lines having two accented and three or four unaccented syllables.

malapropism (F *mal à propos* 'not to the purpose') So called after Mrs Malaprop, a character in Sheridan's *The Rivals* (1775), who had a habit of using polysyllabic words incorrectly. There are some characteristic examples in the following passage from the opening Act:

> Then, sir, she should have a supercilious knowledge in accounts; – and as she grew up, I would have her instructed in geometry, that she might know something of the contagious countries . . . and likewise that she might reprehend the true meaning of what she is saying. This, Sir Anthony, is what I would have a woman know; – and I don't think there is a superstitious article in it.

But malapropisms were by no means new in 1775. Dogberry, the Watch in *Much Ado About Nothing* (*c.* 1598–9), was addicted to them. So was Mrs Slipslop in Fielding's *Joseph Andrews* (1742). One of the most amusing malapropists was Mrs Winifred Jenkins in Smollett's *Humphry Clinker* (1771), who was capable of writing: 'I have already made very creditable correxions in this here place; where, to be sure, we have the very squintasense of satiety'.

Another adept was Mrs Heidelberg in *The Clandestine Marriage* (1766) by George Colman (the Elder).

Fortunately malapropisms are a feature of everyday life and people continue to produce endearing gems. Traditionally, loquacious charwomen are a fruitful source, as these samples testify: 'He rides the motor bike and she sits on the pavilion'; 'I'd like you to meet my daughter's fiasco'; 'I've always been thin. When I was a girl I had infantile paraphernalia'.

Medical conditions have caused bizarre afflictions, such as 'malingering' tumours, 'hysterical rectums', and 'teutonic' ulcers. There have been severed 'juggler' veins and 'Cistercian' childbirths. A middle-aged man believed he had undergone a 'midwife' crisis, and a lady declined to volunteer as a 'blood doughnut'.

mal mariée (F 'unhappily married') An OF form of song or poem in which a married woman laments her marriage and calls upon her lover. In some cases the lover comes to rescue her. A variant is the lament of a nun who wants to be taken away from her convent by a lover. The poems were often written in *ballade* (*q.v.*) meter.

Manchester school Originally a term used by Benjamin Disraeli (1804–81) to describe the political party led by Richard Cobden (1804–65) and John Bright (1811–89), both advocates of free trade. Later the term was used of a group of Mancunian dramatists whose plays were produced at the Gaiety Theatre, Manchester, in the period 1907–14 when it was run by Annie Horniman (1860–1937), the founder of the Manchester Repertory Theatre. Three dramatists in particular are associated with this 'school'; namely, Allan Monkhouse (1858–1936), William Houghton (1881–1913) and Harold Brighouse (1882–1958). Many of the plays are about the trials and tribulations of Lancashire domestic life and reveal the influence of Ibsen. A handful of them have long since been part of the standard repertoire of theatrical companies, especially Houghton's *The Dear Departed* (1908) and his *Hindle Wakes* (1912) and Brighouse's *Hobson's Choice* (1916).

manifesto (L *manu festus* 'struck by hand') A public declaration, usually of political, religious, philosophical or literary principles and beliefs. Literary movements are also given to publishing manifestos. For instance, Wyndham Lewis's *Blast: The Review of the Great English Vortex* (1914–15), a manifesto for Vorticism (*q.v.*), and André Breton's *Manifeste du surréalisme* (1924).

mannerism A term developed in the 20th c. to describe various manifestations of painting and architecture (chiefly Italian) in the period 1520–1600. The word *maniera* (from which *mannerism* derives) was used by Vasari (author of *Le Vite de' più eccelenti Architetti, Pittori et Scultori Italiani*, 1550) to describe 'the schematic quality of much of the work produced which was based on intellectual preconceptions rather than direct visual perceptions. Much of mannerism consists of deliberately flouting the "Rules" deduced from classical art and established during the Renaissance' (*A Dictionary of Art and Artists* by Peter and Linda Murray). Like baroque (*q.v.*), mannerism has been applied to particular styles of writing characterized by ornateness of language, strange syntax, far-fetched images and elaborate periods. The writers (like the painters and architects) can be called *manneristi*. Two authors in particular are associated with mannerism in the 16th c. They are the Spaniard Antonio de Guevara (1480?–1545) and John Lyly (1554–1606) famous for his euphuism (*q.v.*).

More generally speaking mannerism may denote the idiosyncratic element of an author's style. Any peculiarity, affectation or quality which sets it apart and makes it easily recognizable. For example, the Latinistic syntax of Milton, the balanced and antithetical cadences of Gibbon, the quaint archaisms of C. M. Doughty, the pseudo-biblical rhythms of Hemingway. *See* GONGORISM; MARINISM.

man of letters A well-educated, well-read, civilized and perhaps learned person – who may also be a writer (e.g. a belle-lettrist). 'A man of capital letters', on the other hand, is one who thinks he is these things but is, in fact, very limited. Pope's victims in *The Dunciad* might be called 'men of capital letters'. *See also* BELLES LETTRES; LITERATI.

mantra An Indian religious chant (*q.v.*). The *Mantrapatha*, a prayerbook, contains about six hundred *mantras*. It is a kind of manual of prayer for all occasions, especially domestic ceremonials.

manual *See* HANDBOOK AND MANUAL.

manuscript (L *codex manu scriptus* 'book written by hand') Strictly a book or document of any kind written by hand rather than printed or typed. True, a typewritten document is often called a manuscript. It is, in fact, a *typescript*.

maqāma An Arabic term for stories in rhymed prose. The two great masters of the form were Abu al-Fadl Ahmed ibn al-Husain al-Hamadhani (967–1007) and Abu Mohammed al-Qasim al-Hariri (1054–1122). Most of the tales come into the category of picaresque (*q.v.*).

Märchen A German term for a folk tale or fairy story (*qq.v.*). The classic collection is that made by the Grimm brothers early in the 19 c. – the *Kinder- und Hausmärchen* (1812, 1814, 1822).

marginalia Notes written in the margin of a manuscript or book by a reader or annotator. Coleridge (in 1832) was the first English man of letters to use this term. *See also* ANNOTATION.

Marian legends Legends about the Virgin Mary were popular and widespread in Europe in the Middle Ages and produced a considerable literature. Collections of Marian legends were formed in Latin in the 11th c. and they proliferated during the next three hundred years. Gradually they were popularized through different vernaculars. *See* LEGEND.

Marienklage A genre of German poetry in monologue form composed in the 13th, 14th and 15th c. Their theme was the suffering and lamentation of the Virgin Mary as she watched her Son suffering on the Cross. *Marienklagen* were sometimes dramatized for performance in church.

Marinism The affected style of the Italian poet Giovanni Battista Marini (1569–1625). Writing characterized by an exaggerated and rather artificial language and imagery. *See* EUPHUISM; GONGORISM; MANNERISM; SECENTISMO.

Marivaudage A manner of writing similar to that of Pierre Marivaux (1688–1763), the dramatist and novelist. Marivaux's style was often affected by being strained, over-elegant, too subtle and too nice by half. Voltaire said of him rather cruelly that he had spent his life weighing nothing in scales made of spiders' webs. Thus Marivaudage is usually a pejorative term. Nevertheless he had a considerable (and by no means wholly harmful) influence on a number of French writers, especially Alfred de Musset and Giraudoux.

Marxist criticism Karl Marx (1818–83) and Friedrich Engels (1820–95) were primarily concerned with economic, political and philosophical issues and worked out explanations of the capitalist theory and mode of production. They did not develop an 'aesthetic' of culture or literature, although they did say quite traditional things about Greek art which suggest that Marx himself believed in the relative autonomy of art (cf. Marx's *Introduction to the Critique of Political Economy*, 1857, and Hans Robert Jauss's article in *New Literary History*, titled *The Idealist Embarrassment*). However, Marxist principles and attitudes and modes of thought and inquiry have been adapted to create a Marxist theory of literature: what it has been, and what it might and, perhaps, should be. The Marxist critic (who tends to be primarily interested in content) writes from the definite standpoint of Marx's philosophical ideas, and from his view of history in which the class struggle is fundamental, or in terms of socio-historical factors.

Much earlier Marxist criticism has been devoted to a reconstruction of the past on the basis of historical evidence in order to find out to what extent a text (say, a novel) is a truthful and accurate representation of social reality at any given time. As Trotsky suggested in *Literature and Revolution* (1924): 'Artistic creation is a changing and a transformation of reality in accordance with the peculiar laws of art'.

The concept of 'socialist realism' (*q.v.*) marked an important advance in the development of Marxist and, *ipso facto*, Communist views on literature – and art in general. Basically, socialist realism required a writer (or any artist) to be committed to the working-class cause of the Party. And it required that literature should be 'progressive' and should display a progressive outlook on society. This necessitated forms of optimism and realism. Moreover, doctrine demanded that literature should be accessible to the masses. This was particularly true of the novel.

Modernism (*q.v.*) in Western literature was deemed to be decadent (especially by critics such as Georg Lukács) because it was, among other things, subjective, introverted and introspective and displayed a fragmented vision of the world. By contrast, the 19th c. realist novel was extolled. However, a certain amount of squaring of circles and an element of double-think was involved, especially in relation to such novelists as Dostoievski and Goncharov, for example, who were profoundly pessimistic and introverted.

A key figure is the first major Marxist critic, namely the Hungarian Georg Lukács (1885–1971). He developed the critical theory of 'reflection', seeing literary works as reflections of a kind of system that was gradually unfolding. In his view, the novel, for instance (and he had much to say about this genre) revealed or ought to reveal underlying patterns in the social order and provide a sense of the wholeness of existence with all its inherent contradictions, tensions and conflicts. Like many Marxist critics he was mainly concerned with content; hence his adverse comments on writers who were preoccupied with form, technique, literary ingenuity and innovation. Lukács created his own idea of realism and failed (or declined) to see that modernist writers were also capable of realism – albeit of other and different kinds. Hence his disagreement with the modernist techniques of Brecht (and with Theodor Adorno, too), another Marxist and a didactic dramatist who was at pains to show social injustice. Brecht made clear his attitude to socialist realism thus: 'We shall take care not to ascribe realism to a particular period, Balzac's or Tolstoy's, for instance, so as to set up purely formal and literary criteria of realism'. He rejected anything formulaic on the grounds that reality changes, and in order to represent it the means of representation must also change. Thus, it follows that Lukács and his followers would hardly approve of formalism, futurism, epic theatre (*qq.v.*) and many other innovative theories and developments.

The Frankfurt school of Marxist aesthetics is associated with the Institute of Social Research founded in 1923 and affiliated to the University of Frankfurt. During the Nazi period it was exiled (in 1933) to New York, from where it returned to Frankfurt in 1949–50. This school (whose chief spirits were Theodor Adorno, Max Horkheimer and Herbert Marcuse) rejected realism more or less completely and developed what is known as 'Critical Theory'. They were much influenced by: (a) their experience of a totalitarian régime and Fascism; (b) their experience of American mass culture, capitalism and commercialism. Both the Nazi and American societies were regarded as 'one-dimensional'.

Adorno advanced the theory that literature does not have direct contact with reality. He favoured modernism in literature because it was 'distanced' from the reality it seeks to describe, and this 'distancing' enhances its critical reality. Thus, knowledge of reality is achieved indirectly or obliquely. As he put it: 'Art is the negative knowledge of the actual world'. Horkheimer was in favour of the *avant-garde* (*q.v.*) and modernism because they are hostile to passivity, acquiescence and submission to the political and artistic status quo, and thus to any form of inhibitive or repressive ideology. Their views were worked out in terms of Marxist beliefs and principles. Marcuse works through the idea that the autonomous work of art negates a repressive society.

Walter Benjamin, for a while associated with Adorno, took a contrary view to him and was pro-Brecht. He surveyed the importance of technology in 19th and 20th c. urban and industrialized society, and also the enormous development of the media. As a Marxist he is interested in 'mass culture' and in the way in which culture is packaged and consumed by the masses. In his view the media – in close contact with reality – has the power to eliminate the ritual and bourgeois élitism of art and literature and give it a kind of political 'freedom'. He is more concerned with technique and with artistic forces at work than with the correct position of art and literature socially and economically. So, the emphasis is on the relation of a work of art to the ever changing conditions of the production of art itself. In his essay *The Work of Art in the Age of Mechanical Reproduction* he suggests that modern technological innovations (e.g. the cinema [especially], radio, photography and the gramophone) have radically transformed the whole idea of a work of art: the very concept, status and value of such an object. Technology enables individual works of art to be reproduced in various ways, by various means, indefinitely, thus making them 'available' to the masses rather than to a minority élite.

Yet other theories and attitudes were expressed by the Rumanian critic Lucien Goldmann, who developed a theory of 'homologies'. The term 'homology' is more commonly used to denote a concept in the natural sciences. For example, the pectoral fins of a fish, a bird's wing and a mammal's forelimbs are 'homologous' because they occupy morphologically equivalent positions in the body and are genetically cognate. Thus, affinity of structure and origin apart from form or use. Goldmann's 'homologies' are structural parallels between literature, ideas and social groups. In his view literary texts are not the work of individual geniuses but are based on 'trans-individual mental structures' which belong to groups or classes. The ideas which exist in these structures are discovered and then re-created in literary form by outstanding writers. Goldmann elaborates this theory through *The Hidden God* (1964) in a discussion of Racine's tragedies, Pascal's philosophy and the social group called *noblesse de la robe*. In his book *Towards a Sociology of the Novel* (1964) he pursues the 'homology' idea in an analysis of the structure of the modern novel in relation to the structure of market economy.

The French Marxist philosopher Louis Althusser (1918–) developed a theory of different 'levels' within the social formation and argued that these 'levels' possess no overall unity. They have a 'relative autonomy'.

'Relative autonomy' is a recent attempt by Marxists to get round the problem posed by Marx's view that Greek art was eternally beautiful. This 'idealist embarrassment' can be overcome if we recognize that art is relatively autonomous.

Althusser argues that at any point one 'level' may be dominant and that level is determined (in the last instance) by the economic level; or, it may be free of it as well – hence it is relative. Althusser's views on literature differ from those of any traditional Marxist. In his opinion great works of literature do not express an ideology nor do they provide a 'conceptual understanding of reality'. He sees literature as an ideological form/state apparatus. In *Letter on Art to André Daspre* and *Ideology and Ideological State Apparatuses* (in his book *Lenin and Philosophy*, 1971), he attempts to show (with the help of Jacques Lacan's psychoanalytic theory) how ideology works in society. Althusser, Pierre Macherey (see below) and Etienne Balibar all emphasize that literature is part of an ideological imposition (cf. P. Macherey and E. Balibar in *On Literature as an Ideological Form* in *Untying the Text*, 1981).

Macherey, a follower of Althusser, in *A Theory of Literary Production* (1966) advances the idea that a literary text, by virtue of its form and its fiction, distances itself from its ideology and also, by the 'silences' or 'gaps' in the text, by what is *not* said. These silences/gaps, he contends, not only conceal but also expose ideological contradictions. Such absences are suppressions, so to speak, within the text of its own 'unconscious'. As he puts it: 'There is a conflict within the text between the text and its ideological content'. In Macherey's view, the task of the Marxist critic is to make vocal those silences and expose the text's unconscious content. Thus, he is concerned with a kind of 'sub-text' (*q.v.*).

Marxist criticism in Britain has not flourished to the extent it has elsewhere. The first English Marxist critic of note was Christopher Caudwell (1907–37). In *Illusion and Reality* (1937) and *Studies in a Dying Culture* (1938) he attempted definitions of Marxist theories of art. More important since has been Raymond Williams (1921–88), who attempted an historical assessment of culture and literature in Marxist terms. His relevant works are, notably, *Culture and Society 1780–1950* (1958), *The Long Revolution* (1961), *The Country and the City* (1973) and *Marxism and Literature* (1977).

The principal theorist of Marxist criticism in Britain is Terry Eagleton, who has developed various views of Althusser and Macherey and suggests that a basic problem is to make clear the relationship between an ideology (e.g. Marxism) and literature. In his view texts do not reflect reality but influence an ideology to produce the effect or impression of reality. By ideology he does not necessarily mean political or Marxist ideology but all systems and theories of representation which help to make up a picture of a person's experience. He examines ideologies 'outside' the text and also the ideology *of the text*. In developing his ideas he has displayed flexibility and tactical open-mindedness and revises his position. Apart from *Literary Theory* (1983), a witty and challenging exposition of and commentary on many modern ideas and '-isms', some of his main books have been *Marxism and Literary Criticism* (1976), *Criticism and Ideology* (1976) and *Aesthetics and Ideology* (1990).

The leading exponent of Marxist criticism in America is Fredric Jameson, who makes eclectic use of a range of theories (including structuralism, deconstruction, archetypal criticism, *qq.v.*, allegorical interpretation and Jacques Lacan's interpretations [or reinterpretations] of Freud), any or all of which he may find useful in the critical interpretation of a literary text, and which he does use in *The Political Unconscious: Narrative as a Socially Symbolic Act* (1981). It is his contention that Marxism 'subsumes' other interpretative modes when it comes to a political interpretation which exposes the 'political unconscious' of a text. Like Macherey he is concerned with the 'sub-text' but more specifically with that sub-text which historically and ideologically constitutes the 'unspoken', the concealed and suppressed. Thus a Marxist interpretation looks for levels of meaning in the mode of allegory (*q.v.*).

masculine caesura A caesura (*q.v.*) which comes after a stressed syllable, as after 'moles' in the second of these lines from Matthew Arnold's *To a Republican Friend*:

> The barren optimistic sophistries
> Of comfortable moles, || whom what they do
> Teaches the limit of the just and true.

See FEMININE CAESURA.

masculine rhyme A single monosyllabic rhyme, like *thorn/scorn* at the end of a line. It is the commonest type of rhyme in English verse. In French verse it frequently alternates with feminine rhyme. *See* FEMININE RHYME; TRIPLE RHYME.

masque (F 'mask') What is probably the first use of the term occurs in Hall's Chronicle for 1512 where 'maske' applies to a dance of masked figures. According to Ben Jonson, masques were formerly called 'disguisings'. John Lydgate, in the period 1427–35, composed seven of these entertainments which he called 'mummings' or 'mummings by way of disguisings'. These may well be the first specimens of the genre to survive.

A masque was a fairly elaborate form of courtly entertainment which was particularly popular in the reigns of Elizabeth I, James I and Charles I, as it was in Italy (where the masque first acquired a distinctive form), and in France. In fact, *Circe* (1581), first produced in Paris, had a considerable influence on English masque.

The masque combined poetic drama, song, dance and music. The costumes were often sumptuous. The structure was usually simple. A Prologue introduced a group of actors known to the audience. They entered in disguise or perhaps in some kind of decorated vehicle. Plot and action were slight. Usually the plot consisted of mythological and allegorical elements. Sometimes there might be a sort of 'debate'. At the end there was a dance of masked figures in which the audience joined. In short, it was a kind of elegant, private pageant (*q.v.*).

In the Tudor period masques accompanied many festive occasions. Towards the end of Elizabeth's reign the poetic element, thanks to the influence of Gascoigne and Daniel, began to predominate. In the reign of James I Ben Jonson perfected the genre with the help of Inigo Jones who (like Brunelleschi in Italy) created lavish sets and costumes and performed many ingenious and spectacular feats with stage machinery. By this time masques had become so elaborate that they could almost be described as forerunners of the musical. They were extremely expensive. For example, Jonson's *Love Freed from Ignorance and Folly* (1611) cost a little under £1,000, and his *Oberon* (1611) cost over £2,000 – huge sums of money for those days.

As time went on they became more and more spectacular, and operatically splendid; to such an extent that even Jonson was disillusioned and felt that they were merely obscuring truth. As he put it in *An Expostulation with Inigo Jones* (1631):

> Oh, to make boards to speak! There is a task!
> Painting and carpentry are the soul of masque!

> Pack with you peddling poetry to the stage!
> This is the money-get, mechanic age.

In the development of the theatre the masque was particularly important because it was Inigo Jones who was responsible for the technique of proscenium staging. Moreover, the masque had considerable influence on contemporary drama, as we can see from Shakespeare's *Love's Labour's Lost* (*c.* 1593), *Dekker's Old Fortunatus* (1600), John Ford's *The Sun's Darling* (1624) and Nabbes's *Microcosmus* (1637). The most famous instance was the masque of Juno and Ceres within the fourth act of *The Tempest* (*c.* 1611), rivalled only by Milton's *Comus* presented at Ludlow Castle in 1634.

Further development was prevented by the outbreak of civil war and the closing of the theatres by the Puritans. Almost the last masque of any note before the ban was Davenant's *Salmacida Spolia* (1640). However, when the theatres re-opened all that had been learned of staging techniques was applied to the production of plays. And Davenant's was by no means the last masque. Shirley's *Cupid and Death* was presented in 1653, Cockayne's *The Masque at Bretby* in 1658, Crowne's *Calisto* in 1675, Davison's *The Masque of Proteus and the Adamantine Rock* in 1688, and Congreve's *The Judgment of Paris* in 1701.

Mention should also be made of the following contributions to the genre: Sir Philip Sidney's *The Lady of May* (1578); Daniel's *The Vision of Twelve Goddesses* (1604); Jonson's *Hymenaei* (1606), *The Masque of Beauty* (1608), *The Masque of Queens* (1609), *The Masque of Augurs* (1621), *Neptune's Triumph for the Return of Albion* (1624?), *The Fortunate Isles and Their Union* (1624); Chapman's *The Masque of the Middle Temple and Lincoln's Inn* (1613?); the anonymous *The Masque of Flowers* (1614); Townsend's *Albion's Triumph* (1632); Shirley's *The Triumph of Peace* (1634); Carew's *Coelum Brittanicum* (1634); Kynaston's *Corona Minervae* (1636); and Nabbes's *The Spring's Glory* (1638). Fletcher, Campion, Beaumont and Middleton also composed masques. *See* ANTI-MASQUE.

maxim (L *propositio maxima* 'greatest theme') A proposition, often barely distinguishable from an *aphorism* (*q.v.*) and closely related to a *pensée* (*q.v.*) which consists of a pithy, succinct statement (usually a sentence or two, though it may run to more) which contains a precept or general truth about human nature and human conduct.

Maxims are to be found scattered about the works of many writers, especially those of Francis Bacon, William Blake, Samuel (*Erewhon*) Butler, Albert Camus, Sebastian Chamfort, Malcolm de Chazal, Chekhov, Lord Chesterfield, Chesterton, Coleridge, Emerson, Goethe, Remy de Gourmont, George Halifax, Hazlitt, Johnson, Kierkegaard, La Bruyère, Lichtenberg, Montaigne, Nietzsche, Ortega y Gasset, Pascal, Cesare Pavese, Pope, Johann-Paul Richter, Santayana, Schopenhauer, Shaw, Stendhal, Thoreau, de Tocqueville, Paul Valéry, Voltaire, Whitehead and Oscar Wilde – to name a handful of the most distinguished makers of maxims. Many maxims are anonymous; not a few echo ancient proverbs (*q.v.*). However, the greatest collection of maxims is unquestionably that of La Rochefoucauld. His work *Maximes* (1665) was the product of a 17th c. salon (*q.v.*) and society 'game'. In this case the diversion took place in the salon of Madame de Sablé in the 1650s and 1660s. At their meetings the members of the *coterie* 'fashioned' these general truths, polished them like gems, and put them into durable shape. They were the result of a group effort, but one may suppose that La Rochefoucauld was the final 'judge' and it was he, it seems, who gave the *Maximes* their discerningly cynical flavour. Here are two instances:

(a) Old people are fond of giving good advice: it consoles them for no longer being capable of setting a bad example.
(b) What men have called friendship is merely association, respect for each other's interests, and exchange of good offices, in fact nothing more than a business arrangement from which self-love is always out to draw some profit.

Less well known but extremely interesting is Vauvenargues's collection of maxims published in 1746 under the title *Introduction à la connaissance de l'esprit humain, suivie de réflexions et maximes.* Vauvenargues is much less cynical than La Rochefoucauld. He sees both good and evil, and makes much more of the virtues and the good impulses of man's passions and heart than does La Rochefoucauld. In fact he is an optimist.

The only equivalent to these collections in English literature is George Halifax's *Maxims of State* (thirty-three in all; circulated in manuscript in 1692, published as a broadsheet in 1693 and finally reprinted in the *Miscellanies* of 1700). To these should be added his *Political Thoughts and Reflections*, *Moral Thoughts and Reflections* and *Miscellaneous Thoughts and Reflections* (none of which was published until 1750, when they came out together).

maximum scene technique A jargon term for stream of consciousness (*q.v.*) technique.

mazarinades Pamphlets (*q.v.*) and satires in prose and verse directed against Cardinal Mazarin (1602–61) at the time of the Fronde (1648–51). These were personal attacks on the venal life of a much hated man.

meaning If we take as an example the following dialogue:

X: Is this a question?
Y: If it is, this is the answer.

we find that in this form it possesses referential or cognitive meaning. If we change it to:

X: Is this a sensible question?
Y: If it is, this is an equally stupid answer.

we introduce an emotive element, and it has what is called emotive meaning.

Under cognitive meaning it is normal to distinguish between two relations: (a) that between a word and the things it names or denotes; hence these things are called the extension or denotation (*q.v.*) of the word; (b) that between a word and certain characteristics; these are the intension of the word, or its connotation (*q.v.*). The word *snake*, for instance, denotes the genus of reptiles; but for many people it also has very strong connotations.

measure Another word for meter (*q.v.*). *See also* LONG MEASURE; POULTER'S MEASURE.

mechanic form *See* ORGANIC FORM.

mechanism In general, it denotes the construction of a work; the relationship of the parts to the whole. We may also speak of the mechanism of a plot (*q.v.*); that is, how it works.

medievalism In a literary work, an emphasis on the attitudes, way of thought, sensibility, themes, style and matter commonly associated with the Middle Ages (*c.* 800–*c.* 1450). The Gothic revival, the Romantic revival and Pre-Raphaelitism (*q.v.*) were all manifestations of medievalism. Keats, for instance, strongly under the influence of Spenser (and of Milton, who in turn had been much influenced by Spenser, a very 'medieval' poet), exhibits many aspects of medievalism.

Meininger The title of a German theatrical company which, under the aegis of and with the backing of Georg II, Duke of Saxe-Meiningen (1826–1914), toured Europe and visited England during the latter part of the 19th c. It was under the directorship of Ludwig Chronegk (1837–91), and had a considerable influence on the development of naturalism (*q.v.*) in the European theatre.

meiosis (Gk 'lessening') A figure of speech which contains an understatement for emphasis: often used ironically, and also for dramatic effect, in the attainment of simplicity. In everyday speech it is sometimes used in gentle irony, especially when describing something very spectacular or impressive as 'rather good', or words to that effect. In *King Lear*, the old king, having suffered the most dreadful disasters, says 'Pray you undo this button'. Meiosis may even pervade the tone and a manner of a work. A particularly good example is Auden's *The Unknown Citizen*. *See also* IRONY; LITOTES.

Meistergesang German poetry for singing to melodies. The Meistersänger were mostly burghers of the 14th, 15th and 16th c. and were organized into guilds on a hierarchical basis. In effect one graduated to the rank of *Meister*. The meetings were informal occasions and the songs were for the most part religious, didactic and moral. In this respect they differed from the Minnesingers (*q.v.*) whose literary descendants they were. Meistersingers were particularly common in southern Germany and in the Rhineland. Two of the most famous were Hans Folz and Hans Sachs.

meiurus (Gk 'tapering') An hexameter (*q.v.*) line in which the first syllable of the last foot is short instead of long. Also known as *teliambos*.

melic poetry Lyric poetry to be sung and danced to. It was mostly composed by Aeolians and Dorians, and the best work dates from the 7th to the 5th c. BC. There were basically two kinds: the monodic and the choral. The former was sung by a single voice and expressed one individual's feelings. The principal writers of monody were Sappho, Alcaeus and Anacreon. The latter expressed the feelings of a group and was sung by a chorus. The main practitioners of this kind were Alcman, Stesichorus, Simonides, Pindar and Bacchylides. *See* LYRIC.

melodrama (Gk 'song drama') The origins of melodrama coincide roughly with the origins of opera (*q.v.*) in Italy very late in the 16th c. Opera developed from an attempt to revive Classical tragedy, and the mixture of music and drama was either opera or melodrama. In the 18th c. Handel called some of his works opera and some melodrama. Towards the end of the 18th c. French dramatists began to develop melodrama as a distinct genre by elaborating the dialogue and making much more of spectacle, action and violence.

Sensationalism and extravagant emotional appeal became popular. One of the main influences from earlier in the century was very probably the gloomy tragedies of Crébillon (*père*). Some of the more notable examples of inchoate melodrama were Rousseau's *Pygmalion* (1775), Gabiot's *L'Auto-da-Fé* (1790) and Gilbert de Pixerécourt's *Caelina, ou l'enfant du mystère* (1800). The French influence, plus the Gothic element in the work of Goethe and Schiller, plus, no doubt, the increasing vogue of the Gothic novel (*q.v.*) and the popularity of M. G. 'Monk' Lewis's melodrama *The Castle Spectre* (1797), all contributed to produce an extraordinary number of melodramas on the English stage during the 19th c., a period during which a very large number of novels (by Scott, Reade, Dickens, Wilkie Collins and others) were adapted for the stage in the form of melodrama. It can be no coincidence that in this period of decadence in the theatre very little original work of any note was created. Writers had lost their 'ear' for dramatic verse and prose.

The flourishing of melodrama in the 19th c. produced a kind of naively sensational entertainment in which the main characters were excessively virtuous or exceptionally evil (hence the luminously good hero or heroine and the villain of deepest and darkest dye), an abundance of blood, thunder, thrills and violent action which made use of spectres, ghouls, witches, vampires and many a skeleton from the supernatural cupboard, and also (in more domestic melodrama) a sordid realism in the shape of extravagant tales of the wickedness of drinking, gambling and murdering.

Among the hundreds of extant examples of the genre, the following are some of the better known: Thomas Holcroft's *A Tale of Mystery* (1802), an unacknowledged translation or adaptation of Pixerécourt's *Caelina*; Douglas Jerrold's *Black-Ey'd Susan* (1829); *Maria Marten; or, The Murder in the Red Barn* (*c.* 1830), a classic story of melodrama which was worked over a number of times; *Sweeney Todd, the Demon Barber of Fleet Street* (1842), which, like *Maria Marten*, provided themes for a number of variations; Miss Braddon's *Lady Audley's Secret* (1863), based on the novel of that title; Tom Taylor's *The Ticket-of-leave Man* (1853); *East Lynne* (1874), which was based on Mrs Henry Wood's novel *The Bells* (1871); Henry Arthur Jones's *The Silver King* (1882); and William Terriss's *The Bells of Hazlemere* (1887).

During the mid-century period Dion Boucicault (1820–90) wrote a number of fine melodramas, some of which have worn well, as was amply shown in 1988 with the National Theatre (*q.v.*) production of *The Shaughraun* (1874). This was one of his best comic melodramas; two others were *The Colleen Bawn* (1860) and *Arrah-na-Pogue* (1864). Boucicault was very prolific. Other successes of his were: *The Corsican Brothers* (1852), *The Vampire* (1852), *Faust and Margaret* (1854), *The Streets of Dublin* (1864), *Jessie Brown; or, The Relief of Lucknow* (1858) and *The Octoroon* (1859).

Mention should also be made of George Bernard Shaw's 'intellectual' melodrama *The Devil's Disciple* (1897), and his short curtain raiser *Passion, Poison, and Petrification, or The Fatal Gazogene* (1905), a hilarious burlesque of some of the more grotesque features of Victorian melodrama. Shaw included this among his *Trifles and Tomfooleries*, but the graver hierophants of the Theatre of the Absurd (*q.v.*) have detected in it certain foreshadowings of 'the absurd'.

At the turn of the century Alfred Jarry (1873–1907) – who died saturated with drink and ether – wrote *Ubu Roi* (1896), a totally original comic melodrama, which influenced the surrealists and the absurdists.

Since about the 1920s the cinema has largely ousted melodrama from the stage, but the melodramatic can still draw big and appreciative audiences (hence the success of *The Shaughraun* in 1988). Between the wars memorable successes were *The Green Goddess* (1923), *Diamond Lil* (1928), Patrick Hamilton's *Rope* (1929) and *Gaslight* (1938), which he followed with *The Governess* (1945). There were also Edgar Wallace's *On the Spot* (1930) and his *The Case of the Frightened Lady* (1931). Post-Second World War varieties of melodrama have been distinguished and include Sartre's 'intellectual' melodrama *Crime passionel* (1948), Maxwell Anderson's *The Bad Seed* (1954), Joe Orton's *The Erpingham Camp* (1966) and *Loot* (1965), Tom Stoppard's parodic *The Real Inspector Hound*

(1968) and Simon Gray's comedy thriller melodrama *Stagestruck* (1979). Orton's *Loot* was an excellent example of a macabre and scintillating burlesque of Victorian melodrama. *See also* GRAND GUIGNOL; THEATRE OF CRUELTY; THRILLER.

melopoeia (Gk 'song making') The musical element in Classical Greek tragedy. Clearly, from its form, it is related to onomatopoeia (*q.v.*) but refers more to the tune and music of the verses, rather than to the specific sounds for certain effects. Tennyson, for instance, achieves some melopoeic effects in the narcotic rhythms of *The Lotos-Eaters*. *See also* LOGOPOEIA; ONOMATOPOEIA; PHANOPOEIA.

memoir-novel A form of novel (*q.v.*) which purports to be a 'true' autobiographical account but which is wholly or mostly fictitious. Thus, a kind of literary convention or fictional device. Daniel Defoe appears to have been the first practitioner with *Robinson Crusoe* (1719) and *Moll Flanders* (1722). Other examples in the 18th c. are Smollett's *Roderick Random* (1748), Goldsmith's *The Vicar of Wakefield* (1766), Mackenzie's *The Man of Feeling* (1771) and Maria Edgeworth's *Castle Rackrent* (1800). In the 19th c. this kind of fiction was much less popular.

memoirs *See* AUTOBIOGRAPHY; DIARY AND JOURNAL.

Menippean satire So called after Menippus, its originator, who was a philosopher and a Cynic of the 3rd c. BC. He satirized the follies of men (including philosophers) in a mixture of prose and verse. He was imitated by Varro (thus this type of satire is sometimes called Varronian) and also by Lucian – especially in his *Dialogues*.

The classic example of this genre in European literature is *Satire Ménippée*, a pamphlet in prose and verse which ridiculed the *États généraux* of 1593 and was published in 1594. It was written by Jean Leroy with the assistance of Jacques Gillot, Nicolas Rapin, Pierre Pithou, Jean Passerat and Florent Chrétien. Its main features were caricature, parody and burlesque (*qq.v.*). It has been suggested by Northrop Frye in his *Anatomy of Criticism* that Burton's *Anatomy of Melancholy* (1621) is in the tradition of Menippus and Varro. Other works which perhaps owe something to this tradition of *satura* or medley are Rabelais's *Gargantua* and *Pantagruel*, Voltaire's *Candide*, Thomas Love Peacock's *Nightmare Abbey*, Aldous Huxley's *Point Counter Point* and *After Many a Summer* and a number of other intellectual charades and fantasies which, through debate and dialogue, serve to ridicule different intellectual attitudes and philosophical postures. *See* SATIRE.

menology (Gk 'record of the month') A form of calendar (*q.v.*) used especially in the Greek Orthodox Church, with biographies of the saints and martyrs. *See* HAGIOGRAPHY; SYNAXARION.

merde, mystique de la Not exactly the 'mystique of shit', but a term denoting a preoccupation with the seamier, muddier, bloodier aspects of life, as well as, excessively, with sex and money. The term was first used by Robert E. Fitch in 1956, and is a coarser version of *nostalgie de la boue.* Among modern writers, Joyce, Genet, Hemingway, Tennessee Williams and William Burroughs have all, from time to time, expoited the possibilities of *merde.*

merismus (Gk 'division into parts') A rhetorical device in which a subject or topic is divided into its various parts. A fairly well-known instance occurs in Shakespeare's *Troilus and Cressida* (III, iii, 171):

> For beauty, wit,
> High birth, vigour of bone, desert in service,
> Love, friendship, charity, are subjects all
> To envious and calumniating Time.

Merz It apparently derives from the word *Kommerz* (commerce); *Merz* was the word which Kurt Schwitters (1887–1948) used as a title for his Dada movement in Hanover in the 1920s. There is also a suggestion that the term is a kind of portmanteau word (*q.v.*) which recalls the French *merde* (*q.v.*) and the German *ausmerzen* ('to extirpate'). Schwitters was a poet as well as a painter, and his work gave rise to *Merz* and a form of concrete poetry (*q.v.*). *See also* ALTAR POEM; PATTERN POETRY.

mesode (Gk 'middle ode') In Greek drama, part of an ode (*q.v.*) between strophe and anti-strophe (*qq.v.*). It has an independent existence.

mesostich *See* ACROSTIC.

messenger In Classical Greek tragedy action which took place off stage was reported by a messenger or herald. In Euripides' *Medea*, for example, a messenger entered to report that the princess was dead, and her death was described in some detail. The messenger often figured in Tudor and Jacobean tragedy and occasionally in comedy. This character was also employed in French Classical drama; or someone performing the function of messenger, like Théramène, the tutor of Hippolyte, reporting the young man's death at the end of Racine's *Phèdre*.

mester de clerecía (Sp 'art of the clerics') After the *epopeya*, the *cantares de gesta* (*q.v.*) chanted by ministrels or *juglares*, and referred to in contrast as the *mester de juglaría*, came the scholars with their learned poetry. This last is what is meant by *mester de clerecía*. At the beginning of the 13th c. attempts were made by the clerics to improve both style and content of the popular verse. Improvements in form led to the *cuaderna vía* (*q.v.*), via the Latin Goliardic verse used by clerics in many countries. But the vehicle was one thing and the intention another. The clerics wished to spread to the ordinary people knowledge of the lives of the saints and other sacred themes. So they used simple methods of composition, a direct style and, so far as possible, the language of the people. The character of the poetry was narrative and real inspiration was rare – as is often the case in didactic poetry (*q.v.*).

mester de juglaría (Sp 'occupation, or art, of the minstrel') The term denotes oral and epic (*q.v.*) narrative poetry of the 12th, 13th and 14th c. It was composed and recited by minstrels and *juglares* and intended to entertain, unlike the *mester de clerecía* (*q.v.*) which was didactic.

mesur tri-thrawiad A Welsh dactylic metre, of half lines.

metalanguage A 'beyond' language. In linguistics it denotes any technical language which describes the properties of language (discussed by Roman Jakobson in his essay *Linguistics and Poetics*, 1960). It is also known as a 'second-order' language which may be used to describe, explain or interpret a 'first-order' language. Given one metalanguage for one explanation it follows that there may be another in turn, and a metalanguage may replace a 'first-order' language. Each order of language implicitly relies on a meta-language by which it is explained. In his book *Elements of Semiology* (1967) Roland Barthes perceives that this could lead to an indefinite regression or *aporia* (*q.v.*), which would ultimately undermine and destroy all metalanguages. In *A Reader's Guide to Contemporary Literary Theory* (1985) Raman Selden summarizes the predicament very succinctly: 'This means that, when we read as critics, we can never step outside discourse and adopt a position invulnerable to a subsequent interrogative reading. All discourses, including critical interpretations, are equally *fictive*; none stands apart in the place of Truth'. *See* DECONSTRUCTION; POST-STRUCTURALISM.

metalepsis (Gk 'after taking, substitution') A form of metonymy (*q.v.*) in which the general idea substituted is considerably removed from the particular detail. As in these lines from *Henry VIII* (II, i):

> Go with me like good angels to my end;
> And as the long divorce of steel falls on me
> Make of your prayers one sweet sacrifice,

See EUPHEMISM; PERIPHRASIS.

metanoia (Gk 'after thought, change of mind') A figurative device in which a statement is made, and then withdrawn or lessened in its impact. For example: 'I'll murder you. You will be punished'.

metaphor (Gk 'carrying from one place to another') A figure of speech in which one thing is described in terms of another. The basic figure in poetry. A comparison is usually implicit; whereas in simile (*q.v.*) it is explicit. There are several metaphors in these lines from the beginning of R. S. Thomas's *Song at the Year's Turning*:

> Shelley dreamed it. Now the dream decays.
> The props crumble. The familiar ways
> Are stale with tears trodden underfoot.
> The heart's flower withers at the root.
> Bury it, then, in history's sterile dust.
> The slow years shall tame your tawny lust.

See ORGANIC METAPHOR; TELESCOPED METAPHOR; TENOR AND VEHICLE.

metaphor/metonymy A theory of binary opposition (*q.v.*) propounded by Roman Jakobson (1896–1982) in *Two Aspects of Language and Two Types of Aphasic Disturbances* (1956). Jakobson uses the distinction developed elsewhere between the two axes of language, syntagmatic and paradigmatic (*q.v.*). The first may be thought of as a horizontal line (here one word is associated with another through contiguity), the second as a vertical line where meanings can be substituted one for another. Through his study of aphasia (a language disorder resulting from memory loss), Jakobson extends this model to metaphor and metonymy (*qq.v.*). Thus, the language disorder acts on the two axes of language in different ways so that those suffering from a 'continuity disorder' tend to use substitution (i.e. metaphor) and those suffering from 'similarity disorder' tend to use association (i.e. metonymy). In Jakobson's words: 'Metaphor is alien to the similarity disorder, and metonymy to the continuity disorder'. Jakobson's point is that some forms of writing use one or the other mode predominantly. Romantic and modernist poetry primarily uses metaphor, and the realist novel uses metonymy. Magic realism (*q.v.*) subverts the mainly metonymic axis of the narrative discourse/novel form, as does post-modernism (*q.v.*). In *The Modes of Modern Writing* (1977) and in *Modern Criticism and Theory* (1988) David Lodge discusses aspects of Jakobson's theories.

metaphysical (L *al* suffixed to Gk 'after [Aristotle's work on] physics') A term now generally applied to a group of 17th c. poets; chiefly Donne, Carew, George Herbert, Crashaw, Henry Vaughan, Marvell, Cleveland and Cowley. It appears that one of the first to use the term was William Drummond of Hawthornden in a letter written to Arthur Johnston *c.* 1630. In his *Discourse of the Original and Progress of Satire* (1692) Dryden said of Donne: 'He affects the metaphysics not only in his satires, but in his amorous verses, where nature only should reign, and perplexes the minds of the fair sex with nice speculations of philosophy'. Later Johnson, in his *Lives of the Poets* (1779–81), established the term more or less permanently as a label. Johnson wrote somewhat disapprovingly of the *discordia concors* in metaphysical imagery, and referred to 'heterogeneous ideas . . . yoked by violence together.'

The marks of 17th c. metaphysical poetry were arresting and original images and conceits (showing a preoccupation with analogies between macrocosm and microcosm), wit, ingenuity, dexterous use of colloquial speech, considerable flexibility of rhythm and meter, complex themes (both sacred and profane), a liking for paradox and dialectical argument, a direct manner, a caustic humour, a keenly felt awareness of mortality, and a distinguished capacity for elliptical thought and tersely compact expression. But for all their intellectual robustness the metaphysical poets were also capable of refined delicacy, gracefulness and deep feeling; passion as well as wit. The following example is Marvell's *The Definition of Love*:

My Love is of a birth as rare
As 'tis for object strange and high:
It was begotten by despair
Upon Impossibility.

Magnanimous Despair alone
Could show me so divine a thing,
Where feeble Hope could ne'r have flown
But vainly flapt its Tinsel Wing.

And yet I quickly might arrive
Where my extended Soul is fixt,
But Fate does Iron wedges drive,
And alwaies crouds it self betwixt.

For Fate with jealous Eye does see
Two perfect Loves; nor lets them close:
Their union would her ruine be,
And her Tyranick pow'r depose.

And therefore her Decrees of Steel
Us as the distant Poles have plac'd,
(Though Loves whole World on us doth wheel)
Not by themselves to be embrac'd.

Unless the giddy Heaven fall,
And Earth some new Convulsion tear;
And, us to joyn, the World should all
Be cramp'd into a *Planisphere*.

As Lines so Loves *oblique* may well
Themselves in every Angle greet:
But ours so truly *Paralel*,
Though infinite can never meet.

Therefore the Love which us doth bind,
But Fate so enviously debarrs,
Is the Conjunction of the Mind,
And Opposition of the Stars.

The Metaphysicals have had a profound influence on the course of English poetry in recent years, thanks, in great measure, to the critical appreciations of Herbert Grierson, T. S. Eliot, J. B. Leishman, H. C. White, Rosemond Tuve, Cleanth Brooks, Louis Martz, George Williamson and Helen Gardner. *See* CONCEIT.

metastasis (Gk 'a changing') A cursory treatment of a matter; a glossing over as if it were of no importance.

metatheatre A term coined by Lionel Abel in 1963 to classify 'serious' plays which, he argues, do not qualify as tragedies, such as Arthur Miller's *Death of a Salesman* (1949), Tennessee Williams's *A Streetcar Named Desire* (1949), John Arden's *Serjeant Musgrave's Dance* (1959) and Robert Bolt's *A Man for All Seasons* (1960). *See also* DRAME; TRAGEDY.

metathesis (Gk 'transposition') The interchanging of consonant sounds, as in *third* from OE *thridda* (cf. G *dritte*).

meter (Gk 'measure') The term refers to the pattern of stressed and unstressed syllables in verse. In English verse, meter is based on stress rather than quantity (*q.v.*). A line may have a fixed number of syllables and yet have a varying number of stresses. As a rule meter keeps to a basic pattern, within which there are many variations. A common form of variation is substitution (*q.v.*).

In English verse the following meters are the commonest: iambic ᴗ /; trochaic / ᴗ; anapaestic ᴗ ᴗ /; dactylic / ᴗ ᴗ; spondaic / /; paeonic / ᴗ ᴗ ᴗ (first paeon).

Coleridge's poem *Metrical Feet* helps to illustrate the first five of these feet:

Tróchěe tríps frŏm lóng tŏ shórt.
Frŏm lóng tŏ lóng ĭn sólĕmn sórt
Slów spóndeé stálks; stróng foót yét íll áblĕ
Evĕr tŏ cóme ŭp wĭth thĕ dáctÿl trĭsýllăblĕ.
Ĭámbĭcs márch frŏm shórt tŏ lóng.
Wĭth ă leáp ănd ă boúnd thĕ swĭft ánăpaĕsts thróng.

The following terms denote the number of feet per line: monometer – 1; dimeter – 2; trimeter – 3; tetrameter – 4; pentameter – 5; hexameter – 6; heptameter – 7; octameter – 8 (*qq.v.*). *See also* FOOT; FREE VERSE; PROSODY; SCANSION; SPRUNG RHYTHM.

metonymy (Gk 'name change') A figure of speech in which the name of an attribute or a thing is substituted for the thing itself. Common examples are 'The Stage' for the theatrical profession; 'The Crown' for the monarchy; 'The Bench' for the judiciary; 'Dante' for his works. *See also* ANTONOMASIA; METALEPSIS; SYNECDOCHE.

metrical romance A story of adventure, love, chivalry, and deeds of derring-do. They quite often contain an element of mystery and the supernatural. A popular form of entertainment from the Middle Ages until the 19th c. when the prose romance, already established in the previous century, gradually superseded it. Among numerous metrical romances, one might mention: *Roman de Troie* (*c.* 1160); *Roman de la Rose* (13th c.); *Sir Orfeo* (mid-14th c.); *Sir Gawain and the Green Knight* (14th c.); Scott's *Lay of the Last Minstrel* (1805) and *The Lady of the Lake* (1810); Byron's *Giaour* (1813) and *The Corsair* (1814); Tennyson's *Idylls of the King* (1842–85) and *The Lady of Shalott* (1852); William Morris's *The Earthly Paradise* (1868–70). *See* ROMANCE.

metrical variations The term covers various techniques used in achieving contrasts in the rhythm and meter of verse. Variations are only possible when there is a basic metrical pattern. Substitution (*q.v.*) is the commonest variation. *See* COUNTERPOINT; FOOT; METER.

metron In Classical prosody the unit of measurement.

mezzo-zeugma (It and Gk 'middle yoke') A figurative device by which a word, usually a verb, refers to two parts of an expression or governs it. As in this example from Pope's *Epistle to Arbuthnot*, in which 'ask'd' governs 'Judgment' and 'place':

> Receiv'd of Wits an undistinguish'd race,
> Who first his Judgment ask'd, and then a Place:

See ZEUGMA.

Middle Comedy This succeeded Old Comedy (*q.v.*) of which the chief writer was Aristophanes. Middle Comedy flourished from *c.* 400 BC to *c.* 330 BC. It contained a good deal of burlesque, parody (*qq.v.*) and literary criticism. Antiphanes and Elixis were the main dramatists in this genre. *See* COMEDY.

middle rhyme *See* INTERNAL RHYME; LEONINE RHYME.

miles gloriosus Originated in a comedy by Plautus (254–184 BC). The *miles gloriosus* was a braggart soldier, the prototype of a stock character (*q.v.*) in comic drama; one who is fundamentally a coward yet boasts of valorous deeds and is often made a fool of by other characters. In English drama he first appeared eponymously in Udall's *Ralph Roister Doister* (*c.* 1553). Bobadill in Ben Jonson's *Everyman in His Humour* (1598) was another such braggart. So was Captain Brazen in Farquhar's *The Recruiting Officer* (1706). The epitome of the braggart was Shakespeare's Falstaff. *See* BRAGGADOCIO.

Miltonic sonnet A form devised by Milton. He retained the octave (*q.v.*) rhyme scheme of the Petrarchan sonnet (*q.v.*) but dispensed with a change of meaning or a turning point or *volta* (*q.v.*) at the beginning of the sestet (*q.v.*). His rhyme scheme in the sestet was also flexible. His sonnet *On the Late Massacre in Piedmont* is an example.

mime (Gk 'imitation') A form of drama in which actors tell a story by gestures, originating in Sicily and southern Italy. Sophron of Syracuse (5th c. BC) composed mime plays. So did Herodas (3rd c. BC) who later influenced Plautus, Terence and Horace. Dumb acting continued as a very popular form of entertainment throughout the Middle Ages and achieved a considerable revival in Italy in the 16th c. when it was much pracised in *commedia dell'arte* (*q.v.*). The influence spread through Europe and in varying degrees mime has been part of the European dramatic tradition ever since.

Nowadays mime denotes acting without words. In France particularly, mime is regarded as an entertainment in its own right. In the 1920s Étienne Decroux encouraged its development and Jean-Louis Barrault aroused much interest in it through his performance in *Les Enfants du paradis*. Jacques Tati has also displayed its possibilities in the cinema. Marcel Marceau is regarded as the greatest mime in the world and has virtually established his own genre of monomime. The 19th c. French mime play *L'Enfant prodigue* (in three acts) is the best known work of the kind. *See* DUMB SHOW; PANTOMIME.

mimesis It has almost the same meaning as mime (*q.v.*) but the concept of imitation (*q.v.*) in this case has wider connotations. Aristotle, in *Poetics*, states that tragedy (*q.v.*) is an imitation of an action, but he uses the term comprehensively to refer to the construction of a play and what is put into it. We should rather use *mimesis* to mean representation, which relates to verisimilitude (*q.v.*). The outstanding work on this topic is Eric Auerbach's *Mimesis* (1957).

Minnesinger (G 'love singer') A German lyric poet who, in the 12th and 13th c., composed poems of courtly love (*q.v.*) or *hohe Minne*. The *Minnesang* was the love-song of homage to a lady. The most renowned of these Minnesingers were Hartmann von Aue and Walther von der Vogelweide. *See also* JONGLEUR; MEISTERGESANG; TROUBADOUR; TROUVERE.

minstrel (MedL *ministerialis* 'pertaining to a minister or servant') The original minstrels were itinerant musicians, professional entertainers, some of whom had fairly permanent positions in courts. The minstrel was the descendant of the *scop*, the *gleeman*, and the *jongleur* (*qq.v.*). Minstrels flourished especially in the 13th and 14th c., but there were many fewer after the invention of printing. They sang old, traditional stories like the *chansons de gestes* (*q.v.*), short epics and folk ballads. Some composed what they sang, but the art of the minstrel, like that of the Slav *guslar* (*q.v.*), is such that it is almost impossible to tell where memory ends and invention begins. *See also* ORAL TRADITION; TROUBADOUR; TROUVERE.

Miracle Play This dramatic genre was a later development from the Mystery Play (*q.v.*). It dramatized saints' lives and divine miracles, and legends of miraculous interventions by the Virgin. Little of note survives in English literature, but in France there is the famous cycle of the *Miracles de Notre Dame*, forty-two plays belonging to the second half of the 14th c. Written in octosyllabic couplets, each dramatizes some aspect of human activity, and each ends with a miraculous intervention by the Blessed Virgin. Other European examples are the German *Marienklage* and the Dutch *Mariken van Nieumeghen* (*c.* 1500). *See also* INTERLUDE; LITURGICAL DRAMA; MORALITY PLAY; PASSION PLAY.

miscellany A medley; a collection of writings in one volume. Probably the most famous in English literature is Tottel's Miscellany (1557). *See also* ANTHOLOGY.

mixed metaphor It arises when there is an incongruous disparity between the two elements of the implied comparison, as in the journalist's assertion that: 'a bottle neck is strangling the traffic flow' or as in Milton's outcry (*Lycidas*, L. 119) against a venal clergy:

> Blind mouths! that scarce themselves know how to hold
> A sheep-hook, or have learned aught else the least
> That to the faithful herdman's art belongs!

See also METAPHOR.

mnemonic (Gk *mneme* 'memory') A device in verse or prose. Well-known examples are: (a) Oxydation Is Loss; Reduction Is Gain. The initial letters make OILRIG; (b) Richard Of York Gave Battle In Vain; and Read Over Your Good Books In Verse. Here the initial letters give the seven prismatic colours: red, orange, yellow, green, blue, indigo, violet. Many mnemonics have been devised for learning Latin, such as this one for masculine nouns:

> Masculine are fons and mons
> chalybs, hydrops, gryps, and pons,
> rudens, torrens, dens, and cliens,
> fractions of the as, as triens,
> Add to Masculine tridens,
> oriens, and occidens,
> bidens (*fork*): but bidens (*sheep*)
> with the Feminines we keep.

See also ACRONYM.

mock-epic A work in verse which employs the lofty manner, the high and serious tone and the supernatural machinery (*q.v.*) of epic (*q.v.*) to treat of a trivial subject and theme in such a way as to make both subject and theme ridiculous. Almost a case of breaking a butterfly upon a wheel. By extension the epic mode is also mocked but this is a secondary consideration.

The acknowledged masterpiece in this genre is Pope's *The Rape of the Lock* (1712, 1714), which he himself describes as an Heroi-comical poem. His subject is the estrangement between two families resulting from Lord Petre's snipping off a lock of Miss Arabella Fermor's hair. With faultless skill Pope minifies the epic scale in proportion to the triviality of his theme:

> What dire Offence from am'rous Causes springs,
> What mighty Contests rise from trivial Things,

I sing – This Verse to *Caryll*, Muse! is due;
This, ev'n *Belinda* may vouchsafe to view:
Slight is the Subject, but not so the Praise,
If She inspire, and He approve my Lays.
  Say what strange Motive, Goddess! cou'd compel
A well-bred *Lord* t'assault a gentle *Belle*?

Pope had precedents in the Homeric *Batrachomyomachia*, or *The Battle of the Frogs and the Mice* (translated by Thomas Parnell as a contemporary satire in 1717); Alessandro Tassoni's *La Secchia Rapita* (The Rape of the Bucket) (1622); Boileau's *Le Lutrin* (1674, 1683); Dryden's *Mac Flecknoe* (1682); and Samuel Garth's *The Dispensary* (1699).

The mock-epic tone of Dryden's opening lines differs from Pope's:

All humane things are subject to decay,
And, when Fate summons, Monarchs must obey:
This Fleckno found, who, like Augustus, young
Was call'd to Empire, and had govern'd long;
In Prose and Verse, was own'd, without dispute
Through all the Realms of Non-sense, absolute.

Mac Flecknoe gave Pope the basic idea for *The Dunciad* (1728–43); also a mock-epic, but more powerful, in a denunciatory manner; and more elaborate than *The Rape of the Lock*. *See* BURLESQUE; PARODY; SATIRE; TRAVESTY.

mock-heroic In the style of mock-epic (*q.v.*), but the term has a slightly wider application. The heroic manner is adopted to make a trivial subject seem grand in such a way as to satirize the style, and it is therefore commonly used in burlesque and parody (*qq.v.*). Fielding's *Tom Thumb* (1730) is a good example of a mock-heroic play, and John Philips's *The Splendid Shilling* (1705) of a burlesque poem.

mode Sometimes approximately synonymous with kind and form, and related to genre (*q.v.*). It is associated with method, manner and style (*q.v.*). Some incline to describe science fiction (*q.v.*) as a mode rather than a genre. Perhaps, too, the horror story (*q.v.*) may be regarded as a mode rather than a genre.

modernism A comprehensive but vague term for a movement (or tendency) which began to get under way in the closing years of the

19th c. and which has had a wide influence internationally during much of the 20th c. The term pertains to all the creative arts, especially poetry, fiction, drama, painting, music and architecture. There have been various theories as to when the movement (or its tendencies) was at its height (some suggest the 1920s for this) and as to whether the modernist movement is actually over. Some have suggested that modernism, as an innovative and revivifying movement, was played out by the late 1940s, and that it was then that post-modernism (*q.v.*) began. In fact, such movements, of their nature, do not just start and stop; the evolution is gradual. The impetus and energy of one diminishes (but continues) as the momentum of another burgeons.

Nevertheless, it is valid to point out certain places and periods where and when modernist tendencies were at their most active and fruitful. For example, in France from the 1890s until the 1940s; in Russia during the pre-revolutionary years and the 1920s; in Germany from the 1890s and on during the 1920s; in England from early in the 20th c. and during the 1920s and 1930s; in America from shortly before the First World War and on during the inter-war period. Thus, it was a European and transcontinental movement, and its principal centres of activity were the capital cities.

Within the general movement or tendency, there were subsidiary and now labelled and identifiable movements (e.g. surrealism, formalism, *qq.v.*). Much that is loosely categorized under modernism is or was *avant-garde* (*q.v.*); but one may distinguish between an 'old' *avant-garde* (e.g. the French symbolist poets) and a 'new' *avant-garde* which is post-modernist (e.g. dramatists of the Theatre of the Absurd, *q.v.*, and the practitioners of the *nouveau roman*, *q.v.*). Professor Frank Kermode made a further distinction: between palaeo-modernism and neo-modernism. The former refers to early manifestations of new movements concluding, perhaps, *c.* 1914–20; the latter to movements since that time.

As far as literature is concerned modernism reveals a breaking away from established rules, traditions and conventions, fresh ways of looking at man's position and function in the universe and many (in some cases remarkable) experiments in form and style. It is particularly concerned with language and how to use it (representationally or otherwise) and with *writing itself*. Thus, structuralism was (and is) from the outset closely connected with modernist tendencies, though the theories of structuralism (*q.v.*) did not gain a strong foothold until the 1960s, by which time post-modernism was well established as a new movement.

Aspects of modernism are touched on in the following entries: CONSTRUCTIVISM; DADAISM; DECADENCE; EXISTENTIALISM; EXPRESSIONISM; FREE VERSE; FUTURISM; IMAGISTS; NEW HUMANISM; STREAM OF CONSCIOUSNESS; SYMBOL AND SYMBOLISM; ULTRAISM; VORTICISM.

modernismo A term coined by the Nicaraguan poet Rubén Darío (1867–1916), it denotes simply 'modernism' (*q.v.*). It was Darío's intention to modernize the language and themes of poetry in the Spanish-American culture. He and his followers were considerably influenced by the Parnassians (*q.v.*).

molossus (from a Greek place-name, Molossós) A metrical foot with three stressed syllables: / / /. Very rare anyway it hardly ever exists as an independent foot. However, some might argue that the last foot in the second of these two lines from Gerard Manley Hopkins's *The Caged Skylark* could be scanned as a molossus:

As a dare-gale skylark scanted in a dull cage
| Mán's moúntĭng | spírĭt ĭn hĭs | bóne-hoúse, | meán hoúse, dwélls–

So the line would scan: palimbacchius/ first paeonic/ spondee/ molossus.

Monk's Tale stanza A stanza of eight iambic pentameters, rhyming ababbcbc, used by Chaucer in *The Monk's Tale*, an *ABC*, and some other poems. In origin it is a French *ballade* (*q.v.*) stanza. It was used quite a lot in the 15th c. and may well have been the model from which Spenser developed what is now known as the Spenserian stanza (*q.v.*).

monodrama A theatrical entertainment in which there is only one character. Recently Ruth Draper, Cornelia Otis Skinner and Joyce Grenfell have excelled in this genre. However, Tennyson also used the term to describe *Maud* (1855). A recent example is *Krapp's Last Tape* (1959) by Samuel Beckett. *See* MONOLOGUE; MONOPOLYLOGUE.

monody (Gk 'alone song') An ode (*q.v.*) sung by a single actor in Greek tragedy, or a poem which mourns someone's death. In his introduction to *Lycidas* Milton described the poem as a monody. And Arnold called *Thyrsis* a monody. *See* DIRGE; ELEGY; EPICEDIUM; LAMENT.

monogatari (J 'tales') Japanese legends and stories in collections; mostly dating from the Middle Ages. Notable examples are: *Taketori Monogatari* (*c.* 850–920), one of the earliest extant works of Japanese fiction; *Utsubo Monogatari* (*c.* 850–1000); *Ise Monogatari* (*c.* 939); *Ochikubo Monogatari* (*c.* 950–990), a novel; *Yamato Monogatari* (*c.* 950), stories illustrated by poems; *Eiga Monogatari* (*c.* 1092); *Okagami* (*c.* 1115); *Hōgen Monogatari* (*c.* 1156), a story of the civil war of the Hōgen period; *Heiji Monogatari* (1159–60); *Tsutsumi Chūnagon Monogatari* (12th c.); *Heike Monogatari* (*c.* 1215–50). *See* NOVEL; SHORT STORY.

monograph (Gk 'single writing') An essay or treatise (*qq.v.*) on a particular subject.

monologic *See* DIALOGIC/MONOLOGIC.

monologue A term used in a number of senses, with the basic meaning of a single person speaking alone – with or without an audience. Most prayers, much lyric verse and all laments are monologues, but, apart from these, four main kinds can be distinguished: (a) monodrama (*q.v.*), as in Strindberg's *The Stronger*; (b) soliloquy (*q.v.*), for instance, the Moor's self-revelations in *Othello*; (c) solo addresses to an audience in a play; for instance, Iago's explanations to the audience (in *Othello*) of what he is going to do; (d) dramatic monologue – a poem in which there is one imaginary speaker addressing an imaginary audience, as in Browning's *Andrea del Sarto*, *My Last Duchess*, *The Bishop orders his tomb at St Praxed's Church*, *Fra Lippo Lippi*, *Caliban upon Setebos.* Browning published some dramatic monologues in *Dramatic Lyrics* (1842). Tennyson also wrote some fine dramatic monologues, notably *Tithonus*, *Ulysses* and *St Simeon Stylites*. Among recent poets who have exploited the possibilities of this form are Thomas Hardy, Rudyard Kipling, W. B. Yeats (e.g. *Crazy Jane* poems), T. S. Eliot (e.g. *Prufrock*, *Portrait of a Lady*, *Journey of the Magi*, *A Song for Simeon*, *Marina*), Conrad Aiken and Robert Frost. *See also* STREAM OF CONSCIOUSNESS.

monometer A line of verse consisting of one metrical foot, as in Herrick's poem *Upon his depature hence*:

I'm made
A shade
And laid

I'th' grave
There have
My cave.

An agreeable humorous example is Ogden Nash's:

Candy
Is dandy
But liquor
Is quicker
Pot
Is not.

See also DIMETER; HEPTAMETER; HEXAMETER; OCTAMETER; PENTAMETER; TETRAMETER; TRIMETER.

monopolylogue An entertainment in which one performer plays many parts, as in some forms of monodrama (*q.v.*).

monorhyme A poem or part of a poem in which all the lines have the same end-rhyme. It is by no means uncommon in Latin, Italian, Arabic, Welsh and Slav poetry. It is very common indeed in Slav poetry of the oral tradition (*q.v.*). In English verse, because English is not a language rich in easy rhymes, monorhyme is fairly uncommon; but Shakespeare achieved a nicely doggerel touch with nine such in 'All that glisters is not gold . . .' (*The Merchant of Venice*, II, vii, 67). *See also* IDENTICAL RHYME.

monostich (Gk 'one line') A single metrical line, or a poem consisting of one line.

mora (L 'delay') A unit of metrical time which denotes the duration (*q.v.*) of a short syllable which is usually represented thus: ∪. This is called a *breve*. The time occupied by a long syllable in quantitative verse is two *morae*. This is represented by /; and this is called a *macron*. *See* FOOT; SCANSION.

moral The lesson to be learnt from a story, poem, fable (*q.v.*), play – or indeed any work which purports to teach anything either directly or obliquely. Thus, the point in any didactic work. As Johnson put it, grandly, in *The Vanity of Human Wishes* (he was referring to the warrior king, Charles XII of Sweden):

But did not Chance at length her Error mend?
Did no subverted Empire mark his End?
Did rival Monarchs give the fatal Wound?
Or hostile Millions press him to the Ground?
His Fall was destin'd to a barren Strand,
A petty Fortress, and a dubious Hand;
He left the Name, at which the World grew pale,
To point a Moral, or adorn a Tale.

See DIDACTIC POETRY.

moral interlude A form of drama which has something in common with both the Morality Play and the Interlude (*qq.v.*). It tended to be didactic but contained more humour than the Morality. Two well-known examples are *Hyckescorner* (1512) and Wever's *Lusty Juventus* (*c.* 1550). But both have been taken to be ordinary Morality Plays.

moralische Wochenschriften German weekly periodicals published throughout much of the 18th c. Their models were English, especially the *Tatler* and the *Spectator*. They were moral in tone and content and concerned with morals, education and matters of taste and aesthetics. They were not political. *See* PERIODICAL.

Morality Play Basically, a Morality Play is an allegory in dramatic form. Its dramatic origins are to be found in the Mystery and Miracle Plays of the late Middle Ages; its allegorical origins in the sermon literature, homilies, *exempla*, romances and works of spiritual edification like the *Lambeth Homilies* (12th c.); *Ancrene Riwle* (1200–50); the homily *Sawles Warde* (13th c.); *Chasteau d'Amour* (14th c.); the *Abbey of the Holy Ghost* (14th c.); *Azenbite of Inwyt* (1340). In essence a Morality Play was a dramatization of the battle between the forces of good and evil in the human soul; thus, an exteriorization of the inward spiritual struggle: man's need for salvation and the temptations which beset him on his pilgrimage through life to death. The main characters in *Everyman* (*c.* 1500) are God, a Messenger, Death, Everyman, Fellowship, Good Deeds, Goods, Knowledge, Beauty and Strength. Everyman is summoned by Death and he finds that no one will go with him except Good Deeds.

In other plays we find the forces of evil (the World, the Flesh and the Devil, the Seven Deadly Sins and various demons) deployed against Man, whose champions are the forces of good (God and his angels, and the four moral and the three theological virtues). Nearly all the Moralities are didactic illustrations of and commentaries on a preoccupation which dominated Christian thought throughout much of the Middle Ages: namely, the war between God and the Devil.

The writing in the plays is often uneven, the characterization is crude and the psychology naive. Nevertheless, in their simplicity, a number of them have a certain robust and impressive power. The better ones show an increasingly sophisticated analysis of character, and point the way to that examination of human nature and morality in depth which makes the best Tudor and Jacobean drama so remarkable.

The most memorable Morality Plays are: *The Castell of Perseverance* (*c.* 1425); *Mind, Will and Understanding* (*c.* 1460); and *Mankind* (*c.* 1475). These three are considered as a group because they occur in the Macro Manuscript. Then comes *Everyman* (*c.* 1500), to which there is a slightly earlier Dutch analogue, *Elckerlijk*. To the same period belong the French Moralities *Bien avisé, Mal avisé* and *L'Homme juste et l'homme mondain*, and *La Condemnation de Banquet*. To the early years of the 16th c. belong *The World and the Child*; *Hyckescorner* (1512); Skelton's *Magnificence* (1516); Rastell's *For Elements* (1519); *Mundus et Infans* (*c.* 1520); Henry Medwall's *Nature* (*c.* 1530); Sir David Lindsay's *Satyre of the Three Estaitis* (1540), an example of a political Morality Play; and Wever's *Lusty Juventus* (*c.* 1550). From about the middle of the 16th c. Morality Plays became less popular, but they were still being written and many plays bore unmistakable marks of their influence, such as Nathaniel Woodes's *The Conflict of Conscience* (1563); Fulwell's *Like Will to Like* (*c.* 1568); Lupton's *All for Money* (*c.* 1578); Marlowe's *Dr Faustus* (*c.* 1588). Even as late as 1625 Ben Jonson's *The Staple of News* showed strong Morality influences, especially in the person of Lady Pecunia, an allegorical figure representing Riches.

The long-term influence of the Moralities is discernible in the pageant and masque (*qq.v.*), and in the label names or aptronymics (*q.v.*) given to characters in 17th and 18th c. comedy (*q.v.*) and also in the names in novels. A modern example of a Morality Play was Jerome K. Jerome's *The Passing of the Third Floor Back* (1908). *See* ALLEGORY; INTERLUDE; MIRACLE PLAY; MORAL INTERLUDE; MYSTERY PLAY.

morology (Gk 'foolish speech') Deliberate foolishness or nonsense for effect. *See* NONSENSE.

morpheme (Gk 'form') A minimal linguistic unit; like *dis-* as a negative prefix. *See also* KENEME.

mosaic rhyme A rhyme of two or more syllables, with more than one word making a part of the rhyme unit. Common in humorous and satirical verse. Swift provides a good example in these lines from *To Dr Sheridan*:

> I went in vain to look for Eupolis,
> Down in the Strand, just where the new pole is;
> For I can tell you one thing, that I can,
> You will not find it in the Vatican.
> He and Cratinus used, as Horace says,
> To take his greatest grandees for asses.
> Poets, in those days, used to venture high;
> But these are lost full many a century.
> Thus you may see, dear friend, ex pede hence,
> My judgment of the old comedians.

mosaic verse A patchwork poem made up of lines from other poems. An ingenious modern example by A. Alvarez occurs in the introduction to *The New Poetry* (rev. ed. 1966). *See* CENTO, where the example by Alvarez is quoted in full.

Moscow Art Theatre Founded in 1898 by Constantin Stanislavsky (1863–1938) and Vladimir Nemirovich-Danchenko (1859–1943). It had its first success with Chekhov's *The Seagull* in 1898. Later the theatre was supported by Lenin, and the world tour of 1922–4 made it very well known. It has continued to be an important theatre whose company has had wide influence.

mot (F 'word') Three phrases commonly used as literary terms employ this word: (a) *bon mot* – an adroitly witty remark; (b) *le mot juste* – the exact or appropriate word for the occasion; (c) *le mot propre* – the precisely necessary term for anything.

mote (Sp 'motto, device, maxim, catchword, nickname') It may also denote a riddle, an enigma and an emblem. In verse, a poem of one or two lines which expresses a complete thought. Often the thought is glossed in verse. The whole composition is then called a *mote* or a *glosa* (*q.v.*). One *mote* may be glossed by several poets, or by one poet in different versions. *See* GLOSS.

motet (F 'little word') A part-song; or harmonized vocal composition. As used in the medieval period it denoted a set of words and a melody to which other melodies and words might be added. The melody might be characterized by variations and counterpoint.

motif One of the dominant ideas in a work of literature; a part of the main theme. It may consist of a character, a recurrent image or a verbal pattern. *See* CARPE DIEM; LEITMOTIF; UBI SUNT.

motion The name given to puppet plays in England in the 16th and 17th c. Originally, the themes were taken from Holy Writ but, as forms of theatrical entertainment became increasingly secular, so the themes became more diverse. In *The Winter's Tale* (IV, iii) there is a reference to a 'motion of the Prodigal Son'. Ben Jonson refers to 'motions' several times, as do other playwrights of that period.

motto (L *muttum* 'murmur') A short sentence or phrase (often in Latin) adopted as representative of a person or family. In such cases it may accompany a shield or coat of arms or other heraldic device. For example: *per ardua ad alta*. Chaucer's Prioresse had the motto *Amor Vincit Omnia* wrought in her gold brooch. Institutions such as schools often have mottoes, as do most regiments and other units of the armed services. They are frequently found on coins and medallions; for instance, the motto on the Welsh one-pound coin is *Pleidiol wyf i'm gwlad* ('Loyal am I to my country'). The term also denotes a passage prefixed to a book or chapter which adumbrates its matter (cf. ARGUMENT) as well as a scrap of verse or prose enclosed in a cracker or accompanying a sweetmeat.

movement A term commonly applied to a trend or development in literature. The Pléiade (*q.v.*), for instance, by dint of their innovations in poetry constituted a movement.

Movement, the A term applied to a tendency rather than a movement which became apparent in the work of a number of British poets in the 1950s. It was a tendency towards traditionalism in form, and also towards empiricism. Some of the main poets associated with the so-called Movement were Kingsley Amis, Donald Davie, Thom

Gunn, Elizabeth Jennings, Philip Larkin and John Wain. A representative selection of their work was published in Robert Conquest's anthology *New Lines* (1956).

Mozarabic lyric The Arabic poetic form *muwashshah* was first developed in Spain *c.* 9th–10th c. Its *kharja* (*q.v.*) or refrain was not in the classical tongue but in Romance or colloquial Arabic, known as the Mozarab dialect. This form was popular in the 11th–12th c.; it may have been the forerunner of the Provençal lyric.

mudanza (Sp 'change, alteration, mood') In Spanish verse, a rhymed triplet used in the *zéjel* (*q.v.*) and followed by a fourth line, known as the *vuelta* (*q.v.*).

multiple or polysyllabic rhyme *See* TRIPLE RHYME.

mumming play A primitive form of folk drama associated with funeral rites and seasonal fertility rites, especially the spring festival. As recently as the middle of the 19th c. it was widespread throughout Britain – there is a description of such a performance in Hardy's *Return of the Native* – and there is reliable evidence that it has been performed regularly as far afield as the islands of Nevis and St Kitts in the West Indies.

Though the 'texts' stem from oral tradition (*q.v.*) there is a good deal of uniformity in the mumming play, which is performed by Mummers. The main characters are St (or Sir) George, a Turkish knight, a doctor, a fool in cap and bells, and a devil (usually Beelzebub). Sometimes there is a Father Christmas and Jack Finney, or Johnny Jack the sweeper. The plot (which is probably not earlier than the 17th c.) and action are very simple: St George introduces himself as a gallant Christian knight and is challenged by the Turk. They duel and one of them (usually St George) is killed. The Doctor then appears and delivers a boastful litany of the ailments he can cure. He finally revives the dead man. There follows a collection of money (often by the devil).

The theme of the mumming play is clearly death and resurrection, which suggests that it may be connected with a pagan spring-festival rite. But there is no evidence for such rites until long after the Middle Ages. *See* PLOUGH MONDAY PLAY; REVESBY PLAY; SWORD DANCE.

Münchener Dichterkreis (G Poets' circle from Munich) A group of German poets who flourished in the middle of the 19th c. and were established by Maximilian II, king of Bavaria, in his court at Munich.

muse One of nine Greek goddesses who were the daughters of Zeus and Mnemosyne (or Memory). Each presided over one activity or art: Calliope, epic poetry; Clio, history; Erato, love poetry; Euterpe, lyric poetry; Melpomene, tragedy; Polyhymnia, songs of praise to the gods; Terpsichore, dancing; Thalia, comedy; Urania, astronomy.

It was the tradition for a poet (especially an epic poet) to invoke the aid of a particular muse to help him with his work. *See* INSPIRATION; INVOCATION; STORM OF ASSOCIATION.

musical comedy A form of theatrical entertainment developed in the United States during the 19th c. It combines song, music and spoken dialogue, and descends from light opera, ballad opera, and vaudeville (*qq.v.*). In the last thirty years musical comedies have become spectacular. Some famous examples of 20th c. musical comedy are *The Arcadians* (1909), *Lady Be Good* (1924), *Me and My Girl* (1937), *Bless the Bride* (1947), *The Boy Friend* (1953) and *My Fair Lady* (1956), adapted from Shaw's *Pygmalion* (1912).

music theatre A form of entertainment related to opera. It is a musical performance presented on a stage with some theatrical props and costume. The emphasis is on the music, but some kind of dramatic text may be included. This sort of entertainment is believed to have originated with the composers György Ligeti and Mauricio Kagel. In 1956 Alexander Goehr and John Cox formed a 'Music Theatre Ensemble' which presented works by Schönberg, Kurt Weill, Peter Maxwell Davies *et al.*

muwashshah *See* MOZARABIC LYRIC.

mycterism (Gk 'turning up of the nose') A subtle form of derision; a sarcasm or irony (*q.v.*) in which the gibe is half hidden.

Mystery Play (L *mi*[*ni*]*sterium* 'handicraft') The Mystery Plays of the Middle Ages were based on the Bible and were particularly concerned with the stories of man's Creation, Fall and Redemption. They antedate Miracle Plays (*q.v.*).

Mystery Plays developed out of the Liturgy of the Church and in particular out of the *Quem Quaeritis trope* (*q.v.*) of Easter Day.

The earliest dramatizations were presented on the greater festivals of the Church: Christmas, Easter, Pentecost and Corpus Christi. At first they were in Latin and performed by the clergy in the church. There then came an increasing admixture of the vernacular, and lay folk also performed in them. This gradual secularization of religious drama was accompanied by a corresponding physical move. The drama moved out of the church through the west door. Thus, what had been sacred drama became, literally, profane (*pro fano* 'before the temple'). From the churchyard to the market-place was the next logical step. The dramatization became more and more elaborate, the plays were written more or less exclusively in the vernacular and their presentation became the concern of the trade guilds, each of which became responsible for a particular episode or episodes. For example, the masons' guild might present the Noah story, and the weavers the Crucifixion. The object of the cycle of plays was to dramatize the Bible from the Creation to the Last Judgement.

Each play was mounted on a wagon with a curtained scaffold. The lower part of the wagon was a dressing room. After the play had been performed the wagon moved on to where another play had just been acted. Thus, in the course of a day or days, the population of a city like York was able to see the complete cycle.

In time the presentation and setting became extremely elaborate. Heaven and Hell were represented; all sorts of mechanical contrivances contributed to theatrical effects. Costume became lavish, and even lighting, for evening performances, was spectacular.

Most of the plays are anonymous (at any rate, we do not know the authors) and show considerable variation in the quality of the writing. For the most part the verse is rough and characterization crude. However, in the later work the beginnings of sophistication and psychological realism are clearly discernible, and this development is intensely interesting.

The principal English Mystery cycles were those of York (48 episodes); Coventry (42); Wakefield – also known as Towneley (32); and Chester (25). There were also the Cornish plays and the *Ludus Coventriae* (which had nothing to do with Coventry), plus one from Newcastle and one from Norwich. There were other cycles at Beverley, Doncaster, Ipswich and Worcester, but these have been lost.

Mystery Plays were widespread in Europe, and in France they were particularly popular. The French preferred a more fixed setting. The *sedes* or mansions (that is, the stages, platforms or scaffoldings on which the plays were performed) were set in two lines facing each other in the yard, square or market-place outside the west door of the church. Each *sedes* represented a particular place, like Hell, Heaven, the House of Caiaphas, the Sepulchre, etc. They were so sited that there was plenty of room for the spectators to gather round.

Other well-known examples are: (a) the Cyprus *Passion Cycle*, a group of Greek prose-plays depicting the events of Holy Week, which originated in Cyprus in the 13th c.; (b) the Oberammergau *Passion Play* of Upper Bavaria which dates from 1633; (c) the Spanish *Autos Sacramentales*, a form of religious drama performed on the feast of Corpus Christi. These allegorical plays were still popular in the 17th c., when they were perfected by Calderón. *See* MORALITY PLAY; PASSION PLAY; SACRA RAPPRESENTAZIONE.

myth (Gk *mūthos* 'anything uttered by word of mouth') It is a term of complex history and meaning. Homer used the word *mūthos* to mean narrative and conversation, but not a fiction. Odysseus tells false stories about himself and uses the term *mūthologenevein* to signify 'telling a story'. Later Greek *mūthos* is used to mean fiction. Plato refers to *mūthoi* to denote something not wholly lacking truth but for the most part fictitious. It has been surmised that the transition of *mūthos* to mean fiction may have been helped by a kind of association with *muein*, 'to initiate into secrets' (hence, mystic, mystery). The word *mūthikos* ('mythical') went into Latin as *mythicus*. *Mūthos* has also been equated with the Latin *fabula* (*q.v.*). Nowadays a myth tends to signify a fiction, but a fiction which conveys a psychological truth.

In general a myth is a story which is not 'true' and which involves (as a rule) supernatural beings – or at any rate supra-human beings. Myth is always concerned with creation. Myth explains how something came to exist. Myth embodies feeling and concept – hence the Promethean or Herculean figure, or the idea of Diana, or the story of Orpheus and Eurydice. Many myths or quasi-myths are primitive explanations of the natural order and cosmic forces.

Classical writers had a 'ready-made' mythology. Others have not been so fortunate and some have felt a great need to invent or somehow contrive a mythology which shall be the vehicle of their beliefs. Poets, especially, have continued to fall back on the Greek and Roman myths and, to a lesser extent, upon Germanic and Scandinavian myths, and in some cases, upon Chinese, Indian,

Egyptian and Latin American myths. As Coleridge put it, 'the old instinct brings back the old names'. A good example of a poet who has 'invented' a mythology akin to the traditional kind is William Blake. He said that he felt obliged to create a system: otherwise he would be enslaved by someone else's. Accordingly he combined his own visionary gleams with what he 'lifted' from established mythologies, plus elements of Christianity and ideas from Swedenborg and Neoplatonism (*q.v.*). A more recent example is W. B. Yeats, who was in the fortunate position of being able to make use of a considerable stock of Celtic lore and legend of a more or less mythical kind. Yeats explained his 'mythology' in *A Vision* (1926). Herman Melville (*Moby-Dick*), James Joyce (*Ulysses*) and D. H. Lawrence (*The Plumed Serpent*) have also used a variety of mythical materials, for the most part those which belong to what Jung described as the 'collective unconscious'. *See* LEGEND; MYTHEME; MYTHOPOEIA; NARRATOLOGY; STRUCTURALISM; SYMBOL AND SYMBOLISM.

mytheme A term coined by Claude Lévi-Strauss, the structuralist anthropologist, by analogy with morpheme and phoneme (*qq.v.*). In his structural analysis of myths a mytheme 'is a set of items which share a single functional trait'. Mythemes are organized in binary oppositions (*q.v.*). Three items in one mytheme for Lévi-Strauss are: (a) Cadmos seeks his sister, ravished by Zeus; (b) Oedipus marries his mother, Jocasta; (c) Antigone buries her brother, Polynices, unlawfully. Lévi-Strauss invented the term 'mytheme' as part of the structural analysis of myths, and it has been of some importance in structuralism (*q.v.*) and in the theory of narratology (*q.v.*). *See also* MYTH.

mythopoeia (Gr 'myth-making') The conscious creation of a myth (*q.v.*). In literature, the appropriation and reworking of mythical material, or the creation of a kind of 'private' mythology.

N

nacimientos Spanish plays and poems about the Nativity of Christ. They were performed/recited at Christmas in churches and private houses, or in the streets. They were common in the 15th c.

nadsat A teenage argot (*q.v.*) devised by Anthony Burgess for his novel *A Clockwork Orange* (1962). The vocabulary comprises about 250 words, many of which are of Slavonic origin. For example: *baboochka* – 'old woman'; *chellovek* – 'man'; *kleb* – 'bread'; *horrorshow (horoshoi)* – 'good'; *malchik* – 'boy'; *sladky* – 'sweet'.

naiv und sentimentalisch (G 'naive and sentimental') A category or distinction made by Schiller in his essay *Über naive und sentimentalische Dichtung* (1795). Schiller divides poets into two classes: (a) the naive (e.g. Homer, Shakespeare, Goethe) who attempt to project nature as they embody it; (b) the sentimental (e.g. Schiller, Wordsworth, Southey) who have lost touch with nature and are trying to depict it as a sought-for ideal. Naive poets create instinctually; the sentimental, formally. Schiller pursued his theory to suggest that sentimental poets try to project an ideal of nature whereas the naive poet cannot and does not do this. He is concerned with nature *as it is*; *not as it may be conceived.* If we compare the work of, say, John Clare, William Barnes, Thomas Hardy, R. S. Thomas and Ted Hughes, with that of, say, John Dyer, Keats, Robert Browning, A. E. Housman and Edmund Blunden, we find that the first group tend to be instinctual in their responses to nature; the second group, formal.

Schiller also elaborated the idea that the poetic genius (*q.v.*) is a sentimental poet by virtue of his feelings and idealisms, and a naive by virtue of his genius. The combination enables him to convey a total vision of nature: the real and the transcendental. Gerard Manley Hopkins might well come into this category. *See* ANTI-

NOMY; APOLLONIAN/DIONYSIAN; CLASSICISM/ROMANTICISM.

narodne pesme (S 'peoples' songs') The poems (*pesma* also means 'poem') belong to the genre of traditional popular narrative poetry based on historical events and created mainly by individual members of an illiterate or semi-literate society and preserved by oral tradition (*q.v.*) in Jugoslavia. They exist in print now because the 19th c. Serbian scholar Vuk Karadžić spent much of his life collecting them from the *guslari* (*q.v.*) while there were still plenty of these itinerant bards in existence.

There are nine epic cycles of these poems. The most famous is the Kosovo cycle, a group of ballads (*q.v.*) and lays which grew up as a result of the battle of Kosovo in 1389 when the Serbs were defeated by the Turks. There is a pre-Kosovo cycle which treats of myth and legend, and a Marko Kraljević cycle which mostly concerns the deeds of a semi-legendary warrior of that name. The fourth main cycle (the most recent) comprises all the poems dealing with the struggles against the Turks in the 19th c. The other five deal with (a) the Serbian nobles and their conflicts after the battle of Kosovo until towards the end of the 15th c.; (b) the exploits of the *hajduks* (bandit-type guerrilla soldiers) against the Turks; (c, d and e) Montenegrin, Bosnian and Dalmatian struggles against invading powers.

The nine cycles constitute one of the most remarkable bodies of oral poetry known. Apart from the Homeric ballads they probably have no equals. *See also* EPIC; JUNACKE PESME; PEVACI; ZENSKE PESME.

narodnost (R 'national character') A requirement demanded of literature under socialist realism (*q.v.*). Literature should express typical national thought and character through a 'national style'. The term also implies 'folk' and 'popular' character; thus there has been much emphasis on folk and popular literature and language and the importance of the contribution it can make to more exalted forms of literature. *See* IDEYNOST; PARTYNOST.

narratee A term invented by Gerald Prince to denote the person to whom a narrator addresses his discourse. The narratee is not to be confused with the reader, who may be the 'virtual reader' (i.e. the kind of reader the narrator has in mind while composing the discourse), or the 'ideal reader' (i.e. the reader who understands everything the writer/narrator is saying and doing). *See also* IMPLIED READER/ACTUAL READER; READER-RESPONSE THEORY.

narrative verse A narrative poem tells a story. Such poetry is widespread in many literatures. The three main kinds are epic, metrical romance and ballad (*qq.v.*) but there are a very large number of narrative poems which cannot be easily classified and which certainly do not fit into any of the above categories, and there is no genre which subsumes works as varied as Smart's *Song to David*, Arnold's *Sohrab and Rustum* and T. S. Eliot's *Journey of the Magi.*

Early examples of narrative poetry are the epic of *Gilgamesh* and the poems of Homer and Hesiod, the narrative odes of Pindar (*c.* 522–442 BC) and the *Argonautica* of Apollonius of Rhodes (end of 3rd c. BC). Callimachus, an older contemporary of Apollonius, wrote short epics called *epyllia* (*q.v.*). The Romans often used narrative verse. Famous examples are: the *Bellum Punicum* of Naevius (*c.* 270–*c.* 199 BC), the first historical epic; the *Annales* of Ennius (239–169 BC); the *Aeneid* of Virgil (70–19 BC) and the *Metamorphoses* of Ovid (43 BC–AD 18). Narrative poems continued to be written in the following five hundred years in both Greek and Latin. For instance, the Gospel story was re-told by Juvencus in *Evangeliorum Libri* (*c.* 330); and early in the 5th c. Sedulius wrote a Paschal Poem. Later, lives of the saints in verse were not uncommon; and historical poems in Latin verse appeared during the Carolingian period. In the early Middle Ages we find the beginnings of romance but it is not until the 12th c. that this is an established form: for example, Benoit de Saint-More's *Roman de Troie* (*c.* 1184), believed to be the first poem in the vernacular (*q.v.*). Between *c.* 1000 and *c.* 1300, for the first time since the 8th c. BC, oral epics were written down – in Western vernaculars and in Greek. Outstanding examples are *Beowulf*, assigned to the middle of the 8th c. (though the MS dates from *c.* 1000), the OHG *Lay of Hildebrand* (*c.* 800), the Greek *Digenes Akritas* (mid-11th c.), the MHG *Nibelungenlied* (*c.* 1200–05), the Spanish *Poema de mío Cid* (*c.* 1200), the ON collection known as the *Elder Edda* (the earliest MS *c.* 1270), plus a large number of *chansons de gestes* (*q.v.*) of which the best known is the *Chanson de Roland* (the earliest manuscript *c.* 1170).

Throughout the later Middle Ages narrative poems were widely written in Europe and increasingly in the vernacular: Dante's

Divina Commedia (c. 1310), Chaucer's *Canterbury Tales* (1385–1400), Langland's *The Vision of Piers Plowman* (c. 1360–99), Chaucer's *Troilus and Criseyde* (c. 1372–86).

The Renaissance period produced a succession of epic narratives, notably: *Orlando Innamorato* by Boiardo (1441–94); *Orlando Furioso* by Ariosto (1474–1533); *Gerusalemme Liberata* by Tasso (1544–95); and the *Os Lusiadas* by Camoëns (1524–80). These four works constitute a revival of national epic.

The turn of the 15th c. saw the beginning of considerable poetic activity in Dalmatia and Croatia, especially in narrative verse. The most notable poets were: Marulić (1450–1524), who wrote *Judita* in Croat and an epic, *Davidijada*, in Latin; Petar Hektorović (1487–1572) of the island of Hvar, the author of *Ribanje* ('Fishing') – a group of poems which may be described as pastorals about fishing: Mavro Vetranić (1482–1576), who wrote an epic called *The Pilgrim*; Petar Zoranić (1508–1569?), the author of a pastoral romance in verse and prose called *Planine* ('The Mountains'); Brno Krnarutić (1520–72), who wrote an epic on a contemporary theme called the *Capture of the City of Sziget*; Juraj Baraković (1549–1628), the author of *Vila Slovinska*, a history of Zadar; and Ivan Gundulić (1588–1638), Dubrovnik's most famous poet, the author of the epic *Osman* – again on a contemporary theme, the battle of the Christians against the Turks.

In the 15th and 16th c. in England narrative poetry also flourished. The 15th c. poets are little read now but Lydgate and Hawes were prolific writers. Lydgate's *Falles of Princes* (1494), based on Boccaccio's *De Casibus Virorum Illustrium*, was a poem of 36,000 lines. Hawes's *Pastime of Pleasure* (1509) was a long allegorical poem concerning the pilgrimage of the soul; a kind of Everyman quest.

Major narrative poems in the 16th c. include Edward Hall's *Chronicle* (c. 1540), Spenser's *The Faerie Queene* (1589, 1596), Marlowe's *Hero and Leander* (1593), Samuel Daniel's *Civil Wars* (1595) and Drayton's *England's Heroicall Epistles* (1597). By the end of the 16th c. the tendency was to write shorter narrative poems; what may be called *epyllia* (*q.v.*).

In the 17th c. the two outstanding narrative poems in English literature are Abraham Cowley's unfinished *Davideis* (1656), and the greatest epic in the language – Milton's *Paradise Lost* (1667). In France in the 17th c. the principal narrative works were Boileau's *Le Lutrin*, a mock-epic (*q.v.*) written between 1673 and 1683, and Fénelon's prose poem (*q.v.*) *Télémaque* (1699).

It is noticeable that in the second half of the 17th c. and during much of the 18th c. longer poems tend to be satire (*q.v.*). In a number of cases these satires were a form of narrative verse. Pope's *The Rape of the Lock* (1712, 1714) is a case in point. Rather than write anything original on an epic scale poets chose to translate. Notable translations of Classical authors were done by Dryden, Pope and Cowper. However, there was one epic work of some merit, namely Voltaire's *Henriade* (1728), a national epic on the religious wars.

Towards the end of the 18th c. we find a recrudescence of the genre. It is probable that the publication of Percy's *Reliques of Ancient Poetry* in 1765 revived interest. It is possible that James Macpherson's Ossianic poems (1760, 1762, 1765) were also an influence. At any rate, towards the turn of the century, and continually thereafter, narrative verse proliferates. In 1785 Cowper published *The Task*. Burns wrote a number of narrative poems and ballads. Scott was very prolific. In 1802–3 he published a collection of Scottish ballads titled *Minstrelsy of the Scottish Border*. This may have encouraged him to write *The Lay of the Last Minstrel* (1805), *Marmion* (1808) and *The Lady of the Lake* (1810). At about the same time George Crabbe made a remarkable contribution to narrative poetry, as a kind of 'regional' poet, with three long works: *The Parish Register* (1807), *The Borough* (1810) and *Tales* (1812). Crabbe was to East Anglia what Thomas Hardy was, as a novelist, to Wessex. Wordsworth, also, was a prolific writer of narrative verse. Among his minor works one should mention *Goody Blake and Harry Gill*; among the major works *Michael* (1800), *The Excursion* (1814) and *The Prelude*, not published until 1850 but written many years earlier. Wordsworth's contemporary Coleridge wrote two of the most famous narrative poems in the language: namely, *The Rime of the Ancient Mariner* (1798) and *Christabel* (1816). Contemporaneously Byron wrote four notable narrative poems of considerable length: *The Giaour* (1813), *Beppo* (1818), *Childe Harold's Pilgrimage* (1809–18) and *Don Juan* (1819–24). Keats's two main narrative poems were *The Eve of St Agnes* (1819) and *Lamia* (1819).

Nearly all the major poets (and many of the minor ones) of the Victorian period (*q.v.*) wrote narrative verse. Here there is only space to mention: Macaulay's *Lays of Ancient Rome* (1842), Aytoun's *Lays of the Scottish Cavaliers* (1849), Matthew Arnold's *Sohrab and Rustum* (1853), Tennyson's *Idylls of the King* (1842–85), and a very large number of works by Browning –

especially: *Through the Metidja to Abd-el-Kadr* (1842), *How they brought the good news from Ghent to Aix* (1845), *Soliloquy of the Spanish Cloister* (1842), *Incident of the French Camp* (1842), *My Last Duchess* (1842), *The Bishop orders his tomb at St Praxed's Church* (1842), *Saul* (1855), *A Grammarian's Funeral* (1855), *Childe Roland to the Dark Tower came* (1855), *Fra Lippo Lippi* (1855), *Andrea del Sarto* (1855), *Rabbi Ben Ezra* (1864), *The Ring and the Book* (1868–9), *Hervé Riel* (1871), to mention only some. William Morris was also a distinguished narrative poet. His two main works are: *Jason* (1867) and *The Earthly Paradise* (1868–70).

Since the Victorian period much narrative verse has been written. Of particular note are Kipling's ballads and Masefield's ballads; also Masefield's *The Everlasting Mercy* (1911), *The Widow in the Bye Street* (1912) and *Reynard the Fox* (1919). Among the shorter narrative poems written in this century mention should be made of Chesterton's *The Ballad of the White Horse* and *Lepanto*; Francis Brett Young's *North-West Passage AD 1497*; Ezra Pound's *Ballad of the Goodly Fere*; W. W. Gibson's *Flannan Isle*, Wilfred Owen's *Strange Meeting*, Edmund Blunden's *Incident in Hyde Park 1803*, Sir John Betjeman's *A Lincolnshire Tale*, Edward Thomas's *Up in the Wind*, T. S. Eliot's *Journey of the Magi*, C. Day Lewis's *Flight to Australia*, Philip Larkin's *Whitsun Weddings*, and a large number of poems by Robert Frost – especially *Death of the Hired Man*, *The Mountain*, *The Black Cottage*, *Blueberries*, *The Code*, *The Fear*, *A Hundred Collars*, *Home Burial* and *Paul's Wife*. Conrad Aiken has also used the narrative form for long, discursive and reflective poems, notably: *Senlin: A Biography*, *Preludes for Memnon*, *Landscape West of Eden* and *Time in the Rock*. W. H. Auden has also written long narrative poems of a reflective nature, in particular *New Year Letter*, *For the Time Being*, *The Sea and the Mirror* and *The Age of Anxiety*.

To this brief selection must be added eleven outstanding narrative poems, all long and all different in style, theme, structure and purpose: Hugh MacDiarmid's *On a Raised Beach*; Patrick Kavanagh's *The Great Hunger*; Andrew Young's *A Traveller in Time*; W. H. Auden's *Letter to Lord Byron*; W. S. Graham's *The Nightfishing*; Vernon Watkins's *The Ballad of the Mari Lwyd*; George Barker's *Goodman Jacksin and the Angel*; Anthony Cronin's *RMS Titanic*; Peter Levi's *The Shearwaters*; Stephen Vincent Benet's *John Brown's Body*; and Kazantzakis's *The Odyssey: A Modern Sequel.*

narratology Theory, discourse or critique of narrative/narration. Structuralist analysis of narrative was begun by Claude Lévi-Strauss (1908–), who, in *Anthropologie structurale* (1958) and elsewhere, advanced a new theory about myth (*q.v.*). He puts forward the idea that myths are variations on basic themes and that in their totality (and there are thousands of them) their narratives contain certain constant, basic and universal structures by which any one myth can be explained. He sees myths as a kind of 'language' which can be broken down into individual units or 'mythemes' – by analogy with phonemes (*q.v.*). Myths can be read in relation to each other rather than as reflecting a particular version. Hence the concept of a kind of 'grammar' or set of relations underneath the surface of the narrative. He also advances the idea that myths have a sort of collective existence independent of individual thought, and posits myths as related to other myths rather than to truth and reality. They are 'outside', so to speak, decentred, and possess their own truth and logic.

This structuralist theory has been brought to bear on the study of narrative in literature, or narratology. In some respects Lévi-Strauss's theory was prefigured by the Russian Formalist Vladimir Propp, who, in his *Morphology of the Folk Tale* (1928), 'reduced' all folk tales to seven 'spheres of action' and thirty-one fixed elements or 'functions' of narrative. The function is the basic unit of the narrative 'language' and denotes or refers to the actions which constitute the narrative, and the functions tend to follow a logical sequence.

A. J. Greimas, in his *Sémantique structurale* (1966), breaks the scheme down still further, and aims at a kind of universal grammar of narrative by attempting a semantic analysis of sentence structure. In place of the 'spheres of action' he proposes the *actant*: a structural unit, which is not even character or narrative. He posits three pairs of binary oppositions (*q.v.*) which include six actants or roles: subject/object; sender/receiver; helper/opponent. These binary oppositions, he proposes, account for or describe three basic patterns which are to be found in narrative: (a) desire, search or aim (subject/object); (b) communication (sender/receiver); (c) auxiliary support or hindrance (helper/opponent). He applies this 'system' to a variety of narrative.

More accessible are Gérard Genette's theories propounded in *Narrative Discourse* (1972) in the context of a detailed analysis of Proust's *A la recherche du temps perdu*. Bearing in mind the distinctions made in Russian Formalism (*q.v.*) between *fabula* ('story') and *syuzhet* ('plot'), he distinguishes between: *récit* (i.e. the chronological order of events in a text/narrative); *histoire* (the sequence in which events actually occur); and *narration* (the act of narrating itself). He then discusses in fascinating depth the various categories of narrative analysis. He also has much of note to say about the narrator (*q.v.*) and the kind of 'voice' he uses, and the relationship of the narrator to the 'narratee' (*q.v.*). Plus an analysis of point of view or viewpoint (*q.v.*). For this aspect he introduces some erudite jargon (*q.v.*) of his own devising. Thus, he distinguishes three basic kinds of narrator: the 'heterodiegetic' (where the narrator is absent from his own narrative); the 'homodiegetic' (the narrator is inside his narrative, as in a story recounted in the first person); the 'autodiegetic' (the narrator is inside the narrative and *also* the main character). Genette's essay *Frontiers of Narrative* (1966) is also of great interest.

Whereas Genette has a relational approach and sees narrative as a product or result of the interaction of its different component levels and all aspects of narrative as dependent units, Roland Barthes (in his essay *Introduction to the Structural Analysis of Narrative*, 1977) presumes a hierarchical arrangement of levels and suggests that, up to a point, they can be discussed separately. He describes narrative as 'a long sentence, just as every constative sentence is in a way the rough outline of a short narrative'. He selects basic units of narrative; for example, 'function' and 'index'. The functions constitute a chain of acts; the indices constitute information about characters. He then amplifies this theory by linguistic analogy, suggesting that the functions are based on metonymic relations and the indices on metaphoric relations. In this distinction he is using Roman Jakobson's theory of metaphor/metonymy (*q.v.*). Barthes also makes use of Emile Benveniste's distinction (discussed in *Problems in General Linguistics*, 1966) between the 'personal' and 'apersonal' aspects of language (*see* SUBJECT OF ENUNCIATION/ SUBJECT OF ENUNCIATING) in order to analyse the 'narration', or the manner in which the story is told.

Lastly, we should mention Northrop Frye's remarkable and original conception of literature proposed in his outstanding book *Anatomy of Criticism* (1957). Frye's theory is not strictly structuralist but it can be seen as structuralist in some respects. He sees literature as an 'autonomous verbal structure' unrelated to anything beyond itself, a world which contains 'life and reality in a system of verbal relationships'. In short, a 'self-contained literary universe'. In this 'universe' there are four radical 'mythoi' – that is to say, plot forms and basic organizing structural principles – which correspond to the four seasons of the natural order and constitute the four main genres of comedy, romance, tragedy and satire (*qq.v.*). He has developed this archetypal theory in many subsequent discourses on a huge range of texts, including the Bible. *See* ARCHETYPAL CRITICISM; STRUCTURALISM.

narrator Plato and Aristotle distinguished three basic kinds of narrator: (a) the speaker or poet (or any kind of writer) who uses his own voice; (b) one who assumes the voice of another person or persons, and speaks in a voice not his own; (c) one who uses a mixture of his own voice and that of others. Out of the thousands of examples available to illustrate the three voices the following will serve: In his poem *The Statue* the poet John Berryman speaks throughout in his own voice. In *The Prisoner of Chillon*, Byron assumes the voice of François de Bonnivard who was imprisoned in the castle of Chillon in the 16th c. A good example of the combination of all three can be found in *Paradise Lost*. Milton begins in his own voice in the first person to invoke the 'Heavenly Muse'. In line 34, Book I, the impression is that the Muse (that is the Holy Spirit) responds to Milton's formal invocation (*q.v.*) thus beginning the main narrative. When Satan first speaks (line 84) the third voice is introduced. Thereafter each different character has his own voice, though all, as it were, are Milton's. At the beginning of Book III Milton draws breath and uses his 'own' voice again.

So anyone telling a story may begin, as narrator, by using his own voice; then introduce a narrator who tells the story – in which there are characters who, in turn, have their own voices and who, in their turn, of course, may narrate. Potentially the progression (or regression) is infinite. Many novelists have employed this technique, one of the most adept being Joseph Conrad.

T. S. Eliot also makes an important distinction in his essay *The Three Voices of Poetry* (1953): 'The first voice is the voice of the poet talking to himself – or to nobody. The second is the voice of the poet addressing an audience, whether large or small. The third is the voice of the poet when he attempts to create a dramatic character speaking in verse; when he is saying, not what he would say in his own person, but only what he can say within the limits of one imaginary character addressing another imaginary character.'

What is known as the 'self-conscious narrator' is one who employs techniques related to the theories of foregrounding and defamiliarization (*qq.v.*). By dint of 'baring the device' (or devices) the writer reveals to and reminds the reader that the narration is a work of fiction while at the same time pointing up or exposing the discrepancies between the fiction and the reality which it purports or seems to represent. Tristram in Sterne's *Tristram Shandy* (1760–67) is a notable instance. Others are Marcel in Proust's *A la recherche du temps perdu* (1913–27) and the narrator in Byron's *Don Juan* (1819–24).

The method of using the self-conscious narrator lends itself to sophisticated and complex refinements in what is known as the 'reflexive novel' (*q.v.*) or the 'involuted novel'. An outstanding example of this is André Gide's *Les Faux-monnayeurs* (1926), in which he uses intricate narrative tactics. This book is the diary of a novelist who is writing a novel – which is going to have the title *Les Faux-monnayeurs* ('The Counterfeiters') – about a novelist who is keeping a diary about the novel he is actually writing. Gide compounded this ingenuity by keeping a journal while he was composing the novel; this was the *Journal of the Counterfeiters*, which he published in the same year as the novel. Vladimir Nabokov's *Pale Fire* (1962) is another and different instance of the involuted narrative method.

There is also what is known as the 'fallible' or 'unreliable narrator'. Such a narrator is one whose perception and interpretation of what he or she narrates does not correspond or coincide with the perceptions, interpretations and opinions of the author who is or purports to be the controlling force in the narration. Thus, there is a kind of contrived discrepancy between the narrator (what James called 'the centre of consciousness') and the actual author. Henry James was a past-master of this technique (e.g. in *The Aspern Papers*, 1888). *See also* AESTHETIC DISTANCE; CONFESSIONAL NOVEL; DIALOGIC/MONOLOGIC; EPISTOLARY NOVEL; NARRATOLOGY; NOVEL; PERSONA; RECIT; STREAM OF CONSCIOUSNESS; SUBJECTIVITY AND OBJECTIVITY; VIEWPOINT.

National Book League Founded in 1925 as the National Book Council by the Society of Bookmen. It is an independent charitable organization whose function is to promote and encourage the use and enjoyment of books. It thus works with all branches of the book trade. It was renamed the National Book League in 1945 and in 1980 moved from its central London premises in Albemarle Street to Book House in Wandsworth, south-west London. It provides many excellent services and administers various literary prizes including the Booker McConnell Prize (*q.v.*).

National Theatre The foundation stone of the British National Theatre was laid on the South Bank of the Thames in 1951. In 1962 a National Theatre board was appointed and Laurence Olivier (1907–89) was put in charge. The Old Vic Theatre (*q.v.*) became the headquarters and an inaugural performance of *Hamlet* was given there in 1962. Eventually the new theatre was built (it took some ten years) with three auditoriums. In March 1976 the Lyttelton opened with a production of Samuel Beckett's *Happy Days*; in October of that year the Olivier opened with a production of Marlowe's *Tamburlaine* (*c.* 1590); and in March 1977 the Cottesloe studio theatre presented Ken Campbell's *Illuminatus*. Before any of the theatres was opened Peter Hall (1930–) had replaced Laurence Olivier as artistic director. Peter Hall held the post from 1973 to 1988 and during those fifteen years a wide variety of plays, from established classics to new work by comparatively unknown dramatists, was presented – often with conspicuous success. Hall was succeeded by Peter Eyre.

naturalism In literary criticism, a word sometimes used loosely as a synonym for realism (*q.v.*), and also in reference to works which show a pronounced interest in, sympathy with and love of natural beauty (e.g. much of the poetry of Wordsworth). Properly speaking, it should be used to describe works of literature which use realistic methods and subjects to convey a philosophical form of naturalism; that is, a belief that everything that exists is a part of nature and can be explained by natural and material causes – and not by supernatural, spiritual or paranormal causes.

In literature naturalism developed out of realism. The main influences that went to forming a different point of view were Darwin's biological theories, Comte's application of scientific ideas to the study of society, and Taine's application of deterministic theories to literature. Those in favour of a naturalistic approach to and interpretation of life concentrated on depicting the social environment and dwelt particularly on its deficiencies and on the shortcomings of human beings. The 'naturalist's' vision of the estate of man tended to be subjective and was very often sombre.

The Goncourt brothers appear to have been the first to establish the naturalistic point of view in literature; namely in *Germinie Lacerteux* (1865). This analytical investigation of the rather squalid life of a servant girl was much admired by Emile Zola, the high priest of the naturalistic movement in literature.

In his preface to *Thérèse Raquin* (1868) he described himself as a *naturaliste*. His method was scientifically clinical, that of the pathologist and physiologist. In his view men's lives and actions were determined by environment and heredity and it was the business of the novelist, as he saw it, to dissect, to perform an autopsy on life. In pursuit of his aims, he 'pulled no punches'. There is much in his work which could be described as sensational and melodramatic, and it has been noted that he concentrated excessively on the seamier aspects of human existence: on the impoverished and underprivileged, on the ugly and the diseased. After *Thérèse Raquin* he planned a cycle of twenty volumes (the cycle is known as *Rougon-Macquart*, 1871–93) which should give the natural and social history of a family. Out of these twenty novels the best known are *L'Assommoir* (1877) and *Germinal* (1885).

Zola's influence has been very considerable and is discernible in many plays and novels of the last hundred years. It is particularly noticeable in the work of Maupassant and J-K. Huysmans, of George Moore and George Gissing. However, he made his greatest impact in Germany, where naturalism as a movement was concentrated in one literary school in Berlin and another in Munich. Here the principal luminaries of the movement were G. M. Conrad, Holz and Schlaf, the Hart brothers, Bleibtreu and Bolsche. The dramatist Gerhart Hauptmann proved to be the most distinguished exponent of German naturalism. Outside France and Germany it was apparent in the works of Ibsen, Strindberg, Chekhov, Tolstoy, Gorki, and across the Atlantic in the novels of Théodore Dreiser, Frank Norris and Stephen Crane. *See also* NATURALISTIC DRAMA; THEATRICALISM; THESIS NOVEL.

naturalistic drama Drama which seeks to mirror life with the utmost fidelity. It became established and popular late in the 19th c., stemming from the naturalism (*q.v.*) of Zola and his followers, and going beyond the realism (*q.v.*) of Ibsen. The main French dramatist was Henri Becque. In the late 1880s Antoine established naturalistic drama in his Théâtre Libre. There Becque and other playwrights, including Strindberg, had their work performed. The movement of naturalism in the theatre spread to Germany, England, Russia and America. A famous instance of ultra-naturalism is Gorki's *Lower Depths* (1902). Gradually, the leading dramatists, like Strindberg and Hauptmann, forsook this kind of play for a more symbolic form. However, naturalism persisted and in its decadence considerably influenced drawing-room comedy (*q.v.*) and much light theatrical entertainment in the 1920s and 1930s. There was a sustained effort to reproduce everyday speech as exactly as possible, and more and more emphasis was placed on surface verisimilitude – especially in décor and setting where no effort was spared to persuade the audience that it was in fact looking at a 'real' set, such an exact representation of a room that they might well use it themselves. Here art was attempting to deceive nature, not reflect it. Thus the theatre was defeating its own ends and, in the abandonment of traditional dramatic conventions, becoming more and more restrictive. Nevertheless, many dramatists exploited the limitations very skilfully. Galsworthy was an outstanding example, and, later, N. C. Hunter and Terence Rattigan. *See* THEATRICALISM.

Natural School, the The name given to an early phase of Russian realism. This particular *-ism* was formulated by Belinsky (1811–48) who was the 'interpreter' of Gogol. It was Belinsky's belief that the writer should eschew anything like romanticism and should depict the social evils of his period, especially the injustices of peasant and serf life. The tenets of the *natural'naya shkola* were strongly opposed to anything artificial or idealistic.

Natureingang A German term for a kind of introductory passage which uses images drawn from the natural order. The images are conventional or 'stock'. The term is usually used in connection with the *Minnesang* (*see* MINNESINGER).

natya A form of Indian dance drama whose plots for the most part derive from the epics *Ramayana* and *Mahabharata*.

near rhyme *See* HALF RHYME.

negation A form of affirmation by denial; sometimes found in litotes (*q.v.*). A famous example occurs in Keats's *Hyperion*:

No stir of air was there,
Not so much life as on a summer's day
Robs not one light seed from the feathered grass,
But where the dead leaf fell, there did it rest.

negative capability A famous phrase used by Keats when writing to his brothers George and Thomas (Dec. 21st, 1817). The relevant passage is:

> I had not a dispute, but a disquisition, with Dilke upon various subjects; several things dove-tailed in my mind, and at once it struck me what quality went to form a man of achievement, especially in literature, and which Shakespeare possessed so enormously – I mean negative capability, that is, when a man is capable of being in uncertainties, mysteries, doubts, without any irritable reaching after fact and reason. Coleridge, for instance, would let go by a fine isolated verisimilitude caught from the penetralium of Mystery, from being incapable of remaining content with half-knowledge. This pursued through volumes would perhaps take us no farther than this; that with a great Poet the sense of beauty overcomes every other consideration, or rather obliterates all consideration.

Accept, therefore, the insight into beauty and be cautious of rationalization. In his *Ode on a Grecian Urn* Keats summarized part of his philosophy in this matter:

> 'Beauty is truth, truth beauty,' – that is all
> Ye know on earth, and all ye need to know.

See SUBJECTIVITY AND OBJECTIVITY.

Negrismo A Latin American movement with strong indigenous traditions particularly associated with black culture. In Cuba it is referred to as Afro-Cubanism. It developed during the 1920s and prominent *negrista* have been Emilo Ballagas and Nicolás Guillén of Cuba, Luis Palés Matos of Puerto Rico and Ildefonso Pereda Valdés of Uruguay. The Cuban novelist Alejo Carpentier (1904–) of Havana (though not a black himself) did much to promote black art and literature. Fernando Ortiz (1881–1969) was a leading light in Afro-Cubanism. *See* NEGRITUDE.

Négritude The term was coined some time in the 1930s by Aimé Césaire (a French poet and dramatist from Martinique) and the Senegalese poet and politician L-S. Senghor. It refers to and connotes the attitudes displayed in some recent writing by African authors and, more particularly, by French-speaking Africans. In literature it represents an aesthetic which seeks to maintain and uphold traditional African culture and sensibilities. The idea of

Négritude has had considerable vogue since the publication of Césaire's *Cahier d'un retour au pays natal* (1939), and as a result of Senghor's work. The latter is now regarded as the chief luminary and he has expressed a part of his philosophy in *Négritude et humanisme* (1964).

nemesis (Gk 'retribution') In Greek thought a personification of the gods' resentment and anger at man's insolence, hubris (*q.v.*), towards themselves. Thus nemesis was punishment; what overtook and befell the tragic hero. *See* TRAGEDY.

neoclassicism The Neoclassic period is usually taken to be the hundred-odd years *c.* 1660–*c.* 1780; in other words, from Dryden's maturity to Johnson's death (1784). Apart from the dramatists the main English authors in this period were: Dryden (1631–1700), Swift (1667–1745), Addison (1672–1719), Steele (1672–1729), Pope (1688–1744), Lord Chesterfield (1694–1773), Fielding (1707–54), Johnson (1709–84), Goldsmith (1730–74) and Gibbon (1737–94). In literary theory and practice most writers of this period were traditionalist, and they had a great respect for the Classical authors, and especially the Romans, who, they believed, had established and perfected the principal literary genres for all time. Literature was regarded as an art, in which excellence could be attained only by prolonged study. Thus the writers of the period were painstaking craftsmen who had a deep respect for the rules of their art. These rules could best be learnt from close study of the Classical authors (Horace was a favourite) and by careful (if not sedulous) imitation of their works. Their approach was thoroughly professional. They thought that reason and judgement were the most admirable faculties (the 18th c. was, after all, the Age of Reason), and that decorum (*q.v.*) was essential. In prose, as in verse, the most desirable qualities were harmony, proportion, balance and restraint. It follows, therefore, that the Neoclassical writers aimed at *correctness*. This was nowhere more evident than in their use of the heroic couplet.

Neoclassical beliefs and ideals generated a definite vision of man and mankind. Man and his activities were regarded as the main subjects of poetry. As Pope put it in *An Essay on Man*:

> Know then thyself, presume not God to scan,
> The proper study of mankind is man.

Man, man in society, man in his social environment – these were to be the preoccupations of the poets. The emphasis tended to be on what men possess in common; the general and representative characteristics of mankind. Johnson summarized it all in *The Vanity of Human Wishes*:

Let observation with extensive view,
Survey mankind, from China to Peru;
Remark each anxious toil, each eager strife,
And watch the busy scenes of crowded life.

There thus evolved a general view of nature and mankind; a general vision of his position and function in the universe, his relationship to the natural order and his relationship with and to God – mid-way in the great chain of being (*q.v.*).

Despite all this the Neoclassicists were not conservative in any pejorative sense. Though they were inclined to settle for the traditional and the typical, they were ready to accept the novel and the particular, and they were much concerned with the importance of invention, and fancy and imagination (*qq.v.*). Johnson often fulminated against the perils of the fanciful, of letting the imagination run away with one. So long as novelty and invention enhanced the subject, adorned the chosen form, it was acceptable; it was, in a sense, 'safe'. *Aurea mediocritas* (the golden mean) was almost a working motto (Horace himself referred to it in one of his *Odes* [II, x, 5]:

aurearn quisquis mediocritatem
diligit tutus, caret obsoleti
sordibus tecti, caret invidenda
  sobrius aula.)

but no one could accuse Pope, Swift or Johnson of lack of originality.

The preservation (as well as the establishment) of order, balance and correctness was dear to them; hence their frequent use of satire (*q.v.*) as a corrective. It was a means of controlling excess (which was especially repugnant to them), folly, stupidity and corruption; indeed, any shortcoming in man and society which threatened to be contrary to the maintenance of good moral order and literary discipline. As Pope wrote, 'Order is Heav'n's first law.' Thus the writer was under some moral and aesthetic obligation to instruct as well as to please. *See also* ABSTRACT; AGE OF REASON; AUGUSTAN AGE; HEROIC COUPLET; POETIC DICTION; ROMANTICISM; ROMANTIC REVIVAL.

neologism (NGk 'innovation in language') A newly coined word; sometimes a phrase. Neologisms are entering languages all the time and are a necessary invigorating influence. They are basically of three kinds: (a) a completely new word (e.g. *hep*; cf. *hippie*, *hepcat*, *hepster*) without any discernible etymological origin or pedigree (*pedigree* was formerly a neologism, formed probably from French *pied de grue*: 'crane's foot', from the arrowhead figure in a stemma, *q.v.*); (b) a word formed from an existing root or prefix (e.g. the many from *stereo-*, *para-*, *hetero-*); (c) an established word (e.g. *beat*, *dig*, *high*) which has been given a completely new meaning.

Many neologisms are acronyms (*q.v.*). In many instances people have forgotten how or why the word was created in the first place by abbreviation using the initial letters. An obvious example of this is quango (Quasi-*A*utonomous *N*on-*G*overnmental – sometimes *N*ational *G*overnment – Organization).

Here follow a handful of neologisms of fairly recent invention: (a) *bubble-headed*: frivolous, flighty; (b) *camcorder*: a video camera and sound recorder combined in one unit; (c) *eurocrat*: an official concerned with any organization within the Common Market (they tend to use a lingo known as 'Euro-babble'); (d) *grammy*: (from gramophone) an award, corresponding to the cinema Oscar, bestowed by the National Academy of Recording Arts and Sciences; (e) *necklacing*: barbaric form of punishment by which a petrol-soaked tyre is placed round the victim's neck and ignited (used in South Africa by blacks against blacks thought to be government sympathizers); (f) *poop scoop/pooper scooper*: an implement/instrument for lifting and removing faeces (especially one used by dog-owners and by environmental statisticians making faecal surveys); (g) *power breakfast/lunch/tea*: high-level business discussion held during such a meal; (h) *quadrella*: an Australian term for a group of four (especially the last four) horse-races at a meeting for which the punter selects the four winners; (i) *Stellenbosch, to*: to relegate to a post where incompetence matters less (from Stellenbosch, Cape of Good Hope, such a dumping ground); (j) *vtol* (pron. vē'tol): an acronym for a system enabling aircraft to land and take off vertically (*v*ertical *t*ake-*o*ff and *l*anding).

Anybody can invent neologisms and anybody does. My own proposed contributions are: (a) *birocrat*: a menial sub-species in the phylum bureaucrat; (b) *sufferingette*: a plaintive and importunate member of the Womens' Liberation movement; (c) *verbocrap*: polysyllabic circumlocutions (the jargon, q.v., of verbocrats, educationalists, sociologists *et al.*). *See also* GHOSTWORD; INKHORN TERMS; LOAN WORD; NONCE-WORD; PORTMANTEAU WORD; VERBOCRAP.

neo-realism A kind of movement in Italy which began in the late 1940s which is particularly associated with the Italian novel (*q.v.*) and also the cinema industry. It is related to the late 19th c. movement in Italy called *verismo* (*q.v.*). Neo-realist novelists of distinction have been Carlo Levi (1902–75), Elio Vittorini (1908–66), Cesare Pavese (1908–50), Beppe Fenoglio (1922–63) and Italo Calvino (1923–85).

neoteric (Gk 'new, modern') Cicero named a group of poets *neoterici*, who found their inspiration in the work of the Greek Alexandrians. Catullus is the best known of the *neoterici*. The word was quite often used in the 17th c. to describe writers who turned to the Classics for their ideas. Nowadays the term is rarely used, unless it be to refer to a writer who is experimenting along new lines. *See* NEOCLASSICISM.

neue Sachlichkeit (G 'new objectivity') Basically, a term for functionalism in architecture. In literature it referred to fiction, journalism and poetry which made social criticism. The inherent attitudes represented a reaction against expressionism (*q.v.*) in the 1920s. *See* GEBRAUCHS-; PROLETARSKAYA KUL'TURA; SOCIALIST REALISM.

New Apocalypse The name of a movement in British poetry during the Second World War. The name derives from the first of three anthologies the movement produced, namely *The New Apocalypse* (1940), edited by J. F. Hendry. The other two were called *The White Horseman* (1941) and *The Crown and the Sickle* (1945). A number of well-known poets contributed, but there was nothing especially apocalyptic about their verse.

New Comedy Greek comedy which flourished in the 3rd and 4th c. BC. It differed from the Old Comedy (*q.v.*) in that there was little or no satire (common in Aristophanes) and both plots and characters were very often stereotyped. The emphasis was on intricate amorous intrigues with a happy ending. Menander, Philemon and Diphilus were the best known playwrights. They were imitated by the Romans Plautus and Terence, who, in turn, had a considerable influence on Elizabethan comedy. *See also* COMEDY; COMEDY OF MANNERS.

New Criticism A term which refers to a kind of 'movement' in literary criticism which developed in the 1920s (for the most part among Americans). However, it was not until 1941 that John Crowe Ransom published a book called *The New Criticism*. In it he criticized the critics I. A. Richards, William Empson, T. S. Eliot and Yvor Winters, and made a plea for what he called the 'ontological critic'.

The New Critics advocated 'close reading' and detailed textual analysis of poetry rather than an interest in the mind and personality of the poet, sources, the history of ideas and political and social implications. The application of semantics to this criticism was also important.

Other leading figures were Allen Tate, R. P. Blackmur, Kenneth Burke, Cleanth Brooks, W. K. Wimsatt and Robert Penn Warren. The last two, in *Understanding Poetry* (1938), helped to spread the principles of the New Criticism throughout the American academic scene. The latest 'new' criticism is, of course, to be found in structuralism and deconstruction (*qq.v.*). However, the traditional methods of criticism and analysis, as in practical criticism (*q.v.*), are still widely employed; not least because structuralist and deconstructive practice tends to be inaccessible to many, and even very abstruse. *See also* FEMINIST CRITICISM; FREUDIAN CRITICISM/PSYCHOANALYTIC CRITICISM; MARXIST CRITICISM; NEW HUMANISM.

Newdigate Prize A prize at Oxford University for English verse, and in all probability the earliest of the literary prizes (*q.v.*) created in England. It was founded in 1805 by Sir Roger Newdigate (1719–1806). Not a few distinguished writers have won it, but if you put all the prize-winning works together the result would be a corpus of unremarkable verse.

Newgate fiction A minor genre or mode which had some vogue in the 1830s; it has been called 'crime fiction' and is, perhaps, an early form of faction (*q.v.*). The so-called Newgate novelists based their stories on actual criminal cases (there was ample source material in the Newgate Calendar). At the time there was an increasing interest in violent crime and in criminal motives, and some of the novelists aroused moral indignation and adverse criticism for presenting criminals and their deeds in a sympathetic light. The two novelists who are particularly associated with this type of fiction are Edward Bulwer Lytton (1803–73) and William Harrison Ainsworth (1805–82). Lytton wrote *Paul Clifford* (1830) and *Eugene Aram* (1832), and Ainsworth wrote *Rookwood* (1834) and *Jack Sheppard* (1839), which considerably glamorized the famous highwayman.

In fact, this sort of fiction was by no means new. Long before, Fielding had dealt with criminal life in detail in *Jonathan Wild* (1743), based on the life of the notorious thief-taker of that name about whom Defoe had already written a biographical account; while in *Caleb Williams* (1794), an early example of the propaganda or thesis novel (*q.v.*) concerned with crime and its detection, Godwin had depicted the ruthless and arrogant criminal Falkland.

In the 1830s Dickens published *Oliver Twist* (1837–8) and Thackeray published *Catherine* (1839–40), and their view of criminal life constituted something of a reaction against the attitudes expressed in Newgate fiction. A few years later Poe was to publish his remarkable stories about crime and murder, thus becoming one of the main progenitors of the detective story (*q.v.*). *See also* CALENDAR; CRIME NOVEL; KRIMINALGESCHICHTE; NOVEL OF SENSATION.

new historicism This term or appelation is relatively new in literary studies and literary theory. The practice of the approach has been described under other names, such as the 'historical method'. There are many kinds of historical method (e.g. those belonging to Marxist criticism and Jauss's reception theory, *qq.v.*). At its simplest, the historical method is not interested in asserting the transcendent or autonomous aesthetic value of literary texts but, to use Marxist terminology, in researching the contexts of their production, consumption and status. It would certainly be true to say that the 'new historicists' are opposed, above all, to the pure formalism of the new criticism, structuralism, post-structuralism and hermeneutics (*qq.v.*) as approaches to literature. They also oppose the old Leavisite preoccupation with moral value, and implicitly question the way that the literary canon in schools and universities has been arrived at, namely through exclusion and suppression. It would not be inaccurate to say that the 'new historicist' work has Marxist sympathies and is also informed by some of the relativism of post-structuralism. Thus, 'new historicists' do not always see what they are doing as incompatible with deconstruction (*q.v.*) since the enemy of both schools is an unrefined and simple idea of value implicit in the canon. New historicism is associated with research being done in two periods – especially in the English-speaking world: the Renaissance and the Romantic period (*qq.v.*). Much of the best research is being done in the USA: for instance, in the Renaissance period by Stephen Greenblatt, and in the Romantic period by Jerome McGann and Marjorie Levinson. In Britain, Marilyn Butler is a distinguished example of a 'new historicist' scholar of the Romantic period. The 'new historicists' tend to question labels and titles and are constantly refining their goals in order to resist being made to seem as crude as 19th c. philological scholars or Marxists trying to give a materialist explanation of literature. They constantly interrogate the relationship between history and literature rather than making dogmatic assertions. *Rethinking Historicism: Critical Readings in Romantic History* (1989), edited by Marjorie Levinson, which includes essays by Marjorie Levinson, Marilyn Butler, Jerome McGann and Paul Hamilton, contains many interesting ideas. There is also *The New Historicism* (1989), a collection of essays, mainly by American academics, edited by H. Aram Veeser.

new humanism A movement in American literary and critical circles which flourished between 1915 and 1933. The prime movers were Irving Babbitt, Paul Elmer More and Norman Foerster. Its programme was intended to uphold human dignity and moral rectitude and extol the importance of the use of reason and the will. New humanists were anti-Romantic, anti-realist and anti-naturalist. Their exemplar and mentor was Matthew Arnold. They had a good deal of influence in their time and some of it was beneficial. In retrospect many of their views seem narrow and bigoted and display the shortcomings of men who, having set themselves up as arbiters, gradually become too big for their books. *See* HUMANISM.

newsbooks Also known as *diurnalls*, they succeeded the *coranto* (*q.v.*). They consisted, first of all, of one printed sheet of eight pages; later of two printed sheets (sixteen pages). They contained domestic or home news and were issued by journalists (under various titles) between 1641 and 1665. They were succeeded by the *Oxford Gazette*, which later became the *London Gazette*. *See* GAZETTE.

newsletters Manuscript records of parliamentary and court news sent twice weekly to subscribers from the London office of a man called

Muddiman (a famous journalist) in the latter half of the 17th c. A relic of these records is the 'London Letter', which still appears in provincial papers.

newspeak A 'language' invented by George Orwell in his novel *Nineteen Eighty-Four* (1949). *See also* EUPHEMISM; JARGON.

Nibelungenstrophe The stanza of the 12th c. MHG epic *Nibelungenlied*. It consists of four lines rhyming aabb. The first three lines have six stressed syllables; the last, seven.

nihilism A word invented by Turgenev in his novel *Fathers and Sons* (1862). It denotes a radical or extreme radical attitude which denies all traditional values, and, not infrequently, moral values as well. Turgenev invented it to describe the radical elements in the Russian intelligentsia who were profoundly disillusioned by lack of reform and believed that the only way to achieve anything was to destroy more or less completely all prevailing systems. The main theorist and ideologist was Pisarev (1840–68), who was depicted by Turgenev as Bazarov in *Fathers and Sons*. Nihilistic ideas spread and nihilism threatened for a time to develop into quite a powerful revolutionary force. Several other novelists took nihilism as a theme in their fiction and through it criticized the nihilists. The main nihilist works were: Pisemski's *Troubled Seas* (1863), Leskov's *No Way Out* (1864), Goncharov's *The Precipice* (1869) and Dostoievski's *The Possessed* (or *The Devils*, 1871–2). Some of the worst aspects of nihilism were exemplified by Dostoievski in the immoral and unscrupulous character Peter Verkhovensky. Few writers were sympathetic to nihilism, but in *What is to be Done?* (1863) Chernyshevski showed some sympathy for the nihilists and portrayed them as self-sacrificing heroes and radical leaders to be emulated.

nihil obstat *See* IMPRIMATUR.

nil volentibus arduum The name taken by a society of Dutch poets founded at Amsterdam in 1669. Their purpose was to establish French Neoclassical rules in the writing of dramatic verse. Their influence did not last long and by the 1680s was declining.

Nine Worthies Caxton, in his preface to Malory's *Le Morte Darthur* (1485) listed the Nine Worthies, or Heroes, of late medieval literature. The pagan heroes are: Hector, Alexander and Julius Caesar; the Jewish: Joshua, David and Judas Maccabeus; the Christian: Arthur, Charlemagne and Godfrey of Bouillon.

Nō (Noh) This form of Japanese drama evolved in the 14th c., probably from ritual dances associated with Shinto worship. They were lyric dramas (there are believed to be about three hundred in all) and were intended for aristocratic audiences. They therefore differed from the 'popular' *kabuki* (*q.v.*). They were traditionally the work of a man named Kwanami and his son Seami. The form became fixed early in the 17th c. It was therefore a 'frozen' or 'fossil' form, like traditional icon paintings, and just about as stylized.

Nō plays are presented on a square stage, raised slightly from the ground, on which the audience sit on two sides. At one side is a balcony accommodating a chorus of ten singers. Upstage there is a smaller platform occupied by four musicians and two stage-hands. The actors enter and leave on a long slanting walk, a sort of bridge, from stage left. There is little or no scenery except for a framework with a roof and three symbolic trees in front of the slanting walk which represent heaven, earth and humanity.

There are usually between two and six actors in a *Nō* play: the hero or leading character, *shite* (or *shtay*); his companion, *tsure*; *waki*, a kind of deuteragonist (*q.v.*), and *waki's* companion. There are also a child, *kokata*, and an extra actor, *ahi*. *Waki* introduces the play with a chant and tells the audience what is going to be performed. *Shite* then appears disguised (in mask and elaborate costume) and delivers a chant. He then converses with *waki* so that the theme of the play is clear and the real character of *shite* is revealed. The rest of the play consists of a series of stylized dances, usually in five movements, by the first actor. These dances are preceded by an interlude in which an actor in ordinary clothes tells the story of the play. All the actors (except the man playing *waki*) usually wear masks and elaborate costumes and they chant in low or high-pitched voices to a musical accompaniment. To Western ears the chanting is reminiscent of the gentle warbling of slightly dispeptic doves, and the gestures which go with it are as arcane as Byzantine cricket.

A full *Nō* entertainment (women never act in it and men take the female roles) lasts about seven hours, and normally consists of five plays separated by three *kyogen* – brief farcical interludes. These are often performed in ordinary costume and actually parody the *Nō* plays themselves; rather as a satyr play (*q.v.*) served as a comic relief to the trilogy in Classical Greek tragedy.

Nō drama has had some influence in the West. W. B. Yeats was very interested in it. Ezra Pound and Fenollosa adapted some *Nō* plays. Arthur Waley did some translations and commentaries. Sturge Moore wrote some *Nō* plays, and Laurence Binyon, Bertolt Brecht and Paul Claudel all used their techniques. Their influence was especially noticeable in the work of Thornton Wilder, particularly in *Our Town* (1938). Two studies by Noel Peri, *Cinq Nō* (1929) and *Le Nō* (1944), have also helped to make *Nō* drama known in Europe.

Nobel Prizes These were established under the will of Alfred Bernhard Nobel (1833–96), the Swedish chemist who made a major contribution to the development of explosives. The terms of his will provided for prizes to be awarded annually for the most important discoveries in physics, chemistry, and physiology or medicine; to the person who has done the most to promote 'the fraternity of nations' (i.e. the Peace Prize); and to the person who has produced in the field of literature 'the most outstanding work of an idealistic tendency'. Some of the awards in literature, at any rate, have, to say the least of it, looked pretty odd. This has led people to believe that awards are made for 'political' reasons; and also that, in a lean year, the judges think that it is 'so-and-so's turn' so he or she (it is *nearly always* a man) had better have it, *faute de mieux*. The award is made to an individual, but some awards appear to have been made on the principle that it is time for a particular country to have one (hence political implications). The first winner for literature was the Frenchman Sully-Prudhomme, a minor poet, in 1901. Thereafter they were: 1902 – Theodor Mommsen; 1903 – Bjørnstjerne Bjørnson; 1904 – José Echegaray and Frédéric Mistral; 1905 – Henryk Sienkiewicz; 1906 – Giosué Carducci; 1907 – Rudyard Kipling; 1908 – Rudolf Eucken; 1909 – Selma Lagerlöf; 1910 – Paul Heyse; 1911 – Maurice Maeterlinck; 1912 – Gerhart Hauptmann; 1913 – Rabindranath Tagore; 1914 – no award; 1915 – Romain Rolland; 1916 – Verner von Heidenstam; 1917 – Karl Kjellerup and Henrik Pontoppidan; 1918 – no award; 1919 – Carl Spitteler; 1920 – Knut Hamsun; 1921 – Anatole France; 1922 – Jacinto Benavente y Martínez; 1923 – W. B. Yeats; 1924 – Wladyslaw Reymont; 1925 – George Bernard Shaw; 1926 – Grazia Deledda; 1927 – Henri Bergson; 1928 – Sigrid Undset; 1929 – Thomas Mann; 1930 – Sinclair Lewis; 1931 – Erik Axel Karlfeldt; 1932 – John Galsworthy;

1933 – Ivan Bunin; 1934 – Luigi Pirandello; 1935 – no award; 1936 – Eugene O'Neill; 1937 – Roger Martin du Gard; 1938 – Pearl S. Buck; 1939 – F. E. Sillanpää; 1940–43 – no awards; 1944 – Johannes V. Jensen; 1945 – Gabriela Mistral; 1946 – Herman Hesse; 1947 – André Gide; 1948 – T. S. Eliot; 1949 – William Faulkner; 1950 – Bertrand Russell; 1951 – Pär Lagerkvist; 1952 – François Mauriac; 1953 – Winston S. Churchill; 1954 – Ernest Hemingway; 1955 – Halldór Laxness; 1956 – Juan Ramón Jiménez; 1957 – Albert Camus; 1958 – Boris Pasternak; 1959 – Salvatore Quasimodo; 1960 – Saint-John Perse; 1961 – Ivo Andrić; 1962 – John Steinbeck; 1963 – George Seferis; 1964 – Jean-Paul Sartre; 1965 – Mikhail Sholokhov; 1966 – S. Y. Agnon and Nelly Sachs; 1967 – Miguel Angel Asturias; 1968 – Yasunari Kawabata; 1969 – Samuel Beckett; 1970 – Alexander Solzhenitsyn; 1971 – Pablo Neruda; 1972 – Heinrich Böll; 1973 – Patrick White; 1974 – Eyvind Johnson and Harry Martinson; 1975 – Eugenio Montale; 1976 – Saul Bellow; 1977 – Vicente Aleixandre; 1978 – Isaac Bashevis Singer; 1979 – Odysseus Elytis; 1980 – Czeslaw Milosz; 1981 – Elias Canetti; 1982 – Gabriel García Márquez; 1983 – William Golding; 1984 – Jaroslav Seifert; 1985 – Claude Simon; 1986 – Wole Soyinka; 1987 – Joseph Brodsky; 1988 – Nagib Mahfouz; 1989 – Camilo José Cela; 1990 – Octavio Paz.

noble savage, the The concept or title which connotes the exemplar of primitive goodness, dignity and nobility uncorrupted by the evil effects of civilization. The origins of the idea of the noble savage are obscure, but one may suppose that they have to do with the belief that in a primitive and 'free' state there existed innocent, prototypal human beings like Milton's Adam and Eve in Eden:

> Two of far nobler shape erect and tall,
> Godlike erect, with native honour clad
> In naked majesty seemed lords of all,
> And worthy seemed, for their looks divine
> The image of their glorious maker shone,
> Truth, wisdom, sanctitude severe and pure.
>
> (*Paradise Lost*, IV, 288)

We find Montaigne touching upon the idea of the noble savage in his essay *Of Cannibals* (1580), but it is not until well on in the 17th c. that it becomes prominent. The concept is handsomely embodied by Dryden in a resonant triplet (*q.v.*) in his heroic play *The Conquest of Granada*, Pt I, I, i (1670):

I am as free as nature first made man,
Ere the base laws of servitude began,
When wild in woods the noble savage ran.

The idea is especially noticeable in Mrs Aphra Behn's *Oroonoko: or, The History of the Royal Slave* (c. 1688). The eponymous hero of this 'romance' is an educated as well as a noble savage (he has learnt French and English), and he is virtuous, young, beautiful, brave and a fine warrior; in short, the 'fair rose i' the state' of his native Africa. Mrs Behn dwelt upon primitive innocence and deplored the effects of civilization and man's inventions. She foreshadowed the 'return to nature' philosophy and doctrine which Rousseau was to elaborate seventy years later in *Emile* (1762). 'Everything is well when it comes fresh from the hands of the Maker', wrote Rousseau, 'everything degenerates in the hands of Man'. Chateaubriand also exploited the noble-savage idea, and it proved a particularly attractive concept to many writers in the late 18th c. and during the Romantic period (*q.v.*). It was a part of the reaction against the growth of industrialism, materialism and capitalism. *See* PRIMITIVISM.

nom de plume (F 'pen-name') A term used in English, but *not* in French, to indicate a fictitious name employed by a writer. For instance: Beachcomber was J. B. Morton; O. Henry was William Sydney Porter; George Eliot was Mary Ann Cross. The French use *nom de guerre* for an author's pen-name or pseudonym. A very large number of writers have pen-names. *See also* ANONYMOUS LITERATURE; PSEUDONYMOUS LITERATURE.

nominatio *See* ONOMATOPOEIA.

nonce-word A word invented and used for a particular purpose, expressly; one used for a specific occasion; for the nonce = for that once, temporarily. Lewis Carroll's *Jabberwocky* is a classic example, but over the centuries numerous neologisms have started life as nonce-words. *See* GHOSTWORD; NEOLOGISM.

nonsense There are basically two kinds of nonsense involving the use of words: (a) the unintentional; (b) the intentional. The former is common in speech and much semi-educated writing (e.g. malaproprisms, *q.v.*). The latter has become a minor genre in literature, especially during the last 150 years. Setting aside gibberish (for example: gibbernog floos tink manga-ha ore doog now less and fly high split in west), true or positive nonsense writing is never intended to make formal sense; nevertheless it has a kind of internal lunatic logic of its own, and often comprises enigmatic variations on the absurd. Most of it is verse, but there is some prose; for example, the patter and punning and intricate witticisms of Shakespearean Fools (especially in *King Lear*, III, ii, iii), James Joyce's epic *Finnegans Wake* and some passages in Thomas Lovell Beddoes's *Death's Jest Book* (1850).

It has a long history in Europe and is to be found in all or nearly all European languages and literatures, and in Russian literature. There are some early instances from the Middle Ages: a poem 'about nothing' by William of Aquitaine (1071–1127), the Middle English poem *The Land of Cockaygne*, a very weird poem in Latin by Cerveri De Girona (14th c.) and some French *fatrasies* (*q.v.*). Another notable fairly early example is *Phyllyp Sparowe*, a lamentation for a sparrow killed by a cat, by John Skelton (1460?–1529). There is quite a lot of anonymous nonsense verse in English, French and Latin dating from the 15th and 16th c. An important pioneer of English nonsense verse was John Taylor, the 'Water-Poet' (1578–1653), who wrote such well-known pieces as *Odcomb's Complaint, Sir Gregory Nonsense His News from No Place* and *Epitaph in the Utopian Tongue*, which begins:

> Nortumblum callimuquash omysteliton quashte burashte . . .

And his *Epitaph in the Bermuda Tongue, which must be pronounced with the accent of the grunting of a hog*, and begins thus:

> Hough gruntough wough Thomough
> Coratough, Odcough robunquogh . . .

The more bizarre imagery and 'far-fet' conceits (*q.v.*) – especially hyperbole and paradox (*qq.v.*) – of the 17th c. metaphysical (*q.v.*) poets begin to approximate to the nonsensical. Satire (*q.v.*), travesty and burlesque (*q.v.*), the drolls (*q.v.*) or droll humours and Bedlamite songs of the mid-17th c. are also forebears of later nonsense.

From the second half of the 17th c. – and through the period of neoclassicism (*q.v.*) – non-sense as a concept, idea or phenomenon can be seen as a contrast to 'good sense' (*q.v.*). When Dryden, Addison, Pope, Fielding and Swift attacked nonsense they were castigating writers whom they regarded as bad or useless, writers with inferior or absurd ideas and inferior powers of communicating them. Hence, for example, Dryden's resounding onslaught in mock-heroic (*q.v.*) style on Shadwell in *Mac Flecknoe* (1682) and Pope's scathing ridicule of dunces in *The Dunciad* (1728). Moreover, it is noticeable that in their more extravagant and grotesque images and conceits both poets achieve a barbed, caricaturing nonsense of their own.

In 1730 Fielding came close to the contrivance of nonsense in his theatrical burlesque *The Author's Farce*. Meanwhile, intentional nonsense writing had flourished. There was a certain amount of anonymous verse and such poems as *A New Song of New Similies* by John Gay (1685–1732), which begins:

My passion is as mustard strong;
  I sit all sober sad;
Drunk as a piper all day long,
  Or like a March-hare mad.

And Henry Carey's *NambyPamby: or, A Panegyric on the New Versificiation* (1725). It was Carey, too, who wrote the ludicrous burlesque tragedy *Chrononhotonthologos* ('the Most Tragical Tragedy that ever was Tragediz'd') in 1734; and he *may* have written 'God Save the King'.

Even Dr Johnson (1709–84), with perhaps slightly unexpected skittishness, composed little verses that might have been written by Edward Lear or Lewis Carroll. For example:

I put my hat upon my head
  And walk'd into the Strand,
And there I met another man
  Whose hat was in his hand.

And Mozart (1756–91) made a contribution with his *Kanontext*:

bona nox; bist a rechter ox;
bona notte, liebe Lotte;
bonne nuit, pfui, pfui;
good night, good night,
heut muss ma no weit;
gute Nacht, gute Nacht,
sch . . . ins Bett, dass's kracht;
gute Nacht; schlaf fei g'sund
und reck'n A . . . zum Mund.

In the 18th c. Christopher Smart, Thomas Holcroft and William

Blake all had a go at nonsense and Samuel Foote (1720–77) produced one of the classic nonsense poems – *The Great Panjandrum*:

So she went into the garden
to cut a cabbage leaf
to make an apple-pie;
and at the same time
a great she-bear, coming down the street,
pops its head into the shop.
What! no soap?
So he died,
and she very imprudently married the Barber:
and there were present
the Picninnies,
and the Joblillies
and the Garyulies,
and the great Panjandrum himself,
with the little round button at top;
and they all fell to playing the game of catch-as-catch-can,
till the gunpowder ran out at the heels of their boots.

During the 19th c. many writers were to compose memorable nonsense verses. For example: Coleridge (*The Devil's Thoughts*); Charles Lamb (*Nonsense Verses*); Thomas Love Peacock (*A Satirical Ballad*, *The Wise Men of Gotham* and *Sir Proteus*); John Keats ('There was a naughty boy . . .'); Thomas Hood, the Elder (*Sally Simpkin's Lament, or John Jones's Kit-Cat-astrophe* – which was a joke about the portraits of the Kit-Cat Club, *q.v.* – *Epicurean Reminiscences of a Sentimentalist*, *The Lament of Toby the Learned Pig* and *A Flying Visit*); Thomas Lovell Beddoes (*The Legend of St Gingulph's Relict* and *The Oviparous Tailor*); Swinburne (*The Higher Pantheism in a Nutshell*); Thackeray (*Foreign Literature*); George du Maurier (*Vers Nonsensiques*); Thomas Hood, the Younger (*The Ballad of the Basking Shark*); and W. S. Gilbert (*The Story of Prince Agib*).

However, the hierophants of nonsense in the 19th c. were beyond question Edward Lear (1812–88) and Lewis Carroll (1832–98). Lear composed *A Book of Nonsense* (1846), which he illustrated, containing a large number of limericks (*q.v.*) of which the following is a representative example:

There was an Old Lady of Chertsey,
Who made a remarkable Curtsey;

She twirled round and round
Till she sunk underground,
Which distressed all the people of Chertsey.

He is probably better known for his *Nonsense Songs*, particularly *The Akond of Swat*, *The Courtship of the Yongby-Bongby-Bò*, *The Dong with the Luminous Nose*, *the Jumblies*, *The Owl and the Pussy-Cat* and *The Pobble Who Has No Toes* – of which one stanza reads:

For his Aunt Jobiska said, 'No harm
Can come to his toes if his nose is warm,
And it's perfectly known that a Pobble's toes
Are safe, provided he minds his nose.

The topsy-turvy world of Lewis Carroll's *Alice's Adventures in Wonderland* (1865) and *Through the Looking-Glass* (1872) contains a form of nonsense in which the logic seems deliberately planned and precise; reason on the spree in a surrealistic funfair. Carroll wrote a number of songs which have become classics: *Melodies*, *The Palace of Humbug*, *The Mad Hatter's Concert Song*, *The Mouse's Tale* (a pattern poem, *q.v.*), *Father William*, *The Duchess's Lullaby*, *How Doth the Little Crocodile*, *The Mock Turtle's Song*, *Jabberwocky* (*q.v.*), *The Walrus and the Carpenter*, *Humpty Dumpty's Poetic Recitation*, *The White Knight's Song* and *The Hunting of the Snark*.

Lear and Carroll both belong to a long tradition of nonsense makers, not least the makers of jingles and nursery rhymes (*qq.v.*). There were plenty of examples in *Mother Goose's Melody* (*c.* 1765), and more later in *Nursery Nonsense, or Rhymes without Reason* (1864). There are many anonymous nonsense verses from the 19th c., including such counting jingles as this:

Ah, ra, chickera,
Roly, poly, pickena,
Kinny, minny, festi,
Shanti-poo,
Ickerman, chickerman, chinee-choo.

During the 20th c. nonsense verse has proliferated. Many major poets have tried their hand at it, often with great success, and many minor writers have made memorable contributions. The Learic and Carrolline tradition has been well sustained. Among British and American writers we should mention the following (with one or two titles): Hilaire Belloc (*Cautionary Tales*, 1907, which verge on satire); G. K. Chesterton (*The Oneness of the Philosopher with Nature*); E. C. Bentley (*Clerihews*, *q.v.*); James Joyce (*The Ballad of Persse O'Reilly*, from *Finnegans Wake*); Marianne Moore (*To Victor Hugo of My Crow Pluto*, which is a kind of macaronic, *q.v.*, nonsense); Edith Sitwell (*Polka*, *The Bat* and *When Sir Beelzebub*); Sacheverell Sitwell (*Rio Grande*); Osbert Sitwell (*On the Coast of Coromandel*, a burlesque of *Rio Grande*); T. S. Eliot (*The Hippopotamus*, and the poems in *Old Possum's Book of Practical Cats*); John Crowe Ransom (*Captain Carpenter*); Ogden Nash (*Oh To Be Odd!*, *The Wombat*, *The Grackle* – and many others); Stevie Smith (*My Hat*, *My Cats*, *Our Bog is Dood*); Kenneth Patchen (*Because It's Good to Keep Things Straight*); Mervyn Peake (*The Frivolous Cake*); John Berryman (*Dream Song*); D. J. Enright (*A Child's Guide to Welfare*); Edwin Morgan (*The First Men on Mercury*); Frank O'Hara (*A Terrestrial Cuckoo*); John Ashbery (*Farm Implements* and *Rutabagas in a Landscape*); Bob Dylan (*Tiny Montgomery*, *Don't Ya Tell Henry*, *Ballad of a Thin Man*); Peter Handke (*The Wrong Way Round*); Hugh Haughton (*The Bollam's Replover: Farewell to Jabberwocky*); James Fenton (*This Octopus Exploits Women*); Paul Muldoon (*Quoof*). There is also a body of 20th c. anonymous nonsense verse.

Among continental and Russian writers and poets who have made notable contributions the following are outstanding: Guillaume Apollinaire (1880–1918), Viktor Khlebnikov (1885–1922), Aleksei Kruchenykh (1886–1968), Philippe Soupault (1897–), Louis Aragon (1897–1982), Lorca (1898–1936), Robert Desnos (1900–45), Jacques Prévert (1900–77), Aleksander Wat (1900–), Rafael Alberti (1902–), Günter Eich (1907–72), Fritz Grasshof (1913–), Vasko Popa (1922–), Miroslav Holub (1923–), Andreas Okopenko (1930–), Jerzy Harasymowicz (1933–), Andrei Voznesensky (1933–) and Mariu Sorescu (1936–).

Of the above perhaps one of the most remarkable inventors of the nonsensical was Viktor Klebnikov, the chief founder of Futurism (*q.v.*) in Russia. A distinguished etymologist, he created his own poetic vocabulary and under his guidance the Futurists tried to create a trans-sense language or *zaumny yazyk* now known as *zaum* (*q.v.*). Khlebnikov composed *Zangesi* (1923), a 'Supersaga in 20 planes' in which the 'characters' (e.g. birds) use an extraordinary onomatopoeic language.

Apart from Lewis Carroll's *Mouse's Tale*, there are other

ingenious examples of nonsense pattern poetry. This is *The Fish's Night Song* by Christian Morgenstern (1871–1914):

—
◡ ◡
— — —
◡ ◡ ◡ ◡
— — —
◡ ◡ ◡ ◡
— — —
◡ ◡ ◡ ◡
— — —
◡ ◡ ◡ ◡
— — —
◡ ◡
—

The fish shape scanned from top to bottom comprises the following feet: half spondee; pyrrhic; molossus and proceleusmatic (*qq.v.*) (alternating); concluding with pyrrhic and half spondee.

A much more ingenious pattern poem is the *Chequered Poem, or Verse for a Chess Piece* (1867). On each of the squares of one chessboard plan are words and syllables. The squares of an adjoining plan are numbered 1 to 64. To 'assemble' the poem (which is in French) the 'reader' makes knight's moves all round the board following the sequence of numbers, each of which corresponds to a word or syllable on the other plan.

There have been a number of theories to explain the greater popularity of nonsense and the absurd. An increasing distrust of the rational and a vision of man as a ludicrous figure in a universe without any identifiable point or purpose seem to have contributed. It is as if sense of man's function and role can be made only by seeing them as nonsensical. Witness the crazier elements in the works of G. K. Chesterton and his use of paradox – especially in *The Napoleon of Notting Hill* (1904); plus those of Getrude Stein, James Thurber, William Saroyan and J. D. Salinger, to name no others; the surrealistic stories of Edward Upward (e.g. *The Railway Accident*), the zany comedy of Spike Milligan's books, the *farfelu* quality of Jacques Tati's films, the buffoonery of 'The Goon Show', the 'freak-out' (and again surreal) nature of the highly successful television show 'Monty Python's Flying Circus', and, perhaps most interesting of all, the grotesque logic and 'happenings' in plays belonging to the Theatre of the Absurd (*q.v.*) – especially those of Ionesco.

In many such works (as in Erasmus's *The Praise of Folly* and Rabelais's *Gargantua and Pantagruel*) nonsense becomes a kind of therapy and protective charm. A particular kind of mirth is evoked to dispel fear and apprehension, to evade and combat the question: To what end?

As long ago as 1901 G. K. Chesterton, one of the 'philosophers' of nonsense, touched upon the teleological theme in *A Defence of Nonsense*:

> This simple sense of wonder at the shapes of things, and at their exuberant independence of our intellectual standards and our trivial definitions, is the basis of spirituality as it is the basis of nonsense. Nonsense and faith (strange as the conjunction may seem) are the two supreme symbolic assertions of the truth that to draw out the soul of things with a syllogism is as impossible as to draw out Leviathan with a hook.

The music-hall comedians of the 20th c. have interpreted human existence in terms of the nonsensical and their humour has become darker and more sardonic with the years. The jokes have become sicker, and it may be that the sick joke and witticism (e.g. 'Is there a life before death?' – allegedly a graffito in a Belfast lavatory), the sick lyric (e.g. the clever songs of Tom Lehrer), sick verse (*q.v.*), and, conceivably, black comedy (*q.v.*), all of which have become increasingly popular in the 20th c., are related to and are a development of the phenomenon of nonsense.

Long before (and better than most) Beaumarchais (1732–99) summarized the spirit of nonsense and the paradox inherent in life in *The Barber of Seville*: 'Je me presse de rire de tout, de peur d'être obligé d'en pleurer'. Hugh Haughton's *The Chatto Book of Nonsense Poetry* (1988) is an outstanding anthology. *See also* BACK SLANG; BARZELLETTA; BURLESQUE; CARNIVALIZATION/CARNIVALESQUE; DOGGEREL; DOUBLE DACTYL; FOLLY LITERATURE; HOLORHYME; LIGHT VERSE; PALINDROME; PATAPHYSICS; PATTER SONG; PUN; RIDDLE; SURREALISM.

notebook *See* DIARY AND JOURNAL.

noucentisme A Catalan literary movement named after the 1900s or 20th c. It started *c.* 1906 when Enric Prat de la Riba published a manifesto (*q.v.*) titled *La nacionalitat catalana*. Members of the movement attempted to create a new humanism (*q.v.*) and they had considerable influence on Catalan literature. Among the main writers were Guereau de Liost, Josep Carner and Carlos Riba.

nouveau roman (F 'new novel') This term appears to have become part of critical jargon in France *c.* 1955 with the publication (in periodicals and reviews) of Robbe-Grillet's essays on the nature and future of the novel (*q.v.*). His theories were later gathered in *Pour un nouveau roman* (1963). The movement, if so it can be called, of the *nouveau roman* was somewhat biblioclastic in the sense that it rejected much that had gone before. In his evangelical role Robbe-Grillet regarded many earlier novelists as *vieux jeu*. Plot, action, narrative, ideas, the delineation and analysis of character . . . such things had little or no place in the novel. On the contrary, the novel should be a form of 'res-istentialism' – to use Paul Jennings's word. It should be about *things*; an individual version and vision of *things*; a systematized and analytical record of objects. And so, in practice, many of the *nouveaux romans* were and are; and hardly anywhere is the practice better displayed than in Michel Butor's outstanding novel *La Modification* (1957).

Such a view of the function of the novel was not entirely new. Long before, Huysmans had suggested what might be done about objects and how the novel might be depersonalized; Kafka had shown that the conventional methods of depicting character were not essential; James Joyce had demonstrated that plot was dispensable; and Louis-Ferdinand Céline, in several novels, but especially in *Voyage au bout de la nuit* (1932), had written of themes which later preoccupied the existentialists and the *hodjas* (mentors) of the cult of the absurd, and especially those of the Theatre of the Absurd (*q.v.*). Proust, William Faulkner, Samuel Beckett and Albert Camus had also shown that it was possible to break with a number of the traditional conventions of the novel form.

In 1939 Nathalie Sarraute published *Tropismes* and this has come to be regarded as a probable prototype of the *nouveau roman*. Later, in 1952, she published a collection of essays called *L'Ere du soupçon* in which she discussed this new form. In the 1940s Maurice Blanchot wrote several *nouveaux romans*: *Aminadab* (1942), *Le Dernier Mot* (1947), *Les Très-Haut* (1948). These he followed with *Le Ressassement éternel* (1951), *Celui qui ne m'accompagnait pas* (1953) and several others. Robbe-Grillet, who has come to be the best known of these novelists, wrote *Les Gommes* (1953), *Le Voyeur* (1955), *La Jalousie* (1957) and *Dans le labyrinthe* (1959). Michel Butor has also experimented in *L'Emploi du temps* (1957) and *Degrés* (1960). One should also mention other works by Nathalie Sarraute; in particular *Portrait d'un inconnu* (1947), *Le Planétarium* (1959) and *Vous les entendez* (1972). Another prominent member among the experimenters is Claude Simon, some of whose best novels are: *Le Tricheur* (1945), *L'Herbe* (1958), *La Route des Flandres* (1960), *Histoire* (1967) and *La Bataille de Pharsale* (1969). *See* ANTI-HERO; ANTI-NOVEL; TROPISM.

nouvelle The *nouvelle* differs from the *roman* or novel (*qq.v.*) in that it deals with a single situation or episode. The event moves to an unexpected climax, and it may be comic or tragic. It is related to the *novella* and the *récit* (*qq.v.*) and seldom exceeds a hundred pages.

The *nouvelle* followed on from the medieval *lais* and *fabliaux* (*qq.v.*), and the form took definite shape in the collection of tales known as *Cent Nouvelles Nouvelles* (1462). Notable examples from near the end of the 15th c. were *Arrêts d'amour* and *Jehan de Paris*. In the next century a collection of stories titled *Nouvelles Récréations et Joyeux Devis* was published *c.* 1558 and ascribed to Des Périers. Thereafter the *nouvelle* was an established form, and in the 19th c. the term *conte* (*q.v.*) was often used as a synonym. The main authors from this period were Flaubert and Maupassant, Alfred de Musset, Alfred de Vigny, Prosper Mérimée, Joseph-Arthur Gobineau and Anatole France. *See also* SHORT STORY.

nouvelle vague (F 'new wave') A term which appears to have come into regular use in the 1950s and 1960s to describe a new trend in the arts. It was particularly applied to experimental work in the cinema (films by Godard and Resnais, for example), and then to experimental novels (for instance, works by Alain Robbe-Grillet, Michel Butor, Nathalie Sarraute, Alan Burns and B. S. Johnson) and also to playwrights like Harold Pinter, Samuel Beckett, Eugène Ionesco. Arthur Adamov, Jean Genet, N. F. Simpson and Ann Jellicoe. *See also* ANTI-NOVEL; AVANT-GARDE; BLACK COMEDY; NOUVEAU ROMAN; NOVEL; THEATRE OF THE ABSURD.

nouvellistes Members of the Parisian population in the 17th c. who held regular meetings at various points in the city in order to pass on news and discuss it. Eventually they were paid to collect news by those in a position of power and influence who needed to know the news. The *nouvellistes* were active even after the establishment of the press. Hand-written newsletters (called *nouvelles à la main* and *gazettes à la main*) were circulated clandestinely. *See also* CORANTO; GAZETTE; NEWSBOOKS; NEWSLETTERS.

novas rimadas A Provençal genre of narrative verse. Normally written in octosyllabic rhymed couplets.

novecentismo A Spanish term denoting the 'spirit' of the 20th c., taken from Massimo Bontempelli's magazine *900* (founded in 1926) and introduced by Eugenio d'Ors. It came to be applied to a group of writers of the post-'98 generation which included Ortega y Gasset, Linares Rivas, Martínez Sierra, Pedro Salinas and Pérez de Ayala. *See* GENERACION DEL 1898.

novel Derived from Italian *novella* 'tale, piece of news', and now applied to a wide variety of writings whose only common attribute is that they are extended pieces of prose fiction. But 'extended' begs a number of questions. The length of novels varies greatly and there has been much debate on how long a novel is or should be – to the *reductio ad absurdum* of when is a novel *not* a novel or a long short-story or a short novel or a *novella* (*q.v.*). There seem to be fewer and fewer rules, but it would probably be generally agreed that, in contemporary practice, a novel will be between 60–70,000 words and, say, 200,000.

The actual term 'novel' has had a variety of meanings and implications at different stages. From roughly the 16th to the 18th c. its meaning tended to derive from the Italian *novella* and the Spanish *novela* (the French term *nouvelle*, q.v., is closely related) and the term (often used in a plural sense) denoted short stories or tales of the kind one finds in Boccaccio's *Decameron* (*c.* 1349–51), Marguerite of Navarre's *Heptaméron* (*c.* 1530), George Pettie's *A petite Pallace of Pettie his pleasure* (1576) and Cervantes's *Novelas ejemplares* (1613). Nowadays we would classify all the contents of the above as short stories. Broadly speaking, the term denoted a prose narrative about characters and their actions in what was recognizably everyday life and usually in the present, with the emphasis on things being 'new' or a 'novelty'. And it was used in contradistinction to 'romance' (*q.v.*). In the 19th c. the concept of 'novel' was enlarged. In Germany the term *Novelle* (*see* NOVELLA) was still associated with the Renaissance *novella*.

As to the quiddity of the novel there has been as much debate. However, without performing contortions to be comprehensive we may hazard that it is a form of story or prose narrative containing characters, action and incident, and, perhaps, a plot (*q.v.*). In fact it is very difficult to write a story without there being *some* sort of plot, however vague and tenuous. So well developed is the average reader's need for a plot (at its simplest the desire to know what is going to happen next) that the reader will look for and find a plot where, perhaps, none is intended. Moreover, as soon as the reader is sufficiently interested in one or more of the characters (one can hardly envisage a novel without a character of some kind) to want to know what is going to happen to them next and to ask why, when and where – then there is a plot. Incident and character are almost inseparable. As Henry James pointed out: 'What is character but the determination of incident? What is incident but the illustration of character?' Thus, plot, even if slight, is likely to develop however much an author may wish to prevent it.

The subject matter of the novel eludes classification, for it is the hold-all and Gladstone bag of literature. No other literary form has proved so pliable and adaptable to a seemingly endless variety of topics and themes. No other literary form has attracted more writers (or more people who are *not* writers), and it continues to do so despite the oft-repeated cry (seldom raised by novelists themselves) that the novel is dead. If proliferation is a sign of incipient death then the demise of the novel must be imminent.

At the moment it seems unlikely. Apart from dramatic comedy (*q.v.*) no other form has been so susceptible to change and development and the literary taxonomist at once finds himself confronted with a wide range of sub-species or categories. For example, we have the epistolary novel, the sentimental novel, the novel of sensation, the condition of England novel, the campus novel, the Gothic novel and the historical novel; we have the propaganda, regional, thesis (or sociological), psychological, proletarian, documentary and time novel; we have the novel of the soil and the saga (or chronicle) novel, the picaresque novel, the key novel (*see* LIVRE A CLEF) and the anti-novel; not to mention the detective novel, the thriller, the crime novel, the police procedural, the spy novel, the novel of adventure and the novelette (*qq.v.*). In French we have various kinds of *roman*, especially the *roman-fleuve*, the *roman à tiroirs*, the *roman-feuilleton*, the *récit*, the *roman policier* (the equivalent of the detective novel), the *nouveau roman* (the equivalent of the anti-novel) and the *roman à clef* or key novel (*qq.v.*). In German we find the *Bildungsroman*, the *Künstlerroman*, the *Ritter- und Räuberroman* (the picaresque), the *Prosaroman*, the *Briefroman* (epistolary), the *Zeitroman*, the *Schauerroman* and the *Schlüsselroman* (key novel) (*qq.v.*). A number of these classifications shade off into each other. For example, psychological novel is a term which embraces many books; proletarian, propaganda and thesis novels tend to have much in common; the picaresque narrative is often a novel of adventure; a saga novel may also be a regional novel. And so on. We should also note that in other literatures and languages similar classifications have been established.

The absolute origins of the genre are obscure, but it seems clear that in the time of the XIIth Dynasty Middle Kingdom (*c.* 1200 BC) Egyptians were writing fiction of a kind which one would describe as a novel today. For instance, *The Princess of Backstaw*, *The Predestined Prince*, and *Sinuhe*. From Classical times other works of fiction have come down to us: notably, *The Milesian Tales* (2nd c. BC), *Daphnis and Chloe* (2nd c. AD) by Longus, *The Golden Ass* (2nd c. AD) by Apuleius, and the *Satyricon* (1st c. AD) of Petronius Arbiter. Most of these are concerned with love of one sort and another and contain the rudiments of novels as we understand them today. This is especially true of the pastoral (*q.v.*) romance *Daphnis and Chloe*.

But it is not until towards the end of the first millennium that we find work more recognizably like the novels we have become accustomed to in the last 200-odd years. These works are in Japanese. For example, the *Taketori Monogatari* (*c.* 850–920), the *Utsubo Monogatari* (*c.* 850–900), a collection of anonymous stories, the *Yamato Monogatari* (*c.* 950), the *Ochikubo Monogatari* (late 10th c.), the *Sumiyoshi Monogatari* (*c.* 1200), a romantic novel, the *Gempei Seisuki* (*c.* 1200–50), a military novel, and the *Taiheiki* (1367–74), a military novel describing the period 1318–67. However, from this period, the most famous of all Japanese works is the tale of *Genji* (*c.* 1000) written by a woman under the pseudonym Murasaki Shikibu. This long story of court life relating the adventures of a Japanese Don Juan at the imperial court is an important work in the history of the genre because of its analysis of character and its study of psychology in love.

It is likely that round about this time of the 10th c. the collection of stories subsequently known as the *Arabian Nights' Entertain-*

ments, or *The Thousand and One Nights*, was in embryonic form. However, they were not collected and established as a group of stories until much later, and then probably by an Egyptian professional story-teller at some time between the 14th and 16th c. These tales did not become known in Europe until early in the 18th c., since when they have had a considerable influence.

In Italy, in the 14th c., there was a vogue for collections of *novelle* or short tales, of which the most famous is Boccaccio's *Decameron*, which had much influence on Chaucer and many of which were later translated by William Painter and published under the title *Palace of Pleasure* (1566, 1567). In the 16th c. Bandello published *Le Novelle* (written between 1510 and 1560), and Marguerite of Navarre published the *Heptaméron*, following the form of Boccaccio. Originally these stories 'of seven days' were called *Contes de la Reine de Navarre*.

These were all short stories but are extremely important because they were in prose, and because in their method of narration and in their creation and development of character they are forerunners of the modern novel.

Until the 14th c. most of the literature of entertainment (and the novel is usually intended as an entertainment) was confined to narrative verse (*q.v.*), particularly the epic (*q.v.*) and the romance. Romance eventually yielded the word *roman*, which is the term for novel in most European languages. In some ways the novel is a descendant of the medieval romances which, in the first place, like the epic, were written in verse and then in prose (e.g. Malory's *Morte Darthur*, 1485). Verse narratives had been supplanted by prose narratives by the end of the 17th c.

Spain was ahead of the rest of Europe in the development of the novel form. At the very beginning of the 14th c. we find a novel called *El Caballero Cifar*; and then, *c.* 1304–12, the *Amadís de Gaula* (publ. 1508), a novel of chivalry which had several sequels and was considerably imitated. The main sequels were *Las sergas de Esplandián* (1510) and *Amadís de Grecia* (1530). Imitations include *Palmerín de Oliva* (1511), *Primaleón* (1512) and *Palmerín de Inglaterra* (1547). Other notable Spanish novels from this period are *La Celestina* (1499–1502), *Abencerraje* (early 16th c.), and two famous Spanish picaresque novels (*q.v.*), *Guzmán de Alfarache* (1599–1604) and *Lazarillo de Tormes* (1554). The greatest of all Spanish novels is Cervantes's *Don Quixote de la Mancha* (1605, 1615) which satirized chivalry and a number of the earlier novels.

After the death of Cervantes the Spanish novel, having begun so promisingly, went into decline until the 19th c.

Apart from *Don Quixote* the only other major work in European literature at this time which could be called a novel is Rabelais's *Gargantua* (1534) and *Pantagruel* (1532). Both these can be classed as novels of phantasy, or mythopoeic. It is a kind which has remained popular until the present day. Some notable instances of this 'line' are *Gulliver's Travels* (1726), *Candide* (1759), *The Shaving of Shagpat* (1856), *Zarathustra* (1883–91), *The First Men in the Moon* (1901) and scores of works which may be loosely described as science fiction (*q.v.*).

In England, at the end of the 16th c., the novel was in its infancy. From the closing years of the century there date two important works in the evolution of the extended prose narrative. They are Lyly's *Euphues* (in two parts, 1578 and 1580), and Sir Philip Sidney's pastoral romance *Arcadia* (1590). Other minor but interesting attempts at prose narrative from this period are Gascoigne's *The Adventures of Master F. J.* (1575), Greene's *The Carde of Fancie* (1587), Nashe's *The Unfortunate Traveller* (1594), and Deloney's three tales: *Jack of Newbury*, *Thomas of Reading* and *The Gentle Craft* (1596–1600).

In the 17th c. there is still no more major advance in prose narrative and the novel form, except for Mme de Lafayette's *La Princesse de Clèves* (1678) – a landmark in the history of the novel. Minor works of note in England were E. Foord's *Ornatus and Artesia* (1634) and Mrs Aphra Behn's *Oroonoko* (*c.* 1688). Bunyan's *Pilgrim's Progress* (1678) can be taken as a kind of allegorical novel. In France there was also D'Urfé's pastoral romance *L' Astrée* (1607–28), which set a vogue satirized by Sorel in *Le Berger extravagant* (1627–8). Minor 17th c. French works were Sorel's *Francion* (1623) and Furetière's *Roman bourgeois* (1666).

Early in the 18th c. Congreve published *Incognita: or, Love and Duty Reconciled* (1713). He called it a novel and in his agreeable preface gives us his conception of what a novel is (an early example of a definition of the genre). First he speaks of romances, which were generally composed 'of the Constant Loves and invincible Courages of Heros, Heroins, Kings and Queens, Mortals of the first Rank', and of the extraordinary things that happen in romances. But novels, he declares, 'are of a more familiar Nature; Come near us, and represent to us Intrigues in Practice, delight us with Accidents and odd Events, but not such as are wholly unusual or unpresidented, such which being not so distant from our Belief bring also the pleasure nearer us. Romances give more Wonder, Novels more Delight.'

Soon after this (1719) Defoe published his story of adventure – *Robinson Crusoe*; one in a long tradition of desert island fiction (*q.v.*). From now on the novel comes of age and within another seventy years is a major and matured form. Defoe's other two main contributions to the novel form were *Moll Flanders* (1722), a sociological novel (*q.v.*), and *A Journal of the Plague Year* (1722) – a reconstruction and thus a piece of historical fiction.

No doubt because the novel form was in an embryonic state, and there were few if any rules for it, the range and variety in the 18th c. is remarkable. Here there is a space to mention only some of the main European works: Lesage's picaresque *Gil Blas* (1715, 1724, 1735), Marivaux's *La Vie de Marianne* (1731–41); Prévost's *Manon Lescaut* (1731); Richardson's *Pamela* (1740), *Clarissa* (1747, 1748) and *Sir Charles Grandison* (1754); Fielding's *Joseph Andrews* (1742), his satirical romance *Jonathan Wild* (1743) and *Tom Jones* (1749); Smollett's *Roderick Random* (1748), *Peregrine Pickle* (1751) and *Humphry Clinker* (1771); Sterne's *Tristram Shandy* (1760–67); Rousseau's *La Nouvelle Héloïse* (1761); Goldsmith's *The Vicar of Wakefield* (1766); Goethe's *Werther* (1774); Laclos's *Les Liaisons dangereuses* (1782); Diderot's *La Religieuse* (1796). To these should be added Voltaire's philosophical tales *Zadig* (1747) and *Candide* (1759) and Johnson's philosophical tale *Rasselas* (1759). A notable characteristic of the novel in the 18th c. is the use of the letter. Several of the above works are classified as epistolary novels (*q.v.*).

Minor but important works in English literature during this period are: Charles Johnstone's *Chrysal, or the Adventures of a Guinea* (1760); Walpole's *The Castle of Otranto* (1764), one of the earliest examples of the Gothic novel (*q.v.*); Henry Brooke's *The Fool of Quality* (1765–70); Henry Mackenzie's *The Man of Feeling* (1771); Richard Graves's *The Spiritual Quixote* (1772); Mrs Clara Reeve's *The Champion of Virtue, a Gothic Tale* (1777); Fanny Burney's *Evelina* (1778); Beckford's *Vathek* (1786); Mrs Charlotte Smith's *The Old Manor House* (1793); William Godwin's *Caleb Williams* (1794); and Robert Bage's *Hermsprong, or Man As He is Not* (1796), a very early instance of the propaganda novel (*q.v.*). Four years later Maria Edgeworth produced what is taken to be the first regional novel (*q.v.*), *Castle Rackrent*.

In the early years of the 19th c. two figures dominate English fiction: Sir Walter Scott and Jane Austen. Scott was the greatest single influence on fiction in the 19th c. and in his time was infinitely more famous than Jane Austen. He was a European figure, an immensely prolific writer – and he established the historical novel (*q.v.*). Some of his better known works are: *Waverley* (1814), *Guy Mannering* (1815), *Old Mortality* (1816), *The Antiquary* (1816), *Rob Roy* (1817), *The Heart of Midlothian* (1818), *The Bride of Lammermoor* (1819), *Ivanhoe* (1819), *Kenilworth* (1821), *Quentin Durward* (1823), *Redgauntlet* (1824), *The Talisman* (1825) and *Woodstock* (1826).

Jane Austen was less prolific. Her major works are: *Sense and Sensibility* (1811), *Pride and Prejudice* (1813), *Emma* (1815) and *Persuasion* (1818).

Minor novelists of note who were active at the beginning of the century were: John Galt (1779–1839), who wrote *Annals of the Parish* (1821); Susan Ferrier (1782–1854), who wrote *Marriage* (1818); Michael Scott (1789–1835), who wrote *Tom Cringle's Log* (1833); and Thomas Love Peacock (1785–1866), author of *Headlong Hall* (1816), *Nightmare Abbey* (1818), *Maid Marian* (1822), *Crotchet Castle* (1831) and *Gryll Grange* (1861). A remarkable curiosity from the period is James Hogg's *The Private Memoirs and Confessions of a Justified Sinner* (1824). We should also mention J. J. Morier's *The Adventures of Hajji Baba* (1824), Mary Russell Mitford's *Our Village* (1824–32) and *Belford Regis* (1835), Frederick Marryat's *Peter Simple* (1834) and his popular adventure stories *Mr Midshipman Easy* (1836) and *Masterman Ready* (1841), Bulwer Lytton's *Falkland* (1827), *Pelham* (1828) and *Eugene Aram* (1832). During the first half of the century, also, Disraeli made a name for himself as a writer of distinguished political novels (among the first of their kind), namely *Vivian Grey* (1826), *Coningsby* (1844), *Sybil* (1845) and *Tancred* (1847). He also wrote a *roman à clef* (*q.v.*), *Venetia* (1837), on the lives of Byron and Shelley.

The middle years of the 19th c. witnessed the most astonishingly prolific output of fiction, especially from Dickens and Anthony Trollope, and it is noticeable that much of this fiction has lasted. The efforts of Dickens included *Sketches by Boz* (1839), *The Posthumous Papers of the Pickwick Club* (1837), *Oliver Twist* (1838), *Nicholas Nickleby* (1839), *The Old Curiosity Shop* (1841), *Barnaby Rudge* (1841), *A Christmas Carol* (1843), *Martin Chuzzlewit* (1844), *Dombey and Son* (1848), *David Copperfield* (1850), *Bleak House* (1853), *Hard Times* (1854), *Little Dorrit* (1857), *A Tale of Two Cities* (1859), *Great Expectations* (1861), *Our Mutual Friend* (1865) and *Edwin Drood* (1870), which was unfinished. Trollope published the Barsetshire chronicles, among which the better known are *The Warden* (1855), *Barchester Towers* (1857) and *The Last Chronicle of Barset* (1867); plus *Dr Thorne* (1858), *Framley Parsonage* (1861), *The Small House at Allington* (1864), *The Belton Estate* (1865), *The Claverings* (1867), *Phineas Finn* (1869) and *The Eustace Diamonds* (1873). Between them Dickens and Trollope produced an English *comédie humaine* to rival that of Balzac.

Thackeray, born a year earlier than Dickens, was active at the same time. His main novels were *Barry Lyndon* (1844), *Vanity Fair* (1847–8), *Pendennis* (1849–50), *Esmond* (1852), *The Newcomes* (1854–5) and *The Virginians* (1858–9). George Eliot, too, began publishing her novels in the 1850s; most famous of which are *Scenes of Clerical Life* (1858), *Adam Bede* (1859), *The Mill on the Floss* (1860), *Silas Marner* (1861), *Romola* (1862–3), *Felix Holt* (1866), *Middlemarch* (1871–2) and *Daniel Deronda* (1874–6).

We should also mention R. S. Surtees, a minor comic novelist of merit who invented two immortal characters of English fiction in the shape of Jorrocks and James Pigg. Some of Surtees's better known books are *Jorrocks's Jaunts and Jollities* (1838), *Hillingdon Hall* (1845), *Hawbuck Grange* (1847), *Mr Sponge's Sporting Tour* (1853) and *Handley Cross* (1843).

To the 1840s belong the classic works of the Brontë sisters: Anne, Emily and Charlotte. In 1847 Emily published *Wuthering Heights*, and in the same year Charlotte published *Jane Eyre* and Anne published *Agnes Grey*, which she followed in the next year with *The Tenant of Wildfell Hall.*

Among minor novelists we should note Mrs Gaskell, who wrote *Mary Barton* (1848), *Cranford* (1853), *North and South* (1855) and *Wives and Daughters* (1864–6); Charlotte M. Yonge, who still has a coterie of devoted readers, who wrote *The Heir of Redclyffe* (1853), *Heartsease* (1854) and *The Daisy Chain* (1856); George Borrow, author of *Lavengro* (1851) and *Romany Rye* (1857), who is still supported by 'Old Borrovians'; Charles Kingsley, who wrote *Alton Locke* (1850), and his brother Henry Kingsley now chiefly remembered for *Geoffrey Hamlyn* (1859); Sheridan Le Fanu, perhaps better known as a writer of good short stories, but who also produced the novels *The House by the Churchyard* (1863) and *Uncle Silas* (1864); Charles Reade, some of whose best works were *It Is Never Too Late to Mend* (1853), *The Cloister and the Hearth* (1861), *Foul Play* (1869) and *Put Yourself in His Place* (1870); George Meredith (whom many consider a major novelist), a prolific writer who is mainly remembered for *The Ordeal of Richard*

Feverel (1859), *Rhoda Fleming* (1865), *Vittoria* (1866), *The Adventures of Henry Richmond* (1871) and *The Egoist* (1879); Wilkie Collins, practically the first English novelist to write a detective story (*q.v.*), whose three most notable works were *The Woman in White* (1860), *Armadale* (1866) and *The Moonstone* (1868).

During approximately the last quarter of the 19th c. the most distinguished English novelist was Thomas Hardy. In 1871 he published *Desperate Remedies*, and in the next twenty-five years wrote the following outstanding novels: *Under the Greenwood Tree* (1872), *Far from the Madding Crowd* (1874), *The Return of the Native* (1878), *The Trumpet-Major* (1880), *The Mayor of Casterbridge* (1886), *The Woodlanders* (1887), *Tess of the D'Urbervilles* (1891) and *Jude the Obscure* (1896). Hardy is England's most eminent regional novelist.

During the 1880s and 1890s R. L. Stevenson published several novels which have become classics: *Treasure Island* (1883), *Kidnapped* (1886), *The Master of Ballantrae* (1889) and the unfinished *Weir of Hermiston* (1896). A contemporary of Stevenson, Mark Rutherford, published two autobiographical-type novels: *The Autobiography of Mark Rutherford* (1881) and *Mark Rutherford's Deliverance* (1885). A little later George Gissing, one of the best of English minor novelists and a powerful portrayer of realism, wrote (among numerous other books): *New Grub Street* (1891), *Born in Exile* (1892), *The Odd Women* (1893) and *The Private Papers of Henry Ryecroft* (1903). And in 1885 George Moore, the Irishman, published *A Mummer's Wife*. This he followed with *Esther Waters* (1894), *The Brook Kerith* (1916) and *Aphrodite in Aulis* (1930).

The development of the novel as a popular form in the 19th c. was a European phenomenon, and one of the most remarkable features of its history is the speed with which it matured. From nowhere, so it seemed, great novelists sprang up and produced novels which became and remained classics. Early in the century there were, for example, Chateaubriand's *René* (1802), Benjamin Constant's *Adolphe* (1816), Manzoni's *I promessi sposi* (1827), Stendhal's *Le Rouge et le Noir* (1830) and his *La Chartreuse de Parme* (1839), Pushkin's *Dubrovsky* (1832–3) and his *A Captain's Daughter* (1836) and Lermontov's *A Hero of Our Times* (1840), and the dominating figure of Balzac who from the 1820s until his death in 1850 produced novel after novel with amazing rapidity; some of the better known being *Les Chouans* (1829), *La Peau de chagrin* (1831), *Eugénie Grandet* (1833), *Le Père Goriot* (1834–5) and *Le Cousin Pons* (1847). At approximately the same time Dumas *père* was achieving immense success with his novels *The Three Musketeers* (1844), *Twenty Years After* (1845) and *The Count of Monte-Cristo* (1844–5). In 1842 Gogol published *Dead Souls*, one of the most outstanding comic novels. In 1846 Dostoievski published *Poor People*, which he was to follow with *Crime and Punishment* (1866), *The Idiot* (1866), *The Possessed* (1871–2) and *The Brothers Karamazov* (1880). The third most famous Russian writer of the mid years of the century was Turgenev, who, as a novelist, is chiefly remembered for *A Nest of Gentlefolk* (1859), *Fathers and Sons* (1862), *Smoke* (1867) and *Virgin Soil* (1876). In 1859 Goncharov published *Oblomov* – a masterpiece among comic novels. In the latter part of the 19th c. the dominating figure was Tolstoy, whose epic novels *War and Peace* (1865–72) and *Anna Karenina* (1875–6) remained unsurpassed in Russian literature.

In France, during the second half of the 19th c. the leading novelists were Flaubert, Victor Hugo, Zola, Guy de Maupassant, Huysmans and Anatole France. Flaubert made his name with *Madame Bovary* (1857). His other principal works were *Salammbô* (1862), *L'Education sentimentale* (1869), *La Tentation de Saint Antoine* (1874) and the unfinished *Bouvard et Pécuchet* (1881). This last was a severe exposure of human stupidity and incorporated Flaubert's ideas about the *idée reçue* (*q.v.*). Victor Hugo, who, long before, had published *Notre-Dame de Paris* (1831), produced three of his finest novels in the 1860s; namely, *Les Misérables* (1862), *Les Travailleurs de la mer* (1866) and *L'Homme qui rit* (1869). Zola, apart from Balzac one of the most prolific novelists in 19th c. France, is particularly important in connection with the theories of realism and naturalism (*qq.v.*). His *magnum opus* was the series of novels *Les Rougon-Macquart*. There were twenty in all and he described them as 'the natural and social history of a family under the Second Empire'. Before embarking on these he wrote *Thérèse Raquin* (1867). Maupassant's two best novels were *Une Vie* (1883) and *Bel-Ami* (1885). Huysmans's two extraordinary novels *A rebours* (1884) and *Là-bas* (1891) have become classics of their kind. Huysmans is especially associated with 19th c. theories of aestheticism and the doctrine of art for art's sake (*qq.v.*). Anatole France, renowned for his irony and wit (*qq.v.*), wrote many novels among which the following are outstanding: *L'Etui de nacre* (1892), *Les Opinions de Jérôme Coignard* (1893), *La Rôtisserie de la Reine Pédauque* (1893), *L'Orme du Mail* (1897), *Le Mannequin d'osier* (1897), *M. Bergeret à Paris* (1901), *L'Ile des pingouins* (1908) and *La Révolte des anges* (1914). Late in the 19th c. and at the beginning of the 20th Maurice Barrès published three didactic trilogies: *Le Culte du moi* (1888–91), *Le Roman de l'énergie nationale* (1897–1902) and *Les Bastions de l'Est* (1905–21), plus the novel *La Colline inspirée* (1913). The trilogies were ambitious and complex chronicles of his times.

During much of the 19th c. the novel form was enriched by a diversity of French writers, among whom we should also give special mention to the following: Prosper Mérimée, who excelled at the *nouvelle* and who also wrote *Chronique du règne de Charles IX* (1829); Alfred de Vigny, one of whose best novels was *Cinq-Mars* (1826); George Sand, a very prolific novelist, some of whose best novels were *Indiana* (1832), *Lélia* (1833) and *La Mare au diable* (1846); Alphonse Kerr, author of nearly a hundred novels of varying quality; and Théophile Gautier, author of *Mademoiselle de Maupin* (1835), *Le Roman de la momie* (1858) and *Le Capitaine Fracasse* (1863).

Other exceptionally gifted European novelists in the second half of the 19th c. were: the Portuguese Queirós, who wrote several fine novels, particularly *O crime do Padre Amaro* (1876), *O primo Basílio* (1878) and *Os Maias* (1888); the Italian Giovanni Verga, whose later work was outstanding, especially *I Malavoglia* (1881) and *Mastro-Don Gesualdo* (1889); and the Pole Sienkiewicz, who became famous for his *Quo Vadis* (1896).

Right at the end of the 18th c. the novel began to be established in Germany. Goethe's *Bildungsroman* (*q.v.*), *Wilhelm Meisters Lehrjahre*, came out in 1795–6. In 1821 the sequel appeared: *Wilhelm Meisters Wanderjahre oder Die Entsagenden*. At the turn of the century several other prominent German writers were active in developing the form. Hölderlin published his only novel, *Hyperion*, in 1797 and 1799 – this was a *Briefroman* (*q.v.*) or epistolary novel. In 1801 Clemens Brentano published *Godwi oder Das steinerne Bild der Mutter*, and in the following year appeared Novalis's unfinished *Heinrich von Ofterdingen*. Jean Paul wrote two notable novels in the same period: *Titan* (1800–03) and *Flegeljahre* (1804–5). At this time Hoffmann and Kleist were establishing the short story (*q.v.*) and the *Novelle*. In fact, the *Novelle* was to become the favoured form in Germany during the 19th c. In 1810 Ludwig Arnim published *Armut, Reichtum, Schuld und Busse der Gräfin Dolores*. Eichendorff's two main works were *Ahnung und Gegenwart* (1815) and *Aus dem Leben eines Taugenichts* (1826). Gottfried Keller was prolific during the 19th c. and is particularly remembered for *Der grüne Heinrich* (1854–5). Later, Theodor

Fontane became one of the outstanding novelists of the era, with such works as *Vor dem Storm* (1878), *L'Adultera* (1882), *Graf Petöfy* (1884), *Cécile* (1887), *Irrungen Wirrungen* (1888), *Stine* (1890), *Unwiederbringlich* (1891), *Frau Jenny Treibel* (1892), *Effi Briest* (1895), *Die Poggenpuhls* (1896) and the conversation piece *Der Stechlin* (1898). Many other German writers published novels during the 19th c.

After falling into desuetude in the 17th c. the Spanish novel was revived with some splendour in the 19th c., during which period the dominating figure was Pérez Galdós, a writer who has often been compared with justice to Balzac and Dickens. He was immensely prolific. In 1873 he published the first of a sequence of forty-six historical novels dealing with the history of Spain from Trafalgar (1805) to the Restoration (1875). The whole series was titled *Episodios nacionales* and is one of the longest novel cycles in existence. Apart from this marathon he is remembered for other individual novels: *Doña Perfecta* (1876), *Fortunata i Jacinta* (1886–7) and *Angel Guerra* (1890–91). Roughly contemporary with Galdós was Juan Valera, author of *Pepita Jiménez* (1874) and *El Comendador Mendoza* (1893). Pereda, born in 1833, was a fine regional novelist. Two of his better known books were *Sotilega* (1884) and *Peñas Arriba* (1894). Born in the same year, Alarcón attained fame with *El sombrero de tres picos* (1874). His *El capitán Veneno* was also impressive. The Countess Emilia Pardo Bazán, famous for her wit, her brains and her ugliness, wrote some distinguished novels about Galician life; in particular *Los Pazos de Ulloa* (1886). Two minor writers, born like the Countess in the 1850s and who lived on into the 20th c., were Leopoldo Alas y Urena, whose best novel is probably *La regenta* (1884–5), and Palacio Valdés, who wrote *La hermana San Sulpicio* (1889) and *La aldea perdida* (1903). The most famous Spanish novelist of the later 19th c. was certainly Vicente Blasco Ibañez, who was considerably influenced by Maupassant and Zola and therefore by the theories of naturalism and realism. He was also influenced by the Spanish schools of *costumbrismo* (*q.v.*) and *regionalismo*. His major novels were *Flor de Mayo* (1896), *La barraca* (1898) and *Cañas y barro* (1902). He wrote many other novels and is one of the few writers in history to have become a millionaire.

At the very end of the 18th c. Charles Brockden Brown helped to establish the American novel with his Gothic romances *Wieland* (1798), *Arthur Mervyn* (1799–1800), *Ormond* (1799) and *Edgar Huntly* (1799). Better known now is James Fenimore Cooper, author of stirring stories of frontier life and the sea. Some of his books are: *The Spy* (1821), one of earliest of spy novels (*q.v.*), *The Pioneers* (1823), *The Last of the Mohicans* (1826), *The Pathfinder* (1840), *The Deerslayer* (1841) and *The Redskins* (1846). In 1851 Herman Melville published *Moby-Dick*, a classic of American literature, with many stylistic peculiarities. To the mid-century, also, belong the major works of Nathaniel Hawthorne – particularly *Twice-Told Tales* (1837), *The Scarlet Letter* (1850), *The House of the Seven Gables* (1851), *The Blithedale Romance* (1852) and *The Marble Faun* (1860). A contemporary was William Dean Howells, an exponent of realism. His principal novels were *Their Wedding Journal* (1872), *The Rise of Silas Lapham* (1885), *Indian Summer* (1886) and *A Hazard of New Fortunes* (1890). In 1884 Sarah Jewett, a neglected writer, published *A Country Doctor*, which she followed with *A Marsh Island* (1885) and *The Country of the Pointed Firs* (1896). At the same time, Frank Norris, also neglected, published an unfinished trilogy of distinction, titled *The Epic of the Wheat*: the two volumes were *The Octopus* (1901) and *The Pit* (1903). In 1899 he had published *McTeague*. During the same period Mark Twain produced *The Adventures of Tom Sawyer* (1876), *The Adventures of Huckleberry Finn* (1885) and *Pudd'nhead Wilson* (1894).

During the last thirty years of the century and in the opening years of the 20th c. the dominating American novelist was Henry James, who spent much of his life in Europe. Out of his many novels the following are of especial excellence: *Washington Square* (1881), *The Portrait of a Lady* (1881), *The Bostonians* (1886), *The Princess Casamassima* (1886), *What Maisie Knew* (1897), *The Spoils of Poynton* (1897), *The Awkward Age* (1899), *The Wings of the Dove* (1902), *The Ambassadors* (1903), *The Golden Bowl* (1904).

In the opening years of the 20th c. three Englishmen and one Pole writing in English were pre-eminent among British novelists. They were Arnold Bennett, E. M. Forster, H. G. Wells and Joseph Conrad. Of the seventy-odd books that Bennett wrote he is now remembered for six of enduring merit; namely, *Anna of the Five Towns* (1901), *The Old Wives' Tale* (1908), *Clayhanger* (1910), *Hilda Lessways* (1911), *These Twain* (1916) and *Riceyman Steps* (1923). During the same period, E. M. Forster, whose total output was slight, published *Where Angels Fear to Tread* (1905), *A Room with a View* (1908), *Howards End* (1910) and *A Passage to India* (1924). The chief novels of H. G. Wells were *Love and Mr Lewisham* (1900), *First Men in the Moon* (1901), *Kipps* (1905), *Ann*

Veronica (1909), *Tono Bungay* (1909) and *The History of Mr Polly* (1910). Conrad had made a name for himself in 1895 with *Almayer's Folly* and then in 1900 produced his first major novel in the shape of *Lord Jim.* This he followed with *Romance* (1903), *Nostromo* (1904), *The Secret Agent* (1907), *Under Western Eyes* (1911), *Chance* (1914) and *Victory* (1915). A minor novel was *The Rover* (1923).

Lesser works of great quality at this time are many and various and certainly include Kipling's *Kim* (1901), George Douglas Brown's *The House with the Green Shutters* (1901), Arthur Morrison's *A Child of the Jago* (1896) and *The Hole in the Wall* (1902), Samuel Butler's *The Way of All Flesh* (1903), May Sinclair's *The Divine Fire* (1904), William de Morgan's *Joseph Vance* (1906), Max Beerbohm's *Zuleika Dobson* (1911), Gilbert Cannon's *Round the Corner* (1913), Compton Mackenzie's *Sinister Street* (1913, 1914), W. L. George's *The Making of an Englishman* (1914), Norman Douglas's *South Wind* (1917) and several novels by J. D. Beresford – especially *Jacob Stahl* (1911), *A Candidate for Truth* (1912), *Goslings* (1913), *The House in Demetrius Road* (1914) and *The Invisible Event* (1915). In 1914 Robert Tressell published *The Ragged Trousered Philanthropists.* The full version of the original text of this remarkable book was not published until 1955. Some would add Hugh Walpole's *Mr Perrin and Mr Traill* (1911) and G. F. Bradby's *The Lanchester Tradition* (1913), classics among school stories; and Ronald Firbank's *Valmouth* (1919).

While most of these authors were drawing towards the end of their writing careers, three other Englishmen were at the same time in the early stages of theirs and all are major though very different figures in the history of the English novel. They were Somerset Maugham, D. H. Lawrence and Wyndham Lewis. Maugham published *Liza of Lambeth* in 1897, and followed it with *Of Human Bondage* (1915) and *The Moon and Sixpence* (1919). Much later came *Cakes and Ale* (1930) and *The Razor's Edge* (1944). Lawrence, championed by F. R. Leavis, has come to be regarded as one of the great English novelists. His principal works were: *The White Peacock* (1911), *Sons and Lovers* (1913), *The Rainbow* (1915), *Women in Love* (1920), *The Plumed Serpent* (1926) and *Lady Chatterley's Lover* (1928). Very different from these two, but highly original and eccentric, was Wyndham Lewis, the inventor of vorticism (*q.v.*). His best known novels are: *Tarr* (1918), *The Childermass* (1928), the first part of the trilogy *The Human Age, The Apes of God* (1930), *The Revenge for Love* (1937); and, in 1955, the second and third parts of *The Human Age.*

In 1915 Dorothy Richardson was the first English novelist to introduce the stream of consciousness technique (*q.v.*). Her marathon sequence of novels *Pilgrimage* ran to twelve volumes, which came out at intervals from 1915 to 1967.

In 1916 James Joyce published *A Portrait of the Artist as a Young Man*, in which he also employed the stream of consciousness technique. He perfected this in *Ulysses* (1922). In *Finnegans Wake* (1939) he pushed it to its probable limits, and also experimented with language to a point where he seemed likely to transcend the limits of his medium. After Joyce the novel was never quite the same again. His influence has been profound and, as one of the great innovators, he has had many imitators.

During the 1920s and 1930s the English novel flourished. So many excellent books were written by so many gifted writers that here there is space to mention only a handful. There was, for example, Ford Madox Ford (in 1915 he had published his admirable *The Good Soldier*), who wrote the Tietjens series: *Some Do Not* (1924), *No More Parades* (1925), *A Man Could Stand Up* (1926) and *The Last Post* (1928). There was L. H. Myers, a rare instance of the 'philosopher' novelist, who wrote *The Orissers* (1922), *The 'Clio'* (1925) and *The Near and the Far* (1929) – this being the first of a tetralogy; the others were *Prince Jali* (1931), *The Root and the Flower* (1935) and *The Pool of Vishnu* (1940). During roughly the same period, Virginia Woolf, influenced by Joyce and Dorothy Richardson, was experimenting with the stream of consciousness technique and she is chiefly remembered for *Jacob's Room* (1922), *Mrs Dalloway* (1925), *To the Lighthouse* (1927), *The Waves* (1931) and *Between the Acts* (1941). In 1922, John Galsworthy, a prolific and much more conventional novelist, published *The Forsyte Saga.* By the 1920s P. G. Wodehouse was well established as a comic novelist with his two main characters Jeeves and Bertie Wooster. His writing career lasted for over seventy years. In the 1920s, too, Aldous Huxley began to publish his novels, among which we should mention *Crome Yellow* (1921), *Antic Hay* (1923) and *Point Counter Point* (1928). In 1932 appeared his anti-utopian tour de force *Brave New World* and, in 1948, *Ape and Essence*. Others who established themselves in the 1930s were James Hilton, author of *The Lost Horizon* (1933) and the *novella*-length *Good-Bye Mr Chips* (1934); James Hanley (a neglected writer), who published fiction for fifty years, including *Drift* (1930), *The Furys* (1935), *Secret Journey* (1936), *Our Time is Gone* (1940) – and many others; and Storm Jameson, who was also prolific and is remembered for

Company Parade (1934), *Love in Winter* (1935) and *None Turn Back* (1936). In 1928 Evelyn Waugh began his career as a witty satirist with *Decline and Fall.* A succession of novels followed: *Vile Bodies* (1930), *Black Mischief* (1932), *A Handful of Dust* (1934), *Scoop* (1938), *Brideshead Revisited* (1945), *The Loved One* (1948) and the trilogy *Sword of Honour*, the first volume of which came out in 1952. Elizabeth Bowen published her first novel, *The Hotel*, in 1927. Later came *To the North* (1932), *The Death of the Heart* (1938) and *The Heat of the Day* (1949). Another distinguished female novelist who started her career at about the same time was Ivy Compton-Burnett. Some of her many novels were: *Brothers and Sisters* (1929), *Men and Wives* (1931), *Daughters and Sons* (1937), *Parents and Children* (1941), *Elders and Betters* (1944) and *Darkness and Day* (1951).

From the late 1920s and 1930s a number of other novels have stood the test of time and changes of taste. For instance, J. B. Priestley's *The Good Companions* (1929) and *Angel Pavement* (1930); Richard Aldington's *Death of a Hero* (1929) and *All Men are Enemies* (1933); H. M. Tomlinson's *All Our Yesterdays* (1930); Vita Sackville-West's *All Passion Spent* (1931); Stella Gibbons's *Cold Comfort Farm* (1932), a clever satire on the novels of Mary Webb (e.g. *Precious Bane*, 1924) and on the novel of the soil (*q.v.*) in general; Lewis Grassic Gibbon's trilogy *A Scot's Quair* (1932), 1933, 1934); Walter Greenwood's *Love on the Dole* (1933), an impressive documentary novel (*q.v.*); Winifred Holtby's regional novel *South Riding* (1936); V. S. Pritchett's *Dead Men Leading* (1932) and *Nothing Like Leather* (1935); the novels of the Powys brothers, especially T. F. Powys's *Mr Weston's Good Wine* (1927), J. C. Powys's *Wolf Solent* (1929) and his *A Glastonbury Romance* (1932); Robert Graves's *I, Claudius* (1934) and his *Claudius the God* (1934); Christopher Isherwood's *Mr Norris Changes Trains* (1935) and *Goodbye to Berlin* (1939); Rebecca West's *The Judge* (1922) and *The Thinking Reed* (1932); Charles Morgan's *The Fountain* (1932) and *Sparkenbroke* (1936); Charles Williams's 'metaphysical thrillers' *War in Heaven* (1930) and *The Place of the Lion* (1931).

Perhaps the most famous English novelist to have begun his career in the 1920s, and to have published novels consistently for some sixty years, is Graham Greene. His first was *Babbling April* (1925). Since then he has published over twenty novels and entertainments (*q.v.*), two of which have been suppressed by the author. Among the more famous works are: *The Man Within*

(1929), *Stamboul Train* (1932), *Brighton Rock* (1938), *The Confidential Agent* (1939), *The Power and the Glory* (1940), *The Heart of the Matter* (1948), *The End of the Affair* (1951), *The Quiet American* (1955), *Our Man in Havana* (1958), *A Burnt-Out Case* (1961), *The Comedians* (1966), *Travels with My Aunt* (1969), *The Honorary Consul* (1973), *The Human Factor* (1978), *Monsignor Quixote* (1982) and *The Captain and the Enemy* (1988).

Henry Green, a more occasional novelist of great gifts, also began in the 1920s with *Blindness* (1926). This he followed with *Living* (1929), *Party Going* (1939), *Loving* (1945), *Nothing* (1950) and *Doting* (1952). An even more occasional novelist is Richard Hughes, who became famous with *A High Wind in Jamaica* (1929). Later came *In Hazard* (1938), and much later *The Fox in the Attic* (1961), the first part of a trilogy. To these should be added Rosamund Lehmann, one of the best modern novelists. Her main works are: *Invitation to the Waltz* (1932), *The Weather in the Streets* (1936), *The Ballad and the Source* (1944) and *The Echoing Grove* (1953).

Since approximately 1940 several other distinguished writers have enhanced the novel in Britain. For example, there are Arthur Koestler's tour de force *Darkness at Noon* (1940); many novels by H. E. Bates, especially *Fair Stood the Wind for France* (1944), *The Purple Plain* (1947) and *Love for Lydia* (1954); several by P. H. Newby, namely *Agents and Witnesses* (1947), *A Season in England* (1951), *The Picnic at Sakkara* (1955), *A Guest and his Going* (1959) and *The Barbary Light* (1962); Gerald Hanley's *The Consul at Sunset* (1951) and *Drinkers of Darkness* (1955); Malcolm Lowry's *Under the Volcano* (1947); L. P. Hartley's *The Shrimp and the Anemone* (1944), *The Sixth Heaven* (1946), *Eustace and Hilda* (1947) and *The Go-Between* (1953); George Orwell's *Nineteen Eighty-Four* (1949). To these should be added Joyce Cary, one of whose earlier works was *The African Witch* (1936). Later came *Mister Johnson* (1939). Then two major trilogies of exceptional merit: first, *Herself Surprised* (1941), *To be a Pilgrim* (1942) and *The Horse's Mouth* (1944); second, *A Prisoner of Grace* (1952), *Except the Lord* (1953) and *Not Honour More* (1955). In 1945 Elizabeth Taylor published her first novel, *At Mrs Lippincote's*. Many excellent novels were to follow, including *A Wreath of Roses* (1950) and *Mrs Palfrey at the Claremont* (1972). She excelled at the depiction of English middle-class life.

The trilogy, the tetralogy, the *roman-fleuve* (*q.v.*) and the chronicle or saga novel (*q.v.*) have proved particularly attractive schemes in the 20th c. No doubt the influences of Balzac and Zola are discernible here. In recent times, as far as the novel in Britain is concerned, three instances of chronicle may be cited: C. P. Snow's *Strangers and Brothers* sequence, which began in 1940 with *Strangers and Brothers*; Henry Williamson's *Chronicle of Ancient Sunlight* (1951–69) in fifteen volumes; and Anthony Powell's twelve-volume sequence *A Dance to the Music of Time*, which started with *A Question of Upbringing* in 1951 and was completed in 1976.

Since James Joyce the main contributions from Irish novelists have come from Liam O'Flaherty, particularly *The Informer* (1926), *Famine* (1937) and *Land* (1946); from Sean O'Faolain, with *A Nest of Simple Folk* (1933) and *Come Back to Erin* (1940); from Flann O'Brien with his remarkable anti-novel (*q.v.*) *At Swim-Two-Birds* (1939); and from Samuel Beckett, who was influenced by Joyce. His four main novels are *Murphy* (1938), *Watt* (1944), *Molloy* (1951) and, best of all, *Malone Dies* (1951). Since the 1950s three of the younger generation of Irish writers have achieved distinction in the novel: Edna O'Brien, Brian Moore and William Trevor. Edna O'Brien, much concerned with the role and position of women in society, published her first novel, *The Country Girls*, in 1960. She followed this success with *The Lonely Girl* (1962), *Girls in Their Married Bliss* (1963), *August is a Wicked Month* (1965), *A Pagan Place* (1971), *Night* (1972) and *Johnny I Hardly Knew You* (1977). Brian Moore wrote a number of outstanding novels, including *Judith Hearne* (1955), *The Feast of Lupercal* (1957), *The Luck of Ginger Coffey* (1960), *I am Mary Dunne* (1968), *Catholics* (1972), *The Mangan Inheritance* (1979), *The Cold Heaven* (1983) and *The Colour of Blood* (1987). Among William Trevor's most memorable novels are *The Old Boys* (1964), *Mrs Eckdorf in O'Neill's Hotel* (1969), *Elizabeth Alone* (1973), *The Children of Dynmouth* (1976) and *Fools of Fortune* (1983).

From the mid-1950s – the period when some people began to claim that the novel was 'dead' – until the late 1980s the novel in Britain continued to show remarkable diversity and resilience, and the form has continued to attract large numbers of gifted writers. Even a 'short' short-list would contain the names of over a hundred. Not a few have tried all sorts of experiments (hence, for instance, the anti-novel). Many novelists have stuck to well-tried conventional methods with minimal devices and a total absence of gimmicks. Some have been influenced by what has come to be called 'magic realism' (*q.v.*). Some have developed a neo-Gothic element. There follow some of the leading writers with mention of a few of their titles.

Kingsley Amis achieved popular renown with *Lucky Jim* in 1954 and thereafter produced novels of variable quality at regular intervals, including *That Uncertain Feeling* (1955), *Take a Girl Like You* (1960), *One Fat Englishman* (1963), *Jake's Thing* (1978) and *The Old Devils* (1986). His contemporaries John Wain and Alan Sillitoe (all three were associated with the so-called angry young man, *q.v.*, phase of the fifties) also received some acclaim. Wain's first novel was *Hurry on Down* (1953), which he followed with *The Contenders* (1958), *A Travelling Woman* (1959) and *Strike the Father Dead* (1962). Sillitoe came to fame with *Saturday Night and Sunday Morning* (1958), but later novels in the sixties and seventies did not live up to the promise of his first; he had more success with short stories (e.g. *The Loneliness of the Long Distance Runner*, 1959). Francis King published two good novels in the fifties: *The Dividing Stream* (1951) and *The Widow* (1957); these he followed with *The Custom House* (1961), *The Action* (1979), the psychological thriller *Act of Darkness* (1983), *Voices in an Empty Room* (1984) and *Visiting Cards* (1990), all impressive. In 1958 Ruth Prawer Jhabvala published *Esmond in India*, which she was to follow with *A New Dominion* (1973), *Heat and Dust* (1975) and *In Search of Love and Beauty* (1983) – all fine novels. In the same period William Golding made a big impact with *Lord of the Flies* (1954), a kind of 'thesis' novel (*q.v.*), completely without humour even though all its characters are young boys, which inspired many theses. He followed this with *The Inheritors* (1955), *Pincher Martin* (1956), *The Spire* (1964) and *Darkness Visible* (1979). Then came *Rites of Passage* (1980), the first of an impressive trilogy completed by *Close Quarters* (1987) and *Fire Down Below* (1989).

In 1957 Lawrence Durrell published the first volume of his *Alexandria Quartet*, a somewhat meretricious tetralogy; later came *Tunc* (1968), *Nunquam* (1970), *Monsieur* (1974) and *Constance* (1982). In 1958 John Berger had some success with *A Painter of Our Time*, which he followed with *The Foot of Clive* (1962), *Corker's Freedom* (1964) and *G* (1972). In 1957 Colin MacInnes published *City of Spades* and followed it with *Absolute Beginners* (1959); he was one of the first to write about black immigrant culture. In 1956 Roy Fuller, better known as a poet, published a good novel called *Image of a Society*. In the same year Sybille Bedford published *The Legacy*, which she followed with *Favourite of the Gods* (1962) and *A Compass Error* (1968). In 1950 William Cooper had won praise with *Scenes from Provincial Life*; this he was to follow with *Scenes from Married Life* (1961) and *Scenes from Metropolitan Life* (1982). During the 1950s Anthony Burgess began to publish his first novels, thus starting a veritable foundry unquenched thirty-odd years later. To the fifties belong *Time for a Tiger* (1956), *The Enemy in the Blanket* (1958) and *Beds in the East* (1959); these were published as *The Malayan Trilogy* in 1972. He also wrote *A Clockwork Orange* (1962), a tour de force, the Enderby novels under the name Joseph Kell, and *Earthly Powers* (1980). Brigid Brophy's main novels were *Hackenfeller's Ape* (1953), *Flesh* (1962), *The Snow Ball* (1962) and *In Transit* (1969). Vladimir Nabokov became famous in 1955 through *Lolita*. At that time few had heard of him. In fact, he had started writing novels in the 1920s. His earlier work was revived, especially *Laughter in the Dark* (1932), *Invitation to a Beheading* (1938) and *Bend Sinister* (1947). After *Lolita* his main works were *Pnin* (1957), *Pale Fire* (1962), *Ada* (1969), *Transparent Things* (1972) and *Look at the Harlequins!* (1972). He was unique in that he wrote equally well in Russian and English and collaborated in the translation of his 'Russian' novels into English, and his 'English' novels into Russian.

Iris Murdoch also began her long career as a novelist in the 1950s with *Under the Net* (1954). She followed this with many other successful novels, including *The Bell* (1958), *A Severed Head* (1961), *The Red and the Green* (1965), *The Time of the Angels* (1968), *Bruno's Dream* (1969), *A Word Child* (1975), *The Sea, the Sea* (1978) and *The Philosopher's Pupil* (1983). By 1989 she had published over twenty novels and shown remarkable consistency in quality. A near contemporary was Angus Wilson, whose main works were *Hemlock and After* (1952), *Anglo-Saxon Attitudes* (1956), *The Middle Age of Mrs Eliot* (1958), *The Old Men at the Zoo* (1961), *No Laughing Matter* (1967), *As if by Magic* (1973) and *Setting the World on Fire* (1980). After a gap of nearly thirty years Antonia White began to publish again in the 1950s with *The Lost Traveller* (1950), *The Sugar House* (1952) and *Beyond the Glass* (1954). This revitalization renewed interest in her excellent novel *Frost in May* of 1933. Barbara Pym also published several well-received novels in the 1950s, including *Excellent Women* (1952), *Less than Angels* (1955) and *A Glass of Blessings* (1958). In 1957 John Braine achieved instant fame with *Room at the Top*, but he was never able to live up to the promise and quality of that novel. Muriel Spark's first novel, *The Comforters*, also came out in 1957. She followed it with a succession of highly accomplished short, witty, satirical novels, such as *Memento Mori* (1959), *The Ballad of Peckham Rye* (1960), *The Prime of Miss Jean Brodie* (1961), *The Girls of Slender Means* (1963), *The Public Image* (1968), *The Abbess of Crewe* (1974) and *The Take Over* (1976). One of the most distinguished novelists to embark on a career in the 1950s was the Trinidad-born V. S. Naipaul. His first two novels were *The Mystic Masseur* (1957) and *The Suffrage of Elvira* (1958). He followed these with the ambitious *A House for Mr Biswas* (1961). In 1967 came *The Mimic Men* and in 1971 *In a Free State*, which won the Booker Prize (*q.v.*). His other most important novels are *A Bend in the River* (1979) and *The Enigma of Arrival* (1987). Naipaul wrote several non-fiction works, including two notable travel books (*q.v.*). Doris Lessing also established herself in the 1950s, first with *The Grass is Singing* (1950), and then with her vast *Bildungsroman The Children of Violence*, which comprises five volumes: *Martha Quest* (1952), *A Proper Marriage* (1954), *A Ripple from the Storm* (1958), *Landlocked* (1965) and *The Four-Gated City* (1969). In 1962 she also published *The Golden Notebook*, a highly complex novel using many different techniques. In the late 1960s and early 1970s she embarked on a very different kind of fiction described as 'inner space fiction', and thereafter began another *magnum opus* which was a form of science fiction: a five-volume sequence titled *Canopus in Argus Archives*.

Olivia Manning published her first novel in 1937 but it was not until the sixties that she became known; firstly with the *Balkan Trilogy: The Great Fortune* (1960), *The Spoilt City* (1962) and *Friends and Heroes* (1965). Later came *The Levant Trilogy*, consisting of *The Danger Tree* (1977), *The Battle Lost and Won* (1978) and *The Sum of Things* (1980). In the early sixties Christine Brooke-Rose wrote some very interesting experimental novels influenced by the then popular French *nouveau roman.* They include *Out* (1964), *Such* (1966), *Between* (1968), and, later, *Thru* (1975) and *Amalgamemnon* (1984). In the same period J. G. Ballard was also making his name with science fiction novels. Many years later he turned away from this to write *Empire of the Sun* (1984). In 1960 Stan Barstow published *A Kind of Loving*, which he was to follow with a number of other regional novels of Yorkshire life such as *Ask Me Tomorrow* (1962) and *Joby* (1964). Barstow, Braine and Sillitoe have often been linked because they wrote realist fiction about northern working-class life. In 1960, too, David Storey published his powerful novel *This Sporting Life*, which he was to follow with *Flight into Camden* (1960), the ambitious *Radcliffe*

(1963) and *Savile* (1976). By this time he had virtually abandoned the novel to write for the stage. Adrian Mitchell wrote one good novel in this period, namely *If You See Me Comin'* (1962); later he published *Wartime* (1973). Julian Mitchell published three successful novels in the 1960s: *Imaginary Toys* (1962), *The White Father* (1964) and *The Undiscovered Country* (1968). Both these writers went on to become distinguished playwrights. B. S. Johnson, a talented experimental novelist, also came to the forefront in the sixties with *Albert Angelo* (1964), *Trawl* (1966), *The Unfortunates* (1969) – a 'novel' which comprised twenty-seven unbound sections in a box – and *Christy Malry's Own Double-Entry* (1973). In 1962 Penelope Mortimer won acclaim with *The Pumpkin Eater*, which she was to follow with *The House* (1971) and *Long Distance* (1974). By *c.* 1960 Paul Scott had already written about ten novels and in 1966 achieved success with *The Jewel in the Crown*, the first of a tetralogy titled the *Raj Quartet*. The other three were *The Day of the Scorpion* (1968), *The Towers of Silence* (1971) and *A Division of the Spoils* (1975). The quartet is a notable account of Anglo-Indian relationships. Raymond Williams produced two good novels in the 1960s, namely *Border Country* (1962) and *Second Generation* (1964). In 1964 A. S. Byatt established herself with *Shadow of a Sun*, which she was to follow with *The Game* (1967) and the ambitious and complex *The Virgin in the Garden* (1978). Her sister, Margaret Drabble, also embarked on her career as a novelist in the 1960s. Her works include *A Summer Birdcage* (1963), *The Garrick Year* (1964), *The Millstone* (1965), *Jerusalem the Golden* (1967), *The Ice Age* (1977) and *The Radiant Way* (1987). An outstanding talent to appear in the sixties was J. G. Farrell, whose second novel was *The Lung* (1965). This he followed with *Troubles* (1969), *The Siege of Krishnapur* (1973) and *The Singapore Grip* (1978). Unhappily, he died when approaching the height of his powers. John Fowles was another to make his name at that time, with *The Collector* (1963), which he followed with *The Magus* (1966), *The French Lieutenant's Woman* (1969), *Daniel Martin* (1977) and *Mantissa* (1982). Piers Paul Read also established himself with *The Junkers* (1968) and *Monk Dawson* (1969); later there came *The Free Frenchman* (1986) and *A Season in the West* (1988). Eva Figes also came to the fore in the sixties with *Equinox* (1966) and *Winter Journey* (1968). Later she produced *Nelly's Version* (1977), *Light* (1983) and *The Seven Ages* (1986). David Lodge, one of the best of the modern comic novelists, published his first, *Ginger, You're Barmy*, in 1962. He followed this with *The British Museum is*

Falling Down (1965), *Changing Places* (1975), an extremely funny campus novel (*q.v.*), a sequel in the form of *Small World* (1983), and then *Nice Work* (1988), which was clever and also very amusing. Malcolm Bradbury's *Stepping Westward* came out in 1965 – his first novel had been *Eating People is Wrong* (1959) – and he followed this with two clever satirical comedies: *The History Man* (1975) and *Rates of Exchange* (1983). Comparatively late in life Edward Upward published his trilogy comprising *In the Thirties* (1962), *Rotten Elements* (1969) and *No Home but the Struggle* (1977). The complete work, titled *The Spiral Ascent*, was published in 1977. In 1967 Simon Raven published the first volume in his *Alms for Oblivion* sequence: a ten-volume *roman-fleuve*, beginning with *Fielding Gray* and ending with *The Survivors* (1967–76), a witty and satirical depiction of middle- and upper-class British life. In 1984 he published the first of a new sequence, *The First-Born of Egypt*, titled *The Morning Star*. In 1967, too, Angela Carter, often associated with the magic realism and the neo-Gothic fantasy element in fiction, published *The Magic Toyshop*. Later came *Heroes and Villains* (1969), and the brilliant *Nights at the Circus* (1984). Susan Hill, a novelist of much promise, published *A Change for the Better* in 1969 and followed this with *I'm the King of the Castle* (1970), *Strange Meeting* (1971) and *Bird of Night* (1972).

Beryl Bainbridge came to the fore in the 1970s with some clever, witty black comedies such as *The Dressmaker* (1973), *The Bottle Factory Outing* (1974) and *Injury Time* (1977). Kingsley Amis's son, Martin, also began to make a name for himself in the seventies with *The Rachel Papers* (1973), *Dark Secrets* (1975), *Success* (1978) and *London Fields* (1989). A popular author of the period was Richard Adams, with his strange allegorical novel *Watership Down* (1972), which he followed with *Shardick* (1974) and *The Plague Dogs* (1977). Tom Sharpe also achieved popularity in the seventies with his satirical novels, such as *Riotous Assembly* (1973), *Porterhouse Blue* (1974), *Wilt* (1976) and, later, *Wilt on High* (1984). Elaine Feinstein proved herself to be a gifted novelist in this period with *The Circle* (1970), *The Amberstone Exit* (1972), which she followed with *The Survivors* (1982) and *The Border* (1984). Two of Peter Vansittart's better novels of this period were *Landlord* (1970) and *Quintet* (1976). Isabel Colegate completed her *Orlando Trilogy* in 1973; later came the successful *The Shooting Party* (1980) and *Deceits of Time* (1988). Salman Rushdie, a writer associated with magic realism, published *Midnight's Children* in 1981. This was followed by *Shame* (1983). Taken up by the literary establishment, he achieved an inflated reputation which became global notoriety in 1988 with the publication of *The Satanic Verses* – a satirical novel which profoundly offended the world's Muslim communities. Another novelist with a somewhat over-rated reputation dating from this period was Anita Brookner, who was prolific through the 1980s, publishing *A Start in Life* (1981), *Providence* (1982), *Look at Me* (1983), *Hotel du Lac* (1984), *Family and Friends* (1985), *A Friend from England* (1987). William Boyd, a talented comic novelist, published four books in the eighties: *Good Man in Africa* (1981), *The Ice-Cream War* (1982), *Stars and Bars* (1984) and *The New Confessions* (1987). Yet another writer to acquire an inflated reputation in the eighties was D. M. Thomas with *The White Hotel* (1981), which he followed with *Ararat* (1983) and *Swallow* (1984). However, Peter Ackroyd displayed considerable originality in technique and ideas in three unusual novels: *The Last Testament of Oscar Wilde* (1983), *Hawksmoor* (1985) and *Chatterton* (1987). He followed these with *First Light* (1989). Julian Barnes also revealed notable originality in *Flaubert's Parrot* (1984) and *Staring at the Sun* (1986). Two excellent novels came from Paul Bailey in the 1980s, namely *At the Jerusalem* (1980) and *Gabriel's Lament* (1986). There were also two good ones by J. L. Carr: *A Month in the Country* (1980) and *The Battle of Pollock's Crossing* (1985). And one good one by Bruce Chatwin: *On the Black Hill* (1982).

During the 1980s a number of women apart from those mentioned above made distinguished contributions in fiction. Some achieved success late in life. For example, Molly Keane (M. J. Farrell), who had first published in the late 1930s (as M. J. F.) and was approaching eighty when she produced *Good Behaviour* (1981), followed by *Time after Time* (1983) and *Loving and Giving* (1988). Mary Wesley was over seventy when she published *Jumping the Queue* (1983), which she followed swiftly with *Camomile Lawn* (1984), *Not That Sort of Girl* (1986) and *Second Fiddle* (1988). A little younger were Monica Dickens, who wrote *Dear Doctor Lily* (1988), and Penelope Fitzgerald, who wrote *At Freddie's* (1982), *Innocence* (1986) and *The Beginning of Spring* (1988). Nina Bawden, well known for her children's stories, published *The Ice House* (1983) and *Circles of Deceit* (1987). In 1982 Elizabeth Jane Howard produced *Getting it Right*. Penelope Lively, also well known for her children's stories, produced three novels: *Judgement Day* (1980), *According to Mark* (1984) and *Moon Tiger* (1987). Alice Thomas Ellis published *The Twenty-Seventh Kingdom* (1982) and *Unexplained Laughter* (1985). Emma Tennant made some impact with *The House of Hospitalities* (1988) and *A Wedding of Cousins* (1988). And Fay Weldon, a militant feminist, published three witty and satirical novels: *The President's Child* (1982), *The Life and Loves of a She-Devil* (1983) and *The Hearts and Lives of Men* (1987).

A large number of other novelists of talent achieved varying degrees of success during the 1980s. They include Iain Banks, Noël Barber, Caroline Blackwood, Charlotte Bingham, Dirk Bogarde, David Cook, Jennifer Dawson, Carlo Gebler, Maggie Gee, Alasdair Gray, Alan Hollinghurst, David Hughes, Howard Jacobson, Jennifer Johnston, Sarah Maitland, Ian McEwan, Timothy Mo, Anita Mason, Bel Mooney, Carolyn Slaughter, Rose Tremain, Barry Unsworth, Marina Warner, and several descendants in the Waugh dynasty: Harriet, Daisy, Teresa and Auberon Waugh.

There was little of note in Australia in the 19th c., if we except the short stories of Henry Lawson and Marcus Clarke's powerful novel about a penal settlement, *For the Term of His Natural Life* (1874). However, in the 20th c. a number of gifted novelists have written memorable work. For example, Henry Handel Richardson (the pen-name of Ethel Florence Richardson), whose two early novels of distinction were *Maurice Guest* (1908) and *The Getting of Wisdom* (1910). She followed these with a trilogy titled *The Fortunes of Richard Mahoney: Australia Felix* (1917), *The Way Home* (1925) and *Ultima Thule* (1929). Later came *The Young Cosima* (1939). Her near contemporary Walter Turner wrote three novels of note: *The Aesthetes* (1927), *Blow for Balloons* (1935) and *The Duchess of Popocatapetl* (1939). Christina Stead is chiefly remembered for *The Man Who Loved Children* (1940), *For Love Alone* (1945), *Letty Fox: Her Luck* (1946) and *Cotter's England* (1967). The main novelist with an international reputation is undoubtedly Patrick White, who was awarded the Nobel Prize (*q.v.*) in 1973. Apart from his two superb epic novels *The Tree of Man* (1955) and *Voss* (1957), his main achievements have been *The Aunt's Story* (1948), *Riders in the Chariot* (1961), *The Solid Mandala* (1966), *The Vivisector* (1970), *The Eye of the Storm* (1973), *A Fringe of Leaves* (1976) and *The Twyborn Affair* (1979). During the 1970s Thomas Keneally established himself with *A Dutiful Daughter* (1971) and *Schindler's Ark* (1972). In 1981 he published *The Playmaker*. In the 1980s Peter Carey produced two notable novels: *Illywhacker* (1985) and *Oscar and Lucinda* (1988).

Three Canadian novelists have made a name for themselves in the 20th c.: Robertson Davies, Margaret Atwood and Mordecai

Richler. Among Davies's main books we should mention particularly *Tempest Tost* (1951), *Leaven of Malice* (1952), *A Mixture of Frailties* (1958) and *What's Bred in the Bone* (1986). In 1971 Mordecai Richler published *St Urbain's Horseman* and there have been several others since, including *Solomon Gursky was Here* (1990). In 1969 Margaret Atwood published *The Edible Woman*, which she followed with *Surfacing* (1972), *Lady Oracle* (1976), *Life before Man* (1979), *Bodily Harm* (1981) and *The Handmaid's Tale* (1985).

In the 20th c., too, several South African novelists have made a wide impression; especially William Plomer, author of *Turbott Wolfe* (1926), *The Case is Altered* (1932) and *A Shot in the Park* (1955); Stuart Cloete, author of *Turning Wheels* (1937), *Watch for the Dawn* (1939), *Congo Song* (1943) and *The Curve and the Tusk* (1952); Alan Paton, who wrote the magnificent and best-selling *Cry, the Beloved Country* (1948) and *Too Late the Phalarope* (1953); Nadine Gordimer, who wrote *A World of Strangers* (1958), *Occasion for Loving* (1963), *A Guest of Honour* (1970), *The Conservationist* (1974), *Burger's Daughter* (1979) and the novella *July's People* (1981). Slightly less well known, perhaps, are: Dan Jacobson, author of *Dance in the Sun* (1956), *The Beginners* (1966) and *The Rape of Tamar* (1970); André Brink, whose main novels have been *Looking on Darkness* (1973–4), *Rumour of Rain* (1978), *A Dry White Season* (1979) and *A Chain of Voices* (1982); and John Coetzee, whose three main novels have been *In the Heart of the Country* (1977), *Waiting for the Barbarians* (1980) and *The Life and Times of Michael K* (1983).

Apart from Rabindranath Tagore, who wrote two novels of merit early in the 20th c. (*Home and the World*, 1919, and *Gora*, 1924), half a dozen novelists in India have made distinguished contributions to the genre. Mulk Raj Anand is especially remembered for his novel *Coolie* (1936), which he followed with a trilogy: *The Village* (1939), *Across the Black Waters* (1940) and *The Sword and the Sickle* (1942). His contemporary R. K. Narayan published his first novel, *Swami and Friends*, in 1935 and then developed as a regional novelist in the creation of his imaginary town of Malgudi. For some forty years he published novels regularly. Some of the best are *The Bachelor of Arts* (1937), *The English Teacher* (1945), *Mr Sampath* (1949), *The Financial Expert* (1952), *The Vendor of Sweets* (1967) and *The Painter of Signs* (1977). Of the same generation are Raja Rao and G. V. Desani. Two of Rao's best novels were *Kanthapura* (1938) and *The Serpent and the Rope* (1960). Desani is chiefly known for his eccentric comic novel *All About H. Hatterr* (1948).

Kamala Markandaya was born and brought up in India and ultimately settled in England. Her main novels have been *Nectar in a Sieve* (1954), *A Silence of Desire* (1960), *Possession* (1963), *A Handful of Rice* (1966), *The Coffer Dams* (1969), *Two Virgins* (1973), *The Golden Honeycomb* (1977) and *Pleasure City* (1982). Anita Desai has been as prolific with such novels as *Cry, the Peacock* (1963), *Voices in the City* (1965), *Bye-Bye Blackbird* (1971), *Where Shall We Go This Summer?* (1975), *Fire on the Mountain* (1977), *Clear Light of Day* (1980) and *Baumgartner's Bombay* (1988).

During the 1950s something approaching a 'school' of gifted Caribbean novelists developed and they, in company with a number of poets, began to create a literature in a region which, hitherto, had lacked virtually any native expression. Among the most eminent writers there have been Edgar Mittelholzer (Guyana), who wrote *A Morning at the Office* (1950), *Children of Kaywana* (1952), *The Harrowing of Hubertus* (1954), *Kaywana Blood* (1958), *The Mad MacMullochs* (1959) and *The Pilkington Drama* (1965); Wilson Harris (Guyana), author of the *Guiana Quartet*, a tetralogy comprising *Palace of the Peacock* (1960), *The Far Journey of Oudin* (1961), *The Whole Armour* (1962) and *The Secret Ladder* (1963), plus the novels *The Waiting Room* (1967), *The Age of the Rainmakers* (1971) and *The Tree of the Sun* (1978); George Lamming (Barbados), who wrote *The Castle of the Skin* (1953), *Of Age and Innocence* (1958) and *Season of Adventure* (1960); Roger Mais (Jamaica), author of *The Hills were Joyful Together* (1953), *Brother Man* (1954) and *Black Lightning* (1955); John Hearne (Jamaica), who wrote *Voices under the Window* (1955), *Stranger at the Gate* (1956), *The Faces of Love* (1957), *Land of the Living* (1961) and *The Sure Salvation* (1981); Samuel Selvon (Trinidad), prolific for over thirty years with such novels as *A Brighter Sun* (1952), *An Island is a World* (1955), *Turn Again, Tiger* (1958), *I Hear Thunder* (1963), *The Housing Lark* (1965), *The Plains of Caroni* (1969), *Those Who Eat the Cascadura* (1973), *Moses Ascending* (1975) and *Moses Migrating* (1983).

The most prominent East African novelist has been the Kenyan Ngugi wa Thiong'o, three of whose main works are *Weep Not, Child* (1964), *A Grain of Wheat* (1967) and *Devil on the Cross* (1982). Four West African novelists (all Nigerians) have won distinction since the 1950s, namely: Amos Tutuola, who virtually inaugurated West African literature in English with *The Palm-Wine Drunkard* (1952), which he followed, drawing on Yoruba folk tales, with *Simbi and the Satyr of the Dark Jungle* (1955), *The Brave African Huntress* (1958), *Feather Woman of the Jungle* (1962), *Ajaiji and His Inherited Poverty* (1967) and *The Witch-Herbalist of the Remote Town* (1981); Chinua Achebe, who made his name with *Things Fall Apart* (1958) and later produced *No Longer at Ease* (1960), *Arrow of God* (1964) and *A Man of the People* (1966); Wole Soyinka, also well known as a playwright, two of whose main novels are *The Interpreters* (1965) and *Season of Anomy* (1973); and Cyprian Ekwensi, whose most notable novels have been *People of the City* (1954), *Jagua Nana* (1962), *Iska* (1966) and *Survive the Peace* (1976). The Ghanaian poet and dramatist Ama Ata Aidoo published a good novel, *Our Sister Killjoy* (1977), and she is one of the very few women African writers.

In America, during the 20th c., the novel has flourished on the same scale as it has in Britain and other European countries. Many distinguished writers have exploited the possibilities of the form. One of the first American woman novelists was the formerly neglected Ellen Glasgow. Her first was *The Descendant* (1897). For the next forty years she published regularly. Some of her main works are *The Voice of the People* (1900), *Virginia* (1913), *Barren Ground* (1925), *The Romantic Comedians* (1926), *They Stooped to Folly* (1929), *The Sheltered Life* (1932) and *Vein of Iron* (1935). Better known now is her near contemporary Edith Wharton, whose *House of Mirth* (1905) remains a minor classic. She also wrote *Ethan Frome* (1911), *The Reef* (1912), *The Custom of the Country* (1913) and *The Age of Innocence* (1920). Early in the century Jack London published *The Call of the Wild* (1903), *White Fang* (1905) and *Iron Heel* (1907). About the same period Upton Sinclair began to make his name with *The Jungle* (1906), *King Coal* (1917), followed by *Boston* (1928). Later he embarked on a huge *roman-fleuve* titled *World's End*. The first volume, *World's End*, came out in 1940. During the next thirteen years ten more were added. Willa Cather came to the fore at the same time, with *O Pioneers!* (1913), *My Antonia* (1918), *A Lost Lady* (1923) and *Death Comes for the Archbishop* (1927). Contemporary with Willa Cather was Sinclair Lewis, whose chief novels were: *Main Street* (1920), *Babbitt* (1922), *Arrowsmith* (1925) and *Anne Vickers* (1933). Theodore Dreiser made his name in 1900 with *Sister Carrie*, which he followed with *Jennie Gerhardt* (1911), and a trilogy comprising *The Financier* (1912), *The Titan* (1914) and, finally, *The Stoic* (1947). His most famous novel was *An American Tragedy* (1925). This remains one of the best novels by an American. In 1921 John Dos Passos published *Three Soldiers*, which he followed with *Manhattan Transfer* (1925) and then an impressive trilogy comprising *The 42nd Parallel* (1930), *1919* (1932) and *The Big Money* (1936); the whole work was published in 1938 as *USA*. In the 1920s Elinor Wylie published two good novels: *The Venetian Glass Nephew* (1925) and *The Orphan Angel* (1926). During the 1920s Scott Fitzgerald spoke for a new generation (and for the 'lost generation', *q.v.*) with *This Side of Paradise* (1920), *The Beautiful and the Damned* (1922) and *The Great Gatsby* (1925). Later he wrote *Tender is the Night* (1934) and *The Last Tycoon* (1941). In 1929 Thomas Wolfe published a minor classic in the shape of *Look Homeward, Angel*. In that year, too, Ernest Hemingway made a great impact with *A Farwell to Arms*. This had been preceded by his satirical *The Torrents of Spring* (1926) and *The Sun also Rises* (1926) – in England titled *Fiesta* – which also spoke for the 'lost generation'. He was to write several other impressive novels, including *For Whom the Bell Tolls* (1940) and the *novella*-length story *The Old Man and the Sea* (1950). In 1929 Dashiell Hammett published *Red Harvest*, which he followed with *The Maltese Falcon* (1930), *The Glass Key* (1931) and *The Thin Man* (1932). Hammett raised the American type of detective story to new levels of distinction in these books. In 1933 Nathaniel West published a minor masterpiece – *Miss Lonelyhearts*. Later came *The Day of the Locust* (1939).

In the 1920s perhaps the most famous and original of all 20th c. American novelists began his long career; namely William Faulkner, who, apart from Thomas Hardy, is probably the best regional novelist to date. Faulkner employed many experimental techniques in novels of remarkable power. Some of his better known books are: *Soldier's Pay* (1926), *The Sound and the Fury* (1929), *Sartoris* (1929), *As I Lay Dying* (1930), *Sanctuary* (1931), *Light in August* (1932), *Wild Palms* (1938), *The Unvanquished* (1938), *The Hamlet* (1940), *The Town* (1957) and *The Mansion* (1959).

Other eminent Americans who began their writing careers between the wars and carried on writing long after the Second World War were: Thornton Wilder, author of *The Bridge of San Louis Rey* (1927), *The Woman of Andros* (1930) and *The Ides of March* (1948); James Gould Cozzens, author of *SS San Pedro* (1931), *Castaway* (1934), *The Just and the Unjust* (1942), *Guard of Honour* (1948) and *By Love Possessed* (1956); John Steinbeck, author of *The Pastures of Heaven* (1932), *Tortilla Flat* (1935), *Of Mice and Men* (1937), *The Grapes of Wrath* (1939), *Cannery Row* (1944) and *The Winter of Our Discontent* (1961); William Saroyan, author of *The Human Comedy* (1943); John O'Hara, author of *Appointment in Samarra* (1934), *Butterfield 8* (1935) and *From the Terrace* (1958); and a strange and rather lonely masterpiece by Carson McCullers titled *The Heart is a Lonely Hunter* (1940). Richard Wright is remembered for *Native Son* (1940) and *The Outsider* (1953). In 1948 Carl Sandburg published *Remembrance Rock*, a work on an epic scale.

After the war many American writers were intent upon compiling the great American war epic. There were some 250 attempts to achieve this. Norman Mailer, who subsequently wrote a picture book about the Marilyn Monroe doctrine, was responsible for what may prove to be the best of that 250-odd. It was called, appropriately enough, *The Naked and the Dead* (1948). During the 1940s an agreeable contrast to these grandiose excesses was the fiction of Raymond Chandler, whose detective stories compared favourably with many supposedly 'serious' novels. He made his name with *The Big Sleep* in 1939, and followed this with *Farewell, My Lovely* (1940), *The High Window* (1942), *The Lady in the Lake* (1943) and, later, *The Long Good-Bye* (1953).

Since *c.* 1950 a dozen or more American novelists have attained distinction and, in some instances, more or less enduring reputations. Pre-eminent has been Saul Bellow, who was awarded the Nobel Prize in 1976. Among his earliest novels was *The Victim* (1947). This he followed with *The Adventures of Augie March* (1953), *Henderson the Rain King* (1959), *Herzog* (1964), *Dr Sammler's Planet* (1969), *Humboldt's Gift* (1974) and *The Dean's December* (1982). His contemporary Mary McCarthy came to the fore with a campus novel *The Groves of Academe* (1952), which she followed with *A Charmed Life* (1955), *The Group* (1963), *Birds of America* (1971) and *Cannibals and Missionaries* (1980). In 1951 Herman Wouk published a fine realistic novel, *The Caine Mutiny*, but did not follow up this success. In the same year J. D. Salinger produced *The Catcher in the Rye*, an unusually good example of a 'mood-of-the-moment' book which became a classic. He also could not follow this success, though *For Esme, with Love and Squalor* suggested he might. David Karp wrote one brilliant cautionary tale, *One* (1953), which rivalled Orwell's *Nineteen Eighty-Four*. His only other novel of distinction was *Day of the Monkey* (1955). In 1955 J. P. Donleavy achieved a rather inflated reputation with *The Ginger Man*, which he later followed with *The Beastly Beatitudes of Balthazar B* (1968) and *The Destinies of Darcy Dancer, Gentleman* (1977). Isaac Bashevis Singer, the Polish-born Yiddish author, wrote several novels of merit, including *The Family Moscat* (1950), *The Magician of Lublin* (1960), *The Slave* (1962), *The Manor* (1967) and the sequel *The Estate* (1969). In the 1950s William Burroughs became notorious with his extraordinary novels about drug addiction, for his experimental techniques in forms of anti-novel and, later, for his fantasies of homosexuality. Some of his best known novels are *Junkie* (1953), *The Naked Lunch* (1959), *Nova Express* (1964) and *The Wild Boys* (1971). James Baldwin also made an impact in the 1950s with *Go Tell It on the Mountain* (1953) and *Giovanni's Room* (1956). Later he published *Another Country* (1962) and *Just Above My Head* (1979). Ray Bradbury, better known now as a writer of short stories, attained renown in 1953 with his frightening futuristic novel *Fahrenheit 451*. In 1962 he published *Something Wicked This Way Comes*. In 1958 Truman Capote published *Breakfast at Tiffany's*, and followed this with a notable example of the documentary or faction (*q.v.*) novel, *In Cold Blood* (1966).

During the 1960s several other novelists established themselves and continued to build reputations. In 1960 John Updike produced *Rabbit, Run*. A succession of novels followed, including *The Centaur* (1963), *Couples* (1968), *Rabbit Redux* (1971), *The Coup* (1979), *Rabbit is Rich* (1981), *The Witches of Eastwick* (1984) and *Roger's Version* (1986). In 1961 Joseph Heller published *Catch-22*, a fine comic war-novel which helped to adjust the balance of the 250 epics. He followed this success with *Something Happened* (1974), *Good as Gold* (1979) and *Picture This* (1988). John Cheever wrote four good novels, namely: *The Wapshot Chronicle* (1957), *The Wapshot Scandal* (1964), *Bullet Park* (1969) and *Falconer* (1977). Distinctive originality has been shown by Robert Coover with several novels, particularly *The Origin of the Brunists* (1966), *The Universal Baseball Association, Inc., J. Henry Waugh, Prop.* (1968) – an ingenious allegorical novel – *The Public Burning* (1977) and *Spanking the Maid* (1981). Allison Lurie wrote a successful campus novel in the shape of *The War between the Tates* (1974), which was preceded by *Love and Friendship* (1962) and *Imaginary Friends* (1967). The novels of Thomas Pynchon have displayed elements of magic realism, especially *Gravity's Rainbow* (1973). His novel *V* (1963) showed the possibilities of allegory. His other principal novel was *The Crying of Lot 49* (1966). Joyce Carol Oates is one of the number of modern novelists who have introduced neo-Gothic elements in fiction. Three of her best known works are *A Garden of Earthly Delights* (1967), *Wonderland* (1971) and *A Bloodsmoor*

Romance (1982). Paul Theroux, long resident in England, has displayed remarkable versatility in his fiction. Three of his best novels are *The Mosquito Coast* (1981), *O-Zone* (1986), a futuristic fantasy, and *My Secret History* (1989).

In Europe, since the beginning of the century, the novel has proliferated as it has in America and elsewhere; especially in France where dozens of gifted writers have made it one of their main modes of expression. André Gide, for example, who wrote *L'Immoraliste* (1902), *La Porte étroite* (1909), *La Symphonie pastorale* (1919) and *Les Faux-monnayeurs* (1926). Gide made a clear distinction between the *roman* and the *récit* (*q.v.*). *Les Faux-monnayeurs* was a *roman*; *L'Immoraliste* and *La Porte étroite* were *récits*. During that period Alain-Fournier produced his solitary masterpiece *Le Grand Meaulnes* (1912), Barbusse wrote a fine war novel *Le Feu* (1916), Proust began the long quest *A la recherche du temps perdu* (1913–27), and Romain Rolland created his huge *Bildungsroman* in ten volumes called *Jean-Christophe* (1906–12). Colette had also embarked on her prolific career, and of her many books the following deserve special mention: *L'Ingénue libertine* (1909), *La Vagabonde* (1911), *L'Entrave* (1913), *Chéri* (1920), *Le Blé en herbe* (1923), *La Fin de Chéri* (1926) and *La Chatte* (1933). The early 1920s produced two masterpieces by an infant prodigy: Raymond Radiguet, who died aged twenty. They were *Le Diable au corps* (1923) and *Le Bal du comte d'Orgel* (1924). In 1928 another brilliant novel was *Nadja* by André Breton, the surrealist. In the same year André Malraux published *Les Conquérants* which he was to follow with a classic, *La condition humaine* (1933), and then *Le Temps du mépris* (1935). In the same period Montherlant was coming to the fore with *Le Songe* (1922) and *Les Bestiaires* (1926). Between 1936 and 1939 he produced his masterpiece of comic fiction – the tetralogy *Les Jeunes Filles*. In 1928 Saint-Exupéry, a rare poet of the skies and of aviation, published *Courrier-Sud*. Later came *Vol de nuit* (1931) and *Pilote de guerre* (1942). In the 1920s, also, François Mauriac, one of the most famous and distinguished of all French novelists, published his early work: *Le Baiser au lépreux* (1922), *Genitrix* (1923), *Le Désert de l'amour* (1925) and *Thérèse Desqueyroux* (1927). *Le Nœud de vipères* followed in 1932. In 1935 came a sequel to *Thérèse* in the shape of *La fin de la nuit* (1935). Other exceptional novels by Mauriac were *Le Mystère Frontenac* (1933), *La Pharisienne* (1941) and *Le Sagouin* (1950). Two other French novelists born in the 1880s have made notable contributions towards the study of mankind in the shape of the *roman-fleuve* or *roman cycle*. Like Zola and Balzac they are documentary encyclopaedists. Georges Duhamel published *Vie et Aventures de Salavin* in five volumes (1920–32), and followed this with a ten-volume saga – *La Chronique des Pasquier* (1933–45). An even vaster panoramic work was carried out by Jules Romains with his *Les Hommes de bonne volonté*, the generic title of a *roman cycle* in twenty-seven volumes (1932–47). Romains wrote several other novels. George Bernanos, born in 1888, was much less prolific and is now best represented by *Sous le soileil de Satan* (1926), *Un Crime* (1935), *Journal d'un curé de campagne* (1936) and *Monsieur Ouine* (1943). Two fine novelists born near the turn of the 19th c. were Jean Giono and Julien Green. Giono is a good example of a regional novelist and his main early works are: *Colline* (1929), *Un de Baumugnes* (1929), *Regain* (1930) – the trilogy titled *Pan*. There followed *Le Grand Troupeau* (1931), *Les Vraies Richesses* (1936), *Batailles dans la montagne* (1939), and, more recently, several novels which Giono called 'chroniques'. Green, influenced by Zola, wrote *Adrienne Mesurat* (1927), *Léviathan* (1928), *Epaves* (1932), *Le Visionnaire* (1934), *Minuit* (1936) and *Varouna* (1940). In 1938 Sartre published *La Nausée*, which, by virtue of the intensity of its personal vision and its philosophy, is one of the most remarkable novels of the century. In 1945 came the first volume of his tetralogy titled *Les Chemins de la liberté*, namely *L'Age de raison*. This was followed by *Le Sursis* (1945) and *La Mort dans l'âme* (1949). The last volume was to be called *La Dernière Chance* but this was never completed or published. Sartre's theories of existentialism (*q.v.*) pervade these novels. The other most important philosopher/novelist of modern times was Albert Camus, the mullah of the cult philosophy of the absurd. He wrote three outstanding novels which have had considerable influence: *L'Etranger* (1942), *La Peste* (1947) and *La Chute* (1956), this last being a fine example of the *récit* and so-called confessional literature. Jean Genet was also making his name in the 1940s with such novels as *Notre-Dame des Fleurs* (1944) and *Querelle de Brest* (1947). In 1945 Julien Gracq published *Un beau ténébreux*, an outstanding work of fiction; he followed this with *Le Rivage des Syrtes* (1951) and *Un balcon en forêt* (1958). Jean-Louis Curtis published *Les Forêts de la nuit* in 1947 and followed this with *Les Justes Causes* (1954), plus several others since.

The 1950s produced a group of talented practitioners of the *nouveau roman* (*q.v.* for details and names of authors). A forerunner of the *nouveau roman* was *Le Chiendent* (1933) by

Raymond Queneau (Robbe-Grillet remarked that it was 'twenty years before its time'). Queneau later wrote *Le Dimanche de la vie* (1952) and *Zazie dans le métro* (1959). In 1950 the Belgian novelist Françoise Mallet-Joris published a distinguished novel in the shape of *Le Rempart des Béguines.* In the following year Marguerite Yourcenar published *Memoirs of Hadrian*, which she followed with *Coup de Grâce* (1957). By this stage Simone de Beauvoir was becoming prominent. In 1943 she had published *L'Invitée*, which was followed by *Le Sang des autres* (1944), and in 1954 she published *Les Mandarins*. Marguerite Duras also became prominent in the early fifties with *Le Marin de Gilbraltar*, which she was to follow with *Le Square* (1955) and *Moderato Cantabile* (1958). In 1954 Françoise Sagan (then aged eighteen) published *Bonjour Tristresse* and at once became a cult figure among the young because of her amoral cynicism and pessimism. Later came *Aimez-vous Brahms?* (1959). For the next thirty years she published novels at regular intervals. In the 1950s Pierre Klossowski produced a distinguished trilogy in the form of *Les Lois de l'hospitalité* (1953–60), which was followed by *Un si funeste désir* (1963) and *Baphomet* (1965). Christine Rochefort wrote two notable novels: *Le Repos du guerrier* (1958) and *Les Stances à Sophie* (1963). In 1957 Claude Simon, winner of the Nobel Prize in 1985, came to the fore with *Le Vent.* Simon was clearly influenced by the *nouveau roman* and also by William Faulkner. Later, he produced several distinguished novels: *La Route de Flandres* (1960), *Le Palace* (1962), *La Bataille de Pharsale* (1969) and *The Georgics* (1989). In 1966 Hélène Cixous, well known now for her feminist criticism (*q.v.*) and literary theories, published *Le Prénom du Dieu*. In the 1970s Michel Tournier became prominent with *Le Roi des aulnes* (1970) and *Les Météores* (1972).

Among many other French novelists who have achieved distinction we should mention Emile Ajar, Elizabeth Barille, Nicolas Bouvier, Louis Ferdinand Celine, Blaise Cendrars, Bernard Clavel, Regine Deforges, Romain Gary, Valéry Larbaud, Violette Leduc, Yves Navarre, Yann Queffelec and Monique Wittig. For Georges Simenon see ROMAN POLICIER.

In Germany the most eminent 20th c. novelist is Thomas Mann, who came to the fore with his *Bildungsroman, Buddenbrooks*, in 1900. In 1924 appeared *Der Zauberberg*, then the huge tetralogy *Joseph und seine Brüder: Die Geschichten Jaakobs* (1933), *Der junge Joseph* (1934), *Joseph in Aegypten* (1936) and *Joseph der Ernährer* (1942). There were also *Lotte in Weimar* (1939), *Doktor Faustus*

(1947) and the unfinished picaresque novel *Confessions of Felix Krull* (1954), plus some splendid *novelle*. His brother, Heinrich Mann, wrote *Professor Unrat* (1905), which was made into the film *The Blue Angel* (1932), *Die kleine Stadt* (1909) and *Der Untertan* (1921). Somewhat less well known now is Alfred Döblin, who wrote a number of distinguished novels such as *Die drei Sprünge des Wang-lun* (1915), *Berge, Meere and Giganten* (1924) and *Berlin Alexanderplatz* (1929). He also produced two important trilogies: *Amazones-Trilogie* (1947–8) and *November 1918* (1948–50). At the beginning of the century his contemporary Robert Walser had published three notable novels: *Jakob von Gunten* (1904), *Geschwister Tanner* (1906) and *Der Gehülfe* (1908). Hermann Hesse, another contemporary, published several outstanding novels, including *Unterm Rad* (1906), *Gertrud* (1910), *Der Steppenwolf* (1927), *Narziss und Goldmund* (1930) and *Das Glasperlenspiel* (1943) – a famous example of an utopian novel. Lion Feuchtwanger was also prolific. He is particularly remembered for *Jud Süss* (1925), but there were many others, including the notable tetralogy *Der Wartesaal. Zyklus aus dem Zeitgeschehen* (1930–44). Hermann Broch is likewise especially well known for his trilogy titled *Die Schlafwandler* (1930–32), plus *Bergroman* (1935) and *Der Tod des Vergil* (1945). In the 1930s Hans Fallada wrote three memorable novels: *Bauern, Bonzen und Bomben* (1931), *Kleiner Mann – was nun?* (1932) and *Wer einmal aus dem Blechnapf frisst* (1934), a study of criminal psychology. In a short life Joseph Roth was prolific in the 1920s and 1930s. In less than twenty years he published as many books. Some of the better known are: *Savoy Hotel* (1924), *Die Rebellion* (1924), *Die Flucht ohne Ende* (1927), *Zipper und sein Vater* (1928), *Hiob* (1930), *Radetzkymarsch* (1932), *Die hundert Tage* (1936), *Das falsche Gewicht* (1937) and *Die Kapuzinergruft* (1938). If there is one German novel from the inter-war period that everyone has heard of, then it is Erich Remarque's *Im Westen nichts Neues* (1929), a best-seller known in English as *All Quiet on the Western Front* – and a novel which inspired a great German film.

Of the generation who came to the fore in the 1950s Heinrich Böll has been pre-eminent. He shares some characteristics with Thomas Mann and François Mauriac and wrote a number of fine novels, some of which are satirical and most of which are highly critical of Nazism and its evils. We should mention particularly: *Wo warst du, Adam?* (1951), a cycle of war stories, *Und sagte kein einziges Wort* (1953), *Haus ohne Huter* (1954), *Das Brot der frühen Jahre* (1955), *Billard um halb zehn* (1959), *Die Ansichten eines*

Clowns (1963) and *Gruppenbild mit Dame* (1971). Johannes Bobrowski, a contemporary of Böll's, wrote two good novels in the sixties: *Levins Mühle* (1964) and *Litauische Klaviere* (1966). Besides being an outstanding writer of short stories, Siegried Lenz has also written some notable novels, chiefly *Es waren Habichte in der Lufte* (1950), *Duell mit dem Schatten* (1953), *Stadtgespräch* (1963) and *Deutschstunde* (1968). Since 1959, when he published *Die Blechtrommel* ('The Tin Drum'), Günter Grass has achieved an international reputation comparable with that of Mann and Böll. He followed *Die Blechtrommel* with *Katz und Maus* (1961), *Hundejahre* (1963), and *Aus dem Tagebuch einer Schnecke* (1972). There have been several other novels. In the 1960s Peter Handke, of a younger generation, began to make a name with *Die Hornissen* (1966) and *Der Hausierer* (1967). He followed these with *Die Angst des Tormanns beim Elfmeter* (1970). Stefan Heym (1913–), most of whose works were first published in English, became prominent in 1981 with *The Wandering Jew* – one of many treatments in German of this theme. We should also mention Arnold Zweig, of an earlier vintage, who has had belated recognition outside Germany with two novels: *Der Streit um den Sergeanten Grischa* (1927) and *De Vriendt kehrt heim* (1932).

Two Austrian novelists with international reputations are Robert Musil, author of a number of fine novels, including *Der Mann ohne Eigenschaften* in three volumes (1930–33), and Max Brod, whose trilogy *Ein Kampf um die Wahrheit* was published in 1916, 1925 and 1948. Brod wrote several other novels, of which *Eine Frau, die nicht enttäuscht* (1933) was especially notable. Stefan Zweig, also Austrian, eventually became famous with *Ungeduld des Herzens* (1939).

Elias Canetti is an example of a writer who, though not German, favoured that language. Canetti was born in Bulgaria of a Spanish/Jewish family, settled in England but wrote in German. He produced one masterpiece: *Die Blendung* (1935) better known in English as *Auto da Fé*.

Lastly one must mention the mysterious and egregious B. Traven, who wrote variously in German and English. He had many aliases and pseudonyms and acquired many identities. At various stages of his long life (1882–1969) he was thought to be Jack London, Ambrose Bierce, a leper, President Adolfo Lopez Mateos, President Elias Calles, a group of leftist Hollywood scriptwriters and a group of writers in Honduras (there were several other identities). He was eventually found to have been Otto Feige, born in Schwiebus. He remains famous for the classic *Der Schatz der Sierra Madre* (1927) and *Das Totenschiff* (1926). There were nine other novels at least, in German and English.

Among Italian, Sardinian and Sicilian novelists a number have achieved world-wide repute in the 20th c. Before turning to the theatre, Pirandello was a prolific novelist, now best represented by *I vecchi e i giovani* (1913) and *Uno, nessuno e centomila* (1926). Italo Svevo was also prolific. An early novel was *Una vita* (1893). This he followed with *La coscienza di Zeno* (1923) and *La novella del buon vecchio e della bella fanciulla* (1929). Antonio Fogazzaro achieved some fame fairly late in life with *Piccolo mondo antico* (1895), followed by *Il santo* (1905) and *Leila* (1910). Two of Ignazio Silone's excellent novels were *Fontamara* (1930) and *Pane e vino* (1937). These he followed with *Il seme sotto la neve* (1941) and *Il segreto di Luca* (1956). Mario Soldati is chiefly famous for *La verità sul caso Motta* (1941), *Lettere da Capri* (1954), *La confessione* (1955), *Il vero Silvestri* (1959) and *Le due città* (1964). Vasco Pratolini's main works have been *Cronache di poveri amanti* (1949), *Un eroe de nostro tempo* (1949), *Le ragazze di Sanfrediano* (1951), plus a trilogy comprising *Metello* (1955), *Lo scialo* (1960) and *La costanza della ragione* (1963). Three of the best novels by Carlo Gadda are *Il castello di Udine* (1934), *Adalgisa* (1944) and *Cognizione del dolore* (1963). Natalia Ginzburg's two best known novels are *È sato così* (1947) and *Le voci della sera* (1961). In his short career Cesare Pavese wrote four outstanding works of fiction, namely: *Il compagno* (1947), *Prima che il gallo canti* (1949), *La bella estate* (1949) and *La luna e i falò* (1950). Pier Paolo Pasolini, who also had a comparatively short life, was perhaps better known for his films; but he wrote two notable novels: *Ragazzi di vita* (1955) and *Una vita violenta* (1958). His almost exact contemporary, Italo Calvino, wrote several novels of distinction, including *Il visconte dimezzato* (1952), *Il barone rampante* (1957), *Il cavaliere inesistente* (1959) and *Palomar* (1983). Carlo Cassola's three main novels are *La ragazza di Bube* (1960), *Un cuore arido* (1961) and *Il cacciatore* (1964). Luigi Meneghello also wrote three memorable novels: *Libera nos a malo* (1963), *I piccoli maestri* (1964)' and *Pomo pero* (1974). Carlo Levi's reputation appears to depend on his masterpiece *Cristo si è fermato a Eboli* (1945). Quite as famous is Giuseppe di Lampedusa's only novel – the fine *Il gattopardo* (1958). Like Pirandello, Lampedusa was a Sicilian. In Britain, at least, the most famous 20th c. Italian novelist has been Alberto Moravia, who has been prolific over a long career. His first novel, *Gli indifferenti*, appeared in 1929. Fifty years later he was still publishing. Among his best known works are: *La romana* (1947), *La ciociara* (1957), *La noia* (1960), *Il conformista* (1951) and *1934* (1983). The only Sardinian novelist of renown is Grazia Deledda. A regional novelist, she has been compared to Thomas Hardy. Her chief works were: *Il vecchio della montagna* (1900), *Elias Portolu* (1903), *Cenere* (1904), *Nostalgia* (1905), *L'ombra del passato* (1907), *L'edera* (1908) and *Canne al vento* (1913).

Among well-known Spanish novelists of the 20th c. mention should be made of Ramón del Valle-Inclán, who wrote *Flor de santidad* (1904), *La corte de los milagros* (1926) and *Viva mi dueño* (1926). Also Pío Baroja, author of *El árbol de la ciencia* (1911), Camilo José Cela, who had much success with his first novel, *La familia de Pascual Duarte* (1942), and scarcely less with *La colmena* (1951), and Juan Goytisolo, some of whose most distinguished novels are *Juegos de manos* (1954), *Duelo en el Paraíso* (1955), *Fiestas* (1958), *Sẽnas de identidad* (1966), *Count Julian* (1970) and *Juan sin tierra* (1975). The Catalan writer Mercè Rodoreda is chiefly known for *La Plaça del Diamant* (1962); and the Mallorcan Llorence Villalonga is well known for *Bearn* (1961).

Of the many Jugoslav novelists easily the most famous is Ivo Andrić, winner of the Nobel Prize in 1961. He was primarily a regional novelist who wrote mostly about his native Bosnia. Three of his finest books are *Bridge on the Drina* (1945), *Bosnian Story* (1945) and *The Woman from Sarajevo* (1945). He also wrote *Devil's Yard* (1954). Other Jugoslav novelists of note are: Miroslav Krleža, who wrote *The Great God Mars* (1922), *The Return of Philip Latinovitz* (1932) and *On the Edge of Reason*; Danilo Kis, author of *Garden Ashes* (1965) and *Tomb for Boris Davidović* (1978); and Poderegin, who wrote *The Dawning* (1986).

The main Czech novelists of the 20th c. are Franz Kafka, Jaroslav Hašek, Karel Čapek and Milan Kundera. Kafka wrote in German and achieved world fame with his short stories and his strange novels *The Trial* (1925) and *The Castle* (1926). Čapek, better known now for his plays, wrote utopian romances and three realistic novels: *Hordubal*, *The Meteor* and *An Ordinary Life* (1933–4). Hašek's reputation depends on his picaresque, comic masterpiece *The Good Soldier Schweik* (1920–23). Latterly, Milan Kundera, in exile, has won renown in Britain and elsewhere with his novels *The Farewell Party* (1976), *The Book of Laughter and Forgetting* (1979) and *The Unbearable Lightness of Being* (1984). Another exiled Czech, Josef Skvorecky, has also attained prominence with such novels as *The Cowards* (1958), *Miss Silver's Past* (1969) and *The Engineer of Human Souls* (1977).

Polish novelists have tended to be little known outside Europe or even outside their own country, but a few of their works have been translated. For example, Ignacy Stanislaw Witkiewicz's *Insatiability* (1930), a dystopian satirical novel; and Witold Gombrowicz's novels, such as *Ferydurke* (1937), *Possessed, or The Secret of Myslotch* (1939) and *Pornografia* (1960). Tadeusz Konwicki also wrote several novels of merit: *Dreambook of Our Time* (1963), *Nothing, or Nothing* (1971), *The Chronicle of Love Events* (1974) and *The Polish Complex* (1977). Czeslaw Milosz, who won the Nobel Prize in 1980, is chiefly known for *Issa Valley* (1955).

Three Hungarian writers have come to the fore, namely, Jozsef Lengyel, who wrote *Prenn Drifting* (1966), Laszlo Nemeth, who wrote *Guilt* (1935), and George Konrad, author of *The Caseworker* (1969) and *The Loser* (1980). Among Rumanians we should mention Livin Rebreanu, author of *The Uprising* (1907) and *The Forest of the Hanged* (1922), Zahariah Stancu, chiefly known for *A Gamble with Death* (1962), and Dmitriu, author of *The Royal Hunt* (1973).

The outstanding Albanian novelist of the era – and he is one of the best novelists in Europe – is Ismail Kadare. He became well known with *The General of the Dead Army* (1964), and followed this with a succession of distinguished novels: *Chronicle in Stone* (1970), *The Bridge with Arcs* (1978), *The Great Winter* (1977), *November of a Capital City* (1975), *Broken April* (1978), *The Twilight of the Gods of the Steppe* (1978) and *Concert in Winter* (1988).

The only 20th c. Greek novelist of international standing is Kazantzakis, who made a great impact with *Zorba the Greek* (1946). This he followed with *Christ Re-crucified* (1954), *The Last Temptation* (1955) and *The Fratricides* (1967).

Several Scandinavian writers have produced notable novels. Two of them have been Nobel Prize winners: Knut Hamsun (1920) and Pär Lagerkvist (1951). Among Hamsun's best known works are *Hunger* (1890), *Mysteries* (1892), *Pan* (1894), *Victoria* (1898) and *Growth of the Soil* (1917). Lagerkvist remains known for *The Dwarf* (1944) and *Barabbas* (1950). Cora Sandel, a Norwegian, wrote three novels of distinction: *Alberta and Freedom* (1931), *Alberta Alone* (1939) and *Krane's Café* (1945). Terjei Vesaas, also Norwegian, made a big impression with the tetralogy comprising

Father's Journey (1930), *Sigrid Stallbrokk* (1931), *The Unknown Men* (1932) and *The Heart Hears its Native Music* (1938).

Since the 1950s the best known Turkish novelist has been Yaşar Kemal, who made his name with *Mehmed, My Hawk* (1955), which he followed with *The Wind from the Plain* (1961) and several other novels of distinction, such as *Iron Earth and Copper Sky* and *Legend of Ararat.*

In 1988 the Egyptian writer Nagib Mahfuz, whom few had heard of, was awarded the Nobel Prize. For much of a long life he has been a practitioner of what has been called 'the urban novel'. Most of his beguiling fiction is about life in Cairo. One of his main works is a trilogy comprising *Bayn al Qasrayn* (1956), *Qasr ash-Shawq* (1957) and *as-Sukkar-iyya* (1957). Each title is the name of a Cairo district.

Half a dozen or more Hebrew novelists have been prolific in the 20th c. Sholem Aleichem remains known for *Tevye's Daughters* (1894), and there were other books thereafter. Shmuel Yosef Agnon, who was awarded the Nobel Prize in 1966, wrote a number of fine novels, including *The Bridal Canopy* (1930) and *A Guest for the Night* (1945). Of a later generation is Yehudah Amichal, whose main novel is *Not of this Time, Not of this Place* (1963). Uri Orlov is remembered particularly for *The Lead Soldiers* (1956). His near contemporary Aharon Appelfeld has written several novels, including *Skin and Clothes* (1971), *Badenheim 1939* (1975) and *The Age of Wonders* (1982). Abraham Yehoshua is known for *A Late Divorce* (1982). Amos Oz has produced four novels of distinction: *Elsewhere Perhaps* (1966), *My Michael* (1968), *The Hill of Evil Counsel* (1973) and *Touch the Water, Touch the Wind* (1973).

A number of Latin American writers have attained fame and distinction in the 20th c. The best known is probably Gabriel García Márquez, a Colombian, who won the Nobel Prize in 1982. His masterpiece is *Cien años de soledad* (1967). He wrote two other notable novels, *La mala hora* (1966) and *El otoño del patriarca* (1975), plus another masterpiece in the shape of *El amor en los tiempos del cólera* (1985). Luis Borges, of the Argentine, is famous for his short stories and his *ficciones* (*q.v.*), as well as his verse and essays. However, there is one notable novel, *Historia universal de la infamia* (1935) – in the tradition of Latin American 'magic realism'. The Mexican Carlos Fuentes has also achieved an international name with some novels, including *La región más transparente* (1958), *Las buenas conciencas* (1964) and *La muerte de Artemio Cruz* (1964). Of an earlier generation, the Argentinian Ricardo

Güiraldes remains famous for a classic novel, *Don Segundo Sombra* (1926). The Cuban Guillermo Carbrera Infante is likewise famous for one novel in particular: *Très tristes tigres* (1967). One Peruvian novelist, Mario Vargas Llosa, has achieved international renown with four novels: *La cuidad y los perros* (1962), *La casa verde* (1966), *Los cachorros: Pichula Cuéllar* (1967) and *Conversación en 'La Catedral'* (1969).

In Russia the novel has continued to flourish on much the same scale as in the 19th c. The most venerable figure was Maxim Gorki, who published *The Mother* (1907), *A Confession* (1908), *The Artamanov's Business* (1925), and then his unfinished cycle of novels *The Life of Klim Samgin*, of which four volumes appeared between 1927 and 1936. Later, Moscow 'beatified' him when it discovered that *The Mother* was the first great novel of socialist realism (*q.v.*). Mikhail Bulgakov made his name with *The White Guard* (1924). He followed this with two fine novels: *Black Snow* (1937) and *The Master and Margarita* (1940). There have been several other major Russian novelists in the 20th c. Firstly Ilya Ehrenburg, author of *The Loves of Jeanne Ney* (1923), *A Street in Moscow* (1930), *The Fall of Paris* (1942), *The Storm* (1949) and *The Thaw* (1954). Next, chronologically, Sholokhov, who wrote *Tales of the Don* (1925), *And Quiet Flows the Don* (1928–38) and *The Don Flows Home to the Sea* (1941). In 1957 Boris Pasternak published *Dr Zhivago*, an epic novel often compared to the work of Tolstoy. In the same year Dudintsev produced *Not by Bread Alone*. More recently, Alexander Solzhenitsyn has emerged as a novelist of heroic stature, but as with Pasternak his reputation has been inflated by political propaganda. Among his best known novels are: *One Day in the Life of Ivan Denisovich* (1962), *The First Circle* (1968), *Cancer Ward* (1968) and *The Gulag Archipelago*, in three volumes (1973–5). In 1969 he was expelled from the Union of Soviet Writers (*q.v.*) and in 1970 received the Nobel Prize. In the following year he began a panoramic cycle of novels with *August 1914*.

A large number of other Russian novelists have achieved varying degrees of distinction in the 20th c. For instance: Andrei Bely, who wrote *Petersburg* (1913–16) and *Kotik Letaev* (1915–16); M. Ageyev, who wrote *Novel with Cocaine* (1920s); Zamyatin, author of the remarkable dystopia *We* (1920–21); Leonid Leonov, who was prolific, with *The Badger* (1924), *The Thief* (1927), *The River Sot* (1929), *Shutarevsky* (1932), *The Road to the Ocean* (1935) and *The Russian Forest* (1953); Nikolai Ostrovsky, who wrote *How the Steel was Tempered* (1932–4); Alexander Fadeyev, author of *The*

Young Guard (1945); Yuri Trifonov, whose four main novels were: *Students* (1950), *The Quenching of a Thirst* (1963), *The Exchange* (1969) and *The Long Goodbye* (1971); Yury Dombrovski, who wrote *The Keeper of Antiquities* (1964); Vasily Grossman, whose two main novels were *Forever Flowing* (1964) and *Life and Fate*; Anatoli Kuznetsov, who made a big impact with *Babi-Yar* (1966); Georgi Vladimov, who wrote *Three Minutes Silence* (1969); Alexander Zinoviev, who wrote *The Madhouse*; Vladimir Voinovich, who wrote the powerful dystopian novel *Moscow 2042*; Sergei Yuryenen, author of *The Marksman*; Jula Voznesenskaya, whose two main books have been *The Women's Decameron* and *The Star Chernobyl* (1988); Vasily Aksynov, who wrote *The Island of Crimea* (1981); and Zinovy Zinik, author of *The Mushroom Pickers* (1987).

In the course of the 20th c. the novel has been richly served by a succession of Japanese writers, not a few of whom were born in the last twenty or thirty years of the 19th c. and lived well into the second half of the 20th. Japan's novelists have, incidentally, been rather better covered by translators into English than some who have written in other languages. Japan's first 'modern' novel is often said to be Futabatei Shimei's *Drifting Clouds* (1887). At the turn of the century Mori Ogai was active and his main work was *The Wild Geese* (1911–13). His contemporary Natsume Soseki wrote four memorable novels: *Young Master* (1906), *Pillow of Grass* (1906), *The Heart* (1914) and *Grass on the Wayside* (1916). Another almost exact contemporary was Tokutomi Roka, chiefly remembered for *Footprints in the Snow* (1901). Of the same vintage was Shimazaki Toson, whose five principal novels were: *Broken Commandment* (1906), *Spring* (1908), *When the Cherries Ripen* (1917), *A New Life* (1919) and *Before the Dawn* (1935). Tayama Katai's chief work was a trilogy comprising *The Quilt* (1907), *The Wife* (1908) and *Karma En* (1908). Masamune Hakucho and Nagai Kafu were both born in 1879 and both lived into their eighties. Hakucho's chief novel was *The Clay Doll* (1911); Kafu's two main works were *Flowers of Hell* (1902) and *The River Sumida* (1909). Later came Shiga Naoya with *A Dark Night's Passing* (1922–37). Two of Japan's most famous novelists are Tanizaki Junichiro and Yasunari Kawabata. The latter is Japan's only Nobel Prize winner (1968). Junichiro's main novels were: *A Fool's Love* (1924–5), *Some Prefer Nettles* (1928), *The Makioka Sisters* (1943–8), *The Mother of Captain Shigemoto* (1950) and *Diary of a Mad Old Man* (1962). Three of Yasunari's most distinguished novels are *The Izu Dancer* (1926),

The Snow Country (1935–47) and *Thousand Cranes* (1949–51). Another outstanding writer of more recent times was Yukio Mishima, who brought his career to an end by ritual suicide at the age of forty-five. Before this he had published several notable novels, including *Confessions of a Mask* (1949), *The Sea of Fertility* – a fine tetralogy – (1965–71) and *Temple of the Golden Pavilion* (1956). Lesser known 20th c. novelists have been: Takiji Kobayashi, who wrote *The Cannery Boat* (1929); Hayashi Fumiko, Japan's most distinguished modern woman writer, who wrote *Journal of a Vagabond* (1922–7) and *Drifting Clouds* (1948); Dazai Osamu, author of *A Clown's Flowers* (1935), *No Longer Human* (1937) and *The Setting Sun* (1947); and Ooka Shohei, who wrote *Fire on the Plain* (1951). Latterly, Kazuo Ishiguro, who writes in English, has made a considerable impact with two fine novels: *An Artist of the Floating World* (1986) and *The Remains of the Day* (1989), which won the Booker McConnell Prize that year.

novelette A work of fiction shorter than a novel but longer than a short story (*q.v.*). Often used derogatorily of 'cheap' fiction, sentimental romances and thrillers of popular appeal but little literary merit. In America the term applies to a long short-story somewhere between the short story and the *novella* (*q.v.*).

novella (It 'tale, piece of news') Originally a *novella* was a kind of short story, a narrative in prose of the genre developed by Boccaccio. His *Decameron* (*c.* 1349–51) was a collection of such stories. Later there appeared Tomassa Guardati's *Novellino* (1467). In the 16th c. Bandello published a collection of 214 *novelle*. Tudor dramatists often used *novelle* as source-books for plots. Thereafter, there was little sign of the *novella* developing for some time; unless one were to include in this category some of the narratives of Deloney and Greene, Nashe's *Unfortunate Traveller* (1594), Emanuel Ford's *Irnatus and Artesia* (1634), Mrs Behn's *Oroonoko* (*c.* 1688) and Congreve's *Incognita* (1713). But such works may also be regarded as romances (*q.v.*), or embryonic novels. It was not until late in the 18th and early in the 19th c. that the *novella* was fashioned into a particular form according to certain precepts and rules. Then the Germans became the most active practitioners, and the *Novelle* has since flourished in Germany more than anywhere else.

Basically, the *Novelle* is a fictional narrative of indeterminate length (a few pages to two or three hundred), restricted to a single event, situation or conflict, which produces an element of suspense and leads to an unexpected turning point (*Wendepunkt*) so that the conclusion surprises even while it is a logical outcome. Many *Novellen* contain a concrete symbol which is the steady point, as it were, at the heart of the narrative.

Goethe attempted to summarize the quiddity of the *Novelle* when he said: 'What else is a *Novelle* about but an event which is unheard of but has taken place?' Or, more concisely, 'an event without precedent' ('eine sich ereignete unerhörte Begebenheit').

The first of its kind, in all probability, was Goethe's *Unterhaltungen deutscher Ausgewanderten* (1795), derived from the *novella* form used by Boccaccio. It is a *Novelle* with a cyclic frame or *Rahmen*. There has been a good deal of debate and theory ever since as to what precisely a *Novelle* is or should be. August Schlegel theorized about it and stressed the importance of the *Wendepunkt* in the narrative. Tieck also stressed the importance of this. Later, Paul Heyse worked out his *Falkentheorie* (*q.v.*) in *Deutscher Novellenschatz* (1871–6). In 1828 Goethe had observed that the genre harboured 'many a wonderful thing'.

Among the principal practitioners were Goethe himself, Kleist (a vital influence in the creation of the short story, *q.v.*, who published his stories as *Erzählungen*), Hoffmann, Tieck, Theodor Storm, Fontane, Paul Heyse, Hermann Hesse and Thomas Mann. The Swiss writers Gottfried Keller and Conrad Meyer were also prolific; as were the Austrians Ferdinand Saar and Arthur Schnitzler.

Nowadays the term is often used to distinguish a long short-story from a short story and a short novel from a full-dress novel (*q.v.*). Stories which might be placed in this middle-distance category are Tolstoy's *The Cossacks* (1852) and *The Death of Ivan Ilyich* (1886); Thomas Mann's *Tonio Kröger* and *Tod in Venedig* (1913); Aldous Huxley's *Two or Three Graces* (1926); Alberto Moravia's *Conjugal Love* (1951); Hemingway's *The Old Man and the Sea* (1952); and H. E. Bates's trilogy *The Nature of Love* (1953). Some would also include Conrad's three long short-stories *Youth*, *Heart of Darkness* (1902) and *Typhoon* (1903). *See* NOVELETTE.

novellat A form of folk tale of the Semitic tradition which is of a particular time and place. It lacks universality (*q.v.*) and thus differs from the *chimerat* (*q.v.*).

Novelle *See* NOVELLA.

novel of adventure Literature in English is particularly rich in this form of fiction, which is seldom to be found in other languages. Daniel Defoe appears to have been its main pioneer with *The Life and Strange and Surprising Adventures of Robinson Crusoe* (1719). This produced many imitations known as 'Robinsonades' (*q.v.*) and a large quantity of what is called 'desert island fiction' (*q.v.*). The novel of adventure is also related to the picaresque novel and the romance (*qq.v.*). Among the numerous British exponents the following are some of the more notable: Captain Marryat, R. M. Ballantyne, G. A. Henty, P. C. Wren, Stanley Weyman, R. L. Stevenson, Anthony Hope, Arthur Conan Doyle, John Buchan, Dornford Yates, Hammond Innes, C. S. Forester, Alistair Maclean, Nevil Shute, Willard Price and John Masters. Two famous Americans in this field are James Fenimore Cooper and Mark Twain.

novel of ideas A vague category of fiction in which conversation, intellectual discussion and debate predominate, and in which plot, narrative, emotional conflict and psychological depth in characterization are deliberately limited. Such a form of novel is perhaps best exemplified by Aldous Huxley's *Crome Yellow* (1921), *Point Counter Point* (1928) and *After Many a Summer* (1939). *See* NOVEL.

novel of sensation A form of fiction which had some vogue from *c.* 1860 onwards. As the term suggests, the themes and action of the novels were improbable, melodramatic and lurid. The guilty secret was a favourite theme. One of the forerunners among the authors was Mrs Clive (1801–73), who in 1855 published *Paul Ferroll* and in 1860 followed it with *Why Paul Ferroll Killed His Wife.* Mrs Clive died sensationally, being burnt to death while she was writing in her boudoir. Well-known examples of the novel of sensation are: Wilkie Collins's *The Woman in White* (1860), Mrs Henry Wood's *East Lynne* (1861) and Mary Braddon's *Lady Audley's Secret* (1862). Mary Braddon wrote over seventy sensation novels, many of them lurid accounts of crime and violence. It is more than likely that the novel of sensation was eventually to influence the evolution of the thriller and the detective story (*qq.v.*). *See also* CRIME NOVEL; GOTHIC NOVEL/FICTION; NEWGATE FICTION.

novel of sensibility *See* SENTIMENTAL NOVEL.

novel of the soil A work of fiction whose main theme is the struggle of human beings against the natural forces of the earth as in Ellen Glasgow's *Barren Ground* (1925), the Norwegian O. E. Rolvagg's *Giants in the Earth* (1927), Erskine Caldwell's *Tobacco Road* (1932) and *God's Little Acre* (1933), John Steinbeck's *Grapes of Wrath* (1939) and Patrick White's *The Tree of Man* (1956). Many would include D. H. Lawrence's *The Rainbow* (1915), the novels of Mary Webb and some of the work of Thomas Hardy, as well as Jean Giono's descriptions of pastoral life in Provence (e.g. *Colline*, 1929; *Un de Baumugnes*, 1929; *Regain*, 1930; *Batailles dans la montagne*, 1939). *See also* NOVEL; THESIS NOVEL.

novelty A good deal was made of the importance of novelty in literature by such writers as Addison, Akenside and Dr Johnson. Johnson approved of it so long as it was a means to an end and provided variation and freshness. Writers of the Romantic period (*q.v.*) were also preoccupied with the matter. Coleridge takes much the same point of view as Johnson. The judicious test of the value of novelty must be whether or not it is an end in itself or a means to an end. Novelty intended solely to shock or surprise will probably run the risk of being meretricious or melodramatic and may, in some cases, have an unbalancing effect. T. S. Eliot's sober observations in his essay *Tradition and the Individual Talent* (1919) show a sense of proportion on this issue. *See* IMITATION; ORIGINALITY.

Nudelverse *See* MACARONIC.

number The term may refer to poems (poetry in general), verses or metrical feet. When Shakespeare writes in the 17th Sonnet:

> If I could write the beauty of your eyes
> And in fresh numbers number all your graces,

he is probably using it in the first sense. On the other hand, when Wordsworth, in *The Solitary Reaper*, writes:

> Will no one tell me what she sings? –
> Perhaps the plaintive numbers flow
> For old, unhappy, far-off things,

he may well be referring to verses.

Pope uses 'numbers' at least twice, and in *Essay on Criticism* is almost certainly using the term in the sense of metrical feet, thus:

But most by numbers judge a poet's song,
And smooth or rough with them is right or wrong.

nursery rhyme Such rhymes belong to oral tradition (*q.v.*) of literature. A nursery rhyme consists of a verse or verses recited or sung by a mother (or other adult) to the very young members of the family. The origins of most nursery rhymes are very obscure and are thought to be of considerable antiquity. Certainly a large number of them are known to have been alive in the oral tradition for two or three hundred years. They range from a very nearly meaningless jingle (*q.v.*) like:

Tae titly,
Little fitty,
Shin sharpy,
Knee knapy.
Hinchie pinchy,
Wymie bulgy,
Breast berry,
Chin cherry,
Moo merry,
Nose nappy,
Ee winky,
Broo brinky.
Ower the croon,
And awa' wi'it.

to quite a sophisticated poem in semi-ballad form like 'What can the matter be?'

O dear, what can the matter be?
Dear, dear, what can the matter be?
O dear, what can the matter be?
Johnny's so long at the fair.

He promised he'd buy me a fairing
  should please me,
And then for a kiss, oh! he vowed
  he would tease me,
He promised he'd bring me a bunch of blue ribbons
To tie up my bonny brown hair.

Somewhat more than eight hundred nursery rhymes are known to exist in English. Many of them are counting jingles, weather rhymes, songs from games, riddles, tongue-twisters and so forth. Apart from these there are ballads, or rhymes in more or less ballad (*q.v.*) form, like: *Aiken Drum, Willy Wood, Ten Little Nigger Boys, The Lover's Tasks, The Twelve Days of Christmas, Tom the Piper's Son, Cock Robin, The Love-Sick Frog, The Milk Maid, The Derby Ram* and *Bobby Shaftoe.* A score or more of the others could be described as extremely well known and many children are still brought up on them. For example: *Ring-a-Ring o' Roses, Humpty Dumpty, Goosey Gander, Ding, Dong, Bell, Old Mother Hubbard, Solomon Grundy, The Queen of Hearts, Miss Muffet, Little Jack Horner, Jack and Jill, Simple Simon, The House that Jack Built, Sing a Song of Sixpence, Old King Cole, Little Bo-Peep, Oranges and Lemons, London Bridge.*

The earliest known collection is *Tom Thumb's Pretty Song Book* (1744). *Mother Goose's Melody* (*c.* 1765) is another famous compilation. Mention should also be made of *Gammer Gurton's Garland* (1784); *Nursery Rhymes of England* (1842); *Popular Rhymes and Nursery Tales* (1849); and *The Oxford Dictionary of Nursery Rhymes* (1951), compiled by Iona and Peter Opie. Another collection by the same editors is *The Oxford Nursery Rhyme Book* (1955). *See* LULLABY.

O

obiter dicta (L 'things said by the way') A vaguely comprehensive term for remarks 'shed' in conversation (or in writing). The aphorism (*q.v.*) or *aperçu* is often an *obiter dictum.* The table-talk (*q.v.*) of great men like Goethe contains many examples. Boswell was an assiduous gleaner of Dr Johnson's *obiter dicta. See* -ANA; ANALECT; PENSEE.

objective and objectivity *See* SUBJECTIVITY AND OBJECTIVITY.

objective correlative A term first used apparently by the American painter Washington Allston in *c.* 1840 and subsequently revived and made famous by T. S. Eliot in an essay on *Hamlet* (1919). The relevant passage is: 'The only way of expressing emotion in the form of art is by finding an "objective correlative"; in other words, a set of objects, a situation, a chain of events which shall be the formula of that *particular* emotion; such that when the external facts, which must terminate in sensory experience, are given, the emotion is immediately evoked.' Eliot goes on to suggest that in Lady Macbeth's sleep-walking speech and in the speech that Macbeth makes when he hears of his wife's death, the words are completely adequate to the state of mind; whereas in Hamlet the prince is 'dominated by a state of mind which is inexpressible, because it is in *excess* of the facts as they appear.' These observations have provoked a good deal of debate.

In other (if Thomistic) terms a successful artistic creation requires an exquisite balance between, and coalescence of, form and matter. If the matter (thought, feeling, action) is 'too much' ('in excess of') the form (in this case words) we have a discrepancy, strain, a lack of unity (that is, insufficient correlation; they don't 'fadge'). Vice versa, another kind of discrepancy and strain: the experience is overwhelmed by the words. Colloquially we say 'I was speechless', 'It was indescribable'. In other words we have not found the 'formula'. In reverse, lacking the 'formula', again we over-describe, say too much. *See* SYMBOL AND SYMBOLISM.

objectivism A term coined by William Carlos Williams (1883–1963) *c.* 1930 and the name bestowed on a short-lived movement among American poets in the 1930s. Williams's early work was imagist. Later he moved to objectivism, which he described thus: 'It looks at the poem with a special eye to its structural aspects, how it has been constructed . . .' It was an attempt at greater precision. Other objectivist poets of the period were George Oppen (founder of the Objectivist Press) Carl Rakosi, Luis Zukovsky and Charles Reznikoff. *See* IMAGISTS.

obligatory scene The English version of the French *scène à faire.* It usually denotes a scene, probably of fairly intense emotional content, which the audience anticipates and which the dramatist feels obliged to include. For instance, one expects, sooner or later, a 'confrontation' between Hamlet and his mother (III, iv). One certainly could hardly expect Shakespeare to have contrived the play without it. When it comes it is an emotional climax.

oblique rhyme *See* HALF RHYME.

obscurity Obscurity in literature may be deliberate or involuntary. In either case an 'obscure' writer is one whose meaning is difficult to discern. Some 19th c. French poets like Mallarmé and Rimbaud were found obscure, but seem less so now. In this century Ezra Pound and T. S. Eliot and David Jones have been charged with obscurity. Marks of obscurity are: an elliptical style (loose syntax; anacoluthon; asyndeton, *qq.v.*), recondite allusion and reference, archaic or ornate language, private and subjective imagery, and the use of the words and phrases from foreign languages. A writer who wilfully disguises the fact that he has little or nothing to say is usually found out in the end. *See* HERMETICISM.

occasional verse Verse written for a particular occasion, perhaps to celebrate some incident or event. It may be light or serious. The elegy and the ode (*qq.v.*) have been used to produce some memorable occasional verse. The Poet Laureate (*q.v.*) is obliged to write a certain amount of it (e.g. for a coronation or a royal wedding). Notable examples are: Milton's *Lycidas* (1637) and his sonnet *On the Late Massacre in Piedmont*; Marvell's *Horatian Ode* *upon Cromwell's Return from Ireland* (1650); Dryden's *Alexander's Feast* (1697); Tennyson's *Charge of the Light Brigade* (1854); Hopkins's *The Wreck of the Deutschland* (c. 1875); Yeats's *Easter 1916*; and Auden's *September 1st 1939*.

octameter A line of eight feet; rare in Classical verse; rarer still in English verse. Swinburne's *March* provides instances; so, in the opinion of some, does Poe's *The Raven*. Tennyson attempted octameters in *Frater Ave atque Vale*:

Row us out from Desenzano, to your Sirmione row!
So they rowed, and there we landed – 'O venusta Sirmio!'
There to me through all the groves of olive in the summer
glow,
There beneath the Roman ruin where the purple flowers grow,
Came that 'Ave atque Vale' of the Poet's hopeless woe,
Tenderest of Roman poets nineteen-hundred years ago,
'Frater Ave atque Vale' – as we wandered to and fro
Gazing at the Lydian laughter of the Garda Lake below
Sweet Catullus's all-but-island, olive-silvery Sirmio!

It can be seen (and heard) at once what a difficult meter it is to manage because of the length of line. The meter is trochaic. Incidentally, the poem also illustrates the use of monorhyme (*q.v.*).

octastich (Gk 'eight rows') A group or stanza of eight lines. Also *huitain* (*q.v.*). A poem of eight lines. *See also* OCTAVE.

octateuch (Gk 'containing eight books') Specifically, the first eight books of the Old Testament; namely, the Pentateuch (*q.v.*), together with Joshua, Judges and Ruth.

octave also known as octet. A group of eight lines – either in stanza form, in which case it is *ottava rima* (*q.v.*), or as the first eight lines of a sonnet (*q.v.*). The octave in a sonnet usually rhymes abbaabba.

octavo A book in which the printer's sheets have been folded three times to produce eight leaves or sixteen pages. Abbrev. 8vo. *See also* DUODECIMO; FOLIO; QUARTO.

octonarius (L 'of eight each') In Latin verse a line of eight feet. Also a stanza of eight lines. *See also* OCTASTICH; OCTAVE; OTTAVA RIMA.

octosyllabic verse A tetrameter (*q.v.*) line containing eight syllables and usually consisting of iambic and/or trochaic feet. Often used in couplets (*q.v.*). In all probability the octosyllabic couplet derives from late medieval French poetry. It was well established in England by the 14th c. when it was used by Chaucer and Gower. Many British poets have since employed it, including Milton, Jonson, Dyer, Collins, Samuel (*Hudibras*) Butler, Wordsworth, Coleridge, Byron, Scott and William Morris. These lines are from Milton's *Il Penseroso*:

> But let my due feet never fail,
> To walk the studious cloister's pale,
> And love the high embowed roof,
> With antique pillars massy proof,
> And storied windows richly dight,
> Casting a dim religious light.

ode (Gk 'song') A lyric poem, usually of some length. The main features are an elaborate stanza-structure, a marked formality and stateliness in tone and style (which make it ceremonious), and lofty sentiments and thoughts. In short, an ode is rather a grand poem; a full-dress poem. However, this said, we can distinguish two basic kinds: the public and the private. The public is used for ceremonial occasions, like funerals, birthdays, state events; the private often celebrates rather intense, personal, and subjective occasions; it is inclined to be meditative, reflective. Tennyson's *Ode on the Death of the Duke of Wellington* is an example of the former; Keats's *Ode to a Nightingale*, an example of the latter.

The earliest odes of any note – or at any rate poems which could be put into the ode category – were written by Sappho (fl. *c.* 600 BC) and Alcaeus (fl. *c.* 611–580 BC). Fragments of Sappho's *Ode to Aphrodite* and Alcaeus's *Ode to Castor and Polydeuces* still survive.

Next, and more important, was Pindar (522–442 BC), a native of Thebes, whose odes were written for public occasions, especially in honour of victors in the Greek games. Modelled on the choric songs of Greek drama, they consisted of strophe, antistrophe and epode (*qq.v.*); a patterned stanza movement intended for choral song and dance.

Pindar's Latin counterpart was Horace (65–8 BC), but his odes were private and personal. They were stanzaically regular and based on limited metrical patterns, especially Alcaics and Sapphics (*qq.v.*). Between them Pindar and Horace were the begetters of the ode and both influenced the development of the form in Renaissance Europe. Meantime, the Provençal *canso* and the Italian *canzone* came near to the ode. Dante described the *canzone* as a composition 'in the tragic style, of equal stanzas without choral interludes, with reference to one subject'. This form, as used by Dante, Guinicelli and their contemporaries, survived and flourished into that period known as the High Renaissance, when Spenser's *Epithalamion* (1595) and *Prothalamion* (1596) showed the loftiness and majesty of the fully blown ode. *Epithalamion* consists of twenty-three regularly rhymed eighteen-line stanzas, followed by an *envoi* (*q.v.*). The stanzas are of ten-syllable lines interspersed with six-syllable lines and each concludes with an alexandrine (*q.v.*). Precedents for *Epithalamion* (Gk 'at the bridal chamber') can be found in the works of Sappho and Catullus. *Prothalamion* (Gk 'before the bridal chamber') is in the same stanzaic form as *Epithalamion* but without the *envoi*.

Late in the 16th c. and early in the 17th William Drummond of Hawthornden, Samuel Daniel and Michael Drayton all attempted odes, but Ben Jonson was the first to write one in the Pindaric tradition; namely, *Ode to Sir Lucius Cary and Sir H. Morison* (1629) which contains the following famous lines:

It is not growing like a tree
In bulk, doth make man better be;
Or standing long an Oak, three hundred year,
To fall a log at last, dry, bald, and sear.
A Lily of a day
Is fairer far, in May
Although it fall and die that night;
It was the plant and flower of light.
In small proportions we just beauties see;
And in short measure, life may perfect be.

Later Andrew Marvell wrote his Horatian *Ode upon Cromwell's Return from Ireland* (1650), and Abraham Cowley published his so-called Pindaric Odes, dispensing with the strophic arrangement. His stanzas were free and varied; so are the lines and meters. This flexibility had much influence on later writers, including Dryden. His four main contributions to the form all come into the Pindaric and public phylum and are among the finest odes in our language. They are: *Threnodia Augustalis* (1685); *Ode to the Memory of Mrs Anne Killigrew* (1686); *Song for St Cecilia's Day* (1687); and

Alexander's Feast (1697). One would have expected Milton to favour the ode form, but he never described any of his poems as such. However, his *On the Morning of Christ's Nativity* is all that one would expect of an ode, and Milton's conception of the grander type of lyric (*q.v.*) had much influence on poets in the 18th c. and during the Romantic period (*q.v.*).

Because of its architectonic possibilities (the elaborate rules, formality and decorum) one would expect the 18th c. poets to be attracted to the ode form, and indeed that period produced many distinguished examples.

Lady Winchilsea (1661–1720) wrote a Pindaric poem on *The Spleen*, and, early in his life, Pope composed an *Ode on Solitude* in the Horatian style. He also attempted the Pindaric manner in *Ode for Music on St Cecilia's Day.* Congreve, too, surprisingly attempted the ode and even wrote a discourse on the Pindaric ode. Isaac Watts, Akenside and Young also tried with varying degrees of success, but it was Collins and Gray, and, to a lesser extent, Cowper who wrote the great odes of the Augustan Age. Collins experimented with several metrical arrangements. The main works were: *Ode to Evening* and *Ode to Simplicity* (both in the Horatian mood), *Ode to Fear*, *Ode to Mercy*, *Ode on the Poetical Character*, *Ode to Liberty* (all in the Pindaric tradition and all published in 1747). Gray's odes also showed considerable variety and versatility. Four of them were relatively short and in simple stanza forms. These were the *Ode on Spring* (1742), *Ode on a Distant Prospect of Eton College* (1742), *Ode on Adversity* (1742) and *Ode on the Death of a Favourite Cat* (1747). To these should be added his two Pindarics: *The Bard* (1757) and *The Progress of Poesy* (1754).

Then followed: Coleridge's *France* (1798) and *Dejection* (1802); Wordsworth's magnificent *Ode on Intimations of Immortality* (1802–04) and his *Ode to Duty* (1805); Shelley's *Ode to the West Wind* (1819); and six superb odes by Keats (*c.* 1819): *On a Grecian Urn*; *To a Nightingale*; *To Autumn*; *On Melancholy*; *On Indolence*; and *To Psyche*.

After that grand constellation of poems most odes have looked a little pale. However, four notable instances must be mentioned. They are Tennyson's *Ode on the Death of the Duke of Wellington* (1854), in the Pindaric manner; and, much more recently, Allen Tate's splendid *Ode to the Confederate Dead*; and Auden's *In Memory of W. B. Yeats* and *In Praise of Limestone*, both in the Horatian manner.

Other well-known English poets to have essayed this kind of

lyric are: Robert Herrick, Landor, Matthew Arnold, Coventry Patmore, Francis Thompson and Algernon Charles Swinburne.

Outside England the ode has flourished particularly in Italy, France and Germany. In Italy experiments in the Pindaric mode were made by Trissinio, Minturno and Alamanni during the Renaissance period; and in France the members of the Pléiade (*q.v.*) tried the form. The most successful of these poets was Ronsard, who, in 1550, published *The First Four Books of Odes.* Later in the 16th c., very probably influenced by Ronsard, the Italian poets Tasso and Chiabrera also published some notable odes. Since their day Manzoni, Leopardi, Carducci and D'Annunzio have all written fine odes. In France the main follower of Ronsard was Boileau (in the 17th c.). In the Romantic period Lamartine, de Musset and Victor Hugo all attempted this lyric form. So, more recently, did Verlaine and Valéry. In Germany the ode was established by Weckherlin early in the 17th c., with *Oden und Gesänge* (1618–19). In the following century Goethe, Klopstock and Schiller revived the use of Classical models. Hölderlin, too, wrote some notable odes. *See also* ANTODE; OCCASIONAL VERSE.

off-Broadway The term denotes drama produced in New York City away from the main theatre 'stem'. It is often experimental drama. There is also a sub-species known as off-off-Broadway, which is clearly even further removed. Much of this kind of drama is in the 'happening' (*q.v.*) category, and may also be skit and revue (*qq.v.*). However, much of it is not. An outstanding repertory company has been the Living Theater (*q.v.*) founded in 1947 by Julian Beck and Judith Malina in order to present new and experimental plays.

officialese A term coined by Sir Ernest Gowers in *Plain Words* (1948) to denote the pompous, abstract, euphemistic, polysyllabic, periphrastic and circumlocutory language often used by officials, bureaucrats, politicians, sociologists, educationists and others. It is a form of verbocrap (*q.v.*), and ranges from semi-literate letters like:

> . . . We are in receipt of your esteemed order of the 29th inst. and beg to inform you that the articles in question have been discontinued. We shall cause you to be informed if any such articles are to be found in alternative sources.

to obfuscating 'Whitehallese' like:

> The efflorescence of a host of specialists in commerce and industry and the ever widening inroad that the Government is

> forging into our business lives are carcinogens of effective communication; for the jargon of, on the on the one hand, such people as computer programmers, systems analysts, cyberneticians, psychologists and, on the other hand, the complex prose of Whitehall constitute an invidious growth which is challenging our ability to express ourselves in clear simple terms.

Other works by Sir Ernest Gowers on the subject are: *The ABC of Plain Words* (1951) and *The Complete Plain Words* (1954). *See* EUPHEMISM; JARGON; LOGORRHEA; PERIPHRASIS.

Old Comedy Greek and of the 5th c. BC, this kind of drama developed from fertility rites in honour of Dionysus. It was fantastic, bawdy and scurrilous, and at times obscene. Invective and satire (*qq.v.*) were essential elements in it. Much of the verse was finely lyrical. The Chorus (*q.v.*) took an important part in the action and represented the dramatist's point of view. In what is known as New Comedy (*q.v.*) the Chorus disappeared. Unhappily only the plays of Aristophanes survive from this period. The best known are *Clouds*, *Knights* and *Frogs*. *See* COMEDY; MIDDLE COMEDY; PARABASIS.

Old French (OF) and Provençal forms Between about 850 to about 1300 most French and Provençal literature was in verse and belonged to oral tradition (*q.v.*). From the 12th c. many of the main forms were becoming established. Metrically elaborate, a great many of them were worked out by the troubadour (*q.v.*) poets. In succeeding centuries most of them were adopted in England and were particularly used by the Victorian poets. The principal forms are: *ballade, chant royal, conte, dit, flamenca, lai, motet, rondeau, rondel, sestina, villanelle* and *virelai* (*qq.v.*). *See also* CHANSON DE GESTES; FIXED FORM; OCTOSYLLABIC VERSE; ROMANCE.

Old Vic Theatre Opened in 1818, it was formerly known as the Coburg and was for many years associated with melodrama (*q.v.*). It was renamed the Royal Victoria and soon came to be known as the 'Old Vic'. A troubled financial period ensued and it was closed in 1880. Soon after, it was bought by Emma Cons, a crusader of the temperance movement, who turned it into an amusement hall. In 1898 Emma Cons was joined by Lilian Baylis (her niece), who became manager in 1912 and made it famous as a theatre for the production of Shakespeare. Between the wars it flourished. War damage put it out of action, but it was restored and from 1947 to 1952 was the headquarters of the Old Vic School under the director Michel Saint-Denis. Between 1953 and 1958 the complete First Folio of Shakespeare's work was presented, and in 1963 it became the home of the National Theatre Company (*q.v.*), which remained there until 1976. Thereafter it had a chequered career and was empty from 1981 to 1983 when it was bought by the Canadian millionaire Ed Mirvish, who had it completely renovated. After it reopened it began another successful career with a range of classics, musicals and new plays.

Omar Khayyám quatrain A stanza of four ten-syllable lines rhyming aaba, as used in Edward Fitzgerald's translation from the Persian of *The Rubá'iyát of Omar Khayyám*, first published anonymously in 1859. *See also* QUATRAIN.

omnibus edition Such an edition of an author's works includes in one volume everything that he has written. The works of Oscar Wilde and Robert Service, among others, have been concentrated in such a form.

one-act play Self-evidently a dramatic work consisting of only one act. Usually short (a playing time of fifteen to forty minutes is about normal). Very rare before late in the 19th c. though there are many earlier examples of shortish plays which could qualify as one-act plays, and the after-piece popular in the 18th c. was a kind of one-act play. However, towards the end of the 19th c. an increasing number of small experimental theatres greatly encouraged the development of the one-act drama as a form in its own right and it was often used as a curtain raiser (*q.v.*). Since that period it has flourished and is as popular as ever, though seldom used as a curtain raiser. A more common practice now is to present two or three one-act plays by way of a double or triple bill. Two recent examples of this are Harold Pinter's *Landscape* and *Silence* (1970) and John Mortimer's *Come As You Are* (1971).

A one-act play is the dramatic equivalent of a short story and tends to concentrate on a single episode or situation and as a general rule has only two or three characters. In theme, mood and subject the range is considerable – from farce to tragedy. Many famous dramatists have attempted the form, including Chekhov, Strindberg, Shaw, Hauptmann, Synge, J. M. Barrie, Eugene O'Neill, Samuel Beckett and Harold Pinter. Of the hundreds of examples that exist the following are some of the better known: J. M. Morton's farce *Box and Cox* (1847); Chekhov's *The Bear* (1888), *The Proposal* (1889), and *The Wedding* (1890); Strindberg's *The Stronger* (1890), *Playing with Fire* (1892) and *The Link* (1897); Oscar Wilde's *Salomé* (1896); Yeats's *The Pot of Broth* (1902); Synge's *Riders to the Sea* (1904); Lady Gregory's *The Gaol Gate* (1906) and *The Rising of the Moon* (1907); O'Neill's group of one-act plays about the sea (1916–18) later produced as *SS Glencairn* (1924); J. M. Barrie's *Shall We Join the Ladies?* (1922); Noël Coward's *Tonight at 8.30* (1936), a series of nine one-act plays, eight of which were first performed in various combinations.

Some more recent ones are: Sartre's *Huis-clos* (1944); Genet's *The Maids* (1947) and *Deathwatch* (1949); Rattigan's *The Browning Version* (1948); Ionesco's *The Bald Prima Donna* (1950), *The Lesson* (1951) and *The Chairs* (1952); Wolf Mankowitz's *The Bespoke Overcoat* (1953); Ionesco's *The New Tenant* (1955); Harold Pinter's *The Room* (1957); David Campton's *The Lunatic View* (1957); Tennessee Williams's *Suddenly Last Summer* (1958), with *Something Unspoken* in a double bill titled *Garden District*; John Mortimer's *Dock Brief* (1958) and *What Shall We Tell Caroline?* (1958); Beckett's monodrama *Krapp's Last Tape* (1958); Albee's *The Zoo Story* (1959); Rattigan's *Separate Tables* (1959), a double one-act bill; Pinter's *The Dumb Waiter* (1960); David Campton's *Four Minute Warning* (1960); Alan Ayckbourn's *Intimate Exchanges* (1984), a series of nine plays all interconnected and to be presented in various combinations; Harold Pinter's *Mountain Language* (1988); and Alan Bennett's double bill of *An Englishman Abroad* and *A Question of Attribution* (1988).

onomasticon A Greek term for a book of names or a vocabulary. Formerly used sometimes for lexicon and dictionary (*qq.v.*).

onomatopoeia (Gk 'name-making') The formation and use of words to imitate sounds. For example: *dong*, *crackle*, *moo*, *pop*, *whizz*, *whoosh*, *zoom*. It is a figure of speech in which the sound reflects the sense. It is very common in verse and fairly common in prose and is found in many literatures at all times. As a rule it is deliberately used to achieve a special effect, as in these lines from Eliot's *Dry Salvages*:

> When the train starts, and the passengers are settled
> To fruit, periodicals and business letters

(And those who saw them off have left the platform)
Their faces relax from grief into relief,
To the sleepy rhythm of a hundred hours.

The whole passage is subtly onomatopoetic; the rhythm of the second line is a beautifully skilful evocation of the clickety-click of wheels on rails.

Pope's *obiter dictum* that the 'sound must seem an echo to the sense' is profoundly true of poetry in general. The following lines from D. H. Lawrence's poem *Snake* illustrate the point:

He reached down from a fissure in the earth-wall in the gloom
And trailed his yellow-brown slackness soft-bellied down, over
the edge of the stone trough
And rested his throat upon the stone bottom,
And where the water had dripped from the tap, in a small
clearness,
He sipped with his straight mouth,
Softly drank through his straight gums, into his slack long body,
Silently.

In the rhythm, motion and length of the lines and in the totality of the sound effects Lawrence has suggested very well the sinuous and slow progression of the reptile. The sound effects are, so to speak, visual as well as aural. This is phanopoeia (*q.v.*). *See also* ALLITERATION; ASSONANCE; CACOPHONY; CONSONANCE; EUPHONY; LOGOPOEIA; MELOPOEIA; SYNAESTHESIA; TONE COLOUR.

ontology A philosophical term which denotes the study of being. As a literary term it has a special meaning, thanks to John Crowe Ransom. According to him the texture (*q.v.*) and structure (*q.v.*) of a poem, which, combined, provide the meaning, combine also to give it 'ontology' – that quality or property peculiar to itself which distinguishes it from anything that is *not* poetry.

open couplet A couplet (*q.v.*) in which the sense is not completed in the second line, but is carried forward into the third or fourth line; or perhaps for several, though this is rare. This example comes from Pope's *Epistle to Augustus*:

Our rural Ancestors, with little blest,
Patient of labour when the end was rest,

> Indulg'd the day that hous'd their annual grain,
> With feasts, and off 'rings, and a thankful strain.

See CLOSED COUPLET; END-STOPPED LINE; ENJAMBEMENT; HEROIC COUPLET.

open stage The term was first used by Richard Southern, the theatre historian, in 1953 to describe any form of staging in which the performers are not separated from the audience by a proscenium arch. Open stage techniques were developed in the first part of the 20th c., particularly by William Poel (1852–1934), Max Reinhardt (1873–1943), Vsevolod Meyerhold (1874–1942), Jacques Copeau (1879–1949) and Nikolai Okhlopkov (1900–67). The main forms are: (a) 'thrust stage', with an audience on three sides; (b) 'end stage', with an audience facing it from one end; (c) 'transverse stage', with an audience on two opposite sides. There is also theatre-in-the-round (*q.v.*), where the audience sits all round the acting area.

opera (L *opera* 'exertion, service', collective feminine from plural of neuter noun *opus* 'work') Originally opera was chanted tragedy, and what is generally agreed to be the first, Rinuccini's *Dafne* (1594), was an attempt to revive Classical Greek tragedy – a form which has had a profound influence on opera. The masque (*q.v.*) influenced the development of opera. Surprisingly few writers (and very few poets) have been attracted to opera *as* writers (except, of course, for those whose expertise and business it is to compose libretti). On the other hand, librettists and composers have drawn freely upon plays and other works for their operas. An interesting example of a collaboration between dramatist and composer is that between Bertolt Brecht and Kurt Weill, which produced *The Threepenny Opera* (1928), *The Rise and Fall of the City of Mahagonny* (1927–9) and *The Seven Deadly Sins* (1933). More recently Auden and Kallman collaborated with Stravinsky to create *The Rake's Progress* (1951). Some notable modern examples of adaptation are Benjamin Britten's operas from Henry James's *The Turn of the Screw* (1953), Herman Melville's *Billy Budd* (1951) and George Crabbe's story of Peter Grimes in his poem *The Borough* (1945). *See also* BALLAD OPERA; LIBRETTO; MELODRAMA; OPERETTA.

opéra-comique A form of drama set to music. Music alternates with spoken dialogue and thus it is akin to ballad opera (*q.v.*). It originated in the *comédies à ariettes* which were comedies (or farces) punctuated with lyrical passages sung to music. They became popular early in the 18th c. and were performed at the Théâtre de la Foire in Paris. In *c.* 1780 the company at the theatre became known as the Opéra-Comique and in 1783 moved to the Salle Favart.

opere citato (L 'in the work cited') Often abbreviated to *op. cit.*, it refers to a book to which reference has already been made. *See* IBIDEM; IDEM; LOCO CITATO.

operetta (It 'little opera') a light drama (for all practical purposes synonymous with F *opéra bouffe*, It *opera buffa*). It consists of musical interludes and spoken dialogue, often satirical. Famous examples are Gay's *Beggar's Opera* (1728), Sheridan's *The Duenna* (1775) and the numerous works of Gilbert and Sullivan. *See also* BALLAD OPERA; OPERA.

oral tradition Poetry belonging to this tradition is composed orally, or made up as the poet goes along. As a rule, it is the product of illiterate or semi-literate societies. It is usually sung or chanted (often to musical accompaniment) and is the earliest of all poetry, in the sense that it precedes written poetry. It is still alive in many parts of the world, and in some regions of Europe: for instance, Sicily, the remoter parts of Greece, and in the central Balkans (especially Bosnia, Serbia and Macedonia). In the upland districts of Jugoslavia it is still possible to find a *guslar* (*q.v.*) reciting verses on recent events. *See also* BALLAD; BYLINA; EPIC; FOLKSONG; NARODNE PESME.

oratio obliqua See INDIRECT SPEECH.

oratio recta *See* INDIRECT SPEECH.

organic form That form which derives from the nature and materials of a writer's subject and theme, as opposed to mechanic form, which derives from rules and conventions imposed on the nature and materials. Shakespeare and his fellow dramatists might be claimed to favour organic form, while the French classical dramatists (like Racine) had a predilection for mechanic form (indeed, in France you were *expected* to follow the rules). However, if a poet chooses to express himself by means of a fixed form (e.g. a *villanelle*, *q.v.*) or by means of an established stanzaic or metrical scheme (e.g. *quatrain, terza rima, qq.v.*) then the result may be a coalescence of organic and mechanic form.

The idea of organic form is to be found in Plato's *Phaedrus* where Socrates draws an analogy between making a speech and the growth of a living creature. It was the German romantics and Coleridge who worked out the analogy in considerable detail. The implications of organic form are that a work 'grows' from a seminal concept, like a living organism. So declared Henry James, Croce and many others. *See* CONVENTION; DONNEE; INSPIRATION; LIGNE DONNEE.

organic metaphor Also known as a functional or structural metaphor; in this figure of speech the vehicle (*see* TENOR AND VEHICLE) is symbolic and carries an implicit tenor. If we examine the following passage from Robinson Jeffers's poem *Hurt Hawks* we may be able to disentangle sense from this thicket of jargon. He has described the wounded hawk and his feelings about it. He comes to the point where he decides that the creature must be put out of its misery:

I gave him the lead gift in the twilight.
What fell was relaxed,
Owl-downy, soft feminine feathers; but what
Soared: the fierce rush: the night-herons by the flooded river
Cried for fear at its rising
Before it was quite unsheathed from reality.

The periphrasis and euphemism (*qq.v.*) of 'lead gift' clearly denote a bullet. What follows suggests that the released 'spirit' of the hawk soars heavenwards; the reversal of stooping to its prey. 'Unsheathed from reality' suggests parting from this life; the sheath being the heap of 'feminine feathers'. Thus the vehicle is the event of death; the tenor, the image (very nearly abstract in this case), the soaring of the hawk's 'soul'. *See also* METAPHOR; TELESCOPED METAPHOR.

orientalism A term pertaining to the Orient as discovered, recorded, described, defined, imagined, produced and, in a sense, 'invented' by Europe and the West. As far as literature is concerned it refers to the discourse by the West about the East, which comprises a vast corpus of texts – literary, sociological, scientific, historical, linguistic/philological, political, anthropological and topographical – which has been accumulating since the Renaissance and particularly since the 18th c. and to which there is no counterpart in the East about the West. In all, this discourse aggregates to a 'textual universe', as Edward Said puts it in his remarkable book *Orientalism* (1978). It also refers to the attitudes of the West towards the East; to the Occident (the outsiders) looking in/on/at the Orient – in fact 'watching' the East and endeavouring to explain and interpret it. A parallel to this image – a parallel nearer home and on a more modest scale – is afforded by Albania, a country for the most part sealed from the West and closed to visitors (especially writers and journalists) during the régimes of Enver Hoxha and his successor Ramiz Alia. For many years there have been the 'Albania watchers', a minority group of Albanian-speaking experts (mostly academics who have never been to Albania) who have created a discourse about the country.

As for what the East consists of, the profusion, in the West, of topographical/geographical terms suggests a certain difficulty in coping with it, in 'containing' it, so to speak, in giving it shape, boundaries, limits. So vast and multitudinous an area (and, with it, equally broad concepts) has led to vague sub-divisions. In Britain we have long been accustomed to such loose categories as the Near East, the Middle East and the Far East (with other sub-divisions such as the Levant and Asia Minor). These categories have their counterparts in, for instance, German (*der Nahe Osten, der Mittlere Osten* and *der Ferne Osten*) and in French (*l'Orient, proche Orient* and *moyen Orient*). This vagueness is compounded by the vexed and disputed matter of 'where East meets West' (and vice versa). No one has yet proposed a junction point of general satisfaction. A number have been suggested: Aden, Suez, Alexandria, Istanbul and even Prijedor (in north-west Bosnia), where, until relatively recently, there stood, from the British point of view, almost the next mosque after Woking. The likeliest candidate is perhaps Sarajevo: an important cultural, commercial and political centre during the period of the Ottoman Islamic Empire and where even today there are some eighty mosques and numerous public 'oriental' buildings. Moreover, it was at Sarajevo that the great camel trains carrying merchandise from Turkestan and Baluchistan, from Persia, Syria and Arabia, finally came to a halt. Further north and west the climate was (and is) unsuitable for camels because they developed sore throats, bronchitis and other pulmonary afflictions. In the ethnographical museum there is a brass instrument for funnelling linctus down the throats of ailing camels.

Orientalism as discourse is believed to have begun its formal existence with the decision of the Church Council of Vienne in 1312 to found a series of chairs in Arabic, Greek, Hebrew and Syriac at Oxford, Paris, Bologna, Avignon and Salamanca. In the Middle Ages (or the late Middle Ages) the East became of increasing interest to the West. It was remote, inaccessible, inscrutable and exotic. Curiosity and speculation were stimulated by travellers' tales and improbably tall stories. Marco Polo (*c.* 1254–*c.* 1324) is a prime example of an author who began to introduce the East to the West with his immensely popular book of travels which was translated into many European languages and first 'Englished' by John Frampton in 1579. And there was Sir John Mandeville, the supposed author of a famous travel book also found in many European languages after its first appearance in Anglo-Norman French in 1356–7. Ostensibly a guide for pilgrims to the Holy Land, it peregrinates (with notable fabulations) through India, Egypt, Persia, Turkey and Tartary.

By early in the 17th c. orientalism as a discourse was well under way. The rise and spread of Islam (and thus the advent of the 'Infidel' and the 'Heathen') had threatened Christianity and led to the Crusades, thus bringing East nearer to West. The battle of Kosovo in 1389 enabled the Turks to establish themselves in the Balkans and the fall of Constantinople in 1453 was virtually the end of Christianity in much of Asia Minor. The gradual spread of Islam and the expansion of the Ottoman Empire threatened the West and Christianity even more. At the height of its power and development the Ottoman Empire's furthest western and eastern frontiers, on the Adriatic and the Caspian respectively, were nearly two thousand miles apart and at one stage the Ottoman Empire incorporated what is now Jugoslavia, Hungary, Bulgaria, Albania, Greece, the islands of the eastern Mediterranean, the Levant, Egypt, the North African littoral as far as Morocco and modern Turkey itself. The West became fearful of this encroachment, and how to deal with it became a matter of urgent military necessity. Numerous city states (especially Venice) were actively involved in combating the Turks. By degrees the expansion ceased and over a period of some four hundred years or more the administration of the Empire became steadily more unwieldy, incompetent and corrupt. By the 18th c. travel through it, though often hazardous, became possible for the intrepid. Travellers' accounts began to proliferate. During the 18th c. interest in the East (Near, Middle and Far) burgeoned and influenced literature in Europe and England. A version of the *Arabian Nights' Entertainments*, or *The Thousand and One Nights*, by Antoine Galland appeared in 1704 and 1717 and aroused much interest in Europe. It also contributed to the vogue of the oriental tale (*q.v.*) in the 18th c. The Grand Tour (*q.v.*) became fashionable and the more adventurous travellers went far beyond the generally prescribed itineraries of the Tour. During the latter part of the century Sir William Jones, one of the first great British orientalists, translated many works from Arabic and Persian and these were to influence the oriental themes of Romantic poets such as Byron, Southey and Thomas Moore. Richard Knolles's *The Generall Historie of the Turkes* (1603) was much admired during the 18th c., not least by Johnson and, later, by Byron.

The rise and expansion of the British Empire vastly increased the archives of oriental studies. So, to a lesser extent, did French colonial enterprises in the Near East and Egypt (during the Napoleonic period); and, later in Indo-China. The 19th c. was the outstanding period of oriental studies. Numerous learned and cultural societies were established in Europe to advance them. The East, as Disraeli suggested in his novel *Tancred* (1847), could be regarded as a 'career'. Countless colonial officials, statesmen, explorers, soldiers, diplomats, doctors, missionaries, travellers, writers, navigators and merchant adventurers contributed memoirs, autobiographies, commentaries, government reports (and what not?) to the corpus of oriental studies. So did scholars, not a few of whom never went anywhere near any part of the East. Encyclopaedic records of oriental studies were published. One of the first important ones was the *Bibliothèque orientale* (1697), a vast compendium of virtually all that was then known about the East, by Barthélemy d'Herbelot (1625–95). Another notable example was Jules Mohl's *Vingt-sept ans d'histoire des études orientales*, a two-volume logbook of everything of note that took place in orientalism between 1840 and 1867. Other outstanding French orientalists were Abraham-Hyacinthe Anquetil-Duperron (1731–1805), Silvestre de Sacy (1758–1838) and Louis Massignon, who made invaluable contributions in the inter-war period in the 20th c. Ernest Renan (1823–92) also achieved fame but was frequently at fault in his judgement and assumptions. German orientalism was largely in the hands of scholars such as Steinthal, Müller, Becker, Goldziher, Brockelmann and Nöldeke. Numerous British adventurers, explorers and scholars have added to the store of oriental studies. For example, Edward Lane, the Arabist, who published his classic work *An Account of the Manners and Customs of the Modern Egyptians* in 1836, Alexander Kinglake, Sir Richard Burton, C. M. Doughty, W. G. Palgrave, T. E. Lawrence, D. G. Hogarth, Gertrude Bell,

Ronald Storrs, Wilfrid Scawen Blunt, St John Philby, H. A. R. Gibb, Edward Henry Palmer and Wilfred Thesiger. We should also mention Lafcadio Hearn, half-Irish, half-Greek, who wrote some memorable books about Japan late in the 19th c. French poets and novelists were also particularly attracted to and influenced by the Orient, especially Chateaubriand, Lamartine, Victor Hugo, Gérard de Nerval, Flaubert and Pierre Loti. Chateaubriand, Hugo and Loti were responsible, among others, for fabricating and projecting a 'romantic' view of it, and it is true that much that belongs to the field of orientalism has remarkably little to do with the actualities and realities of life in the Orient – wherever it be. It is the product of 'myth', legend, assumption and theory. It is as if the magnetism of the East, the spell it cast, inspired Europeans to create or re-create an East which would accord with what the West wanted it to be: mysterious, wonderful, bizarre and perhaps even immoral. Chateaubriand 'invented' an Orient which suited him and what Stendhal called his 'stinking egoism'. Hugo's collection of lyrics, *Les Orientales* (1829), evokes a personal view of an Orient which is exotic, languorous and barbaric. Loti used Constantinople as a picturesque setting for sentimental romance novels.

In the 20th c. miscellaneous British novelists – Kipling, E. M. Forster, Anthony Burgess, Paul Scott and J. G. Farrell, for example – attempted to depict the British and Asians under the imperial régime.

The relationship of the United States with the Orient only really began with the Second World War and thus in terms of political and military action. Since that war the military/political factor has been pre-eminent and American orientalism is largely concerned with policies, with data, statistics, trends and commerce. Culture and literature seldom come in to it.

The bibliography of European orientalism and oriental studies multiplies yearly. Apart from Edward Said's highly original critical analysis, there have been many scholarly works in recent years. Of special note are Raymond Schwab's *La Renaissance orientale* (1950), Johann W. Fück's *Die arabischen Studien in Europa bis in den Anfang des 20. Jahrhunderts* (1955) and Dorothy Metlitzki's *The Matter of Araby in England* (1977). Plus traditional-type travel books (*q.v.*) by such authors as Freya Stark, Wilfred Thesiger, Colin Thubron, Paul Theroux, William Dalrymple and V. S. Naipaul, whose excursion into Islam, *Among the Believers* (1981), is a considered attempt to assess Islamic movements and feelings today.

Much of the discourse of orientalism has been partial and prejudiced and often condescending (especially that originating from government servants, colonial officers, political agents/rulers *et al.*). Much, too, reveals a certain arrogance and sense of superiority – a 'we know best' attitude – on the part of the West towards the East. Much of it is marred by racism, naïvety, presumption and plain ignorance, and there are often facile generalizations by people who should know better (e.g. Ernest Renan, T. E. Lawrence) as in vague statements about 'the Arab mind', 'the Asian sensibility', 'the Semitic temperament'. Moreover, not a little of it has been repetitive and reductive in so far as writers/scholars have merely recycled the ideas and views of predecessors to create a body of *idées reçues* of the kind that Flaubert called 'bromides': platitudes and trite generalizations which purport to embody a truth.

oriental tale/novel A form of fiction which had a considerable vogue in the 18th c. and early in the 19th c. They tended to be rather exotic and extravagant tales of adventure with 'Eastern' settings (more particularly those of the Near East). The heroes were luminously good and virtuous; the villains suitably double-dyed and wicked. Supernatural and/or magical elements were a prominent feature in this literature of diversion and entertainment.

The vogue is partly explained by the fact that the *Arabian Nights* appeared in an English translation in 1705–8 and these tales became extremely popular. Sir William Jones (1746–94), an outstanding orientalist, also made available translations of Indian and Arabic literature of which most people knew nothing. There was another reason: by *c.* 1750 there was a sizeable quantity of travel books (*q.v.*) giving accounts of journeys to the Levant and Near East and through the Ottoman Empire, which by that stage was huge. These travels aroused considerable interest in the 'East' and everything to do with it. The more intrepid travellers (e.g. Lady Mary Wortley Montague) who undertook the Grand Tour (*q.v.*) roved as far as Constantinople (as Istanbul was then known) and beyond.

The fiction produced displays variety, and ranges from Johnson's sober didactic romance *The History of Rasselas, Prince of Abyssinia* (1759) to Beckford's improbable fantasia *Vathek* (1786). Other notable examples are: John Hawkesworth's *Almoran and Hamlet* (1761); James Ridley's *Tales of the Genii* (1764); Frances Sheridan's *The History of Nourjahad* (1767); Alexander Dow's *Tales . . . of*

Inatulla of Delhi (1768); and James Morier's *The Adventures of Hajji Baba of Ispahan* (1824).

There were also oriental narrative tales in verse, such as Southey's *The Curse of Kehama* (1810), Byron's *The Giaour* (1813) and *The Corsair* (1814), and Thomas Moore's enormously popular *Lalla Rookh* (1817), which had run to twenty editions by 1840. Moore used the frame story (*q.v.*) method with a series of tales in verse which were connected by a narrative in prose.

originality A work may be said to possess this quality if, as a result of the author's invention (*q.v.*), he innovates a new form or mode; or, perhaps, uses hitherto undiscovered or unexploited themes and subjects. *See* CONVENTION; FANCY AND IMAGINATION; INSPIRATION; NOVELTY; PLAGIARISM.

orismology (Gk 'definition of knowledge') The explanation of technical terms, which this dictionary is in aid of. *See* LEXICOGRAPHY.

ornamentalism A term which, in Russian literary history, denotes an intricate, mannered and ostentatious prose style. It is usually related to prose of the early part of the 20th c. and particularly to a school of writers led by Andrei Bely (1880–1934) and Alexei Remizov.

orta oyunu (T 'middle play') A kind of Turkish folk drama (*q.v.*) not dissimilar to *commedia dell'arte* (*q.v.*). The characters are Turkish regional 'types' and the actors imitate their dialects while depicting their occupations. The stage is usually an open space with an audience all round. Occasionally a platform is used. Scenery is limited and the actors normally sit with the audience. Each actor has his own piece of music and introduces himself with a song or a dance. There are two main characters – Pişekâr and Kavuklu. The former wears a brightly coloured costume and carries a club which he uses to hit the other actors. Pişekâr is on stage nearly all the time. The latter is the comic character and the dialogues between them form the basis of the play. There is also a woman (Zenne) played by a man, and perhaps one or two other subsidiary characters. Each *orta oyunu* normally consists of two parts. In the first Pişekâr and Kavuklu do their comic turn (reminiscent of Punch and Judy), and in the second the Turkish character types are 'taken off'. *See* KARAGOZ.

orthotone A word which is normally unstressed, but which, because it occupies a certain position in a metrical line, may receive stress. Likely words are: and, but, the, a, an, to. Orthotonic words are fairly common in ballad (*q.v.*).

Oscan Fable *See* FABULA.

Ossianism Ossian is the name normally given to Oisin, a legendary Gaelic warrior and poet, who is supposed to have lived in the 3rd c. In 1760 James Macpherson (1736–96) published *Fragments of Ancient Poetry Collected in the Highlands of Scotland, and Translated from the Gaelic or Erse Language*. In 1762 he produced *Fingal*, and in 1763 *Temora*. Both purported to be translations of epic poems in Gaelic by a poet named Ossian. In fact they were a sort of fabulation of Gelic ballads mixed with Macpherson's own work. Notwithstanding this, his evocation of a remote past, a Gaelic twilight of myth and legend, had a considerable influence on writers in Europe and made some contribution to romanticism (*q.v.*). Goethe was particularly interested in the Ossianic poems; so were Herder and Schiller. They were widely translated, and the long-term effects of the so-called Ossianic movement are discernible late in the 19th c. *See* LITERARY FORGERIES.

ostranenie *See* DEFAMILIARIZATION.

ottava rima (It 'eighth rhyme') An eight-line iambic stanza rhyming abababcc. It is almost certainly of Italian or Sicilian origin, and it may have developed from the *canzone* (*q.v.*) or the *strambotto* (*q.v.*). A number of medieval Italian poets employed it, including Boccaccio, who, by using it in *Teseida* (*c.* 1340) and *Filostrato* (*c.* 1340), helped to establish it as the main form for Italian narrative verse (*q.v.*). Other poets who developed it were Boiardo, Pulci and Poliziano in the 15th c. Ariosto used it for *Orlando Furioso* (1516) and Tasso for *Gerusalemme Liberata* (1575). Spanish and Portuguese poets followed their example, particularly Ercilla in *La Araucana* (1569, 1578, 1589) and Camoëns in *Os Lusiadas* (1570). The form was introduced into English verse by Sir Thomas Wyatt early in the 16th c. Later Spenser and Drayton used it. It was not favoured much thereafter until Shelley and Keats experimented. It proved the ideal vehicle for Byron's narrative poems. He used it for *Beppo* (1818) and *The Vision of Judgment* (1822), and, most notably, in *Don Juan* (1819–24). From time to time since, other poets have employed the form. Yeats's *Sailing to Byzantium* is an outstanding example. He also wrote *ottava rima* for *Among School Children*, from which the following stanza (the last) comes:

> Labour is blossoming or dancing where
> The body is not bruised to pleasure soul,
> Nor beauty born of its own despair,
> Nor blear-eyed wisdom out of midnight oil.
> O chestnut tree, great-rooted blossomer,
> Are you the leaf, the blossom or the bole?
> O body swayed to music, O brightening glance,
> How can we know the dancer from the dance?

See HUITAIN; SICILIAN OCTAVE; SPENSERIAN STANZA.

outrides *See* SPRUNG RHYTHM.

outsider A term and concept which had some vogue in the late 1950s as a result of a much publicized and much talked-of book called *The Outsider* (1956) by Colin Wilson. An 'outsider' may be seen as a person (especially a creative artist) who is, in some respects, above and 'outside' the society in which he or she lives and perhaps even superior to it. There have always been the unconventional, the eccentric and the egregious; the outsider is all these; perhaps even a kind of 'superman'. Those endowed with what is loosely known as genius (*q.v.*) might be regarded as outsiders. The German romantics seem to have had some concept of such a being with their image of the *Kraftgenie* (*q.v.*). Anybody can make their own selection of outsiders. Among Wilson's are Nietzsche, Kierkegaard, Kafka, T. E. Lawrence and Ernest Hemingway. Another list might include James Joyce, Jean Genet, Samuel Beckett, Wilfred Thesiger and Jack Kerouac. In a different way there are outsiders as 'characters' in literature. For example, the hero of Camus's novel *L'Etranger* (1942). A further category might be the *lishni chelovek* or 'superfluous man' (*q.v.*) of 19th c. Russian novelists. In short it is one of those concepts and terms which may be made to serve a variety of theses.

ovillejo A ten-line Spanish stanza form with three paired rhymes (each pair comprises one octosyllabic and one shorter line) followed by a quatrain or *redondilla* (*qq.v.*) of three octosyllables and a fourth line repeating the three short lines. It was so named by Francisco de Cascales (1564–1642).

Oxford movement Also known as the Tractarian movement, it originated in July 1833 as a result of a sermon by Keble on the subject of national apostasy; a sermon against the Latitudinarian and Erastian attitudes of the time. Men who shared Keble's views supported him, and in 1833 there appeared the first of the famous *Tracts for the Times*. The most notable figures in the movement were Newman, Froude and Pusey. The main object was to revive the position and role of the Church of England and to re-emphasize its sacramental and divine mission. Ironically, in the course of this reforming effort, doctrines akin to those of Roman Catholicism were adopted.

The movement caused a very considerable disturbance and involved several leading literary figures – especially Charles Kingsley and Matthew Arnold. Kingsley attacked Newman and the latter replied in *Apologia pro Vita Sua* (1864), a major work in English literature. *See* TRACT.

oxymoron (Gk 'pointedly foolish') A figure of speech which combines incongruous and apparently contradictory words and meanings for a special effect. As in Lamb's celebrated remark: 'I like a smuggler. He is the only honest thief'.

It is a common device, closely related to antithesis and paradox (*qq.v.*), especially in poetry, and is of considerable antiquity. There are many splendid instances in English poetry. It was particularly popular in the late 16th c. and during the 17th. A famous example occurs in *Romeo and Juliet*, when Romeo jests about love:

> Here's much to do with hate, but more with love.
> Why then, O brawling love! O loving hate!
> O anything! of nothing first create!
> O heavy lightness! serious vanity!
> Mis-shapen chaos of well-seeming forms!

Other well-known examples are Milton's description of hell in *Paradise Lost*:

> No light, but rather darkness visible

And Pope's reference to man in *Essay on Man*:

> Plac'd on this isthmus of a middle state,
> A being darkly wise, and rudely great.

Goldsmith has some striking ones in *The Deserted Village*:

> Where grey-beard mirth and smiling toil retired

> The toiling pleasure sickens into pain

A particularly well-known example comes in Tennyson's *Lancelot and Elaine*:

The shackles of an old love straiten'd him
His honour rooted in dishonour stood,
And faith unfaithful kept him falsely true.

Almost as well-known are these lines in Francis Thompson's *The Hound of Heaven*:

I tempted all His servitors, but to find
My own betrayal in their constancy,
In faith to him their fickleness to me,
Their traitorous trueness, and their loyal deceit.

And a very arresting one in Gerard Manley Hopkins's *The Wreck of the Deutschland*:

[She] Was calling 'O Christ, Christ, come quickly':
The cross to her she calls Christ to her, christens her wild-worse Best.

Probably the most famous instance of sustained oxymoron is Sir Thomas Wyatt's version of Petrarch's 134th sonnet, which begins:

I find no peace, and all my war is done;
I fear and hope, I burn and freeze like ice;
I flee above the wind, yet can I not arise;
And nought I have and all the world I season.

Other English poets who have used the figure extensively are Keats and Crashaw. The Italian Marino and the Spaniard Góngora also had a predilection for it.

oxytone (Gk 'sharp strain') A word or line of verse with the accent (*q.v.*) on the last syllable. Every iambic or anapaestic line bears the accent or stress on the last syllable. *See* ANAPAEST; FOOT; IAMB.

P

ꕥꕥꕥꕥꕥꕥ

pace-egging play A mumming play (*q.v.*); usually the play of St George (or Sir George) which used to be performed (and occasionally still is) in the north of England, especially Lancashire. The Mummers called themselves 'pace-eggers' after the Eastertide custom of staining hard-boiled eggs and rolling them against one another until they broke, after which they were eaten. Easter Monday is the traditional day for this. *Pace* is northern dialect for *Pasch* from Heb. *pesakh* 'Passover'. *See also* PLOUGH MONDAY PLAY; REVESBY PLAY.

paean (Gk 'striking' from *paiein* 'to strike') A song or hymn of joy, exultation or praise. In ancient Greece it was an invocation (*q.v.*) or thanksgiving addressed to Apollo the Striker, 'one who strikes blows in order to heal mankind'.

paeon In Classical prosody a foot of one stressed and three unstressed syllables. It is known as the first, second, third or fourth paeon depending on the position of the stressed syllable: (a) / ∪ ∪ ∪; (b) ∪ / ∪ ∪; (c) ∪ ∪ / ∪; (d) ∪ ∪ ∪ /. Paeonic verse is found in Greek poetry, and especially in comedy. Rare in English verse. Gerard Manley Hopkins is one of the few poets to use it successfully and he experimented with it a good deal. This example is taken from *The Windhover: To Christ Our Lord*:

Ĭ caúght | thĭs mór|nĭng mór|nĭng's mí|nĭŏn, kíng-
  dŏm ŏf dáylĭght's | daúphĭn, | dápplĕ | dáwn-dráwn |
    Fálcŏn, ĭn hĭs | rídĭng
  Ŏf thĕ róllĭng | lévĕl | úndĕr|neáth hĭm | steádў | áir, ănd |
    strídĭng
Hígh thĕre, hŏw hĕ | rúng ŭpŏn thĕ | reín ŏf ă wímp|lĭng wíng
Ĭn hĭs écstă|sў! thĕn óff, | óff fórth ón swíng,
  Ăs ă skáte's hĕel | sweéps smoóth | ŏn ă bów-bĕnd: | thĕ
    húrl ănd glídĭng

Rĕbúffed | thĕ bíg wínd. | Mў heárt | ĭn hídĭng
Stírred fŏr ă bírd, | – thĕ ăchiéve ŏf, | thĕ mástĕrў | ŏf thĕ
thíng!

This is only one of several possible ways of scanning this piece of verse. However it is scanned, it contains pronounced variations. The first line is fairly even iambics with an anapaest to end. The second line scans: paeon c | trochee | trochee | spondee | trochee. 'In his riding' is paeon c. Line three scans: paeon c | followed by six trochees. Line four scans: paeon a | paeon a | choriam | iamb. Line five scans: paeonic | anapaest | spondee | spondee (but 'off forth on swing', depending on how it is read, might be paeonic in two or possibly three different ways. It might also be antispast: ∪ / / ∪). Line six scans: paeon c | spondee | paeon c | iamb. 'And gliding' is amphibrach. Line seven scans: iamb | bacchius | iamb | amphibrach. Line eight scans: choriambus | poeon c | paeon b | anapaest. *See also* EPITRITE; SPRUNG RHYTHM.

pageant Originally the movable stage or platform on which the medieval Mystery Plays (*q.v.*) were presented, it was built on wheels and consisted of two rooms: the lower was used as a dressing room, the upper as a stage. Later, the term was applied to plays acted on this platform. In modern usage it describes any sort of spectacular procession which presents tableaux and includes songs, dances and dramatic scenes. This sort of entertainment was fashionable in the early decades of the 20th c., especially in depicting local history. The annual Lord Mayor's Show in London carries on the tradition. A recent and interesting example of a kind of dramatic pageant was John Arden's *Left-Handed Liberty* (1965), a play commemorating the six-hundredth anniversary of the signing of the Magna Carta. *See also* MASQUE; MORALITY PLAY.

palaeography (Gk 'ancient writing') The study of and the art of deciphering ancient manuscripts, inscriptions and writings.

paleface and redskin Terms appropriated in 1939 by Philip Rahv and used by him to distinguish two 'poles' (as in north and south, but in this case in no sense regional). The polarization, which is a kind of antinomy (*q.v.*), sees a grouping of writers according to their attitude, style, subject matter and so forth. Thus, Herman Melville (1819–91) and Henry James (1843–1916) may be regarded as 'palefaces', whereas Walt Whitman (1819–92) and Mark Twain

(1835–1910) may be regarded as 'redskins'. 'Palefaces' have cultured and patrician attitudes and write in a mannered style using symbolism and lofty themes. 'Redskins' write of frontier life, working men, the plebs, low life in cities, etc., and are more colloquial and naturalistic in style. Among more recent writers, William Faulkner might be regarded as a redskin; John Updike as a paleface; with writers such as Saul Bellow and Bernard Malamud somewhere in between.

palilogy (Gk 'speaking over again') A deliberate repetition of a word or words for emphasis. A common rhetorical device. The following example is from Beckett's play *Waiting for Godot*, and comes from Lucky's long speech in Act I:

> . . . so fast I resume the skull to shrink waste and concurrently simultaneously what is more for reasons unknown in spite of the tennis on on the beard the flames the tears the stones so blue so calm alas alas on on the skull the skull the skull the skull in Connemara in spite of the tennis the labours abandoned left unfinished graver still abode of stones in a word I resume alas alas abandoned unfinished the skull the skull in Connemara in spite of the tennis the skull alas the stones Cunard . . .

palimbacchius Also known as the anti-bacchius. In Greek prosody a foot of two stressed syllables and one unstressed: / / ∪. In other words, the reverse of bacchius (*q.v.*). Rare in English verse, but occasional examples occur in the work of Tennyson, Swinburne, Browning, Gerard Manley Hopkins, Ezra Pound, W. B. Yeats, and more recent poets.

palimpsest (Gk 'again rubbed away') A surface, usually vellum or parchment, which has been used more than once for writing on, the previous writing having been rubbed out or somehow removed. Medieval parchment, being expensive, was often used two or three times.

palindrome (Gk 'running back again') A word or sentence (occasionally a verse) which reads the same both ways. Common words are: *civic*, *level*, *minim*, *radar*, *rotor*. Famous examples of such phrases or sentences are: (a) 'Madam, I'm Adam', to which the reply was 'Sir, I'm Iris'; (b) Able was I ere I saw Elba (attributed apocryphally to Napoleon who, alas, spoke no English); (c) Sums are not set as a test on Erasmus; (d) A man, a plan, a canal – Panama!; (e) 'In girum imus nocte et consumimur igni', said by Latin-speaking moths in flight; (f) Straw? No, too stupid a fad; I put soot on warts!; (g) 'Deliver desserts', demanded Nemesis, emended, named, stressed, reviled; (h) T. Eliot, top bard, notes putrid tang emanating, is sad. I'd assign it a name: 'Gnat dirt upset on drab pot toilet' (by W. H. Auden); (i) Stop Syrian! I start at rats in airy spots; (j) Sex at noon taxes; (k) *Νίψον' ἀνόμηματα, μὴ μόνανοψιν* ('Wash not only my face, but also my sins' – an inscription on the phiale in St Sophia, Istanbul); (k) SIROMORIS – this was the telegraphic address on the writing paper of Edward Elgar (1857–1934), who was knighted and appointed OM. There are also numerical palindromes. A simple example is: add 132 to 321 for the total 363.

The best known collection of verses was that produced by one Ambrose Pamperis in 1802. It consists of 416 palindromic verses recounting the campaigns of Catherine the Great. *See also* ACROSTIC.

palinode (Gk 'singing over again') A recantation in song or verse. Usually a poem in which a writer retracts or counter-balances a statement made in an earlier poem. The first palinode was a lyric by the Greek poet Stesichorus (*c.* 640–655 BC) in which he withdrew his attack on Helen as the cause of the Trojan war. Ovid is supposed to have written his *Remedia Amoris* in order to retract his *Ars Amatoria*. As a theme the palinode is not uncommon in love poetry. A well-known instance of a palinode in English literature is Chaucer's *Legend of Good Women* (*c.* 1372–86), written to atone for the story of the false Criseyde in *Troilus and Criseyde*.

palinodic Adjective of palinode (*q.v.*). It describes a verse where two similar stanzas or stanzaic groups (e.g. strophe and antistrophe, *qq.v.*) are interrupted by another matched pair.

palliata *See* FABULA.

pamphlet (AL *panfletus*, possibly from a Latin erotic poem *Pamphilus* – from Greek *Pamphilos* 'beloved of all' – very popular in the Middle Ages) A small unbound book, usually with paper covers. Originally a pamphlet was a sort of treatise or tract (*qq.v.*). It then came to mean a short work written on a topical subject on which an author feels strongly. Many outstanding writers have used the pamphlet to express vigorous political or religious views. The pamphlet has flourished most notably in England in the hands of such authors as Sir Thomas More, Tyndale, Greene, Dekker, Gerard Winstanley, Milton, Defoe, Swift and Shelley, plus the 19th c. Chartists. During the 18th and 19th c. many political controversies were dealt with in pamphlets. In France, too, the pamphlet has been much used – especially during times of unrest like the Revolutionary period from 1789 to 1848.

pandect (Gk *pan* 'everything' + *dektēs* 'a receiver') A book that purports to include everything possible on a topic; originally Justinian's encyclopaedia of Roman civil law in fifty volumes.

panegyric (Gk 'pertaining to public assembly') A speech or poem in fulsome praise of an individual, institution or group of people. Originally panegyric was a branch of rhetoric (*q.v.*) whose rules were laid down in the rhetorical works of Menander and Hermogenes. Scaliger also provides its rules in *Poetices Libri Septem* (1561). Two famous examples from Classical times are the festival oration delivered by Isocrates (436–338 BC) on the occasion of the Olympian games in 380, and Pliny the Younger's (AD 61–*c.* 113) eulogy on Trajan. Mark Antony's funeral oration in Shakespeare's *Julius Caesar* (1599) could be described as panegyric. *See* ENCOMIUM.

panoramic method A term for the omniscient viewpoint (*q.v.*) in authorship, especially in writing fiction.

pantaloon The old man in harlequinade (*q.v.*) who is the butt of the clown's practical jokes. Pantalone was an elderly Venetian in *commedia dell'arte* (*q.v.*) renowned for being greedy, suspicious, gullible and amorous. In Elizabeth times, a term applied to an old man. Hence the reference by Jaques to 'the lean and slippered pantaloon' in his speech on the seven ages of man in *As You Like It* (II, vii, 158).

pantomime (Gk 'all imitator') It may be merely a synonym for mime (*q.v.*), but its principal modern meaning is an exotic and spectacular entertainment particularly suitable for children. It first became popular in England in the 18th c., when it was a variation on the harlequinade. By the 19th c. it had become the main item on a bill. Modern pantomime is based on fairy tales, and it includes popular songs and topical comedy. Tradition requires the hero or principal boy to be played by a girl, and the comic older woman, the dame, to be played by a man. Favourite subjects are Cinderella, Aladdin, Dick Whittington, the Babes in the Wood and Jack and the Bean Stalk.

The term has also been used to describe mime plays, dumb show, melodrama (*qq.v.*), and 18th c. mythical ballets. In ancient Rome actors sometimes performed a kind of pantomime, with the aid of masks, in the dramatization of fabulous tales called *fabula Atellana*. *See* FABULA.

pantun A verse form of Malayan origin. A poem of no determinate length, composed of quatrains (*q.v.*) with internal assonance (*q.v.*) and rhyming abab. The second and fourth lines of each stanza become the first and third lines of the next. In the last quatrain the first line of the poem re-appears as the last, and the third line as the second. *Pantun běrkait* and *pantun běrikat* are terms which denote sets of quatrains; and a *pantun sindiran* is an epigram (*q.v.*). The form was introduced into Western poetry by Ernest Fouinet in the 19th c. Some distinguished French poets used it, notably Victor Hugo, Leconte de Lisle and Baudelaire. It never proved popular in England. One of the better known versions is Austin Dobson's *In Town*.

parabasis (Gk 'going aside, stepping forward') Part of the choral performance in Greek Old Comedy (*q.v.*). Usually near the end of a play the Chorus, without masks, came forward and addressed the audience directly in a speech which contained the personal views of the author on some topical matter of religion or politics. *See* ANTODE; EPIRRHEMA.

parable (Gk 'side throwing, comparison') A short and simple story, related to allegory and fable (*qq.v.*), which points a moral. Our Lord's forty parables are recorded in the synoptic Gospels only. *See* EXEMPLUM.

paradiastole (Gk 'side separation') A form of euphemism (*q.v.*) where the force and tone of a description is deliberately weakened – often in irony (*q.v.*). For example: 'unattractive' for 'ugly', 'perceptive' for 'sharp', 'uncivilized' for 'savage'. *See* LITOTES.

paradigm (Gk 'example') A pattern, exemplar or model which, as a literary device, points up a resemblance, as in this stanza from Cleveland's poem *To the State of Love, or, The Senses' Festival*:

My sight took pay, but (thank my charms)
I now impale her in my arms,
(Love's compasses) confining you,
Good angels, to a circle too.
Is not the universe strait-laced
When I can clasp it in the waist?
My amorous folds about thee hurled,
With Drake I girdle in the world.
I hoop the firmament and make
This my embrace the zodiac.
  How would thy centre take my sense
  When admiration doth commence
  At the extreme circumference?

See CONCEIT; METAPHYSICAL.

paradigmatic *See* SYNTAGMATIC/PARADIGMATIC.

paradox (Gk 'beside/beyond opinion') Originally a paradox was merely a view which contradicted accepted opinion. By round about the middle of the 16th c. the word had acquired the commonly accepted meaning it now has: an apparently self-contradictory (even absurd) statement which, on closer inspection, is found to contain a truth reconciling the conflicting opposites. Basically, two kinds may be distinguished: (a) particular or 'local'; (b) general or 'structural'. Examples of the first are short, pithy statements which verge on the epigrammatic – such as Hamlet's line: 'I must be cruel only to be kind'; Milton's description of God: 'Dark with excessive bright thy skirts appear'; Sir Thomas Browne's magnificent image: 'The sun itself is the dark simulacrum and light is the shadow of God'; and Congreve's neat turn of phrase in *Amoret*:

Careless she is with artful care,
Affecting to seem unaffected.

The second kind is more complex. For instance, there is a paradox at the heart of the Christian faith: that the world will be saved by failure. A structural paradox is one which is integral to, say, a poem. The works of the metaphysical (*q.v.*) poets, especially Donne and Marvell, abound in them. In fact Donne has been regarded as the first major English poet to develop the possibilities of paradox as a fundamental structural device which sustains the dialectic and argument (*qq.v.*) of a poem. Notable examples are to be found in *The Will*, *Good Friday, 1613, Riding Westward* and the sonnet beginning:

> Death be not proud, though some have called thee
> Mighty and dreadful, for, thou art not so . . .

Marvell's poem *The Garden* depends on a central paradoxical idea. Other good instances are to be found in Milton's *Lycidas*; and in *Paradise Lost* Milton is concerned with that other general paradox at the centre of Christian belief: the *felix culpa*, or 'happy fault', how good grows from evil. In *An Essay on Man* Pope combined a general statement about the paradoxical nature and condition of man with a series of particular paradoxes:

> Placed on this isthmus of a middle state
> A being darkly wise, and rudely great:
> With too much knowledge for the Sceptic side,
> With too much weakness for the Stoic's pride,
> He hangs between; in doubt to act, or rest,
> In doubt to deem himself a God, or Beast,
> In doubt his Mind or Body to prefer,
> Born but to die, and reasoning but to err . . .
> Created half to rise, and half to fall;
> Great lord of all things, yet a prey to all;
> Sole judge of Truth, in endless Error hurl'd:
> The glory, jest, and riddle of the world!

In modern times, apart from George Bernard Shaw (an incorrigible paradoxer of the more inconoclastic kind), an expert is G. K. Chesterton. He uses paradox (to a fault) like a comedian who has discovered an almost inexhaustible source of humour, and in his hands the device becomes a stunt in verbal and conceptual acrobatics.

In recent verse one of the most striking series of paradoxes can be found at the beginning of T. S. Eliot's *Little Gidding*:

> Midwinter spring is its own season
> Sempiternal though sodden towards sundown,
> Suspended in time, between pole and tropic.
> When the short day is brightest, with frost and fire,
> The brief sun flames the ice, on pond and ditches,

In windless cold that is the heart's heat,
Reflecting in a watery mirror
A glare that is blindness in the early afternoon.
And glow more intense than blaze of branch, or brazier,
Stirs the dumb spirit: no wind, but pentecostal fire
In the dark time of the year.

Some critical theory goes so far as to suggest that the language of poetry is the language of paradox. This idea has been elaborated persuasively by, among others, Cleanth Brooks in his book *The Well-Wrought Urn* (1947).

A paradoxical vision of the behaviour and state of human kind is inherent in much nonsense (*q.v.*) poetry and also in plays belonging to the Theatre of the Absurd (*q.v.*).

The ultimate logic of deconstructive criticism implies a paradoxical state of affairs, for such criticism suggests that the meaning of any text is indefinitely in doubt and it follows, therefore, that by using language in *another* text in order to interpret the meaning and language of the *first* text the meaning of the second text is, *ipso facto*, indefinitely in doubt – and so on. *See* DECONSTRUCTION; DEFAMILIARIZATION; FOLLY LITERATURE; METALANGUAGE; OXYMORON; PATAPHYSICS.

paragram (Gk 'letter joke') A play on words by alteration of a letter or letters. Quite often a facetious and low form of humour, of traditional 'schoolboy' kind – for example: 'What's homicidal and lives in the sea?' Answer: Jack the Kipper'. However, it may attain respectability and sense on occasion – for example: 'The straw that breaks the *hamal's* back' (author's example). *See also* PUN; SPOONERISM.

paragraph (Gk 'side writing') Originally a short, horizontal stroke drawn below the beginning of a line in which there was a break in the sense. Now, for all practical purposes, a passage, or section, or subdivision in a piece of writing. Usually a paragraph deals with one particular point or aspect of the subject presented. It may vary greatly in length.

paralipomena (Gk 'things left out') Matter left out of the main body of a work and included in appendices.

paralipsis (Gk 'leaving aside') A figurative device by which a speaker or writer feigns to ignore or pass over a matter and thus draws attention to it. A famous example occurs when Mark Anthony is addressing the mob in *Julius Caesar* (III, ii, 130).

parallelism (Gk 'alongside one another') A very common device in poetry (especially Hebrew poetry) and not uncommon in the more incantatory types of prose. It consists of phrases or sentences of similar construction and meaning placed side by side, balancing each other, as in Isaiah (9:2):

> The people that walked in darkness have seen a great light: they that dwell in the land of the shadow of death, upon them hath the light shined.
>
> Thou hast multiplied the nation, and not increased the joy: they joy before thee according to the joy in harvest, and as men rejoice when they divide the spoil.

Parallelism is common in poetry of the oral tradition (*q.v.*) – for instance, in *Beowulf* and the *narodne pesme* (*q.v.*) – and often the effect is that of a litany (*q.v.*). Other interesting examples can be found in the work of Langland, T. S. Eliot, D. H. Lawrence, and especially in the verse of Walt Whitman, who probably used the device more than any other poet.

paraphrase (Gk 'tell in other words') A version in other words of the sense of any passage or text. It may be a free rendering or amplification of a passage (not to be confused with précis, *q.v.*). As Dryden put it: 'translation with latitude where the author is kept in view . . . but his words are not so strictly followed as his sense'. Paraphrase is often used nowadays in re-writing technical books and articles in language which the layman can understand.

para-rhyme *See* HALF-RHYME.

parataxis (Gk 'beside arrangement') Co-ordination of clauses without conjunctions; the opposite of hypotaxis (*q.v.*). Common in Latin and not unusual in English. The effect is terseness and compression. Pope was expert in its use within the exacting form of the heroic couplet (*q.v.*), as these lines from his *Epistle IV*: *To Richard Boyle* suggest:

> Still follow Sense, of ev'ry Art the Soul,
> Parts answ'ring parts shall slide into a whole,

Spontaneous beauties all around advance,
Start ev'n from Difficulty, strike from Chance;
Nature shall join you, Time shall make it grow
A work to wonder at – perhaps a STOW.

See ELLIPSIS; POLYSYNDETON.

parenthesis (Gk 'put in beside') A word, phrase or clause put into a sentence which is grammatically complete without the insertion. It is usually marked by brackets, dashes or commas. For example: Parenthesis – usually marked by brackets, dashes or commas – is often used when a writer wishes to qualify or add to a statement.

parison (Gk 'almost equal, evenly balanced') A sequence of clauses or sentences which have a symmetrical structure.

Parnassians Parnassianism was an influential literary movement in France in the second half of the 19th c. It was a kind of reaction against the romanticism (*q.v.*) of Victor Hugo, de Vigny and Lamartine, against subjectivism and 'artistic socialism'. Some scholars take Théophile Gautier (1811–72) as the founder and star of the movement. Others hold that Leconte de Lisle (1818–94) was the 'chef d'orchestre'. They both had much influence. In the Preface to *Mademoiselle de Maupin* (1835) Gautier put forward the belief that art was an end in itself, not a means to an end. In Gautier's view a poet was like a sculptor, a craftsman who must be strictly objective and fashion his poem into something almost tangible. Hence analogies with the plastic arts, and imagery drawn from them. And hence the idea of objective poetry from which the personality of the poet is eliminated. This looks forward to Eliot's dictum that the 'progress of an artist is a continual self-sacrifice, a continual extinction of personality'. *L'art pour l'art* can be taken as one of the slogans of *les Parnassiens*. For them poetry achieved the status of a religion.

Most of *les Parnassiens* were born round about 1840, and the main movement started with Catulle Mendès and L-X. de Ricard in the early 1860s. At their meetings Leconte de Lisle was the oracular figure (one might say the Lenin of the movement, to Gautier's Marx). Apart from him the important figures were: Théodore de Banville (1823–91), Sully Prudhomme (1839–1907), François Coppée (1842–1908), Léon Dierx (1838–1912), Jean Lahor (1840–1909), and J-M. de Heredia (1842–1905).

By the 1870s the theories of this Parnassian School were beginning to be felt in England, largely through the influence of de Banville whose *Petit traité de poésie française* (1872) was widely known. De Banville corresponded with Austin Dobson, Swinburne, Edmund Gosse and Andrew Lang, and the so-called English Parnassians became enthusiastic followers of the French cult, especially in matters of style and form and in the use of older French forms like *ballade*, *rondeau* and *villanelle* (*qq.v.*). However, the doctrines of 'art for art's sake' (*q.v.*) never really caught on in England. *See also* AESTHETICISM; PERSONAL HERESY; SYMBOL AND SYMBOLISM.

parody (Gk 'beside, subsidiary or mock song') The imitative use of the words, style, attitude, tone and ideas of an author in such a way as to make them ridiculous. This is usually achieved by exaggerating certain traits, using more or less the same technique as the cartoon caricaturist. In fact, a kind of satirical mimicry. As a branch of satire (*q.v.*) its purpose may be corrective as well as derisive.

If an author has a propensity for archaic or long words, double-banked adjectives, long, convoluted sentences and paragraphs, strange names, quaint mannerisms of expression, is sentimental, bombastic, arch or pompous, then these are some of the features that the would-be parodist will seek to exploit.

Parody is difficult to accomplish well. There has to be a subtle balance between close resemblance to the 'original' and a deliberate distortion of its principal characteristics. It is, therefore, a minor form of literary art which is likely to be successful only in the hands of writers who are original and creative themselves. In fact, the majority of the best parodies are the work of gifted writers.

The origins of parody are ancient. Aristotle refers to it in *Poetics* and attributes its invention to Hegemon of Thasos who used an epic style to represent men as being inferior to what they are in real life. Hegemon was supposed to have been the first man to introduce parody in the theatre, in the 5th c. BC. However, the 6th c. poet Hipponax has also been credited with this.

Aristophanes used parody in the *Frogs* where he took off the style of Aeschylus and Euripides. Plato also caricatured the style of various writers in the *Symposium*. Lucian used parody in his *Dialogues*. It was so common among Latin authors that Cicero listed its varieties. In the Middle Ages parodies of the liturgy, hymns and the Bible were fairly frequent. One of the first and best known English parodies was Chaucer's *Tale of Sir Thopas* (*c.*

1383), a skit on some of the more absurd characteristics of medieval romances (Chaucer was in turn to be well parodied by Alexander Pope and W. W. Skeat).

Late in the Renaissance period Cervantes parodied the whole tradition of medieval romances in *Don Quixote* (1605, 1615). Erasmus in *Moriae Encomium* (1509) and Rabelais in *Gargantua* and *Pantagruel* (1534, 1532) turned scholasticism upside down. Shakespeare parodied the euphuism (*q.v.*) of John Lyly in *Henry IV*, Pt I (1597), Marlowe's bombastic manner in *Hamlet* (*c.* 1603) and the general style of Nashe in *Love's Labour's Lost* (*c.* 1595). Later Sir John Suckling took off Donne splendidly as a love poet, and in 1701 John Philips parodied Milton very cleverly in *The Splendid Shilling*. Somewhat earlier Buckingham produced one of the few dramatic parodies which have survived contemporary interest; namely *The Rehearsal* (1671) which mocked Dryden's *The Conquest of Granada*.

In 1736 Isaac Hawkins's *A Pipe of Tobacco* created a precedent because it was the first collection of parodies of various authors' supposed attempts on a single subject. Fielding's burlesque drama *Tom Thumb* appeared in 1730; and Fielding's *Shamela* (1741) was a complete parodic novel at the expense of Richardson's *Pamela* (1740). To the 18th c. also belongs Sheridan's *The Critic* (1779), a successful parody of sentimental drama and the malicious literary criticism of the period.

The Romantic period and the 19th c. provided a succession of ample targets for literary inconoclasts. In 1812 James and Horace Smith published *Rejected Addresses* in which Scott, Wordsworth, Byron, Coleridge, Dr Johnson and others were parodied very successfully. Thereafter, Burns, Byron, Wordsworth, Poe, Longfellow, Tennyson, Browning, William Morris, the Rossettis, Swinburne, Southey, Whitman, Hopkins and Kipling were quite frequently parodied, often by writers equally distinguished. For example, Keats on Wordsworth, Byron on Wordsworth, James Hogg on Wordsworth, Swinburne on Tennyson, C. S. Calverley on Browning, Lewis Carroll on Swinburne, Hogg on Coleridge – and so forth. The favourite victims were Southey, Wordsworth, Browning and Swinburne.

Max Beerbohm refined parody to art, and his collection of his own parodies in *A Christmas Garland* (1912), which includes pieces in the manner of Kipling, Galsworthy, Hardy, Arnold Bennett, Edmund Gosse and others, is generally agreed to have set a standard which may never be surpassed.

In what has been described as the 'post Beerbohm' period of parody there is to be found as much variety as in the 19th c. and often as much skill. James Joyce was a gifted parodist, some of whose best efforts can be found in the 'Oxen of the Sun' episode of *Ulysses.* A classic parody of the 1930s was Stella Gibbons's *Cold Comfort Farm* (1932), a clever caricature of the primitivism (*q.v.*) of Mary Webb's novels – and also, for that matter, of the primitivism of Hardy, J. C. Powys and D. H. Lawrence. More recent and talented instances are C. Day Lewis's parodies in Part V of *An Italian Visit*, Cyril Connolly on Aldous Huxley, Paul Jennings on Resistentialism, Kenneth Tynan on Thornton Wilder – plus a whole school of American parodists much of whose work has appeared in *The New Yorker.* The best known of these are Robert Benchley, Peter De Vries, Wolcott Gibbs, S. J. Perelman, Frank Sullivan, James Thurber and E. B. White. In 1960 Dwight MacDonald published *Parodies: an Anthology from Chaucer to Beerbohm and After*, an admirable collection of vintage pieces. An accomplished contemporary parodist in verse is Wendy Cope. There are some good examples in her collection of poems *Making Cocoa for Kingsley Amis* (1986). *See* BURLESQUE; LAMPOON; MOCK-EPIC; MOCK-HEROIC; SKIT.

parole *See* LANGUE AND PAROLE.

paronomasia *See* PUN.

paronym (Gk 'beside word') A word from the same root as another, especially a word taken from another language with slight modifications. For example: Gk *ekstasis* – OF *ecstasie* – MedL *extasis* – English *ecstasy.*

paroxytone A word, or line of verse, with the accent on the penultimate syllable. *See* OXYTONE.

partimen A form of *jeu parti* (*q.v.*) and related to the *tenson* (*q.v.*). A kind of poetic debate in which, for example, a poet presents a proposition. A stock instance is: it is better to love a woman than be loved by her. A second poet then defends or rejects the proposition; after which the first again defends his proposition. The issue is then referred to an arbiter for settlement. There are occasional instances of a triple *partimen* with three poets engaged. *See* POETIC CONTESTS.

partitio *see* MERISMUS.

part-song A song whose parts are sung by different voices to create a harmony, with or without instrumental accompaniment.

partynost (R 'party spirit') One of the main requirements in literature in socialist realism (*q.v.*). Writers are expected to express a 'party spirit' in accordance with the objectives and methods of the Communist Party in the Soviet Union. It is believed that Lenin was the first to point out that this was necessary. *See also* IDEYNOST; NARODNOST.

paso (Sp 'passage') A procession representing part of the Passion of Christ. The term has also been applied to a short dramatic piece and a comic interlude.

pasquinade (It *pasquinata* 'lampoon') *Pasquinata* derives from the name Pasquino or Pasquillo given to a damaged statue discovered in Rome in 1501. The custom developed that it was honoured on St Mark's Day by having satirical Latin verses hung on it. Hence, a lampoon (*q.v.*) hung up in some public place.

Passion Play A religious drama presenting the Crucifixion of Christ, usually performed on Good Friday. The first was performed in *c.* 1200 at Siena. In 1244 *The Passion* and *The Resurrection* were presented together at Padua. In some places Passion Plays were incorporated in the Corpus Christi cycle; in others they remained separate. Long after the Reformation they were performed in Southern Germany, Austria and Switzerland. The most famous survival is at Oberammergau, Bavaria, where the villages have performed the play every ten years since 1633. *See* MIRACLE PLAY; MYSTERY PLAY.

passus (L 'step') A division in a story or poem; a chapter, a canto (*q.v.*). Langland used the term for the sections of *The Vision of Piers Plowman.*

pastiche (It *pasta* 'paste') A patchwork of words, sentences or complete passages from various authors or one author. It is, therefore, a kind of imitation (*q.v.*) and, when intentional, may be a form of parody (*q.v.*). An elaborate form of pastiche is a sustained work (say, a novel) written mostly or entirely in the style and manner of another writer. A good modern example is Peter Ackroyd's brilliant *The Last Days of Oscar Wilde* (1983), which is a diary. *See* CENTO; COLLAGE.

pastoral (L 'pertaining to shepherds') A minor but important mode which, by convention, is concerned with the lives of shepherds. It is of great antiquity and interpenetrates many works in Classical and modern European literature. It is doubtful if pastoral ever had much to do with the daily working-life of shepherds, though it is not too difficult to find shepherds in Europe (in Montenegro, Albania, Greece and Sardinia, for instance) who compose poetry, sing songs and while away the hours playing the flute. For the most part pastoral tends to be an idealization of shepherd life, and, by so being, creates an image of a peaceful and uncorrupted existence; a kind of pre-lapsarian world.

The origins of pastoral with many of its conventions are to be found in the works of Theocritus (*c.* 316–*c.* 260 BC), a native of Syracuse in Sicily, who wrote pastorals for the sophisticated Greeks of Alexandria. He wrote what are called *Idylls* or *Epyllia* (*qq.v.*), short mythological narratives, and pastoral or bucolic poems: dialogues or monologues which treated of the lives of shepherds, goatherds, neatherds, farmers and fishermen. His shepherds are involved in the contests of piping and the improvisation of songs. They also descant on the attractions of girls. An important figure in his poems was Daphnis, a shepherd who married the nymph Chloe, and was killed by Aphrodite for being so uxoriously faithful. Nature mourned the death of Daphnis, and this became the prototype of the pastoral elegy (*q.v.*) of which an outstanding example is Milton's *Lycidas*.

Theocritus's successors were Bion (*c.* 100 BC) and Moschus (*c.* 150 BC), whose poems were similar. Virgil (70–19 BC) modelled his *Eclogues* on Theocritus and in them evoked that 'golden age' in which innocent shepherds lived in primitive bliss.

The next work of note in the tradition is the Greek pastoral romance *Daphnis and Chloe* (3rd–5th c. AD) by Longus, the model of the romance favoured by writers in the Renaissance. Latin poets of the Middle Ages wrote eclogues but little of note survives except for a poem in dialogue form by Alcuin (735–804). This is an early instance of the medieval form of *débat* (*q.v.*). In the later Middle Ages we find poems of a dramatic character which are associated with Whitsuntide and May Day games; especially a form known as the *pastourelle* (*q.v.*). An interesting instance of a pastoral poem in this tradition is Henryson's *Robene and Makyne* (15th c.).

One may suppose that by the late Middle Ages the pastoral imagery which was an important feature of the Christian and Hebrew teaching may well have had some influence on pastoral. After all, Christ was the shepherd and human beings were His flock. Such knowledge enhanced the conviction that the shepherd's life was a paradigm of tranquillity and harmonious love. In this connection one should note that *The Adoration of the Shepherds* was a popular medieval Mystery Play (*q.v.*). The veneration accorded to Virgil in the Middle Ages resulted from the famous lines in the *Fourth Eclogue*, which were interpreted as a prophecy of the advent of Christ, and which accordingly had some influence on the concept of pastoral and the pastoral life.

Petrarch and Boccaccio wrote eclogues in Latin; but more influential than these were the Latin pastorals of Mantuan (1448–1516). These had some vogue throughout Europe and were texts for schoolboys in England in the Elizabethan period. Alexander Barclay's five *Eclogues* (*c.* 1515–21) were also influential. Two were translations from Mantuan, and three were adaptations from the *Miseriae Curialium* (15th c.) of Aeneas Sylvius who became Pope Pius II.

By this time the pastoral 'novel' was also beginning to be established. In the 14th c. Boccaccio wrote one called *Ameto*, and in 1504 Sannazaro published *Arcadia*. It comprised twelve verse eclogues linked by prose and set a fashion which Montemayor followed with *Diana* (*c.* 1559), and this in its turn was a kind of model for Sidney's pastoral romance *Arcadia* (1590). Meantime, Spenser's *Shepheard's Calender* was closely modelled on the eclogues of Theocritus, Virgil and Mantuan. It consisted of twelve poems (one for each month of the year), all of which showed great metrical variety and skill. The elements of allegory (*q.v.*), pastoral elegy and the *débat* were apparent. In this *Calender* Spenser combined the idealized world of Classical pastoral with the everyday world of English shepherds and gave this combination a unity by projecting the inner world of his own imagination. Pastoral conventions were also noticeable in other works by Spenser, especially in *Colin Clout's Come Home Again*, in *Daphnaïda* (an elegy on the death of Sir Arthur Gorges's wife) and *Astrophil* (an elegy on the death of Sir Philip Sidney).

In the late 16th c. many other works amplified the pastoral tradition, such as Marlowe's *The Passionate Shepherd to His Love*, which evoked a memorable reply from Sir Walter Ralegh. Michael Drayton also wrote some eclogues (1593) in which he introduced an earthier and more realistic quality to pastoralism, particularly in *Daffodil*, *The Shepherd's Sirena* and *The Muses' Elysium.*

At about this time pastoral drama appeared in Italy with Tasso's *Aminta* (1581) and Guarini's *Il Pastor Fido* (1585). The influence of these works is discernible in a number of Shakespeare's plays; also in Ben Jonson's unfinished play *The Sad Shepherd* (1641). This was a descendant of the Whitsuntide pastorals. James Shirley also wrote a pastoral play called *The Arcadia* (1640) which was a kind of adaptation from Sidney's work. But probably the most distinguished pastoral play in English literature was John Fletcher's *The Faithful Shepherdess* (1608). Masques (*q.v.*) of the period also used pastoral themes. One of the last to do so was Milton's *Comus* (1634).

Pastoral and pastoral drama also flourished in France in the latter part of the 16th c. and during the 17th. We find early traces of Italian influence in the poets of the Pléiade (*q.v.*) and Belleau wrote a *Bergerie* which used a pastoral framework for some complimentary poems. The first major works are Nicolas Filleul's *Ombres* (1566) and Belleforest's *Pastorale amoureuse* (1569). In 1585 Nicolas de Montreux started the publication of *Bergeries de Juliette*, a pastoral romance which had several sequels. He also wrote pastoral dramas, notably *Diane* (1594) and *Arimine* (1596). From then on pastoral in one form or another proliferated in France. Some of the more important works are: Montchrétien's *Bergerie* (1600); Nicolas Chreestien de Croix's *Les Amantes ou la grande pastourelle* (1613); Honoré d'Urfé's *L'Astrée* (1607–27); Racan's *Bergeries* (1625); Mairet's *Sylvie et Silvanire* (*c.* 1625–9); Gombauld's *Amaranthe* (1631). Hereabouts pastoral is becoming decadent, as we can see from Pichou's *Folies de Cardenio* (1629) and Mareschal's *Inconstance d'Hylas* (1630), both of which were based on *L'Astrée.* In 1627 Sorel parodied *L'Astrée* in *Le Berger extravagant.* Some time later Molière wrote some successful pastoral comedies, notably *Mélicerte* (1666) and *Les Amants magnifiques* (1670).

In England, in the 17th c., broadly speaking, the pastoral undergoes modifications in form and content. Like Ralegh, John Donne 'replied' to Marlowe with *The Bait*. In this poem Donne tilts laconically at the conventions and assumptions of pastoral.

William Browne, on the other hand, a friend of Drayton and Jonson, settled for the well-established Elizabethan tradition. For the most part his pastoralism is 'romantic' (he appealed to poets of the romantic period, *q.v.*, especially Keats), and his main works,

Britannia's Pastorals (1613, 1616, 1852) and *Shepherd's Pipe* (1614), are rather anaemic and diffuse.

Phineas Fletcher, a contemporary of Browne, also worked in the Spenserian Elizabethan tradition. His *Piscatorie Eclogs* (1633) deal with the lives of fishermen rather than shepherds. Sannazaro had already done this with his piscatory eclogues in 1526, and in 1555 the Dalmatian poet Petar Hektorović had published *Ribanje i ribarsko prigovaranje*, a realistic fishing pastoral.

Apart from these the main name in connection with the pastoral convention in the 17th c. is Milton – who was influenced by Phineas Fletcher and Spenser. Pastoral elements occur in his *Hymn on the Morning of Christ's Nativity*, *L'Allegro*, *Arcades*, *Comus* and, above all, in *Lycidas* (1637). Minor works of note by contemporaries of Milton are those by Marvell, especially his *Damon the Mower*, *The Mower against Gardens*, *The Mower to the Glow-worms*, and *The Mower's Song*. Marvell's use of pastoral is highly individual.

Later in the 17th c. Sir Charles Sedley and Dryden wrote verses which sustained the pastoral convention. For instance, a slight work by Sedley called *Phyllis Knotting*, and Dryden's *The Lady's Song*. One should note also that Dryden wrote some good pastoral verse for the sub-plot of *Marriage à la Mode*. In this play Leonidas and Palmyra have been brought up as shepherds though they are of noble birth. In these verses they look back to the old days.

Fundamentally, this is what pastoral is about: it displays a nostalgia for the past, for some hypothetical state of love and peace which has somehow been lost. The dominating idea and theme of most pastoral is the search for the simple life away from the court and town, away from corruption, war, strife, the love of gain, away from 'getting and spending'. In a way it reveals a yearning for a lost innocence, for a pre-Fall paradisal life in which man existed in harmony with nature. It is thus a form of primitivism (*q.v.*) and a potent longing for things past. Hence the myth of the golden age which, in Classical literature, is diffused in Hesiod, Virgil and Ovid. In the Middle Ages Boethius, Jean de Meung, Dante and Chaucer used it as an image or metaphor for the Garden of Eden. During the Renaissance period the expression of a longing for this Arcadian world was worked out in greater detail. But it is probably not entirely a coincidence that, as the mythopoetic attractions of pastoral happiness diminish, so utopia (*q.v.*) begins to acquire a particular interest for people.

In the 18th c. pastoral was further modified. It remained a popular mode, but too often became effete, precious, 'Dresdenesque'.

In 1709 Pope published four pastoral poems in imitation of Spenser. These showed considerable elegance and technical virtuosity. In the same year Ambrose Philips also published some pastorals. Between the two poets there was some rivalry and envy over the respective merits of their poems. John Gay took Pope's part and in *Shepherd's Week* (1714) attempted a parody of Philips's work. This misfired because Gay, in his efforts to show what rustic life was really like, produced a realistic 'home-spun' type pastoral. Gay also composed several ironical eclogues.

Apart from these, most 18th c. poems in the pastoral tradition were descriptions of particular places, and thus were topographical poetry (*q.v.*). One of the earliest examples of this kind of poem was Denham's *Cooper's Hill* (1642). Others of note were Pope's *Windsor Forest* (1713) and Dyer's *Grongar Hill* (1726). Wordsworth's *Tintern Abbey* belonged to this kind. Longer and more ambitious descriptive poems were James Thomson's *The Seasons* (1726–30) which derives from Virgil's *Georgics*. A century later John Clare wrote something rather similar in the form of *The Shepherd's Calendar* (1827). Other major minor works, so to speak, of the 18th c. which employ pastoral elements are: Alan Ramsay's pastoral drama *The Gentle Shepherd* (1725); William Shenstone's *A Pastoral Ballad* (1755); William Collins's *The Persian Eclogues* (1724); and Thomas Chatterton's *The African Eclogues* (*c.* 1777).

In his *Shepherd's Week*, John Gay had shown how it was possible to treat rural subjects in a realistic manner instead of with a stylized and rose-tinted formalism. When George Crabbe published *The Village* in 1783 he painted the cot

As Truth will paint it and as bards will not.

Most of Crabbe's verse annals were outstanding for their realistic treatment of rural scenes.

For Blake the shepherd was still a symbol of an innocent and unspoilt way of life; and for Wordsworth also the country, unblemished nature and the uncorrupted existence of countrymen, were in many ways ideal. However, Wordsworth, like Crabbe, had no liking for the formal pastoral and was realistic in his treatment of rural themes and scenes. In his topographical and narrative poems we have what amounts to a new version of pastoral even though he still stresses the simplicity and innocence of country life. This is evident in *The Pet Lamb*, *The Idle Shepherd Boys* and *Michael*. Wordsworth is fully aware of the pastoral tradition and in *Michael* (1800), which is a kind of narrative idyll, he shows the destruction of the traditional pastoral way of life. It is a mournful, almost tragic poem and is a counterpart to Goldsmith's lament in *The Deserted Village* (1770). In a remarkable passage (lines 173 ff.) in Book VIII of *The Prelude* Wordsworth evoked the whole history of pastoral, contrasting the old idea of the shepherd's 'smooth life' with rough reality. Nevertheless, the 19th c. produced two great pastoral elegies in Shelley's *Adonais* (1821) and Matthew Arnold's *Thyrsis* (1867). Moreover Landor returned to the pastoral manner of Theocritus in his *Hellenics* (1846–7).

From about the middle of the 19th c. onwards the pastoral tradition fissiparated, and the main results, as a rule interesting experiments, display much variety. Later attempts at a kind of pastoralism were made by Tennyson in *Dora*, *The Northern Farmer* and *The Princess*; by William Barnes in his dialect *Poems of Rural Life*; by John Davidson in *The Fleet Street Eclogues*; and by Edward LeFroy in *Echoes from Theocritus*, a series of sonnets in the tradition of Theocritus's Idylls. To these we should add a number of poems by the French Parnassians, the poems in A. E. Housman's *A Shropshire Lad*, miscellaneous poems by W. B. Yeats and Eduardo Marquina's *Eglogas*.

Other noteworthy works which, in various ways, are associated with the pastoral, the eclogue and pastoralism are: Ezra Pound's *An Idyll for Glaucus*; Roy Campbell's satirical pastiche *A Veld Eclogue: The Pioneers*, and his *Jungle Eclogue*; Auden's *The Age of Anxiety*; MacNeice's *Eclogue for Christmas*; George Barker's long narrative poem in *débat* (*q.v.*) form, *Goodman Jacksin and the Angel*; Norman Cameron's *Shepherds and Shepherdesses*; and William Bell's *Elegies*.

Though pastoral may die in one form it is likely to be reincarnated, and the traditional primitivist themes reanimated. To support this one may cite the novels of Jean Giono, and the fine lyrics of R. S. Thomas, whose austerely compassionate eye has done for the Welsh rural scene what Crabbe, in a totally different way, did for his parish.

pastourelle A short narrative poem of the Middle Ages (in Provençal *pastorela*) whose typical subject is a meeting between a knight and a shepherdess. A kind of 'debate' follows, and the shepherdess may or may not succumb; or she may outwit the knight, or be rescued by shepherds. *Pastourelle* was a popular form of entertainment in OF in the 13th c. *See also* DEBAT; PASTORAL.

pataphysics A pseudo-philosophical system devised by Alfred Jarry (1873–1907), and known as the 'science of imaginary solutions'. Jarry was a precursor of surrealism (*q.v.*), and after the Second World War a number of devotees founded the *Collège de Pataphysique*. With solemn whimsy they invented rules and regulations and in fact produced a sort of parody of the conventional college of learning. The main spirits in this 'joke' were Ionesco, Raymond Queneau, Boris Vian, Jacques Prévert and Jean Dubuffet. Pataphysics are the metaphysics of nonsense (*q.v.*) and the absurd, and are anti-reason. The influence of the ideas can most clearly be seen in the Theatre of the Absurd (*q.v.*).

patavinity A rare term which denotes dialect peculiarities in writing. It also denotes a 'provincial' style. The word derives from the place-name *Patavium* – where Livy was born. The historian's writings were said to possess such oddities.

patent theatres Letters patent were issued in 1662 by Charles II to William Davenant (1606–68) and Thomas Killigrew (1612–83), which allowed them the sole right to present plays in public within the City of Westminster. After their deaths the letters patent were the source of numerous legal disputes, squabbles and sales; ultimately they were settled on the Drury Lane and Covent Garden theatres. Legitimate (*q.v.*) drama was confined to the patent theatres, but there was much dispute as to exactly what legitimate drama was. The patents existed until 1843 when the Theatres Act made them inoperative.

pathetic fallacy A phrase invented by John Ruskin in 1856 (*Modern Painters*, Vol. III, Pt IV). According to Ruskin a writer was pathetically fallacious when he ascribed human feelings to the inanimate. For Ruskin it was a derogatory term because it applied, so he said, not to the 'true appearances of things to us', but to the 'extraordinary, or false appearances, when we are under the influence of emotion of contemplative fancy'. To illustrate his point Ruskin quotes from Kingsley's *The Sands of Dee*:

> They rowed her in across the rolling foam –
> The cruel, crawling foam.

And from Coleridge's *Christabel*:

> The one red leaf, the last of its clan
> That dances as often as dance it can.

Such passages are, according to Ruskin, 'morbid', however beautiful they may be.

Such a form of personification (*q.v.*) has been used countless times from Homer onwards, and still is. By Ruskin's criterion, therefore, many of the greatest poets would qualify as morbid. Nowadays the phrase is used in a non-pejorative and therefore neutral way to define this common poetic phenomenon.

pathopoeia (Gk 'making of feeling') A scene or passage intended to arouse feelings: anger, grief or passion. For example, Henry V's pre-battle speeches in *Henry V*.

pathos (Gk 'suffering, feeling') That quality in a work of art which evokes feelings of tenderness, pity or sorrow. For example: in *Hamlet*, Gertrude's speech describing the death of Ophelia; in *Othello*, the death of Desdemona.

patois A word of unknown origin which denotes a local dialect, especially in France and French Switzerland. We find it in OF as *patois* 'rough speech'; perhaps from the OF *patoier* 'to handle roughly'. Often used loosely as an equivalent of cant, lingo, slang (*qq.v.*). *See also* ARGOT.

patronage A patron is a person of wealth and position (often of power and rank, also) who bestows bounty on an artist and thus supports him. In return the artist dedicates his work to the patron and thus honours him. Two of the most famous patrons were the Emperor Augustus, and his friend Maecenas. Both were much celebrated for their patronage of learning and letters. Maecenas was benefactor to Virgil and Horace. Patronage was common in classical times and throughout the medieval and Renaissance periods. As the power of printers and publishers increased, patronage became less frequent. Nevertheless, quite a large number of writers continued to enjoy the advantages of benefactors during the 17th and 18th c. *See also* POET LAUREATE.

pattern As a literary term, a model, design, plan or precedent – with the implication of being worthy of imitation. Pope's *Imitations* of Horace are based on the Roman's pattern. *See also* ARCHETYPE; SYMBOL AND SYMBOLISM.

pattern poetry Probably Oriental in origin, this kind of poem has its lines arranged to represent a physical object, or to suggest action/

motion, mood/feeling; but usually shape and motion. Thus geometric figures are common; other shapes are wings, egg and spear. Pattern poems first appear in the works of Greek bucolic poets, particularly those of Simias of Rhodes (4th c. BC). It seems that the Planudean version of the *Greek Anthology* passed on the idea. In English literature pattern poems begin to appear in the 16th c.; for instance, in Puttenham's *The Arte of English Poesie* (1589). George Herbert's *Easter Wings* is one of the most famous examples. Among modern poets to attempt the form are Apollinaire, Mayakovsky, e. e. cummings and Dylan Thomas. This example comes from Dylan Thomas's series of twelve pattern poems entitled *Vision and Prayer*:

Who
Are you
Who is born
In the next room
So loud to my own
That I can hear the womb
Opening and the dark run
Over the ghost and the dropped son
Behind the wall thin as a wren's bone?
In the birth bloody room unknown
To the burn and turn of time
And the heart print of man
Bows no baptism
But dark alone
Blessing on
The wild
Child.

See ALTAR POEM; CONCRETE POETRY/VERSE; EMBLEM-BOOK; PRUNING POEM; RHOPALIC VERSE.

patter song Usually a kind of comic lyric (*q.v.*) half spoken, half sung – or chanted. In ancient Greek comedy (*q.v.*) it was known as *pnigos* (*q.v.*). A large number of patter songs developed during service life in the First World War and lasted thereafter. The Cockney tradition of a quick-fire line of guff, and the music hall tradition of a jokey story half sung, half told, were both strong influences. Two famous ones are:

Today is my daughter's wedding day,
Ten thousand pounds I'll give away. (Three cheers)

On second thoughts I think it best
To put it away in the old oak chest.
You mingy bastard! Chuck him out! etc. etc.

And

Help, help, there's a woman overboard!
Who will save her?
I will!
Who are you?
Ballocky Bill the sailor, just returned from sea!

Such more or less nonsense patters might be recited for no reason at all, perhaps only to relieve tension or create a diversion. A famous example of service patter (still to be heard in training depots) is the drill sergeant's admonitory chant to recruits:

> And while you're resting I'll tell you a little tale. When I was a lad I had a box of wooden soldiers. They were beautiful wooden soldiers and I thought the world of them. Well, one day I lost them and the loss nearly broke my poor little heart. So I went to my mother and I told her what had happened. 'Never mind, son,' she said, 'never mind. 'You'll find your wooden soldiers again one day.' (Pause for effect, and balefully appraising glance from sergeant.) And, by God, I have, too!!

Not a few of the best patters are bawdy. One of the most famous is *The Showman* (or *The Wild West Show*). It was known before the First World War, but became very popular during it.

Most patter songs belong to the oral tradition (*q.v.*). An instance of a 'written' one is Gilbert and Sullivan's 'nightmare' in *Iolanthe*.

Patter probably derives from *Pater Noster*; from the rapid recitation of the prayer when, for example, saying the rosary. *See also* JINGLE.

pause In prose fiction a kind of resting point which allows the reader to reflect. Trollope uses the device quite often in his recapitulations. In verse, the equivalent of a caesura (*q.v.*). In drama, an indication that there is to be a silence – often of no determined length. Some modern dramatists (e.g. Jean-Jacques Bernard, Montherlant, Samuel Beckett and Harold Pinter) have made extensive use of the pause: an exploitation of the dramatic principle that what people do not say may be quite as important as what they do say. *See also* THEATRE OF SILENCE.

payada In Spanish-American *una paya* is an improvised song accompanied by a guitar. *Un payo* is 'a rustic', and *un payaso* 'a clown or buffoon', A *payada* has come to denote a dialogued poetical composition which the *payadores* improvise and accompany on the guitar. Two *payadores* may play in counterpoint; hence *payada de contrapunto*. In the Argentine this is a popular form of contest between gauchos. In Argentina the *payador* is akin to our strolling player, and thus related to the *jongleur, trouvère* and troubadour (*qq.v.*).

Peking opera It dates from the 18th c. during the reign of the Emperor Ch'ien Lung (1736–95), who personally collected the best actors and singers in his realm. As a form of drama it incorporates a wide range of traditional theatrical modes, including music, song, dance, dialogue and acrobatics. *See also* WEN AND WU.

PEN An international association of Poets, Playwrights, Editors, Essayists and Novelists founded in 1921 by Mrs Dawson-Scott under the presidency of John Galsworthy. Its function is to promote co-operation among writers world-wide, in the interests of international goodwill and freedom of expression and literature in general. There are regular conferences in various parts of the world.

penny dreadful A novel or novelette (*qq.v.*) of mystery, adventure, crime and action. Without any literary pretensions. Bound in paper and cheaply printed. A penny, from the cost; dreadful, presumably, because they were regarded as low, vulgar, sensational, etc. Known among schoolboys as 'bloods', and the equivalent of the American dime novel (*q.v.*). G. K. Chesterton wrote a celebrated defence of penny dreadfuls. *See also* BLUE BOOK; DETECTIVE STORY; MELODRAMA; ROMAN A DEUX SOUS; THRILLER.

pensée (F 'thought') A thought (or reflection) put in literary form. It may be only a short sentence – like the average aphorism or maxim (*qq.v.*) – or it may run to several pages. The most famous collection of *pensées* is unquestionably Pascal's. It constituted the notes and framework for an uncompleted *Defence of the Christian Religion* (1670). According to how they are numbered and classified there are between eight hundred and a thousand of Pascal's *pensées*. They display a profoundly original and acute mind and constitute one of the great works of European literature. A brief example is: 'Memory and joy are intuitive; and even mathematical propositions become so. For reason creates natural intuitions, and natural intuitions are erased by reason.'

Many writers keep notebooks, diaries, journals, daybooks and other memoranda in which they jot down thoughts, but relatively few have chosen to make the *pensée* the main vehicle of their thinking. Indeed, had Pascal lived to complete his work the result would have been an *apology* (*q.v.*) for the Christian faith rather than a diversity of thoughts. However, outstanding examples of those who followed in the Pascal tradition are Diderot, whose *Pensées philosophiques* (1746) were intended as a kind of reply to Pascal's work, and Joseph Joubert (1754–1824), who took the *pensée* as his principal form. His observations on a wide variety of subjects were edited by Chateaubriand as *Receuil des pensées* (1838).

English writers have not been given so much to the *pensée* habit, though many of their journals and notebooks abound in them, and many survive in collections of table-talk (*q.v.*). However, there have been some notable contributions. First, Ben Jonson's *Timber, or Discoveries made upon Men and Matters* (1640), a collection of *obiter dicta, sententiae* and reflections on miscellaneous subjects. Some are only a line or two; some as long as short essays. George Savile, Marquess of Halifax, composed three collections of 'thoughts' towards the end of the 17th c. but they were not published until 1750, when they appeared as *Political, Moral and Miscellaneous Reflexions*.

To these one may add three other notable collections from more recent years: *Speculations* (1924), the result of Herbert Read's editing of T. E. Hulme's notebooks; Paul Valéry's *Rhumbs* (1926), thus called in reference to the navigational sense of the word *rhumb* or *rumb* (the angular distance between two successive points of the compass); and *The Unquiet Grave* (1944) by Palinurus, alias Cyril Connolly, an assembly of quotations and sage *aperçus* on a wide range of topics. *See also* CHARACTER; COMMONPLACE BOOK; DIARY AND JOURNAL; ESSAY; OBITER DICTA; SENTENTIA.

pentameter (Gk 'of five measures') The five-foot line and the basic line in much English verse; especially in blank verse and the heroic couplet (*qq.v.*). It was probably introduced by Chaucer, and was certainly established by him. For the next five hundred years it was the line unit commonly favoured by scores of poets. Late in the 19th c. poets began to experiment in freer forms, hence free verse (*q.v.*). It was Ezra Pound, as much as anyone, who helped to loosen its traditional hold ('to break the pentameter,' he said, 'that was the first heave'). In the 20th c. poets have experimented a great deal with lines of varying length, yet the pentameter has remained a most convenient unit.

The first two lines from this poem, *Mr Edwards and the Spider*, by Robert Lowell, are pentameters; the following three are not.

> Ĭ sáw | thĕ spí|dĕrs már|chĭng thróugh | thĕ áir,
> Swímmĭng | frŏm trée | tŏ trée | thăt míl|dĕwed dáy
> Ĭn láttĕr | Aúgŭst | whĕn thĕ háy
> Căme créakĭng | tŏ thĕ bárn. | Bŭt whére
> Thĕ wínd | ĭs wéstĕrlў . . .

The basic foot in English pentameters is iambic. In antiquity the pentameter was a dactylic-spondaic line of two equal parts: two and a half feet + two and a half feet. Coleridge illustrates this use neatly in *Ovidian Elegiac Meter*:

> Ín thĕ hĕx|ámĕtĕr | rísĕs thĕ | fóuntaĭn's | sílvĕrў | cólŭmn,
> Ín thĕ pĕn|támĕtĕr | áye fáll ĭng ĭn mélŏdў báck.

See DACTYL; HEXAMETER; IAMB.

pentapody (Gk 'five feet') A group or line of five feet.

pentarsic (Gk 'five rises') A line with five metrical beats, like an iambic pentameter (*q.v.*). *See* ARSIS AND THESIS.

pentastich (Gk 'five lines) A stanza or poem of five lines. *See* CINQUAIN; QUINTET.

pentateuch (Gk 'containing five books') The first five books of the Old Testament: Genesis, Exodus, Leviticus, Numbers and Deuteronomy. They are taken together as a connected group and ascribed (traditionally) to Moses. *See* OCTATEUCH.

penthimimer (Gk 'of five halves') In Greek and Latin verse a metrical unit consisting of two feet; as that forming either half of a pentameter (*q.v.*) or the first part of a hexameter (*q.v.*).

pereval (R 'the pass') A group or society of Russian writers formed in 1923 whose leader was Alexander Voronski (1884–1937?). Their work was published in his journal *Red Virgin Soil.* They were against the concept and practice of proletarian literature. The group was abolished in 1932 when all literary organizations were compulsorily amalgamated in the Union of Soviet Writers (*q.v.*).

perfect rhyme Also known as true or full rhyme, it occurs when there is an exact correspondence between vowel sounds and the following consonants, but not of the consonants preceding the vowel. It may be single, double or triple: haunch – launch; dollar – collar; podium – sodium. *See also* RIMES RICHES; RIMES SUFFISANTES.

performance *See* COMPETENCE/PERFORMANCE.

performance art A vague term for theatrical presentations or events of the 'happenings' (*q.v.*) kind in which there is emphasis on spectacular visual effects. Some of the work done by, for instance, the Living Theater, the International Centre of Theatre Research and the Bread and Puppet Theatre (*qq.v.*) might be categorized as performance art. *See also* TOTAL THEATRE.

period A term commonly used in the history of literature for convenient if sometimes arbitrary classification and reference. For example: Renaissance period, Restoration period, Augustan, Romantic and Victorian period (*qq.v.*). Renaissance is associated with all the creative arts and the history of art. Restoration has political connotations. Augustan suggests a certain style (*q.v.*) as well as having political connotations. Romantic derives from a literary term and implies a certain attitude and feeling. Victorian is a matter of chronology: roughly coincident with the sovereign's reign. Such classifications have little to do with literary norms and are often misleading.

For the grammatical sense of period, *see* LOOSE AND PERIODIC SENTENCE.

periodical A magazine or journal published at regular intervals: monthly, quarterly, etc. The periodical, as we understand it today, dates from the middle of the 17th c. The exclusively literary periodical is more recent. The first of any note to appear was the French *Journals des Scavans* [*Savants*] in 1665. Then came the Italian *Giornale de Letterati* (1668–81), and the British *Mercurius Librarius* (1668–1711). The *Athenian Mercury* (1690–97) and the *Gentleman's Journal* (1692–4) were then precursors of the *Spectator*. The opening years of the 18th c. were vital in the evolution of the periodical and the essay (*q.v.*) because of Defoe's *Review of the*

Affairs of France and All Europe (1704–12) – and the *Tatler* (1709–11), the *Spectator* (1711–12) and the *Guardian* (1713), all three of which were established by Addison and Steele. In 1731 the *Gentleman's Magazine* first came out and was to last until 1907. Boswell was one of its more famous contributors. Similar publications were the *London Magazine* (1732–84), the *Scots* (1739–1817), which became the *Edinburgh* for seven years after that, the *Oxford* (1768–82), and the *European* (1782–1826). The *Museum* (1746–7) and the *Monthly Review* (1749–1845) were landmarks in the development of the literary periodical. The latter was a Whig journal and from this time politics were to influence the genre for many years. Three important Tory periodicals from about the same period were: the *Critical Review* (1756–1817), the *London Review* (1775–80) and the *British Critic* (1793–1843). In 1802 was published the *Edinburgh Review*, one of the most famous and influential of all periodicals. It lasted until 1929. The *Quarterly Review*, a Tory publication, began in 1809 and is still published. From this period, too, dates the foundation of Blackwood's *Edinburgh Magazine*. From the beginning of the 19th c. there was a steadily increasing number of periodicals until the First World War. Since then, and especially since the Second World War, the number has steadily decreased, largely because they are too expensive to produce. Some of the more famous publications in the 19th c. were the *London Magazine*, *Fraser's Magazine*, *Dublin University Magazine*, *The Cornhill Magazine*, *Longman's Magazine*, *London Quarterly Review*, *The Athenaeum*, *Spectator*, *Saturday Review*, *The Examiner*, *Truth* and *The Speaker*. In the 20th c. some of the landmarks in periodical literature have been the publication of *The Times Literary Supplement*, *Saturday Westminster Gazette*, *Week-End Review*, *New Statesman*, *Time and Tide*, *New Age*, *T. P.'s Weekly*, *G. K.'s Weekly* and *John o' London's Weekly*. Sir John Squire's *London Mercury* was a literary magazine of prime importance. Also *Horizon*. In more recent years the *London Magazine* has been revived, and *Encounter* has established itself.

Outside Britain the periodical has flourished also, especially in France, Germany, Italy and America.

peripeteia (Gk 'sudden change') Peripety is a reversal of fortune; a fall. In drama, usually the sudden change of fortune from prosperity to ruin; but it can be the other way about. A much debated term, it was first used by Aristotle in *Poetics* (Chap. VI). The relevant passage, in Bywater's translation, is:

> [Peripety] is the change from one state of things within the play to its opposite of the kind described, and that too in the way we are saying, in the probable or necessary sequence of events; as it is for instance in *Oedipus*: here the opposite of things is produced by the Messenger, who, coming to gladden Oedipus and to remove his fears as to his mother, reveals the secret of his birth.

See ANAGNORISIS; TRAGEDY; TURNING POINT.

periphrasis (Gk 'roundabout speech') A roundabout way of speaking or writing; known also as circumlocution; thus, using many or very long words where a few or simple words will do. For example: Her olfactory system was suffering from a temporary inconvenience (i.e. her nose was blocked). Much periphrasis comes from an over-nice regard for 'politeness', in the pejorative sense. Semi-literate people are also tempted to this sort of pomp and verbosity. It is also much loved by lawyers, politicians, officials, bureaucrats and verbocrats. What Sir Ernest Gowers described as 'officialese' (*q.v.*) is laden with the periphrastic. It is very often the result of slack thinking, but it may be used deliberately – usually for comic effect, especially in the depiction of character. In the 18th c., particularly, propriety and poetic decorum required periphrastic usage. *See* DECORUM; EUPHEMISM; HOMERIC EPITHET; JARGON; KENNING; METALEPSIS; PLEONASM; POETIC DICTION; TAUTOLOGY.

peroration The concluding part of an oration, speech or discourse; a summing or rounding up of what has gone before. It suggests the grand manner favoured by Greek and Roman orators and 18th and 19th c. statesmen. In written works Dr Johnson, Gibbon and Macaulay, for instance, were inclined to perorate.

perqué (It *perché* 'why') A Spanish verse form comprising a series of octosyllabic couplets to ask rhetorical questions. Usually preceded by a *redondilla* or *quintilla* (*qq.v.*). The first on record is by Hurtado de Mendoza in the 14th c.

persona (L 'mask') Originally a mask or false face of clay or bark worn by actors. From it derives the term *dramatis personae* (*q.v.*) and, later, the word *person.* In literary and critical jargon *persona* has come to denote the 'person' (the 'I' of an 'alter ego') who speaks in a poem or novel or other form of literature. For instance, the narrator of Chaucer's *Canterbury Tales*, the speaker in Keats's *Ode* *to a Nightingale*, the different speakers in Browning's dramatic monologues, the Gulliver of *Gulliver's Travels*, Marlow in Conrad's *Heart of Darkness* and other stories by him. *See also* AESTHETIC DISTANCE; MONOLOGUE; NARRATOR; VIEWPOINT.

personal heresy, the In 1934 C. S. Lewis contributed an article on *The Personal Heresy in Criticism* to *Essays and Studies*. In this he expressed disquiet at and disapproval of the then fairly widely held belief that poetry is or should be the expression of a poet's personality. In the course of this he referred to a book by E. M. W. Tillyard on Milton in which, according to Lewis, Tillyard stated the premise that all poetry is about the poet's state of mind. Tillyard 'replied' to this in an essay. Lewis 'replied' to that. And so on. The two men then decided to publish their three essays apiece in one volume (publ. 1939). *The Personal Heresy*, erudite, urbane, courteous and continuously stimulating, is, in its way, a model of how people should agree to differ in their search after truth. *See also* AESTHETICISM; PARNASSIANS; SINCERITY.

personification The impersonation or embodiment of some quality or abstraction; the attribution of human qualities to inanimate objects. Personification is inherent in many languages through the use of gender, and it appears to be very frequent in all literatures – especially in poetry. This example is from Sylvia Plath's *The Moon and the Yew Tree*:

> The moon is no door. It is a face in its own right,
> White as a knuckle and terribly upset.
> It drags the sea after it like a dark crime; it is quiet
> With the O-gape of complete despair. I live here.
> Twice on Sunday, the bells startle the sky –
> Eight great tongues affirming the Resurrection.
> At the end, they soberly bong out their names.

See PATHETIC FALLACY.

Petrarchan sonnet Also known as the Italian sonnet, the form originated in Italy in the 13th c. and was perfected by Petrarch (1304–74). It is a fourteen-line poem divided into two parts: the first eight lines comprise the octave (*q.v.*) or octet and rhyme abbaabba; the following six lines or sestet (*q.v.*) usually rhyme cdecde. Rhyme variations in the sestet are admissible, but rhymes are limited to five. As a rule the octave presents the theme or problem of the poem, the thesis; the sestet resolves it. It was imported to England in the 16th c. This example is by Sir Thomas Wyatt, translating Petrarch:

> The pillar perisht is whereto I leant,
> The strongest stay of mine unquiet mind;
> The like of it no man again can find,
> From East to West still seeking though he went.
> To mine unhap! for hap away hath rent
> Of all my joy the very bark and rind;
> And I, alas, by chance am thus assigned
> Daily to mourn till death do it relent.
> But since that thus it is by destiny,
> What can I more but have a woful heart –
> My pen in plaint, my voice in careful cry,
> My mind in woe, my body full of smart,
> And I myself myself always to hate –
> Till dreadful death do ease my doleful state?

Wyatt here has the traditional rhyming couplet to round off the poem. *See* SONNET.

Petrarchism In a broad sense the imitation of Petrarch's style. Petrarch (1304–74) was considerably plagiarized and imitated during and after his life and he had a considerable influence on European poets: Bembo, Michelangelo, Tasso, Ronsard, du Bellay, Lope de Vega, Góngora, Camoëns, Wyatt, Surrey, Sidney, Spenser and Shakespeare (and some other Elizabethans). The influence was by no means entirely beneficial, as can be seen from the more mannered and elaborate sonnets of Spenser and Shakespeare (especially the former). On the other hand, Petrarch helped to develop the use of the vernacular and established the sonnet (*q.v.*) form. *See* BLAZON; PETRARCHAN SONNET.

pevači Muslim ballad-singers or chanters in Bosnia, where the ballad tradition was under strong Turkish influence. They were professional minstrels of the oral tradition (*q.v.*) and thus kin to the Greek *rhapsodes*, the Old English *scopas*, the Scandinavian *skalds* and the Serbian *guslari* (*qq.v.*). The *pevači* differed from the Christian *guslari* in that they accompanied their chant or recitation on a *tambura*, whereas the *guslar* used a *gusle* – a one-stringed fiddle.

phallocentric Centred on the phallus. Phallocentrism denotes a system which privileges the phallus as the symbol and source of power. A patriarchal society is phallocentric. The term has frequently been used in feminist literary criticism (*q.v.*) – for example, by Julia Kristeva and Hélène Cixous – in attempts to dismantle such binary oppositions (*q.v.*) as male/female, masculine/feminine. *See also* PHALLOGOCENTRIC.

phallogocentric A term invented by the French philosopher Jacques Derrida. It is a conflation of *phallocentric* ('phallus-centred') and *logocentric* ('word-centred'; epistemologically, 'truth-centred'). Terry Eagleton has translated it (happily) as 'cock-sure'. Applied to, for example, society, it denotes one which controls or attempts to control by means of sexual/social influence and power. Thus, a patriarchal society would be predominantly logocentric as well as phallocentric. Post-structuralists would describe modern Western society (or some aspects of such societies) as phallogocentric. As far as literature is concerned, the term might be applied to novels in which the male characters have the upper hand and the female characters are sex objects. The more macho features of Ernest Hemingway's novels might be called phallogocentric. *See* PHALLOCENTRIC.

phanopoeia (Gk 'making something visible') A figurative or verbal device by which the writer conveys the image of the object (be it fixed or moving) to the visual imagination. Ezra Pound discussed this in *ABC of Reading* (1934). In these lines from Philip Larkin's *The Whitsun Weddings* the rhythm and stress sequences skilfully suggest the physical motion of the train and produce a visual image:

> All afternoon, through the tall heat that slept
> For miles inland,
> A slow and stopping curve southwards we kept.
> Wide farms went by, short-shadowed cattle, and
> Canals with floatings of industrial froth;

The heavily stressed paeonic rhythms of the first two lines relax into iambs in the third line (except for the spondaic 'southwards'). The fourth line is also heavily stressed; the fifth is a relatively brisk combination of two iambs and two anapaests. *See* LOGOPOEIA; MELOPOEIA.

phantom word A word that exists through the error of scribe, printer or lexicographer, or merely through some corruptive influence. Examples are: *willy-nilly* for *will he? nill he?*; *whatnot; dacious* for *audacious*; *obstropolous* for *obstreperous*; *brecksus* for *breakfast. Bacon and eggs* and *ham and eggs* are inclined to appear on European menus as *bekendecks* and *hemenex*, and in other variations. The OED Supplement has a list of such words. *See* GHOSTWORD.

phatic language *Phatic* derives from Greek *phasis* 'utterance'. A term in linguistics which derives from the phrase 'phatic communion' invented by the anthropologist Bronislaw Malinowski (1884–1942). It was applied to language used for establishing an atmosphere and the communication of feelings rather than of ideas, and of logical and rational thoughts. Phatic words and phrases have been called 'idiot salutations'; and, when they generate to a form of dialogue, 'two-stroke conversations'. Exchanges about the state of the weather and a person's health fall into this category. It seems that the term may also be applied to the kind of noises that a mother makes to her baby, a lover to his mistress and a master to his dog.

phenomenology (Gk *phenomena* 'things appearing' + *logos* 'knowledge') A method of philosophical inquiry which lays stress on the perceiver's vital and central role in determining meaning. It derives from the thinking of Edmund Husserl (1859–1938), the German philosopher. In his view the proper object of philosophical inquiry is not the objects in the world that are perceivable through the senses but, rather, the *a priori* contents of our consciousness. Thus, the method demands a close inspection of mental and intellectual states and processes. By using this method, he believed, it is possible to reveal the underlying nature of consciousness and phenomena, and to do so in an *a*temporal and *a*historical way – the point being to establish a trans-subjective theory of understanding. The implication is that an individual human mind is the centre and origin of meaning. As far as literature and literary theory are concerned, the phenomenologist's critical approach involves an entry to and investigation of the underlying nature and essence of a work of literature under scrutiny and thus a kind of access to the author's consciousness.

A different – and perhaps more 'vulgar' – version of the phenomenological approach is the exploration of the unique personality behind a work of literature. In order to do this the phenomenological critic needs to empty his or her mind of all preconceptions and presuppositions about the author and the text he or she is to study. Having done this, the critic is or ought to be in a highly receptive and sensitive state, a state which may enable him or her to share the mode of consciousness of the author. This state of mind has been described as 'consciousness of the consciousness of another'. It is probably doubtful if any critic could actually bring about such a state of mind. With the best will and intentions in the world the consciousness of the critic would, sooner or later, intervene.

The influence of phenomenology has been widespread since Husserl put forward his theories in 1900 and thereafter. Concepts of phenomenology were developed by Martin Heidegger in Germany and by Maurice Merleau-Ponty and, in turn, by Hans-Georg Gadamer. The Polish theorist Roman Ingarden developed Husserl's ideas in *The Literary Work of Art* (1931, trans. 1973) and in *The Cognition of the Literary Work of Art* (1937, trans. 1973). Important German critics affected by Ingarden are Wolfgang Iser and Hans Robert Jauss. The influence is especially clear in Iser's reader-response theory (*q.v.*) and Jauss's reception theory (*q.v.*). The term 'phenomenological criticism' has also been applied to the theory and practice of the Geneva School of critics. The long-term effects of the various theories are also evident in post-structuralism (*q.v.*). *See* HERMENEUTICS.

Pherecretean A classical meter named after the poet Pherecrates (5th c. BC). It is a catalectic form of the glyconic (*q.v.*). Basically, it allowed a resolved foot only in the first two syllables. It is to be found with one or more glyconics in Anacreon and the choruses of Greek tragedy.

philippic A denunciation in speech or writing and couched in vituperative language. The term derives from Demosthenes's orations in denunciation of Philip of Macedon. *See* DIATRIBE; INVECTIVE.

Philistine The Philistines were an alien and aggressive tribe who inhabited the southern coast of Palestine. From there they continually raided the Israelites. The term *Philister* was applied by German students to a person who was a 'townsman' in the sense that he was not a member of the university. From this probably derives the notion that a Philistine is a person devoted to money, material objects, the commonplace, the prosaic and the uncultured. He has little concern for art (of any kind), beauty or the nobler aspirations and achievements of mankind. Matthew Arnold, in his last lecture as Professor of Poetry at Oxford (1867), criticized those whom he regarded as the Philistines of England – namely the bourgeois classes who accepted wealth as the measure of greatness. Arnold argued that culture 'helps us by means of its spiritual standard of perfection, to regard wealth as but machinery . . . If it were not for this purging effect wrought upon our minds by culture, the whole world, the future as well as the present, would inevitably belong to the Philistines.' *See* AESTHETICISM; DECADENCE.

philology (Gk 'love of speech, or learning') The study of literature and scholarship. More particularly, now, the science of language and linguistics (*q.v.*).

Philosophes, les Broadly speaking, men of letters, philosophers, writers, scientists *et al.* of 18th c. France. Though many of them differed considerably in their individual attitudes and convictions, they were united in their belief and trust in the power and value of reason. They were also united in their antagonism to outmoded creeds, superstitions and institutions. Many distinguished writers and intellectuals were numbered among them, including: Montesquieu, Voltaire, Diderot, Rousseau, Buffon, Condillac, Turgot, Condorcet, d'Alembert, Morellet, d'Holbach, Marmontel, Helvétius and Raynal. Their *magnum opus* was the *Encyclopédie* (1751–66). They were frequently attacked by different and powerful groups, particularly the Jansenists and Jesuits (who themselves were in a state of dispute). The overall influence of their independence of mind and rebellious spirit was immeasurable and their attitudes and doctrines did much to bring about the Revolution.

phoneme (Gk 'speech sound') A basic sound unit in a language. For example, in English 't' and 'd' are separate phonemes; 'c' and 'k' may be the same or different (compare *cider*, *caulk*, *kirk*); 'c' and 's' may be the same or different (compare *sump*, *cork* and *civet*); 'ph' and 'f' in English are the same.

phonocentrism The word *phonocentric* means 'centred on sound/speech'; hence, phonocentrism denotes 'sound centring' or 'sound-centredness'. Jacques Derrida (1930–), the French philosopher, uses the term 'logocentrism' (*q.v.*) to describe all forms of thought which base themselves on notions of truth. 'Phonocentrism' is a sub-category of logocentrism, and consists of privileging speech over writing; this logocentric bias is based on the view that speech is closer to truth than writing is. Derrida talks about writing not in terms of *speech* (the opposite of Plato who gives speech precedence over writing), and counters with the idea of language as a kind of writing – what he calls 'archi-écriture'. This is his way of emphasizing that philosophy is only a kind of writing, and is a 'quasi-science' of language. The basic point is that for Derrida language is a tissue of what is written and philosophy therefore can make no pretensions to being anything more than 'a kind of writing'. *See also* GRAMMATOLOGY.

picaresque novel (Sp *picaro* 'rogue') It tells the life of a knave or picaroon who is the servant of several masters. Through his experience this picaroon satirizes the society in which he lives. The picaresque novel originated in 16th c. Spain, the earliest example being the anonymous *Lazarillo de Tormes* (1553). The two most famous Spanish authors of picaresque novels were Mateo Alemán, who wrote *Guzmán de Alfarache* (1599–1604), and Francisco Quevedo, who wrote *La vida del Buscón* (1626). Both books were widely read in Europe. Other picaresque novels included Thomas Nashe's *The Unfortunate Traveller* (1594), Lesage's *Gil Blas* (1715), Defoe's *Moll Flanders* (1722), Fielding's *Jonathan Wild* (1743) and Smollett's *Roderick Random* (1748). A more recent example is Thomas Mann's unfinished *Confessions of Felix Krull* (1954). The German term for this kind of story is *Räuberroman*.

picaroon *See* PICARESQUE NOVEL.

Piccolo Teatro, Milan Opened in 1947, the Piccolo was the first Italian theatre to be supported by public funds. For forty years it had continual success under the direction of Giorgio Strehler (1921–) and achieved an international reputation with a company which has visited over thirty countries. It has been particularly well known for many notable productions of Brecht's plays.

picturesque During the 18th c. there was a steadily increasing interest in rural scenery, and in the 'scenic'. This interest was closely connected with landscape gardening (by, for example, William Kent, 'Capability' Brown and Humphry Repton) and landscape in general, and with a growing amount of travel in Britain and abroad (it is noticeable that travel books, *q.v.*, begin to proliferate in the 18th c.). In due course the Grand Tour (*q.v.*) was also to have an influence on peoples' sensibilities and responses. Artists and writers looked at scenery in new and different ways. The work of three painters in particular became very popular in Britain: namely, Nicolas Poussin (1594–1665), Claude Lorrain (1600–82) and Salvator Rosa (1615–73). Landscape gardeners copied scenes from Claude's compositions. The poet Thomas Gray (1716–71) carried what was called a 'Claude glass', a kind of mirror, convex and blackened, which gave the impression of a 'Claudian' view. Writers re-experienced the natural order through the individual vision of these painters and others. Almost a case of visual defamiliarization (*q.v.*). They began to describe scenery in detail, and the wilder, more remote and unspoilt it was (e.g. Wales, the Lake District), the better they like it. Thus there developed what may be called a 'cult of the picturesque'. Gardens were landscaped to look 'wild' and 'natural', fake ruins were built to adorn them, the grander and more awe-inspiring aspects of the natural order were admired and extolled. It was a matter of aesthetic taste and fashion of which people became connoisseurs, or affected to be connoisseurs. This cult is discernible early in the 18th c. in, for instance, Addison's *Remarks on Several Parts of Italy* (1705) and Pope's *Eloisa to Abelard* (1717). In the course of the 18th c. and early in the 19th c. the cult produced a certain amount of literature of interest. For example, William Mason's poem *The English Garden* (1771–81), Thomas Gray's travel journal (1775), Richard Payne Knight's *The Landscape: A Didactic Poem* (1794), and, of course, the delightful topographical poetry (*q.v.*) of the period which relished the rural scene. There were various essays on the matter, too, among them William Gilpin's *Three Essays: On Picturesque Beauty; On Picturesque Travel; On Sketching Landscape* (1792) and Sir Uvedale Price's *Essay on the Picturesque* (1794). The Gothic novelists went in for descriptions of picturesque scenery and their influence becomes discernible in Walter Scott's novels. Eventually there came those who made fun of it and satirized it. For instance, Jane Austen in *Mansfield Park* (1814), Peacock in *Headlong Hall* (1816) and William Combe in *The Tour of Dr Syntax in Search of the Picturesque* (1809). The cult of the picturesque is related to romanticism and also to the concept of the sublime (*q.v.*). *See also* GOTHIC NOVEL/FICTION.

pièce à thèse *See* THESIS PLAY.

pièce bien faite *See* WELL-MADE PLAY.

pièces noires *See* BLACK COMEDY.

pie quebrado (Sp *pie* 'foot', *quebrado* 'broken' – from *quebrar* 'to break') In Spanish prosody a short line of five syllables at the most, but usually four; longer in certain combinations and thus known as *copla de pie quebrado*. In general *pie* denotes verse, foot or syllable as in English use, and there are therefore many ways in which *pie* + adjective or past participle could be used. The first known examples date from the 14th c. in Pedro de Veragie and Juan Ruiz, Arcipreste de Hita. *See* COPLA; REDONDILLA.

pillow book A form of commonplace book (*q.v.*) which appears to have originated in Japan. It is a compilation of notes, jottings, 'occasional' writings; the sort of thing that might go into an extended diary (*q.v.*) or journal. A classic example, and one of the earliest extant, is *The Pillow Book of Sei Shōnagon* which is titled *Makura no Sōshi* ('notes of the pillow') and was composed *c.* 1000. Sei Shōnagon was a lady-in-waiting to the Empress Sadako during the last decade of the 10th c. The story of its origin is that when a bundle of unused notebooks was brought to the Empress she wondered what to do with them. The lady-in-waiting suggested that she should have them and make them into a pillow. That may have meant putting them into the drawers of a wooden pillow. She subsequently filled the notebooks with random facts and jottings, lists and so forth. This early pillow book is the forerunner of a traditional Japanese genre called *zuihitsu* ('occasional writings') which still exists.

pillow dictionary A euphemism (*q.v.*) for a tutor in a foreign language or languages who, as the term implies, gives tuition in bed. A term more commonly used by men of women than vice versa. Those who practise hypnopaedic techniques use a different kind of dictionary. *See also* LEXICON; PILLOW BOOK.

Pindaric ode *See* ODE.

p'ing hua A Chinese term for a type of popular tale or yarn (*qq.v.*) which is dominated by the narrator's presence and by the use of colloquial and idiomatic language. The *p'ing hua* tends to be fantastic in content but is realistic in tone. It is akin to the Russian *skaz* and to the tall story (*qq.v.*).

pivot word A word or phrase which has the effect of modifying what precedes or follows, especially in repetition. A recent example is the use of the word 'something' by Jon Silkin in *Death of a Son* (*who died in a mental hospital aged one*). The poem begins:

Something has ceased to come along with me.
Something like a person: something very like one.
And there was no nobility in it
Or anything like that.

piyyut A form of Hebrew liturgical poem especially written to celebrate a festival. They sometimes taken an acrostic (*q.v.*) form. They were common between the 3rd and 7th c. Seven are known to have been written by Yose ben Yose, the Hebrew religious poet.

plagiarism (L *plagiarius* 'kidnapper, seducer, literary thief') Hence *plagiary*, the noun; and *plagiarize*, the verb. C. T. Onions defined plagiarism as 'wrongful appropriation and publication as one's own'. As such it is *scelus semper et ubique*. Much plagiarism has been the lifting, filching or pirating of other people's works; a very common practice among dramatists during the Elizabethan period when hackwriters blatantly stole the plays of others and presented them as their own. These days (and for long past) such thieving is rare and authors are now fairly well protected by copyright (*q.v.*).

There are other forms of literary felony and pilfering which have been regarded as less reprehensible. These may be conscious or unconscious borrowing. In his conversations with Eckermann, Goethe once pointed out (on Jan. 4th, 1827) that through all art 'there is filiation i.e. descent or transmission from. If you see a great master, you will always find that he has used what was good in his predecessors, and that it was this which made him great. Men like Raphael do not spring out of the ground. They took their root in the antique and in the best that has been done before them.' This is a point of view with which many would agree, from Aristotle onwards. Imitation (*q.v.*) was a practice fully approved by the Classical authors (e.g. Aristotle, Cicero and Quintilian) and it has been legitimate ever since Homer, who himself borrowed from the ballads then alive in oral tradition (*q.v.*). In fact, the ballad-maker, almost by definition, is a borrower in the more acceptable sense of the term. The good ballad-maker studies carefully what has already been achieved, learns from it and then attempts to adapt and improve it on his own account. He assimilates, refines, modifies and, if he is gifted, he then produces an original work of his own which will embellish the existing tradition. This is progress. The ballad *The Unquiet Grave* exists in several versions over a considerable period of time and each is equally good. There are no fewer than thirty-nine variants of *Mary Hamilton* – and again many of them are equally good. To support the point we may cite Luther's highly successful re-using of the old Church hymns, and Burns's use of traditional material which he shaped anew to his own purpose.

Ballad-making is a popular art and entertainment. By analogy so are the Punch and Judy show, music hall, proverbs, games, dance songs, festival rituals, fertility rites, folksongs and folk dramas (e.g. the Mumming Play and the Plough Monday Play, *qq.v.*). All borrow.

Another form of borrowing involves the use of source-books. Shakespeare, for instance, took many of his plots from chronicles and well-established stories. Many of his contemporaries did the same. Very often they transformed the source into an original work.

A less obvious example of the influence of source material can be seen in the plays of Molière, who made such notable use of the traditions and techniques of *commedia dell'arte* (*q.v.*).

Other kinds of source are legend and myth. The pervasive influence of these, in European literature especially, has been considerable (e.g. Oedipus, Ulysses, Faustus, Don Juan, The Wandering Jew).

There are also innumerable instances of verbal 'borrowing'. Consider, for example, from Munday and Chettle's *Death of Robert, Earl of Huntingdon* (*c.* 1598):

> The multitudes of seas dyed red with blood

from Munday's *Downfall of Robert, Earl of Huntingdon* (*c.* 1598):

> And made the green sea red with Pagan blood

and Shakespeare's (from *Macbeth*):

> The multitudinous seas incarnadine,
> Making the green one red.

All are fine; Shakespeare's the best by half a length.

In general nearly all artists live off each other. They borrow from each other. Ultimately the only true test is whether or not it is justifiable. Occasionally a man appears who is virtually a law unto himself, the genius (*q.v.*). After him nothing is quite the same ever again. Lesser mortals are content to follow the rules and conventions, but to use them skilfully and with as much originality as they are capable of. Occasionally there appears the literary iconoclast; the man who doesn't want to know about tradition, who wants to make a completely clean start on the fabulous *tabula rasa*. They are nearly always of inferior talents and achieve little that lasts. In fact, literary iconoclasm (like most other forms of iconoclastic activity) usually creates a paltry mess.

In broader senses yet, the writer (the artist) is a borrower. Using what Coleridge, himself a noted plagiarist, referred to as 'the hooks-and-eyes of memory' he stores and stocks his mind with the experience and creations of other writers. He teaches himself from them and through them. The creative mind matures this knowledge, allows it to macerate, so to speak, in what Henry James described as the 'deep well of unconscious cerebration'. One can detect the results clearly enough in many works. To take a few notable examples: Seneca was much influenced by the Greek tragedians; so was Racine. Hosts of writers of all kinds have 'lived off' Aristotle and Plato. Milton was much influenced by Spenser who owed much to Chaucer who, in turn, had borrowed from French and Italian writers. Keats was much influenced by all three of these Englishmen. Pope, who had a profound knowledge and understanding of the Classical authors, 'imitated' Horace. Dr Johnson, who had a comparable knowledge and understanding, 'imitated' Juvenal. The Pre-Raphaelites borrowed extensively from medieval authors (hence medievalism, *q.v.*). And one can hardly imagine Dylan Thomas and Ted Hughes being the fine poets they are if they had not learnt much from Gerard Manley Hopkins. W. H. Auden is an outstanding example of a poet who has used many long-established poetic forms and adapted them to his own individual needs and purposes.

Such men (and there are scores of others) are examples of good borrowers; the kind that Jonson was thinking of (he understood the matter very well) when, in *Discoveries*, he spoke of the writer who learns from his predecessors 'not as a creature that swallows what it takes in, crude, raw, or undigested; but that feeds with an appetite, and hath a stomach to concoct, divide and turn all into nourishment.' Jonson followed precept with practice, and no one could accuse him of lacking orginality (*q.v.*).

There are also plentiful examples of bad borrowing. This was particularly common in the 18th c., largely as a result of the influence of Milton. Wordsworth in turn was to exert a great influence for a hundred or more years, and even in the 1930s poets were still writing ponderous 'Wordsworthese'. Another notable example of wholly unsuccessful borrowing was the kind practised by 19th c. verse dramatists who adopted the styles, conventions and even attitudes of the Elizabethan playwrights and attempted to write dramatic blank verse like Shakespeare. Basically, writers like James Sheridan Knowles, Shelley, Tennyson and Browning did not understand the conventions.

Self-plagiarism is not uncommon among writers, and is often unconscious. When conscious, it usually involves the re-working of a poem, as in Collins's *How Sleep the Brave*, which he 'lifted' and re-shaped from *Ode on Colonel Ross.*

Plain thieving has always been fairly rare, probably because the risks of the detection are too great. However, Sterne was often unscrupulous; so was Disraeli. *See* INVENTION; SPONTANEITY.

plaint A lament (*q.v.*) in verse. *See* COMPLAINT; DIRGE; ELEGY; PLANH.

plaisir/jouissance Terms used with a special signification by Roland Barthes in his book *Le Plaisir du texte* (1973), a discussion of the *lisible/scriptible* or readerly/writerly (*q.v.*) text. The writerly text, he opines, offers two kinds of enjoyment: *plaisir*, 'pleasure'; and *jouissance*, 'bliss'. *Jouissance* carries connotations of ecstasy and sexual delight, and Barthes offers an aesthetics based on the pleasure of the body. To clarify his distinction he suggests that the *plaisir* taken in a text comes through the more or less straightforward processes of reading, while the *jouissance*, a heightened form of pleasure, derives from a sense of interruption, a 'breakdown' or gap, where, perhaps, something unorthodox or unexpected occurs. The comforts of *plaisir* are compatible with texts which are *lisible*; while the comforts and surprises of *jouissance* arise from the *scriptible.* He elaborates with a kind of erotic analogy, suggesting that the focus of erotic pleasure is the place where naked flesh meets a garment, where 'the garment gapes'. This is analogous to *jouissance.* However, he also suggests that the 'text of bliss' may impose a 'state of loss'; it is a text that discomforts and 'unsettles the reader's historical, cultural, psychological assumptions, the consistency of his tastes, values, memories, brings to a crisis his relation with language'.

planh A funeral lament (*q.v.*) in Old Provençal. Some forty-odd are believed to be extant. Most of them are laments for the death of some distinguished person, a patron or patroness. *See* COMPLAINT; DIRGE; ELEGY.

plateresco (Sp *platero* 'silversmith') Thus, an ornamental, 'filigreed' style of writing in Spanish 16th c. romances. The English version is *plateresque* 'silversmith-like'. Primarily an architectural term, and applied to an ornate style of architecture popular in Spain during the 16th c. *See also* BAROQUE; GONGORISM; MARINISM.

platitude A dull, commonplace statement. A trite and obvious remark. Many proverbial expressions and idioms have become platitudes. For example: 'You cannot have your cake and eat it.'

Platonism Paradoxically, Platonism has been a continual, pervasive and powerful influence on poets and poetry (and other forms of literature) down the ages. 'Paradoxically' because Plato would not 'allow' most forms of poetry in his *Republic*. The point is made uncompromisingly clear towards the end of Book X: 'But you will know that the only poetry that ought to be allowed in a state is praise to the gods and paeans to virtuous men; as soon as you go beyond that and admit lyric or epic poetry, then pleasure and pain become your rulers instead of the law and the principles that are commonly accepted as best'. However, Plato believed that poetry might serve the community by helping to educate it, and poetry which praised the gods and good men would show people who and what they should emulate. The didactic virtues of poetry were invoked in late Classical and medieval times to defend the art against those who objected to it on moral grounds. During the Renaissance (*q.v.*) period such a Platonic idea influenced the belief that the poet had a special role as a kind of 'celebrant' of nationalism. Much epic (*q.v.*) in the Renaissance is national epic. For example, Camoëns in *Os Lusiadas* composed a kind of historical manifesto of Portuguese nationalism, and Camoëns would have had a passport to the Republic because he sang the praises of noble men.

Plato saw the world as an imperfect imitation of a divine ideal, a shadowy and even distorted simulacrum of a heavenly prototype. It followed that the poet imitated this (because he imitated nature) and thus his work was merely an imitation of an imitation. As such, in the Platonic view, poetry could not arrive at truth. Aristotle attempted to deal with this problem in *Poetics* and advanced the theory that poetry did indeed convey the truth by a form of acceptable imitation or feigning (*q.v.*). Neoplatonic philosophers (the most distinguished was Plotinus, 3rd c.) thought that poetry was the most estimable form of imitation because it 'copied' not nature but a divine archetype. Such theories had much influence at the Renaissance and during the Romantic period (*q.v.*).

Plato, like Homer, also claimed that the poet was an inspired person. The idea of inspiration (*q.v.*) found great favour in later ages and there developed the belief that the poet was different from ordinary mortals; that the Muse had visited him; that he had vatic powers; that, in short, in the creation of poetry, he was in an exalted state as the result of divine insufflation. The image of the poet as visionary and prophet (even, according to Shelley, as an unacknowledged legislator) had a considerable vogue during the Romantic period.

Many of Plato's works (especially *Symposium*, *Timaeus*, *Parmenides* and the *Republic*) also include myths, symbols and images through whose similitudes (*q.v.*) he sought to express his ideas of Truth, Beauty and the Good, all of which, in his view, were One: a form of aesthetic and philosophic Trinity. These concepts were a powerful influence from the early Middle Ages onwards, and especially during the Renaissance when the influence of Platonism was at its greatest, thanks in great measure to Marsilio Ficino's Latin translation of Plato's works towards the end of the 15th c. and his attempted 'reconciliation' of Platonic and Christian philosophy in *Theologia Platonica*. Indeed, it was Ficino who used the term *Amor Platonicus* more or less synonymously with *Amor Socraticus* to denote spiritual love. Platonic love has become the best known idea or aspect of Platonism, and the ideal of Platonic love has influenced Western literature and life to such an extent that the most unlettered person may be presumed to have some acquaintance with it. In its origin (and the source is Plato's *Symposium*) it was the contemplation of the idea of perfect and absolute beauty; separate, simple and infinite beauty. By contrast, terrestrial beauty was a shadowy reflection of it. The chief Neoplatonist philosophers were Plotinus, Porphyry, Proclus and Hypatia; they combined Platonic ideas with oriental mysticism and drew on the theory of Platonic love and influenced Christian philosophy through St Augustine. Renaissance thinkers developed it into a theory that physical beauty was an outward expression of the inward grace and spiritual beauty of the soul, and this spiritual radiance was an extension of the effulgent beauty of God Himself. The Platonic lover therefore paid devotion and adoration to a physical beauty of his mistress only in so far as that beauty reflected her soul. From earthly and physical desire he aspired to the contemplation of the beatific vision. Such an attitude informed much lyric and love poetry of the late Middle Ages and during the Renaissance. Spenser elaborated the idea in his *Four Hymns.* There is a notable exposition in the fourth book of Castiglione's *Il Libro del Cortegiano* (The Book of the Courtier), 1528.

During the Romantic period there was a marked revival of interest in the concept of Platonic love, and a great interest in Platonism in general. Blake, Wordsworth, Shelley and Hölderlin especially were strongly influenced by it. This is particularly noticeable in Shelley's *Epipsychidion* and Wordsworth's *Intimations of Immortality.*

Between the end of the 16th c. and the beginning of the Romantic period Platonism as a force and influence is not much marked in Western thought and literature. However, mention should be made of the Cambridge Platonists – a group of philosophers who flourished during the middle of the 17th c. and whose headquarters were at Cambridge University. The main members of the group were Ralph Cudworth, Henry More, John Smith and Nathanael Culverwel. This group reacted against Puritan dogmatism and against the materialistic philosophies of Hobbes and Descartes. They were idealists who believed in the essentially spiritual constitution of the world. Henry More wrote some philosophical poetry which propounded some of the ideas of the group.

Platonism has continued to be a strong fertilizing influence in the minds of various poets, especially Coleridge, Rilke, Yeats and Wallace Stevens. There can be little doubt that Benjamin Jowett's translations of Plato (1871) did much to encourage the study of Platonism throughout the English-speaking world, though nowadays he has come under criticism for inaccuracy and pseudo-archaic English.

Plato's manifold influences have pervaded much political and utopian (*see* UTOPIA) thinking. Modern Fascism and Marxist Communism would have been repugnant to Plato, but his *Republic* depicts a prototypical totalitarian state and has had incalculable influence.

The form in which he chose to express many of his ideas was the dialogue (*q.v.*), of which there have been many celebrated examples since. We should also note the continual influence he has had on modes of thinking, methods of teaching and education in general.

play A dramatic work designed to be presented on a stage (or in a television studio) and performed by actors and actresses. An exception is a closet play (*q.v.*). *See* CHRONICLE PLAY; COMEDY; COMEDY OF MANNERS; HIGH COMEDY; LOW COMEDY; MIRACLE PLAY; MORALITY PLAY; MYSTERY PLAY; PASSION PLAY; THESIS PLAY; TRAGEDY; WELL-MADE PLAY.

Pléiade A group of 16th c. French poets named after the constellation of the seven daughters of Atlas. Ronsard originated the term in 1556. Until that time he had used the term *Brigade*. He adopted *Pléiade* from the Alexandrine group of poets who had borne that name. Membership of the group varied over the years but never exceeded seven. In 1556, besides Ronsard, it included Joachim du Bellay, Pontus de Thiard, Jean-Antoine de Baïf, Jacques Pelletier, Etienne Jodelle and Rémy Belleau. They were innovators who wished to abandon the medieval poetic tradition, and their innovations were based on a study of Greek and Latin poetry. They established the sonnet, the ode and the alexandrine (*qq.v.*) in France. Their theories were expounded in du Bellay's *Deffense et Illustration de la langue françoise* (1549), in Ronsard's preface to his *Odes* (1550) and in his *Abrégé de l'art poétique* (1565).

pleonasm (Gk 'superfluity') Redundant use of words. It may be deliberate but is usually involuntary. A common fault in much writing. For example: 'In this day and age', instead of 'now', 'today' or 'nowadays'. *See* PERIPHRASIS; POETIC DICTION; TAUTOLOGY.

pliego suelto (Sp 'loose sheet') Sheets of paper used for printing Spanish ballads from early in the 16th c. Also known as *literatura de cordel* ('writings hanging from a string') because vendors strung the broadsheets from cords in stationers' shops or tents on market days. Collections of them formed *cancioneros* (*q.v.*), nowadays normally in book form. The first (undated) *cancionero de romances* was published in Antwerp; presumably before 1550 – the date of the second. Followed by *romanceros* (*q.v.*), beginning in 1551 with Sepúlveda's. There were also *silvas de romances* and *rosas de romances*.

ploce (Gk 'plaited, woven') A figurative device in which the same word (or words) is repeated. It also denotes the complication of a dramatic plot. *See also* INCREMENTAL REPETITION.

plot The plan, design, scheme or pattern of events in a play, poem or work of fiction; and, further, the organization of incident and character in such a way as to induce curiosity and suspense (*q.v.*) in the spectator or reader. In the space/time continuum of plot the continual question operates in three tenses: Why did that happen? Why is this happening? What is going to happen next – and why? (To which may be added: And – is *anything* going to happen?)

In *Poetics*, Aristotle includes plot as one of the six elements in tragedy (*q.v.*). For Aristotle it is the 'first principle' and 'the soul of a tragedy'. He calls plot 'the imitation of the action', as well as the arrangement of the incidents. He required a plot to be 'whole' (that is, to have a beginning, a middle and an end) and that it should have unity, namely 'imitate one action and that a whole, the structural union of the parts being such that, if any one of them is displaced or removed, the whole will be disjointed and disturbed'.

This is the ideal, well-knit plot which Aristotle distinguished from the episodic plot in which the acts succeed one another 'without probable or necessary sequence', and which he thought was inferior. Aristotle also distinguished between simple and complex plots: in the simple the change of fortune occurs without peripeteia (*q.v.*) and without anagnorisis (*q.v.*), whereas in the complex there is one or the other or both. Aristotle also emphasized the importance of plot as opposed to character.

His views will be adequate for some Greek tragedy, some Elizabethan and Jacobean tragedy and some French Classical tragedy, and elements of the application of Aristotle's theories can be found in many plays – and novels.

However, a plot has come to denote something much more flexible than that envisaged by Aristotle. The decline of tragedy, the rise of comedy, the development of the novel – all have contributed to a much looser conception and many varied theories.

A more homely approach than Aristotle's is that of E. M. Forster. In *Aspects of the Novel* (1927) he provided a simple but very serviceable description of plot: 'We have defined a story as a narrative of events arranged in their time-sequence. A plot is also a narrative of events, the emphasis falling on causality. "The king died and the queen died," is a story. "The king died and then the queen died of grief," is a plot. The time-sequence is preserved, but the sense of causality overshadows it. Or again: "The queen died, no one knew why, until it was discovered that it was through grief at the death of the king." This is a plot with a mystery in it, a form capable of high development. It suspends the time-sequence, it moves as far away from the story as its limitations will allow.'

Such a description will suffice to cover a very large number of plots, especially those in which causality among episodes is explicit or implied. It will certainly cover an enormous number of novels. On the other hand no theory or definition of plot can now cover adequately the variety of works by, say, Joyce, Bulgakov, Graham Greene, Ivy Compton-Burnett, Heinrich Böll, Michel Butor, William Burroughs, Robbe-Grillet and Len Deighton – to take a handful of very different writers at random; or, for that matter, Kafka, Arnold Bennett, Malcolm Lowry, Ivo Andrić, Eric Ambler, Nabokov, Saul Bellow, Grass, Bykov, Claude Simon and V. S. Naipaul. *See* SUB-PLOT.

Plough Monday play, the In English folk-festivals Plough Monday is the Monday after Twelfth Night. The play, which is related to the Mumming (or St George) Play, survives in a few fragmentary texts from the East Midlands. The play differs from the Mumming Play in several respects. The characters are Tom the Fool, a Recruiting Sergeant, a Ribboner or Recruit, three farm servants, a Doctor and Beelzebub; plus two women, the Young Lady and old Dame Jane. The play (like the St George play) in all probability symbolizes the death and resurrection of the year and may well be the survival of a fertility rite. *See also* MUMMING PLAY; PACE-EGGING PLAY; REVESBY PLAY.

pluralist criticism This entails a critical approach to literature by which a text is studied with an open mind and thus without any necessary or apparent commitment to an ideological position or stance. Most importantly it expresses the willingness to hold more than one position. Structuralist critics have expressed disapproval of this approach. Many Marxist critics – who tend to be committed to a position – would also disapprove. *See* MARXIST CRITICISM; STRUCTURALISM.

plurisignation A term (it means, literally, several or many signs or marks) used by Wheelwright in *The Burning Fountain* (1954) to indicate that a word, a passage or a whole work may have various levels and meanings of what is described as 'semantic thrust'. This instrument of critical jargon can be useful in the work of close analysis. *See* ALLEGORY; ALLUSION; AMBIGUITY; FOUR LEVELS OF MEANING.

pnigos (Gk 'strangler') A sort of patter song (*q.v.*) in Greek Old Comedy (*q.v.*). Traditionally in anapaestic dimeters and recited without pause; thus liable to make the reciter run out of breath. *See* ANAPAEST; DIMETER.

poem (Gk *poiēma* 'something made, created'. Thus, a work of art) A composition, a work of verse, which may be in rhyme (*q.v.*) or may be blank verse (*q.v.*) or a combination of the two. Or it may depend on having a fixed number of syllables, like the *haiku* (*q.v.*).

In the final analysis what makes a poem different from any other kind of composition is a species of magic, the secret to which lies in the way the words lean upon each other, are linked and interlocked in sense and rhythm, and thus elicit from each other's syllables a kind of tune whose beat and melody varies subtly and which is different from that of prose (*q.v.*) – 'the other harmony'. *See also* POESIE; POETRY.

poëme A genre invented by Alfred de Vigny. In 1837 he defined his *poëmes*, in a preface, as compositions in which philosophic thought is presented under an epic (*q.v.*) or dramatic form. Thus, *poëmes philosophiques*.

poesie (Gk *poíēsis*, from *poieîn* 'to make') Thus *poíēsis* denotes 'making' in general, but in particular the making of poetry. The word came into the English language in the 14th c. Later in that century the word 'poetrie' (from L *poetria*) was also introduced. They were frequently used synonymously. Eventually *poetry* supplanted *poesy*. The latter produced *posy*, 'a motto verse'. *See* POEM.

poetaster A hack poet; an inferior versifier. The word is a combination of 'poet' and '-aster'; *aster* being a suffix of substantives and adjectives expressing an incomplete resemblance. The word is always derogatory. Its usage dates from the 16th c.

poète maudit A phrase which became current as a result of Verlaine's collection of essays *Les Poètes maudits* (1884, 1888). These were brief critical and biographical studies of six poets who, in his view, were insufficiently appreciated and understood. They were: Marceline Desbordes-Valmore (1786–1859), Villiers de l'Isle-Adam (1838–89), Stéphane Mallarmé (1842–98), Tristan Corbière (1845–75), Arthur Rimbaud (1854–91) and 'Pauvre Lelian', Paul

Verlaine's anagram of his own name. The phrase 'poètes maudits' may be a reference to Baudelaire's *Bénédiction*, the first poem in *Les Fleurs du mal* (1857). *See also* TEL QUEL SCHOOL.

poetic contests There are two basic kinds: (a) a formal competition in which poets enter and compete for a prize. This form of competition goes back to the festivals in Athens. In the Middle Ages there were comparable contests, mostly in France at Valenciennes, Arras, Douai, Tournai, Lille, Rouen and Dieppe. In Germany, from the 14th to the 16th c., the Meistersinger guilds held singing contests. The Academy of the Jocs Florals, which originated in Toulouse in the 14th c., still has festivals. Probably the best known of all is the National Eisteddfod (*q.v.*) of Wales, which dates at least from the 13th c. and is still held annually; (b) an imaginary debate or contest in a play or poem. An early example is to be found in Aristophanes's *Frogs*, in which Aeschylus and Euripides argue the merits of their poetry. The device, if such it is, occurs in Latin, Provençal, OF and ME works. One of the most interesting examples of a poetic contest in Europe is to be witnessed at Nuoro in central Sardinia where, at midsummer or later, shepherds compete with one another in the improvisation of poems in dialect. For some time before the final there have been eliminating contests. *See also* BARD; DEBAT; DIALOGUE; FLYTING; LAUDA; PARTIMEN; PUY; TENSON.

poetic contractions *See* SYNAERESIS; SYNCOPE.

poetic diction In general, diction denotes the vocabulary used by a writer. Poetic diction usually refers to that rather particular kind of language and artificial arrangement employed by many poets in the 18th c. who were guided by the theory and practice of neoclassicism (*q.v.*). Thomas Gray observed that 'the language of the age is never the language of poetry', and by this he meant that language must be selected and adapted according to its appropriateness for the work in hand. This is the principle of decorum (*q.v.*). Satire, for instance, a favoured mode of expression in the 18th c., required an urbane, cultivated and somewhat formal language; the style and diction of a gentleman. Pope was the supreme exponent of this. An ode (*q.v.*), on the other hand, or a pastoral (*q.v.*) required a more specialized diction. Probably the most notable characteristic of poetic diction in the 18th c. was periphrasis (*q.v.*) for the sake of elegance and politeness. Stock examples are: 'finny tribe' for 'fish'; 'feathered breed' for 'birds'; 'wingy swarm' for 'bees'; and 'foodful brine' for 'sea'. Taken to extremes this kind of expression could become absurd, a mere contortion. Excessive use of Latinism (*q.v.*) in 18th c. poetic diction *did* on occasion become absurd, as in these examples: 'purple groves pomaceous' for 'orchards'; 'rich saponaceous loam' for 'good soil'; 'nectareous streams' for 'sheep's milk'; 'hyperborean' for 'belonging to the far north', 'mantling bliss' for 'ale' – and so on. Other features of Neoclassical poetic diction were archaism (*q.v.*) and frequent use of personification (*q.v.*).

At its best the judicious use of poetic diction could produce agreeable results, as in these lines from Gray's *Ode on a Distant Prospect of Eton College* (1747):

> Say, Father Thames, for thou hast seen
> Full many a sprightly race
> Disporting on thy margent green
> The paths of pleasure trace;
> Who foremost now delight to cleave
> With pliant arm thy glassy wave?
> To captive linnet which enthrall?
> Why idle progeny succeed
> To chase the rolling circle's speed,
> Or urge the flying ball?

At the turn of the century there set in a strong reaction against poetic diction. This was expressed with vigour by Wordsworth, in his preface to the second edition of the *Lyrical Ballads* (1800). He was for the language of the common man, for everyday colloquial speech in poetry, what Shakespeare meant by 'russet yeas and honest kersey noes'; but even Wordsworth found this difficult to achieve in practice, and the problem of what language is appropriate for poetry and what not has exercised writers ever since Wordsworth and Coleridge addressed themselves to the matter. Throughout the 19th c. we find many poets trying to work out a mode and idiom and, often enough, failing to develop an individual one of their own. Much verse written in that age was laboured and stilted, encumbered by archaism and strange syntax. Gerard Manley Hopkins tried to break free of these clogs and, in his highly idiosyncratic fashion, proved a profoundly influential innovator. But even as late as the 1920s there were poets who had still not solved the problem of how to use colloquial language.

T. S. Eliot asked for an 'easy commerce of the old and new',

> The common word exact without vulgarity,
> The formal word precise but not pedantic

And Wallace Stevens introduced the idea of the 'anti-poetic' as a counter to the concept that there had to be something special about the language of poetry.

It may be argued that any word is a suitable tool for the poet, and that its suitability will depend on how it is used. But this immediately raises the difficulty of technical language, jargon (*q.v.*) and obscure words. Consider the opening lines of Hugh MacDiarmid's *On a Raised Beach*:

> All is lithogenesis – or lochia,
> Carpolite fruit of the forbidden tree,
> Stones blacker than any in the Caaba,
> Cream-coloured caen-stone, chatoyant pieces,
> Celadon and corbeau, bistre and beige,
> Glaucous, hoar, enfouldered, cyathiform,
> Making mere faculae of the sun and moon,
> I study you glout and gloss, but have
> No cadrans to adjust you with, and turn again
> From optik to haptik and like a blind man run
> My fingers over you, arris by arris, burr by burr,
> Slickensides, truité, rugas, foveoles

And so forth for a dozen more lines, before the language becomes simpler. The general sense of the passage is clear but the average reader would not know many of the words. MacDiarmid was a poet who was much preoccupied with finding an ideal diction and idiom. *See also* AUREATE LANGUAGE.

poetic justice A term invented by Thomas Rymer in *Tragedies of the Last Age Considered* (1678) to convey the idea that the evil are punished appropriately and the good rewarded as they should be. It was a widely held belief that literature should reflect a moral point of view and that a work of literature should reward the virtuous and punish the wicked. Towards the end of the 17th c. it was going out of fashion. Corneille rejected it; so, later, did Addison. However, it seems that many people still think a work of literature should show *some* sense of justice: at its simplest, that the villain should get his deserts.

poetic licence The liberty allowed to the poet to wrest the language according to his needs in the use of figurative speech, archaism (*q.v.*), rhyme (*q.v.*), strange syntax (*q.v.*), etc. But this liberty depends on the end justifying the means. Dryden defined it as 'the liberty which poets have assumed to themselves in all ages, of speaking things in verse, which are beyond the severity of prose'.

poetic prose Prose (*q.v.*) which approximates to verse in the use of rhythm, perhaps even a kind of meter (*q.v.*), in the elaborate and ornate use of language, and especially in the use of figurative devices like onomatopoeia, assonance and metaphor (*qq.v.*). Poetic prose is usually employed in short works or in brief passages in longer works in order to achieve a specific effect and to raise the 'emotional temperature'. Many writers have attempted it. For example: Lyly, Sir Thomas Browne, Jeremy Taylor, de Quincey, Lautréamont, Melville, Rimbaud, Oscar Wilde, James Joyce, Virginia Woolf, William Faulkner and Lawrence Durrell. There are some examples of it in the narrator's part in Dylan Thomas's radio play *Under Milk Wood* (1954). *See also* EUPHUISM; GONGORISM; MARINISM; POLYPHONIC PROSE; PROSE POEM; PURPLE PASSAGE.

poetischer Realismus (G 'poetic realism') This -ism, coined by Friedrich Schelling in 1802, is, somewhat surprisingly perhaps, peculiar to German literature. It is a rather vague term associated with, approximately, the period 1840–80 and denoting narrative poetry of a plain and realistic kind, traditionalist in attitude and moral and humane in tone and feeling. The principal writers associated with poetic realism were: Annette von Droste-Hülshoff (1797–1848); Jeremias Gotthelf (1797–1854); Adalbert Stifter (1805–68); Otto Ludwig (1813–65); Theodor Storm (1817–88); Gottfried Keller (1819–90); Conrad Meyer (1825–98); and Wilhelm Raabe (1831–1910).

poet laureate The origin of the term lies in the myth of Apollo who tried to seize Daphne, whereupon she turned into a laurel tree. Apollo ordained that the laurels should be the prize for poets and victors. It is likely that the tradition of the court poet and professional entertainer is the forebear of the modern poet laureate. The epithet *laureate* was applied to a number of poets (e.g. Petrarch, Chaucer, Skelton, Ben Jonson, Davenant, and others) before the first official appointment was made, namely Dryden in 1668. Since Dryden's removal (1688) there have been sixteen poets laureate: Thomas Shadwell (1689–92); Nahum Tate (1692–1715); Nicholas Rowe (1715–18); Laurence Eusden (1718–30); Colley Cibber (1730–57); William Whitehead (1757–85); Thomas Warton (1785–90); Henry James Pye (1790–1813); Robert Southey (1813–43); William Wordsworth (1843–50); Alfred Lord Tennyson (1850–92); Alfred Austin (1896–1913); Robert Bridges (1913–30); John Masefield (1930–68); Cecil Day Lewis (1968–72); John Betjeman (1973–84); Ted Hughes (1984–). Of these only three can be accounted major poets: namely, Dryden, Wordsworth and Tennyson.

poetry (MedL *poetria* based on Gk *poētēs* 'doer, creator') It is a comprehensive term which can be taken to cover any kind of metrical composition. However, it is usually employed with reservations, and often in contradistinction to verse. For example, we should describe Shakespeare's sonnets as poetry, and the wittily ingenious creations of Ogden Nash as verse; though both are *in* verse. We speak of 'light verse' rather than 'light poetry'. The implications are that poetry is a superior form of creation; not necessarily, therefore, more serious. Aristophanes, Chaucer, Ben Jonson, Donne, Marvell, Pope, Byron and Auden, to name a few, have all written witty and humorous poems.

poet's corner A part of the south transept of Westminster Abbey, London, which contains the tombs (or monuments) of a number of famous English poets: notably, Shakespeare, Edmund Spenser, Ben Jonson, Milton, Michael Drayton, Samuel Butler, Mrs Aphra Behn, John Gay, Lord Byron and W. H. Auden.

point of attack The moment in a play or story when the main action begins.

point of rest *See* PAUSE.

point of turning *See* CLIMAX.

polemic (Gk 'pertaining to war') A vigorous dispute. A controversy, especially in politics and religion. A famous example of a polemic is Milton's *Areopagitica* (1664). British polemicists of note are Richard Bentley, Jonathan Swift, Sydney Smith, Cardinal Newman, Bernard Shaw, Hilaire Belloc and G. K. Chesterton.

police procedural A sub-genre of the detective story (*q.v.*). Until its advent the police were often on the side-lines and were not infrequently depicted as cumbersome, inept and dull-witted (very nearly joke coppers in some instances) in contrast to the sagacious and quasi-omniscient amateur sleuth or private detective whose greatest exemplar is Sherlock Holmes.

Police procedurals deal realistically with crime from the point of view of the police and how they solve crimes and catch criminals. The central figure is a professional police officer (such as Commander Gideon).

A move away from what was regarded as the classic type of detective story towards the police procedural took place in the late 1920s with the development of the private eye, an investigator of the 'hard-boiled school' (of which there have been countless descendants, not least on television). Raymond Chandler (1888–1959) and Dashiell Hammett (1894–1961) were the pioneers. Later came the stories of professional policemen using traditional police methods and resources (increasingly sophisticated in the technological age). But they were a long time coming. Laurence Treat's *V as in Victim* (1945) is generally regarded as the first American police procedural. The next was Hillary Waugh's *Last Seen Wearing* (1952). The development of the genre in the USA was much influenced by a very popular radio show called 'Dragnet'. Notable practitioners have been Thomas Chastain with such books as *High Voltage* (1980) and *The Diamond Exchange* (1981), Elizabeth Linnington (1921–) with her Glendale and Los Angeles Police novels, and, most famous of all, Ed McBain (1926–) with his 87th Precinct (New York City) police procedural series introduced in 1956 with *Cop Hater* and *The Mugger*.

One of the first British police procedurals was *The Lonely Magdalen* (1940) by Henry Wade (1887–1969), pseudonym of Sir Aubrey Fletcher, who as chairman of the Buckinghamshire CC committee that oversaw the police learnt much about their procedures. Later he was Lord Lieutenant of Buckinghamshire (1954–61). Major British practitioners in the genre have been Maurice Procter (1906–73); John Creasey (1908–73), who, under the pseudonym J. J. Marric, created the Commander Gideon series of twenty-one books; Michael Gilbert (1912–), author of the Petrella police procedural series; Jonathan Ross (1916–), who wrote a series about crime in a provincial city; John Wainwright (1921–); Jack Scott (1922–); Laurence Henderson (1928–); Bill Knox (1928–); Roger Busby (1941–), who writes extremely well-informed procedurals; and Freny Olbrich, one of the few woman exponents of the genre, whose series features Chief Inspector Desouza of the Bombay CID.

The procedural is predominantly a British and American genre but mention should be made of the two Swedish writers – Per Wahloo (1926–75) and Maj Sjowall (1935–), a husband-and-wife team – who wrote ten novels about the work of the Stockholm police and who created quite a well-known anti-hero (*q.v.*) type policeman named Martin Beck.

politico-military thriller *See* THRILLER.

polyphonic prose A kind of poetic prose (*q.v.*) developed by Amy Lowell (1874–1925) and named by John Gould Fletcher (1886–1950). Amy Lowell got the idea from the *Ballades* (1886) of the French poet Paul Fort. Her most notable work is *Can Grande's Castle* (1918). Fletcher also used this style in *Breakers and Granite* (1921). This sort of prose has many of the attributes of verse: elaborate cadences and tuneful rhythms, assonance, alliteration and rhyme (*qq.v.*). *See also* FREE VERSE; PROSE POEM; VERS LIBRES.

polyptoton (Gk *poly* 'many' + *ptosis* 'a falling, fall') A rhetorical figure; a case or grammatical inflexion of any kind (e.g. of the adverb from the adjective). The idea is that one ending (e.g. nominative case) 'falls off' the end of the word to be replaced by another (e.g. accusative). So, the term has come to mean the repetition of a word in a different form. For instance: 'The live give life to the living'. A well-known example occurs in Shakespeare's *Troilus and Cressida* (I, i, 7–8):

> The Greeks are strong, and skilful to their strength,
> Fierce to their skill, and to their fierceness valiant;

polyrhythmic (Gk 'of many rhyms') Applied to a poem which has different metrical patterns. Pindar was well known for his polyrhythms.

polyschematic (Gk 'of many forms') In Classical prosody, varying combinations of the trochee and the choriambus (*qq.v.*).

polysyllabic rhyme *See* TRIPLE RHYME.

polysyndeton (Gk 'much compounded') The opposite of asyndeton (*q.v.*) and thus the repetition of conjunctions. Common in poetry and prose. The most frequently used conjunction in English is 'and'. Ernest Hemingway, for instance, was particularly addicted to this device in the use of 'and'. In the more extreme instances of his pseudo-biblical style it becomes the equivalent of a verbal tic. *See* HYPOTAXIS; PARATAXIS.

popular novel A loose term for a novel which has a wide readership; it often carries slightly pejorative connotations which suggest a middle- or low-brow 'audience' and imply that such a novel may not possess much literary merit. Many a best-seller, historical novel, novel of sensation, thriller and novel of adventure (*qq.v.*) has been so described. Some of the well-known British popular novelists have been: Warwick Deeping, Howard Spring, R. F. Delderfield, Dornford Yates, Angela Thirkell, Daphne du Maurier and Dennis Wheatley. Such a list might be greatly extended.

pornography (Gk 'writing of harlots') In all probability the term derives from the sign hung outside a brothel or whore's establishment.

A pornographer is a writer of pornography, and a *pornograph* is a work of fiction (in the broadest sense of that term) in which there is a considerable emphasis on sexual activity and which is, as a rule, written in such a way as to arouse sexual excitement. It may be funny, serious, bizarre or horrific, and, like any other kind of fiction, it may be well or badly written.

We may distinguish two basic sorts of pornography: (a) *erotica* – this concentrates on the physical aspects of heterosexual love and may describe them in great detail; (b) *exotica* – this concentrates on what are known as abnormal or deviationist sexual activities, and thus the emphasis is on sexual perversion. Common subjects for this kind of pornography are: sadism, masochism, fetishism, transvestism, voyeurism (or scoptolagnia), narcissism, pederasty and necrophilia. Less common subjects are: coprophilia, kleptolagnia, zoophilia and pyrolagnia.

Under phylum (a) we can put such classics as Ovid's *Ars Amatoria* (1st c. BC); Vatsayana's *Kama-Sutra* (4th c. AD) and other Indian love manuals; and Casanova's *Memoirs* (1826–38). Under phylum (b) Sade's *Justine* (17681) and his *The 120 Days of Sodom* (1785), Sacher-Masoch's *Venus in Furs* (*c.* 1870) and *The Whippingham Papers* (late 1880s).

As society has become more 'permissive', so the conception of what is obscene (and pornographic) has become more flexible. There was a time when Joyce's *Ulysses* (first published in a limited and numbered edition in 1922) and Lawrence's *Lady Chatterley's Lover* (1928) and Radclyffe Hall's *The Well of Loneliness* (1928) were regarded as obscene and pornographic. They provoked abusive and scandalized comment and legal action. Lawrence Durrell's *Black Book* (1936) was also thought pornographic; so, in 1955, was Nabokov's *Lolita*. Anyone who now described these books as pornographic would be regarded as loudly ridiculous.

In the final analysis judgement must depend on the individual, on his moral and aesthetic conscience, because pornographic elements (or what some would describe as such) are to be found in many books. As a serviceable guide in the matter one can hardly do better than take Lehmann's precept that we must distinguish between works which have an *intent* to corrupt and those which have a *tendency* to do so.

The subject is further complicated by such terms as 'straight porn', 'hard porn' and 'soft porn'. And works like *The Pearl, A Monthly Journal of Facetiae and Voluptuous Reading, The Naked Lunch* and *Last Exit to Brooklyn* might be put under any of those subheadings according to taste and different criteria.

Discounting for the moment the enormous quantities of 'pulp' literature (illustrated and otherwise) which explores and exploits most conceivable aspects of sexual behaviour, especially the deviant and perverted, and much of which is aesthetically crude, we can find some kinds of pornography which either are literature (*q.v.*) or have pretensions to being so.

In general the literature of pornography is vast, and some of it is of considerable antiquity. At the outset, however, we must distinguish between pornography and the pornographic. Actually it is only since the second half of the 18th c. that pornography has been produced on a large scale and much of this has been the pornography of *exotica*. Pornographic elements, however, are to be found much earlier and in many literatures.

There is plentiful material in the Old Testament on the subject of pornography in its original sense. There are pornographic elements in the plays of Aristophanes (especially *Lysistrata*), in *The Satyricon* of Petronius Arbiter (1st c. AD), in *The Letters of Alciphron* (*c.* 200 AD), the *Deipnosophistai* of Athenaus (2nd c. AD), and the *Dialogues* of Lucian (2nd c. AD). The *Milesian Tales* of Aristides of the 2nd c. BC were also believed to be pornographic, but they do not survive.

In Europe, after the fall of the Roman Empire, there appears to be no pornography and no literature with pornographic elements, though there is quite a lot of erotic poetry (*q.v.*) until late in the Middle Ages. Then, we find bawdy or innocuously obscene elements in, for instance, the *fabliaux* (*q.v.*) and some of Chaucer's tales.

The first major work of modern pornography is Boccaccio's *Decameron* (*c.* 1349–51). Other works of note in the Renaissance period which have been described as pornographic are: Poggio's *Facetiae* (15th c.), Rabelais's *Gargantua* (1534) and *Pantagruel* (1532), Cellini's *Memoirs* (begun in 1558), Aretino's *Ragionamenti* (1600), Brantôme's *Vies des dames Galantes* (1665–6) and Beroalde de Verville's *Le Moyen de pervenir* (1610). There are also some instances of pornographic scenes in Elizabethan and Jacobean drama, and scurrilous or bawdy elements in much verse (e.g. Skelton's poetry).

The same could be said of some Restoration comedy (*q.v.*) and several 18th c. novels. From the 18th c. dates what many have regarded as the first masterpiece of English pornography, namely John Cleland's *Memoirs of a Woman of Pleasure*, or *Memoirs of the Life of Fanny Hill* (1748–9). After that, an increasing number of pornographic works were published. The full details and titles are to be found in H. S. Ashbee's *Notes on Curious and Uncommon Books* (1877–85) and the *Register Librorum Eroticorum* by R. S. Reade (1936). Some notable examples are: *New Atlantis for the Year* (1762), *Useful Hints to Single Gentlemen respecting Marriage, Concubinage and Adultery. In Prose and Verse. With Notes Moral, Critical and Explanatory* (1792); *The Merry Muses of Caledonia, a Collection of Favourite Scots Songs, ancient and modern, selected for us of the Chrochallan Fencibles* (*c.* 1800); *The Voluptuarian Cabinet* (*c.* 1820).

Between 1820 and 1840, and then from *c.* 1860 onwards, a colossal amount of erotic pornography was published (much of it illustrated). Some notable examples are: *The Bedfellows: or Young Misses' Manual* (1820); *The Adventures, Intrigues and Amours of a Lady's Maid* (1822); *The Modern Rake* (1824); *The Lustful Turk* (1828); *The Seducing Cardinale* (1830); *The Favourite of Venus* (1830); *The Festival of Love, or Revels at the Fount of Venus* (1860); *Intrigues and Confessions of a Ballet Girl* (1868–70); *The Romance of Lust* (1873); *The Power of Mesmerism, a highly erotic narrative of Voluptuous Facts and Fancies* (1880); *Laura Middleton, her Brother and her Lover* (1890); *Venus in India, or Love Adventures in*

Hindustan (1890); *Raped on the Railway: A True Story of a Lady who was first ravished and then flagellated on the Scotch Express* (1894); *Flossie, A Venus of Fifteen: By one who knew this Charming Goddess and worshipped at her shrine* (1897).

Other well-known curiosities of erotic pornography are *A Night in a Moorish Harem* by 'Lord George Herbert' (late 1890s); the works of Edward Sellon, one of the most famous English pornographers – particularly *The New Epicurean* (1865), *The Ups and Downs of Life* (1867) and *Letters from a Friend in Paris* (1874). To these should be added the anonymous *My Secret Life* (*c.* 1885) and *My Life and Loves* (1925–9) by Frank Harris. There are also many works in German and French dating from the 19th c.

Most of these could be placed in the category of *erotica*. There are quite as many under *exotica*, or the pornography of perversion. Many are concerned with flagellation practices, incest and various forms of fetishism. Two celebrated names are always associated with this kind of pornography, namely the Marquis de Sade and Leopold von Sacher-Masoch, from whom derive the words *sadist* and *masochist*. Sade's principal works are: *Justine* (1781); *The 120 Days of Sodom* (1785); *Aline and Valcour* (1788); *The Philosopher in the Boudoir* (1795); *Juliette* (1796); and *The Crimes of Love* (1800). Sacher-Masoch's *Venus in Furs* (*c.* 1870) is his masterpiece.

Other notable works connected with flagellation practices are *Venus School-Mistress; or Birchen Sports* (*c.* 1810); *The Romance of Chastisement* (1866); *The Whippingham Papers* (late 1880s), to which Swinburne contributed; *Gynecocracy* (1893); *The Memoirs of Dolly Morton* (*c.* 1900).

In the 20th c. so much pornographic literature of every kind has been published that there is no space to give an account of it. Innumerable works, especially novels, contain pornographic elements. Much of it is to be found in 'girlie' and 'cutie' magazines and glossy periodicals. Most such publications combine articles and stories case histories, diaries and so forth with a variety of photographs. For many of these one might coin a portmanteau word (*q.v.*) like *phorntography* or *porntography*.

As a rule the subject is taken seriously, and good comic pornography is rare. A distinguished exception in recent times is D. D. Bell's novel *Dicky, or The Midnight Ride of Dicky Vere* (1970).

A minor and innocuous branch of pornography (or perhaps more accurately scatology) is the bawdy ballads of the oral tradition (*q.v.*) kept alive in the Armed Forces and among sporting fraternities (especially rugby clubs). Many of them are 'shit without wit', as has been remarked, but some have style and originality and only in the perfervid mind of Puritans could they be described as potentially corruptive.

Whether such verses are obscene or merely bawdy is again largely a matter of opinion and taste, and it is next to impossible (and perhaps not particularly useful) to categorize them. However, one might suggest as a general pointer that those in category (a) are obscene and those in (b) bawdy: (a) *Eskimo Nell*, *The Wheel*, *The Great Plenipotentiary*, *The Whole World Over*, *The One-Eyed Riley*, *The Ball of Kirriemuir*, *The Good Ship Venus*, *The Street of the Thousand Arseholes*, *The Cowpuncher's Whore*, *The Rajah of Astrakhan*, *The Harlot of Jerusalem*, *Nightfuck*, *The Great Farting Contest*, *Diamond Lily*, *The Keyhole in the Door* and *The Travelling Man*; (b) *Abdul Abulbul Emir*, *Arseholes are Cheap Today*, *The Virgin Sturgeon*, *Sonia Snell*, *The Portions of the Female*, *The Hedgehog Song*, *A Clean Story*, *If I were the marrying sort*, *The Happy Family*, *Father's Grave*, *The Farmer's Dog* and *My Jenny Wren Bride*. *See also* LOW COMEDY.

portmanteau word (F *porter* 'to carry' + *manteau* 'cloak') A word formed by combining two or more words. Also known as a telescope word. Lewis Carroll applied this term to combined words in *Through the Looking-Glass* in explanation of some words in *Jabberwocky* (*q.v.*). James Joyce, in *Finnegans Wake*, coined a large number of such words. The following passage suggests how Joyce did it:

> Hence when the clouds roll by, jamey, a proudseye view is enjoyable of our mounding's mass, now Wallinstone national museum, with, in some greenish distance, the charmful waterloose country and the two quitewhite villagettes who hear show of themselves so gigglesomes minxt the follyages, the prettilees! Penetrators are permitted into the museomound free. Welsh and the Paddy Patkinses, one shelenk! Redismembers invalids of old guard find poussepousse pousseypram to sate the sort of their butt. For her passkey supply to the janitrix, the mistress Kathe. Tip.

See also GHOSTWORD; NEOLOGISM; NONCE-WORD.

post-modernism A general (and sometimes controversial) term used to refer to changes, developments and tendencies which have taken place (and are taking place) in literature, art, music, architecture, philosophy, etc. since the 1940s or 1950s. Post-modernism is different from modernism (*q.v.*), even a reaction against it. It is no easier to define than many other -isms. Like them, it is amorphous by nature.

To talk of post-modernism is to imply that modernism is over and done with. This is not so. There never is a neat demarcation line. Originally, *avant-garde* (*q.v.*) movements in literature and the arts in general were modernist; *avant-garde* influences continue. It might be said that there is a new *avant-garde*. Besides, post-modernism is still happening. When something else develops from it or instead of it, it will, perhaps, be easier to identify, describe and classify.

As far as literature is concerned it is possible to descry certain features in post-modernism. For instance, there is literature which tends to be non-traditional and against authority and signification. Here one may cite experimental techniques, in fiction as displayed in the *nouveau roman* and the anti-novel (*qq.v.*). In some cases these looked perilously close to mere gimmickry. There have also been experiments with what is called concrete poetry (*q.v.*), though there is nothing particularly post-modernist about that (or even modernist, for that matter) since Simias of Rhodes was experimenting with pattern poems (*q.v.*) in the 4th c. BC. In drama one might cite experiment with form, content and presentation in such developments as the Theatre of the Absurd, Total Theatre, the 'happening' and, latterly, the Théâtre de Complicité (*qq.v.*).

Other discernible features of post-modernism are an eclectic approach, aleatory writing, parody and pastiche (*qq.v.*). Nor should we forget the importance of what is called magic realism (*q.v.*) in fiction, new modes in science fiction (*q.v.*), the popularity of neo-Gothic and the horror story (*q.v.*).

The burgeoning of Marxist, feminist and psychoanalytic criticism since the 1970s is yet another aspect of post-modernism. It also refers to a critical position in criticism, in which a complete relativism exists – hence its proximity to post-structuralism (*q.v.*). Perhaps most important of all are the revolutionary theories in philosophy and literary criticism expressed in structuralism and deconstruction (*qq.v.*). A helpful analysis of various aspects is Jean-François Lyotard's *The Postmodern Condition: A Report on Knowledge* (1984). *See also* ALTERNATIVE LITERATURE; ALTERNATIVE THEATRE; FEMINIST CRITICISM; GOTHIC NOVEL/FICTION; MARXIST CRITICISM; SUB-CULTURE.

post-structuralism Late in the 1960s, structuralism (*q.v.*) became subject to a rigorous and lasting critique of its thinking and methods. Post-structuralism is a more rigorous working out of the possibilities, implications and shortcomings of structuralism and its basis in Saussurean linguistics itself. In a sense it complements structuralism by offering alternative modes of inquiry, explanation and interpretation.

Post-structuralism doubts the adequacy of structuralism and, as far as literature is concerned, tends to reveal that the meaning of any text is, of its nature, unstable. It reveals that signification is, of its nature, unstable.

Saussure's fundamental distinction between signifier and signified (*q.v.*) is at the heart of the instability. Without realizing it, Saussure, in making the distinction, exposed not coherence between signs, but an inherent incoherence. Post-structuralism pursues further the Saussurean perception that in language there are *only differences without positive terms* and shows that the signifier and signified are, as it were, not only oppositional but plural, pulling against each other, and, by so doing, creating numerous deferments of meaning, apparently endless criss-crossing patterns and sequences of meaning. In short, what are called 'disseminations' (*q.v.*).

A belief in the incommensurate qualities of language (a form of inadequacy) is basic to post-structuralist thinking. Hence the idea of indeterminacy (*q.v.*), which is an important element in deconstructive practice and in Jacques Derrida's theory of *différance* (*q.v.*). The extreme position of post-structuralist theory is that meaning is inherently unstable, whereas a structuralist would hold that an explanation/understanding is conceivable and possible, provided that the conventions and codes of any literary text or cultural message are analysed.

In post-structuralist theory Roland Barthes is of particular importance because he bridges the structuralist and post-structuralist movements. In his book *Elements of Semiology* (1967) he proposed that structuralism is capable of an explanation of any sign system of any culture (i.e. all systems of signification). But he also perceives that such an explanation necessitates a theory of meaning/explanation. This gives rise to the idea of a 'metalanguage' (*q.v.*); that is to say, a 'beyond' language or 'second-order language' which is used to describe/explain/interpret a 'first-order' language. Given one metalanguage for one explanation, it follows that there may be another in turn, and a metalanguage may replace a 'first-order' language. Each order of language implicitly relies on a metalanguage by which it is explained, and ironically, therefore, deconstruction is placed precariously in the position of becoming (against its principles and design) a metalanguage itself. Thus, discourse upon discourse in regression; and all discourses are exposed to interrogation. This is one aspect of Barthes's post-structuralist thinking and is, fundamentally, deconstructive.

Barthes's later theories (post-1968) lead him to other challenging caveats: (a) that the Author (or the concept of the Author) is dead; this idea he elaborates in his essay *The Death of the Author* (1968); (b) that there are two basic experiences to be had in reading: namely, *plaisir* and *jouissance* (*q.v.*); (c) that texts may be either *lisible* or *scriptible* (i.e. 'readerly' or 'writerly', *q.v.*); and (d) that given the application of certain codes a text may be analysed and interpreted as either 'readerly' or 'writerly' (or even as both).

Further important contributions to post-structuralist theory in the French tradition (and the French have been the principal innovators) have been made by Julia Kristeva. Hers is fundamentally a psychoanalytic approach and, though of considerable complexity, is fascinating. In *La Révolution du langage poétique* (1974) she discusses the relationship between the orderly/rational and the heterogeneous/irrational, between the conscious and the unconscious, the 'normal' and the 'poetic'. She suggests that semiotic material is irrational and illogical, the material of impulse and rhythm; while reason creates logic, syntax and coherence and brings about the symbolic element. There are implied antinomies such as feelings/thoughts, heart/brain and, to reverse the sequence in the binary opposition (*q.v.*), Apollonian/Dionysiac.

Basically, she conceives the 'semiotic' element (which is linked with the concept of infant – a word which means 'speechless' – in the pre-Oedipal phase) as being opposed to the 'symbolic' and sees it as a means of undermining symbolic order, thus causing confusion, through its fluidity and plurality, its pulsions, in any attempt at precise meaning. Like water, the semiotic element is opposed to anything fixed or static; and it is opposed to any binary opposition such as masculine/feminine. Though, of course, there is more than a hint of binary opposition in fluid/fixed. In a sense, 'semiotic' writing is bisexual (the pre-Oedipal phase is genderless). In English literature, James Joyce and Virginia Woolf are instances of 'semiotic' writers, using a fluid, diffuse, disseminated 'writerly' mode and style; and in those respects different from anything fixed, rigid, conventional or realistic.

Julia Kristeva goes so far as to relate sound in poetry to primary sexual impulse and suggests that combinations of consonantal sounds, for example, may be either feminine or masculine. There is a suggestion that 'semiotic' material might be equated with a feminine tendency, and the symbolic with the masculine. This raises the possibility for feminist theory of the idea of *écriture feminine* (*q.v.*).

Even this very brief résumé of complex matters makes it clear that the approaches of Roland Barthes and Kristeva are very different.

The main aspect of post-structuralist theory used in literary practice is deconstruction, for which Jacques Derrida has been primarily responsible. His essay *Structure, Sign and Play* (1966) is the first critique of structuralism and it was he who initiated the techniques of particularly close reading which latterly have been largely practised in the USA. *See also* DECONSTRUCTION.

potboiler A work written merely to gain a livelihood. The term is at least as old as the 18th c. A classic example of the potboiler that transcends its immediate end is Johnson's philosophical 'novel' or didactic 'romance' (*qq.v.*) *Rasselas* (1759), which was written in the evenings of a week to defray the expenses of his mother's funeral and to pay her debts. *See* KITSCH.

poulter's measure Rhyming couplets consisting of one iambic hexameter (*q.v.*) followed by an iambic heptameter (*q.v.*). To be found in the *Towneley Mystery Plays* and some Morality Plays (*q.v.*) and used quite frequently in the 16th c. (by Sir Thomas Wyatt, the Earl of Surrey and Sir Philip Sidney, among others) but little thereafter because it was found that the hexameter and the heptameter are lines too long to be easily manageable. The term derives from the poulterer's traditional practice of giving fourteen eggs in the second dozen, a point recorded by Gascoigne in *Steele Glas* (1576). These lines come from the Earl of Surrey's *Youth and Age*:

Laid in my quiet bed, in study as I were,
I saw within my troubled head a heap of thoughts appear.
And every thought did show so lively in mine eyes,
That now I sigh'd, and then I smiled, as cause of thought did rise.
I saw the little boy in thought how oft that he
Did wish of God to scape the rod, a tall young man to be.

povest A Russian term for a fictional narrative. It denotes the sum of facts and events connected with an individual or a particular incident. Alexander Pushkin (1799–1837), who mastered all the Western literary forms and genres, referred to a '*povest* of myself', meaning the sum total of what had happened to him. His *Povesti Belkin* (1830) are notable examples of the form. Terseness and compression are characteristic of *povesti*, which have less complex plots than novels and are shorter. It is perhaps the Russian equivalent of the German *Novelle* (*see* NOVELLA) and by virtue of its length, at any rate, comparable with the French *récit* (*q.v.*). The Bulgarians use the term *povest* for a reasonably long short-story; and in Croatian (which has the 'ije' dialect of what is commonly called Serbo-Croatian) the word *povijest* denotes history or records or a chronicle. In Serbian *povest* means history and story.

power, literature of In an essay titled *The Poetry of Pope* (published in the *North British Review*, Aug. 1848), Thomas de Quincey made any interesting distinction between the literature of knowledge and the literature of power:

> There is, first, the literature of *knowledge*; and, secondly, the literature of *power*. The function of the first is – to *teach*; the function of the second is – to *move*: the first is a rudder, the second an oar or a sail. The first speaks to the *mere* discursive understanding; the second speaks ultimately, it may happen, to the higher understanding or reason, but always *through* affections of pleasure and sympathy.

De Quincey elaborates the idea at some length. What he is getting at is that an encyclopaedia instructs and is therefore didactic; a great play, on the other hand, moves by appealing to be emotions – and thereby also instructs but in a totally different way.

practical criticism Criticism based on close analysis of a text in isolation. Such criticism was pioneered by I. A. Richards (1893–1979) and the term was given currency by him. His book *Practical Criticism: A Study of Literary Judgment* (1929) was to revolutionize the teaching and study of English and his methods were to have an immeasurable influence: not least on the acceptance of modernism (*q.v.*) and the development of what came to be called the New Criticism (*q.v.*). Other important books by Richards were *The Meaning of Meaning* (1923), *Principles of Literary Criticism* (1924) and *Science and Poetry* (1926). F. R. Leavis was an outstanding exponent of practical criticism and influenced a complete generation of critics.

praecisio *See* APOSIOPESIS.

praeposteratio *See* HYSTERON PROTERON.

Prague school Also known as the Prague Linguistic Circle. It was founded in 1926 and remained active in the 1920s and the early 1930s. Leading figures were Roman Jakobson, Boris Eikenbaum, Trubetskoy, Viktor Shklovsky and Mukařovský. They were influenced by Russian Formalism (*q.v.*) and by futurism (*q.v.*), and developed the theory of phonology in which sounds are analysed in sets of oppositions.

praxis A Gk term used by Aristotle in *Poetics* (it is normally rendered by the word 'action') to denote the first principle and soul of tragedy (*q.v.*).

préciosité, la The term denotes that refinement of language and manners which became the concern of civilized and sophisticated French men and women early in the 17th c. The Marquise de Rambouillet appears to have been one of the prime movers in this matter. From 1608, and for forty years thereafter, she established salon (*q.v.*) life at her town house. To this venue came many of those who wished to refine and polish manners and literary style. Honoré d'Urfé's pastoral (*q.v.*) novel *L'Astrée* (1607) inspired many aspects of their urbane code. The main sources for a knowledge of *les précieuses* are A. B. de Somaize's *Dictionnaire des précieuses* (1660), Madeleine de Scudery's *Le Grand Cyrus* (1649–53) and *Clélie* (1654–60), and Tellemant des Réaux's *Historiettes.* The pursuit of elegance was a civilizing influence, but it also led to affectation. Some of the *habitués* of this salon helped to found the Académie Française in 1635. Their affectations were satirized by Molière in *Les Précieuses ridicules* (1659). *See also* BLUE STOCKING CIRCLE/SOCIETY; SECENTISMO.

précis A summary or synopsis of a work. A shortened version of a passage.

preface An introduction to a literary work. Some famous examples are: Johnson's *Preface* to his *Dictionary* (1755), one of the finest pieces of prose in the language; Shaw's prefaces to many of his plays (in some cases they were much longer than the plays and contained all that he could not express dramatically); Harley Granville-Barker's *Preface to Shakespeare* (4 vols., 1927–48), a most valuable contribution to an understanding of the plays. *See also* FOREWORD.

pregunta (Sp 'question', from *preguntar* 'to ask') A form of poetic debate practised by Spanish court-poets in the late 14th c. and in the 15th c. A poet put a question (*recuesta*) on some theme concerned with morals, love, philosophy or religion, and a second poet provided an answer (*respuesta*) in exactly the same form and using the same rhymes.

Pre-Raphaelites, the The mid-19th c. self-styled brotherhood of London artists, all young, who united to resist current artistic conventions and to create, or re-create, art forms in use before the period of Raphael (1483–1520). They expressed their views in the magazine *The Germ* (1850). The members of the group were John Everett Millais, William Holman Hunt, Dante Gabriel Rossetti, William Michael Rossetti, Thomas Woolner, Frederick George Stephens and James Collinson. Their 'movement' subsequently influenced the writers William Morris, Christina Rossetti and Swinburne, and the artist Burne-Jones. The poetry of the Pre-Raphaelites showed a distinct liking for medievalism (*q.v.*), 18th c. ballads, archaic diction, symbolism and sensuousness. The poets were considerably under the influence of Spenser. Tennyson had already stimulated their interest in medievalism. Rossetti and his followers were dubbed 'the fleshly school of poetry' (*q.v.*). *See also* AESTHETCISM; PARNASSIANS; PRIMITIVISM; SYMBOL AND SYMBOLISM.

press (L *pressare* 'to press') The term denotes, variously: printing; a printing machine; a printing organization; a publishing house; printing activities; newspapers and periodicals collectively; the journalistic profession; a newspaper; a favourable (or unfavourable) reception in a newspaper or periodical (e.g. a review; hence a 'good' press, a 'bad' press).

There are numerous phrases and terms which are derivative: (a) press agent – a person who arranges for newspaper advertising and publicity; (b) press association – an association of newspapers formed to act as a news agency for the members of the association, supplying local news etc.; (c) press-book – a book printed at a private press (*q.v.*); (d) press-box – an erection provided for the use of reporters (e.g. at sports, games, shows, etc.); (e) press conference – a meeting of a public personage with members of the press in order to make an announcement or answer questions; (f) press-cutting – a paragraph or article cut out of a newspaper, periodical (*q.v.*) or magazine; (g) press gallery – a gallery for reporters (e.g. in the House of Commons); (h) pressman – one who works at a printing press, a journalist or reporter; (i) press-mark – a mark on a book to show its place in a library; (j) press-proof – the last proof before printing; (k) press release – an official statement or report supplied to the press; (l) press-room – a room where printing presses are worked or a room for the use of journalists and reporters; (m) press-work – the operation of a printing press; (n) at press, in press – in the course of printing or about to be published; (o) go to press – to begin to print or to be printed; (p) liberty, freedom, of the press – the right of publishing material without submitting it to a government authority for permission; (q) printed matter in general (especially newspapers) and journalists as a group or class.

priamel (L *praeambulum* 'preamble') It denotes a form of German folk verse which had some vogue from the 12th to the 16th c. It appears to have developed from a kind of improvised epigram (*q.v.*). Basically a *priamel* comprised a variety of disconnected ideas and observations with a surprise conclusion.

priapean From the god Priapus, a god of fertility often represented as a grotesque figure with an exaggerated phallus. He gives his name to a classical Greek meter comprising a glyconic and a pherecretean (*qq.v.*). Anacreon used the measure, and it was also used for the choruses in satyr plays (*q.v.*).

primary accent and secondary accent The primary accent or 'primary' falls clearly on the first or main syllable of a word. The secondary tends to come on the third syllable. As in *secondary*, where the 'a' is not so heavily stressed. *See also* STRESS.

primer Originally a prayer-book for the laity before the Reformation, and for some time after it. The medieval primer consisted of translations and/or copies from various sections of the breviary (*q.v.*). In the 16th c. the name was given to similar works. After the Reformation the name was used of books in which the offices for daily prayers had been based on orders in the *Book of Common Prayer*. Gradually there developed the sense of an elementary school-book. In his *Dictionary* (1755) Johnson defined a primer as a small prayer-book for teaching children to read.

primer couplet A fixed verse form of dipodic couplets rhyming aa, bb, cc and so on. As in the anonymous *Obadiah*:

> Obadiah
> Jumped in the fire,
> The fire was hot,
> He jumped in the pot . . .

primitivism In the history of art the 'primitives' are taken to be those painters of the Netherlandish and Italian schools who flourished before *c.* 1500. That is to say, all the Netherlandish painters of the late 14th c. and the 15th c., and all Italian painters between Giotto (1276–1337) and Raphael (1483–1520). The term 'primitive' is also applied to the work of many artists belonging to many periods and *milieux* which displays a naive vision, a technically 'simple' conception and presentation of reality, even a certain crudeness of style. Perhaps a kind of untutored art.

As far as literature is concerned primitivism has very different connotations. Fundamentally, the so-called primitivist writer is, in Horace's words, *a laudator temporis acti*, 'an extoller of things in the past' (though not necessarily either testy or querulous), and primitivism is, and expresses, a form of nostalgia for a primitive (or pre-civilized) way of life. The *laudator temporis acti* is an observably common phenomenon since there seems to be a deeply rooted awareness and conviction in mankind that once upon a time there was a paradisal era, a 'golden age' to which there are plentiful allusions in Classical literature). At its simplest, such an awareness is expressed in clichés like: 'It wasn't like that in my day'; 'In the old days'; 'In good King Charles's golden days'. Thus, in the past, in youth, in a time when all was well, in that 'never never land'. In jargon language these are barely concealed allusions to a pre-lapsarian state, the awareness of which is heightened by the burden of post-Fall guilt. The Bible and many writers of antiquity exalt this hypothetical *saturnia regna* ('age of Saturn'); so do many works of the Renaissance period when there was a remarkable resurgence of interest in Classical learning and literature.

The kind of atavistic nostalgia to which I have referred has impelled man to look for his origins, for that lost 'innocence', for 'the good old days'. Such impulses moved the Italian primitives and, later, the Pre-Raphaelites (*q.v.*). In fact the apotheosis or glorification of this mythical state of well-being is common in art and literature; and primitive themes are even commoner, as is evident from a study of utopianism (*see* UTOPIA), the pastoral (*q.v.*) tradition and convention, and what may be called 'desert island fiction' (*q.v.*).

Basically, then, the primitivist is anti-civilization, anti-materialism, anti-industrialism, anti-progress and pro-Nature; pro-, at its crudest, a getting back to 'grass roots'. Thus he yearns for that time when he would have been: 'As free as Nature first made man'.

And the cultural primitivist, as he has been called, finds that peoples isolated from civilization ('wild in woods') are preferable to those living in civilized and urbanized *milieux* (under the 'base laws of servitude'). The cult of the 'Noble Savage' (*q.v.*) in European and American literature (a cult closely associated with some aspects of romanticism, *q.v.*), is part of the ideal.

Primitivist themes are found in many literatures of the world; they are plentiful in Classical and medieval literature. As far as Europe is concerned it is very noticeable that, with the growth of civilization, with the advance of technology, and with the development of an urban and industrialized way of life, so these themes become more frequent and obvious; just as, with the decline of orthodox Christian beliefs in an afterworld, utopian schemes proliferate.

Here there is space to mention only a few instances. Montaigne's observations on the life of savages in his essay *Of Cannibals* (1580) is one of the earlier suggestions of an interest in a more natural way of life. Sir Philip Sidney's pastoral romance *Arcadia* (1590) is a fine evocation of 'the golden age'. In general, pastoral verse contains strong undertones of nostalgia for bucolic bliss. Pastoral drama, also, of the Tudor and Jacobean periods depicts on occasions the ideal existence. This is particularly noticeable in Shakespeare's *The Winter's Tale* and *As You Like It*. In fact, in the latter play Shakespeare refers to the whole idea (or primitivist syndrome, again to use the current jargon) at the very beginning of the piece when Charles the wrestler speaks of the old Duke in exile in the forest of Arden: 'They say many young gentlemen flock to him every day, and fleet the time carelessly, as they did in the golden world'. In both plays Shakespeare contrasts the sophistications (and corruptions) of court life with the simpler and healthier life of the countryside.

The primitivist concept of simplicity and felicity is even better expressed in Traherne's lyric *Eden*:

> Only what Adam in his first estate
> Did I behold;
> Hard silver and dry gold
> As yet lay underground; my happy fate
> Was more acquainted with the old
> And innocent delights which he did see
> In his original simplicity.
>
> Those things which first his Eden did adorn,
> My infancy did crown; simplicity
> Was my protection when I first was born.

Here we have a notable synthesis of the myth of the pre-Fall childhood innocence, the myth of the golden age and the myth of the paradisal garden. Dante, Tasso, Guarini, Spenser, Milton and many other poets expressed similar ideas.

During the 18th c. and especially in the latter part, there was a reaction against neoclassicism (*q.v.*), civilization, luxury, sophistication, materialism, industrialism and urban corruption, and the reactionaries were in favour of a natural, unsophisticated way of life and upbringing. People became interested in the idea of primitive, simple man. Travellers brought back tales of primitive societies totally different from anything hitherto known in Europe. They even brought back actual 'specimens' of primitive man, such as the native of Haiti who, in 1776, became the object of much curiosity and respect among the learned in London.

Miscellaneous writers contributed in various ways to this cult. For example, there was Mrs Aphra Behn's *Oroonoko: or, The History of the Royal Slave* (*c.* 1688), which became popular reading and had considerable influence. It achieved even more influence through Richard Southern's stage adaptation (1695) which remained popular in the theatre for many years. Rousseau, perhaps more than anyone, was responsible for a powerful resurgence of primitivist feelings. With him the 'Noble Savage' cult becomes fully grown. In *Julie ou la Nouvelle Héloïse* (1761) Rousseau attempted to reconcile heterosexual relationships with the natural order. In *Emile* (1762) he expounded his theories of natural education. In *Du contrat social* (1762) he provided his blue-print for the organization of an ideal society. The eccentric Scottish peer, Lord Monboddo (1714–99), judge and anthropologist, propagated the merits of primitive societies and kept a pet orang-utan as a kind of mascot or emblem of the infantine state of the human species. In Cumberland's play *The West Indian* (1771) the young hero Belcour is 'a child of nature' and symbolizes the untainted and simple virtues of a persona unsullied by decadent civilization. The moral of the romantic musical comedy *Inkle and Yarico* (1787) by George Colman (the Younger) is that you do not marry for wealth and position but for beauty, simplicity and goodness, here exemplified by the heroine, a black Barbadian. Mrs Inchbald (1753–1821) wrote two prose romances – *A Simple Story* (1791) and *Nature and Art* (1796) – in which she propounds her faith in natural upbringing. And Robert Bage's *Hermsprong, or Man as He is Not* (1796) is the story of a 'natural' man brought up among American Indians.

The primitivist yearning is implicit in much 18th c. pastoralism and in the 18th c. interest in peasant poetry. For example, the self-educated farm labourer Stephen Duck (1705–56) attracted much attention with his depictions of peasant life – especially his poem *The Thresher's Labour* – as did the work of Ann Yearsley, a dairywoman, who wrote *The Rural Lyre* (1796). The immense enthusiasm for the work of the fake primitives Macpherson and Chatterton and the cult of Ossianism (*q.v.*) late in the 18th c. is a further aspect of primitivism. The revival of interest in early English poetry achieved by the scholars Thomas Percy and Joseph Ritson is yet another. Another important figure is Thomas Gray, whose poems *The Bard* and *The Progress of Poesy* reflect strong feelings for a non-classical past. Primitivism is implicit, too, in Oliver Goldsmith's eloquent and moving lament for a vanishing way of life in *The Deserted Village* (1770). And though in the 18th c. there was not much sympathy with or understanding of the academic, old-fashioned pastoral, a strong feeling of nostalgia pervades much of the poetry written in that age. This is especially noticeable in the minor poets, and a pre-Romantic feeling for Nature is apparent early in the century (e.g. a number of poems by Lady Winchilsea).

Critical theory, too, of that period underlines a taste for primitivism. This is clear in the work of Vico, Blair, Blackwell and others who reacted against neoclassicism and admired the works of 'primitives' such as Homer, Shakespeare, Ossian and the peasant poets. It should be noted, as well, that when writers such as William Cowper and Thomas Day came to attack slavery and the slave trade they defended the concept of the Noble Savage. It was Day, incidentally, who wrote *The History of Little Jack* (1787), the tale of a young wild boy suckled by goats. Instances of 'savage' or 'wild children' aroused particular curiosity in the 18th c.

Apart from the nostalgia for a simple rustic life and for the putative *saturnia regna*, primitivism has other manifestations in literature. A number of writers have 'tapped' the primitive response in attempts to locate or re-locate the primitivist world, not in some remote retreat or paradise, but in the individual. This has involved the re-creation of different modes of feeling and different attitudes; in other words, animistically; by the use of symbol (*q.v.*) and mythopoeia.

This is apparent in the way Wordsworth feels about and responds to Nature. In his mode of sensibility he vivifies and re-vivifies the natural scene and re-animates the thoughts and feelings in communal myths and folklore. This re-animation is also apparent in Coleridge's *Rime of the Ancient Mariner* (1798), in Fenimore Cooper's *Leatherstocking Tales* (1826–41), in Melville's stories *Typee* (1846), *Omoo* (1847) and *Mardi* (1849), and above all in that author's *Moby-Dick* (1851).

In the 20th c. animistic and mythopoeic primitivism can be profitably and extensively studied in many poems by W. B. Yeats, in T. S. Eliot's *The Waste Land*, in a number of poems by Robert Frost and in a few by D. H. Lawrence (particularly *The Ship of Death*).

As far as fiction is concerned a number of works by novelists should be cited: Conrad's *Lord Jim* (1900) and his *Heart of Darkness* (1902); Joyce's *Ulysses* (1922); Mary Webb's *Gone to Earth* (1917) and *Precious Bane* (1924); D. H. Lawrence's *The Rainbow* (1915) and *The Plumed Serpent* (1926), most of William Faulkner's novels and those of the French regional novelist Jean Giono; Saul Bellow's *Henderson the Rain King* (1959); William Golding's *Lord of the Flies* (1954). *The Inheritors* (1955) and *Pincher Martin* (1956); Patrick White's *Voss* (1957).

private press Such a press is usually set up and run by an individual or a small group in order to publish works which might not otherwise get into print. The most famous in England have been: the Strawberry Hill Press established by Horace Walpole in his home in 1757; Dr Daniel's press at Oxford in 1845; the Kelmscott Press founded by William Morris, in 1890; the Golden Cockerel Press (1921); the Nonesuch Press established by Francis Meynell in 1923; and finally Eric Gill's press set up in 1933. There have been few outside England. The best known is probably the Cranach founded at Weimar in 1913. *See also* PRESS.

proairetic code *See* CODE.

problem play *See* THESIS PLAY.

proceleusmatic (Gk 'arousing to action in advance') A metrical foot comprising four unstressed syllables: ∪ ∪ ∪ ∪. Rare in Greek lyric poetry and tragedy; but not uncommon in Latin comedy. *Very* occasional as an isolated foot in English verse.

prochronism *See* ANACHRONISM.

proem (Gk 'prelude') Colloquially a 'limbering up' or 'warming up'; a preface; an introduction; a preamble. Milton sounds his proem at the beginning of *Paradise Lost*. It is the literary equivalent of an overture.

Professorenroman (G 'professor novel') Not, as might be thought, a campus novel (*q.v.*) of the kind that Professors Bradbury, Lodge and Wain have excelled at, but historical novels and novels with archaeological themes and subjects which display a range of recondite erudition but are short on style, character and imaginative recreation. Exponents were the distinguished German professors Felix Dahn (1834–1912), George Ebers (1837–98) and Adolf Hausrath (1837–1909).

prohemio A Spanish term denoting an introduction to a collection of poems. There is a well-known example by Santillana (1398–1458), addressed to the Constable of Portugal and giving a personal view of Spanish poetry to date.

prolegomenon (Gk 'something said in advance') A preface (*q.v.*) or introduction; perhaps an introductory treatise. The equivalent of clearing the ground in preparation for building. A good recent example is R. B. McKerrow's *Prolegomena for the Oxford Shakespeare* (1939).

prolepsis (Gk 'a taking beforehand, anticipation') A figurative device by which a future event is presumed to have happened. A very famous example occurs in Keats's *Isabella* (stanza 27):

So the two brothers and their *murder'd man*
Rode past fair Florence, to where Arno's stream
Gurgles through straitened banks

Lorenzo, the 'murder'd man', has not yet been murdered but he is being taken into a forest by Isabella's two brothers where he *will* be murdered.

The term also denotes a pre-emptive strike in argument in the shape of raising an objection beforehand in order to dispose of it. Also the summary of a detailed account of something to come. *See also* HYPALLAGE.

proletarian novel A novel (*q.v.*) about the working classes and working-class life; perhaps with the intention of making propaganda (*q.v.*) in pointing out poor economic conditions. An excellent example is Walter Greenwood's *Love on the Dole* (1933). *See also* DOCUMENTARY NOVEL; THESIS NOVEL.

proletarskaya kul'tura (R 'proletarian culture') Abbreviated to the rather barbarous *proletcult*, which refers to a Soviet movement started by Bogdanov in 1917. The group was made up of militant writers strongly in favour of a proletarian culture. The results of such organizations (the Smithy Poets, *q.v.*, was another) are only too apparent in some Communist states today, including the renegade Albania. Many of the contributors to their publications were pick and shovel hackwriters. *See also* CONSTRUCTIVISM; SOCIALIST REALISM.

prologue (Gk 'before speech') The opening section of a work; a kind of introduction which is part of the work and not prefatory. It was common in drama in the 17th and 18th c., when it was often in verse. Occasionally found in novels. In plays the prologue is usually a chorus (*q.v.*). The most famous example in English is Chaucer's *General Prologue* to *The Canterbury Tales*. *See also* EPILOGUE; INDUCTION.

promythium *See* EPIMYTHIUM.

pronominatio *See* ANTONOMASIA.

pro-ode In Greek dramatic and lyric poetry a strophe (*q.v.*) without a matching antistrophe (*q.v.*) which preceded the strophe and antistrophe of a choral ode (*q.v.*). It may also denote a short verse before a longer one.

propaganda ' term 'lifted' from the title *Congregatio de propaganda fide* (now the APF – Association for the Propagation of the Faith), a committee of the Roman Church responsible for foreign missions and the dissemination of the faith. It was set up in 1622.

When literature is propaganda and when it is not is a much debated issue. If an author sets out to make a case for a particular religious, social or political point of view, through the medium of a play or a novel, for example, and he is *seen* to be doing this, and perhaps in the process he sacrifices verisimilitude (*q.v.*) by contriving character and situation to suit his thesis, then it might be said that the result is a work of propaganda. If what he has to say is worth reading or listening to long after the issue which provoked the propaganda is dead, then his art has transcended the contingent needs of the propagandist.

Basically propaganda is devoted to the spreading of a particular idea or belief. Much pamphlet (*q.v.*) literature and journalism (*q.v.*) has precisely this purpose. It is partial. Pamphleteering in the 18th c., for instance, was openly propagandist. Later, notable polemicists like H. G. Wells, Bernard Shaw, Hilaire Belloc and G. K. Chesterton wrote a lot of propaganda to support and promulgate their political, social and religious beliefs. Though proselytizing is forbidden to the layman, Belloc and Chesterton came very near it at times. Ibsen might fairly be described as propagandist in some of his plays; so might Galsworthy. And Brecht certainly was. There have also been a number of plays presented to spread the doctrines of Moral Re-Armament. Many writers in the Communist bloc have been overtly propagandist in aid of socialism, in novels, as well as in plays and verse. *See* COMMITMENT; COMMUNICATION FALLACY; THESIS NOVEL; THESIS PLAY.

propaganda novel *See* THESIS NOVEL.

propaganda play *See* THESIS PLAY.

propos (F 'chat') A minor form invented by Emile-Auguste Chartier (1868–1951), whose pen-name was 'Alain'. In 1906, this distinguished teacher started a daily series of *Propos d'un Normand* in the *Dépêche de Rouen*. They were short essays of about eight hundred to a thousand words on a wide variety of subjects. He continued them for many years and in 1933 published *Propos de littérature*. *See* CAUSERIE; ESSAY.

proposition That part of a work in which the author states his theme (*q.v.*) or intention, and introduces the burden of the work. It may be explicit or implicit and is likely to come at or near the beginning. Some famous examples of propositions are: (a) the opening lines of Milton's *Paradise Lost*; (b) the first sentence of Rousseau's *Du contrat social*; (c) the opening sentences of Tolstoy's *Anna Karenina*. *See* PROEM.

propriety The canons of propriety are the canons of good taste, good manners and correctness; thus, in writing, conformity with what is suitable and appropriate. A virtue especially prized in the 18th c. when the suiting of style and form to subject matter was studied with more than usual care. Hence the regard for decorum (*q.v.*). *See also* POETIC DICTION.

Prosaroman A German term for prose versions of courtly verse romances (*q.v.*). Most of them belong to the 15th c. They are distinguished from the *Volksbücher* which developed at the end of that century from the *Prosaroman*. *See* VOLKSBUCH.

prose The word derives from the Latin *prosa* or *proversa oratio* 'straightforward discourse'. Thus, a direct, unadorned form of language, written or spoken, in ordinary usage. It differs from poetry or verse (*qq.v.*) in that it is not restricted in rhythm, measure or rhyme (*qq.v.*). However, there are such things as poetic prose and the prose poem (*qq.v.*).

In theory there are as many different kinds of prose as there are people to write it, as becomes plain from a cursory study of such different practitioners as: Sir Walter Ralegh, Sir Francis Bacon, Sir Thomas Browne, Hobbes, George Savile Marquess of Halifax, Swift, Locke, Addison, Johnson, Fielding, Goldsmith, Hume, Berkeley, Macaulay, Jane Austen, Gibbon, Coleridge, Scott, Dickens, Carlyle, George Eliot, Hardy, Lytton Strachey, Jack London, Henry James, Conrad, James Joyce, Virginia Woolf, Ernest Hemingway, William Faulkner, Graham Greene, Nabokov and Samuel Beckett.

prose poem A composition printed as prose (*q.v.*) but distinguished by elements common in poetry (*q.v.*): such as elaborately contrived rhythms, figures of speech, rhyme (*q.v.*), internal rhyme (*q.v.*), assonance (*q.v.*), consonance (*q.v.*) and startling images. Aloysius Bertrand (1807–41) appears to have been one of the first writers to establish it as a minor genre. His *Gaspard de la nuit* (1842) was a collection of fantasies in the manner of Rembrandt and Callot written in very ornate and rhythmical language. It contains many dazzling images, a number of which are grotesque. Later, Baudelaire was influenced by this work, as is apparent from his *Petits poèmes en prose* (1869). It is likely that Bertrand's work had some influence on the symbolist poets and on the surrealists. Other writers of note to have attempted the prose poem are Rimbaud, Oscar Wilde, Amy Lowell and T. S. Eliot; plus, latterly, Peter Redgrove and David Wevill. A remarkable recent example is Heathcote Williams's *Whale Nation* (1988), a long work which is a celebration of the existence and way of life of whales and a plea for their preservation. *See also* POETIC PROSE; SURREALISM; SYMBOL AND SYMBOLISM.

prose rhythm What Dryden called the 'other harmony of prose' has its own rhythms which vary from writer to writer, according to their nature, style, subject matter and purpose.

prosodion A form of religious song used in devotions to the god Apollo in ancient Greece. It was sung by a Chorus (*q.v.*) to the accompaniment of music.

prosody The study or science of versification and every aspect of it. It thus includes meter, rhythm, rhyme and stanza (*qq.v.*) forms.

prosopopoeia (Gk 'face making') The term is still used sometimes for personification (*q.v.*).

prospect poem *See* TOPOGRAPHICAL POETRY.

protagonist (Gk 'first combatant') The first actor in a play; thence the principal actor or character. In Greek tragedy (*q.v.*) the playwright was limited to the protagonist (first actor), deuteragonist (second actor) and tritagonist (third actor). It is probable that in the first place Greek drama consisted of a Chorus (*q.v.*) and the leader of the Chorus. Thespis (6th c. BC) is believed to have added the first actor to give greater variety to the dialogue and action. The second and third were added by Aeschylus and Sophocles respectively. The protagonist has come to be the equivalent of the hero (*q.v.*). *See* AGON; ANTAGONIST.

protasis (Gk 'stretching forward') Thus, a proposition or something put forward. In Greek drama the opening section of a play in which the characters are introduced and the situation explained. The protasis is followed by the epitasis and the catastrophe (*qq.v.*). *See* CATASTASIS; FREYTAG'S PYRAMID.

protatic character A character introduced at the beginning of a play, usually for the purpose of exposition (*q.v.*). Probably a development of the Chorus (*q.v.*). In drawing-room comedy often a servant.

prothalamion A term invented by Spenser (by analogy with epithalamion, *q.v.*) for his poem (1596) in celebration of the double wedding of the Lady Elizabeth and the Lady Katherine Somerset. It thus means a 'spousal verse' or something written 'before the bridal chamber'.

protozeugma *See* ZEUGMA.

protreptic A kind of discourse designed to persuade or hortate. Not unusual in Classical literature. Aristotle wrote one called *Protreptikos.*

Proustian In the style or manner or with the technique of Marcel Proust (1871–1922), and also referring to his whole attitude towards and feeling for what he describes. It particularly refers to his remarkable novel *A la recherche du temps perdu* (1913–27).

proverb A short pithy saying which embodies a general truth. It is related in form and content to the maxim and the aphorism (*qq.v.*). Common to most nations and peoples, it is a form of expression of great antiquity. Many writers have made use of them. The best known collection is The Book of Proverbs which follows The Psalms in the Old Testament. The following examples indicate the nature of a proverb: Send a fool to close the shutters and he'll close them all over the town (Yiddish); We cannot step twice into the same river (Classical Greek); When you want a drink of milk you don't buy the cow (Cretan); If vinegar is free it is sweeter than honey (Serbian); An uninvited guest is worse than a Tatar

(Russian); There is but an hour a day between a good housewife and a bad one (English); It is better to wear out one's shoes than one's sheets (Genoese); The wife carries her husband on her face; the husband carries the wife on his linen (Bulgarian); Watch the faces of those who bow low (Polish); If it is not in the head it is in the feet (Czech); Visits always give pleasure – if not the arrival, the departure (Portuguese); To tell a woman what she may not do is to tell her what she can (Spanish); Every invalid is a physician (Irish). A fine collection of English proverbs is the *Oxford Dictionary of English Proverbs* (1935).

proverbe dramatique A short dramatic sketch which illustrates a proverbial saying. The genre had some vogue in the French salons of the 17th and 18th c. Their precursors were *jeux des proverbes* – parlour games in which a conversation had to be sustained by using proverbs. *Proverbes dramatiques* were then written for private theatricals. In the first place these were much the same as charades and the audience had to guess the proverb. Then writers disclosed the proverb and illustrated it in their little play, which was normally a one-act comedy.

Towards the end of the 17th c. a collection of *Proverbes* by Mme Durand was published. About this time Mme de Maintenon composed *proverbes* to be acted by the young ladies of Saint-Cyr. Such pieces had their greatest vogue in the mid-18th c. Collé, Carmontelle and Moissy were the main authors in this period. After the Revolution the *proverbe* tradition was revived in salons. In the 1820s and 1830s the best known authors were Antoine-Marie, Baron Roederer, Hyacinthe de Latouche and Octave Feuillet. However, it was Alfred de Musset who mastered this genre in the middle of the 19th c. Two well-known works by him are: *On ne badine pas avec l'amour*, and *Il faut qu'une porte soit ouverte ou fermée*.

pruning poem More accurately a 'pruned' poem. In this verse form, which is very rare, the second and third rhymes of each stanza are formed by pruning the first consonant of the preceding rhyme. George Herbert's *Paradise* is an example. The first two stanzas are:

> I blesse thee, Lord, because I GROW
> Among thy trees, which in a ROW
> To thee both fruit and order OW.

What open force, or hidden CHARM
Can blast my fruit, or bring me HARM
While the inclosure is thine ARM.

See also ALTAR POEM; PATTERN POETRY; RHOPALIC VERSE.

psalm A sacred song or hymn (*q.v.*), especially one of the collection in the Bible: The Book of Psalms.

psalter A book which contains psalms; a psalm-book; not to be confused with psaltery, an ancient or medieval musical instrument. *See* PSALM.

pseudepigrapha (Gk 'false inscription') A term for books or writings which have a false title or are ascribed to an author who is not the real one. *See also* FORGERY.

pseudonym (Gk 'false name') A name other than his own taken by a writer. Also known as a pen-name and a nom de plume (*q.v.*).

pseudonymous literature The use of a pseudonym, pen-name or nom de plume (*q.v.*) is a well-established practice; as well established as publishing work anonymously. Here are just a few: Montcorbier – François Villon; Gerard – Desiderius Erasmus; François-Marie Arouet – Voltaire; Jean Baptiste Poquelin – Molière; Friedrich von Hardenberg – Novalis; Marie Henri Beyle – Stendhal; the Brontë sisters – Currer, Ellis and Acton Bell; Thackeray – Michael Angelo Titmarsh; Dickens – Boz; Mary Ann Evans – George Eliot; Edward Bradley – Cuthbert Bede; Samuel Clemens – Mark Twain; Louis Marie Julien Viaud – Pierre Loti; Jacques Anatole François Thibault – Anatole France; William Sydney Porter – O. Henry; Edgar Allison Peers – Bruce Truscot; H. H. Munro – Saki; C. Day Lewis – Nicholas Blake; J. I. M. Stewart – Michael Innes.

pseudo-statement A term used by I. A. Richards to distinguish 'scientific' from 'poetic' truth. By 'statement' Richards means a scientific expression of fact which is verifiable as such. A pseudo-statement, on the other hand, is found in poetry and is not necessarily verifiable or even logical. Such statements have the function of ordering and organizing the receptor's (*q.v.*) attitudes and feelings. The implications of this concept and distinction are that poetry tells the truth and its own truth in its own way by feigning (*q.v.*). In other words, verisimilitude (*q.v.*) and a kind of truth can be attained and conveyed by emotive as well as referential language (*qq.v.*). The idea that poetry can convey a particular kind of knowledge not conveyable by any other means is of great antiquity.

psittacism (L 'parrot-like speech') Meaningless and repetitive speech. Mosque servants who memorize thousands of *suras* (*q.v.*) of the *Koran* and repeat them suffer from psittacism.

psychic distance *See* AESTHETIC DISTANCE.

psychoanalytic criticism *See* FREUDIAN CRITICISM/PSYCHOANALYTIC CRITICISM.

psychobabble A term coined by R. D. Rosen in *Psychobabble: Fast Talk and Quick Cure in the Era of Feeling* (1977) – a critique of DIY ego-psychology – and defined as: 'a set of repetitive verbal formalities that kills off the very spontaneity, candour and understanding it pretends to promote. It's an idiom that reduces psychological insight to a collection of standardized observations, that provides a frozen lexicon to deal with an infinite variety of problems'. Common in everyday speech and re-created/reproduced in fiction (e.g. Cyra McFadden's clever satirical novel *The Serial: A Year in the Life of Marin County*, 1977). It is discussed by David Lodge in a witty essay in *Working with Structuralism* (1981) in which he cites such instances as: 'get centred', 'get in on with', 'into the pits', 'hang in on', 'flash on', 'blow away', 'off the wall', 'wig out', 'upfront', 'spaced/spaced out/spacey'. All have metaphorical or semi-metaphorical meanings, in some cases a good deal removed from literal sense. For example, 'off the wall' signifies 'spontaneously'. *See also* NEOLOGISM.

psychobiography A form of biography which is clinical in its treatment of its subject, which stresses the subject's psychological development and applies psychoanalytical knowledge and principles. For example, Erik H. Erikson's biography of Martin Luther – *Young Man Luther* (1958) – makes use of Freud's discoveries and theories in examination of Luther's adolescent 'identity crisis'. Notable examples of literary psychobiography are Leon Edel's *Henry James* (1953–72) and Justin Kaplan's *Mark Twain and*

His World (1974). *See also* FREUDIAN CRITICISM/PSYCHOANALYTIC CRITICISM; PSYCHOGRAPHY.

psychography (Gk 'writing of souls') A term apparently applied by George Saintsbury to Sainte-Beuve, who described himself as a 'naturalist of souls'. As a jargon term it refers to the importance of an author's life in a work of art. The psychographer, therefore, will be in search of revealing details in the life of an author in order to see what bearing they may have on his art.

psychological novel A vague term to describe that kind of fiction which is for the most part concerned with the spiritual, emotional and mental lives of the characters and with the analysis of character rather than with the plot and the action. Many novelists during the last two hundred years have written psychological novels.

public lending right This was secured by an Act of Parliament in 1979. It was the result of a long campaign (twenty-eight years) initiated by the novelist John Brophy in 1951. The Society of Authors (*q.v.*) and the Writers' Action Group were closely associated with it. By this statute authors receive annually a payment for the loan of books from public libraries. The amount depends on the number of books they have in print and the frequency with which they are borrowed. The scheme (which has reciprocal arrangements in other countries) is financed by a central grant from the Treasury and in Britain is administered by a registrar in Stockton-on-Tees.

puffery The kind of criticism which is the product of literary cliques. Authors who belong to such cliques laud one another's works. 'To puff' is to overpraise, to 'blow up'. The term no doubt derives from the character Mr Puff, the bogus and verbose critic of Sheridan's play *The Critic*. In publishers' jargon a puff is the equivalent of a blurb (*q.v.*). *See* LOG-ROLLING.

pulp literature (L *pulpa* 'flesh') 'Pulp' is a pejorative term for certain kinds of fiction (and its authors). Pulp magazines began to appear during the First World War or earlier and got their name from the fact that they were printed on wood pulp, which gave the content a coarse, grainy appearance. They were about 7 × 10 inches in size, had gaudy covers and comprised about 120 pages. They published short stories and occasional extracts from novels. During the 1920s they became extremely popular (there were well over 200 in existence) and they remained popular in the 1930s. Eventually, television brought about their demise.

They are of some importance in literary history because the American detective story (*q.v.*) was born in them. Well-known examples were *The Black Mask*, *Dime Detective*, *Thrilling Detective* and the *Detective Story Magazine*. Pulp magazines also published examples of the horror story (*q.v.*), and many tales of the weird and wonderful, the supernatural and the fantastic. Science fiction (*q.v.*) stories also became very popular through the pulp magazine, especially *Amazing Stories* (first published in 1926), though this was by no means the first SF magazine.

Pulp literature is basically trash, or something very close to it; what Aldous Huxley would have described as 'inconceivable twaddle' or 'semi-minus epsilon'. It includes soft porn, the kitsch (*q.v.*), potboilers (*q.v.*), poor Westerns (*q.v.*), many novelettes (*q.v.*), the lower forms of crime fiction and third-rate sentimental romances.

pun A figure of speech which involves a play upon words. The Greek term is paronomasia. One of the earliest types of wordplay, the pun is widespread in many literatures and gives rise to a fairly universal form of humour. Puns are very often intended humorously but not always. Donne, for example, puns elaborately and quite seriously in his *Hymn to God the Father* thus:

> I have a sin of fear, that when I have spun
>   My last thread, I shall perish on the shore;
> But swear by Thy self, that at my death Thy Son
> Shall shine as he shines now, and heretofore;
>   And having done that, Thou hast done;
>   I fear no more.

Here 'Son' means both Christ and 'the sun', and the word 'done' is a pun on the poet's name.

A famous pun in dramatic literature is Mercutio's laconic crack as he is dying: 'Ask for me tomorrow and you shall find me a grave man' (*Romeo and Juliet*, III, i).

A pun form known as *asteismus* involves a reply to earlier words used in a different sense. This example occurs in *Cymbeline* (II, i):

CLOTEN: Would he had been one of my rank!
LORD: To have smell'd like a fool.

A kind of sylleptic pun is contained in the following admonitory notice seen by the author outside a London church: 'Are you going to sleep with the wise virgins, or wake with the foolish ones?'

James Joyce is generally regarded as one of the most compulsive and incorrigible of punners in English literature. *Ulysses* and *Finnegans Wake* abound in them. *See* PARAGRAM.

pure poetry A question-begging term because of the ambiguities and connotations of 'pure', and very nearly as loose, at times, as the banality of 'sheer poetry'. However, if, in Valéry's words, we 'cleanse the verbal situation', we can say with a degree of truth that poetry aspires to the state of purity in the sense that it aspires to an excellence and by so doing is refined to all dross and impurity.

It may also be said to aspire 'towards the condition of music', as Walter Pater, in an essay on Giorgione in 1873, said all art does. If poetry does this, then the idea is suggested that the beauty of the poem's words and its content would be in unsurpassable harmony with the melody and sound the words conveyed.

As it happens, the theory and idea of pure poetry manifests itself in the middle of the 19th c. Edgar Allan Poe was hinting at it in *The Poetic Principle* (1850). Baudelaire, who was much influenced by Poe, was referring to it in his *Notes nouvelles sur Edgar Poe* (1857). Hereafter there seems gradually to have developed the idea that pure poetry was a form of music; that it expressed the essence of whatever it was the poet needed to express. Baudelaire, Mallarmé, Verlaine and Rimbaud, and, later, Valéry, all explored the possibilities of this kind of purity in verse. Thus, the theories of pure poetry are closely associated with symbolism and the symbolist poets.

In the 20th c. the most notable advocates of pure poetry were George Moore and the Abbé Bremond. In an introduction to his anthology of *Pure Poetry* (1924) Moore esteemed the works of Poe because they were 'almost free from thought'. In 1926 Abbé Bremond published *La Poésie pure*. The Abbé associated poetry with prayer; it aspired to an ineffable and incantatory condition.

T. S. Eliot also regarded pure poetry as a notable development in 19th c. verse, as he pointed out in his essay *From Poe to Valéry* (1949). *See* AESTHETICISM; CREATIONISM; HERMETICISM; SYMBOL AND SYMBOLISM.

purism At its worst the doctrine of precisionists and pedagogues who, to a fault, are devoted to the maintenance of absolute standards of correctness in writing; and an absolute observance of the rules of expression. However, the letter killeth and in the end such purism defeats its own object because words, as instruments, are as imperfect as the human beings who use them.

In a wider sense purism refers to those periodic efforts that have been made to purify languages – especially in the exclusion of foreign terms. In this respect the Greek Atticists were purists. The Romans, too, were not sympathetic to Greek coinages. The most notable attempt ever at purism was that made by the Académie Française, who received a commission in 1635 to purify the French language. This task they undertook and their dictionary was published in 1694. Fortunately, the English language, like many others, has not been subjected to the misguided proprietorship, however well-meaning, of similar custodians. It has remained, to its great advantage, a permeable and assimilative language of whose usage and abusage the common man and the pundit are co-equal arbiters.

It was Johnson who, in the *Preface* to his *Dictionary* (1755), entered the most eloquent of all claims for a language to be free of legislators:

> When we see men grow old and die at a certain time one after another, from century to century, we laugh at the elixir that promises to prolong life to a thousand years; and with equal justice may the lexicographer be derided, who, being able to produce no example of a nation that has preserved their words and phrases from mutability, shall imagine that his dictionary can embalm his language and secure it from corruption and decay, that it is in his power to change sublunary nature, and clear the world at once from folly, vanity, and affectation.
>
> With this hope, however, academies have been instituted to guard the avenues of their languages, to retain fugitives, and repulse intruders. But their vigilance and activity have hitherto been vain: sounds are too volatile and subtle for legal restraints; to enchain syllables, and to lash the wind, are equally the undertakings of pride, unwilling to measure its desires by its strength.

purple patch In *Ars Poetica* (2, 3, 14–19) Horace refers to *purpureus . . . pannus*, the purple piece of cloth which is an irrelevant insertion of a grandiloquent passage into a work. Thus the term now denotes an ornate, florid or over-written piece of writing which is incongruous. It is nearly always used pejoratively.

puy The title of medieval fraternities of *jongleurs* (*q.v.*) and also the ordinary citizens of towns in northern and western France. The *puys* held poetry contests at which lyric poets competed. The title may derive from the place-name Le Puy-en-Velay (where such contests were believed to have begun), or from *puy* denoting a raised stage on which the poets recited their verses in front of a president and panel of judges. The *puys* date, in all probability, from the 12th c., and the poems usually had a religious theme. For example, at the *puy* of Rouen poets presented poems in honour of the Immaculate Conception. There were similar *puys* at Caen and Dieppe.

puyyut (Gk *poietes* 'maker, poet') A Hebrew psalm of the early Christian era, mostly associated with the Baghdad region.

pyrrhic (Gk 'war dance') A metrical foot comprising two short syllables: ∪ ∪. Also known as a dibrach. The shortest metrical foot in Classical verse. In English prosody the pyrrhic of two unstressed syllables often occurs but it is regarded as belonging to adjacent feet or as a substitution (*q.v.*).

pysma A Greek term denoting a question which requires an answer and not merely 'yes' or 'no'. A rhetorical device by which a speaker or writer asks a series of questions which require various forms of answer. The Latin rhetoricians used the term *quaestium*. A well-known example is Hamlet's outburst to Gertrude (*Hamlet*, III, iv):

> Have you eyes?
> Could you on this fair mountain leave to feed,
> And batten on this moor? . . . what judgement
> Would step from this to this?

pythiambic verse A combination of dactylic hexameters (*q.v.*) and iambic dimeters of trimeters (*qq.v.*). There are some examples in Horace's *Epodes*. *See* PYTHIAN METER.

pythian meter Also known as *versus pythius*. A name given to the dactylic hexameter (*q.v.*) because it was the meter used in the Pythian or Delphic oracles. *See* PYTHIAMBIC VERSE.

Q

qasida A type of formal ode (*q.v.*) believed to have originated in the 6th c., and used by Arabic, Persian, Turkish and Urdu poets. The themes were varied: elegy, eulogy, panegyric or satire (*qq.v.*). The length varied also – between thirty to two or three hundred lines. The form was imitated by Tennyson in *Locksley Hall*, using couplets in octameters (*q.v.*), for the most part trochaic. Also used by Flecker in his poetic drama *Hassan* (published 1922).

In Spanish verse the *qasida* is probably of Bedouin Arab origin, and was a kind of elegy in which the meter might vary whereas the subjects (and their order) were fixed. The poet began with a nostalgic reference to a re-discovery of a place which recalled his love; then dwelt on this love; then on the ensuing sufferings it caused. There followed a lengthy account of the various journeys he had undertaken. Finally, he sang the praises of one who, he hoped, would become the patron of his efforts. The verses were transmitted orally at first; later they were written down.

quadrivium In the Middle Ages the seven liberal arts were divided into the *quadrivium* and the *trivium*. The former, being the more advanced, comprised the mathematical sciences, namely: arithmetic, geometry, astronomy and music; the latter, grammar, logic and rhetoric (which included oratory).

quaestium *See* PYSMA.

quantity The duration (*q.v.*) of the sound of a syllable; thus, the time needed for its pronunciation. Most Classical verse is based on quantities in accordance with certain rules. In English verse the duration of the vowels and syllables is important aesthetically but is of no metrical importance. Compare the first line of Virgil's *Aeneid* with the first line of Milton's *Paradise Lost*:

Ármă vĭrúmquĕ cănó, Troíaĕ qŭi prímŭs ăb órĭs
Of Man's first disobedience, and the fruit

The quantities of Virgil's dactylic hexameter (*q.v.*) are fixed; those of Milton's pentameter (*q.v.*) are flexible and the line might be read in more ways than one according to different degrees of emphasis. *See also* ACCENT; BEAT; HOVERING ACCENT; STRESS; VARIABLE SYLLABLE.

quart d'heure (F 'quarter of an hour') A short one-act play (*q.v.*); a curtain raiser (*q.v.*), common in the French theatre, rare in England.

quartet Four lines of verse, either as a separate quatrain (*q.v.*) or as a non-separate part of a poem. For example, the Shakespearean sonnet (*q.v.*), which consists of three groups of four lines concluded by a 'binding' couplet.

quarto (Short for Latin *in quarto* 'in fourth') (a) A book made from printer's sheets folded twice to form four leaves or eight pages. Abbrev. 4to; (b) The form in which about twenty of Shakespeare's plays were printed. Such versions are known as First Quarto, Second Quarto, and so forth. *See* DUODECIMO; FOLIO.

quaternarius *See* IAMB.

quatorzain Any poem of fourteen lines, which usually follows the sonnet (*q.v.*) pattern, but not always regularly.

quatrain A stanza of four lines, rhymed or unrhymed. The commonest of all stanzaic forms in European poetry, it lends itself to wide variation in meter and rhyme. Most rhyming quatrains fall into the following patterns:

(a) abab, as in Charles Causley's *The Prisoners of Love*:

Trapped in their tower, the prisoners of love
Loose their last message on the failing air.
The troops of Tyre assault with fire the grove
Where Venus veils with light her lovely hair.

(b) xbyb, as in the same writer's *The Life of the Poet*:

Lock the door, Schoolmaster,
  Keep the children in.
The river in spate at the schoolyard gate
  Roars like original sin.

(c) aabb, as in Causley's *Timothy Winters*:

> Timothy Winters comes to school
> With eyes as wide as a football pool,
> Ears like bombs and teeth like splinters:
> A blitz of a boy is Timothy Winters.

(d) abba, the so-called envelope stanza (*q.v.*) which Tennyson used in *In Memoriam*:

> Strong Son of God, immortal Love,
> Whom we, that have not seen thy face,
> By faith, and faith alone, embrace,
> Believing where we cannot prove;

(e) aaxa, a form which is less common but well known as the Omar Khayyám stanza:

> Awake! for Morning in the Bowl of Night
> Has flung the Stone that puts the Stars to flight:
> And Lo! the Hunter of the East has caught
> The Sultan's Turret in a Noose of light.

It is also possible to have a monorhymed stanza. Other complexities are: alternate use of masculine and feminine rhymes and irregular line lengths. Some special names have been acquired by some quatrains. The heroic or elegiac stanza (*q.v.*), used by Gray in his *Elegy*, consists of iambic pentameters rhyming abab. Ballad (*q.v.*) meter consists of iambic tetrameter (*q.v.*), trimeter (*q.v.*), tetrameter trimeter, usually rhymed abcb or xbyb. Hymn (*q.v.*) forms have also received special names: common meter, which is the same as ballad meter, or 'eights-and-sixes'; long meter, which is iambic tetrameters; short meter, which is trimeter, trimeter, tetrameter, trimeter.

The quatrain has been used a great deal in European poetry, usually in long and narrative poems. The term can also be applied to the two components of the octave (*q.v.*) of a sonnet (*q.v.*). In epigrammatic utterance the quatrain has been used successfully as a poem by itself by many writers, for example: Prior, Landor, Yeats and Ogden Nash. Nash wrote a lot of them, like:

> Sure, deck your lower limbs in pants;
> Yours are the limbs, my sweeting.
> You look divine as you advance –
> Have you seen yourself retreating?

Not a few are anonymous. For example:

Mary Ann has gone to rest,
Safe at last on Abraham's breast,
Which may be nuts for Mary Ann
But is certainly rough on Abraham.

See also QUARTET; TETRASTICH.

quem quaeritis trope A trope (*q.v.*) of vital importance in the evolution of European drama. Part of the Easter *Introit*, it was adapted and elaborated into a dialogue and so became the source of liturgical drama. E. K. Chambers goes into the matter in great detail in his classic work *The Medieval Stage* (1903).

querelle des anciens et des modernes *See* ANCIENTS AND MODERNS.

question, epic A device in epic poetry by which the poet invokes the aid of a muse, patroness or superior power to explain what has happened. Milton uses it to considerable effect at the beginning of Books I, VII and IX of *Paradise Lost*.

questione della lingua (It 'dispute, problem, question or quarrel of the language') A controversy or debate about the suitability of the vernacular as opposed to Latin as the language of literature. It also raised the problem of which Italian dialects should be used. This was a medieval debate in origin, to which Dante contributed. In *De vulgari eloquentia* he rejected all dialects and argued for an eclectic language composed from the best elements of all the dialects. In his *Divina Commedia* he used the Florentine dialect; which Petrarch and Boccaccio also used. The argument went on long after this, even though Florentine had become the literary language of Italians. In the 16th c. Castiglione was in favour of the language spoken in courts; others reverted to Dante's eclectic theory. Two schools of thought developed, and produced an 'ancients versus moderns' conflict. Bembo insisted on 14th c. Florentine in his *Prose della volgar lingua* (1525). Castelvetro and Machiavelli opted for the contemporary Florentine. The debate was still going on in the 19th c. when Leopardi favoured 14th c. Florentine. In the 19th c. Manzoni also tackled the problem.

quidproquo (L *quid pro quo* 'something for something') A term usually limited to the drama in reference to some kind of blunder or misunderstanding on the part of the characters, perhaps from the misinterpretation of a word of situation. Frequent in comedy; for example: situations in Shakespeare's *The Comedy of Errors*, Jonson's *The Alchemist*, Goldsmith's *She Stoops to Conquer* and Sheridan's *School for Scandal.*

quinary A metrical line of five syllables, as in William Blakes's *The Sick Rose*:

O Rose! thou art sick!
The invisible worm,
That flies in the night,
In the howling storm

quintain A stanza or verse group of five lines, as in Jack Clemo's *The Plundered Fuchsias*:

They lie all around the lawn
  And on the furrowed wall
Like little red bombs winged and splayed.
  No gale has made them fall:
  A child's whim, that is all.

See also QUINTET.

quintet A five-line stanza of varying rhyme scheme and line length. A common rhyme scheme is ababb. Shelley, for instance, used this in *To a Skylark*:

Hail to thee, blithe spirit!
  Bird thou never wert,
That from Heaven, or near it,
  Pourest thy full heart
In profuse strains of unpremeditated art.

See also QUINTAIN.

quinteto In Spanish prosody a verse of five lines of *arte mayor* (*q.v.*).

quintilla (Sp 'little fifth') A five-line stanza of eight syllables and two rhymes; or any five-line stanza with two rhymes. Verses or lines with other numbers of syllables do exist. In Castilian, the *quintilla* is one of the commonest octosyllabic strophes. It was used by dramatists (e.g. Lope de Vega), but perhaps the most famous instance is Fernández de Moratín's *Fiesta de toros en Madrid* of the 18th c. *See also* REDONDILLA.

quinzain A fifteen-line stanza. Rare because of its length.

quod semper quod ubique (L 'which always and which everywhere') This remains the hallmark of great literature in time and place. The words occur in the so-called Vincentian canon framed by St Vincent of Lérins (near Cannes) in the 5th c. The sentence runs: *Id teneo quod semper quod ubique et quod ab omnibus creditum est.* It applies the test of eternity, ubiquity and consensus. *See* UNIVERSALITY.

quotation titles Titles of books echoing famous phrases from earlier literature and evoking known associations in the mind of the reader. This kind of title has achieved considerable popularity in the 20th c. when the fashion was set by E. M. Forster in *Where Angels Fear to Tread* (1905), recalling Pope's *Essay on Criticism* (l. 625):

> No place so sacred from such fops is barr'd,
> Nor is Paul's church more safe than Paul's churchyard:
> Nay, fly to altars, there they'll talk you dead;
> For fools rush in where angels fear to tread.

But this practice was by no means new to our century. After all, Thackeray's *Vanity Fair* (1848) reproduced that fair in Bunyan's *The Pilgrim's Progress* which was held in Vanity town by Beelzebub, Apollyon and Legion, and through which all pilgrims passed on their way to the Eternal City. *Household Words*, a weekly periodical launched by Dickens only two years later (1850), harked back to King Henry's speech before the Battle of Agincourt in Shakespeare's *Henry V* (IV, iii, 52). Robert Louis Stevenson's *Virginibus Puerisque* (1881) was taken direct from the third book of Horace's *Odes*.

In the 20th c., however, Forster has had so many followers in this respect that space allows us to select only a few: Ford Madox Ford's *Ladies Whose Bright Eyes* (1911) from Milton's *L'Allegro* (l. 121); A. S. M. Hutchinson's *If Winter Comes* (1921) from Shelley's *Ode to the West Wind* (l. 57); Rose Macaulay's *Told by an Idiot* (1923) from Shakespeare's *Macbeth* (V, i, 26); William Faulkner's *The Sound and the Fury* (1931) from Shakespeare's *Macbeth* (V, v, 27); Aldous Huxley's *Brave New World* (1932) from Shakespeare's *The Tempest* (V, i, 183); and that same author's *Eyeless in Gaza* (1936) from Milton's *Samson Agonistes* (l. 41); Anthony Powell's *From a View to a Death* (1933) from John Woodcock Graves's hunting song *John Peel*; Eric Linklater's *Ripeness is All* (1935) from Shakespeare's *King Lear* (V, ii, 9); John Steinbeck's *The Grapes of Wrath* (1940) from Julia Ward Howe's *Battle Hymn of the Republic*; Ernest Hemingway's *For Whom the Bell Tolls* (1940) from Donne's *Meditation* (l. 17); Graham Greene's *The Power and the Glory* (1940) from St Matthew's Gospel (6: 13); Joyce Cary's *To be a Pilgrim* (1942) from Bunyan's *The Pilgrim's Progress*; H. E. Bates's *Fair Stood the Wind for France* (1944) from Michael Drayton's *Agincourt*; Iris Murdoch's *Unofficial Rose* (1962) from Rupert Brooke's *The Old Vicarage, Grantchester*; Anthony Burgess's *Nothing Like the Sun* (1970) from Shakespeare's 130th Sonnet.

R

Ꮥ

Rabelaisian From the name of François Rabelais (*c.* 1490–1553). The term usually denotes ribald humour, but can also cover fantastical and exuberant writing.

rabinal achí A form of ballet-drama found among the Quiche Indians of Guatemala. Its theme is the heroic exploits and legend of the princes of Rabinal. It is performed at traditional festivals.

Rahmen (G 'frame') There are two basic forms of frame story technique: the *zyklischer* or 'cyclic' and the *Einzelrahmen* or 'single frame'. The former combines a series of stories into a unified entity; the latter constitutes a self-contained story linked to the frame by a narrator. *See* RAHMENERZAHLUNG.

Rahmenerzählung (G 'frame story') Some of the better known are Ovid's *Metamorphoses, The Arabian Nights*, Boccaccio's *Decameron* and Chaucer's *Canterbury Tales*. Goethe, Hoffmann and Tieck all used the frame story, or stories within a story. The Swiss writers C. F. Meyer and Gottfried Keller are regarded as the most accomplished users of the frame story in recent times. Among their main works are: Meyer's *Der Heilige* (1880) and *Die Hochzeit des Mönchs* (1884); Keller's *Züricher Novellen* (1876) and *Das Sinngedicht* (1881). *See also* NOVELLA; STORY WITHIN A STORY.

raisonneur (F 'reasoner') An equivalent of confidant (*q.v.*).

rannaigheacht bheag An Irish verse form similar to the *rannaigheacht mhor*, except that the line endings are disyllabic. *See* RANNAIGHEACHTS.

rannaigheachts An Irish syllabic verse form. The *rannaigheacht ghairid* is a quatrain (*q.v.*) stanza in which the first line has three syllables and the rest seven. It rhymes aaba, and the third line cross-rhymes with the fourth. There are variations. For example, if lines end in disyllables instead of monosyllables, the form is called *rannaigheacht chetharchubaid garit recomarcach*. *Rannaigheacht mhor* is a quatrain stanza of heptasyllable lines which consonate abab. In this form there are at least two cross-rhymes in each couplet and the final word of the third line rhymes with a word in the middle of the fourth. In the second couplet rhymes must be exact. In each line two words alliterate.

RAPP An acronym for Russian Association of Proletarian Writers. This organization was created in 1929 and was an off-shoot of the *proletarskaya kul'tura* (*q.v.*) movement during the first Five-Year Plan. It was violently anti-bourgeois and strongly in favour of proletarian culture and literature. Its militant chairman was Leopold Averbakh (1903–?). RAPP was disbanded in 1932 and merged with the Union of Soviet Writers (*q.v.*).

rasa A Sanskrit term for one of the nine so-called flavours of a work of art. The desirable nine are: the erotic, heroic, furious, piteous, comic, fearful, repulsive, marvellous and peaceful.

rationalism At least three basic meanings may be distinguished: (a) the theory or doctrine that human reason can provide *a priori* knowledge without intermediary sense data; (b) the theory or doctrine that reason can pursue and attain truth for its own sake; (c) the idea or conviction that a rational order can be found in reality; and, alternatively, that reason can impose an order on reality.

Rationalism, rationalist and rational are often used fairly loosely. For example, the 18th c. is referred to as a period of rationalism; a rationalist may be a person who depends on reason rather than feeling and intuitive perception; being rational may mean using the brain and ratiocinative processes rather than any others. All three terms are occasionally used pejoratively.

Räuberroman *See* RITTER- UND RAUBERROMAN.

Raumbühne The German term for theatre-in-the-round (*q.v.*).

readerly/writerly Terms devised by Roland Barthes (1915–80), the French critic, to make a distinction between two basic kinds of text: the *lisible* ('readerly') and the *scriptible* ('writerly'). He expounds on this in his book *S/Z* (1970). By a 'readerly' text he means a book (a novel, say) to which a reader's response is more or less passive. For example, a 'realistic' novel (or any 'classic text' as Barthes terms them), presents to us a recognizable world with easily recognizable characters and events. The reader accepts the meaning without needing to make much effort. A writerly' text, however, makes demands on the reader; he or she has to work things out, look for and provide meaning. Obvious examples of writerly texts are Joyce's *Ulysses* and *Finnegans Wake*. A writerly text tends to focus attention on how it is written, on the mechanics of it, the particular use of language. A writerly text tends to be self-conscious; it calls attention to itself as a work of art. It also makes the reader into a producer. Barthes makes the point that the writerly text is of value because the goal of literary work (of literature as work) is to make the reader no longer a consumer, but a producer of the text. However, as Barthes demonstrates in his analysis of Balzac's short story *Sarrasine* (which is basically a readerly story but which Barthes discusses as a writerly one), a critic may, if he or she wishes, read any story as either writerly or readerly. A readerly or writerly reading is not inherent in the text but may be a part of the reading. *See also* AUTHOR, DEATH OF; CODE; POST-STRUCTURALISM; STRUCTURALISM.

reader-oriented theory *See* READER-RESPONSE THEORY; RECEPTION THEORY.

reader-response theory Theory concerned with the relationship between text and reader and reader and text, with the emphasis on the different ways in which a reader participates in the course of reading a text and the different perspectives which arise in the relationship. Thus, reader-response theory is concerned with the reader's contribution to a text, and it challenges, with varying degrees of plausibility and conviction, the text-oriented theories of Formalism and the New Criticism (*qq.v.*), which have tended to ignore or underestimate the reader's role.

Fundamentally, a text, whatever it be (poem, short story, essay, scientific exposition), has no real existence until it is read. Its meaning is *in potentia*, so to speak. A reader completes its meaning by reading it. The reading is complementary; it *actualizes potential meaning*. Thus, the reader does not have, as has been traditionally thought and accepted, a passive role; on the contrary, the reader is an active agent in the creation of meaning. By applying codes and strategies the reader decodes the text.

Various theories about this 'collaboration' have been advanced since the mid to late 1970s. For example, in his book *The Act of Reading: A Theory of Aesthetic Response* (1976, trans. 1978) Wolfgang Iser puts the proposition that all literary texts have *Leerstellen* ('blanks', 'gaps' or 'lacunae'). These blanks have to be filled in or 'concretized' by the reader in order to interpret the text. But this proposition poses a basic question: is the text itself the cause of the reader's interpretation, or does the reader impose, as it were, an interpretation on the text? A possible answer to this is that the reader supplies a set of social, historical and cultural norms but the text calls them forth and in a sense contains them.

In 1979 Umberto Eco, the Italian semiotician and novelist, published *The Role of the Reader*. In this he proposes a distinction between what he calls 'open' and 'closed' texts. An 'open' text (e.g. *Finnegans Wake*, Eliot's *The Waste Land* or Jacques Lacan's theories of the unconscious) requires the reader's close and active collaboration in the creation of meaning; whereas a 'closed' text (e.g. a whodunit by Agatha Christie, a thriller by Frederick Forsyth or a scientific treatise on lice) more or less determines or predetermines a reader's response; though, of course, in a detective story the interpretation of clues would be an important part of a reader's response.

Yet another reader-response theory is that advanced by the Americans Norman Holland and David Bleich. In their view reading is a form of covert wish-fulfilment, so the reader engages with a text as with any other form of desire. In their books – *Five Readers Reading* (1975) by Holland and *Subjective Criticism* (1978) by Bleich – they analyse in depth the reading habits and responses of individual readers.

In *Semiotics of Poetry* (1978) Michael Riffaterre postulates what he describes as the 'Superreader', who analyses a text in a search for meanings beyond and below surface meanings. The 'Superreader' represents the sum of reactions to the language of a text manifested in the published work of its interpreters, translators and so on. Riffaterre believes that the stylistic function of a text can be analysed objectively, that style has a constant trans-subjective tone. He suggests that the task of the stylistician is to reveal what is ungrammatical or in any other way unconventional or 'abnormal' in the way a text (e.g. a poem) is composed.

In examination of the conventions of reading, Jonathan Culler (in

The Pursuit of Signs: Semiotics, Literature, Deconstruction, 1981) attempts a structuralist theory of interpretation in the analysis of readers' strategies, with an emphasis on the operation of interpretive moves rather than the content of the moves.

Another theory about the reader and reader responses has been proposed by Gerald Prince, who coins the term 'narratee' (*q.v.*). The 'narratee' is not the reader but the kind of person who is addressed by the narrator.

The American critic Stanley Fish evolved a reader-oriented theory which he calls 'affective stylistics'. He is concerned with the ways a reader's responses develop and change in relation to the words or sentences *as they succeed each other in time*.

Yet another aspect of reader-response theory is contained in what is known as 'reception theory' (*q.v.*), discussed by Hans Robert Jauss in connection with what he calls the 'horizon of expectations' (*q.v.*).

Reader-oriented theory is fundamental to phenomenology (*q.v.*) and phenomenological criticism and also to theories of hermeneutics (*q.v.*). *See also* IMPLIED READER/ACTUAL READER; READERLY/WRITERLY.

realism An exceptionally elastic critical term, often ambivalent and equivocal, which has acquired far too many qualifying (but seldom clarifying) adjectives, and is a term which many now feel we could do without.

Philosophy distinguishes two basic concepts concerning reality: correspondence and coherence. The correspondence theory suggests that the external world is knowable by scientific inquiry, by the accumulation of data, by documentation, by definition. The coherence theory suggests that the external world is knowable (or perhaps can be understood) by intuitive perception, by insight. Thus, correspondence will require referential language; coherence, emotive language. The former will imply an objective point of view; the latter a subjective. But, as language interpenetrates, no absolute divisions are possible.

To simplify here are two approximations to reality on the subject of a song thrush:

1. SONG THRUSH *Turdus philomelos*

Identification: 9″. A brown-backed bird, with a spotted breast. Distinguished from Mistle Thrush and Fieldfare by much smaller size, uniform *brown* upper-parts and yellowish-buff breast and flanks with *small spots*; from Redwing by lack of chestnut on flanks and beneath wings and lack of prominent supercilium. Shows *buff* beneath wings. Often feeds on open ground, running spasmodically. Voice: a loud '*tchuck*,' or '*tchick*,' repeated rapidly as alarm; flight-call a soft '*sip*' (shorter than Redwing's call). Song loud and musical, the short, varied phrases *repeated* 2–4 *times*, between brief pauses. Habitat: Around human habitations, parks, woods and hedges. Nests in bushes, hedges, ivy, etc., occasionally in buildings.

2. Terrifying are the attent sleek thrushes on the lawn,
More coiled steel than living – a poised
Dark deadly eye, those delicate legs
Triggered to stirrings beyond sense – with a start, a bounce,
a stab
Overtake the instant and drag out some writhing thing.
No indolent procrastinations and no yawning stares,
No sighs or head-scratchings. Nothing but bounce and stab
And a ravening second.

The first is an extract from Collins's *Field Guide to Birds of Britain and Europe*; the second is a quotation from Ted Hughes's poem *Thrushes*. Each is concerned with reality. Each is realistic within the limits of what it sets out to achieve: to give an impression or idea of a thrush to the receptor (*q.v.*). So different are the methods employed that it would be superfluous to point them out.

Fundamentally, in literature, realism is the portrayal of life with fidelity. It is thus not concerned with idealization, with rendering things as beautiful when they are not, or in any way presenting them in any guise as they are not; nor, as a rule, is realism concerned with presenting the supranormal or transcendental, though, of course, the writings of Richard Rolle of Hampole, for example, or the mystical poems of St John of the Cross, are realistic enough if we believe in God and the spiritual order. The writings of the mystic and the visionary perhaps belong to a rather special category which might be called 'super-reality'. On the whole one tends to think of realism in terms of the everyday, the normal, the pragmatic. More crudely, it suggests jackets off, sleeves rolled up, a 'no nonsense' approach.

One may suppose that most writers have been concerned with reality (and therefore with some attempt at some form of realism) since the year dot. Much of the world's literature can be accounted realistic; much epic (*q.v.*) for example, though it is often about supermen and improbably heroic deeds; most drama, even when it is very stylized, as in *Nō* (*q.v.*); a great deal of lyric (*q.v.*) poetry; the vast majority of fictional works . . . and so forth. In general this enormous body of literature displays what H. Levin has described as that 'willed tendency of art to approximate reality'. However, one can suggest that some literature is *more* realistic than other literature. For instance, most of the poetry written by George Crabbe, Kipling and Robert Frost is more realistic than most of the poetry written by, say, Spenser, Keats and Conrad Aiken. The novels of Zola, Gissing and Theodore Dreiser are much more realistic than the works of Huysmans, Firbank and Ivy Compton-Burnett. 'More realistic' in the sense of more down to earth, closer to everyday life, and thus well within the experience of the legendary man on the Clapham bus, or Clapham Man.

The use of the terms real and realistic clearly implies their antitheses, like unreal, unrealistic, fantastic, improbable, fanciful, of the dream world. The imaginative flights of bizarre invention that we find in some of Lucian's works, in Rabelais, in Voltaire's *Candide*, in H. G. Wells's *The War of the Worlds*, in Ray Bradbury's science fiction (*q.v.*) stories, are not realistic, though they are excellent fantasy based on reality. Occasionally a writer (e.g. Roald Dahl) manages to keep a beautiful and breathtaking balance on that high wire that joins both worlds.

In the end realism, as a literary term, is about as clear and bendable a term as, say, Romanticism (*q.v.*) and, as it happens, they are the -isms of two very different camps – if not campuses. In the last hundred years or so there have developed a large number of theories about realism, and about what is to be regarded as realistic or not. We can hardly avoid using the term on occasions, particularly when we mean to state or suggest that a work of literature has verisimilitude (*q.v.*) or in some way possesses that kind of authenticity which is generally believed to be an essential quality in a work of literature, however fantastic or improbable (in some cases) it might be – or *seems* to be.

The issue has been much confused by the fact that in the 19th c. – a period almost too fertile in antinomies, schools, movements and, to use the current jargon, 'cultural fissiparation' – there was a recognizable and conscious movement in literature which was subsequently tagged 'realism'. The French were responsible for this movement. It began some time in the 1830s and had gathered momentum by the 1850s. During the latter part of the century realism was a definite trend in European literature.

One of the earlier instances of the use of the term *le réalisme* is to be found in the *Mercure français du XIXe siècle* (1826). Here it refers to a point of view or doctrine which states that realism is a copy of nature and reveals to us the literature of truth. Realism rejects Classicism (*q.v.*), Romanticism and the doctrine of art for art's sake (*q.v.*).

It is clear that the realist thought an artist should concern himself with the here and now, with everyday events, with his own environment and with the movements (political, social, etc.) of his time. The anti-Romantic movements in Germany also concentrated attention on the lot of the common man and on the need to present life with all its warts. In general we can see clearly enough in the works of Immermann, Balzac and Dickens, for instance, what forms the realist attitude was likely to take.

Theory combined with practice in the 19th c. to produce a large body of literature which presented an altogether different view of the so-called *condition humaine*. The practice was almost certainly influenced by philosophical thought, and most notably by Comte's *Cours de philosophie positive* (1830). Comte's positivism made sociology a prime science. Later, the inquiries of Feuerbach and Darwin induced many people to re-appraise assumptions about their origin and to take a very different view of the environment. Later, also, Comte's theories were applied by Taine to the sphere of literature, especially in *Histoire de la littérature anglaise* (1863–4) and in *Nouveaux essais de critique et d'histoire* (1865). One may also suppose that the invention of photography in 1839 had an immense effect on the way people looked at the world and existence in general. Here was precision; the scene, the fact, the episode were faithfully recorded. The paintings of Courbet, too, had an incalculable influence. Courbet was strongly opposed to any kind of idealization in art. He rejected both Classical and Romantic precepts and tastes, and maintained that only realism was democratic. For him the peasant and the worker were the fittest and most estimable subjects for a painter. Champfleury, in *Le Réalisme* (1857), applied Courbet's point of view to literature and suggested that the hero in the novel should be an ordinary man. Here, no doubt, we have the egg of the so-called anti-hero (*q.v.*) whose genesis *appears* to have been of a later date.

It is a noteworthy curiosity of this realistic movement that in the first place realism was either defined negatively or rejected as undesirable. Courbet himself did not like it as a label though he used it himself. Champfleury expressed disapproval of it in his essays *Le Réalisme* (1857). Baudelaire described it as an 'injure dégoutante' and as a 'mot vague et élastique'. Edmond de Goncourt also expressed dislike of it in his preface to *Les Frères Zemganno* (1879). Distaste for the term seems to have arisen from a fear that realism would be regarded as a school or movement, which is how we are inclined to think of it now. As it happened Champfleury was the prime mover behind a trend already very apparent in the novels of Balzac and Stendhal. Champfleury's *Le Réalisme* was virtually a manifesto of a new doctrine.

In the same year in which Champfleury published this, Flaubert produced *Madame Bovary*, which was greeted as a great work of realism (later it was greeted as a great work of naturalism, *q.v.*). Flaubert, too, disliked the label. Other so-called realistic novels to appear at this period were *Germinie Lacerteux* (1865) by Edmond and Jules de Goncourt, and minor works by Ernest Feydeau, who wrote *Fanny* (1858), and Duranty, who wrote *Le Malheur d'Henriette Gérard* (1860).

The realist novelists paid particular attention to exact documentation, to getting the facts right, and in many ways were continuing in a more intensive and conscientious fashion what Balzac had been doing years before in *La Comédie humaine*. Balzac regarded man (and analysed character) as a zoologist might and he expressed the intention of following Buffon's work on zoology in order to write a natural history of man. This was a scientific approach which, at times, came near to the method of the field guide quoted above.

Zola and Maupassant have also been taken as exponents of realism but it is perhaps more correct to regard them as the supreme analysts of the school of naturalism. Zola's essays in *Le Roman expérimental* (1880) are one of the main statements about naturalism.

Outside France the effects of realism are to be seen in the works of Tolstoy, Gogol and Gorki, and, to a lesser extent, in Turgenev. Also in the work of Gissing and the American novelist William Dean Howells.

The long-term effects of what the French writers achieved are difficult to assess. In recent years attempts at more acute realism have quite often led to the kind of excesses to which Zola himself proved vulnerable in, for example, *Thérèse Raquin* (1868) and *Germinal* (1885). In fact the quest for truth and accuracy has degenerated on occasions into mere sensationalism, as in Mailer's *The Naked and the Dead* (1948) and James Jones's *From Here to Eternity* (1951). William Burroughs's 'junky' novels and the masturbatory fantasies of Roth's *Portnoy's Complaint* (1969) provide other instances of realism carried to extremes. There are scores of other works of less merit but comparable pretensions.

As far as drama is concerned, realism in the 19th c. was a less extreme form of naturalism. Playwrights who favoured realism – Ibsen is a key figure – rejected the concept of the well-made play (*q.v.*) with its mechanical artifices and its altogether too slick plotting, and rejected also exaggerated theatricalism. Ibsen's influence was very great, especially on Shaw and Strindberg, and subsequently on a whole generation of prominent 20th c. dramatists; not to mention Stanislavsky and the various adaptations of his teachings in method acting.

What is known as socialist realism (*q.v.*) in the theatre is largely a Russian phenomenon. Anatoli Lunacharsky (1875–1933) invented the theory of it. This involved the development of specifically Soviet theatre. Classics were to be interpreted in contemporary terms so that they became more relevant to the people. New plays should be about life lived by ordinary people. The effects of his teachings in Communist countries have been considerable, even where the Kremlin faith has been thrown over with consequent excommunication – as in Albania. Now, socialist realism suggests the committed propaganda (*q.v.*) of writers submissive to a particular political régime.

Realism occurs in another important context, namely psychological realism. This denotes fidelity to the truth in depicting the inner workings of the mind, the analysis of thought and feeling, the presentation of the nature of personality and character. Such realism also requires a fictional character to behave *in* character. The ultimate in psychological realism is the use of the stream of consciousness (*q.v.*) method. This kind of realism, too, has often resulted in a kind of decadence (*q.v.*) as authors dig deeper and further and with greater relish into the scatological and orectic chaos of the conscious and subconscious territories. *See also* ROMAN DOCUMENTAIRE; SLICE OF LIFE; VERISM.

recension A critical revision of a literary work.

reception theory A school of literary theory which is associated particularly with the University of Konstanz and the journal *Poetik and Hermeneutik* (published from 1964). One theorist, namely Hans Robert Jauss, is especially associated with the theory. He is concerned with the general response to literature in terms of reception-aesthetics rather than the individual's response, and he suggests that literary work should be studied in terms of the impression or impact it makes on its contemporary audience, and that literary value is judged according to how much the view of a text alters over time. 'Aesthetic distance' (*q.v.*) is the term used by Jauss to denote the difference between the contemporary view of a work of art (at the time of its first publication) and the present-day view. But still the idea holds that the reader has a contribution to make in the process. So there is a kind of balance and co-operation between text and what it provides and what the reader contributes. However, all readers are different and therefore may be supposed to bring a different response to any text.

More recently a number of American critics (e.g. Edward Said, Jonathan Culler and Stanley Fish) have become interested in 'reading communities' and institutions as determining forces in the reading of texts. Fish, for instance, holds that it is only within a given community or institution that the facts of literary study (i.e. genres, periods, authors, texts) are available and that these 'facts' are as much a product of the community as they are of the interpreters. Fish contends that all interpreters are extensions of communities. His collection of essays *Is There a Text in This Class?* (1980) is relevant. *See* FORMALISM, RUSSIAN; HORIZON OF EXPECTATIONS; PHENOMENOLOGY; READER-RESPONSE THEORY.

receptor A jargon term for the person (or group of persons) experiencing a work of art.

recessive accent This occurs when a word usually accented on its final syllable is followed by another heavily accented word. For the sake of meter and rhythm the accent is shifted to the beginning of the preceding word. A common practice in writing blank verse.

récit (F 'narration, narrative, accounts of events, recital') A form of fictional narrative which is related to the *novella*, the *Novelle*, the *roman* and the *nouvelle* (*qq.v.*). André Gide, one of its most notable practitioners, made a clear distinction between his *romans* and his *récits*. *Les Faux-monnayeurs* (1926), for instance, is a *roman*; *L'Immoraliste* (1902) and *La Porte étroite* (1909) are outstanding examples of the *récit*. Gide theorized about both forms, and debate as to precisely what a *récit* is and is not continues. Typically, a *récit* has a high degree of compression and concentration and the narrative is related from one point of view (two in *La Porte étroite*).

It has a single theme and very few characters, apart from the central character on whom attention is focused almost exclusively. Events and actions should speak for themselves and the reader is left to draw his or her own conclusions. Thus, there is no intervention on the part of the author to explain motives, pass judgements or draw conclusions. Gide's *récits* combine intimate personal experience with a technique which is aimed to exclude the presence of the author. His elimination of the author in some ways prefigures Roland Barthes's celebrated exposition *The Death of the Author* (*see* AUTHOR, DEATH OF). In order to achieve the required effacement he uses the first-person narrator device, but the first person is 'borrowed'. The author effaces himself behind his narrator (who is also his hero/heroine or one of the main characters). Whereas in a novel events tend to unfold in a chronological sequence and are described as they occur, the events in a *récit* are depicted by an oblique, reflective and associative method. *Récits* may be as long as novels and a plot may extend over a longer period of time than does the single and significant episode of the *nouvelle*. The *récit* seems to have a kind of intermediary position between novel and *nouvelle*. Apart from those cited, other examples which might fall into the *récit* category are Samuel Beckett's *Malone Dies* (1951) and Albert Camus's *La Chute* (1956). *See also* NARRATOLOGY.

recognition *See* ANAGNORISIS.

recoil A term used when speaking of tragedy (*q.v.*) to indicate that the protagonist has brought about his own doom.

recto and verso The *recto* is the right-hand page in a book; the *verso* the left-hand page.

recuesta (Sp 'request') A type of poetry written on request or commission by a *trovador*, the Spanish equivalent of the troubadour (*q.v.*). *See also* PREGUNTA.

redaction the editing or revising of a work for publication.

rederijkers Members of the chambers of rhetoric in the Netherlands in the 15th and 16th c. They were poets and students of poetry and are comparable to the Meistersingers (*q.v.*). Their main interests were dramatic and lyric poetry. *See* REFREIN; RHETORIQUEURS; STOCK.

redondilla (Sp 'little round', diminutive of *redondo* 'round, clear, straightforward'; or 'a round, ring, circle') An eight-syllable quatrain (*q.v.*) rhyming either abba or abab, but in the latter rhyme scheme is usually called *serventesio*. Sometimes *redondilla* is referred to as *redondilla mayor*, *cuarteta* and *cuartilla*. Formerly the term included the *quintilla* (*q.v.*) and was also applied to any eight-syllable strophe in which all the verses rhymed in consonance. This is an important form because it was adapted by one poet after another until Lope de Vega and Calderón used it very widely and often for specific purposes (for example, to create mood) in drama. In the verses of King Alfonso the Wise *redondillas* of *pie cruzado* are also to be found.

redundant verse *See* ACATALECTIC.

reduplicatio *See* ANADIPLOSIS.

reference, point of An idea developed by Coventry Patmore (*Principle in Art*, 1889) and first applied to painting. It was gradually adopted as a literary term, partly owing to Quiller Couch, and as such now denotes a figure, a character, who may be regarded as 'normal' or balanced in the sense that he keeps a sense of proportion amidst excesses. A sound example is the sane, good and pragmatic Kent in *King Lear. See also* IDEAL SPECTATOR.

referent *See* SIGNIFIER/SIGNIFIED.

referential language *See* EMOTIVE LANGUAGE.

reflexive novel A novel in which the author calls the reader's attention to the fact that he or she is writing (or has written) a novel. Thus, what Roland Barthes would call a 'writerly' novel. A classic and early example of such a work is Laurence Sterne's *Tristram Shandy* (1760–67), an attempt at autobiography in which virtually no progress is made. Sterne uses many devices to show that there is a discrepancy between reality/life and art, and that it is not possible to provide a coherent and rational picture of anything so complex as life and reality. Other reflexive novels of that period are Fielding's *Joseph Andrews* (1742) and his *Tom Jones* (1749).

In the 19th c. most novelists tried to give form, shape and rationality to their versions of reality, though this often tended to falsify reality in the cause of artistic and aesthetic coherence. Periodically, one can see that novelists were well aware of the inherent shortcomings of the endeavour to impose form on the disorderly or chaotic.

In the 20th c. numerous novelists have developed various forms of reflexive novel. James Joyce (with *Ulysses*, 1922) is an outstanding example. So is Gide's *Les Faux-monnayeurs* (1926). Since the 1950s we should also mention the work of Vladimir Nabokov, Flann O'Brien, William Burroughs, Christine Brooke-Rose, Samuel Beckett, Alain Robbe-Grillet, Thomas Pynchon and John Fowles. This kind of fiction is also sometimes called 'self-conscious' or 'self-referential'. *See* ANTI-NOVEL; NOUVEAU ROMAN; READERLY/WRITERLY; STREAM OF CONSCIOUSNESS.

refrain A phrase, line or lines repeated at intervals during a poem and especially at the end of a stanza. A device of great antiquity, it is found in the Egyptian *Book of the Dead*, the Bible, Greek and Latin verse, in Provençal and Renaissance verse and in many ballads (*q.v.*). Very often it is an exact repetition. Sometimes it serves to work out an 'argument' (*q.v.*) in a poem, in which case it will undergo slight modifications, as in this fine lyric by Sir Thomas Wyatt:

Disdain me not without desert,
  Nor leave me not so suddenly;
Since well ye wot that in my heart
  I mean ye not but honestly.
    Disdain me not.

Refuse me not without cause why,
  Nor think me not to be unjust;
Since that by lot of fantasy
  This careful knot needs knit I must.
    Refuse me not.

Mistrust me not, though some there be
  That fain would spot my steadfastness;
Believe them not, since that we see
  The proof is not as they express.
    Mistrust me not.

Forsake me not till I deserve
  Nor hate me not till I offend;
Destroy me not till that I swerve;
  But since ye know what I intend,
    Forsake me not.

Disdain me not that am your own:
  Refuse me not that am so true:
Mistrust me not till all be known:
  Forsake me not ne for no new.
    Disdain me not.

See REPETEND; REPETITION.

refrán (Sp 'refrain') But not a refrain in the English sense. It is, rather, equivalent to a saying, proverb (*q.v.*), saw, or popular maxim (*q.v.*); and synonymous with the French *dicton*. In Spanish verse it often comprises two short phrases rhyming in consonance or assonance (*qq.v.*) and containing alliteration. Usually, too, it has some sonic device which makes it easily memorable (like the alliteration and assonance in the English phrase 'as cool as a cucumber'). The word may be of French provenance and came into general use in the 15th c. Much Spanish literature of that period stemmed from *refranes*, which dealt with many subjects and aspects of life. The poet, the Marqués de Santillana (1398–1458), at the king's request, made a collection of these nuggets of wisdom.

refrein A poetic form very popular among the *rederijkers* (*q.v.*) in the Netherlands. It consists of four or more stanzas of the same length and rhyme scheme, each of which concludes with an identical line. It derived from the French *refrain* (*q.v.*) and very probably originates in the French *ballade* (*q.v.*). *See* STOCK.

regional novel A regional writer is one who concentrates much attention on a particular area and uses it and the people who inhabit it as the basis for his or her stories. Such a locale is likely to be rural and/or provincial. Among the earliest of regional novelists was Maria Edgeworth (1767–1849), an Anglo-Irish woman who was one of the first to perceive the possibilities of relating characters to a particular environment. Her most notable novels were *Castle Rackrent* (1800), *Belinda* (1801) and *The Absentee* (1812).

Castle Rackrent is generally believed to have been the first of its kind. It was followed quite soon by novels by the Irish writer Lady

Morgan (1776–1859). The Scottish novels of John Galt (1779–1839) and Sir Walter Scott (1771–1832) were also closely dependent on regional study and atmosphere. Once established, the regional novel began to interest a number of writers, and soon the regions described became smaller and more specifically defined. For example, the novels of Mrs Gaskell (1810–65) and George Eliot (1819–80) centred on the Midlands, and those of the Brontë sisters were set in Yorkshire. Other novelists to concentrate on particular areas were Charles Kingsley (1819–75) and R. D. Blackmore (1825–1900), who set their scenes in Devon, Richard Jefferies (1848–87), who concentrated on his native Hampshire (and Wiltshire), Robert Louis Stevenson (1850–94), who wrote about the Highlands and Lowlands, and J. M. Barrie (1860–1937), who was devoted to Angus.

The four outstanding regional novelists were: Thomas Hardy (1840–1928), who re-created the West Country (especially Dorset) in many of his novels and short stories and revived the name Wessex; Arnold Bennett (1867–1931), who centred many of his stories on the Potteries – 'the five towns'; D. H. Lawrence (1885–1930), who evoked his native Nottinghamshire; and William Faulkner (1897–1962), whose main focus was the Deep South in the USA.

There were also 'urban' or 'industrial' novels, set in a particular town or city, some of which had considerable fame in the 19th c. and some of which remain major novels. Notable instances are Mrs Gaskell's *Mary Barton* (1848) and her *North and South* (1854–5), Charles Dickens's *Hard Times* (1854) and George Eliot's *Middlemarch* (1871–2).

The tradition of the regional novel in Britain is by no means defunct. Latterly, Stanley Middleton and Stanley Barstow have both written a number of such novels; the former about his native Nottinghamshire and the latter about his native Yorkshire. Alan Sillitoe has also contributed to this form of fiction.

Other distinguished writers of this kind were the Spanish Countess Emilia Pardo Bazán, who wrote about Galician life in the 19th c.; Grazia Deledda (1871–1936), who wrote mostly about Sardinia and its people; Ivan Cankar (1876–1918), the Slovene dramatist and writer of short stories whose native Slovenia was the scene of much of his work; Ivo Andrić (1892–1975), a number of whose novels and short stories are about his native Bosnia, and in particular the small townships of Travnik and Višegrad; and Jean Giono (1895–1970), who re-created the region of Provence in several of his books. *See* CONDITION OF ENGLAND NOVEL; COSTUMBRISMO; LOCAL COLOUR; NOVEL; REALISM.

register A list of facts or names. A precise record. A volume into which information is entered systematically. Early examples of register were the *Doomsday Book* and a bead-roll. *See* ROLL.

regressio *See* EPANADOS.

Reimrede (G 'rhyme speech') A form of poetry comprising continuous rhyming couplets not in strophic form. To be spoken rather than sung. Fairly common in the 14th and 15th c.

rejet A term in French prosody which denotes that the sense in one line of verse is completed in the next; that part 'run over' is the *rejet. See also* ENJAMBEMENT; RUN-ON LINE.

relativism In aesthetics the term refers to a situation in which it is logically possible for two contradictory 'value judgements' to be true and known to be true. For instance: (a) this is a good novel; (b) this novel is bad. Apart from the subjective nature of the critic's opinion and tastes it must be remembered that sensibility changes from age to age, and what was regarded as a good novel in 1900 may be thought much otherwise fifty years later. *See* ABSOLUTISM.

remate (Sp 'end, finish, finishing touch', from the verb *rematar* 'to end, to stop, to finish off') The last and shortest stanza of a *canción* or song. It goes under other names: *commiato*, *despido*, *envio*, *contera*, *vuelta*, *ripressa. See also* ENVOI.

Renaissance (F 'rebirth', from Italian *rinascenza*, *rinascimento*) The original meaning of the Italian *rinascimento* for those who actually took part in it was the 'rebirth' of Classical Greek and Latin literature. The term is commonly applied to the historical period which follows the Middle Ages, but when the Middle Ages ended and when the Renaissance began has been a source of much debate. A long-accepted view was that the Renaissance began in the latter half of the 14th c. and that it continued throughout the 15th and 16th c. and perhaps even later. In order to make the issues more manageable historians have identified periods within the period; hence, early, middle, high and late Renaissance.

In the course of time a variety of misconceptions about the

Middle Ages (as opposed to the Renaissance) developed. These became particularly apparent in the 19th c. when, among some, there evolved an image of the Middle Ages as being ignorant, narrow, priest-ridden, backward, superstitious, uncultured and inhibitied by dogmatic theology. By contrast, the Renaissance was extolled as learned, civilized, broadminded, progressive, enlightened and free-thinking. The derogatory view of the Middle Ages was encouraged by such writers as Jules Michelet (1798–1874), J. A. Symonds (1840–93) and G. G. Coulton (1858–1947). J. A. Symonds was even capable of saying that: 'The arts and the inventions, the knowledge and the books which suddenly became vital at the Renaissance, had long been neglected on the shores of the Dead Sea which we call the Middle Ages.' Moreover, misconceptions about the Renaissance (and, *ipso facto*, the Middle Ages) were presented by Jacob Burckhardt (1818–97) and Walter Pater (1839–94).

Nor have the terms 'medieval' and 'middle ages' by any means lost their pejorative connotations. People still use them to suggest the backward and the primitive. The late Sir Julian Huxley was capable of doing so. Such implied attitudes overlook the facts that the period 1100–1400 produced such men as (and this is a random selection): Abelard, Hartmann von der Aue, Walther von der Vogelweide, Wolfram von Eschenbach, Albert the Great, St Bernard, Thomas Aquinas, Peter Lombard, Roger Bacon, Guinicelli, Ramon Llull, Giovanni Pisano, Vincent of Beauvais, Meister Eckhart, William Langland and Chaucer . . . And such cathedrals as those of Piacenza, Rochester, Chartres, Mainz, Lisbon, Modena, Verona, Siena, Notre Dame de Paris, Rheims, Amiens, Salisbury, Burgos, Toledo and Cologne . . .

Opinions like those of J. A. Symonds have been totally discredited during the 20th c. and in recent years historians' views about the Renaissance have been considerably modified. Moreover, there has been a tendency to think in terms of several renaissances, each succeeding the other and each gathering a kind of momentum from its predecessor(s). Such a view has, for instance, been put persuasively by Irwin Panofsky in *Meaning in the Visual Arts* (1955). The beginnings of the Renaissance have been pushed further and further back, even as far as the 12th c. – and not without justice. At that time Romanesque architecture was at a high point of development and Gothic architecture was beginning. Vernacular literatures were developing. There was a revival of the Latin classics, Latin poetry and Roman law. Greek philosophy and Greek and

Arab scientific discoveries were becoming known. The first European universities were being founded. In short, intellectual and creative activity abounded.

Italy is customarily taken as the starting place of the Renaissance but authorities differ as to when. As far as literature is concerned, some settle for the 14th c. (even though this omits a considerable part of Dante's life, 1265–1321). Others prefer the 13th c. and cite the Sicilian School (*q.v.*), that group of talented poets who flourished at the Palermo court of the Hohenstaufen monarchs from *c.* 1200. We should also note that there was a modest literary Renaissance in Bohemia (and other parts of what is now Czechoslovakia) during the 14th c.

It may be that attempts to identify a beginning to the Renaissance are not particularly helpful or fruitful. We might cite the problems inherent in tracing the development of painting from *c.* 1150. For instance, Cimabue (*c.* 1240–*c.* 1302), Duccio (*c.* 1255/60–*c.* 1318/19) and Giotto (*c.* 1266/7–1337) are often taken to be important pioneers of the Renaissance in Italy (and so they were), but what they attempted and achieved in their work had *already* been anticipated by court painters (e.g. Dimitrije, Djordje and Teodor) in the churches built under the Nemanjić dynasty in the Balkans (usually referred to as the 'Raška School') late in the 12th c. and early in the 13th c., and was later often excelled by the successors (e.g. Astrapas, Mihajlo and Eutihije) of those painters in the late 13th c. and early 14th c.

Broadly speaking it may be said that between *c.* 1200 and *c.* 1600 man's opinions about the nature and structure of the universe (and the role of man in it) brought about profound and far-reaching changes. But the gradualness of these changes must be emphasized. Many attitudes, beliefs and convictions which were commonplace in, say, the 15th c. were still widespread in the 17th. Whether these changes were for good or evil can be argued endlessly.

The gradualness may perhaps be underlined by referring to two outstanding personalities: Ramon Llull and Sir Thomas More. Llull was a Catalan; a gifted poet, a scholar, philosopher, linguist, theologian and encyclopaedist, a prolific author in many fields (his extant works number 243). He spent between 30 and 40 years of his, for those days, exceptionally long life, in travelling over Europe and North Africa in the promotion of the cause of Catholicism. Sir Thomas More's achievements are too well known to need reiteration. Ramon Llull was born in 1235 and died *c.* 1315. More was born in 1478 and executed in 1535. Llull was beatified by the Church and

More was canonized. One cannot help feeling that, had they been contemporaries, they would have found much in common. They were both 'Renaissance men'.

Again, broadly speaking, it may be suggested that a survey of the achievements of painters, writers, sculptors and architects (not to mention scientists, philosophers and astronomers) between say, 1200 and 1600, reveals almost continuous creative and intellectual activity of an excellence which may never be equalled. To catalogue the names is to intone a litany of geniuses.

Among writers those invariably mentioned are: Dante, Petrarch, Boccaccio, Machiavelli and Sanazzaro in Italy; Erasmus in the Netherlands; Montaigne, Rabelais and the poets of the Pléiade (*q.v.*) in France; Lope de Vega and Cervantes in Spain; Sir Thomas More, Sir Thomas Wyatt, Edmund Spenser, Sir Philip Sidney, Shakespeare and Sir Francis Bacon in England. *See* HUMANISM; SCHOLASTICISM.

renga A Japanese verse form; a kind of linked verse in which successive half *tanka* (*q.v.*) are composed by different poets.

repartee A witty or clever rejoinder, as in the story of Bernard Shaw meeting a very fat man on a narrow staircase. Shaw shoved his way past him. 'Pig!' said the fat man angrily. Shaw raised his hat and replied: 'Shaw. Good afternoon.'

repetend A repeated element in a poem; a word, a phrase or a line. The term can be used as a synonym for a refrain (*q.v.*), but a repetend is usually more varied than a refrain and occurs at different and unexpected points in a poem. It is a kind of echo and a common device. A number of excellent examples are to be found in T. S. Eliot's *The Love Song of J. Alfred Prufrock*. *See* INCREMENTAL REPETITION; REPETITION.

repetitio *See* ANAPHORA.

repetition An essential unifying element in nearly all poetry and much prose. It may consist of sounds, particular syllables and words, phrases, stanzas, metrical patterns, ideas, allusions and shapes. Thus refrain, assonance, rhyme, internal rhyme, alliteration and onomatopoeia (*qq.v.*) are frequent in repetition. *Hoarding* by Roger McGough contains some ordinary repetitive elements:

all too busy boarding

thirty year old numbskull
with a change of dirty coats
every single day gets porridge
but never gets his oats

all too busy boarding
the xmas merry-go-round

old lady sits by the firegrate
knitting a pudding with twine
dreams of brandy sauce
drinks methylated wine

all too busy boarding
the xmas merry-go-round
hoarding hoarding hoarding

girl in the secondhand nightie
with bruises on her brain
dips her thumb in the coldcream
sucks it over again

all too busy boarding
the xmas merry-go-round
hoarding hoarding hoarding
forgodssake giveusapound

This example in prose comes from the closing pages of Samuel Beckett's novel *Malone Dies*:

This tangle of grey bodies is they. Silent, dim, perhaps clinging to one another, their heads buried in their cloaks, they lie together in a heap, in the night. They are far out in the bay. Lemuel has shipped his oars, the oars trail in the water. The night is strewn with absurd

absurd lights, the stars, the beacons, the buoys, the lights of earth and in the hills the faint fires of the blazing gorse. Macmann, my last, my possessions, I remember, he is there too, perhaps he sleeps. Lemuel.

Lemuel is in charge, he raises his hatchet on which the blood will never dry, but not to hit anyone, he will not hit anyone, he will not hit anyone any more, he will not touch anyone any more, either with it or with it or with it or with or or with it or with his hammer or with his stick or with his fist or in thought in dream I mean never he will never

or with his pencil or with his stick or

or light light I mean

never there he will never

never anything

there

any more

replevin (OF *replevir*, from *plevir* 'to pledge') Of legal origin, it denotes an inquiry intended to restore to the owner goods which have been in some way wrongfully distrained. As a literary term it denotes an inquiry intended to secure for a writer recognition which has been denied.

resolution Those events which form the outcome of the climax of a play or story. The equivalent of falling action (*q.v.*).

rest A metrical term adopted from music. It indicates where a pause seems to compensate for the absence of an unstressed syllable (or syllables) in a foot.

Restoration comedy That kind of drama which prevailed between the restoration of the English monarchy in 1660 and the advent of sentimental comedy (*q.v.*) early in the 18th c. It is also referred to as artificial comedy or comedy of manners (*q.v.*) and was chiefly concerned with presenting a society of elegance and stylishness. Its characters were gallants, ladies and gentlemen of fashion and rank, fops, rakes, social climbers and country bumpkins. Witty, urbane and sometimes licentious, it dealt with the intricacies of sexual and marital intrigue and therefore also with adultery and cuckoldry. A five-star constellation of gifted playwrights were largely responsible for this resurgence of theatrical life after the Puritan period. They were Wycherley, Etheredge, Congreve, Vanbrugh and Farquhar. The main plays were: Wycherley's *The Country Wife* (1672 or 1673) and *The Plain Dealer* (1674); Etheredge's *The Man of Mode* (1676); Congreve's *The Double Dealer* (1694), *Love for Love* (1895) and *The Way of the World* (1700); Vanbrugh's *The Relapse* (1697) and *The Provoked Wife* (1697); Farquhar's *The Recruiting Officer*

(1706) and *The Beaux' Stratagem* (1707). These last two were somewhat less mannered and artificial than their predecessors. *See* COMEDY; RESTORATION PERIOD.

Restoration period It is usually taken to apply to the period from 1660 (the year Charles II was re-established as monarch) to the end of the century. The outstanding writers in this age were John Aubrey, Dryden, Congreve, Sir John Vanbrugh, Farquhar, Etheredge, Wycherley, Pepys, George Savile Marquess of Halifax, Otway, Samuel Butler, the Earl of Rochester, and Sir William Temple. Dryden was the major writer of the period in both verse and prose. *See also* RESTORATION COMEDY.

resumptio *See* EPANALEPSIS.

retroencha A Provençal lyric form which had a refrain (*q.v.*) at the end of each stanza.

revenge tragedy A form of tragic drama in which someone (usually a hero or a villain) rights a wrong. Perhaps the earliest instance of a kind of revenge tragedy is the *Oresteia* of Aeschylus. During the Renaissance period two main 'revenge' traditions are discernible: first, the French–Spanish tradition, best exemplified in the work of Lope de Vega (1562–1635), Calderón (1600–81) and Corneille (1606–84). In their treatment of revenge themes the emphasis is on the point of honour (*see* CALDERONIAN HONOUR) and the conflict between love and duty. English revenge tragedy owed much to Senecan tragedy (*q.v.*). The Elizabethan dramatists took Seneca as a model and the Roman stoic's influence can be seen in a considerable body of drama between *c.* 1580 and *c.* 1630. His plays were sensational, melodramatic and savage and emphasised bloodshed and vengeance. One of the earliest English Senecan-type tragedies was *Gorboduc* (1561), in which there is a revenge element: Porrex, one of the sons of King Gorboduc and Queen Videna, kills his brother Ferrex. The mother revenges the murder by killing Porrex. However, it was Thomas Kyd who established the genre of revenge tragedy in England with *The Spanish Tragedy* (*c.* 1586). This play contains many of the basic features of the genre. It begins with the introduction of a ghost and with the character of Revenge. In the course of the play they function as Chorus (*q.v.*) to an elaborate intrigue in which Hieronomo seeks revenge for his murdered son. Hieronomo pretends to be mad and presents a play in dumb show (*q.v.*) at court. *The Spanish Tragedy* was a sensational play which pleased the Elizabethan taste for blood, melodrama and rhetoric. It was popular (though ridiculed by writers of the period) and had a wide influence.

Shakespeare's first attempt at the genre was *Titus Andronicus* (1594). This is similar in construction to *The Spanish Tragedy* and deeply under its influence. It is one of the bloodiest and most horrific of all plays. Later, Shakespeare was to raise the genre to its highest level with *Hamlet* (1603–4). He may have been influenced by what is known as the *Ur-Hamlet*, a play not extant.

A different kind of revenge tragedy was Marlowe's *The Jew of Malta* (*c.* 1592), a kind of chronicle history concerned with the siege of Malta in which the central character is Barabas, a revengeful Jew, and a Machiavel (*q.v.*) type. John Marston's *Antonio's Revenge* (1600) carried on the Kyd tradition and was unmarked by Marlowe's influence; but Marston's play *The Malcontent* (1604) – a rare example of comedy involving revenge in the tragic tradition – has a plurality of revenging characters and also a revenger in disguise. In *Hoffman* (1602), Henry Chettle had already achieved a further development by making his hero revenger a villain (*q.v.*) who has no good cause, who is morally corrupt and exults in his villainous deeds rather as Iago does in *Othello* (1604). *Othello* is not a revenge tragedy but Iago is the supreme villain of the period and much of the play is concerned with the way in which he takes his revenge on the Moor. Cyril Tourneur's *The Revenger's Tragedy* (1607) is the last of the major tragedies in the tradition of Kyd but the villain revenger is a different kind of person from any of the villains hitherto. From about this time the villain became more and more prominent. In many plays the protagonist was a villain and the themes of revenge and motives of revenge became more and more complex.

In its decadence revenge tragedy became increasingly sensational and macabre. Ghosts, apparitions, graveyards, charnel houses, incest, insanity, adultery, rape, murder, infanticide, suicide, arson, poisoning and treachery were commonplace elements. Moral and political corruption were displayed in lurid detail. The characters inhabited microcosms of hell in which the plotting villains went about their work with sardonic relish, devising ever more bizarre methods of destroying people. Death was the main subject on their syllabus and murder their recreation.

Among other major works which have revenge themes mention should be made of: George Chapman's *The Revenge of Bussy*

D'Ambois (1607); Tourneur's *The Atheist's Tragedy* (1611); Webster's *The White Devil* (1612) and *The Duchess of Malfi* (*c.* 1613–14); and Middleton and Rowley's *The Changeling* (1622).

Of the many minor works in this tradition, some of the more outstanding are: John Fletcher's *The Bloody Brother* (*c.* 1616); Thomas Drue's *The Bloody Banquet* (1620); Massinger's *The Duke of Milan* (1620); James Shirley's *The Maid's Revenge* (1626); and Henry Glapthorne's *Revenge for Honour* (1640).

This kind of drama did not become wholly extinct. Shelley's closet drama (*q.v.*) *The Cenci* (1819) is in the revenge tradition. So are Victor Hugo's *Hernani* (1830) and his *Ruy Blas* (1838). In more recent times Lorca's *Blood Wedding* (1933) continued the form. Arthur Miller's *A View from the Bridge* (1955) treated of the Sicilian point-of-honour revenge in a modern setting. David Rudkin's *Afore Night Come* (1962) also contained revenge elements. *See* TRAGEDY.

reverdie An OF dance form which celebrated the advent of spring. In structure it is similar to the *chanson* (*q.v.*) and has five or six stanzas without a refrain (*q.v.*).

reversal *See* PERIPETEIA.

reversio *See* ANASTROPHE.

Revesby play A remarkable example of English folk drama which comes from Revesby, Lincolnshire. It is akin to the Mumming Play and the Plough Monday Play (*qq.v.*). The characters are the Fool and his sons (Pickle Herring, Blue Breeches, Pepper Breeches and Ginger Breeches) and Mr Allspice and Cicely. The Fool has a battle with a hobby-horse and a dragon. The sons perform a ritual killing of the Fool. But the Fool is revived and there follows a sword dance (*q.v.*) and the wooing of Cicely by the Fool and his sons. In all probability this is a dramatic survival of a fertility rite which symbolizes the death of the old year and the resurrection in the spring. *See also* PACE-EGGING PLAY.

review (a) A short notice or discussion or critical article in a paper, journal or periodical; (b) A journal or periodical containing articles on literature, art and philosophy. The *Edinburgh Review* is a famous example: so is the *Quarterly Review*. Publications like *Horizon*, *Scrutiny*, the *London Magazine*, *Essays in Criticism* and *Encounter* might well be placed in this category. *See also* PERIODICAL.

revolving stage Often called merely a 'revolve', it is a turntable stage which dates from Roman theatres in the 1st c. BC. In modern times it was first used *c.* 1760 in the Japanese *kabuki* (*q.v.*) theatre. In Europe, the first dates from 1896 in Munich. Such a stage is now a standard piece of equipment in most large theatres and is a great help in bringing about rapid scene changes.

revue A theatrical entertainment comprising dance, song, sketches, mime (*q.v.*) and improvisation. It is usually satirical and topical. Reference to the form is first found in Planché's *Recollections* (1872) when he claims to have been responsible for the first revue on the English stage: a work called *Success: or, a Hit if You Like It* (1825). But this was no more than a review (*q.v.*) of productions in the previous season. The first revue in the modern sense of the term was *Under the Clock* (1893), by Seymour Hicks and Charles Brookfield. In the early 20th c. this kind of entertainment became very popular, and so it continued to be during the First World War. In America revue started up with the *Ziegfeld Follies* in 1907. Since then the vogue for revue has waned little. Famous names associated with it have been C. B. Cochran, Noël Coward and Herbert Farjeon. Notable successes have been *Apple Sauce* (1940); *New Faces* (1940); *Rise Above It* (1941); *Sweet and Low* (1943); *Oranges and Lemons* (1949); *Airs on a Shoestring* (1953).

In 1961 was produced *Beyond the Fringe*, a highly successful attempt at satirical revue which had considerable influence; especially, for instance, on *The Royal Commission Revue* (1964).

Other well-known instances have been *At the Drop of a Hat* (1956) and *At the Drop of Another Hat* (1962), both devised and performed by Michael Flanders and Donald Swann. *See also* EXTRAVAGANZA.

rhapsody (Gk 'stitch song') In ancient Greece a rhapsodist was an itinerant minstrel who recited epic poetry. Part came from memory: part was improvised. A rhapsodist was thus a poet who 'stitched' together various elements.

In a more general sense a rhapsody may be an effusive and emotional (perhaps even ecstatic) utterance in verse or, occasionally, in prose. *See also* GUSLAR; SCOP; SKALD; TROUBADOUR; TROUVERE.

rhetoric (Gk *rhētōr* 'speaker in the assembly') Rhetoric is the art of using language for persuasion, in speaking or writing; especially in oratory. The Classical theoreticians codified rhetoric very thoroughly. A knowledge and command of it was regarded as essential. The major textbooks included Aristotle's *Rhetoric*; Quintilian's *Institutio Oratoria*; Cicero's *De Inventione*, *De Optimo Genere Oratorum* and *De Oratore*. Cicero himself was an accomplished rhetorician. So great was the influence of these men (and, later, of Longinus in the work ascribed to him, *On the Sublime*) that in the Middle Ages rhetoric became part of the *trivium*, together with logic and grammar.

The rules for oral and written composition (these rules altered little from Cicero's day until well on in the 19th c.) were divided into five processes in a logical order: invention, arrangement (or disposition), style, memory and delivery (each had a large number of sub-divisions). 'Invention' (*q.v.*) was the discovery of the relevant material; 'arrangement' was the organization of the material into sound structural form; under 'style' (*q.v.*) came the consideration of the appropriate manner for the matter and the occasion (e.g. the grand style, the middle and the low or plain); under 'memory' came guidance on how to memorize speeches; the section devoted to 'delivery' elaborated the technique for actually making a speech (*q.v.*).

rhetorical figure An artful arrangement of words to achieve a particular emphasis and effect, as in apostrophe, chiasmus and zeugma (*qq.v.*). A rhetorical figure does not alter the meanings of words, as a metaphor (*q.v.*) may do. The repetitions in these lines from Gerard Manley Hopkins's *St Winefred's Well* are rhetorical in their emphasis and echoing:

T. What is it, Gwen, my girl?| why do you hover and haunt me?
W. You came by Caerwys, sir?|
V. I came by Caerwys.
W. There
Some messenger there might have | met you from my uncle.
T. Your uncle met the messenger – | met me; and this the message:
Lord Bueno comes to night.|
W. To night, sir!

See RHETORIC.

rhetorical irony A form of irony (*q.v.*) in which the attitude and tone of the speaker or writer is the exact opposite of what is expressed.

Such irony is common in the work of Swift, Voltaire, Samuel (*Erehwon*) Butler and Anatole France.

rhetorical question Basically a question not expecting an answer, or one to which the answer is more or less self-evident. It is used primarily for stylistic effect, and is a very common device in public speaking – especially when the speaker is trying to work up the emotional temperature. For example (a politician on the hustings):

> Are we going to tolerate this intrusion upon our freedom? Are we going to accept these restrictions? Are we to be intimidated by time-serving bureaucrats? Are we to be suppressed by sycophantic and supine jackals waiting for dead men's shoes?

Or the writer may argue with himself (and in a different way work upon the emotions of the reader) as Sir Philip Sidney does in the 47th sonnet of the sequence *Astrophil and Stella*:

> What, have I thus betrayed my libertie?
> Can those blacke beames such burning markes engrave
> In my free side? or am I borne a slave,
> Whose necke becomes such yoke of tyranny?
> Or want I sense to feele my miserie?
> Or sprite, disdained of such disdaine to have?

Another fundamental form of rhetorical question is that to which an answer is at once supplied. A particularly good example of this is Falstaff's disquisition on 'honour' in *King Henry IV*, Pt I (V, i, 131).

Two other kinds of rhetorical question (both having something in common with the above) are: (a) a series of questions in quick succession for emphasis (e.g. 'Can we make it? If so, will it work? Where can we market it? Where can we market it cheaply?' and so on); (b) a question put to another person or oneself which expresses surprise, astonishment or anger and which is not easily answered. A good example is Bolingbroke's outburst in *Richard II* (I, iii, 294) after he has been banished:

> O, who can hold a fire in his hand
> By thinking on the frosty Caucasus?
> Or cloy the hungry edge of appetite
> By bare imagination of a feast?
> Or wallow naked in December snow
> By thinking on fantastic summer's heat?

See also RHETORIC; RHETORICAL FIGURE; RHETORICAL IRONY.

rhétoriqueurs A group of French poets who flourished late in the 15th and early in the 16th c. at the court of Burgundy and in Paris. They were obscure, difficult poets who went in for complex allegory, intricate rhyme and meter, involved rhetoric and a high degree of formalism. Among the better known are Alain Chartier, Jean Lemaire de Belges, Molinet, Crétin and Jean Marot. They have no counterparts in England or elsewhere.

rhopalic verse (Gk *rhopalon* 'cudgel') Thus, verse thicker at one end than the other, by dint of each word being a syllable longer than its predecessor, or each line a foot longer. So, for example, Crashaw's *Wishes to His Supposed Mistress* begins:

> Whoe'er she be
> That not impossible She
> That shall command my heart and me;

The first line is a dimeter, the second a trimeter, the third a tetrameter (*qq.v.*) – and so the poem continues for forty-two stanzas in all. *See also* PATTERN POETRY; PRUNING POEM.

rhozzum A word of obscure origin which denotes a short humorous tale (*q.v.*), often about a local character. They tend to belong (or *have* belonged) to oral tradition (*q.v.*). Students of folklore, historians of folk literature, and anthropologists (among others) have recorded many of them. They tend also to belong to rural communities and some are very old indeed. Like many other kinds of folk tale they have been classified into types and enjoy a degree of universality. A well-known example is 'The Irishman's Hat' (also called 'The Hat that Paid' and 'The Hat that Pays for Everything'). The theme is guile and gullibility. In various forms it is known all over Europe, Asia and the New World. Other instances fairly widespread in Britain are: 'The Farmer and the "Parson"'; 'The Three Foreigners' (also widely known in Europe, India and the New World); 'The Deaf Man and the Pig Trough' (also known in India and North America); 'The Borrowdale Cuckoo' (a very funny story which has variants in different parts of Britain and varies in length considerably); and 'Growing the Church' – known in Somerset, Herefordshire, Oxfordshire and Suffolk as well as in New York. The rhozzum is a relative of, among other things, the tall story, the shaggy dog story, fable, *fabliau*, *Märchen* and *fatrasie* (*qq.v.*).

rhupunt A Welsh syllabic verse form. It comprises lines of three, four or five sections and each section contains four syllables. All but the last section rhyme with each other. The last section carries the main rhyme from line to line.

rhyme (OF *rime* 'series') Rhyme has two main functions: (a) it echoes sounds and is thus a source of aesthetic satisfaction. There is pleasure in the sound itself and in the coincidence of sounds, and this pleasure must be associated with the sense of music, of rhythm (*q.v.*) and beat; the pulse sense which is common to all human beings. Part of the pleasure often consists of the surprise that a successful and unexpected rhyme evokes; this is especially true of comic verse where ingenious rhymes make an important contribution to the humour; (b) Rhyme assists in the actual structure of verse. It helps to organize the verse, simultaneously opening up and concluding the sense. Thus it is a rhythmical device for intensifying the meaning as well as for 'binding' the verse together. The rhythmical effects are particularly noticeable with head and internal rhyme (*qq.v.*). Rhyme also helps to make verse easier to remember. Though many poets have not used rhyme – and some have spoken against it – it is unquestionably the commonest and most ancient form of metrical devices. *See also* RIME.

rhyme counterpoint A poetic device in which line length is opposed to rhyme scheme. The rhymed lines are of unequal length; the unrhymed of equal length.

rhyme royal A stanza form of seven decasyllabic lines rhyming ababbcc and so called, in all probability, from its use by James I of Scotland in *Kingis Quair* (1423). Because Chaucer was the first to use it in *Complaint unto Pity* it is also known as the Chaucerian stanza. Chaucer employed it in *Troilus and Criseyde*, *The Parlement of Foules* and several of *The Canterbury Tales*. Other poets who have experimented with it include Sir Thomas Wyatt, Edmund Spenser, Shakespeare, Michael Drayton, William Morris and John Masefield. *See* HEPTASTICH; RHYME; SCOTTISH CHAUCERIANS; SEPTET.

rhyme scheme Used to denote the pattern of rhymes in a stanza or poem. It is usually represented by small letters, thus: ababbcc (the rhyme royal, *q.v.*, scheme). *See* RHYME.

rhyming slang A form of cryptic speech devised and used by cockney people. It is based on a trick rhyme, in which a phrase is substituted for the word; as in, 'apples and pears' for 'stairs'. Occasionally the word is twice removed from its name in rhyming slang, as in 'use your loaf' from 'use your head' which rhymes with 'bread'. Other well-known examples are: trouble and strife/wife; plates of meat/feet; Hampstead Heath/teeth; titfor (titfortat)/hat; tea-leaf/thief; north and south/mouth. There are hundreds of such phrases, many of which have been gathered in Julian Franklyn's *A Dictionary of Rhyming Slang* (1960). *See also* BACK SLANG; CANT; COCKNEY RHYMES; SLANG.

rhythm (Gk 'flowing') In verse or prose, the movement or sense of movement communicated by the arrangement of stressed and unstressed syllables and by the duration (*q.v.*) of the syllables. In verse the rhythm depends on the metrical pattern. In verse the rhythm is regular: in prose it may or may not be regular. *See* CADENCE; FALLING RHYTHM; METER; RISING RHYTHM; ROCKING RHYTHM; SPRUNG RHYTHM.

rhythmical pause By some used as the equivalent of a caesura (*q.v.*), and thus it occurs during a line of verse rather than at the end of it.

riddle (OE 'opinion, advice') An ancient and universal form of literature, in its commonest form it consists of a puzzle question: the equivalent of a conundrum or an enigma. For example:

> Brothers and sisters have I none.
> This man's father is my father's son.
> Who am I?

The earliest known English riddles are recorded in the *Exeter Book* (8th c.). Some are brief, while others run to many lines of verse.

There are collections of riddles also in Sanskrit, Hebrew, Arabic and Persian literature, not to mention Greek riddles in the *Greek Anthology* and the Latin riddles of Symphosius. Other authors of Anglo-Latin riddles were Aldhelm of Sherborne, Tatwine, Archbishop of Canterbury, and Eusebius, Abbot of Wearmouth. One of the largest collections is Nicolas Reusner's *Aenigmatographia* (1602).

riding rhyme A term for the heroic couplet (*q.v.*) and its meter. So named in all probability because Chaucer used it for *The Canterbury Tales*, related by the pilgrims while riding to the shrine at Canterbury.

rime The word derives from the Greek *rhythmos*. In Late Latin the word *rithmi* was used of accented verse and *metra* of quantitative verse. The word *rithmus* (conceivably influenced by the OHG word *rim*, 'number') became *rime*. By the 17th c. there was a clear distinction between rhyme and rhythm. But the term *rime* is by no means defunct. *See* RHYME.

rime couée *See* TAIL-RHYME STANZA.

rimes croisées In French prosody, the alternation of masculine and feminine rhymes (*qq.v.*) for an abab rhyme scheme. *See also* ALTERNANCE DES RIMES.

rimes embrassées In French prosody, the alternation of masculine and feminine rhymes (*qq.v.*) for an abba rhyme scheme. *See also* ALTERNANCE DES RIMES.

rimes équivoquées In French prosody, a scheme in which the rhyming syllables are identical in spelling and sound but the words they make up in various combinations are puns. *Les rhétoriqueurs* (*q.v.*) were fond of this kind of word play.

rimes mêlées In French prosody this denotes a random rhyming scheme. Even so, the rule pertaining to the alternation of masculine and feminine rhymes (*qq.v.*) is still observed. It is common in light verse, madrigal, fable and *chanson* (*qq.v.*) in the 17th c.

rimes plates *See* ALTERNANCE DES RIMES.

rimes riches In French (and later English) prosody rhyming syllables in which accented vowels and the consonants before and after them sounded identical. When spelt the same they are homographs (e.g. well/well); when spelt differently they are homophones (e.g. stare/stair). Also known as identical rhyme. *See* PERFECT RHYME.

rimes suffisantes In French prosody, rhyming syllables in which the accented vowel and one identical consonant sound. *See* RIMES RICHES.

rimes suivies *See* ALTERNANCE DES RIMES.

rímur A form of Icelandic metrical romance (*q.v.*) which originated in the 14th c. They were narrative poems based on heroic tales and composed, for the most part, in alliterative four-line stanzas. They were complex in meter and the kenning (*q.v.*) occurs frequently.

rionnaird tri-nard An Irish syllabic verse form. It consists of a quatrain (*q.v.*) stanza with hexasyllabic lines with disyllabic endings. The second and fourth lines rhyme and the third line consonates with them. The second couplet has two cross-rhymes.

rising action That part of a play which precedes the climax (*q.v.*). *See* FALLING ACTION; FREYTAG'S PYRAMID.

rising rhythm This occurs when the stress pattern is thrown *forward* in a line of verse, so that it falls on the last syllable of the feet. Iambic and anapaestic feet are basic to rising rhythm. Most English verse is composed in it. The following example comes from the Prologue to Vernon Watkins's *The Ballad of the Mari Lwyd.* 'Midnight' is trochaic, then he moves into a mixture of iambics and anapaests:

> Mídnĭght. | Mídnĭght. | Mídnĭght. | Mídnĭght.
> Hárk | ăt thĕ hánds | ŏf thĕ clóck:
> Nŏw deád | mĕn ríse | ĭn thĕ fróst | ŏf thĕ stárs
> Ănd físts | ŏn thĕ cóf|fĭns knóck.
> Thĕy drópped | ĭn theĭr gráves | wĭthóut | óne sóund:
> Thén thĕy wĕre | steádў | ănd stíff.
> Bŭt nów | thĕy teár | thróugh thĕ fróst | ŏf thĕ gróund
> Ăs hérĕtĭc, drún|kărd ănd thíef.

See ANAPAEST; FALLING RHYTHM; IAMB; TROCHEE.

rispetto (It 'respect') An eight-line stanza, usually rhyming abababcc. Probably of Tuscan origin, it is now general in Italy. Well-known Italian poets who have used this form (the themes are often related to love, honour and respect) are Lorenzo de Medici, Carducci and Pascoli. *See* SICILIAN OCTAVE; STRAMBOTTO.

ritornello (It 'little return') Two lines (occasionally three) which have the function equivalent to a refrain (*q.v.*) at the end (or beginning) of a stanza.

Ritter- und Räuberroman (G 'knight and robber novel') As the term suggests, such novels were tales of adventure and derring-do; basically historical novels, which were elaborately contrived, melodramatic and sensational. Some of them were extremely successful. The *Sturm und Drang* (*q.v.*) movement had some influence on their development. Their closest counterpart in Britain was the Gothic novel (*q.v.*). Some of the main authors were Benedikte Naubert (1756–1819), one of the few female novelists of the period, Friedrich Schlenkert (1757–1826), who wrote *Das Petermännchen* (1791–2), Karl Cramer (1758–1817), author of *Hasper a Spada* (1792–3), and Christian Vulpius (1762–1827), who wrote the very popular *Rinaldo Rinaldini, der Räuberhauptmann* (1798). *See* PICARESQUE NOVEL.

Robinsonade The German term for stories which derived from Defoe's ever popular *The Life and Strange and Surprising Adventures of Robinson Crusoe* (1719). The first German translation appeared the following year and there were numerous imitations. Among the more notable examples were Johann Schnabel's *Die Insel Felsenburg* (1731–43), Johann Campe's *Robinson der Jüngere* (1779–80) and Johann Wyss's *Der schweizerische Robinson* (1812–27) which, as *The Swiss Family Robinson*, became a much loved classic in Britain. *See* DESERT ISLAND FICTION.

rocking rhythm A term used by Gerard Manley Hopkins in his *Preface* to *Poems* (1918). A metrical device which occurs when a stressed syllable comes between two unstressed syllables, as in the first of these two lines from the poet's *The Wreck of the Deutschland*:

> Bŭt hĕ scóres ĭt ĭn scárlĕt hĭmsélf ŏn hĭs ówn bĕspókĕn,
> Bĕfóre-tíme-tákĕn, deárĕst prízĕd ănd príced –

See RUNNING RHYTHM; SPRUNG RHYTHM.

rococo (F *rocaille* 'rock work') An architectural term used to describe decorative scroll-work. As a literary term it may be used judiciously to describe something which is light, gay and graceful, and perhaps embellished by elegant twirls and flourishes of wit, image or verbal dexterity. The rococo period belongs to the 18th c. Pope's *The Rape of the Lock* might qualify as a specimen.

rodomontade The term derives from a character called Rodomonte (literally 'roll-mountain'), a bragging Saracen king in Ariosto's *Orlando Furioso*. As a literary term it can be applied to a style which is inflated, bombastic and generally strives for exotic or meretricious effect. *See also* BOMBAST.

rogue literature A genre concerned with the underworld and thus with criminal and quasi-criminal life and activities. It was particularly popular in the 16th and 17th c. and at its best gives a vivid and memorable impression of the seamier sides of existence among vagrants, vagabonds, beggars, cutpurses, con-men *et al.* – the Autolycuses of this world. Some fairly renowned examples are: *Hye Way to the Spyttel House* (16th c.) by Robert Copland, *Caveat for Commen Cursetors* (1567) by Thomas Harman, *A Notable Discovery of Coosnage* (1592) by Robert Greene and *Lanthorne and Candle-light* (1608) by Thomas Dekker. In the field of modern criminology there is a plentiful literature in the 'rogue' tradition. Jean Genet's *Journal du voleur* (1949) is a well-known instance.

roll A piece of parchment made into a cylindrical form which usually bears official records. Thus, a kind of register (*q.v.*). Rolls are to be found in any public-record office. Famous examples are: *The Ragman Roll*, the *Pipe Rolls*, and the *Rolls Series* (or *Chronicles and Memorials of Great Britain and Ireland from the Invasion of the Romans to the Reign of Henry VIII*).

roman A word used in most European languages (including the Slav languages) to denote a novel. French in origin, it first denoted a common language, as opposed to Latin. There is a reference in 813 to *roman* meaning the vernacular tongue, while Latin was the learned language. In literary history, one of the earliest dates it appears is 1140, when *roman* denoted a story in verse adapted from Latin legends. Originally, *roman* referred to imaginative works in the vernacular; mainly the medieval French verse epics. By the 16th c. it was applied to works in prose.

In French there are various categories of *roman*: *roman-fleuve*, *roman à tiroirs*, *roman noir*, *roman-feuilleton*, *roman policier*, *roman documentaire*, *nouveau roman* (*qq.v.*), *roman à clef* (see LIVRE A CLEF) and *roman d'aventure*. The French also use the terms *récit* and *nouvelle* (qq.v.) to denote particular kinds of novel. Various other classifications have come into use in the 20th c.: (a) *roman réaliste* – which covers *romans sur la guerre, romans réalistes à thèse révolutionnaire, romans documentaires, romans populistes et prolétariens, romans régionalistes* and *romans documentaires sur le pays de l'Union Française et sur les pays étrangers*; (b) *roman psychologique* – which covers *psychologues catholiques, psychologues humanistes* and *psychologues de la passion et de la volonté*; (c) *roman d'imagination* – which covers *roman merveilleux, roman d'adventure, roman historique* and *roman policier.* There is also the *roman existentialiste.*

roman à clef *See* LIVRE A CLEF.

roman à deux sous French equivalent of a penny dreadful (*q.v.*).

roman à tiroirs (F 'novel with drawers') A novel (*q.v.*) which consists of a series of episodes which have no very obvious connecting link or theme. A noteworthy instance is Lesage's *Gil Blas de Santillane*, a picaresque (*q.v.*) romance which came out in four volumes between 1715 and 1735.

romance (i) (MedL *romanice* 'in the Romantic tongue') In OF *romaunt* and *roman* meant, approximately, 'courtly romance in verse' or a 'popular book'. Thus romances in verse (and to start with most of them were in verse) were works of fiction, or non-historical. In the 13th c. a romance was almost any sort of adventure story, be it of chivalry or of love. Gradually more and more romances were written in prose.

Whatever else a romance may be (or have been) it is principally a form of entertainment. It may also be didactic but this is usually incidental. It is a European form which has been influenced by such collections as *The Arabian Nights.* It is usually concerned with characters (and thus with events) who live in a courtly world somewhat remote from the everyday. This suggests elements of fantasy, improbability, extravagance and naïvety. It also suggests elements of love, adventure, the marvellous and the 'mythic'. For the most part the term is used rather loosely to describe a narrative of heroic or spectacular achievements, of chivalry, of gallant love, of deeds of derring-do.

In medieval romance there were three main cycles: (a) the matter of Britain, which included Arthurian matter derived from Breton lays; (b) the matter of Rome, which included stories of Alexander, the Trojan wars and Thebes; (c) the matter of France, most of which was about Charlemagne and his knights.

The medieval metrical romances were akin to the *chansons de gestes* and to epic (*qq.v.*). There were a very large number of them, as we might expect in a form of popular literature. Chrétien de Troyes, who flourished in the latter half of the 12th c., was one of their most distinguished composers. His works were widely translated and imitated and he showed remarkable skill in combining the love story with the adventure story. His characterization was subtle and his style graceful. He wrote for a well-educated and mostly aristocratic audience, in which women played an important role. Courtly love was the main theme of his poems: *Erec*, *Cligès*, *Chevalier à Charrette*, *Lancelot*, *Yvain* and *Perceval.*

Three 13th c. German poets produced one notable romance each: Hartmann von Aue's *Iwein* (*c.* 1203); Gottfried von Strassburg's *Tristan und Isult* (*c.* 1210); and Wolfram von Eschenbach's *Parzifal* (*c.* 1210).

England produced two great romances in the 14th c.: the popular *Lay of Havelok the Dane* and the aristocratic romance of *Sir Gawain and the Green Knight.* Later came Sir Thomas Malory's prose work *Le Morte Darthur* in the latter half of the 15th c., printed by Caxton in 1485. By this time prose had become increasingly the medium for romance.

The traditions and codes of romance remained evident during the Renaissance period, in the poems of Ariosto and Tasso, in Spenser's *Faerie Queene* and in numerous other works. The Elizabethans had a penchant for stories of all kinds, especially the folktale sort, and the many different rather debased varieties of romance. A major pastoral (*q.v.*) romance of the period is Sir Philip Sidney's *Arcadia* (1590), in prose; a minor work of importance is Greene's *Pandosto* (1588), also in prose. Romance elements are also to be found at this time in some drama, particularly romantic comedy (*q.v.*).

Near the end of the 14th c. Chaucer satirized romance by means of burlesque (*q.v.*) in his *Tale of Sir Thopas*. Occasionally, after Chaucer, we find examples of satire on the conventions and sensibilities of the romance, but not until Cervantes's *Don Quixote* was the whole idea and tradition 'sent up'. The first part of *Don Quixote* was published in 1605, the second in 1615. It was published in English 1612–20; in French 1614–18; in Italian 1622–5; in German 1683. This suggests its wide popularity and helps to explain its influence. Though the book is many other things besides being a satire it is unquestionably the principal work to display the incongruities of romance. It does so by making fun of the conventions of chivalry and contrasting them with the realities of ordinary life.

Beaumont's comedy *The Knight of the Burning Pestle* (*c.* 1607) may well have been influenced by it. However, the preface to the play claims that Beaumont had the idea of the absurd knight. At any rate this play is a burlesque of knight-errantry (the Grocer Errant has a burning pestle on his shield and is involved in absurd adventures) and is very probably the first play meant as a parody of another play – namely Thomas Heywood's *The Foure Prentices of London.* Later in the 17th c. Samuel Butler modelled his splendid mock-heroic (*q.v.*) poem *Hudibras* (1663, 1664, 1678) on *Don Quixote.* And in the following century Fielding described his novel *Joseph Andrews* (1742) as an imitation of *Don Quixote*. In fact, Cervantes's masterpiece had a considerable influence on the picaresque (*q.v.*) narrative of adventure and on the novel in general during the 19th c. In many ways Don Quixote is an early example of the anti-hero (*q.v.*) – or non-hero.

After *Don Quixote* romance could never be quite the same; nevertheless, the appetite for the old-fashioned knight-errantry type of story has remained unsatiated, as much fiction of the 20th c. clearly proves. And the traditional kind of romance remained popular in the 17th c., especially in France and England. A notable instance in French literature is *Artamène ou le Grand Cyrus* (1649–53) by Madeleine de Scudéry.

In the 18th c. romance elements are still evident, but the novel is already tending to concentrate on the everyday, the social and domestic – except when picaresque. With the advent of the Gothic novel (*q.v.*) a new kind of romance appears, one which makes use of the more bizarre and extravagant characteristics of the medieval romance.

During the Romantic period (*q.v.*), a more unstable and, at times, turbulent age, the concept of the romance (and what is romantic) underwent a further modification. In the 18th c. the term 'romantic' meant something that could happen in a romance (or, to use the French word, it was *romanesque*) but towards the end of the 18th c. and at the beginning of the 19th it becomes clear that romance connotes those flights of fancy and imagination (*q.v.*) which had been regarded with suspicion in the Augustan Age (*q.v.*). Hence the renewed interest in ballads, especially the Border ballads, the popularity of Chatterton's work and Macpherson's Ossianic poems, the interest in folk tales and fairy tales and in *The Arabian Nights*, and the rather conscious revival of medievalism (*q.v.*) – a revival that was to gather momentum during the 19th c. It may well be that the modern connotations of 'to romance' and 'romancing' (i.e. the telling of stories or tales of a tallish kind in which there is a strong element of make-believe) were established during the Romantic period.

At this time a number of major works illustrate a new conception of the romance as a revitalizing force. The poets re-create a remote past, an 'old world' of romance which reveals a potent nostalgia and the considerable influence of Spenser. It is almost as if romance has come to symbolize something which is at once ancient, ideal and liberating, and, periodically, an evocation of lost youth. We can hardly read Keats's *The Eve of St Agnes* or Coleridge's *Kubla Khan* or Sir Walter Scott's *Marmion* (or indeed any of Scott's long poems) or Shelley's *Queen Mab* without receiving a strong impression of an introspective and imaginative world, a *paysage intérieur*, reminiscent at times of the illustrations to be found in medieval books of hours, the world of 'golden-tongued' romance and all that resounds (to use Milton's words in *Paradise Lost*):

> In fable or romance of Uther's son
> Begirt with British and Armoric knights;
> And all who since, baptized or infidel
> Jousted in Aspramont or Montalban,
> Damasco, or Marocco, or Trebisond,
> Or whom Biserta sent from Afric shore
> When Charlemain with all his peerage fell
> By Fontarabbia.

Later in the 19th c. we find other evidence of the long-term influences of the medieval romance, more especially in Tennyson, who re-worked the matter of Arthur in *The Idylls of the King* – a labour which occupied him on and off for forty years. William Morris, a distinguished translator of Icelandic sagas and old French romances, also turned to the traditional sources of romance in *The Earthly Paradise* (1868–70). Morris, like the Pre-Raphaelites (*q.v.*), was a kind of *laudator temporis acti*, 'an extoller of things in the past', and much of his work was an attempt to re-create the medieval as a corrective and alternative to 19th c. industrialism and materialism.

In the 19th c. three very different novelists wrote a large number of works which can be variously classified as kinds of romance.

They were Sir Walter Scott, Nathaniel Hawthorne and George Meredith. Most of Scott's historical novels had their roots in the kind of material of which older forms of romance were composed but Scott's approach was realist and he sought to make his characters permanent. Hawthorne and Meredith set their romances in the contemporary scene. Hawthorne's more notable works are *The House of the Seven Gables* (1851) and *The Marble Faun* (1860). A good representative example of the kind of romance Meredith wrote is *The Adventures of Henry Richmond* (1871).

By this time realism, to be followed by naturalism (*qq.v.*), was the main trend in fiction, and romance was scarcely compatible with it. The more popular kinds of 'romance', an entertainment and form of escapist literature, remained in demand, but more serious novelists, like H. G. Wells, for example, attempted a reconciliation between romance and realism. *Kipps* (1905), *Tono-Bungay* (1909) and *The History of Mr Polly* (1910) show an acute awareness of the qualities that enable the circulating library romance to survive, but are also didactic and 'socially realistic' novels.

There is nothing airy or 'faery' about Conrad's novels but many would probably agree that Conrad was a supreme 'romancer', especially in *Lord Jim* (1900), *Romance* (1903) and *The Shadow Line* (1917). No one knew better than Conrad how to relate an extraordinary and improbable tale of adventure. He is an expert in dealing with the exotic, the remote and the extravagant.

A score of other writers in the last 80-odd years might be cited as romancers. Much of their work may be regarded as ephemeral, and much of it would more or less fit Congreve's description of romance, in the preface of his novel *Incognita* (1713):

> Romances are generally composed of the Constant Loves and invincible Courages of Heros, Heroins, Kings and Queens, Mortals of the first Rank, and so forth; where lofty Language, miraculous Contingencies and impossible Performances, elevate and surprize the Reader into a giddy Delight whenever he gives of, and vexes him to think how he had suffer'd himself to be pleased and transported, concern'd and afflicted at the several Passages which he has Read, viz. these Knights Success to their Damozels Misfortunes, and such like, when he is forced to be very well convinced that 'tis all a lye.

See also CHANTE-FABLE; GESTA; LAI.

romance (ii) This Spanish term should not be confused with the English and French words similarly spelled (though the same derivation is common to all three). In Spanish it is pronounced approximately *ro – mahn – thay*, with the middle syllable stressed and the last very short.

In Spanish the original use of the word was for the language, as in the English 'romance languages'. When literary poetic forms of Provençal or French or other Latin-language origin arrived in Spain they were referred to as *romance* for that reason. The term can also refer to the type of meter used in the medieval poems.

The background to the *romance* is essentially popular, being generally connected with oral tradition (*q.v.*), and there is some similarity with the English ballad and the French *ballade* (*qq.v.*). As to the origin of the first romances, there are two main schools of thought. Both Menéndez y Pelayo and Menéndez Pidal support the suggestion put forward in 1874 by Milá y Fontanals that they are surviving fragments of medieval epic songs. This fits in with the lack of division into strophes, as well as with the type of assonance. Before 1874 it was thought that the romances had been the precursors of the *cantares de gesta* – the counterpart of the French *chansons de gestes* (*qq.v.*). It seems probable that the form developed concurrently with the Spanish language itself, yet the first mention of the term appears to be *c.* 1445–8 when the Marqués de Santillana referred to 'those songs and romances the lower classes so much enjoy'. It may well be that the romances developed along with the growth of Spanish national feeling. From the second half of the 16th c. onwards a number of poets have composed romances. They can be broadly classified as follows: *romance viejo* (the popular type); *romance artístico* (those composed by cultured poets); *romance histórico* (on various historical periods, in cycles); *romance fronterijo* (concerned with the 'frontier wars' in which the Arabs were beaten back from Granada); *romance morisco* (similar to the preceeding); and *romance juglaresco* (on subjects about which the *juglares* sang). Some of the better known writers have been Castillejo, Montemayor, Silvestre and Espinel. Lope de Vega, Cervantes, Quevedo and, later, the Duque de Rivas and Zorrilla, also composed romances.

romance languages A collective term for the group of languages descended from Latin. The main ones are: French, Italian, Spanish, Portuguese, Provençal, Rumanian and Romansch.

romancero (Sp 'collection of romances') A collection of ballads which had previously been gathered on loose sheets known as *pliegos* *sueltos* (*q.v.*). The first of these was Sepúlveda's in 1551. There were many different types of collection from the highly specialized (e.g. *Poema de mío Cid*) to *romanceros generales* (1600 onwards).

romance-six A six-syllable line acting as a tail to the octosyllabic couplet of the OF romance.

roman cycle A series of interconnected novels (but each novel is independent and self-contained) with a central hero, heroine or family. It is kin to the *roman-fleuve* and the saga novel (*qq.v.*). Well-known examples are Georges Duhamel's five Salavin novels, *Vie et Aventures de Salavin* (1920–32), and his *Chronique des Pasquier* (1933–45).

roman documentaire This form of fiction was invented by the Goncourt brothers, Edmond (1822–96) and Jules (1830–70), in the 1860s. The brothers, in collaboration, set out to write history 'which might have happened'. It was a form of realism and naturalism (*qq.v.*), and the Goncourts are often cited in connection with those two -isms. Using the research methods of the historian and also of the anthropologist working in the field, they aimed for the highest possible degree of fidelity to life, to fact. They describe their approach in their famous *Journal*, which was begun in 1851 and continued by Edmond after Jules died. An entry for Oct. 24th, 1864 reads: 'Le roman actuel se fait avec des *documents* racontés, ou relevés d'après nature, comme l'histoire se fait avec des documents écrits'. For the most part the novels were not well received, but they are important in the development of fictional techniques. The brothers developed a particular style which they called *écriture artiste* (*q.v.*). The main novels are *Les Hommes de lettres* (1860), *Sœur Philomène* (1861), *Renée Mauperin* (1864), *Germinie Lacerteux* (1864), *Manette Salomon* (1867) and *Madame Gervaisais* (1869). In 1879 Edmond published *Les Frères Zemganno*, a study of circus life. *Germinie Lacerteux* remains one of the best known; it is a detailed history of their faithful servant who led a double life: off-duty she devoted her time to debauchery and corruption. *Sœur Philomène* is a remarkable account of hospital life. Later, Emile Zola was to apply comparable methods of documentary 'fieldwork' to achieve maximum realism and accuracy.

roman-feuilleton A novel published in instalments in a daily paper. The fashion began *c.* 1830. In 1836 a translation of the Spanish picaresque novel *Lazarillo de Tormes* first appeared in the newspaper *Le Siècle*. In the late 19th c. many authors took advantage of such serialization. It is still done occasionally when a newspaper is absolutely sure than an author's book is going to sell well.

roman-fleuve A term used in modern fiction for a series of novels, each of which exists as a separate novel in its own right but all of which are inter-related because the characters (some or all) reappear in each succeeding work. The vogue for this kind of encyclopaedic and epic chronicle was established in the 19th c. Balzac planned and in part executed his vast scheme of *La Comédie humaine*; Zola wrote his twenty-volume series *Les Rougon-Macquart* (1871–93) and the Spaniard Pérez Galdós produced his monumental *Episodios nacionales* (1873–1912), a cycle of historical novels covering the history of Spain from Trafalgar (1805) to the Restoration (1875). In the 20th c. four Frenchmen have undertaken works on a similar scale. Romain Rolland wrote *Jean-Christophe* (1906–12) in ten volumes. Later he returned to the *roman-fleuve* scheme with *L'Ame enchantée* (1922–33) in seven volumes. Proust's monumental *A la recherche du temps perdu* (1913–27) consists of seven inter-related sections and occupied him for at least twelve years. Georges Duhamel began with the *Vie et Aventures de Salavin* (1920–32) in five novels, and followed this with *Chronique des Pasquier* (1933–45) in ten volumes. Jules Romains was even more ambitious with his *Les Hommes de bonne volonté* (1932–47), the generic title of a series of twenty-seven novels covering a wide range of French life from 1908 to 1933. Galsworthy attempted the same sort of thing with *The Forsyte Saga* (1922). More recently there have been C. P. Snow's *Strangers and Brothers* sequence (1940–70), which gives a documentary chronicle of English social history from 1925; Henry Williamson's *A Chronicle of Ancient Sunlight* (1951–69) in fifteen volumes; and Anthony Powell's *A Dance to the Music of Time* (1951–76) in twelve volumes. A number of other novelists have used the trilogy and the tetralogy (*qq.v.*) to achieve a comparable continuity. *See* BILDUNGSROMAN; NOVEL; SAGA NOVEL.

roman noir (F 'black novel') The equivalent of the English Gothic novel (*q.v.*).

roman policier The French equivalent of the detective story (*q.v.*) and novel about crime. It is generally agreed that the first practitioner was Emile Gaboriau (1832–73). Gaboriau was ahead of his time, for he created a policeman as his detective, namely Lecoq. He also had an amateur sleuth in the shape of an old pawnbroker, Père Tabaret, called 'Tir-au-clair'. Gaboriau's long-term influence on British and Amerian writers of detective fiction was considerable, and in some ways he was the first to see the possibilities of the police procedural (*q.v.*), which was not to be fully developed until the 1950s. His *Le Crime d'Orcival* (1867) was the first full-length detective novel. This he followed with *Le Dossier no. 113* (1867), *L'Affair Lerouge* (1868) and *Monsieur Lecoq* and *Les Esclaves de Paris* (both 1869). Later, Fortuné du Boisgobey wrote stories similar to Gaboriau's, the most notable being his *Le Crime de l'Opéra* (1880). Another distinguished crime novelist of that era was Gaston Leroux (1868–1927), who wrote over thirty crime novels and is chiefly remembered for *Le Mystère de la chambre jaune* (1907). Better known now than those is Maurice Leblanc. The detective story was well established in Britain by 1900 and it was beginning to proliferate in the first ten years of the 20th c. Sherlock Holmes was a household name. Leblanc followed English practice in creating his detective as the hero. Some of his most memorable stories are *Arsène Lupin* (1907), *Arsène Lupin contre Sherlock Holmes* (1908) and *Arsène Lupin, gentleman cabrioleur* (1914).

Later there was Sebastien Japrisot (1931–), a prolific writer of ingenious crime novels, many of which have been filmed. More recently Yves Jacquemard (1943–) and Jean Michel Senecal (1943–) have collaborated in crime novels. Easily the most famous writer of the *policier* is Georges Simenon (1903–90), whose detective inspector Jules Maigret has become universally famous, almost as famous as Sherlock Holmes himself. The Maigret novels were written between 1931 and 1973. Maigret finally 'retired' from fiction on Feb. 7th, 1973, after he had become *Commissaire* at the Quay des Orfèvres, the headquarters of the Paris police. Simenon also wrote a large number of crime novels in which there is no particular hero. His total output was huge.

romans bretons Romances (usually in octosyllabic couplets) composed in the period *c.* 1150–1250. Their subjects for the most part are 'the matter' of Brittany. Two of the most famous authors were Marie de France and Chrétien de Troyes. *See also* METRICAL ROMANCE; ROMANCE; ROMANS COURTOIS; ROMANS D'ANTIQUITE; ROMANS D'AVENTURE.

romans courtois A general term which denotes medieval romances, *romans bretons*, *romans d'aventure* (*qq.v.*). Such works were nearly always in verse and composed in octosyllabic couplets. They were usually intended to be read aloud. *See also* METRICAL ROMANCE; ROMANS D'ANTIQUITE.

romans d'antiquité Medieval metrical romances (*q.v.*) whose themes and subjects were mostly taken from the works of Roman authors. Notable examples from the 12th c. are *Roman de Troie*, *Roman de Thèbes* and *Eneas*. *See also* ROMANS BRETONS; ROMANS COURTOIS; ROMANS D'AVENTURE.

romans d'adventure Fictional narratives of the 12th and 13th c. They were usually in verse (commonly octosyllabic couplets), but were sometimes composed in prose, or in a mixture of prose and verse. The principal themes were love and chivalry and, like most romances (*q.v.*), they were intended solely as entertainment (largely for women). In this period some of the more distinguished works were: *Ipomedon*; *Partenopeu*; *Guillaume de Dole*; *Aucassin et Nicolette*; *Le Châtelain de Coucy*; *Guillaume de Palerme*; *Floire et Blancheflor*; *Robert le Diable*. *Aucassin et Nicolette* is an outstanding instance of the mixture of prose and verse. Two well-known prose romances were *Conte du roi Constant l'empereur* and *Le Roi Flore et la belle Jeanne*. *See also* METRICAL ROMANCE; ROMANS BRETONS; ROMANS COURTOIS; ROMANS D'ANTIQUITE.

romantic comedy A somewhat vague term which denotes a form of drama (it may, occasionally, be applied to a novel) in which love is the main theme – and love which leads to a happy ending, as in Shakespeare's *A Midsummer Night's Dream*, *As You Like It* and *Twelfth Night*. *See* COMEDY.

romantic irony Novalis (alias Friedrich von Hardenberg, 1772–1801) described irony as 'genuine consciousness, true presence of mind'. The writer who employs what is called romantic irony (a concept for which Schlegel was largely responsible) exhibits true presence of mind by showing an awareness, a sensibility, that he does not expect his work to be taken wholly seriously – and does not wish it to be. He conveys this tone and attitude (thus inviting a complementary tone and attitude in his reader) by being at once critically aware of what he is doing and why he is doing it, even while he may be impelled by a strong dynamic creative purpose. Thus he is fully conscious of the comic implication of his own seriousness.

This form of irony is often at its best when the author is *showing* us what he is doing while he is doing it, so to speak. It may occur, for instance, when he comments on literary composition and perhaps also on the composition in hand. The novel is the main vehicle of romantic irony, but dramatists and poets have also used it. Notable examples are: (a) Fielding's interruptions and comments as author in *Tom Jones* and *Joseph Andrews*; (b) Pirandello's awareness of the ambivalent nature of drama in *Six Characters in Search of an Author*; and (c) Byron's continual breaking of the serious tone in *Don Juan*.

Among other outstanding exponents of this kind of irony are Aristophanes, Chaucer, Cervantes, Marivaux, Sterne, Diderot, Goethe, Hoffman, Heine, Henry James, Gide and Nabokov. Perhaps the most accomplished of all is Thomas Mann, especially in *Joseph und seine Brüder* and *Der Zauberberg* where the ironic tone produces a gradual and cumulative joke, a growing sense of comic innuendo. It is mirth brought about by subtle and elaborate teasing. *See* COMEDY; DRAMATIC IRONY; IRONY; SATIRE.

romanticism The American scholar A. O. Lovejoy once observed that the word 'romantic' has come to mean so many things that, by itself, it means nothing at all. It may seem that repetition has wrung the life out of the term, yet it still appears to be as potentially sustaining as a twist of pemmican. It is a word at once indispensable and useless. The variety of its actual and possible meanings and connotations reflect the complexity and multiplicity of European romanticism. In *The Decline and Fall of the Romantic Ideal* (1948) F. L. Lucas counted 11,396 definitions of 'romanticism'. In *Classic, Romantic and Modern* (1961) Barzun cites examples of synonymous usage for *romantic* which show that it is perhaps the most remarkable example of a term which can mean many things according to personal and individual needs. Barzun gives: 'attractive', 'bombastic', 'conservative', 'emotional', 'exuberant', 'fanciful', 'formless', 'futile', 'heroic', 'irrational', 'materialistic', 'mysterious', 'nordic', 'ornamental', 'realistic', 'stupid', 'unreal', and 'unselfish'. To which one might add: 'adventurous', 'daring', 'extraordinary', 'gallant', 'melodramatic', 'passionate' and 'wild'.

We are 'stuck' with the words *romantic* and *romanticism* which, today, as much as ever before, evoke all manner of varied responses ranging from repugnance to enthusiastic approval. In the same way we are 'stuck' with the closely allied terms *classic, classicism* and *neoclassicism* (*qq.v.*).

The word *romantic (ism)* has a complex and interesting history. In the Middle Ages 'romance' denoted the new vernacular languages derived from Latin – in contradistinction to Latin itself, which was the language of learning. *Enromancier*, *romancar*, *romanz* meant to compose or translate books in the vernacular. The work produced was then called *romanz*, *roman*, *romanzo* and *romance* (*q.v.*). A *roman* or *romant* came to be known as an imaginative work and a 'courtly romance'. The terms also signified a 'popular book'. There are early suggestions that it was something new, different, divergent. By the 17th c. in Britain and France, 'romance' had acquired the derogatory connotations of fanciful, bizarre, exaggerated, chimerical. In France a distinction was made between *romanesque* (also derogatory) and *romantique* (which meant 'tender', 'gentle', 'sentimental' and 'sad'). It was used in the English form in these latter senses in the 18th c. In Germany the word *romantisch* was used in the 17th c. in the French sense of *romanesque*, and then, increasingly from the middle of the 18th c., in the English sense of 'gentle', 'melancholy'.

Friedrich Schlegel is generally held to have been the person who first established the term *romantisch* in literary contexts. However, he was not very clear as to what he meant by it. That which is romantic depicts emotional matter in an imaginative form, he said. It would not be easy to be much vaguer than that. At the same time, in fairness, it should be said that the baffling and, very often, irritating part about anything to do with the romantic and romanticism is that it *is* vague and formless. Schlegel also equated 'romantic' with 'Christian'. His brother August implied that romantic literature is in contrast to that of classicism, thus producing the famous antimony (*q.v.*).

Madame de Staël knew the Schlegels and she appears to have been responsible for popularizing the term *romantique* in literary contexts in France. She made a distinction between the literature of the north and of the south. The northern was medieval, Christian and romantic; the southern, Classical and pagan.

Many hold to the theory that it was in Britain that the romantic movement really started. At any rate, quite early in the 18th c. one can discern a definite shift in sensibility and feeling, particularly in relation to the natural order and Nature. This, of course, is hindsight. When we read Keats, Coleridge and Wordsworth, for instance, we gradually become aware that many of their sentiments and responses are foreshadowed by what has been described as a 'pre-romantic sensibility'.

The British influence travelled to the continent via Thomson's *Seasons* (1726–30), Young's *Night Thoughts* (1742–5), Blair's *The Grave* (1743), Hervey's *Meditations among the Tombs* (1748), Gray's *Elegy* (1750), Macpherson's Ossianic poetry, much of which was published in the 1760s, and Percy's *Reliques* (1765). Most of these works (and especially Young's *Night Thoughts*) show a preoccupation with death and decay, with ruins and graveyards; they display a grieving melancholy, a mournful reflectiveness and a quantity of self-indulgent sentimentality. Hence the title 'Graveyard School of Poetry' (*q.v.*).

New modes of feeling are also evident in sentimental comedy, *comédie larmoyante* and the sentimental novel (*qq.v.*). The novel is particularly important in tracing the history of romanticism. Especially the following works: Richardson's *Pamela* (1740), *Clarissa Harlowe* (1747) and *Sir Charles Grandison* (1754); Goldsmith's *The Vicar of Wakefield* (1766); Sterne's *Sentimental Journey* (1768); Henry Mackenzie's *The Man of Feeling* (1771); and Henry Brooke's *Juliet Grenville; or the History of the Human Heart* (1774). On the continent three major works of fiction are a counterpart – namely: Prévost's *Manon Lescaut* (1735), Rousseau's *La Nouvelle Héloïse* (1761) and Goethe's *Die Leiden des jungen Werthers* (1774). One should add that the Gothic novel (*q.v.*) and a considerable revival of Shakespeare's plays round about the middle of the 18th c. also contributed to the movement subsequently known as 'romantic'.

Other aspects of romanticism in the 18th c. are: (a) an increasing interest in Nature, and in the natural, primitive and uncivilized way of life: (b) a growing interest in scenery, especially its more untamed and disorderly manifestations; (c) an association of human moods with the 'moods' of Nature – and thus a subjective feeling for it and interpretation of it; (d) a considerable emphasis on natural religion; (e) emphasis on the need for spontaneity in thought and action and in the expression of thought; (f) increasing importance attached to natural genius and the power of the imagination; (g) a tendency to exalt the individual and his needs and emphasis on the need for a freer and more personal expression; (h) the cult of the Noble Savage (*q.v.*).

In all these connections Rousseau is the major figure in the 18th c. and his influence in the pre-romantic period was immense; especially through the following works: *Discours sur l'origine de l'inégalité parmi les hommes* (1755); *Du contrat social* (1762); *Rêveries du promeneur solitaire* (1778); and *Les Confessions* (published after his death in 1781 and 1788). *La Nouvelle Héloïse* has been mentioned above.

Notable works by other authors which expressed a new vision of man and his role in the world are: Goethe's *Götz von Berlichingen* (1773); Herder's *Stimmen der Völker* (1778); Schiller's *Die Räuber* (1781); Bernardin de Saint-Pierre's *La Chaumière indienne* (1790) and *Paul et Virginie* (1788); Chateaubriand's *Atala* (1801) and his *René* (1805).

To these should be added the extremely influential *Conjectures on Original Composition* by Young, which was published in 1759 and published in a German translation the following year. Young's aesthetic theories considerably affected the so-called *Sturm und Drang* (*q.v.*) movement.

The German romantics belong to roughly two generations known as the *Frühromantik* ('Early Romantics') and the *Hochromantik* ('High Romantics'). The *Frühromantik* formed a group from the late 1790s until early in the 18th c. which was based first on Berlin and then on Jena. The two central figures of the group were the brothers Schlegel: Friedrich (1759–1805) and August Wilhelm (1767–1845). The other main personalities in the group were Wackenroder (1773–98), Tieck (1773–1853) and Novalis (1772–1801). These were all poets. There were also the philosophers Schelling and Baader, the theologian Schleiermacher and the physicist Ritter.

The *Hochromantik* group comprised principally Arnim (1781–1831), Brentano (1778–1842), Chamisso (1781–1838), Eichendorff (1788–1857), Fouqué (1777–1843), Heine (1797–1856), Hoffmann (1776–1822) and Mörike (1804–75).

Grossly to simplify the matter one can say that the earlier group were the philosophers and aestheticians of the new movement and revolution; while their followers practised as poets and writers of stories more than they preached. Both were movements of intense activity and national importance.

In Britain romanticism was much more diffused and never really associated with a movement, but then literary movements have been rare in Britain. There was no British romantic campaign and the literary and cultural revolution was a much more gradual and informal affair than on the continent. The main figures associated with it are primarily Coleridge, Wordsworth, Keats, Shelley, Byron and Sir Walter Scott. The political and social beliefs of Wordsworth, Coleridge and Shelley were quite often expressed in their poems as well as their prose works.

Partly because of the Revolution and partly because of the French devotion to classicism and neoclassicism, the Romantic movement came considerably later to France. There the works of Lamartine, Victor Hugo and de Vigny were the main influence to start with; later came de Musset and Dumas (*père*).

As to the long-term after-effects of romanticism, there is scarcely more agreement about these than there has been about what it actually was. Greatly to simplify two opposite points of view – there are those who in general support Goethe's later attitude that it was a sickness of the spirit and a disorganizing irruption of subjectivism; others who hold that it was a kind of renaissance, a re-discovery, a wholly beneficial upheaval, and a much needed rejection of defunct standards and beliefs which resulted in a creative freedom of mind and spirit. No doubt the truth, as usual, lies somewhere in between: yet only attainable in the ideal reconciliation of opposites. *See* PARNASSIANS; PRE-RAPHAELITES; REALISM.

romantic period *See* ROMANTIC REVIVAL.

romantic revival A term loosely applied to a movement in European literature (and other arts) during the last quarter of the 18th c. and the first twenty or thirty years of the 19th c. It was marked by a rejection of the ideals and rules of classicism and neoclassicism (*qq.v.*) and by an affirmation of the need for a freer, more subjective expression of passion, pathos and personal feelings. At its narrowest, the Romantic period in Britain is usually taken to run between 1798, the year in which Coleridge and Wordsworth published the first edition of *Lyrical Ballads*, and 1832, when Sir Walter Scott and Goethe died and the Reform Bill was passed. The major British writers in this period, apart from Coleridge, Wordsworth and Scott, were Byron, Shelley, Keats, Jane Austen, Hazlitt and de Quincey. Abroad, the movement was widely embracing: Goethe, Schlegel, Wackenroder, Tieck, Schelling, Novalis and Hölderlin in Germany; Chateaubriand and Madame de Staël in France; Leopardi, Manzoni and Foscolo in Italy; Espronceda in Spain; Slowacki in Poland; Pushkin and Lermontov in Russia; Petöfi in Hungary; and Oehenschläger in Denmark. *See* ROMANCE; ROMANTICISM.

romería Of 12th c. Galician origin, a kind of festival at a local shrine. The *cantiga de romería* is a type of *cossante* (*q.v.*) composed by local minstrels in honour of their shrine.

rondeau (OF *rond* 'round') An OF form, consisting of a thirteen- or fifteen-line poem, usually octosyllabic, in three stanzas. The opening words became the refrain (*q.v.*). Usually there were only two rhymes. It was popular in 16th c. France. Among distinguished French poets who have since used it one may mention Clément Marot, Alfred de Musset and Théodore de Banville. The form did not catch on in England until late in the 19th c. when Dobson and Swinburne, among others, experimented extensively with it. The following example, *In Rotten Row*, by W. E. Henley, illustrates the basic principles:

In Rotten Row a cigarette
I sat and smoked, with no regret
  For all the tumult that had been.
  The distances were still and green,

And streaked with shadows cool and wet.
Two sweethearts on a bench were set,
Two birds among the bows were met;
So love and song were heard and seen
          In Rotten Row.

A horse or two there was to fret
The soundless sand; but work and debt,
  Fair flowers and falling leaves between,
  While clocks are chiming clear and keen,
A man may very well forget
          In Rotten Row.

See also RONDEAU REDOUBLE; RONDEL.

rondeau redoublé A rare poetic form akin to OF forms but little used, apparently, before the 16th c. It consists of six quatrains and only two rhymes are worked, as in the *rondeau* (*q.v.*). Marot, La Fontaine and Théodore de Banville are among the few poets known to have experimented with it. A good, witty modern example is Wendy Cope's *Rondeau Redoublé* (in the collection *Making Cocoa for Kingsley Amis*, 1986).

rondel A French fixed form of considerable antiquity and known from the 13th c. In its earliest form it appears to have been an eight-line poem rhyming AB aA ab AB (A and B represent repeated lines). A variation was the *rondel doublé* rhyming ABBA abBA abba ABBA. The most usual *rondel* form consisted of three stanzas working on two rhymes, thus: ABba abAB abba (B); a thirteen-line poem in which the refrain came twice in the first eight lines and the opening line was repeated as the last line. If it was of fourteen lines, the refrain was repeated three times. Among British poets who attempted the form were W. E. Henley, Edmund Gosse, Austin Dobson and R. L. Stevenson. *See also* RONDEAU; ROUNDEL.

rondelet A short fixed form, usually consisting of one stanza of five or seven lines, on two rhymes. If of seven lines, the first part of the opening line is used as a refrain (*q.v.*) thus: abRabbR (R is the refrain).

round character *See* FLAT AND ROUND CHARACTERS.

roundel As developed by Swinburne and published in his *A Century of Roundels* (1883), this form was an eleven-line poem in three stanzas, the twice repeated refrain consisting of the opening lines of the poem, and rhyming thus: abaR, bab, abaR (R is the refrain). Swinburne at once described and illustrated the form in *The Roundel*:

> A Roundel is wrought as a ring or a starbright sphere,
> With craft of delight and with cunning of sound unsought,
> That the heart of the hearer may smile it to pleasure his ear
> A roundel is wrought

See also RONDEAU; RONDEL.

roundelay A short simple song with a refrain. A kind of ditty (*q.v.*) popular in medieval times, to which people danced. The term also covers, variously, fixed forms like *rondeau*, *rondel* and *villanelle* (*qq.v.*) where refrain and repetition are used extensively.

roundlet A short form of roundel (*q.v.*).

Royal Literary Fund A benevolent society founded in 1790 to help authors and their dependants. It began as the Literary Fund Society and in 1818 was granted a royal charter. It added 'Royal' to its title in 1845. The fund has always depended on donations of one kind and another. Well-known beneficiaries have been Coleridge, Thomas Love Peacock, James Hogg, John Clare, James Joyce, D. H. Lawrence and Dylan Thomas.

Royal Shakespeare Company Thanks to the initiative and financial backing of a brewing family, the Flowers, the first Shakespeare Memorial Theatre in Stratford-upon-Avon, Warwickshire, was opened in 1879, and F. R. Benson (1858–1939) was appointed as director of an annual Shakespeare festival there. He remained associated with the theatre until 1919. The original theatre was destroyed by fire in 1926 and a second one was opened on the same site in 1932. After the Second World War the theatre prospered under three distinguished directors: Barry Jackson, Anthony Quayle and Glen Byam Shaw. In 1960 the Royal Shakespeare Company was formed and Peter Hall was made director. The RSC then took on the Aldwych Theatre in London. In 1970 Trevor Nunn replaced Peter Hall, who, in 1973, was to become artistic direct of the National Theatre (*q.v.*). The RSC also has a smaller theatre – the Other Place – at Stratford, plus the theatres in the Barbican Centre (opened in 1982). For the most part the company has concentrated on presentations of Shakespeare, often with great success (e.g. *The Wars of the Roses Cycle* in 1963, devised by Peter Hall and John Barton); but at the Other Place and at the Barbican a wide range of work by other playwrights, ancient and modern, has been produced.

Royal Society of Literature Founded in 1823 under the patronage of George IV. It awarded pensions to 'Associates' who were elected by the Society's council. It had regular meetings at which papers were read to members and thereafter published as *Transactions*. The Society has Members and Fellows, and also Companions (dating from 1961).

rubá'iyát (A *rubai* 'quatrain') A name given to a collection of quatrains. The best known example is the *Rubá'iyát of Omar Khayyám*, translated by Edward Fitzgerald. *See* QUATRAIN.

Rührstücke (G 'melodrama, tear-jerker') A genre of German drama which had some vogue among middle-class theatre-goers late in the 18th c. and early in the 19th c. August Iffland (1759–1814), an outstanding actor, wrote a number of them; as did August von Kotzebue (1761–1819).

rules In literary theory and history, those precepts and conventions which by custom and usage have come to be regarded and accepted as norms, if not actually ordained and thus taken as a body of dogma. For instance, those concerned with the dramatic unities (*q.v.*), with the composition of epic and tragedy, eclogue and sonnet (*qq.v.*), with the kind of subject matter suitable for, say, comedy, with the appropriateness of style to subject matter (e.g. the grand and fully canonical manner for epic; a much 'lower' style for farcical comedy).

Many of the rules originated in Classical theory: for instance, Aristotle's *Poetics*, Horace's *Ars Poetica*; and, later, in that work ascribed to Longinus called *On the Sublime*. The 'rules' of many forms and genres were established during the Middle Ages and in the 16th c., but it was during the 17th c. especially and in the first half of the 18th that writers paid particular attention to the 'rules'. Witness Racine's devotion to the conventions governing the Classical form of tragedy, or Pope's exacting and professional regard for decorum (*q.v.*) in language and genre (*q.v.*).

Since the end of the 18th c. fidelity to the rules has been taken to be of less and less importance. However, the best writers still tend to be those who have learnt the rules so thoroughly (this is particularly true of poets) that they are then in a position to modify them (and break them) and make rules of their own.

rune (ON and OE *run* 'whisper, mystery') A character of the earliest Germanic alphabet, *run* denoted a cryptic sign signifying something secret, mysterious or pertaining to hidden lore. It thus had associations with magic. The Runic alphabet, consisting of twenty-four letters, was adapted from Greek and Latin and devised by the Scandinavians and Anglo-Saxons for carving on slabs of beechwood. The 9th c. poet Cynewulf 'signed' his name by means of runes in four of his poems. The rune names were: *cen* 'torch', *yr* 'bow', *ned* 'need', *eoh* 'horse', *wyn* 'joy', *ur* 'bison', *lagu* 'sea', *feoh* 'wealth'.

running rhythm A term used by Gerard Manley Hopkins in his *Preface* to *Poems* (1918). It denotes a rhythm measured by feet of two or three syllables (excluding imperfect feet at the beginning and end of lines, and feet which seem to be paired together and double or composite feet which seem to arise). Each foot has one main stress or accent. The remaining one or two unaccented syllables are known as 'the slack'. The term is synonymous with common English rhythm. Hopkins distinguishes this from sprung rhythm (*q.v.*). *See* FALLING RHYTHM; RISING RHYTHM; ROCKING RHYTHM.

run-on line A line of verse which runs into the next line without any grammatical break. Also known as *enjambement* (*q.v.*), it is common in English poetry. This example is from Auden's *Letter to Lord Byron*:

> It is a commonplace that's hardly worth
>   A poet's while to make profound or terse,
> That now the sun does not go round the earth,
>   That man's no centre of the universe.

See also REJET.

S

saber A Provençal term which, in origin, probably meant 'wisdom' and then came to mean 'poetic skill'. It refers to the art of the troubadour (*q.v.*), which was codified in the Toulouse treatise *Leys d'amours* of the 14th c. *See* GAI SABER; TROUVERE.

sacra rappresentazione (It 'sacred representation') A dramatic form originating in medieval Italy, and akin to the Mystery Plays (*q.v.*) in England and elsewhere. Its usual subjects were the passion of Christ. It was a devotional entertainment or diversion which was presented after Mass and might be accompanied by sermons.

sacred books Literature connected with any specific religion; works of spiritual guidance, rules, hymn books, liturgies, any kind of record made of the utterances of holy men, prophets or sages. Obvious and well-known examples are: the Old and New Testaments; *Vedas*, *Brahmanas* and *Upanishads*; the *Kijoki* and *Nihongi*; the *Talmud*; the *Qur'an* (or *Koran*); the *Analects* of Confucius; *The Rule of St Benedict*; Walter Hilton's *The Scale of Perfection*; Thomas à Kempis's *Imitation of Christ*. To which might be added *The Confessions* of St Augustine, *The Cloud of Unknowing*, *The Steps of Humility* by St Bernard of Clairvaux, the works of Meister Eckhart and Jakob Boehme, Nicolas of Cusa's *Vision of God*, the Tibetan *Book of the Dead*, Thomas Traherne's *Centuries of Meditation*, and the works of St François de Sales and William Law. *See also* HAGIOGRAPHY.

saga (ON 'saw, saying') The sagas were medieval Icelandic and Scandinavian prose narratives usually about a famous hero or family or the exploits of heroic kings and warriors. Until the 12th c. most of them belonged to the oral tradition (*q.v.*) and thereafter scribes wrote them down. They can be divided into approximately five groups: (a) Sagas of the Kings, mainly about the early Norwegian kings; for instance, *Heimskringla* and *Sverris saga*. But there are some about the earls of Orkney known as the *Orkneyinga saga*. Others are about the Danish kings, like *Skjöldunga saga* and *Knýtlinga saga*. One, the *Jómsvíkinga saga*, treats of both Danish and Norwegian kings; (b) The Icelandic sagas, concerned with the period when Iceland was first settled; that is *c*. 930–*c*. 1030. Some of the more famous Icelandic sagas are: *Gísla saga Súrssonar*; *Víga-Glúms saga*; *Grettis saga*; *Hallfreðar saga*; *Egils saga*; *Laxdœla saga*; *Vatnsdœla saga*; *Njáls saga*; *Eyrbyggja saga*; *Hrafnkels saga*; and *Bandamanna saga*. These are anonymous works and are believed to have been first written down in the first half of the 12th c.; (c) Contemporary Sagas, about Icelandic chieftains and bishops. They date from the end of the 12th c. and later, and in some cases the authors are known. Moreover the authors were contemporaries of the people they wrote about. The main works are: the *Sturlunga saga*, the *Islendinga saga* and the *Hungrvaka*. There are also separate sagas devoted to several bishops whose episcopal reigns covered the period of *c*. 1178 to *c*. 1330; (d) What are known as the Fornaldarsögur, about legendary times, with little historical basis. The best known is the *Völsunga saga*; (e) During the 12th and 13th c. a number of romances were translated into Norse. The main works are: *Alexander's saga* (a version of a Latin poem on Alexander the Great; the *þiðriks saga* (from a German original); and *Karlamagnús saga* (which stems mostly from stories in French about Charlemagne). There have been many versions of these sagas in English literature, especially by William Morris. Longfellow, too, used the *Heimskringla saga* as a basis for his *Saga of King Olaf*. *See also* SCOP; SKALD.

saga novel So called from the Icelandic sagas (*q.v.*) because it is a narrative about the life of a large family. The most notable example in English literature is Galsworthy's *Forsyte Saga*, a series of novels – written over a long period – which are all linked together by the Forsyte family. The main ones are: *The Man of Property* (1906), *In Chancery* (1920), *To Let* (1921) and *A Modern Comedy* (1929). One of the most remarkable saga novels of European literature is Thomas Mann's tetralogy (*q.v.*) *Joseph und seine Brüder* (1933, 1934, 1936, 1942). *See also* BILDUNGSROMAN; ROMAN CYCLE; ROMAN-FLEUVE.

sainete (Sp diminutive of *sain* 'piquant sauce') A term used to describe one-act sketches which were developed to form the main kind of *género chico* (*q.v.*). They remain popular in Spain.

salon (F 'reception room') A social gathering *and* the place where it occurs. An informal meeting of writers, artists, scientists *et al.* at a private house. The *salon* was particularly popular in France in the 17th and 18th c. The prototype was very probably the Hôtel de Rambouillet (that is, town house) where, between 1610 and 1650, literary men and aristocrats were wont to assemble in the 'Blue Room' of the Marquise de Rambouillet. Other famous *salons* were run by Mesdames de Scudéry, Scarron, de Tencin and Récamier. After the French Revolution the influence and importance of the *salon* declined. In England it was never a popular institution, though Mrs Vesey and Mrs Elizabeth Montagu tried to establish it. In England the pub, the club and the coffee house were preferred.

samizdat (R *sam* 'self' + *izdatelstvo* 'publishing') The term now denotes a form of underground writing ('self-publication') and has been in general use since *c.* 1966 to denote articles and books which are circulated in typescript (or are run off on duplicating machines and then circulated) without the knowledge of the authorities and certainly without their approval. *Samizdat* is literature which expresses views contrary to those of the state. In 1966 the trial of Andrei Sinyavsky revealed the existence of a large body of underground literature (*q.v.*) in the Soviet Union. In that year Sinyavsky and another writer, Yuri Daniel, were sent to prison for publishing works abroad under pseudonyms. More famous writers than these have incurred the disapproval of the state by making use of *samizdat*. They included Solzhenitsyn and Andrei Sakharov. Solzhenitsyn's *The First Circle*, published in English in 1968, started life as underground literature. Sakharov published his political treatise *Progress, Coexistence and Intellectual Freedom* in the same way.

A reverse process named *tamizdat* (R *tam* 'there' + *izdatelstvo* 'publishing') is the publication of work in Russian in the West. This is then taken into the Soviet Union secretly. Pasternak's *Dr Zhivago* was banned in the Soviet Union, then published in Russian in Milan in 1957. Later, copies found their way back into the USSR.

Magnitizdat denotes material recorded on tapes which are then circulated illegally.

Sapphic ode Named after the poetess Sappho (7th c. BC). An ode (*q.v.*) written in regular stanza form. Sapphics, as they are called, are written in a quatrain (*q.v.*) stanza with a particular metrical scheme thus:

/ ∪ | / ⏓ | / ∪ ∪ | / ∪ | / ⏓ |

repeated thrice, and a fourth line:

/ ∪ ∪ | / ⏓ |

In the fourth and eleventh syllables of the first three lines the foot may be trochaic or spondaic; and on the last syllable of the fourth line the same applies.

Despite (or, perhaps, because of) the difficulties of this form a large number of European poets have used it. Among Englishmen the best known are Sir Philip Sidney, Cowper, Watts, Southey, Tennyson, Swinburne and Ezra Pound. This example is Pound's *Apparuit*, and it shows the strain of using dactyls and trochees as the basic feet in English verse:

> Góldĕn | róse thĕ | hoúse, ĭn thĕ | pórtăl Í sắw |
> theé, ă | márvĕl, | cárvĕn ĭn | súbtlĕ | stúff, ă |
> pórtĕnt. | Lífe diéd | dówn ĭn thĕ | lámp ănd | flíckĕred, |
>   caúght ăt thĕ | wóndĕr. |
>
> Crimson, frosty with dew, the roses bend where
> thou afar, moving in the glamorous sun,
> drinkst in life of earth, of the air, the tissue
>   golden about thee.
>
> Green the ways, the breath of the fields is thine there,
> open lies the land, yet the steely going
> darkly hast thou dared and the dreaded æther
>   parted before thee.
>
> Swift at courage thou in the shell of gold, cast-
> ing a-loose the cloak of the body, camest
> straight, then shone thine oriel and the stunned light
>   faded about thee.
>
> Half the graven shoulder, the throat aflash with
> strands of light inwoven about it, loveli-
> est of all things, frail alabaster, ah me!
>   swift in departing.
>
> Clothed in goldish weft, delicately perfect,
> gone as wind! The cloth of the magical hands!
> Thou a slight thing, thou in access of cunning
>   dar'dst to assume this?

See also ALCAICS; ODE.

satanic school The term was originated by Southey in his preface to *A Vision of Judgment* (1821), a poem which made a fairly violent attack on Shelley and Keats and, especially, on Byron. In the preface Southey refers to Byron's works as 'monstrous combinations of horrors and mockery, lewdness and impiety'. Southey attacked these poets because he thought them immoral (in their lives as well as in their work), because they rejected orthodox Christianity and because he strongly disapproved of their interest in the exotic and passionate. Byron got his own back with a splendid satirical parody (*q.v.*) called *The Vision of Judgment* (1822). However, Southey was poet laureate (*q.v.*) and the law was on his side. Byron's publisher was fined.

satire (L *satira* later from of *satura* 'medley') It may be a cooking term in origin or, as Juvenal called it, *ollapodrida* 'mish-mash', 'farrago'. Quintillian used the term to refer to the kind of poem written by Lucilius – a poem in hexameters (*q.v.*) on various themes; a poem with the tone of the work of Lucilius and Horace. Later the term widened its meaning to include works that were satirical in tone but not in form. At some stage a confusion came about between the Greek *satyros* and *satura* which led to the word being written *satyra* and then, in English, *satyre*. Elizabethan writers, misled by the etymology, supposed that it derived from the Greek *satyr* 'woodland demon'. The situation was finally cleared up in 1605 by the French Huguenot scholar, Isaac Casaubon.

In his *Dictionary* Johnson defined *satire* as a poem 'in which wickedness or folly is censured'. This, clearly, is limiting. Dryden claimed that the true end of satire was 'the amendment of vices'; and Defoe thought that it was 'reformation'. One of the most famous definitions is Swift's. 'Satire', he wrote, 'is a sort of glass wherein beholders do generally discover everybody's face but their own, which is the chief reason for that kind of reception it meets in the world, and that so very few are offended with it.' In *Epilogue to the Satires* (1738), Pope apostrophized satire thus:

> O sacred Weapon! left for Truth's defence,
> Sole dread of Folly, Vice, and Insolence!
> To all but Heav'n-directed hands deny'd,
> The Muse may give thee, but the Gods must guide.
> Rev'rent I touch thee!

The satirist is thus a kind of self-appointed guardian of standards, ideals and truth; of moral as well as aesthetic values. He is a man (women satirists are *very* rare) who takes it upon himself to correct, censure and ridicule the follies and vices of society and thus to bring contempt and derision upon aberrations from a desirable and civilized norm. Thus satire is a kind of protest, a sublimation and refinement of anger and indignation. As Ian Jack has put it very adroitly: 'Satire is born of the instinct to protest; it is protest become art.'

In *Essays in Satire* (1928) Ronald Knox likened the satirist to a small boy who goes about with a water pistol charged with vitriol. He also suggests that the satirist is a kind of spiritual therapist whose function is to destroy the root causes of the major diseases of the spirit, like hypocrisy, pride and greed. But the satirist does not necessarily confine himself to such moral cancers. Juvenal had taken a much wider view in *Satires* I (ll. 85–6):

> quidquid agunt homines, votum timor ira voluptas
> gaudia discursus, nostri farrago libelli est.

Juvenal was particularly severe on the Roman society of his time. However, very often the satirist does attack on a narrow front (is highly selective rather than going in for the 'saturation bombing' of Juvenal), but his chosen targets are sufficiently representative to give his satire universality (*q.v.*) and this is all-important. Good examples are Jonson's ferocious exposure of the evils of cupidity in *Volpone*, Molière's sardonic ridicule of religious hypocrisy in *Tartuffe*, Pope's scathing epistle *Of the Characters of Women* and Samuel Butler's ironical condemnation of complacency and materialism in *The Way of All Flesh*.

The history of satire begins with the early Greek poets. With Archilochus, for example (7th c. BC), and with Hipponax (6th c. BC). The former is said to have been so savage that one, Lycambes, and his daughters hanged themselves. Pliny tells us that Hipponax was so maliciously cruel at the expense of two artists who had made a statue which ridiculed his ugliness that they, too, hanged themselves in despair. But the great satirist of Greece was Aristophanes (*c.* 448–*c.* 380 BC), who used invective, ridicule and abuse to excellent effect in several plays.

In Rome satire began, as suggested above, with Lucilius (180–102 BC), while Varro, Horace, Petronius and Seneca practised the other kind, *satura*, of whom the first composer was probably Ennius (239–169 BC). There appears to be no satire in the modern sense in his *Saturae*. On the other hand we do find some elements of *satura* in Lucilius, who had a considerable influence on Horace, who in turn influenced Persius – the acknowledged 'master' of Juvenal. Grossly to simplify the complex development of a genre, we can say that Horace and Juvenal between them are the 'father' figures of two basic classes of satire. Horace is the tolerant, urbane and amused spectator of the human scene; Juvenal is bitter, misanthropic and consumed with indignation. Pope's *Moral Essays* are in the tradition of Horace; his *Dunciad* in that of Juvenal.

From the 1st c. AD until near the end of the 12th there appears to be little satire of any note in European literature, though one can detect satirical elements and tones here and there in the occasional work. In medieval literature and thereafter it becomes quite plentiful; in, for instance, *Livre des Manières* (*c.* 1170) and in *fabliaux* (*q.v.*); and in such works as *Reynard the Fox* and *Till Eulenspiegel.* It is plentiful, also, in Chaucer's *Canterbury Tales* (late 14th c.) and Langland's *Piers Plowman* (late 14th c.), in Goliardic verse (*q.v.*) and in Villon's *Ballades.* We find it becoming more overt later in, for example, *satire bernesque* (*q.v.*), in Brandt's *Narrenschiff* (1494), Erasmus's *Moriae Encomium* (1509) and Sir Thomas More's *Utopia* (1516). Quite sustained satire, though rough and swingeing, and perhaps better described as invective, is a feature of much verse by Dunbar and Skeleton.

The first adaptation of Classical satire appears to have been Thomas Drant's *Medicinable Morall* (1566), two books of translations from Horace; which he followed in the next year with *Arte of Poetrie*, further translations from Horace.

From late in the 16th c. and early in the 17th we find an increasing propensity towards satirical modes and means, rather than the *occasional* satire of Dante, Barclay or Cervantes. Examples in English literature are Thomas Lodge's *A Fig for Momus* (1595), a collection of satires in the Horatian manner. The satires of Donne, Marston and Hall are more bitter and sardonic and thus nearer to Juvenal. Marston's pessimism produced some notable satire, particularly in *The Scourge of Villainie* (1598). Hall claimed to be the first English satirist, but this now seems presumptuous on his part. From this period too we should mention the satirical comedy (*q.v.*) of Ben Jonson.

From round about the middle of the 17th c. the closed or heroic couplet (*q.v.*) tends to be the favourite form of the verse satirist. The couplet was developed by Sir John Denham and Edmund Waller and perfected, in turn, by Marvell, Dryden and Pope. Marvell's satires are vigorous and denunciatory to the point of being savage. *The Last Instructions to a Painter* (not published until

1689 but written much earlier) is one of his most notable works. Milton only very occasionally wrote satirical verse.

The major English satirist of the second half of the 17th c. was Dryden, whose most notable satires were *Absalom and Achitophel* (1681), *The Medal* (1682), *Mac Flecknoe* (1682) and *The Hind and the Panther* (1687); plus his admirable translations of satires by Persius and Juvenal (1693) to which he wrote an important preface called 'Discourse concerning the Original and Progress of Satire'.

John Oldham, a younger contemporary of Dryden, wrote some satires and so, later, did Rochester. During approximately the same period Samuel Butler published his mock-heroic poem *Hudibras* (1663, 1664, 1678). In France Molière was producing a succession of satirical comedies which have become classics. The finest satire of the period in verse was written by Boileau. From 1660 onwards he published a large number of satires. One of his main works was *Le Lutrin* (1674, 1683), a mock-heroic (*q.v.*) poem.

In European literature, the last part of the 17th c. and much of the 18th is generally regarded as the golden age of satire. Various reasons are adduced for this. Those commonly put forward are that it was a period of fairly highly developed civilization and culture (at any rate, for a minority) which bred the satirists whose need and purpose was to protect this culture from abuse, aberration and corruption. The satirist's aim was to keep it intact by ridiculing and bringing scorn upon those who threatened to impair it. Thus we find Pope satirizing materialism, excess and bad writing; Swift ferociously attacking hypocrisy, pride, cruelty and political expedience; Voltaire ridiculing credulity, religious humbug and naive optimism; and Dr Johnson, with sombre magnificence, arraigning the world with folly, vanity and affectation. With their moral weight and unblinking scrutiny of the truth, such men sought to be the cleansers and guardians of civilization – such as it was; for there can be no doubt that the 18th c. (like any other century) was, for the majority, from China to Peru, an era of poverty, misery and pain.

One could say that during the period in question one of the major preferred modes of expression, in prose and verse, was satire. The debate as to whether verse or prose is the most suitable vehicle for satire is unresolved. On balance it seems that both have equal claims, but satirists have tended to use prose more – very probably because it is very difficult indeed to write good satire in verse.

In the first half of the 18th c. there flourished the two greatest satirists in the history of literature; namely, Swift and Pope. Swift excelled in prose, Pope in verse. The Dean's principal works were *A Tale of a Tub* (1704), *The Battle of the Books* (1704), *Gulliver's Travels* (1726) and *A Modest Proposal* (1729). He was also an accomplished verse satirist, as he showed, for example, in *Verses on the Death of Dr Swift* (1739). Pope's main works were *The Rape of the Lock* (1714), miscellaneous *Satires, Epistles* and *Moral Essays* published during the 1730s and *The Dunciad* (1728, 1729, 1742 and 1743). Other notable instances of satire in English literature from the mid-18th c. onwards were Fielding's burlesque play *Tom Thumb* (1730) – burlesque (*q.v.*) was a particularly favoured means of satire at this time – his *Shamela* (1741) and his *Jonathan Wild* (1743). To these examples one should add Johnson's great poems *London* (1738) and *The Vanity of Human Wishes* (1749), Charles Churchill's *Rosciad* (1761) and *The Prophecy of Famine* (1763) and other works, and the anonymous *Letters of Junius* (1769–71). In France the greatest prose satirist of the period was unquestionably Voltaire. Minor verse satirists of the later 18th c. were John Wolcot, Christopher Anstey, Allan Ramsay and Robert Burns.

Most of the major poets who flourished at the turn of the century and during the Romantic period (*q.v.*) wrote satire occasionally. Crabbe, for instance, in his narrative poems; Shelley in *Masque of Anarchy* (1832); Keats in his unfinished *The Cap and Bells* (1848). However, the major satirist of this period was undoubtedly Byron, who was outstandingly successful in the satiric mode in *Don Juan* (1819–24) and *The Vision of Judgment* (1822).

Many 19th c. poets wrote satire on occasions, notably Praed, Bulwer-Lytton, Tennyson, Browning, Coventry Patmore, and Alfred Austin. In France the main verse satirist was Victor Hugo whose collection *Les Châtiments* (1853) is a major work. For the most part, during the 19th c. (and thereafter) prose was the chosen medium for satire. The principal writers were Thackeray, Flaubert, Anatole France and Samuel Butler. Thackeray's main achievements were *Barry Lyndon* (1844) and *Vanity Fair* (1847–8). Flaubert's chief satire was *Bouvard et Pécuchet* (1881). Anatole France wrote *L'Histoire contemporaine* (1896–1901) and *L'Ile des pingouins* (1908). Butler's most famous works were *Erewhon* (1872), *Erewhon Revisited* (1901) and *The Way of All Flesh* (1903).

During the 20th c. satire has been rare. Two of the main reasons for this lack are that it has been a period of much instability and violent change, and the humour industry has grown to such an extent that the satirist can hardly make himself felt except in the caricature and the cartoon. Sustained verbal satire of merit has been very unusual. Verse satire is very uncommon, though we find occasional instances in Belloc, Chesterton, Wyndham Lewis, W. H. Auden, Julian Bell and Hugh MacDiarmid. The only poet to attempt satire on a considerable scale was Roy Campbell in *The Georgiad* and *The Wayzgoose*.

To these instances we should add some of Aldous Huxley's early novels (e.g. *Antic Hay*), several novels by Evelyn Waugh (e.g. *Vile Bodies*, *Black Mischief*, *A Handful of Dust*, *Scoop*, *Put Out More Flags* and *The Loved One*) and George Orwell's *Animal Farm* – a political satire in the beast-fable tradition. Anti-utopianism or dystopianism has also produced a kind of satire: the creation of a futuristic society whose shortcomings and evils are then exposed. The most famous examples of these in English literature are Huxley's *Brave New World* and Orwell's *Nineteen Eighty-Four*. *See also* CARICATURE; INVECTIVE; LAMPOON; MENIPPEAN SATIRE; UTOPIA.

satire bernesque A type of satire (*q.v.*) named after the Italian poet Berni (1490–1536). Its main feature is grotesque caricature of manners, in which paradox, fantasy and bizarre comparisons are the commonest elements.

satirical comedy A form of comedy (*q.v.*), usually dramatic, whose purpose is to expose, censure and ridicule the follies, vices and shortcomings of society, and of individuals who represent that society. It is often closely akin to burlesque, farce and comedy of manners (*qq.v.*). Some of the best and earliest examples of satirical comedy are to be found in the plays of Aristophanes, especially his *Acharnians*, *Knights*, *Clouds*, *Wasps*, *Birds*, *Frogs* and *Lysistrata*. In English literature classic examples of the genre are Ben Jonson's *Volpone* (1606) and *The Alchemist* (1610); Sheridan's *The School for Scandal* (1777); Shaw's *The Doctor's Dilemma* (1906). Apart from Aristophanes and Jonson, the supreme exponent of satirical comedy in the theatre is Molière, as in *Les Précieuses ridicules* (1659); *Le Misanthrope* (1666); *Le Médecin malgré lui* (1666); *Tartuffe* (1669); *L'Avare* (1669); *Le Bourgeois Gentilhomme* (1670); *Le Malade imaginaire* (1673). Other such works include Machiavelli's *Mandragola* (*c.* 1520); Gogol's *The Government Inspector* (1836); Benavente's *Gente conocida* (1896), *La noche del sábado* (1903), *Los intereses creados* (1907); Kanin's *Born Yesterday* (1946); and Sartre's *Nekrassov* (1955). Since the Second World War there have been Nigel Dennis's *Cards of Identity* (1956), *The Making of Moo*

(1957) and *August for the People* (1961); Alan Bennett's *Forty Years On* (1968); Tom Stoppard's *Jumpers* (1972) and *Dirty Linen* (1976); David Hare's *Teeth 'n' Smiles* (1975); David Mamet's *American Buffalo* (1975) and *Glengarry Glen Ross* (1983); Michael Frayn's *Liberty Hall* (1979); David Hare and Howard Brenton's *Pravda* (1985); and Caryl Churchill's *Serious Money* (1987).

satura *See* SATIRE.

Saturnian meter An early Latin meter chiefly used by Livius Andronicus and Naevius, and so called because Roman writers related it to the age of Saturn. There are about 160 examples of it. Whether it was scanned accentually or by quantity is not certain.

satyr play The Greek tragic poet was expected to present four plays at once: three tragedies (whether a trilogy or not) and a satyr play, which came as a kind of after-piece (*q.v.*). It was a form of burlesque (*q.v.*) in which a mythical hero (perhaps the hero of the foregoing tragedies) was presented as a ridiculous personage with a chorus of satyrs, perhaps led by Silenus. The satyrs were creatures that were half man and half goat, or half man and half horse, and bore prominent, erect phalluses. In Greek art and pottery satyri were often depicted thus; and the goat has for centuries been regarded as a symbol of lust. The satyr plays were ribald in speech and action as well as in costume, and their dramatic function was clearly a form of comic relief (*q.v.*) after matters of high seriousness. Such a play had the effect of 'earthing' an audience, so to speak, after it had had the exalting spiritual experience of tragedy. It was a reaffirmation of the senses and of the sensual pleasures of life. Their origin is obscure, though Aristotle contends that tragedy developed out of the satyric. It is possible that the satyr play first formed part of the tragic contest instituted by Pisistratus at the festival of Dionysus.

There were a great many satyr plays. Aeschylus is believed to have written 90 plays altogether, including about 20 satyr plays. Sophocles's output is believed to have been 123 plays all told, including perhaps 30 satyr plays. And Euripides probably wrote 80 plays, 15 of which were satyr plays. We may conclude that we have lost over 60 satyr plays in all. As to what became of them there has been much speculation. Perhaps they were destroyed/repressed for socio-political reasons; or perhaps they were destroyed/repressed during the early centuries of Christian culture. Tony Harrison, in his introduction to his play *The Trackers of Oxyrhynchus* (publ. 1990), suggests that the latter reason may be the relevant one when he writes: 'The unease that is felt and has long been felt at the idea of the bloated celebrant following hard on the heels of the sufferer, has been responsible, along with natural oblivion, for the loss of these plays . . .'

Pratinas and Aeschylus were regarded as the masters of the form. Only one play survives complete, namely the *Cyclops* of Euripides. In 1907 Grenfell and Hunt, the Oxford classical scholars and papyrologists, while excavating a rubbish mound at Oxyrhynchus (a former town about 100 miles south of modern Cairo) discovered fragments of Sophocles's satyr play the *Ichneutai*. It comprises about 400 lines.

In 1987 Tony Harrison's remarkable play *The Trackers of Oxyrhynchus* was presented at Delphi. This is based on Sophocles's *Ichneutai* and is a free adaptation and development (in verse) of its ideas and themes in such a way as to give them contemporary relevance. In 1990 it was performed at the National Theatre, London.

There is no connection of any kind between satyric drama and satire (*q.v.*); or, apparently, between it and Greek comedy. *See* TETRALOGY.

saudosismo A Portuguese term for a blend of pantheism and the cult of the Portuguese sentiment *saudade* or 'yearning'. The movement, such as it was, to which the term refers was initiated shortly before the First World War by Teixeira de Pascoais (1878–1952). It was inspired by a kind of mystical nationalism and was retrogressive in that it harked back to folklore, fantasy and national myth. Neither realistic nor rational, it promoted the bizarre idea that a 'new world' would emerge under the leadership of Portugal and was so far out of touch with reality that its more eccentric advocates actually thought that King Sebastian (killed in Morocco in 1578) was destined to return and lead Portugal to greatness in the putative new era. The poet Fernando Pessoa (1885–1935) was closely associated with it and his collection of poems *Mensagem* (1934) expressed some of the cult's fundamental yearnings.

savoyard In the 18th c. natives of Savoy (near Lake Geneva) were well known as itinerant musicians with hurdy-gurdy and monkey. Today the term is more likely to denote a devotee of Gilbert and

Sullivan operas, for which, in 1881, D'Oyly Carte built the Savoy Theatre in London. He opened it with a production of *Patience*.

scansion (L *scandere* 'to climb') The analysis of the metrical patterns of verse. It includes the arrangement of accented and unaccented syllables into metrical feet and the grouping of lines according to the number of feet. Also, the classification of stanza according to rhyme scheme and the number of lines per stanza.

There are three basic methods of scanning English verse: graphic, musical and acoustic. The graphic is the most commonly used. The conventional symbols are: × or ∪ to denote a syllable which is unstressed (or short); / or — to denote a stressed (or long) syllable; | to indicate a foot division; || to indicate a caesura (*q.v.*).

When scanning, the normal practice is to mark in the stressed and unstressed syllables according to the natural emphasis in the words. Thus, this first stanza from Kingsley Amis's *Beowulf* reads:

> Só, || bóred wĭth drágŏns, || hĕ láy dówn tŏ sléep,
> Lóckĭng fŏr góod || hĭs mássĭve hóard ŏf wórds
> (Dĭscúss ănd íllŭstrăte), || fŏrgéttĭng nów
> Thĕ hópe ŏf héathĕns, || múddlĕd thóughts ŏn fáte.

Scansion helps to reveal rhythm and gives the reader a representation of the 'tune' underlying and supporting the words.

Stanzaic structure may be analyzed by indicating the rhyme scheme in letters and by the number of feet per line in the numbers. For example, the following stanza from Thomas Hood's *A Reflection*:

> When Eve upon the first of Men
> The apple press'd with specious cant,
> Oh, what a thousand pities then
> That Adam was not Adamant.

may be notated thus: abab – $a^4b^4a^4b^4$.

Some prosodists prefer musical symbols, using eighth for unstressed syllables and quarter or half notes for stressed syllables. Caesuras may be indicated by musical rests of varying lengths. The acoustic method has been developed by linguists using the kymograph and the oscillograph. A small minority prefer to indicate rhythmical movements and sound units by wavy lines and brackets. *See* FOOT; METER; SPRUNG RHYTHM.

Scapigliatura Derived from the Italian word *scapigliati* 'dishevelled', it refers to a group of artists and writers who flourished in Milan and Turin in the 1860s. They led an excessively Bohemian life and rebelled against prevailing literary and artistic modes and conventions. Their vitality and experimental approach had a considerable influence on the immediate course of Italian literature.

scatology (Gk 'dung knowledge') In pathology, diagnosis by a study of the faeces. As a literary term used occasionally for obscene or bawdy literature. *See* LOW COMEDY; PORNOGRAPHY.

scazon *See* CHOLIAMBUS.

scenario An outline of a theatrical or cinematic work, giving the sequence of scenes, the characters involved and so forth.

scene A sub-division of an act (*q.v.*) in a play or an opera or other theatrical entertainment.

scène à faire French for 'obligatory scene' (*q.v.*).

Schauerroman (G 'shudder novel') The German equivalent of the Gothic novel (*q.v.*) in English and related to the horror story (*q.v.*). 'Shudder' because it is a spine-chiller which gives you 'the shivers'. *See also* RITTER- UND RAUBERROMAN.

Schauspiel (G 'spectacle, sight') A term for any public performance or visual entertainment. More specifically it denotes a play which is neither comedy nor tragedy (*qq.v.*) but which is a serious play whose resolution is positive and hopeful or optimistic. It does not end with the death of the hero or heroine. The term was first used for the performance of a stage play by Niklaus Manuel (1484–1530). During the 18th c. it acquired its modern sense. Examples of a *Schauspiel* are Goethe's *Iphigenie auf Tauris* (1779), Schiller's *Die Räuber* (1782) and Brecht's *Leben des Galilei* (1943). *See also* DRAME; TRAGI-COMEDY.

Schelmenroman The German term for picaresque novel (*q.v.*).

Schicksalstragödie (G 'fate/destiny tragedy') A form of tragedy (*q.v.*) which had some vogue in Germany early in the 19th c. In such a play the hero or heroine (in some instances a complete family) was driven towards crime or destruction by a kind of fate or nemesis from which there was no escape. The sequence of tragic events might be the result of some crime. The victims might be destroyed on a particular fated day or through a fated/fatal weapon (or both). The sombre and doom-laden quality of these plays owes something to Greek tragedy, the Gothic novel (*q.v.*) and to the more bizarre extravagances of Gothic type romances. Crime and its disastrous consequences were themes that were to become of increasing interest to writers during the 19th c., as may be seen in a variety of fiction (e.g. Newgate fiction and the detective story, *qq.v.*). The first example of *Schicksalstragödie* is generally believed to be Moritz's *Blunt, oder der Gast* (1781). Later came Zacharias Werner's *Der vierundzwanzigste Februar* (1806). Others are *Der neunundzwanzigste* (1815) by Adolf Müllner and his *Die Schuld* (1816). Baron von Houwald wrote *Das Bild* (1821), *Die Heimkehr* (1821) and *Der Leuchtturm* (1821). Grillparzer's *Die Ahnfrau* (1816) has also been regarded as a fate tragedy. After the 1820s this form of drama fell into desuetude.

Schlüsselroman A German term for a 'key novel' or *roman à clef*. *See* LIVRE A CLEF.

scholasticism The teachers of the liberal arts in the medieval schools were known as *doctores scholastici*; theologians and philosophers were also so called. Scholasticism now refers, loosely, to the methods and matter of theological and philosophical thought in the Middle Ages. St Thomas Aquinas, Duns Scotus, Peter Lombard and Albertus Magnus were all scholastics – the principal luminaries in an exceptional constellation of metaphysicians. The influence of scholasticism since the Middle Ages has been enormous, and its spirit has been kept alive in more recent times by T. E. Hulme, Jacques Maritain, Etienne Gilson and Gabriel Marcel. *See also* HUMANISM; RENAISSANCE.

school The term may be applied to a group of writers who combine as an influential unit and who are broadly agreed on the principles upon which their work should be based. Sometimes the principles are published as a manifesto (*q.v.*). A school may produce a movement whose influence spreads to several countries. Schools are usually shortlived but their fertilizing impact may last many years, especially when the principles which guided them have been of a revolutionary nature. Well-known examples of literary schools are: the Pléiade, the Göttinger Dichterbund, the Pre-Raphaelite

Brotherhood, the Parnassians, the school of Spenser and the Bloomsbury Group (*qq.v.*).

school drama A term applied to an academic and educational genre of plays which were written by scholars and performed by schoolboys. Early in the 16th c. there was a great deal of dramatic activity in schools and colleges in England. In *c.* 1553 *Ralph Roister Doister* was written by Nicholas Udall or Uvedale, headmaster of Westminster, and performed by the boys of the school. In 1566 *Gammer Gurton's Needle*, of uncertain authorship, was acted at Christ's College, Cambridge. The tradition of the annual school play very probably derives from school drama. One of the best known examples is the annual Greek play at Bradfield. Originally the plays were in Latin; then the vernacular was used more and more. The Jesuits, above all, were responsible for the popularization of this form in Europe and were the major influence in the 17th c. Jesuit drama (*q.v.*) is a genre of its own. *See* ACADEMIC DRAMA; JESUIT DRAMA.

school of Spenser A group of English poets who, in the earlier part of the 17th c., were considerably under the influence of Edmund Spenser. The main poets were: Browne, Wither, Giles and Phineas Fletcher, and the Scots Drummond of Hawthornden and Sir William Alexander. In imagery, meter and diction, as well as in theme and subject matter, they were imitators of Spenser.

Schüttelreim (G 'jolting verse') The German equivalent of the Spoonerism (*q.v.*), which depends for its comic effect on the transposition or 'jolting' of initial letters.

Schwank A German term for an anecdote or tale in a rather simple literary form. They became popular in the late Middle Ages and proliferated in collections after the invention of printing. Hans Sachs composed many in verse. The jest book (*q.v.*) is an example. *Schwänke* are by no means extinct.

Schwellvers A German term for what are known as expanded lines in OE alliterative verse (*q.v.*). The verse 'swells' when the normal metrical scheme is departed from and extra syllables and words are put in. In these lines from the OE poem *The Seafarer* the last three are clearly different from the first two, which are in the basic meter:

Sē gestaþelade stīþe grundas,
Eorþan scēatas and ūprodor.
Dol biþ sē þe him his Dryhten ne ondrǣdeþ: cumeð him sē dēað unþinged.
Ēadig bið sē þe ēaþmōd leofað: cymeð him sēo ār of heofonum:
Meotod him þaet mōd gestaþelað, for þon hē in his meahte gelȳfeð.

science fiction A science fiction story is a narrative (usually in prose) of short story, *novella* or novel (*qq.v.*) length. As to what it is about, this is not easily classifiable. Such stories are about an amazing variety of things, topics, ideas. They include trips to other worlds, quests, the exploration of space, visits to other planets and interplanetary warfare. Some SF stories are concerned with utopia (*q.v.*) and utopist visions, and also with dystopia. Others are set in the future but are not utopian. Still others are set in the past. Many have a contemporary setting which is somehow influenced by the arrival or invasion of alien beings (alienation in various ways is a common theme) or by some invention which profoundly alters normality. They are also concerned with technological change and development, with scientific experiment, with social, climatic, geological and ecological change. Some are concerned with supernatural forces and agencies. They are often fantastic, though they may be rooted in reality. They stretch the imagination.

The term 'science fiction' was first used, it seems, in 1851, the year of the Great Exhibition, in William Wilson's *A Little Earnest Book upon a Great Old Subject*. Having cited Thomas Campbell's remark that 'Fiction in Poetry is not the reverse of truth, but her soft and enchanting resemblance', Wilson goes on to say: 'Now this applies especially to Science-Fiction, in which the revealed truths of Science may be given, interwoven with a pleasant story which itself may be poetical and true . . .'

There have been many other definitions of this particular mode of fiction, including two by one of the acknowledged experts – Brian Aldiss (1925–), author of *Billion Year Spree* (1973), which was later expanded and updated in the sequel *Trillion Year Spree* (1986). Aldiss defines thus: 'Science fiction is the search for a definition of mankind and his status in the universe which will stand in our advanced but confused state of knowledge (science) and is characteristically cast in the Gothic or post-Gothic mode'. He also defines it more succinctly as 'Hubris clobbered by nemesis'.

New science fiction titles are published by the hundred each year and they are bought and read by the million. It is so diversified a mode, has such a range of form and content, that, ultimately, it eludes definition. As Johnson said of light (April 10th, 1776): 'We all *know* what light is; but it is not easy to *tell* what it is'.

The term was eventually put into circulation in the late 1920s by Hugo Gernsback (1894–1967), who had originally coined the word 'scientifiction'. 'Science fiction' gradually replaced the term 'scientific romance', and science fiction is quite often categorized as 'speculative fiction'.

The ancestors of modern science fiction are many and various and they reveal, among other things, mankind's remarkable need and capacity for inventing 'alternative worlds'. Myth, legend, travellers' tales, the eschatological order . . . all have made their contributions. There are domains, realms, cities, islands, never-never lands, cloud-cuckoo lands, castles in Spain, lands of Cockaigne, utopias and dystopias. In their *Dictionary of Imaginary Places* (1981) Alberto Manguel and Gianni Guadalopi listed and described about a thousand such microcosms, some not so small. Whether, fundamentally, this propensity and capacity for alternative worlds represent an expression of dissatisfaction with the world men and women actually live in and on is a debatable issue.

Notable predecessors of modern science fiction are too numerous to list in full. An early example is the *Vera Historia* or 'True History' (*c.* AD 150) of Lucian of Samosata, a parody (*q.v.*) of the tall stories (*q.v.*) of adventure presented as truth by former historians. The hero of this work visits the moon and the sun and is involved in interplanetary warfare. The 'vision literature' of the Middle Ages was very popular and widespread in Europe. It is about the exploration of metaphysical worlds: heaven, hell and purgatory. Especially hell, largely, one suspects, because it was more interesting and, anyway, was easier to describe. Trips to the abode of the damned (and conducted tours therein) were, in some cases, an early form of horror story (*q.v.*), and were forerunners of a later kind of 'scientific romance'. Gradually the attraction of such escapist tales palled, to be replaced by utopianism. Thomas More's *Utopia* was published in 1516 and was to be a kind of prototype of all sorts of utopia and utopian schemes, plus adventure quests, including expeditions into space. For instance, Francis Godwin's *The Man in the Moone: or, A Discourse of a Voyage Thither by Domingo Gonsales* (1638), John Wilkins's *Discovery of a New World in the Moone* (1638) and the fantastic stories of Cyrano de

Bergerac, namely *Histoire comique des états et empires de la Lune* (1656) and *Histoire comique des états et empires du Soleil* (1661). In 1668 Margaret Cavendish, Duchess of Newcastle, published *The Description of a New World, called The Blazing World* – an extraordinary Wellsian fantasy in the course of which the Duchess advanced the then improbable idea that mankind might be ruled by a non-human, animal 'intelligence'. Other 17th c. curiosities among the 'ancestors' are Kepler's *Somnium* (1634), also concerned with lunar exploration; and a guided tour of heaven somewhat in the medieval tradition of vision literature in the form of Kircher's *Itinerarium Exstaticum* (1656). In this the author uses Virgil as a guide. To have a guide had been standard practice in medieval grand tours of heaven, hell and purgatory.

The 18th c. was no less fecund in the creation of other worlds and fictional voyages of discovery. Two key works were Swift's *Gulliver's Travels* (1726) and Defoe's *Robinson Crusoe* (1719). These two books were to have a profound and long-lasting influence on fiction in general. *Robinson Crusoe* was the prototype of a genre of novel subsequently described as desert island fiction (*q.v.*) and was the progenitor of the Robinsonade (*q.v.*). There were scores of imitations in Europe during the next two hundred years. Less well known adventure stories of the 18th c. are Ludwig Holberg's *A Journey to the World Underground*, published in 1741 (he wrote it in Latin under the title *Nicolai Klimii Iter Subterraneum*), Robert Paltock's *The Life and Adventures of Peter Wilkins* (1751) and Ralph Morris's *The Life and Astonishing Adventures of John Daniel* (1751). By this stage the novel of adventure and the travel book (*qq.v.*) were well established as separate genres. Voltaire's *Candide* (1759), a philosophical and satirical adventure story, was a combination of both. By this stage, too, there had been a number of utopian fantasies – and many were to follow.

A key work – perhaps *the* key work – in the evolution of science fiction was Mary Shelley's *Frankenstein* (1818). The long-term effect of this novel has been extraordinary. *Frankenstein* is a completely original work, an innovation. The anonymous, identikit monster created by Dr Frankenstein is the product of scientific research, knowledge and skills. The doctor imparts life to a composite being constructed from bits of corpses. The scientific experiment goes disastrously wrong and Frankenstein rejects his creation. That is the basis of the fiction but it is about many other things as well.

Frankenstein produced countless imitations and variations. It was almost immediately dramatized (and continued to be until the films of the 1930s). Since then the monster has been inseparably associated with the name of Boris Karloff – a gentle and humane man whose principal interest was cricket, a game about which he was deeply knowledgeable. During 170 or so years the Frankenstein story has taken secure hold on the popular imagination, but it is perhaps unfortunate that Mary Shelley did not give the monster a name; many who know the basic story but have not read the book refer to it/him as Frankenstein.

During the 19th c. a number of other writers showed a predilection for the scientific romance, akin to what we might now loosely describe as science fiction. Mary Shelley wrote a much less well known book, *The Last Man* (1826), there were yet more utopian novels, the influence of the Gothic novel became pervasive, and Edgar Allan Poe published a number of stories in which one can see him feeling his way towards a science fiction mode. Examples are: *The Conversation of Eiros and Charmion, The Unparalleled Adventures of One Hans Pfaall, The Balloon-Hoax, Mellonta Tauta* and *The Colloquy of Monos and Una.*

By the mid-19th c. (Poe died in 1849), one could say that science fiction was on the move; things were happening, so to speak. In an entry in their *Journal* (for July 16th, 1856) the Goncourt brothers (Edmond and Jules) displayed remarkably astute prescience in commenting on 'a new literary world pointing to the literature of the twentieth century. Scientific miracles, fables on the pattern A+B; a clear-sighted, sickly literature. No more poetry, but analytic fantasy . . . Things playing a more important part than people . . .'

The ever popular Jules Verne (1828–1905), who was considerably influenced by Poe, made a major contribution to a new kind of fiction which combined adventure and exploration and the popularization of science. Immensely prolific, he is now best remembered for *Voyage au centre de la terre* (1864), *Vingt mille lieues sous les mers* (1869) and *Le Tour du monde en quatre-vingts jours* (1873). A major part of Verne's success was his ability to make scientific expertise plausible.

Something of a landmark in the evolution of new kinds of fiction was Colonel Chesney's *The Battle of Dorking* (1871), an account of an imaginary invasion of England. This produced many imitations of the war-scare kind. The First World War pretty well put an end to that kind of fiction, but not entirely. In 1978 General Sir John Hackett published *The Third World War*, which was a best-seller.

Such fiction is of only marginal importance in terms of the development of SF.

Three minor writers (now seldom read) who experimented with scientific romance at the turn of the 19th c. were M. P. Shiel (1865–1947), William Hope Hodgson (1877–1918) and J. D. Beresford. One of Shiel's first books was *The Yellow Danger* (1898), a future war/invasion story (for his generation 'the yellow peril' was a realistic threat). He followed this with *The Purple Cloud* (1901), *The Lord of the Sea* (1901), *The Last Miracle* (1906) and, much later, *The Young Men are Coming* (1973). Hodgson is now best remembered for his visionary allegory (*q.v.*) *The House on the Borderland* (1908) and also *The Night Land* (1912). Beresford wrote *The Hampdenshire Wonder* (1912). Kipling, Ouida and Arthur Conan Doyle all wrote stories which showed they were aware of other possibilities apart from traditional realism (*q.v.*) in fiction. Doyle's *The Lost World* (1912) is an obvious example. Grant Allen wrote *The British Barbarians* (1895), a story about a scientist from the future working as an anthropologist in England. In Germany Kurt Lasswitz published a remarkable novel called *Auf zwei Planeten* (1897) about Martians.

In the 1890s H. G. Wells, one of the great originators of science fiction ideas – many of which have been refashioned by other writers since – made his impact on the world with such stories as *The Time Machine* (1895), *The Wonderful Visit* (1895), *The Island of Dr Moreau* (1896), *The War of the Worlds* (1898) and the *First Men in the Moon* (1901). Wells was prophetic and showed the way to many possibilities in SF. He had the advantage of being a trained scientist with a profound understanding of scientific matters (he prophesied the atom bomb and lived to see it a reality).

Edgar Rice Burroughs (1875–1950) was also an important figure at the beginning of the 20th c. Apart from inventing Tarzan and all those adventure stories, he wrote many interplanetary fantasies and popularized his own brand of SF in the early pulp (*q.v.*) magazines. Edgar Wallace (1875–1932), better known for his contribution to the thriller (*q.v.*), also wrote SF (e.g. *The Day of Uniting*, 1926, and *Planetoid 127*, 1929), and shortly before he died was responsible for the screenplay for one of the most notable science fiction film successes – *King Kong*.

The First World War affected everyone in Britain to a greater or lesser degree, not least the creators of futuristic scientific romance. There was a steadily burgeoning idea (and even a conviction) that another world war would spell the end of civilization and that mankind was approaching irreversible disaster leading to another epoch of barbarianism. This would be the ultimate horror story. More or less concurrent with this idea was another – that the *terminus post quem* catastrophe/holocaust/Armageddon etc. might somehow lead to the establishment of a new race of human beings; or, that, because mankind was on the brink of comprehensive disaster, a 'new race' would be desirable. A further instance of alternative worlds. These were dominant ideas between the wars. After the Second World War the advent of the nuclear/hydrogen bomb age and the increasing possibility that the whole world might be written off by a lunatic megalomaniac or even by mere carelessness or inefficiency inspired spates of post-nuclear disaster fantasies, and for years tens of thousands of schoolboys read the stuff avidly and indulged their speculative powers on such themes in their weekly compositions. The spectre of the 100-megaton 'bomb' cast an enormous shadow for some twenty years. By the 1980s the fact that a single submarine in the Irish Sea had enough nuclear firepower in its missiles to wipe out all the major cities of Europe was taken entirely for granted and hardly raised an eyebrow.

In the inter-war period not a few British authors wrote books concerned with the effects of a new war. Notable examples are Edward Shanks's *People of the Ruins* (1920), Cicely Hamilton's *Theodore Savage* (1922) and H. G. Wells's *The Shape of Things to Come* (1933). The idea of a new race, a new species of humanity, was developed by a number of writers, and principally by Olaf Stapledon (1886–1950). He introduced an ethical and philosophical element – almost a mystical element – to his extraordinary scientific romances which display a cosmic vision at once grand, spectacular and despairing. His two main books were *Last and First Men* (1930) – a history of man's descendants over some billions of years – and *Star Maker* (1937). He also wrote *Odd John* (1935), *Sirius* (1944), *The Flames* (1947) and *A Man Divided* (1950). Other writers to explore comparable themes about the future of man were E. V. Odle in *The Clockwork Man* (1923), John Gloag in *Tomorrow's Yesterday* (1930), M. P. Shiel in *The Young Men are Coming* and J. D. Beresford in *What Dreams May Come . . .* (1941).

By the 1920s utopian visions were unfashionable. Dystopian visions began to replace them. For example, Zamyatin's *We* (1920–21) and Muriel Jaeger's *The Question Mark* (1923). Later, in 1932, came Aldous Huxley's *Brave New World*: a brilliantly witty and deeply depressing picture of a possible future society in a book whose popularity has remained undiminished after nearly sixty years. From the late 1940s onwards there was to come a succession of anti-utopian or dystopian fictions which examined various kinds of repressive régimes. George Orwell's *Nineteen Eighty-Four* (1949) remains the most famous. Other notable instances are: H. F. Heard's *Doppelgangers* (1947); B. F. Skinner's *Walden Two* (1948); George R. Stewart's *Earth Abides* (1949); Kurt Vonnegut's *Player Piano* (1952); David Karp's *One* (1953), a most sinister depiction of a totalitarian system; Evelyn Waugh's *Love among the Ruins* (1953); Pohl and Kornbluth's *The Space Merchants* (1953); Ray Bradbury's *Fahrenheit 451* (1953); Anthony Burgess's *A Clockwork Orange* (1962) and *The Wanting Seed* (1962); Harry Harrison's *Make Room! Make Room!* (1966); James Blish and Norman L. Knight's *A Torrent of Faces* (1967); John Brunner's *Stand on Zanzibar* (1968); and Philip K. Dick's *Flow My Tears, the Policeman Said* (1974). Some of these novels are concerned with the nightmare of overcrowding on an over-populated planet.

In the 1920s scientific romance in America received a big boost through magazines and through the popularity of, for example, Edgar Rice Burroughs's space fiction stories, or space operas. Hugo Gernsback popularized a number of writers through magazines. The American authors were not much concerned with global catastrophes or the advantages of a 'new' *homo sapiens*, partly, no doubt, because the American continent had not been affected by the First World War. They were more interested in new technologies and interplanetary travel. Much of it was pulp literature in the full pejorative sense. In short, it was often naïve trash.

During the 1930s and 1940s American science fiction continued to be confined to the magazines, but gradually it became more intellectual and sophisticated. This was largely due to the impact of John W. Campbell, a third-rate writer but a fine editor. He took over the magazine *Astounding* in 1937 and edited it for thirty-four years. It was he who recruited such writers as Isaac Asimov, Robert A. Heinlein, Clifford D. Simak, Theodore Sturgeon, A. E. van Vogt and Fritz Leiber.

Asimov, prodigiously prolific, has been a dominant figure for nearly fifty years and has written a wide variety of fiction. His early stories were the three-volume *Foundation* series (1942–50), which came out in book form in 1951–3. In 1951 he published what has become a classic collection: *I, Robot*. He followed with science fiction detective stories such as *The Caves of Steel* (1954) and *The Naked Sun* (1956), plus robot stories in the collection *The*

Bicentennial Man and Other Stories (1976). Other novels include *The Currents of Space* (1952), *The End of Eternity* (1955), *The Gods Themselves* (1972), *Foundation's Edge* (1982), *The Robots of Dawn* (1983) and *Robots and Empires* (1985). Robert A. Heinlein began his long career in the pulp magazines in 1939. Many of those stories were collected in *The Past through Tomorrow* (1967). He has written numerous novels, including *Double Star* (1956), the future war story *Starship Troopers* (1959) and *Stranger in a Strange Land* (1961). A. E. van Vogt wrote several distinguished short stories and memorable novels, including *Slan* (1940), *The Weapon Ships of Isher* (1941), *The World of Null-A* (1945) and its sequel *The Pawns of Null-A* (1948–9). Among Simak's best known books is *Way Station* (1963). One of Sturgeon's best early novels is *More than Human* (1953). Leiber's two outstanding novels are *The Big Time* (1958) and *The Wanderer* (1964).

Science fiction became even more popular in America with the arrival of paperbacks. Many short stories were still written, but the novel (and series of novels) attracted writers more and more. The American modes of science fiction became dominant in Britain and elsewhere during the 1950s.

In Britain, C. S. Lewis had already made highly individual contributions in the late 1930s with *Out of the Silent Planet* (1938), and *Perelandra* (1939) – which he followed with *That Hideous Strength* (1945). This trilogy has remained immensely popular. J. R. R. Tolkien's *The Lord of the Rings* (1954–5) was read avidly by SF buffs, but whether or not it is science fiction, however that flexible term is interpreted, is debatable. Perhaps it is scientific romance. In the 1950s John Wyndham published a series of highly original books which combined elements of the old-fashioned romance with those of more modern science fiction. He depicted ordinary people exposed to weird and terrifying circumstances which involve a desperate struggle for survival. His main and continuously popular novels are *The Day of the Triffids* (1951), *The Kraken Wakes* (1953), *The Chrysalids* (1955), *The Midwich Cuckoos* (1957) and *The Trouble with Lichen* (1960). Even more successful was Arthur C. Clarke, whose early work showed the influence of Olaf Stapledon. Clarke made his name with *Childhood's End* (1953) and *The City and the Stars* (1956). Other notable books have been *Rendezvous with Rama* (1973), *Imperial Earth* (1975) and *The Fountains of Paradise* (1979). He is particularly associated with *2001: A Space Odyssey* (1968) and *2010: Space Odyssey Two* (1982), from which spectacular films were made. Apart from writing the brilliant and encyclopaedically knowledgeable surveys of SF already mentioned – *Billion Year Spree* and *Trillion Year Spree* – Brian Aldiss has made an outstanding contribution to British SF with a series of adventurous novels and many short stories. His first two main books were *Non-Stop* (1958) and *Greybeard* (1964). Gradually his work became more and more varied; for example, *Hothouse* (1962), *Report on Probability A* (1968) and *Barefoot in the Head* (1969). His most ambitious and inventive work was the trilogy *Helliconia Spring* (1982), *Helliconia Summer* (1983) and *Helliconia Winter* (1985). J. G. Ballard has been scarcely less inventive and original. A specialist in the catastrophic, his early novels were *The Drowned World* (1962), *The Drought* (1965) and *The Crystal World* (1966). He followed these with the 'fragmented novels' *The Atrocity Exhibition* (1970) and the novel *Crash* (1973). His short stories, collected in *The Four-Dimensional Nightmare* (1963) and *The Terminal Beach* (1964), are generally regarded as among the best in science fiction.

Basically, since the 1950s, American authors have dominated the scene – in their dozens. Here there is space to mention only a handful. For example, Paul Anderson, who wrote *Brain Wave* (1954) and, much later, *Tan Zero* (1970); Alfred Beston, author of *The Demolished Man* (1953) and *The Stars My Destination* (1956); Clifford Simak, author of *Ring around the Sun* (1952) and *Time and Again* (1951); Kornbluth, author of *Wolfbane* (1959), who collaborated with Frederik Pohl to write the famous story *The Space Merchants.* Pohl also wrote a number of successful novels in the 1970s and 1980s – namely, *Man Plus* (1976), *Gateway* (1977), *Jem* (1979), *Beyond the Blue Event Horizon* (1980) and *The Years of the City* (1985). A classic SF novel is Walter M. Miller's *A Canticle for Leibowitz* (1960). Among James Blish's best achievements were *The Frozen Year* (1957), *Cities in Flight* (1970), *A Case of Conscience* (1958) and *The Day after Judgment* (1971). Ray Bradbury wrote many short stories, a number with science fiction themes, which have been published in various collections. Two of his best known works are *The Martian Chronicles* (1950) and *Fahrenheit 451*. Three of Robert Sheckley's most famous books are *A Journey beyond Tomorrow* (1963), *Dimension of Miracles* (1968) and *Dramocles* (1983). Robert Silverberg was also prolific; some of his best books are *Nightwings* (1967), *Downward to the Earth* (1970), *A Time of Changes* (1971) and *Dying Inside* (1972).

The 1970s saw many more women writers attempting science fiction. For example, Alice Sheldon, Anne McCaffrey, Kate

Wilhelm, Kit Reed, Josephine Saxton, Marion Zimmer Bradley, Vonda McIntyre, Suzy Mckee Charnas, Joan Vinge, Pamela Sargent and Ursula Le Guin. Ursula Le Guin has been particularly successful and highly regarded. Some of her best known works are *The Earthsea Trilogy* (1968–72), *The Left Hand of Darkness* (1969) and *The Dispossessed* (1974).

New developments in science fiction took place in the mid-1960s and many of these have been attributed to the so-called new wave under the influence of Michael Moorcock, who took over the important magazine *New Worlds* in 1964. Moorcock wrote some outstanding books, especially his series about Jerry Cornelius. His tetralogy comprising *The Final Programme* (1968), *A Cure for Cancer* (1971), *The English Assassin* (1972) and *The Condition of Muzak* (1977) was particularly highly thought of. Moorcock regarded William Burroughs as a kind of archetype for a new kind of science fiction. The American Harlan Ellison had some effect on the 'new wave' in his anthologies begun with *Dangerous Visions* (1967). Ellison also wrote some notable short stories, such as *I Have No Mouth and I Must Scream* (1967) and *A Boy and His Dog* (1969). There were many new experimental writers. Among them we should mention particularly: Roger Zelazny, author of *A Rose for Ecclesiastes* (1963), *The Dream Mask* (1966), *This Immortal* (1966) and *Lord of Light* (1967); Philip K. Dick, who wrote a number of memorable novels, including *The Man in the High Castle* (1962), *Martian Time-Slip* (1964), *Now Wait for Last Year* (1966), *Do Androids Dream of Electric Sheep?* (1969) and *A Scanner Darkly* (1977); Thomas M. Disch, author of *Camp Concentration* (1968); Samuel R. Delaney, author of *Nova* (1968), *Dhalgren* (1975) and short stories collected in the title *Driftglass* (1971); John Sladek, who wrote *The Muller-Fokker Effect* (1970); Barry Malzberg, author of *Beyond Apollo* (1972), *The Men Inside* (1973) and *Herovit's World* (1973); Frank Herbert, who published the immensely successful series of *Dune* novels in the 1960s and 1970s; and Kurt Vonnegut, author of *Slaughterhouse-5* (1969), which helped to make science fiction 'respectable' on American university campuses.

Professional practitioners of the modern horror story (e.g. Stephen King) have recently tended to introduce science fiction elements in their work. Some writers who have for the most part written fairly traditional and realistic fiction have also turned to science fiction for new ideas and techniques. A notable instance is Doris Lessing with her space fiction series *Canopus in Argos:*

Archives (1979–83), which comprises five novels. Others are Thomas Pynchon, Gore Vidal and Jeremy Leven. Pynchon's *Gravity's Rainbow* (1973) was particularly successful.

scolion A type of Greek lyric poetry. Its etymology and origin are uncertain, but it seems to have been a kind of drinking song, sung by choruses and accompanied by a lyre. Tradition ascribes the invention of the *scolion* to a famous musician called Terpander, a native of Lesbos, who lived in the first half of the 7th c. BC.

scop (OE 'jester, one who scoffs') An Anglo-Saxon minstrel; also known as a gleeman. A professional entertainer (poet and singer) of an ancient and honoured calling. The *scopas* were the conservers of the OE oral tradition (*q.v.*) and they were makers of poetry as well as reciters. A number of them were members of royal households, like the *skalds* (*q.v.*). Few are known by name, but in the OE poem *Widsith* 'far traveller' we see the *scop* travelling from court to court and reciting his lays. The poem *Deor* 'animal brave' also affords us glimpses of the *scop's* life. The art of the *scop* is still perpetuated by ballad-makers in many parts of the world, and especially by the *guslar* (*q.v.*) in the South Slav lands. *See also* EPIC; SAGA; TROUBADOUR; TROUVERE.

Scottish Chaucerians The traditional title of a group of Scottish poets whose work apparently shows the influence of Chaucer. In fact, the influence was slight, though it is true that in his poem *The Kingis Quair* King James I (1394–1437) did use the rhyme royal (*q.v.*) scheme that Chaucer had used in *Troilus and Criseyde* and elsewhere, and Robert Henryson (1424?–1506?) wrote a fine sequel to Chaucer's poem in the shape of *The Testament of Cresseid.* Henryson and the King were two of the main Scottish Chaucerians. The others were William Dunbar (1456?–1513?) and Gawin Douglas (1475?–1522). *See also* SCOTTISH RENAISSANCE.

Scottish Enlightenment The term denotes an intellectual movement which originated in Glasgow early in the 18th c. and was thereafter at its most active in Edinburgh from *c.* 1750 to 1800. It is mostly associated with philosophers and scientists, and the leading lights in the movement had considerable influence in Britain, France and America. Some of them were: Francis Hutcheson (1694–1746); Thomas Reid (1710–96); David Hume (1711–76); Adam Smith

(1723–90); Adam Ferguson (1723–1816); and Dugald Stewart (1753–1828). *See* ENLIGHTENMENT.

Scottish renaissance A movement in Scottish literature which was at its most active between the wars. Those who belonged to it wished to revive Scots (or Lallans as it is now called) as a literary language. They aimed to achieve the revival through the use of regional dialects and also by harking back to the styles and traditions of the Scottish poets of the 15th and 16th c. The principal moving spirit of the movement was Hugh MacDiarmid (1892–1978) – his actual name was C. M. Grieve – who was politically committed (he was a Communist) and wanted to re-create Scots as a national language. He also wanted to reanimate Scottish political and social institutions. By these means he aimed to counter what he described as the 'English ascendancy'. Other prominent members of the movement were William Soutar (1898–1943), Lewis Grassic Gibbon (1901–1935) and Sorley Maclean (1911–). *See also* SCOTTISH CHAUCERIANS.

Scriblerus Club A club founded *c.* 1713 whose principal members were Pope, Swift, Gay, Congreve, Arbuthnot, Parnell and Lord Oxford. It was so called after an imaginary antiquarian Martinus Scriblerus, a German of Münster, who had the reputation of being a man who had read almost everything but who had no judgement at all. He became the subject of 'memoirs', mostly written by Dr John Arbuthnot, and published in 1741. The 'memoirs' were a kind of satire (*q.v.*) against pretentious learning and false tastes.

scriptible *See* READERLY/WRITERLY.

scriptorium (L 'writing room') A room in a monastery or abbey which is devoted to the writing and copying of books.

Scythians A group of Russian writers and intellectuals led by the socialist revolutionary Ivanov-Ruzumnik (pseudonym of R. V. Ivanov, 1878–1945) who, with various followers, supported the Bolsheviks in the 1917 October Revolution. They stressed the fundamental differences between Russia and the West and maintained that the Russians were not Europeans but Scythians: that is, half Asiatic and half European. They sought to do away with European influence and purge Russia of it. They had mystical beliefs in the nature and future of Russia and the Russians, and they greatly admired the poetry of Yesenin (1895–1925) and Klyuyev (1885–1937), which presented a kind of mystical acceptance of the Russian Revolution as the ultimate destiny of the Russian people. A number of notable writers were influenced by the Scythians' point of view, including Alexander Blok (1880–1921) and Andrei Bely (1880–1934). *See also* SLAVOPHILES; WESTERNERS.

séadna An Irish syllabic verse form with a quatrain (*q.v.*) stanza of alternating octosyllabic lines with disyllabic endings, and heptasyllabic lines with monosyllabic endings. The second and fourth lines rhyme. The third line rhymes with the stressed word which precedes the final word of the fourth line. In the second couplet there are two crossed rhymes (*q.v.*). Alliteration is also a standard feature of the form.

sea shanty (F *chantez* (imperative) 'sing!') Sea shanties were the working songs of sailors aboard the old square-rigged sailing vessels. Their origins are not known, but it would not be too fanciful to suppose that sailors have chanted songs to ease their labour since early times. One can easily imagine the Vikings doing so. The shanty *Haul on the Bowline* dates from Tudor times. Most of the best shanties were recorded in the 19th c., the age of the clippers. Their function was to co-ordinate group activity and to maintain morale. Their rhythms and words are therefore dictated by the kind of work being done. Negroes and Irishmen were particularly good at devising them. Some famous examples are *Hanging Johnny*, *Blow the Man Down*, *Boney*, *Haul Away* and *The Fair Maid of Amsterdam*. *See also* ORAL TRADITION.

secentismo (An Italianism from *seicento* 'six hundred' = 17th c.) Connoting a reaction against classicism and a taste for the elaborate conceit (*q.v.*). It was the counterpart of baroque (*q.v.*) and its literary relations are Gongorism, *préciosité* and euphuism (*qq.v.*). In Italian *secentismo* is more or less synonymous with Marinism (*q.v.*) – from Marino (1569–1625), who wrote *L'Adone*, a long poem full of flamboyance and stylistic conceits; a bizarre work in every respect. Marinism is evident in the work of English writers like Richard Crashaw and Sir Thomas Browne.

seci A Turkish term for a feature of prose style in which the last words of a clause or sentence rhyme. The *Koran* contains a number of examples of it.

sedoka A Japanese verse form comprising two *katautas* (*q.v.*) with a syllable count of five, seven, seven, five, seven, seven.

seer One who sees visions of divine things; and, in a broader sense, a person endowed with precognitive and prophetic powers. Virgil was credited with the vatic gift because he would seem to have foretold the birth of Christ in his *Fourth Eclogue*:

> Ultima Cumaei venit iam carminis aetas;
> Magnus ab integro saeclorum nascitur ordo.
> Iam redit et virgo . . . (ll. 4–6)

('The last age, heralded in Cumean song, is come, and the great march of the centuries begins anew. Now the Virgin returns . . .')

William Blake was often vouchsafed a visionary gleam of the supranormal and the divine. H. G. Wells was a prophet in his writings in a more literal sense. One of the most remarkable of all prophetic writers (at any rate outside the Old Testament) was Nostradamus (1503–66), the Provençal astrologer. His work in verse named *Centuries* achieved considerable popularity in his time, and because of the fulfilment of some of his forecasts of major events in the 20th c. (e.g. the rise of Hitler, the assassination of the Kennedys, the flight of yellow men over London and the death of two Popes in quick succession) his predictions are again under scrutiny.

segrel A Galician term for Castilian *juglar*, the equivalent of the French *jongleur* (*q.v.*) and the English minstrel.

seguidilla (Sp 'little series', diminutive of *seguido* 'series') A Spanish poetic form of popular origin which may have begun life as a dance song. To start with, it probably consisted of a four-line strophe with alternating long and short lines (seven or eight syllables in the long lines; five or six in the short). Later, very probably during the 17th c., three lines were added and it became established as a seven-line form, alternating seven and five syllables in the first part, and five, seven, five in the second. It is regarded as the most elegant of the popular Spanish metrical forms and is the only generalized form of the seven-line verse. *See* FOLIA.

semantics A branch of linguistics (*q.v.*) which deals with the meanings of words, and particularly with changes in the meanings. It involves, moreover, the study of the relationship between words and things; and between language, thought and behaviour. That is, how behaviour is influenced by words uttered by others or to oneself.

semic code *See* CODE.

semiotics/semiology Both terms have a common Greek root: *semeion* 'sign'. Hence, the science of signs. The basic founders of modern semiotics and semiology were the philosopher C. S. Peirce (1839–1914) and the linguistician Ferdinand de Saussure (1857–1913). Strictly speaking, semiology is the science of signs (and signals) in general; semiotics refers to the theory of sign systems in language. For all practical purposes they are both concerned with the means of communication as conventions, with particular emphasis on language. But, *not just language*. The study of animal behaviour is known as *zoosemiotics*. Human bodily communication (*kinsemics* and *proxemics*) and communication by olfactory signs (i.e. the codes of scent) are branches of semiotics.

The term 'semiology' was taken over and used by Saussure in a manuscript dated 1894. He defines semiology as 'a science that studies the life of signs within a society'. Semiotics is the older of the two terms and its use is traceable to the ancient Greeks. Broadly speaking, semiotics is associated with the North American tradition of sign study, whereas semiology is associated with the European tradition. In literary criticism semiotics is concerned with the complete signifying system of a text and the codes and conventions we need to understand in order to be able to read it.

Peirce made two main contributions to the science: (a) he demonstrated that a sign can never possess or arrive at a definite meaning; definition has always to be qualified; (b) he distinguished between various types of sign; for example, as summarized by Raman Selden in *A Reader's Guide to Contemporary Literary Theory* (1985): (i) the 'iconic' – a sign which resembles its referent (*see* SIGNIFIER/SIGNIFIED), as in a road sign for a double bend; (ii) the 'indexical' – when the sign is associated with its referent: for instance, smoke = fire; (iii) the 'symbolic' – when sign and referent have an arbitrary relationship. Language signs are arbitrary, except in ideographic/ideogrammatic signs (e.g. those used in Chinese) or in onomatopoeic signs. The above examples of Peirce's system (which come under his heading of 'triadic relations of performance') are only three of his nine types of sign, all of which are susceptible to various possible combinations which would produce, all told, ten classes of sign. Ogden, I. A. Richards, Wimsatt and the behaviourist and semiotician Charles Morris have all discussed semiotic schemes related to Peirce's theories.

Saussure's classic work is *Cours de linguistique générale* (1915) – a text constructed from students' notes. It was his belief that beyond language there lies a range of sign systems. He made the primary distinctions of: (a) *langue* and *parole* (*q.v.*); (b) signifier and signified (*q.v.*). His theories have been fundamental to all developments in structuralism and post-structuralism (*qq.v.*) and have also influenced psychoanalytic criticism as developed by, for instance, the French philosopher Jacques Lacan (1901–81). Julia Kristeva, in *The System and the Speaking Subject*, tries to describe a semiotics which goes beyond Saussure, Peirce and structuralism towards a displacement of the subject – *à la* Freud. 'Semanalysis', as Kristeva calls it, conceives of meaning not as a sign system but as a signifying process. Jonathan Culler argues that a semiotics of literature should be concerned with signifying practices and interpretative conventions which make it possible for literary texts to communicate with readers. *See* NARRATOLOGY.

senarius A metrical line which has six feet or six stresses. The Roman equivalent of the Greek iambic trimeter (*q.v.*) and the meter commonly used for dramatic dialogue. The alexandrine (*q.v.*) is its 'descendant'. *See also* HEXAMETER.

Senecan tragedy The closet dramas (*q.v.*) of the Roman Seneca (4 BC–AD 65) had a considerable influence on the Elizabethan tragedians who accepted them as stage plays.

The themes of Seneca's plays *Hercules Furens*, *Medea*, *Troades*, *Phaedra*, *Agamemnon*, *Oedipus*, *Hercules Oetaeus*, *Phoenissae* and *Thyestes* were taken from the whole field of Greek drama and contained little or no action in the true sense of the word. The characters rarely voiced feelings similar to those experienced by most human beings, and Seneca was better fitted to express ideas than put life into his characters. The illusion of action was evoked by words, and the whole burden was thrown on to the language. Rhetorical devices were plentiful: stichomythia (*q.v.*) was a favourite device.

The plays had a five-act structure with a Chorus (*q.v.*) marking the end of each act. The subject matter of these choric speeches, often little more than mythological catalogues, was often remote from the action of the play.

Other and important features were: the theme of revenge, usually introduced by the ghost of a wronged person (obvious Shakespearean parallels are Hamlet's father and Banquo's ghost in *Macbeth*); the messenger figure whose speeches usually report the culminating activity or disaster and fall into a stereotyped pattern, e.g. the bleeding captain in *Macbeth*; and a striving to extract the utmost effect from the spoken word.

One of the earliest Senecan tragedies was *Gorboduc* (1561) by Thomas Norton and Thomas Sackville. With its bloody plot, long, static and declamatory speeches, sensational events and high emotions its debt to Seneca was obvious; and nowhere more so than in the purely mechanical juxtaposition of speeches and the constant striving for balance and counterbalance in language. Thomas Kyd's *The Spanish Tragedy* (*c.* 1586) also owed much to Seneca. But Kyd did not allow Seneca's influence to overcome his own sense of theatrical technique. The Senecan elements were all present: the revenge theme was supplied by the death of Horatio, though other characters also called for revenge; the characters were disproportionate and the emotions were taken too far (Hieronomo kills innocent people as well as those deserving death); the language was heavily rhetorical. Unlike Seneca, Kyd presented his atrocities on stage, and he had a good instinct for ironic juxtapositions. Shakespeare's *Titus Andronicus* (1594) was considerably influenced by Kyd's play and has a full complement of blood-curdling deeds.

Tudor and Jacobean dramatists owed many other debts to Seneca, whose influence extended through Marlowe and Shakespeare to Webster, who, like him, was fascinated by states of extreme suffering and by stoic virtues. For example, in *The Duchess of Malfi* (*c.* 1613–14) Webster followed Seneca in investigating the role of madness in society; as did Middleton and Rowley in *The Changeling* (1622). *See* REVENGE TRAGEDY; TRAGEDY; VILLAIN.

senhal A fanciful name used to address people in Old Provençal poems. Perhaps we should now call it a pet name.

sensation novel *See* NOVEL OF SENSATION.

sense In the first place it concerns what is said and the meaning of what is said (e.g. 'What is the sense?'; 'Does it make sense?'). In critical terminology 'sense' has acquired some more flexible connotations. When we speak of a 'man of good sense' we imply someone whose judgement is sound, a man who has some capacity for appreciation. Good sense equals more or less the French *bon sens*. Jane Austen contrasted sense with sensibility (*q.v.*), in *Sense and Sensibility*.

The 18th c. has been described as 'the age of good sense' – for its balance, its feeling for proportion, its regard for the superiority of reason, its good taste and awareness of decorum (*q.v.*). *See also* NEOCLASSICISM; PROPRIETY.

sensibility The term became popular in the 18th c., when it acquired the meaning of 'susceptibility to tender feelings'; thus, a capacity not for feeling sorry for oneself so much as being able to identify with and respond to the sorrows of others – and to respond to the beautiful. This quality of empathy was probably a reaction against 17th c. stoicism and Hobbes's theory that man is innately selfish and motivated by self-interest and the power drive. In sermon, essay (*qq.v.*), fiction and philosophical writing (in the early 18th c.) it was averred, on the contrary, that man was innately benevolent and thus wished others well. The Earl of Shaftesbury's *Characteristicks* (1711) proclaimed this view. In the periodical *The Prompter* (1735) a writer defended the human attitude that is not content merely with good-natured actions 'but feels the misery of others with inward pain'. This was deservedly termed 'sensibility'. By mid-century such feelings were an accepted part of social ethics and public morality. It was a sign of good breeding and good manners to shed a sympathetic tear, as indeed in Gray's *Elegy* (1750), Goldsmith's *The Deserted Village* (1770) and Cowper's *The Task* (1785), not to mention the various odes to sensibility from the 1760s onwards. Two other relevant works in the history of this attitude were Sterne's *A Sentimental Journey* (1768) and Mackenzie's *The Man of Feeling* (1771). 'Dear sensibility!' writes Sterne (in an almost ode-like tone), 'source inexhausted of all that's precious in our joys, or costly in our sorrows!' In *The Man of Feeling* sensibility became self-indulgent. It declined into sentimentalism, and showed a propensity for 'the luxury of grief'. Jane Austen and Dr Johnson both criticized it; particularly Jane Austen in *Sense and Sensibility* (1811).

In the 19th c. the term was more or less replaced by 'sensitivity', but the latter never established itself as a literary term. In fact, sensibility received a renewed and vigorous life in the critical essays of T. S. Eliot, for whom it represented the creative faculty and the quality of temperament in a poet. *See also* SENTIMENTAL COMEDY; SENTIMENTALITY; SENTIMENTAL NOVEL.

sententia (L 'feeling, opinion, judgement') Closely related to, if not actually synonymous with, the apophthegm, maxim and aphorism (*qq.v.*), a *sententia* is customarily a short, pithy statement which expresses an opinion; hence the term 'sententious', now as a rule used pejoratively. One of the most famous collections of *sententiae* is that by Peter Lombard, who was known as *Magister sententiarum*. His *Sententiae* (12th c.) was an important theological textbook in the later Middle Ages. *See also* PENSEE.

sentimental comedy Also known as the drama of sensibility, it followed on from Restoration comedy (*q.v.*) and was a kind of reaction against what was regarded as immorality and licence in the latter. Jeremy Collier (1650–1726) severely criticized Restoration comedy in *A Short View of the Immorality and Profaneness of the English Stage* (1698). Sentimental comedy was rather anaemic by comparison and is seldom produced now. It arose because a rising middle class enjoyed this kind of drama, in which, as Goldsmith put it, 'the virtues of private life are exhibited, rather than the vices exposed, and the distresses rather than the frailty of mankind . . .'. The characters, both good and bad, were luminously simple; the hero was ever magnanimous and honourable and hypersensitive to the sensibilities of other people – rather like the hero in Hampton's *The Philanthropist* (1971). Good representative examples from the period are Richard Steele's *The Conscious Lovers* (1722), Hugh Kelly's *False Delicacy* (1768), Goldsmith's *The Good-Natured Man* (1768) and several works by Richard Cumberland – notably *The Brothers* (1769) and *The West Indian* (1771). In the same period Sheridan was attempting to revive comedy of manners (*q.v.*). *See also* COMEDIE LARMOYANTE; SENSIBILITY; SENTIMENTAL NOVEL.

sentimentality For the most part a pejorative term to describe false or superficial emotion, assumed feeling, self-regarding postures of grief and pain. In literature it denotes overmuch use of pathetic effects and attempts to arouse feeling by 'pathetic' indulgence. It was not often found earlier than the 18th c., though Crashaw might fairly be described as sentimental at times. It showed itself in Cowper and Gray and, later, in Shelley. It was also evident in sentimental comedy (*q.v.*) and in *comédie larmoyante* (*q.v.*) and in the sentimental novel (*q.v.*). It was particularly apparent in the thinking and attitudes of Rousseau and Shaftesbury. Cowper's poem *To Mary* illustrates some of its more obvious characteristics:

> The twentieth year is well-nigh past,
> Since our first sky was overcast;
> Ah would that this might be the last!
> My Mary!
>
> Thy needles, once a shining store,
> For my sake restless heretofore,
> Now rust disus'd, and shine no more,
> My Mary!
>
> Partakers of thy sad decline,
> Thy hands their little force resign;
> Yet, gently press'd, press gently mine,
> My Mary!

sentimental novel A form of fiction popular in 18th c. England. It concentrated on the distresses of the virtuous and attempted to show that a sense of honour and moral behaviour were justly rewarded. It also attempted to show that effusive emotion was evidence of kindness and goodness. The classic example was Richardson's *Pamela, or Virtue Rewarded* (1740), the story of a servant girl who withstood every attack on her honour. Comparable but more readable novels in this category were Goldsmith's *The Vicar of Wakefield* (1766), Henry Brooke's *The Fool of Quality* (1765–70), Mackenzie's *The Man of Feeling* (1771) and Maria Edgeworth's *Castle Rackrent* (1800). Sentimentality (*q.v.*) was very apparent in Sterne. In this period scores of sentimental novels were published and read avidly. *See also* BATHOS; COMEDIE LARMOYANTE; PATHOS; SENSIBILITY; SENTIMENTAL COMEDY.

septenarius (L 'of seven each') A metrical line consisting of seven feet or seven stresses. More commonly known as the septenary, which is the same as the heptameter and fourteener (*qq.v.*). The term is now usually restricted to MedL verse and to ME poems like *Orm*, *Poema Morale* and Robert of Gloucester's *Chronicle*.

septet A seven-line stanza (Italian *septette* and French *septain*) of varying meter and rhyme. A large number of English poets have used it, including Chaucer, Lydgate, Hoccleve, Skelton, Sir Thomas

Wyatt and William Morris – plus the Scot, Dunbar. *See* RHYME ROYAL.

sequence A composition sung after the Epistle at Mass. Sequences were incorporated into the Liturgy at an early stage and certainly by the end of the 19th c. Many sequences were of impressive beauty.

Serapionovy bratya (R 'Serapion brothers') A group of young Soviet writers formed in 1921. They were followers of Zamyatin (author of *We*) and took their name from E. T. A. Hoffmann's story *The Serapion Brothers*, about an individualist who dedicates himself to non-conformist art. The Serapion fraternity claimed a right to create literature independent of political ideology. Their articles of faith were drawn up by Lev Lunts in 1922. Other members of the group were Zoshchenko, Tikhonov, Fedin, Vsevolod Ivanov, Nikolay Nikitin, and Slonimiski.

serenade (It *serenata* 'made serene, purified', associated with *sera* 'evening') Traditionally a song sung at night beneath a lady's window; or an imitation of such a song, like Shelley's *Indian Serenade*. Its meaning has now become vague, but it is a musical rather than a literary term. One should mention Mozart's *Serenata notturna*, Vaughan Williams's *Serenade to Music*, and Benjamin Britten's *Serenade*.

sermon (L *sermo* 'talk, discourse') As a form of literature the sermon dates from the sub-Apostolic age. One of the earliest examples is the so-called *Second Epistle* of Clement (*c.* 100–200). Throughout the Middle Ages many of the Fathers (Origen, Basil, Gregory of Nazianzus, John Chrysostom, Ambrose, Augustine *et al.*) helped to develop the sermon into something like a work of art, with definite rules of composition. By the late Middle Ages the *ars predicandi* was something which had to be learnt and worked at (as Chaucer's Pardoner implied). Hence, in part, the growth of the preaching orders, like the Dominicans and Franciscans; and also the number of manuals for preachers. John Bromyard's *Summa Praedicantium* (printed in 1485), for instance, was an encyclopaedic reference work for the preacher.

The sermon became one of the principal sources of instruction and 'entertainment' in a period when the Church had much control over the diversions available to the public. The great age of sermon literature runs from the 13th to the 17th c., and throughout Europe the 'literature of the pulpit' had considerable influence on the establishment of ethnic languages and the development of allegory, *exemplum*, fable, dialogue (*qq.v.*), verse and drama. Religious reformers like Wycliffe and Luther used the sermon to publicize their beliefs. The invention of printing allowed countless volumes of sermons to be published, though there are vast collections of manuscript sermons still lying unread in the cathedral libraries of Europe.

Between 1550 and 1700 the sermon attained its apogee in England and France. Notable preachers of the period were Latimer, Lancelot Andrewes, Joseph Hall, John Donne and Jeremy Taylor in England; Bossuet, Bourdaloue and Massillon in France. John Donne, as Dean of St Paul's Cathedral in London, could command an audience of perhaps 10,000 at St Paul's Cross, in the open air, with an extremely learned and closely argued sermon lasting up to two hours or more.

Since these times sermons have been published in large quantities and have been much read. Among many famous preachers one should mention Wesley (reputed to have preached over 40,000 sermons), Frederick Robertson, Cardinal Newman and Cardinal Manning. As a literary form the sermon is almost defunct today, and the extent to which the art of preaching has deteriorated is shown by the fact that the average contemporary preacher has difficulty in keeping the interest of a few hundred people for ten minutes in a church equipped with a microphone and a public-address system. *See* HOMILY.

sermon joyeux A kind of mock sermon which was popular in medieval times, especially in France. It was delivered in churches during the period associated with the traditional Feast of Fools (i.e. between Christmas and the Octave of the Epiphany – Jan. 13th). In this period revels, sometimes of a semi-dramatic nature, were permitted in church. A *sermon joyeux* played a part in these and was often a satirical and/or ribald diversion. Later (by the 15th c.) these profane interpolations in the Mass and the Liturgy were abolished and were eventually succeeded in the developing drama by farces, Morality Plays and *soties* (*qq.v.*). *See also* CARNIVALIZATION/CARNIVALESQUE.

serpentine verse A line or a stanza of poetry which begins and ends with the same word.

serranilla (Sp 'little highland, mountain') A lyric song which may have had its origin among highlanders in Spain. Usually composed in *arte mayor* (*q.v.*) and the theme was normally the meeting of a gentleman and a country wench. Such lyrics were common in the late medieval period. The best known were composed by the Archpriest Hita (*c.* 1283–*c.* 1350) and the Marqués de Santillana.

sesquipedalian (L 'of a foot and a half') A term used humorously of polysyllabic words or verses.

sestet The sub-division or last six lines of the Italian sonnet (*q.v.*) following the octet or octave (*q.v.*). Sometimes the sestet resolves the proposition made in the octave, just as the final couplet in the Shakespearean sonnet (*q.v.*) rounds off the propositions in the three preceding quatrains (*q.v.*). *See* HEXASTICH; SESTINA; SEXAIN.

sestina A complex verse form first worked out by the troubadours (*q.v.*), it consists of six stanzas of six lines apiece with an *envoi* (*q.v.*) of three lines. The rhyming scheme requires that the same six end words occur in each stanza but in a different order according to a fixed pattern. The invention of the form is attributed to Arnaut Daniel (*c.* 1200). It was practised by many Provençal poets and also by Dante and Petrarch. Examples are to be found in Sir Philip Sidney's *Arcadia* (1590). From time to time since then various European and English poets have used it. One of the best known examples in English verse is Swinburne's *Complaint of Lisa.* Kipling, Pound, Eliot and Auden have also cultivated it. *See* HEXASTICH; SESTET; SEXAIN.

setting The where and when of a story or play; the locale. In drama the term may refer to the scenery or props.

sevdalinke Bosnian love-songs. The word is Serbian, based on the Turkish *sevda* 'love'. *Sev* is love as a verb, *sevdali* means 'one who is in love'; so, *sevda*, *sevdali*. There are at least two other words for each meaning. Reminiscent of the Moorish love-songs, *sevdalinke* are fatalistic in mood and tone, and sometimes bitter. They often express a helpless or hopeless yearning and lament the pangs of unrequited or disprized love. Their influence on music and song in the Balkans has been considerable, as any traveller there can verify. In Bosnia itself, in such towns as Foča and Sarajevo, one may easily hear modern *sevdalinke*. Similarly in Serbia and across Bulgaria and in other parts where the Ottoman Empire prevailed.

seven arts, the *See* QUADRIVIUM.

7:84 Theatre Company Founded in 1971 by John McGrath (1935–) and so called on the basis of a then current statistic that 7 per cent of the British population owned 84 per cent of the wealth. The first production was McGrath's *Trees in the Wind* at the 1971 Edinburgh Festival. He followed that up with several other plays in the 1970s. Other notable dramatists to have work performed by the company were John Arden (1930–) and David Edgar (1948–). In 1973 the company was divided into two groups: 7:84 England and 7:84 Scotland. Avowedly political and left-wing, the company sought to bring drama to working-class audiences. *See also* AGITPROP DRAMA; THEATRE WORKSHOP; UNITY THEATRE.

sexain A six-line stanza, also known variously as a sixain, sextain, sextet, sestet (*q.v.*) and hexastich.

sextilla A Spanish verse form of six octosyllabic or shorter lines with a varying rhyme scheme.

shadow show A puppet show in a shadow theatre. The puppets are manipulated between a strong light and a translucent screen. *See also* KARAGOZ.

shaggy dog story An improbable kind of yarn, often long and spun out, which, as a rule, does *not* have a witty or surprise ending; but comes, rather, to a deflating and quasi-humorous conclusion. Colloquially, 'a groaner'. A tolerably well-known example concerns the Australian bee which had a consuming ambition to become a ballet dancer. It presented itself to the authorities in Sydney and was advised to go to Covent Garden, London. But how was it to get there? Eventually it persuaded a racing pigeon bound for London to transport it. After many hazards (all detailed in the story) they arrived and the bee made a 'bee-line' for the Covent Garden Opera House. It explained its ambition and the powers that be were so impressed that they decided that a 'pigeon-towed' bee would be a unique addition to the corps. In fiction, Joseph Heller's digressive and crazily funny novel *Catch-22* (1961) might be taken as an example. *See also* TALL STORY.

Shakespearean sonnet A fourteen-line poem in iambic pentameters (with subtle variations on the iambic pattern) consisting of three quatrains (*q.v.*) and a concluding couplet. It is so named because Shakespeare was its greatest practitioner. Also known as the English sonnet, it is a variant of the Petrarchan sonnet (*q.v.*). It was developed, particularly, by Sir Thomas Wyatt and the Earl of Surrey during the Tudor period. The rhyme scheme is normally (a) abab, cdcd, efef, gg; or (b) abba, cddc, effe, gg. The following example is Shakespeare's 46th Sonnet:

Mine eye and heart are at a mortal war,
How to divide the conquest of thy sight;
Mine eye my heart thy picture's sight would bar,
My heart mine eye the freedom of that right.
My heart doth plead that thou in him dost lie
A closet never pierc'd with crystal eyes;
But the defendant doth that plea deny,
And says in him thy fair appearance lies.
To 'cide this title is impannelled
A quest of thoughts, all tenants to the heart;
And by their verdict is determined
The clear eye's moiety and the dear heart's part –
    As thus: mine eye's due is thine outward part,
    And my heart's right thine inward love of heart.

It will be seen from this that each quatrain deals with a separate aspect of the theme introduced in the first line, and that the 'argument' (*q.v.*) is resolved in the final couplet. *See* SONNET.

sharacans (Ar 'rows of gems') Armenian verse forms which consist of chants and hymns. Composed in either free verse (*q.v.*) or according to metrical schemes, they constitute the main part of Armenian church music. Most of them were composed between the 5th and the 7th c. but occasional additions were made up until *c.* 1500. Some of the poets are known by name.

Shavian Characteristic of the style, tone and attitudes of George Bernard Shaw (1856–1950). Thus, witty, irreverent, paradoxical, eloquent, stimulating and socialist. However, Shaw could also be verbose.

shelta A term of unknown origin, it denotes a kind of cryptic language used by Irish tinkers and gipsies. Also known among them as *sheldrū* and *shelter*. *See also* ARGOT; CANT; PATOIS; SLANG.

shih (Ch 'songs') In Chinese there is no word for poetry, but there are words for different kinds of poetry. *Shih* is the basic Chinese verse, and the term was first used to designate folksongs, hymns and libretti. The earliest examples of *shih* in regular five-word lines date from *c.* 1st c. BC.

shimpa A form of Japanese dance drama which developed late in the 19th c. and derives in some respects from *kabuki* (*q.v.*).

short couplet A tetrameter (*q.v.*) couplet, usually either iambic or trochaic, like the following from Belloc's *Henry King*:

The Chief Defect of Henry King
Was chewing little bits of String.
At last he swallowed some which tied
Itself in ugly Knots inside.

short measure Often abbreviated to SM, in Anglican hymn books, it consists of a quatrain (*q.v.*) rhyming abab or abxb. The first, second and fourth lines are iambic trimeters (*q.v.*), the third an iambic tetrameter (*q.v.*), as in the opening stanza of this hymn by Edwin Hatch (1835–89):

Breathe on me, Breath of God,
Fill me with life anew,
That I may love what thou dost love,
And do what thou wouldst do.

See also HYMNAL STANZA; POULTER'S MEASURE.

short meter *See* SHORT MEASURE.

short novel A work of fiction which is longer than a short story (*q.v.*) and shorter than a novel (*q.v.*). We tend to use the Italian word *novella* (*q.v.*) for this 'middle-distance' type of book. Novelette is another term sometimes used. Examples are: Conrad's *Heart of Darkness* and Aldous Huxley's *Two or Three Graces*. However, many people would classify these as merely long short-stories.

short story When it comes to classification this is one of the most elusive forms. It is doubtful, anyway, whether classification is helpful. Certainly there seems to be little point in measuring it. One is confronted with the question: how long (or short) is short? In athletic terms, if we take the *novella* (*q.v.*) as a 'middle-distance' book/story, then the short story comes into the 100/200 meter class. Nevertheless, there are very long short-stories and very short ones. D. H. Lawrence's *The Fox* (1923) is about 30,000 words; Kleist's ghost story *Das Bettelweib von Locarno* (1810) is only 800 words. In his preface to his *Complete Short Stories* Somerset Maugham remarks that the shortest item runs to about 1,600 words and the longest to about 20,000 words. The vast majority of short stories would fall somewhere between the two.

It may be argued that the forefathers of the short story, however rude in some cases, are myth, legend, parable, fairy tale, fable, anecdote, *exemplum*, essay, character study and *Märchen*; plus the *lai*, the *fabliau* and even the ballad (*qq.v.*). The term 'short story' has relatives in the shape of the French *conte* and *nouvelle*, the Spanish *novela*, the Italian *novella*, the German *Novelle* and *Kurzgeschichte* (a word used to translate the English 'short story'), the yarn, the sketch, the tale and the Russian *skaz* (*qq.v.*).

Historically, we find many inset stories or digressions in Classical literature which amount to short stories. In the Bible the accounts of Cain and Abel, the Prodigal Son, Ruth, Judith and Suzannah are all short stories. In the Norse sagas (*q.v.*) we find inset tales or episodes, the *þættir*. Chaucer's *Canterbury Tales* (1385–1400), albeit in verse, are short stories. So are the tales in Boccaccio's *Decameron* (*c.* 1349–51) and in Marguerite of Navarre's *Heptaméron* (*c.* 1530). George Pettie's collection *A petite Pallace of Pettie his pleasure* (1576) is comparable. In 1613 Cervantes published his *Novelas ejemplares*, and these are short stories more or less as we understand the term today. In France, a form of the short story, the *conte* (*q.v.*), was established in the 17th c. by La Fontaine's *Amours de Psyché et de Cupidon* (1669) and Perrault's *Contes de ma mère l'Oye* (1697). Later, Crébillon (*fils*) followed with *Le Sopha* (1745) and other tales. As early as 1772 Denis Diderot, the encyclopaedist, wrote *Ceci n'est pas un conte* (published in 1784), which anticipates by two centuries some recent theory of narratology, reception theory and reader-response theory (*qq.v.*). He introduces into the story (which he claims at the beginning is *not* a story) a listener, a character whose role is more or less that of the reader.

In the second half of the 18th c. the short story was being developed and established in Britain, partly as a result of the popularity of the oriental tale (*q.v.*) but more so as a result of the popularity of the Gothic novel (*q.v.*). Such was the appetite for the then new kind of horror story (*q.v.*) and the 'literature of terror' that by *c.* 1800 a large number of short Gothic stories had been published, as well as the numerous novels. By the end of the 18th c. the German *Novelle* (*see* NOVELLA) had become established both as a term and as a genre of fiction. In the opening years of the 19th c. the short story as a form was highly evolved, especially in the shape of the ghost story (*q.v.*) and the horror story, and stories which had to do with the supernatural. The two major influences at this stage were E. T. A. Hoffmann (1776–1822) and Heinrich von Kleist (1777–1811). Hoffmann's first collection of stories, *Fantasiestücke*, appeared in 1814. He followed this with several more between 1816 and 1821. Kleist's all-important stories were collected in two volumes in 1810 and 1811. One can scarcely underestimate their contribution to the foundation of the short story. Other important pioneers were Sir Walter Scott (1771–1832) and the Americans Washington Irving (1783–1859) and Nathaniel Hawthorne (1804–64). Scott wrote some excellent ghost stories. Irving is particularly remembered for his adaptations of German folk tales (e.g. *Rip Van Winkle* and *The Legend of Sleepy Hollow*) and for his tales in *The Sketch Book* (1819–20). Hawthorne's short stories were collected in *Twice-Told Tales* (1837), *Mosses from an Old Manse* (1846) and *The Snow-Image and Other Twice-Told Tales* (1851).

Edgar Allan Poe (1809–49) was for long regarded (inaccurately) as the originator of the modern short story. Certainly, as a practitioner he excelled – especially in the detective story (e.g. *The Murders in the Rue Morgue*), though he was by no means the first to write a detective story (*q.v.*). He also excelled with a kind of Gothic spine-chiller (e.g. *The Pit and the Pendulum*) and composed a form of early science fiction (*q.v.*) tale (e.g. *The Gold Bug*). Poe was affected by the German romantics and their Gothic stories, and particularly by Hoffmann and also, of course, by his fellow Americans Irving, Brockden Brown and Hawthorne. In the mid-19th c. Poe was a major influence. *Tales of the Grotesque and Arabesque* appeared in 1839 and *The Murders in the Rue Morgue* in 1841. *The Gold Bug* followed in 1843. Among his other remarkable stories were *The Fall of the House of Usher* (1839), *A Descent into the Maelstrom* (1841), *The Masque of the Red Death* and *The Mystery of Marie Roget* (1842), and *The Cask of Amontillado* (1846).

With practice came comment and theory. In 1842 Poe himself (reviewing Hawthorne's *Twice-Told Tales*) expressed some serviceable general precepts on the short story, by which he meant a prose narrative (of indeterminate length) requiring anything from half an hour to one or two hours in its 'perusal'; a story that concentrates on a unique or single effect and one in which the totality of effect is the main objective.

In the end the form has shown itself to be so flexible and susceptible of so much variety that its possibilities seem almost endless. For example, it may be concerned with a scene, an episode, an experience, an action, the exhibition of a character or characters, the day's events, a meeting, a conversation, a fantasy . . . And what not? In the course of the 19th c. many of the possibilities were explored and there was a great deal of experiment.

Early in the 19th c. the German *Novelle* rapidly became a developed form which attracted many writers and also inspired quite a lot of theory. Apart from interest in this narrative prose form (of the short or shorter kind), there was also wide interest in German folk tales and folklore. There were two famous collections: *Des Knaben Wunderhorn* (1805, 1808), which comprised songs gathered by Achim von Arnim and Clemens Brentano, and the *Kinder- und Hausmärchen* (1812, 1814, 1822) gathered by the Grimm brothers. Numerous *Kunstmärchen* (or 'Art' Tales) were composed by such writers as Brentano, Hoffmann and Tieck. Such stories were often about strange and mysterious events, and there was a supernatural element. Later more realistic stories were written by, among others, Stifter, Keller and Storm.

The realistic short story also became highly developed in Russia. Alexander Pushkin was among the first to exploit it in the 1830s with *The Tales of Belkin* (1830), *The Queen of Spades* (1834) and *The Captain's Daughter* (1836). Gogol's stories were being published during the same period. He wrote about everyday things and events and ordinary people. Among his most famous works are *Nevsky Prospekt* (1835), *Notes of a Madman* (1835), *The Portrait* (1835), *The Nose* (1836) and *The Overcoat* (1842). This last has been regarded as a seminal story for later writers and evoked Turgenev's celebrated observation: 'We have all come out from under Gogol's "Overcoat"'. Turgenev himself composed some notable stories, namely *Asya* (1858), *First Love* (1860) and *Torrents of Spring* (1870), and published the collection *A Sportman's Sketches* (1847–51), also known as *A Hunter's Notes*. Tolstoy, too, wrote a number of short stories which are regarded as among the greatest in Russian literature; notably, *Happy Ever After* (1859), *The Cossacks* (1863), *The Death of Ivan Ilyich* (1884) and *The Kreutzer Sonata* (1890). Chekhov, who was to have a profound and universal influence on the short story, published several collections, including *Motley Stories* (1886) and *In the Twilight* (1888). Among his greatest are *A Dreary Story* (1889), *Ward No. Six* (1892), *My Life* (1896), *Ionych, The Man in a Case, Gooseberries, About Love* (1898) and *The Lady with the Little Dog* (1899).

In France the short story was established in 1829–31 with the publication of a dozen *contes* by Prosper Mérimée, Balzac and Gautier. There were considerable developments later. Among Mérimée's main works were *Mosaïque* (1833), *Colomba* (1841), *Nouvelles* (1852) and *Dernières Nouvelles* (1873). Alphonse Daudet wrote a variety of delightful short stories, published in his collections *Lettres de mon moulin* (1868), the *Tartarin* burlesques (1872–90) and *Les Contes du lundi* (1873). Flaubert's contribution was *Trois Contes* (1877). Other notable authors who were practitioners of the genre were Alfred de Vigny, Jules Barbey d'Aurevilly, Arthur de Gobineau, Auguste Villiers de l'Isle-Adam and Anatole France. The outstanding French writer of short stories in the 19th c. was unquestionably Guy de Maupassant, among whose main collections were *La Maison Tellier* (1881), *Mademoiselle Fifi* (1882), *Contes de la bécasse* (1883), *Les Sœurs Rondoli* (1884), *Miss Harriet* (1884), *Contes du jour et de la nuit* (1885), *Toine* (1885), *Yvette* (1885). Chekhov and Maupassant are generally accounted the masters of the genre in this period. Their combined influenced has been immeasurable.

By the middle of the 19th c. the ghost story and the horror story were very well established. Many hundreds of short stories during the second half of the century were one or the other (or both combined). There were also hundreds of short stories with supernatural or supranormal themes; often tales of suspense and mystery. This popularity was to continue in the 20th c.

In America, during the second half of the 19th c., eight writers made a considerable name for themselves in the short story form: Herman Melville, Mark Twain, Bret Harte, Ambrose Bierce, O. Henry, Stephen Crane, Jack London and Sherwood Anderson. Melville's three most famous are *Bartleby the Scrivener*, *Benito Cereno* and *The Encantadas*. These were published in his collection *The Piazza Tales* (1856). One of Mark's Twain's best known is *The Celebrated Jumping Frog of Calveras County*. This is an example of the tall tale or tall story (*q.v.*), a kind of fiction which was popular in America in the 19th c. Twain's main collection is *The Celebrated Jumping Frog of Calaveras County and Other Sketches* (1867). Francis Bret Harte was a prolific writer of short stories and helped to popularize the Western (*q.v.*). One of his best collections is *The Luck of Roaring Camp and Other Sketches* (1870). Ambrose Bierce is still well remembered for his collection *Tales of Soldiers and Civilians* (1891). Stephen Crane published two distinguished collections – *The Open Boat and Other Tales of Adventure* (1898) and *The Monster and Other Stories* (1899). O. Henry was very prolific and, like many of his contemporaries, wrote tight, well-crafted stories, almost slick in their adroit contrivance, and was a master of the surprise ending or 'twist in the tail'. Among his main collections are *Cabbages and Kings* (1904), *The Four Million* (1906), *The Trimmed Lamp* (1907) and *The Roads of Destiny* (1909). Jack London was equally prolific. Two of his main collections are *The Son of the Wolf* (1900) and *Tales of the Far North* (1900). His *Two Thousand Dozen* is one of the best of all tall stories. Sherwood Anderson's collections include *The Triumph of the Egg* (1921) and *Horses and Men* (1923).

Meanwhile, another American, Henry James, had for some twenty-five years been writing very different types of short story (including remarkable ghost stories) and made a lasting contribution to the genre. Apart from *The Turn of the Screw* (1898) there were four main collections: *A Passionate Pilgrim* (1875), *Daisy Miller* (1879), *Tales of Three Cities* (1884) and *The Aspern Papers* (1888).

Thomas Hardy, an almost exact contemporary of Henry James, was equally active. His four main collections of short stories are *Wessex Tales* (1888), *A Group of Noble Dames* (1891), *Life's Little Ironies* (1894) and *A Changed Man and Other Tales* (1913). Many other writers were active during the same period. In the 1890s Arthur Conan Doyle established the detective story with *The Adventures of Sherlock Holmes* (1892) and *The Memoirs of Sherlock Holmes* (1894). In the 1890s, too, H. G. Wells burst upon the scene with *The Time Machine* (1895), which he was to follow with *The Island of Dr Moreau* (1896) and *The Invisible Man* (1897) and many other compulsively readable tales, including ghost stories, horror stories and science fiction stories. *The Country of the Blind* came out in 1911. In the same year Chesterton published a collection of his detective stories, *The Innocence of Father Brown*, and E. M. Forster produced his first collection, *The Celestial Omnibus*. It was followed in 1928 by a collection of pre-war stories – *The Eternal Moment*; in 1972, posthumously, there was a further collection of earlier stories titled *The Life to Come*. In 1911, as well, Katherine Mansfield, one of the most important figures in the evolution of the short story (her stories were the first in English to show the influence of Chekhov), published *In a German Pension*, which she was to follow with *Prelude* (1918), *The Garden Party* (1922) and *The Aloe* (1930), plus several other collections.

During the 1890s and across the turn of the century Conrad, R. L. Stevenson, Kipling, W. W. Jacobs, George Moore and Saki (pseudonym of H. H. Munro) were all regular practitioners of the form. Conrad's *Tales of Unrest* came out in 1898, which he followed with *Youth, Heart of Darkness* and *Typhoon* in 1902. Stevenson published *The Merry Men and Other Tales* in 1887. Kipling's main collections were *Traffics and Discoveries* (1904), *Actions and Reactions* (1909) and *A Diversity of Creatures* (1917). W. W. Jacobs published his first collection *Many Cargoes* in 1896; there followed *Sea Urchins* (1898), *Light Freights* (1901), *The Lady of the Barge* (1902) and *Night Watches* (1914). He is particularly famous for his macabre horror story *The Monkey's Paw.* George Moore's collection *The Untilled Field* (1903) showed traces of Turgenev. Saki's short stories, sardonic, witty and elegant, remain perennially popular. There were four main collections: *Reginald* (1904), *Reginald in Russia* (1910), *The Chronicles of Clovis* (1911) and *Beasts and Superbeasts* (1914).

Scores of other writers were equally industrious at the turn of the century, exploiting the possibilities of the form and often producing original work. The advent of the pulp (*q.v.*) magazine early in the 20th c. boosted the output of short stories and provided an outlet for many professional and occasional writers. It was to continue to do so for the next thirty or more years. Many of the early science fiction short stories were published in such magazines. The ghost and the horror story and stories of the uncanny continued to be very popular at this time, but impressionistic stories of everyday life in the tradition of Gogol, Turgenev and Chekhov were equally popular. In 1914 Joyce published *Dubliners*, something of a landmark in the genre. Meanwhile Somerset Maugham had been establishing himself as a highly accomplished craftsman, very much in the tradition of Maupassant, and he was to go on writing short stories for nearly fifty years. In 1899 he had produced his first collection, *Orientations.* This was to be followed by *The Trembling of a Leaf* (1921) – which contained the well-known *Rain* – *The Casuarina Tree* (1926), *Cosmopolitans* (1936), *The Mixture as Before* (1940) and *Creatures of Circumstance* (1947). In 1928 he published his *Ashenden* stories, which were important in the evolution of the spy story (*q.v.*).

Two notable European short story writers in the early part of the

20th c. were the Slovene Ivan Cankar and the Czech Franz Kafka. Cankar was the Slovene counterpart of Thomas Hardy and wrote highly original short stories about a variety of people and themes. His work includes social parables, symbolic and psychological tales and miscellaneous sketches. There were a number of collections: *Vinjete* (1899), *Knjiga za lahkomiselne ljudi* (1901), *Ob zori* (1903), *Za križem* (1908), *Zgodbe iz doline šentflorjanske* (1908), *Volja in moč* (1911) and several others. Kafka wrote nearly eighty short stories and they display a remarkable variety of length, style, theme and technique. Some are barely a hundred words long. They include fable, parable, sketch, report, letter, dialogue, dramatic dialogue and essay, but all qualify as short stories. He remains especially famous for *Metamorphosis* (1915), *The Judgement* (1913) and *In the Penal Colony* (1919). His weird and enigmatic vision makes his stories unlike anything else in the genre. Between them, Cankar and Kafka considerably broadened the possibilities of what might be achieved in the form.

However, for the most part, short story writers have settled for the realistic or naturalistic manner. Since *c.* 1920 numerous British authors have made memorable contributions. Between 1914 and 1934 D. H. Lawrence wrote and published a large number of short stories which were presented as a collection in 1934. Some of his main works were *The Prussian Officer*, *Odour of Chrysanthemums*, *The White Stocking*, *England, My England*, *The Fox* and *The Woman Who Rode Away*. In 1922 Aldous Huxley published a group of five stories titled *Mortal Coils*, which contained two of his best: *The Gioconda Smile* and *The Tillotson Banquet*. In 1926 he published his very long short-story (or *novella*) *Two or Three Graces*, in company with three others. In 1923 A. E. Coppard published *The Black Dog and Other Tales*, and David Garnett produced his well-known *Lady into Fox* (1922). Elizabeth Bowen, a notable practitioner, published her first collection, *Encounters*, in 1923. She continued to write short stories for many years, and her *Collected Stories* were published in 1980. In 1923, too, T. F. Powys, a writer of highly unusual and idiosyncratic stories, published his first two collections: *The Left Leg* and *Black Bryony*. In the next year came two others: *Mr Tasker's Gods* and *Mark Only*. Later were to come two more: *Bottle's Path* (1946) and *God's Eyes A-Twinkle* (1947). L. P. Hartley published his first collection, *Night Fears*, in 1924. Both these authors wrote outstanding ghost and horror stories. Richard Hughes produced three collections: *A Moment of Time* (1926), *The Spider's Palace* (1926) and *Don't*

Blame Me (1940). In 1931 M. R. James's collected ghost stories came out under the title *Ghost Stories of an Antiquary*. He had begun writing ghost stories in the 1890s and had produced two earlier separate volumes, in 1904 and 1911. Graham Greene's short stories cover some forty years of work, and there are four collections: *The Basement Room and Other Stories* (1935), *Nineteen Stories* (1947), *Twenty-One Stories* (1954) and *May We Borrow Your Husband?* (1967). V. S. Pritchett has long been regarded as one of the finest exponents in the genre, and his are mostly in the Chekhovian tradition and manner. There have been four main collections: *The Spanish Virgin and Other Stories* (1930), *You Make Your Own Life* (1938), *When My Girl Comes Home* (1961), *The Camberwell Beauty* (1974) – plus the two volumes of *Collected Stories* (1982, 1983). H. E. Bates also excelled in this form and his main collections are: *The Woman Who Had Imagination* (1934), *The Flying Goat* (1939), *The Beauty of the Dead* (1940), *Country Tales* (1940) and *The Daffodil Sky* (1955). Bates wrote a very good book about the genre – *The Modern Short Story* (1941). In 1934 Isak Dinesen (Karen Blixen) published *Seven Gothic Tales*, which reveal the long-term influence of the Gothic novel and Gothic short stories. Sylvia Townsend Warner published two main collections: *A Garland of Straw* (1943) and *Museum of Cheats* (1947). Through the 1940s and 1950s William Sansom was one of the most prolific authors. His first collection, *Fireman Flower* (1944), was followed by seven others. During the same period Angus Wilson was also active, and had three main collections: *The Wrong Set* (1949), *Such Darling Dodos* (1950) and *A Bit off the Map* (1957). Dylan Thomas produced *Portrait of the Artist as a Young Dog* (1940) and *Adventures in the Skin Trade* (1955). In the 1950s Elizabeth Taylor published her first accomplished collection, titled *Hester Lilly* (1954); three more followed: *The Blush* (1958), *A Dedicated Man* (1965) and *The Devastating Boys* (1972). Nabokov's first collection, *Nabokov's Dozen*, appeared in 1958 and was later followed with *Nabokov's Quartet* (1966). Muriel Spark also produced her first collection, *The Go-Away Bird*, in 1958; her collected short stories came out in 1967. Other authors who published collections in the 1960s are: Joyce Cary (*Spring Song and Other Stories*, 1960); Malcolm Lowry (*Hear Us, O Lord, from Heaven Thy Dwelling Place*, 1961); and V. S. Naipaul (*A Flag on the Island*, 1967). Roald Dahl's immensely successful collection *Kiss, Kiss* (1959) was followed with *Switch Bitch* (1974). These two collections, plus his first (*Someone Like You*, 1954), contain some of the best of modern short stories: clever, witty, macabre and sardonic. In 1971 Susan Hill made a considerable impact with her first collection – *The Albatross and Other Stories.* In the same period Jean Rhys came out with two notable collections: *Tigers are Better Looking* (1968) and *Sleep it off, Lady* (1976). In the 1960s and 1970s Kingsley Amis wrote a number of excellent short stories and his *Collected Short Stories* were published in 1980. Paul Theroux, more British than American, published two fine collections: *The Consul's File* (1977) and *The London Embassy* (1982). Angela Carter's first collection, *Bloody Chamber*, came out in 1979. In the 1970s and 1980s Alex Hamilton was prolific with four collections; his fifth – *The Christmas Pudding that Shook the World* – was published in 1988.

Several Irish writers, apart from Moore and Joyce, have made outstanding contributions to the genre. Namely, Liam O'Flaherty (*Spring Sowing*, 1926), Frank O'Connor (*Guests of the Nation*, 1931, plus no fewer than nine other collections), Sean O'Faolain (*Midsummer Night's Madness*, 1932), Edna O'Brien (*The Love Object*, 1968, *A Scandalous Woman and Other Stories*, 1974, *Mrs Reinhardt and Other Stories*, 1978, and *Lantern Slides*, 1990) and William Trevor (*The Day We Got Drunk on Cake*, 1969, *Angels at the Ritz*, 1975, *Beyond the Pale*, 1981). One of the leading Scottish writers in the genre has been George Mackay Brown, who published *A Calendar of Love* (1967). Frank Sargeson, a New Zealander, had two notable collections: *Conversations with My Uncle* (1936) and his *Collected Short Stories* (1965). The Australian Patrick White published *The Burnt Ones* (1964) and *The Cockatoos* (1974).

Since the 1920s writers of short stories in America have been scarcely less prolific. Among the more famous have been Scott Fitzgerald, who published *Flappers and Philosophers* (1920), *Tales of the Jazz Age* (1922) and *All the Sad Young Men* (1926); William Faulkner, who wrote some of the best short stories in existence, and whose three main collections were *These 13* (1931), *Idyll in the Desert* (1931) and *Go Down, Moses, and Other Stories* (1942); Katherine Anne Porter, one of the most gifted of short story writers, whose main collections were *Flowering Judas* (1930), *Hacienda* (1934), *Pale Horse, Pale Rider* (1939) and *The Leaning Tower* (1944); William Saroyan, who published several collections, including *The Daring Young Man on the Flying Trapeze* (1934); Damon Runyon, whose first collection *Guys and Dolls* came out in 1931 and was to be followed by several more; James Thurber, who published several collections of short stories and sketches, including

The Owl in the Attic, and Other Perplexities (1931), *The Seal in My Bedroom, and Other Predicaments* (1932), *The Middle-Aged Man on the Flying Trapeze* (1935), *Let Your Mind Alone* (1937) and *The Beast in Me, and Other Animals* (1948); John Hara, author of *The Doctor's Son and Other Stories* (1935), *Pal Joey* (1940) and *Pipe Night* (1945); Carson McCullers, whose major collection was *The Ballad of the Sad Café* (1951), which contains the *novella*-length story *The Member of the Wedding*; Ernest Hemingway, whose main collection is *The First Forty-Nine Stories* (1938); Raymond Chandler, who produced *Trouble is My Business* (1950), *Killer in the Rain* (1964) and *The Smell of Fear* (1965); Bernard Malamud, whose main collections were *The Magic Barrel* (1958), *Idiots First* (1963) and *Rembrandt's Hat* (1973); Isaac Bashevis Singer, who wrote for the most part in Yiddish and whose main collections are *Gimpel the Fool* (1957), *The Spinoza of Market Street* (1961), *Zlateh the Goat* (1966) and *A Friend of Kafka* (1970); Ray Bradbury, brilliantly inventive and versatile, published numerous collections, including: *The Illustrated Man* (1951), *The Golden Apples of the Sun* (1953), *The October Country* (1955), *A Medicine for Melancholy* (1959) – in Britain this collection had the title *The Day It Rained Forever* – *The Machineries of Joy* (1964), *The Last Circus and the Electrocution* (1980) and *A Memory of Murder* (1984); and John Updike, whose three main collections are *Pigeon Feathers and Other stories* (1962), *Museums and Women* (1972) and *Problems and Other Stories* (1979). Flannery O'Connor had her complete stories published posthumously in 1971.

From the 1890s and during the 20th c. a number of Russian authors have also enriched the genre. Gorki published his first story *Makur Chudra* in 1892, which he followed with *Chelkash* (1895) and *Twenty-Six Men and a Girl* (1899). Later came his series of stories about New York called *The City of the Yellow Devil* (1906). His contemporary Leonid Andreyev wrote a few which have been regarded as outstanding; for example, *Thought* (1902), *In The Fog* (1902), *The Governor* (1906), *Seven that were Hanged* (1908). Ivan Bunin remains famous for his collection *The Gentleman from San Francisco and Other Stories* (1914). Isaak Babel's *Red Cavalry* (1923–5) is another notable collection; as is Andrei Platonov's *The Locks of Yepifan* (1927).

Somewhat less well known, perhaps, were: Vera Inber, who was prolific and published her first collection, *Tales*, in 1925; Ilf and Petrov (pseudonyms of Ilya Arnoldovich Fainzilberg and Yergevny Petrovich Katayev), who published a number, including *On the*

Grand Scale; Sergei Nikitin, who produced several collections, among them *Seven Elephants* (1954), *Tales* (1955), *Old Men* (1958), *A Sleepless Night* (1959) and *Bonfire in the Wind* (1960); Yuri Nagibin, known for three main collections: *Before the Holiday* (1960), *In Early Spring* (1961) and *People, My Friends* (1961); Yuri Laptyev, who also had three main collections: *The People's Court* (1956), *Tales and Stories* (1958) and *There is a Little Town* (1961). Konstantin Paustovsky, Yuri Oyesha and Sergei Antonov also wrote notable short stories.

In Italy, too, the short story has become an established form and some of the most distinguished 20th c. writers have enriched it. For example, Carlo Gadda with a number of collections, including *La madonna dei filosofi* (1931), *Il castello di Udine* (1934) and *L'Adalgisa* (1944). Mario Soldati's main collections were *A cena col commendatore* (1950), *La messa dei villeggianti* (1959) and *Storie di spettri* (1962). Alberto Moravia produced two main collections: *Racconti romani* (1954) and *Nuovi racconti romani* (1959). In 1960 Cesare Pavese published *I racconti.* Two important collections were Vasco Pratolini's *Via de' Magazzini* (1942) and *Le amiche* (1943). Natalie Ginzburg produced her first collection, titled *La strada che va in città*, in 1942, and followed this with *Tutti i nostri ieri* (1952), plus two long stories, *Valentino* and *La madre*, in 1957. Carlo Cassola produced several volumes of short stories and a big collection *I racconti* in 1958. Italo Calvino was also prolific with several volumes, and the collection *I racconti* in 1959.

German writers of the 20th c. have been no less prolific in the genre. For example, the East German writer Anna Seghers, a notable exponent of the *Novelle* and the short narrative. Some of her collections are *Der Ausflug der toten Mädchen* (1948), *Die Hochzeit von Haiti* (1949), *Die Linie* (1950), *Friedensgeschichten* (1950) and *Die Kinder* (1951). Luise Rinser published three collections: *Ein Bündel weisser Narzissen* (1956), *Vom Sinn der Traurigkeit* (1962) and *Septembertag* (1964). Heinrich Böll wrote some of the best stories in the language, especially the cycle of short ones collected under the title *Wo warst du, Adam?* (1951), followed by the collection *Der Bahnhof von Zimpren* (1952), *So ward Abend und Morgen* (1955) and *Unberechenbare Gäste* (1956). Wolfgang Borchert's first collection was *Hundeblume* (1947), which he followed with *An einem Dienstag* (1947); and there was a posthumous collection in 1962, titled *Die traurigen Geranien.* Ingeborg Bachmann wrote a number of notable stories and she is particularly remembered for the collection *Das dreissigste Jahr*

(1961) and *Simultan* (1972), which contains five stories. One of the most highly regarded writers in this genre in the 20th c. has been Siegfried Lenz, who has published several memorable collections, including *Jäger des Spotts* (1958), *Das Feuerschiff* (1960), *Der Spielverderber* (1965) and *So war das mit dem Zirkus* (1971). Martin Walser's two main collections so far have been *Ein Flugzeug über dem Haus* (1955) – where the influence of Kafka is discernible – and *Lügengeschichten* (1964).

French writers, it seems, have not been so prolific. Colette, Jules Supervielle and Vercors all wrote occasional short stories. Marcel Aymé wrote quite a few, including some well-known ones for children. Jean Paul Sartre's main (and remarkable) contribution was the collection *Le Mur* (1939), which comprised five longish short stories. Albert Camus wrote six memorable ones gathered together under the title *L'Exil et le royaume* (1957), and Pierre Gascar wrote a number published under the titles *Les Bêtes* and *Le Temps des morts* (1953), and *Les Femmes* (1958).

Some others of note are Jean Ferry, whose best known collection was *Le Mécanicien* (1950), Henri Thomas, who published the collection *La Cible* in 1955, Philippe Sollers, Marcel Jouhandeau and Alain Robbe-Grillet, who wrote the remarkable *La Plage* (published in *Instantanés* in 1962).

Two Spanish American authors who have attained international renown are Luis Borges and Gabriel García Márquez. Borges devised a form of his own, the *ficción*: a kind of story-essay. His ideas, themes and technique are highly idiosyncratic and reminiscent, at times, of both Cankar and Kafka. His three collections were: *Ficciones* (1944), *El Aleph* (1949) and *Labyrinths* (1953). In 1974 Márquez published eleven stories in the collection *Ojos de perro azul.* Two other collections were *Los funerales de Mamá Grande* (1962) and *La increíble y triste historia de la cándida Eréndira y su abuela desalmada* (1972). The Cuban novelist Alejo Carpentier has also published a few short stories which have been highly regarded.

In 1989 there were well over a hundred general anthologies of short stories available in English alone (including a fair number of translations into English). Regularly, well-established stories, or classics of the genre, are recycled in new anthologies, often just cobbled together by an editor, with minimal or no introduction, their *raison d'être* being little more than commercial enterprise.

Short-Title Catalogue Published by the Bibliographical Society in

1926; an indispensable guide and reference work to English books published between 1475 and 1640.

sic (L 'so') put in brackets after a word or expression or even perhaps a sentence from a quoted passage to indicate that it is quoted accurately even though it may be incorrect, absurd or grotesque.

Sicilian octave An eight-line Italian stanza (rhyming abababab) of hendecasyllabic (*q.v.*) verses. Also called *strambotto* (*q.v.*) *popolare*, it is believed to have been used in Southern Italy and Sicily in the 13th c., and also in Tuscany. It is related to the medieval French *estrabot* and to *ottava rima* (*q.v.*), which may have developed from it. It was in fairly general use in the 15th c. *See also* RISPETTO; SONNET.

Sicilian school A term applied to a group of poets associated with the court of Emperor Frederick II (1220–50) in Palermo. The poets used the vernacular and were very probably the first to establish Italian as a literary language. The school flourished for about fifty years.

sick verse Sick verse (the term is a modern neologism) is kin to black comedy (*q.v.*); it is queasily, uneasily funny, mordant, sardonic and occasionally macabre. Its themes are misfortune, death, disease, cruelty, love-sickness and morbid preoccupations related to mental illness (sometimes masochistic and sadistic). It is the product of melancholy, ennui, despair and nausea of the world. At its strongest it displays horror and necrophiliac urges. It ranges from the apocalyptically sombre vision of James Thomson's *City of Dreadful Night* to the comparatively light-hearted jingle of W. S. Gilbert's *Nightmare*.

A very large number of poets have written verse which qualifies as sick. Some would find parts of Juvenal's more misanthropic satires fairly sick, but there is little of note until the 15th c. when the disastrous wars and plagues which devastated Europe inspired poets to express disgust and regret. Some notable examples from this period of what we might now describe as sick verse are: Villon's *Regrets de la belle heaulmière*, *Ballade des dames du temps jadis*, and *Ballade des pendus*; Chastellain's *Le Pas de la Mort*; and Olivier de la Marche's *Parement et Triumphe des Dames*. A preoccupation with death, decay and disease sometimes inspired Elizabethan and Jacobean dramatists (especially Webster and

Tourneur) to write appropriately sick verse for some scenes. A macabre and 'sick' element is particularly noticeable in revenge tragedy (*q.v.*).

Sick verse becomes rare after the middle of the 17th c., but a certain blackness of spirit and a dwelling upon the gloomy and horrific re-appears towards the middle of the 18th c. in the Graveyard School of Poetry (*q.v.*), and during the 19th c. sick verse of one kind and another is common. Out of the many examples available one should mention George Crabbe's *Peter Grimes* and *Sir Eustace Grey*; many works by Thomas Lovell Beddoes (especially his play *Death's Jest-Book*); *The City of Dreadful Night* by James Thomson, already referred to, and the same author's *Insomnia*; Edgar Allan Poe's poems *The Raven*, *The Bells*, *The Conqueror Worm, The Sleeper*; Robert Browning's poems *Madhouse Cells, Soliloquy of the Spanish Cloister*, *The Laboratory*, *Sibrandus Schafnaburgensis* and *Childe Roland to the Dark Tower Came*; Swinburne's *Faustine* and *After Death*. The works of some 19th c. French poets also qualify as sick. For instance, Baudelaire's *Les Fleurs du mal* and *Spleen*; Rimbaud's *Le Bateau ivre* and *Une saison en enfer*. In more recent years some of the more notable contributions have been made by Robert Graves (*The Halls of Bedlam*, *The Castle*, *The Suicide in the Copse*); Robert Service (*The Cremation of Sam McGee*); W. H. Auden (*Miss Gee*); John Betjeman (*Death in Leamington*; *Late-Flowering Lust*); Sylvia Plath (*Surgeon at 2 a.m.*, *In Plaster*). One should also mention Tom Lehrer's witty 'sick' lyrics. *The Penguin Book of Sick Verse* (1963), edited by George MacBeth, is a sufficiently emetic collection. *See also* NONSENSE.

sigmatism A term deriving from the Greek letter *sigma* 's'. It denotes the marked use (or repetition) of the letter 's'. In English it is a very common letter and the use of sibilance, especially in verse, in order to achieve certain effects is also very common. From among many well-known instances one may cite Wordsworth's celebrated description of skating in *The Prelude*:

All shod with steel,
We hissed along the polished ice in games
Confederate, imitative of the chase
And woodland pleasures – the resounding horn,
The pack loud chiming, and the hunted hare.
So through the darkness and the cold we flew,

And not a voice was idle; with the din
Smitten, the precipices rang aloud;
The leafless trees and every icy crag
Tinkled like iron; while far distant hills
Into the tumult sent an alien sound
Of melancholy not unnoticed, while the stars
Eastward were sparkling clear, and in the west
The orange sky of evening died away.
Not seldom from the uproar I retired
Into a silent bay, or sportively
Glanced sideway, leaving the tumultuous throng,
To cut across the reflex of a star
That fled, and, flying still before me, gleamed
Upon the glassy plain.

See ONOMATOPOEIA.

signature The printer's original sheet with four or more pages printed on it. Folded and bound, this forms a section. *See* GATHERING.

signifiant *See* SIGNIFIER/SIGNIFIED.

signifié *See* SIGNIFIER/SIGNIFIED.

signifier/signified In his classic work *Cours de linguistique générale* (1915) Ferdinand de Saussure describes a language system as 'a series of differences of sound combined with a series of differences of ideas'. In elaboration, he makes the famous distinction between *signifiant* ('signifier') and *signifié* ('signified'). Each sign in language is a union of *signifier* (i.e. a sound image or its graphic equivalent) and a *signified* (i.e. the referent; the concept referred to). The letters or marks *h-o-u-s-e* form a signifier which evoke the signified 'house'. There is no inherent reason why the letters or marks should mean 'house'. The association of signifier and signified is the product of linguistic convention and not of any natural link. The relation between the whole sign and what it refers to (i.e. the referent, or actual house with walls, roof, doors, windows, etc.) is arbitrary in that there is no natural link between the sign and the actuality to which it refers. Each sign in a linguistic system possesses 'meaning' by virtue of the fact that it is different from any other sign rather than because of any linguistic reason why this should be so. House is different from 'louse' and 'mouse'. Thus a word can be identified because of how it is related to, and differentiated from, other words in the linguistic system. As Saussure puts it: 'in language there are only differences without positive terms'. *See* DECONSTRUCTION; LANGUE AND PAROLE; POST-STRUCTURALISM; STRUCTURALISM.

sijo (K 'melody of the times') A Korean verse form, originally sung or chanted to the accompaniment of music. A complex form, the conventional *sijo* comprises three lines, each being composed of four groups of syllables. The first two lines had either fourteen or fifteen syllables, the third fifteen. There were slight variations, but a *sijo* was usually of forty-three, forty-four or forty-five syllables. Head rhyme (*q.v.*) is common. The *sijo* is of great antiquity and dates back at least to the 14th c. It is still used by Korean poets.

sillographer A writer of *silloi* (Gk 'squint-eyed') pieces: poems which satirize particular schools of thought or an individual's doctrines. A famous sillographer of antiquity was Xenophanes of Colophon who satirized the mythology of Homer and Hesiod. Samuel Butler's *Hudibras* (1663–78) might be described as a sillographic work. So might Pope's *Dunciad* (1728–43). Belloc and Chesterton were other writers who excelled at trenchant debunking of this kind. *See also* SATIRE.

silva A Spanish poetic form, apparently first developed in the 16th c. and related to the *canción* (*q.v.*). It consisted of hendecasyllabic or heptasyllabic lines arranged in strophic form and with a variable rhyme scheme. Lope de Vega wrote a number of them.

silver fork school *See* FASHIONABLE NOVEL.

simile (L neuter of *similis* 'like') A figure of speech in which one thing is likened to another, in such a way as to clarify and enhance an image. It is an explicit comparison (as opposed to the metaphor, *q.v.*, where the comparison is implicit) recognizable by the use of the words 'like' or 'as'. It is equally common in prose and verse and is a figurative device of great antiquity. The following example in prose comes from Graham Greene's *Stamboul Train*:

> The great blast furnaces of Liège rose along the line like ancient castles burning in a border raid.

And this instance in verse from Ted Hughes's poem *February*:

> The wolf with its belly stitched full of big pebbles;
> Nibelung wolves barbed like black pine forest
> Against a red sky, over blue snow . . .

See also EPIC SIMILE.

similiter desinens *See* HOMEOTELEUTON.

similitude (from L 'likeness') For all practical purposes a synonym for parable and allegory (*qq.v.*); and thus in the sense 'in the guise of'. As the prophet Hosea put it (12: 10): 'I have multiplied visions, and used similitudes'. Occasionally it is used to mean a simile (*q.v.*), as Macaulay intended in his attack on Robert Montgomery's poems (1830); he derides the poet for a comparison: 'We take this to be, on the whole, the worst similitude in the world'.

simultanéisme A short-lived movement in French poetry early in the 20th c. The writers aimed at a kind of 'simultaneousness' of image and sound to represent or reproduce human sounds mingled with other sounds (e.g. those made by animals, birds, etc.) and also the sounds of cities (e.g. traffic). It was an attempt at a complex form of onomatopoeia (*q.v.*) and also at a form of synaesthesia and the kinaesthetic image (*qq.v.*). Representative examples are to be found in *La Trilogie des forces* (1908–14) by H-M. Barzun, the leader of the movement, and *Naissance du poème* (1918) by Fernand Divoire. *See also* KINETIC POEM; PHANOPOEIA; UNANIMISME.

sincerity A term commonly used in the 19th c. to denote a criterion of aesthetic excellence and truthfulness, even of moral integrity. Matthew Arnold, for example, held that the test of greatness in poetry was whether or not it possessed the 'high seriousness which comes from absolute sincerity'. Later critical thinking dispensed with the term as being too vague, and because it implied or presupposed a knowledge of the author's intentions and feelings which no one but the author himself could be fully aware of. *See* PERSONAL HERESY; SPONTANEITY.

single-moulded line An end-stopped line, fairly frequent in early blank verse (*q.v.*). Three of the following lines from Marlowe's *Jew of Malta*, III, iv (*c.* 1592) are end-stopped:

Barabas: O trusty Ithamore; no servant, but my friend!*
I here adopt thee for mine only heir,
All that I have is thine when I am dead,
And, whilst I live, use half; spend as myself;
Here take my keys, I'll give 'em thee anon.*
Go buy thee garments; but thou shalt not want.*
Only know this, that thus thou art to do:
But first go fetch me in the pot of rice
That for our supper stands upon the fire.

single rhyme A one-syllable or masculine rhyme (*q.v.*). For instance: stuff/muff.

Singspiel A German term for a simple form of opera in which strophic songs are linked by spoken dialogue. In Germany it dates from the 18th c. with imitations of John Gay's *The Beggar's Opera* (1728). The term also denotes musical comedy. Bertolt Brecht experimented with *Singspiel*; for instance, *Mahagonny* (1927), described as a *Songspiel*. *See* BALLAD OPERA.

sirventes A Provençal poetic form (not fixed) used by the troubadours (*q.v.*). It is like a *canso* (*q.v.*) but the themes were usually political or moral, and the intention was very often satirical. Also used for personal lampoon (*q.v.*).

skald An ON word of unknown origin. A Scandinavian bard or court singer. Many of them were Icelanders who settled in Norway. Skaldic poetry differs from the Elder Edda lays because most of the authors are known by name. Much of the poetry deals with the deeds of contemporary chieftains and kings. The verse forms are complicated; mostly the *dróttkvaett* (*q.v.*). The kenning (*q.v.*) was used liberally. Among the better known *skalds* are: Bragi Boddason (*c.* 800–50); Þjóðólfr ór Hvini (9th c.); Þorbjörn Hornklofi (*c.* 900); Eyvindr Finnson (10th c.); Egill Skallagrímsson (9th c.); Kormákr Ögmundarson (10th c.); Gunnlaugr Ormstunga Illugason (10th–11th c.); Hallfreðr Ottarsson Vandrae Askald (10th–11th c.); Þórmóðr Kolbrúnarskáld (11th c.); Sigvatr Þórðarson (*c.* 995–1045); Arnórr Þórðarson Jarlaskáld (11th c.). From late in the 11th c. the *skald* became less and less important. The oral tradition (*q.v.*) declined and poetry came to be written down more and more. *See also* GUSLAR; SAGA; SCOP; TROUBADOUR; TROUVERE.

skaz A Russian term (from *skazat* 'to tell') applied to a genre of folk literature. It usually consists of an eyewitness account of an episode in peasant or provincial life. More specifically it is a narrative related by a fictitious narrator rather than by the author directly. Such a device allows the author considerable scope in the use of speech forms such as dialect, slang, neologism (*qq.v.*), mispronunciation and so forth, which give a naturalistic vigour and colourfulness which might not be attainable in a more conventional narrative told solely from the author's viewpoint (*q.v.*). The possibilities of this technique were exploited very successfully by Nikolai Leskov (1831–95), many of whose tales are told in *skaz*. Early in the 20th c. the *skaz* style was often used as a form of ornamentalism (*q.v.*) and Leskov's influence is apparent in the work of such authors as Remizov, Babel and Zoshchenko. *See also* TALL STORY.

skazka Russian folk tales. *See* SKAZ.

Skeltonics Or Skeltonic verse (also known as 'tumbling verse', *q.v.*), named after John Skelton (1460?–1529), a poet of the Tudor period. It is a headlong, kettle-drum, tumultuous verse related to doggerel (*q.v.*) whose chief stylistic features are short lines, multiple rhyme, alliteration and parallelism (*qq.v.*). Pejoratively called 'rude rayling', Skeltonics have become admired and respectable. The following lines come from *The World Nowadays* (*c.* 1512):

So many newes and knackės,
So many naughty packės,
And so many that money lackės,
  Saw I never:
So many maidens with child
And wilfully beguiled,
And so many places untiled,
  Saw I never . . .

So much striving
For goodės and for wiving,
And so little thriving,
  Saw I never:
So many capacities,
Offices and pluralities,
And changing of dignities,
  Saw I never:

Various influences have been adduced to explain Skelton's highly individual style: some of them may have been the OE rhyming poem and alliterative verse (*q.v.*), and medieval rhymed accentual verse.

sketch Two basic categories of sketch may be distinguished: (a) a short piece of prose (often of perhaps a thousand to two thousand words) and usually of a descriptive kind. Commonly found in newspapers and magazines. In some cases it becomes very nearly a short story (*q.v.*). A well-known example is Dickens's *Sketches by Boz* (1839), a series of sketches of life and manners; (b) a brief dramatic piece of the kind one might find in a revue (*q.v.*) or as a curtain raiser (*q.v.*) or as part of some other kind of theatrical entertainment. A good example is Harold Pinter's *Last Bus*.

The sketch has also been developed into a particular dramatic form, as a kind of monodrama (*q.v.*) by monologists like Hetty Hunt, Ruth Draper and Joyce Grenfell. The solo mime Marcel Marceau has worked out his own form of dramatic sketch. *See also* CHARACTER.

skit (ON 'shooting') A skit aims to 'shoot' or caricature a person or a style of writing or a mode of performance and interpretation. It is thus very closely related to, if not actually synonymous with, parody and burlesque (*qq.v.*). It is common in musical revue (*q.v.*) and comparable entertainments where famous people are 'taken off' by humorous impersonation, or where the style of a composer or author is 'guyed'.

slack The unaccented syllable(s) in a metrical foot. In a dactyl (*q.v.*) like *métrĭcăl*, the slack consists of the second and third syllables.

slang (ON *slyngva* 'to sling') The present meaning comes close to Norwegian dialect *sleigeord* 'offensive language'. *Slengjenamn* means 'nickname', and the phrase *slengje kjœften* means 'to sling the jaw' – or utter offensive language – which smacks of slang.

'The world of slang', wrote G. K. Chesterton, 'is a kind of topsy-turvydom of poetry, full of blue moons and white elephants, of men losing their heads, and men whose tongues run away with them – a whole chaos of fairy tales.'

Common to many languages, it is the lingo of the gutter, the street, the market-place, the saloon, the stable, the workshop, the theatre, the fo'c'sle, the barrack room and the ranch – indeed almost anywhere where men work or play. It is the poetry of the common man, the tuppence-coloured of everyday life, and is indispensable to the well-being of a language. A thriving and developing language has plentiful slang. Slang provides its calories, its energy and its vigour.

One can readily distinguish between slang, formal language and colloquial (*q.v.*) language: 'He dresses in a contemporary fashion' is formal; 'He's always got the latest clothes' is colloquial; 'He's a snappy dresser' is slangy.

Again: 'We have had a week of many misfortunes'; 'It's been a bad week'; 'It's been a dark seven'. In the growth of language the movement is thus: – colloquialism > standard speech > idiom > cliché> archaism (*qq.v.*). Take the phrase 'our withers are unwrung' which Shakespeare uses in *Hamlet* (III, ii, 255). Shakespeare may have heard this, or invented it himself. It could have been a slang phrase. At any rate, as a result of his usage it became colloqial and passed into standard speech. Persistent usage gave it the rank of idiom; overusage has put it in the cliché class; and it may soon become a dead metaphor (*q.v.*) or an archaism (*q.v.*).

So slang is the language of intimacy, of everyday conversation, and much of it is ephemeral. However, if it passes the hard tests of vitality and originality it may survive for centuries. It *can* date very rapidly, like fashions in clothes, and the writer, therefore, is obliged to be judicious in his use of current slang in order to remain natural and unaffected. Examples of long-established slang phrases are: smudge = plumber's black; chancellor's egg = a day-old barrister; bear = broker who works to lower the price of stock; haggis debate = discussion on Scottish affairs; sea pheasant = bloater or kipper; resistance piece = chief attraction; butter boys = fledgling cabbies; yell play = a bad play which relies on jokes to keep it going; a man with muscles on his eyebrows = a strong man.

Sex, money, food and drink are responsible for a large proportion of slang terms. Those relating to sex are so plentiful and many of them so commonly used that most people may be expected to know them. One may refer to money as: cash, dough, rhino, folding, green, cabbage, ready, bread, spondulicks, blunt, off, splosh, chink, dibs, plunks, bucks, bones, siller, dust, tin, the necessary, the needful, the wherewithal, lolly or jack; plus, greenbacks (old £1 notes), bluebacks (£5 notes), brownbacks (old 10/- notes). And to food as: nosh, grub, scoff, chop, prog, chow, chuck, toke, belly-timber, prov. A man may be intoxicated or drunk, or he may be: canned, smashed, stoned, squiffy, foxed, blotto, pissed, plastered, sloshed, sozzled, pickled, corned, raddled, boiled, tiddly, stinking, lit-up, groggy, top-heavy, whiffled, screwed, lushy, oiled, muzzy, tight, stewed to the eyeballs, half-seas over, three sheets in the wind, with back teeth awash, under the table, drunk as a piper, drunk as a fiddler's bitch, or drunk as a lord.

Much slang from trades and professions 'graduates' from being private and esoteric to becoming public and open. However, school slang has a habit of remaining private. English public schools are well known for their domestic or parochial slang. Slang has been studied in some detail in the 20th c. and the most celebrated expert on the subject is Eric Partridge, one of whose main works is *A Dictionary of Slang and Unconventional English* (1937; 1961). *See also* ARGOT; BACK SLANG; CANT; EUPHEMISM; JARGON; KING'S ENGLISH; PATOIS; RHYMING SLANG; STANDARD ENGLISH.

slant rhyme A rhyme that is not true. It may be deliberate or the result of incompetence. In this stanza from Peter Redgrove's *The Archaeologist* the second and third line contain a form of slant rhyme, and the first and fourth have pure rhymes:

> So I take one of those thin plates
> And fit it to a knuckled other,
> Carefully, for it trembles on the edge of powder,
> Restore the jaw and find the fangs their mates.

slapstick Low, knockabout comedy, involving a good deal of physical action and farcical buffoonery like the throwing of custard pies. A slapstick consisted of two pieces of wood which, when applied, for instance, to somebody's buttocks, produced a cracking or slapping sound. It was used by the Harlequin in *commedia dell'arte* (*q.v.*). There *may* be some connection between this and the tradition of the Vice (*q.v.*) cudgelling the devil; and, further back, the demons of the medieval Mystery Plays (*q.v.*) coming on with fire-crackers exploding from their tails. *See also* FARCE; LOW COMEDY.

slavophiles Members of a Russian intellectual movement active from *c.* 1840 to the 1860s. They were in favour of preserving and nurturing Russian cultural roots and in maintaining tradition. They were opposed to many of the influences of Western Europe (its culture, rationalism, materialism and democratic systems) and were thus opposed to the contrary movement of the 'Westerners' (*q.v.*) in Russia. *See* SCYTHIANS.

slice of life A direct translation of the French phrase *tranche de vie* (attributed to the French playwright Jean Jullien, 1854–1919), and applied to the works of Zola and other 'realistic' writers. It suggests that a work presents life 'in the raw', factual, visceral and unadulterated by art. It is not a particularly helpful or clear term since it might be variously applied to Chaucer's *Miller's Tale*, Defoe's *Journal of the Plague Year* (1722), George Gissing's *New Grub Street* (1891), Walter Greenwood's *Love on the Dole* (1933) and John Braine's *Room at the Top* (1957), without telling us very much about any of them. *See* NATURALISM; REALISM.

Slipslop After Mrs Slipslop, a character in Fielding's *Joseph Andrews* (1742). She had a habit of misusing words in a ridiculous way: 'delemy' for dilemma; 'confidous' for confident; 'indicted to wenching' for addicted to wenching; and 'ragmaticallest mophrodites' – which is anyone's guess. This is better known as a Malapropism (*q.v.*).

slogan The term derives from the Gaelic compound *sluagh-ghairm*; *sluagh* 'host' or 'army', *ghairm* 'cry' or 'shout'. Thus, a war-cry; the cry of a political party. It is related to watchword and motto.

šloka A Sanskrit verse form consisting of two hemistichs (*q.v.*), each of sixteen syllables organized in four units of four syllables each. It was used in many epic Sanskrit works.

smithy poets A pejorative term applied to a group of Soviet poets (formed about 1920) who wrote crude verse as a sort of jingoistic propaganda (*q.v.*) on behalf of the proletariat. The *kuznitsa* 'the smithy' was a branch of the *proletarskaya kul'tura* (*q.v.*). There were also 'Cosmists' who believed in universal power for the 'proles'. The Smithies could be better described as 'hammer and tongs' poets.

soap opera A pejorative term for films, television serials and radio programmes which are facile, shallow and melodramatic and, though superficially realistic, often bear little relationship to the actualities of most people's lives (though there are honourable exceptions to this). Often abbreviated to 'a soap', the term is also applied to fiction which displays the characteristics listed. The term dates from the early 1930s when American radio serials were sponsored by soap manufacturers.

socialist realism A kind of artistic credo, developed in Russia to implement Marxist doctrine, which has spread into other Communist countries. It requires art to promote the cause of the socialist society and looks upon the artist (whatever his medium) as a kind of servant of the state, or, in Stalin's emetic phrase, as 'the engineer of human souls'. At its worst it has produced the so-called smithy poets (*q.v.*) and the *proletarskaya kul'tura* (*q.v.*); at its best some writers who have succeeded in transcending many of its impositions (e.g. Alexander Fadeyev and Mikhail Sholokov). It has also produced the notorious colonies of writers, artists, composers, etc. who are dedicated to the propaganda (*q.v.*) of social realism which in Russia has been regarded as a reaction against naturalism (*q.v.*) or what is described as bourgeois realism. Opponents maintain that to force the artist to commit himself to an ideology is to impugn his freedom. Two famous Russian rebel writers have been Pasternak and Solzhenitsyn, both of whom were used unashamedly for propaganda purposes by the Western press. The Hungarian Marxist critic George Lukács has investigated aspects of socialist realism in *Studies in European Realism* (1950) and *The Meaning of Contemporary Realism* (1963). *See also* COMMITMENT; IDEYNOST; NARODNOST; PARTYNOST; REALISM; THESIS NOVEL.

Society of Authors It was founded in 1884 by Sir Walter Besant (1836–1901) to help authors stand up for their rights, especially in matters of copyright (*q.v.*). Within thirty years the society had achieved a good deal in the protection of authors, more particularly in dealing with publishers' contracts. George Bernard Shaw became a militant supporter, especially over the rights of dramatists. In 1931 the League of Dramatists was created as an autonomous section of the society. Other sections were formed in due course. Membership of the society enables an author to receive help in such matters as taxation, contracts, libel and social security. The society made an outstanding contribution in the campaign (which lasted for twenty-eight years) to establish the Public Lending Right (*q.v.*).

society verse *See* VERS DE SOCIETE.

sociological novel *See* THESIS NOVEL.

sociometry The study and measurement of attitudes in various groups. As far as literature is concerned, study of what sort of readers buy particular books and why.

Socratic irony So called after Socrates whose favourite device was to simulate ignorance in discussion, especially by asking a series of apparently innocuous questions in order to trap his interlocutor into error. *See* IRONY.

solecism (Gk *soloikismos*, from *soloikos* 'barbarous') A deviation from conventional usage in grammar, syntax or pronunciation. For example: 'I ain't done nothing'; 'I never ought to have come'; 'You didn't ought to do it'.

soliloquy It is possible that St Augustine of Hippo coined this compound in Latin: *soliloquium*, from *solus* 'alone' and *loqui* 'to speak'.

A soliloquy is a speech, often of some length, in which a character, alone on the stage, expresses his thoughts and feelings. The soliloquy is an accepted dramatic convention (*q.v.*) of great importance and the various uses it has been put to show the strengths and advantages of such a convention. Its advantages are inestimable because it enables a dramatist to convey direct to an audience important information about a particular character: his state of mind and heart, his most intimate thoughts and feelings, his motives and intentions.

In Classical drama the soliloquy is rare, but the playwrights of the Elizabethan and Jacobean periods used it extensively and with great skill. They achieved an excellence in the use of this convention which has not been equalled. *Hamlet*, *Macbeth* and *Othello* all have major soliloquies (those in *King Lear* are somewhat less important), and so does Marlowe's *Dr Faustus*.

A particular use of the convention is to be found in the development of the villain (*q.v.*) at this time. The soliloquies given to the villains are more like prolonged asides and often take the form of a direct address to the audience. The villains are manipulators of the plot and commentators on the action. Often they deliver these self-revelatory statements of invention rather in the manner of the devils in the Morality Plays (*q.v.*). Examples are to be found in *Othello* (from Iago), *The Jew of Malta* (from Barabas), in *Titus Andronicus* (from Aaron), *Richard III* (from Gloucester), *The Duchess of Malfi* (from Bosola), *The White Devil* (from Flamineo), *The Revenger's Tragedy* (from Vendice), *Antonio's Revenge* (from Piero) and *Lust's Dominion* (from Eleazar).

In a modified form dramatists continued to use the soliloquy during the Restoration period and during the 18th and 19th c. With the advent of a more naturalistic drama towards the end of the 19th c. it was no longer feasible, though dramatists who persisted in writing verse plays still exploited its possibilities. In the last eighty-odd years it has been very rare. However, fairly recent exceptions may be found in Auden's *The Ascent of F6*, Eliot's *Murder in the Cathedral* and Robert Bolt's *A Man for All Seasons*. *See* MONOLOGUE.

somonka A Japanese syllabic verse form. It comprises two *tankas* (*q.v.*) with a syllable count of five, seven, five, seven, seven. It is a kind of epistolary love poem, usually composed by two authors. The first part is a declaration or statement of love, the second part is a reply.

son et lumière French in origin. A form of theatrical, mixed-media entertainment, usually out of doors, in which spectacular lighting and sound effects are combined with music, narration and dramatic presentation, sometimes with an element of pageant (*q.v.*). Not infrequently used to present major historical events (e.g. the French Revolution). A famous building, such as Windsor Castle or the Tower of London, which has a long and colourful history, lends itself particularly well to *son et lumière*.

song Many poems, even if not set to music, may be called songs (e.g. Smart's *A Song to David*; Blake's *Songs of Innocence*; Robert Service's *Songs of a Sourdough*), but the term, in its literary sense, usually denotes a poem and its musical setting; a poem for singing or chanting, with or without musical accompaniment. Music and words may be composed together; or the music may be 'fitted' to the words and vice versa.

It seems that in the earlier stages of civilization (in many parts of the world) much of the poetry created was designed to be sung or chanted (much of it still is) and the oral tradition (*q.v.*) sustained the union of music and poetry. In fact, up until the 16th c., in Europe, poet and composer/musician were often one and the same. The epic (*q.v.*), the war-song, the ballad (*q.v.*), the madrigal (*q.v.*) and the lyric (*q.v.*) were in many cases the works of professional musician/poets who were also composers (for example, the *skalds*, *scops*, troubadours, *trouvères* and *Minnesänger*, *qq.v.*). During the 16th c. (or perhaps a little earlier) a kind of fissiparation took place. The poet and composer/musician began to part company, and the classifying of literary forms or genres put the song in an individual category. Lyrics were written in the expectation of their being set to music and composers made extensive use of the great variety of poetry available.

Paradoxically, though the poet and composer/musician were parting company (and the term 'song' increasingly meant a literary composition in verse form rather than words for music) the 16th and 17th c. in England produced a great many good songs for music. Sir Thomas Wyatt, for example, an important innovator in the Tudor period, wrote some beautiful songs. These two stanzas are from one of his better known pieces:

My lute awake! perform the last
Labour that thou and I shall waste,
  The end that I have now begun;
For when this song is sung and past,
  My lute be still, for I have done.

As to be heard where the ear is none,
As lead to grave in marble stone,
  My song may pierce her heart as soon;
Should we then sigh or sing or moan?
  No, no, my lute, for I have done.

Much of Wyatt's work (and Surrey's) was published with other poems in *Songes and Sonnettes*, a collection made by Richard Tottel the publisher and published in 1557 (this is better known as Tottel's Miscellany).

Many of the poets of the Elizabethan and Jacobean periods wrote fine songs as well as poems that might be set to music. The two most famous composer/poets of the period were Thomas Campion (1559?–1619) and John Dowland (1563?–1626?). Campion, who was a theoretician as well as a practitioner (he wrote an interesting treatise called *Observations in the Art of English Poesie*, 1602), published four *Books of Ayres* (1601–17). The fourth one contained one of his best known songs 'There is a Garden in Her Face'. Dowland, one of the most famous musicians and composers of his time, published three volumes called *Songes or Ayres of Foure Partes* (1597, 1600, 1603). The third book contained the anonymous 'Weep you no more, sad fountains', an exquisite piece which illustrates many of the merits of the song lyric of the period:

Weep you no more, sad fountains;
  What need you flow so fast?

Look how the snowy mountains
  Heaven's sun doth gently waste.
    But my son's heavenly eyes
      View not your weeping,
      That now lies sleeping
    Softly, now softly lies
      Sleeping.

Sleep is a reconciling,
  A rest that peace begets:
Doth not the sun rise smiling
  When fair at ev'n he sets?
    Rest you then, rest, sad eyes,
      Melt not in weeping
      While she lies sleeping
    Softly, now softly lies
      Sleeping.

The period immediately each side of 1600 saw a number of other publications besides those of Campion and Dowland. Among the more notable were: William Byrd's *Songs of Sundry Natures* (1589); Thomas Morley's *Canzonets or Little Short Songs to Three Voices* (1593); John Mundy's *Songs and Psalms* (1594); Thomas Morley's *First Book of Ballets to Five Voices* (1595); Thomas Weelkes's *Madrigals of 6 Parts* (1600); Robert Jones's *First Book of Songs and Airs* (1600); Tobias Hume's *The First Part of Airs* (1605); and J. Wilbye's *Second Set of Madrigals* (1609).

In the 17th c. many poets composed songs. Suckling, Herrick, Lovelace, Jonson, Milton and Dryden created some of the best known of all. In *Arcades* (1633) and *Comus* (1634) Milton produced some outstanding songs. These lines come from the masque (*q.v.*) of *Comus* – the song to Echo:

Sweet Echo, sweetest nymph that liv'st unseen
        Within thy airy shell
    By slow Meander's margent green,
And in the violet-embroidered vale
    Where the love-lorn nightingale
Nightly to thee her sad song mourneth well.
Canst thou not tell me of a gentle pair
    That likest thy Narcissus are?
        O if thou have
    Hid them in some flowery cave,
        Tell me but where

Sweet queen of parley, daughter of the sphere
  So mayst thou be translated to the skies,
And give resounding grace to all heaven's harmonies.

The dramatists of the period 1580–1640 often used songs in their plays to sustain or create a particular mood. In many cases the song was an integral – one might say an essential – part of the dramatic structure (e.g. Desdemona's 'Willow' song in *Othello*; Ophelia's songs in *Hamlet*; Iago's drinking song in *Othello*). A large number of the best and most famous Elizabethan and Jacobean songs are to be found in the drama. The following are notable instances (I give the first line in each case): 'Who is Silvia? what is she?' (*The Two Gentlemen of Verona*, 1594–5); 'When icicles hang by the wall' (*Love's Labour's Lost*, *c.* 1595); 'Over hill, over dale' and 'You spotted snakes, with double tongue' and several others (*A Midsummer Night's Dream*, 1595–6); 'Tell me where is fancy bred' (*The Merchant of Venice*, 1596); 'Sigh no more, ladies, sigh no more' (*Much Ado About Nothing*, 1598–9); 'Blow, blow thou winter wind' and 'It was a lover and his lass' (*As You Like It*, *c.* 1599); 'O Mistress mine! where are you roaming' and 'Come away, come away, death' (*Twelfth Night*, 1600); 'Take, O take those lips away' (*Measure for Measure*, *c.* 1604); 'Fear no more the heat o' the sun' (*Cymbeline*, 1610–11); 'When daffodils begin to peer' and 'Jog on, jog on, the footpath way' (*The Winter's Tale*, 1609–10); 'Full fathom five thy father lies' (*The Tempest*, 1611); 'Orpheus with his lute made trees' (*Henry VIII*, 1613).

To this selection from Shakespeare one may add: 'Golden slumbers kiss your eyes' (Thomas Dekker's *Patient Grissell*, 1603); 'Come, Sleep, and with thy sweet deceiving' (Beaumont and Fletcher's *The Woman-Hater*, 1607); 'Weep no more, nor sigh, nor groan' (Beaumont and Fletcher's *The Queen of Corinth*, *c.* 1608); 'Still to be neat, still to be drest' (Ben Jonson's *Epicœne*, 1609); 'Take, O take those lips away' (Fletcher's *The Bloody Brother*, 1616); 'Why so pale and wan, fond lover?' (Sir John Suckling's *Aglaura*, 1638); 'Hence all you vain delights' (Fletcher and Middleton's *The Nice Valour*, printed in 1647); 'The glories of our blood and state' (James Shirley's *The Contention of Ajax and Ulysses*, 1659).

The influence of the masque on song-writing in the 1620s and 1630s was considerable. Many masques contained good songs (or lyrics) and the authors were fortunate in having two English composers who well understood the techniques of allying music and words. They were Henry Lawes (1596–1662) and his brother William (1602–45). Later Purcell was to make an even greater contribution in setting words to music.

When the theatres re-opened after the Puritan ban, Dryden sustained the tradition of the Elizabethans and Jacobeans in song-writing. A notable example is 'Beneath a myrtle shade' (*The Conquest of Granada*, 1670); and his *Ode for St Cecilia's Day* is one of the great songs in English literature. However, by the end of the 17th c. the poet no longer used the theatre. Dramatic prose was the desired medium for comedy of manners (*q.v.*) and the art of song-writing very nearly died in the 18th c., except, of course, in opera and ballad opera (*qq.v.*) at which Gay and Dibdin excelled, and in the occasional play: for instance, Goldsmith wrote a successful song 'Let schoolmasters puzzle their brain' for *She Stoops to Conquer* (1773), and another one for his novel *The Vicar of Wakefield* (1766) which begins 'When lovely woman stoops to folly'. Sheridan, too, showed that he still had the knack with his rousing catch 'Here's to the maiden of bashful fifteen' in *School for Scandal* (1777). This might have been expected of Sheridan for he had showed considerable aptitude for the sung lyric in his comic opera *The Duenna* (1775). Thereafter there is almost nothing of note, for a long time, in drama. When Robert Bell published his *Songs from the Dramatists* (1854) he printed over three hundred songs, and Sheridan was the last author to be represented. In fact, Sheridan's last song 'Yes, yes, be merciless thou tempest dire' in his unsuccessful tragedy *Pizarro* (1799) shows how the art of song-making had declined.

This is not to say that the song in general was defunct, but if we compare the 18th with the 17th c. the former has little to show for its efforts – except two major collections of earlier songs: namely, Thomas D'Urfey's *Pills to Purge Melancholy* (1719), which contained over a thousand songs, and Bishop Percy's *Reliques of Ancient English Poetry* (1765).

A handful of poets, only, kept the tradition of song-writing alive. Notable examples are Thomas Moore, Robert Burns, William Blake, Thomas Haynes Bayly, plus the anonymous makers of ballad and folksong (*qq.v.*). Of the poets just mentioned the two most important are Moore and Burns. Thomas Moore (1779–1852) was a musician as well as poet, and became the national lyrist of Ireland through the publication of his *Irish Melodies* (1807–35). He also published *National Airs* (1815) and *Sacred Songs* (1816). Burns (1759–96) did for Scotland what Moore did for Ireland, and wrote some of the finest songs ever created. Many of them were published in James Thomsons's *Scots Musical Museum* (1787–1803) and George Thomson's *Select Collection of Scottish Airs* (1793–1805).

In the 19th c. there was no revival of song-writing in England, though Thomas Lovell Beddoes and Thomas Hardy both showed a considerable gift for the song lyric. In more recent times dramatists have again become aware of the importance of songs in plays. The work of W. B. Yeats, Sean O'Casey, T. S. Eliot, W. H. Auden, Brendan Behan and John Arden – among a number of others – illustrates the point. *See* DITTY; LYRIC.

songbook As a rule a collection of verses set to music. A famous instance is the *Carmina Burana* (*q.v.*). Scores of manuscript collections survive in Europe and many have been printed. *See* AIR; CANCIONEIROS; CAROL; DITTY; LAUDA; MADRIGAL; MINNESINGER; SONG; TROUBADOUR.

sonnet The term derives from the Italian *sonetto* a 'little sound' or 'song'. Except for the curtal sonnet (*q.v.*) the ordinary sonnet consists of fourteen lines, usually in iambic pentameters (*q.v.*) with considerable variations in rhyme scheme. The three basic sonnet forms are: (a) the Petrarchan (*q.v.*), which comprises an octave (*q.v.*) rhyming abbaabba and a sestet (*q.v.*) rhyming cdecde or cdcdcd, or in any combination except a rhyming couplet (*q.v.*); (b) the Spenserian (*q.v.*) of three quatrains and a couplet, rhyming abab, bcbc, cdcd, ee; (c) the Shakespearean, again with three quatrains and a couplet, rhyming abab, cdcd, efef, gg.

The Italian form is the commonest. The octave develops one thought; there is then a 'turn' or *volta*, and the sestet grows out of the octave, varies it and completes it.

In the other two forms a different idea is expressed in each quatrain; each grows out of the one preceding it; and the argument, theme and dialect (*qq.v.*) are concluded, 'tied up' in the binding end-couplet.

The Petrarchan sonnet probably developed from the Sicilian *strambotto* (*q.v.*). It consisted of two quatrains to which were added two tercets (*q.v.*). The earliest sonnets are attributed to Giacomo da Lentino (*c.* 1215–33) of the Sicilian School. But the form may have been invented by another poet at the court of the Emperor Frederick II in Sicily. At any rate, throughout the later Middle Ages, the form was used by all the Italian lyric poets, notably Guinicelli, Cavalcanti and Dante. They usually used it for love poetry and more particularly for that semi-Platonic and semi-religious devotion to the Lady or *Donna* which subsequently became a cliché of love poetry. It was Petrarch, more than anyone, who established the sonnet as one of the major poetic forms. His *Canzoniere* were a kind of encyclopaedia of love and passion. Thereafter, several Italian poets composed sonnets which have remained famous. They include Serafino dall'Aquila (1466–1500), Bembo (1470–1547), Michelangelo (1475–1564), Castiglione (1478–1529) and Tasso (1544–95). In the 16th c. there was also an outburst of sonneteering in France where the most notable sequences were du Bellay's *L'Olive* (1549) and his *Regrets* and *Antiquités de Rome* (1558), and Ronsard's *Amours* (1552) and his *Sonnets pour Hélène* (1578). Philippe Desportes (1546–1606) was less important, but Malherbe (1555–1628) was largely responsible for establishing the alexandrine (*q.v.*) through his sonnets. In Spain the sonnet was introduced by the Marquis de Santillana (1398–1458). Notable Spanish sonneteers who followed him were Juan Boscán (1490–1552) and Garcilaso de la Vega (1503–36). Two poets who established the sonnet in Portugal in the 16th c. were Sá de Miranda and Antonio Ferreira. The sonnet did not become established in Germany until somewhat later and then mostly through the work of Weckherlin (1584–1653).

The sonnet came into the English language via Sir Thomas Wyatt and the Earl of Surrey early in the 16th c. and it was the Petrarchan form which they imported. However, it was not until the last decade of the 16th c. that the sonnet was finally established in England.

Surrey established the rhyming scheme of abab, cdcd, efef, gg and it was this form that was most used in England in the later 16th c. George Gascoigne described it succinctly in 1575:

> Sonnets are of fourteene lynes, every lyne conteyning tenne syllables. The first twelve do ryme in staves of foure lynes by crosse metre, and the last two ryming together do conclude the whole.

The first major sonnet cycle was *Astrophil and Stella*, written by Sir Philip Sidney (*c.* 1580–83) and printed in 1591. There followed in rapid succession Daniel's *Delia* (1592), Lodge's *Phillis* (1593), Constable's *Diana* (1594), Drayton's *Idea's Mirror* (1594) and Spenser's *Amoretti* (1595). There were many other sequences of lesser note.

The greatest sequence of all was Shakespeare's sonnets, not

printed until 1609, but some had circulated in manuscript for at least eleven years before. He wrote 154 sonnets, from which I choose No. 94 to illustrate the form:

They that have power to hurt and will do none,
That do not do the thing they most do show,
Who, moving others, are themselves as stone,
Unmovèd, cold, and to temptation slow –
They rightly do inherit Heaven's graces,
And husband Nature's riches from expense;
They are the lords and owners of their faces,
Others but stewards of their excellence.
The summer flow'r is to the summer sweet
Though to itself it only live and die;
But if that flow'r with base infection meet,
The basest weed outbraves his dignity.
    For sweetest things turn sourest by their deeds:
    Lilies that fester smell far worse than weeds.

By early in the 17th c. the vogue for love sonnets was already over. Ben Jonson was not interested in the form, and hardly any lyric poet in the Jacobean and Caroline periods (*qq.v.*) wrote a sonnet of note. However, Donne did write nineteen very fine sonnets on religious themes, grouped together under the title of *Holy Sonnets*.

Thereafter it was not until Milton that the sonnet received much attention. Milton did not write a sequence and he did not write about love. His sonnets belong to the genre of occasional verse (*q.v.*), and thus are about a particular event, person or occasion, like *When the Assault was Intended to the City*, *To the Lord General Cromwell* and *On the Late Massacre in Piedmont*.

After Milton the sonnet was virtually extinct for well over a hundred years. In the whole of the 18th c. there were few of merit, apart from Thomas Gray's *Ode on the Death of Richard West*, Thomas Warton's *To the River Lodon* and William Bowles's *At Ostend*.

There was a very considerable revival of interest during the Romantic period (*q.v.*). Wordsworth, Keats and Shelley all wrote splendid sonnets. Wordsworth's are generally thought to be the best, especially his *Composed upon Westminster Bridge, September 3, 1802*, *To Toussaint L'Ouverture* and *On the Extinction of the Venetian Republic.* Wordsworth wrote two sequences titled *The River Duddon* and *Ecclesiastical Sonnets* – but these must be accounted almost complete failures. Keats's most distinguished sonnets are *On First Looking into Chapman's Homer*, and his late poem: *Bright star! would I were steadfast as thou art*. Shelley also wrote two splendid sonnets: *Ozymandias* and *England in 1819*.

The resurgence of interest in the sonnet during the Romantic period in England is paralleled in other countries towards the end of the 18th c. and during the 19th c. In Italy Ugo Foscolo (1778–1827) and Carducci (1835–1907) were distinguished sonneteers. In France the sonnet was revived by Théophile Gautier (1811–72) and Baudelaire (1821–67). Other French poets who wrote outstanding sonnets were Lecomte de Lisle, Valéry, Mallarmé and Rimbaud. The sonnet was revived in Germany by Gottfried Bürger (1747–94) and the form was later used by several German Romantic writers, including Tieck, Eichendorff and August Graf von Platen-Hallermünde, whose *Sonette aus Venedig* remain highly regarded.

During the Victorian period (*q.v.*) a large number of poets re-established the sonnet form, and in particular the sonnet sequence about love. The major works are: Elizabeth Barrett Browning's *Sonnets from the Portuguese* (1847–50), Robert Bridges's *The Growth of Love* (1876), D. G. Rossetti's *The House of Life* (1881). Rossetti's sister Christina also wrote some very fine sonnets, especially a sequence of three on her unhappiness. There was also George Meredith's sequence *Modern Love* (1862). Meredith used a sixteen-line form, and this was a departure; but the main innovator in Victorian times was Gerard Manley Hopkins, whose poems were not published until after his death, in 1918. His experiments with the sonnet are extremely interesting and he made something new in the form. Particularly remarkable works of his are *Spelt from Sibyl's Leaves* (an experiment in combining the alexandrine with sprung rhythm, *q.v.*), and four poems whose first lines are respectively:

> No worst, there is none. Pitched past pitch of grief,
>
> I wake and feel the fell of dark, not day.
>
> Patience, hard thing! the hard thing but to pray,
>
> My own heart let me more have pity on; let

In the 20th c. a number of poets writing in English have composed a variety of sonnets on many different themes. Those by Rupert Brooke are little read now, but his droll tour de force *Sonnet Reversed* (1911) is well worth noting. It is a kind of anti-sonnet, *beginning* with a couplet, which sends up the tradition of idealized love (Verlaine had preceded him in writing such 'inverted sonnets'). Robert Frost, John Crowe Ransom and W. H. Auden all composed memorable sonnets. Some of Auden's best are on public affairs and famous men: for instance, *The Ship*, his sonnets on A. E. Housman, Arthur Rimbaud and Edward Lear, and his *Sonnets from China* (1937). Dylan Thomas and George Barker also wrote notable sonnets, as did Robert Lowell (e.g. his sequence *The Dolphin*). Edwin Morgan, the Scottish poet, achieved two fine long sequences with *Glasgow Sonnets* (1972) and *Sonnets from Scotland* (1984). Patrick Kavanagh, the Irish poet, composed a score or more of great merit. Two other distinguished modern poets who have composed sequences are Geoffrey Hill and Seamus Heaney. Hill's are *Funeral Music* (in *King Log*, 1968) and *Lachrimae* (in *Tenebrae*, 1978). Heaney's are *Glanmore Sonnets* (in *Field Work*, 1979) and *Clearances* (in *The Haw Lantern*, 1987). Apart from those Hill also wrote *Two Formal Elegies for the Jews in Europe*, *Requiem for the Plantagenet Kings*, *Asmodeus* (in *For the Unfallen*, 1959), *Annunciations* (in *King Log*) and *Apology for the Revival of Christian Architecture in England* (in *Tenebrae*). Some of Heaney's other sonnets are *The Forge* and *Requiem for the Croppies* (in *Door into the Dark*, 1969), *The Lead Cutters*, *Strange Fruit* and *Act of Union* (in *North*, 1975), plus *In Memoriam: Robert Fitzgerald* and *The Old Team* (in *The Haw Lantern*). In the late 1970s Tony Harrison emerged as an outstandingly talented sonneteer. His sonnet sequence *The School of Eloquence* (1978) takes language as a kind of 'site' in the class-war conflict. Many of his best sonnets are concerned with his native Yorkshire land and there are especially moving ones about his father. He is particularly skilled in the use of colloquial and idiomatic language. James Fenton composed a number of fine sonnets in *Our Western Furniture* (1968), and we should also mention Roy Fuller's *Mythological Sonnets* (1969).

During over 700 years the 'narrow room of the sonnet' has been adapted to a remarkable variety of experiment and development and an astonishing range of feeling and themes. Its apparently limitless inherent possibilities have been recently revealed once again: by John Updike in his clever and laconic 'love' sonnet which begins:

> In Love's rubber armor I come to you,

and thereafter has no words, but merely the rhyme scheme ingeniously contrived and punctuated to create onomatopoeic effects which suggest coition.

One of the most remarkable of all modern experiments in sonnet form is Vikram Seth's 'Novel' *The Golden Gate* (1986). The 'novel' (it tells a story) comprises 13 chapters and 590 sonnets. They are in tetrameters (*q.v.*) and have varying rhyme schemes. A wide range of tone and mood is achieved: elegiac, comic, satirical and parodic. Even the acknowledgements and the biographical note about the author are in sonnet form. *See also* CROWN OF SONNETS; QUATORZAIN; SONNET CYCLE.

sonnet cycle A series of sonnets on a particular theme to a particular individual. Love is the commonest theme and the advantages of the cycle are that they enable the poet to explore many different aspects and moods of the experience, to analyse his feelings in detail and to record the vicissitudes of the affair. At the same time each individual sonnet lives as an independent poem. Of the many cycles the following are the most famous: Dante's *Vita Nuova* (1292–4), in which there are extensive prose links; Petrarch's *Canzoniere* (*c.* 1328–74); du Bellay's *L'Olive* (1549); Ronsard's *Amours* (1552); Sidney's *Astrophil and Stella* (1591); Spenser's *Amoretti* (1595); Shakespeare's *Sonnets* (1609); Donne's *Holy Sonnets* (1635–9); Wordsworth's *Ecclesiastical Sonnets* (1822); Rossetti's *The House of Life* (1881); Elizabeth Barrett Browning's *Sonnets from the Portuguese* (1850); Rilke's *Sonette an Orpheus* (1923). *See also* CROWN OF SONNETS; CURTAL SONNET; SONNET.

soraismus (Gk 'mingle-mangle') A mixture of terms from various tongues, usually used for comic effect. A particularly good example is Skelton's *Speak, Parrot* (1521), from which this example comes:

> *Moderata juvant*, but *toto* doth exceed:
> Discretion is mother of noble virtues all.
> *Myden agan* in Greeke tongue we read.
> But reason and wit wanteth their provincial
> When wilfulness is vicar general.
> *Haec res acu tangitur*, Parrot, *par ma foy*:
> *Taisez-vous*, Parrot, *tenez-vous coy!*

See FATRASIE; MACARONIC.

sotadean A verse form named after Sotades, an Alexandrian poet of the 3rd century BC. Basically an ionic (*q.v.*) tetrameter (*q.v.*).

sotie (or sottie) The term derives from the French *sot, sotte* 'fool', and applies to a kind of dramatic entertainment which was popular in

France in the late Middle Ages. Not genuine farce (*q.v.*) but a knockabout satirical jollification which sometimes served as a curtain raiser (*q.v.*) to Mystery and Morality Plays (*qq.v.*). The actors wore fool's costume and derided society, manners and political events. Two well-known *soties* were: *Le Jeu du Prince de Sots et Mère Sotte* (1512) and *Les Trois Pèlerins* (*c.* 1521). At the end of the 19th c. André Gide brought his individual genius to the creation of a new kind of *sotie*; a type of *récit* (*q.v.*) 'arbitraire et volontiers bouffon'. Examples are *Paludes* (1896), *Le Prométhée mal enchaîné* (1899) and *Les Caves du Vatican* (1914).

source-book Any work from which an author has 'lifted' or borrowed an idea, plot or story. Holinshed's *Chronicles* (1577) was a much used source-book for Elizabethan dramatists. *See also* PLAGIARISM.

spasmodic school A group of minor 19th c. poets who achieved considerable popularity in England and America in the 1840s and 1850s. The three main ones were P. J. Bailey, Sydney Dobell and Alexander Smith. Among their better known works are Bailey's epic drama *Festus* (1839), Dobell's *The Roman* (1850) and Alexander Smith's *A Life Drama* (1853). These turgid verse plays of inordinate length were written in an extravagant, bombastic 'neo-romantic' verse and they had little formal discipline or structure. In 1853 Charles Kingsley described their work as 'spasmodic'. Later William Aytoun parodied and derided them successfully in *Firmilian, or, The Student of Badajoz: A Spasmodic Tragedy* (1854). He also attacked them in *Blackwood's Magazine.*

speech, divisions of These divisions were first laid down by the Classical rhetoricians. They did not all agree, but the basic parts are: (a) introduction – (proem or exordium); (b) statement of the case; (c) argument (or agon); (d) conclusion (epilogue or peroration). Some sub-divided 'statement' into: (i) agreed points; (ii) points in controversy; (iii) points the speaker intends to establish. 'Argument' is sometimes sub-divided into: (i) proof; (ii) refutation. These divisions are still taught today. *See* ARGUMENT; RHETORIC.

Spenserian sonnet Developed by and named after Edmund Spenser, it has a rhyme scheme abab, bcbc, cdcd, ee. It is also known as the link sonnet – because of the rhyme scheme. It has the binding couplet of the Shakespearean sonnet (*q.v.*) at the end. This example is No. LXX from Spenser's sonnet cycle *Amoretti* (1595):

> Fresh spring, the herald of love's mighty king,
> In whose coat-armour richly are displayed
> All sorts of flowers, the which on earth do spring,
> In goodly colours gloriously arrayed;
> Go to my love, where she is careless laid,
> Yet in her winter's bower not well awake;
> Tell her the joyous time will not be stayed,
> Unless she do him by the forelock take;
> Bid her therefore herself soon ready make,
> To wait on Love amongst his lovely crew;
> Where every one, that misseth then her make,
> Shall be by him amerced with penance due.
>   Make haste, therefore, sweet love, whilst it is prime;
>   For none can call again the passèd time.

See PETRARCHAN SONNET; SONNET; SONNET CYCLE.

Spenserian stanza A form invented by Edmund Spenser and an important innovation in the history of English poetry. It consists of nine iambic lines, the first eight being pentameters and the last a hexameter or alexandrine (*qq.v.*), with a rhyme scheme ababbcbcc. Spenser invented it for his long allegorical poem *The Faerie Queene* (1589, 1596). This is the last stanza from Canto III in Book I:

> Nought is there under heaven's wide hollowness,
> That moves more dear compassion of mind,
> Than beauty brought to unworthy wretchedness
> Through envy's snares, or fortune's freaks unkind.
> I, whether lately through her brightness blind,
> Or through allegiance, and fast fealty,
> Which I do owe unto all womankind,
> Feel my heart pierced with so great agony,
> When such I see, that all for pity I could die.

Oddly enough, this stanza form, which is related to *ottava rima* (*q.v.*), and the octave used by Chaucer in *The Monk's Tale*, was little used in the 17th c., though the Fletcher brothers, Giles and Phineas, attempted it; and it was not until the 18th c. that its possibilities in narrative were fully appreciated. Three works from that period display notable use of it: namely, Shenstone's *The Schoolmistress* (1742), James Thomson's *Castle of Indolence* (1748) and James Beattie's *The Minstrel* (Book I, 1771; Book II, 1774). The Romantic poets proved its most successful exponents, their major works being Byron's *Childe Harold's Pilgrimage* (1812, 1816, 1818); Keats's *Eve of St Agnes* (1820); Shelley's *Revolt of Islam* (1818) and *Adonais* (1821). *See also* MONK'S TALE STANZA.

Spielmannsdichtung (G 'minstrel poetry') A general term for medieval German epics of the more popular kind which, it was formerly believed, were composed and written down by itinerant and professional poet minstrels. Well-known examples are *Herzog Ernst, König Rother, Orendel, Ortnit* and *Salman und Morolf* (12th and 13th c.).

spondee (Gk 'libation') A metrical foot of two stressed or long syllables, so named because it was used in Greek melodies accompanying libations. Not particularly common in accentual verse (poems written wholly or mostly in spondaics are very rare), but often used sparingly to slow the rhythm of a line, thus making it 'heavier' for a particular effect. There is skilful use of spondees to suggest dead weight in this extract from Ted Hughes's *View of a Pig*:

Thĕ píg | láy ŏn ă | bárrŏw deád.
Ĭt weíghed, | thĕy saíd, | ăs múch | ăs threé mén.
Ĭts éyes | clósed, pínk | whíte éye|láshĕs.
Ĭts trót|tĕrs stúck | straíght oút.

Sŭch weíght | ănd thíck | pínk búlk
Sét ĭn deáth | seémed nót | jŭst deád.
Ĭt wăs léss | thăn lífelĕss, | fúrthĕr óff.
Ĭt wăs líke | ă sáck | ŏf wheát.

See also DISPONDEE; FOOT; SCANSION.

spontaneity As a critical term, linked with the idea that the creative act is (or should be) unpremeditated, a sudden precipitation of verse or prose. Perhaps what Shelley had in mind when he described the skylark pouring forth its full heart in 'profuse strains of unpremeditated art'. In fact, poets of the Romantic period (*q.v.*) regarded spontaneity as one of the more reliable marks of the true poet. The most celebrated remark on the matter was Wordsworth's, that 'Poetry is the spontaneous overflow of powerful feelings'. Coleridge, rather more cautiously, distinguished between poets who write from inspiration and those who do it by an act of will.

This attitude has long been unfashionable and has been replaced by the view that the poet is much more like a patient and painstaking artificer or craftsman; that the poem is shaped, worked at, revised over and over again until it is well wrought. Auden averred you may have a few lines 'given' to you, but the rest is just 'plugging away': a point of view that Shelley would have deplored. It was error, Shelley claimed, to assert that 'the finest passages of poetry are produced by labour and study'.

The term may still be used judiciously, perhaps to describe what *appears* to be unpremeditated. *See* DONNEE; INSPIRATION; LIGNE DONNEE; SINCERITY.

spoof A neologism (*q.v.*) invented by the comedian Arthur Roberts (1852–1933). Originally it described any sort of hoaxing game, or jape. Also applied to a round game of cards in which certain cards when occurring together are called 'spoof'. As a literary term it may be used of the sort of hoax that pokes fun by use of parody, satire and burlesque (*qq.v.*). Well-known examples are: *1066 and All That* (1931) by W. C. Sellar and R. J. Yeatman; Richard Armour's *It All Started with Columbus* (1953), and several other 'it all started' books by that author; R. M. Myer's *From Beowulf to Virginia Woolf* (1952); Robert Nathan's *The Weans* (1960); and Nabokov's novel *Pale Fire* (1962).

Spoonerism So called after the Rev. W. A. Spooner (1844–1930), dean and warden of New College, Oxford. It consists of a transposition between the consonant sounds (especially the initial sounds) of two words; a practice to which Spooner was addicted. 'The queer old dean', for 'the dear old queen' is a famous example attributed to him. So are these valedictory words he is alleged to have addressed to an undergraduate pupil: 'You have tasted your worm, hissed my mystery lectures, and you must catch the first town drain.'

sporting verse/fiction There is a modest corpus of such verse in British and American literature. In view of the fact that the British have been responsible for the invention and development of a high proportion of the world's games and sports, the surprising thing is that there is not more of it; and also that it is not of better quality.

If we except the splendid description of the hunt in *Sir Gawain and the Green Knight* (14th c.), there is not much of note until the 18th c., from which period date a few anonymous poems on curling, boxing and bowls. The only memorable poem of the period about a game is *Cricket* by James Love (1722–74). It celebrates Kent's victory over All-England at the Artillery in June 1744. The poem comprises three short books each prefaced by an argument (*q.v.*). Love adopts an epic 'stance' and, naturally, writes in the standard heroic couplets (*q.v.*) of the period in which the influence of Pope's *Rape of the Lock* (1714) is easily discernible.

Most sporting verse is about cricket, hunting, curling, swimming, running, football and boxing. From the 19th c. date a number of broadside (*q.v.*) poems about pugilism and notable prize-fights of the era, and such legendary pugilists as Tom Cribb, Dick Curtis, Mendoza, John Randall, James Burke, 'Bendigo' Thomson, William Perry 'the Tipton Slasher', Charles Freeman, Brassey, Caunt, Tom Sayers and John Heenan.

The most prolific sporting poet of the 19th c. was George Whyte-Melville (1821–78), who was an authority on field sports and wrote copiously about them, especially fox-hunting. He was a facile versifier capable of the occasional memorable descriptive piece.

Many distinguished poets have sometimes composed on a sporting theme, or a theme very closely related to a sport or game. A roll-call of names is impressive: Wordsworth (on skating), Coleridge (climbing), Byron (swimming), Swinburne (swimming), Andrew Lang (cricket), Francis Thompson (cricket), W. B. Yeats (horse-racing), John Masefield (fox-hunting), Alfred Noyes (swimming), J. C. Squire (rugby union), Ezra Pound (fencing), Hart Crane (swimming), John Betjeman (golf), Louis MacNeice (cycling), John Arlott (cricket), Norman Nicholson (cricket), Gavin Ewart (cricket), Vernon Scannell (boxing), Alan Ross (cricket), Dannie Abse (football), James Kirkup (rugby league), Ted Hughes (football), Douglas Dunn (running) and Roger McGough (tennis).

There are some quite ingenious examples of concrete poetry (*q.v.*) on sports and games. For example, Roger McGough's *40–Love*, Maxine Kumin's *400-Meter Freestyle*, Stephen Morris's *High Jump Poem* and *Long Jump Poem* and Michael Horowitz's *The Game*.

Only two sportsmen of national or international fame have displayed any facility whatever as poets. They are John Snow, the Sussex and England fast bowler, and Muhammed Ali, whose jingles are no more than self-advertisements for 'the Greatest'.

A handful of writers have written sporting novels. There have been few of distinction. However, R. S. Surtees made the world of fox-hunting his own and produced a number of fine comic novels (which at their best rival those of Dickens), including *Handley*

Cross (1843), *Mr Sponge's Sporting Tour* (1853) and *Mr Facey Romford's Hounds* (1865). Of his many comic characters three are outstanding: Jorrocks, the sporting cockney grocer, James Pigg, his dour and morose huntsman, and Mr Soapy Sponge. George Whyte-Melville also wrote a number of sporting novels of merit, especially *Market Harborough* (1861); like Surtees he was especially interested in and knowledgeable about the hunting scene.

In the 20th c. there has been little of note in fiction (apart from a few good short stories such as Edmund Blunden's *The Flower Show Match*), but David Storey's *This Sporting Life* (1960) was a novel of considerable distinction. He also wrote *The Changing Room* (1972), a play which, like *This Sporting Life*, is set in the world of rugby league football.

Sprachgesellschaften German literary societies founded in the 17th c. Their aim was to 'purify' the German language and encourage its use in poetry. The main ones were: the Fruchtbringende Gesellschaft (founded 1617); the Tannengesellschaft (1643); the Teutschgesinnte Genossenschaft (1643); the Hirten- und Blumenorden an der Pegnitz (1644) and the Elbschwanenorden (1660). It should be noted that Latin and French prevailed in Germany early in the 17th c.

Sprechspruch *See* SPRUCH.

Spruch (G 'saying, epigram') A short lyrical poem set to music. Walther von der Vogelweide (*c.* 1170–1230), generally regarded as the best of the Minnesingers (*q.v.*), wrote a number of them.

The *Spruch* has to be distinguished from the *Sprechspruch*, a form of gnomic verse (*q.v.*) designed to be spoken and read. The *Sprüche* first appear in the 12th c., and there was a 13th c. collection called *Bescheidenheit* 'modesty', which remained popular until the 16th c. Other poets who composed *Sprüche* were Goethe and Stefan George.

sprung rhythm The thing is old but the term is comparatively new. The term was invented by Gerard Manley Hopkins to describe his own metrical system, and his re-discovery of the techniques involved in sprung rhythm have had a wide influence on the development of English poetry. Hopkins's own words on the subject (in *Preface* to *Poems*, 1918) can hardly be improved upon:

> [It] is measured by feet of from one to four syllables, regularly, and for particular effects any number of weak or slack syllables may be used. It has one stress, which falls on the only syllable, if there is only one, or, if there are more, then scanning as above, on the first, and so gives rise to four sorts of feet, a monosyllable and the so-called accentual Trochee, Dactyl, and the First Paeon [*qq.v.*]. And there will be four corresponding natural rhythms; but nominally the feet are mixed and any one may follow any other. And hence Sprung Rhythm differs from Running Rhythm [*q.v.*] in having or being only one nominal rhythm, a mixed or "logaoedic" one, instead of three, but on the other hand in having twice the flexibility of foot, so that any two stresses may either follow one another running or be divided by one, two, or three slack syllables . . . It is natural in Sprung Rhythm for the lines to be *rove over*, that is for the scanning of each line immediately to take up that of the one before, so that if the first has one or more syllables at its end the other must have so many the less at its beginning . . . Two licences are natural to Sprung Rhythm. The one is rests, as in music . . . The other is *hangers* or *outrides*, that is one, two, or three slack syllables added to a foot and not counted in the nominal scanning. They are so called because they seem to hang below the line or ride forward or backward from it in another dimension than the line itself . . .

Some analysis of his poem *Harry Ploughman* may help to clarify the main points:

Hárd as hurdle arms, with a bróth of góldish flúe
Breáthed roúnd: the ráck of ríbs; the scoóped flank; lank
Rópe-over thígh; knée-nave; and bárrelled shánk –
Héad and fóot, shóuldér and shánk –
By a gréy eye's heed stéered wéll, one créw, fall to;
Stand at stréss. Each límb's bárrowy bráwn, his théw
That onewhere cúrded, onewhere súcked or sánk
Sóared ór sánk – ,
Though as a beéchbóle firm, finds his, as at a róll cáll, rank
And feátures, ín flesh, whát deéd he each must dó –
His sínew-sérvice where do.

He leans to it, Harry bends, look. Back, elbow, and liquid wâist
In him, all quâil to the wallowing o' the plough: 'S cheék crímsons; cúrls

Wág or cróssbrídle, in a wind lífted, wíndláced –
                                                  Seé his wind-lilylocks-láced;
Chûrlsgrace, too, chîld of Amansstrength, how it hangs or húrls
Them – broad ín bluff híde his frówning feét láshed! raced
With, along them, crágiron under and cóld fúrls –
                                                  With-a-fountain's shíning-shót
                                                                                furls.

The symbols used by Hopkins indicate the following:

(a) ʹ = metrical stress.
(b) ∧ = strong stress.
(c) ⌒ = a pause or dwelling on a syllable.
(d) ~ = a quiver or circumflexion; a drawing out of one syllable to make it almost two.
(e) ⌢ = slur; a tying or binding together of syllables into the time of one.
(f) ⌣ = hanger or outride.
(g) ⌐¬ over adjacent words indicates that, though one word has the metrical stress and the other has not, in recitation they are to be taken as more or less equal.

This re-discovery of Hopkins (sprung rhythm was not unknown in OE and ME alliterative verse) has had a considerable influence on the work of, among others, T. S. Eliot, Dylan Thomas and Ted Hughes. *See also* FOOT; ICTUS; INSCAPE AND INSTRESS; SCANSION.

spy story A form of fiction devoted to various kinds of espionage. Since late in the 19th c., and increasingly so since the 1920s, it has been kin to novels of adventure (e.g. Anthony Hope's *The Prisoner of Zenda*, 1894; Baroness Orczy's *The Scarlet Pimpernel*, 1905), the thriller (e.g. the stories of Edgar Wallace), and the politico-military thriller (e.g. some works by Eric Ambler, some of Graham Greene's 'entertainments', *q.v.*, and novels by Lionel Davidson, Frederick Forsyth and Francis Clifford). In fact, the spy story has subsumed many of the best elements of such tales, and has evolved into a specialized and sophisticated form of fiction which, at its best, is skilfully plotted, contains well-drawn characters, exciting action and a high degree of suspense and tension, and is extremely authentic in all technical detail. In the hands of an accomplished writer like Len Deighton it becomes a distinguished sub-species of the novel (*q.v.*).

The use of spies is an ancient practice. There is evidence of it in the Bible, in Classical and Byzantine history; and it becomes more evident in the history of the late Middle Ages and the Renaissance period. For example, the rival states of Renaissance Italy used spies continually for military and political purposes. The diplomatic corps of Europe then (as now) were frequently involved in espionage. Ambassadors, legates and envoys were known to be agents for their governments and accepted as such. In England, in the 16th c., Walsingham built up a very efficient and ruthless secret service organization. The Church, too, used priests as spies and these in turn were spied upon by anti-papal agents. It became a commonplace for people to spy upon each other. Kings, princes and tyrants, guided by the needs of expediency, employed agents to watch their enemies. Like Macbeth, in every house they kept an agent fee'd.

From that time forwards espionage of all kinds has proliferated in most countries, until, in the 20th c., we find huge secret service agencies and secret police organizations operating all over the world. A world influential pioneer of such organizations was Fouché, Napoleon's chief of police. He was a gifted secret agent and built up a powerful system of espionage. In the East spying has been an accepted practice for centuries. Perhaps the earliest *vade mecum* (*q.v.*) of all on the skills of espionage and the arts of war was the Chinese *Ping Fa* (510 BC) by Sun-tzû. This has remained required reading for Chinese agents and was even issued in translation (suitably abridged and simplified) to the RAF in Ceylon during the Second World War; though it is by no means clear why the RAF there should have been so favoured. From China, too, came *San Kuo* by Lo Kuan-chung (1260–1341), a novel much concerned with espionage. It is said that Mao Tse-tung and the Vietcong guerrillas consulted it frequently. In China, the study of the literature of espionage is part of general education.

The industrial revolution, a succession of wars in the 19th c., and more and more wars in the 20th c. have meant the development of ever more sophisticated weapons and lethal substances. Inevitably there has been a genuine threat of secret documents being stolen: a favourite theme in espionage novels. In fact, to adapt Parkinson's law, one could say that spies have accumulated to fill the roles that technology requires of them. It is not surprising, therefore, that the spy story has matured concurrently.

One of the earliest examples of such a story is *The Spy* (1821) by James Fenimore Cooper. It is not of much merit, but it made clear that spying was a hazardous activity for which the penalty was very likely to be execution – usually without trial. After Cooper, there is little of note (except for Dickens's *A Tale of Two Cities*, 1859, which contributed to the development of the genre) until the tales of William Le Queux (1864–1927), who was probably a spy himself. His first book, *Guilty Bonds* (1890), described the intricacies of political conspiracy. His second, *A Secret Service* (1896), dealt with anti-Jewish activities after the assassination of Alexander III. Other works included *England's Peril* (1899), *The Invasion of 1910* (1905) and *Spies of the Kaiser* (1909); in this last he warned of a German invasion in the near future. Out of the hundred odd books which Le Queux wrote, some thirty were concerned with espionage, but they are seldom read now and most of them are poor stuff. However, he was a pioneer of the spy story.

In 1905 Baroness Orczy (1865–1947), creator of the improbable hero Sir Percy Blakeney, achieved great success with her espionage romance *The Scarlet Pimpernel*, set during the French Revolution. She followed this with several other Pimpernel yarns: *I Will Repay* (1906), *Eldorado* (1913) and *Sir Percy Hits Back* (1927). In 1921 Rafael Sabatini (1875–1950) published *Scaramouche*, a spy tale in the Orczy style. Such books are more or less unreadable now (except as curiosity 'period pieces'), but they enjoyed a great vogue at the time.

A much more distinguished author was Erskine Childers (1870–1922), who wrote *The Riddle of the Sands* (1903), one of the first spy stories to gain respect in literary circles. He was the first to provide the expert technical background and knowledge of the kind which is now commonplace (*and* expected) in spy stories.

Edgar Wallace (1875–1932), who wrote 173 books, also contributed to the development of spy fiction – particularly with his story *Code No. 2* (1916), which anticipates the technological advances of a later period. Wallace also wrote a series of secret service stories in which the central character was Major Haynes.

In the pre-war period Joseph Conrad (1857–1924) published two books about revolutionary agents, both of which involved espionage and secret service activities. The first was *The Secret Agent* (1907), an account of anarchist activities in London; the second was *Under Western Eyes* (1911). The spies in both books (Verloch and Razumov) were Russians and double agents; and in both books Conrad was more interested in the depiction of 'the very soul of things Russian' than in spying.

The First World War produced a number of spy stories of

nationalistic and right-wing tone in Britain, in which, inevitably, the Germans were the 'baddies'. This is noticeable in the books of John Buchan (1875–1940) and Sapper – pseudonym of Herman Cyril McNeile (1888–1937). Among Buchan's best known spy stories are *The Thirty-Nine Steps* (1915) and *Greenmantle* (1916), which he followed with others of considerable quality. Sapper published *Bulldog Drummond* in 1916. Bulldog Drummond must rank as one of the most ludicrous and disagreeable characters ever invented: a prototypal MCP, right-wing, racialist and Fascist. Sapper was a very poor writer, but his Bulldog Drummond series (later to be continued by Gerard Fairlie, 1899–) was extremely popular.

In 1928 Somerset Maugham (1874–1965) published his *Ashenden* stories, something of a landmark in the genre. They were based on the author's experiences as an intelligence officer and are notable for their detachment and neutrality and also for their quiet tone. Maugham presented spies who were very ordinary and quite amiable people doing a job. There is a complete absence of anything sensational in the stories.

Between the world wars several other writers published spy fiction of varying quality. For example, Taffrail, pseudonym of Capt. Henry Dorling, RN (1883–1968), who put his experience of sea and warfare to good use in several readable spy stories, among them *The Lonely Bungalow* (1931), *Operation 'MO'* (1938) and *The Shetland Plan* (1939). Another was Francis Beeding, the pen-name of a partnership of two authors: John Palmer (1885–1944) and Hilary Saunders (1898–1951). As Francis Breeding they wrote some forty novels, including the Granby secret service stories – such as *The League of Discontent* (1930), *The Three Fishers* (1931), *The Four Armourers* (1931), *Take It Crooked* (1932), *The One Sane Man* (1934), *The Black Arrows* (1938) and *The Secret Weapon* (1940), this last being very topical since it concerned a quest for the formula of one of Hitler's secret weapons. A third was Sydney Horler (1888–1954), a popular thriller writer who produced a spate of spy stories in the 1930s, and Bernard Newman (1897–1968), who concentrated on espionage in Europe with a series of topical but not particularly well-written stories.

Others active during the 1920s and 1930s were: E. Phillips Oppenheim (1866–1946), who was immensely prolific but an indifferent writer; Valentine Williams (1883–?), who published a number of successful secret service stories; Martha McKenna (*c.* 1893–1969), who was a spy in the First World War and wrote a dozen successful novels; Sax Rohmer (1883–1959), author of the notorious (and idiotic) Dr Fu Manchu series; and John Creasey (1908–73), who wrote 562 books, a handful of which were devoted to espionage.

Between the wars some of the very best spy stories were those by Eric Ambler (1909–) – especially *The Dark Frontier* (1936), *Epitaph for a Spy* (1938) and *The Mask of Dimitrios* (1939). Ambler's books remain compulsively readable. He was original because of his detachment and his exceptional gift for creating and sustaining tension without being melodramatic.

As good, but different in his approach, was Graham Greene (1904–), who classified his spy stories (like some of his other books) as 'entertainments'. *England Made Me* (1935) contains some espionage. *The Confidential Agent* (1939) was more successful, and *Ministry of Fear* (1943) showed Greene as a supremely capable contriver of a wholly realistic spy story.

Together, Maugham, Ambler and Greene deglamorized the spy and the whole business of espionage, but, even so, the realism begun by Maugham was somewhat reversed during the Second World War, which produced much third-rate 'nationalistic' spy fiction. An exception to this generalization is *The Secret Vanguard* (1940) by Michael Innes, a novel in which orders are provided by way of an additional stanza to Swinburne's *Forsaken Garden.*

In the 1950s there began the James Bond era of spy fiction written by Ian Fleming (1908–64). In many ways unreadable, the Bond stories achieved enormous success, first as books, then as films. As a character Bond was only marginally less ridiculous than Bulldog Drummond. Some of Fleming's books were *Casino Royale* (1953), *Moonraker* (1955), *Diamonds are Forever* (1956), *From Russia with Love* (1957), *Doctor No* (1958) and *Goldfinger* (1959). In 1958 a salutary contrast to these melodramatic excesses was Graham Greene's *Our Man in Havana*, a fine piece of droll comedy which 'sent up' the secret agent business. Twenty years later he published *The Human Factor*, a very different account of secret service activity.

From the 1950s the spy story burgeoned, and so it was to continue for the next thirty or more years. Dozens of writers (most of them British) applied themselves to tales of espionage. Many produced good or excellent novels, but there were quantities of run-of-the-mill derivative stuff in which there was far too much gratuitous violence and brutality – plus gratuitous 'sex'. The burgeoning took place alongside extensive coverage in the media of actual spy 'scandals' of one kind and another. There were lurid stories of defection, treachery and exposure. The Burgess and Maclean affair was plugged year in, year out; there were also the levanting of Philby and the unmasking of Blunt. Numerous books about the CIA, MI5, DI5, MI6, DI6 and secret service activities in general were published. In 1988 there was a big controversy about *Spycatcher* – and so on.

By 1960, if not earlier, many people had had more than enough of James Bond; certainly most writers interested in spy fiction had had enough. During the 1960s an anti-Bond image developed; in fact a kind of anti-hero (*q.v.*) agent/spy/operator evolved. This was noticeable in the fiction of Len Deighton (1929–) and John Le Carré (1931–). Both excellent writers (Deighton having the finer style), they between them established an even more realistic form of spy story than that conceived by Maugham, Ambler and Greene. They revealed the squalor, cynicism, treachery, expediency and corruption of the world of espionage and in their novels confirmed the actualities of that world in real life. Some of Deighton's best known books are: *The Ipcress File* (1963), *Funeral in Berlin* (1964), *Billion Dollar Brain* (1966), *Twinkle, Twinkle, Little Spy* (1976) and the trilogy *Game, Set and Match* (1986). John Le Carré made his name with *The Spy Who Came in from the Cold* (1963), and followed this success with *The Looking-Glass War* (1965), *A Small Town in Germany* (1968), *Tinker, Tailor, Soldier, Spy* (1974), *Smiley's People* (1980) and *A Perfect Spy* (1986).

Since the late 1950s numerous other writers have produced notable spy fiction (the list that follows is in no particular order of merit or chronology), for instance: Richard Condon (1915–) – *The Manchurian Candidate* (1959); Edward Weismiller (1915–) – *The Serpent Sleeping* (1962); Adam Bell (1920–) – *The Quiller Memorandum* (1965), which he was to follow with *Berlin Memorandum*, *Quiller's Run* and *The Pekin Target* (1981); Helen MacInnes (1907–) – *The Venetian Affair* (1963), *The Salzburg Connection* (1968); John Gardner (1927–) – *The Liquidator* (1964) and several others; Francis Clifford (1917–75) – *The Naked Runner* (1966) and *The Blind Side* (1971); Ted Allbeury (1917–) – *A Choice of Enemies* (1971), *The Man with the President's Mind* (1977), *The Judas Factor* (1984), *Children of Tender Years* (1985), *A Wilderness of Mirrors* (1988); Charles McCarry (1929–) – *The Miernik Dossier* (1974), *Tears of Autumn* (1975), *The Secret Lovers* (1977); Evelyn Anthony (1928–) – *The Tamarind Seed* (1971), *No Enemy but Time* (1987), *The House of Vandelias* (1988); William Haggard (1907–) –

The Arena (1961), *The Unquiet Sleep* (1962), *The Antagonists* (1964), *The Conspirators* (1967), *The Protectors* (1972); Anthony Price (1928–) – *Our Man in Camelot* (1975) and several others; Nicholas Luard (1937–) – *The Robespierre Serial* (1975), *Travelling Horseman* (1975), *The Orion Line* (1976), *The Dirty Area* (1977); Gerald Seymour (1941–) – *Harry's Game* (1979), *In Honour Bound* (1984), *Field of Blood* (1985), *At Close Quarters* (1987); Alan Williams (1935–) – *The Beria Papers* (1973), *Gentleman Traitor* (1975); Brian Freemantle (1936–) – *Charlie Muffin* (1977); Frederick Forsyth (1938–) – *The Odessa File* (1972); Brian Garfield (1939–) – *Hopscotch* (1974); Kenneth Follett (1949–) – *The Shakeout* (1975), *The Bear Raid* (1976); Trevanian – *The Eiger Sanction* (1972), *The Loo Sanction* (1973).

Apart from these, many other writers in the 20th c. (not a few of whom also produced detective stories, thrillers and miscellaneous tales of mystery and suspense) have been attracted to the possibilities of espionage in fiction. Some of them have been what are loosely called 'popular novelists' who could turn their hand to pretty well anything and were immensely prolific. Obvious examples are Peter Cheyney (1876–1951), Dennis Wheatley (1897–1977) and Leslie Charteris (1907–), who all wrote spy stories of variable quality.

Others – by and large less well known – are: Simon Harvester (1909–75), Kenneth Benton (1909–), Robert Harling (1910–), Ronald Seth (1911–), Victor Canning (1911–), Stephen Coulter (1914–), Chapman Pincher (1914–), Philip Atlee (1915–), Harry Hossent (1916–), Sarah Gainham (1922–), Donald Seaman (1922–), John Leasor (1923–), Leon Uris (1924–), Walter Wager (1924–), R. Wright Campbell (1927–), Angus Ross (1927–), Noël Behn (1928–), Wilson McCarthy (1930–), Douglas Hurd (1930–), well known as a politician, Eric Clark (1937–), Andrew Osmond (1938–), John Howlett (1940–) and Diana Winsor (1946–).

Hurd and Osmond collaborated successfully with three books which are basically political (or politico-military) thrillers with espionage undertones. The partnership produced *Send Him Victorious* (1968), *Smile on the Face of the Tiger* (1969) and *Scotch on the Rocks* (1971). Hurd also wrote *The Truth Game* (1972) and *Vote to Kill* (1975). Osmond's best novel was *Saladin* (1975).

Very surprisingly, the spy story has not flourished in other languages and literatures. In fact, the British (and, to a lesser extent, the Americans) have been and are overwhelmingly the main practitioners. Between the wars the only continental Europeans were Darwin and Hildegarde Teilhet. The former wrote some spy novels in the 1930s. As a partnership they produced some more in the 1940s. Two solitary Frenchmen have also contributed to the genre: Hubert Monteilhet (1928–) and Pierre Nord, who were both quite prolific in the 1960s and 1970s. One Communist-bloc author has made some name in the genre. In about 1960 Andrei Gulyashki, a Bulgarian novelist, was 'invited' by the KGB to refurbish the image of Soviet espionage which had been tarnished by the successes of James Bond (a figure who, incredible though it may seem, was actually taken seriously by some members of the KGB). Gulyashki very sensibly accepted the KGB 'invitation' (otherwise he might have had twisted *moshonki*) and created a proletarian Bond in the shape of Avakum Zakhov, a crack spy, one of whose main missions was to liquidate 007. Gulyashki's most successful novel was *Avakum Zakhov versus 07* (*sic*), published in 1966. *See* THRILLER.

stage directions Notes incorporated in or added to the script of a play to indicate the moment of a character's appearance, character and manner; the style of delivery; the actor's movements; details of location, scenery and effects. Printed texts of Elizabethan and Jacobean dramatists keep them to an absolute minimum (e.g. Enter two servants; Music; Dies; *Exit*; Sings; *Manet*; *Exeunt omnes*; Stabs him). Over the years they became more detailed and complex and by the end of the 19th c. dramatists were providing elaborate directions and instructions. Shaw, perhaps more than anyone, exploited their possibilities very skilfully and usually at considerable length, often indicating *exactly* how he wanted anything to be said or done. In recent years there has been a reaction against this kind of elaboration. Some dramatists have gone to the other extreme and pared direction to an austere simplicity. A notable exponent of such frugal practice is Harold Pinter.

standard English That English, spoken or written, which is regarded as generally accepted and correct in grammar, syntax and spelling, and which is a fit model for imitation. *See* COLLOQUIALISM; KING'S ENGLISH; SLANG.

stanza (It 'standing, stopping place') A group of lines of verse. It may be of any number but more than twelve is uncommon; four is the commonest. A stanza pattern is determined by the number of lines, the number of feet in each line and the metrical and rhyming schemes. The stanza is the unit of structure in a poem and most poets do not vary the unit within a poem. Exceptions can be found in Spenser's *Epithalamion* and Coleridge's *Rime of the Ancient Mariner*. Earlier English terms are batch, fit and stave (*qq.v.*). *See also* CANTO; OTTAVA RIMA; QUATRAIN; RHYME ROYAL; SPENSERIAN STANZA; TERZA RIMA; VERSE PARAGRAPH.

stasimon (Gk 'stationary song') An ode (*q.v.*) sung by the Chorus (*q.v.*) in a Greek play after taking its position in the orchestra. The *stasima* alternated with dialogue delivered by other actors.

statement A division of a speech (*q.v.*). Also used by I. A. Richards in a special sense to refer to a scientifically verifiable discourse. *See* PSEUDO-STATEMENT.

Stationendrama (G 'station drama') The walls of Roman Catholic churches are usually adorned by pictures or carvings (customarily fourteen in number) which represent the stages of Christ's journey to Calvary, the 'Stations of the Cross'. Thus, they are a series of tableaux; separate but inter-related episodes. This form of representation is analogous to the *Stationendrama*, which was basically expressionist. Among the better known exponents were Georg Kaiser (1878–1945), Reinhard Sorge (1892–1916) and Ernst Toller (1893–1939).

stave A back formation from *staves*, plural of *staff*. A synonym for stanza (*q.v.*). *See* BATCH; CANTO; FIT; VERSE PARAGRAPH.

stemma (Gk 'garland') The term has come to denote the recorded genealogy of a family; hence, family tree. By transference, it also denotes the tree of descent or lineage of a text (*q.v.*). A manuscript (*q.v.*) may exist in several versions. There are 'good' texts and 'bad' (or 'corrupt') texts. A scholarly edition of a text will take into account all the available data, readings, versions and emendations. A published text may in turn be subject to re-editing, hence recension and redaction (*qq.v.*). *See also* FOLIO; TEXTUAL CRITICISM.

stichomythia (Gk 'line talk') Dialogue of alternate single lines, especially in drama. Usually a kind of verbal parrying accompanied by antithesis (*q.v.*) and repetitive patterns. It is highly effective in the creation of tension and conflict. It is frequent in Classical drama, not so common since. Well-known examples occur in *Hamlet* (III, iv) and *Richard III* (IV, iv) and in many scenes in *Love's Labour's*

Lost. Molière used it several times in *Les Femmes savantes* (III, v) and he sometimes used double lines. The following example comes from Milton's *Comus* (1634):

> Comus: What chance good lady hath bereft you thus?
> Lady: Dim darkness, and this leavy labyrinth.
> Comus: Could that divide you from near-ushering guides?
> Lady: They left me weary on a grassy turf.
> Comus: By falsehood, or discourtesy, or why?
> Lady: To seek i' the valley some cool friendly spring.
> Comus: And left your fair side all unguarded lady?
> Lady: They were but twain, and purposed quick return.
> Comus: Perhaps forestalling night prevented them.

See ALTERCATIO; AMOEBEAN; HEMISTICH; SENECAN TRAGEDY.

stichos (Gk 'line, row') A line of Greek or Latin verse. A single line or a poem of one line. Verse is stichic when composed in homogeneous lines (e.g. iambic pentameters) in which case it is not stanzaic. *See* STANZA.

stock The identical line which ends each stanza of the *refrein* (*q.v.*) in the poetry of the *rederijkers* (*q.v.*). It contains the main theme of the poem.

stock character A recurrent type, like the *miles gloriosus* in Roman drama, the characters in *commedia dell'arte* (*q.v.*) and the villain and heroine in melodrama (*q.v.*). Other examples are the golden-hearted whore, Colonel Blimp, the oaf, the clown, the coward, the hypochondriac, the procrastinator, the nagging wife, the absent-minded professor and the man whose life is always beset with misfortune. A writer of creative originality can take such stock figures and transform them into individuals. Falstaff was the outstanding example of the braggart soldier; the braggadocio (*q.v.*). Jonson's Volpone was the supreme instance of the miser. *See also* ARCHETYPE; FABULA; FLAT AND ROUND CHARACTERS.

stock response A reaction on the part of a reader or spectator according to a standard pattern of behaviour. No critical judgement is involved. Obvious examples are cheering the hero and booing the villain.

stock situation A well-tried, recurrent pattern in fiction or drama. For example: mistaken identity; the eternal triangle; dramatic irony (*q.v.*); deception based on disguise; imposture. *See also* ARCHETYPE.

storm and stress *See* STURM UND DRANG.

storm of association A phrase used by Wordsworth in connection with the power of inspiration (*q.v.*). He suggests that a kind of external force impels or compels the poet to write. In this respect he believes in the traditional idea of the Muse (*q.v.*).

stornello (It 'turning aside') An Italian folk verse form of three lines, often beginning with an invocation to a flower. It originated in Tuscany in the 17th c. and thereafter spread through much of Italy. *See also* FOLKSONG.

story within a story An enclosed narrative; a story which occurs as part of, or as a digression in, a longer story. Of many examples one may mention *The Arabian Nights*, Voltaire's *Zadig* and Dickens's *Nicholas Nickleby*. *See* FRAME STORY; RAHMENERZAHLUNG.

stracittà (It 'over or across city') A form of literary movement in Italy which developed after the First World War. The leader of the movement was Massimo Bontempelli (1878–1960), who elaborated a literary creed known as *novecentismo*. He advocated a break with traditional 19th c. forms and attitudes and sought for what he called 'magic realism'. Yet another attempt to elucidate the essence of reality. *See also* STRAPAESE.

strambotto (It *strambo* 'eccentric, queer, whimsical') One of the oldest of Italian verse forms, it is a one-stanza composition in hendecasyllables (*q.v.*); usually either an octave (*q.v.*) or a sestet (*q.v.*). *See* OTTAVA RIMA; RISPETTO; SICILIAN OCTAVE; SONNET.

strapaese (It 'across, over country') An Italian literary movement which attained some prominence in the 1920s. Its origins appear to have been related to the Nationalist Party manifesto of 1904 by Giovanni Papini. Its principal periodical was *Il Selvaggio*, and one of its leading lights was the Roman novelist Curzio Malaparte (1878–1957). *See also* STRACITTA.

strategy A jargon (*q.v.*) term which appears to have come into literary criticism some time in the 1930s. It can mean either (a) an author's attitude towards his theme and subject; or (b) his method or technique of dealing with it. *See* SYMBOLIC ACTION.

stream of consciousness A term coined by William James in *Principles of Psychology* (1890) to denote the flow of inner experiences. Now an almost indispensable term in literary criticism, it refers to that technique which seeks to depict the multitudinous thoughts and feelings which pass through the mind. Another phrase for it is 'interior monologue'. Something resembling it is discernible in Sterne's *Tristram Shandy* (1760–67), and long self-communing passages to be found in some 19th c. novels (e.g. those of Dostoievski) are also kin to interior monologue. In 1901 the German playwright and novelist Arthur Schnitzler published a *Novelle* called *Leutnant Gustl*, a satire on the official code of military honour. In this the interior monologue technique is highly developed. However, it seems that it was a minor French novelist, Edouard Dujardin, who first used the technique (in a way which was to prove immensely influential) in *Les Lauriers sont coupés* (1888). James Joyce, who is believed to have known this work, exploited the possibilities and took the technique almost to a point *ne plus ultra* in *Ulysses* (1922) which purports to be an account of the experiences (the actions, thoughts, feelings) of two men, Leopold Bloom and Stephen Daedalus, during the twenty-four hours of June 16th, 1904, in Dublin. The following lines give some idea of the method:

> Yes. Thought so. Sloping into the Empire. Gone. Plain soda would do him good. Where Pat Kinsella had his Harp theatre before Whitbread ran the Queen's. Broth of a boy. Dion Boucicault business with his harvestmoon face in a poky bonnet. Three Purty Maids from School. How time flies eh? Showing long red pantaloons under his skirts. Drinkers, drinking, laughed spluttering, their drink against their breath. More power, Pat. Coarse red: fun for drunkards: guffaw and smoke. Take off that white hat. His parboiled eyes. Where is he now? Beggar somewhere. The harp that once did starve us all.

The climax to this extraordinary work is the forty-odd page interior monologue of Molly Bloom, a passage which has only one punctuation mark.

The beginning of Joyce's *A Portrait of the Artist as a Young Man* (1916) is an early indication of his interest in this technique.

Meantime, Dorothy Richardson had begun to compile her twelve-volume *Pilgrimage* (1915–67) and Marcel Proust was at work on the equally ambitious *A la recherche du temps perdu* (1913–27). Henry James and Dostoievski had already indicated, through long passages of introspective writing, that they were aware of something like the stream of consciousness technique. So it seems that several original minds had been working, independently, towards a new method of writing fiction.

Since the 1920s many writers have learned from Joyce and emulated him. Virginia Woolf (*Mrs Dalloway*, 1925; *To the Lighthouse*, 1927) and William Faulkner (*The Sound and the Fury*, 1931) are two of the most distinguished developers of the stream of consciousness method. There have been hundreds of others and it has long been a commonplace literary technique. *See also* ANTI-NOVEL; FREE ASSOCIATION; IMPRESSIONISM; NOUVELLE VAGUE; VIEWPOINT.

street songs Most of these are anonymous and some are very old, though not many are extant from earlier than the 17th c. Unhappily, they are also dying out though traditional ones may still be heard very occasionally in markets or in the old-fashioned pub where locals gather for a sing-song. Cockneys tend to know them more than most people. At their best they are racy, witty and slangy, as this first stanza from *A Leary Mot* suggests:

Rum old Mog was a leary flash mot, and she was round and fat,
With twangs in her shoes, a wheelbarrow too, and an oilskin round her hat;
A blue bird's-eye o'er dairies fine – as she mizzled through Temple Bar,
Of vich side of the way, I cannot say, but she boned it from a Tar –
Singing tol-lol-lol-lido.

Other fairly well-known ones are *The Ploughman's Wooing*, *Unfortunate Miss Bailey*, *The Ratcatcher's Daughter*, *She was poor but she was honest*, *Under the Drooping Willow Tree*, *Bung Your Eye*, *Polly Perkins*, *Darky Sunday School*, *The Man on the Flying Trapeze* and *Wot Cher! or, Knocked 'em in the Old Kent Road*. The last two were certainly music-hall songs. *See* BALLAD; FOLKSONG; JINGLE; NONSENSE; PATTER.

stress As a metrical term, stress is interchangeable with accent (*q.v.*). A metrical foot usually comprises one stressed syllable and one or more unstressed syllables; for example, the dactyl (*q.v.*) — ∪ ∪. *See* BEAT; FOOT; ICTUS; PRIMARY AND SECONDARY ACCENT; QUANTITY; SCANSION.

strict meter poetry A 14th c. Welshman, Einion the Priest, is regarded as the first person to have analysed the meter of Welsh poetry. He defined twenty-four different meters and classified them under three categories: *awdl*, *cywydd*, *englyn* (*qq.v.*). These are known as strict meter poetry. *See* FREEMETER.

strophe (Gk 'turning') Originally the first part of a choral ode (*q.v.*) in Greek drama which the Chorus chanted while moving from one side of the stage to the other. It was followed by the antistrophe (*q.v.*), a reverse movement, and then by the epode (*q.v.*) of a different metrical structure which was chanted by the Chorus when standing still. The term came to be used as a synonym for stanza (*q.v.*) especially in the ode (*q.v.*). More recently it has been applied to a unit or verse paragraph (*q.v.*) in free verse (*q.v.*).

structural metaphor *See* ORGANIC METAPHOR.

structure The sum of the relationships of the parts to each other; thus, the whole. Even as the Germans speak of *Gestalt* (*q.v.*), we can speak of the structure of a word, a sentence, a paragraph, a chapter, a book, and so forth. The formal structure of a play consists of its acts and scenes and their interdependent balance. The non-formal structure comprises the events and actions which take place. John Crowe Ransom makes a distinctive use of the term when he holds that the structure of a poem is its central statement or argument (its logical structure) while everything else (the words, their sounds, the images, the connotations suggested by the 'in-load' of the words, etc.) is texture (*q.v.*) or 'local texture'. *See* FORM; STYLE.

Stuart period 1603–1714, during which time the Stuart family ruled England (except for the Cromwellian period). *See* CAROLINE; CAVALIER; JACOBEAN; RESTORATION (PERIODS).

Sturm und Drang (G 'storm and stress') The phrase first occurred in the title of the play *Der Wirrwarr, oder Sturm und Drang* (1776) by

Friedrich Maximilian von Klinger (1732–1831). It gave its name to the revolutionary literary movement which was stirring in Germany at that time. Adherents of anti-Enlightenment and anti-Classicism, its supporters preferred inspiration to reason. They were also unduly nationalistic. A number of famous German authors were influenced by the movement, including Goethe, Schiller, Herder and Lenz. *See* CLASSICISM/ROMANTICISM; ENLIGHTENMENT; GOTTINGER DICHTERBUND; ROMANTICISM.

style The characteristic manner of expression in prose or verse; how a particular writer says things. The analysis and assessment of style involves examination of a writer's choice of words, his figures of speech, the devices (rhetorical and otherwise), the shape of his sentences (whether they be loose or periodic), the shape of his paragraphs – indeed, of every conceivable aspect of his language and the way in which he uses it. Style defies complete analysis or definition (Remy de Gourmont put the matter tersely when he said that defining style was like trying to put a sack of flour in a thimble) because it is the tone and 'voice' of the writer himself; as peculiar to him as his laugh, his walk, his handwriting and the expressions on his face. The style, as Buffon put it, *is* the man.

However, styles have been roughly classified and these crude categories are sometimes helpful: (a) according to period: Metaphysical, Augustan, Georgian, etc.; (b) according to individual authors: Chaucerian, Miltonic, Gibbonian, Jamesian, etc.; (c) according to level: grand, middle, low and plain; (d) and according to language: scientific, expository, poetic, emotive, referential, journalistic, etc. *See also* DECORUM; PROPRIETY.

stylistics Akin to linguistics and semantics (*qq.v.*), it is an analytical science which covers all the expressive aspects of language: phonology, prosody, morphology, syntax and lexicology.

structuralism A movement of thought in the human sciences, widespread in Europe, which has affected a number of fields of knowledge and inquiry – especially philosophy, anthropology, history, sociology and literary criticism. It has led to a fundamental reconsideration of mankind's and womankind's position, behaviour, function and attitude historically – and now.

Broadly speaking it is concerned with 'language' in a most general sense: not just the language of utterance in speech and writing. It is concerned with signs and thus with signification.

Structuralist theory considers all conventions and codes of communication; for example, all forms of signal (smoke, fire, traffic lights, Morse, flags, gesture), body language, clothes, artefacts, status symbols and so on. In theory, at any rate, it is to do with any or all of the means by which human beings convey information to each other: from a railway timetable to a thumbs-up sign; from a PR brochure to a siren.

The biologist's and zoologist's study of animal, insect, fish and bird behaviour, for instance, is equally concerned with 'language' signs and signification (zoosemiotics). In the non-human order communication is astonishingly refined and complex, not least through scent. For example, the female silk moth (*Bombyx mori*) secretes a chemical substance (a pheromone) into the air whose scent is so alluring that it can attract a male moth over a distance of half a mile; and the secretion weighs but the thousandth part of a gram. Indeed, even the *antennae of a disembodied male*, monitored by electrodes, will respond to a mere molecule of *Bombykol.*

Everything, then, in the theory of structuralism, is the product of a system of signification or code (*q.v.*). The relationships between the elements of the code give it signification. Codes are arbitrary (all signs are arbitrary) and without them we cannot apprehend reality.

As far as literature and literary criticism are concerned, structuralism challenges the long-standing belief that a work of literature (or any kind of literary text) reflects a given reality; a literary text is, rather, constituted of other conventions and texts.

Structuralism began in the science of linguistics and, more particularly, in the work of Ferdinand de Saussure (1857–1913), whose most influential text is *Cours de linguistique générale* (1915), a treatise which forms the basis of 20th c. linguistics and which has ultimately influenced much literary criticism.

Saussure made a number of important original contributions: (a) the concept of language as a sign system or structure whose individual components can be understood only in relation to each other and to the system as a whole rather than to an external 'reality'; (b) a distinction between *langue* and *parole* (*q.v.*), *langue* representing a language as a whole (e.g. French, English, German), and *parole* representing utterance, a particular use of individual units of *langue*; (c) a distinction between diachronic and synchronic (*q.v.*), diachronic denoting the historical study of the growth and development of a language (namely through philology), and synchronic denoting the study of a language as a system at any given moment of its life (Saussure put most emphasis on synchronic study); (d) a distinction between the signifier and the signified (*q.v.*).

The concept of language as a sign system was developed in the science of semiotics (*q.v.*), and especially by the American founder of semiotics, C. S. Peirce (1839–1914). Saussure's ideas were further developed by Charles Bally (1865–1947), by the Geneva School (*q.v.*) of phenomenology (*q.v.*) and by the Prague Linguistic Circle (*q.v.*). The theories of Russian Formalism (*q.v.*) are also associated with structuralist theory.

Claude Lévi-Strauss (1908–) developed a structural theory in a consideration of myth, ritual and kinship, especially in his classic work *Anthropologie structurale* (1958), and in his earlier *Elementary Structures of Kinship* (1949). He sees social structure as a kind of model and is at pains to show that the behaviour patterns of kinship and the existence of institutions depend on methods of communication that are all characteristic of how the human mind works. Thus, he analyses modes of thought as well as modes of action, looking for the system of differences which underlie practice, rather than their origins and causes. His theories about myths had considerable influence in the development of the theory of narratology (*q.v.*), a further aspect of structuralism.

The structuralist theories of Roland Barthes (1915–80), expressed in, for example, *Mythologies* (1957) and *Système de la mode* (1967), reveal a very general interpretation of the term 'language' as social practice. Early Barthes is Marxist and he had a rather different view of myth and kinship – perhaps more as bourgeois ideology. He is also concerned with, for instance, *haute cuisine* and clothes. His quest is for a kind of 'grammar' and 'syntax' of such modes of communication. He interprets social practices involving food and clothes as sign systems which function on the same model as language. Thus, he elaborates the idea that there is a 'garment system' which works like a language. Garments in general are the system (what Saussure would call *langue* and Chomsky would call 'competence'); a particular set of garments is the equivalent of a 'sentence' (what Saussure denotes as *parole* and Chomsky as 'performance'). The same distinction applies to food. Foodstuffs in general constitute the system; a particular menu and meal constitute the 'sentence'. It should be added that after 1968 and his celebrated discourses *S/Z* (1970) and *The Death of the Author* (1968), Barthes was associated with post-structuralism.

Noam Chomsky (1928–) made another contribution to structuralist theory which is of importance in linguistics and should be mentioned here. He made a distinction between 'surface structures' and 'deep structures'. A surface structure consists of the collection of words and sounds that we articulate and hear in a sentence; a deep structure is the abstract and underlying structure in language. A single sentence may have many different surface forms and features and yet have the same meaning. The underlying or deep structure regulates the meaning. These are central theoretical distinctions in generative grammar (*q.v.*). The main current theory, as summarized by David Crystal, is that 'a grammar operates by generating a set of abstract deep structures in its phrase-structure rules, subsequently converting these underlying representations into surface structures by applying a set of transformational rules'. Crystal points out that this two-level conception of grammatical structure has been questioned.

A theory of structuralist poetics has been developed by Jonathan Culler in his book *Structuralist Poetics: Structuralism, Linguistics and the Study of Literature* (1975). He advances the idea that the real object of poetics 'is not the work itself but its intelligibility. One must attempt to explain how it is that works can be understood; the implicit knowledge, the conventions that enable readers to make sense of them, must be formulated . . .' Culler focuses on the reader rather than the text, suggesting that whereas it is possible to determine the rules which govern the interpretation of texts, it is not possible to determine the rules which govern the composition of texts. Thus, the structure resides in the system that underlies the reader's interpretation or 'literary competence' rather than in the text. The idea of 'literary competence' is questionable, but Culler does not seek to identify a set of predictable rules of reading through it; as an articulation of a theory of codes and conventions it is internalized.

The work of Roman Jakobson (1896–1982), especially his two essays *Linguistics and Poetics* (1960) and *Two Aspects of Language* (1956), provides other forms of structuralist theory. He developed a theory based on the concept of binary opposition (*q.v.*) in the structure of language. He was particularly concerned with the metaphor/metonymy (*q.v.*) opposition and its implication in the analysis of realism and symbolism. In *The Modes of Modern Writing* (1977) Professor David Lodge applies the theory to modern literature, and in his fine comic novel *Nice Work* (1988) makes some drolly witty 'play' with the concept. *See also* DECONSTRUCTION; POST-STRUCTURALISM.

structuralist poetics *See* STRUCTURALISM.

sub-culture All societies are diverse in that none has a common or uniform system of values, codes, rituals, conventions, taboos, ethics, behaviour, dress, food, ideologies, religious beliefs, worship, recreations, creative activities, artefacts . . . And so on. The list might be considerably extended.

One may refer loosely to the culture of, say, England, Japan and the Caribbean islands and by so doing imply that the civilizations of those regions are very different from each other in scores of ways that might be described, analysed and explained, and any educated person may be supposed to have some inkling of fundamental points of contrast and comparison. However, culture is a 'hold-all' term which may subsume any and every aspect of the way of life of a society. It is not surprising that Hans Johst remarked, 'When I hear the word culture I reach for my gun'. The term 'sub-culture' is even less amenable to anything resembling definition.

The prefix 'sub-' inevitably implies something going on below or underneath . . . A culture below the surface of an overall, prevailing or 'first-order' culture. There is a connotation of it being different from, apart from, that other and prevalent culture. It also carries with it the concepts of 'alternative' and secrecy; and it includes an idea of popular culture.

A classic and historical example of a sub-culture developing and being maintained during a very long period is that of Slovenia. Despite Germanic influence (sometimes very repressive) extending over the greater part of a millennium, the Slovenes kept intact their own language, literature, conventions, customs, traditions, etc. Another and rather different instance is the sub-culture nurtured by the Catholic Church in Poland during the ruthless Nazi régime. For example, the Polish 'identity' and the education of Polish children were kept alive during the Nazi occupation, and in some respects this was achieved literally underground. Yet another instance is the *samizdat* (*q.v.*) organization of publishing in the USSR and elsewhere.

More generally speaking, sub-culture pertains to miscellaneous social groups within a society. For example, ghettos tend to produce sub-cultures. So do ethnic minorities. And so do many institutions (e.g. the prison system, schools). Sub-cultures are to be found in fairly 'closed' or tightly knit groups and communities associated with a particular activity (e.g. coal-miners). Specialist minorities tend to develop a kind of sub-culture (e.g. rat-catchers, bookies). There are also organizations (e.g. the services, the police force), and the 'learned' professions (whose members are, traditionally, lawyers, doctors, clergymen and teachers). To these few one might add the 'Turf'; the whole world of horse-racing has a kind of sub-culture. And there are all the professionals who operate on 'circuits' (in fact, rather 'closed' circuits), such as snooker players, golfers and tennis players. To these one might add hippies, punks, mods, rockers, skinheads, flower peoples *and* the Beat generation (*q.v.*), whose influence, through many followers, went far beyond regional and social boundaries.

What sub-cultures tend to have in common are their own slang, jargon, argot, patois (*qq.v.*), scale of values, accepted and typical codes and modes of dress and behaviour, ethical conventions, recreations and creative activities (e.g. in music, poetry, song and dance).

In some instances, a sub-culture is a real or symbolic resistance to a real or imagined authority or establishment, and all those who are, willy-nilly, upholders of conformity and tradition.

The term is also associated with youth, with pop culture, and with related terms such as 'counter-culture', 'alternative society', 'alternative literature' (*q.v.*) and 'alternative theatre' (*q.v.*). *See also* UNDERGROUND LITERATURE/POETRY.

subdued metaphor *See* TELESCOPED METAPHOR.

subintellectio *See* SYNECDOCHE.

subjectivity and objectivity The terms subjective and objective were imported into England from the post-Kantian German critics of the late 18th c. and are, in many ways, as Ruskin put it, 'two of the most objectionable words . . . ever coined by the troublesomeness of metaphysicians'. Subjectivity, when applied to writing, suggests that the writer is primarily concerned with conveying personal experience and feeling – as in autobiography (*q.v.*) or in fiction which is thinly concealed autobiography (e.g. Joyce's *A Portrait of the Artist as a Young Man*, Samuel Butler's *The Way of All Flesh* and Thomas Wolfe's *Look Homeward, Angel*). Objectivity suggests that the writer is 'outside' of and detached from what he is writing about, has expelled himself from it, is writing about other people rather than about himself, and by so doing is exercising what Keats called 'negative capability' (*q.v.*), and preserving what is described as 'aesthetic distance' (*q.v.*). The novels of Henry James and, to a certain extent, the poems of Philip Larkin show marked objectivity.

In fact, any writer of any merit is simultaneously subjective and objective. He is subjectively engrossed in his work and the quality and intensity of his personal vision will be dictated in a subjective way. At the same time he must be removed from and in control of his material. Thus he is involved in a paradoxical activity: an intellectually creative balancing act in which invention (*q.v.*) and judgement coalesce or co-ordinate to achieve and preserve equilibrium. *See also* PERSONAL HERESY; VIEWPOINT.

subject of enunciation/subject of enunciating Terms used in linguistic theory to denote two concepts of the pronoun 'I'. For instance, in the sentence 'I am writing this sentence' there are two 'I's: (a) in one sense 'I' is a point of reference, a self-designation by the use of the pronoun ('I' here is the 'subject of enunciation'); (b) in another sense the 'I' stands for what might be called the *aggregate of the self*, the sum total of the entire being – of all that 'I' am (this is the 'subject of enunciating'). This second 'I' is self-evidently permanently elusive by virtue of the fact that it is 'plurisignificative' (i.e. it bears meanings which are multiple).

The French linguist Emile Benveniste discusses the matter at length in *Problems in General Linguistics* (1966). He distinguishes between the 'personal' and 'apersonal' aspects of language. In one sense 'I' is personal; in another, apersonal. When apersonal, '*I*' is nothing other than 'the person who utters the present instance of discourse containing the linguistic instance "*I*" '. Roland Barthes elaborates on Benveniste in his discourse *The Death of the Author*, pointing out that linguistically the author is never more than 'the instance writing, just as *I* is nothing other than the instance saying *I*: language knows a "subject", not a "person", and this subject, empty outside of the very enunciation which defines it, suffices to make language "hold together", suffices, that is to say, to exhaust it'.

It is perhaps worth noting that this is a matter of narrative theory, and also of psychoanalytic/ideological criticism. The 'theory of the subject' in literary theory is anti-Cartesian. The 'I' is an ideological construct associated with the individualist ethos of capitalistic and bourgeois society; so, the redefinition of the 'I' is part of a critique of a realist aesthetic. *See also* NARRATOLOGY.

subjunctio *See* EPIZEUXIS.

sublime (L 'elevated, lofty') As a critical and aesthetic term it owes its existence to a treatise, *On the Sublime*, originally entitled in Greek *Peri Hypsous* (*hypsos*, 'height', 'elevation'), ascribed to Longinus.

The idea of sublimity stems from the rhetoricians' distinctions of various styles of speech: namely, high, middle and low. From the 17th c. onwards it held a particular fascination for people. As an intellectual concept and as an attainable quality in art and literature it was especially attractive to writers during the 18th c. and during the Romantic period (*q.v.*). Sublimity came to connote a surpassing excellence, an Everest of achievement, where great thoughts, noble feeling, lofty figures (i.e. figurative language), diction and arrangement (the five sources of sublimity established by Longinus) all coincided. Edmund Burke's *A Philosophical Inquiry into the Origin of our Ideas of the Sublime and the Beautiful* (1757) was an important contribution to thinking on the subject and the ideas were of great interest to literary critics and those concerned with aesthetics. Burke distinguished between the sublime and the beautiful. The former is associated with the infinite, solitude, emptiness, darkness and terror; the latter with brightness, smoothness and smallness.

The sublime also came to be associated with powerful emotions, with spiritual and religious awe, with vastness and immensity, with the natural order in its grander manifestations and with the concept of genius (*q.v.*).

What Burke had to say about terror and the inspiration of terror and the terrible in his *Inquiry* excited people's imaginations and this was to have some influence on the Gothic novel (*q.v.*), which became extremely popular in the last forty-odd years of the 18th c. During that time there was a kind of cult of the sublime, considerably stimulated by Macpherson's Ossianic poems. James Macpherson (1736–96) created a sensation with these fake poems in Gaelic and, in company with Homer and Milton, he was regarded as one of the great poets of the sublime. His works were widely read, not least in Germany, where Goethe, Schiller and Klopstock, among others, praised them loudly. Artists, too, were inspired by the sublime (e.g. Fuseli, Barry, Mortimer, Salvator Rosa and the mad John Martin). The Grand Tour (*q.v.*) introduced people to sublime scenery: the Alps, abysses, forests, mountain ravines and torrents. Travellers waxed lyrical on the grandeurs of Nature: the more awe-inspiring it was the better.

Many writers were affected by the cult, which was to have a far-reaching influence during the Romantic revival (*q.v.*). In 1781 Kant developed Burke's ideas in his *Critique of Pure Reason* and equated beauty with the finite and the sublime with the infinite. As Byron was to put it later in *Childe Harold*:

> Dark-heaving – boundless, endless, and sublime,
> The image of eternity.

Shelley and Wordsworth were particularly susceptible to intimations of the sublime and were profoundly stirred by the mysteries and dynamic forces of Nature.

submutatio *See* HYPALLAGE.

sub-plot A subsidiary action in a play or story which coincides with the main action. Very common in Tudor and Jacobean drama, it is usually a variation of or counterpoint to the main plot. For example, the comic sub-plot involving Stefano and Trinculo in *The Tempest*; and the serious one involving Gloucester, Edmund and Edgar in *King Lear*. The sub-plot became increasingly rare after the 17th c. *See* PLOT.

subscription publishing A method or system by which authors get together a list of buyers who are prepared to pay for their books in advance. In other words, before publication and, conceivably, before they even embark on writing. William Caxton (*c.* 1422–91), the English printer, is known to have got advances, or at any rate promises, of money for some of his major works. Early in the 17th c. John Minsheu achieved the same for his lexicographical *Guide into Tongues* (1617). The system became popular in the 18th c. and worked tolerably well, partly through the influence of patronage (*q.v.*). In this period writers issued what were called 'Proposals' for books and toted for subscribers. Pope and Johnson both did this; so did many others. Subscription publishing has worked sporadically since then with varying success and is still used by authors who produce specialist books on, perhaps, arcane subjects which would have a very limited readership.

substitution In verse, the replacement of one kind of metrical foot (*q.v.*) by another. Usually done as a deliberate variation in order to produce a particular counterpoint (*q.v.*) effect of sound and sense. A common form of substitution in English verse is putting a trochee (*q.v.*) for an iamb (*q.v.*) at the beginning of a line. In this first stanza from Geoffrey's Hill's *God's Little Mountain* the basic foot is an iamb (though there are one or two variations), but the first word of the third line is a trochee carefully placed for emphasis:

Bĕlów, | thĕ rí|vĕr scrám|blĕd líke | ă goát
Dĭslód|gĭng stónes. | Thĕ móun|taĭn stámped| ĭts fóot,
Shákĭng, | ăs fróm | ă tránce. | Ănd Í | wăs shút
Wĭth wáds | ŏf sóund | ĭntŏ ă súd|dĕn quíĕt.

See also CHOLIAMBUS.

sub-text The 'under' or 'below' text; what is not said or done. The term has a wide application to literature in general; particularly, perhaps, to the novel and short story, and other fictional genres, and to poetry. A reader tends to construct a sub-text for herself or himself, imagining or interpreting what is *not* said or *not* done (and *how* it is not said or done), what may be implied, suggested or hinted, what is ambiguous, marginal, ambivalent, evasive, emphasized or not emphasized – and so on. In doing all this the reader exercises insight into the 'unconscious' elements in the work itself and thus elicits additional meanings. Psychoanalytical criticism involves a quest for such concealed or partially concealed meanings.

The term is often associated with drama to denote the unspoken in a play; what is implied by pause and by silence. And perhaps also what Harold Pinter means by 'the pressure behind the words'. The term may also apply to the shape of the plot and the patterns of imagery.

Another and perhaps somewhat arcane concept of the sub-text is to be found in the work of two prominent Marxist critics: Pierre Macherey and Fredric Jameson. Macherey is concerned with the 'silences' or 'gaps' in a text which both conceal and expose ideological contradictions, and he believes that the critic's task is to reveal the text's unconscious content. Jameson is concerned with the 'political unconscious' of a text: that sub-text which, historically and ideologically, constitutes the 'unspoken', the concealed and repressed. *See* HERMENEUTIC OF SUSPICION; INDETERMINACY; MARXIST CRITICISM; RECEPTION THEORY; THEATRE OF SILENCE.

succès (F 'success') A *succès d'estime* means that the critics have given their blessing; *succès fou* is a popular hit; *succès de scandale*, a popular hit because of some notoriety or scandalous element. A *roman à clef* or *livre à clef* (*q.v.*) might produce a *succès de scandale*.

suggestion The term covers those ideas, feelings and impulses that a word or an arrangement of words may evoke over and above their actual sense and sound. Suggestion may be achieved by literary association (and, perhaps, allusion) as well as through subjective links in the receptor (*q.v.*) – to use a jargon (*q.v.*) term. Much writing is 'suggestive' in various ways for different people, especially in the use of allegory (*q.v.*), symbol (*q.v.*), and particular images. Both the poet and the writer of prose may 'suggest'. It is largely a matter of subjectivity (*q.v.*). These lines from John Berryman's *The Dispossessed* might trigger all sorts of associations through suggestion for various readers:

> 'and something that . . . that is theirs – no longer ours'
> stammered to me the Italian page. A wood
> seeded & towered suddenly. I understood. –
>
> The Leading Man's especially, and the Juvenile Lead's,
> and the Leading Lady's thigh that switches & warms,
> and their grimaces, and their flying arms:
>
> *our* arms, our story. Every seat was sold.
> A crone met in a clearing sprouts a beard
> and has a tirade. Not a word we heard.
>
> Movement of stone within a woman's heart,
> abrupt & dominant. They gesture how
> fings really are. Rarely a child sings now.
>
> My harpsichord weird as a koto drums
> *adagio* for twilight, for the storm-worn dove
> no more de-iced, and the spidery business of love.
>
> The Juvenile Lead's the Leader's arms, one arm
> running the whole bole, branches, roots, (O watch)
> and the faceless fellow waving from her crotch,
>
> Stalin-unanimous! who procured a vote
> and care not use it, who have kept an eye
> and care not use it, percussive vote, clear eye.

See also CONNOTATION.

summary A précis (*q.v.*) or résumé of the main points of a book or part of it. Also known as a synopsis. To be found in abridged works and also by way of introduction. It used to be a common practice but is now fairly rare. *See* ARGUMENT.

superfluous man (R *lishni chelovek*) The name given to an important and recurrent character type in 19th c. Russian literature. It denotes an idealistic but inactive hero who is aware of and sensitive to moral and social problems but who does not take action; in part because of personal weakness and lassitude, in part because of social and political restraints to freedom of action. Pushkin was the first to use the word *lishni* in this sense, in so describing the character Onegin in *Eugene Onegin* (1823–31). Eugene is regarded as the prototype, closely followed by Griboyedov's Chatski in *Woe from Wit* (1825). Pushkin's Onegin influenced Lermontov in his creation of Pechorin in *A Hero of Our Times* (1840). A development of the type was achieved by Turgenev in Rudin (*Rudin*, 1856). Turgenev's short story *The Diary of a Superfluous Man* (1850) popularized the term. His character Rakitin in his play *A Month in the Country* is a comparable type, as is the character in *The Hamlet of the Shchigrovsky District* in *Sketches from a Hunter's Album.* Turgenev tried to document and justify the existence of this type in Russian society, seeing him as a kind of tragi-comic figure, a compound of Hamlet and Don Quixote, unable to reconcile the impulses of heart and head, given to over-much introspectiveness, intellectualizing and indecision. Perhaps the most famous of all superfluous men is the endearing and totally ineffectual Oblomov in Goncharov's *Oblomov* (1859). Descendants of Onegin *et al.* are to be found in Tolstoy (e.g. Count Vronski in *Anna Karenina*, 1875–6) and in Chekhov's plays and stories, where they abound. By contrast, the heroines involved with superfluous men were strong, determined and decisive (e.g. Tatyana in *Eugene Onegin* and Natalya in *Rudin*). A contrast was aesthetically desirable and necessary anyway; hence the energetic and ebullient figure, Stolz, in *Oblomov*. *See also* CHARACTER; FABULA; STOCK CHARACTER.

supernatural story A very comprehensive term which may be applied to any sort of story which in some way makes use of ghosts, ghouls, spectres, apparitions, poltergeists, good and evil spirits and things that go bump in the night; not to mention magic, witchcraft, marvels, talismans, the eerie atmosphere and the presence of the uncanny; anything supranormal, and beyond sensory perception; what makes the flesh creep and the hair stand on end; the 'spooky', the numinous; that which conveys the sense of the preternatural (to use Coleridge's word) powers. In short anything which belongs to that world so powerfully suggested by Milton in *Comus* when he wrote of:

Calling shapes and beckoning shadows dire,
And airy tongues that syllable men's names
On sands, and shores, and desert wildernesses.

In verse, of the thousands of examples available, one may mention the supernatural and supranormal elements in *Beowulf*, *Sir Gawain and the Green Knight*, *Sir Orfeo*, Spenser's *Faerie Queene*, Milton's *Paradise Lost* and *Comus*, Coleridge's *Rime of the Ancient Mariner* and *Christabel*, Keats's *La Belle Dame Sans Merci*, E. A. Poe's *The Raven*, Browning's *Childe Roland to the Dark Tower Came*, Walter de la Mare's *The Listeners*, W. W. Gibson's *Flannan Isle*, Alfred Noyes's *Sherwood*, Vernon Watkins's *The Ballad of the Mari Lwyd*, as well as a large number of ballads (e.g. *The Wee Wee Man*, *The Wife of Usher's Well*, *The Daemon Lover*).

Two classic collections of supernatural stories are *The Arabian Nights* and the brothers Grimm *Fairy Tales*. Mention should also be made of Perrault's collection of fairy stories which includes Sleeping Beauty, Cinderella and Red Riding Hood; Defoe's *True Relation of the Apparition of one Mrs Veal*; Horace Walpole's *Castle of Otranto*; Ann Radcliffe's *Mysteries of Udolpho*; M. G. ('Monk') Lewis's *The Monk* and *The Castle Spectre*; C. R. Maturin's *Melmoth the Wanderer*; Mary Shelley's *Frankenstein*; Hoffmann's *Tales*; Poe's *Tales of Mystery and Imagination*; Hawthorne's *The Scarlet Letter*; James Hogg's *Confessions of a Justified Sinner*; Dostoievski's *The Possessed*; Dickens's *A Christmas Carol*; Stevenson's *Dr Jekyll and Mr Hyde* and *The Bottle Imp*; Oscar Wilde's *The Picture of Dorian Gray*; Ambrose Bierce's *An Occurrence at Owl Creek Bridge*; W. W. Jacobs's *The Monkey's Paw*; Sheridan Le Fanu's *In a Glass Darkly* (a collection which contains the famous *Green Tea*); Henry James's *The Turn of the Screw*; Conan Doyle's *The House of the Baskervilles*; H. G. Wells's *The Invisible Man*. Plus a large number of stories by French and Russian 19th c. writers – principally Gautier, Mérimée, Villiers de l'Isle-Adam, Huysmans, Balzac, Gogol, Pushkin and Turgenev.

More recent writers of note who have made memorable use of supernatural elements are: G. K. Chesterton, Walter de la Mare, Algernon Blackwood, H. P. Lovecraft, W. F. Harvey, A. M. Burrage, A. N. L. Munby, Georges Bernanos, L. P. Hartley, M. R. James (his *Ghost Stories of an Antiquary* is a classic), Dennis Wheatley, Ray Bradbury and Roald Dahl. *See also* GHOST STORY; GOTHIC NOVEL/FICTION; HORROR STORY.

superreader *See* READER-RESPONSE THEORY.

superstructuralism A term coined by Richard Harland in *Superstructuralism: the Philosophy of Structuralism and Post-Structuralism* (1987). He uses it to cover the whole field of structuralism, post-structuralism, semiotics (*qq.v.*), Althusserian Marxists, Foucaultians, etc. He suggests that in relation to structuralism, 'superstructuralism' appears as '*super*-Structuralism' – a larger intellectual phenomenon over and above structuralism (taking 'super' in its strict Latin sense). He also suggests that the term can be read in another and more important sense, as '*superstructure*-alism', and elaborates the idea that 'superstructuralists' invert our ordinary 'base-and-superstructure models until what we used to think of as superstructural takes precedence over what we used to think of as basic'.

supplément The French word *suppléer* means 'to take the place of, to substitute' as well as 'to supplement'. The noun *supplément* can mean 'substitute' as well as 'addition'. The term *supplément* is used by the French philosopher Jacques Derrida to denote, for example, the unstable equilibrium and thus a constantly shifting relationship which exists between speech and writing. Each term both replaces and supplements the other. But not only this relationship or opposition. The idea of '*supplément*' is part of a Derridan critique of the simple structuralist binary opposition (*q.v.*) in which a term is defined by its opposite. Derrida uses the idea of the supplement to emphasize that there is no priority in any of these oppositions but only *différance* (*q.v.*). Speech, nature, truth, for instance, are themselves supplements, substitutions and deferrals of traces; they are not stable or logocentric in the way that structuralists use them. In *Of Grammatology* (1967, trans. 1976) Derrida writes: 'It is the strange essence of the supplement not to have essentiality: it may always not have taken place. Moreover, literally, it has never taken place: it is never present, here and now. If it were, it would not be what it is, a supplement, taking and keeping the place of the other'. In the same book his reading of Rousseau depends on the ambiguity of the word *supplément*, in relation to the nature/culture opposition which Rousseau discusses. In *Deconstruction: An Advanced Reader*, Vincent B. Leitch clarifies: 'Derrida notes the emergence of an undecidable concept (the supplement), tracing its pervasive operations throughout the text of Rousseau. The effect is to deconstruct nature and culture, showing that culture does not supplement nature but that nature [*sic*] is always already a supplemented entity'. The point is that since the term 'nature' needs its opposite 'culture' in order to exist, the supplement is always already there. It is not simply that the supplement *comes after* but that the supposed priority of the term nature is itself supplementary (i.e. the process of the supplement is an aspect of *différance*, difference and deferral). *See* DECONSTRUCTION; LOGOCENTRISM.

sura A section or 'chapter' in the *Koran*. Each *sura* contains a variable number of verses.

surprise ending The twist in the tail of a story; a sudden and unexpected turn of fortune or action. Some writers of the short story (*q.v.*) have proved expert at this device; notably, O. Henry and Maupassant.

surrealism This movement originated in France in the 1920s and was a development of Dadaism (*q.v.*). The surrealists attempted to express in art and literature the workings of the unconscious mind and to synthesize these workings with the conscious mind. The surrealist allows his work to develop non-logically (rather than illogically) so that the results represent the operations of the unconscious.

The term 'super-realism' was coined by Guillaume Apollinaire (1880–1918), but it was not until 1924 that the poet André Breton issued the first manifesto (there were three altogether) of surrealism which recommended that the mind should be liberated from logic and reason. Breton had been influenced by Freudian analysis and had experimented with automatic writing under hypnosis. The surrealists were particularly interested in the study and effects of dreams and hallucinations and also in the interpenetration of the sleeping and waking conditions on the threshold of the conscious mind, that kind of limbo where strange shapes materialize in the gulfs of the mind. In his second manifesto (1929) Breton explained how the surrealist idea was to revitalize the psychic forces by a 'vertiginous descent' into the self in quest of that secret and hidden territory where all that is apparently contradictory in our everyday lives and consciousness will be made plain. There was a 'point' in the mind, he thought, where, beyond realism, one attained a new knowledge.

Distinguished writers who experimented with surrealistic methods were mostly Frenchmen: principally (apart from Breton) Louis Aragon, Paul Eluard, Benjamin Péret and Philippe Soupault. The main surrealistic painters have become much more famous: chiefly, Chirico, Max Ernst, Picasso and Salvador Dali.

The long-term influence of surrealism all over the world has been enormous. Apart from poetry, it has affected the novel, the cinema, the theatre, painting and sculpture. A great many writers have continued to explore the territories of the conscious and semi-conscious mind; delving into and exposing the private chaos, the individual hell. In doing so they have often experimented with stream of consciousness (*q.v.*) techniques. Surrealistic poetry is now rare, but plays and novels often show the influence of surrealism. From the scores of examples available, one may mention the work of Antonin Artaud, Eugène Ionesco, Jean Genet, Samuel Beckett, William Burroughs, Julien Gracq, Alain Robbe-Grillet, Nathalie Sarraute, Alan Burns and B. S. Johnson. *See also* EXPRESSIONISM; NONSENSE; PATAPHYSICS; REALISM; THEATRE OF THE ABSURD; VORTICISM.

suspended rhyme *See* ANALYSED RHYME.

suspense A state of uncertainty, anticipation and curiosity as to the outcome of a story or play, or any kind of narrative in verse or prose. The suspense in *Hamlet*, for instance, is sustained throughout by the question of whether or not the Prince will achieve what he has been instructed to do and what he intends to do. *See* PLOT.

sutra A Sanskrit term for (a) a mnemonic rule; (b) a poetic treatise in verse.

sweetness and light A phrase probably used for the first time by Swift in his preface to *The Battle of the Books* (1697): 'Instead of dirt and poison we have rather chosen to fill our hives with honey and wax; thus furnishing mankind with the two noblest of things, which are sweetness and light'. Matthew Arnold, in *Culture and Anarchy* (1869), regarded these as the basic contributions of the artist: '. . . He who works for sweetness and light united, works to make reason and the will of God prevail.'

sword dance A dramatic ritual of ancient origin; in the first place probably a fertility rite symbolizing the death and resurrection of the year. It is widespread in central Europe. In England also, especially in Yorkshire, Durham and Northumberland. Often enough the practice of the dance survives in mining areas. There are many variations. An element common to a large number of them is the symbolic death of one of the characters and his revival. There are some stock characters (*q.v.*): notably a Fool and a man dressed in woman's clothes. The sword dance is one of the origins of the Mumming Play (*q.v.*). A famous European example is the *Moreška*, a traditional dramatic spectacle at least a thousand years old, performed on the Jugoslav Adriatic island of Korčula (it also used to be done at Split, Zadar, Dubrovnik, Vis and Budva). It is performed by the young men of the island (boat-builders, farmers, masons *et al.*) and is basically an amalgam of masque, melodrama (*qq.v.*) and dance. One form of it symbolizes the war between the Christians and Arabs, to which there is a more or less peaceful ending; the other a struggle between Moorish forces (hence the name *Moreška*) and the Turks, at the end of which the Moorish leader is conquered. The latter version is the one staged on Korčula. *See* FOLK DRAMA; PLOUGH MONDAY PLAY; REVESBY PLAY.

syllaba anceps (L 'twofold, fluctuating syllable') A syllable that may be read as either long or short according to the requirements of the meter. This especially refers to a syllable at the end of a line of verse.

syllabic verse Verse measured not by stress (*q.v.*) or quantity (*q.v.*) but by the number of syllables in each line. The more conservative English poets, like Dryden, Pope and Johnson, were fairly strict about the number of syllables they would allow in the pentameter (*q.v.*) line. The term is also applied to a type of verse which became fairly common in the late 1950s and 1960s which was based merely on a syllable count, regardless of duration (*q.v.*). Among well-known poets who experimented were W. H. Auden, Thom Gunn and George MacBeth. Roy Fuller's *Owls and Artificers* (1971) is a discussion of syllabics. *See also* FOOT; SCANSION.

syllepsis (Gk 'a taking together, comprehension') A figure of speech in which the same word (verb or preposition) is applied to two others in different senses. For example: 'she looked at the object with suspicion and a magnifying glass'; or 'Miss Bolo went home in a flood of tears and a sedan chair' (Charles Dickens); or Evelyn's description of Charles I as 'Circled with his royal diadem and the affections of his people'. *See also* ZEUGMA.

syllogism (Gk 'reckoning together') Deduction, from two propositions containing three terms of which one appears in both, of a conclusion that is true *if* they are true. A stock example is: All men are mortal; Greeks are men; so all Greeks are mortal. 'Men' is the middle term. 'Mortal', the second term in the conclusion, is the major term and the premise in which it occurs is the major premise. 'Greeks' is the minor term and its premise the minor premise.

symbol and symbolism The word symbol derives from the Greek verb *symballein* 'to throw together', and its noun *symbolon* 'mark', 'emblem', 'token' or 'sign'. It is an object, animate or inanimate, which represents or 'stands for' something else. As Coleridge put it, a symbol 'is characterized by a translucence of the special [i.e. the species] in the individual'. A symbol differs from an allegorical (*see* ALLEGORY) sign in that it has a *real* existence, whereas an allegorical sign is arbitrary.

Scales, for example, symbolize justice; the orb and sceptre, monarchy and rule; a dove, peace; a goat, lust; the lion, strength and courage; the bulldog, tenacity; the rose, beauty; the lily, purity; the Stars and Stripes, America and its States; the Cross, Christianity; the swastika (or crooked Cross) Nazi Germany and Fascism; the gold, red and black hat of the Montenegrin symbolizes glory, blood and mourning. The scales of justice may also be allegorical; as might, for instance, a dove, a goat or a lion.

Actions and gestures are also symbolic. The clenched fist symbolizes aggression. Beating of the breast signifies remorse. Arms raised denote surrender. Hands clasped and raised suggest suppliance. A slow upward movement of the head accompanied by a closing of the eyes means, in Turkish, 'no'. Moreover, most religious and fertility rites are rich with symbolic movements and gestures, especially the Roman Mass.

A literary symbol combines an image with a concept (words themselves are a kind of symbol). It may be public or private, universal or local. They *exist*, so to speak. As Baudelaire expressed it in his sonnet *Correspondances*:

> La Nature est un temple où de vivants piliers
> Laissent parfois sortir de confuses paroles;
> L'homme y passe à travers des forêts de symboles . . .

In literature an example of a public or universal symbol is a journey into the underworld (as in the work of Virgil, Dante and James Joyce) and a return from it. Such a journey may be an interpretation of a spiritual experience, a dark night of the soul and a kind of redemptive odyssey. Examples of private symbols are those that recur in the works of W. B. Yeats: the sun and moon, a tower, a mask, a tree, a winding stair and a hawk.

Dante's *Divina Commedia* is structurally symbolic. In *Macbeth* there is a recurrence of the blood image symbolizing guilt and violence. In *Hamlet* weeds and disease symbolize corruption and decay. In *King Lear* clothes symbolize appearances and authority; and the storm scene in this play may be taken as symbolic of cosmic and domestic chaos to which 'unaccommodated man' is exposed. The poetry of Blake and Shelley is heavily marked with symbols. The shooting of the albatross in Coleridge's *Rime of the Ancient Mariner* is symbolic of all sin and stands for a lack of respect for life and a proper humility towards the natural order. In his *Four Quartets* T. S. Eliot makes frequent use of the symbols of Fire and the Rose. To a lesser extent symbolism is an essential part of Eliot's *Ash Wednesday* (especially Pt III) and *The Waste Land*.

In prose works the great white whale of Melville's *Moby-Dick* (the 'grand god') is a kind of symbolic creature – a carcass which symbol-hunters have been dissecting for years. Much of the fiction of William Golding (especially *Lord of the Flies*, *Pincher Martin* and *The Spire*) depends upon powerful symbolism capable of more interpretations than one. To these examples should be added the novels and short stories of Kafka, and the plays of Maeterlinck, Andreyev, Hugo von Hofmannsthal, Synge and O'Neill.

In all these works we find instances of the use of a concrete image to express an emotion or an abstract idea; or, as Eliot put it when explaining his term 'objective correlative' (*q.v.*), finding 'a set of objects, a situation, a chain of events, which shall be the formula of that particular emotion'.

There is plentiful symbolism in much 19th c. French poetry. In *Oeuvres complètes* (1891) Mallarmé explained symbolism as the art of evoking an object 'little by little so as to reveal a mood' or, conversely, 'the art of choosing an object and extracting from it an *état d'âme*'. This 'mood', he contended, was to be extracted by 'a series of decipherings'.

Mallarmé's follower Henri Régnier made the additional point that a symbol is a kind of comparison between the abstract and the concrete in which one of the terms of the comparison is only suggested. Thus it is implicit, oblique; *not* spelt out.

As far as particular objects are concerned, this kind of symbolism is often private and personal. Another kind of symbolism is known as the 'transcendental'. In this kind, concrete images are used as symbols to represent a general or universal ideal world of which the real world is a shadow. Sir Thomas Browne, long before theories of symbolism were abundant, suggested the nature of this in his magnificent neo-Platonic phrase: 'The sun itself is the dark simulacrum, and light is the shadow of God'.

The 'transcendental' concept is Platonic in origin, was elaborated by the neo-Platonists in the 3rd c. and was given considerable vogue in the 18th c. by Swedenborg. In the 19th c. there developed the idea that this 'other world' was attainable, not through religious faith or mysticism, but, as Baudelaire expressed it in *Notes nouvelles sur Edgar Poe*, 'à travers la poésie'. Through poetry the soul perceives 'les splendeurs situées derrière le tombeau'.

Baudelaire and his followers created the image of the poet as a kind of seer (*q.v.*) or *voyant*, who could see through and beyond the real world to the world of ideal forms and essences. Thus the task of the poet was to create this 'other world' by suggestion and symbolism; by transforming reality into a greater and more permanent reality.

The attainment, in transcendental symbolism, of the vision of the essential Idea was to be achieved by a kind of deliberate obfuscation or blurring of reality so that the ideal becomes clearer. This, according to symbolist theory, could be best conveyed by the fusion of images and by the musical quality of the verse; by, in short, a form of so-called pure poetry (*q.v.*). The music of the words provided the requisite element of suggestiveness. Verlaine, in his poem *Art poétique* (1874), for instance, says that verse must possess this musical quality 'avant toute chose'. Such a point of view was also expressed, in other words, by Mallarmé, Valéry and Rimbaud.

Theory and practice led the French symbolist poets to believe that the evocativeness and suggestiveness could best be obtained by verse forms that were not too rigid. Hence *vers libérés* and *vers libres* (*qq.v.*). Rimbaud and Mallarmé were the main experimenters in these forms; Rimbaud the chief practitioner of the 'prose poem' (*q.v.*). Such verse enabled the poet to achieve what Valéry described as 'cette hésitation prolongée entre le son et le sens'.

The definitive manifesto of symbolism was published in September 1886 in an article in *Le Figaro* by Jean Moréas, contending that romanticism, naturalism and the movement of *les Parnassiens* were over and that henceforth symbolic poetry 'cherche à vêtir l'idée d'une forme sensible'. Moréas founded the Symbolist School whose progenitors were Baudelaire, Mallarmé, Verlaine and Rimbaud; and whose disciples were, among others, René Ghil, Stuart Merrill, Francis Viélé-Griffin and Gustave Khan.

Some of the major symbolists poems by Baudelaire are *Les Correspondences*, *Harmonie du soir*, *Spleen*, *La Chevelure*, *L'Invitation au voyage*, *Bénédiction*, *Au lecteur*, *Moesta et Errabunda*, *Elévation*, *Les Sept Vieillards*, *Le Voyage*, *Le Cygne*. His main work is the collection known as *Les Fleurs du mal* (1857).

From Verlaine's work one should mention *Poèmes saturniens* (1866), *Fêtes galantes* (1869), *La Bonne Chanson* (1872), *Romances sans paroles* (1874) and *Sagesse* (1881). From Rimbaud *Le Bateau ivre* (1871), *Une saison en enfer* (1873) and *Les Illuminations* (1886). From Mallarmé, these poems particularly: *Apparition*, *Les Fenêtres*, *Sonnet allégorique de lui-même*, *Ses purs ongles*, *Un coup de dés*, *Grand oeuvre*. His main collection is *Poésies* (1887).

These poets were later to influence the work of Valéry very considerably, as can be seen from a study of *Le Cimetière marin*, *L'Abeille*, *Le Rameur*, *Palme*, *Les Grenades*, *La Jeune Parque* and in various poems in the collection *Charmes* (1922).

Other influences of symbolist theory and practice are discernible in Lautréamont's prose poem *Chants de Maldoror* (1868, 1869), in several works by Laforgue, in a number of plays by Villiers de l'Isle Adam, Maurice Maeterlinck and Claudel, in J-K. Huysmans's novel *A rebours* (1884), and, most of all, in Proust's *A la recherche du temps perdu* (1913–27).

The main 'heirs' of the symbolist movement outside France are W. B. Yeats, the Imagist group of English and American poets (especially T. E. Hulme and Ezra Pound), and T. S. Eliot; and, in Germany, Rainer Maria Rilke and Stefan George. The ideas of the French symbolists were also adopted by Russian writers in the 1870s and the early years of the 20th c.; notably by Bryusov, Volynsky and Bely. *See also* ALLEGORY; CORRESPONDENCE OF THE ARTS; IMAGERY; IMAGISTS; IMPRESSIONISM; METONYMY; PARNASSIANS; PRIMITIVISM; SUGGESTION; SYMBOLIC ACTION; SYNECDOCHE; TROPE.

symbolic action This jargon term denotes the conscious or unconscious 'ritual' which the writer experiences while creating a work. The work is a 'strategy' (*q.v.*) for controlling his own problems. The writer disguises his identity and, by so doing, performs a symbolic action. For example, a writer may 'write out of himself' aggressive impulses, guilt complexes, sex complexes, through the symbolic action. These theories were introduced and elaborated by Kenneth Burke in *Attitudes towards History* (1937) and *The Philosophy of Literary Form: Studies in Symbolic Action* (1941).

symbolic code *See* CODE.

symbolistes, les *See* SYMBOL AND SYMBOLISM.

sympathy *See* EMPATHY.

symposium (Gk 'drinking together') The term derives from the most famous of Plato's Dialogues, *The Symposium*, and, by transference, it now applies to a collection of essays or articles by various scholars on some special topic. Sometimes such a collection of monographs is presented to a person as a homage volume. *See also* FESTSCHRIFT.

synaeresis (Gk 'seizing together') It occurs when two normally separate vowels are combined into one syllable. For example: 'see-est' becomes 'seest'. *See* CONTRACTION; ELISION.

synaesthesia (Gk 'perceiving together') The mixing of sensations; the concurrent appeal to more than one sense; the response through several senses to the stimulation of one. For instance: 'hearing' a 'colour', or 'seeing' a 'smell'. Dr Johnson once remarked on the discovery of a blind man that scarlet represented 'the clangour of a trumpet'.

It is probable that the word was first used by Jules Millet in 1892 in a thesis on *Audition colorée*. Before that, Huysmans's character Des Esseintes and Rimbaud had consciously attempted synaesthetic effects. Earlier, Baudelaire had deliberately attempted the same sort of impression in many of his poems. As he put it in his sonnet *Correspondances*:

> Les parfums, les couleurs et les sons se répondent.
>
> Il est des parfums frais comme des chairs d'enfant,
> Doux comme les hautbois, verts comme les prairies

Synaesthetic effects are frequent in Baudelaire's *Les Fleurs du mal*, especially in those poems addressed to Jeanne Duval. But there was nothing new about synaesthesia, except that it had not been theorized over so intensely before or so consciously used. Homer, Aeschylus, Horace, Donne, Crashaw, Shelley and dozens of other poets had used synaesthetic effects. We use them in everyday speech when we talk of 'a cold eye', 'a soft wind', 'a heavy silence', 'a hard voice', 'a black look', and so forth. *See also* CORRESPONDENCE OF THE ARTS; LOGOPOEIA; ONOMATOPOEIA; TONE COLOUR.

synaloepha (Gk 'coalescence') In Classical prosody the contraction of a long vowel or diphthong at the end of one word with a vowel or diphthong at the beginning of the next. Thus, the making of one long syllable. In effect, elision (*q.v.*). In Spanish verse *sinalefa* is more complex and has been known to combine six vowels. Spanish has rather more words *beginning* with vowels and ending with them than other languages.

synathroesmus (Gk 'collection, union') An accumulation of words of different meaning in a sentence or a sequence of clauses, as in these lines from *Macbeth* (II, iii):

> Who can be wise, amaz'd, temp'rate and furious,
> Loyal and neutral, in a moment?

synaxarion In the Eastern Church, a brief account of a saint or feast appointed to be read at the early morning service of *Orthros*. It also denotes the book which contains such passages, arranged according to the Calendar (the Greater Synaxarion). Synaxaries therefore belong to hagiography (*q.v.*). *See also* CALENDAR.

synchronic *See* DIACHRONIC/SYNCHRONIC.

syncopation (MedL 'striking together') In verse and in music it occurs when the metrical pattern goes contrary to the natural stress of normal speech. Common in ballad meter, as in these two opening stanzas from *Sir Patrick Spens*:

> The King sits in Dumfermline toune,
>   Drinking the blude-red wine:
> 'O whar will I get a skeely skipper
>   To sail this ship o' mine?'
>
> Up and spak an eldern knicht,
>   Sat at the king's richt kne:
> 'Sir Patrick Spens is the best sailor
>   That sails upon the se.'

'Sailor' in line 7 is a trochaic word, but the meter clearly requires the stress to fall upon the second syllable, making it iambic. *See* FOOT; RHYTHM; SCANSION; WRENCHED ACCENT.

syncope (Gk 'cutting') The cutting short of a word by omitting a letter or syllable, as in 'e'er' for 'ever', 'e'en' for 'even'. *See* CONTRACTION; ELISION.

synecdoche (Gk 'taking up together'). A figure of speech in which the part stands for the whole, and thus something else is understood within the thing mentioned. For example: in 'Give us this day our daily bread', 'bread' stands for the meals taken each day. In these lines from Thomas Campbell's *Ye Mariners of England*, 'oak' represents the warships as well as the material from which they are made:

> With thunders from her native oak,
> She quells the flood below.

Synecdoche is common in everyday speech. In 'Chelsea won the match', Chelsea stands for the Chelsea Football Team. *See also* ANTONOMASIA; METALEPSIS; METONYMY.

syneciosis (Gk 'lining of opposites') An antithetical device quite frequent in satire (*q.v.*) which was often used by practitioners of the heroic couplet (*q.v.*). This example comes from part of Dryden's description of Shimei in *Absalom and Achitophel*:

> His Cooks, with long disuse, their Trade forgot;
> Cool was his Kitchen, tho' his Brains were hot.

See ANTITHESIS; OXYMORON; ZEUGMA

synizesis *See* SYNALOEPHA.

synonym (Gk 'together name') A word similar in meaning to another. It is rare to find an exact synonymous meaning. It is usually a matter of 'shades' of meaning, as in: insane, mad, demented, daft, loopy, psychotic, barpoo, crazy, nutty, maghnoon, off one's coconut, etc. *See.* ANTONYM.

synonymous parallelism Jargon for a couplet in which each line expresses the same idea in different terms.

synopsis *See* SUMMARY.

syntagmatic/paradigmatic The structuralist Ferdinand de Saussure (1857–1913) described language as 'a system of interdependent terms in which the value of each term results solely from the simultaneous presence of the others'. From this principle or premise he elaborates the idea that there are two dimensions in the relationships of words: (a) the syntagmatic or 'horizontal' relations; (b) the associative or 'vertical' relations, more usually described as paradigmatic. By this distinction he means that each word has a linear relationship with the words that may go before it and come after it. It is axiomatic that in any linguistic communication terms are arranged in sequences. For example, in the sentence 'The batsman hit the ball to the boundary' there is a perceptible relationship between each word. The paradigmatic relationship entails a consideration of the fact that each word in, say, a sentence (like the one above) has a relationship with other words that are *not* used but are *capable of being used* – and by being capable are thus associated. Obvious associative words in this instance would be pads, gloves, bat, bowler – or even the whole concept of cricket.

In *A Survey of Structural Linguistics* (1972) G. C. Lepschy analyses the distinction very concisely:

> A sign is in contrast with other signs which come before and after it in a sentence. It has with the preceding and following signs a syntagmatic relationship. This is a relationship *in praesentia*, i.e. between elements (the sign in question, and the preceding and following ones) which are all present in the message. But a sign is also opposed to other signs not because they are in the message but because they belong to the language; it is associated (through similarity or difference) with these other signs, it has with them an associative relationship. This is a relationship *in absentia*, i.e. between the element in question which is there, and other elements, which are not there in that particular message.

Thus, the syntagmatic is concerned with combination; the paradigmatic with substitution.

The concept of the 'language of presence' and the 'language of absence' creates a kind of fundamental opposition or antinomy (*q.v.*), which Jacques Derrida has been at pains to question; he sees no resolution, only an instability. *See* DIACHRONIC/SYNCHRONIC; DIFFERANCE; GRAMMATOLOGY; METAPHOR/METONYMY; SIGNIFIER/SIGNIFIED.

syntax (Gk 'together arrangement') Sentence construction.

synthesis *See* ANALYSIS.

synthetic rhyme This occurs when words are distorted in any way in order to give an approximate phonetic identity. It is common in humorous verse. For example, Ogden Nash's *Requiem*:

> There was a young belle of old Natchez
> Whose garments were always in patchez.
> When comment arose
> On the state of her clothes,
> She drawled, 'When Ah itchez Ah scratchez'.

And:

> For the over fifties
> And the not-so-nifties
> A discotheque
> Is a risk to tek. (J. A. Cuddon)

synthetic rhythm The repetition of a word or phrase to fill up a line. It is common in folksong, nonsense verse and ballad (*qq.v.*). The second and third stanzas from *The Wife of Usher's Well* illustrate the effect:

> They hadna been a week from her,
> A week but barely ane,
> When word came to the carline wife
> That her three sons were gane.
>
> They hadna been a week from her,
> A week but barely three,
> When word came to the carline wife
> That her sons she'd never see.

See also INCREMENTAL REPETITION; REFRAIN.

system In Greek prosody, a sequence of *cola* (*q.v.*) in the same meter (*q.v.*).

systrophe A rhetorical device which contains an accumulation of definitions, or repetition by definition. A classic example is Macbeth's apostrophe (*q.v.*) to Sleep (*Macbeth*, II, ii.).

syzygy (Gk 'yoke') A term in Classical prosody to describe the combination of two feet into a single metrical unit. Phonetic *syzygy* describes consonant sound patterns and repetitions not covered by alliteration (*q.v.*). *See also* CONSONANCE; IAMBIC TRIMETER.

T

tableau (F 'little table, picture') Primarily a theatrical term, though deriving from graphic art. Current from the 19th c. and frequently used in stage directions in 19th c. plays. To create a tableau actors took up positions and held them until the curtain came down or applause finished. Sometimes, when the curtain went up again, the actors would be regrouped into another tableau. Sometimes an actual picture was copied and there would be a copy of the picture on stage for rehearsal to guide the performers. The musical *My Fair Lady* (adapted from Shaw's *Pygmalion*) has a fine tableau for the Ascot scene which is not in the original play. *See also* DUMB SHOW.

tableaux vivants A development of the tableau (*q.v.*) in the theatre in the 19th c. and also frequent as a form of elegant private entertainment (in a drawing room, for instance). A mythical topic, a notable work of art or a famous historical event was 'dramatized' in a series of fixed tableaux. The whole thing was highly 'theatrical'. Attitudes and groupings were exaggerated and authentic costume was an important part of the presentation. A kind of static choreography was needed. Vivid animation was essential. Nelson's mistress, Lady Hamilton, was a well-known presenter of *tableaux vivants* and as a form of private entertainment they became popular. Frances Trollope (mother of the novelist Anthony) in *The Mother's Manual* (1842) actually recommends the *tableau vivant* as an acceptable way of luring suitors to marriageable daughters. In the theatre James Robinson Planché (1796–1880), who designed extravaganzas (*q.v.*) for Madame Vestris (1797–1856), and Gilbert and Sullivan made use of them. In the 1820s Andrew Ducrow presented 'living statues' at Astley's Amphitheatre. During the 1830s *tableaux vivants* were a feature of music-hall entertainments, where they were called *poses plastiques*. In the long run their influence is easily discernible in 20th c. musicals, in chorus-line routines and in the kind of film musicals that Busby Berkeley excelled at creating.

table-talk A form of literary biography (*q.v.*) which consists of a person's sayings, opinions, *obiter dicta* (*q.v.*), *aperçus*, etc. These are recorded by the person to whom they are addressed. Table talk may constitute extremely valuable material for biographers (e.g. the biography of Ben Jonson would be meagre without his conversations recorded by William Drummond of Hawthornden).

This type of literature (often known as '-ana', *q.v.*, as in *Walpoliana*) is of great antiquity. A notable paradigm in Greek literature is *Deipnosophistai* ('Sophists at Dinner' or 'Connoisseurs in Dining'), by Athenaeus (*c.* AD 200), a work of fifteen books in which twenty-three learned men meet at dinner in Rome on various occasions and discuss food and other subjects. The author was a diligent gleaner of excerpts, conversations and anecdotes which he reproduced in the form of dialogue; rather as Landor did in his *Imaginary Conversations.* In Latin literature the *Noctes Atticae* of Aulus Gellius (*c.* 200) is a collection of writings in 'essay' (*q.v.*) form based on quotations, conversations, discourses. Comparable are the 'Lectures' (*Diatribai*) of Epictetus (*c.* 60–140), which are verbatim notes on Stoic writings; and the lives of eminent philosophers compiled by Diogenes Laërtius (*c.* 200–250). The works of Athenaeus and Gellius are more akin to dialogue (*q.v.*) – as in Oliver Wendell Holmes's 'breakfast table' series of conversations – but they are a form of table-talk and we find not dissimilar collections in several European literatures, and also in Persian, Hebrew, Arabic and Turkish literature.

Two early instances of table-talk in modern European literature were *De Dictis et factis Alphonsi regis Aragonum* (i.e. Alphonso of Aragon) compiled by Antonio Beccadelli *c.* 1455, and the *Facezie et molti arguti* (*c.* 1475) which was ascribed to Poliziano; but by far the most important of the early records of table-talk, brutally frank and intimate, were Martin Luther's *Tischreden* or *Colloquia Mensalia* (1566).

In 1618 Ben Jonson visited (on foot) William Drummond of Hawthornden in Scotland. The laird recorded many of his observations and left them in manuscript. Though not published in full until 1833, they comprise one of the earliest and most valuable instances of table-talk in English literature.

A vogue for recording table-talk established itself during the 17th c. For instance, in 1627 was published a collection (made by

J.L.S.) of observations made by James I, entitled *Flores Regii. Or Proverbs and Aphorisms, Divine and Moral, of James I.* Another collection of the King's *sententiae* was made by his servant Benjamin Agar and published in 1643 as *King James His Apophthegms; Or Table-Talk* (1643). In 1650 came out Worcester's *Apophthegms or Witty Sayings of the Right Honourable Henry (late) Marquess and Earl of Worcester*; and in 1667, the 'Essays and Discourses Gather'd from the Mouth of my Noble Lord and Husband', which are contained in the fourth book of *The Life of William Duke of Newcastle.*

Clearly, by now, table-talk and '-ana' were 'in', and it is worth noting that as far back as *c.* 1569 the term 'table-talk' meaning conversation at the dinner table had been used, and in Camden's *Remains* (1605) the term 'table-talker' occurs. It is also worth noting that during the 17th c. the practice of keeping diaries, journals and notebooks became widespread. To this time belong the famous diaries of Pepys and John Evelyn, also various collections of apophthegms, *pensées* and aphorisms (*qq.v.*). Even John Aubrey's *Brief Lives* are almost a form of table-talk because Aubrey, as a biographer, depended so much on his ears and therefore on what people said, rather than on books and what people wrote.

The greatest table-talker of the 17th c. was John Selden (1584–1654), a friend of Jonson's. Fortunately, his secretary Richard Milward had spent twenty years in the assiduous collection of his master's *obiter dicta.* These, for diplomatic and political reasons, were not finally published until 1689 under the title of *Table-Talk: Being the Discourses of John Selden Esq*; *or His Sense of Various Matters of High Consequence Relating Especially to Religion and State.* These discourses, in Dr Johnson's opinion, were better than all the French '-ana' put together.

There was already a fashion for '-ana' because of the publication in 1666 of *Scaligerana*, a collection of the sayings of Joseph Scaliger made by François Vertunien the physician, and Scaliger's friend. These were followed by *Perroniana*, *Thuana* and *Colomesiana*. The gathering of '-ana' was by this stage becoming popular in France where friends of distinguished scholars were in the habit of collecting their conversations and publishing them as tributes. One notable example is *Ménagiana* (1693), the cherished verbal crumbs of Ménage, who was renowned as a scholar and conversationalist. Actually, '-ana' remained predominantly a French fashion and few English scholars have been so well reported as were Ménage, Charpentier and Boileau. However, the fashion began to die out fairly early in the 18th c. in France and by *c.* 1750 '-ana' were so *démodés* that collectors disguised them as 'Recueils' or 'Mélanges'. *Mélanges* were much more like *Festschriften* (*q.v.*) or 'homage volumes': collections of essays by colleagues and quondam students (e.g. *Mélanges de philologie offerts à Ferdinand Brunot*).

Meanwhile, in England, Joseph Spence (1699–1768) was gathering material for his *Anecdotes*, many of which were reports of things that Pope had said. They were eventually published in 1822 under the title *Anecdotes, Observations, and Characters of Men. Collected from the Conversation of Mr Pope, and other eminent Persons of his time.*

In 1763 Boswell began laying down the vintage Johnsoniana and, not to be outdone, also bottled his own *Boswelliana* – as well as the abrasive remarks of his caustic wife which he titled *Uxoriana.* At Strawberry Hill Horace Walpole had his Boswell in the shape of J. Pinkerton, who published *Walpoliana* in 1799. Two other famous 18th c. English writers went into the books of the 'Ana-ists'. Samuel Foote was recorded by William Cooke, who published *Memoirs of the Life of Samuel Foote* (1778) and *Memoirs of Samuel Foote Esq.* (1805). The dramatist Sheridan was reported by Kelly, who published *Sheridaniana; Or, Anecdotes of the Life of Richard Brinsley Sheridan; his Table-Talk, and Bon Mots* in 1826. Richard Porson, the Classical scholar, also had a kind of Boswell in William Maltby, whose *Porsoniana* were published in *Recollections of the Table-Talk of Samuel Rogers* in 1856. In the same year Dyce produced *Recollections of the Table-Talk of Samuel Rogers.*

Sydney Smith, one of the wittiest of all English talkers, had much reported by his daughter Lady Holland in *A Memoir of the Reverend Sydney Smith* (1855), and by Thomas Moore, whose *Memoirs, Journal, and Correspondence* was published in 1856. At about the time that Smith was most famous Eckermann arrived in Weimar (*c.* 1823) and when Goethe was already an old man. However, Eckermann was able to jot down many of the sage's most interesting observations before the poet died in 1832. The first two volumes of the *Conversations* were published in 1836, the third in 1848. Again at about the same period H. N. Coleridge was recording the table-talk of S. T. Coleridge. Specimens of this came out in 1835. Apart from Selden, Johnson and Goethe, Coleridge was about the best table-talker of all time.

Three other notable collections of table-talk dating from the first half of the 19th c. are: Hazlitt's conversations with James Northcote the painter (which Hazlitt had published in 1830 under the title *Conversations of James Northcote Esq. RA*), Thomas Medwin's record of things said by Byron when the poet was at Pisa in 1821–2 (which was published in 1824) and Leigh Hunt's *Table-Talk* (1851). Leigh Hunt, table-talking on table-talk, provides us with a pleasing and serviceable description of what it is at its best:

> Table-talk, to be perfect, should be sincere without bigotry, differing without discord, sometimes grave, always agreeable, touching on deep points, dwelling most on seasonable ones, and letting everybody speak and be heard . . .The perfection of conversational intercourse is when the breeding of high life is animated by the fervour of genius . . . Luckily for table-talkers in general, they need be neither such fine gentlemen as Chesterfield, nor such oracles as Jonson, nor such wits as Addison and Swift, provided they have nature and sociability, and are not destitute of reading and observation.

See also ANECDOTE.

Tabulatur The code of rules which regulated the composition of *Meistergesang* (*q.v.*). The rules were on a board (tabula) or *Tafel.*

Tafelspel A dramatic form popular in the Netherlands from the 15th to the 18th c. It was a kind of interlude (*q.v.*) during a banquet or a wedding and appears to have been connected with festivals like the Epiphany.

tag Something added to a piece of writing by way of ornament; commonly a quotation. It may also apply to a saying, proverb or adage. The addition of a quotation is quite a common device among modern poets. T. S. Eliot made good use of it. Ezra Pound was addicted to the practice, as can be seen in his *Cantos.*

Tagelied (G 'dawn song') A form of German Minnesang derived from the *alba* of the troubadours. The earliest example dates from the 12th c. Wolfram von Eschenbach (*c.* 1200) is generally regarded as one of its finest practitioners. *See* AUBADE.

tail-rhyme A tailed caudate rhyme is our term for F *rime couée* (L *rhythmus caudatus*). It denotes a unit of verse in which a short line, followed by a group of longer lines, e.g. couplet, triolet or stanza (*qq.v.*), rhymes with a preceding short line. The tail-rhyme stanza has a number of variants. Well-known instances can be found in

Chaucer's *Sir Thopas*, Drayton's *Ballad of Agincourt* and Shelley's *To Night*, from which the following example is taken:

> Swiftly walk o'er the western wave,
>   Spirit of Night!
> Out of the misty eastern cave,
> Where, all the long and lone daylight,
> Thou wovest dreams of joy and fear,
> Which make thee terrible and dear, –
>   Swift be thy flight!

See CAUDA; CAUDATE SONNET.

tale A narrative, written (in prose or verse) or spoken. When in prose, barely distinguishable from a short story (*q.v.*). If there *is* a difference, then a tale perhaps suggests something written in the tone of voice of someone speaking. Usually the theme of a tale is fairly simple but the method of relating it may be complex and skilled. Much depends on the writer's viewpoint (*q.v.*). One might perhaps say that the kind of narratives which R. L. Stevenson, Rudyard Kipling, W. W. Jacobs, Joseph Conrad, Somerset Maugham and William Faulkner liked to write and excelled at are tales, whereas the kind preferred by Henry James, E. M. Forster, Aldous Huxley, Katherine Mansfield and Elizabeth Bowen are short stories. However, any such classifications may be wholly misleading, and such a division would not be serviceable in classifying the shorter works of Poe, Saki, Chekhov, Maupassant and D. H. Lawrence or a dozen other writers.

The tale in verse has a long and venerable history in English literature (the term includes ballad, epic and lay, *qq.v.*) from Chaucer's *Canterbury Tales* to C. Day Lewis's *The Nabara*. Among shorter tales the following are notable: Thomas Parnell's *The Hermit*, William Cowper's *John Gilpin*, George Crabbe's *Peter Grimes*, Robert Burns's *Tam o'Shanter*, Wordsworth's *Michael*, Coleridge's *Ancient Mariner*, Byron's *Prisoner of Chillon*, Keats's *Eve of St Agnes*, Macaulay's *The Keeping of the Bridge*, Tennyson's *Maud* and *Morte d'Arthur*, Browning's *Childe Roland to the Dark Tower Came*, Matthew Arnold's *Sohrab and Rustum*, Dante Gabriel Rossetti's *The White Ship*, Swinburne's *St Dorothy*, Dobson's *The Ballad of 'Beau Brocade'*, Hardy's *The Sacrilege*, R. L. Stevenson's *Ticonderoga*, Kipling's *Tomlinson*, Robert Service's *The Shooting of Dan Macgrew*, Laurence Binyon's *The Battle of Stamford Bridge*, Masefield's *The Rider at the Gate* and *Reynard,*

Alfred Noyes's *The Highwayman* (not to mention many by Sir Walter Scott and William Morris) – plus: Edmund Blunden's *Incident in Hyde Park, 1803*, W. S. Graham's *The Nightfishing*, Patrick Kavanagh's *The Great Hunger*, Anthony Cronin's *RMS Titanic*, Vernon Watkins's *The Ballad of the Mari Lwyd*, and a considerable number of poems by Robert Frost. *See also* CONTE; FAIRY TALE; FOLK TALE; NARRATIVE VERSE; SHORT STORY; TALL STORY; YARN.

tall story A story which is extravagant, outlandish or highly improbable. Usually regarded as false, however good it may be. They are of the same family as fantasy and fairy tale (*q.v.*). The epic (*q.v.*) tradition, and especially the primary epic, contains a good many episodes which are classifiable as tall stories: e.g. the deeds of Odysseus, Beowulf's swimming match with Breca, the feats of Marko Kraljević in the South Slav *narodne pesme* (*q.v.*) and the exploits of Skandarbeg in the Albanian epic cycles. They abound in legend and hagiography (*qq.v.*). Often enough the 'traveller's tale' is virtually the same as a tall story. Early and very entertaining examples of these are to be found in Pliny the Elder's *Natural History* (1st c. AD), and in Lucian's *Dialogues* (2nd c. AD), particularly Icaromenippus. Medieval 'Vision' literature is full of splendid tall stories (e.g. the 12th c. *Vision of Tundale*) and medieval collections of *exempla*, like the *Gesta Romanorum*, also contain many. Some of the early authors (especially Pliny) believed them. Sir John Mandeville's *Book of Travels* (14th c.) is a classic of its kind. Chaucer's *Miller's Tale* is as good an example as one can hope to meet. In Rabelais's *Gargantua* and *Pantagruel* (1534, 1532) we find some of the more prodigious instances of the tall story. Another Renaissance writer to make much of its possibilities was Cellini, in his *Autobiography* (*c.* 1560). Utopian literature also provides memorable instances, for example Gabriel de Foigny's *La Terre Australe Connue* (1676). But for sustained invention, wit and panache it is difficult to find anything to equal Voltaire's *Zadig* (1747), and, even better, *Candide* (1759). That age which, for all its devotion to reason, took much delight in fantasia also produced Raspe's *Baron Munchausen: Narrative of his Marvellous Travels* (1785). There have been few taller stories than Munchausen's tale of the horse that was cut in two, drank from a fountain, and was sewn up again.

More recent examples are: T. B. Thorpe's *The Big Bear of Arkansas*; Sheridan Le Fanu's *The Ghost and the Bone-Setter*;

Francis Bret Harte's *Plain Language from Truthful James*; Mark Twain's *The Celebrated Jumping Frog of Calaveras County*; Jack London's *One Thousand Dozen* (i.e. eggs); John Russell's *The Price of the Head*; T. F. Powys's *Lie Thee Down, Oddity*; William Faulkner's *A Rose for Emily*; Stephen Vincent Benét's *The Devil and Daniel Webster*; Marcel Aymé's *The Ubiquitous Wife*; James Thurber's *The Catbird Seat*; and J. G. Ballard's *The Lost Leonardo* – a brilliant tour de force (*q.v.*) of the genre.

Ambrose Bierce wrote twenty-three 'tall tales' which he called 'negligible' stories. They are satirical, blackly comic and inclined to the grotesque and in some cases are extremely funny. His tale *An Imperfect Conflagration* begins: 'Early one morning in June 1872 I murdered my father – an act which made a deep impression on me at the time . . . My father and I were in the library of our home, dividing the proceeds of a burglary which we had committed that night.' Other notable contributors to the genre are O. Henry, J. C. Powys and William Saroyan.

The tall story has also flourished in the environments and atmospheres of frontier life, 'bad lands', pioneering endeavours (e.g. the Gold Rush in the Yukon and Australia), among sporting fraternities, among fishermen and sailors, and in general in rural areas (hence, for instance, the rhozzum, *q.v.*, which is kin to the tall tale). A very large number of folk tales, which are usually the product of rural environments, have all the traditional elements of a good tall one (e.g. Jack the Giant Killer). Not a few of the best belong to oral tradition (*q.v.*), such as this famous one from the Second World War: the *Luftwaffe*, seeking to deceive the RAF, put wooden dummy planes on some of their major airfields. RAF reconnaissance photographed these planes. Bomber Command were not impressed by them as dummies. At the next opportunity a bomber squadron attacked the airfields – dropping high-explosive on the installations and *wooden bombs on the dummies.* The Germans were not amused.

The ghost story (*fact* rather than fiction), the Russian *skaz* and the Chinese *p'ing hua* (*qq.v.*) are also sources of tall tales. *See also* FOLK LITERATURE; SHAGGY DOG STORY; WESTERN; YARN.

tamizdat *See* SAMIZDAT.

tanka A Japanese lyric form of thirty-one syllables, in lines of five/seven/five/seven/seven syllables. Also known as a *Waka* or an *uta*, it originated in the 7th c. and is regarded as the classic Japanese poetic form. It has not had so much influence on Western poetry as the *haiku* (*q.v.*). A few poets (e.g. Amy Lowell and Adelaide Crapsey) have imitated it.

tantra (Skt 'thread, fundamental doctrine') Any of a number of Hindu and Buddhist writings of a religious didactic nature. They give ritual instructions, including the use of incantations and diagrams. Many *tantras* are ascribed to Buddha and thousands have been composed since *c.* 500 AD. The Tibetan *Book of the Dead* (8th c.) – a spiritual guide for the dying – contains numerous *tantras*.

tapinosis (Gk 'lowering') A figurative device, expression or epithet which belittles by exaggeration; for instance, Pope's lines about Timon's villa in *Moral Essays, Epistle IV*:

> Greatness, with Timon, dwells in such a draught
> As brings all Brobdignag before your thought.
> To compass this, his building is a Town,
> His pond an Ocean, his parterre a Down:
> Who but must laugh, the Master when he sees,
> A puny insect, shiv'ring at a breeze!
> Lo, what huge heaps of littleness around!

See HYPERBOLE.

taste We first find the word used as a critical term towards the end of the 17th c. La Bruyère, for example, in *Les Caractères* (1688) argued that in artistic matters 'il y a donc un bon et un mauvais goût'. Joseph Addison, in his *Spectator* papers on taste (1712), defined it as 'that faculty of the soul which discerns the beauties of an author with pleasure, and the imperfections with dislike'. The term became well established in the 18th c. and, in criticism, was thereafter used in a bewildering variety of senses especially in the philosophy and science of aesthetics. How bewildering may be gauged from Coleridge's definition of it as 'the intermediate faculty which connects the active with the passive powers of our nature, the intellect with the senses; and its appointed function is to elevate the *images* of the latter, while it realizes the *ideas* of the former'. In fact, the history of the word exemplifies the truism: *quot homines, tot sententiae*.

Every man may be expected to possess at any rate an inchoate idea of taste, about which, in all probability, there can be no dispute – or a great deal. To establish a polarity: some hold that matters of taste are subjective; others that they are objective. In either case the judgements may be universally valid, but it is more than likely that, owing to what Dr Johnson referred to as 'the wild vicissitudes of taste', few works survive to pass a hypothetical absolute test of excellence or inferiority; that is, the test of universality (*q.v.*). Even Shakespeare's works have been regarded as lacking in taste, and have suffered a period of being 'out of fashion'. The issue is further complicated by the fact that any arbiter is immediately vulnerable when he arrogates to himself the power of discriminating between what is in good or bad taste. *See* VULGARITY.

tautology (Gk 'the same saying') Redundant words or ideas. Repetition of words or ideas, as in the common phrase 'I myself personally'. *See also* PERIPHRASIS.

tawddgyrch cadwynog A Welsh syllabic verse form similar to the *rhupunt* (*q.v.*).

telescoped metaphor Also known as a complex metaphor. In such a figure of speech the vehicle of one metaphor becomes the tenor of another (*see* TENOR AND VEHICLE). Consider the following lines from *King Lear* (IV, vi, 141–8):

> And the creature run from the cur? There thou mightst behold
> The great image of authority: a dog's obeyed in office . . .
> . . . The usurer hangs the cozener.
> Through tatter'd clothes small vices do appear;
> Robes and furr'd gowns hide all. Plate sin with gold,
> And the strong lance of justice hurtless breaks;
> Arm it in rags, a pigmy's straw does pierce it.

The vehicle here may be taken as the image or concept of authority whose shortcomings can be concealed by rich apparel (a thematic image in *King Lear* and an idea central to the tragedy; thus it is doubly an organic metaphor, *q.v.*). This vehicle becomes the personification of sin armoured in gold like a knight at tourney; or, again, like a beggar. Thus we have one vehicle elaborated in three tenors.

The passage also contains what are sometimes called 'subdued metaphors'; in this case they are implied images of justice in a court of law, and the conflict in a jousting tournament. The interlocking images support each other; the 'sword' of justice becomes a lance and then a straw. *See* IMAGERY; METAPHOR.

telescope word *See* PORTMANTEAU WORD.

telestich *See* ACROSTIC.

Tel Quel school In 1960 the French novelist and critic Phillipe Sollers (1936–) founded the literary periodical *Tel Quel*, and later he outlined its objectives in his discourse *Logiques* (1968). The aims are basically ideological and activist, as well as aesthetic. One of its aims is to restore to language its original revolutionary power; and it advances the principle that 'literature is language made with language'. The school, which has been influenced by, among others, Roland Barthes, and also by theories of semiotics and semiology (*q.v.*), has been particularly concerned to promote interest in and more understanding of such French writers as the Marquis de Sade (1740–1814), Stéphane Mallarmé (1842–98), Lautréamont (1846–70) and Antonin Artaud (1896–1948), who had a considerable influence on theatre and drama in the 20th c. *See also* POETE MAUDIT; THEATRE OF CRUELTY.

tema con variazioni (It 'theme with variations') A musical term occasionally used in literary criticism to denote a humorous verse or parody (*q.v.*).

tenor and vehicle Terms coined by I. A. Richards. By 'tenor' he meant the purport or general drift of thought regarding the subject of a metaphor; by 'vehicle', the image which embodies the tenor. In these lines from R. S. Thomas's *A Blackbird Singing* the tenor is the bird's song, its tune; the vehicle is the fine smelting image in the fifth and sixth lines:

> It seems wrong that out of this bird,
> Black, bold, a suggestion of dark
> Places about it, there yet should come
> Such rich music, as though the notes'
> Ore were changed to a rare metal
> At one touch of that bright bill.

tension A term used in a particular sense by Allen Tate to designate the totality of meaning in a poem. He derives it from the logical terms 'extension' and 'intension' by removing the prefixes. Extension = literal meaning; intension = metaphorical meaning. The simultaneous co-existence of these sets of meaning constitutes tension. It may also refer to 'conflict structures'. For example, the counterpoint (*q.v.*) between the rhythm and meter of a poem and speech rhythms; or between the concrete and the abstract. Some critics, following the theories of Anaximander and Heraclitus, take it to mean the balance of mental and emotional tensions which help to give shape and unity to a work.

tenson A type of poetic composition (also known as *tenzone* and *tencon*) which originated in Provence in the 12th c. It usually consisted of a debate between two poets, or with a poet versus an imaginary opponent. The subjects were various: love, politics, literary criticism. It developed into the *partimen* (*q.v.*) and the *jeu parti* (*q.v.*) and as a poetic device spread to Italy and Sicily. *See* DEBAT.

ten-year test A term devised by Cyril Connolly to denote a book (usually a novel) which, ten years after its first publication, is still regarded as being of unusual literary merit, is still being widely read, and is still well thought of in literary and critical circles. Recent instances in English have been William Golding's *Lord of the Flies* (1954), Kingsley Amis's *Lucky Jim* (1954), V. S. Naipaul's *A House for Mr Biswas* (1961), J. G. Farrell's *The Siege of Krishnapur* (1973), Malcolm Bradbury's *The History Man* (1975) and Iris Murdoch's *The Sea, the Sea* (1978). *See also* BEST-SELLER.

tercerilla In Spanish prosody a three-line stanza of *arte menor* (*q.v.*): two to eight syllables of one or more rhythmic stresses.

tercet (F 'triplet') A stanza of three lines linked by rhyme, as in *terza rima* (*q.v.*). Also as one of a pair of triplets which makes up the sestet (*q.v.*) of a sonnet (*q.v.*) or as three consecutive rhyming lines (known as a triplet in a poem which is largely written in couplets). These tercets are from Tennyson's *Two Voices*:

A still small voice spake unto me:
'Thou art so full of misery,
Were it not better not to be?'

Then to the still small voice I said:
'Let me not cast in endless shade
What is so wonderfully made.'

tern A group of three stanzas, especially in a *ballade* (*q.v.*) consisting of a tern and an *envoi* (*q.v.*). *See* TERCET.

ternaire (F 'three at one time') A three-line stanza on one rhyme. The French poet Auguste Brizeux (1803–55) claimed to be the first to use it.

tertulia A type of Spanish literary salon (*q.v.*) which gradually replaced the formal literary academy of the 18th c. The term is believed to derive from the word *tertuliantes* – the educated classes and clergy among theatre-goers. They were so called because they frequently quoted Tertullian, and the *tertulia* in a theatre was an upper circle or gallery. Tertullian (born *c.* 150) was one of the most famous early Christian writers in Latin. He wrote *Apologeticus* (197) and a number of treatises on the Christian life.

terza rima (It 'third rhyme') The measure adopted by Dante for his *Divina Commedia*, consisting of a series of interlocking tercets (*q.v.*) in which the second line of each one rhymes with the first and third lines of the one succeeding, thus: aba, bcb, cdc. At the end of the canto (*q.v.*) a single line rhymes with the second from last: wxyx, as in the conclusion of the first canto of the *Inferno*:

Ed io a lui: Poeta, io ti richieggio
  per quello Dio che tu non conoscesti,
  acciocch'io fugga questo male e peggio
Che tu mi meni là dov'or dicesti,
  sì ch'io vegga la porta di san Pietro,
  e color cui tu fai cotanto mesti.
Allor si mosse, ed io li tenni retro.

Terza rima was also used by Petrarch and Boccaccio. Chaucer used it for part of *A Complaint to his Lady*, but it was Sir Thomas Wyatt who pioneered its use in England. This example comes from the beginning of his *Second Satire*:

My mother's maids, when they did sew and spin,
They sang sometimes a song of the field mouse,
That for because her livelihood was but thin

Would needs go seek her townish sister's house.
She thought herself endured to much pain:
The stormy blasts her cave so sore did souse . . .

Because it is a difficult form to manage (few Italian poets have used it successfully) it has never been very adaptable or popular outside Italy. A few 19th and 20th c. Dutch and German poets employed it; some French (notably Gautier); and some English – principally Byron in *The Prophecy of Dante*, Shelley in *Prince Athanese*, *The Triumph of Life* and *Ode to the West Wind*, Browning in *The Statue and The Bust*. More recently, Auden attempted it (with variations) in *The Sea and the Mirror*. *See also* CAPITOLO; TERZA RIMA SONNET.

terza rima sonnet A term occasionally used to describe a quatorzain (*q.v.*) whose rhyme uses the interlocking method of *terza rima* (*q.v.*). The rhyme pattern of aba, bcb, cdc, ded, ee (the same form as the sections in Shelley's *Ode to the West Wind*) is similar to the Spenserian sonnet (*q.v.*).

terzina An Italian term for a stanza of three lines, especially in *terza rima* (*q.v.*). Also applied to a continuous (non-stanzaic) poem rhymed aba, bcb, cdc, and so on. Fairly common in early Romance languages (*q.v.*), but rare in English.

testament (L 'witnessing') A document which bears witness; an affirmation. For instance, the Old and New Testaments. A number of well-known secular works come into the category. Among the better known are: Thomas Usk's allegorical prose work *The Testament of Love* (1387); Henryson's beautiful *Testament of Cresseid* (15th c. but printed in 1593); Villon's highly personal *Petit Testament* (1456) and *Grand Testament* (c. 1461), both of which (and especially the first) contain a strong element of mockery; Bridges's philosophical poem *The Testament of Beauty* (1929). In view of the general meaning of the term, numerous other writings might be put into this genre. For example, St Augustine's *Confessions*, or Newman's *Apologia pro Vita Sua*, or Camus's remarkable *Lettres à un ami allemand*. *See also* CONFESSIONAL LITERATURE.

tetralogy (Gk 'set of four') Four plays (three tragedies and a satyr play) were submitted for the prize in tragedy (*q.v.*) at the drama competitions in Athens in the 5th c. The term may now be applied to any four connected works. Eight of Shakespeare's ten History Plays are sometimes divided into two tetralogies: (a) *Henry VI* (Pts

I, II and III) and *Richard III*; (b) *Richard II*, *Henry IV* (Pts I and II) and *Henry V*. *See also* SATYR PLAY; TRILOGY.

tetrameter (Gk 'of four measures') A line of four metrical feet. In English verse usually iambic or trochaic. Used extensively by many English poets, including Milton, Scott and Byron. These lines are from Milton's *L'Allegro*:

> Haste thee nymph, and bring with thee
> Jest and youthful Jollity,
> Quips and Cranks, and wanton wiles,
> Nods, and becks, and wreathed smiles

tétramètre The twelve-syllable French Classical alexandrine (*q.v.*). It was already in use in the 12th c. and is seen at its best in the tragedies of Corneille and Racine. *See also* TRIMETRE.

tetrapody (Gk 'four feet') A group or line of four feet.

tetrastich (Gk 'four lines') A group, stanza or poem of four lines. A synonym for quatrain (*q.v.*).

text (L *texere*, *textum* 'to weave') A number of meanings may be distinguished: (a) the actual words of a book in their original form or any form they have been transmitted in or transmuted to; (b) a book of such words; (c) the main body of matter in a book – apart from notes, commentary, glosses, index, appendices, etc.; (d) a short passage taken from the Bible as the theme or subject or a sermon. *See* MANUSCRIPT; TEXTUAL CRITICISM.

textual criticism A branch of scholarship which is devoted to the study and analysis of extant texts in order to determine authorship and authenticity and, where there is a multiplicity of texts of one work, to determine which one is the 'best' or the 'original'.

texture A jargon term derived from the plastic arts which denotes the surface qualities of a work, as opposed to its shape and structure. In modern literary criticism it tends to designate the concrete qualities of a poem as opposed to its ideas; thus, the verbal surface of a work, its sensuous qualities, the density of its imagery. In these lines from John Crowe Ransom's *Dog* (Ransom, incidentally, uses 'texture' to refer also to the variations on the basic metrical pattern or structure) the texture varies a good deal:

Cock-a-doodle-doo the brass-lined rooster says,
Brekekekex intones the fat Greek frog –
These fantasies do not terrify me as
The bow-wow-wow of dog.

I had a little doggie who used to sit and beg,
A pretty little creature with tears in his eyes
And anomalous hand extended on his leg;
Housebroken was my Huendchen, and so wise.

Tentative analysis suggests that the general springiness and resilience of the rhythms is varied by a certain abrasiveness in 'brekekekex', a plumpness in 'fat Greek frog', and a pronounced brittleness in 'a pretty little creature'. The alliteration in the fourth line of the second stanza helps to knot the line together; while the nap on the mellifluous third line of that stanza is relieved by slight asperity of 'intertexture' in the word 'extended'.

Théâtre de Complicité A London-based theatrical company founded in 1983 by Annabel Arden, Simon McBurney and Marcello Magni. The company has developed a highly experimental form of total theatre (*q.v.*) which makes extensive use of mime, clown techniques, improvisation, the techniques of *commedia dell'arte* (*q.v.*), acrobatics and most traditional theatrical styles and modes, including *Nō* (*q.v.*). Movement is taken to be as important as the text, and performance makes much use of the absurd. Tragedy (*q.v.*) is regarded as basic material – for that is where the comedy lies. In 1988 a notable version of Dürrenmatt's *The Visit* (1956) was presented. *See also* THEATRE OF THE ABSURD.

theatre-in-the-round A form of theatrical presentation in which the acting area is surrounded by the audience. It is far from being a new idea, though it has had some vogue since the 1930s. It seems very probable that some of the Cornish Mystery Plays were performed in the open air with an audience ranged round the actors on banks. One may suppose, too, that Mumming Plays (*q.v.*) and related dramatic entertainments were thus presented. In modern times theatre-in-the-round achieved prominence in Russia in the 1930s where Okhlopov, using his realistic theatre, even involved the audience in the drama. At that time, too, Robert Atkins was producing Shakespeare in The Ring at Blackfriars. In America it has been a particularly popular form of presentation, especially in the universities. Margo Jones was the main American exponent. In

France, also, it has had some success, particularly in the hands of André Villiers who, in 1954, founded the Théâtre en Rond in Paris. In England the leading light and dedicated crusader was Stephen Joseph, who established something of a tradition for theatre-in-the-round at Stoke-on-Trent. Joseph also worked on it in London, Southampton and Scarborough.

Theatre Laboratory A Polish theatre company founded in 1959 under the directorship of Jerzy Grotowski (1933–). It was highly experimental and many of the productions were adaptations of classic Polish works little known outside Poland. Grotowski created a troupe with *avant-garde* (*q.v.*) attitudes and his techniques had considerable influence on the Living Theater and the Third Theatre (*qq.v.*), and on such directors as Peter Brook. The company became defunct in 1984. *See also* TOTAL THEATRE.

Théâtre Libre A theatre company created by André-Léonard Antoine (1858–1943) in Paris in 1887. It lasted for ten years and was to have an immeasurable influence on playwrights, directors and actors for a very long time; it was thus an important landmark in the evolution of the modern theatre. It was highly naturalistic in presentation and performance and concentrated on 'slice-of-life' (*q.v.*) plays known as *comédies rosses* ('cynical comedies'). Eugène Brieux (1858–1932) wrote a number of these. Antoine also presented work by Ibsen, Strindberg, Verga and Hauptmann, and his achievement helped to bring about the formation of similar theatres – such as Otto Brahm's Freie Bühne (*q.v.*) in Berlin.

Théâtre Nationale Populaire The theatre was founded in 1920, when Firmin Gémier (1865–1933) chose it as the name of his touring company. In 1937 it was established at the Palais de Chaillot. Jean Vilar (1912–71) became director in 1951. As a state-subsidized theatre it was and is expected to provide a wide variety of 'popular' theatre in many parts of France. Georges Wilson was director from 1963 to 1971, and in 1972 Roger Planchon (1931–) took the post.

theatre of cruelty This derives from the theories of the French dramatist Antonin Artaud (1896–1948), who, in 1938, published *Le Théâtre et son double*, in which he formulated his principles. In his view the theatre must disturb the spectator profoundly, pierce him heart and soul in such a way as to free unconscious repressions and oblige men to view themselves as they really are. In it mime (*q.v.*), gesture and scenery are more important than words, and the director is a kind of maker of magic, 'a master of sacred ceremonies'. Much depends on spectacle, lighting effects and the exploitation of the full range of the 'theatrical'. Prior to 1938 Artaud had published two manifestos (in 1923 and 1933) and also had produced *Les Cenci* (1935), based on versions by Shelley and Stendhal, which was an attempt to put his theories into practice. Artaud's influence has been very considerable, especially on the work of Adamov, Genet, Camus and Audiberti. English dramatists have not been affected anything like as much. A recent and well-known example of *Théâtre de la cruauté* is Weiss's drama *The Persecution and Assassination of Marat as Performed by the Inmates of the Asylum of Charenton under the Direction of the Marquis de Sade* (1964). *See also* GRAND GUIGNOL; MELODRAMA.

theatre of panic The term *théâtre panique* was invented in 1962 by the Spanish-born dramatist Fernando Arrabal (1932–), a playwright of the theatre of the absurd (*q.v.*) who writes in French. Arrabal, who was much influenced by Samuel Beckett and Antonin Artaud, sought to create a kind of ritualistic drama which combines elements of tragedy and buffoonery with religious (or quasi-religious) ceremonial. It is intended to surprise and frighten as well as to arouse laughter. Two notable examples of such drama have been *The Architect and the Emperor of Assyria* (1967) and *And They Handcuffed the Flowers* (1969). *See also* GRAND GUIGNOL; THEATRE OF CRUELTY.

theatre of silence A theory of drama, more accurately called the theatre of the unspoken (*Théâtre de l'inexprimé*) devised by Jean-Jacques Bernard (1888–1972) in the 1920s. In his view dialogue was not sufficient; equally important was what characters *could* not and *did* not say. Though this may always have been obvious, and certainly has been since Bernard's experiments, very few dramatists had deliberately exploited the possibilities of silence before. Chekhov is a clear exception. Bernard's influence has been considerable. Some of his main works are: *Le Feu qui reprend mal* (1921), *Martine* (1922), *Le Printemps des autres* (1924), *L'Ame en peine* (1926). Among recent English dramatists the master of the prolonged pause (*q.v.*) and sustained silence is unquestionably Harold Pinter (especially in *Landscape* and *Silence*, 1970). *See* SUBTEXT.

theatre of the absurd A term applied to many of the works of a group of dramatists who were active in the 1950s: Adamov, Beckett, Genet, Ionesco and Pinter. Among the less known were Albee, Arrabal, Günter Grass, Pinget and N. F. Simpson. The phrase 'theatre of the absurd' was probably coined by Martin Esslin, who wrote *The Theatre of the Absurd* (1961).

The origins of this form of drama are obscure, but it would be reasonable to suppose that its lineage is traceable from Roman mime plays, through to aspects of comic business and technique in medieval and Renaissance drama and *commedia dell'arte* (*q.v.*), and thence to the dramatic works of Jarry, Strindberg and Brecht. The work of Jarry is vital and the possibilities of a theatre of the absurd are already apparent in *Ubu Roi* (1896), *Ubu Cocu* (1897–8) and *Ubu enchaîné* (*c.* 1898); as they are also in Apollinaire's *Les Mamelles de Tirésias* (completed in 1917). Moreover, it is conceivable that the increasing popularity of nonsense verse (*q.v.*) from about the mid-19th c. onwards is connected with this concept of the absurd. Almost certainly dadaism and surrealism (*qq.v.*) influenced the development of the theatre of the absurd, and so have Artaud's theories on the theatre of cruelty (*q.v.*).

In the evolution of a new vision of mankind in relation to his environment and the universe one may expect to see a large number of cross-fertilizing influences. Clearly, the idea that man is absurd is by no means new. An awareness of the essential absurdity of much human behaviour has been inherent in the work of many writers. Aristophanes, Plautus, Terence, Chaucer, Erasmus, Cervantes, Molière, Swift, Pope, both Samuel Butlers, Anatole France, Balzac, Dickens, Goncharov, Thurber, Chesterton, Belloc, Damon Runyon, William Saroyan – to cite only a handful – have all shown an acute feeling for man's comicality.

However, the concept of *homo absurdus* has acquired a rather more specific meaning in the last hundred years or so. This is partly, no doubt, owing to the need to provide an explanation of man's apparently purposeless role and position in a universe which is popularly imagined to have no discernible reason for existence.

Mathematically, a surd is that which cannot be expressed in finite terms of ordinary numbers of quantities. Hence irrational rather than ridiculous. It is in the mathematical sense that the 'philosophy' of the absurd has been mostly expressed. But it is a *pervasive attitude rather than a system of thought.*

In his *La Tentation de l'occident* (1926) André Malraux, who has expatiated at length about 'the human condition', remarked that 'at the centre of European man, dominating the great moments of his life, there lies an essential absurdity'. The theme recurs in a number of works by Malraux, and is apparent, particularly, in the works of Sartre and Camus. The latter's collection of essays *The Myth of Sisphus* (1942) contains some of the most interesting statements on the theme. Camus expounded in some detail a vision of life which was essentially absurd, without apparent purpose, out of harmony with its surroundings, sad to the point of anguish, and at the same time, in a laconic fashion, funny. He stresses the destructive nature of time, the feeling of solitude in a hostile world, the sense of isolation from other human beings. The dominant symbolism of the title is perfectly appropriate.

In the early 1950s many diffused conceptions of the absurd began to be resolved and articulated in a series of remarkable plays which dramatized the kind of vision which Camus had projected – fundamentally, human beings struggling with the irrationality of experience, in a state of what has been described as 'metaphysical anguish'. The plays themselves lack a formal logic and conventional structure, so that both form and content support (while emphasizing the difficulty of communicating) the representation of what may be called the absurd predicament. The major works are: (the dramatists in alphabetical order) *La Parodie* and *L'Invasion* (1950), *Le Professeur Taranne* (1953), *Le Ping-Pong* (1955), *Paolo Paoli* (1957) by Adamov; *Waiting for Godot* (1953), *Endgame* (1957), *Happy Days* (1961) by Beckett; *Le Balcon* (1957), *Les Nègres* (1959), *Les Paravents* (1961) by Genet; *La Cantatrice chauve* (1950), *La Leçon* (1951), *Les Chaises* (1952), *Amédée* (1954), *Le Nouveau Locataire* (1955), *Rhinocéros* (1960), *Le Roi se meurt* (1961) by Ionesco; *Lettre Morte* (1960), *La Manivelle* (1960) by Pinget; *The Room* (1957), *The Birthday Party* (1958), *The Dumb Waiter* and *The Caretaker* (1960), *The Homecoming* (1965), *Landscape* and *Silence* (1970) and *No Man's Land* (1975) by Pinter; *Next Time I'll Sing to You* (1962) by James Saunders; *A Resounding Tinkle* (1957), *The Hole* (1958) and *One Way Pendulum* (1959) by N. F. Simpson; to these should be added minor works, namely: *Pique-nique en campagne* (1952) by Arrabal; *The Lunatic View* (1957) by David Campton; *The Sport of My Mad Mother* (1958) by Ann Jellicoe. *See also* FARCE; HAPPENING; PATAPHYSICS.

Theatre Workshop A theatrical company founded in 1945 by Joan Littlewood (1914–) and Ewan MacColl (1915–1989). From 1953 its headquarters were at the Theatre Royal, Stratford East, London. It was a notable success and proved a life-giving force in the theatre for over twenty years. The policy was that left-wing writers and writers with working-class backgrounds were given special encouragement. One of its most famous and memorable productions was *Oh! What a Lovely War!* (1963).

theatricalism A concept and theory of dramatic presentation which developed in Russia and Germany in the early years of the 20th c. It was strongly opposed to naturalism (*q.v.*) and was in favour of the principle that theatre *is* theatre and is a representation of life – and is *not* life itself. Nevertheless, naturalistic drama (*q.v.*), like the well-made play (*q.v.*), has continued to be popular.

theme Properly speaking, the theme of a work is not its subject but rather its central idea which may be stated directly or indirectly. For example, the theme of *Othello* is jealousy. *See* LEITMOTIF; MOTIF.

theogony A Greek term for an account of the origin and genealogy of the gods. Probably the most famous is the *Theogonia*, a poem in hexameters attributed to Hesiod (8th c. BC). In it he recounts the genealogy and mythological history of the gods.

thesaurus (Gk 'treasure') A repository of information, like a dictionary or encyclopaedia (*qq.v.*). Well-known examples are: the *Thesaurus Linguae Latinae*, the German dictionary of the Latin language begun in 1900. Roget's *Thesaurus of English Words and Phrases*, first published in 1852, has been revised and enlarged many times since.

thesis Three meanings may be distinguished: (a) a long essay (*q.v.*) or treatise (*q.v.*) presented for a degree; (b) a proposition to be proved; (c) the unstressed syllable of a metrical foot (e.g. *thesis* itself is a trochaic word on which the second syllable is unstressed). *See* ARSIS.

thesis novel One which treats of a social, political or religious problem with a didactic and, perhaps, radical purpose. It certainly sets out to call people's attention to the shortcomings of a society. Some outstanding examples of the genre are: Charles Kingsley's *Alton Locke* (1850); Harriet Beecher Stowe's *Uncle Tom's Cabin* (1852); Dickens's *Hard Times* (1854); Charles Reade's *Hard Cash*

(1863); Samuel Butler's *The Way of All Flesh* (1903); Upton Sinclair's *The Jungle* (1906); Robert Tressell's *The Ragged Trousered Philanthropists* (1914, abbreviated text; full text, 1955); Walter Greenwood's *Love on the Dole* (1933); Winifred Holtby's *South Riding* (1936); John Steinbeck's *The Grapes of Wrath* (1939); and Alan Paton's *Cry, the Beloved Country* (1948). Some would include William Golding's *Lord of the Flies* (1954) in this category. Utopian and dystopian visions in fictional form might also be included. *See also* PROLETARIAN NOVEL; THESIS PLAY; UTOPIA.

thesis play A drama which deals with a specific problem and, very probably, offers a solution. This form appears to have originated in France in the 19th c. Both Dumas (*fils*) and Brieux wrote a considerable number between 1860 and 1900. Elsewhere Ibsen was a major influence on the genre, for example *A Doll's House* (1879). In England Shaw (*Widowers' Houses*, 1892, *Mrs Warren's Profession*, 1902, *Major Barbara*, 1905) and Galsworthy (*The Silver Box*, 1907, *Strife*, 1909, *Justice*, 1910) made notable contributions. This type of drama is also known as a problem or propaganda play. Arnold Wesker has also written something approximating to thesis plays (e.g. *Chicken Soup with Barley*, 1958, *Roots*, 1959, and *I'm Talking about Jerusalem*, 1960). A sub-species of the problem play is what has been called the 'discussion play'. This is more like a debate in which characters put forward different points of view. Shaw employed this method of dramatizing issues in *Getting Married*, *The Apple Cart* and in Act III of *Man and Superman* – perhaps the best known example.

During the 1960s and from then onwards, some playwrights developed a rather different approach to the problem play about a social issue, very different from the intense but narrow focus achieved by, for instance, Ibsen in *An Enemy of the People* (1882). They have been concerned with broad political and social issues and have been influenced by the example of agitprop drama, the Living Theater, documentary theatre and the Living Newspaper (*qq.v.*) and by such dramatists as Brecht and Ewan MacColl. The dramatists have addressed themselves (often in a spirit of protest and reform) to such matters as the class system in Britain, racism, sexism, chauvinism, Thatcherism, crime, violence, moral values, poverty and the condition of the deprived, the press and political corruption and hypocrisy. Many of the plays have thus been about 'the state of Britain'. Outstanding among these playwrights are

John McGrath, David Edgar, Howard Brenton, David Hare, Edward Bond, Howard Barker and Caryl Churchill.

third theatre A term coined in 1976 by Eugenio Barba (1936–) to describe his own theatrical group, the Odin Teatret founded in 1964 in Oslo. So called by analogy with the term 'Third World' – deprived, neglected and short of money and resources. It is a kind of fringe (*q.v.*) theatre company and has a good deal in common with Theatre Laboratory and Total Theatre (*qq.v.*).

threnody (Gk 'wailing song') Originally a choral ode (*q.v.*), it changed to a monody (*q.v.*) which was strophic in form. It can now be applied to any lamentation; for instance, Tennyson's *In Memoriam* (1850) has been described as 'the great threnody of our language'. *See* COMPLAINT; DIRGE; ELEGY; EPICEDIUM; LAMENT; UBI SUNT.

thriller A vague term, perhaps no longer particularly useful for purposes of categorization, yet frequently used for a wide variety of fiction, and also for plays and films. In fiction it is a tense, exciting, tautly plotted and sometimes sensational type of novel (occasionally a short story) in which action is swift and suspense continual. Sex and violence may often play a considerable part in such a narrative, and they have tended to do so (often gratuitously) since the 1960s. *Very* broadly speaking, such fiction might include the crime novel, the police procedural, the *roman policier*, the cloak-and-dagger story, some ghost and horror stories, a multitude of novels of adventure (*qq.v.*) and, of course, what is known as the politico-military (thriller). Most of the best spy stories (*q.v.*) are *ipso facto* thrillers. Some detective stories, or forms of detective story, might also be described as thrillers; particularly, perhaps, those belonging to the 'hard-boiled school' of private-eye detection at which Dashiell Hammett and Raymond Chandler excelled. But the classic type of detective story (*q.v.*) as practised by, for instance, Agatha Christie and Dorothy L. Sayers, does not really qualify as a thriller though it may be very tense and exciting. There are also numerous novels which do not fall readily into any particular category but which depend to a high degree on suspense, mystery and adventure. 'Suspense writer' and 'mystery writer' are sub-species, as it were, often so described in reference books.

In the broad sense the thriller is one of the most remarkable literary phenomena of the 20th c. Since the turn of the 19th c. more than six hundred writers (the vast majority of them British and American) have written thrillers of one kind and another. Some of them have been immensely prolific, publishing a hundred or more titles in their professional careers (John Creasey is thought to have produced over six hundred books). Not a few have used several pseudonyms. Thriller writers in languages other than English can be counted on a few hands.

Professionalism has been an increasing feature of thriller writers (many of whom make a good living from their work), and a large, well-informed and critical reading public which includes many thriller addicts (just as there are detective story addicts) has come to expect certain standards from their writers. Output on a vast scale has inevitably meant a superfluity of potboilers (*q.v.*) and there has been a great deal of hackwork which has sunk without trace. Some thriller writers who were famous in the first half of the 20th c. have been out of print for many years.

The origins of the thriller go back to the Gothic novel (*q.v.*) and the 'literature of terror' which was so popular during the latter part of the 18th c. and at the beginning of the 19th c. From that period its evolution can be plotted via the development of the crime story, the ghost, horror and detective story, the so-called novel of sensation (*q.v.*) and what came to be known as Newgate fiction (*q.v.*). It was particularly developed by Edgar Allan Poe in his short stories and by Wilkie Collins in such novels as *The Woman in White* (1860) and *The Moonstone* (1868). Collins was something of an expert in mystery, suspense and crime.

Near the turn of the century Rider Haggard achieved great popularity (it has waned little in a hundred years) with some fine adventure novels, especially *King Solomon's Mines* (1886) and *She* (1887). Anthony Hope, too, had great success with his two famous Ruritanian adventure stories: *The Prisoner of Zenda* (1894) and its sequel *Rupert of Hentzau* (1898). His contemporary Stanley Weyman produced a succession of romances and adventure novels of the thriller kind. In fact, at this time the modern thriller was coming of age, so to speak. A. E. W. Mason was a prolific writer of them; for example, *The Four Feathers* (1902), *At the Villa Rose* (1910) and *The House of the Arrow* (1924). Contemporaneous, too, was E. W. Hornung (brother-in-law of Arthur Conan Doyle), who wrote a number of successful thriller/crime short stories as well as novels. He invented one of the better known characters in such fiction: A. J. Raffles, the public school, cricketing, gentleman burglar – intended in part as a contrast to Sherlock Holmes, who, by 1900, was becoming world famous. All these writers could tell a 'rattling good yarn' (*q.v.*).

Roughly contemporary with them, John Buchan became a specialist in comparable tales. For instance: *The Watcher by the Threshold* (1902), *Prester John* (1910), *The Thirty-Nine Steps* (1915), *Greenmantle* (1916), *The Three Hostages* (1924) and a number of others. In 1903 Erskine Childers published his single work of fiction, *The Riddle of the Sands*, which remains a classic of the thriller genre. Childers later joined the IRA and was caught and shot in 1922. During the early part of the 19th c. the supreme exponent of the 'pure' thriller was Edgar Wallace, an immensely prolific writer who made his name with *The Four Just Men* (1906) and followed this up with a succession of gripping stories, including *Sanders of the River*, *The Angel of Terror*, *The Green Archer*, *The Mind of Mr J. G. Reeder*, *The Fellowship of the Frog*, *The Dark Eyes of London* and *The Hand of Power*. In his era the novel of espionage and the detective story were fully established and the pulp (*q.v.*) magazines featured miscellaneous kinds of thriller. Raymond Le Queux's thrillers (now very dated) had a great vogue early in the 20th c., as did Nathaniel Gould's 'racing' thrillers. Eventually (from 1962) Dick Francis was to take on Gould's mantle and become *the* 'racing thriller' writer, producing a series of highly accomplished stories in which the world of the 'Turf' is an important or central element (Francis himself was a distinguished jockey).

In the inter-war period Sydney Horler, Sapper, Sax Rohmer and Dornford Yates, to name a few, all achieved fame, but much of their work soon became very dated and is scarcely readable now – except for curiosity and period interest.

An outstanding talent to come to the fore in the 1930s and 1940s was Eric Ambler. Regarded by many (including Graham Greene) as 'the master' of the genre, he produced, over a period of fifty years, a succession of finely written and well-constructed thrillers. He remains particularly famous for *The Mask of Dimitrios* (1939), but there are a number of other excellent books: *The Schismer Inheritance* (1953), *The Night-Comers* (1956), *Passage of Arms* (1959), *The Light of Day* (1962), *The Intercom Conspiracy* (1969), *The Levanter* (1972) and *Care of Time* (1981). Greene himself also wrote some good ones: *A Gun for Sale* (1936), *Ministry of Fear* (1943) – which he classed as 'entertainments' (*q.v.*); plus *The Third Man* (1950) and the comic espionage thriller *Our Man in Havana* (1958). Their slightly older contemporary, Geoffrey Household, became famous with *Rogue Male* (1939) – long regarded as a classic of the genre. He never quite matched this novel, but in the course of his eighty-eight years wrote others of distinction, including *Rough Shoot* (1951), *Watcher in the Shadows* (1960) and *Summon the Bright Water* (1981).

In America, in the 1920s, Dashiell Hammett established the private-eye type of crime thriller (the 'hard-boiled school' of detective fiction with the 'hard-nosed' detective). Besides many short stories Hammett wrote five novels: *Red Harvest* (1929), *The Dain Curse* (1929), *The Maltese Falcon* (1930), *The Glass Key* (1931), *The Thin Man* (1934). Of these *The Maltese Falcon* has gradually established itself as a classic of its kind. Hammett had many imitators, most of whom have long since sunk without trace. His most distinguished 'successor' in the private-eye thriller form was Raymond Chandler. Chandler began with pulp stories, but his reputation rests on seven novels, of which the following are probably the best: *The Big Sleep* (1939), *The High Window* (1942), *The Little Sister* (1949), *The Long Good-Bye* (1953). *Farewell, My Lovely* (1940) is also highly regarded. Chandler's reputation has grown steadily and he has made many a so-called serious novelist with greater pretensions look very ordinary. In turn, he has had many aspiring imitators. Latterly, among American writers, Ross Macdonald and Elmore Leonard have shown they are unusually gifted in the Chandler tradition.

Less talented contemporaries of Ambler, Household and Chandler were Peter Cheyney, John Creasey, Rex Stout, James Hadley Chase, Leslie Charteris, Erle Stanley Gardner, Dennis Wheatley, Nevil Shute, Nigel Balchin and George Bagby. All were highly successful and in some cases extremely prolific.

Since the 1950s a large number of other thriller writers have become prominent or famous. Julian Symons and Hammond Innes were by then well established. Symons published his thriller *Broken Penny* in 1953 and thereafter tended to write his particular kind of crime novel, often very exciting. He also published an excellent history of crime fiction: *Bloody Murder* (1972). Innes specialized in the adventure/thriller novel and had steady success. The 1950s was the era of Ian Fleming's James Bond stories, a species of cloak-and-dagger and espionage. Averaging about fifteen clichés per page, they were scarcely readable then and became even less so as the years went by. Their phenomenal success was compounded by the universally popular Bond films. The Bond film industry was still flourishing in the late 1980s.

Many of the best thrillers from the 1950s onwards have been concerned with espionage. Pre-eminent in this field are Len Deighton and John Le Carré (*see* SPY STORY for details). Of these two Deighton proved to be somewhat the better writer. During the sixties Lionel Davidson made a big impact with several well-written and witty thrillers, such as *The Night of Wenceslas* (1960), *The Rose of Tibet* (1962), *A Long Way to Shiloh* (1966) and *Making Good Again* (1968). In the 1970s Frederick Forsyth achieved enormous success with several brilliantly constructed, well-researched and complex thrillers, notably *The Day of the Jackal* (1971), *The Odessa File* (1972) and *The Dogs of War* (1974). Later books such as *The Devil's Alternative* and *The Fourth Protocol* were somewhat disappointing. Francis Clifford also wrote a number of excellent spy novels and thrillers, and he is particularly remembered for *The Naked Runner* (1966), *Amigo, Amigo* (1973) and *Drummer in the Dark* (1976). Also during the 1970s Gerald Seymour became well known with such thrillers as *Harry's Game* (1979) and *Red Fox* (1979). Douglas Hurd (who later became British Home and then Foreign Secretary) wrote some good political thrillers in collaboration with Andrew Osmond, namely *Send Him Victorious* (1968), *Smile on the Face of the Tiger* (1969) and *Scotch on the Rocks* (1971). Hurd's solo efforts were *The Truth Game* (1972) and *Vote to Kill* (1975). A consistently high standard has been set by Patricia Highsmith in her suspense thrillers: stories which feature the anti-hero (*q.v.*) Tom Ripley. Adam Hall has also been prolific, as have Jack Higgins and Gavin Lyall. In Lyall's earlier books aviation played an important role. Three of his better known novels are: *The Wrong Side of the Sky* (1961), *Judas Country* (1975) and *The Secret Servant* (1980). James Barlow, who died prematurely, wrote one outstanding thriller in the shape of *The Patriots* (1960). William Garner, Robert Ludlum, James Leasor and Martin Cruz Smith are others who have written a variety of notable thrillers. Scores of other writers active, with varying degrees of success, since the 1950s might be cited. The public demand for such fiction appears unabated.

In the theatre the thriller derived from the 19th c. tradition of melodrama (*q.v.*). There has been a large number of successful plays of the thriller kind in the 20th c. Here again Edgar Wallace excelled with *The Ringer* (1926), *On the Spot* (1930) and *The Case of the Frightened Lady* (1931). Other notable instances were John Willard's *The Cat and the Canary* (1922); Frederick Lonsdale's *The Last of Mrs Cheyney* (1925); Patrick Hamilton's *Rope* (1929),

Gaslight (1938) and *The Governess* (1945); Emlyn Williams's *Night Must Fall* (1935) and *Some One Waiting* (1953); Barré Lyndon's *The Amazing Dr Clitterhouse* (1936); Frederick Knott's *Dial 'M' for Murder* (1952); Agatha Christie's *Ten Little Niggers* (1943), *The Mousetrap* (1952) – a play still running thirty-eight years later – and *Witness for the Prosecution* (1953). Since the 1950s good stage thrillers have been rare, but Simon Gray's comedy thriller *Stage-struck* (1979) was a success.

time novels A term used occasionally to denote those novels which employ the stream of consciousness (*q.v.*) technique and in which the use of time and time as a theme is of pre-eminent importance. Famous instances are: Proust's *A la recherche du temps perdu* (1913–27), Dorothy Richardson's *Pilgrimage* (1915–67); Joyce's *Ulysses* (1922) and Thomas Mann's *Der Zauberberg* (1924). More recently there has been Anthony Powell's twelve-volume series *A Dance to the Music of Time* (named after Poussin's painting), which began with *A Question of Upbringing* (1951) and concluded with *Hearing Secret Harmonies* (1975). Time is thematically central to the sequence. Nicholas Jenkins, the narrator, observes that all human beings are driven 'at different speeds by the same Furies'. *See also* BILDUNGSROMAN; KUNSTLERROMAN; ROMAN CYCLE; ROMAN-FLEUVE; SAGA NOVEL; TIME PLAY.

time play A loose category for a form of drama which in some way exploits chronological sequence by various means: the flashback, and what might be called the 'flash-forward'. It entails the exploitation of dramatic convention (*q.v.*). Numerous playwrights have used various devices. For instance, in *The Winter's Tale* the Chorus asks us to accept the fact that sixteen years have elapsed since Perdita was 'lost'. J. B. Priestley (1894–1984) is the most notable example of a dramatist who experimented with the space/time continuum. In this he was influenced by J. W. Dunne's theories expounded in *An Experiment with Time* (1927) and *The Serial Universe* (1934). Priestley wrote four plays in which he experimented with space/time: *I Have Been Here Before* (1937), *Time and the Conways* (1937), *Johnson over Jordan* (1939) and *An Inspector Calls* (1946). In *Time and the Conways*, for instance, he ingeniously allows eighteen years to elapse between Acts I and II, and in the third act reverts to 1919. Many writers have been deeply interested in the nature of time. H. G. Wells is an obvious example. Another is Graham Greene, who, in his autobiographical *Ways of*

Escape, wonders whether or not it is possible to take symbols from the future as well as from the past. Writers of science fiction (*q.v.*) are particularly preoccupied with the question of time.

tirade (F 'volley of words') A long speech, usually vehement, and perhaps abusive and censorious. Timon delivers several remarkable tirades in Act IV of Shakespeare's *Timon of Athens* (*c.* 1607).

tmesis (Gk 'a cutting') The separation of the parts of a word by the insertion of another word or words. Not unusual in abusive speech. For example: 'Neverthebloodyless, I won't accept that.'

toddaid A Welsh syllabic verse form comprising quatrain (*q.v.*) stanzas which alternate between nine- and ten-syllable lines. Cross-rhyming is characteristic.

tonada *See* TONADILLA.

tonadilla *Tonada* is a Spanish term for a type of ballad poem performed in the intervals between acts of *autos sacramentales* (*q.v.*). They were often bawdy or obscene. The diminutive *tonadilla* came to denote an operetta with two to four characters and lasting about fifteen minutes. They were presented between the acts of serious plays in the 18th c. *See also* ENTREMES.

tone The reflection of a writer's attitude (especially towards his readers), manner, mood and moral outlook in his work; even, perhaps, the way his personality pervades the work. The counterpart of tone of voice in speech, which may be friendly, detached, pompous, officious, intimate, bantering and so forth. For example, in the following poem by David Holbrook *Living? Our Supervisors Will Do That For Us!* the skilfully contrived rhythm almost slouches and preserves the tune of slightly jerky, elliptical speech. The shrugging, 'throw-away' language, very colloquial, suggests laconic detachment. As a sketch of two contrasting characters it is most adroit in its economy and largely sympathetic to both:

> Dankwerts, scholarship boy from the slums,
> One of many, studied three years for the Tripos,
> Honours, English; grew a beard, imitated the gesture
> And the insistent deliberate (but not dogmatic)
> 'There!' of his supervisor. For a time

The mimesis was startling. Dankwerts knew
Uncannily what was good, what bad.
Life and earning a living, extra muros, for a time
afterwards,
Left him hard up: people in their ambiguity
Nuisances. A bracing need for self-justification
(And spot cash) drove some of the nonsense out of him:
He found a foothold in films, the evening papers,
With his photograph, up to the ears in steaks, or ivy,
In 'art' magazines. Passing over the metropolis
He ejaculates like a satellite, evaporates, and falls,
Albeit on to a fat bank balance of amoral earnings.

Whereas his supervisor can be seen any Friday
Walking up Trumpington Street with an odd movement
of the feet,
Still looking like an old corm, lissom, and knowing
Uncannily what's good, what's bad,
And probably rather hard up out of the bargain.

tone colour Jargon for the auditory quality of speech sounds, what Ezra Pound meant by melopoeia (*q.v.*). It covers kinaesthetic and synaesthetic experience. For instance, despair may be a 'black' word; hope, a 'white'. We speak of a 'hard' tone and a 'soft' tone. Words may seem 'smooth' or 'rough'. *Mellifluous* is 'soft' and euphonious, whereas *crag* is 'hard' and harsh. *See* EUPHONY; LOGOPOEIA; ONOMATOPOEIA; SYNAESTHESIA.

tongue-twister Associated with nonsense verse, nursery rhyme and patter songs (*qq.v.*) the tongue-twister is an alliterative jingle (*q.v.*) of some antiquity. Also known as a tongue-tripper. The following is a fairly well-known example:

Theophilus Thistledown, the successful thistle sifter,
In sifting a sieve of unsifted thistles,
Thrust three thousand thistles
Through the thick of his thumb.
If, then, Theophilus Thistledown, the successful
thistle sifter,
In sifting a sieve full of unsifted thistles,
Thrust three thousand thistles
Through the thick of his thumb,
See that thou, in sifting a sieve of unsifted thistles,
Do not get the unsifted thistles stuck in thy tongue.

topographical poetry Writing of Denham in *Lives of the Poets* (1779–81) Johnson aptly described this genre as 'local poetry, of which the fundamental subject is some particular landscape, to be poetically described, with the addition of such embellishments as may be supplied by historical retrospection, or incidental meditation'. One of the earliest examples was, in fact, Sir John Denham's *Cooper's Hill* (1642). In the next 150 years the genre flourished in England (it seems to be a very English phenomenon) like a counterpart to landscape painting. Not a few of them are what are known as 'prospect poems': the poet views a broad scene from a high vantage point and describes, for instance, a park or estate (perhaps in the hope of gaining patronage from a rich and powerful owner who was very likely to belong to the peerage). Apart from one or two slight pieces by Lady Winchilsea (e.g. *Fanscomb Barn*), some of the principal works were: Pope's *Windsor Forest* (1713); Samuel Garth's *Claremont* (1715); Dyer's *Grongar Hill* (1726), one of the most agreeable poems of the kind; James Thomson's delightful poem *The Seasons* (1726–30), which Wordsworth later remarked offered new images of 'external nature'; Gray's *Ode on a Distant Prospect of Eton College* (1742); Collins's *Ode on the Popular Superstitions of the Highlands of Scotland* (written in 1749, but not published until 1788); Richard Jago's *Edge-hill* (1767); Goldsmith's *The Deserted Village* (1770); plus several works by George Crabbe, who might be described as a regional poet of East Suffolk: most notably, *The Village* (1783), *The Parish Register* (1807), *The Borough* (1810), *Tales* (1812) and *Tales of the Hall* (1819). Wordsworth also wrote topographical poetry; an obvious example is *Tintern Abbey* (1798). After Wordsworth and Crabbe few seriously attempted the form on any scale. However, one encounters the occasional poem which is in the general tradition, not infrequently displaying nostalgia and elegiac regret for a vanishing rural scene, and in the 20th c. Sir John Betjeman (who remarked on his 'topographical predilection') achieved something of a revival of such poetry with many evocative descriptions (tinged with melancholy) of rural, urban, suburban and provincial scenes. Ted Hughes also wrote two memorable poems of the topographical type in the shape of *Remains of Elmet* (1979) and *River* (1983). *See also* PASTORAL.

tornada A short concluding stanza, similar to the *envoi* (*q.v.*), added to Old Provençal poems by way of complimentary dedication to a patron or friend. *See also* CHANSON.

total theatre The German term *Totaltheater* was first used in the mid-1920s for a form of theatrical presentation planned by Walter Gropius for the director Erwin Piscator (1893–1966). Piscator's approach was highly individual. He altered texts to suit his own ends and was the first to introduce film and animated cartoons on stage to speed up the action. He was in favour of spectacle to get his messages (often propagandist) across. The text was subordinated to effects which could be achieved by arresting lighting, music, dance, acrobatics, startling sets and costumes. All the mechanical resources of the theatre were put to use. Total theatre developed into epic theatre (*q.v.*). In France the concept of total theatre was put into practice by Jean-Louis Barrault in the 1950s. One of his notable productions was Claudel's *Christophe Colombe* (1953). More recently the Italian director Luca Ronconi has enlarged the possibilities of total theatre by involving spectators and audience in the action. For example, his travelling version of Ariosto's *Orlando Furioso* (1970). In England the leading exponent was Joan Littlewood at the Theatre Workshop. One of her most successful productions was *Oh! What a Lovely War!* (1963). There have been many others in the total theatre style. One of the most brilliant and spectacular was Bill Bryden's version of the *Wakefield Mystery Plays* in the promenade productions at the National Theatre and the Lyceum in 1985–6.

touchstone A touchstone is a dark flinty schist, jasper or basanite, and so called because gold is tried by it. Matthew Arnold used the word in his essay *The Study of Poetry* (1880) in connection with literary criteria and standards:

> Indeed there can be no more useful help for discovering what poetry belongs to the class of the truly excellent, and can therefore do us most good, than to have always in one's mind lines and expressions of the great masters, and to apply them as a touchstone to other poetry. Of course we are not to require this other poetry to resemble them; it may be very dissimilar. But if we have any tact we shall find them, when we have lodged them well in our minds, an infallible touchstone for detecting the presence or absence of high poetic quality, and also the degree of this quality, in all other poetry which we may place beside them.

Arnold goes on to quote lines from Homer, Dante, Shakespeare and Milton to demonstrate his point. He suggests that his touchstone method should be the basis of a 'real' rather than an 'historic' or 'personal' estimate of poetry. He also contends that a passage has 'high poetic quality' if it has high seriousness and the grand style. Such a view is now regarded as somewhat limiting and exclusive.

Arnold was by no means the first critic to have suggested such criteria. John Dennis (1657–1734) had presented a comparable point of view in *The Advancement and Reformation of Modern Poetry* (1701) and *The Grounds of Criticism in Poetry* (1704).

tour de force (F 'turn of force') As a literary term it may be applied to a work which provides an outstanding illustration of a writer's skill and mastery; a sort of 'one-off' brilliant display. Among modern examples one might suggest: Hemingway's short story *The Short and Happy Life of Francis Macomber* (1938); Arthur Koestler's novel *Darkness at Noon* (1940); Orwell's fable *Animal Farm* (1945); Anthony Burgess's novel *A Clockwork Orange* (1962); Daniel Keyes's short story *Flowers for Algernon* (1965); and Vikram Seth's extraordinary 'novel' *The Golden Gate* (1986) – a narrative which consists of 590 sonnets in rhyming tetrameters.

trace A term used in a particular sense by the French philosopher Jacques Derrida (1930–) to signify his view that there is no simple sense in which linguistic signs are either present or absent. According to Derrida, every sign (e.g. a word such as 'dwelling') contains a 'trace' of other signs which differ from itself. But, paradoxically, the 'trace' is *not* there; it is *potentially inherent*, or *present by virtue of its absence*, just as absence denotes the possibility of presence. No sign is complete in itself. One sign leads to another via the 'trace' – indefinitely. The word/sign 'dwelling' carries with it scores of traces (i.e. connotations) and other signs associated with dwelling. The 'trace' is one aspect of Derrida's theory of *différance* (*q.v.*). In his discourse *Positions* (1972, trans. 1981) he elaborates:

> The play of differences involves syntheses and referrals [*renvois*] which prevent there from being at any moment or in any way a simple element which is *present* in and of itself and refers only to itself. Whether in written or spoken discourse, no element can function as a sign without relating to another element which itself is not simply present. This linkage means that each element – phoneme or grapheme – is constituted with reference to the trace in it of the other elements of the sequence

or system . . . Nothing, in either the elements or the system, is anywhere ever simply present or absent.

See CONNOTATION; DECONSTRUCTION; DENOTATION; DISSEMINATION; POST-STRUCTURALISM; SIGNIFIER/SIGNIFIED; STRUCTURALISM; SYNTAGMATIC/PARADIGMATIC.

tract Usually a short pamphlet (*q.v.*) on a religious or political subject. Two famous examples are the *Marprelate Tracts* issued in 1588–9, which were an attack on the bishops and a defence of Presbyterian discipline, and *Tracts for the Times* (1833–41), a series on religious subjects written by, among others, Cardinal Newman, Keble, R. H. Froude and Pusey. Their object was to revive certain doctrines of the Church. *See* OXFORD MOVEMENT.

tractarian movement *See* OXFORD MOVEMENT.

tradition This denotes the inherited past which is available for the writer to study and learn from. Thus, the writer's native language, literary forms, codes, devices, conventions (*q.v.*) and various cultures from the past. We may, for example, refer to the Neoclassical tradition or the French Classical tradition or to the tradition of the English essay, or the Irish tradition of dramatic comedy, or the Scottish ballad tradition, or the Welsh tradition of religious lyric poetry and many others, and in each case mean something fairly specific in spirit, matter and style. Anything traditional is established, has often been tried and is constantly returned to.

And every writer begins with some sort of tradition behind him (even if only that provided by his language) and every writer in some way modifies or influences that tradition, even when being imitative. Though some poems by Keats might have been written by Milton, and some by Dylan Thomas are almost indistinguishable from work by Gerard Manley Hopkins, there are differences.

Arbitrary classification of writers according to differing traditions is obviously a more perilous undertaking, but, bearing in mind the primary meaning of tradition (that which is passed down from generation to generation through custom and practice), we may distinguish certain traditions in English poetry (or poetry written by English speaking peoples). Basically, there are (a) the native tradition, as exemplified in the work of Chaucer and the Scottish

Chaucerians, Wyatt, Shakespeare (and the majority of his contemporary poets and dramatists), Donne and most of the 17th c. lyric poets, and, thereafter, Burns, Blake, Clare, Barnes, Browning, Hopkins, Yeats, Pound, Eliot, W. H. Auden, Dylan Thomas and Ted Hughes – to mention only some of the major writers, and; (b) the Italianate tradition of Surrey, Sidney, Spenser, Milton, Keats, Shelley, Tennyson, Matthew Arnold and Francis Thompson. Linking these two, and owing a good deal to both, is the Neoclassical tradition from the Renaissance through to the 18th c., whose finest representatives are Dryden, Pope, Johnson and Crabbe, though all four are peculiarly *English* poets. Pope, for example, is much nearer in spirit and style to Donne than to Tennyson. As always there are poets who appear not to belong to (or who are not easily identified with) any specific tradition. Wordsworth, Coleridge and Byron are obvious examples.

Among prose writers definite traditions are much less distinguishable. For example, in the novel the main tradition seems to lie through the work of Jane Austen, George Eliot, Charles Dickens, Thomas Hardy, Henry James, Conrad, Arnold Bennett and D. H. Lawrence, but clearly this is not a tradition in which one could include major writers like James Joyce, Dorothy Richardson, Virginia Woolf, William Faulkner and Samuel Beckett, and dozens of others who have flourished recently.

tragedy (Gk 'goat song') In the first place it almost certainly denoted a form of ritual sacrifice accompanied by a choral song in honour of Dionysus, the god of the fields and the vineyards. Out of this ritual developed Greek dramatic tragedy.

In his *Poetics*, Aristotle defined tragedy as:

> The imitation of an action that is serious and also, as having magnitude, complete in itself; in language with pleasurable accessories, each kind brought in separately in the parts of the work; in a dramatic, not in a narrative form; with incidents arousing pity and fear, wherewith to accomplish its catharsis of such emotions.

Later he spoke of the plot:

> Plots are either simple or complex, since the actions they represent are naturally of this twofold description. The action, proceeding in the way defined, as one continuous whole, I call simple, when the change in the hero's fortunes takes place

> without Peripety or Discovery, and complex when it involves one or the other, or both. These should each of them arise out of the structure of the Plot itself, so as to be the consequence, necessary or probable, or the antecedents.

Subsequently, Aristotle spoke of the tragic hero:

> There remains, then, the intermediate kind of personage, a man not pre-eminently virtuous and just, whose misfortune, however, is brought upon him not by vice and depravity but by some error of judgement, of the number of those in the enjoyment of great reputation and prosperity; e.g. Oedipus, Thyestes, and the men of note of similar families. The perfect Plot, accordingly, must have a single, and not (as some tell us) a double issue; the change in the hero's fortunes must be not from misery to happiness, but on the contrary from happiness to misery; and the cause of it must lie not in any depravity, but in some great error on his part; the man himself being either such as we have described, or better, not worse, than that. (Bywater's translation)

There is little of note between him and the writers of the Renaissance period. Diomedes (4th c. AD), for example, remarks that tragedy is a narrative about the fortunes of heroic or semi-divine characters. Isidore of Seville (*c.* 6th–7th c.) observes that tragedy comprises sad stories about commonwealths and kings. John of Garland (12th c.) describes tragedy as a poem written in the grand style about shameful and wicked deeds; a poem which begins in joy and ends in grief. And Chaucer, in the prologue to *The Monk's Tale*, gives a representative medieval view:

> Tragedie is to seyn a certeyn storie,
> As olde bookes maken us memorie,
> Of hym that stood in greet prosperitee
> And is yfallen out of heigh degree
> Into myserie, and endeth wrecchedly.

Later, Sir Philip Sidney eloquently refers to 'high and excellent Tragedy' that opens the greatest wounds and displays the ulcers covered with tissue; tragedy which makes kings fear to be tyrants and tyrants to 'manifest their tyrannical humours'. Sidney goes on to say that it stirs 'the affects of admiration and commiseration, teacheth the uncertainty of this world, and upon how weak foundations gilden roofs are builded.'

In the end it becomes fairly clear, from both theory and practice, that, hitherto, tragedy has tended to be a form of drama concerned with the fortunes and misfortunes, and, ultimately, the disasters, that befall human beings of title, power and position. For example: Oedipus, Agamemnon, Antigone, Hecuba, Romeo and Juliet, Antony and Cleopatra, Hamlet, the Duchess of Malfi, Samson, Phèdre, Jaffier and Belvidera, Cato, Don Carlos, Brand, Deirdre . . . What makes them tragic figures is that they have qualities of excellence, of nobleness, of passion; they have virtues and gifts that lift them above the ordinary run of mortal men and women. In tragedy these attributes are seen to be insufficient to save them either from self-destruction or from destruction brought upon them. And there is no hope for them. There is hope, perhaps, *after* the tragedy, but not *during* it. The overwhelming part about tragedy is the element of hopelessness, of inevitability. This aspect of tragedy is nowhere better expressed than by the Chorus at the beginning of Anouilh's play *Antigone*:

> . . . The machine is in perfect order; it has been oiled ever since time began, and it runs without friction. Death, treason and sorrow are on the march; and they move in the wake of storm, of tears, of stillness . . . Tragedy is clean, it is restful, it is flawless . . . In tragedy nothing is in doubt and everyone's destiny is known. That makes for tranquillity. There is a sort of fellow-feeling among characters in a tragedy: he who kills is as innocent as he who gets killed: it's all a matter of what part you are playing. Tragedy is restful; and the reason is that hope, that foul, deceitful thing, has no part in it.

Tragedy is the disaster which comes to those who represent and who symbolize, in a peculiarly intense form, those flaws and shortcomings which are universal in a lesser form. Tragedy is a disaster that happens to other people; and the greater the person, so it seems, the more acute is their tragedy. Put at its crudest – the bigger they are the harder they fall.

In a way, also, tragedy is a kind of protest; it is a cry of terror or complaint or rage or anguish to and against whoever or whatever is responsible for 'this harsh rack', for suffering, for death. Be it God, Nature, Fate, circumstance, chance or just something nameless. It is a 'cry' about the tragic situation in which the tragic hero or heroine find themselves.

On the plane of reality, the life and death of Christ have all the basic traditional elements of tragedy – especially inevitability. His death was foreseen and forecast, and was a 'foregone conclusion'. And even Christ was very nearly without hope. His cry of agony and despair from the Cross was the final proof, so to speak, of the authenticity of his human nature.

By participating vicariously in the grief, pain and fear of the tragic hero or heroine, the spectator, in Aristotle's words, experiences pity and fear and is purged. Or, again crudely, he has a good cry and feels better. But then, comedy (*q.v.*) purges, too – through laughter. And laughter and tears are so closely associated physically and physiologically that often we do not know whether to laugh or to cry. And comic relief (*q.v.*) in tragedy serves many purposes, not least preventing the spectator from being overcharged with tragic emotion.

Classical Greek tragedy is almost wholly devoid of comedy (though the occasional grim observation or rejoinder might raise a laconic smile), but the Greek tragedians made up for this by having a satyr play (*q.v.*) to make the fourth part of the tetralogy (*q.v.*) and this was a kind of palliative burlesque after the full cathartic experience of pity and fear.

The Greeks were the first of the tragedians and it was upon their work only that Aristotle formed his conclusions. Unhappily, owing to Aristotle's immense prestige and authority, his theories were later misapplied and misused: either by trying to make them fit all forms of tragedy; or by doing the opposite and excluding all those works which did not fit his descriptions. Both misapplications were equally harmful.

The principal writers of tragedy before Aeschylus, Sophocles and Euripides, were Phrynicus, Pratinas and Choerilus, and the semi-legendary Thespis (fl. *c.* 354 BC). Thespis is believed to have made a major innovation by introducing an actor into tragic performances which formerly were given by a Chorus (*q.v.*) alone. To this Aeschylus (525–456 BC) added a second, and Sophocles (496–406 BC) a third; namely, protagonist, deuteragonist and tritagonist (*qq.v.*). Both these playwrights and Euripides (480–406 BC) made other modifications and improvements to the structure of tragedy.

Aeschylus wrote about ninety plays of which seven are extant, namely: *Suppliants*, *Persians*, *Seven Against Thebes*, *Prometheus Bound*, and the Oresteian trilogy which comprises *Agamemnon*, *Choephori* and *Eumenides*. Sophocles was even more prolific. He is credited with 120 plays and at the dramatic festivals won eighteen times with eighteen different tetralogies. Only seven of his works are also extant, namely: *Antigone*, *Oedipus Tyrannus*, *Electra*, *Ajax*, *Trachiniae*, *Philoctetes* and *Oedipus at Colonus*. The output of Euripides was almost as great. Eighty or ninety plays are ascribed to him, and eighteen of these (if we include *Rhesus*) survive. Of these the main works are: *Alcestis*, *Medea*, *Hippolytus*, *Trojan Women*, *Orestes*, *Iphigenia at Aulis*, *Bacchae*, *Andromache*, *Hecuba*, *Electra* and *Iphigenia in Tauris*.

By 400 BC Greek tragedy seems to have run itself out, but a hundred-odd years had produced a tragic corpus that has certainly not been surpassed.

There is relatively little of note in Roman tragedy except for the work of Seneca which, fifteen hundred years after his death, was to have a very considerable influence on Elizabethan tragedy. In 240 BC Livius Andronicus first presented rough adaptations of Greek tragedy, and he continued to do that. Naevius, a younger contemporary, composed tragedies on Greek subjects and themes, and also *fabulae praetextae* (*see* FABULA). His main successors were Ennius, Pacuvius and Accius who also wrote occasional *praetextae*. After them tragedy declined and it was not until the age of Nero that Seneca (*c.* 4 BC–AD 65) made any notable contribution to the genre. He was a prolific writer of tragedies who took the bulk of his subjects from Greek sources; but his tragedies were not intended for the stage.

Thereafter, for 1,500 years, there appears to be no tragedy of any kind anywhere. It seems almost incredible that a thousand years of Byzantine civilization produced no drama. We can only surmise that the liturgy of the Church satisfied the dramatic and histrionic needs of the Byzantine Greeks.

In the Middle Ages Classical drama was not known; nor were Aristotle's theories. In that period tragedy was a story of the kind that Chaucer described in his Prologue to *The Monk's Tale*. The greatest tragedy of all (namely the Passion and death of Christ) had been played in real life. From it grew the richly complex, symbolic drama of church ritual. In the absence of drama this must have been theatre and spectacle enough. However, out of the Mystery Plays (*q.v.*), some of which dealt with the Passion and Death of Christ, the secular drama evolved; and in the Elizabethan period tragedy as a form was revived. Seneca provided the model for a formal five-act play in a rhetorical style.

An early and important example of this was *Gorboduc* (1561) by Thomas Sackville and Thomas Norton. Often regarded as the first Elizabethan tragedy, it was also a kind of political Morality Play (*q.v.*) on the proper government of a kingdom.

The Senecan model produced approximately two kinds of tragedy: academic drama (*q.v.*), based on Classical rules and often using a Chorus (*q.v.*) of the type used by the Greeks and Romans; and the much more important genre of revenge tragedy (*q.v.*). A notable early instance of the latter is Thomas Kyd's *Spanish Tragedy* (*c.* 1586). To this tradition and convention also belong Marlowe's *The Jew of Malta* (*c.* 1592), and Shakespeare's *Titus Andronicus* (1594) and *Hamlet* (*c.* 1603–4). There are many other well-known instances.

During the latter part of the 16th c. and until approximately 1640, dramatists paid less attention to the Classical rules and conventions and worked out what was suitable for their individual needs. In fact we find a large number of tragedies in this period whose form and structure show considerable variations. In rough chronological order some of the more famous and notable works are: Thomas Preston's *Cambyses* (1569); Marlowe's *Dr Faustus* (*c.* 1588), a play which used some of the conventions of the Morality; the anonymous *Arden of Faversham* (*c.* 1592), a very early instance of what has been described as domestic tragedy (*q.v.*); several major works by Shakespeare, namely: *Romeo and Juliet* (*c.* 1595), *Othello* (1604), *King Lear* (1606), *Macbeth* (*c.* 1606), *Antony and Cleopatra* (*c.* 1606–7) and *Coriolanus* (*c.* 1608); George Peele's *David and Bethsabe* (1599); John Marston's *Antonio and Mellida* (1602) and his *Antonio's Revenge* (1602); Chettle's *The Tragedy of Hoffman* (1602); Thomas Heywood's *A Woman Killed with Kindness* (1603); Ben Jonson's *Sejanus* (1603) and his *Catiline* (1611), both of which were influenced by Classical models; Chapman's *Bussy D'Ambois* (1607), *The Revenge of Bussy D'Ambois* (1613), *Caesar and Pompey* (1631) and *The Tragedy of Chabot* (1639); Tourneur's *The Revenger's Tragedy* (1607) and his *The Atheist's Tragedy* (1611); Webster's *The White Devil* (*c.* 1608), *Appius and Virginia* (*c.* 1609) and *The Duchess of Malfi* (*c.* 1613–14); the anonymous *A Yorkshire Tragedy* (1608), a curiosity in its way; Beaumont and Fletcher's *The Maid's Tragedy* (*c.* 1610), plus several other works by this very prolific pair of partners; Middleton's *Women Beware Women* (*c.* 1621); Middleton and Rowley's *The Changeling* (1622); Massinger's *The Roman Actor* (1626); John Ford's *The Broken Heart* (1633) and his *'Tis Pity She's a Whore* (1633).

During approximately the same period tragedy burgeoned in Spain, where the main writers were Lope de Vega (1562–1635), Molina (1571–1648) and Calderón (1600–81), and just as a declension began in England and Spain so the form began to flourish in France where the two finest exponents were Corneille and Racine. This was tragedy in a traditional grand manner, in an heroic manner. As Racine expressed it in his Preface to *Bérénice* (1668): 'Ce n'est point une nécessité qu'il y ait du sang et des morts dans une tragédie; il suffit que l'action en soit grande, que les acteurs en soient héroïques, que les passions y soient excitées, et que tout s'y ressente de cette tristesse majestueuse qui fait tout le plaisir de la tragédie'. And both these dramatists conceived the tragic form in Classical terms. The major works of Corneille are: *Médée* (1635), *Le Cid* (1636), *Horace, Cinna* and *Polyeucte* (all 1640), *La Mort de Pompée* (1643?), and *Rodogune* (1644). Those of Racine are: *Andromaque* (1667), *Iphigénie* (1674), *Phèdre* (1677), *Britannicus* (1669), *Bérénice* (1670), *Mithridate* (1673), *Esther* (1689) and *Athalie* (1691).

In the latter part of the 17th c. there was a slight revival of tragedy in England, but it was very slight. The most notable work of the period (belonging to the category heroic drama, *q.v.*), was Dryden's *All for Love* (1678), a highly successful re-working of the story of Antony and Cleopatra. Minor works were Milton's *Samson Agonistes* (1671); Thomas Otway's *Venice Preserved* (1682); and Thomas Southerne's *The Fatal Marriage* (1694).

It is a commonplace of dramatic history that from *c.* 1700 onwards relatively little tragedy of note was written; or, to put it another way, little that has survived has proved of durable interest. There seems to be a definite connection between the decline of verse drama and the inferiority of tragedy. In the 18th c. playwrights tended to write under the influence of Classical rules and models, or they attempted something like domestic or bourgeois tragedy. Prose and verse were used. But verse drama was seldom successful. This is true also of the 19th c. Dramatic prose was usually serviceable; verse was too often like an unconscious parody or deliberate imitation of Elizabethan and Jacobean blank verse (*q.v.*). These faults are very noticeable in the works of, for example, quite a talented dramatist like James Sheridan Knowles (1784–1862), whose best tragedy was *Caius Gracchus* (1815), and in plays by Keats, Tennyson, Browning and Swinburne.

Nevertheless, during the 18th and 19th c. a large number of European playwrights did experiment with tragic formulae, and in some cases with considerable or varying success. Among the more notable achievements one should mention Nicholas Rowe's *The Fair Penitent* (1703) and his *The Tragedy of Jane Shore* (1714); Addison's *Cato* (1713); Lillo's *The London Merchant* (1731); Johnson's *Irene* (1749); Edward Moore's *The Gamester* (1753); Lessing's *Miss Sara Simpson* (1755); John Home's *Douglas* (1756);

Lessing's *Emilia Galotti* (1772) and his *Nathan the Wise* (1783); Alfieri's *Saul* (1784) and his *Mirra* (1786); Schiller's *Don Carlos* (1787); George Colman the Younger's *The Iron Chest* (1796); Schiller's *Maria Stuart* (1800); Kleist's *Penthesilea* (1808) and *Prince of Homburg* (1811); Shelley's *Cenci* (written in 1818, but first performed in 1886); Victor Hugo's *Hernani* (1830) and *Ruy Blas* (1838); Büchner's *Danton's Death* (1835) and his incomplete *Woyzeck* (1836–7).

Near the end of the 19th c. two Scandinavian dramatists brought about a wholly unexpected revolution of tragic form and subject. Their works displayed the tragedy of disease, of eccentricity, of bad heredity, of madness and more or less psychotic and emotionally morbid states. Their tragic vision revealed a society that was diseased; spiritually and morally corrupt and decadent. In Ibsen's case the vision gave great and bitter offence. What he exposed was too near the truth for almost anybody's comfort. One can say that their tragedies were unlike anything written hitherto, and, like many that followed, far removed from Classical and Aristotelian concepts. Some of their major works in the tragic mode were: Strindberg's *The Father* (1887) and *Miss Julie* (1889); Ibsen's *A Doll's House* (1879), *Brand* (1885), *Hedda Gabler* (1891) and *John Gabriel Borkman* (1897).

Since then a large number of dramatists have attempted different kinds of tragedy; or serious plays which are tragic in tone, import and intention. Notable instances are: Synge's *Riders to the Sea* (1904) and his *Deirdre of the Sorrows* (1910); Granville-Barker's *Waste* (1907); Eugene O'Neill's *Emperor Jones* (1920) and *All God's Chillun* (1924); O'Casey's *Juno and the Paycock* (1924); Lorca's *Blood Wedding* (1933), *Yerma* (1934) and *The House of Bernarda Alba* (1945); T. S. Eliot's *Murder in the Cathedral* (1935); Maxwell Anderson's *Winterset* (1935); Clifford Odets's *Golden Boy* (1937); Anouilh's *Antigone* (1944); Tennessee Williams's *A Streetcar Named Desire* (1947); Arthur Miller's *Death of a Salesman* (1948) and his *A View from the Bridge* (1955); John Arden's *Serjeant Musgrave's Dance* (1959); and John McGrath's *Events while Guarding the Bofors Gun* (1966).

If tragedy, like other major art forms, is to be taken as an expression and reflection of man's nature, and his vision of the universe and his role and position in it, in any society or period, then the concept of tragedy has changed greatly since the 16th c. The scale and tone of tragedy or anything resembling it has been modified. We now have the grief, the misery, the disaster, of the ordinary man. Not a king or a queen or a prince, but an everyday mother, tramp, peasant or salesman.

Two powerful influences in the 20th c. theatre have been the Theatre of the Absurd and the Theatre of Silence (*qq.v.*). Nowadays the potentially tragic dramatist is more likely to express the sadness and wrechedness of man's position by understatement; even to the point of saying nothing. What a world of difference there is between the magnificent, articulate, self-conscious and deeply moving valedictory speech of Othello, and the broken, barely articulate concluding words of Davies in Pinter's *The Caretaker* – a farewell which just rambles away into a long silence (the stage direction is *Long Silence*). *See* ANAGNORISIS; DRAME; HAMARTIA; HUBRIS; METATHEATRE; PERIPETEIA; TRAGIC FLAW.

tragedy of blood *See* REVENGE TRAGEDY.

tragic flaw Traditionally that defect in a tragic hero or heroine which leads to their downfall. To all intents and purposes a synonym for the Greek *hamartia* (*q.v.*). The *locus classicus* is *Hamlet*, I, iv, 23–36. *See also* HUBRIS; TRAGEDY.

tragic irony *See* IRONY.

tragi-comedy The term derives from a reference by Plautus (254–184 BC) to the unconventional mixture of kings, gods and servants in his own play *Amphitruo* as *tragico-comoedia*. However, the idea of tragi-comedy was not new even then since Euripides's *Alcestis* and *Iphigenia* (both tragedies) had happy endings; and Aristotle had made it clear in *Poetics* that audiences preferred the kind of endings where poetic justice (*q.v.*) was seen to be done.

From the late Middle Ages (or early Renaissance) there are two roughly identifiable genres of tragi-comedy in drama: the Neo-classical and the popular. Some Italian playwrights, of whom the best known is Giraldi Cinthio, wrote several tragedies with happy endings which he called *tragedie miste* ('mixed tragedies'). Others wrote what Polonius might have called tragical comedies (or comical tragedies) which had serious main plots and comic sub-plots (*q.v.*). By the end of the 16th c. these two kinds had drawn together and were more or less indistiguishable. By this time, anyway, we find an increasing mingling of tragic and comic elements, the use of comic relief (*q.v.*) in tragedy, and what might be called tragic aggravation or heightening in comedy.

A different kind of tragi-comedy was that devised by the Italian Guarini (1537–1612), author of the pastoral drama *Il pastor fido* (*c.* 1585). Guarini drew on the pastoral (*q.v.*) tradition. Like Cinthio he had characters of rank and nobility and also tragic elements; but he also presented comic episodes and characters and used appropriate comic diction. His play had a mixed reception and some critics attacked it. As a result he wrote his *Compendio della poesia tragicomica* (1601) to defend and explain what he was aiming at. He stressed particularly the need for a style of poetry which should be midway between that suitable for tragedy and comedy. *Il pastor fido* had a considerable vogue in England in the 17th c. It was often translated and also acted in a Latin version at Cambridge. The dramatist most influenced by Guarini in England was John Fletcher, whose version of Guarini was *The Faithful Shepherdess* (*c.* 1608). His preface, following Guarini, describes the genre: 'A tragicomedy is not so called in respect of mirth and killing, but in respect it wants deaths, which is enough to make it no tragedy, yet brings some near it, which is enough to make it no comedy . . .' Beaumont and Fletcher between them created several tragi-comedies for courtly audiences in private theatres.

Shakespeare also wrote tragi-comedies. All are different from each other and from anything that preceded them: namely, *Troilus and Cressida* (1602), *All's Well that Ends Well, Measure for Measure* (1604), *The Winter's Tale* (1609–10), *Cymbeline* (*c.* 1610) and *The Tempest* (*c.* 1611). Ben Jonson seems not to have approved of tragi-comedy (he describe it as 'mongrel') but late in life he wrote *The Sad Shepherd* (1641), of which only two acts were completed, and this is a tragi-comedy. Other works of note were: Beaumont and Fletcher's *Philaster, or Love Lies Bleeding* (*c.* 1610) and Chapman's *The Widow's Tears* (1612). John Marston, Thomas Heywood, Massinger, Shirley, Dryden and Davenant also wrote tragi-comedies.

It is noticeable that by the turn of the 16th c. something like a theory of tragi-comedy is evolving. We find John Florio referring to 'tragi-comedia' and Sir Philip Sidney, in his *Apologie for Poetrie* (1595), speaking of 'mungrell Tragi-comedie'. In 1603 Samuel Harsnet alludes to Plautus's classification thus: 'Our Daemonopoiia or Devill-fiction is Tragico-Comoedia, a mixture of both as Amphitryo in Plautus is . . .' And William Drummond of Hawthornden refers to this tragi-comedy called life.

The pioneer of tragi-comedy in France was Robet Garnier (1534–90), who wrote *Bradamante* (1582). Thereafter the genre was developed by Jean Schelandre, who wrote *Tyr et Sidon*, first produced in 1608 and later re-written under the influence of Alexandre Hardy (*c.* 1569–1632), a prolific writer of tragi-comedies who borrowed his plot materials from Spanish sources: notably Cervantes, who had been influenced by the novel *Tragicomédia de Calisto y Melibea*. Something like two hundred tragi-comedies were produced in France in the period *c.* 1620–70. Outstanding examples were Rotrou's *Don Bernard de Cabrère* (1647), Corneille's *Don Sanche d' Aragon* (1649) and Molière's *Le Misanthrope* (1666).

With the demise of verse drama, dramatic tragi-comedy virtually disappeared, but occasionally a playwright has combined tragic and comic elements in such a way as to warrant his work being called tragi-comedy. Notable examples are Rostand's *Cyrano de Bergerac* (1897); Chekhov's *Uncle Vanya* (1900) and *The Cherry Orchard* (1904); J. M. Synge's *The Shadow of the Glen* (1903); Ashley Duke's *Jew Süss* (1929); Giraudoux's *La Folle de Chaillot* (1945); Marcel Aymé's *The Count of Clerembard* (1950); Brendan Behan's *The Quare Fellow* (1954); and Samuel Beckett's *Waiting for Godot* (1955), which the author described as a tragi-comedy. More recently, David Hare's *Secret Rapture* (1989) might also come into the category.

But distinctions between between tragi-comedy, black comedy (*q.v.*) and what Jean Anouilh calls *pièces noires* and *pièces grinçantes* are difficult to make. From the 18th c. onwards the French have tended to use the term *drame* (*q.v.*) to denote a serious play which contains some comedy; and there are literally hundreds of plays extant from, say, 1800 which are now loosely called 'dramas' because they do not fit into any easily identifiable category.

One may conclude that the Elizabethan and Jacobean conception of life as a tragi-comedy was an attempt to balance and reconcile a conflict of vision. This would help to explain the mordant wit and the more macabre elements; also the sudden and sombre events which unexpectedly overshadow the radiance of plays like *Much Ado About Nothing*. It is a commonplace that surprisingly little tragedy of note has been produced since the 17th c. whereas there have been many excellent plays with tragic qualities and tragic potentialities.

It should also be noted that since early in the 20th c. the theatre of the absurd (*q.v.*) has been a major influence in drama; perhaps partly as a result of this the 'darker' comedies of the Elizabethan and Jacobean playwrights have become particularly popular.

tranche de vie *See* SLICE OF LIFE.

transcendentalism A New England movement which flourished from *c.* 1835 to 1860. It had its roots in romanticism (*q.v.*) and in post-Kantian idealism by which Coleridge was influenced. It had a considerable influence on American art and literature. Basically religious, it emphasized the role and importance of the individual conscience, and the value of intuition in matters of moral guidance and inspiration. The actual term was coined by opponents of the movement, but accepted by its members (e.g. Ralph Waldo Emerson, 1803–82, one of the leaders, published *The Transcendentalist* in 1841) The group were also social reformers. Some of the members, besides Emerson, were famous and included Bronson Alcott, Henry David Thoreau and Nathaniel Hawthorne.

transferred epithet *See* HYPALLAGE.

transgressio *See* HYPERBATON.

translatio *See* METAPHOR.

translation Despite the truth of the Italian aphorism 'traduttore traditore', there have been many praiseworthy and successful (and, in some cases, superlative) translations across a large number of languages – not least from foreign tongues into English. Three basic kinds of translation may be distinguished: (a) a more or less literally exact rendering of the original meaning at the expense of the syntax, grammar, colloquialism and idiom of the language into which it is put (e.g. Lang, Leaf and Myers' famous translation of the *Iliad*, 1883); (b) an attempt to convey the spirit, sense and style of the original by finding equivalents in syntax, grammar and idiom (e.g. Dryden's *Virgil*, 1697); (c) a fairly free adaptation which retains the original spirit but may considerably alter style, structure, grammar and idiom (e.g. Edward Fitzgerald's free versions of six of Calderón's plays, 1853; the same author's version of *Omar Khayyám*, 1859).

Notable landmarks in the history of translation are: King Alfred's translation of Boethius's *De Consolatione* and of Bede's *Ecclesiastical History* (9th c.); Luther's version of the Bible (1522–34); William Adlington's translation of *The Golden Ass* by Apuleius (1566); North's version of *Plutarch's Lives* (1579); Marlowe's of Ovid's *Elegies* (1590); George Chapman's of the *Iliad*

(1598–1611); Florio's of Montaigne's *Essays* (1603); The English Authorized Version of the Bible (1611); Dryden's *Virgil* (1687); Pope's *Iliad* (1715–20); Schlegel's *Shakespeare* (1797–1810); Jowett's version of Plato (1871). Other outstanding translators are: C. M. R. Leconte de Lisle, Ezra Pound, Arthur Waley, Scott Moncrieff, E. V. Rieu and Robert Graves.

transmutatio *See* METONYMY.

travel book A neglected and much varied genre of great antiquity to which many famous, more or less professional or 'full-time' writers have contributed, but which has also been enriched by a number of occasional writers. For the most part these have been diplomats, scholars, missionaries, soldiers of fortune, doctors, explorers and sailors. The genre subsumes works of exploration and adventure as well as guides and accounts of sojourns in foreign lands and includes such various works as: Pausanias's *Hellados Periegesis* or 'guide' to Greece (2nd c. AD); Giraldus Cambrensis's *Itinerarium Cambriae* (*c.* 1188); the extravaganzas of Sir John Mandeville or Jean d'Outremeuse (namely, his *Travels*, printed 1496), and Baron Munchausen (namely, *Narrative of his Marvellous Travels by Rudolph Raspe*, 1785); Friedrich Humboldt's immense output of travel narratives combined with scientific reports (thirty volumes in all, produced in the 19th c.), Curzon's classic work on Persia (*Persia and the Persian Question*, 1892); Scott's record of Polar exploration (*The Voyage of the Discovery*, 1905); D. H. Lawrence's personal and highly subjective account of a brief trip to Sardinia (*Sea and Sardinia*, 1923); and the well-documented and scholarly descriptions of his journey's in Russia and the Balkans by Sir Fitzroy Maclean (*Eastern Approaches*, 1949).

Some of the earliest records of travels come from Egypt; for instance, an anonymous 14th c. BC record known as *The Journeying of the Master of the Captains of Egypt*; and an account by Cosmas of Alexandria (*c.* AD 548) of travels in Ethiopia and the Indian Ocean. From China we have early accounts of travels in India by Fa-Hian (*c.* AD 399–414), and by Shaman Hwui-Li (*c.* AD 630) of journeys in the Far East. The Histories of Herodotus (*c.* 485–425 BC) are a fascinating record of extensive travels in Egypt, Africa and elsewhere. And in Greek literature there is the almost epic narrative of Xenophon (*c.* 430 BC) about the return of the Ten Thousand from Sardis. Among Roman authors Horace (65–8 BC) has left a record of a journey to Brundisium, and there are interesting accounts by Gaius Solinus (3rd c. AD) of journeys to Britain and Asia. A notable Arabian traveller was Ibn Battutah (1304–78), who for twenty-eight years travelled round the Far East, India, Africa, South Russia, Egypt, Spain and elsewhere and who in 1354 compiled a copious description of his journeyings. In the 16th c. Al Hassan Ibn Mohammed Al Wezas Al Fasi (a Moor), later known as Leo Africanus, left an account of his travels in the Mediterranean. Two Persian travellers of importance were Abd-Er-Razzak Samarqandi (1413–82) and Don Juan of Persia (1560–1605). The former described a journey to Samarkand; the latter, an expedition to Muscovy. One of the earlier German travellers was Albert de Mandelslo (*c.* 1614) whose record of a trip to Muscovy and Persia is particularly interesting. An enterprising Russian traveller of the Middle Ages was the man known as Abbot Daniel of Kiev (*c.* 1107) who recorded a journey to the Holy Land. Among Dutchmen one should mention Jan Huygen van Linschoten (*c.* 1563–1611), who made a long trip to the East Indies in 1576. One of the earlier travellers of French origin was St Silvia of Aquitaine, who, *c.* AD 400, made an extensive journey to the Near East. And in the 14th c. a French friar, Jordanus of Séverac, also went to the Near East, Armenia and India. Apart from Columbus and Vasco da Gama, an early Portuguese traveller of some note was Francisco de Alvarez (*c.* 1465–1541) who set off *c.* 1487 for the land of the legendary Prester John. In the 16th c. another Portguese, Fernao Mendes Pinto (1509–83), travelled to the Far East. A much more famous contemporary of his, Fr Mathew Ricci, the Jesuit (1552–1610), went to China and spent many years there. He left an absorbing account of this, which a modern writer, Vincent Cronin, used in his equally interesting narrative called *The Wise Man from the West.* A well-known 17th c. Portuguese explorer and traveller was Jeronimo Lobo (1593–1678), who ventured to Ethiopia. Early Spanish travellers have also left us memorable accounts of their voyages. Ruy Gonzalez de Clavijo, for example, who also took that legendary 'golden road' to Samarkand *c.* 1403; and Antonio de Herrera y Tordesillas (1559–1625), who travelled to Darien, and the great Cortés (1485–1547), the conqueror of Mexico. A contemporary, Garcilaso Inca de la Vega, also left an account of travels in Central America – *c.* 1539–42. Another contemporary was a man who signed himself 'A Gentleman of Elvas' and gave a version of Don Ferdinando's travels in Florida (*c.* 1540–42). Among Italians one should mention the record of John of Pian de Carpine's journey to Russia (in 1245). This was written by a man known as Friar

Benedict the Pole. A little later the legendary Marco Polo (*c.* 1254–*c.* 1324) made his famous journeys to the East. In the middle of the 14th c. John de Marignolli travelled to see the Emperor of the Tatars. In the following century and a half the Cabots (John and Sebastian) made their journeys to the South American seas and the Far East. And in the 16th c. Cellini wrote extensive accounts in his *Memoirs* of his various peregrinations.

These are only a handful of the many who, in Classical times, in the Middle Ages and during the Renaissance period, explored the then known world and opened up the unknown.

From the 16th c. onwards the Near East, the Middle East and the Far East, Asia and parts of Africa were increasingly explored and travelled, and the world of the Americas was gradually charted. As the world became more navigable and better known, so travel books of every kind proliferated. Here there is only space to mention a few of the hundreds that exist.

One of the earliest extant accounts of an Englishman's travels abroad are those concerning one Willibald who set out for Rome with his father, brother and sister in *c.* AD 718. This record is anonymously written by a nun of Heidenheim.

But it is not until the 16th c. that we find plentiful narratives by Englishmen travelling abroad. For example, Anthony Jenkinson's account of a trip to Russia in 1557; and Thomas Dallam's account of a journey to Constantinople in 1599. Dallam was organist to Queen Elizabeth.

In the last half of the 16th c. a number of accounts of exploratory journeys began to appear. A random selection of these is: Martin Frobisher's *Third Voyage to the North-West* (1578); Barlowe's account of the *Discovery of Virginia* (1584); John Davis's *Voyage to the Straits of Magellan* (1591–3); Henry May's *Voyage to the East and West Indies* (1591–4); Richard Hawkins's *Voyage in the Pacific* (1594); Ralegh's account of the discovery of Guinea (1595); Fynes Moryson's trip to the Levant (1596–7); James Lancaster's *Voyage to the East Indies* (1601–3); Sylvester Jourdan's account of the discovery of the Bermudas (1609); and Habbakuk Prickett's narrative of Hudson's last voyage about the return of the *Discovery* from the northwest (1611).

From this period two great collections of travel records survive. The first is Hakluyt's *Principall Navigations, Voiages, and Discoveries of the English Nation* (1598); and the successor to this work, known as *Hakluytus Posthumus, or Purchas his Pilgrimes, contayning a History of the World in Sea Voyages and Land Travell by*

Englishmen and others (1625). Purchas made use of MSS left by Hakluyt.

Other works from the 15th to the 17th c. worthy of particular mention are: Pero Tafur's *Las andancas e viajes* (1435–9); Flavio Biondo's *Italia Instaurata* (*c.* 1500); Nicolas de Nicolay's *Quatres Premiers Livres* (1567); *The Travels of John Sanderson in the Levant* (1584–1602); *A Relation of a Journey begun An. Dom. 1610* (1615) by George Sandys; *Coryat's Crudities and Coryat's Cramb* (1611) by Thomas Coryat; *A voiag of ambasad* (1618) by John Tradescant; *The Totall Discourse of the Rare Adventures and Painefull Peregrinations, Etc.* of William Lithgow (1632); *A Voyage into the Levant* by Sir Henry Blount (1636); *A New Voyage around the World* (1697) by William Dampier, which he followed with *Voyages and Descriptions* (1698) and *A Voyage to New Holland* (1703–9); *A Journey from Aleppo to Jerusalem at Easter AD 1697* by Henry Maundrell (*c.* 1703); *A Faithful Account of the Religion and Manners of the Mahometans* (1704) by Joseph Pitts; and, perhaps the best of all 17th c. travel books, the ten volumes written by Evliya Celebi in the course of his travels through the Ottoman Empire in Europe, Asia and Africa. Evliya was born in Istanbul in 1611 and died in 1682. He is one of the great travel-writers and his works give an extraordinary amount of information on the history, geography, customs, folklore etc. of the many countries he visited.

Travel became easier in the 18th c. (hence the popularity of the Grand Tour, *q.v.*) and thus there is a steadily increasing number of works. The following are a few of the more notable instances: Aaron Hill's *Account of the Present State of the Ottoman Empire* (1709); Jean Chardin's *Voyage en Perse et aux Indes Orientales* (1711); Woodes Rogers's *A Cruizing Voyage round the World* (*c.* 1720); Montesquieu's *Lettres Persanes* (1721); Defoe's *A Tour through the Whole Island of Great Britain* (1724–6); Thomas Shaw's *Travels or Observations relating to Several Parts of Barbary and the Levant* (1738); The Earl of Sandwich's *A Voyage performed . . . round the Mediterranean in the Years 1738 and 1739* (1739); Charles Perry's *A View of the Levant* (1734); Richard Pococke's *A Description of the East* (1743–5); Robert Wood's *The Ruins of Palmyra* (1753); and the same author's *The Ruins of Balbec* (1757); Henry Fielding's *Journal of a Voyage to Lisbon* (1755); Lady Mary Wortley Montagu's *Letters . . . During Travels in Europe, Asia and Africa* (1763–7); Smollet's *Travels in France and Italy* (1766); Sterne's *Sentimental Journey through France and Italy* (1768); James Boswell's *An Account of Corsica* (1768); Bougainville's

Voyage autour du monde (1771); James Cook's accounts of his voyages, published in 1773, 1777 and 1784; Johnson's *Journey to the Western Islands of Scotland* (1775); Henry Swinburne's *Travels through Spain* (1775–6); and the same author's *Travels in the Two Sicilies* (1779–80); Boswell's *Journal of a Tour to the Hebrides* (1785); Arthur Young's *Travels in France* (1792); Mungo Park's *Travels in the Interior of Africa* (1799); plus many other works by European writers.

Early in the 19th c. Alexander von Humboldt, the great German explorer, geographer, botanist and mineralogist, began to publish the voluminous accounts of his global travels. All told they amount to the biggest body of travel literature in existence composed by a single person. Between 1808 and 1827 he published thirty-five volumes, finally gathered together under the title *Voyage aux régions équinoxiales du Nouveau Continent.* These were translated by Helen Williams in the period 1814–29. Humboldt wrote several other travel books apart from this *magnum opus.*

In the 19th and 20th c. there is a positive flood of one sort and another which shows no signs of abating. Since the Second World War, 'arm-chair' travelling has become an occupation for many people; and, as travelling has become easier and easier, so people read more books about the places they have heard of, have been to or are going to.

Here follow some of the outstanding works of the last 190-odd years: Nikolai Karamzin's *Letters of a Russian Traveller* (1801), translated into English in 1957; Abraham Parsons's *Travels in Asia and Africa* (1808); James Morier's *A Journey through Persia, Armenia and Asia Minor to Constantinople in the Years 1808–1809* (1812) and his *A Second Journey through Persia* (1818); Prince Pückler-Muskau's *Letters from a Dead Man* (1830), later published as *The Adventures of Prince Pückler-Maskau in England, Wales and Ireland*; William Cobbett's *Rural Rides* (1830); George Sand's *Lettres d'un voyageur* (1834–6); William Beckford's *Recollections of an Excursion to the Monasteries of Alcobaça and Batalha* (1835); Lamartine's *Souvenirs, Impressions, Pensées et Paysages pendant un voyage en Orient* (1835); E. W. Lane's *Account of the Manners and Customs of the Modern Egyptians* (1836); James Wellstead's *Travels in Arabia* (1838); Charles Darwin's *Voyage of the Beagle* (1839); Richard Dana's *Two Years before the Mast* (1840); George Borrow's *The Bible in Spain* (1843); Kinglake's *Eothen* (1844); Eliot Warburton's *The Crescent and the Cross* (1845); Richard Ford's *A Handbook for Travellers in Spain* (1845); Thackeray's *Cornhill to*

Grand Cairo (1846); Robert Curzon's *Visits to Monasteries in the Levant* (1849); Sir Richard Burton's *Scinde, or The Unhappy Valley* (1851); Edward Lear's *Journal of a Landscape Painter in Southern Calabria* (1852); Laurence Oliphant's *A Journey to Khatmandu* (1852) and his *The Russian Shores of the Black Sea* (1853–4); Alfred Wallace's *Travels on the Amazon and Rio Negro* (1853); Sir Richard Burton's *Personal Narrative of a Pilgrimage to El-Medinah and Meccah* (1855); C. T. Newton's *First Footsteps in East Africa* (1856); David Livingstone's *Missionary Travels in S. Africa* (1857); George Borrow's *Wild Wales* (1862); J. H. Speke's *Journal of the Discovery of the Source of the Nile* (1863); David Livingstone's *The Zambesi and its Tributaries* (1865); Lady Duff Gordon's *Letters from Egypt* (1863–5); W. G. Palgrave's *Narrative of a Journey through Central and Eastern Arabia* (1865); C. T. Newton's *Travels and Discoveries in the Levant* (1869); Alfred Wallace's *The Malay Archipelago* (1869); Sir Henry Stanley's *How I Found Livingstone* (1872); Sir Richard Burton's *Unexplored Syria* (1872); Sir Arthur Evans's *Through Bosnia and Herzegovina on Foot during the Insurrection 1875* (1876); R. L. Stevenson's *Inland Voyage* (1878); Sir Henry Stanley's *Through the Dark Continent* (1878); Sir Richard Burton's *Goldmines of Midian and Ruined Midianite Cities* (1878); and that author's *The Land of Midian Revisited* (1879); R. L. Stevenson's *Travels with a Donkey* (1879); Sir Adolphus Slade's *Travels in Turkey, Greece etc.* (1883); W. H. Hudson's *The Purple Land* (1885) and *Idle Days in Patagonia* (1893), plus, later, his *Afoot in England* (1909); C. M. Doughty's *Travels in Arabia Deserta* (1888); Nansen's *The First Crossing of Greenland* (1888); Lafcadio Hearn's *Two Years in the French West Indies* (1890), *Glimpses of Unfamiliar Japan* (1894) and *Out of the East* (1895); W. B. Harris's *A Journey through the Yemen* (1893); Pierre Loti's *Le Désert* (1895); D. G. Hogarth's *A Wandering Scholar in the Levant* (1896); Mary Kingsley's *Travels in West Africa* (1897); Hilaire Belloc's *Path to Rome* (1902); Pierre Loti's *Vers Ispahan* (1904); Edith Durham's *The Burden of the Balkans* (1905) and *High Albania* (1909); Gertrude Bell's *The Desert and the Sown* (1907); W. H. Davies's *Autobiography of a Super-Tramp* (1908); H. M. Tomlinson's *The Sea and the Jungle* (1912); Pierre Loti's *Un pélérin d'Angkor* (1912); R. F. Scott's *Scott's Last Expedition* (1913); W. H. Hudson's *Far Away and Long Ago* (1918); Norman Douglas's *Old Calabria* (1915); H. St John B. Philby's *The Heart of Arabia* (1922); Apsley Cherry Garrard's *The Worst Journey in the World* (1922); Aldous Huxley's *Jesting Pilate* (1926); H. St John B. Philby's *Arabia of the*

Wahabis (1928); Olive Murray Chapman's *Across Lapland* (1932); Bertram Thomas's *Arabia Felix* (1932); H. St John B. Philby's *The Empty Quarter* (1933); Peter Fleming's *Brazilian Adventure* (1933); Aldous Huxley's *Across the Mexique Bay* (1934); Anne Lindbergh's *North to the Orient* (1935); T. E. Lawrence's *The Seven Pillars of Wisdom* (1935); Geoffrey Gorer's *Africa Dances* (1935); Freya Stark's *The Southern Gates of Arabia* (1936); Peter Fleming's *News from Tartary* (1936); Ella Maillart's *Forbidden Journey* (1937); Robert Byron's *The Road to Oxiana* (1937); Graham Greene's *Lawless Roads* (1939); Freya Stark's *Winter in Arabia* (1940); Henry Miller's *The Colossus of Maroussi* (1941); Rebecca West's *Black Lamb and Grey Falcon* (1942); Denton Welch's *Maiden Voyage* (1943); H. St John B. Philby's *A Pilgrim in Arabia* (1946); Evelyn Waugh's *When the Going was Good* (1946) – a selection of all he wished to preserve from four previous travel books; Gerald de Gaury's *Arabia Phoenix* (1946); R. A. B. Hamilton's *The Kingdom of Melchior* (1949); André Dupeyrat's *Mitzinari* (1949); Thor Heyerdahl's *The Kon-Tiki Expedition* (1950); Laurens van der Post's *Venture into the Interior* (1952); Sir Arthur Grimble's *A Pattern of Islands* (1952); Heinrich Harrer's *Seven Years in Tibet* (1953); Peter Mayne's *The Alleys of Marrakesh* (1953); V. S. Pritchett's *The Spanish Temper* (1954); Lord Kinross's *Within the Taurus* (1954); Vincent Cronin's *The Golden Honeycomb* (1954); Alberto Denti di Pirajno's *A Cure for Serpents* (1955); Eric Newby's *The Last Grain Race* (1956); Lawrence Durrell's *Bitter Lemons* (1957); Gavin Maxwell's *A Reed Shaken by the Wind* (1957); Gerald Brenan's *South from Granada* (1957); Laurens van der Post's *The Lost World of the Kalahari* (1958); Patrick Leigh Fermor's *Mani* (1959); Thor Heyerdahl's *Aku-Aku* (1958); Eric Newby's *A Short Walk in the Hindu Kush* (1958), which he followed with *Slowly Down the Ganges* (1966) and *The Big Red Train Ride* (1978); Wilfred Thesiger's *Arabian Sands* (1959) and several others; James Morris's *Venice* (1960), plus several others; V. S. Naipaul's *An Area of Darkness* (1964), which he followed with *A Turn in the South* (1989); John Hillaby's *Journey to the Jade Sea* (1964) and *Through Britain* (1968); Sir Harry Luke's *Cyprus, a Portrait and Appreciation* (1965); Patrick Leigh Fermor's *Rumeli* (1966); Wally Herbert's *Across the Top of the World* (1969); Geoffrey Moorhouse's *Calcutta* and *The Fearful Void* (1974); Paul Theroux's *The Great Railway Bazaar* (1975) and *The Old Patagonian Express* (1979); Patrick Leigh Fermor's *A Time of Gifts* (1977), the first volume of an autobiographical account of his travels which he followed with *Between Woods and Water* (1986); Gavin Young's *Return to the Marshes* (1977), followed by *Iraq: Land of Two Rivers* (1980), *Slow Boats to China* (1981) and *Slow Boats Home* (1985); Bruce Chatwin's *In Patagonia* (1978) and *The Songlines* (1987); Jonathan Raban's *Old Glory* (1981); Colin Thubron's *Among the Russians* (1983) and *Behind the Wall* (1987), plus some on the Near East; Philip Glazebrook's *Journey to Kars* (1984); Redmond O'Hanlon's *Into the Heart of Borneo* (1984) and *In Trouble Again* (1988); Michael Asher's *Impossible Journey* (1988); Ronald Sinclair's *Adventures in Persia: To India by the Back Door* (1988), written in Sinclair's ninety-eighth year about travels made in the 1920s; Richard West's *The Diamonds and the Necklace* (1989); and William Dalrymple's *In Xanadu: A Quest* (1989).

This selection suggests the remarkable richness and variety of travel literature. There are, in addition, numerous books by explorers, navigators, mountaineers, anthropologists, archaeologists *et al.* Plus an increasing number of books on *how* to travel, as it were. These are the 'survival-kit' books for those venturing into out-of-the-way places. The classic and compendious *vade mecum* (*q.v.*), a prototype of this kind, is still Francis Galton's handbook *Art of Travel; or Shifts and Contrivances Available in Wild Countries* (1872). This includes advice for virtually every conceivable need and contingency, ranging from how to write in the dark or how to use a disused termites' nest as an oven to the 'Management of Savages', who, as Galton points out, 'are not half such fools as strangers usually account them'. *See also* GUIDEBOOK.

travesty *See* BURLESQUE.

treatise A formal work containing a systematic examination of a subject and its principles. The commonest subjects are philosophical, religious, literary, political, scientific and mathematical. Notable examples of the genre are: Aristotle's *Poetics* and *Metaphysics*, (4th c. BC); Quintilian's *Institutio* (1st c. AD); Peter Lombard's *Sententiae* (*Liber Sententiarum*) (1145–50); Calvin's *Institution de la religion chrétienne* (1535); Sir Philip Sidney's *Apologie for Poetrie* (1595); Francis Bacon's *Novum Organum* (1620); William Harvey's *Exercitatio Anatomica de Motu Cordis et Sanguinis in Animalibus* (1628); Isaac Newton's *Principia Mathematica* (1687); Locke's *Essay concerning Human Understanding* (1690); Bossuet's *Traité de la connaissance de Dieu et de soi-même* (1722); David Hume's

Treatise of Human Nature (1739–40); Montesquieu's *Esprit des lois*; Rousseau's *Du Contrat Social* (1762); Bentham's *Introduction to Principles of Morals and Legislation* (1789); Malthus's *An Essay on the Principle of Population* (1798); J. S. Mill's *System of Logic* (1843) and his *Principles of Political Economy* (1848); Darwin's *Origin of Species* (1859); A. N. Whitehead's *A Treatise of Universal Algebra* (1898) and his *The Concept of Nature* (1920); Louis Aragon's *Traité du Style* (1928). *See also* TRACT; PAMPHLET.

tremendismo A characteristic of some Spanish fiction since the late 1940s. Authors using *tremendista* techniques stress violence and terror, the violent tendencies of modern society and the damaging influences of social and religious upbringing on behaviour. Early notable examples of novels of this kind are Camilo José Cela's *La familia de Pascual Duarte* (1942) and Carmen Laforet's *Nada* (1944).

treno The Spanish term for threnody (*q.v.*).

triad (Gk 'three') In Classical Greek poetry a group of three lyric stanzas: strophe, antistrophe and epode (*qq.v.*). This arrangement was probably introduced by Stesichorus (*c.* 650–*c.* 555 BC) and was followed by Simonides and Pindar. *See* ODE.

tribe of Ben Or the sons of Ben. A title adopted by a group of English poets early in the 17th c. who were considerably influenced by Ben Jonson – and thus by Classicism (*q.v.*). Their lyrics were often epigrammatical, witty and satirical and were modelled on the lyrics of *The Greek Anthology*. The main members of the 'tribe' were Herrick, Carew, Sir John Suckling, Lovelace, Randolph and Godolphin. *See also* METAPHYSICAL; SCHOOL OF SPENSER.

tribrach (Gk 'three short') A metrical foot containing three unstressed syllables: ∪ ∪ ∪. Usually a resolved iamb or trochee (*qq.v.*) and seldom found as an independent foot.

trilogy (Gk 'set of three') A group of three tragedies presented by individual authors at the drama festivals in Athens in the 5th c. BC. The practice was introduced by Aeschylus, whose *Oresteia* is the only complete trilogy extant from that time. More recent examples are Shakespeare's *Henry VI* (*c.* 1592); Schiller's *Wallenstein* (1799); Eugene O'Neill's *Mourning Becomes Electra* (1931), which was a reworking of the Oresteian theme; and Arnold Wesker's *Chicken Soup with Barley*, *Roots* and *I'm Talking about Jerusalem* (1960). The term may also be applied to a group of three novels linked by a common theme and characters. A good modern example is Joyce Cary's *Herself Surprised*, *To be a Pilgrim* and *The Horse's Mouth* (1941–4). *See* TETRALOGY.

trimeter (Gk 'three measure') A line of verse containing three metrical feet, as in the second and fourth lines of these verses from W. S. Gilbert's *The Yarn of the 'Nancy Bell'*:

> 'Twas on the shores that round our coast
>   Frŏm Déal | tŏ Ráms|găte spán,
> That I found alone on a piece of stone
>   Ăn él|dĕrlў́ návăl mán.
>
> His hair was weedy, his beard was long,
>   Ănd wéé|dў̆ ănd lóng | wăs hé,
> And I heard this wight on the shore recite,
>   Ĭn ă sín|gŭlăr mí|nŏr kéy:

Line 2 contains three iambs; line 4 an iamb, an anapaest and an iamb; line 6 is the same as line 4; line 8 is anapaest, anapaest, iamb. *See* ANAPAEST; IAMB.

trimètre A French metrical term for the twelve-syllable alexandrine (*q.v.*) which has *three* divisions to the line. Common in the 16th c., it was later used by Molière and La Fontaine, and extensively revived by the 19th c. romantic poets.

triolet (F 'little three') A French fixed form, it has eight lines and two rhymes. The first line is repeated as the fourth, and the second and eighth are alike. The first and fourth lines are repeated in the seventh. It has been used occasionally by various poets, mostly French: Deschamps and Froissart in the late Middle Ages, La Fontaine in the 17th c., Daudet and Théodore du Banville in the 19th c. Few English poets have attempted it, but Austin Dobson, W. E. Henley and Robert Bridges all experimented quite successfully. The following piece is by Bridges:

> When first we met, we did not guess
>   That Love would prove so hard a master;
> Of more than common friendliness
> When first we met we did not guess

Who could foretell the sore distress,
  The inevitable disaster,
When first we met? We did not guess
  That Love would prove so hard a master.

An agreeable recent example is Wendy Cope's *Triolet* (in *Making Cocoa for Kingsley Amis*, 1986).

triple meter This occurs when a metrical scheme requires a three-syllable foot. It is common in anapaestic meter, and also with dactyls; though dactylic metrical schemes are fairly rare. *See* ANAPAEST; DACTYL; DUPLE RHYTHM.

triple rhyme Multiple or polysyllabic rhyme. A three-syllable rhyme, like prettily | wittily, rosily | cosily. Rare except in comic and bawdy verse. Four-syllable rhymes, like risibility | visibility, are rarer still but can be found or invented.

triple rhythm A synonym for triple meter (*q.v.*).

triplet A run of three lines in the same pattern, as a stanza, an individual poem, or, in particular, in a poem whose basic scheme is different: especially three successive rhyming lines in a poem of rhyming couplets. Dryden was fond of the occasional triplet, as in *Absalom and Achitophel*, Pt I, 150:

Of these the false Achitophel was first,
A name to all succeeding ages curst:
For close designs and crooked counsels fit,
Sagacious, bold, and turbulent of wit,
Restless, unfixed in principles and place,
In power unpleas'd, impatient of disgrace;
A fiery soul, which working out its way,
Fretted the pigmy body to decay
And o'er-informed the tenement of clay.

The interlinking *sestine* of Dante's *Divina Commedia* is the major example of triplet composition. Other notable users of it are Donne, in his verse epistles; Shelley, in *Ode to the West Wind* and *The Triumph of Life*; and William Carlos Williams in *The Desert Music*. *See* TERCET; TERZA RIMA; TERZINA.

tripody A line of three feet or three feet treated as one unit. *See* TRIMETER.

trisemic (Gk 'of three time units') The term denotes the principle whereby three syllables are equivalent to three morae. *See* MORA.

tristich (Gk 'three rows') A group of three lines of verse or a stanza of three lines, as in a triplet (*q.v.*).

tritagonist (Gk 'third contestant') The third actor in Greek tragedy, probably introduced by Sophocles. *See* ANTAGONIST; PROTAGONIST; TRAGEDY.

triversen stanza A stanza with three lines which comprise a complete sentence. The sentence is broken into three parts, each part being one line. This form was developed by William Carlos Williams (1883–1963).

trivium *See* QUADRIVIUM.

trobar (Pr) The profession, act or art of composing poetry. The word appears to derive from the Latin *tropare* 'to make tropes'. *See* TROBAR CLUS; TROPE.

trobar clus (Pr) An esoteric form of 12th c. Provençal poetry marked by complex language, enigmatic treatment and ingenious rhyming. In many cases technical virtuosity seems to have been more important than having anything to say. This style was opposed to *trobar clar*, or 'open' writing. *See* TROBAR.

trochee (Gk 'running') A metrical foot containing a stressed, followed by an unstressed, syllable: / ◡. The reverse of an iamb (*q.v.*) and thus producing a falling rhythm (*q.v.*) as opposed to a rising rhythm (*q.v.*). In Classical verse trochaics were used from the time of Archilochus onwards, especially in lyric and drama. The commonest form was the trochaic tetrameter (*q.v.*) catalectic – known as the *septenarius* by the Romans. Not much used in English verse before the 16th c., the trochee (also known sometimes as a *choree*) was used increasingly thereafter in blank verse to provide variations in the iambic line. Many subtle examples of this substitution (*q.v.*) can be found, for instance, in Milton's *L'Allegro* and *Il Penseroso*. It is rare to find English verse composed exclusively of trochaics. When employed as the basic foot, as in Longfellow's *Hiawatha*, the effect can become monotonous. In these two lines from Robert Lowell's *The Holy Innocents* the first words are trochaic:

Lístĕn, | thĕ háy-bélls | tínklĕ | ăs thĕ cárt
Wávĕrs | ŏn rúb|bĕr týres | ălóng | thĕ tár

Troilus stanza *See* RHYME ROYAL.

trope (Gk 'turn') In general it still denotes any rhetorical or figurative device, but a special development in its use occurred during the Middle Ages when it came to be applied to a verbal amplification of the liturgical text. An early example was the elaboration of the *Kyrie eleison*:

Kyrie,
magnae Deus potentiae,
liberator hominis,
transgressoris mandati,
eleison.

However, the most famous instance of such an interpolation was the *Quem quaeritis* (*q.v.*) trope preceding the *Introit* on Easter Sunday. This developed into a dramatized form and became detached from the sacred Liturgy. *See* LITURGICAL DRAMA; MYSTERY PLAY.

tropism A term popularized by the French novelist Nathalie Sarraute (1902–) which refers to mental and imaginative life as perceived by her. Thus perceived, it comprises millions of tiny little responses to innumerable stimuli. In her experimental fictional narratives, such as *Tropismes* (1939) – regarded as one of the prototypes of the *nouveau roman* (*q.v.*) – she attempts to translate her vision of reality with a highly unconventional use of language to give the impression of a different kind of reality. *See also* STREAM OF CONSCIOUSNESS.

troubadour (Pr 'finder, inventor') The troubadours were poets who flourished in the south of France between *c.* 1100 and 1350. They were attached to various courts and were responsible for the phenomenon known as courtly love (*q.v.*). Most of their lyrics were amorous; some satirical and political. They cultivated five main genres: the *canso d'amor* (*see* CHANSON); the *pastorela* (*see* PASTOURELLE); the *alba* (*see* AUBADE); the *tenso*, *partimen* or *jeu parti* (*q.v.*); and the *sirventes* (*q.v.*). Some troubadours were known by name: Guillaume d'Aquitaine, Arnaut Daniel and Bertrand de Born. The troubadours (who composed in *langue d'oc*) had a very considerable influence on Dante and Petrarch, and indeed on the whole development of the lyric (*q.v.*), especially the love lyric, in Europe. *See* MINNESINGER; PAYADA; TROUVERE.

trouvère (OF 'finder, inventor') A medieval poet of northern France, especially Picardy. The *trouvères*, who were contemporary with the southern troubadour poets, wrote lyrics on similar topics in *langue d'oïl*. They also composed *chansons de gestes* (*q.v.*) and *romans bretons* (*q.v.*). As with the troubadours, some were known by name: for instance, Jean Bodel, Blondel de Nesle, Conon de Béthune. *See* MINNESINGER; PAYADA; TROUBADOUR.

truncation *See* CATALEXIS.

Tudor period The period of 1485–1603 during which the Tudor family ruled England. Among the hundreds of writers who flourished during this time of almost unparalleled creative activity in literature, the following are some of the most famous: John Lydgate, William Caxton, John Skelton, William Dunbar, Alexander Barclay, William Tyndale, Sir Thomas More, Sir David Lindsay, John Bale, John Heywood, Sir Thomas Elyot, Sir Thomas Wyatt, Nicholas Udall, Roger Ascham, the Earl of Surrey, George Puttenham, Thomas Sackville, George Gascoigne, Thomas Deloney, Sir Philip Sidney, Richard Hakluyt, Edmund Spenser, Sir Walter Ralegh, John Florio, John Lyly, Richard Hooker, Robert Greene, Thomas Kyd, George Peele, Thomas Lodge, George Chapman, Sir Francis Bacon, Robert Southwell, Samuel Daniel, Michael Drayton, Christopher Marlowe, William Shakespeare, Thomas Campion, Thomas Nashe, Henry Chettle, Barnabe Barnes, Thomas Dekker, Thomas Middleton, Ben Jonson, John Donne, Thomas Heywood, John Marston, Robert Burton, Cyril Tourneur, John Fletcher, John Webster.

tumbling verse A term apparently first used by James VI of Scotland in *Reulis and Cautelis* (1585) to describe a four-foot line of trisyllabic feet (dactyls and anapaests); a line form which developed from the alliterative verse (*q.v.*) of the Middle Ages. Skelton, among others, experimented with this. The following stanza comes from *Speak, Parrot* (1521):

> My name is Parrot, a bird of Paradise,
> By nature devisèd of a wonderous kind,

Daintily dieted with divers delicate spice
  Till Euphrates, that flood, driveth me into Ind;
  Where men of that countrý by fortune me find
And send me to greatë ladyés estate:
Then Parrot must have an almond or a date.

Most of the feet are dactylic or anapaestic.

However, the term is also applied to another kind of verse at which Skelton again was particularly adept. It consists of short lines of two or three stresses which move at a brisk, almost helter-skelter (one might say helter-Skelton) pace, as in his *Colin Clout* (1519–20). *See* DOGGEREL; SKELTONICS.

turning point The observable moment when, in a story or a play (or indeed in many kinds of narrative), there is a definite change in direction and one becomes aware that it is now about to move towards its end. This is a change of fortune; what Aristotle described as *peripeteia* (*q.v.*), or reversal. It is the equivalent of reaching a peak and beginning the descent beyond. In tragedy (*q.v.*), especially, one is conscious of this crucial or fulcral point. Thomas Hardy, for example, underlines the moment in *The Mayor of Casterbridge*:

> Small as the police-court incident had been in itself, it formed the edge or turn in the incline of Henchard's fortunes. On that day – almost at that minute – he passed the ridge of prosperity and honour, and began to descend rapidly on the other side.

In the same way, Chaucer, when he begins Book IV of *Troilus and Criseyde*, makes it clear that the wheel of fortune is about to turn:

From Troilus she [Fortune] gan hire brighte face
Awey to writhe, and tok of hym non heede,
But caste hym clene out of his lady grace,
And on hire whiel she sette up Diomede;
For which right now myn herte gynneth blede,
And now my penne, allas! with which I write,
Quaketh for drede of that I moste endite.

See CLIMAX; FREYTAG'S PYRAMID.

typological *See* ALLEGORY; CONCEIT.

tz'u A Chinese poetic form created during the T'ang period. It was a kind of song libretto with a tonal pattern similar to that found in the *lu-shih* (*q.v.*), and its meters were irregular.

U

ubi sunt (L 'where are they?') The opening words of a number of MedL poems, they are now used to classify a particular kind of poem that dwells on and laments the transitory nature of life and beauty. Sometimes the words open a poem, or begin each stanza, or serve as a refrain (*q.v.*). The elegiac mood to which they are a keynote is present in some early OE poems like *The Seafarer* and *The Wanderer*, and in ME lyrics like the 13th c. *Ubi Sount Qui Ante Nos Fuerount* which begins:

> Uuere be þey beforen us weren,
> Houndes ladden and hauekes beren
> And hadden feld and wode?
> Þe riche leuedies in hoere bour,
> Þat wereden gold in hoere tressour
> Wiþ hoere briȝtte rode . . .

A number of French poets made considerable use of the motif. In the 14th c. Deschamps composed several *ballades* on the theme. In the 15th c. Chastellain used it in a long poem called *Le Pas de la Mort*, and in the same period Olivier de la Marche worked it through the allegorical *Parement et Triumphes des Dames.* Probably the best known of all is Villon's *Ballade des Dames du Temps Jadis* (also of the 15th c.) with its famous refrain 'Mais où sont les neiges d'antan?'. The motif recurs regularly in Tudor and Elizabethan lyric poetry, and nowhere more eloquently than in Thomas Nashe's magnificent *In Time of Pestilence* whose third stanza runs:

> Beauty is but a flower
> Which wrinkles will devour:
> Brightness falls from the air,
> Queens have died young and fair,
> Dust hath closed Helen's eye.

Followed by the knell-like refrain:

> I am sick, I must die.
> Lord have mercy on us!

The motif is present in many elegies, but today one is unlikely to find it except in a fixed form; as in, for example, Edmund Gosse's *Ballade of Dead Cities*. *See also* CARPE DIEM; CORONACH; DANSE MACABRE; DIRGE; ELEGY; EPICEDIUM; LAMENT; THRENODY.

Ultra Grupo A group of seven Spanish poets who began the *ultraismo* movement in 1919 and published a manifesto the following year. The name was invented by Guillermo de Torre, one of the poets. The others were Xavier Bóveda, César A. Comet, Pedro Garfías, Fernando Iglesias Caballero, J. Rivas Panedas and J. de Aroca. Like many such movements of that period it aimed at a complete break with the past and traditionalism, and advocated the creation of the 'pure' poem without formal or narrative structure and without any eroticism.

ultraism A radical attitude whose quest and objective in literature (and art) is for a kind of *reductio ad absurdum*, or for an expression of experience which seeks to go beyond the limitations of the medium. Hence phenomena like 'happenings', the use of different coloured pages in a novel to suggest tone and mood, gimmick books in which the pages can be re-arranged as the reader wishes. In this century there have been many experiments in ultraistic modes. If we accept that language is 'public' but that 'private' languages are also possible, then Joyce, in *Finnegans Wake*, was pushing language near the limits of comprehensibility in the 'public' sense. Orwell was clearly experimenting 'ultraistically' in *Nineteen Eighty-Four*. Likewise Anthony Burgess with *nadsat* in *A Clockwork Orange*; and B. S. Johnson in several of his novels. Ultraism is particularly noticeable in the Theatre of the Absurd (*q.v.*). *See also* DADAISM; EXPRESSIONISM; NADSAT; SURREALISM.

unanimisme A French poetic movement developed *c.* 1908–11 by Jules Romains. It was probably inspired by Whitman's concepts of universal brotherhood and had a kind of didactic and reforming purpose and spirit: to reveal the soul of the group and the collective society. Hence the idea of unanimity. There were several poets involved, principally Georges Duhamel (1884–1966), Luc Durtain,

Charles Vildrac, René Arcos and Georges Chennevière. They favoured what was called 'poésie immédiate', a poetry shorn of anything symbolic or allegorical, without assonance (*q.v.*) or end-rhyme (*q.v.*) and possessing distinctive accentual rhythms. The main statements of intention and practice were *Notes sur la technique poétique* (1910) and *Petit traité de versification* (1923). Jules Romains explained his ideas in *Les Hommes de bonne volonté* (1932–47).

unconscious, the A region or state of mind assumed to exist without any evidence other than that adduced by conscious action. Alternatively, by assumption, the sum of the dynamic elements which constitute a personality (the individual may be aware of some of these and unaware of others). Or, again by assumption, a mental process wholly different from a conscious process but at the same time one which influences and modifies the conscious processes; also known as endopsychic processes.

The term 'unconscious', like subconscious and, to a much lesser extent, pre-conscious, co-conscious and extra-conscious, has become a part of literary critical jargon; for example, in the phrase 'creative unconscious', which Koestler says works by a 'bisociation of matrices'.

underground literature/poetry The adjective 'underground' suggests something illegal, subversive and clandestine. This is all true of *samizdat* (*q.v.*) literature but does not accurately describe the work of a number of British writers active from the late 1950s to the 1970s to which the term 'underground' has been applied. Some of the writers so classified are Alexander Trocchi (1925–84), Adrian Mitchell (1932–), Jeff Nuttall (1933–), Heathcote Williams (1941–) and Tom Pickard (1946–). Plus the Liverpool Poets (*q.v.*), whose works have for many years been esteemed in the most conservative classrooms. There was a time when the writings of the Beat generation (*q.v.*) might easily have been described as 'underground'. They have long since been 'mainstream'.

The so-called underground poets were predominantly anti-war, anti-establishment, non-traditional and experimental, and quite often wrote a kind of poetry of protest which was clearly influenced by traditional folksong. The poets tended to reach their audiences through public readings and they published their work in little magazines (*q.v.*). This was deliberate policy; they declined to go through the standard publishing channels. A notable one was *New*

Departures, founded in 1959 and edited by Michael Horowitz. He also published an anthology of their work titled *Children of Albion: Poetry of the 'Underground' in Britain* (1969). *See also* JAZZ POETRY; SUB-CULTURE.

understatement *See* LITOTES.

Union of Soviet Writers Formed in April 1932 by order of the Central Committee of the Communist Party. By decree all existing literary organizations were abolished, and a new uniform, literary policy was established. Socialist realism (*q.v.*) was to be the dogma. Those who did not conform were to be expelled from the union. If you were expelled you could not function as a writer. If you toed the Party line then you could expect good working conditions, a high salary, rewards and respect. *See also* IDEYNOST; NAROD-NOST; PARTYNOST.

unities Aristotle was the first to consider the problem of the dramatic unities of action, time and space, but he did not invent them. In *Poetics* (writing of action) he says: 'The fable should be the imitation of one action, and of the whole of this and the parts of the transactions should be so arranged, that any one of them being transposed, or taken away, the whole would become different and changed'. Of time he writes: 'Tragedy endeavours to confine itself to one revolution of the sun, or but slightly to exceed this limit'. On space he is less explicit, merely saying (when contrasting epic and tragedy, *qq.v.*) that tragedy should be confined to a narrow compass.

In the 16th and 17th c. Neoclassic critics of the drama in Italy and France required adherence to the unities. In all probability it was Jean Mairet (1604–86) who established the doctrine of unities (though Ronsard and Jean de la Taille had made earlier statements) which French dramatists were to follow (almost unquestioningly) for two hundred years. Mairet's play *Sophonisbe* (1634) was the first French play to conform strictly to the unity rules.

The supporters of the Classical precepts required that a play should be a unified whole, that the time of action should be limited to twenty-four hours (though some allowed thirty-six) and that the scene should be unchanged (or at any rate confined to one town or city).

These rules were largely ignorerd by English and Spanish dramatists – probably to the lasting gain of drama – though, oddly, the French called them *les unités scaligeriennes* after Julius Caesar Scaliger, the eminent classical scholar, who had referred to them in *Poetices Libri Septem* (1561) when speaking of verisimilitude (*q.v.*). *See* CONVENTION; UNITY.

unity The concept of artistic unity was first worked out by Plato in *Phaedrus*. A work which possesses the quality of unity has an internal logic of structure wherein each part is interdependent. The work coheres, is self-contained and is free of any element (digression, ornament or episode) which might distract attention from its main purpose. The concept of perfect unity presupposes a work from which nothing can be taken away without marring it, and to which nothing can be added without introducing a blemish. *See also* PLATONISM; UNITIES.

Unity Theatre An amateur membership theatre group of great enterprise founded in 1935–6 as a result of a merger of Red Radio and the Rebel Players. It was a left-wing company, part of the Labour movement, and based in London. The policy was to present socialist and Communist plays and the group pioneered the Living Newspaper (*q.v.*) in England. Its first production was a version of Clifford Odets's *Waiting for Lefty* (1935). In 1937 the group took over and converted a missionary hall at St Pancras, London, where, in 1938, they presented Brecht's *Senora Carrar's Rifles* – the first Brecht play to be produced in Britain. In the war members of Unity gave entertainments to people sheltering from the blitz in London tube stations. During and after the war numerous regional branches were established. Notable productions were: *Black Magic* (1947), *Matchgirls* (1947), *Cyanamide* (1957), British premières of plays by Brecht and Sartre, and Adamov's *Spring '71*. In 1975 Unity became defunct when its theatre was burnt down. *See* AGITPROP DRAMA; COMMITMENT; PROPAGANDA.

universality That quality in a work of art which enables it to transcend the limits of the particular situation, place, time, person and incident in such a way that it may be of interest, pleasure and profit (in the non-commercial sense) to all men at any time in any place. As it was expressed in the treatise *On the Sublime* – 'lofty and true greatness in art pleases all men in all ages'. The writer who aspires to universality therefore concerns himself with, primarily, aspects of human nature and behaviour which seldom or never change. Thus the good satirist concentrates on the major diseases of the mind and spirit – like pride and avarice, envy, hypocrisy and lust for power. This explains why the satires of Aristophanes, Juvenal, Erasmus, Ben Jonson, Molière, Dryden, Swift, Voltaire, Pope and Samuel (*Erewhon*) Butler are so successful. *See also* QUOD SEMPER QUOD UBIQUE; TASTE.

university wits A name given to a group of writers who flourished in London in the last twenty years or so of the 16th c. The most notable members (all Oxford or Cambridge men) were: Marlowe, Nashe, Greene, Lyly, Lodge and Peele. They are reputed to have used the Mermaid Tavern in Bread Street off Cheapside. Shakespeare was not a university man and in his romantic comedy *Love's Labour's Lost* (*c.* 1595) there is a certain amount of mirth and wit at the expense of the university wits.

untranslatableness A word used by Coleridge in a fairly famous passage in *Biographia Literaria* (Chap. XXII): 'In poetry, in which every line, every phrase, may pass the ordeal of deliberation and deliberate choice, it is possible, and barely possible, to attain that *ultimatum* which I have ventured to propose as the infallible test of a blameless style; namely; its *untranslatableness* in words of the same language without injury to the meaning.'

urbanitas *See* ASTEISMUS.

usage The generally accepted mode of expression in words, as established by custom, tradition and practice. Words, idioms, colloquialisms, syntax, grammar in common everyday use. Two classic works on the subject are H. W. & F. G. Fowler's *The King's English* (1906) and H. W. Fowler's *A Dictionary of Modern English Usage* (1926). *See* KING'S ENGLISH.

utopia Sir Thomas More was the first to apply this word (from Gk *ou* 'not' + *topos* 'place') to a literary genre when he named his imaginary republic *Utopia* (1516), a pun on *eutopia* 'place (where all is) well'.

The idea of a place where all is well is of great antiquity. In the Sumerian epic of *Gilgamesh*, for example, of the second millennium BC, we find a description of a kind of earthly paradise: 'The croak of the raven was not heard, the bird of death did not utter the cry of death, the lion did not devour, the wolf did not tear the lamb, the dove did not mourn, there was no widow, no sickness, no old age, no lamentation'. Homer described the Elysian Fields in the *Odyssey*. So, later, did Lucian in a slightly more comic fashion. There were various versions of the Greek myth of the Isles of the Blessed, which Hesiod described (also Pindar and Horace). Christianity reinforced the notion of an attainable paradise which, in St Augustine's terms, was the heavenly city (as opposed to the earthly city) and for the next thousand years at least, in both 'official' and popular literature, the kingdom of heaven was a more than possible objective. The Church exhorted the faithful to lead holy lives in order to go there. The popular conception was fed on visions of paradise and accounts of journeys there, just as it was nourished on extremely dissuasive accounts of hell and purgatory. Many of the paradises are reminiscent of garden cities and the descriptions are materialistic in tone.

It is probably no coincidence that as traditional religious beliefs were modified, so the number of earthly utopian schemes proliferated. Since More's *Utopia*, which (if we except Ramon Llull's utopia in *Blanquerna*, c. 1285) can probably be taken as the first of modern times, there have been at least a hundred similar ideas. Some are mere pipe-dreams, little more than Butlin castles in Spain; others are carefully thought-out working models.

Long before More, however, the very first ideal commonwealth was devised by Plato. In his *Republic* (4th c. BC), Plato depicted a state in which rulers are philosophers, goods and women are communally owned, slavery is taken for granted, and the breeding of children is controlled on eugenic lines. There was to be no art or drama and next to no poetry. It was a Spartan utopia; indeed, the prototype of the totalitarian state.

More's welfare state was also communistic. No private property, free universal education, six hours' manual work a day, utility clothes, free medical treatment, meals in civic restaurants (meals accompanied by reading or music). All religions were to be tolerated, but the penal code, especially in sexual matters, was harsh; adultery led to slavery; repeated offences to death.

The next utopian plan of note was the *Christianopolis* (1619) of Andreae and this was not dissimilar to More's conception. A remarkable feature was the town-planning scheme which provided houses with bathrooms. Campanella's *La Città del Sole* (1623) has many features of Plato's and More's régimes, but the ruler is an executive – O or Metaphysic – assisted by three subordinates named Love, Power and Knowledge. In 1626 Francis Bacon published his *New Atlantis*, which is akin to a treatise on political philosophy in the form of a fable and is particularly noteworthy because it contains the 'blueprint' for the Royal Society and mentions inventions which suggest the future development of aeroplanes, submarines and telephones. In Samuel Gott's *New Jerusalem* (1648) there is great emphasis on ideal education, and in Gerrard Winstanley's *The Law of Freedom in a Platform* (1649) there are detailed plans for communal property and free education. Winstanley and others were leaders of a 17th c. group of Levellers (called 'Diggers') who were in favour of applying communistic principles to land ownership. From this period also dates Hobbes's *Leviathan* (1651) and Harrington's *Oceana* (1656). Hobbes's work is a treatise on political philosophy; *Oceana* a counter and a contrast to it, a kind of political romance (*q.v.*).

From this time on many contributions to utopian literature were made (not a few of them frivolous and extravagant) but there is nothing of great importance or merit until the 19th c. when there was not only a spate of literary utopias, but an increasing number of experiments in putting utopian schemes into actual practice.

The influence of the French and Industrial Revolutions suggested again that some form of earthly paradise was attainable. For example, Southey and Coleridge were stimulated by the concept of Pantisocracy (a utopia in which all rule and all are equal).

The most original utopias were created towards the end of the century: Bulwer Lytton's *The Coming Race* (1871); Edward Bellamy's *Looking Backward* (1888); William Morris's *A Dream of John Bull* (1888) and his utopian romance *News from Nowhere* (1890); Theodor Hertzka's *Freeland, a Social Anticipation* (1891). But the major contribution was H. G. Wells's *A Modern Utopia* (1905). Wells was the first to conceive utopia as a world state: international government; central bureaucracy; state-controlled land, capital and industry; and population control. This global utopia was ruled by a voluntary 'nobility' called Samurai – the equivalent of Plato's guardian Philosophers. Wells, a compulsive utopist, followed this up with *Men Like Gods* (1925), a further plan for harmonious living. In 1962 Aldous Huxley published *Island*, a genuinely constructive utopia which has been misunderstood.

The seeming impossibility of utopia (and the many failures to create it) has produced its converse: dystopia or anti-utopia; in some cases almost chiliastic forecasts of the doom awaiting mankind. They range from the whimsical fantasy of Joseph Hall's *Mundus Alter et Idem* (1600), very probably the first of its kind, to the unrelievedly depressing vision of Orwell's *Nineteen Eighty-*

Four (1949). In between come Zamyatin's *My* (1920), a Wellsian fantasy set in the 26th c., Aldous Huxley's *Brave New World* (1932), the wittiest and most urbane of all anti-utopian worlds, and *Ape and Essence* (1949). Political dystopia is also well represented by Orwell's *Animal Farm* (1945) and David Karp's *One* (1953).

In some instances utopian worlds are almost indistinguishable from those in SF, desert island fiction (*qq.v.*) and tall traveller's tales of the kind that Pliny, Lucian and Sir John Mandeville delighted in (and sometimes combine elements of all three). Some works which owe a good deal to the classic examples of utopia are: Francis Godwin's *The Man in the Moone* (1638); Gabriel de Foigny's *La Terre Australe Connue* (1676); Samuel Butler's *Erewhon* (1872); H. G. Wells's *When the Sleeper Wakes* (1899), *The Time Machine* (1895) and *The First Men in the Moon* (1901); E. M. Forster's *The Machine Stops* (1947); Mary McCarthy's *A Source of Embarrassment* (1950); Evelyn Waugh's *Love among the Ruins* (1953); William Golding's *Lord of the Flies* (1954); and John Wyndham's *From Pillar to Post* (1956). Since the 1950s new visions of dystopia have flourished in the cinema and in somewhat apocalyptic fiction, often of considerable and disturbing power. Examples in fiction are: Kurt Vonnegut's *Player Piano* (1952), F. Pohl and C. M. Kornbluth's *The Space Merchants* (1953), Anthony Burgess's *A Clockwork Orange* (1962), William Burrough's *Nova Express* (1964) and J. G. Ballard's *The Terminal Beach* (1964) and *The Disaster Area* (1967). *See also* APOCALYPTIC LITERATURE.

ut pictura poesis (L 'as is painting so is poetry') A phrase invented by Horace (*Ars Poetica* 361), though the idea was not new, suggesting that painting and poetry are comparable or similar arts. The idea provoked some discussion during the 16th, 17th and 18th c. Shaftesbury may well have been right when, in *Plastics* (1712), he remarked that comparisons 'between painting and poetry are almost ever absurd and at best constrained, lame and defective'. As an aesthetic theory (it was probably little more than a casually tentative *obiter dictum* by Horace – like Aristotle's remarks on the dramatic unities, *q.v.*) it is not often held now. *See* CORRESPONDENCE OF THE ARTS.

V

vade mecum (L 'go with me') A manual (*q.v.*) or handbook carried for frequent and regular reference. For example, *The Fisherman's Vade Mecum* (1942) by G. W. Maunsell. Field guides for birds, trees, mammals, insects etc. are also vade mecums. *See also* GUIDEBOOK.

variable syllable One which may be stressed or unstressed according to the needs of the metrical pattern. Also known as 'distributed stress' and 'hovering accent'. Take these lines from the beginning of Pope's *Second Epistle: Of the Characters of Women*:

> Nothing so true as what you once let fall,
> Most Women have no Characters at all.
> Matter too soft a lasting mark to bear,
> And best distinguish'd by black, brown or fair.

The first line is regularly iambic, except for the substituted trochaic foot at the beginning ('nothing' is trochaic) and scans thus:

> Nóthĭng | sŏ trué | ăs whát | yŏu ónce | lĕt fáll,

The second line, however, might be scanned in three different ways, according to where the emphases are placed in order to get a particular sense:

> Móst Wó|mĕn hăve nŏ | Chárăctĕrs | ăt áll.

That is: spondee/tribrach (which is rare)/dactyl/iamb. Or:

> Mŏst Wó|mĕn hăve nó | Chárăctĕrs | ăt áll.

That is: iamb/anapaest/dactyl/iamb. Or:

> Móst wó|mĕn háve nó | Chárăcters | ăt áll.

That is: spondee/bacchius (which is rare)/dactyl/iamb.

The third line is exactly the same as the first, with a substituted trochaic 'matter'. The fourth has a variable syllable in 'distinguish'd'. The line may be scanned either:

Ănd bést | dĭstíngúish'd | bў blácк, | brówn ŏr fáir.

That is: iamb/bacchius/iamb/cretic (or amphimacer). Or:

Ănd bést | dĭstíngŭish'd | bў bláck, | brówn ŏr fáir.

In this version 'distinguish'd is an amphibrach.

It should be noted that each of the above lines has ten syllables and that in each the basic stress pattern tends to comprise five stresses per line – as one would expect in iambic pentameters. But Pope had such a sensitive ear for the delicate nuances of words that he often eludes scansion, and technical exegesis of the kind displayed here verges on impertinence. *See* DURATION; FOOT; HOVERING STRESS; SUBSTITUTION.

variorum (Short for, 'an edition with the notes of various persons' from L *editio cum notis variorum*) A *variorum* contains the complete works of an author accompanied by the notes of previous commentators and editors; and, in all probability, indications of the textual changes made during successive printings. An outstanding recent example is the *Twickenham Edition* of Pope's works.

vates (L 'poet, bard') Especially one of the theopneustic or prophetic kind. Hence *vatic* means characteristic of a prophet or seer. A class of Gaulish druids were known as *vates.* Perhaps the most famous of classical times was the Sibyl. Virgil has been credited with vatic powers because, in the *Fourth Eclogue*, he prophesied the birth of a boy under whose rule the world would be peaceful. This was later interpreted as a prophecy of the birth of Christ.

vaudeville (Shortened alteration of OF *chanson du vau de Vire* 'song of the vale of Vire') In all probability the term derives from the fact that, in the 15th c., Olivier Basselin, who lived in the valley of the river Vire in Calvados, Normandy, wrote satirical songs. Such songs were later incorporated in comedies; thus, comedy with vaudevilles. Later, it was adopted in America to describe comic, musical and acrobatic turns in the theatre; the equivalent of the British music hall. The period of its greatest popularity coincided with that of the music hall (*c.* 1890–1930). Thereafter vaudeville could not compete with the cinema. The term is still used in France and England to describe light, theatrical entertainment of a knockabout kind, with musical interludes. *See also* ZARZUELA.

vehicle *See* TENOR AND VEHICLE.

venedotian code An extremely complex code dating from the 15th c. which lays down the rules of Welsh versification and classifies twenty-four different measures.

Venus and Adonis stanza So named because Shakespeare used it for *Venus and Adonis* (1593). A six-lined stanza rhyming ababcc. But a number of poets had used it earlier, e.g. Sidney in *Arcadia* (1590). However, it has a 'curiosity' interest because Shakespeare used it in *Love's Labour's Lost* (*c.* 1595) and *Romeo and Juliet* (*c.* 1595) where its effect is to produce dramatic stylization of an almost operatic kind.

verbocrap A type of jargon (*q.v.*) language commonly used by verbocrats, and thus dear to bureaucrats and semi-literate officials of all kinds. It is marked by polysyllabic circumlocutions, crude syntax, faulty grammar and a self-important, orotund tone; what A. P. Herbert called 'Jungle English' or 'Dolichologia'. An example (from an ILEA educational publication) is:

> Due to increased verbalization the educationist desires to earnestly see school populations achieve cognitive clarity, auracy, literacy and numeracy both within and without the learning situation. However, the classroom situation (and the locus of evaluation *is* the classroom) is fraught with so many innovative concepts (e.g. the problem of locked confrontation between pupil and teacher) that the teaching situation is, in the main, inhibitive to any meaningful articulacy. It must now be fully realized that the secondary educational scene has embraced the concept that literacy has to be imparted and acquired via humanoid-to-humanoid dialogue. This is a break-through.

One may well ask – from what and to what. *See also* OFFICIALESE; PERIPHRASIS.

Verfremdung *See* ALIENATION EFFECT.

verisimilitude Likeness to the truth, and therefore the appearance of being true or real even when fantastic. But then fantasy is, or should be, rooted in reality. What might be called the inherent authenticity of a work (as well as its intrinsic probability), having made allowances for premisses, conventions and codes, will be the criterion by which its 'truth' can be assessed. If the writer has done his work well, then the reader will find the result an acceptable presentation of reality. Thus, works which may strain ordinary credulity (e.g. Rabelais's *Gargantua* and *Pantagruel*, Swift's *Gulliver's Travels*, Voltaire's *Candide*, Wells's *The First Men in the Moon*) will be as credible as those which purport to be mundanely realistic (e.g. most of the novels of writers like Jane Austen, Zola, Thomas Hardy, Henry James and Arnold Bennett). In the end, verisimilitude will depend as much on the reader's knowledge, intelligence and experience (and his capacity for make-believe) as upon the writer's use of those same resources. *See* BIENSEANCES; MIMESIS; VRAISEMBLANCE.

verism The doctrine that literature or art should represent the truth (reality), however disagreeable that truth might be. A verist believes this. *See* REALISM; VERISMO.

verismo A literary movement in Italy which occurred late in the 19th c. and early in the 20th c. In part it derived from the movement of naturalism (*q.v.*) in France. Theories of naturalism had been discussed by Francesco De Sanctis (1817–83) in his two works *La scienza e la vita* (1872) and *Studio sopra Emilio Zola* (1878), but the chief theorist in the *verismo* movement was Luigi Capuana (1839–1915). The main emphasis was on 'truthfulness', truth at any price, so to speak. This in effect meant a great deal of stress on the more squalid aspects of life: poverty, despair and violence, among other things. The main novelists involved were Giovanni Verga (1840–1922), De Roberto (1866–1927) and Capuana himself. The term *verismo* was also applied to the rather violent and melodramatic operas composed by Puccini and Mascagni *c.* 1900.

vernacular (L *vernaculus* 'domestic, native, indigenous') Domestic or native language. Now applied to the language used in one's native country. It may also be used to distinguish between a 'literary' language and a dialect; for instance, William Barnes's 'vernacular poems', an outstanding example of dialect (*q.v.*) poetry.

vers A kind of song in Old Provençal. Almost indistinguishable from the *chanson* (*q.v.*), but *vers* is the older term.

vers de société Literally 'society verse', a sub-species of light verse (*q.v.*). It is usually epigrammatic or lyrical verse dealing with the superficial problems and events of a sophisticated and polite society. It is often satirical and characterized by technical virtuosity, wit, elegance and a conversational tone. Often intricate forms like *triolet*, *villanelle* and *rondeau* (*qq.v.*) are used. The ballads, the limerick and the clerihew (*qq.v.*) are also favourite forms. A great many English poets have produced such verse; outstanding among them are Alexander Pope, Matthew Prior, Winthrop Mackworth Praed, Theodore Hook, C. S. Calverley, W. E. Henley, Andrew Lang, Austin Dobson, W. S. Gilbert, Hilaire Belloc, G. K. Chesterton, A. P. Herbert, John Betjeman and W. H. Auden. Less notable contributions have been made by George Wither, the Cavalier Poets (*q.v.*), John Wilmot Earl of Rochester, and Thomas Gray. Among Americans the better known are Ogden Nash, Morris Bishop, Phyllis McGinley and Richard Armour. Many French poets have essayed *vers de société*, including Léon-Paul Fargue, Jules Laforgue, Tristan Corbière and Théophile Gautier.

Betjeman's *In Westminster Abbey* is a good modern example of the genre. The first verses run:

Let me take this other glove off
  As the *vox humana* swells
And the beauteous fields of Eden
  Bask beneath the Abbey bells.
Here, where England's statesmen lie,
Listen to a lady's cry.

Gracious Lord, oh bomb the Germans.
  Spare their women for Thy Sake,
And if that is not too easy
  We will pardon Thy Mistake.
But gracious Lord, whate'er shall be,
Don't let anyone bomb me.

Keep our Empire undismembered
  Guide our Forces by Thy Hand,
Gallant blacks from far Jamaica,
  Honduras and Togoland;
Protect them Lord in all their fights,
And, even more, protect the whites.

Think of what our Nation stands for,
  Books from Boots' and country lanes,
Free speech, free passes, class distinction,
  Democracy and proper drains.
Lord, put beneath Thy special care
One-eighty-nine Cadogan Square.

A more recent witty example is Philip Larkin's *Vers de Société* (in *High Windows*, 1974).

verse Three main meanings may be distinguished: (a) a line of metrical writing; (b) a stanza (*q.v.*); (c) poetry in general.

verse paragraph A group of lines (often in blank verse) which forms a unit. Common in long narrative poems, like Milton's *Paradise Lost* and Wordsworth's *Prelude*. In fact, Milton developed the verse paragraph so skilfully that it is unlikely that anyone will ever surpass him. *See* LAISSE; VERSET.

verset A form derived from the kind of verse formations to be found in the Old Testament (e.g. *The Song of Songs*). Usually several long lines forming a group or 'paragraph', the whole characterized by a strong rhythm and many figurative and rhetorical devices. A number of European poets have explored the possibilities of this flexible form. Notable instances are Hölderlin, Péguy, Rimbaud and Claudel. Among English poets: Ezra Pound, T. S. Eliot and D. H. Lawrence. The following lines from Lawrence's *Kangaroo* give some idea of the verset:

Still she watches with eternal, cocked wistfulness!
How full her eyes are, like the full, fathomless, shining eyes of an Australian black-boy
Who has been lost so many centuries on the margins of existence!

She watches with insatiable wistfulness.
Untold centuries of watching for something to come,
For a new signal from life, in that silent lost land of the South.

Where nothing bites but insects and snakes and the sun, small life.
Where no bull roared, no cow ever lowed, no stag cried, no leopard screeched, no lion coughed, no dog barked,
But all was silent save for parrots occasionally, in the haunted blue bush.

Wistfully watching, with wonderful liquid eyes.
And all her weight, all her blood, dripping sack-wise down towards the earth's centre,
And the live little-one taking in its paw at the door of her belly.

Leap then, and come down on the line that draws to the earth's deep, heavy centre.

See VERSE PARAGRAPH.

versicle Usually a liturgical term. Four meanings can be distinguished: (a) a short sentence said or sung antiphonally; (b) a little verse; (c) a verse of the Psalms or Bible; (d) a short or single metrical line.

versification Three meanings may be distinguished: (a) the action of composing a verse (*q.v.*) or the art or practice of versifying; (b) the form of a poetical composition – its structure and meter; (c) a metrical version of some prose work.

vers libérés (F 'freed verse') The French *symbolistes*, most notably Verlaine, *c.* 1880, introduced new metrical forms and modifications of traditional ones. The intention was to free French versification from Classical conventions. But this 'liberated' verse was still syllabic and still rhymed. *See also* FREE VERSE; VERS LIBRES; SYMBOL AND SYMBOLISM.

vers libres (F 'free verse') (1) A term used to denote verse forms commonly employed in the 17th c. in which there were subtle variations of line and stanza length and alternations of masculine and feminine rhymes in order to achieve special effects. La Fontaine's *Fables* (1668–94) contain many examples. *See also* FREE VERSE; VERS LIBERES.

(2) An important innovation in French prosody dating, like *vers libérés* (*q.v.*), from *c.* 1880. It abandoned certain traditional principles; especially the rules which prescribed recurrent metrical patterns and a certain number of syllables per line. Rhythm, and the division of verse into rhythmical units, was held to be the essential foundation of poetic form. This rhythm was to be personal, the particular expression of the individual poet. Thus, his own voice or tune. The rhythm had also to be appropriate to the subject. Any poet worthy of the name had always been keenly aware of the nature and importance of rhythm, and any poet anyway has his own voice and tune. The theories of the French poets and

prosodists helped to enforce a heightened awareness of the essential; and the innovations were, in many cases, beneficial.

Among the earliest poems to be written in *vers libres* were two by Rimbaud: namely, *Marine* and *Mouvement* (*c.* 1872–3). Other important *vers-libristes* were Paul Verlaine, Jules Laforgue, Edouard Dujardin, Francis Jammes, Henri de Regnier and Emile Verhaeren. The innovations had considerable influence upon American and English poets. How much is a matter of dispute; but it is a fact that Walt Whitman, Ezra Pound, T. S. Eliot and D. H. Lawrence (among many others) were all, at some stage or another, affected by them. Poets continue to experiment with *vers libres*. For example: Gregory Corso, Lawrence Ferlinghetti, Allen Ginsberg, Roger McGough, John Berryman, Ted Hughes, Michael Hamburger, Peter Redgrove, Thom Gunn, Sylvia Plath and Anne Sexton – to name a handful of American and English poets. Their counterparts on the European continent are as numerous.

verso piano (It 'plain verse') In Italian prosody, any line that has a feminine ending (*q.v.*) with the stress on the penultimate syllable. *Verso piano* is the basic narrative line in Italian verse, corresponding to our iambic pentameter. *See* IAMB; PENTAMETER; VERSO SCIOLTO; VERSO TRONCO.

verso sciolto (It 'free, easy, loose verse') An unrhymed hendecasyllabic line with the main accent on the tenth syllable. Italian poets were using it in the 13th c. and by the Renaissance period it was established as the equivalent of the Classical hexameter (*q.v.*) used for epic poetry. It served as the basis for blank verse (*q.v.*) in English poetry. *See also* VERSO PIANO; VERSO TRONCO.

verso sdrucciolo (It 'sliding, slippery verse') In Italian prosody, a line with the principal accent on the tenth syllable and ending with a word accented on the antepenultimate syllable – thus giving the line twelve syllables.

verso tronco (It 'truncated verse') In Italian prosody, any line ending with an accented syllable, especially one with the principal accent on the tenth syllable and a masculine ending. *See also* VERSO PIANO; VERSO SCIOLTO.

Verstehen A German term used from late in the 19th c. to denote understanding achieved from within by means of empathy (*q.v.*). It is commonly associated with hermeneutics (*q.v.*).

Vice, the A kind of fool or buffoon who appeared as a character in the Interludes and Morality Plays (*qq.v.*) in the 16th c. The Vice was often borne on the devil's back and he carried a dagger of lath or a stick. *See also* SLAPSTICK.

Victorian period The era of Queen Victoria's reign (1837–1901). The period is sometimes dated from 1832 (the passage of the first Reform Bill). A period of intense and prolific activity in literature, especially by novelists and poets, philosophers and essayists. Dramatists of any note are few. Much of the writing was concerned with contemporary social problems; for instance, the effects of the industrial revolution, the influence of the theory of evolution, movements of political and social reform. The following are among the most notable British writers of the period: Thomas Love Peacock, Keble, Carlyle, William Barnes, Cardinal Newman, Disraeli, R. S. Surtees, Bulwer Lytton, J. S. Mill, Elizabeth Barrett Browning, Kinglake, Tennyson, Charles Darwin, Thackeray, Robert Browning, Edward Lear, Dickens, Aytoun, Charles Reade, Trollope, Charlotte Brontë, Emily Brontë, Anne Brontë, Charles Kingsley, George Eliot, Ruskin, Matthew Arnold, Wilkie Collins, T. H. Huxley, George Meredith, Dante Gabriel Rossetti, Christina Rossetti, Lewis Carroll, William Morris, Lord Acton, Samuel Butler, Swinburne, Pater, Dobson, Thomas Hardy, Gerard Manley Hopkins, Andrew Lang, Alice Meynell, W. E. Henley, Robert Louis Stevenson, Henry Arthur Jones, Oscar Wilde, Pinero, Francis Thompson, Rudyard Kipling, Synge.

Famous American writers of the period were Emerson, Hawthorne, Longfellow, Melville, Mark Twain and Henry James.

vidalita A Spanish verse form common in gaucho literature (*q.v.*). It consists of four- or six-line stanzas of four, six or eight syllables each. The rhymes are customarily on the second and fourth lines, or the third and sixth.

viewpoint The position of the narrator in relation to his story; thus the outlook from which the events are related. There are many variations and combinations but three basic ones may be distinguished. Firstly, the omniscient – the author moves from character to character, place to place, and episode to episode with complete freedom, giving himself access to his characters' thoughts and feelings whenever he chooses and providing information whenever he wishes. This is probably the commonest point of view and one which has been established for a very long time. Chaucer used the method very successfully in *Troilus and Criseyde* (*c.* 1385); Fielding employed it in *Tom Jones* (1749); Huxley in *Brave New World* (1932); Gabriel Fielding in *The Birthday King* (1962). Such a point of view does not require the author to stay outside his narrative. He may interpolate his own commentaries. Secondly, the third person – the author chooses a character and the story is related in terms of that character in such a way that the field of vision is confined to him or her alone. A good example of this is Strether in Henry James's *The Ambassadors* (1903). Thirdly, first person narrative – here the story is told in the first person by one of the characters. Well-known examples are Defoe's *Moll Flanders*, Melville's *Moby-Dick*, Dickens's *Great Expectations*, Mark Twain's *The Adventures of Huckleberry Finn*, Conrad's *Heart of Darkness* and Scott Fitzgerald's *The Great Gatsby*. This method has become increasingly popular and has been used by many authors during this century. A recent instance is Graham Greene's *Travels with My Aunt* (1969). Various combinations of these methods have been attempted by many authors; in some cases deliberately; in some, apparently, haphazardly. For example: Dickens shifts his viewpoint continually in *Bleak House* (1852–3). So does Tolstoy in *War and Peace* (1865–72). In many cases the viewpoint is restricted to a minor character within the story. Examples of this method are to be found in Emily Brontë's *Wuthering Heights* (1847), Conrad's *Victory* (1915) and Somerset Maugham's *The Razor's Edge* (1944).

Percy Lubbock's *The Craft of Fiction* (1926), E. M. Forster's *Aspects of the Novel* (1927) and Henry James's prefaces to his novels (eventually collected and published as *The Art of the Novel*, 1934) are important discourses on the matter of point of view. Since those days theory on this aspect of the novelist's art, and, indeed, of the story-teller's art in general, has proliferated. *See also* AESTHETIC DISTANCE; CONFESSIONAL NOVEL; EPISTOLARY NOVEL; NARRATOLOGY; NARRATOR; NOVEL; PERSONA; RECIT; STREAM OF CONSCIOUSNESS; SUBJECTIVITY AND OBJECTIVITY.

vignette (F 'little vine') A small ornamental design on a blank page in a book, especially at the beginning or end of a chapter. Today it may also be applied to a sketch or short composition which shows considerable skill (e.g. Virginia Woolf's short story *Kew Gardens*). Moreover, it may describe part of a longer work (e.g. Faulkner's extraordinary description of the wild spotted horses in *The*

Hamlet). A further example is Turgenev's *Sketches of a Sportsman* (1847–51), vignettes of country life in Russia.

villain The bad man in a story, and, in an important and special sense, the evil machinator or plotter in a play. Not to be found in Classical literature, the villain, as a particular character type, was developed in the 16th c. in drama. During this period the devils who played a prominent part in the medieval Mystery Plays (*q.v.*) and the Tudor Moralities (*q.v.*) suffered a kind of metamorphosis into the full-scale villains of Elizabethan and Jacobean tragedy (the majority of the villains are to be found in revenge tragedy, *q.v.*). In effect the devils were humanized and the villains diabolized. This process of evolution, in which two of the major formative influences were the concept of 'Senecal man' and the philosophy of expediency culled from Machiavelli (hence Machiavel, *q.v.*, Machiavellian), can be seen in the *Digby Plays* (*c.* 1512), *The Castell of Perseverance* (1425), *Mind, Will and Understanding* (1460), in Bale's *The Temptation of Our Lord* (1547), in Wever's *Lusty Juventus* (*c.* 1559), in *The Conflict of Conscience* (1563), in Fulwell's *Like Will to Like* (1568), in Lupton's *All For Money* (1578) and in Marlowe's *Dr Faustus* (*c.* 1588) – plus a number of other works. In most of these (and in similar plays) the devils are comic or semi-comic figures – devils continued to appear as devils in comedy until late in the 16th c. and early in the 17th c. e.g. Greene's *Friar Bacon and Friar Bungay* (1594), Haughton's *Grim the Collier of Croydon* (1600), the anonymous *The Merry Devil of Edmonton* (1608), Dekker's *If this be not good the Devil is in it* (1610), Ben Jonson's *The Devil is an Ass* (1616) and the anonymous *The Witch of Edmonton* (1623); but *Dr Faustus* is one of the few tragedies of the period in which the devil appears *as* a devil. Other examples are Barnabe Barnes's *Devil's Charter* (1607) and Chapman's *Bussy D'Ambois* (1607).

The villains (and some of the villainous characters) of Elizabethan and Jacobean tragedy (*q.v.*) exhibit the characteristics of devils incarnate. Of the many instances that might be cited the following are among the most notable: Barabas in Marlowe's *The Jew of Malta* (*c.* 1592), Aaron in Shakespeare's *Titus Andronicus* (1594), and Gloucester in his *Richard III* (*c.* 1594), Piero in John Marston's *Antonio's Revenge* (1599), Hoffman in Chettle's *Tragedy of Hoffman* (*c.* 1600), Eleazar in *Lust's Dominion* (1600), Iago in Shakespeare's *Othello* (1604), Vendici in Tourneur's *The Revenger's Tragedy* (1607), Flamineo in Webster's *The White Devil* (*c.* 1608), the husband in the anonymous *Yorkshire Tragedy* (1608), D'Amville in Tourneur's *The Atheist's Tragedy* (1607–11), Bosola in Webster's *The Duchess of Malfi* (*c.* 1613–14), De Flores in Middleton and Rowley's *The Changeling* (1622) and Eleazar in William Heminge's *The Jewe's Tragedy* (*c.* 1637).

In these plays, and in many others of the period, the dramatists explored and exploited the possibilities of the evil antagonist as something like an incarnate devil, thus achieving an increased realism.

The summit and apotheosis, so to speak, of the villain in literature (and a devilish villain at that) is attained in Milton's portrayal of Satan in *Paradise Lost* (1667). Satan, as a figure and character, combines many of the characteristics of the devils and villains of the preceding three hundred years.

Thereafter, the villain as a character is not prominent until 19th c. melodrama when, for the most part, he has deteriorated into a grotesque if not buffoonish 'baddy' to be hissed and booed. The outstanding exception to this generalization is the Mephistopheles of Goethe's *Faust* (Pt I: 1808; Pt II: 1832), but this character does not really belong to the same tradition of the Elizabethan and Jacobean villain. *See* SENECAN TRAGEDY; SOLILOQUY.

villancico A Spanish song and verse form believed to derive from the Arabic *zéjel* (*q.v.*) and often used by Spanish court poets in the early Renaissance period. The term derives from *villano* 'villein, peasant' and so we may suppose that it has a rustic origin. It is a popular poetic form often with a religious content which is sung in churches at Christmas and on other feast days. In some cases it can be taken as a kind of carol, though, properly, a Christmas carol is *verso de Nochebuena* or *verso de Navidad.*

villanelle (It 'rural, rustic' from *villano* 'peasant') Originally used for pastoral (*q.v.*) poetry in various forms. Jean Passerat (1534–1602) very probably fixed the standard form: five three-lined stanzas or tercets (*q.v.*) and a final quatrain (*q.v.*). The first and third lines of the first tercet recur alternately in the following stanzas as a refrain (*q.v.*) and form a final couplet. A number of English poets have experimented with it, notably Oscar Wilde, W. E. Henley and W. H. Auden. Auden's *If I Could tell You* is a good example:

> Time will say nothing but I told you so,
> Time only knows the price we have to pay;
> If I could tell you I would let you know.

If we should weep when clowns put on their show,
If we should stumble when musicians play,
Time will say nothing but I told you so.

There are no fortunes to be told, although,
Because I love you more than I can say,
If I could tell you I would let you know.

The winds must come from somewhere when they blow,
There must be reasons why the leaves decay;
Time will say nothing but I told you so.

Perhaps the roses really want to grow,
The vision seriously intends to stay;
If I could tell you I would let you know.

Suppose the lions all get up and go,
And all the brooks and soldiers run away;
Will Time say nothing but I told you so?
If I could tell you I would let you know.

See CHAIN VERSE.

vireli A Provençal verse form (it also appears as *virelai*, *virelais*) which varies in length and the number of stanzas. There are two kinds: *vireli ancien* and *vireli nouveau*. A rare form. Austin Dobson experimented with it.

virgule A slanting stroke / often used to mark foot divisions in a line of verse. *See* SCANSION.

vísa Half-line unit in ON poetry.

vocalic assonance *See* VOWEL RHYME.

voice *See* NARRATOR; PERSONA; VIEWPOINT.

volapük An artificial international language invented by J. M. Schleyer in 1879. It was superseded by Esperanto (*q.v.*). *See also* BASIC ENGLISH; IDO.

Volksbuch A German term for 'popular' literature of the prose narrative type. The term was coined by Johann Görres, who in 1807 published *Die teutschen Volksbücher. Volksbücher* were very popular during the 16th c. and remained so until well on in the 18th c. Many derived from French and German verse romances of the Middle Ages. During the Romantic revival (*q.v.*) there was renewed interest in them.

Volksbühne (G 'people's stage') A German theatre association founded in 1890 by Bruno Wille which was of considerable importance in the 'people's theatre' movement of the period. It opened a theatre in 1914 in Berlin, where Erwin Piscator (1893–1966), the pioneer of epic and documentary theatre (*qq.v.*), became director in 1924. The Nazis suppressed the theatre but it reopened after the war. Until October 1990 there was one *Volksbühne* in West Berlin and one in East Berlin.

Volkslied (G 'folk poem/song') A poem of unknown origin belonging to oral tradition (*q.v.*). Usually in a simple stanza (*q.v.*) form rhyming abab, abcb. The term was invented by the great German scholar Johann Herder and first used in his essay *Auszug aus einem Briefwechsel über Ossian und die Lieder alter Völker* (1773). Interest in this kind of poetry became widespread in the late 18th c. (it was an aspect of nationalism) and was to continue in the 19th c. Percy's *Reliques of Ancient English Poetry* (1765) had a considerable influence in Germany and elsewhere. Herder published a collection of folksongs in 1778–9 and many were to follow through the work of others.

Volksmärchen (G 'folk tale') A tale which belongs to the oral tradition (*q.v.*), and thus differs from the *Kunstmärchen* (*q.v.*) which is written down.

Volksstück (G 'folk play') A play in local dialect for 'popular' audiences. *Volksstücke* originated in Vienna early in the 18th c. There were two main forms: the 'magic play' or *Zauberstück*; and the *Lokalstück* (*q.v.*). The former presented a somewhat extravagant and fairy-like world in which the central character was the 'common man'; perhaps an ordinary Viennese tradesman, somewhat dim-witted or something of a comic, who would experience various adventures. The latter tended to be broad or knockabout comedy, with plentiful jokes at the expense of local society, characters, celebrities, fashions, customs, language and so forth. A development of the genre was the *Besserungsstück* (*q.v.*).

Such plays (which were often presented with elaborate stage

machinery and scenic splendour and often included music and song) remained popular until the turn of the 19th c., and were always particularly associated with Vienna and its environs. Karlweis (1850–1901), a Viennese railway inspector, was one of the last dramatists to write them successfully.

volta (It 'turn') The change in thought or feeling which separates the octave (*q.v.*) from the sestet (*q.v.*) in a sonnet (*q.v.*). *See also* MILTONIC SONNET.

vorticism A movement in art and literature begun *c.* 1912 by the painter and writer Wyndham Lewis. It produced a magazine, *Blast: The Review of the Great English Vortex*, which came out twice, in 1914 and 1915. These publications carried the manifestoes of Wyndham Lewis, the poet Ezra Pound and the sculptor Henri Gaudier-Brzeska. Some of the early poems of Pound and T. S. Eliot were also published in *Blast* and Pound used it to elaborate his theory of the image. The movement lost momentum after 1920. *See also* IMAGISTS; SURREALISM.

vowel rhyme When two words rhyme because their vowel or vowels are the same. For instance: boot/roof; ease/peace. Some accept it as a form of rhyme in which any vowel sound is allowed to agree with any other. Emily Dickinson used it quite often, as in these two stanzas from *A bird came down the walk*:

> . . . Cautious,
> I offered him a Crumb,
> And he unrolled his feathers
> And rowed him softer home –
>
> Than Oars divide the Ocean,
> Too silver for a seam –
> Or Butterflies, off Banks of Noon,
> Leap, plashless, as they swim.

See also ASSONANCE.

vraisemblance The French equivalent of verisimilitude (*q.v.*). 17th c. French criticism distinguished between *vraisemblance ordinaire* and *extraordinaire*. The former covered appropriateness of behaviour and motive; the latter, supernatural or extraneous action – the element of surprise in plot or word. *See* BIENSEANCES.

vuelta (Sp 'turn, return') In the Spanish *zéjel* (*q.v.*) the *vuelta* is a fourth line which follows a rhymed triplet called the *mudanza* (*q.v.*).

vulgarity Of the large number of synonyms available in English for vulgar, 'loud', partly because of its sartorial associations, is one of the most suitable. Vulgarity in literature usually occurs when a writer strains himself and protests too much. He then becomes boorish, ill-bred, bullying, crude, conceivably tawdry, or just plain silly or absurd. Thus vulgarity occurs where there is a serious discrepancy between tone, matter and form; where there is incongruity; where the feelings are contrived or forced; where the language is not apt for the emotional content; where there is pretension or self-indulgence in the shape of meretricious ornament, effect for the sake of effect, and 'display' of emotions which are not really felt.

A good deal of dramatic verse written during the Elizabethan and Jacobean periods is in poor taste because it is bombast (*q.v.*). This kind of vulgarity was skilfully parodied by Shakespeare on a number of occasions (especially, for example, in the Players' speeches in *Hamlet*, and in Pistol's rant in *Henry IV* and *Henry V*). Crashaw, in his more syrupy moods (there are a good many instances in *Steps to the Temple*, 1646, and *The Delights of the Muses*, 1646) is also guilty of vulgarity. For example, these lines from *The Weeper*:

Upwards thou dost weep,
Heav'n's bosom drinks the gentle stream,
Where the milky rivers creep
Thine floats above, and is the cream.
Waters above the heavens, what they be,
We're taught best by thy tears, and thee.
Every morn from hence,
A brisk cherub something sips,
Whose sacred influence
Adds sweetness to his sweetest lips,
Then to his music, and his song
Tastes of this breakfast all day long.

Crashaw was a poet susceptible to the more bathetic forms of vulgarity, and so were a number of poets and novelists during the 18th c., a period when writers were particularly sensitive to what was fitting, and to aberrations from decorum (*q.v.*). An attitude and sensibility (*q.v.*) conveyed in Lord Chesterfield's remark that audible laughter was illiberal and ill-bred, and in Johnson's *obiter dictum* that cow-keeper and hogherd were not to be used in our language (though, he added, there were no finer words in the Greek language). Thomas Parnell, a minor 18th c. poet, conveys the then prevailing view tersely at the beginning of his *Essay on the Different Styles of Poetry* (1713):

> I hate the vulgar with untuneful mind;
> Hearts uninspir'd, and senses unrefin'd.

To this century belongs a particularly good example of a certain kind of vulgarity – Dyer's *The Fleece* (1757). He begins his four-book poem on sheep farming in the high and serious manner of Virgil and Milton:

> The care of sheep, the labours of the loom,
> And arts of trade, I sing. Ye rural nymphs,
> Ye swains, and princely merchants, aid the verse.

And so on. Some lines at the beginning of the second book are a good example of a discrepancy between style, tone and matter:

> Through all the brute creation, none, as sheep,
> To lordly man such ample tribute pay.
> For him their udders yield nectareous streams;
> For him the downy vestures they resign;
> For him they spread the feast; ah! ne'er may he
> Glory in wants which doom to pain and death
> His blameless fellow creatures.

The vulgarity of over-much sentimentality is a notable feature of some 18th c. novels, especially Richardson's *Pamela* (1740) and Mackenzie's *The Man of Feeling* (1771).

Some of the more flamboyant 'musicesque' poems of Edgar Allan Poe display another kind of vulgarity. Consider the beginning of *Ulalume* (1847):

> The skies they were ashen and sober;
>   The leaves they were crisped and sere –
>   The leaves they were withering and sere;
> It was night in the lonesome October
>   Of my most immemorial year;
> It was hard by the dim lake of Auber,
>   In the misty mid region of Weir –

It was down by the dank tarn of Auber
  In the ghoul-haunted woodland of Weir.

This anapaestic word-thumping is crude.

Many other examples can be found. Swinburne often tries strenuously to be 'poetical'. Balzac, frequently a bad writer, is quite often guilty of vulgarity (for example, in *Séraphita*, 1834–5). So is Dickens, especially in the death scene of Little Nell in *The Old Curiosity Shop* (1841). Hardy comes perilously near to 'overdoing it' in the horrors of *Jude the Obscure* (1895). Among more recent writers examples can be found in the work of Henry Miller, Lawrence Durrell, William Burroughs and Ian Fleming; not to mention many instances in the purveyors of cheap, popular 'pulp' (*q.v.*) literature: the third-rate erotica and the fourth-rate thrillers. *See* TASTE.

waka A Japanese verse form related to the *tanka* (*q.v.*) consisting of alternate five- and seven-syllable lines. The *waka* form was standard for hundreds of years and survives.

Waldeinsamkeit (G 'forest loneliness') A 'mode' word (apparently coined by Tieck) during the German romantic period which was frequently used. It implies a turning away from reality into a dream world, a yearning for distant countries (of the mind as well as of actuality), a yearning for remoteness of time and place. The concept of the forest is important because forests are remote, wild, dark, lonely places where the spirit may commune with Nature. A good deal of poetry and fiction of the period dwells on this quasi-mystical longing. It is apparent in the work of, among others, Novalis (1772–1801), Ludwig Tieck (1773–1853) and Clemens Brentano (1778–1842). Goethe's poem *Wanderers Nachtlied* is a well-known example of the expression of the feelings involved. *See also* ROMANTICISM; ROMANTIC REVIVAL.

Wappendichtung *See* HEROLDSDICHTUNG.

war literature *See* WAR POETS.

war poets, the A title ultimately bestowed on, primarily, a number of writers who 'soldiered' in various capacities during the First World War and who recorded very memorably their feelings about their experience. Some seventy British poets wrote about that war and more than fifty of them were actively engaged in it. Not a few of them were killed. A handful (e.g. Rupert Brooke and Julian Grenfell) expressed patriotic and quasi-romantic views. The majority expressed varying degrees of disgust, disenchantment, cynicism, revulsion, anger and horror. It was often poetry of protest and it deglamorized war for ever. The strongest feelings were often leavened by a grim and laconic humour. Pre-eminent among the poets were (and are) Wilfred Owen, Siegfried Sassoon, Edmund Blunden, Charles Sorley, Isaac Rosenberg, W. N. Hodgson, Edward Shanks, Edward Thomas, Robert Nichols, Wilfred Gibson, Alan Seeger, Herbert Asquith and David Jones. One of the major poems is *In Parenthesis* (1937) by David Jones. It is on an epic scale and was begun by him in 1927. Passages of prose are combined with the verse.

The Second World War, and its aftermath, was recorded (somewhat less memorably) by another generation of writers: notably, Sidney Keyes, Keith Douglas, Alun Lewis, Roy Fuller, Roy Campbell, Charles Causley and Alan Ross.

Most of the poets of both world wars have been well represented in a number of fine anthologies. Two of the best concerned with the First World War are *Up the Line to Death* (1964), edited by R. B. Gardner, and *Men Who March Away* (1965), edited by I. M. Parsons. The Second World War yielded *The Poetry of War: 1939–1945* (1965), edited by I. Hamilton, *The Components of the Scene* (1966), edited by R. Blythe, and *The Terrible Rain* (1966), edited by R. B. Gardner. It is noticeable that all five anthologies appeared within two years of each other in the 1960s, nearly fifty years after the First World War ended and twenty years after the end of the Second World War. This is some indication of the length of the shadow that both cataclysms cast across the world. In 1988, the seventieth anniversary of the original armistice year, half a dozen volumes of verse and prose about the 1914–18 war were published.

Not a few of those classed as war poets also contributed to a copious quantity of literature (novels, short stories, autobiography, biography, diaries, journals, *qq.v.*, memoirs, and stories of escape from prisoner-of-war camps) which appeared steadily in the inter-war period and continued unabated from the late 1940s onwards. Three writers in particular published memoirs of the First World War which, over the years, have become more or less established as classics of their kind: namely, *Undertones of War* (1928) by Edmund Blunden, *Goodbye to All That* (1929) by Robert Graves and *Memoirs of a Fox-Hunting Man* (1928) by Siegfried Sassoon. Two lesser known works of considerable merit are Frank Richards's *Old Soldiers Never Die* (1933) and *With a Machine Gun to Cambrai* (1969) by George Coppard (a brother of A. E. Coppard). *See also* LITERATURE OF ESCAPE; LOST GENERATION.

weak-ending One that is unaccented. *See* FEMININE ENDING.

well-made play Eugène Scribe (1791–1861), the French dramatist, is usually credited with the concept of the well-made play. The term is now normally pejorative and refers to a neatly and economically constructed play which works with mechanical efficiency. Scribe was a very successful dramatist and exerted considerable influence in the theatre for many years. Well-made plays were still common in the 1930s and not infrequent until the late fifties. There may always be a commercial market for them. Witness the phenomenal run of Agatha Christie's *The Mousetrap* (1952).

Weltanschauung (G 'world outlook') As a literary term it may be used judiciously in reference to a particular author's attitude to the world, or to the prevailing spirit and vision of a period. For instance, Thomas Hardy's view of the human being as the victim of fate, destiny, impersonal forces and circumstances; or the disillusioned and laconic cynicism so often expressed by poets in the 1930s. W. H. Auden, Louis MacNeice, Stephen Spender, Cecil Day Lewis, William Empson, Francis Scarfe, Michael Roberts, Bernard Spencer, Norman Cameron, David Gascoyne and others.

Weltliteratur A term coined by Goethe which means, approximately (Goethe did not define it), that literature which is of all nations and peoples, and which, by a reciprocal exchange of ideas, mediates between nations and helps to enrich the spirit of man. Carlyle spoke of 'World literature'. *See also* COMPARATIVE LITERATURE.

Weltschmerz (G 'world pain') Vague yearning and discontent, a weariness of life, and a melancholy pessimism. Many of the poems of Giacomo Leopardi (1798–1837) suggest such a feeling of unease and despair. The term may also apply to the spirit of a period like the 15th c. when there was widespread despondency and pessimism throughout Europe: feelings frequently manifest in the literature and art of that time. *See also* WELTANSCHAUUNG; ZEITGEIST.

wên and wu The two main classes of traditional Chinese drama. *Wên* denotes civil, and *wu* military drama. The 'book' for these plays is more like a roughly outlined scenario than a dramatic text as we understand it in the West. In China the actors fill out the scenario framework as required, and this gives flexibility. The plays are a mixture of dialogue in prose and verse, acrobatics, dancing, mime and operatic singing. They are divided into many different scenes of variable length and are usually performed on a square stage. The dramatic conventions are prescribed and elaborate. Stage props are simple and symbolic: a table, for instance, may represent variously an altar, a wall, a bridge, a hill or a judge's bench; four black flags waved vigorously represent a strong wind; a hat done up in red cloth signifies a decapitated head; a cube wrapped in yellow silk is an official seal – and so on.

There are four main types of character: *shêng* – males in general; *tan* – females in general; *ching* or *hua-lien* – strong, vigorous men whose faces are painted like masks; *ch'ou* – comedians. Within these categories there are a number of sub-divisions.

Both speech and song are delivered in a high-pitched voice, though the comedians render a kind of bass. The noises are reinforced by not dissimilar musical accompaniment from a fiddle; but the Chinese orchestra (which is on stage) also has brass and percussion instruments.

Costume and make-up are of the greatest importance. Costumes tend to be lavish and are adapted from the styles of the T'ang, Sung, Yüan and Ming dynastic periods. Convention prescribes the significance of particular colours (emperors wear red, important officials yellow, and so forth) and also prescribes particular uses of the clothes (for example, a sleeve held up to the eyes denotes weeping). Comparable rules apply in the use of complicated make-up. Character and temperament are expressed by lines on the face and varied combinations of colour. For instance, white denotes a treacherous disposition; red, loyalty and courage; black, candour and integrity; yellow, guile; green for demons, brigands and outlaws . . . and so on. The beard, an important prestige and status symbol in ancient China, is also an integral part of make-up. A very long beard signifies heroism and wealth; a blue or red beard signifies a supernatural being.

The movements of the actors are according to convention and their tempo is set by the orchestra.

Most of the *wên* and *wu* plays are based on traditional material like legends and historical events. They tend to point a moral, or give that impression. They possess a timeless quality in that they depict Chinese life over many centuries, and they are as stylized as *Nō* (*q.v.*) and puppet-theatre like *karagöz* (*q.v.*).

Wendepunkt (G 'turning point') An important element in the theory and practice of the *Novelle*. *See* NOVELLA.

Wertherism An *-ism* deriving from the title of Goethe's *Die Leiden des jungen Werthers* (1774), an autobiographical and epistolary novel and also a kind of *Künstlerroman* (*qq.v.*). The hero, Werther, is a hypersensitive, highly strung and melancholy young man who is a social misfit and is engaged in a hopeless love affair; the prototype of the pale, love-lorn, romantic, 'interesting' youth. The novel was an enormous success in Europe and created a cult which influenced male fashion (a blue coat and yellow breeches were *de rigueur* among young men who were well-off) and such artefacts as China tea-sets which were decorated with scenes and motifs from the story. 'Wertherism' became a popular term in English. A young man suffering from 'Wertherism' was subject to fits of melancholia, and what Goethe described (in the novel) as *Weltschmerz* ('a feeling of being ill-at-ease with the world') and *Ichschmerz* ('a feeling of self-dissatisfaction').

Western A genre of fiction – usually in short story or novel (*qq.v.*) form – associated with the western states of the USA (sometimes called the 'Wild West'), and more particularly the South-west (i.e. the region encompassing the border states of Arizona, New Mexico and Western Texas) and what was known as the 'Old South-west', which included the area between the Savannah River and the Mississippi which formed the south-western frontier from colonial times to the 19th c. It is also associated with the great plains and prairies of Nebraska, Kansas, Oklahoma and Texas, plus parts of Montana, Wyoming, Colorado, the western parts of North and South Dakota, and New Mexico. These territories were inhabited by famous tribes of American Indians. White pioneer settlers (some of whom were called 'crackers' because their chief diet was cracked corn) created a folklore of the regions. This in turn produced frontier stories and sketches about hunting, trapping, ranching, cowboys, conflicts with Indians, cattle-rustling, sheriffs, gun-law, prospecting, brigandage and so forth. There were also ballads and other verse which were part of local gaucho literature (*q.v.*), and many a tall story (*q.v.*) or tall tale.

James Fenimore Cooper (1789–1851) was one of the first to write of such ways of life memorably – especially in his *Leatherstocking Tales* (*q.v.*) – between 1823 and 1841. A number of other lesser known writers contributed numerous stories, sketches and yarns which were forerunners of the traditional and timeless Western which proved such a boon to the cinema industry. Some of these writers were cowboys. Among the better known were Davy Crockett (1786–1836), A. B. Longstreet (1790–1870), Sol Smith (1801–69), J. M. Field (1810–56), G. W. Harris (1814–69), author of the *Sut Lovingwood Yarns* (1867), Joseph Baldwin (1815–64), J. J. Hooper (1815–62) and T. B. Thorpe (1815–78), author of the famous tall story *The Big Bear of Arkansas*.

Francis Bret Harte (1836–1902) made a considerable contribution to the genre. In 1868 he helped to establish *Overland Monthly* as an outlet for Western writers and he printed a number of his own stories in it. In 1870 he published *The Luck of Roaring Camp and Other Sketches* – a collection of Western stories about frontier life and the fortunes and misfortunes of the individual in frontier society. Harte (and the other writers mentioned above) were eventually to have some influence on Mark Twain and, much later, William Faulkner.

One of the best known writers of a traditional type of Western was Andy Adams (1859–1935), author of *The Log of a Cowboy* (1903), *The Outlet* (1905) and *Cattle Brands* (1906). Eugene Manlove Rhodes (1869–1934) wrote ten or more novels on comparable themes. Another who became popular was Harold Bell Wright (1872–1944), author of *The Shepherd of the Hills* (1907), *The Calling of Dan Matthews* (1909) and *When a Man's a Man* (1916). The most famous in the 20th c. has been Zane Grey (1872–1939), who wrote over sixty novels and is particularly remembered for *Riders of the Purple Sage* (1912), *To the Last Man* (1922), *Nevada* (1928), *Wild Horse Mesa* (1928) and *Code of the West* (1934). He presents the West as a kind of moral landscape in which and against which characters fight and struggle. Their destruction or salvation/redemption depends on how they cope with and respond to the codes of violence which prevail. Over a hundred Western films were based on Grey's stories, and during the 1920s and 1930s he was the most popular author in America. Latterly Jack Shaefer has written books in the same tradition; for instance, *The Big Range* (1953). Other recent writers who have contributed are: Winifred Blevins, Bill Gulick, Donald Hamilton, Dorothy M. Johnson, Louis L'Amour and Peggy S. Curry.

Westerners Russian intellectuals who created a movement *c.* 1840. They were opposed to the ideology of the Czar and to the Russian Slavophiles (*q.v.*). These two groups were in contention over the matter of Russia's relationship with the West. The Westerners maintained that it was essential to belong to European civilization, to be a part of its culture and to use its progressive forms of government and technological progress. Turgenev's novel *Smoke* (1867) depicts the controversy from the point of view of the

Westerners. Other 'Westernist' writers were Nikolai Ogaryov (1813–77), Yakov Polonski (1819–98) and Alexander Druzhinin (1824–64).

wheel *See* BOB AND WHEEL.

whodunnit An illiterate form of 'who did it?' (i.e. the crime). A crime story closely akin to the thriller, the detective story and the *roman policier* (*qq.v.*), and often synonymous with these terms.

willing suspension of disbelief One of the most famous phrases ever coined. Like 'negative capability' and 'dissociation of sensibility' (*qq.v.*) it has almost the utility of an indispensable talisman. Coleridge invented it and used it in Chapter XIV of *Biographia Literaria* to describe that state of receptivity and credulity desirable in a reader or member of an audience (in current jargon, 'the receptor'). The reader must 'grant' that he or she is about to read a story; a person in the audience is 'asked' to accept the dramatic conventions of the theatre and stage. In explaining one of the more remarkable *aperçus* in literary criticism Coleridge writes:

> In this idea [he has been speaking of two possible subjects for poetry] originated the plan of the LYRICAL BALLADS; in which it was agreed, that my endeavours should be directed to persons and characters supernatural, or at least romantic; yet so as to transfer from our inward nature a human interest and a semblance of truth sufficient to procure for these shadows of imagination that willing suspension of disbelief for the moment, which constitutes poetic faith.

It is possible that Coleridge got the original idea from the French sceptic François de La Mothe le Vayer (1588–1672), who composd a number of dialogues and discourses (e.g. *Les Problèmes sceptiques*, 1666, *Les Solitudes sceptiques*, 1670) and referred to the wisdom of the sceptic in his phrase 'cette belle suspension d'esprit de la sceptique'. *See also* ALS OB.

wit (OE *witan* 'to know') The word has acquired a number of accretions in meaning since the Middle Ages, and in critical and general use has changed a good deal. Wit formerly meant 'sense' or 'the five senses'; thus common sense. (Cf. the phrase 'out of one's wits'.) During the Renaissance period it meant 'intelligence' or 'wisdom'; thus intellectual capacity; even, perhaps, 'genius' (*q.v.*).

Roger Ascham and Lyly, for example, associated quick wit with intellectual liveliness. To Sir Philip Sidney it suggested an aptitude for writing poetry. Later, during the 17th c., the word came to mean 'fancy', dexterity of thought and imagination. Boyle and Locke understood it in those terms. Hobbes, however, in *Leviathan* (1651) thought that judgement rather than fancy was the main element. 'Judgement without fancy is wit, but fancy without judgement not.' Dryden, Cowley and Pope (among others) held that wit was primarily a matter of propriety. As Pope put it in his *Essay on Criticism* (he uses the term forty-six times in at least five different senses):

> True wit is Nature to advantage dressed,
> What oft was thought, but ne'er so well expressed.

Johnson, however, growled disapprovingly at Cowley's conception and referred to his 'heterogeneous ideas . . . yoked by violence together . . .' Hazlitt distinguished between wit, which is artificial, and imagination, which is valid. During the 19th c., imagination was the term generally used to designate the ability to invent and find resemblances. Wit was associated with levity. Matthew Arnold would not allow Chaucer or Pope on his list of the greatest poets because of their wittiness, and lack of 'high seriousness'. T. S. Eliot adjusted the balance by preferring witty poets like Donne and Marvell because they were able to combine wit with seriousness. The majority of modern critics agree with Eliot. For the most part wit now suggests intellectual brilliance and ingenuity; verbal deftness, as in the epigram (*q.v.*). Wit is commonly verbal, while humour need not be. *See* FANCY AND IMAGINATION; JEU D'ESPRIT.

wrenched accent This occurs in verse when the requirements of metrical stress prevail over the natural stress of a word or words. Common in ballads, as in this verse from the 18th c. Scots ballad *Mary Hamilton*:

> He's courted her in the kitchen,
> He's courted her in the ha',
> He's courted her in the laigh cellar,
> And that was warst of a'.

Cellar is a trochaic word, but for the sake of the stress pattern is here made iambic – thus *cellár*.

writerly *See* READERLY/WRITERLY.

Writers' Guild of Great Britain Founded in 1959 as the Screenwriters' Guild. It is the writer's trade union, affiliated to the TUC, and represents writers' interests in film, radio, theatre, publishing and television. It is by constitution non-political, has no involvement with any political party and does not pay a political levy. There is an executive council of twenty-nine members and regional committees represent Scotland and Wales and the North and West of England.

X

Xanaduism A form of academic research which entails the quest for sources behind works of imagination. John Livingston Lowes set a fashion for it in 1927 with the publication of *The Road to Xanadu*, which was inspired by Coleridge's 'visionary' poem about Xanadu.

Xenophanic Xenophanes (6th c. BC) was a native of Ionia and an itinerant poet who visited many parts of the Greek world. He was also a sillographer (*q.v.*). Thus 'Xenophanic' may be used to describe a wandering poet with a witty and satirical talent. The Goliards were Xenophanic. *See also* GOLIARDIC VERSE.

Y

Yale school A group of literary critics associated with deconstruction (*q.v.*) in America, centred on Yale University, Connecticut, and also, more recently at Irvine, California (Irvine is a branch of the University of California). The Yale school flourished particularly during the 1970s. The chief luminaries were Harold Bloom, Paul de Man, Geoffrey Hartman, J. Hillis Miller and the French philosopher Jacques Derrida. The so-called Yale Manifesto to which all five contributed essays was published in 1979 under the title *Deconstruction and Criticism*. The essays were all initially responses to Shelley's poem *The Triumph of Life*. They were much influenced by Freud and by the deconstruction theories of Derrida.

yarn A story or tale (*q.v.*). The term derives from the nautical slang phrase 'to spin a yarn'. It often has the connotation of a tallish or slightly improbable story. One who 'yarns' is inclined to be a romancer, with the attitude of 'believe it if you will'. Among the many distinguished yarners in English and American literature one should mention R. L. Stevenson, Rudyard Kipling, W. W. Jacobs, Joseph Conrad, Somerset Maugham, A. E. Coppard, John Masefield, T. F. Powys, Mark Twain and William Faulkner. Some poets, too, have been fine yarners. For example: John Masefield, Robert Frost, Robert Service; plus the Australian poets Charles Harpur, Adam Lindsay Gordon, A. B. 'Banjo' Paterson, Henry Lawson and Christopher Brennan. *See* SHORT STORY; TALL STORY.

year book In particular the reports of English Common Law cases for the period 1292–1534. These were succeeded by the Law Reports. In general a year book is an annual publication; usually a reference work – like *The Writers' and Artists' Year Book*.

yellow-backs Cheap editions of novels bound in yellow boards, including the 'railway novels' of the latter years of the 19th c.

Yellow Book, The An illustrated quarterly which appeared in 1894–7. Many distinguished writers and artists contributed. Among the better known were Aubrey Beardsley, Max Beerbohm, Henry James and Walter Sickert.

yellow journalism A name given to a particularly sensational kind of journalism which flourished in America in the 1880s. The term derives from an 1895 number of the *New York World* in which a child in a yellow dress ('The Yellow Kid') was the central figure of a cartoon. This was an experiment in colour printing. In England the term 'yellow press' is applied to sensational periodicals.

yüeh-fu (Ch 'music bureau') A form of Chinese poetry so named because the music bureau collected popular songs and ballad-type lyrics. The *yüeh-fu* poems were in mixed meters and short lines (a five-word line was common), and the number of stanzas was variable. The poem usually consisted of monologue or dialogue which presented, in dramatic form, some misfortune.

Z

zany (It *zani, zanni*; a Venetian form of Gianni or Giovanni) A servant-clown in *commedia dell'arte* (*q.v.*). More generally, any kind of jester or clown; also a comedian's stooge. Currently used on occasions to describe an idea (or person) which is off-beat, odd, crazily funny.

zapadnichestvo *See* WESTERNERS.

zarzuela (Sp, after La Zarzuela, a hunting lodge near the Pardo Palace near Madrid) A form of 17th c. Spanish drama first composed by Calderón de la Barca with the help of composers such as Juan Risco. *Zarzuelas* were a form of musical comedy (*q.v.*) in one to three acts. Thus a sort of hybrid of drama and opera. Music became an increasingly important element in which recitative alternated with song. The themes were usually mythological and the plays were stylized in structure and language. Early examples (both by Calderón) were *El mayor encanto amor* (1635) and *El jardín de Falerina*. In the 1650s the plays were performed at the hunting lodge. *Zarzuelas* became particularly popular in the 17th c. After a period of desuetude in the 18th c. they were revived in the 19th and continue to be popular to this day.

Zauberstück *See* VOLKSSTUCK.

zaum A Russian term for 'trans-sense' language (*zaumny yazyk*), a language which would be 'beyond sense'. For example, neologisms (*q.v.*), onomatopoeic effects, arbitrary combinations of sounds and play with the morphological components of ordinary words. It was a notable feature of work produced by Russian Futurist poets, especially Ḳhlebnikov and Kruchenykh. *See* FUTURISM; NONSENSE.

Zeitgeist (G 'spirit of the times') The trend, fashion or taste of a particular period. For instance, a preoccupation with the more morbid aspects of dying and death was characteristic of some English literature in the Jacobean period (*q.v.*), especially in the works of dramatists like Webster and Tourneur. *See also* DECADENCE; WELTANSCHAUUNG.

Zeitroman (G 'era, period, times, novel') In German the term denotes a novel which is mainly concerned with an author's critical analysis of the age in which he or she lives. There are many such novels. Notable examples in German literature are Gutzkow's *Die Ritter vom Geiste* (1850–51), Freytag's *Soll und Haben* (1855), Thomas Mann's *Der Zauberberg* (1924), and Günter Grass's *Die Blechtrommel* (1959) and his *Aus dem Tagebuch einer Schnecke* (1972). *See also* BILDUNGSROMAN.

zéjel A Spanish poetic form (believed to be of Arabic origin) which was popular in Spain in the late Middle Ages. It consists of an introductory strophe (*q.v.*) followed by a series of strophes. At its simplest the strophic form is four verses rhyming aaab, cccb. The b rhyme runs throughout. *See also* ESTRIBILLO; MUDANZA; VUELTA.

ženske pesme (S 'women's songs') Songs or poems of oral tradition and of the ballad (*qq.v.*) type frequently sung and chanted by South Slav women, especially peasant women. Their themes are often love, death, marriage, home life and romance. *See* JUNACKE PESME; NARODNE PESME.

zeugma (Gk 'yoking, bonding') A figure of speech in which a verb or an adjective is applied to two nouns, though appropriate only to one of them. A well-known example occurs in *Henry V* when Fluellen says, 'Kill the poys and the luggage'. The verb 'kill' cannot apply to luggage. *See* SYLLEPSIS.

Zhdanovshchina (R 'the Zhdanov time') The period of 1946–8 during which Andrei Zhdanov, secretary of the Central Committee in control of ideology, brought heavy pressure to bear on prominent Soviet writers who were deemed not to be following Party doctrine. Among the most prominent were Anna Akhmatova, Mikhail Zoshchenko and Boris Pasternak. Later, comparable pressures were put on Alexander Solzhenitsyn, who in 1969 was expelled from the Union of Soviet Writers (*q.v.*) and in 1974 was deported to West Germany. *See also* DISSIDENT WRITERS.